2002 DOCUMENTS SUPPLEMENT TO

LEGAL PROBLEMS OF INTERNATIONAL ECONOMIC RELATIONS

Fourth Edition

By

John H. Jackson
University Professor,
Georgetown Law Center

William J. Davey
Edwin M. Adams Professor of Law,
University of Illinois

Alan O. Sykes, Jr.
Frank and Bernice Greenberg Professor of Law,
University of Chicago

AMERICAN CASEBOOK SERIES®

WEST GROUP
A THOMSON COMPANY

Mat #17208640

American Casebook Series, and the West Group symbol
are registered trademarks used herein under license.

COPYRIGHT © 1977, 1986, 1989, 1995 By WEST PUBLISHING CO.
COPYRIGHT © 2002 By WEST GROUP
        610 Opperman Drive
        P.O. Box 64526
        St. Paul, MN 55164–0526
        1–800–328–9352

ISBN 0–314–24661–4

 TEXT IS PRINTED ON 10% POST CONSUMER RECYCLED PAPER

1st Reprint — 2003

Introduction

This Documents Supplement contains the basic international agreements on trade in goods and services and the principal U.S. statutes regulating international trade, as well as the North American Free Trade Agreement and the Articles of Agreement of the International Monetary Fund. Because it is impossible to predict which provisions of an agreement may turn out to be of interest in the years to come or in specific classroom discussions, we have tried to include complete sets of documents, even though comprehensiveness comes at a price, including additional weight to carry.

We have divided the Documents Supplement into four parts:

Part I: The World Trade Organization, including the General Agreement on Tariffs and Trade and all of the Uruguay Round Agreements now in force

Part II: The International Monetary Fund, including its Articles of Agreement

Part III: The North American Free Trade Agreement, including the side agreements on the environment, labor and safeguards

Part IV: U.S. trade laws

In order to simplify use of the Supplement, each part has its own introduction to explain the organization of that part.

By organizing the Documents Supplement on the basis of agreements, it is inevitable that specific subjects will be treated in several parts of the Supplement. In order to further simplify use of the Supplement, in the following chart we indicate the provisions on several important subjects that are found in the various parts of the Documents Supplement. We have included cross references to the casebook as well.

We have used the following abbreviations:

AD Agreement	Agreement on Implementation of Article VI (Antidumping)
GATS	General Agreement on Trade in Services
GATT	General Agreement on Tariffs and Trade
NAFTA	North American Free Trade Agreement
SCM Agreement	Agreement on Subsidies and Countervailing Measures
TBT Agreement	Agreement on Technical Barriers to Trade
TRIPS Agreement	Agreement on Trade-Related Aspects of Intellectual Property Rights
Valuation Agreement	Agreement on Implementation of Article VII
UR	Uruguay Round

Table of Contents

PART I. THE WORLD TRADE ORGANIZATION

2002 DOCUMENTS SUPPLEMENT TO

LEGAL PROBLEMS OF INTERNATIONAL ECONOMIC RELATIONS

*

Part I

THE WORLD TRADE ORGANIZATION

Introduction to Part I

Part I contains the constituent documents of the Agreement Establishing the World Trade Organization. The documents are arranged as they appear in the annexes to that agreement, with the exception that the General Agreement on Tariffs and Trade 1947, with its accompanying notes, is reproduced as the first document in Annex IA—Multilateral Agreements on Trade in Goods. It is followed (and modified) by the General Agreement on Tariffs and Trade 1994, which is based on the 1947 text, but with some specified modifications (including 6 understandings relating to specific GATT articles and the Marrakesh Protocol). We have included only one of the plurilateral agreements listed in Annex 4—the Agreement on Government Procurement. The Dairy and Beef Agreements were terminated in 1997. The 1979 Tokyo Round Civil Aircraft agreement remains in force; efforts to renegotiate it did not succeed in the Uruguay Round. We have also included the Ministerial Decisions, Declarations and Understandings that were reached at the time the WTO Agreement was signed at Marrakesh on April 15, 1994. In addition, we have included the Singapore and Doha ministerial declarations and an important documents related to GATS (the telecoms reference paper).

Table of Contents

Item 1

AGREEMENT ESTABLISHING THE WORLD TRADE ORGANIZATION

The *Parties* to this Agreement,

Recognizing that their relations in the field of trade and economic endeavour should be conducted with a view to raising standards of living, ensuring full employment and a large and steadily growing volume of real income and effective demand, and expanding the production of and trade in goods and services, while allowing for the optimal use of the world's resources in accordance with the objective of sustainable development, seeking both to protect and preserve the environment and to enhance the means for doing so in a manner consistent with their respective needs and concerns at different levels of economic development,

Recognizing further that there is need for positive efforts designed to ensure that developing countries, and especially the least developed among them, secure a share in the growth in international trade commensurate with the needs of their economic development,

Being desirous of contributing to these objectives by entering into reciprocal and mutually advantageous arrangements directed to the substantial reduction of tariffs and other barriers to trade and to the elimination of discriminatory treatment in international trade relations,

Resolved, therefore, to develop an integrated, more viable and durable multilateral trading system encompassing the General Agreement on Tariffs and Trade, the results of past trade liberalization efforts, and all of the results of the Uruguay Round of Multilateral Trade Negotiations,

Determined to preserve the basic principles and to further the objectives underlying this multilateral trading system,

Agree as follows:

Article I

Establishment of the Organization

The World Trade Organization (hereinafter referred to as "the WTO") is hereby established.

Article II

Scope of the WTO

1. The WTO shall provide the common institutional framework for the conduct of trade relations among its Members in matters related to the agreements and associated legal instruments included in the Annexes to this Agreement.

2.   The agreements and associated legal instruments included in Annexes 1, 2 and 3 (hereinafter referred to as "Multilateral Trade Agreements") are integral parts of this Agreement, binding on all Members.

3.   The agreements and associated legal instruments included in Annex 4 (hereinafter referred to as "Plurilateral Trade Agreements") are also part of this Agreement for those Members that have accepted them, and are binding on those Members. The Plurilateral Trade Agreements do not create either obligations or rights for Members that have not accepted them.

4.   The General Agreement on Tariffs and Trade 1994 as specified in Annex 1A (hereinafter referred to as "GATT 1994") is legally distinct from the General Agreement on Tariffs and Trade, dated 30 October 1947, annexed to the Final Act Adopted at the Conclusion of the Second Session of the Preparatory Committee of the United Nations Conference on Trade and Employment, as subsequently rectified, amended or modified (hereinafter referred to as "GATT 1947").

Article III

Functions of the WTO

1.   The WTO shall facilitate the implementation, administration and operation, and further the objectives, of this Agreement and of the Multilateral Trade Agreements, and shall also provide the framework for the implementation, administration and operation of the Plurilateral Trade Agreements.

2.   The WTO shall provide the forum for negotiations among its Members concerning their multilateral trade relations in matters dealt with under the agreements in the Annexes to this Agreement. The WTO may also provide a forum for further negotiations among its Members concerning their multilateral trade relations, and a framework for the implementation of the results of such negotiations, as may be decided by the Ministerial Conference.

3.   The WTO shall administer the Understanding on Rules and Procedures Governing the Settlement of Disputes (hereinafter referred to as the "Dispute Settlement Understanding" or "DSU") in Annex 2 to this Agreement.

4.   The WTO shall administer the Trade Policy Review Mechanism (hereinafter referred to as the "TPRM") provided for in Annex 3 to this Agreement.

5.   With a view to achieving greater coherence in global economic policy-making, the WTO shall cooperate, as appropriate, with the International Monetary Fund and with the International Bank for Reconstruction and Development and its affiliated agencies.

Article IV

Structure of the WTO

1.   There shall be a Ministerial Conference composed of representatives of all the Members, which shall meet at least once every two years. The Ministerial Conference shall carry out the functions of the WTO and take actions necessary to this effect. The Ministerial Conference shall have the authority to take decisions on all matters under any of the Multilateral Trade Agreements, if so requested by a Member, in accordance with the specific

requirements for decision-making in this Agreement and in the relevant Multilateral Trade Agreement.

2.   There shall be a General Council composed of representatives of all the Members, which shall meet as appropriate.   In the intervals between meetings of the Ministerial Conference, its functions shall be conducted by the General Council.   The General Council shall also carry out the functions assigned to it by this Agreement.   The General Council shall establish its rules of procedure and approve the rules of procedure for the Committees provided for in paragraph 7.

3.   The General Council shall convene as appropriate to discharge the responsibilities of the Dispute Settlement Body provided for in the Dispute Settlement Understanding.   The Dispute Settlement Body may have its own chairman and shall establish such rules of procedure as it deems necessary for the fulfilment of those responsibilities.

4.   The General Council shall convene as appropriate to discharge the responsibilities of the Trade Policy Review Body provided for in the TPRM. The Trade Policy Review Body may have its own chairman and shall establish such rules of procedure as it deems necessary for the fulfilment of those responsibilities.

5.   There shall be a Council for Trade in Goods, a Council for Trade in Services and a Council for Trade–Related Aspects of Intellectual Property Rights (hereinafter referred to as the "Council for TRIPS"), which shall operate under the general guidance of the General Council.   The Council for Trade in Goods shall oversee the functioning of the Multilateral Trade Agreements in Annex 1A.   The Council for Trade in Services shall oversee the functioning of the General Agreement on Trade in Services (hereinafter referred to as "GATS").   The Council for TRIPS shall oversee the functioning of the Agreement on Trade–Related Aspects of Intellectual Property Rights (hereinafter referred to as the "Agreement on TRIPS").   These Councils shall carry out the functions assigned to them by their respective agreements and by the General Council.   They shall establish their respective rules of procedure subject to the approval of the General Council.   Membership in these Councils shall be open to representatives of all Members.   These Councils shall meet as necessary to carry out their functions.

6.   The Council for Trade in Goods, the Council for Trade in Services and the Council for TRIPS shall establish subsidiary bodies as required. These subsidiary bodies shall establish their respective rules of procedure subject to the approval of their respective Councils.

7.   The Ministerial Conference shall establish a Committee on Trade and Development, a Committee on Balance-of-Payments Restrictions and a Committee on Budget, Finance and Administration, which shall carry out the functions assigned to them by this Agreement and by the Multilateral Trade Agreements, and any additional functions assigned to them by the General Council, and may establish such additional Committees with such functions as it may deem appropriate.   As part of its functions, the Committee on Trade and Development shall periodically review the special provisions in the Multilateral Trade Agreements in favour of the least-developed country Members and report to the General Council for appropriate action.   Membership in these Committees shall be open to representatives of all Members.

8. The bodies provided for under the Plurilateral Trade Agreements shall carry out the functions assigned to them under those Agreements and shall operate within the institutional framework of the WTO. These bodies shall keep the General Council informed of their activities on a regular basis.

Article V

Relations With Other Organizations

1. The General Council shall make appropriate arrangements for effective cooperation with other intergovernmental organizations that have responsibilities related to those of the WTO.

2. The General Council may make appropriate arrangements for consultation and cooperation with non-governmental organizations concerned with matters related to those of the WTO.

Article VI

The Secretariat

1. There shall be a Secretariat of the WTO (hereinafter referred to as "the Secretariat") headed by a Director–General.

2. The Ministerial Conference shall appoint the Director–General and adopt regulations setting out the powers, duties, conditions of service and term of office of the Director–General.

3. The Director–General shall appoint the members of the staff of the Secretariat and determine their duties and conditions of service in accordance with regulations adopted by the Ministerial Conference.

4. The responsibilities of the Director–General and of the staff of the Secretariat shall be exclusively international in character. In the discharge of their duties, the Director–General and the staff of the Secretariat shall not seek or accept instructions from any government or any other authority external to the WTO. They shall refrain from any action which might adversely reflect on their position as international officials. The Members of the WTO shall respect the international character of the responsibilities of the Director–General and of the staff of the Secretariat and shall not seek to influence them in the discharge of their duties.

Article VII

Budget and Contributions

1. The Director–General shall present to the Committee on Budget, Finance and Administration the annual budget estimate and financial statement of the WTO. The Committee on Budget, Finance and Administration shall review the annual budget estimate and the financial statement presented by the Director–General and make recommendations thereon to the General Council. The annual budget estimate shall be subject to approval by the General Council.

2. The Committee on Budget, Finance and Administration shall propose to the General Council financial regulations which shall include provisions setting out:

(a) the scale of contributions apportioning the expenses of the WTO among its Members; and

(b) the measures to be taken in respect of Members in arrears.

The financial regulations shall be based, as far as practicable, on the regulations and practices of GATT 1947.

3.   The General Council shall adopt the financial regulations and the annual budget estimate by a two-thirds majority comprising more than half of the Members of the WTO.

4.   Each Member shall promptly contribute to the WTO its share in the expenses of the WTO in accordance with the financial regulations adopted by the General Council.

Article VIII

Status of the WTO

1.   The WTO shall have legal personality, and shall be accorded by each of its Members such legal capacity as may be necessary for the exercise of its functions.

2.   The WTO shall be accorded by each of its Members such privileges and immunities as are necessary for the exercise of its functions.

3.   The officials of the WTO and the representatives of the Members shall similarly be accorded by each of its Members such privileges and immunities as are necessary for the independent exercise of their functions in connection with the WTO.

4.   The privileges and immunities to be accorded by a Member to the WTO, its officials, and the representatives of its Members shall be similar to the privileges and immunities stipulated in the Convention on the Privileges and Immunities of the Specialized Agencies, approved by the General Assembly of the United Nations on 21 November 1947.

5.   The WTO may conclude a headquarters agreement.

Article IX

Decision-Making

1.   The WTO shall continue the practice of decision-making by consensus followed under GATT 1947.[1]   Except as otherwise provided, where a decision cannot be arrived at by consensus, the matter at issue shall be decided by voting.   At meetings of the Ministerial Conference and the General Council, each Member of the WTO shall have one vote.   Where the European Communities exercise their right to vote, they shall have a number of votes equal to the number of their member States[2] which are Members of the WTO. Decisions of the Ministerial Conference and the General Council shall be

---

1. The body concerned shall be deemed to have decided by consensus on a matter submitted for its consideration, if no Member, present at the meeting when the decision is taken, formally objects to the proposed decision.

2. The number of votes of the European Communities and their member States shall in no case exceed the number of the member States of the European Communities.

taken by a majority of the votes cast, unless otherwise provided in this Agreement or in the relevant Multilateral Trade Agreement.[3]

2.   The Ministerial Conference and the General Council shall have the exclusive authority to adopt interpretations of this Agreement and of the Multilateral Trade Agreements. In the case of an interpretation of a Multilateral Trade Agreement in Annex 1, they shall exercise their authority on the basis of a recommendation by the Council overseeing the functioning of that Agreement. The decision to adopt an interpretation shall be taken by a three-fourths majority of the Members. This paragraph shall not be used in a manner that would undermine the amendment provisions in Article X.

3.   In exceptional circumstances, the Ministerial Conference may decide to waive an obligation imposed on a Member by this Agreement or any of the Multilateral Trade Agreements, provided that any such decision shall be taken by three fourths[4] of the Members unless otherwise provided for in this paragraph.

   (a) A request for a waiver concerning this Agreement shall be submitted to the Ministerial Conference for consideration pursuant to the practice of decision-making by consensus. The Ministerial Conference shall establish a time-period, which shall not exceed 90 days, to consider the request. If consensus is not reached during the time-period, any decision to grant a waiver shall be taken by three fourths[4] of the Members.

   (b) A request for a waiver concerning the Multilateral Trade Agreements in Annexes 1A or 1B or 1C and their annexes shall be submitted initially to the Council for Trade in Goods, the Council for Trade in Services or the Council for TRIPS, respectively, for consideration during a time-period which shall not exceed 90 days. At the end of the time-period, the relevant Council shall submit a report to the Ministerial Conference.

4.   A decision by the Ministerial Conference granting a waiver shall state the exceptional circumstances justifying the decision, the terms and conditions governing the application of the waiver, and the date on which the waiver shall terminate. Any waiver granted for a period of more than one year shall be reviewed by the Ministerial Conference not later than one year after it is granted, and thereafter annually until the waiver terminates. In each review, the Ministerial Conference shall examine whether the exceptional circumstances justifying the waiver still exist and whether the terms and conditions attached to the waiver have been met. The Ministerial Conference, on the basis of the annual review, may extend, modify or terminate the waiver.

5.   Decisions under a Plurilateral Trade Agreement, including any decisions on interpretations and waivers, shall be governed by the provisions of that Agreement.

3. Decisions by the General Council when convened as the Dispute Settlement Body shall be taken only in accordance with the provisions of paragraph 4 of Article 2 of the Dispute Settlement Understanding.

4. A decision to grant a waiver in respect of any obligation subject to a transition period or a period for staged implementation that the requesting Member has not performed by the end of the relevant period shall be taken only by consensus.

Article X

Amendment

1. Any Member of the WTO may initiate a proposal to amend the provisions of this Agreement or the Multilateral Trade Agreements in Annex 1 by submitting such proposal to the Ministerial Conference. The Councils listed in paragraph 5 of Article IV may also submit to the Ministerial Conference proposals to amend the provisions of the corresponding Multilateral Trade Agreements in Annex 1 the functioning of which they oversee. Unless the Ministerial Conference decides on a longer period, for a period of 90 days after the proposal has been tabled formally at the Ministerial Conference any decision by the Ministerial Conference to submit the proposed amendment to the Members for acceptance shall be taken by consensus. Unless the provisions of paragraphs 2, 5 or 6 apply, that decision shall specify whether the provisions of paragraphs 3 or 4 shall apply. If consensus is reached, the Ministerial Conference shall forthwith submit the proposed amendment to the Members for acceptance. If consensus is not reached at a meeting of the Ministerial Conference within the established period, the Ministerial Conference shall decide by a two-thirds majority of the Members whether to submit the proposed amendment to the Members for acceptance. Except as provided in paragraphs 2, 5 and 6, the provisions of paragraph 3 shall apply to the proposed amendment, unless the Ministerial Conference decides by a three-fourths majority of the Members that the provisions of paragraph 4 shall apply.

2. Amendments to the provisions of this Article and to the provisions of the following Articles shall take effect only upon acceptance by all Members:

Article IX of this Agreement;

Articles I and II of GATT 1994;

Article II:1 of GATS;

Article 4 of the Agreement on TRIPS.

3. Amendments to provisions of this Agreement, or of the Multilateral Trade Agreements in Annexes 1A and 1C, other than those listed in paragraphs 2 and 6, of a nature that would alter the rights and obligations of the Members, shall take effect for the Members that have accepted them upon acceptance by two thirds of the Members and thereafter for each other Member upon acceptance by it. The Ministerial Conference may decide by a three-fourths majority of the Members that any amendment made effective under this paragraph is of such a nature that any Member which has not accepted it within a period specified by the Ministerial Conference in each case shall be free to withdraw from the WTO or to remain a Member with the consent of the Ministerial Conference.

4. Amendments to provisions of this Agreement or of the Multilateral Trade Agreements in Annexes 1A and 1C, other than those listed in paragraphs 2 and 6, of a nature that would not alter the rights and obligations of the Members, shall take effect for all Members upon acceptance by two thirds of the Members.

5. Except as provided in paragraph 2 above, amendments to Parts I, II and III of GATS and the respective annexes shall take effect for the Members

that have accepted them upon acceptance by two thirds of the Members and thereafter for each Member upon acceptance by it. The Ministerial Conference may decide by a three-fourths majority of the Members that any amendment made effective under the preceding provision is of such a nature that any Member which has not accepted it within a period specified by the Ministerial Conference in each case shall be free to withdraw from the WTO or to remain a Member with the consent of the Ministerial Conference. Amendments to Parts IV, V and VI of GATS and the respective annexes shall take effect for all Members upon acceptance by two thirds of the Members.

6. Notwithstanding the other provisions of this Article, amendments to the Agreement on TRIPS meeting the requirements of paragraph 2 of Article 71 thereof may be adopted by the Ministerial Conference without further formal acceptance process.

7. Any Member accepting an amendment to this Agreement or to a Multilateral Trade Agreement in Annex 1 shall deposit an instrument of acceptance with the Director–General of the WTO within the period of acceptance specified by the Ministerial Conference.

8. Any Member of the WTO may initiate a proposal to amend the provisions of the Multilateral Trade Agreements in Annexes 2 and 3 by submitting such proposal to the Ministerial Conference. The decision to approve amendments to the Multilateral Trade Agreement in Annex 2 shall be made by consensus and these amendments shall take effect for all Members upon approval by the Ministerial Conference. Decisions to approve amendments to the Multilateral Trade Agreement in Annex 3 shall take effect for all Members upon approval by the Ministerial Conference.

9. The Ministerial Conference, upon the request of the Members parties to a trade agreement, may decide exclusively by consensus to add that agreement to Annex 4. The Ministerial Conference, upon the request of the Members parties to a Plurilateral Trade Agreement, may decide to delete that Agreement from Annex 4.

10. Amendments to a Plurilateral Trade Agreement shall be governed by the provisions of that Agreement.

Article XI
Original Membership

1. The contracting parties to GATT 1947 as of the date of entry into force of this Agreement, and the European Communities, which accept this Agreement and the Multilateral Trade Agreements and for which Schedules of Concessions and Commitments are annexed to GATT 1994 and for which Schedules of Specific Commitments are annexed to GATS shall become original Members of the WTO.

2. The least-developed countries recognized as such by the United Nations will only be required to undertake commitments and concessions to the extent consistent with their individual development, financial and trade needs or their administrative and institutional capabilities.

Article XII
Accession

1. Any State or separate customs territory possessing full autonomy in the conduct of its external commercial relations and of the other matters

provided for in this Agreement and the Multilateral Trade Agreements may accede to this Agreement, on terms to be agreed between it and the WTO. Such accession shall apply to this Agreement and the Multilateral Trade Agreements annexed thereto.

2.   Decisions on accession shall be taken by the Ministerial Conference. The Ministerial Conference shall approve the agreement on the terms of accession by a two-thirds majority of the Members of the WTO.

3.   Accession to a Plurilateral Trade Agreement shall be governed by the provisions of that Agreement.

Article XIII

Non-Application of Multilateral Trade Agreements Between Particular Members

1.   This Agreement and the Multilateral Trade Agreements in Annexes 1 and 2 shall not apply as between any Member and any other Member if either of the Members, at the time either becomes a Member, does not consent to such application.

2.   Paragraph 1 may be invoked between original Members of the WTO which were contracting parties to GATT 1947 only where Article XXXV of that Agreement had been invoked earlier and was effective as between those contracting parties at the time of entry into force for them of this Agreement.

3.   Paragraph 1 shall apply between a Member and another Member which has acceded under Article XII only if the Member not consenting to the application has so notified the Ministerial Conference before the approval of the agreement on the terms of accession by the Ministerial Conference.

4.   The Ministerial Conference may review the operation of this Article in particular cases at the request of any Member and make appropriate recommendations.

5.   Non-application of a Plurilateral Trade Agreement between parties to that Agreement shall be governed by the provisions of that Agreement.

Article XIV

Acceptance, Entry into Force and Deposit

1.   This Agreement shall be open for acceptance, by signature or otherwise, by contracting parties to GATT 1947, and the European Communities, which are eligible to become original Members of the WTO in accordance with Article XI of this Agreement.   Such acceptance shall apply to this Agreement and the Multilateral Trade Agreements annexed hereto.   This Agreement and the Multilateral Trade Agreements annexed hereto shall enter into force on the date determined by Ministers in accordance with paragraph 3 of the Final Act Embodying the Results of the Uruguay Round of Multilateral Trade Negotiations and shall remain open for acceptance for a period of two years following that date unless the Ministers decide otherwise.   An acceptance following the entry into force of this Agreement shall enter into force on the 30th day following the date of such acceptance.

2.   A Member which accepts this Agreement after its entry into force shall implement those concessions and obligations in the Multilateral Trade

Agreements that are to be implemented over a period of time starting with the entry into force of this Agreement as if it had accepted this Agreement on the date of its entry into force.

3.   Until the entry into force of this Agreement, the text of this Agreement and the Multilateral Trade Agreements shall be deposited with the Director–General to the CONTRACTING PARTIES to GATT 1947. The Director–General shall promptly furnish a certified true copy of this Agreement and the Multilateral Trade Agreements, and a notification of each acceptance thereof, to each government and the European Communities having accepted this Agreement. This Agreement and the Multilateral Trade Agreements, and any amendments thereto, shall, upon the entry into force of this Agreement, be deposited with the Director–General of the WTO.

4.   The acceptance and entry into force of a Plurilateral Trade Agreement shall be governed by the provisions of that Agreement. Such Agreements shall be deposited with the Director–General to the CONTRACTING PARTIES to GATT 1947. Upon the entry into force of this Agreement, such Agreements shall be deposited with the Director–General of the WTO.

Article XV

Withdrawal

1.   Any Member may withdraw from this Agreement. Such withdrawal shall apply both to this Agreement and the Multilateral Trade Agreements and shall take effect upon the expiration of six months from the date on which written notice of withdrawal is received by the Director–General of the WTO.

2.   Withdrawal from a Plurilateral Trade Agreement shall be governed by the provisions of that Agreement.

Article XVI

Miscellaneous Provisions

1.   Except as otherwise provided under this Agreement or the Multilateral Trade Agreements, the WTO shall be guided by the decisions, procedures and customary practices followed by the CONTRACTING PARTIES to GATT 1947 and the bodies established in the framework of GATT 1947.

2.   To the extent practicable, the Secretariat of GATT 1947 shall become the Secretariat of the WTO, and the Director–General to the CONTRACTING PARTIES to GATT 1947, until such time as the Ministerial Conference has appointed a Director–General in accordance with paragraph 2 of Article VI of this Agreement, shall serve as Director–General of the WTO.

3.   In the event of a conflict between a provision of this Agreement and a provision of any of the Multilateral Trade Agreements, the provision of this Agreement shall prevail to the extent of the conflict.

4.   Each Member shall ensure the conformity of its laws, regulations and administrative procedures with its obligations as provided in the annexed Agreements.

5.   No reservations may be made in respect of any provision of this Agreement. Reservations in respect of any of the provisions of the Multilater-

al Trade Agreements may only be made to the extent provided for in those Agreements. Reservations in respect of a provision of a Plurilateral Trade Agreement shall be governed by the provisions of that Agreement.

6. This Agreement shall be registered in accordance with the provisions of Article 102 of the Charter of the United Nations.

DONE at Marrakesh this fifteenth day of April one thousand nine hundred and ninety-four, in a single copy, in the English, French and Spanish languages, each text being authentic.

————

Explanatory Notes:

The terms "country" or "countries" as used in this Agreement and the Multilateral Trade Agreements are to be understood to include any separate customs territory Member of the WTO.

In the case of a separate customs territory Member of the WTO, where an expression in this Agreement and the Multilateral Trade Agreements is qualified by the term "national", such expression shall be read as pertaining to that customs territory, unless otherwise specified.

LIST OF ANNEXES

ANNEX 1

ANNEX 1A: Multilateral Agreements on Trade in Goods

 General Agreement on Tariffs and Trade 1994

 Agreement on Agriculture

 Agreement on the Application of Sanitary and Phytosanitary Measures

 Agreement on Textiles and Clothing

 Agreement on Technical Barriers to Trade

 Agreement on Trade–Related Investment Measures

 Agreement on Implementation of Article VI of the General Agreement on
  Tariffs and Trade 1994

 Agreement on Implementation of Article VII of the General Agreement
  on Tariffs and Trade 1994

 Agreement on Preshipment Inspection

 Agreement on Rules of Origin

 Agreement on Import Licensing Procedures

 Agreement on Subsidies and Countervailing Measures

 Agreement on Safeguards

ANNEX 1B: General Agreement on Trade in Services and Annexes

ANNEX 1C: Agreement on Trade–Related Aspects of Intellectual Property
 Rights

ANNEX 2

Understanding on Rules and Procedures Governing the Settlement of Disputes

ANNEX 3

Trade Policy Review Mechanism

ANNEX 4

Plurilateral Trade Agreements

Agreement on Trade in Civil Aircraft

Agreement on Government Procurement

International Dairy Agreement

International Bovine Meat Agreement

ANNEX 1

ANNEX 1A

MULTILATERAL AGREEMENTS ON TRADE IN GOODS

General interpretative note to Annex 1A:

In the event of conflict between a provision of the General Agreement on Tariffs and Trade 1994 and a provision of another agreement in Annex 1A to the Agreement Establishing the World Trade Organization (referred to in the agreements in Annex 1A as the "WTO Agreement"), the provision of the other agreement shall prevail to the extent of the conflict.

Item 2

GENERAL AGREEMENT ON TARIFFS
AND TRADE 1947, AS AMENDED

The following is the text of the General Agreement on Tariffs and Trade, as amended and in force on January 1, 1995. The original GATT Agreement can be found at 55 U.N.T.S. 194, as well as in GATT Documents, "Basic Instruments and Selected Documents." The current version of the General Agreement can be found in BISD Vol. IV. A list of the various amending agreements can be found in Jackson, World Trade and the Law of GATT, Appendix C at 888–897, Bobbs–Merrill (1969), and since the general articles of the General Agreement have not been amended since 1969, that list contains all agreements which changed the text of the General Agreement. The following note is contained in the GATT, BISD Vol. IV (March, 1969):

The General Agreement is applied "provisionally" by all contracting parties. The original contracting parties, and also those former territories of Belgium, France, the Netherlands and the United Kingdom which, after attaining independence, acceded to the General Agreement under Article XXVI: 5(c), apply the GATT under the Protocol of Provisional Application, the text of which is reproduced in this volume. Chile applies the General Agreement under a Special Protocol of September 1948. The contracting parties which have acceded since 1948 apply the General Agreement under their respective Protocols of Accession.

For the convenience of the reader, asterisks mark the portions of the text which should be read in conjunction with notes and supplementary provisions in Annex I to the Agreement. In accordance with Article XXXIV, Annexes A to I are an integral part of the Agreement. The Schedules of tariff concessions annexed to the General Agreement (not here reproduced) are also, in accordance with Article II:7, an integral part of the Agreement.

By the Decision of 23 March 1965, the CONTRACTING PARTIES changed the title of the head of the GATT secretariat from "Executive Secretary" to "Director–General". However, in the absence of an amendment to the General Agreement to take account of this change, the title "Executive Secretary" has been retained in the text of Articles XVIII:12(e), XXIII:2, and XXVI:4, 5 and 6. The Decision of 23 March 1965 provides that the duties and powers conferred upon the Executive Secretary by the General Agreement "shall be exercised by the person holding the position of Director–General, who shall, for this purpose, also hold the position of Executive Secretary".

The General Agreement was terminated as of January 1, 1996 (see BISD, 41S/6). The text was incorporated by reference into GATT 1994 (see Item 3).

Table of Contents

Text of the General Agreement on Tariffs and Trade.

THE GENERAL AGREEMENT ON TARIFFS AND TRADE

The Governments of the Commonwealth of Australia, the Kingdom of Belgium, the United States of Brazil, Burma, Canada, Ceylon, the Republic of

Chile, the Republic of China, the Republic of Cuba, the Czechoslovak Republic, the French Republic, India, Lebanon, the Grand–Duchy of Luxemburg, the Kingdom of the Netherlands, New Zealand, the Kingdom of Norway, Pakistan, Southern Rhodesia, Syria, the Union of South Africa, the United Kingdom of Great Britain and Northern Ireland, and the United States of America:

Recognizing that their relations in the field of trade and economic endeavour should be conducted with a view to raising standards of living, ensuring full employment and a large and steadily growing volume of real income and effective demand, developing the full use of the resources of the world and expanding the production and exchange of goods,

Being desirous of contributing to these objectives by entering into reciprocal and mutually advantageous arrangements directed to the substantial reduction of tariffs and other barriers to trade and to the elimination of discriminatory treatment in international commerce,

Have through their Representatives agreed as follows:

PART I

Article I

General Most–Favoured–Nation Treatment

1.   With respect to customs duties and charges of any kind imposed on or in connection with importation or exportation or imposed on the international transfer of payments for imports or exports, and with respect to the method of levying such duties and charges, and with respect to all rules and formalities in connection with importation and exportation, and with respect to all matters referred to in paragraphs 2 and 4 of Article III,* any advantage, favour, privilege or immunity granted by any contracting party to any product originating in or destined for any other country shall be accorded immediately and unconditionally to the like product originating in or destined for the territories of all other contracting parties.

2.   The provisions of paragraph 1 of this Article shall not require the elimination of any preferences in respect of import duties or charges which do not exceed the levels provided for in paragraph 4 of this Article and which fall within the following descriptions:

(*a*) Preferences in force exclusively between two or more of the territories listed in Annex A, subject to the conditions set forth therein;

(*b*) Preferences in force exclusively between two or more territories which on July 1, 1939, were connected by common sovereignty or relations of protection or suzerainty and which are listed in Annexes B, C and D, subject to the conditions set forth therein;

(*c*) Preferences in force exclusively between the United States of America and the Republic of Cuba;

(*d*) Preferences in force exclusively between neighbouring countries listed in Annexes E and F.

3.   The provisions of paragraph 1 shall not apply to preferences between the countries formerly a part of the Ottoman Empire and detached from it on

July 24, 1923, provided such preferences are approved under paragraph 5 [†] of Article XXV, which shall be applied in this respect in the light of paragraph 1 of Article XXIX.

4. The margin of preference* on any product in respect of which a preference is permitted under paragraph 2 of this Article but is not specifically set forth as a maximum margin of preference in the appropriate Schedule annexed to this Agreement shall not exceed:

(*a*) in respect of duties or charges on any product described in such Schedule, the difference between the most-favoured-nation and preferential rates provided for therein; if no preferential rate is provided for, the preferential rate shall for the purposes of this paragraph be taken to be that in force on April 10, 1947, and, if no most-favoured-nation rate is provided for, the margin shall not exceed the difference between the most-favoured-nation and preferential rates existing on April 10, 1947;

(*b*) in respect of duties or charges on any product not described in the appropriate Schedule, the difference between the most-favoured-nation and preferential rates existing on April 10, 1947.

In the case of the contracting parties named in Annex G, the date of April 10, 1947, referred to in sub-paragraphs (*a*) and (*b*) of this paragraph shall be replaced by the respective dates set forth in that Annex.

Article II

Schedules of Concessions

1. (*a*) Each contracting party shall accord to the commerce of the other contracting parties treatment no less favourable than that provided for in the appropriate Part of the appropriate Schedule annexed to this Agreement.

(*b*) The products described in Part I of the Schedule relating to any contracting party, which are the products of territories of other contracting parties, shall, on their importation into the territory to which the Schedule relates, and subject to the terms, conditions or qualifications set forth in that Schedule, be exempt from ordinary customs duties in excess of those set forth and provided for therein. Such products shall also be exempt from all other duties or charges of any kind imposed on or in connection with importation in excess of those imposed on the date of this Agreement or those directly and mandatorily required to be imposed thereafter by legislation in force in the importing territory on that date.

(*c*) The products described in Part II of the Schedule relating to any contracting party which are the products of territories entitled under Article I to receive preferential treatment upon importation into the territory to which the Schedule relates shall, on their importation into such territory, and subject to the terms, conditions or qualifications set forth in that Schedule, be exempt from ordinary customs duties in excess of those set forth and provided for in Part II of that Schedule. Such products shall also be exempt from all other duties or charges of any kind imposed on or in connection with importation in excess of those imposed on the date of this Agreement or those directly and mandatorily required to be imposed thereafter by legislation in force in the importing territory on that date. Nothing in this Article shall

† The authentic text erroneously reads "sub-paragraph 5(a)".

prevent any contracting party from maintaining its requirements existing on the date of this Agreement as to the eligibility of goods for entry at preferential rates of duty.

2.   Nothing in this Article shall prevent any contracting party from imposing at any time on the importation of any product:

(*a*) a charge equivalent to an internal tax imposed consistently with the provisions of paragraph 2 of Article III* in respect of the like domestic product or in respect of an article from which the imported product has been manufactured or produced in whole or in part;

(*b*) any anti-dumping or countervailing duty applied consistently with the provisions of Article VI;*

(*c*) fees or other charges commensurate with the cost of services rendered.

3.   No contracting party shall alter its method of determining dutiable value or of converting currencies so as to impair the value of any of the concessions provided for in the appropriate Schedule annexed to this Agreement.

4.   If any contracting party establishes, maintains or authorizes, formally or in effect, a monopoly of the importation of any product described in the appropriate Schedule annexed to this Agreement, such monopoly shall not, except as provided for in that Schedule or as otherwise agreed between the parties which initially negotiated the concession, operate so as to afford protection on the average in excess of the amount of protection provided for in that Schedule.   The provisions of this paragraph shall not limit the use by contracting parties of any form of assistance to domestic producers permitted by other provisions of this Agreement.*

5.   If any contracting party considers that a product is not receiving from another contracting party the treatment which the first contracting party believes to have been contemplated by a concession provided for in the appropriate Schedule annexed to this Agreement, it shall bring the matter directly to the attention of the other contracting party.   If the latter agrees that the treatment contemplated was that claimed by the first contracting party, but declares that such treatment cannot be accorded because a court or other proper authority has ruled to the effect that the product involved cannot be classified under the tariff laws of such contracting party so as to permit the treatment contemplated in this Agreement, the two contracting parties, together with any other contracting parties substantially interested, shall enter promptly into further negotiations with a view to a compensatory adjustment of the matter.

6.   (*a*) The specific duties and charges included in the Schedules relating to contracting parties members of the International Monetary Fund, and margins of preference in specific duties and charges maintained by such contracting parties, are expressed in the appropriate currency at the par value accepted or provisionally recognized by the Fund at the date of this Agreement.   Accordingly, in case this par value is reduced consistently with the Articles of Agreement of the International Monetary Fund by more than twenty per centum, such specific duties and charges and margins of preference may be adjusted to take account of such reduction; *Provided* that the

CONTRACTING PARTIES (i.e., the contracting parties acting jointly as provided for in Article XXV) concur that such adjustments will not impair the value of the concessions provided for in the appropriate Schedule or elsewhere in this Agreement, due account being taken of all factors which may influence the need for, or urgency of, such adjustments.

(b) Similar provisions shall apply to any contracting party not a member of the Fund, as from the date on which such contracting party becomes a member of the Fund or enters into a special exchange agreement in pursuance of Article XV.

7.   The Schedules annexed to this Agreement are hereby made an integral part of Part I of this Agreement.

PART II
Article III*
National Treatment on Internal Taxation and Regulation

1.   The contracting parties recognize that internal taxes and other internal charges, and laws, regulations and requirements affecting the internal sale, offering for sale, purchase, transportation, distribution or use of products, and internal quantitative regulations requiring the mixture, processing or use of products in specified amounts or proportions, should not be applied to imported or domestic products so as to afford protection to domestic production.*

2.   The products of the territory of any contracting party imported into the territory of any other contracting party shall not be subject, directly or indirectly, to internal taxes or other internal charges of any kind in excess of those applied, directly or indirectly, to like domestic products. Moreover, no contracting party shall otherwise apply internal taxes or other internal charges to imported or domestic products in a manner contrary to the principles set forth in paragraph 1.*

3.   With respect to any existing internal tax which is inconsistent with the provisions of paragraph 2, but which is specifically authorized under a trade agreement, in force on April 10, 1947, in which the import duty on the taxed product is bound against increase, the contracting party imposing the tax shall be free to postpone the application of the provisions of paragraph 2 to such tax until such time as it can obtain release from the obligations of such trade agreement in order to permit the increase of such duty to the extent necessary to compensate for the elimination of the protective element of the tax.

4.   The products of the territory of any contracting party imported into the territory of any other contracting party shall be accorded treatment no less favourable than that accorded to like products of national origin in respect of all laws, regulations and requirements affecting their internal sale, offering for sale, purchase, transportation, distribution or use. The provisions of this paragraph shall not prevent the application of differential internal transportation charges which are based exclusively on the economic operation of the means of transport and not on the nationality of the product.

5.   No contracting party shall establish or maintain any internal quantitative regulation relating to the mixture, processing or use of products in

specified amounts or proportions which requires, directly or indirectly, that any specified amount or proportion of any product which is the subject of the regulation must be supplied from domestic sources. Moreover, no contracting party shall otherwise apply internal quantitative regulations in a manner contrary to the principles set forth in paragraph 1.*

6. The provisions of paragraph 5 shall not apply to any internal quantitative regulation in force in the territory of any contracting party on July 1, 1939, April 10, 1947, or March 24, 1948, at the option of that contracting party; *Provided* that any such regulation which is contrary to the provisions of paragraph 5 shall not be modified to the detriment of imports and shall be treated as a customs duty for the purpose of negotiation.

7. No internal quantitative regulation relating to the mixture, processing or use of products in specified amounts or proportions shall be applied in such a manner as to allocate any such amount or proportion among external sources of supply.

8. (*a*) The provisions of this Article shall not apply to laws, regulations or requirements governing the procurement by governmental agencies of products purchased for governmental purposes and not with a view to commercial resale or with a view to use in the production of goods for commercial sale.

(*b*) The provisions of this Article shall not prevent the payment of subsidies exclusively to domestic producers, including payments to domestic producers derived from the proceeds of internal taxes or charges applied consistently with the provisions of this Article and subsidies effected through governmental purchases of domestic products.

9. The contracting parties recognize that internal maximum price control measures, even though conforming to the other provisions of this Article, can have effects prejudicial to the interests of contracting parties supplying imported products. Accordingly, contracting parties applying such measures shall take account of the interests of exporting contracting parties with a view to avoiding to the fullest practicable extent such prejudicial effects.

10. The provisions of this Article shall not prevent any contracting party from establishing or maintaining internal quantitative regulations relating to exposed cinematograph films and meeting the requirements of Article IV.

Article IV

Special Provisions Relating to Cinematograph Films

If any contracting party establishes or maintains internal quantitative regulations relating to exposed cinematograph films, such regulations shall take the form of screen quotas which shall conform to the following requirements:

(*a*) Screen quotas may require the exhibition of cinematograph films of national origin during a specified minimum proportion of the total screen time actually utilized, over a specified period of not less than one year, in the commercial exhibition of all films of whatever origin, and shall be computed on the basis of screen time per theatre per year or the equivalent thereof;

(b) With the exception of screen time reserved for films of national origin under a screen quota, screen time including that released by administrative action from screen time reserved for films of national origin, shall not be allocated formally or in effect among sources of supply;

(c) Notwithstanding the provisions of sub-paragraph (b) of this Article, any contracting party may maintain screen quotas conforming to the requirements of sub-paragraph (a) of this Article which reserve a minimum proportion of screen time for films of a specified origin other than that of the contracting party imposing such screen quotas; *Provided* that no such minimum proportion of screen time shall be increased above the level in effect on April 10, 1947;

(d) Screen quotas shall be subject to negotiation for their limitation, liberalization or elimination.

Article V

Freedom of Transit

1. Goods (including baggage), and also vessels and other means of transport, shall be deemed to be in transit across the territory of a contracting party when the passage across such territory, with or without trans-shipment, warehousing, breaking bulk, or change in the mode of transport, is only a portion of a complete journey beginning and terminating beyond the frontier of the contracting party across whose territory the traffic passes. Traffic of this nature is termed in this Article "traffic in transit".

2. There shall be freedom of transit through the territory of each contracting party, via the routes most convenient for international transit, for traffic in transit to or from the territory of other contracting parties. No distinction shall be made which is based on the flag of vessels, the place of origin, departure, entry, exit or destination, or on any circumstances relating to the ownership of goods, of vessels or of other means of transport.

3. Any contracting party may require that traffic in transit through its territory be entered at the proper custom house, but, except in cases of failure to comply with applicable customs laws and regulations, such traffic coming from or going to the territory of other contracting parties shall not be subject to any unnecessary delays or restrictions and shall be exempt from customs duties and from all transit duties or other charges imposed in respect of transit, except charges for transportation or those commensurate with administrative expenses entailed by transit or with the cost of services rendered.

4. All charges and regulations imposed by contracting parties on traffic in transit to or from the territories of other contracting parties shall be reasonable, having regard to the conditions of the traffic.

5. With respect to all charges, regulations and formalities in connection with transit, each contracting party shall accord to traffic in transit to or from the territory of any other contracting party treatment no less favourable than the treatment accorded to traffic in transit to or from any third country.*

6. Each contracting party shall accord to products which have been in transit through the territory of any other contracting party treatment no less favourable than that which would have been accorded to such products had

they been transported from their place of origin to their destination without going through the territory of such other contracting party. Any contracting party shall, however, be free to maintain its requirements of direct consignment existing on the date of this Agreement, in respect of any goods in regard to which such direct consignment is a requisite condition of eligibility for entry of the goods at preferential rates of duty or has relation to the contracting party's prescribed method of valuation for duty purposes.

7.   The provisions of this Article shall not apply to the operation of aircraft in transit, but shall apply to air transit of goods (including baggage).

Article VI

Anti-dumping and Countervailing Duties

1.   The contracting parties recognize that dumping, by which products of one country are introduced into the commerce of another country at less than the normal value of the products, is to be condemned if it causes or threatens material injury to an established industry in the territory of a contracting party or materially retards the establishment of a domestic industry. For the purposes of this Article, a product is to be considered as being introduced into the commerce of an importing country at less than its normal value, if the price of the product exported from one country to another

(a) is less than the comparable price, in the ordinary course of trade, for the like product when destined for consumption in the exporting country, or,

(b) in the absence of such domestic price, is less than either

(i) the highest comparable price for the like product for export to any third country in the ordinary course of trade, or

(ii) the cost of production of the product in the country of origin plus a reasonable addition for selling cost and profit.

Due allowance shall be made in each case for differences in conditions and terms of sale, for differences in taxation, and for other differences affecting price comparability.*

2.   In order to offset or prevent dumping, a contracting party may levy on any dumped product an anti-dumping duty not greater in amount than the margin of dumping in respect of such product. For the purposes of this Article, the margin of dumping is the price difference determined in accordance with the provisions of paragraph 1.*

3.   No countervailing duty shall be levied on any product of the territory of any contracting party imported into the territory of another contracting party in excess of an amount equal to the estimated bounty or subsidy determined to have been granted, directly or indirectly, on the manufacture, production or export of such product in the country of origin or exportation, including any special subsidy to the transportation of a particular product. The term "countervailing duty" shall be understood to mean a special duty levied for the purpose of offsetting any bounty or subsidy bestowed, directly or indirectly, upon the manufacture, production or export of any merchandise.*

4.   No product of the territory of any contracting party imported into the territory of any other contracting party shall be subject to anti-dumping or

countervailing duty by reason of the exemption of such product from duties or taxes borne by the like product when destined for consumption in the country of origin or exportation, or by reason of the refund of such duties or taxes.

5.   No product of the territory of any contracting party imported into the territory of any other contracting party shall be subject to both anti-dumping and countervailing duties to compensate for the same situation of dumping or export subsidization.

6.   (*a*) No contracting party shall levy any anti-dumping or countervailing duty on the importation of any product of the territory of another contracting party unless it determines that the effect of the dumping or subsidization, as the case may be, is such as to cause or threaten material injury to an established domestic industry, or is such as to retard materially the establishment of a domestic industry.

(*b*) The CONTRACTING PARTIES may waive the requirement of sub-paragraph (*a*) of this paragraph so as to permit a contracting party to levy an anti-dumping or countervailing duty on the importation of any product for the purpose of offsetting dumping or subsidization which causes or threatens material injury to an industry in the territory of another contracting party exporting the product concerned to the territory of the importing contracting party.   The CONTRACTING PARTIES shall waive the requirements of sub-paragraph (*a*) of this paragraph, so as to permit the levying of a countervailing duty, in cases in which they find that a subsidy is causing or threatening material injury to an industry in the territory of another contracting party exporting the product concerned to the territory of the importing contracting party.*

(*c*) In exceptional circumstances, however, where delay might cause damage which would be difficult to repair, a contracting party may levy a countervailing duty for the purpose referred to in sub-paragraph (*b*) of this paragraph without the prior approval of the CONTRACTING PARTIES; *Provided* that such action shall be reported immediately to the CONTRACTING PARTIES and that the countervailing duty shall be withdrawn promptly if the CONTRACTING PARTIES disapprove.

7.   A system for the stabilization of the domestic price or of the return to domestic producers of a primary commodity, independently of the movements of export prices, which results at times in the sale of the commodity for export at a price lower than the comparable price charged for the like commodity to buyers in the domestic market, shall be presumed not to result in material injury within the meaning of paragraph 6 if it is determined by consultation among the contracting parties substantially interested in the commodity concerned that:

    (*a*) the system has also resulted in the sale of the commodity for export at a price higher than the comparable price charged for the like commodity to buyers in the domestic market, and

    (*b*) the system is so operated, either because of the effective regulation of production, or otherwise, as not to stimulate exports unduly or otherwise seriously prejudice the interests of other contracting parties.

Article VII

Valuation for Customs Purposes

1.   The contracting parties recognize the validity of the general principles of valuation set forth in the following paragraphs of this Article, and they undertake to give effect to such principles, in respect of all products subject to duties or other charges* or restrictions on importation and exportation based upon or regulated in any manner by value.   Moreover, they shall, upon a request by another contracting party review the operation of any of their laws or regulations relating to value for customs purposes in the light of these principles.   The CONTRACTING PARTIES may request from contracting parties reports on steps taken by them in pursuance of the provisions of this Article.

2.   (*a*) The value for customs purposes of imported merchandise should be based on the actual value of the imported merchandise on which duty is assessed, or of like merchandise, and should not be based on the value of merchandise of national origin or on arbitrary or fictitious values.*

(*b*) "Actual value" should be the price at which, at a time and place determined by the legislation of the country of importation, such or like merchandise is sold or offered for sale in the ordinary course of trade under fully competitive conditions.   To the extent to which the price of such or like merchandise is governed by the quantity in a particular transaction, the price to be considered should uniformly be related to either (i) comparable quantities, or (ii) quantities not less favourable to importers than those in which the greater volume of the merchandise is sold in the trade between the countries of exportation and importation.*

(*c*) When the actual value is not ascertainable in accordance with subparagraph (*b*) of this paragraph, the value for customs purposes should be based on the nearest ascertainable equivalent of such value.*

3.   The value for customs purposes of any imported product should not include the amount of any internal tax, applicable within the country of origin or export, from which the imported product has been exempted or has been or will be relieved by means of refund.

4.   (*a*) Except as otherwise provided for in this paragraph, where it is necessary for the purposes of paragraph 2 of this Article for a contracting party to convert into its own currency a price expressed in the currency of another country, the conversion rate of exchange to be used shall be based, for each currency involved, on the par value as established pursuant to the Articles of Agreement of the International Monetary Fund or on the rate of exchange recognized by the Fund, or on the par value established in accordance with a special exchange agreement entered into pursuant to Article XV of this Agreement.

(*b*) Where no such established par value and no such recognized rate of exchange exist, the conversion rate shall reflect effectively the current value of such currency in commercial transactions.

(*c*) The CONTRACTING PARTIES, in agreement with the International Monetary Fund, shall formulate rules governing the conversion by contracting parties of any foreign currency in respect of which multiple rates of exchange are maintained consistently with the Articles of Agreement of the International Monetary Fund. Any contracting party may apply such rules in respect of such foreign currencies for the purposes of paragraph 2 of this Article as an alternative to the use of par values. Until such rules are adopted by the CONTRACTING PARTIES, any contracting party may employ, in respect of any such foreign currency, rules of conversion for the purposes of paragraph 2 of this Article which are designed to reflect effectively the value of such foreign currency in commercial transactions.

(d) Nothing in this paragraph shall be construed to require any contracting party to alter the method of converting currencies for customs purposes which is applicable in its territory on the date of this Agreement, if such alteration would have the effect of increasing generally the amounts of duty payable.

5. The bases and methods for determining the value of products subject to duties or other charges or restrictions based upon or regulated in any manner by value should be stable and should be given sufficient publicity to enable traders to estimate, with a reasonable degree of certainty, the value for customs purposes.

Article VIII

*Fees and Formalities Connected With Importation and Exportation**

1. (a) All fees and charges of whatever character (other than import and export duties and other than taxes within the purview of Article III) imposed by contracting parties on or in connexion with importation or exportation shall be limited in amount to the approximate cost of services rendered and shall not represent an indirect protection to domestic products or a taxation of imports or exports for fiscal purposes.

(b) The contracting parties recognize the need for reducing the number and diversity of fees and charges referred to in sub-paragraph (a).

(c) The contracting parties also recognize the need for minimizing the incidence and complexity of import and export formalities and for decreasing and simplifying import and export documentation requirements.*

2. A contracting party shall, upon request by another contracting party or by the CONTRACTING PARTIES, review the operation of its laws and regulations in the light of the provisions of this Article.

3. No contracting party shall impose substantial penalties for minor breaches of customs regulations or procedural requirements. In particular, no penalty in respect of any omission or mistake in customs documentation which is easily rectifiable and obviously made without fraudulent intent or gross negligence shall be greater than necessary to serve merely as a warning.

4. The provisions of this Article shall extend to fees, charges, formalities and requirements imposed by governmental authorities in connexion with importation and exportation, including those relating to:

(a) consular transactions, such as consular invoices and certificates;

(b) quantitative restrictions;

(c) licensing;

(d) exchange control;

(*e*) statistical services;

(*f*) documents, documentation and certification;

(*g*) analysis and inspection; and

(*h*) quarantine, sanitation and fumigation.

Article IX

Marks of Origin

1. Each contracting party shall accord to the products of the territories of other contracting parties treatment with regard to marking requirements no less favourable than the treatment accorded to like products of any third country.

2. The contracting parties recognize that, in adopting and enforcing laws and regulations relating to marks of origin, the difficulties and inconveniences which such measures may cause to the commerce and industry of exporting countries should be reduced to a minimum, due regard being had to the necessity of protecting consumers against fraudulent or misleading indications.

3. Whenever it is administratively practicable to do so, contracting parties should permit required marks of origin to be affixed at the time of importation.

4. The laws and regulations of contracting parties relating to the marking of imported products shall be such as to permit compliance without seriously damaging the products, or materially reducing their value, or unreasonably increasing their cost.

5. As a general rule, no special duty or penalty should be imposed by any contracting party for failure to comply with marking requirements prior to importation unless corrective marking is unreasonably delayed or deceptive marks have been affixed or the required marking has been intentionally omitted.

6. The contracting parties shall co-operate with each other with a view to preventing the use of trade names in such manner as to misrepresent the true origin of a product, to the detriment of such distinctive regional or geographical names of products of the territory of a contracting party as are protected by its legislation. Each contracting party shall accord full and sympathetic consideration to such requests or representations as may be made by any other contracting party regarding the application of the undertaking set forth in the preceding sentence to names of products which have been communicated to it by the other contracting party.

Article X

Publication and Administration of Trade Regulations

1. Laws, regulations, judicial decisions and administrative rulings of general application, made effective by any contracting party, pertaining to the classification or the valuation of products for customs purposes, or to rates of duty, taxes or other charges, or to requirements, restrictions or prohibitions on imports or exports or on the transfer of payments therefor, or affecting their sale, distribution, transportation, insurance, warehousing, inspection,

exhibition, processing, mixing or other use, shall be published promptly in such a manner as to enable governments and traders to become acquainted with them. Agreements affecting international trade policy which are in force between the government or a governmental agency of any contracting party and the government or governmental agency of any other contracting party shall also be published. The provisions of this paragraph shall not require any contracting party to disclose confidential information which would impede law enforcement or otherwise be contrary to the public interest or would prejudice the legitimate commercial interests of particular enterprises, public or private.

2. No measure of general application taken by any contracting party effecting an advance in a rate of duty or other charge on imports under an established and uniform practice, or imposing a new or more burdensome requirement, restriction or prohibition on imports, or on the transfer of payments therefor, shall be enforced before such measure has been officially published.

3. (*a*) Each contracting party shall administer in a uniform, impartial and reasonable manner all its laws, regulations, decisions and rulings of the kind described in paragraph 1 of this Article.

(*b*) Each contracting party shall maintain, or institute as soon as practicable, judicial, arbitral or administrative tribunals or procedures for the purpose, *inter alia*, of the prompt review and correction of administrative action relating to customs matters. Such tribunals or procedures shall be independent of the agencies entrusted with administrative enforcement and their decisions shall be implemented by, and shall govern the practice of, such agencies unless an appeal is lodged with a court or tribunal of superior jurisdiction within the time prescribed for appeals to be lodged by importers; *Provided* that the central administration of such agency may take steps to obtain a review of the matter in another proceeding if there is good cause to believe that the decision is inconsistent with established principles of law or the actual facts.

(*c*) The provisions of sub-paragraph (*b*) of this paragraph shall not require the elimination or substitution of procedures in force in the territory of a contracting party on the date of this Agreement which in fact provide for an objective and impartial review of administrative action even though such procedures are not fully or formally independent of the agencies entrusted with administrative enforcement. Any contracting party employing such procedures shall, upon request, furnish the CONTRACTING PARTIES with full information thereon in order that they may determine whether such procedures conform to the requirements of this sub-paragraph.

Article XI*

General Elimination of Quantitative Restrictions

1. No prohibitions or restrictions other than duties, taxes or other charges, whether made effective through quotas, import or export licenses or other measures, shall be instituted or maintained by any contracting party on the importation of any product of the territory of any other contracting party or on the exportation or sale for export of any product destined for the territory of any other contracting party.

2. The provisions of paragraph 1 of this Article shall not extend to the following:

(*a*) Export prohibitions or restrictions temporarily applied to prevent or relieve critical shortages of foodstuffs or other products essential to the exporting contracting party;

(*b*) Import and export prohibitions or restrictions necessary to the application of standards or regulations for the classification, grading or marketing of commodities in international trade;

(*c*) Import restrictions on any agricultural or fisheries product, imported in any form,* necessary to the enforcement of governmental measures which operate:

(i) to restrict the quantities of the like domestic product permitted to be marketed or produced, or, if there is no substantial domestic production of the like product, of a domestic product for which the imported product can be directly substituted; or

(ii) to remove a temporary surplus of the like domestic product, or, if there is no substantial domestic production of the like product, of a domestic product for which the imported product can be directly substituted, by making the surplus available to certain groups of domestic consumers free of charge or at prices below the current market level; or

(iii) to restrict the quantities permitted to be produced of any animal product the production of which is directly dependent, wholly or mainly, on the imported commodity, if the domestic production of that commodity is relatively negligible.

Any contracting party applying restrictions on the importation of any product pursuant to sub-paragraph (*c*) of this paragraph shall give public notice of the total quantity or value of the product permitted to be imported during a specified future period and of any change in such quantity or value. Moreover, any restrictions applied under (i) above shall not be such as will reduce the total of imports relative to the total of domestic production, as compared with the proportion which might reasonably be expected to rule between the two in the absence of restrictions. In determining this proportion, the contracting party shall pay due regard to the proportion prevailing during a previous representative period and to any special factors* which may have affected or may be affecting the trade in the product concerned.

Article XII*

Restrictions to Safeguard the Balance of Payments

1. Notwithstanding the provisions of paragraph 1 of Article XI, any contracting party, in order to safeguard its external financial position and its balance of payments, may restrict the quantity or value of merchandise permitted to be imported, subject to the provisions of the following paragraphs of this Article.

2. (*a*) Import restrictions instituted, maintained or intensified by a contracting party under this Article shall not exceed those necessary:

(i) to forestall the imminent threat of, or to stop, a serious decline in its monetary reserves, or

(ii) in the case of a contracting party with very low monetary reserves, to achieve a reasonable rate of increase in its reserves.

Due regard shall be paid in either case to any special factors which may be affecting the reserves of such contracting party or its need for reserves, including, where special external credits or other resources are available to it, the need to provide for the appropriate use of such credits or resources.

(*b*) Contracting parties applying restrictions under sub-paragraph (*a*) of this paragraph shall progressively relax them as such conditions improve, maintaining them only to the extent that the conditions specified in that sub-paragraph still justify their application. They shall eliminate the restrictions when conditions would no longer justify their institution or maintenance under that sub-paragraph.

3. (*a*) Contracting parties undertake, in carrying out their domestic policies, to pay due regard to the need for maintaining or restoring equilibrium in their balance of payments on a sound and lasting basis and to the desirability of avoiding an uneconomic employment of productive resources. They recognize that, in order to achieve these ends, it is desirable so far as possible to adopt measures which expand rather than contract international trade.

(*b*) Contracting parties applying restrictions under this Article may determine the incidence of the restrictions on imports of different products or classes of products in such a way as to give priority to the importation of those products which are more essential.

(*c*) Contracting parties applying restrictions under this Article undertake:

(i) to avoid unnecessary damage to the commercial or economic interests of any other contracting party;*

(ii) not to apply restrictions so as to prevent unreasonably the importation of any description of goods in minimum commercial quantities the exclusion of which would impair regular channels of trade; and

(iii) not to apply restrictions which would prevent the importation of commercial samples or prevent compliance with patent, trade mark, copyright, or similar procedures.

(*d*) The contracting parties recognize that, as a result of domestic policies directed towards the achievement and maintenance of full and productive employment or towards the development of economic resources, a contracting party may experience a high level of demand for imports involving a threat to its monetary reserves of the sort referred to in paragraph 2(*a*)of this Article. Accordingly, a contracting party otherwise complying with the provisions of this Article shall not be required to withdraw or modify restrictions on the ground that a change in those policies would render unnecessary restrictions which it is applying under this Article.

4. (*a*) Any contracting party applying new restrictions or raising the general level of its existing restrictions by a substantial intensification of the measures applied under this Article shall immediately after instituting or intensifying such restrictions (or, in circumstances in which prior consultation

is practicable, before doing so) consult with the CONTRACTING PARTIES as to the nature of its balance of payments difficulties, alternative corrective measures which may be available, and the possible effect of the restrictions on the economies of other contracting parties.

(*b*) On the date to be determined by them,* the CONTRACTING PARTIES shall review all restrictions still applied under this Article on that date. Beginning one year after that date, contracting parties applying import restrictions under this Article shall enter into consultations of the type provided for in sub-paragraph (*a*)of this paragraph with the CONTRACTING PARTIES annually.

(*c*) (i) If, in the course of consultations with a contracting party under sub-paragraph (*a*) or (*b*) above, the CONTRACTING PARTIES find that the restrictions are not consistent with the provisions of this Article or with those of Article XIII (subject to the provisions of Article XIV), they shall indicate the nature of the inconsistency and may advise that the restrictions be suitably modified.

(ii) If, however, as a result of the consultations, the CONTRACTING PARTIES determine that the restrictions are being applied in a manner involving an inconsistency of a serious nature with the provisions of this Article or with those of Article XIII (subject to the provisions of Article XIV) and that damage to the trade of any contracting party is caused or threatened thereby, they shall so inform the contracting party applying the restrictions and shall make appropriate recommendations for securing conformity with such provisions within a specified period of time. If such contracting party does not comply with these recommendations within the specified period, the CONTRACTING PARTIES may release any contracting party the trade of which is adversely affected by the restrictions from such obligations under this Agreement towards the contracting party applying the restrictions as they determine to be appropriate in the circumstances.

(*d*) The CONTRACTING PARTIES shall invite any contracting party which is applying restrictions under this Article to enter into consultations with them at the request of any contracting party which can establish a *prima facie* case that the restrictions are inconsistent with the provisions of this Article or with those of Article XIII (subject to the provisions of Article XIV) and that its trade is adversely affected thereby. However, no such invitation shall be issued unless the CONTRACTING PARTIES have ascertained that direct discussions between the contracting parties concerned have not been successful. If, as a result of the consultations with the CONTRACTING PARTIES, no agreement is reached and they determine that the restrictions are being applied inconsistently with such provisions, and that damage to the trade of the contracting party initiating the procedure is caused or threatened thereby, they shall recommend the withdrawal or modification of the restrictions. If the restrictions are not withdrawn or modified within such time as the CONTRACTING PARTIES may prescribe, they may release the contracting party initiating the procedure from such obligations under this Agreement towards the contracting party applying the restrictions as they determine to be appropriate in the circumstances.

(e) In proceeding under this paragraph, the CONTRACTING PARTIES shall have due regard to any special external factors adversely affecting the export trade of the contracting party applying restrictions.*

(f) Determinations under this paragraph shall be rendered expeditiously and, if possible, within sixty days of the initiation of the consultations.

5.   If there is a persistent and widespread application of import restrictions under this Article, indicating the existence of a general disequilibrium which is restricting international trade, the CONTRACTING PARTIES shall initiate discussions to consider whether other measures might be taken, either by those contracting parties the balances of payments of which are under pressure or by those the balances of payments of which are tending to be exceptionally favourable, or by any appropriate intergovernmental organization, to remove the underlying causes of the disequilibrium. On the invitation of the CONTRACTING PARTIES, contracting parties shall participate in such discussions.

Article XIII*

Non-discriminatory Administration of Quantitative Restrictions

1.   No prohibition or restriction shall be applied by any contracting party on the importation of any product of the territory of any other contracting party or on the exportation of any product destined for the territory of any other contracting party, unless the importation of the like product of all third countries or the exportation of the like product to all third countries is similarly prohibited or restricted.

2.   In applying import restrictions to any product, contracting parties shall aim at a distribution of trade in such product approaching as closely as possible the shares which the various contracting parties might be expected to obtain in the absence of such restrictions, and to this end shall observe the following provisions:

(a) Wherever practicable, quotas representing the total amount of permitted imports (whether allocated among supplying countries or not) shall be fixed, and notice given of their amount in accordance with paragraph 3(b) of this Article;

(b) In cases in which quotas are not practicable, the restrictions may be applied by means of import licences or permits without a quota;

(c) Contracting parties shall not, except for purposes of operating quotas allocated in accordance with sub-paragraph (d) of this paragraph, require that import licences or permits be utilized for the importation of the product concerned from a particular country or source;

(d) In cases in which a quota is allocated among supplying countries, the contracting party applying the restrictions may seek agreement with respect to the allocation of shares in the quota with all other contracting parties having a substantial interest in supplying the product concerned. In cases in which this method is not reasonably practicable, the contracting party concerned shall allot to contracting parties having a substantial interest in supplying the product shares based upon the proportions, supplied by such contracting parties during a previous representative period, of the total quantity or value of imports of the product, due account being taken of any special factors which may have affected or may be affecting the trade in the product. No conditions or formalities shall be imposed which would prevent any contracting party from utilizing fully the share of any such total quantity or value which has been allotted to it, subject to importation being made within any prescribed period to which the quota may relate.*

3. (a) In cases in which import licences are issued in connection with import restrictions, the contracting party applying the restrictions shall provide, upon the request of any contracting party having an interest in the trade in the product concerned, all relevant information concerning the administration of the restrictions, the import licences granted over a recent period and the distribution of such licences among supplying countries; *Provided* that there shall be no obligation to supply information as to the names of importing or supplying enterprises.

(b) In the case of import restrictions involving the fixing of quotas, the contracting party applying the restrictions shall give public notice of the total quantity or value of the product or products which will be permitted to be imported during a specified future period and of any change in such quantity or value. Any supplies of the product in question which were *en route* at the time at which public notice was given shall not be excluded from entry; *Provided* that they may be counted so far as practicable, against the quantity permitted to be imported in the period in question, and also, where necessary, against the quantities permitted to be imported in the next following period or periods; and *Provided* further that if any contracting party customarily exempts from such restrictions products entered for consumption or withdrawn from warehouse for consumption during a period of thirty days after the day of such public notice, such practice shall be considered full compliance with this sub-paragraph.

(c) In the case of quotas allocated among supplying countries, the contracting party applying the restrictions shall promptly inform all other contracting parties having an interest in supplying the product concerned of the shares in the quota currently allocated, by quantity or value, to the various supplying countries and shall give public notice thereof.

4. With regard to restrictions applied in accordance with paragraph 2(*d*) of this Article or under paragraph 2(*c*) of Article XI, the selection of a* representative period for any product and the appraisal of any special factors affecting the trade in the product shall be made initially by the contracting party applying the restriction; *Provided* that such contracting party shall, upon the request of any other contracting party having a substantial interest in supplying that product or upon the request of the CONTRACTING PARTIES, consult promptly with the other contracting party or the CONTRACTING PARTIES regarding the need for an adjustment of the proportion determined or of the base period selected, or for the reappraisal of the special factors involved, or for the elimination of conditions, formalities or any other provisions established unilaterally relating to the allocation of an adequate quota or its unrestricted utilization.

5. The provisions of this Article shall apply to any tariff quota instituted or maintained by any contracting party, and, in so far as applicable, the principles of this Article shall also extend to export restrictions.

Article XIV*

Exceptions to the Rule of Non-discrimination

1. A contracting party which applies restrictions under Article XII or under Section B of Article XVIII may, in the application of such restrictions, deviate from the provisions of Article XIII in a manner having equivalent effect to restrictions on payments and transfers for current international transactions which that contracting party may at that time apply under Article VIII or XIV of the Articles of Agreement of the International Monetary Fund, or under analogous provisions of a special exchange agreement entered into pursuant to paragraph 6 of Article XV.*

2. A contracting party which is applying import restrictions under Article XII or under Section B of Article XVIII may, with the consent of the CONTRACTING PARTIES, temporarily deviate from the provisions of Article XIII in respect of a small part of its external trade where the benefits to the contracting party or contracting parties concerned substantially outweigh any injury which may result to the trade of other contracting parties.*

3. The provisions of Article XIII shall not preclude a group of territories having a common quota in the International Monetary Fund from applying against imports from other countries, but not among themselves, restrictions in accordance with the provisions of Article XII or of Section B of Article XVIII on condition that such restrictions are in all other respects consistent with the provisions of Article XIII.

4. A contracting party applying import restrictions under Article XII or under Section B of Article XVIII shall not be precluded by Articles XI to XV or Section B of Article XVIII of this Agreement from applying measures to direct its exports in such a manner as to increase its earnings of currencies which it can use without deviation from the provisions of Article XIII.

5. A contracting party shall not be precluded by Articles XI to XV, inclusive, or by Section B of Article XVIII, of this Agreement from applying quantitative restrictions:

    (a) having equivalent effect to exchange restrictions authorized under Section 3(b) of Article VII of the Articles of Agreement of the International Monetary Fund, or

    (b) under the preferential arrangements provided for in Annex A of this Agreement, pending the outcome of the negotiations referred to therein.

Article XV

Exchange Arrangements

1. The CONTRACTING PARTIES shall seek co-operation with the International Monetary Fund to the end that the CONTRACTING PARTIES and the Fund may pursue a co-ordinated policy with regard to exchange questions within the jurisdiction of the Fund and questions of quantitative restrictions and other trade measures within the jurisdiction of the CONTRACTING PARTIES.

2. In all cases in which the CONTRACTING PARTIES are called upon to consider or deal with problems concerning monetary reserves, balances of

payments or foreign exchange arrangements, they shall consult fully with the International Monetary Fund. In such consultations, the CONTRACTING PARTIES shall accept all findings of statistical and other facts presented by the Fund relating to foreign exchange, monetary reserves and balances of payments, and shall accept the determination of the Fund as to whether action by a contracting party in exchange matters is in accordance with the Articles of Agreement of the International Monetary Fund, or with the terms of a special exchange agreement between that contracting party and the CONTRACTING PARTIES. The CONTRACTING PARTIES in reaching their final decision in cases involving the criteria set forth in paragraph 2(*a*) of Article XII or in paragraph 9 of Article XVIII, shall accept the determination of the Fund as to what constitutes a serious decline in the contracting party's monetary reserves, a very low level of its monetary reserves or a reasonable rate of increase in its monetary reserves, and as to the financial aspects of other matters covered in consultation in such cases.

3. The CONTRACTING PARTIES shall seek agreement with the Fund regarding procedures for consultation under paragraph 2 of this Article.

4. Contracting parties shall not, by exchange action, frustrate* the intent of the provisions of this Agreement, nor, by trade action, the intent of the provisions of the Articles of Agreement of the International Monetary Fund.

5. If the CONTRACTING PARTIES consider, at any time, that exchange restrictions on payments and transfers in connexion with imports are being applied by a contracting party in a manner inconsistent with the exceptions provided for in this Agreement for quantitative restrictions, they shall report thereon to the Fund.

6. Any contracting party which is not a member of the Fund shall, within a time to be determined by the CONTRACTING PARTIES after consultation with the Fund, become a member of the Fund, or, failing that, enter into a special exchange agreement with the CONTRACTING PARTIES. A contracting party which ceases to be a member of the Fund shall forthwith enter into a special exchange agreement with the CONTRACTING PARTIES. Any special exchange agreement entered into by a contracting party under this paragraph shall thereupon become part of its obligations under this Agreement.

7. (*a*) A special exchange agreement between a contracting party and the CONTRACTING PARTIES under paragraph 6 of this Article shall provide to the satisfaction of the CONTRACTING PARTIES that the objectives of this Agreement will not be frustrated as a result of action in exchange matters by the contracting party in question.

(*b*) The terms of any such agreement shall not impose obligations on the contracting party in exchange matters generally more restrictive than those imposed by the Articles of Agreement of the International Monetary Fund on members of the Fund.

8. A contracting party which is not a member of the Fund shall furnish such information within the general scope of section 5 of Article VIII of the Articles of Agreement of the International Monetary Fund as the CON-

TRACTING PARTIES may require in order to carry out their functions under this Agreement.

9.   Nothing in this Agreement shall preclude:

(*a*) the use by a contracting party of exchange controls or exchange restrictions in accordance with the Articles of Agreement of the International Monetary Fund or with that contracting party's special exchange agreement with the CONTRACTING PARTIES, or

(*b*) the use by a contracting party of restrictions or controls on imports or exports, the sole effect of which, additional to the effects permitted under Articles XI, XII, XIII and XIV, is to make effective such exchange controls or exchange restrictions.

Article XVI*

Subsidies

Section A—Subsidies in General

1.   If any contracting party grants or maintains any subsidy, including any form of income or price support, which operates directly or indirectly to increase exports of any product from, or to reduce imports of any product into, its territory, it shall notify the CONTRACTING PARTIES in writing of the extent and nature of the subsidization, of the estimated effect of the subsidization on the quantity of the affected product or products imported into or exported from its territory and of the circumstances making the subsidization necessary.   In any case in which it is determined that serious prejudice to the interests of any other contracting party is caused or threatened by any such subsidization, the contracting party granting the subsidy shall, upon request, discuss with the other contracting party or parties concerned, or with the CONTRACTING PARTIES, the possibility of limiting the subsidization.

Section B—Additional Provisions on Export Subsidies*

2.   The contracting parties recognize that the granting by a contracting party of a subsidy on the export of any product may have harmful effects for other contracting parties, both importing and exporting, may cause undue disturbance to their normal commercial interests, and may hinder the achievement of the objectives of this Agreement.

3.   Accordingly, contracting parties should seek to avoid the use of subsidies on the export of primary products.   If, however, a contracting party grants directly or indirectly any form of subsidy which operates to increase the export of any primary product from its territory, such subsidy shall not be applied in a manner which results in that contracting party having more than an equitable share of world export trade in that product, account being taken of the shares of the contracting parties in such trade in the product during a previous representative period, and any special factors which may have affected or may be affecting such trade in the product.*

4.   Further, as from 1 January 1958 or the earliest practicable date thereafter, contracting parties shall cease to grant either directly or indirectly any form of subsidy on the export of any product other than a primary product which subsidy results in the sale of such product for export at a price

lower than the comparable price charged for the like product to buyers in the domestic market. Until 31 December 1957 no contracting party shall extend the scope of any such subsidization beyond that existing on 1 January 1955 by the introduction of new, or the extension of existing, subsidies.*

5. The CONTRACTING PARTIES shall review the operation of the provisions of this Article from time to time with a view to examining its effectiveness, in the light of actual experience, in promoting the objectives of this Agreement and avoiding subsidization seriously prejudicial to the trade or interests of contracting parties.

Article XVII

State Trading Enterprises

1*. (a) Each contracting party undertakes that if it establishes or maintains a State enterprise, wherever located, or grants to any enterprise, formally or in effect, exclusive or special privileges,* such enterprise shall, in its purchases or sales involving either imports or exports, act in a manner consistent with the general principles of non-discriminatory treatment prescribed in this Agreement for governmental measures affecting imports or exports by private traders.

(b) The provisions of sub-paragraph (a) of this paragraph shall be understood to require that such enterprises shall, having due regard to the other provisions of this Agreement, make any such purchases or sales solely in accordance with commercial considerations,* including price, quality, availability, marketability, transportation and other conditions of purchase or sale, and shall afford the enterprises of the other contracting parties adequate opportunity, in accordance with customary business practice, to compete for participation in such purchases or sales.

(c) No contracting party shall prevent any enterprise (whether or not an enterprise described in sub-paragraph (a) of this paragraph) under its jurisdiction from acting in accordance with the principles of sub-paragraphs (a) and (b) of this paragraph.

2. The provisions of paragraph 1 of this Article shall not apply to imports of products for immediate or ultimate consumption in governmental use and not otherwise for resale or use in the production of goods* for sale. With respect to such imports, each contracting party shall accord to the trade of the other contracting parties fair and equitable treatment.

3. The contracting parties recognize that enterprises of the kind described in paragraph 1(a) of this Article might be operated so as to create serious obstacles to trade; thus negotiations on a reciprocal and mutually advantageous basis designed to limit or reduce such obstacles are of importance to the expansion of international trade.*

4. (a) Contracting parties shall notify the CONTRACTING PARTIES of the products which are imported into or exported from their territories by enterprises of the kind described in paragraph 1(a) of this Article.

(b) A contracting party establishing, maintaining or authorizing an import monopoly of a product, which is not the subject of a concession under Article II, shall, on the request of another contracting party having a substantial trade in the product concerned, inform the CONTRACTING PARTIES of the import mark-up* on the product during a recent representative period, or, when it is not possible to do so, of the price charged on the resale of the product.

(c) The CONTRACTING PARTIES may, at the request of a contracting party which has reason to believe that its interests under this Agreement are being adversely affected by the operations of an enterprise of the kind described in paragraph 1(a), request the contracting party establishing, maintaining or authorizing such enterprise to supply information about its operations related to the carrying out of the provisions of this Agreement.

(d) The provisions of this paragraph shall not require any contracting party to disclose confidential information which would impede law enforcement or otherwise be contrary to the public interest or would prejudice the legitimate commercial interests of particular enterprises.

Article XVIII*

Governmental Assistance to Economic Development

1.   The contracting parties recognize that the attainment of the objectives of this Agreement will be facilitated by the progressive development of their economies, particularly of those contracting parties the economies of which can only support low standards of living* and are in the early stages of development.*

2.   The contracting parties recognize further that it may be necessary for those contracting parties, in order to implement programmes and policies of economic development designed to raise the general standard of living of their people, to take protective or other measures affecting imports, and that such measures are justified in so far as they facilitate the attainment of the objectives of this Agreement. They agree, therefore, that those contracting parties should enjoy additional facilities to enable them (a) to maintain sufficient flexibility in their tariff structure to be able to grant the tariff protection required for the establishment of a particular industry* and (b) to apply quantitative restrictions for balance of payments purposes in a manner which takes full account of the continued high level of demand for imports likely to be generated by their programmes of economic development.

3.   The contracting parties recognize finally that, with those additional facilities which are provided for in Sections A and B of this Article, the provisions of this Agreement would normally be sufficient to enable contracting parties to meet the requirements of their economic development. They agree, however, that there may be circumstances where no measure consistent with those provisions is practicable to permit a contracting party in the process of economic development to grant the governmental assistance required to promote the establishment of particular industries* with a view to raising the general standard of living of its people. Special procedures are laid down in Sections C and D of this Article to deal with those cases.

4.   (a) Consequently, a contracting party the economy of which can only support low standards of living* and is in the early stages of development* shall be free to deviate temporarily from the provisions of the other Articles of this Agreement, as provided in Sections A, B and C of this Article.

(*b*) A contracting party the economy of which is in the process of development, but which does not come within the scope of sub-paragraph (*a*) above, may submit applications to the CONTRACTING PARTIES under Section D of this Article.

5.   The contracting parties recognize that the export earnings of contracting parties, the economies of which are of the type described in paragraph 4(*a*) and (*b*) above and which depend on exports of a small number of primary commodities, may be seriously reduced by a decline in the sale of such commodities.   Accordingly, when the exports of primary commodities by such a contracting party are seriously affected by measures taken by another contracting party, it may have resort to the consultation provisions of Article XXII of this Agreement.

6.   The CONTRACTING PARTIES shall review annually all measures applied pursuant to the provisions of Sections C and D of this Article.

Section A

7.   (*a*) If a contracting party coming within the scope of paragraph 4(*a*) of this Article considers it desirable, in order to promote the establishment of a particular industry* with a view to raising the general standard of living of its people, to modify or withdraw a concession included in the appropriate Schedule annexed to this Agreement, it shall notify the CONTRACTING PARTIES to this effect and enter into negotiations with any contracting party with which such concession was initially negotiated, and with any other contracting party determined by the CONTRACTING PARTIES to have a substantial interest therein.   If agreement is reached between such contracting parties concerned, they shall be free to modify or withdraw concessions under the appropriate Schedules to this Agreement in order to give effect to such agreement, including any compensatory adjustments involved.

(*b*) If agreement is not reached within sixty days after the notification provided for in sub-paragraph (*a*) above, the contracting party which proposes to modify or withdraw the concession may refer the matter to the CONTRACTING PARTIES, which shall promptly examine it.   If they find that the contracting party which proposes to modify or withdraw the concession has made every effort to reach an agreement and that the compensatory adjustment offered by it is adequate, that contracting party shall be free to modify or withdraw the concession if, at the same time, it gives effect to the compensatory adjustment.   If the CONTRACTING PARTIES do not find that the compensation offered by a contracting party proposing to modify or withdraw the concession is adequate, but find that it has made every reasonable effort to offer adequate compensation, that contracting party shall be free to proceed with such modification or withdrawal.   If such action is taken, any other contracting party referred to in sub-paragraph (*a*) above shall be free to modify or withdraw substantially equivalent concessions initially negotiated with the contracting party which has taken the action.*

Section B

8.   The contracting parties recognize that contracting parties coming within the scope of paragraph 4(*a*) of this Article tend, when they are in rapid process of development, to experience balance of payments difficulties arising

mainly from efforts to expand their internal markets as well as from the instability in their terms of trade.

9.   In order to safeguard its external financial position and to ensure a level of reserves adequate for the implementation of its programme of economic development, a contracting party coming within the scope of paragraph 4(*a*) of this Article may, subject to the provisions of paragraphs 10 to 12, control the general level of its imports by restricting the quantity or value of merchandise permitted to be imported; *Provided* that the import restrictions instituted, maintained or intensified shall not exceed those necessary:

  (*a*) to forestall the threat of, or to stop, a serious decline in its monetary reserves, or

  (*b*) in the case of a contracting party with inadequate monetary reserves, to achieve a reasonable rate of increase in its reserves.

Due regard shall be paid in either case to any special factors which may be affecting the reserves of the contracting party or its need for reserves, including, where special external credits or other resources are available to it, the need to provide for the appropriate use of such credits or resources.

10.   In applying these restrictions, the contracting party may determine their incidence on imports of different products or classes of products in such a way as to give priority to the importation of those products which are more essential in the light of its policy of economic development; *Provided* that the restrictions are so applied as to avoid unnecessary damage to the commercial or economic interests of any other contracting party and not to prevent unreasonably the importation of any description of goods in minimum commercial quantities the exclusion of which would impair regular channels of trade; and *Provided* further that the restrictions are not so applied as to prevent the importation of commercial samples or to prevent compliance with patent, trade mark, copyright or similar procedures.

11.   In carrying out its domestic policies, the contracting party concerned shall pay due regard to the need for restoring equilibrium in its balance of payments on a sound and lasting basis and to the desirability of assuring an economic employment of productive resources.   It shall progressively relax any restrictions applied under this Section as conditions improve, maintaining them only to the extent necessary under the terms of paragraph 9 of this Article and shall eliminate them when conditions no longer justify such maintenance; *Provided* that no contracting party shall be required to withdraw or modify restrictions on the ground that a change in its development policy would render unnecessary the restrictions which it is applying under this Section.*

12.   (*a*) Any contracting party applying new restrictions or raising the general level of its existing restrictions by a substantial intensification of the measures applied under this Section, shall immediately after instituting or intensifying such restrictions (or, in circumstances in which prior consultation is practicable, before doing so) consult with the CONTRACTING PARTIES as to the nature of its balance of payment difficulties, alternative corrective measures which may be available, and the possible effect of the restrictions on the economies of other contracting parties.

(*b*) On a date to be determined by them,* the CONTRACTING PARTIES shall review all restrictions still applied under this Section on that date. Beginning two years after that date, contracting parties applying restrictions under this Section shall enter into consultations of the type provided for in sub-paragraph (*a*) above with the CONTRACTING PARTIES at intervals of approximately, but not less than, two years according to a programme to be drawn up each year by the CONTRACTING PARTIES; *Provided* that no consultation under this sub-paragraph shall take place within two years after the conclusion of a consultation of a general nature under any other provision of this paragraph.

(*c*) (i) If, in the course of consultations with a contracting party under sub-paragraph (*a*) or (*b*) of this paragraph, the CONTRACTING PARTIES find that the restrictions are not consistent with the provisions of this Section or with those of Article XIII (subject to the provisions of Article XIV), they shall indicate the nature of the inconsistency and may advise that the restrictions be suitably modified.

(ii) If, however, as a result of the consultations, the CONTRACTING PARTIES determine that the restrictions are being applied in a manner involving an inconsistency of a serious nature with the provisions of this Section or with those of Article XIII (subject to the provisions of Article XIV) and that damage to the trade of any contracting party is caused or threatened thereby, they shall so inform the contracting party applying the restrictions and shall make appropriate recommendations for securing conformity with such provisions within a specified period. If such contracting party does not comply with these recommendations within the specified period, the CONTRACTING PARTIES may release any contracting party the trade of which is adversely affected by the restrictions from such obligations under this Agreement towards the contracting party applying the restrictions as they determine to be appropriate in the circumstances.

(*d*) The CONTRACTING PARTIES shall invite any contracting party which is applying restrictions under this Section to enter into consultations with them at the request of any contracting party which can establish a *prima facie* case that the restrictions are inconsistent with the provisions of this Section or with those of Article XIII (subject to the provisions of Article XIV) and that its trade is adversely affected thereby. However, no such invitation shall be issued unless the CONTRACTING PARTIES have ascertained that direct discussions between the contracting parties concerned have not been successful. If, as a result of the consultations with the CONTRACTING PARTIES no agreement is reached and they determine that the restrictions are being applied inconsistently with such provisions, and that damage to the trade of the contracting party initiating the procedure is caused or threatened thereby, they shall recommend the withdrawal or modification of the restrictions. If the restrictions are not withdrawn or modified within such time as the CONTRACTING PARTIES may prescribe, they may release the contracting party initiating the procedure from such obligations under this Agreement towards the contracting party applying the restrictions as they determine to be appropriate in the circumstances.

(*e*) If a contracting party against which action has been taken in accordance with the last sentence of sub-paragraph (*c*)(ii) or (*d*) of this paragraph, finds that the release of obligations authorized by the CONTRACTING PARTIES adversely affects the operation of its programme and policy of economic development, it shall be free, not later than sixty days after such action is taken, to give written notice to the Executive Secretary to the CONTRACTING PARTIES of its intention to withdraw from this Agreement and such withdrawal shall take effect on the sixtieth day following the day on which the notice is received by him.

(*f*) In proceeding under this paragraph, the CONTRACTING PARTIES shall have due regard to the factors referred to in paragraph 2 of this Article. Determinations under this paragraph shall be rendered expeditiously and, if possible, within sixty days of the initiation of the consultations.

Section C

13.   If a contracting party coming within the scope of paragraph 4(*a*) of this Article finds that governmental assistance is required to promote the establishment of a particular industry* with a view to raising the general standard of living of its people, but that no measure consistent with the other provisions of this Agreement is practicable to achieve that objective, it may have recourse to the provisions and procedures set out in this Section.*

14.   The contracting party concerned shall notify the CONTRACTING PARTIES of the special difficulties which it meets in the achievement of the objective outlined in paragraph 13 of this Article and shall indicate the specific measure affecting imports which it proposes to introduce in order to remedy these difficulties.   It shall not introduce that measure before the expiration of the time-limit laid down in paragraph 15 or 17, as the case may be, or if the measure affects imports of a product which is the subject of a concession included in the appropriate Schedule annexed to this Agreement, unless it has secured the concurrence of the CONTRACTING PARTIES in accordance with the provisions of paragraph 18; *Provided* that, if the industry receiving assistance has already started production, the contracting party may, after informing the CONTRACTING PARTIES, take such measures as may be necessary to prevent, during that period, imports of the product or products concerned from increasing substantially above a normal level.*

15.   If, within thirty days of the notification of the measure, the CON-TRACTING PARTIES do not request the contracting party concerned to consult with them,* that contracting party shall be free to deviate from the relevant provisions of the other Articles of this Agreement to the extent necessary to apply the proposed measure.

16.   If it is requested by the CONTRACTING PARTIES to do so,* the contracting party concerned shall consult with them as to the purpose of the proposed measure, as to alternative measures which may be available under this Agreement, and as to the possible effect of the measure proposed on the commercial and economic interests of other contracting parties.   If, as a result of such consultation, the CONTRACTING PARTIES agree that there is no measure consistent with the other provisions of this Agreement which is practicable in order to achieve the objective outlined in paragraph 13 of this Article, and concur* in the proposed measure, the contracting party concerned shall be released from its obligations under the relevant provisions of the

other Articles of this Agreement to the extent necessary to apply that measure.

17.   If, within ninety days after the date of the notification of the proposed measure under paragraph 14 of this Article, the CONTRACTING PARTIES have not concurred in such measure, the contracting party concerned may introduce the measure proposed after informing the CONTRACTING PARTIES.

18.   If the proposed measure affects a product which is the subject of a concession included in the appropriate Schedule annexed to this Agreement, the contracting party concerned shall enter into consultations with any other contracting party with which the concession was initially negotiated, and with any other contracting party determined by the CONTRACTING PARTIES to have a substantial interest therein.   The CONTRACTING PARTIES shall concur* in the measure if they agree that there is no measure consistent with the other provisions of this Agreement which is practicable in order to achieve the objective set forth in paragraph 13 of this Article, and if they are satisfied:

(a) that agreement has been reached with such other contracting parties as a result of the consultations referred to above, or

(b) if no such agreement has been reached within sixty days after the notification provided for in paragraph 14 has been received by the CONTRACTING PARTIES, that the contracting party having recourse to this Section has made all reasonable efforts to reach an agreement and that the interests of other contracting parties are adequately safeguarded.*

The contracting party having recourse to this Section shall thereupon be released from its obligations under the relevant provisions of the other Articles of this Agreement to the extent necessary to permit it to apply the measure.

19.   If a proposed measure of the type described in paragraph 13 of this Article concerns an industry the establishment of which has in the initial period been facilitated by incidental protection afforded by restrictions imposed by the contracting party concerned for balance of payments purposes under the relevant provisions of this Agreement, that contracting party may resort to the provisions and procedures of this Section; *Provided* that it shall not apply the proposed measure without the concurrence* of the CONTRACTING PARTIES.*

20.   Nothing in the preceding paragraphs of this Section shall authorize any deviation from the provisions of Articles I, II and XIII of this Agreement. The provisos to paragraph 10 of this Article shall also be applicable to any restriction under this Section.

21.   At any time while a measure is being applied under paragraph 17 of this Article any contracting party substantially affected by it may suspend the application to the trade of the contracting party having recourse to this Section of such substantially equivalent concessions or other obligations under this Agreement the suspension of which the CONTRACTING PARTIES do not disapprove;* *Provided* that sixty days' notice of such suspension is given to the CONTRACTING PARTIES not later than six months after the measure has been introduced or changed substantially to the detriment of the

contracting party affected. Any such contracting party shall afford adequate opportunity for consultation in accordance with the provisions of Article XXII of this Agreement.

Section D

22. A contracting party coming within the scope of sub-paragraph 4(*b*) of this Article desiring, in the interest of the development of its economy, to introduce a measure of the type described in paragraph 13 of this Article in respect of the establishment of a particular industry* may apply to the CONTRACTING PARTIES for approval of such measure. The CONTRACT-ING PARTIES shall promptly consult with such contracting party and shall, in making their decision, be guided by the considerations set out in paragraph 16. If the CONTRACTING PARTIES concur* in the proposed measure the contracting party concerned shall be released from its obligations under the relevant provisions of the other Articles of this Agreement to the extent necessary to permit it to apply the measure. If the proposed measure affects a product which is the subject of a concession included in the appropriate Schedule annexed to this Agreement, the provisions of paragraph 18 shall apply.*

23. Any measure applied under this Section shall comply with the provisions of paragraph 20 of this Article.

Article XIX

Emergency Action on Imports of Particular Products

1. (*a*) If, as a result of unforeseen developments and of the effect of the obligations incurred by a contracting party under this Agreement, including tariff concessions, any product is being imported into the territory of that contracting party in such increased quantities and under such conditions as to cause or threaten serious injury to domestic producers in that territory of like or directly competitive products, the contracting party shall be free, in respect of such product, and to the extent and for such time as may be necessary to prevent or remedy such injury, to suspend the obligation in whole or in part or to withdraw or modify the concession.

(*b*) If any product, which is the subject of a concession with respect to a preference, is being imported into the territory of a contracting party in the circumstances set forth in sub-paragraph (*a*) of this paragraph, so as to cause or threaten serious injury to domestic producers of like or directly competitive products in the territory of a contracting party which receives or received such preference, the importing contracting party shall be free, if that other contracting party so requests, to suspend the relevant obligation in whole or in part or to withdraw or modify the concession in respect of the product, to the extent and for such time as may be necessary to prevent or remedy such injury.

2. Before any contracting party shall take action pursuant to the provisions of paragraph 1 of this Article, it shall give notice in writing to the CONTRACTING PARTIES as far in advance as may be practicable and shall afford the CONTRACTING PARTIES and those contracting parties having a substantial interest as exporters of the product concerned an opportunity to consult with it in respect of the proposed action. When such notice is given in relation to a concession with respect to a preference, the notice shall name the

contracting party which has requested the action. In critical circumstances, where delay would cause damage which it would be difficult to repair, action under paragraph 1 of this Article may be taken provisionally without prior consultation, on the condition that consultation shall be effected immediately after taking such action.

3. (*a*) If agreement among the interested contracting parties with respect to the action is not reached, the contracting party which proposes to take or continue the action shall, nevertheless, be free to do so, and if such action is taken or continued, the affected contracting parties shall then be free, not later than ninety days after such action is taken, to suspend, upon the expiration of thirty days from the day on which written notice of such suspension is received by the CONTRACTING PARTIES, the application to the trade of the contracting party taking such action, or, in the case envisaged in paragraph 1(*b*) of this Article, to the trade of the contracting party requesting such action, of such substantially equivalent concessions or other obligations under this Agreement the suspension of which the CONTRACTING PARTIES do not disapprove.

(*b*) Notwithstanding the provisions of sub-paragraph (*a*) of this paragraph, where action is taken under paragraph 2 of this Article without prior consultation and causes or threatens serious injury in the territory of a contracting party to the domestic producers of products affected by the action, that contracting party shall, where delay would cause damage difficult to repair, be free to suspend, upon the taking of the action and throughout the period of consultation, such concessions or other obligations as may be necessary to prevent or remedy the injury.

Article XX

General Exceptions

Subject to the requirement that such measures are not applied in a manner which would constitute a means of arbitrary or unjustifiable discrimination between countries where the same conditions prevail, or a disguised restriction on international trade, nothing in this Agreement shall be construed to prevent the adoption or enforcement by any contracting party of measures:

(*a*) necessary to protect public morals;

(*b*) necessary to protect human, animal or plant life or health;

(*c*) relating to the importation or exportation of gold or silver;

(*d*) necessary to secure compliance with laws or regulations which are not inconsistent with the provisions of this Agreement, including those relating to customs enforcement, the enforcement of monopolies operated under paragraph 4 of Article II and Article XVII, the protection of patents, trade marks and copyrights, and the prevention of deceptive practices;

(*e*) relating to the products of prison labour;

(*f*) imposed for the protection of national treasures of artistic, historic or archaeological value;

(*g*) relating to the conservation of exhaustible natural resources if such measures are made effective in conjunction with restrictions on domestic production or consumption;

(*h*) undertaken in pursuance of obligations under any intergovernmental commodity agreement which conforms to criteria submitted to the CONTRACTING PARTIES and not disapproved by them or which is itself so submitted and not so disapproved;*

(*i*) involving restrictions on exports of domestic materials necessary to ensure essential quantities of such materials to a domestic processing industry during periods when the domestic price of such materials is held below the world price as part of a governmental stabilization plan; *Provided* that such restrictions shall not operate to increase the exports of or the protection afforded to such domestic industry, and shall not depart from the provisions of this Agreement relating to non-discrimination;

(*j*) essential to the acquisition or distribution of products in general or local short supply; *Provided* that any such measures shall be consistent with the principle that all contracting parties are entitled to an equitable share of the international supply of such products, and that any such measures, which are inconsistent with the other provisions of this Agreement shall be discontinued as soon as the conditions giving rise to them have ceased to exist. The CONTRACTING PARTIES shall review the need for this sub-paragraph not later than 30 June 1960.

Article XXI

Security Exceptions

Nothing in this Agreement shall be construed

(*a*) to require any contracting party to furnish any information the disclosure of which it considers contrary to its essential security interests; or

(*b*) to prevent any contracting party from taking any action which it considers necessary for the protection of its essential security interests

(i) relating to fissionable materials or the materials from which they are derived;

(ii) relating to the traffic in arms, ammunition and implements of war and to such traffic in other goods and materials as is carried on directly or indirectly for the purpose of supplying a military establishment;

(iii) taken in time of war or other emergency in international relations; or

(*c*) to prevent any contracting party from taking any action in pursuance of its obligations under the United Nations Charter for the maintenance of international peace and security.

Article XXII

Consultation

1. Each contracting party shall accord sympathetic consideration to, and shall afford adequate opportunity for consultation regarding, such representations as may be made by another contracting party with respect to any matter affecting the operation of this Agreement.

2.   The CONTRACTING PARTIES may, at the request of a contracting party, consult with any contracting party or parties in respect of any matter for which it has not been possible to find a satisfactory solution through consultation under paragraph 1.

Article XXIII

Nullification or Impairment

1.   If any contracting party should consider that any benefit accruing to it directly or indirectly under this Agreement is being nullified or impaired or that the attainment of any objective of the Agreement is being impeded as the result of

(*a*) the failure of another contracting party to carry out its obligations under this Agreement, or

(*b*) the application by another contracting party of any measure, whether or not it conflicts with the provisions of this Agreement, or

(*c*) the existence of any other situation,

the contracting party may, with a view to the satisfactory adjustment of the matter, make written representations or proposals to the other contracting party or parties which it considers to be concerned. Any contracting party thus approached shall give sympathetic consideration to the representations or proposals made to it.

2.   If no satisfactory adjustment is effected between the contracting parties concerned within a reasonable time, or if the difficulty is of the type described in paragraph 1(c) of this Article, the matter may be referred to the CONTRACTING PARTIES. The CONTRACTING PARTIES shall promptly investigate any matter so referred to them and shall make appropriate recommendations to the contracting parties which they consider to be concerned, or give a ruling on the matter, as appropriate. The CONTRACTING PARTIES may consult with contracting parties, with the Economic and Social Council of the United Nations and with any appropriate inter-governmental organization in cases where they consider such consultation necessary. If the CONTRACTING PARTIES consider that the circumstances are serious enough to justify such action, they may authorize a contracting party or parties to suspend the application to any other contracting party or parties of such concessions or other obligations under this Agreement as they determine to be appropriate in the circumstances. If the application to any contracting party of any concession or other obligation is in fact suspended, that contracting party shall then be free, not later than sixty days after such action is taken, to give written notice to the Executive Secretary to the CONTRACTING PARTIES of its intention to withdraw from this Agreement and such withdrawal shall take effect upon the sixtieth day following the day on which such notice is received by him.

PART III

Article XXIV

Territorial Application—Frontier Traffic—Customs Unions and Free-Trade Areas

1.   The provisions of this Agreement shall apply to the metropolitan customs territories of the contracting parties and to any other customs

territories in respect of which this Agreement has been accepted under Article XXVI or is being applied under Article XXXIII or pursuant to the Protocol of Provisional Application. Each such customs territory shall, exclusively for the purposes of the territorial application of this Agreement, be treated as though it were a contracting party; *Provided* that the provisions of this paragraph shall not be construed to create any rights or obligations as between two or more customs territories in respect of which this Agreement has been accepted under Article XXVI or is being applied under Article XXXIII or pursuant to the Protocol of Provisional Application by a single contracting party.

2. For the purposes of this Agreement a customs territory shall be understood to mean any territory with respect to which separate tariffs or other regulations of commerce are maintained for a substantial part of the trade of such territory with other territories.

3. The provisions of this Agreement shall not be construed to prevent:

(*a*) Advantages accorded by any contracting party to adjacent countries in order to facilitate frontier traffic;

(*b*) Advantages accorded to the trade with the Free Territory of Trieste by countries contiguous to that territory, provided that such advantages are not in conflict with the Treaties of Peace arising out of the Second World War.

4. The contracting parties recognize the desirability of increasing freedom of trade by the development, through voluntary agreements, of closer integration between the economies of the countries parties to such agreements. They also recognize that the purpose of a customs union or of a free-trade area should be to facilitate trade between the constituent territories and not to raise barriers to the trade of other contracting parties with such territories.

5. Accordingly, the provisions of this Agreement shall not prevent, as between the territories of contracting parties, the formation of a customs union or of a free-trade area or the adoption of an interim agreement necessary for the formation of a customs union or of a free-trade area; *Provided* that:

(*a*) with respect to a customs union, or an interim agreement leading to the formation of a customs union, the duties and other regulations of commerce imposed at the institution of any such union or interim agreement in respect of trade with contracting parties not parties to such union or agreement shall not on the whole be higher or more restrictive than the general incidence of the duties and regulations of commerce applicable in the constituent territories prior to the formation of such union or the adoption of such interim agreement, as the case may be;

(*b*) with respect to a free-trade area, or an interim agreement leading to the formation of a free-trade area, the duties and other regulations of commerce maintained in each of the constituent territories and applicable at the formation of such free-trade area or the adoption of such interim agreement to the trade of contracting parties not included in such area or not parties to such agreement shall not be higher or more restrictive than the corresponding duties and other regulations of commerce existing in the same constituent territories prior to the formation of the free-trade area, or interim agreement, as the case may be; and

(c) any interim agreement referred to in sub-paragraphs (a) and (b) shall include a plan and schedule for the formation of such a customs union or of such a free-trade area within a reasonable length of time.

6.   If, in fulfilling the requirements of sub-paragraph 5(a), a contracting party proposes to increase any rate of duty inconsistently with the provisions of Article II, the procedure set forth in Article XXVIII shall apply.   In providing for compensatory adjustment, due account shall be taken of the compensation already afforded by the reductions brought about in the corresponding duty of the other constituents of the union.

7.   (a) Any contracting party deciding to enter into a customs union or free-trade area, or an interim agreement leading to the formation of such a union or area, shall promptly notify the CONTRACTING PARTIES and shall make available to them such information regarding the proposed union or area as will enable them to make such reports and recommendations to contracting parties as they may deem appropriate.

(b) If, after having studied the plan and schedule included in an interim agreement referred to in paragraph 5 in consultation with the parties to that agreement and taking due account of the information made available in accordance with the provisions of sub-paragraph (a), the CONTRACTING PARTIES find that such agreement is not likely to result in the formation of a customs union or of a free-trade area within the period contemplated by the parties to the agreement or that such period is not a reasonable one, the CONTRACTING PARTIES shall make recommendations to the parties to the agreement.   The parties shall not maintain or put into force, as the case may be, such agreement if they are not prepared to modify it in accordance with these recommendations.

(c) Any substantial change in the plan or schedule referred to in paragraph 5(c) shall be communicated to the CONTRACTING PARTIES, which may request the contracting parties concerned to consult with them if the change seems likely to jeopardize or delay unduly the formation of the customs union or of the free-trade area.

8.   For the purposes of this Agreement:

(a) A customs union shall be understood to mean the substitution of a single customs territory for two or more customs territories, so that

(i) duties and other restrictive regulations of commerce (except, where necessary, those permitted under Articles XI, XII, XIII, XIV, XV and XX) are eliminated with respect to substantially all the trade between the constituent territories of the union or at least with respect to substantially all the trade in products originating in such territories, and,

(ii) subject to the provisions of paragraph 9, substantially the same duties and other regulations of commerce are applied by each of the members of the union to the trade of territories not included in the union;

(b) A free-trade area shall be understood to mean a group of two or more customs territories in which the duties and other restrictive regulations of commerce (except, where necessary, those permitted under Articles XI, XII, XIII, XIV, XV and XX) are eliminated on substantially all the trade between the constituent territories in products originating in such territories.

9.   The preferences referred to in paragraph 2 of Article I shall not be affected by the formation of a customs union or of a free-trade area but may be eliminated or adjusted by means of negotiations with contracting parties affected.* This procedure of negotiations with affected contracting parties shall, in particular, apply to the elimination of preferences required to conform with the provisions of paragraph 8(a)(i) and paragraph 8(b).

10.   The CONTRACTING PARTIES may by a two-thirds majority approve proposals which do not fully comply with the requirements of paragraphs 5 to 9 inclusive, provided that such proposals lead to the formation of a customs union or a free-trade area in the sense of this Article.

11.   Taking into account the exceptional circumstances arising out of the establishment of India and Pakistan as independent States and recognizing the fact that they have long constituted an economic unit, the contracting parties agree that the provisions of this Agreement shall not prevent the two countries from entering into special arrangements with respect to the trade between them, pending the establishment of their mutual trade relations on a definitive basis.*

12.   Each contracting party shall take such reasonable measures as may be available to it to ensure observance of the provisions of this Agreement by the regional and local governments and authorities within its territory.

Article XXV
Joint Action by the Contracting Parties

1.   Representatives of the contracting parties shall meet from time to time for the purpose of giving effect to those provisions of this Agreement which involve joint action and, generally, with a view to facilitating the operation and furthering the objectives of this Agreement. Wherever reference is made in this Agreement to the contracting parties acting jointly they are designated as the CONTRACTING PARTIES.

2.   The Secretary–General of the United Nations is requested to convene the first meeting of the CONTRACTING PARTIES, which shall take place not later than March 1, 1948.

3.   Each contracting party shall be entitled to have one vote at all meetings of the CONTRACTING PARTIES.

4.   Except as otherwise provided for in this Agreement, decisions of the CONTRACTING PARTIES shall be taken by a majority of the votes cast.

5.   In exceptional circumstances not elsewhere provided for in this Agreement, the CONTRACTING PARTIES may waive an obligation imposed upon a contracting party by this Agreement; *Provided* that any such decision shall be approved by a two-thirds majority of the votes cast and that such majority shall comprise more than half of the contracting parties. The CONTRACTING PARTIES may also by such a vote

(i) define certain categories of exceptional circumstances to which other voting requirements shall apply for the waiver of obligations, and

(ii) prescribe such criteria as may be necessary for the application of this paragraph.[†]

Article XXVI

Acceptance, Entry into Force and Registration

1.　The date of this Agreement shall be 30 October 1947.

2.　This Agreement shall be open for acceptance by any contracting party which, on 1 March 1955, was a contracting party or was negotiating with a view to accession to this Agreement.

3.　This Agreement, done in a single English original and in a single French original, both texts authentic, shall be deposited with the Secretary–General of the United Nations, who shall furnish certified copies thereof to all interested governments.

4.　Each government accepting this Agreement shall deposit an instrument of acceptance with the Executive Secretary[1] to the CONTRACTING PARTIES, who will inform all interested governments of the date of deposit of each instrument of acceptance and of the day on which this Agreement enters into force under paragraph 6 of this Article.

5.　(*a*) Each government accepting this Agreement does so in respect of its metropolitan territory and of the other territories for which it has international responsibility, except such separate customs territories as it shall notify to the Executive Secretary[1] to the CONTRACTING PARTIES at the time of its own acceptance.

(*b*) Any government, which has so notified the Executive Secretary[1] under the exceptions in sub-paragraph (*a*) of this paragraph, may at any time give notice to the Executive Secretary[1] that its acceptance shall be effective in respect of any separate customs territory or territories so excepted and such notice shall take effect on the thirtieth day following the day on which it is received by the Executive Secretary.[1]

(*c*) If any of the customs territories, in respect of which a contracting party has accepted this Agreement, possesses or acquires full autonomy in the conduct of its external commercial relations and of the other matters provided for in this Agreement, such territory shall, upon sponsorship through a declaration by the responsible contracting party establishing the above-mentioned fact, be deemed to be a contracting party.

6.　This Agreement shall enter into force, as among the governments which have accepted it, on the thirtieth day following the day on which instruments of acceptance have been deposited with the Executive Secretary[1] to the CONTRACTING PARTIES on behalf of governments named in Annex H, the territories of which account for 85 per centum of the total external trade of the territories of such governments, computed in accordance with the applicable column of percentages set forth therein.　The instrument of

---

† The authentic text erroneously reads "sub-paragraph".　　**1.**　See Preface.

acceptance of each other government shall take effect on the thirtieth day following the day on which such instrument has been deposited.

7.   The United Nations is authorized to effect registration of this Agreement as soon as it enters into force.

Article XXVII

Withholding or Withdrawal of Concessions

Any contracting party shall at any time be free to withhold or to withdraw in whole or in part any concession, provided for in the appropriate Schedule annexed to this Agreement, in respect of which such contracting party determines that it was initially negotiated with a government which has not become, or has ceased to be, a contracting party. A contracting party taking such action shall notify the CONTRACTING PARTIES and, upon request, consult with contracting parties which have a substantial interest in the product concerned.

Article XXVIII*

Modification of Schedules

1.   On the first day of each three-year period, the first period beginning on 1 January 1958 (or on the first day of any other period* that may be specified by the CONTRACTING PARTIES by two-thirds of the votes cast) a contracting party (hereafter in this Article referred to as the "applicant contracting party") may, by negotiations and agreement with any contracting party with which such concession was initially negotiated and with any other contracting party determined by the CONTRACTING PARTIES to have a principal supplying interest* (which two preceding categories of contracting parties, together with the applicant contracting party, are in this Article hereinafter referred to as the "contracting parties primarily concerned"), and subject to consultation with any other contracting party determined by the CONTRACTING PARTIES to have a substantial interest* in such concession, modify or withdraw a concession* included in the appropriate Schedule annexed to this Agreement.

2.   In such negotiations and agreement, which may include provision for compensatory adjustment with respect to other products, the contracting parties concerned shall endeavour to maintain a general level of reciprocal and mutually advantageous concessions not less favourable to trade than that provided for in this Agreement prior to such negotiations.

3.   (a) If agreement between the contracting parties primarily concerned cannot be reached before 1 January 1958 or before the expiration of a period envisaged in paragraph 1 of this Article, the contracting party which proposes to modify or withdraw the concession shall, nevertheless, be free to do so and if such action is taken any contracting party with which such concession was initially negotiated, any contracting party determined under paragraph 1 to have a principal supplying interest and any contracting party determined under paragraph 1 to have a substantial interest shall then be free not later than six months after such action is taken, to withdraw, upon the expiration of thirty days from the day on which written notice of such withdrawal is received by the CONTRACTING PARTIES, substantially equivalent concessions initially negotiated with the applicant contracting party.

(*b*) If agreement between the contracting parties primarily concerned is reached but any other contracting party determined under paragraph 1 of this Article to have a substantial interest is not satisfied, such other contracting party shall be free, not later than six months after action under such agreement is taken, to withdraw, upon the expiration of thirty days from the day on which written notice of such withdrawal is received by the CONTRACTING PARTIES, substantially equivalent concessions initially negotiated with the applicant contracting party.

4.   The CONTRACTING PARTIES may, at any time, in special circumstances, authorize* a contracting party to enter into negotiations for modification or withdrawal of a concession included in the appropriate Schedule annexed to this Agreement subject to the following procedures and conditions:

(*a*) Such negotiations* and any related consultations shall be conducted in accordance with the provisions of paragraphs 1 and 2 of this Article.

(*b*) If agreement between the contracting parties primarily concerned is reached in the negotiations, the provisions of paragraph 3(*b*) of this Article shall apply.

(*c*) If agreement between the contracting parties primarily concerned is not reached within a period of sixty days* after negotiations have been authorized, or within such longer period as the CONTRACTING PARTIES may have prescribed, the applicant contracting party may refer the matter to the CONTRACTING PARTIES.

(*d*) Upon such reference, the CONTRACTING PARTIES shall promptly examine the matter and submit their views to the contracting parties primarily concerned with the aim of achieving a settlement. If a settlement is reached, the provisions of paragraph 3(*b*) shall apply as if agreement between the contracting parties primarily concerned had been reached. If no settlement is reached between the contracting parties primarily concerned, the applicant contracting party shall be free to modify or withdraw the concession, unless the CONTRACTING PARTIES determine that the applicant contracting party has unreasonably failed to offer adequate compensation.* If such action is taken, any contracting party with which the concession was initially negotiated, any contracting party determined under paragraph 4(*a*) to have a principal supplying interest and any contracting party determined under paragraph 4(*a*) to have a substantial interest, shall be free, not later than six months after such action is taken, to modify or withdraw, upon the expiration of thirty days from the day on which written notice of such withdrawal is received by the CONTRACTING PARTIES, substantially equivalent concessions initially negotiated with the applicant contracting party.

5.   Before 1 January 1958 and before the end of any period envisaged in paragraph 1 a contracting party may elect by notifying the CONTRACTING PARTIES to reserve the right, for the duration of the next period, to modify the appropriate Schedule in accordance with the procedures of paragraphs 1 to 3. If a contracting party so elects, other contracting parties shall have the right, during the same period, to modify or withdraw, in accordance with the same procedures, concessions initially negotiated with that contracting party.

Article XXVIIIbis

Tariff Negotiations

1. The contracting parties recognize that customs duties often constitute serious obstacles to trade; thus negotiations on a reciprocal and mutually advantageous basis, directed to the substantial reduction of the general level of tariffs and other charges on imports and exports and in particular to the reduction of such high tariffs as discourage the importation even of minimum quantities, and conducted with due regard to the objectives of this Agreement and the varying needs of individual contracting parties, are of great importance to the expansion of international trade. The CONTRACTING PARTIES may therefore sponsor such negotiations from time to time.

2. (*a*) Negotiations under this Article may be carried out on a selective product-by-product basis or by the application of such multilateral procedures as may be accepted by the contracting parties concerned. Such negotiations may be directed towards the reduction of duties, the binding of duties at then existing levels or undertakings that individual duties or the average duties on specified categories of products shall not exceed specified levels. The binding against increase of low duties or of duty-free treatment shall, in principle, be recognized as a concession equivalent in value to the reduction of high duties.

(*b*) The contracting parties recognize that in general the success of multilateral negotiations would depend on the participation of all contracting parties which conduct a substantial proportion of their external trade with one another.

3. Negotiations shall be conducted on a basis which affords adequate opportunity to take into account:

(*a*) the needs of individual contracting parties and individual industries;

(*b*) the needs of less-developed countries for a more flexible use of tariff protection to assist their economic development and the special needs of these countries to maintain tariffs for revenue purposes; and

(*c*) all other relevant circumstances, including the fiscal,* developmental, strategic and other needs of the contracting parties concerned.

Article XXIX

The Relation of This Agreement to the Havana Charter

1. The contracting parties undertake to observe to the fullest extent of their executive authority the general principles of Chapters I to VI inclusive and of Chapter IX of the Havana Charter pending their acceptance of it in accordance with their constitutional procedures.*

2. Part II of this Agreement shall be suspended on the day on which the Havana Charter enters into force.

3. If by September 30, 1949, the Havana Charter has not entered into force, the contracting parties shall meet before December 31, 1949, to agree whether this Agreement shall be amended, supplemented or maintained.

4. If at any time the Havana Charter should cease to be in force, the CONTRACTING PARTIES shall meet as soon as practicable thereafter to agree whether this Agreement shall be supplemented, amended or main-

tained. Pending such agreement, Part II of this Agreement shall again enter into force; *Provided* that the provisions of Part II other than Article XXIII shall be replaced, *mutatis mutandis,* in the form in which they then appeared in the Havana Charter; and *Provided* further that no contracting party shall be bound by any provisions which did not bind it at the time when the Havana Charter ceased to be in force.

5. If any contracting party has not accepted the Havana Charter by the date upon which it enters into force, the CONTRACTING PARTIES shall confer to agree whether, and if so in what way, this Agreement in so far as it affects relations between such contracting party and other contracting parties, shall be supplemented or amended. Pending such agreement the provisions of Part II of this Agreement shall, notwithstanding the provisions of paragraph 2 of this Article, continue to apply as between such contracting party and other contracting parties.

6. Contracting parties which are Members of the International Trade Organization shall not invoke the provisions of this Agreement so as to prevent the operation of any provision of the Havana Charter. The application of the principle underlying this paragraph to any contracting party which is not a Member of the International Trade Organization shall be the subject of an agreement pursuant to paragraph 5 of this Article.

Article XXX

Amendments

1. Except where provision for modification is made elsewhere in this Agreement, amendments to the provisions of Part I of this Agreement or to the provisions of Article XXIX or of this Article shall become effective upon acceptance by all the contracting parties, and other amendments to this Agreement shall become effective, in respect of those contracting parties which accept them, upon acceptance by two-thirds of the contracting parties and thereafter for each other contracting party upon acceptance by it.

2. Any contracting party accepting an amendment to this Agreement shall deposit an instrument of acceptance with the Secretary–General of the United Nations within such period as the CONTRACTING PARTIES may specify. The CONTRACTING PARTIES may decide that any amendment made effective under this Article is of such a nature that any contracting party which has not accepted it within a period specified by the CONTRACT-ING PARTIES shall be free to withdraw from this Agreement, or to remain a contracting party with the consent of the CONTRACTING PARTIES.

Article XXXI

Withdrawal

Without prejudice to the provisions of paragraph 12 of Article XVIII, of Article XXIII or of paragraph 2 of Article XXX, any contracting party may withdraw from this Agreement, or may separately withdraw on behalf of any of the separate customs territories for which it has international responsibility and which at the time possesses full autonomy in the conduct of its external commercial relations and of the other matters provided for in this Agreement. The withdrawal shall take effect upon the expiration of six months from the day on which written notice of withdrawal is received by the Secretary–General of the United Nations.

Article XXXII
Contracting Parties

1. The contracting parties to this Agreement shall be understood to mean those governments which are applying the provisions of this Agreement under Articles XXVI or XXXIII or pursuant to the Protocol of Provisional Application.

2. At any time after the entry into force of this Agreement pursuant to paragraph 6 of Article XXVI, those contracting parties which have accepted this Agreement pursuant to paragraph 4 of Article XXVI may decide that any contracting party which has not so accepted it shall cease to be a contracting party.

Article XXXIII
Accession

A government not party to this Agreement, or a government acting on behalf of a separate customs territory possessing full autonomy in the conduct of its external commercial relations and of the other matters provided for in this Agreement, may accede to this Agreement, on its own behalf or on behalf of that territory, on terms to be agreed between such government and the CONTRACTING PARTIES. Decisions of the CONTRACTING PARTIES under this paragraph shall be taken by a two-thirds majority.

Article XXXIV
Annexes

The annexes to this Agreement are hereby made an integral part of this Agreement.

Article XXXV
Non-application of the Agreement Between Particular Contracting Parties

1. This Agreement, or alternatively Article II of this Agreement, shall not apply as between any contracting party and any other contracting party if:

(a) the two contracting parties have not entered into tariff negotiations with each other, and

(b) either of the contracting parties, at the time either becomes a contracting party, does not consent to such application.

2. The CONTRACTING PARTIES may review the operation of this Article in particular cases at the request of any contracting party and make appropriate recommendations.

PART IV*
TRADE AND DEVELOPMENT
Article XXXVI
Principles and Objectives

1*. The contracting parties,

(a) recalling that the basic objectives of this Agreement include the raising of standards of living and the progressive development of the economies of all contracting parties, and considering that the attainment of these objectives is particularly urgent for less-developed contracting parties;

(*b*) considering that export earnings of the less-developed contracting parties can play a vital part in their economic development and that the extent of this contribution depends on the prices paid by the less-developed contracting parties for essential imports, the volume of their exports, and the prices received for these exports;

(*c*) noting, that there is a wide gap between standards of living in less-developed countries and in other countries;

(*d*) recognizing that individual and joint action is essential to further the development of the economies of less-developed contracting parties and to bring about a rapid advance in the standards of living in these countries;

(*e*) recognizing that international trade as a means of achieving economic and social advancement should be governed by such rules and procedures—and measures in conformity with such rules and procedures—as are consistent with the objectives set forth in this Article;

(*f*) noting that the CONTRACTING PARTIES may enable less-developed contracting parties to use special measures to promote their trade and development;

agree as follows.

2. There is need for a rapid and sustained expansion of the export earnings of the less-developed contracting parties.

3. There is need for positive efforts designed to ensure that less-developed contracting parties secure a share in the growth in international trade commensurate with the needs of their economic development.

4. Given the continued dependence of many less-developed contracting parties on the exportation of a limited range of primary products,* there is need to provide in the largest possible measure more favourable and acceptable conditions of access to world markets for these products, and wherever appropriate to devise measures designed to stabilize and improve conditions of world markets in these products, including in particular measures designed to attain stable, equitable and remunerative prices, thus permitting an expansion of world trade and demand and a dynamic and steady growth of the real export earnings of these countries so as to provide them with expanding resources for their economic development.

5. The rapid expansion of the economies of the less-developed contracting parties will be facilitated by a diversification* of the structure of their economies and the avoidance of an excessive dependence on the export of primary products. There is, therefore, need for increased access in the largest possible measure to markets under favourable conditions for processed and manufactured products currently or potentially of particular export interest to less-developed contracting parties.

6. Because of the chronic deficiency in the export proceeds and other foreign exchange earnings of less-developed contracting parties, there are important inter-relationships between trade and financial assistance to development. There is, therefore, need for close and continuing collaboration between the CONTRACTING PARTIES and the international lending agencies so that they can contribute most effectively to alleviating the burdens these less-developed contracting parties assume in the interest of their economic development.

7. There is need for appropriate collaboration between the CONTRACTING PARTIES, other intergovernmental bodies and the organs and agencies of the United Nations system, whose activities relate to the trade and economic development of less-developed countries.

8. The developed contracting parties do not expect reciprocity for commitments made by them in trade negotiations to reduce or remove tariffs and other barriers to the trade of less-developed contracting parties.*

9. The adoption of measures to give effect to these principles and objectives shall be a matter of conscious and purposeful effort on the part of the contracting parties both individually and jointly.

Article XXXVII

Commitments

1. The developed contracting parties shall to the fullest extent possible—that is, except when compelling reasons, which may include legal reasons—give effect to the following provisions:

(*a*) accord high priority to the reduction and elimination of barriers to products currently or potentially of particular export interest to less-developed contracting parties, including customs duties and other restrictions which differentiate unreasonably between such products in their primary and in their processed forms;*

(*b*) refrain from introducing, or increasing the incidence of, customs duties or non-tariff import barriers on products currently or potentially of particular export interest to less-developed contracting parties; and

(*c*) (i) refrain from imposing new fiscal measures, and

(ii) in any adjustments of fiscal policy accord high priority to the reduction and elimination of fiscal measures,

which would hamper, or which hamper, significantly the growth of consumption of primary products, in raw or processed form, wholly or mainly produced in the territories of less-developed contracting parties, and which are applied specifically to those products.

2. (*a*) Whenever it is considered that effect is not being given to any of the provisions of sub-paragraph (*a*), (*b*) or (*c*) of paragraph 1, the matter shall be reported to the CONTRACTING PARTIES either by the contracting party not so giving effect to the relevant provisions or by any other interested contracting party.

(*b*) (i) The CONTRACTING PARTIES shall, if requested so to do by any interested contracting party, and without prejudice to any bilateral consultations that may be undertaken, consult with the contracting party concerned and all interested contracting parties with respect to the matter with a view to reaching solutions satisfactory to all contracting parties concerned in order to further the objectives set forth in Article XXXVI. In the course of these consultations, the reasons given in cases where effect was not being given to the provisions of sub-paragraph (*a*), (*b*) or (*c*) of paragraph 1 shall be examined.

(ii) As the implementation of the provisions of sub-paragraph (*a*), (*b*), or (*c*) of paragraph 1 by individual contracting parties may in some cases be more readily achieved where action is taken jointly with other developed contracting parties, such consultation might, where appropriate, be directed towards this end.

(iii) The consultations by the CONTRACTING PARTIES might also, in appropriate cases, be directed towards agreement on joint action designed to further the objectives of this Agreement as envisaged in paragraph 1 of Article XXV.

3. The developed contracting parties shall:

(*a*) make every effort, in cases where a government directly or indirectly determines the resale price of products wholly or mainly produced in the territories of less-developed contracting parties, to maintain trade margins at equitable levels;

(*b*) give active consideration to the adoption of other measures* designed to provide greater scope for the development of imports from less-developed contracting parties and collaborate in appropriate international action to this end;

(*c*) have special regard to the trade interests of less-developed contracting parties when considering the application of other measures permitted under this Agreement to meet particular problems and explore all possibilities of constructive remedies before applying such measures where they would affect essential interests of those contracting parties.

4. Less-developed contracting parties agree to take appropriate action in implementation of the provisions of Part IV for the benefit of the trade of other less-developed contracting parties, in so far as such action is consistent with their individual present and future development, financial and trade needs taking into account past trade developments as well as the trade interests of less-developed contracting parties as a whole.

5. In the implementation of the commitments set forth in paragraphs 1 to 4 each contracting party shall afford to any other interested contracting party or contracting parties full and prompt opportunity for consultations under the normal procedures of this Agreement with respect to any matter or difficulty which may arise.

Article XXXVIII
Joint Action

1. The contracting parties shall collaborate jointly, within the framework of this Agreement and elsewhere, as appropriate, to further the objectives set forth in Article XXXVI.

2. In particular, the CONTRACTING PARTIES shall:

(*a*) where appropriate, take action, including action through international arrangements, to provide improved and acceptable conditions of access to world markets for primary products of particular interest to less-developed contracting parties and to devise measures designed to stabilize and improve conditions of world markets in these products including measures designed to attain stable, equitable and remunerative prices for exports of such products;

(b) seek appropriate collaboration in matters of trade and development policy with the United Nations and its organs and agencies, including any institutions that may be created on the basis of recommendations by the United Nations Conference on Trade and Development;

(c) collaborate in analysing the development plans and policies of individual less-developed contracting parties and in examining trade and aid relationships with a view to devising concrete measures to promote the development of export potential and to facilitate access to export markets for the products of the industries thus developed and, in this connexion, seek appropriate collaboration with governments and international organizations, and in particular with organizations having competence in relation to financial assistance for economic development, in systematic studies of trade and aid relationships in individual less-developed contracting parties aimed at obtaining a clear analysis of export potential, market prospects and any further action that may be required;

(d) keep under continuous review the development of world trade with special reference to the rate of growth of the trade of less-developed contracting parties and make such recommendations to contracting parties as may, in the circumstances, be deemed appropriate;

(e) collaborate in seeking feasible methods to expand trade for the purpose of economic development, through international harmonization and adjustment of national policies and regulations, through technical and commercial standards affecting production, transportation and marketing, and through export promotion by the establishment of facilities for the increased flow of trade information and the development of market research; and

(f) establish such institutional arrangements as may be necessary to further the objectives set forth in Article XXXVI and to give effect to the provisions of this Part.

Annex A

List of Territories Referred to in Paragraph 2(a) of Article I

United Kingdom of Great Britain and Northern Ireland

Dependent territories of the United Kingdom of Great Britain and Northern Ireland

Canada

Commonwealth of Australia

Dependent territories of the Commonwealth of Australia

New Zealand

Dependent territories of New Zealand

Union of South Africa including South West Africa

Ireland

India (as on April 10, 1947)

Newfoundland

Southern Rhodesia

Burma

Ceylon

Certain of the territories listed above have two or more preferential rates in force for certain products. Any such territory may, by agreement with the other contracting parties which are principal suppliers of such products at the most-favoured-nation rate, substitute for such preferential rates a single preferential rate which shall not on the whole be less favourable to suppliers at the most-favoured-nation rate than the preferences in force prior to such substitution.

The imposition of an equivalent margin of tariff preference to replace a margin of preference in an internal tax existing on April 10, 1947 exclusively between two or more of the territories listed in this Annex or to replace the preferential quantitative arrangements described in the following paragraph, shall not be deemed to constitute an increase in a margin of tariff preference.

The preferential arrangements referred to in paragraph 5(b) of Article XIV are those existing in the United Kingdom on April 10, 1947, under contractual agreements with the Governments of Canada, Australia and New Zealand, in respect of chilled and frozen beef and veal, frozen mutton and lamb, chilled and frozen pork, and bacon. It is the intention, without prejudice to any action taken under sub-paragraph (h)[†] of Article XX, that these arrangements shall be eliminated or replaced by tariff preferences, and that negotiations to this end shall take place as soon as practicable among the countries substantially concerned or involved.

The film hire tax in force in New Zealand on April 10, 1947, shall, for the purposes of this Agreement, be treated as a customs duty under Article I. The renters' film quota in force in New Zealand on April 10, 1947, shall, for the purposes of this Agreement, be treated as a screen quota under Article IV.

The Dominions of India and Pakistan have not been mentioned separately in the above list since they had not come into existence as such on the base date of April 10, 1947.

Annex B

List of Territories of the French Union Referred to in Paragraph 2(b) of Article I

France

French Equatorial Africa (Treaty Basin of the Congo [1] and other territories)

French West Africa

Cameroons Under French Trusteeship [1]

[†] The authentic text erroneously reads "part I(*h*)".

[1.] For imports into Metropolitan France and Territories of the French Union.

French Somali Coast and Dependencies

French Establishments in Oceania

French Establishments in the Condominium of the New Hebrides [1]

Indo–China

Madagascar and Dependencies

Morocco (French zone) [1]

New Caledonia and Dependencies

Saint–Pierre and Miquelon

Togo under French Trusteeship [1]

Tunisia

Annex C

List of Territories Referred to in Paragraph 2(b) of Article I as Respects the Customs Union of Belgium, Luxemburg and the Netherlands

The Economic Union of Belgium and Luxemburg

Belgian Congo

Ruanda Urundi

Netherlands

New Guinea

Surinam

Netherlands Antilles

Republic of Indonesia

For imports into the territories constituting the Customs Union only.

Annex D

List of Territories Referred to in Paragraph 2(b) of Article I as Respects the United States of America

United States of America (customs territory)

Dependent territories of the United States of America

Republic of the Philippines

The imposition of an equivalent margin of tariff preference to replace a margin of preference in an internal tax existing on April 10, 1947, exclusively between two or more of the territories listed in this Annex shall not be deemed to constitute an increase in a margin of tariff preference.

Annex E

List of Territories Covered by Preferential Arrangements Between Chile and Neighbouring Countries Referred to in Paragraph 2(d) of Article I

Preferences in force exclusively between Chile on the one hand, and

1. Argentina

1. For imports into Metropolitan France and Territories of the French Union.

2. Bolivia

3. Peru

on the other hand.

Annex F

List of Territories Covered by Preferential Arrangements Between
Lebanon and Syria and Neighbouring Countries Referred to
in Paragraph 2(d) of Article I

Preferences in force exclusively between the Lebano–Syrian Customs Union, on the one hand, and

1. Palestine

2. Transjordan

on the other hand.

Annex G

Dates Establishing Maximum Margins of Preference
Referred to in Paragraph 4 [†] of Article I

Australia	October 15, 1946
Canada	July 1, 1939
France	January 1, 1939
Lebano–Syrian Customs Union	November 30, 1938
Union of South Africa	July 1, 1938
Southern Rhodesia	May 1, 1941

Annex H

Percentage Shares of Total External Trade to Be Used for the Purpose
of Making the Determination Referred to in Article XXVI

(based on the average of 1949–1953)

If, prior to the accession of the Government of Japan to the General Agreement, the present Agreement has been accepted by contracting parties the external trade of which under column I accounts for the percentage of such trade specified in paragraph 6 of Article XXVI, column I shall be applicable for the purposes of that paragraph. If the present Agreement has not been so accepted prior to the accession of the Government of Japan, column II shall be applicable for the purposes of that paragraph.

	Column I (Contracting parties on 1 March 1955)	*Column II* (Contracting parties on 1 March 1955 and Japan)
Australia	3.1	3.0
Austria	0.9	0.8
Belgium–Luxemburg	4.3	4.2
Brazil	2.5	2.4
Burma	0.3	0.3

[†] The authentic text erroneously reads "Paragraph 3".

	Column I (Contracting parties on 1 March 1955)	Column II (Contracting parties on 1 March 1955 and Japan)
Canada	6.7	6.5
Ceylon	0.5	0.5
Chile	0.6	0.6
Cuba	1.1	1.1
Czechoslovakia	1.4	1.4
Denmark	1.4	1.4
Dominican Republic	0.1	0.1
Finland	1.0	1.0
France	8.7	8.5
Germany, Federal Republic of	5.3	5.2
Greece	0.4	0.4
Haiti	0.1	0.1
India	2.4	2.4
Indonesia	1.3	1.3
Italy	2.9	2.8
Netherlands, Kingdom of the	4.7	4.6
New Zealand	1.0	1.0
Nicaragua	0.1	0.1
Norway	1.1	1.1
Pakistan	0.9	0.8
Peru	0.4	0.4
Rhodesia and Nyasaland	0.6	0.6
Sweden	2.5	2.4
Turkey	0.6	0.6
Union of South Africa	1.8	1.8
United Kingdom	20.3	19.8
United States of America	20.6	20.1
Uruguay	0.4	0.4
Japan	—	2.3
	100.0	100.0

Note: These percentages have been computed taking into account the trade of all territories in respect of which the General Agreement on Tariffs and Trade is applied.

Annex I

Notes and Supplementary Provisions

Ad *Article I*

Paragraph 1

The obligations incorporated in paragraph 1 of Article I by reference to paragraphs 2 and 4 of Article III and those incorporated in paragraph 2(*b*) of Article II by reference to Article VI shall be considered as falling within Part II for the purposes of the Protocol of Provisional Application.

The cross-references, in the paragraph immediately above and in paragraph 1 of Article I, to paragraphs 2 and 4 of Article III shall only apply after Article III has been modified by the entry into force of the amendment provided for in the Protocol Modifying Part II and Article XXVI of the General Agreement on Tariffs and Trade, dated September 14, 1948.[1]

Paragraph 4

The term "margin of preference" means the absolute difference between the most-favoured-nation rate of duty and the preferential rate of duty for the like product, and not the proportionate relation between those rates. As examples:

(1) If the most-favoured-nation rate were 36 per cent *ad valorem* and the preferential rate were 24 per cent *ad valorem,* the margin of preference would be 12 per cent *ad valorem,* and not one-third of the most-favoured-nation rate;

(2) If the most-favoured-nation rate were 36 per cent *ad valorem* and the preferential rate were expressed as two-thirds of the most-favoured-nation rate, the margin of preference would be 12 per cent *ad valorem*;

(3) If the most-favoured-nation rate were 2 francs per kilogramme and the preferential rate were 1.50 francs per kilogramme, the margin of preference would be 0.50 franc per kilogramme.

The following kinds of customs action, taken in accordance with established uniform procedures, would not be contrary to a general binding of margins of preference:

(i) The re-application to an imported product of a tariff classification or rate of duty, properly applicable to such product, in cases in which the application of such classification or rate to such product was temporarily suspended or inoperative on April 10, 1947; and

(ii) The classification of a particular product under a tariff item other than that under which importations of that product were classified on April 10, 1947, in cases in which the tariff law clearly contemplates that such product may be classified under more than one tariff item.

Ad *Article II*

Paragraph 2 (a)

The cross-reference, in paragraph 2(*a*) of Article II, to paragraph 2 of Article III shall only apply after Article III has been modified by the entry into force of the amendment provided for in the Protocol Modifying Part II and Article XXVI of the General Agreement on Tariffs and Trade, dated September 14, 1948.[1]

Paragraph 2 (b)

See the note relating to paragraph 1 of Article I.

Paragraph 4

Except where otherwise specifically agreed between the contracting parties which initially negotiated the concession, the provisions of this paragraph will be applied in the light of the provisions of Article 31 of the Havana Charter.

---

1. This Protocol entered into force on 14 December 1948.

1. This Protocol entered into force on 14 December 1948.

Ad *Article III*

Any internal tax or other internal charge, or any law, regulation or requirement of the kind referred to in paragraph 1 which applies to an imported product and to the like domestic product and is collected or enforced in the case of the imported product at the time or point of importation, is nevertheless to be regarded as an internal tax or other internal charge, or a law, regulation or requirement of the kind referred to in paragraph 1, and is accordingly subject to the provisions of Article III.

Paragraph 1

The application of paragraph 1 to internal taxes imposed by local governments and authorities within the territory of a contracting party is subject to the provisions of the final paragraph of Article XXIV. The term "reasonable measures" in the last-mentioned paragraph would not require, for example, the repeal of existing national legislation authorizing local governments to impose internal taxes which, although technically inconsistent with the letter of Article III, are not in fact inconsistent with its spirit, if such repeal would result in a serious financial hardship for the local governments or authorities concerned. With regard to taxation by local governments or authorities which is inconsistent with both the letter and spirit of Article III, the term "reasonable measures" would permit a contracting party to eliminate the inconsistent taxation gradually over a transition period, if abrupt action would create serious administrative and financial difficulties.

Paragraph 2

A tax conforming to the requirements of the first sentence of paragraph 2 would be considered to be inconsistent with the provisions of the second sentence only in cases where competition was involved between, on the one hand, the taxed product and, on the other hand, a directly competitive or substitutable product which was not similarly taxed.

Paragraph 5

Regulations consistent with the provisions of the first sentence of paragraph 5 shall not be considered to be contrary to the provisions of the second sentence in any case in which all of the products subject to the regulations are produced domestically in substantial quantities. A regulation cannot be justified as being consistent with the provisions of the second sentence on the ground that the proportion or amount allocated to each of the products which are the subject of the regulation constitutes an equitable relationship between imported and domestic products.

Ad *Article V*

Paragraph 5

With regard to transportation charges, the principle laid down in paragraph 5 refers to like products being transported on the same route under like conditions.

Ad *Article VI*

Paragraph 1

1. Hidden dumping by associated houses (that is, the sale by an importer at a price below that corresponding to the price invoiced by an exporter

with whom the importer is associated, and also below the price in the exporting country) constitutes a form of price dumping with respect to which the margin of dumping may be calculated on the basis of the price at which the goods are resold by the importer.

2. It is recognized that, in the case of imports from a country which has a complete or substantially complete monopoly of its trade and where all domestic prices are fixed by the State, special difficulties may exist in determining price comparability for the purposes of paragraph 1, and in such cases importing contracting parties may find it necessary to take into account the possibility that a strict comparison with domestic prices in such a country may not always be appropriate.

Paragraphs 2 and 3

1. As in many other cases in customs administration, a contracting party may require reasonable security (bond or cash deposit) for the payment of anti-dumping or countervailing duty pending final determination of the facts in any case of suspected dumping or subsidization.

2. Multiple currency practices can in certain circumstances constitute a subsidy to exports which may be met by countervailing duties under paragraph 3 or can constitute a form of dumping by means of a partial depreciation of a country's currency which may be met by action under paragraph 2. By "multiple currency practices" is meant practices by governments or sanctioned by governments.

Paragraph 6 (b)

Waivers under the provisions of this sub-paragraph shall be granted only on application by the contracting party proposing to levy an anti-dumping or countervailing duty, as the case may be.

Ad *Article VII*

Paragraph 1

The expression "or other charges" is not to be regarded as including internal taxes or equivalent charges imposed on or in connexion with imported products.

Paragraph 2

1. It would be in conformity with Article VII to presume that "actual value" may be represented by the invoice price, plus any non-included charges for legitimate costs which are proper elements of "actual value" and plus any abnormal discount or other reduction from the ordinary competitive price.

2. It would be in conformity with Article VII, paragraph 2(*b*), for a contracting party to construe the phrase "in the ordinary course of trade * * * under fully competitive conditions", as excluding any transaction wherein the buyer and seller are not independent of each other and price is not the sole consideration.

3. The standard of "fully competitive conditions" permits a contracting party to exclude from consideration prices involving special discounts limited to exclusive agents.

4. The wording of sub-paragraphs (a) and (b) permits a contracting party to determine the value for customs purposes uniformly either (1) on the basis of a particular exporter's prices of the imported merchandise, or (2) on the basis of the general price level of like merchandise.

Ad *Article VIII*

1. While Article VIII does not cover the use of multiple rates of exchange as such, paragraphs 1 and 4 condemn the use of exchange taxes or fees as a device for implementing multiple currency practices; if, however, a contracting party is using multiple currency exchange fees for balance of payments reasons with the approval of the International Monetary Fund, the provisions of paragraph 9(a) of Article XV fully safeguard its position.

2. It would be consistent with paragraph 1 if, on the importation of products from the territory of a contracting party into the territory of another contracting party, the production of certificates of origin should only be required to the extent that is strictly indispensable.

Ad *Articles XI, XII, XIII, XIV and XVIII*

Throughout Articles XI, XII, XIII, XIV and XVIII, the terms "import restrictions" or "export restrictions" include restrictions made effective through state-trading operations.

Ad *Article XI*

Paragraph 2 (c)

The term "in any form" in this paragraph covers the same products when in an early stage of processing and still perishable, which compete directly with the fresh product and if freely imported would tend to make the restriction on the fresh product ineffective.

Paragraph 2, last sub-paragraph

The term "special factors" includes changes in relative productive efficiency as between domestic and foreign producers, or as between different foreign producers, but not changes artificially brought about by means not permitted under the Agreement.

Ad *Article XII*

The CONTRACTING PARTIES shall make provision for the utmost secrecy in the conduct of any consultation under the provisions of this Article.

Paragraph 3 (c)(i)

Contracting parties applying restrictions shall endeavour to avoid causing serious prejudice to exports of a commodity on which the economy of a contracting party is largely dependent.

Paragraph 4 (b)

It is agreed that the date shall be within ninety days after the entry into force of the amendments of this Article effected by the Protocol Amending the Preamble and Parts II and III of this Agreement. However, should the CONTRACTING PARTIES find that conditions were not suitable for the application of the provisions of this sub-paragraph at the time envisaged, they may determine a later date; *Provided* that such date is not more than thirty days after such time as the obligations of Article VIII, Sections 2, 3 and 4, of the Articles of Agreement of the International Monetary Fund become applicable to contracting parties, members of the Fund, the combined foreign trade of which constitutes at least fifty per centum of the aggregate foreign trade of all contracting parties.

Paragraph 4 (e)

It is agreed that paragraph 4(*e*) does not add any new criteria for the imposition or maintenance of quantitative restrictions for balance of payments reasons. It is solely intended to ensure that all external factors such as changes in the terms of trade, quantitative restrictions, excessive tariffs and subsidies, which may be contributing to the balance of payments difficulties of the contracting party applying restrictions, will be fully taken into account.

Ad *Article XIII*

Paragraph 2 (d)

No mention was made of "commercial considerations" as a rule for the allocation of quotas because it was considered that its application by governmental authorities might not always be practicable. Moreover, in cases where it is practicable, a contracting party could apply these considerations in the process of seeking agreement, consistently with the general rule laid down in the opening sentence of paragraph 2.

Paragraph 4

See note relating to "special factors" in connexion with the last sub-paragraph of paragraph 2 of Article XI.

Ad *Article XIV*

Paragraph 1

The provisions of this paragraph shall not be so construed as to preclude full consideration by the CONTRACTING PARTIES, in the consultations provided for in paragraph 4 of Article XII and in paragraph 12 of Article XVIII, of the nature, effects and reasons for discrimination in the field of import restrictions.

Paragraph 2

One of the situations contemplated in paragraph 2 is that of a contracting party holding balances acquired as a result of current transactions which it finds itself unable to use without a measure of discrimination.

Ad *Article XV*

Paragraph 4

The word "frustrate" is intended to indicate, for example, that infringements of the letter of any Article of this Agreement by exchange action shall not be regarded as a violation of that Article if, in practice, there is no appreciable departure from the intent of the Article. Thus, a contracting party which, as part of its exchange control operated in accordance with the Articles of Agreement of the International Monetary Fund, requires payment to be received for its exports in its own currency or in the currency of one or more members of the International Monetary Fund will not thereby be deemed to contravene Article XI or Article XIII. Another example would be that of a contracting party which specifies on an import licence the country from which the goods may be imported, for the purpose not of introducing any additional element of discrimination in its import licensing system but of enforcing permissible exchange controls.

Ad *Article XVI*

The exemption of an exported product from duties or taxes borne by the like product when destined for domestic consumption, or the remission of such duties or taxes in amounts not in excess of those which have accrued, shall not be deemed to be a subsidy.

Section B

1. Nothing in Section B shall preclude the use by a contracting party of multiple rates of exchange in accordance with the Articles of Agreement of the International Monetary Fund.

2. For the purposes of Section B, a "primary product" is understood to be any product of farm, forest or fishery, or any mineral, in its natural form or which has undergone such processing as is customarily required to prepare it for marketing in substantial volume in international trade.

Paragraph 3

1. The fact that a contracting party has not exported the product in question during the previous representative period would not in itself preclude that contracting party from establishing its right to obtain a share of the trade in the product concerned.

2. A system for the stabilization of the domestic price or of the return to domestic producers of a primary product independently of the movements of export prices, which results at times in the sale of the product for export at a price lower than the comparable price charged for the like product to buyers in the domestic market, shall be considered not to involve a subsidy on exports within the meaning of paragraph 3 if the CONTRACTING PARTIES determine that:

> (a) the system has also resulted, or is so designed as to result, in the sale of the product for export at a price higher than the comparable price charged for the like product to buyers in the domestic market; and

> (b) the system is so operated, or is designed so to operate, either because of the effective regulation of production or otherwise, as not to stipulate exports unduly or otherwise seriously to prejudice the interests of other contracting parties.

Notwithstanding such determination by the CONTRACTING PARTIES, operations under such a system shall be subject to the provisions of paragraph 3 where they are wholly or partly financed out of government funds in addition to the funds collected from producers in respect of the product concerned.

Paragraph 4

The intention of paragraph 4 is that the contracting parties should seek before the end of 1957 to reach agreement to abolish all remaining subsidies as from 1 January 1958; or, failing this, to reach agreement to extend the application of the standstill until the earliest date thereafter by which they can expect to reach such agreement.

Ad *Article XVII*

Paragraph 1

The operations of Marketing Boards, which are established by contracting parties and are engaged in purchasing or selling, are subject to the provisions of sub-paragraphs (*a*) and (*b*).

The activities of Marketing Boards which are established by contracting parties and which do not purchase or sell but lay down regulations covering private trade are governed by the relevant Articles of this Agreement.

The charging by a state enterprise of different prices for its sales of a product in different markets is not precluded by the provisions of this Article, provided that such different prices are charged for commercial reasons, to meet conditions of supply and demand in export markets.

Paragraph 1 (a)

Governmental measures imposed to ensure standards of quality and efficiency in the operation of external trade, or privileges granted for the exploitation of national natural resources but which do not empower the government to exercise control over the trading activities of the enterprise in question, do not constitute "exclusive or special privileges".

Paragraph 1 (b)

A country receiving a "tied loan" is free to take this loan into account as a "commercial consideration" when purchasing requirements abroad.

Paragraph 2

The term "goods" is limited to products as understood in commercial practice, and is not intended to include the purchase or sale of services.

Paragraph 3

Negotiations which contracting parties agree to conduct under this paragraph may be directed towards the reduction of duties and other charges on imports and exports or towards the conclusion of any other mutually satisfactory arrangement consistent with the provisions of this Agreement. (See paragraph 4 of Article II and the note to that paragraph.)

Paragraph 4 (b)

The term "import mark-up" in this paragraph shall represent the margin by which the price charged by the import monopoly for the imported product (exclusive of internal taxes within the purview of Article III, transportation, distribution, and other expenses incident to the purchase, sale or further processing, and a reasonable margin of profit) exceeds the landed cost.

Ad *Article XVIII*

The CONTRACTING PARTIES and the contracting parties concerned shall preserve the utmost secrecy in respect of matters arising under this Article.

Paragraphs 1 and 4

1. When they consider whether the economy of a contracting party "can only support low standards of living", the CONTRACTING PARTIES shall take into consideration the normal position of that economy and shall not base their determination on exceptional circumstances such as those which may result from the temporary existence of exceptionally favourable conditions for the staple export product or products of such contracting party.

2. The phrase "in the early stages of development" is not meant to apply only to contracting parties which have just started their economic development, but also to contracting parties the economies of which are undergoing a process of industrialization to correct an excessive dependence on primary production.

Paragraphs 2, 3, 7, 13 and 22

The reference to the establishment of particular industries shall apply not only to the establishment of a new industry, but also to the establishment of a new branch of production in an existing industry and to the substantial transformation of an existing industry, and to the substantial expansion of an existing industry supplying a relatively small proportion of the domestic demand. It shall also cover the reconstruction of an industry destroyed or substantially damaged as a result of hostilities or natural disasters.

Paragraph 7 (b)

A modification or withdrawal, pursuant to paragraph 7(*b*), by a contracting party, other than the applicant contracting party, referred to in paragraph 7(*a*), shall be made within six months of the day on which the action is taken by the applicant contracting party, and shall become effective on the thirtieth day following the day on which such modification or withdrawal has been notified to the CONTRACTING PARTIES.

Paragraph 11

The second sentence in paragraph 11 shall not be interpreted to mean that a contracting party is required to relax or remove restrictions if such relaxation or removal would thereupon produce conditions justifying the intensification or institution, respectively, of restrictions under paragraph 9 of Article XVIII.

Paragraph 12 (b)

The date referred to in paragraph 12(*b*) shall be the date determined by the CONTRACTING PARTIES in accordance with the provisions of paragraph 4(*b*) of Article XII of this Agreement.

Paragraphs 13 and 14

It is recognized that, before deciding on the introduction of a measure and notifying the CONTRACTING PARTIES in accordance with paragraph 14, a contracting party may need a reasonable period of time to assess the competitive position of the industry concerned.

Paragraphs 15 and 16

It is understood that the CONTRACTING PARTIES shall invite a contracting party proposing to apply a measure under Section C to consult with them pursuant to paragraph 16 if they are requested to do so by a contracting party the trade of which would be appreciably affected by the measure in question.

Paragraphs 16, 18, 19 and 22

1.   It is understood that the CONTRACTING PARTIES may concur in a proposed measure subject to specific conditions or limitations. If the measure as applied does not conform to the terms of the concurrence it will to that extent be deemed a measure in which the CONTRACTING PARTIES have not concurred. In cases in which the CONTRACTING PARTIES have concurred in a measure for a specified period, the contracting party concerned, if it finds that the maintenance of the measure for a further period of time is required to achieve the objective for which the measure was originally taken, may apply to the CONTRACTING PARTIES for an extension of that period in accordance with the provisions and procedures of Section C or D, as the case may be.

2.   It is expected that the CONTRACTING PARTIES will, as a rule, refrain from concurring in a measure which is likely to cause serious prejudice to exports of a commodity on which the economy of a contracting party is largely dependent.

Paragraphs 18 and 22

The phrase "that the interests of other contracting parties are adequately safeguarded" is meant to provide latitude sufficient to permit consideration in each case of the most appropriate method of safeguarding those interests. The appropriate method may, for instance, take the form of an additional concession to be applied by the contracting party having recourse to Section C or D during such time as the deviation from the other Articles of the Agreement would remain in force or of the temporary suspension by any other contracting party referred to in paragraph 18 of a concession substantially equivalent to the impairment due to the introduction of the measure in question. Such contracting party would have the right to safeguard its interests through such a temporary suspension of a concession; *Provided* that this right will not be exercised when, in the case of a measure imposed by a contracting party coming within the scope of paragraph 4(a), the CONTRACTING PARTIES have determined that the extent of the compensatory concession proposed was adequate.

Paragraph 19

The provisions of paragraph 19 are intended to cover the cases where an industry has been in existence beyond the "reasonable period of time" referred to in the note to paragraphs 13 and 14, and should not be so construed as to deprive a contracting party coming within the scope of paragraph 4(*a*) of Article XVIII, of its right to resort to the other provisions of Section C, including paragraph 17, with regard to a newly established industry even though it has benefited from incidental protection afforded by balance of payments import restrictions.

Paragraph 21

Any measure taken pursuant to the provisions of paragraph 21 shall be withdrawn forthwith if the action taken in accordance with paragraph 17 is withdrawn or if the CONTRACTING PARTIES concur in the measure proposed after the expiration of the ninety-day time limit specified in paragraph 17.

Ad *Article XX*

Sub-paragraph (h)

The exception provided for in this sub-paragraph extends to any commodity agreement which conforms to the principles approved by the Economic and Social Council in its resolution 30(IV) of 28 March 1947.

Ad *Article XXIV*

Paragraph 9

It is understood that the provisions of Article I would require that, when a product which has been imported into the territory of a member of a customs union or free-trade area at a preferential rate of duty is re-exported to the territory of another member of such union or area, the latter member should collect a duty equal to the difference between the duty already paid and any higher duty that would be payable if the product were being imported directly into its territory.

Paragraph 11

Measures adopted by India and Pakistan in order to carry out definitive trade arrangements between them, once they have been agreed upon, might depart from particular provisions of this Agreement, but these measures would in general be consistent with the objectives of the Agreement.

Ad *Article XXVIII*

The CONTRACTING PARTIES and each contracting party concerned should arrange to conduct the negotiations and consultations with the greatest possible secrecy in order to avoid premature disclosure of details of prospective tariff changes. The CONTRACTING PARTIES shall be informed immediately of all changes in national tariffs resulting from recourse to this Article.

Paragraph 1

1. If the CONTRACTING PARTIES specify a period other than a three-year period, a contracting party may act pursuant to paragraph 1 or paragraph 3 of Article XXVIII on the first day following the expiration of such other period and, unless the CONTRACTING PARTIES have again specified

another period, subsequent periods will be three-year periods following the expiration of such specified period.

2.   The provision that on 1 January 1958, and on other days determined pursuant to paragraph 1, a contracting party "may * * * modify or withdraw a concession" means that on such day, and on the first day after the end of each period, the legal obligation of such contracting party under Article II is altered; it does not mean that the changes in its customs tariff should necessarily be made effective on that day. If a tariff change resulting from negotiations undertaken pursuant to this Article is delayed, the entry into force of any compensatory concessions may be similarly delayed.

3.   Not earlier than six months, nor later than three months, prior to 1 January 1958, or to the termination date of any subsequent period, a contracting party wishing to modify or withdraw any concession embodied in the appropriate Schedule, should notify the CONTRACTING PARTIES to this effect. The CONTRACTING PARTIES shall then determine the contracting party or contracting parties with which the negotiations or consultations referred to in paragraph 1 shall take place. Any contracting party so determined shall participate in such negotiations or consultations with the applicant contracting party with the aim of reaching agreement before the end of the period. Any extension of the assured life of the Schedules shall relate to the Schedules as modified after such negotiations, in accordance with paragraphs 1, 2 and 3 of Article XXVIII. If the CONTRACTING PARTIES are arranging for multilateral tariff negotiations to take place within the period of six months before 1 January 1958, or before any other day determined pursuant to paragraph 1, they shall include in the arrangements for such negotiations suitable procedures for carrying out the negotiations referred to in this paragraph.

4.   The object of providing for the participation in the negotiations of any contracting party with a principal supplying interest, in addition to any contracting party with which the concession was initially negotiated, is to ensure that a contracting party with a larger share in the trade affected by the concession than a contracting party with which the concession was initially negotiated shall have an effective opportunity to protect the contractual right which it enjoys under this Agreement. On the other hand, it is not intended that the scope of the negotiations should be such as to make negotiations and agreement under Article XXVIII unduly difficult nor to create complications in the application of this Article in the future to concessions which result from negotiations thereunder. Accordingly, the CONTRACTING PARTIES should only determine that a contracting party has a principal supplying interest if that contracting party has had, over a reasonable period of time prior to the negotiations, a larger share in the market of the applicant contracting party than a contracting party with which the concession was initially negotiated or would, in the judgment of the CONTRACTING PARTIES, have had such a share in the absence of discriminatory quantitative restrictions maintained by the applicant contracting party. It would therefore not be appropriate for the CONTRACTING PARTIES to determine that more than one contracting party, or in those exceptional cases where there is near equality more than two contracting parties, had a principal supplying interest.

5. Notwithstanding the definition of a principal supplying interest in note 4 to paragraph 1, the CONTRACTING PARTIES may exceptionally determine that a contracting party has a principal supplying interest if the concession in question affects trade which constitutes a major part of the total exports of such contracting party.

6. It is not intended that provision for participation in the negotiations of any contracting party with a principal supplying interest, and for consultation with any contracting party having a substantial interest in the concession which the applicant contracting party is seeking to modify or withdraw, should have the effect that it should have to pay compensation or suffer retaliation greater than the withdrawal or modification sought, judged in the light of the conditions of trade at the time of the proposed withdrawal or modification, making allowance for any discriminatory quantitative restrictions maintained by the applicant contracting party.

7. The expression "substantial interest" is not capable of a precise definition and accordingly may present difficulties for the CONTRACTING PARTIES. It is, however, intended to be construed to cover only those contracting parties which have, or in the absence of discriminatory quantitative restrictions affecting their exports could reasonably be expected to have, a significant share in the market of the contracting party seeking to modify or withdraw the concession.

Paragraph 4

1. Any request for authorization to enter into negotiations shall be accompanied by all relevant statistical and other data. A decision on such request shall be made within thirty days of its submission.

2. It is recognized that to permit certain contracting parties, depending in large measure on a relatively small number of primary commodities and relying on the tariff as an important aid for furthering diversification of their economies or as an important source of revenue, normally to negotiate for the modification or withdrawal of concessions only under paragraph 1 of Article XXVIII, might cause them at such a time to make modifications or withdrawals which in the long run would prove unnecessary. To avoid such a situation the CONTRACTING PARTIES shall authorize any such contracting party, under paragraph 4, to enter into negotiations unless they consider this would result in, or contribute substantially towards, such an increase in tariff levels as to threaten the stability of the Schedules to this Agreement or lead to undue disturbance of international trade.

3. It is expected that negotiations authorized under paragraph 4 for modification or withdrawal of a single item, or a very small group of items, could normally be brought to a conclusion in sixty days. It is recognized, however, that such a period will be inadequate for cases involving negotiations for the modification or withdrawal of a larger number of items and in such cases, therefore, it would be appropriate for the CONTRACTING PARTIES to prescribe a longer period.

4. The determination referred to in paragraph 4(*d*) shall be made by the CONTRACTING PARTIES within thirty days of the submission of the matter to them, unless the applicant contracting party agrees to a longer period.

5.   In determining under paragraph 4(*d*) whether an applicant contracting party has unreasonably failed to offer adequate compensation, it is understood that the CONTRACTING PARTIES will take due account of the special position of a contracting party which has bound a high proportion of its tariffs at very low rates of duty and to this extent has less scope than other contracting parties to make compensatory adjustment.

Ad *Article XXVIIIbis*

Paragraph 3

It is understood that the reference to fiscal needs would include the revenue aspect of duties and particularly duties imposed primarily for revenue purposes or duties imposed on products which can be substituted for products subject to revenue duties to prevent the avoidance of such duties.

Ad *Article XXIX*

Paragraph 1

Chapters VII and VIII of the Havana Charter have been excluded from paragraph 1 because they generally deal with the organization, functions and procedures of the International Trade Organization.

Ad *Part IV*

The words "developed contracting parties" and the words "less-developed contracting parties," as used in Part IV are to be understood to refer to developed and less-developed countries which are parties to the General Agreement on Tariffs and Trade.

Ad *Article XXXVI*

Paragraph 1

This Article is based upon the objectives set forth in Article I as it will be amended by Section A of paragraph 1 of the Protocol Amending Part I and Articles XXIX and XXX when that Protocol enters into force.[1]

Paragraph 4

The term "primary products" includes agricultural products, *vide* paragraph 2 of the note ad Article XVI, Section B.

Paragraph 5

A diversification programme would generally include the intensification of activities for the processing of primary products and the development of manufacturing industries, taking into account the situation of the particular contracting party and the world outlook for production and consumption of different commodities.

Paragraph 8

It is understood that the phrase "do not expect reciprocity" means, in accordance with the objectives set forth in this Article, that the less-developed contracting parties should not be expected, in the course of trade negotiations,

1. This Protocol was abandoned on January 1, 1968.

to make contributions which are inconsistent with their individual development, financial and trade needs, taking into consideration past trade developments.

This paragraph would apply in the event of action under Section A of Article XVIII, Article XXVIII, Article XXVIIIbis (Article XXIX after the amendment set forth in Section A of paragraph 1 of the Protocol Amending Part I and Articles XXIX and XXX shall have become effective[1]), Article XXXIII, or any other procedure under this Agreement.

Ad *Article XXXVII*

Paragraph 1 (a)

This paragraph would apply in the event of negotiations for reduction or elimination of tariffs or other restrictive regulations of commerce under Articles XXVIII, XXVIIIbis (XXIX after the amendment set forth in Section A of paragraph 1 of the Protocol Amending Part I and Articles XXIX and XXX shall have become effective[1]), and Article XXXIII, as well as in connection with other action to effect such reduction or elimination which contracting parties may be able to undertake.

Paragraph 3 (b)

The other measures referred to in this paragraph might include steps to promote domestic structural changes, to encourage the consumption of particular products, or to introduce measures of trade promotion.

---

1. This Protocol was abandoned on January 1, 1968.

Item 3

GENERAL AGREEMENT ON TARIFFS AND TRADE 1994

1. The General Agreement on Tariffs and Trade 1994 ("GATT 1994") shall consist of:

(a) the provisions in the General Agreement on Tariffs and Trade, dated 30 October 1947, annexed to the Final Act Adopted at the Conclusion of the Second Session of the Preparatory Committee of the United Nations Conference on Trade and Employment (excluding the Protocol of Provisional Application), as rectified, amended or modified by the terms of legal instruments which have entered into force before the date of entry into force of the WTO Agreement;

(b) the provisions of the legal instruments set forth below that have entered into force under the GATT 1947 before the date of entry into force of the WTO Agreement:

(i) protocols and certifications relating to tariff concessions;

(ii) protocols of accession (excluding the provisions (a) concerning provisional application and withdrawal of provisional application and (b) providing that Part II of GATT 1947 shall be applied provisionally to the fullest extent not inconsistent with legislation existing on the date of the Protocol);

(iii) decisions on waivers granted under Article XXV of GATT 1947 and still in force on the date of entry into force of the WTO Agreement [1];

(iv) other decisions of the CONTRACTING PARTIES to GATT 1947;

(c) the Understandings set forth below:

(i) Understanding on the Interpretation of Article II:1(b) of the General Agreement on Tariffs and Trade 1994;

(ii) Understanding on the Interpretation of Article XVII of the General Agreement on Tariffs and Trade 1994;

(iii) Understanding on Balance-of-Payments Provisions of the General Agreement on Tariffs and Trade 1994;

(iv) Understanding on the Interpretation of Article XXIV of the General Agreement on Tariffs and Trade 1994;

(v) Understanding in Respect of Waivers of Obligations under the General Agreement on Tariffs and Trade 1994;

---

1. The waivers covered by this provision are listed in footnote 7 on pages 11 and 12 in Part II of document MTN/FA of 15 December 1993 and in MTN/FA/Corr.6 of 21 March 1994. The Ministerial Conference shall establish at its first session a revised list of waivers covered by this provision that adds any waivers granted under GATT 1947 after 15 December 1993 and before the date of entry into force of the WTO Agreement, and deletes the waivers which will have expired by that time.

(vi) Understanding on the Interpretation of Article XXVIII of the General Agreement on Tariffs and Trade 1994; and

(d) the Marrakesh Protocol to GATT 1994.

2. *Explanatory Notes*

(a) The references to "contracting party" in the provisions of GATT 1994 shall be deemed to read "Member". The references to "less-developed contracting party" and "developed contracting party" shall be deemed to read "developing country Member" and "developed country Member". The references to "Executive Secretary" shall be deemed to read "Director–General of the WTO".

(b) The references to the CONTRACTING PARTIES acting jointly in Articles XV:1, XV:2, XV:8, XXXVIII and the Notes *Ad* Article XII and XVIII; and in the provisions on special exchange agreements in Articles XV:2, XV:3, XV:6, XV:7 and XV:9 of GATT 1994 shall be deemed to be references to the WTO. The other functions that the provisions of GATT 1994 assign to the CONTRACTING PARTIES acting jointly shall be allocated by the Ministerial Conference.

(c) (i) The text of GATT 1994 shall be authentic in English, French and Spanish.

(ii) The text of GATT 1994 in the French language shall be subject to the rectifications of terms indicated in Annex A to document MTN.TNC/41.

(iii) The authentic text of GATT 1994 in the Spanish language shall be the text in Volume IV of the Basic Instruments and Selected Documents series, subject to the rectifications of terms indicated in Annex B to document MTN.TNC/41.

3. (a) The provisions of Part II of GATT 1994 shall not apply to measures taken by a Member under specific mandatory legislation, enacted by that Member before it became a contracting party to GATT 1947, that prohibits the use, sale or lease of foreign-built or foreign-reconstructed vessels in commercial applications between points in national waters or the waters of an exclusive economic zone. This exemption applies to: (*a*) the continuation or prompt renewal of a non-conforming provision of such legislation; and (*b*) the amendment to a non-conforming provision of such legislation to the extent that the amendment does not decrease the conformity of the provision with Part II of GATT 1947. This exemption is limited to measures taken under legislation described above that is notified and specified prior to the date of entry into force of the WTO Agreement. If such legislation is subsequently modified to decrease its conformity with Part II of GATT 1994, it will no longer qualify for coverage under this paragraph.

(b) The Ministerial Conference shall review this exemption not later than five years after the date of entry into force of the WTO Agreement and thereafter every two years for as long as the exemption is in force for the purpose of examining whether the conditions which created the need for the exemption still prevail.

(c) A Member whose measures are covered by this exemption shall annually submit a detailed statistical notification consisting of a five-year moving average of actual and expected deliveries of relevant vessels as well as additional information on the use, sale, lease or repair of relevant vessels covered by this exemption.

(d) A Member that considers that this exemption operates in such a manner as to justify a reciprocal and proportionate limitation on the use, sale, lease or repair of vessels constructed in the territory of the Member invoking the exemption shall be free to introduce such a limitation subject to prior notification to the Ministerial Conference.

(e) This exemption is without prejudice to solutions concerning specific aspects of the legislation covered by this exemption negotiated in sectoral agreements or in other fora.

UNDERSTANDING ON THE INTERPRETATION OF ARTICLE II:1(b) OF THE GENERAL AGREEMENT ON TARIFFS AND TRADE 1994

Members hereby *agree* as follows:

1. In order to ensure transparency of the legal rights and obligations deriving from paragraph 1(b) of Article II, the nature and level of any "other duties or charges" levied on bound tariff items, as referred to in that provision, shall be recorded in the Schedules of concessions annexed to GATT 1994 against the tariff item to which they apply. It is understood that such recording does not change the legal character of "other duties or charges".

2. The date as of which "other duties or charges" are bound, for the purposes of Article II, shall be 15 April 1994. "Other duties or charges" shall therefore be recorded in the Schedules at the levels applying on this date. At each subsequent renegotiation of a concession or negotiation of a new concession the applicable date for the tariff item in question shall become the date of the incorporation of the new concession in the appropriate Schedule. However, the date of the instrument by which a concession on any particular tariff item was first incorporated into GATT 1947 or GATT 1994 shall also continue to be recorded in column 6 of the Loose–Leaf Schedules.

3. "Other duties or charges" shall be recorded in respect of all tariff bindings.

4. Where a tariff item has previously been the subject of a concession, the level of "other duties or charges" recorded in the appropriate Schedule shall not be higher than the level obtaining at the time of the first incorporation of the concession in that Schedule. It will be open to any Member to challenge the existence of an "other duty or charge", on the ground that no such "other duty or charge" existed at the time of the original binding of the item in question, as well as the consistency of the recorded level of any "other duty or charge" with the previously bound level, for a period of three years after the date of entry into force of the WTO Agreement or three years after the date of deposit with the Director–General of the WTO of the instrument incorporating the Schedule in question into GATT 1994, if that is a later date.

5. The recording of "other duties or charges" in the Schedules is without prejudice to their consistency with rights and obligations under GATT 1994 other than those affected by paragraph 4. All Members retain the right to challenge, at any time, the consistency of any "other duty or charge" with such obligations.

6. For the purposes of this Understanding, the provisions of Articles XXII and XXIII of GATT 1994 as elaborated and applied by the Dispute Settlement Understanding shall apply.

7. "Other duties or charges" omitted from a Schedule at the time of deposit of the instrument incorporating the Schedule in question into GATT 1994 with, until the date of entry into force of the WTO Agreement, the Director–General to the CONTRACTING PARTIES to GATT 1947 or, thereafter, with the Director–General of the WTO, shall not subsequently be added to it and any "other duty or charge" recorded at a level lower than that prevailing on the applicable date shall not be restored to that level unless such additions or changes are made within six months of the date of deposit of the instrument.

8. The decision in paragraph 2 regarding the date applicable to each concession for the purposes of paragraph 1(b) of Article II of GATT 1994 supersedes the decision regarding the applicable date taken on 26 March 1980 (BISD 27S/24).

UNDERSTANDING ON THE INTERPRETATION OF ARTICLE XVII OF THE GENERAL AGREEMENT ON TARIFFS AND TRADE 1994

Members,

Noting that Article XVII provides for obligations on Members in respect of the activities of the state trading enterprises referred to in paragraph 1 of Article XVII, which are required to be consistent with the general principles of non-discriminatory treatment prescribed in GATT 1994 for governmental measures affecting imports or exports by private traders;

Noting further that Members are subject to their GATT 1994 obligations in respect of those governmental measures affecting state trading enterprises;

Recognizing that this Understanding is without prejudice to the substantive disciplines prescribed in Article XVII;

Hereby *agree* as follows:

1. In order to ensure the transparency of the activities of state trading enterprises, Members shall notify such enterprises to the Council for Trade in Goods, for review by the working party to be set up under paragraph 5, in accordance with the following working definition:

> "Governmental and non-governmental enterprises, including marketing boards, which have been granted exclusive or special rights or privileges, including statutory or constitutional powers, in the exercise of which they influence through their purchases or sales the level or direction of imports or exports."

This notification requirement does not apply to imports of products for immediate or ultimate consumption in governmental use or in use by an enterprise as specified above and not otherwise for resale or use in the production of goods for sale.

2. Each Member shall conduct a review of its policy with regard to the submission of notifications on state trading enterprises to the Council for Trade in Goods, taking account of the provisions of this Understanding. In

carrying out such a review, each Member should have regard to the need to ensure the maximum transparency possible in its notifications so as to permit a clear appreciation of the manner of operation of the enterprises notified and the effect of their operations on international trade.

3.   Notifications shall be made in accordance with the questionnaire on state trading adopted on 24 May 1960 (BISD 9S/184–185), it being understood that Members shall notify the enterprises referred to in paragraph 1 whether or not imports or exports have in fact taken place.

4.   Any Member which has reason to believe that another Member has not adequately met its notification obligation may raise the matter with the Member concerned. If the matter is not satisfactorily resolved it may make a counter-notification to the Council for Trade in Goods, for consideration by the working party set up under paragraph 5, simultaneously informing the Member concerned.

5.   A working party shall be set up, on behalf of the Council for Trade in Goods, to review notifications and counter-notifications. In the light of this review and without prejudice to paragraph 4(c) of Article XVII, the Council for Trade in Goods may make recommendations with regard to the adequacy of notifications and the need for further information. The working party shall also review, in the light of the notifications received, the adequacy of the above-mentioned questionnaire on state trading and the coverage of state trading enterprises notified under paragraph 1. It shall also develop an illustrative list showing the kinds of relationships between governments and enterprises, and the kinds of activities, engaged in by these enterprises, which may be relevant for the purposes of Article XVII. It is understood that the Secretariat will provide a general background paper for the working party on the operations of state trading enterprises as they relate to international trade. Membership of the working party shall be open to all Members indicating their wish to serve on it. It shall meet within a year of the date of entry into force of the WTO Agreement and thereafter at least once a year. It shall report annually to the Council for Trade in Goods.[2]

UNDERSTANDING ON THE BALANCE–OF–PAYMENTS PROVISIONS OF THE GENERAL AGREEMENT ON TARIFFS AND TRADE 1994
(followed by 1979 Declaration)

Members,

Recognizing the provisions of Articles XII and XVIII:B of GATT 1994 and of the Declaration on Trade Measures Taken for Balance-of-Payments Purposes adopted on 28 November 1979 (BISD 26S/205–209, referred to in this Understanding as the "1979 Declaration") and in order to clarify such provisions [3];

2.   The activities of this working party shall be coordinated with those of the working group provided for in Section III of the Ministerial Decision on Notification Procedures adopted on 15 April 1994.

3.   Nothing in this Understanding is intended to modify the rights and obligations of Members under Articles XII or XVIII:B of GATT 1994. The provisions of Articles XXII and XXIII of GATT 1994 as elaborated and applied by the Dispute Settlement Understanding may be invoked with respect to any matters arising from the application of restrictive import measures taken for balance-of-payments purposes.

Hereby *agree* as follows:

Application of Measures

1. Members confirm their commitment to announce publicly, as soon as possible, time-schedules for the removal of restrictive import measures taken for balance-of-payments purposes. It is understood that such time-schedules may be modified as appropriate to take into account changes in the balance-of-payments situation. Whenever a time-schedule is not publicly announced by a Member, that Member shall provide justification as to the reasons therefor.

2. Members confirm their commitment to give preference to those measures which have the least disruptive effect on trade. Such measures (referred to in this Understanding as "price-based measures") shall be understood to include import surcharges, import deposit requirements or other equivalent trade measures with an impact on the price of imported goods. It is understood that, notwithstanding the provisions of Article II, price-based measures taken for balance-of-payments purposes may be applied by a Member in excess of the duties inscribed in the Schedule of that Member. Furthermore, that Member shall indicate the amount by which the price-based measure exceeds the bound duty clearly and separately under the notification procedures of this Understanding.

3. Members shall seek to avoid the imposition of new quantitative restrictions for balance-of-payments purposes unless, because of a critical balance-of-payments situation, price-based measures cannot arrest a sharp deterioration in the external payments position. In those cases in which a Member applies quantitative restrictions, it shall provide justification as to the reasons why price-based measures are not an adequate instrument to deal with the balance-of-payments situation. A Member maintaining quantitative restrictions shall indicate in successive consultations the progress made in significantly reducing the incidence and restrictive effect of such measures. It is understood that not more than one type of restrictive import measure taken for balance-of-payments purposes may be applied on the same product.

4. Members confirm that restrictive import measures taken for balance-of-payments purposes may only be applied to control the general level of imports and may not exceed what is necessary to address the balance-of-payments situation. In order to minimize any incidental protective effects, a Member shall administer restrictions in a transparent manner. The authorities of the importing Member shall provide adequate justification as to the criteria used to determine which products are subject to restriction. As provided in paragraph 3 of Article XII and paragraph 10 of Article XVIII, Members may, in the case of certain essential products, exclude or limit the application of surcharges applied across the board or other measures applied for balance-of-payments purposes. The term "essential products" shall be understood to mean products which meet basic consumption needs or which contribute to the Member's effort to improve its balance-of-payments situation, such as capital goods or inputs needed for production. In the administration of quantitative restrictions, a Member shall use discretionary licensing only when unavoidable and shall phase it out progressively. Appropriate

justification shall be provided as to the criteria used to determine allowable import quantities or values.

Procedures for Balance-of-Payments Consultations

5.   The Committee on Balance-of-Payments Restrictions (referred to in this Understanding as the "Committee") shall carry out consultations in order to review all restrictive import measures taken for balance-of-payments purposes.   The membership of the Committee is open to all Members indicating their wish to serve on it.   The Committee shall follow the procedures for consultations on balance-of-payments restrictions approved on 28 April 1970 (BISD 18S/48–53, referred to in this Understanding as "full consultation procedures"), subject to the provisions set out below.

6.   A Member applying new restrictions or raising the general level of its existing restrictions by a substantial intensification of the measures shall enter into consultations with the Committee within four months of the adoption of such measures.   The Member adopting such measures may request that a consultation be held under paragraph 4(a) of Article XII or paragraph 12(a) of Article XVIII as appropriate.   If no such request has been made, the Chairman of the Committee shall invite the Member to hold such a consultation.   Factors that may be examined in the consultation would include, *inter alia*, the introduction of new types of restrictive measures for balance-of-payments purposes, or an increase in the level or product coverage of restrictions.

7.   All restrictions applied for balance-of-payments purposes shall be subject to periodic review in the Committee under paragraph 4(b) of Article XII or under paragraph 12(b) of Article XVIII, subject to the possibility of altering the periodicity of consultations in agreement with the consulting Member or pursuant to any specific review procedure that may be recommended by the General Council.

8.   Consultations may be held under the simplified procedures approved on 19 December 1972 (BISD 20S/47–49, referred to in this Understanding as "simplified consultation procedures") in the case of least-developed country Members or in the case of developing country Members which are pursuing liberalization efforts in conformity with the schedule presented to the Committee in previous consultations.   Simplified consultation procedures may also be used when the Trade Policy Review of a developing country Member is scheduled for the same calendar year as the date fixed for the consultations. In such cases the decision as to whether full consultation procedures should be used will be made on the basis of the factors enumerated in paragraph 8 of the 1979 Declaration.   Except in the case of least-developed country Members, no more than two successive consultations may be held under simplified consultation procedures.

Notification and Documentation

9.   A Member shall notify to the General Council the introduction of or any changes in the application of restrictive import measures taken for balance-of-payments purposes, as well as any modifications in time-schedules for the removal of such measures as announced under paragraph 1.   Significant changes shall be notified to the General Council prior to or not later than

30 days after their announcement. On a yearly basis, each Member shall make available to the Secretariat a consolidated notification, including all changes in laws, regulations, policy statements or public notices, for examination by Members. Notifications shall include full information, as far as possible, at the tariff-line level, on the type of measures applied, the criteria used for their administration, product coverage and trade flows affected.

10.   At the request of any Member, notifications may be reviewed by the Committee. Such reviews would be limited to the clarification of specific issues raised by a notification or examination of whether a consultation under paragraph 4(a) of Article XII or paragraph 12(a) of Article XVIII is required. Members which have reasons to believe that a restrictive import measure applied by another Member was taken for balance-of-payments purposes may bring the matter to the attention of the Committee. The Chairman of the Committee shall request information on the measure and make it available to all Members. Without prejudice to the right of any member of the Committee to seek appropriate clarifications in the course of consultations, questions may be submitted in advance for consideration by the consulting Member.

11.   The consulting Member shall prepare a Basic Document for the consultations which, in addition to any other information considered to be relevant, should include: *(a)* an overview of the balance-of-payments situation and prospects, including a consideration of the internal and external factors having a bearing on the balance-of-payments situation and the domestic policy measures taken in order to restore equilibrium on a sound and lasting basis; *(b)* a full description of the restrictions applied for balance-of-payments purposes, their legal basis and steps taken to reduce incidental protective effects; *(c)* measures taken since the last consultation to liberalize import restrictions, in the light of the conclusions of the Committee; *(d)* a plan for the elimination and progressive relaxation of remaining restrictions. References may be made, when relevant, to the information provided in other notifications or reports made to the WTO. Under simplified consultation procedures, the consulting Member shall submit a written statement containing essential information on the elements covered by the Basic Document.

12.   The Secretariat shall, with a view to facilitating the consultations in the Committee, prepare a factual background paper dealing with the different aspects of the plan for consultations. In the case of developing country Members, the Secretariat document shall include relevant background and analytical material on the incidence of the external trading environment on the balance-of-payments situation and prospects of the consulting Member. The technical assistance services of the Secretariat shall, at the request of a developing country Member, assist in preparing the documentation for the consultations.

Conclusions of Balance-of-Payments Consultations

13.   The Committee shall report on its consultations to the General Council. When full consultation procedures have been used, the report should indicate the Committee's conclusions on the different elements of the plan for consultations, as well as the facts and reasons on which they are based. The Committee shall endeavour to include in its conclusions proposals for recommendations aimed at promoting the implementation of Articles XII

and XVIII:B, the 1979 Declaration and this Understanding. In those cases in which a time-schedule has been presented for the removal of restrictive measures taken for balance-of-payments purposes, the General Council may recommend that, in adhering to such a time-schedule, a Member shall be deemed to be in compliance with its GATT 1994 obligations. Whenever the General Council has made specific recommendations, the rights and obligations of Members shall be assessed in the light of such recommendations. In the absence of specific proposals for recommendations by the General Council, the Committee's conclusions should record the different views expressed in the Committee. When simplified consultation procedures have been used, the report shall include a summary of the main elements discussed in the Committee and a decision on whether full consultation procedures are required.

1979 DECLARATION ON TRADE MEASURES TAKEN FOR BALANCE–OF–PAYMENTS PURPOSES

Adopted on 28 November 1979.
GATT Doc. L/4904, 26th Supp. BISD 205 (1980).

The CONTRACTING PARTIES,

Having regard to the provisions of Articles XII and XVIII:B of the General Agreement;

Recalling the procedures for consultations on balance-of-payments restrictions approved by the Council on 28 April 1970 [4] and the procedures for regular consultations on balance-of-payments restrictions with developing countries approved by the Council on 19 December 1972; [5]

Convinced that restrictive trade measures are in general in inefficient means to maintain or restore balance-of-payments equilibrium;

Noting that restrictive import measures other than quantitative restrictions have been used for balance-of-payments purposes;

Reaffirming that restrictive import measures taken for balance-of-payments purposes should not be taken for the purpose of protecting a particular industry or sector;

Convinced that the contracting parties should endeavor to avoid that restrictive import measures taken for balance-of-payments purposes stimulate new investments that would not be economically viable in the absence of the measures;

Recognizing that the less-developed contracting parties must taken into account their individual development, financial and trade situation when implementing restrictive import measures taken for balance-of-payments purposes;

Recognizing that the impact of trade measures taken by developed countries on the economies of developing countries can be serious;

Recognizing that developed contracting parties should avoid the imposition of restrictive trade measures for balance-of-payments purposes to the maximum extent possible.

4. BISD 18S/48–53   **5.** BISD 20S/47–49.

Agree as follows:

1.   The procedures for examination stipulated in Articles XII and XVIII shall apply to all restrictive import measures taken for balance-of-payments purposes. The application of restrictive import measures taken for balance-of-payments purposes shall be subject to the following conditions in addition to those provided for in Article XII, XIII, XV and XVIII without prejudice to other provisions of the General Agreement:

(a) In applying restrictive import measures contracting parties shall abide by the disciplines provided for in the GATT and give preference to the measure which has the least disruptive effect on trade; [6]

(b) The simultaneous application of more than one type of trade measure for this purpose should be avoided;

(c) Whenever practicable, contracting parties shall publicly announce a time schedule for the removal of the measures.

The provisions of this paragraph are not intended to modify the substantive provisions of the General Agreement.

2.   If, notwithstanding the principles of this Declaration, a developed contracting party is compelled to apply restrictive import measures for balance-of-payments purposes, it shall, in determining the incidence of its measures, take into account the export interests of less-developed contracting parties and may exempt from its measures products of export interest to those contracting parties.

3.   Contracting parties shall promptly notify to the GATT the introduction or intensification of all restrictive import measures taken for balance-of-payments purposes. Contracting parties which have reason to believe that a restrictive import measure applied by another contracting party was taken for balance-of-payments purposes may notify the measure to the GATT or may request the GATT secretariat to seek information on the measure and make it available to all contracting parties if appropriate.

4.   All restrictive import measures taken for balance-of-payments purposes shall be subject to consultation in the GATT Committee on Balance-of-Payments Restrictions (hereafter referred to as "Committee").

5.   The membership of the Committee is open to all contracting parties indicating their wish to serve on it. Efforts shall be made to ensure that the composition of the Committee reflects as far as possible the characteristics of the contracting parties in general in terms of their geographical location, external financial position and stage of economic development.

6.   The Committee shall follow the procedures for consultations on balance-of-payments restrictions approved by the Council on 28 April 1970 [7] (hereinafter referred to as "full consultation procedures") or the procedures for regular consultations on balance-of-payments restrictions with developing countries approved by the Council on 19 December 1972 [8] (hereinafter re-

6. It is understood that the less-developed contracting parties must taken into account their individual development, financial and trade situation when selecting the particular measure to be applied.

7. BISD 18S/48–653.

8. BISD 20S/47–49.

ferred to as "simplified consultation procedures") subject to the provisions set out below.

7.   The GATT secretariat, drawing on all appropriate sources of information, including the consulting contracting party, shall with a view to facilitating the consultations in the Committee prepare a factual background paper describing the trade aspects of the measures taken, including aspects of particular interests to less-developed contracting parties. The paper shall also cover such other matters as the Committee may determine. The GATT secretariat shall give the consulting contracting party the opportunity to comment on the paper before it is submitted to the Committee.

8.   In the case of consultations under Article XVIII:12(b) the Committee shall base its decision on the type of procedure on such factors as the following:

(a) the time elapsed since the last full consultations;

(b) the steps the consulting contracting party has taken in the light of conclusions reached on the occasion of previous consultations;

(c) the changes in the overall level or nature of the trade measures taken for balance-of-payments purposes;

(d) the changes in the balance-of-payments situation or prospects;

(e) whether the balance-of-payments problems are structural or temporary in nature.

9.   A less-developed contracting party may at any time request full consultations.

10.   The technical assistance services of the GATT secretariat, shall, at the request of a less-developed consulting contracting party, assist it in preparing the documentation for the consultations.

11.   The Committee shall report on its consultations to the Council. The reports on full consultations shall indicate:

(a) the Committee's conclusions as well as the facts and reasons on which they are based;

(b) the steps the consulting contracting party has taken in the light of conclusions reached on the occasion of previous consultations;

(c) in the case of less-developed contracting parties, the facts and reasons on which the Committee based its decision on the procedure followed; and

(d) in the case of developed contracting parties, whether alternative economic policy measures are available.

If the Committee finds that the consulting contracting party's measures

(a) are in important respects related to restrictive trade measures maintained by another contracting party[9] or

(b) have a significant adverse impact on the export interests of a less-developed contracting party,

9. It is noted that such a finding is more likely to be made in the case of recent measures than of measures in effect for some considerable time.

it shall so report to the Council which shall take such further action as it may consider appropriate.

12. In the course of full consultations with a less-developed contracting party the Committee shall, if the consulting contracting party so desires, give particular attention to the possibilities for alleviating and correcting the balance-of-payments problem through measures that contracting parties might take to facilitate an expansion of the export earnings of the consulting contracting party, as provided for in paragraph 3 of the full consultation procedures.

13. If the Committee finds that a restrictive import measure taken by the consulting contracting party for balance-of-payments purposes is inconsistent with the provisions of Articles XII, XVIII:B or this Declaration, it shall, in its report to the Council, make such findings as will assist the Council in making appropriate recommendations designed to promote the implementation of Articles XII and XVIII:B and this Declaration. The Council shall keep under surveillance any matter on which it has made recommendations.

UNDERSTANDING ON THE INTERPRETATION OF ARTICLE XXIV OF THE GENERAL AGREEMENT ON TARIFFS AND TRADE 1994

Members,

Having regard to the provisions of Article XXIV of GATT 1994;

Recognizing that customs unions and free trade areas have greatly increased in number and importance since the establishment of GATT 1947 and today cover a significant proportion of world trade;

Recognizing the contribution to the expansion of world trade that may be made by closer integration between the economies of the parties to such agreements;

Recognizing also that such contribution is increased if the elimination between the constituent territories of duties and other restrictive regulations of commerce extends to all trade, and diminished if any major sector of trade is excluded;

Reaffirming that the purpose of such agreements should be to facilitate trade between the constituent territories and not to raise barriers to the trade of other Members with such territories; and that in their formation or enlargement the parties to them should to the greatest possible extent avoid creating adverse effects on the trade of other Members;

Convinced also of the need to reinforce the effectiveness of the role of the Council for Trade in Goods in reviewing agreements notified under Article XXIV, by clarifying the criteria and procedures for the assessment of new or enlarged agreements, and improving the transparency of all Article XXIV agreements;

Recognizing the need for a common understanding of the obligations of Members under paragraph 12 of Article XXIV;

Hereby *agree* as follows:

1. Customs unions, free-trade areas, and interim agreements leading to the formation of a customs union or free-trade area, to be consistent with

Article XXIV, must satisfy, *inter alia*, the provisions of paragraphs 5, 6, 7 and 8 of that Article.

Article XXIV:5

2. The evaluation under paragraph 5(a) of Article XXIV of the general incidence of the duties and other regulations of commerce applicable before and after the formation of a customs union shall in respect of duties and charges be based upon an overall assessment of weighted average tariff rates and of customs duties collected. This assessment shall be based on import statistics for a previous representative period to be supplied by the customs union, on a tariff-line basis and in values and quantities, broken down by WTO country of origin. The Secretariat shall compute the weighted average tariff rates and customs duties collected in accordance with the methodology used in the assessment of tariff offers in the Uruguay Round of Multilateral Trade Negotiations. For this purpose, the duties and charges to be taken into consideration shall be the applied rates of duty. It is recognized that for the purpose of the overall assessment of the incidence of other regulations of commerce for which quantification and aggregation are difficult, the examination of individual measures, regulations, products covered and trade flows affected may be required.

3. The "reasonable length of time" referred to in paragraph 5(c) of Article XXIV should exceed 10 years only in exceptional cases. In cases where Members parties to an interim agreement believe that 10 years would be insufficient they shall provide a full explanation to the Council for Trade in Goods of the need for a longer period.

Article XXIV:6

4. Paragraph 6 of Article XXIV establishes the procedure to be followed when a Member forming a customs union proposes to increase a bound rate of duty. In this regard Members reaffirm that the procedure set forth in Article XXVIII, as elaborated in the guidelines adopted on 10 November 1980 (BISD 27S/26–28) and in the Understanding on the Interpretation of Article XXVIII of GATT 1994, must be commenced before tariff concessions are modified or withdrawn upon the formation of a customs union or an interim agreement leading to the formation of a customs union.

5. These negotiations will be entered into in good faith with a view to achieving mutually satisfactory compensatory adjustment. In such negotiations, as required by paragraph 6 of Article XXIV, due account shall be taken of reductions of duties on the same tariff line made by other constituents of the customs union upon its formation. Should such reductions not be sufficient to provide the necessary compensatory adjustment, the customs union would offer compensation, which may take the form of reductions of duties on other tariff lines. Such an offer shall be taken into consideration by the Members having negotiating rights in the binding being modified or withdrawn. Should the compensatory adjustment remain unacceptable, negotiations should be continued. Where, despite such efforts, agreement in negotiations on compensatory adjustment under Article XXVIII as elaborated by the Understanding on the Interpretation of Article XXVIII of GATT 1994 cannot be reached within a reasonable period from the initiation of negotiations, the customs union shall, nevertheless, be free to modify or withdraw

the concessions; affected Members shall then be free to withdraw substantially equivalent concessions in accordance with Article XXVIII.

6. GATT 1994 imposes no obligation on Members benefiting from a reduction of duties consequent upon the formation of a customs union, or an interim agreement leading to the formation of a customs union, to provide compensatory adjustment to its constituents.

Review of Customs Unions and Free–Trade Areas

7. All notifications made under paragraph 7(a) of Article XXIV shall be examined by a working party in the light of the relevant provisions of GATT 1994 and of paragraph 1 of this Understanding. The working party shall submit a report to the Council for Trade in Goods on its findings in this regard. The Council for Trade in Goods may make such recommendations to Members as it deems appropriate.

8. In regard to interim agreements, the working party may in its report make appropriate recommendations on the proposed time-frame and on measures required to complete the formation of the customs union or free-trade area. It may if necessary provide for further review of the agreement.

9. Members parties to an interim agreement shall notify substantial changes in the plan and schedule included in that agreement to the Council for Trade in Goods and, if so requested, the Council shall examine the changes.

10. Should an interim agreement notified under paragraph 7(a) of Article XXIV not include a plan and schedule, contrary to paragraph 5(c) of Article XXIV, the working party shall in its report recommend such a plan and schedule. The parties shall not maintain or put into force, as the case may be, such agreement if they are not prepared to modify it in accordance with these recommendations. Provision shall be made for subsequent review of the implementation of the recommendations.

11. Customs unions and constituents of free-trade areas shall report periodically to the Council for Trade in Goods, as envisaged by the CONTRACTING PARTIES to GATT 1947 in their instruction to the GATT 1947 Council concerning reports on regional agreements (BISD 18S/38), on the operation of the relevant agreement. Any significant changes and/or developments in the agreements should be reported as they occur.

Dispute Settlement

12. The provisions of Articles XXII and XXIII of GATT 1994 as elaborated and applied by the Dispute Settlement Understanding may be invoked with respect to any matters arising from the application of those provisions of Article XXIV relating to customs unions, free-trade areas or interim agreements leading to the formation of a customs union or free-trade area.

Article XXIV:12

13. Each Member is fully responsible under GATT 1994 for the observance of all provisions of GATT 1994, and shall take such reasonable measures as may be available to it to ensure such observance by regional and local governments and authorities within its territory.

14.   The provisions of Articles XXII and XXIII of GATT 1994 as elaborated and applied by the Dispute Settlement Understanding may be invoked in respect of measures affecting its observance taken by regional or local governments or authorities within the territory of a Member. When the Dispute Settlement Body has ruled that a provision of GATT 1994 has not been observed, the responsible Member shall take such reasonable measures as may be available to it to ensure its observance. The provisions relating to compensation and suspension of concessions or other obligations apply in cases where it has not been possible to secure such observance.

15.   Each Member undertakes to accord sympathetic consideration to and afford adequate opportunity for consultation regarding any representations made by another Member concerning measures affecting the operation of GATT 1994 taken within the territory of the former.

UNDERSTANDING IN RESPECT OF WAIVERS OF OBLIGATIONS UNDER THE GENERAL AGREEMENT ON TARIFFS AND TRADE 1994

Members hereby *agree* as follows:

1.   A request for a waiver or for an extension of an existing waiver shall describe the measures which the Member proposes to take, the specific policy objectives which the Member seeks to pursue and the reasons which prevent the Member from achieving its policy objectives by measures consistent with its obligations under GATT 1994.

2.   Any waiver in effect on the date of entry into force of the WTO Agreement shall terminate, unless extended in accordance with the procedures above and those of Article IX of the WTO Agreement, on the date of its expiry or two years from the date of entry into force of the WTO Agreement, whichever is earlier.

3.   Any Member considering that a benefit accruing to it under GATT 1994 is being nullified or impaired as a result of:

(a) the failure of the Member to whom a waiver was granted to observe the terms or conditions of the waiver, or

(b) the application of a measure consistent with the terms and conditions of the waiver

may invoke the provisions of Article XXIII of GATT 1994 as elaborated and applied by the Dispute Settlement Understanding.

UNDERSTANDING ON THE INTERPRETATION OF ARTICLE XXVIII OF THE GENERAL AGREEMENT ON TARIFFS AND TRADE 1994

Members hereby *agree* as follows:

1.   For the purposes of modification or withdrawal of a concession, the Member which has the highest ratio of exports affected by the concession (i.e. exports of the product to the market of the Member modifying or withdrawing the concession) to its total exports shall be deemed to have a principal supplying interest if it does not already have an initial negotiating right or a principal supplying interest as provided for in paragraph 1 of Article XXVIII. It is however agreed that this paragraph will be reviewed by the Council for

Trade in Goods five years from the date of entry into force of the WTO Agreement with a view to deciding whether this criterion has worked satisfactorily in securing a redistribution of negotiating rights in favour of small and medium-sized exporting Members. If this is not the case, consideration will be given to possible improvements, including, in the light of the availability of adequate data, the adoption of a criterion based on the ratio of exports affected by the concession to exports to all markets of the product in question.

2. Where a Member considers that it has a principal supplying interest in terms of paragraph 1, it should communicate its claim in writing, with supporting evidence, to the Member proposing to modify or withdraw a concession, and at the same time inform the Secretariat. Paragraph 4 of the "Procedures for Negotiations under Article XXVIII" adopted on 10 November 1980 (BISD 27S/26–28) shall apply in these cases.

3. In the determination of which Members have a principal supplying interest (whether as provided for in paragraph 1 above or in paragraph 1 of Article XXVIII) or substantial interest, only trade in the affected product which has taken place on an MFN basis shall be taken into consideration. However, trade in the affected product which has taken place under non-contractual preferences shall also be taken into account if the trade in question has ceased to benefit from such preferential treatment, thus becoming MFN trade, at the time of the negotiation for the modification or withdrawal of the concession, or will do so by the conclusion of that negotiation.

4. When a tariff concession is modified or withdrawn on a new product (i.e. a product for which three years' trade statistics are not available) the Member possessing initial negotiating rights on the tariff line where the product is or was formerly classified shall be deemed to have an initial negotiating right in the concession in question. The determination of principal supplying and substantial interests and the calculation of compensation shall take into account, *inter alia,* production capacity and investment in the affected product in the exporting Member and estimates of export growth, as well as forecasts of demand for the product in the importing Member. For the purposes of this paragraph, "new product" is understood to include a tariff item created by means of a breakout from an existing tariff line.

5. Where a Member considers that it has a principal supplying or a substantial interest in terms of paragraph 4, it should communicate its claim in writing, with supporting evidence, to the Member proposing to modify or withdraw a concession, and at the same time inform the Secretariat. Paragraph 4 of the above-mentioned "Procedures for Negotiations under Article XXVIII" shall apply in these cases.

6. When an unlimited tariff concession is replaced by a tariff rate quota, the amount of compensation provided should exceed the amount of the trade actually affected by the modification of the concession. The basis for the calculation of compensation should be the amount by which future trade prospects exceed the level of the quota. It is understood that the calculation of future trade prospects should be based on the greater of:

(a) the average annual trade in the most recent representative three-year period, increased by the average annual growth rate of imports in that same period, or by 10 per cent, whichever is the greater; or

(b) trade in the most recent year increased by 10 per cent.

In no case shall a Member's liability for compensation exceed that which would be entailed by complete withdrawal of the concession.

7. Any Member having a principal supplying interest, whether as provided for in paragraph 1 above or in paragraph 1 of Article XXVIII, in a concession which is modified or withdrawn shall be accorded an initial negotiating right in the compensatory concessions, unless another form of compensation is agreed by the Members concerned.

MARRAKESH PROTOCOL TO THE GENERAL AGREEMENT ON TARIFFS AND TRADE 1994

Members,

Having carried out negotiations within the framework of GATT 1947, pursuant to the Ministerial Declaration on the Uruguay Round,

Hereby *agree* as follows:

1. The schedule annexed to this Protocol relating to a Member shall become a Schedule to GATT 1994 relating to that Member on the day on which the WTO Agreement enters into force for that Member. Any schedule submitted in accordance with the Ministerial Decision on measures in favour of least-developed countries shall be deemed to be annexed to this Protocol.

2. The tariff reductions agreed upon by each Member shall be implemented in five equal rate reductions, except as may be otherwise specified in a Member's Schedule. The first such reduction shall be made effective on the date of entry into force of the WTO Agreement, each successive reduction shall be made effective on 1 January of each of the following years, and the final rate shall become effective no later than the date four years after the date of entry into force of the WTO Agreement, except as may be otherwise specified in that Member's Schedule. Unless otherwise specified in its Schedule, a Member that accepts the WTO Agreement after its entry into force shall, on the date that Agreement enters into force for it, make effective all rate reductions that have already taken place together with the reductions which it would under the preceding sentence have been obligated to make effective on 1 January of the year following, and shall make effective all remaining rate reductions on the schedule specified in the previous sentence. The reduced rate should in each stage be rounded off to the first decimal. For agricultural products, as defined in Article 2 of the Agreement on Agriculture, the staging of reductions shall be implemented as specified in the relevant parts of the schedules.

3. The implementation of the concessions and commitments contained in the schedules annexed to this Protocol shall, upon request, be subject to multilateral examination by the Members. This would be without prejudice to the rights and obligations of Members under Agreements in Annex 1A of the WTO Agreement.

4. After the schedule annexed to this Protocol relating to a Member has become a Schedule to GATT 1994 pursuant to the provisions of paragraph 1, such Member shall be free at any time to withhold or to withdraw in whole or in part the concession in such Schedule with respect to any product for which the principal supplier is any other Uruguay Round participant the schedule of

which has not yet become a Schedule to GATT 1994. Such action can, however, only be taken after written notice of any such withholding or withdrawal of a concession has been given to the Council for Trade in Goods and after consultations have been held, upon request, with any Member, the relevant schedule relating to which has become a Schedule to GATT 1994 and which has a substantial interest in the product involved. Any concessions so withheld or withdrawn shall be applied on and after the day on which the schedule of the Member which has the principal supplying interest becomes a Schedule to GATT 1994.

5.   (a) Without prejudice to the provisions of paragraph 2 of Article 4 of the Agreement on Agriculture, for the purpose of the reference in paragraphs 1: (b) and 1(c) of Article II of GATT 1994 to the date of that Agreement, the applicable date in respect of each product which is the subject of a concession provided for in a schedule of concessions annexed to this Protocol shall be the date of this Protocol.

(b) For the purpose of the reference in paragraph 6(a) of Article II of GATT 1994 to the date of that Agreement, the applicable date in respect of a schedule of concessions annexed to this Protocol shall be the date of this Protocol.

6.   In cases of modification or withdrawal of concessions relating to non-tariff measures as contained in Part III of the schedules, the provisions of Article XXVIII of GATT 1994 and the "Procedures for Negotiations under Article XXVIII" adopted on 10 November 1980 (BISD 27S/26–28) shall apply. This would be without prejudice to the rights and obligations of Members under GATT 1994.

7.   In each case in which a schedule annexed to this Protocol results for any product in treatment less favourable than was provided for such product in the Schedules of GATT 1947 prior to the entry into force of the WTO Agreement, the Member to whom the schedule relates shall be deemed to have taken appropriate action as would have been otherwise necessary under the relevant provisions of Article XXVIII of GATT 1947 or 1994. The provisions of this paragraph shall apply only to Egypt, Peru, South Africa and Uruguay.

8.   The Schedules annexed hereto are authentic in the English, French or Spanish language as specified in each Schedule.

9.   The date of this Protocol is 15 April 1994.

[The agreed schedules of participants will be annexed to the Marrakesh Protocol in the treaty copy of the WTO Agreement.]

Item 4

AGREEMENT ON AGRICULTURE

Members,

Having decided to establish a basis for initiating a process of reform of trade in agriculture in line with the objectives of the negotiations as set out in the Punta del Este Declaration;

Recalling that their long-term objective as agreed at the Mid–Term Review of the Uruguay Round "is to establish a fair and market-oriented agricultural trading system and that a reform process should be initiated through the negotiation of commitments on support and protection and through the establishment of strengthened and more operationally effective GATT rules and disciplines";

Recalling further that "the above-mentioned long-term objective is to provide for substantial progressive reductions in agricultural support and protection sustained over an agreed period of time, resulting in correcting and preventing restrictions and distortions in world agricultural markets";

Committed to achieving specific binding commitments in each of the following areas: market access; domestic support; export competition; and to reaching an agreement on sanitary and phytosanitary issues;

Having agreed that in implementing their commitments on market access, developed country Members would take fully into account the particular needs and conditions of developing country Members by providing for a greater improvement of opportunities and terms of access for agricultural products of particular interest to these Members, including the fullest liberalization of trade in tropical agricultural products as agreed at the Mid–Term Review, and for products of particular importance to the diversification of production from the growing of illicit narcotic crops;

Noting that commitments under the reform programme should be made in an equitable way among all Members, having regard to non-trade concerns, including food security and the need to protect the environment; having regard to the agreement that special and differential treatment for developing countries is an integral element of the negotiations, and taking into account the possible negative effects of the implementation of the reform programme on least-developed and net food-importing developing countries;

Hereby *agree* as follows:

Part I

Article 1

Definition of Terms

In this Agreement, unless the context otherwise requires:

(a) "Aggregate Measurement of Support" and "AMS" mean the annual level of support, expressed in monetary terms, provided for an agricultural product in favour of the producers of the basic agricultural product or non-product-specific support provided in favour of agricultural producers in general, other than support provided under programmes that qualify as exempt from reduction under Annex 2 to this Agreement, which is:

(i) with respect to support provided during the base period, specified in the relevant tables of supporting material incorporated by reference in Part IV of a Member's Schedule; and

(ii) with respect to support provided during any year of the implementation period and thereafter, calculated in accordance with the provisions of Annex 3 of this Agreement and taking into account the constituent data and methodology used in the tables of supporting material incorporated by reference in Part IV of the Member's Schedule;

(b) "basic agricultural product" in relation to domestic support commitments is defined as the product as close as practicable to the point of first sale as specified in a Member's Schedule and in the related supporting material;

(c) "budgetary outlays" or "outlays" includes revenue foregone;

(d) "Equivalent Measurement of Support" means the annual level of support, expressed in monetary terms, provided to producers of a basic agricultural product through the application of one or more measures, the calculation of which in accordance with the AMS methodology is impracticable, other than support provided under programmes that qualify as exempt from reduction under Annex 2 to this Agreement, and which is:

(i) with respect to support provided during the base period, specified in the relevant tables of supporting material incorporated by reference in Part IV of a Member's Schedule; and

(ii) with respect to support provided during any year of the implementation period and thereafter, calculated in accordance with the provisions of Annex 4 of this Agreement and taking into account the constituent data and methodology used in the tables of supporting material incorporated by reference in Part IV of the Member's Schedule;

(e) "export subsidies" refers to subsidies contingent upon export performance, including the export subsidies listed in Article 9 of this Agreement;

(f) "implementation period" means the six-year period commencing in the year 1995, except that, for the purposes of Article 13, it means the nine-year period commencing in 1995;

(g) "market access concessions" includes all market access commitments undertaken pursuant to this Agreement;

(h) "Total Aggregate Measurement of Support" and "Total AMS" mean the sum of all domestic support provided in favour of agricultural producers, calculated as the sum of all aggregate measurements of support for basic agricultural products, all non-product-specific aggregate measurements of support and all equivalent measurements of support for agricultural products, and which is:

(i) with respect to support provided during the base period (i.e. the "Base Total AMS") and the maximum support permitted to be provided during any year of the implementation period or thereafter (i.e. the "Annual and Final Bound Commitment Levels"), as specified in Part IV of a Member's Schedule; and

(ii) with respect to the level of support actually provided during any year of the implementation period and thereafter (i.e. the "Current Total AMS"), calculated in accordance with the provisions of this Agreement, including Article 6, and with the constituent data and methodology used in the tables of supporting material incorporated by reference in Part IV of the Member's Schedule;

(i) "year" in paragraph (f) above and in relation to the specific commitments of a Member refers to the calendar, financial or marketing year specified in the Schedule relating to that Member.

Article 2

Product Coverage

This Agreement applies to the products listed in Annex 1 to this Agreement, hereinafter referred to as agricultural products.

Part II

Article 3

Incorporation of Concessions and Commitments

1. The domestic support and export subsidy commitments in Part IV of each Member's Schedule constitute commitments limiting subsidization and are hereby made an integral part of GATT 1994.

2. Subject to the provisions of Article 6, a Member shall not provide support in favour of domestic producers in excess of the commitment levels specified in Section I of Part IV of its Schedule.

3. Subject to the provisions of paragraphs 2(b) and 4 of Article 9, a Member shall not provide export subsidies listed in paragraph 1 of Article 9 in respect of the agricultural products or groups of products specified in Section II of Part IV of its Schedule in excess of the budgetary outlay and quantity commitment levels specified therein and shall not provide such subsidies in respect of any agricultural product not specified in that Section of its Schedule.

Part III

Article 4

Market Access

1. Market access concessions contained in Schedules relate to bindings and reductions of tariffs, and to other market access commitments as specified therein.

2.   Members shall not maintain, resort to, or revert to any measures of the kind which have been required to be converted into ordinary customs duties [1], except as otherwise provided for in Article 5 and Annex 5.

Article 5
Special Safeguard Provisions

1.   Notwithstanding the provisions of paragraph 1(b) of Article II of GATT 1994, any Member may take recourse to the provisions of paragraphs 4 and 5 below in connection with the importation of an agricultural product, in respect of which measures referred to in paragraph 2 of Article 4 of this Agreement have been converted into an ordinary customs duty and which is designated in its Schedule with the symbol "SSG" as being the subject of a concession in respect of which the provisions of this Article may be invoked, if:

(a) the volume of imports of that product entering the customs territory of the Member granting the concession during any year exceeds a trigger level which relates to the existing market access opportunity as set out in paragraph 4; or, but not concurrently:

(b) the price at which imports of that product may enter the customs territory of the Member granting the concession, as determined on the basis of the c.i.f. import price of the shipment concerned expressed in terms of its domestic currency, falls below a trigger price equal to the average 1986 to 1988 reference price [2] for the product concerned.

2.   Imports under current and minimum access commitments established as part of a concession referred to in paragraph 1 above shall be counted for the purpose of determining the volume of imports required for invoking the provisions of subparagraph 1(a) and paragraph 4, but imports under such commitments shall not be affected by any additional duty imposed under either subparagraph 1(a) and paragraph 4 or subparagraph 1(b) and paragraph 5 below.

3.   Any supplies of the product in question which were *en route* on the basis of a contract settled before the additional duty is imposed under subparagraph 1(a) and paragraph 4 shall be exempted from any such additional duty, provided that they may be counted in the volume of imports of the product in question during the following year for the purposes of triggering the provisions of subparagraph 1(a) in that year.

4.   Any additional duty imposed under subparagraph 1(a) shall only be maintained until the end of the year in which it has been imposed, and may

---

1.   These measures include quantitative import restrictions, variable import levies, minimum import prices, discretionary import licensing, non-tariff measures maintained through state-trading enterprises, voluntary export restraints, and similar border measures other than ordinary customs duties, whether or not the measures are maintained under country-specific derogations from the provisions of GATT 1947, but not measures maintained under balance-of-payments provisions or under other general, non-agriculture-specific provisions of GATT 1994 or of the other Multi- lateral Trade Agreements in Annex 1A to the WTO Agreement.

2.   The reference price used to invoke the provisions of this subparagraph shall, in general, be the average c.i.f. unit value of the product concerned, or otherwise shall be an appropriate price in terms of the quality of the product and its stage of processing. It shall, following its initial use, be publicly specified and available to the extent necessary to allow other Members to assess the additional duty that may be levied.

only be levied at a level which shall not exceed one third of the level of the ordinary customs duty in effect in the year in which the action is taken. The trigger level shall be set according to the following schedule based on market access opportunities defined as imports as a percentage of the corresponding domestic consumption [3] during the three preceding years for which data are available:

(a) where such market access opportunities for a product are less than or equal to 10 per cent, the base trigger level shall equal 125 per cent;

(b) where such market access opportunities for a product are greater than 10 per cent but less than or equal to 30 per cent, the base trigger level shall equal 110 per cent;

(c) where such market access opportunities for a product are greater than 30 per cent, the base trigger level shall equal 105 per cent.

In all cases the additional duty may be imposed in any year where the absolute volume of imports of the product concerned entering the customs territory of the Member granting the concession exceeds the sum of (x) the base trigger level set out above multiplied by the average quantity of imports during the three preceding years for which data are available and (y) the absolute volume change in domestic consumption of the product concerned in the most recent year for which data are available compared to the preceding year, provided that the trigger level shall not be less than 105 per cent of the average quantity of imports in (x) above.

5.   The additional duty imposed under subparagraph 1(b) shall be set according to the following schedule:

(a) if the difference between the c.i.f. import price of the shipment expressed in terms of the domestic currency (hereinafter referred to as the "import price") and the trigger price as defined under that subparagraph is less than or equal to 10 per cent of the trigger price, no additional duty shall be imposed;

(b) if the difference between the import price and the trigger price (hereinafter referred to as the "difference") is greater than 10 per cent but less than or equal to 40 per cent of the trigger price, the additional duty shall equal 30 per cent of the amount by which the difference exceeds 10 per cent;

(c) if the difference is greater than 40 per cent but less than or equal to 60 per cent of the trigger price, the additional duty shall equal 50 per cent of the amount by which the difference exceeds 40 per cent, plus the additional duty allowed under (b);

(d) if the difference is greater than 60 per cent but less than or equal to 75 per cent, the additional duty shall equal 70 per cent of the amount by which the difference exceeds 60 per cent of the trigger price, plus the additional duties allowed under (b) and (c);

3. Where domestic consumption is not taken into account, the base trigger level under subparagraph 4(a) shall apply.

(e) if the difference is greater than 75 per cent of the trigger price, the additional duty shall equal 90 per cent of the amount by which the difference exceeds 75 per cent, plus the additional duties allowed under (b), (c) and (d).

6.   For perishable and seasonal products, the conditions set out above shall be applied in such a manner as to take account of the specific characteristics of such products.   In particular, shorter time periods under subparagraph 1(a) and paragraph 4 may be used in reference to the corresponding periods in the base period and different reference prices for different periods may be used under subparagraph 1(b).

7.   The operation of the special safeguard shall be carried out in a transparent manner.   Any Member taking action under subparagraph 1(a) above shall give notice in writing, including relevant data, to the Committee on Agriculture as far in advance as may be practicable and in any event within 10 days of the implementation of such action.   In cases where changes in consumption volumes must be allocated to individual tariff lines subject to action under paragraph 4, relevant data shall include the information and methods used to allocate these changes.   A Member taking action under paragraph 4 shall afford any interested Members the opportunity to consult with it in respect of the conditions of application of such action.   Any Member taking action under subparagraph 1(b) above shall give notice in writing, including relevant data, to the Committee on Agriculture within 10 days of the implementation of the first such action or, for perishable and seasonal products, the first action in any period.   Members undertake, as far as practicable, not to take recourse to the provisions of subparagraph 1(b) where the volume of imports of the products concerned are declining.   In either case a Member taking such action shall afford any interested Members the opportunity to consult with it in respect of the conditions of application of such action.

8.   Where measures are taken in conformity with paragraphs 1 through 7 above, Members undertake not to have recourse, in respect of such measures, to the provisions of paragraphs 1(a) and 3 of Article XIX of GATT 1994 or paragraph 2 of Article 8 of the Agreement on Safeguards.

9.   The provisions of this Article shall remain in force for the duration of the reform process as determined under Article 20.

Part IV

Article 6

Domestic Support Commitments

1.   The domestic support reduction commitments of each Member contained in Part IV of its Schedule shall apply to all of its domestic support measures in favour of agricultural producers with the exception of domestic measures which are not subject to reduction in terms of the criteria set out in this Article and in Annex 2 to this Agreement.   The commitments are expressed in terms of Total Aggregate Measurement of Support and "Annual and Final Bound Commitment Levels".

2.   In accordance with the Mid–Term Review Agreement that government ment measures of assistance, whether direct or indirect, to encourage agricul-

tural and rural development are an integral part of the development programmes of developing countries, investment subsidies which are generally available to agriculture in developing country Members and agricultural input subsidies generally available to low-income or resource-poor producers in developing country Members shall be exempt from domestic support reduction commitments that would otherwise be applicable to such measures, as shall domestic support to producers in developing country Members to encourage diversification from growing illicit narcotic crops. Domestic support meeting the criteria of this paragraph shall not be required to be included in a Member's calculation of its Current Total AMS.

3.   A Member shall be considered to be in compliance with its domestic support reduction commitments in any year in which its domestic support in favour of agricultural producers expressed in terms of Current Total AMS does not exceed the corresponding annual or final bound commitment level specified in Part IV of the Member's Schedule.

4.   (a) A Member shall not be required to include in the calculation of its Current Total AMS and shall not be required to reduce:

(i) product-specific domestic support which would otherwise be required to be included in a Member's calculation of its Current AMS where such support does not exceed 5 per cent of that Member's total value of production of a basic agricultural product during the relevant year; and

(ii) non-product-specific domestic support which would otherwise be required to be included in a Member's calculation of its Current AMS where such support does not exceed 5 per cent of the value of that Member's total agricultural production.

(b) For developing country Members, the *de minimis* percentage under this paragraph shall be 10 per cent.

5.   (a) Direct payments under production-limiting programmes shall not be subject to the commitment to reduce domestic support if:

(i) such payments are based on fixed area and yields; or

(ii) such payments are made on 85 per cent or less of the base level of production; or

(iii) livestock payments are made on a fixed number of head.

(b) The exemption from the reduction commitment for direct payments meeting the above criteria shall be reflected by the exclusion of the value of those direct payments in a Member's calculation of its Current Total AMS.

Article 7

General Disciplines on Domestic Support

1.   Each Member shall ensure that any domestic support measures in favour of agricultural producers which are not subject to reduction commitments because they qualify under the criteria set out in Annex 2 to this Agreement are maintained in conformity therewith.

2.   (a) Any domestic support measure in favour of agricultural producers, including any modification to such measure, and any measure that is subsequently introduced that cannot be shown to satisfy the criteria in Annex 2 to this Agreement or to be exempt from reduction by reason of any other provision of this Agreement shall be included in the Member's calculation of its Current Total AMS.

(b) Where no Total AMS commitment exists in Part IV of a Member's Schedule, the Member shall not provide support to agricultural producers in excess of the relevant *de minimis* level set out in paragraph 4 of Article 6.

Part V

Article 8

Export Competition Commitments

Each Member undertakes not to provide export subsidies otherwise than in conformity with this Agreement and with the commitments as specified in that Member's Schedule.

Article 9

Export Subsidy Commitments

1.   The following export subsidies are subject to reduction commitments under this Agreement:

(a) the provision by governments or their agencies of direct subsidies, including payments-in-kind, to a firm, to an industry, to producers of an agricultural product, to a cooperative or other association of such producers, or to a marketing board, contingent on export performance;

(b) the sale or disposal for export by governments or their agencies of non-commercial stocks of agricultural products at a price lower than the comparable price charged for the like product to buyers in the domestic market;

(c) payments on the export of an agricultural product that are financed by virtue of governmental action, whether or not a charge on the public account is involved, including payments that are financed from the proceeds of a levy imposed on the agricultural product concerned or on an agricultural product from which the exported product is derived;

(d) the provision of subsidies to reduce the costs of marketing exports of agricultural products (other than widely available export promotion and advisory services) including handling, upgrading and other processing costs, and the costs of international transport and freight;

(e) internal transport and freight charges on export shipments, provided or mandated by governments, on terms more favourable than for domestic shipments;

(f) subsidies on agricultural products contingent on their incorporation in exported products.

2.   (a) Except as provided in subparagraph (b), the export subsidy commitment levels for each year of the implementation period, as specified in a Member's Schedule, represent with respect to the export subsidies listed in paragraph 1 of this Article:

(i) in the case of budgetary outlay reduction commitments, the maximum level of expenditure for such subsidies that may be allocated or incurred in that year in respect of the agricultural product, or group of products, concerned; and

(ii) in the case of export quantity reduction commitments, the maximum quantity of an agricultural product, or group of products, in respect of which such export subsidies may be granted in that year.

(b) In any of the second through fifth years of the implementation period, a Member may provide export subsidies listed in paragraph 1 above in a given year in excess of the corresponding annual commitment levels in respect of the products or groups of products specified in Part IV of the Member's Schedule, provided that:

(i) the cumulative amounts of budgetary outlays for such subsidies, from the beginning of the implementation period through the year in question, does not exceed the cumulative amounts that would have resulted from full compliance with the relevant annual outlay commitment levels specified in the Member's Schedule by more than 3 per cent of the base period level of such budgetary outlays;

(ii) the cumulative quantities exported with the benefit of such export subsidies, from the beginning of the implementation period through the year in question, does not exceed the cumulative quantities that would have resulted from full compliance with the relevant annual quantity commitment levels specified in the Member's Schedule by more than 1.75 per cent of the base period quantities;

(iii) the total cumulative amounts of budgetary outlays for such export subsidies and the quantities benefiting from such export subsidies over the entire implementation period are no greater than the totals that would have resulted from full compliance with the relevant annual commitment levels specified in the Member's Schedule; and

(iv) the Member's budgetary outlays for export subsidies and the quantities benefiting from such subsidies, at the conclusion of the implementation period, are no greater than 64 per cent and 79 per cent of the 1986–1990 base period levels, respectively. For developing country Members these percentages shall be 76 and 86 per cent, respectively.

3. Commitments relating to limitations on the extension of the scope of export subsidization are as specified in Schedules.

4. During the implementation period, developing country Members shall not be required to undertake commitments in respect of the export subsidies listed in subparagraphs (d) and (e) of paragraph 1 above, provided that these are not applied in a manner that would circumvent reduction commitments.

Article 10

Prevention of Circumvention of Export Subsidy Commitments

1. Export subsidies not listed in paragraph 1 of Article 9 shall not be applied in a manner which results in, or which threatens to lead to, circumvention of export subsidy commitments; nor shall non-commercial transactions be used to circumvent such commitments.

2. Members undertake to work toward the development of internationally agreed disciplines to govern the provision of export credits, export credit guarantees or insurance programmes and, after agreement on such disciplines, to provide export credits, export credit guarantees or insurance programmes only in conformity therewith.

3. Any Member which claims that any quantity exported in excess of a reduction commitment level is not subsidized must establish that no export

subsidy, whether listed in Article 9 or not, has been granted in respect of the quantity of exports in question.

4. Members donors of international food aid shall ensure:

(a) that the provision of international food aid is not tied directly or indirectly to commercial exports of agricultural products to recipient countries;

(b) that international food aid transactions, including bilateral food aid which is monetized, shall be carried out in accordance with the FAO "Principles of Surplus Disposal and Consultative Obligations", including, where appropriate, the system of Usual Marketing Requirements (UMRs); and

(c) that such aid shall be provided to the extent possible in fully grant form or on terms no less concessional than those provided for in Article IV of the Food Aid Convention 1986.

Article 11

Incorporated Products

In no case may the per-unit subsidy paid on an incorporated agricultural primary product exceed the per-unit export subsidy that would be payable on exports of the primary product as such.

Part VI

Article 12

Disciplines on Export Prohibitions and Restrictions

1. Where any Member institutes any new export prohibition or restriction on foodstuffs in accordance with paragraph 2(a) of Article XI of GATT 1994, the Member shall observe the following provisions:

(a) the Member instituting the export prohibition or restriction shall give due consideration to the effects of such prohibition or restriction on importing Members' food security;

(b) before any Member institutes an export prohibition or restriction, it shall give notice in writing, as far in advance as practicable, to the Committee on Agriculture comprising such information as the nature and the duration of such measure, and shall consult, upon request, with any other Member having a substantial interest as an importer with respect to any matter related to the measure in question. The Member instituting such export prohibition or restriction shall provide, upon request, such a Member with necessary information.

2. The provisions of this Article shall not apply to any developing country Member, unless the measure is taken by a developing country Member which is a net-food exporter of the specific foodstuff concerned.

Part VII

Article 13

Due Restraint

During the implementation period, notwithstanding the provisions of GATT 1994 and the Agreement on Subsidies and Countervailing Measures (referred to in this Article as the "Subsidies Agreement"):

(a) domestic support measures that conform fully to the provisions of Annex 2 to this Agreement shall be:

(i) non-actionable subsidies for purposes of countervailing duties [4];

(ii) exempt from actions based on Article XVI of GATT 1994 and Part III of the Subsidies Agreement; and

(iii) exempt from actions based on non-violation nullification or impairment of the benefits of tariff concessions accruing to another Member under Article II of GATT 1994, in the sense of paragraph 1(b) of Article XXIII of GATT 1994;

(b) domestic support measures that conform fully to the provisions of Article 6 of this Agreement including direct payments that conform to the requirements of paragraph 5 thereof, as reflected in each Member's Schedule, as well as domestic support within *de minimis* levels and in conformity with paragraph 2 of Article 6, shall be:

(i) exempt from the imposition of countervailing duties unless a determination of injury or threat thereof is made in accordance with Article VI of GATT 1994 and Part V of the Subsidies Agreement, and due restraint shall be shown in initiating any countervailing duty investigations;

(ii) exempt from actions based on paragraph 1 of Article XVI of GATT 1994 or Articles 5 and 6 of the Subsidies Agreement, provided that such measures do not grant support to a specific commodity in excess of that decided during the 1992 marketing year; and

(iii) exempt from actions based on non-violation nullification or impairment of the benefits of tariff concessions accruing to another Member under Article II of GATT 1994, in the sense of paragraph 1(b) of Article XXIII of GATT 1994, provided that such measures do not grant support to a specific commodity in excess of that decided during the 1992 marketing year;

(c) export subsidies that conform fully to the provisions of Part V of this Agreement, as reflected in each Member's Schedule, shall be:

(i) subject to countervailing duties only upon a determination of injury or threat thereof based on volume, effect on prices, or consequent impact in accordance with Article VI of GATT 1994 and Part V of the Subsidies Agreement, and due restraint shall be shown in initiating any countervailing duty investigations; and

(ii) exempt from actions based on Article XVI of GATT 1994 or Articles 3, 5 and 6 of the Subsidies Agreement.

Part VIII

Article 14

Sanitary and Phytosanitary Measures

Members agree to give effect to the Agreement on the Application of Sanitary and Phytosanitary Measures.

---

4. "Countervailing duties" where referred to in this Article are those covered by Article VI of GATT 1994 and Part V of the Agreement on Subsidies and Countervailing Measures.

Part IX

Article 15

Special and Differential Treatment

1. In keeping with the recognition that differential and more favourable treatment for developing country Members is an integral part of the negotiation, special and differential treatment in respect of commitments shall be provided as set out in the relevant provisions of this Agreement and embodied in the Schedules of concessions and commitments.

2. Developing country Members shall have the flexibility to implement reduction commitments over a period of up to 10 years. Least-developed country Members shall not be required to undertake reduction commitments.

Part X

Article 16

Least–Developed and Net Food–Importing Developing Countries

1. Developed country Members shall take such action as is provided for within the framework of the Decision on Measures Concerning the Possible Negative Effects of the Reform Programme on Least–Developed and Net Food–Importing Developing Countries.

2. The Committee on Agriculture shall monitor, as appropriate, the follow-up to this Decision.

Part XI

Article 17

Committee on Agriculture

A Committee on Agriculture is hereby established.

Article 18

Review of the Implementation of Commitments

1. Progress in the implementation of commitments negotiated under the Uruguay Round reform programme shall be reviewed by the Committee on Agriculture.

2. The review process shall be undertaken on the basis of notifications submitted by Members in relation to such matters and at such intervals as shall be determined, as well as on the basis of such documentation as the Secretariat may be requested to prepare in order to facilitate the review process.

3. In addition to the notifications to be submitted under paragraph 2, any new domestic support measure, or modification of an existing measure, for which exemption from reduction is claimed shall be notified promptly. This notification shall contain details of the new or modified measure and its conformity with the agreed criteria as set out either in Article 6 or in Annex 2.

4. In the review process Members shall give due consideration to the influence of excessive rates of inflation on the ability of any Member to abide by its domestic support commitments.

5.   Members agree to consult annually in the Committee on Agriculture with respect to their participation in the normal growth of world trade in agricultural products within the framework of the commitments on export subsidies under this Agreement.

6.   The review process shall provide an opportunity for Members to raise any matter relevant to the implementation of commitments under the reform programme as set out in this Agreement.

7.   Any Member may bring to the attention of the Committee on Agriculture any measure which it considers ought to have been notified by another Member.

Article 19

Consultation and Dispute Settlement

The provisions of Articles XXII and XXIII of GATT 1994, as elaborated and applied by the Dispute Settlement Understanding, shall apply to consultations and the settlement of disputes under this Agreement.

Part XII

Article 20

Continuation of the Reform Process

Recognizing that the long-term objective of substantial progressive reductions in support and protection resulting in fundamental reform is an ongoing process, Members agree that negotiations for continuing the process will be initiated one year before the end of the implementation period, taking into account:

(a) the experience to that date from implementing the reduction commitments;

(b) the effects of the reduction commitments on world trade in agriculture;

(c) non-trade concerns, special and differential treatment to developing country Members, and the objective to establish a fair and market-oriented agricultural trading system, and the other objectives and concerns mentioned in the preamble to this Agreement; and

(d) what further commitments are necessary to achieve the above mentioned long-term objectives.

Part XIII

Article 21

Final Provisions

1.   The provisions of GATT 1994 and of other Multilateral Trade Agreements in Annex 1A to the WTO Agreement shall apply subject to the provisions of this Agreement.

2.   The Annexes to this Agreement are hereby made an integral part of this Agreement.

ANNEX 1

PRODUCT COVERAGE

1.   This Agreement shall cover the following products:

  (i) HS Chapters 1 to 24 less fish and fish products, plus*

(ii)	HS Code	2905.43	(mannitol)
	HS Code	2905.44	(sorbitol)
	HS Heading	33.01	(essential oils)
	HS Headings	35.01 to 35.05	(albuminoidal substances, modified starches, glues)
	HS Code	3809.10	(finishing agents)
	HS Code	3823.60	(sorbitol n.e.p.)
	HS Headings	41.01 to 41.03	(hides and skins)
	HS Heading	43.01	(raw furskins)
	HS Headings	50.01 to 50.03	(raw silk and silk waste)
	HS Headings	51.01 to 51.03	(wool and animal hair)
	HS Headings	52.01 to 52.03	(raw cotton, waste and cotton carded or combed)
	HS Heading	53.01	(raw flax)
	HS Heading	53.02	(raw hemp)

2.   The foregoing shall not limit the product coverage of the Agreement on the Application of Sanitary and Phytosanitary Measures.

* The product descriptions in round brackets are not necessarily exhaustive.

ANNEX 2

DOMESTIC SUPPORT: THE BASIS FOR EXEMPTION FROM THE REDUCTION COMMITMENTS

1.   Domestic support measures for which exemption from the reduction commitments is claimed shall meet the fundamental requirement that they have no, or at most minimal, trade-distorting effects or effects on production. Accordingly, all measures for which exemption is claimed shall conform to the following basic criteria:

  (a) the support in question shall be provided through a publicly-funded government programme (including government revenue foregone) not involving transfers from consumers; and,

  (b) the support in question shall not have the effect of providing price support to producers;

plus policy-specific criteria and conditions as set out below.

Government Service Programmes

2.   General services

Policies in this category involve expenditures (or revenue foregone) in relation to programmes which provide services or benefits to agriculture or the rural community. They shall not involve direct payments to producers or processors. Such programmes, which include but are not restricted to the following list, shall meet the general criteria in paragraph 1 above and policy-specific conditions where set out below:

(a) research, including general research, research in connection with environmental programmes, and research programmes relating to particular products;

(b) pest and disease control, including general and product-specific pest and disease control measures, such as early-warning systems, quarantine and eradication;

(c) training services, including both general and specialist training facilities;

(d) extension and advisory services, including the provision of means to facilitate the transfer of information and the results of research to producers and consumers;

(e) inspection services, including general inspection services and the inspection of particular products for health, safety, grading or standardization purposes;

(f) marketing and promotion services, including market information, advice and promotion relating to particular products but excluding expenditure for unspecified purposes that could be used by sellers to reduce their selling price or confer a direct economic benefit to purchasers; and

(g) infrastructural services, including: electricity reticulation, roads and other means of transport, market and port facilities, water supply facilities, dams and drainage schemes, and infrastructural works associated with environmental programmes. In all cases the expenditure shall be directed to the provision or construction of capital works only, and shall exclude the subsidized provision of on-farm facilities other than for the reticulation of generally available public utilities. It shall not include subsidies to inputs or operating costs, or preferential user charges.

3. Public stockholding for food security purposes [5]

Expenditures (or revenue foregone) in relation to the accumulation and holding of stocks of products which form an integral part of a food security programme identified in national legislation. This may include government aid to private storage of products as part of such a programme.

The volume and accumulation of such stocks shall correspond to predetermined targets related solely to food security. The process of stock accumulation and disposal shall be financially transparent. Food pur-

---

5. For the purposes of paragraph 3 of this Annex, governmental stockholding programmes for food security purposes in developing countries whose operation is transparent and conducted in accordance with officially published objective criteria or guidelines shall be considered to be in conformity with the provisions of this paragraph, including programmes under which stocks of foodstuffs for food security purposes are acquired and released at administered prices, provided that the difference between the acquisition price and the external reference price is accounted for in the AMS.

5. & 6. For the purposes of paragraphs 3 and 4 of this Annex, the provision of foodstuffs at subsidized prices with the objective of meeting food requirements of urban and rural poor in developing countries on a regular basis at reasonable prices shall be considered to be in conformity with the provisions of this paragraph.

chases by the government shall be made at current market prices and sales from food security stocks shall be made at no less than the current domestic market price for the product and quality in question.

4.   Domestic food aid [6]

Expenditures (or revenue foregone) in relation to the provision of domestic food aid to sections of the population in need.

Eligibility to receive the food aid shall be subject to clearly-defined criteria related to nutritional objectives. Such aid shall be in the form of direct provision of food to those concerned or the provision of means to allow eligible recipients to buy food either at market or at subsidized prices. Food purchases by the government shall be made at current market prices and the financing and administration of the aid shall be transparent.

5.   Direct payments to producers

Support provided through direct payments (or revenue foregone, including payments in kind) to producers for which exemption from reduction commitments is claimed shall meet the basic criteria set out in paragraph 1 above, plus specific criteria applying to individual types of direct payment as set out in paragraphs 6 through 13 below. Where exemption from reduction is claimed for any existing or new type of direct payment other than those specified in paragraphs 6 through 13, it shall conform to criteria (b) through (e) in paragraph 6, in addition to the general criteria set out in paragraph 1.

6.   Decoupled income support

(a) Eligibility for such payments shall be determined by clearly-defined criteria such as income, status as a producer or landowner, factor use or production level in a defined and fixed base period.

(b) The amount of such payments in any given year shall not be related to, or based on, the type or volume of production (including livestock units) undertaken by the producer in any year after the base period.

(c) The amount of such payments in any given year shall not be related to, or based on, the prices, domestic or international, applying to any production undertaken in any year after the base period.

(d) The amount of such payments in any given year shall not be related to, or based on, the factors of production employed in any year after the base period.

(e) No production shall be required in order to receive such payments.

7.   Government financial participation in income insurance and income safety-net programmes

(a) Eligibility for such payments shall be determined by an income loss, taking into account only income derived from agriculture, which exceeds 30 per cent of average gross income or the equivalent in net income terms (excluding any payments from the same or similar schemes) in the preceding three-year period or a three-year average based on the preceding five-year period, excluding the highest and the lowest entry.

Any producer meeting this condition shall be eligible to receive the payments.

(b) The amount of such payments shall compensate for less than 70 per cent of the producer's income loss in the year the producer becomes eligible to receive this assistance.

(c) The amount of any such payments shall relate solely to income; it shall not relate to the type or volume of production (including livestock units) undertaken by the producer; or to the prices, domestic or international, applying to such production; or to the factors of production employed.

(d) Where a producer receives in the same year payments under this paragraph and under paragraph 8 (relief from natural disasters), the total of such payments shall be less than 100 per cent of the producer's total loss.

8. Payments (made either directly or by way of government financial participation in crop insurance schemes) for relief from natural disasters

(a) Eligibility for such payments shall arise only following a formal recognition by government authorities that a natural or like disaster (including disease outbreaks, pest infestations, nuclear accidents, and war on the territory of the Member concerned) has occurred or is occurring; and shall be determined by a production loss which exceeds 30 per cent of the average of production in the preceding three-year period or a three-year average based on the preceding five-year period, excluding the highest and the lowest entry.

(b) Payments made following a disaster shall be applied only in respect of losses of income, livestock (including payments in connection with the veterinary treatment of animals), land or other production factors due to the natural disaster in question.

(c) Payments shall compensate for not more than the total cost of replacing such losses and shall not require or specify the type or quantity of future production.

(d) Payments made during a disaster shall not exceed the level required to prevent or alleviate further loss as defined in criterion (b) above.

(e) Where a producer receives in the same year payments under this paragraph and under paragraph 7 (income insurance and income safety-net programmes), the total of such payments shall be less than 100 per cent of the producer's total loss.

9. Structural adjustment assistance provided through producer retirement programmes

(a) Eligibility for such payments shall be determined by reference to clearly defined criteria in programmes designed to facilitate the retirement of persons engaged in marketable agricultural production, or their movement to non-agricultural activities.

(b) Payments shall be conditional upon the total and permanent retirement of the recipients from marketable agricultural production.

10. Structural adjustment assistance provided through resource retirement programmes

(a) Eligibility for such payments shall be determined by reference to clearly defined criteria in programmes designed to remove land or other resources, including livestock, from marketable agricultural production.

(b) Payments shall be conditional upon the retirement of land from marketable agricultural production for a minimum of three years, and in the case of livestock on its slaughter or definitive permanent disposal.

(c) Payments shall not require or specify any alternative use for such land or other resources which involves the production of marketable agricultural products.

(d) Payments shall not be related to either the type or quantity of production or to the prices, domestic or international, applying to production undertaken using the land or other resources remaining in production.

11. Structural adjustment assistance provided through investment aids

(a) Eligibility for such payments shall be determined by reference to clearly-defined criteria in government programmes designed to assist the financial or physical restructuring of a producer's operations in response to objectively demonstrated structural disadvantages. Eligibility for such programmes may also be based on a clearly-defined government programme for the reprivatization of agricultural land.

(b) The amount of such payments in any given year shall not be related to, or based on, the type or volume of production (including livestock units) undertaken by the producer in any year after the base period other than as provided for under criterion (e) below.

(c) The amount of such payments in any given year shall not be related to, or based on, the prices, domestic or international, applying to any production undertaken in any year after the base period.

(d) The payments shall be given only for the period of time necessary for the realization of the investment in respect of which they are provided.

(e) The payments shall not mandate or in any way designate the agricultural products to be produced by the recipients except to require them not to produce a particular product.

(f) The payments shall be limited to the amount required to compensate for the structural disadvantage.

12. Payments under environmental programmes

(a) Eligibility for such payments shall be determined as part of a clearly-defined government environmental or conservation programme and be dependent on the fulfilment of specific conditions under the government programme, including conditions related to production methods or inputs.

(b) The amount of payment shall be limited to the extra costs or loss of income involved in complying with the government programme.

13.   Payments under regional assistance programmes

(a) Eligibility for such payments shall be limited to producers in disadvantaged regions. Each such region must be a clearly designated contiguous geographical area with a definable economic and administrative identity, considered as disadvantaged on the basis of neutral and objective criteria clearly spelt out in law or regulation and indicating that the region's difficulties arise out of more than temporary circumstances.

(b) The amount of such payments in any given year shall not be related to, or based on, the type or volume of production (including livestock units) undertaken by the producer in any year after the base period other than to reduce that production.

(c) The amount of such payments in any given year shall not be related to, or based on, the prices, domestic or international, applying to any production undertaken in any year after the base period.

(d) Payments shall be available only to producers in eligible regions, but generally available to all producers within such regions.

(e) Where related to production factors, payments shall be made at a degressive rate above a threshold level of the factor concerned.

(f) The payments shall be limited to the extra costs or loss of income involved in undertaking agricultural production in the prescribed area.

ANNEX 3

DOMESTIC SUPPORT: CALCULATION OF AGGREGATE MEASUREMENT OF SUPPORT

1.   Subject to the provisions of Article 6, an Aggregate Measurement of Support (AMS) shall be calculated on a product-specific basis for each basic agricultural product receiving market price support, non-exempt direct payments, or any other subsidy not exempted from the reduction commitment ("other non-exempt policies"). Support which is non-product specific shall be totalled into one non-product-specific AMS in total monetary terms.

2.   Subsidies under paragraph 1 shall include both budgetary outlays and revenue foregone by governments or their agents.

3.   Support at both the national and sub-national level shall be included.

4.   Specific agricultural levies or fees paid by producers shall be deducted from the AMS.

5.   The AMS calculated as outlined below for the base period shall constitute the base level for the implementation of the reduction commitment on domestic support.

6.   For each basic agricultural product, a specific AMS shall be established, expressed in total monetary value terms.

7.   The AMS shall be calculated as close as practicable to the point of first sale of the basic agricultural product concerned. Measures directed at agricultural processors shall be included to the extent that such measures benefit the producers of the basic agricultural products.

8.   Market price support: market price support shall be calculated using the gap between a fixed external reference price and the applied administered price multiplied by the quantity of production eligible to receive the applied

administered price. Budgetary payments made to maintain this gap, such as buying-in or storage costs, shall not be included in the AMS.

9. The fixed external reference price shall be based on the years 1986 to 1988 and shall generally be the average f.o.b. unit value for the basic agricultural product concerned in a net exporting country and the average c.i.f. unit value for the basic agricultural product concerned in a net importing country in the base period. The fixed reference price may be adjusted for quality differences as necessary.

10. Non-exempt direct payments: non-exempt direct payments which are dependent on a price gap shall be calculated either using the gap between the fixed reference price and the applied administered price multiplied by the quantity of production eligible to receive the administered price, or using budgetary outlays.

11. The fixed reference price shall be based on the years 1986 to 1988 and shall generally be the actual price used for determining payment rates.

12. Non-exempt direct payments which are based on factors other than price shall be measured using budgetary outlays.

13. Other non-exempt measures, including input subsidies and other measures such as marketing-cost reduction measures: the value of such measures shall be measured using government budgetary outlays or, where the use of budgetary outlays does not reflect the full extent of the subsidy concerned, the basis for calculating the subsidy shall be the gap between the price of the subsidized good or service and a representative market price for a similar good or service multiplied by the quantity of the good or service.

ANNEX 4

DOMESTIC SUPPORT: CALCULATION OF EQUIVALENT MEASUREMENT OF SUPPORT

1. Subject to the provisions of Article 6, equivalent measurements of support shall be calculated in respect of all basic agricultural products where market price support as defined in Annex 3 exists but for which calculation of this component of the AMS is not practicable. For such products the base level for implementation of the domestic support reduction commitments shall consist of a market price support component expressed in terms of equivalent measurements of support under paragraph 2 below, as well as any non-exempt direct payments and other non-exempt support, which shall be evaluated as provided for under paragraph 3 below. Support at both national and sub-national level shall be included.

2. The equivalent measurements of support provided for in paragraph 1 shall be calculated on a product-specific basis for all basic agricultural products as close as practicable to the point of first sale receiving market price support and for which the calculation of the market price support component of the AMS is not practicable. For those basic agricultural products, equivalent measurements of market price support shall be made using the applied administered price and the quantity of production eligible to receive that price or, where this is not practicable, on budgetary outlays used to maintain the producer price.

3. Where basic agricultural products falling under paragraph 1 are the subject of non-exempt direct payments or any other product-specific subsidy not exempted from the reduction commitment, the basis for equivalent measurements of support concerning these measures shall be calculations as for the corresponding AMS components (specified in paragraphs 10 through 13 of Annex 3).

4. Equivalent measurements of support shall be calculated on the amount of subsidy as close as practicable to the point of first sale of the basic agricultural product concerned. Measures directed at agricultural processors shall be included to the extent that such measures benefit the producers of the basic agricultural products. Specific agricultural levies or fees paid by producers shall reduce the equivalent measurements of support by a corresponding amount.

ANNEX 5

SPECIAL TREATMENT WITH RESPECT
TO PARAGRAPH 2 OF ARTICLE 4

Section A

1. The provisions of paragraph 2 of Article 4 shall not apply with effect from the entry into force of the WTO Agreement to any primary agricultural product and its worked and/or prepared products ("designated products") in respect of which the following conditions are complied with (hereinafter referred to as "special treatment"):

(a) imports of the designated products comprised less than 3 per cent of corresponding domestic consumption in the base period 1986–1988 ("the base period");

(b) no export subsidies have been provided since the beginning of the base period for the designated products;

(c) effective production-restricting measures are applied to the primary agricultural product;

(d) such products are designated with the symbol "ST–Annex 5" in Section I–B of Part I of a Member's Schedule annexed to the Marrakesh Protocol, as being subject to special treatment reflecting factors of non-trade concerns, such as food security and environmental protection; and

(e) minimum access opportunities in respect of the designated products correspond, as specified in Section I–B of Part I of the Schedule of the Member concerned, to 4 per cent of base period domestic consumption of the designated products from the beginning of the first year of the implementation period and, thereafter, are increased by 0.8 per cent of corresponding domestic consumption in the base period per year for the remainder of the implementation period.

2. At the beginning of any year of the implementation period a Member may cease to apply special treatment in respect of the designated products by complying with the provisions of paragraph 6. In such a case, the Member concerned shall maintain the minimum access opportunities already in effect at such time and increase the minimum access opportunities by 0.4 per cent of corresponding domestic consumption in the base period per year for the

remainder of the implementation period. Thereafter, the level of minimum access opportunities resulting from this formula in the final year of the implementation period shall be maintained in the Schedule of the Member concerned.

3. Any negotiation on the question of whether there can be a continuation of the special treatment as set out in paragraph 1 after the end of the implementation period shall be completed within the time-frame of the implementation period itself as a part of the negotiations set out in Article 20 of this Agreement, taking into account the factors of non-trade concerns.

4. If it is agreed as a result of the negotiation referred to in paragraph 3 that a Member may continue to apply the special treatment, such Member shall confer additional and acceptable concessions as determined in that negotiation.

5. Where the special treatment is not to be continued at the end of the implementation period, the Member concerned shall implement the provisions of paragraph 6. In such a case, after the end of the implementation period the minimum access opportunities for the designated products shall be maintained at the level of 8 per cent of corresponding domestic consumption in the base period in the Schedule of the Member concerned.

6. Border measures other than ordinary customs duties maintained in respect of the designated products shall become subject to the provisions of paragraph 2 of Article 4 with effect from the beginning of the year in which the special treatment ceases to apply. Such products shall be subject to ordinary customs duties, which shall be bound in the Schedule of the Member concerned and applied, from the beginning of the year in which special treatment ceases and thereafter, at such rates as would have been applicable had a reduction of at least 15 per cent been implemented over the implementation period in equal annual instalments. These duties shall be established on the basis of tariff equivalents to be calculated in accordance with the guidelines prescribed in the attachment hereto.

Section B

7. The provisions of paragraph 2 of Article 4 shall also not apply with effect from the entry into force of the WTO Agreement to a primary agricultural product that is the predominant staple in the traditional diet of a developing country Member and in respect of which the following conditions, in addition to those specified in paragraph 1(a) through 1(d), as they apply to the products concerned, are complied with:

(a) minimum access opportunities in respect of the products concerned, as specified in Section I–B of Part I of the Schedule of the developing country Member concerned, correspond to 1 per cent of base period domestic consumption of the products concerned from the beginning of the first year of the implementation period and are increased in equal annual instalments to 2 per cent of corresponding domestic consumption in the base period at the beginning of the fifth year of the implementation period. From the beginning of the sixth year of the implementation period, minimum access opportunities in respect of the products concerned correspond to 2 per cent of corresponding domestic consumption in the base period and are increased in equal annual instalments to 4 per cent of corresponding domestic consumption in the base period until the beginning of the 10th year. Thereafter, the level of minimum access opportunities resulting from this formula in the 10th year shall be maintained in the Schedule of the developing country Member concerned;

(b) appropriate market access opportunities have been provided for in other products under this Agreement.

8.   Any negotiation on the question of whether there can be a continuation of the special treatment as set out in paragraph 7 after the end of the 10th year following the beginning of the implementation period shall be initiated and completed within the time-frame of the 10th year itself following the beginning of the implementation period.

9.   If it is agreed as a result of the negotiation referred to in paragraph 8 that a Member may continue to apply the special treatment, such Member shall confer additional and acceptable concessions as determined in that negotiation.

10.   In the event that special treatment under paragraph 7 is not to be continued beyond the 10th year following the beginning of the implementation period, the products concerned shall be subject to ordinary customs duties, established on the basis of a tariff equivalent to be calculated in accordance with the guidelines prescribed in the attachment hereto, which shall be bound in the Schedule of the Member concerned. In other respects, the provisions of paragraph 6 shall apply as modified by the relevant special and differential treatment accorded to developing country Members under this Agreement.

Attachment to Annex 5

Guidelines for the Calculation of Tariff Equivalents for the Specific
Purpose Specified in Paragraphs 6 and 10 of this Annex

1.   The calculation of the tariff equivalents, whether expressed as *ad valorem* or specific rates, shall be made using the actual difference between internal and external prices in a transparent manner. Data used shall be for the years 1986 to 1988. Tariff equivalents:

(a) shall primarily be established at the four-digit level of the HS;

(b) shall be established at the six-digit or a more detailed level of the HS wherever appropriate;

(c) shall generally be established for worked and/or prepared products by multiplying the specific tariff equivalent(s) for the primary agricultural product(s) by the proportion(s) in value terms or in physical terms as appropriate of the primary agricultural product(s) in the worked and/or prepared products, and take account, where necessary, of any additional elements currently providing protection to industry.

2.   External prices shall be, in general, actual average c.i.f. unit values for the importing country. Where average c.i.f. unit values are not available or appropriate, external prices shall be either:

(a) appropriate average c.i.f. unit values of a near country; or

(b) estimated from average f.o.b. unit values of (an) appropriate major exporter(s) adjusted by adding an estimate of insurance, freight and other relevant costs to the importing country.

3.   The external prices shall generally be converted to domestic currencies using the annual average market exchange rate for the same period as the price data.

4.   The internal price shall generally be a representative wholesale price ruling in the domestic market or an estimate of that price where adequate data is not available.

5.   The initial tariff equivalents may be adjusted, where necessary, to take account of differences in quality or variety using an appropriate coefficient.

6.   Where a tariff equivalent resulting from these guidelines is negative or lower than the current bound rate, the initial tariff equivalent may be established at the current bound rate or on the basis of national offers for that product.

7.   Where an adjustment is made to the level of a tariff equivalent which would have resulted from the above guidelines, the Member concerned shall afford, on request, full opportunities for consultation with a view to negotiating appropriate solutions.

Item 5

AGREEMENT ON THE APPLICATION OF SANITARY AND PHYTOSANITARY MEASURES

Members,

Reaffirming that no Member should be prevented from adopting or enforcing measures necessary to protect human, animal or plant life or health, subject to the requirement that these measures are not applied in a manner which would constitute a means of arbitrary or unjustifiable discrimination between Members where the same conditions prevail or a disguised restriction on international trade;

Desiring to improve the human health, animal health and phytosanitary situation in all Members;

Noting that sanitary and phytosanitary measures are often applied on the basis of bilateral agreements or protocols;

Desiring the establishment of a multilateral framework of rules and disciplines to guide the development, adoption and enforcement of sanitary and phytosanitary measures in order to minimize their negative effects on trade;

Recognizing the important contribution that international standards, guidelines and recommendations can make in this regard;

Desiring to further the use of harmonized sanitary and phytosanitary measures between Members, on the basis of international standards, guidelines and recommendations developed by the relevant international organizations, including the Codex Alimentarius Commission, the International Office of Epizootics, and the relevant international and regional organizations operating within the framework of the International Plant Protection Convention, without requiring Members to change their appropriate level of protection of human, animal or plant life or health;

Recognizing that developing country Members may encounter special difficulties in complying with the sanitary or phytosanitary measures of importing Members, and as a consequence in access to markets, and also in the formulation and application of sanitary or phytosanitary measures in their own territories, and desiring to assist them in their endeavours in this regard;

Desiring therefore to elaborate rules for the application of the provisions of GATT 1994 which relate to the use of sanitary or phytosanitary measures, in particular the provisions of Article XX(b) [1];

Hereby agree as follows:

---

1. In this Agreement, reference to Article XX(b) includes also the chapeau of that Article.

Article 1

General Provisions

1. This Agreement applies to all sanitary and phytosanitary measures which may, directly or indirectly, affect international trade. Such measures shall be developed and applied in accordance with the provisions of this Agreement.

2. For the purposes of this Agreement, the definitions provided in Annex A shall apply.

3. The annexes are an integral part of this Agreement.

4. Nothing in this Agreement shall affect the rights of Members under the Agreement on Technical Barriers to Trade with respect to measures not within the scope of this Agreement.

Article 2

Basic Rights and Obligations

1. Members have the right to take sanitary and phytosanitary measures necessary for the protection of human, animal or plant life or health, provided that such measures are not inconsistent with the provisions of this Agreement.

2. Members shall ensure that any sanitary or phytosanitary measure is applied only to the extent necessary to protect human, animal or plant life or health, is based on scientific principles and is not maintained without sufficient scientific evidence, except as provided for in paragraph 7 of Article 5.

3. Members shall ensure that their sanitary and phytosanitary measures do not arbitrarily or unjustifiably discriminate between Members where identical or similar conditions prevail, including between their own territory and that of other Members. Sanitary and phytosanitary measures shall not be applied in a manner which would constitute a disguised restriction on international trade.

4. Sanitary or phytosanitary measures which conform to the relevant provisions of this Agreement shall be presumed to be in accordance with the obligations of the Members under the provisions of GATT 1994 which relate to the use of sanitary or phytosanitary measures, in particular the provisions of Article XX(b).

Article 3

Harmonization

1. To harmonize sanitary and phytosanitary measures on as wide a basis as possible, Members shall base their sanitary or phytosanitary measures on international standards, guidelines or recommendations, where they exist, except as otherwise provided for in this Agreement, and in particular in paragraph 3.

2. Sanitary or phytosanitary measures which conform to international standards, guidelines or recommendations shall be deemed to be necessary to protect human, animal or plant life or health, and presumed to be consistent with the relevant provisions of this Agreement and of GATT 1994.

3. Members may introduce or maintain sanitary or phytosanitary measures which result in a higher level of sanitary or phytosanitary protection than would be achieved by measures based on the relevant international standards, guidelines or recommendations, if there is a scientific justification, or as a consequence of the level of sanitary or phytosanitary protection a Member determines to be appropriate in accordance with the relevant provisions of paragraphs 1 through 8 of Article 5.[2] Notwithstanding the above, all measures which result in a level of sanitary or phytosanitary protection different from that which would be achieved by measures based on international standards, guidelines or recommendations shall not be inconsistent with any other provision of this Agreement.

4. Members shall play a full part, within the limits of their resources, in the relevant international organizations and their subsidiary bodies, in particular the Codex Alimentarius Commission, the International Office of Epizootics, and the international and regional organizations operating within the framework of the International Plant Protection Convention, to promote within these organizations the development and periodic review of standards, guidelines and recommendations with respect to all aspects of sanitary and phytosanitary measures.

5. The Committee on Sanitary and Phytosanitary Measures provided for in paragraphs 1 and 4 of Article 12 (referred to in this Agreement as the "Committee") shall develop a procedure to monitor the process of international harmonization and coordinate efforts in this regard with the relevant international organizations.

Article 4

Equivalence

1. Members shall accept the sanitary or phytosanitary measures of other Members as equivalent, even if these measures differ from their own or from those used by other Members trading in the same product, if the exporting Member objectively demonstrates to the importing Member that its measures achieve the importing Member's appropriate level of sanitary or phytosanitary protection. For this purpose, reasonable access shall be given, upon request, to the importing Member for inspection, testing and other relevant procedures.

2. Members shall, upon request, enter into consultations with the aim of achieving bilateral and multilateral agreements on recognition of the equivalence of specified sanitary or phytosanitary measures.

Article 5

Assessment of Risk and Determination of the Appropriate
Level of Sanitary or Phytosanitary Protection

1. Members shall ensure that their sanitary or phytosanitary measures are based on an assessment, as appropriate to the circumstances, of the risks

---

2. For the purposes of paragraph 3 of Article 3, there is a scientific justification if, on the basis of an examination and evaluation of available scientific information in conformity with the relevant provisions of this Agreement, a Member determines that the relevant international standards, guidelines or recommendations are not sufficient to achieve its appropriate level of sanitary or phytosanitary protection.

to human, animal or plant life or health, taking into account risk assessment techniques developed by the relevant international organizations.

2.   In the assessment of risks, Members shall take into account available scientific evidence; relevant processes and production methods; relevant inspection, sampling and testing methods; prevalence of specific diseases or pests; existence of pest- or disease-free areas; relevant ecological and environmental conditions; and quarantine or other treatment.

3.   In assessing the risk to animal or plant life or health and determining the measure to be applied for achieving the appropriate level of sanitary or phytosanitary protection from such risk, Members shall take into account as relevant economic factors: the potential damage in terms of loss of production or sales in the event of the entry, establishment or spread of a pest or disease; the costs of control or eradication in the territory of the importing Member; and the relative cost-effectiveness of alternative approaches to limiting risks.

4.   Members should, when determining the appropriate level of sanitary or phytosanitary protection, take into account the objective of minimizing negative trade effects.

5.   With the objective of achieving consistency in the application of the concept of appropriate level of sanitary or phytosanitary protection against risks to human life or health, or to animal and plant life or health, each Member shall avoid arbitrary or unjustifiable distinctions in the levels it considers to be appropriate in different situations, if such distinctions result in discrimination or a disguised restriction on international trade. Members shall cooperate in the Committee, in accordance with paragraphs 1, 2 and 3 of Article 12, to develop guidelines to further the practical implementation of this provision. In developing the guidelines, the Committee shall take into account all relevant factors, including the exceptional character of human health risks to which people voluntarily expose themselves.

6.   Without prejudice to paragraph 2 of Article 3, when establishing or maintaining sanitary or phytosanitary measures to achieve the appropriate level of sanitary or phytosanitary protection, Members shall ensure that such measures are not more trade-restrictive than required to achieve their appropriate level of sanitary or phytosanitary protection, taking into account technical and economic feasibility.[3]

7.   In cases where relevant scientific evidence is insufficient, a Member may provisionally adopt sanitary or phytosanitary measures on the basis of available pertinent information, including that from the relevant international organizations as well as from sanitary or phytosanitary measures applied by other Members. In such circumstances, Members shall seek to obtain the additional information necessary for a more objective assessment of risk and review the sanitary or phytosanitary measure accordingly within a reasonable period of time.

8.   When a Member has reason to believe that a specific sanitary or phytosanitary measure introduced or maintained by another Member is

---

3. For purposes of paragraph 6 of Article 5, a measure is not more trade-restrictive than required unless there is another measure, reasonably available taking into account technical and economic feasibility, that achieves the appropriate level of sanitary or phytosanitary protection and is significantly less restrictive to trade.

constraining, or has the potential to constrain, its exports and the measure is not based on the relevant international standards, guidelines or recommendations, or such standards, guidelines or recommendations do not exist, an explanation of the reasons for such sanitary or phytosanitary measure may be requested and shall be provided by the Member maintaining the measure.

Article 6
Adaptation to Regional Conditions, Including Pest- or Disease– Free Areas and Areas of Low Pest or Disease Prevalence

1. Members shall ensure that their sanitary or phytosanitary measures are adapted to the sanitary or phytosanitary characteristics of the area— whether all of a country, part of a country, or all or parts of several countries—from which the product originated and to which the product is destined. In assessing the sanitary or phytosanitary characteristics of a region, Members shall take into account, *inter alia*, the level of prevalence of specific diseases or pests, the existence of eradication or control programmes, and appropriate criteria or guidelines which may be developed by the relevant international organizations.

2. Members shall, in particular, recognize the concepts of pest- or disease-free areas and areas of low pest or disease prevalence. Determination of such areas shall be based on factors such as geography, ecosystems, epidemiological surveillance, and the effectiveness of sanitary or phytosanitary controls.

3. Exporting Members claiming that areas within their territories are pest- or disease-free areas or areas of low pest or disease prevalence shall provide the necessary evidence thereof in order to objectively demonstrate to the importing Member that such areas are, and are likely to remain, pest- or disease-free areas or areas of low pest or disease prevalence, respectively. For this purpose, reasonable access shall be given, upon request, to the importing Member for inspection, testing and other relevant procedures.

Article 7
Transparency

Members shall notify changes in their sanitary or phytosanitary measures and shall provide information on their sanitary or phytosanitary measures in accordance with the provisions of Annex B.

Article 8
Control, Inspection and Approval Procedures

Members shall observe the provisions of Annex C in the operation of control, inspection and approval procedures, including national systems for approving the use of additives or for establishing tolerances for contaminants in foods, beverages or feedstuffs, and otherwise ensure that their procedures are not inconsistent with the provisions of this Agreement.

Article 9
Technical Assistance

1. Members agree to facilitate the provision of technical assistance to other Members, especially developing country Members, either bilaterally or

through the appropriate international organizations. Such assistance may be, *inter alia*, in the areas of processing technologies, research and infrastructure, including in the establishment of national regulatory bodies, and may take the form of advice, credits, donations and grants, including for the purpose of seeking technical expertise, training and equipment to allow such countries to adjust to, and comply with, sanitary or phytosanitary measures necessary to achieve the appropriate level of sanitary or phytosanitary protection in their export markets.

2.   Where substantial investments are required in order for an exporting developing country Member to fulfil the sanitary or phytosanitary requirements of an importing Member, the latter shall consider providing such technical assistance as will permit the developing country Member to maintain and expand its market access opportunities for the product involved.

Article 10
Special and Differential Treatment

1.   In the preparation and application of sanitary or phytosanitary measures, Members shall take account of the special needs of developing country Members, and in particular of the least-developed country Members.

2.   Where the appropriate level of sanitary or phytosanitary protection allows scope for the phased introduction of new sanitary or phytosanitary measures, longer time-frames for compliance should be accorded on products of interest to developing country Members so as to maintain opportunities for their exports.

3.   With a view to ensuring that developing country Members are able to comply with the provisions of this Agreement, the Committee is enabled to grant to such countries, upon request, specified, time-limited exceptions in whole or in part from obligations under this Agreement, taking into account their financial, trade and development needs.

4.   Members should encourage and facilitate the active participation of developing country Members in the relevant international organizations.

Article 11
Consultations and Dispute Settlement

1.   The provisions of Articles XXII and XXIII of GATT 1994 as elaborated and applied by the Dispute Settlement Understanding shall apply to consultations and the settlement of disputes under this Agreement, except as otherwise specifically provided herein.

2.   In a dispute under this Agreement involving scientific or technical issues, a panel should seek advice from experts chosen by the panel in consultation with the parties to the dispute. To this end, the panel may, when it deems it appropriate, establish an advisory technical experts group, or consult the relevant international organizations, at the request of either party to the dispute or on its own initiative.

3.   Nothing in this Agreement shall impair the rights of Members under other international agreements, including the right to resort to the good offices or dispute settlement mechanisms of other international organizations or established under any international agreement.

Article 12

Administration

1. A Committee on Sanitary and Phytosanitary Measures is hereby established to provide a regular forum for consultations. It shall carry out the functions necessary to implement the provisions of this Agreement and the furtherance of its objectives, in particular with respect to harmonization. The Committee shall reach its decisions by consensus.

2. The Committee shall encourage and facilitate ad hoc consultations or negotiations among Members on specific sanitary or phytosanitary issues. The Committee shall encourage the use of international standards, guidelines or recommendations by all Members and, in this regard, shall sponsor technical consultation and study with the objective of increasing coordination and integration between international and national systems and approaches for approving the use of food additives or for establishing tolerances for contaminants in foods, beverages or feedstuffs.

3. The Committee shall maintain close contact with the relevant international organizations in the field of sanitary and phytosanitary protection, especially with the Codex Alimentarius Commission, the International Office of Epizootics, and the Secretariat of the International Plant Protection Convention, with the objective of securing the best available scientific and technical advice for the administration of this Agreement and in order to ensure that unnecessary duplication of effort is avoided.

4. The Committee shall develop a procedure to monitor the process of international harmonization and the use of international standards, guidelines or recommendations. For this purpose, the Committee should, in conjunction with the relevant international organizations, establish a list of international standards, guidelines or recommendations relating to sanitary or phytosanitary measures which the Committee determines to have a major trade impact. The list should include an indication by Members of those international standards, guidelines or recommendations which they apply as conditions for import or on the basis of which imported products conforming to these standards can enjoy access to their markets. For those cases in which a Member does not apply an international standard, guideline or recommendation as a condition for import, the Member should provide an indication of the reason therefor, and, in particular, whether it considers that the standard is not stringent enough to provide the appropriate level of sanitary or phytosanitary protection. If a Member revises its position, following its indication of the use of a standard, guideline or recommendation as a condition for import, it should provide an explanation for its change and so inform the Secretariat as well as the relevant international organizations, unless such notification and explanation is given according to the procedures of Annex B.

5. In order to avoid unnecessary duplication, the Committee may decide, as appropriate, to use the information generated by the procedures, particularly for notification, which are in operation in the relevant international organizations.

6. The Committee may, on the basis of an initiative from one of the Members, through appropriate channels invite the relevant international

organizations or their subsidiary bodies to examine specific matters with respect to a particular standard, guideline or recommendation, including the basis of explanations for non-use given according to paragraph 4.

7.   The Committee shall review the operation and implementation of this Agreement three years after the date of entry into force of the WTO Agreement, and thereafter as the need arises. Where appropriate, the Committee may submit to the Council for Trade in Goods proposals to amend the text of this Agreement having regard, *inter alia*, to the experience gained in its implementation.

Article 13

Implementation

Members are fully responsible under this Agreement for the observance of all obligations set forth herein. Members shall formulate and implement positive measures and mechanisms in support of the observance of the provisions of this Agreement by other than central government bodies. Members shall take such reasonable measures as may be available to them to ensure that non-governmental entities within their territories, as well as regional bodies in which relevant entities within their territories are members, comply with the relevant provisions of this Agreement. In addition, Members shall not take measures which have the effect of, directly or indirectly, requiring or encouraging such regional or non-governmental entities, or local governmental bodies, to act in a manner inconsistent with the provisions of this Agreement. Members shall ensure that they rely on the services of non-governmental entities for implementing sanitary or phytosanitary measures only if these entities comply with the provisions of this Agreement.

Article 14

Final Provisions

The least-developed country Members may delay application of the provisions of this Agreement for a period of five years following the date of entry into force of the WTO Agreement with respect to their sanitary or phytosanitary measures affecting importation or imported products. Other developing country Members may delay application of the provisions of this Agreement, other than paragraph 8 of Article 5 and Article 7, for two years following the date of entry into force of the WTO Agreement with respect to their existing sanitary or phytosanitary measures affecting importation or imported products, where such application is prevented by a lack of technical expertise, technical infrastructure or resources.

ANNEX A

DEFINITIONS [4]

1.   *Sanitary or phytosanitary measure*—Any measure applied:

4. For the purpose of these definitions, "animal" includes fish and wild fauna; "plant" includes forests and wild flora; "pests" include weeds; and "contaminants" include pesticide and veterinary drug residues and extraneous matter.

(a) to protect animal or plant life or health within the territory of the Member from risks arising from the entry, establishment or spread of pests, diseases, disease-carrying organisms or disease-causing organisms;

(b) to protect human or animal life or health within the territory of the Member from risks arising from additives, contaminants, toxins or disease-causing organisms in foods, beverages or feedstuffs;

(c) to protect human life or health within the territory of the Member from risks arising from diseases carried by animals, plants or products thereof, or from the entry, establishment or spread of pests; or

(d) to prevent or limit other damage within the territory of the Member from the entry, establishment or spread of pests.

Sanitary or phytosanitary measures include all relevant laws, decrees, regulations, requirements and procedures including, *inter alia*, end product criteria; processes and production methods; testing, inspection, certification and approval procedures; quarantine treatments including relevant requirements associated with the transport of animals or plants, or with the materials necessary for their survival during transport; provisions on relevant statistical methods, sampling procedures and methods of risk assessment; and packaging and labelling requirements directly related to food safety.

2. *Harmonization*—The establishment, recognition and application of common sanitary and phytosanitary measures by different Members.

3. *International standards, guidelines and recommendations*

(a) for food safety, the standards, guidelines and recommendations established by the Codex Alimentarius Commission relating to food additives, veterinary drug and pesticide residues, contaminants, methods of analysis and sampling, and codes and guidelines of hygienic practice;

(b) for animal health and zoonoses, the standards, guidelines and recommendations developed under the auspices of the International Office of Epizootics;

(c) for plant health, the international standards, guidelines and recommendations developed under the auspices of the Secretariat of the International Plant Protection Convention in cooperation with regional organizations operating within the framework of the International Plant Protection Convention; and

(d) for matters not covered by the above organizations, appropriate standards, guidelines and recommendations promulgated by other relevant international organizations open for membership to all Members, as identified by the Committee.

4. *Risk assessment*—The evaluation of the likelihood of entry, establishment or spread of a pest or disease within the territory of an importing Member according to the sanitary or phytosanitary measures which might be applied, and of the associated potential biological and economic consequences; or the evaluation of the potential for adverse effects on human or animal health arising from the presence of additives, contaminants, toxins or disease-causing organisms in food, beverages or feedstuffs.

5. *Appropriate level of sanitary or phytosanitary protection*—The level of protection deemed appropriate by the Member establishing a sanitary or

phytosanitary measure to protect human, animal or plant life or health within its territory.

NOTE: Many Members otherwise refer to this concept as the "acceptable level of risk".

6. *Pest- or disease-free area*—An area, whether all of a country, part of a country, or all or parts of several countries, as identified by the competent authorities, in which a specific pest or disease does not occur.

NOTE: A pest- or disease-free area may surround, be surrounded by, or be adjacent to an area—whether within part of a country or in a geographic region which includes parts of or all of several countries -in which a specific pest or disease is known to occur but is subject to regional control measures such as the establishment of protection, surveillance and buffer zones which will confine or eradicate the pest or disease in question.

7. *Area of low pest or disease prevalence*—An area, whether all of a country, part of a country, or all or parts of several countries, as identified by the competent authorities, in which a specific pest or disease occurs at low levels and which is subject to effective surveillance, control or eradication measures.

ANNEX B

TRANSPARENCY OF SANITARY AND PHYTOSANITARY REGULATIONS

Publication of regulations

1. Members shall ensure that all sanitary and phytosanitary regulations [5] which have been adopted are published promptly in such a manner as to enable interested Members to become acquainted with them.

2. Except in urgent circumstances, Members shall allow a reasonable interval between the publication of a sanitary or phytosanitary regulation and its entry into force in order to allow time for producers in exporting Members, and particularly in developing country Members, to adapt their products and methods of production to the requirements of the importing Member.

Enquiry points

3. Each Member shall ensure that one enquiry point exists which is responsible for the provision of answers to all reasonable questions from interested Members as well as for the provision of relevant documents regarding:

(a) any sanitary or phytosanitary regulations adopted or proposed within its territory;

(b) any control and inspection procedures, production and quarantine treatment, pesticide tolerance and food additive approval procedures, which are operated within its territory;

5. Sanitary and phytosanitary measures such as laws, decrees or ordinances which are applicable generally.

(c) risk assessment procedures, factors taken into consideration, as well as the determination of the appropriate level of sanitary or phytosanitary protection;

(d) the membership and participation of the Member, or of relevant bodies within its territory, in international and regional sanitary and phytosanitary organizations and systems, as well as in bilateral and multilateral agreements and arrangements within the scope of this Agreement, and the texts of such agreements and arrangements.

4. Members shall ensure that where copies of documents are requested by interested Members, they are supplied at the same price (if any), apart from the cost of delivery, as to the nationals[6] of the Member concerned.

Notification procedures

5. Whenever an international standard, guideline or recommendation does not exist or the content of a proposed sanitary or phytosanitary regulation is not substantially the same as the content of an international standard, guideline or recommendation, and if the regulation may have a significant effect on trade of other Members, Members shall:

(a) publish a notice at an early stage in such a manner as to enable interested Members to become acquainted with the proposal to introduce a particular regulation;

(b) notify other Members, through the Secretariat, of the products to be covered by the regulation together with a brief indication of the objective and rationale of the proposed regulation. Such notifications shall take place at an early stage, when amendments can still be introduced and comments taken into account;

(c) provide upon request to other Members copies of the proposed regulation and, whenever possible, identify the parts which in substance deviate from international standards, guidelines or recommendations;

(d) without discrimination, allow reasonable time for other Members to make comments in writing, discuss these comments upon request, and take the comments and the results of the discussions into account.

6. However, where urgent problems of health protection arise or threaten to arise for a Member, that Member may omit such of the steps enumerated in paragraph 5 of this Annex as it finds necessary, provided that the Member:

(a) immediately notifies other Members, through the Secretariat, of the particular regulation and the products covered, with a brief indication of the objective and the rationale of the regulation, including the nature of the urgent problem(s);

(b) provides, upon request, copies of the regulation to other Members;

6. When "nationals" are referred to in this Agreement, the term shall be deemed, in the case of a separate customs territory Member of the WTO, to mean persons, natural or legal, who are domiciled or who have a real and effective industrial or commercial establishment in that customs territory.

(c) allows other Members to make comments in writing, discusses these comments upon request, and takes the comments and the results of the discussions into account.

7. Notifications to the Secretariat shall be in English, French or Spanish.

8. Developed country Members shall, if requested by other Members, provide copies of the documents or, in case of voluminous documents, summaries of the documents covered by a specific notification in English, French or Spanish.

9. The Secretariat shall promptly circulate copies of the notification to all Members and interested international organizations and draw the attention of developing country Members to any notifications relating to products of particular interest to them.

10. Members shall designate a single central government authority as responsible for the implementation, on the national level, of the provisions concerning notification procedures according to paragraphs 5, 6, 7 and 8 of this Annex.

General reservations

11. Nothing in this Agreement shall be construed as requiring:

(a) the provision of particulars or copies of drafts or the publication of texts other than in the language of the Member except as stated in paragraph 8 of this Annex; or

(b) Members to disclose confidential information which would impede enforcement of sanitary or phytosanitary legislation or which would prejudice the legitimate commercial interests of particular enterprises.

ANNEX C
CONTROL, INSPECTION AND APPROVAL PROCEDURES [7]

1. Members shall ensure, with respect to any procedure to check and ensure the fulfilment of sanitary or phytosanitary measures, that:

(a) such procedures are undertaken and completed without undue delay and in no less favourable manner for imported products than for like domestic products;

(b) the standard processing period of each procedure is published or that the anticipated processing period is communicated to the applicant upon request; when receiving an application, the competent body promptly examines the completeness of the documentation and informs the applicant in a precise and complete manner of all deficiencies; the competent body transmits as soon as possible the results of the procedure in a precise and complete manner to the applicant so that corrective action may be taken if necessary; even when the application has deficiencies, the competent body proceeds as far as practicable with the procedure

---

7. Control, inspection and approval procedures include, *inter alia*, procedures for sampling, testing and certification.

if the applicant so requests; and that upon request, the applicant is informed of the stage of the procedure, with any delay being explained;

(c) information requirements are limited to what is necessary for appropriate control, inspection and approval procedures, including for approval of the use of additives or for the establishment of tolerances for contaminants in food, beverages or feedstuffs;

(d) the confidentiality of information about imported products arising from or supplied in connection with control, inspection and approval is respected in a way no less favourable than for domestic products and in such a manner that legitimate commercial interests are protected;

(e) any requirements for control, inspection and approval of individual specimens of a product are limited to what is reasonable and necessary;

(f) any fees imposed for the procedures on imported products are equitable in relation to any fees charged on like domestic products or products originating in any other Member and should be no higher than the actual cost of the service;

(g) the same criteria should be used in the siting of facilities used in the procedures and the selection of samples of imported products as for domestic products so as to minimize the inconvenience to applicants, importers, exporters or their agents;

(h) whenever specifications of a product are changed subsequent to its control and inspection in light of the applicable regulations, the procedure for the modified product is limited to what is necessary to determine whether adequate confidence exists that the product still meets the regulations concerned; and

(i) a procedure exists to review complaints concerning the operation of such procedures and to take corrective action when a complaint is justified.

Where an importing Member operates a system for the approval of the use of food additives or for the establishment of tolerances for contaminants in food, beverages or feedstuffs which prohibits or restricts access to its domestic markets for products based on the absence of an approval, the importing Member shall consider the use of a relevant international standard as the basis for access until a final determination is made.

2. Where a sanitary or phytosanitary measure specifies control at the level of production, the Member in whose territory the production takes place shall provide the necessary assistance to facilitate such control and the work of the controlling authorities.

3. Nothing in this Agreement shall prevent Members from carrying out reasonable inspection within their own territories.

Item 6

AGREEMENT ON TEXTILES AND CLOTHING

Members,

Recalling that Ministers agreed at Punta del Este that "negotiations in the area of textiles and clothing shall aim to formulate modalities that would permit the eventual integration of this sector into GATT on the basis of strengthened GATT rules and disciplines, thereby also contributing to the objective of further liberalization of trade";

Recalling also that in the April 1989 Decision of the Trade Negotiations Committee it was agreed that the process of integration should commence following the conclusion of the Uruguay Round of Multilateral Trade Negotiations and should be progressive in character;

Recalling further that it was agreed that special treatment should be accorded to the least-developed country Members;

Hereby *agree* as follows:

Article 1

1. This Agreement sets out provisions to be applied by Members during a transition period for the integration of the textiles and clothing sector into GATT 1994.

2. Members agree to use the provisions of paragraph 18 of Article 2 and paragraph 6(b) of Article 6 in such a way as to permit meaningful increases in access possibilities for small suppliers and the development of commercially significant trading opportunities for new entrants in the field of textiles and clothing trade.[1]

3. Members shall have due regard to the situation of those Members which have not accepted the Protocols extending the Arrangement Regarding International Trade in Textiles (referred to in this Agreement as the "MFA") since 1986 and, to the extent possible, shall afford them special treatment in applying the provisions of this Agreement.

4. Members agree that the particular interests of the cotton-producing exporting Members should, in consultation with them, be reflected in the implementation of the provisions of this Agreement.

5. In order to facilitate the integration of the textiles and clothing sector into GATT 1994, Members should allow for continuous autonomous industrial adjustment and increased competition in their markets.

6. Unless otherwise provided in this Agreement, its provisions shall not affect the rights and obligations of Members under the provisions of the WTO Agreement and the Multilateral Trade Agreements.

1. To the extent possible, exports from a least-developed country Member may also ben- efit from this provision.

7.   The textile and clothing products to which this Agreement applies are set out in the Annex.

Article 2

1.   All quantitative restrictions within bilateral agreements maintained under Article 4 or notified under Article 7 or 8 of the MFA in force on the day before the entry into force of the WTO Agreement shall, within 60 days following such entry into force, be notified in detail, including the restraint levels, growth rates and flexibility provisions, by the Members maintaining such restrictions to the Textiles Monitoring Body provided for in Article 8 (referred to in this Agreement as the "TMB"). Members agree that as of the date of entry into force of the WTO Agreement, all such restrictions maintained between GATT 1947 contracting parties, and in place on the day before such entry into force, shall be governed by the provisions of this Agreement.

2.   The TMB shall circulate these notifications to all Members for their information. It is open to any Member to bring to the attention of the TMB, within 60 days of the circulation of the notifications, any observations it deems appropriate with regard to such notifications. Such observations shall be circulated to the other Members for their information. The TMB may make recommendations, as appropriate, to the Members concerned.

3.   When the 12–month period of restrictions to be notified under paragraph 1 does not coincide with the 12–month period immediately preceding the date of entry into force of the WTO Agreement, the Members concerned should mutually agree on arrangements to bring the period of restrictions into line with the agreement year [2], and to establish notional base levels of such restrictions in order to implement the provisions of this Article. Concerned Members agree to enter into consultations promptly upon request with a view to reaching such mutual agreement. Any such arrangements shall take into account, *inter alia*, seasonal patterns of shipments in recent years. The results of these consultations shall be notified to the TMB, which shall make such recommendations as it deems appropriate to the Members concerned.

4.   The restrictions notified under paragraph 1 shall be deemed to constitute the totality of such restrictions applied by the respective Members on the day before the entry into force of the WTO Agreement. No new restrictions in terms of products or Members shall be introduced except under the provisions of this Agreement or relevant GATT 1994 provisions.[3] Restrictions not notified within 60 days of the date of entry into force of the WTO Agreement shall be terminated forthwith.

5.   Any unilateral measure taken under Article 3 of the MFA prior to the date of entry into force of the WTO Agreement may remain in effect for the duration specified therein, but not exceeding 12 months, if it has been reviewed by the Textiles Surveillance Body (referred to in this Agreement as the "TSB") established under the MFA. Should the TSB not have had the opportunity to review any such unilateral measure, it shall be reviewed by the

2. The "agreement year" is defined to mean a 12–month period beginning from the date of entry into force of the WTO Agreement and at the subsequent 12–month intervals.

3. The relevant GATT 1994 provisions shall not include Article XIX in respect of products not yet integrated into GATT 1994, except as specifically provided in paragraph 3 of the Annex.

TMB in accordance with the rules and procedures governing Article 3 measures under the MFA. Any measure applied under an MFA Article 4 agreement prior to the date of entry into force of the WTO Agreement that is the subject of a dispute which the TSB has not had the opportunity to review shall also be reviewed by the TMB in accordance with the MFA rules and procedures applicable for such a review.

6.   On the date of entry into force of the WTO Agreement, each Member shall integrate into GATT 1994 products which accounted for not less than 16 per cent of the total volume of the Member's 1990 imports of the products in the Annex, in terms of HS lines or categories. The products to be integrated shall encompass products from each of the following four groups: tops and yarns, fabrics, made-up textile products, and clothing.

7.   Full details of the actions to be taken pursuant to paragraph 6 shall be notified by the Members concerned according to the following:

(a) Members maintaining restrictions falling under paragraph 1 undertake, notwithstanding the date of entry into force of the WTO Agreement, to notify such details to the GATT Secretariat not later than the date determined by the Ministerial Decision of 15 April 1994. The GATT Secretariat shall promptly circulate these notifications to the other participants for information. These notifications will be made available to the TMB, when established, for the purposes of paragraph 21;

(b) Members which have, pursuant to paragraph 1 of Article 6, retained the right to use the provisions of Article 6, shall notify such details to the TMB not later than 60 days following the date of entry into force of the WTO Agreement, or, in the case of those Members covered by paragraph 3 of Article 1, not later than at the end of the 12th month that the WTO Agreement is in effect. The TMB shall circulate these notifications to the other Members for information and review them as provided in paragraph 21.

8.   The remaining products, i.e. the products not integrated into GATT 1994 under paragraph 6, shall be integrated, in terms of HS lines or categories, in three stages, as follows:

(a) on the first day of the 37th month that the WTO Agreement is in effect, products which accounted for not less than 17 per cent of the total volume of the Member's 1990 imports of the products in the Annex. The products to be integrated by the Members shall encompass products from each of the following four groups: tops and yarns, fabrics, made-up textile products, and clothing;

(b) on the first day of the 85th month that the WTO Agreement is in effect, products which accounted for not less than 18 per cent of the total volume of the Member's 1990 imports of the products in the Annex. The products to be integrated by the Members shall encompass products from each of the following four groups: tops and yarns, fabrics, made-up textile products, and clothing;

(c) on the first day of the 121st month that the WTO Agreement is in effect, the textiles and clothing sector shall stand integrated into GATT 1994, all restrictions under this Agreement having been eliminated.

9. Members which have notified, pursuant to paragraph 1 of Article 6, their intention not to retain the right to use the provisions of Article 6 shall, for the purposes of this Agreement, be deemed to have integrated their textiles and clothing products into GATT 1994. Such Members shall, therefore, be exempted from complying with the provisions of paragraphs 6 to 8 and 11.

10. Nothing in this Agreement shall prevent a Member which has submitted an integration programme pursuant to paragraph 6 or 8 from integrating products into GATT 1994 earlier than provided for in such a programme. However, any such integration of products shall take effect at the beginning of an agreement year, and details shall be notified to the TMB at least three months prior thereto for circulation to all Members.

11. The respective programmes of integration, in pursuance of paragraph 8, shall be notified in detail to the TMB at least 12 months before their coming into effect, and circulated by the TMB to all Members.

12. The base levels of the restrictions on the remaining products, mentioned in paragraph 8, shall be the restraint levels referred to in paragraph 1.

13. During Stage 1 of this Agreement (from the date of entry into force of the WTO Agreement to the 36th month that it is in effect, inclusive) the level of each restriction under MFA bilateral agreements in force for the 12–month period prior to the date of entry into force of the WTO Agreement shall be increased annually by not less than the growth rate established for the respective restrictions, increased by 16 per cent.

14. Except where the Council for Trade in Goods or the Dispute Settlement Body decides otherwise under paragraph 12 of Article 8, the level of each remaining restriction shall be increased annually during subsequent stages of this Agreement by not less than the following:

(a) for Stage 2 (from the 37th to the 84th month that the WTO Agreement is in effect, inclusive), the growth rate for the respective restrictions during Stage 1, increased by 25 per cent;

(b) for Stage 3 (from the 85th to the 120th month that the WTO Agreement is in effect, inclusive), the growth rate for the respective restrictions during Stage 2, increased by 27 per cent.

15. Nothing in this Agreement shall prevent a Member from eliminating any restriction maintained pursuant to this Article, effective at the beginning of any agreement year during the transition period, provided the exporting Member concerned and the TMB are notified at least three months prior to the elimination coming into effect. The period for prior notification may be shortened to 30 days with the agreement of the restrained Member. The TMB shall circulate such notifications to all Members. In considering the elimination of restrictions as envisaged in this paragraph, the Members concerned shall take into account the treatment of similar exports from other Members.

16. Flexibility provisions, i.e. swing, carryover and carry forward, applicable to all restrictions maintained pursuant to this Article, shall be the same as those provided for in MFA bilateral agreements for the 12–month period prior to the entry into force of the WTO Agreement. No quantitative limits

shall be placed or maintained on the combined use of swing, carryover and carry forward.

17.   Administrative arrangements, as deemed necessary in relation to the implementation of any provision of this Article, shall be a matter for agreement between the Members concerned. Any such arrangements shall be notified to the TMB.

18.   As regards those Members whose exports are subject to restrictions on the day before the entry into force of the WTO Agreement and whose restrictions represent 1.2 per cent or less of the total volume of the restrictions applied by an importing Member as of 31 December 1991 and notified under this Article, meaningful improvement in access for their exports shall be provided, at the entry into force of the WTO Agreement and for the duration of this Agreement, through advancement by one stage of the growth rates set out in paragraphs 13 and 14, or through at least equivalent changes as may be mutually agreed with respect to a different mix of base levels, growth and flexibility provisions. Such improvements shall be notified to the TMB.

19.   In any case, during the duration of this Agreement, in which a safeguard measure is initiated by a Member under Article XIX of GATT 1994 in respect of a particular product during a period of one year immediately following the integration of that product into GATT 1994 in accordance with the provisions of this Article, the provisions of Article XIX, as interpreted by the Agreement on Safeguards, will apply, save as set out in paragraph 20.

20.   Where such a measure is applied using non-tariff means, the importing Member concerned shall apply the measure in a manner as set forth in paragraph 2(d) of Article XIII of GATT 1994 at the request of any exporting Member whose exports of such products were subject to restrictions under this Agreement at any time in the one-year period immediately prior to the initiation of the safeguard measure. The exporting Member concerned shall administer such a measure. The applicable level shall not reduce the relevant exports below the level of a recent representative period, which shall normally be the average of exports from the Member concerned in the last three representative years for which statistics are available. Furthermore, when the safeguard measure is applied for more than one year, the applicable level shall be progressively liberalized at regular intervals during the period of application. In such cases the exporting Member concerned shall not exercise the right of suspending substantially equivalent concessions or other obligations under paragraph 3(a) of Article XIX of GATT 1994.

21.   The TMB shall keep under review the implementation of this Article. It shall, at the request of any Member, review any particular matter with reference to the implementation of the provisions of this Article. It shall make appropriate recommendations or findings within 30 days to the Member or Members concerned, after inviting the participation of such Members.

Article 3

1.   Within 60 days following the date of entry into force of the WTO Agreement, Members maintaining restrictions [4] on textile and clothing prod-

---

4. Restrictions denote all unilateral quantitative restrictions, bilateral arrangements and other measures having a similar effect.

ucts (other than restrictions maintained under the MFA and covered by the provisions of Article 2), whether consistent with GATT 1994 or not, shall (a) notify them in detail to the TMB, or (b) provide to the TMB notifications with respect to them which have been submitted to any other WTO body. The notifications should, wherever applicable, provide information with respect to any GATT 1994 justification for the restrictions, including GATT 1994 provisions on which they are based.

2.   Members maintaining restrictions falling under paragraph 1, except those justified under a GATT 1994 provision, shall either:

(a) bring them into conformity with GATT 1994 within one year following the entry into force of the WTO Agreement, and notify this action to the TMB for its information; or

(b) phase them out progressively according to a programme to be presented to the TMB by the Member maintaining the restrictions not later than six months after the date of entry into force of the WTO Agreement. This programme shall provide for all restrictions to be phased out within a period not exceeding the duration of this Agreement. The TMB may make recommendations to the Member concerned with respect to such a programme.

3.   During the duration of this Agreement, Members shall provide to the TMB, for its information, notifications submitted to any other WTO bodies with respect to any new restrictions or changes in existing restrictions on textile and clothing products, taken under any GATT 1994 provision, within 60 days of their coming into effect.

4.   It shall be open to any Member to make reverse notifications to the TMB, for its information, in regard to the GATT 1994 justification, or in regard to any restrictions that may not have been notified under the provisions of this Article. Actions with respect to such notifications may be pursued by any Member under relevant GATT 1994 provisions or procedures in the appropriate WTO body.

5.   The TMB shall circulate the notifications made pursuant to this Article to all Members for their information.

Article 4

1.   Restrictions referred to in Article 2, and those applied under Article 6, shall be administered by the exporting Members. Importing Members shall not be obliged to accept shipments in excess of the restrictions notified under Article 2, or of restrictions applied pursuant to Article 6.

2.   Members agree that the introduction of changes, such as changes in practices, rules, procedures and categorization of textile and clothing products, including those changes relating to the Harmonized System, in the implementation or administration of those restrictions notified or applied under this Agreement should not: upset the balance of rights and obligations between the Members concerned under this Agreement; adversely affect the access available to a Member; impede the full utilization of such access; or disrupt trade under this Agreement.

3.   If a product which constitutes only part of a restriction is notified for integration pursuant to the provisions of Article 2, Members agree that any change in the level of that restriction shall not upset the balance of rights and obligations between the Members concerned under this Agreement.

4.   When changes mentioned in paragraphs 2 and 3 are necessary, however, Members agree that the Member initiating such changes shall inform and, wherever possible, initiate consultations with the affected Member or Members prior to the implementation of such changes, with a view to reaching a mutually acceptable solution regarding appropriate and equitable adjustment.   Members further agree that where consultation prior to implementation is not feasible, the Member initiating such changes will, at the request of the affected Member, consult, within 60 days if possible, with the Members concerned with a view to reaching a mutually satisfactory solution regarding appropriate and equitable adjustments.   If a mutually satisfactory solution is not reached, any Member involved may refer the matter to the TMB for recommendations as provided in Article 8.   Should the TSB not have had the opportunity to review a dispute concerning such changes introduced prior to the entry into force of the WTO Agreement, it shall be reviewed by the TMB in accordance with the rules and procedures of the MFA applicable for such a review.

Article 5

1.   Members agree that circumvention by transshipment, re-routing, false declaration concerning country or place of origin, and falsification of official documents, frustrates the implementation of this Agreement to integrate the textiles and clothing sector into GATT 1994.   Accordingly, Members should establish the necessary legal provisions and/or administrative procedures to address and take action against such circumvention.   Members further agree that, consistent with their domestic laws and procedures, they will cooperate fully to address problems arising from circumvention.

2.   Should any Member believe that this Agreement is being circumvented by transshipment, re-routing, false declaration concerning country or place of origin, or falsification of official documents, and that no, or inadequate, measures are being applied to address and/or to take action against such circumvention, that Member should consult with the Member or Members concerned with a view to seeking a mutually satisfactory solution.   Such consultations should be held promptly, and within 30 days when possible.   If a mutually satisfactory solution is not reached, the matter may be referred by any Member involved to the TMB for recommendations.

3.   Members agree to take necessary action, consistent with their domestic laws and procedures, to prevent, to investigate and, where appropriate, to take legal and/or administrative action against circumvention practices within their territory.   Members agree to cooperate fully, consistent with their domestic laws and procedures, in instances of circumvention or alleged circumvention of this Agreement, to establish the relevant facts in the places of import, export and, where applicable, transshipment.   It is agreed that such cooperation, consistent with domestic laws and procedures, will include: investigation of circumvention practices which increase restrained exports to the Member maintaining such restraints;   exchange of documents, correspon-

dence, reports and other relevant information to the extent available; and facilitation of plant visits and contacts, upon request and on a case-by-case basis. Members should endeavour to clarify the circumstances of any such instances of circumvention or alleged circumvention, including the respective roles of the exporters or importers involved.

4. Where, as a result of investigation, there is sufficient evidence that circumvention has occurred (e.g. where evidence is available concerning the country or place of true origin, and the circumstances of such circumvention), Members agree that appropriate action, to the extent necessary to address the problem, should be taken. Such action may include the denial of entry of goods or, where goods have entered, having due regard to the actual circumstances and the involvement of the country or place of true origin, the adjustment of charges to restraint levels to reflect the true country or place of origin. Also, where there is evidence of the involvement of the territories of the Members through which the goods have been transshipped, such action may include the introduction of restraints with respect to such Members. Any such actions, together with their timing and scope, may be taken after consultations held with a view to arriving at a mutually satisfactory solution between the concerned Members and shall be notified to the TMB with full justification. The Members concerned may agree on other remedies in consultation. Any such agreement shall also be notified to the TMB, and the TMB may make such recommendations to the Members concerned as it deems appropriate. If a mutually satisfactory solution is not reached, any Member concerned may refer the matter to the TMB for prompt review and recommendations.

5. Members note that some cases of circumvention may involve shipments transiting through countries or places with no changes or alterations made to the goods contained in such shipments in the places of transit. They note that it may not be generally practicable for such places of transit to exercise control over such shipments.

6. Members agree that false declaration concerning fibre content, quantities, description or classification of merchandise also frustrates the objective of this Agreement. Where there is evidence that any such false declaration has been made for purposes of circumvention, Members agree that appropriate measures, consistent with domestic laws and procedures, should be taken against the exporters or importers involved. Should any Member believe that this Agreement is being circumvented by such false declaration and that no, or inadequate, administrative measures are being applied to address and/or to take action against such circumvention, that Member should consult promptly with the Member involved with a view to seeking a mutually satisfactory solution. If such a solution is not reached, the matter may be referred by any Member involved to the TMB for recommendations. This provision is not intended to prevent Members from making technical adjustments when inadvertent errors in declarations have been made.

Article 6

1. Members recognize that during the transition period it may be necessary to apply a specific transitional safeguard mechanism (referred to in this Agreement as "transitional safeguard"). The transitional safeguard may

be applied by any Member to products covered by the Annex, except those integrated into GATT 1994 under the provisions of Article 2. Members not maintaining restrictions falling under Article 2 shall notify the TMB within 60 days following the date of entry into force of the WTO Agreement, as to whether or not they wish to retain the right to use the provisions of this Article. Members which have not accepted the Protocols extending the MFA since 1986 shall make such notification within 6 months following the entry into force of the WTO Agreement. The transitional safeguard should be applied as sparingly as possible, consistently with the provisions of this Article and the effective implementation of the integration process under this Agreement.

2. Safeguard action may be taken under this Article when, on the basis of a determination by a Member [5], it is demonstrated that a particular product is being imported into its territory in such increased quantities as to cause serious damage, or actual threat thereof, to the domestic industry producing like and/or directly competitive products. Serious damage or actual threat thereof must demonstrably be caused by such increased quantities in total imports of that product and not by such other factors as technological changes or changes in consumer preference.

3. In making a determination of serious damage, or actual threat thereof, as referred to in paragraph 2, the Member shall examine the effect of those imports on the state of the particular industry, as reflected in changes in such relevant economic variables as output, productivity, utilization of capacity, inventories, market share, exports, wages, employment, domestic prices, profits and investment; none of which, either alone or combined with other factors, can necessarily give decisive guidance.

4. Any measure invoked pursuant to the provisions of this Article shall be applied on a Member-by-Member basis. The Member or Members to whom serious damage, or actual threat thereof, referred to in paragraphs 2 and 3, is attributed, shall be determined on the basis of a sharp and substantial increase in imports, actual or imminent [6], from such a Member or Members individually, and on the basis of the level of imports as compared with imports from other sources, market share, and import and domestic prices at a comparable stage of commercial transaction; none of these factors, either alone or combined with other factors, can necessarily give decisive guidance. Such safeguard measure shall not be applied to the exports of any Member whose exports of the particular product are already under restraint under this Agreement.

5. The period of validity of a determination of serious damage or actual threat thereof for the purpose of invoking safeguard action shall not exceed 90 days from the date of initial notification as set forth in paragraph 7.

5. A customs union may apply a safeguard measure as a single unit or on behalf of a member State. When a customs union applies a safeguard measure as a single unit, all the requirements for the determination of serious damage or actual threat thereof under this Agreement shall be based on the conditions existing in the customs union as a whole. When a safeguard measure is applied on behalf of a member State, all the requirements for the determination of serious damage, or actual threat thereof, shall be based on the conditions existing in that member State and the measure shall be limited to that member State.

6. Such an imminent increase shall be a measurable one and shall not be determined to exist on the basis of allegation, conjecture or mere possibility arising, for example, from the existence of production capacity in the exporting Members.

6. In the application of the transitional safeguard, particular account shall be taken of the interests of exporting Members as set out below:

(a) least-developed country Members shall be accorded treatment significantly more favourable than that provided to the other groups of Members referred to in this paragraph, preferably in all its elements but, at least, on overall terms;

(b) Members whose total volume of textile and clothing exports is small in comparison with the total volume of exports of other Members and who account for only a small percentage of total imports of that product into the importing Member shall be accorded differential and more favourable treatment in the fixing of the economic terms provided in paragraphs 8, 13 and 14. For those suppliers, due account will be taken, pursuant to paragraphs 2 and 3 of Article 1, of the future possibilities for the development of their trade and the need to allow commercial quantities of imports from them;

(c) with respect to wool products from wool-producing developing country Members whose economy and textiles and clothing trade are dependent on the wool sector, whose total textile and clothing exports consist almost exclusively of wool products, and whose volume of textiles and clothing trade is comparatively small in the markets of the importing Members, special consideration shall be given to the export needs of such Members when considering quota levels, growth rates and flexibility;

(d) more favourable treatment shall be accorded to re-imports by a Member of textile and clothing products which that Member has exported to another Member for processing and subsequent reimportation, as defined by the laws and practices of the importing Member, and subject to satisfactory control and certification procedures, when these products are imported from a Member for which this type of trade represents a significant proportion of its total exports of textiles and clothing.

7. The Member proposing to take safeguard action shall seek consultations with the Member or Members which would be affected by such action. The request for consultations shall be accompanied by specific and relevant factual information, as up-to-date as possible, particularly in regard to: (a) the factors, referred to in paragraph 3, on which the Member invoking the action has based its determination of the existence of serious damage or actual threat thereof; and (b) the factors, referred to in paragraph 4, on the basis of which it proposes to invoke the safeguard action with respect to the Member or Members concerned. In respect of requests made under this paragraph, the information shall be related, as closely as possible, to identifiable segments of production and to the reference period set out in paragraph 8. The Member invoking the action shall also indicate the specific level at which imports of the product in question from the Member or Members concerned are proposed to be restrained; such level shall not be lower than the level referred to in paragraph 8. The Member seeking consultations shall, at the same time, communicate to the Chairman of the TMB the request for consultations, including all the relevant factual data outlined in paragraphs 3 and 4, together with the proposed restraint level. The Chairman shall inform the members of the TMB of the request for consultations, indicating the requesting Member, the product in question and the Member having received

the request. The Member or Members concerned shall respond to this request promptly and the consultations shall be held without delay and normally be completed within 60 days of the date on which the request was received.

8. If, in the consultations, there is mutual understanding that the situation calls for restraint on the exports of the particular product from the Member or Members concerned, the level of such restraint shall be fixed at a level not lower than the actual level of exports or imports from the Member concerned during the 12–month period terminating two months preceding the month in which the request for consultation was made.

9. Details of the agreed restraint measure shall be communicated to the TMB within 60 days from the date of conclusion of the agreement. The TMB shall determine whether the agreement is justified in accordance with the provisions of this Article. In order to make its determination, the TMB shall have available to it the factual data provided to the Chairman of the TMB, referred to in paragraph 7, as well as any other relevant information provided by the Members concerned. The TMB may make such recommendations as it deems appropriate to the Members concerned.

10. If, however, after the expiry of the period of 60 days from the date on which the request for consultations was received, there has been no agreement between the Members, the Member which proposed to take safeguard action may apply the restraint by date of import or date of export, in accordance with the provisions of this Article, within 30 days following the 60–day period for consultations, and at the same time refer the matter to the TMB. It shall be open to either Member to refer the matter to the TMB before the expiry of the period of 60 days. In either case, the TMB shall promptly conduct an examination of the matter, including the determination of serious damage, or actual threat thereof, and its causes, and make appropriate recommendations to the Members concerned within 30 days. In order to conduct such examination, the TMB shall have available to it the factual data provided to the Chairman of the TMB, referred to in paragraph 7, as well as any other relevant information provided by the Members concerned.

11. In highly unusual and critical circumstances, where delay would cause damage which would be difficult to repair, action under paragraph 10 may be taken provisionally on the condition that the request for consultations and notification to the TMB shall be effected within no more than five working days after taking the action. In the case that consultations do not produce agreement, the TMB shall be notified at the conclusion of consultations, but in any case no later than 60 days from the date of the implementation of the action. The TMB shall promptly conduct an examination of the matter, and make appropriate recommendations to the Members concerned within 30 days. In the case that consultations do produce agreement, Members shall notify the TMB upon conclusion but, in any case, no later than 90 days from the date of the implementation of the action. The TMB may make such recommendations as it deems appropriate to the Members concerned.

12. A Member may maintain measures invoked pursuant to the provisions of this Article: (*a*) for up to three years without extension, or (*b*) until the product is integrated into GATT 1994, whichever comes first.

13.   Should the restraint measure remain in force for a period exceeding one year, the level for subsequent years shall be the level specified for the first year increased by a growth rate of not less than 6 per cent per annum, unless otherwise justified to the TMB.   The restraint level for the product concerned may be exceeded in either year of any two subsequent years by carry forward and/or carryover of 10 per cent of which carry forward shall not represent more than 5 per cent.   No quantitative limits shall be placed on the combined use of carryover, carry forward and the provision of paragraph 14.

14.   When more than one product from another Member is placed under restraint under this Article by a Member, the level of restraint agreed, pursuant to the provisions of this Article, for each of these products may be exceeded by 7 per cent, provided that the total exports subject to restraint do not exceed the total of the levels for all products so restrained under this Article, on the basis of agreed common units.   Where the periods of application of restraints of these products do not coincide with each other, this provision shall be applied to any overlapping period on a *pro rata* basis.

15.   If a safeguard action is applied under this Article to a product for which a restraint was previously in place under the MFA during the 12–month period prior to the entry into force of the WTO Agreement, or pursuant to the provisions of Article 2 or 6, the level of the new restraint shall be the level provided for in paragraph 8 unless the new restraint comes into force within one year of:

(a)   the date of notification referred to in paragraph 15 of Article 2 for the elimination of the previous restraint; or

(b)   the date of removal of the previous restraint put in place pursuant to the provisions of this Article or of the MFA

in which case the level shall not be less than the higher of (i) the level of restraint for the last 12–month period during which the product was under restraint, or (ii) the level of restraint provided for in paragraph 8.

16.   When a Member which is not maintaining a restraint under Article 2 decides to apply a restraint pursuant to the provisions of this Article, it shall establish appropriate arrangements which: (a) take full account of such factors as established tariff classification and quantitative units based on normal commercial practices in export and import transactions, both as regards fibre composition and in terms of competing for the same segment of its domestic market, and (b) avoid over-categorization.   The request for consultations referred to in paragraphs 7 or 11 shall include full information on such arrangements.

Article 7

1.   As part of the integration process and with reference to the specific commitments undertaken by the Members as a result of the Uruguay Round, all Members shall take such actions as may be necessary to abide by GATT 1994 rules and disciplines so as to:

(a)   achieve improved access to markets for textile and clothing products through such measures as tariff reductions and bindings, reduction or elimination of non-tariff barriers, and facilitation of customs, administrative and licensing formalities;

(b) ensure the application of policies relating to fair and equitable trading conditions as regards textiles and clothing in such areas as dumping and anti-dumping rules and procedures, subsidies and counter-vailing measures, and protection of intellectual property rights; and

(c) avoid discrimination against imports in the textiles and clothing sector when taking measures for general trade policy reasons.

Such actions shall be without prejudice to the rights and obligations of Members under GATT 1994.

2.   Members shall notify to the TMB the actions referred to in paragraph 1 which have a bearing on the implementation of this Agreement. To the extent that these have been notified to other WTO bodies, a summary, with reference to the original notification, shall be sufficient to fulfil the require-ments under this paragraph. It shall be open to any Member to make reverse notifications to the TMB.

3.   Where any Member considers that another Member has not taken the actions referred to in paragraph 1, and that the balance of rights and obligations under this Agreement has been upset, that Member may bring the matter before the relevant WTO bodies and inform the TMB. Any subse-quent findings or conclusions by the WTO bodies concerned shall form a part of the TMB's comprehensive report.

Article 8

1.   In order to supervise the implementation of this Agreement, to examine all measures taken under this Agreement and their conformity therewith, and to take the actions specifically required of it by this Agree-ment, the Textiles Monitoring Body ("TMB") is hereby established. The TMB shall consist of a Chairman and 10 members. Its membership shall be balanced and broadly representative of the Members and shall provide for rotation of its members at appropriate intervals. The members shall be appointed by Members designated by the Council for Trade in Goods to serve on the TMB, discharging their function on an *ad personam* basis.

2.   The TMB shall develop its own working procedures. It is understood, however, that consensus within the TMB does not require the assent or concurrence of members appointed by Members involved in an unresolved issue under review by the TMB.

3.   The TMB shall be considered as a standing body and shall meet as necessary to carry out the functions required of it under this Agreement. It shall rely on notifications and information supplied by the Members under the relevant Articles of this Agreement, supplemented by any additional informa-tion or necessary details they may submit or it may decide to seek from them. It may also rely on notifications to and reports from other WTO bodies and from such other sources as it may deem appropriate.

4.   Members shall afford to each other adequate opportunity for consul-tations with respect to any matters affecting the operation of this Agreement.

5.   In the absence of any mutually agreed solution in the bilateral consultations provided for in this Agreement, the TMB shall, at the request of either Member, and following a thorough and prompt consideration of the matter, make recommendations to the Members concerned.

6.   At the request of any Member, the TMB shall review promptly any particular matter which that Member considers to be detrimental to its interests under this Agreement and where consultations between it and the Member or Members concerned have failed to produce a mutually satisfactory solution. On such matters, the TMB may make such observations as it deems appropriate to the Members concerned and for the purposes of the review provided for in paragraph 11.

7.   Before formulating its recommendations or observations, the TMB shall invite participation of such Members as may be directly affected by the matter in question.

8.   Whenever the TMB is called upon to make recommendations or findings, it shall do so, preferably within a period of 30 days, unless a different time period is specified in this Agreement. All such recommendations or findings shall be communicated to the Members directly concerned. All such recommendations or findings shall also be communicated to the Council for Trade in Goods for its information.

9.   The Members shall endeavour to accept in full the recommendations of the TMB, which shall exercise proper surveillance of the implementation of such recommendations.

10.   If a Member considers itself unable to conform with the recommendations of the TMB, it shall provide the TMB with the reasons therefor not later than one month after receipt of such recommendations. Following thorough consideration of the reasons given, the TMB shall issue any further recommendations it considers appropriate forthwith. If, after such further recommendations, the matter remains unresolved, either Member may bring the matter before the Dispute Settlement Body and invoke paragraph 2 of Article XXIII of GATT 1994 and the relevant provisions of the Dispute Settlement Understanding.

11.   In order to oversee the implementation of this Agreement, the Council for Trade in Goods shall conduct a major review before the end of each stage of the integration process. To assist in this review, the TMB shall, at least five months before the end of each stage, transmit to the Council for Trade in Goods a comprehensive report on the implementation of this Agreement during the stage under review, in particular in matters with regard to the integration process, the application of the transitional safeguard mechanism, and relating to the application of GATT 1994 rules and disciplines as defined in Articles 2, 3, 6 and 7 respectively. The TMB's comprehensive report may include any recommendation as deemed appropriate by the TMB to the Council for Trade in Goods.

12.   In the light of its review the Council for Trade in Goods shall by consensus take such decisions as it deems appropriate to ensure that the balance of rights and obligations embodied in this Agreement is not being impaired. For the resolution of any disputes that may arise with respect to matters referred to in Article 7, the Dispute Settlement Body may authorize, without prejudice to the final date set out under Article 9, an adjustment to paragraph 14 of Article 2, for the stage subsequent to the review, with respect to any Member found not to be complying with its obligations under this Agreement.

Article 9

This Agreement and all restrictions thereunder shall stand terminated on the first day of the 121st month that the WTO Agreement is in effect, on which date the textiles and clothing sector shall be fully integrated into GATT 1994. There shall be no extension of this Agreement.

ANNEX

LIST OF PRODUCTS COVERED BY THIS AGREEMENT

1. This Annex lists textile and clothing products defined by Harmonized Commodity Description and Coding System (HS) codes at the six-digit level.

2. Actions under the safeguard provisions in Article 6 will be taken with respect to particular textile and clothing products and not on the basis of the HS lines *per se*.

3. Actions under the safeguard provisions in Article 6 of this Agreement shall not apply to:

(a) developing country Members' exports of handloom fabrics of the cottage industry, or hand-made cottage industry products made of such handloom fabrics, or traditional folklore handicraft textile and clothing products, provided that such products are properly certified under arrangements established between the Members concerned;

(b) historically traded textile products which were internationally traded in commercially significant quantities prior to 1982, such as bags, sacks, carpetbacking, cordage, luggage, mats, mattings and carpets typically made from fibres such as jute, coir, sisal, abaca, maguey and henequen;

(c) products made of pure silk.

For such products, the provisions of Article XIX of GATT 1994, as interpreted by the Agreement on Safeguards, shall be applicable.

[Product list omitted.]

Item 7

AGREEMENT ON TECHNICAL BARRIERS TO TRADE

Members,

Having regard to the Uruguay Round of Multilateral Trade Negotiations;

Desiring to further the objectives of GATT 1994;

Recognizing the important contribution that international standards and conformity assessment systems can make in this regard by improving efficiency of production and facilitating the conduct of international trade;

Desiring therefore to encourage the development of such international standards and conformity assessment systems;

Desiring however to ensure that technical regulations and standards, including packaging, marking and labelling requirements, and procedures for assessment of conformity with technical regulations and standards do not create unnecessary obstacles to international trade;

Recognizing that no country should be prevented from taking measures necessary to ensure the quality of its exports, or for the protection of human, animal or plant life or health, of the environment, or for the prevention of deceptive practices, at the levels it considers appropriate, subject to the requirement that they are not applied in a manner which would constitute a means of arbitrary or unjustifiable discrimination between countries where the same conditions prevail or a disguised restriction on international trade, and are otherwise in accordance with the provisions of this Agreement;

Recognizing that no country should be prevented from taking measures necessary for the protection of its essential security interest;

Recognizing the contribution which international standardization can make to the transfer of technology from developed to developing countries;

Recognizing that developing countries may encounter special difficulties in the formulation and application of technical regulations and standards and procedures for assessment of conformity with technical regulations and standards, and desiring to assist them in their endeavours in this regard;

Hereby *agree* as follows:

Article 1

General Provisions

1.1 General terms for standardization and procedures for assessment of conformity shall normally have the meaning given to them by definitions adopted within the United Nations system and by international standardizing bodies taking into account their context and in the light of the object and purpose of this Agreement.

1.2 However, for the purposes of this Agreement the meaning of the terms given in Annex 1 applies.

1.3 All products, including industrial and agricultural products, shall be subject to the provisions of this Agreement.

1.4 Purchasing specifications prepared by governmental bodies for production or consumption requirements of governmental bodies are not subject to the provisions of this Agreement but are addressed in the Agreement on Government Procurement, according to its coverage.

1.5 The provisions of this Agreement do not apply to sanitary and phytosanitary measures as defined in Annex A of the Agreement on the Application of Sanitary and Phytosanitary Measures.

1.6 All references in this Agreement to technical regulations, standards and conformity assessment procedures shall be construed to include any amendments thereto and any additions to the rules or the product coverage thereof, except amendments and additions of an insignificant nature.

TECHNICAL REGULATIONS AND STANDARDS
Article 2

Preparation, Adoption and Application of Technical Regulations by Central Government Bodies

With respect to their central government bodies:

2.1 Members shall ensure that in respect of technical regulations, products imported from the territory of any Member shall be accorded treatment no less favourable than that accorded to like products of national origin and to like products originating in any other country.

2.2 Members shall ensure that technical regulations are not prepared, adopted or applied with a view to or with the effect of creating unnecessary obstacles to international trade. For this purpose, technical regulations shall not be more trade-restrictive than necessary to fulfil a legitimate objective, taking account of the risks non-fulfilment would create. Such legitimate objectives are, *inter alia:* national security requirements; the prevention of deceptive practices; protection of human health or safety, animal or plant life or health, or the environment. In assessing such risks, relevant elements of consideration are, *inter alia:* available scientific and technical information, related processing technology or intended end-uses of products.

2.3 Technical regulations shall not be maintained if the circumstances or objectives giving rise to their adoption no longer exist or if the changed circumstances or objectives can be addressed in a less trade-restrictive manner.

2.4 Where technical regulations are required and relevant international standards exist or their completion is imminent, Members shall use them, or the relevant parts of them, as a basis for their technical regulations except when such international standards or relevant parts would be an ineffective or inappropriate means for the fulfilment of the legitimate objectives pursued, for instance because of fundamental climatic or geographical factors or fundamental technological problems.

2.5 A Member preparing, adopting or applying a technical regulation which may have a significant effect on trade of other Members shall, upon the request of another Member, explain the justification for that technical regulation in terms of the provisions of paragraphs 2 to 4. Whenever a technical regulation is prepared, adopted or applied for one of the legitimate objectives explicitly mentioned in paragraph 2, and is in accordance with relevant international standards, it shall be rebuttably presumed not to create an unnecessary obstacle to international trade.

2.6 With a view to harmonizing technical regulations on as wide a basis as possible, Members shall play a full part, within the limits of their resources, in the preparation by appropriate international standardizing bodies of international standards for products for which they either have adopted, or expect to adopt, technical regulations.

2.7 Members shall give positive consideration to accepting as equivalent technical regulations of other Members, even if these regulations differ from their own, provided they are satisfied that these regulations adequately fulfil the objectives of their own regulations.

2.8 Wherever appropriate, Members shall specify technical regulations based on product requirements in terms of performance rather than design or descriptive characteristics.

2.9 Whenever a relevant international standard does not exist or the technical content of a proposed technical regulation is not in accordance with the technical content of relevant international standards, and if the technical regulation may have a significant effect on trade of other Members, Members shall:

2.9.1 publish a notice in a publication at an early appropriate stage, in such a manner as to enable interested parties in other Members to become acquainted with it, that they propose to introduce a particular technical regulation;

2.9.2 notify other Members through the Secretariat of the products to be covered by the proposed technical regulation, together with a brief indication of its objective and rationale. Such notifications shall take place at an early appropriate stage, when amendments can still be introduced and comments taken into account;

2.9.3 upon request, provide to other Members particulars or copies of the proposed technical regulation and, whenever possible, identify the parts which in substance deviate from relevant international standards;

2.9.4 without discrimination, allow reasonable time for other Members to make comments in writing, discuss these comments upon request, and take these written comments and the results of these discussions into account.

2.10 Subject to the provisions in the lead-in to paragraph 9, where urgent problems of safety, health, environmental protection or national security arise or threaten to arise for a Member, that Member may omit such of the steps enumerated in paragraph 9 as it finds necessary, provided that the Member, upon adoption of a technical regulation, shall:

2.10.1 notify immediately other Members through the Secretariat of the particular technical regulation and the products covered, with a brief indication of the objective and the rationale of the technical regulation, including the nature of the urgent problems;

2.10.2 upon request, provide other Members with copies of the technical regulation;

2.10.3 without discrimination, allow other Members to present their comments in writing, discuss these comments upon request, and take these written comments and the results of these discussions into account.

2.11 Members shall ensure that all technical regulations which have been adopted are published promptly or otherwise made available in such a manner as to enable interested parties in other Members to become acquainted with them.

2.12 Except in those urgent circumstances referred to in paragraph 10, Members shall allow a reasonable interval between the publication of technical regulations and their entry into force in order to allow time for producers in exporting Members, and particularly in developing country Members, to adapt their products or methods of production to the requirements of the importing Member.

Article 3

*Preparation, Adoption and Application of Technical Regulations by
Local Government Bodies and Non–Governmental Bodies*

With respect to their local government and non-governmental bodies within their territories:

3.1 Members shall take such reasonable measures as may be available to them to ensure compliance by such bodies with the provisions of Article 2, with the exception of the obligation to notify as referred to in paragraphs 9.2 and 10.1 of Article 2.

3.2 Members shall ensure that the technical regulations of local governments on the level directly below that of the central government in Members are notified in accordance with the provisions of paragraphs 9.2 and 10.1 of Article 2, noting that notification shall not be required for technical regulations the technical content of which is substantially the same as that of previously notified technical regulations of central government bodies of the Member concerned.

3.3 Members may require contact with other Members, including the notifications, provision of information, comments and discussions referred to in paragraphs 9 and 10 of Article 2, to take place through the central government.

3.4 Members shall not take measures which require or encourage local government bodies or non-governmental bodies within their territories to act in a manner inconsistent with the provisions of Article 2.

3.5 Members are fully responsible under this Agreement for the observance of all provisions of Article 2. Members shall formulate and implement positive measures and mechanisms in support of the observance of the provisions of Article 2 by other than central government bodies.

Article 4
Preparation, Adoption and Application of Standards

4.1 Members shall ensure that their central government standardizing bodies accept and comply with the Code of Good Practice for the Preparation, Adoption and Application of Standards in Annex 3 to this Agreement (referred to in this Agreement as the "Code of Good Practice"). They shall take such reasonable measures as may be available to them to ensure that local government and non-governmental standardizing bodies within their territories, as well as regional standardizing bodies of which they or one or more bodies within their territories are members, accept and comply with this Code of Good Practice. In addition, Members shall not take measures which have the effect of, directly or indirectly, requiring or encouraging such standardizing bodies to act in a manner inconsistent with the Code of Good Practice. The obligations of Members with respect to compliance of standardizing bodies with the provisions of the Code of Good Practice shall apply irrespective of whether or not a standardizing body has accepted the Code of Good Practice.

4.2 Standardizing bodies that have accepted and are complying with the Code of Good Practice shall be acknowledged by the Members as complying with the principles of this Agreement.

CONFORMITY WITH TECHNICAL REGULATIONS AND STANDARDS
Article 5
Procedures for Assessment of Conformity by Central Government Bodies

5.1 Members shall ensure that, in cases where a positive assurance of conformity with technical regulations or standards is required, their central government bodies apply the following provisions to products originating in the territories of other Members:

5.1.1 conformity assessment procedures are prepared, adopted and applied so as to grant access for suppliers of like products originating in the territories of other Members under conditions no less favourable than those accorded to suppliers of like products of national origin or originating in any other country, in a comparable situation; access entails suppliers' right to an assessment of conformity under the rules of the procedure, including, when foreseen by this procedure, the possibility to have conformity assessment activities undertaken at the site of facilities and to receive the mark of the system;

5.1.2 conformity assessment procedures are not prepared, adopted or applied with a view to or with the effect of creating unnecessary obstacles to international trade. This means, *inter alia*, that conformity assessment procedures shall not be more strict or be applied more strictly than is necessary to give the importing Member adequate confidence that products conform with the applicable technical regulations or standards, taking account of the risks non-conformity would create.

5.2 When implementing the provisions of paragraph 1, Members shall ensure that:

5.2.1 conformity assessment procedures are undertaken and completed as expeditiously as possible and in a no less favourable order for products originating in the territories of other Members than for like domestic products;

5.2.2 the standard processing period of each conformity assessment procedure is published or that the anticipated processing period is communicated to the applicant upon request; when receiving an application, the competent body promptly examines the completeness of the documentation and informs the applicant in a precise and complete manner of all deficiencies; the competent body transmits as soon as possible the results of the assessment in a precise and complete manner to the applicant so that corrective action may be taken if necessary; even when the application has deficiencies, the competent body proceeds as far as practicable with the conformity assessment if the applicant so requests; and that, upon request, the applicant is informed of the stage of the procedure, with any delay being explained;

5.2.3 information requirements are limited to what is necessary to assess conformity and determine fees;

5.2.4 the confidentiality of information about products originating in the territories of other Members arising from or supplied in connection with such conformity assessment procedures is respected in the same way as for domestic products and in such a manner that legitimate commercial interests are protected;

5.2.5 any fees imposed for assessing the conformity of products originating in the territories of other Members are equitable in relation to any fees chargeable for assessing the conformity of like products of national origin or originating in any other country, taking into account communication, transportation and other costs arising from differences between location of facilities of the applicant and the conformity assessment body;

5.2.6 the siting of facilities used in conformity assessment procedures and the selection of samples are not such as to cause unnecessary inconvenience to applicants or their agents;

5.2.7 whenever specifications of a product are changed subsequent to the determination of its conformity to the applicable technical regulations or standards, the conformity assessment procedure for the modified product is limited to what is necessary to determine whether adequate confidence exists that the product still meets the technical regulations or standards concerned;

5.2.8 a procedure exists to review complaints concerning the operation of a conformity assessment procedure and to take corrective action when a complaint is justified.

5.3 Nothing in paragraphs 1 and 2 shall prevent Members from carrying out reasonable spot checks within their territories.

5.4 In cases where a positive assurance is required that products conform with technical regulations or standards, and relevant guides or recommendations issued by international standardizing bodies exist or their completion is imminent, Members shall ensure that central government bodies use them, or the relevant parts of them, as a basis for their conformity assessment procedures, except where, as duly explained upon request, such guides or recommendations or relevant parts are inappropriate for the Members concerned, for, *inter alia*, such reasons as: national security requirements; the prevention of deceptive practices; protection of human health or safety, animal or plant life or health, or the environment; fundamental climatic or other geographical factors; fundamental technological or infrastructural problems.

5.5 With a view to harmonizing conformity assessment procedures on as wide a basis as possible, Members shall play a full part, within the limits of their resources, in the preparation by appropriate international standardizing bodies of guides and recommendations for conformity assessment procedures.

5.6 Whenever a relevant guide or recommendation issued by an international standardizing body does not exist or the technical content of a proposed conformity assessment procedure is not in accordance with relevant guides and recommendations issued by international standardizing bodies, and if the conformity assessment procedure may have a significant effect on trade of other Members, Members shall:

5.6.1 publish a notice in a publication at an early appropriate stage, in such a manner as to enable interested parties in other Members to become acquainted with it, that they propose to introduce a particular conformity assessment procedure;

5.6.2 notify other Members through the Secretariat of the products to be covered by the proposed conformity assessment procedure, together with a brief indication of its objective and rationale. Such notifications shall take place at an early appropriate stage, when amendments can still be introduced and comments taken into account;

5.6.3 upon request, provide to other Members particulars or copies of the proposed procedure and, whenever possible, identify the parts which in substance deviate from relevant guides or recommendations issued by international standardizing bodies;

5.6.4 without discrimination, allow reasonable time for other Members to make comments in writing, discuss these comments upon request, and take these written comments and the results of these discussions into account.

5.7 Subject to the provisions in the lead-in to paragraph 6, where urgent problems of safety, health, environmental protection or national security arise or threaten to arise for a Member, that Member may omit such of the steps enumerated in paragraph 6 as it finds necessary, provided that the Member, upon adoption of the procedure, shall:

5.7.1 notify immediately other Members through the Secretariat of the particular procedure and the products covered, with a brief indication of the objective and the rationale of the procedure, including the nature of the urgent problems;

5.7.2 upon request, provide other Members with copies of the rules of the procedure;

5.7.3 without discrimination, allow other Members to present their comments in writing, discuss these comments upon request, and take these written comments and the results of these discussions into account.

5.8 Members shall ensure that all conformity assessment procedures which have been adopted are published promptly or otherwise made available in such a manner as to enable interested parties in other Members to become acquainted with them.

5.9 Except in those urgent circumstances referred to in paragraph 7, Members shall allow a reasonable interval between the publication of requirements concerning conformity assessment procedures and their entry into force in order to allow time for producers in exporting Members, and particularly in developing country Members, to adapt their products or methods of production to the requirements of the importing Member.

Article 6

Recognition of Conformity Assessment by Central Government Bodies

With respect to their central government bodies:

6.1 Without prejudice to the provisions of paragraphs 3 and 4, Members shall ensure, whenever possible, that results of conformity assessment procedures in other Members are accepted, even when those procedures differ from their own, provided they are satisfied that those procedures offer an assurance of conformity with applicable technical regulations or standards equivalent to their own procedures. It is recognized that prior consultations may be necessary in order to arrive at a mutually satisfactory understanding regarding, in particular:

6.1.1 adequate and enduring technical competence of the relevant conformity assessment bodies in the exporting Member, so that confidence in the continued reliability of their conformity assessment results can exist; in this regard, verified compliance, for instance through accreditation, with relevant guides or recommendations issued by international standardizing bodies shall be taken into account as an indication of adequate technical competence;

6.1.2 limitation of the acceptance of conformity assessment results to those produced by designated bodies in the exporting Member.

6.2 Members shall ensure that their conformity assessment procedures permit, as far as practicable, the implementation of the provisions in paragraph 1.

6.3 Members are encouraged, at the request of other Members, to be willing to enter into negotiations for the conclusion of agreements for the mutual recognition of results of each other's conformity assessment procedures. Members may require that such agreements fulfil the criteria of paragraph 1 and give mutual satisfaction regarding their potential for facilitating trade in the products concerned.

6.4 Members are encouraged to permit participation of conformity assessment bodies located in the territories of other Members in their conformity assessment procedures under conditions no less favourable than those accorded to bodies located within their territory or the territory of any other country.

Article 7

Procedures for Assessment of Conformity by Local Government Bodies

With respect to their local government bodies within their territories:

7.1 Members shall take such reasonable measures as may be available to them to ensure compliance by such bodies with the provisions of Articles 5 and 6, with the exception of the obligation to notify as referred to in paragraphs 6.2 and 7.1 of Article 5.

7.2 Members shall ensure that the conformity assessment procedures of local governments on the level directly below that of the central government in Members are notified in accordance with the provisions of paragraphs 6.2 and 7.1 of Article 5, noting that notifications shall not be required for conformity assessment procedures the technical content of which is substantially the same as that of previously notified conformity assessment procedures of central government bodies of the Members concerned.

7.3 Members may require contact with other Members, including the notifications, provision of information, comments and discussions referred to in paragraphs 6 and 7 of Article 5, to take place through the central government.

7.4 Members shall not take measures which require or encourage local government bodies within their territories to act in a manner inconsistent with the provisions of Articles 5 and 6.

7.5 Members are fully responsible under this Agreement for the observance of all provisions of Articles 5 and 6. Members shall formulate and implement positive measures and mechanisms in support of the observance of the provisions of Articles 5 and 6 by other than central government bodies.

Article 8

Procedures for Assessment of Conformity by Non–Governmental Bodies

8.1 Members shall take such reasonable measures as may be available to them to ensure that non-governmental bodies within their territories which operate conformity assessment procedures comply with the provisions of Articles 5 and 6, with the exception of the obligation to notify proposed conformity assessment procedures. In addition, Members shall not take measures which have the effect of, directly or indirectly, requiring or encouraging such bodies to act in a manner inconsistent with the provisions of Articles 5 and 6.

8.2 Members shall ensure that their central government bodies rely on conformity assessment procedures operated by non-governmental bodies only if these latter bodies comply with the provisions of Articles 5 and 6, with the exception of the obligation to notify proposed conformity assessment procedures.

Article 9

International and Regional Systems

9.1 Where a positive assurance of conformity with a technical regulation or standard is required, Members shall, wherever practicable, formulate and adopt international systems for conformity assessment and become members thereof or participate therein.

9.2 Members shall take such reasonable measures as may be available to them to ensure that international and regional systems for conformity assessment in which relevant bodies within their territories are members or participants comply with the provisions of Articles 5 and 6. In addition, Members shall not take any measures which have the effect of, directly or indirectly, requiring or encouraging such systems to act in a manner inconsistent with any of the provisions of Articles 5 and 6.

9.3 Members shall ensure that their central government bodies rely on international or regional conformity assessment systems only to the extent that these systems comply with the provisions of Articles 5 and 6, as applicable.

INFORMATION AND ASSISTANCE
Article 10
Information About Technical Regulations, Standards and Conformity Assessment Procedures

10.1 Each Member shall ensure that an enquiry point exists which is able to answer all reasonable enquiries from other Members and interested parties in other Members as well as to provide the relevant documents regarding:

10.1.1 any technical regulations adopted or proposed within its territory by central or local government bodies, by non-governmental bodies which have legal power to enforce a technical regulation, or by regional standardizing bodies of which such bodies are members or participants;

10.1.2 any standards adopted or proposed within its territory by central or local government bodies, or by regional standardizing bodies of which such bodies are members or participants;

10.1.3 any conformity assessment procedures, or proposed conformity assessment procedures, which are operated within its territory by central or local government bodies, or by non-governmental bodies which have legal power to enforce a technical regulation, or by regional bodies of which such bodies are members or participants;

10.1.4 the membership and participation of the Member, or of relevant central or local government bodies within its territory, in international and regional standardizing bodies and conformity assessment systems, as well as in bilateral and multilateral arrangements within the scope of this Agreement; it shall also be able to provide reasonable information on the provisions of such systems and arrangements;

10.1.5 the location of notices published pursuant to this Agreement, or the provision of information as to where such information can be obtained; and

10.1.6 the location of the enquiry points mentioned in paragraph 3.

10.2 If, however, for legal or administrative reasons more than one enquiry point is established by a Member, that Member shall provide to the other Members complete and unambiguous information on the scope of responsibility of each of these enquiry points. In addition, that Member shall ensure that any enquiries addressed to an incorrect enquiry point shall promptly be conveyed to the correct enquiry point.

10.3 Each Member shall take such reasonable measures as may be available to it to ensure that one or more enquiry points exist which are able to answer all reasonable enquiries from other Members and interested parties in other Members as well as to provide the relevant documents or information as to where they can be obtained regarding:

10.3.1 any standards adopted or proposed within its territory by non-governmental standardizing bodies, or by regional standardizing bodies of which such bodies are members or participants; and

10.3.2 any conformity assessment procedures, or proposed conformity assessment procedures, which are operated within its territory by non-governmental bodies, or by regional bodies of which such bodies are members or participants;

10.3.3 the membership and participation of relevant non-governmental bodies within its territory in international and regional standardizing bodies and conformity assessment systems, as well as in bilateral and multilateral arrangements within the scope of this Agreement; they shall also be able to provide reasonable information on the provisions of such systems and arrangements.

10.4 Members shall take such reasonable measures as may be available to them to ensure that where copies of documents are requested by other Members or by interested parties in other Members, in accordance with the provisions of this Agreement, they are supplied at an equitable price (if any) which shall, apart from the real cost of delivery, be the same for the nationals [1] of the Member concerned or of any other Member.

10.5 Developed country Members shall, if requested by other Members, provide, in English, French or Spanish, translations of the documents covered by a specific notification or, in case of voluminous documents, of summaries of such documents.

10.6 The Secretariat shall, when it receives notifications in accordance with the provisions of this Agreement, circulate copies of the notifications to all Members and interested international standardizing and conformity assessment bodies, and draw the attention of developing country Members to any notifications relating to products of particular interest to them.

10.7 Whenever a Member has reached an agreement with any other country or countries on issues related to technical regulations, standards or conformity assessment procedures which may have a significant effect on trade, at least one Member party to the agreement shall notify other Members through the Secretariat of the products to be covered by the agreement and include a brief description of the agreement. Members concerned are encouraged to enter, upon request, into consultations with other Members for the purposes of concluding similar agreements or of arranging for their participation in such agreements.

---

1. "Nationals" here shall be deemed, in the case of a separate customs territory Member of the WTO, to mean persons, natural or legal, who are domiciled or who have a real and effective industrial or commercial establishment in that customs territory.

10.8 Nothing in this Agreement shall be construed as requiring:

10.8.1 the publication of texts other than in the language of the Member;

10.8.2 the provision of particulars or copies of drafts other than in the language of the Member except as stated in paragraph 5; or

10.8.3 Members to furnish any information, the disclosure of which they consider contrary to their essential security interests.

10.9 Notifications to the Secretariat shall be in English, French or Spanish.

10.10 Members shall designate a single central government authority that is responsible for the implementation on the national level of the provisions concerning notification procedures under this Agreement except those included in Annex 3.

10.11 If, however, for legal or administrative reasons the responsibility for notification procedures is divided among two or more central government authorities, the Member concerned shall provide to the other Members complete and unambiguous information on the scope of responsibility of each of these authorities.

Article 11

Technical Assistance to Other Members

11.1 Members shall, if requested, advise other Members, especially the developing country Members, on the preparation of technical regulations.

11.2 Members shall, if requested, advise other Members, especially the developing country Members, and shall grant them technical assistance on mutually agreed terms and conditions regarding the establishment of national standardizing bodies, and participation in the international standardizing bodies, and shall encourage their national standardizing bodies to do likewise.

11.3 Members shall, if requested, take such reasonable measures as may be available to them to arrange for the regulatory bodies within their territories to advise other Members, especially the developing country Members, and shall grant them technical assistance on mutually agreed terms and conditions regarding:

11.3.1 the establishment of regulatory bodies, or bodies for the assessment of conformity with technical regulations; and

11.3.2 the methods by which their technical regulations can best be met.

11.4 Members shall, if requested, take such reasonable measures as may be available to them to arrange for advice to be given to other Members, especially the developing country Members, and shall grant them technical assistance on mutually agreed terms and conditions regarding the establishment of bodies for the assessment of conformity with standards adopted within the territory of the requesting Member.

11.5 Members shall, if requested, advise other Members, especially the developing country Members, and shall grant them technical assistance on mutually agreed terms and conditions regarding the steps that should be taken by their producers if they wish to have access to systems for conformity assessment operated by governmental or non-governmental bodies within the territory of the Member receiving the request.

11.6 Members which are members or participants of international or regional systems for conformity assessment shall, if requested, advise other Members, especially the developing country Members, and shall grant them technical assistance on mutually agreed terms and conditions regarding the establishment of the institutions and legal framework which would enable them to fulfil the obligations of membership or participation in such systems.

11.7 Members shall, if so requested, encourage bodies within their territories which are members or participants of international or regional systems for conformity assessment to advise other Members, especially the developing country Members, and should consider requests for technical assistance from them regarding the establishment of the institutions which would enable the relevant bodies within their territories to fulfil the obligations of membership or participation.

11.8 In providing advice and technical assistance to other Members in terms of paragraphs 1 to 7, Members shall give priority to the needs of the least-developed country Members.

Article 12
Special and Differential Treatment of Developing Country Members

12.1 Members shall provide differential and more favourable treatment to developing country Members to this Agreement, through the following provisions as well as through the relevant provisions of other Articles of this Agreement.

12.2 Members shall give particular attention to the provisions of this Agreement concerning developing country Members' rights and obligations and shall take into account the special development, financial and trade needs of developing country Members in the implementation of this Agreement, both nationally and in the operation of this Agreement's institutional arrangements.

12.3 Members shall, in the preparation and application of technical regulations, standards and conformity assessment procedures, take account of the special development, financial and trade needs of developing country Members, with a view to ensuring that such technical regulations, standards and conformity assessment procedures do not create unnecessary obstacles to exports from developing country Members.

12.4 Members recognize that, although international standards, guides or recommendations may exist, in their particular technological and socio-economic conditions, developing country Members adopt certain technical regulations, standards or conformity assessment procedures aimed at preserving indigenous technology and production methods and processes compatible with their development needs. Members therefore recognize that developing country Members should not be expected to use international standards as a basis for their technical regulations or standards, including test methods, which are not appropriate to their development, financial and trade needs.

12.5 Members shall take such reasonable measures as may be available to them to ensure that international standardizing bodies and international systems for conformity assessment are organized and operated in a way which facilitates active and representative participation of relevant bodies in all Members, taking into account the special problems of developing country Members.

12.6 Members shall take such reasonable measures as may be available to them to ensure that international standardizing bodies, upon request of developing country Members, examine the possibility of, and, if practicable, prepare international standards concerning products of special interest to developing country Members.

12.7 Members shall, in accordance with the provisions of Article 11, provide technical assistance to developing country Members to ensure that the preparation and application of technical regulations, standards and conformity assessment procedures do not create unnecessary obstacles to the expansion and diversification of exports from developing country Members. In determining the terms and conditions of the technical assistance, account shall be taken of the stage of development of the requesting Members and in particular of the least-developed country Members.

12.8 It is recognized that developing country Members may face special problems, including institutional and infrastructural problems, in the field of preparation and application of technical regulations, standards and conformity assessment procedures. It is further recognized that the special development and trade needs of developing country Members, as well as their stage of technological development, may hinder their ability to discharge fully their obligations under this Agreement. Members, therefore, shall take this fact fully into account. Accordingly, with a view to ensuring that developing country Members are able to comply with this Agreement, the Committee on Technical Barriers to Trade provided for in Article 13 (referred to in this Agreement as the "Committee") is enabled to grant, upon request, specified, time-limited exceptions in whole or in part from obligations under this Agreement. When considering such requests the Committee shall take into account the special problems, in the field of preparation and application of technical regulations, standards and conformity assessment procedures, and the special development and trade needs of the developing country Member, as well as its stage of technological development, which may hinder its ability to discharge fully its obligations under this Agreement. The Committee shall, in particular, take into account the special problems of the least-developed country Members.

12.9 During consultations, developed country Members shall bear in mind the special difficulties experienced by developing country Members in formulating and implementing standards and technical regulations and conformity assessment procedures, and in their desire to assist developing country Members with their efforts in this direction, developed country Members shall take account of the special needs of the former in regard to financing, trade and development.

12.10 The Committee shall examine periodically the special and differential treatment, as laid down in this Agreement, granted to developing country Members on national and international levels.

INSTITUTIONS, CONSULTATION AND DISPUTE SETTLEMENT
Article 13
The Committee on Technical Barriers to Trade

13.1 A Committee on Technical Barriers to Trade is hereby established, and shall be composed of representatives from each of the Members. The Committee shall elect its own Chairman and shall meet as necessary, but no less than once a year, for the purpose of affording Members the opportunity of consulting on any matters relating to the operation of this Agreement or the furtherance of its objectives, and shall carry out such responsibilities as assigned to it under this Agreement or by the Members.

13.2 The Committee shall establish working parties or other bodies as may be appropriate, which shall carry out such responsibilities as may be assigned to them by the Committee in accordance with the relevant provisions of this Agreement.

13.3 It is understood that unnecessary duplication should be avoided between the work under this Agreement and that of governments in other technical bodies. The Committee shall examine this problem with a view to minimizing such duplication.

Article 14
Consultation and Dispute Settlement

14.1 Consultations and the settlement of disputes with respect to any matter affecting the operation of this Agreement shall take place under the auspices of the Dispute Settlement Body and shall follow, *mutatis mutandis*, the provisions of Articles XXII and XXIII of GATT 1994, as elaborated and applied by the Dispute Settlement Understanding.

14.2 At the request of a party to a dispute, or at its own initiative, a panel may establish a technical expert group to assist in questions of a technical nature, requiring detailed consideration by experts.

14.3 Technical expert groups shall be governed by the procedures of Annex 2.

14.4 The dispute settlement provisions set out above can be invoked in cases where a Member considers that another Member has not achieved satisfactory results under Articles 3, 4, 7, 8 and 9 and its trade interests are significantly affected. In this respect, such results shall be equivalent to those as if the body in question were a Member.

FINAL PROVISIONS
Article 15
Final Provisions

Reservations

15.1 Reservations may not be entered in respect of any of the provisions of this Agreement without the consent of the other Members.

Review

15.2 Each Member shall, promptly after the date on which the WTO Agreement enters into force for it, inform the Committee of measures in existence or taken to ensure the implementation and administration of this Agreement. Any changes of such measures thereafter shall also be notified to the Committee.

15.3 The Committee shall review annually the implementation and operation of this Agreement taking into account the objectives thereof.

15.4 Not later than the end of the third year from the date of entry into force of the WTO Agreement and at the end of each three-year period thereafter, the Committee shall review the operation and implementation of this Agreement, including the provisions relating to transparency, with a view to recommending an adjustment of the rights and obligations of this Agreement where necessary to ensure mutual economic advantage and balance of rights and obligations, without prejudice to the provisions of Article 12. Having regard, *inter alia,* to the experience gained in the implementation of the Agreement, the Committee shall, where appropriate, submit proposals for amendments to the text of this Agreement to the Council for Trade in Goods.

Annexes

15.5 The annexes to this Agreement constitute an integral part thereof.

ANNEX 1

TERMS AND THEIR DEFINITIONS FOR THE PURPOSE OF THIS AGREEMENT

The terms presented in the sixth edition of the ISO/IEC Guide 2: 1991, General Terms and Their Definitions Concerning Standardization and Related Activities, shall, when used in this Agreement, have the same meaning as given in the definitions in the said Guide taking into account that services are excluded from the coverage of this Agreement.

For the purpose of this Agreement, however, the following definitions shall apply:

1. *Technical regulation*

Document which lays down product characteristics or their related processes and production methods, including the applicable administrative provisions, with which compliance is mandatory. It may also include or deal exclusively with terminology, symbols, packaging, marking or labelling requirements as they apply to a product, process or production method.

Explanatory note

The definition in ISO/IEC Guide 2 is not self-contained, but based on the so-called "building block" system.

2. *Standard*

Document approved by a recognized body, that provides, for common and repeated use, rules, guidelines or characteristics for products or related processes and production methods, with which compliance is not mandatory. It may also include or deal exclusively with terminology, symbols, packaging, marking or labelling requirements as they apply to a product, process or production method.

Explanatory note

The terms as defined in ISO/IEC Guide 2 cover products, processes and services. This Agreement deals only with technical regulations, standards and conformity assessment procedures related to products or processes and production methods. Standards as defined by ISO/IEC Guide 2 may be mandatory or voluntary. For the purpose of this Agreement standards are defined as voluntary and technical regulations as mandatory documents. Standards prepared by the international standardization community are based on consensus. This Agreement covers also documents that are not based on consensus.

3. *Conformity assessment procedures*

Any procedure used, directly or indirectly, to determine that relevant requirements in technical regulations or standards are fulfilled.

Explanatory note

Conformity assessment procedures include, *inter alia*, procedures for sampling, testing and inspection; evaluation, verification and assurance of conformity; registration, accreditation and approval as well as their combinations.

4. *International body or system*

Body or system whose membership is open to the relevant bodies of at least all Members.

5. *Regional body or system*

Body or system whose membership is open to the relevant bodies of only some of the Members.

6. *Central government body*

Central government, its ministries and departments or any body subject to the control of the central government in respect of the activity in question.

Explanatory note

In the case of the European Communities the provisions governing central government bodies apply. However, regional bodies or conformity assessment systems may be established within the European Communities, and in such cases would be subject to the provisions of this Agreement on regional bodies or conformity assessment systems.

7. *Local government body*

Government other than a central government (e.g. states, provinces, Länder, cantons, municipalities, etc.), its ministries or departments or any body subject to the control of such a government in respect of the activity in question.

8. *Non-governmental body*

Body other than a central government body or a local government body, including a non-governmental body which has legal power to enforce a technical regulation.

ANNEX 2

TECHNICAL EXPERT GROUPS

The following procedures shall apply to technical expert groups established in accordance with the provisions of Article 14.

1. Technical expert groups are under the panel's authority. Their terms of reference and detailed working procedures shall be decided by the panel, and they shall report to the panel.

2. Participation in technical expert groups shall be restricted to persons of professional standing and experience in the field in question.

3. Citizens of parties to the dispute shall not serve on a technical expert group without the joint agreement of the parties to the dispute, except in exceptional circumstances when the panel considers that the need for specialized scientific expertise cannot be fulfilled otherwise. Government officials of parties to the dispute shall not serve on a technical expert group. Members of technical expert groups shall serve in their individual capacities and not as government representatives, nor as representatives of any organization. Governments or organizations shall therefore not give them instructions with regard to matters before a technical expert group.

4. Technical expert groups may consult and seek information and technical advice from any source they deem appropriate. Before a technical expert group seeks such information or advice from a source within the jurisdiction of a Member, it shall inform the government of that Member. Any Member shall respond promptly and fully to any request by a technical expert group for such information as the technical expert group considers necessary and appropriate.

5. The parties to a dispute shall have access to all relevant information provided to a technical expert group, unless it is of a confidential nature. Confidential information provided to the technical expert group shall not be released without formal authorization from the government, organization or person providing the information. Where such information is requested from the technical expert group but release of such information by the technical expert group is not authorized, a non-confidential summary of the information will be provided by the government, organization or person supplying the information.

6. The technical expert group shall submit a draft report to the Members concerned with a view to obtaining their comments, and taking them into account, as appropriate, in the final report, which shall also be circulated to the Members concerned when it is submitted to the panel.

ANNEX 3

CODE OF GOOD PRACTICE FOR THE PREPARATION, ADOPTION AND APPLICATION OF STANDARDS

General Provisions

A. For the purposes of this Code the definitions in Annex 1 of this Agreement shall apply.

B. This Code is open to acceptance by any standardizing body within the territory of a Member of the WTO, whether a central government body, a local government body, or a non-governmental body; to any governmental regional standardizing body one or more members of which are Members of the WTO; and to any non-governmental regional standardizing body one or more members of which are situated within the territory of a Member of the WTO (referred to in this Code collectively as "standardizing bodies" and individually as "the standardizing body").

C. Standardizing bodies that have accepted or withdrawn from this Code shall notify this fact to the ISO/IEC Information Centre in Geneva. The notification shall include the name and address of the body concerned and the scope of its current and expected standardization activities. The notification may be sent either directly to the ISO/IEC Information Centre, or through the national member body of ISO/IEC or, preferably, through the relevant national member or international affiliate of ISONET, as appropriate.

SUBSTANTIVE PROVISIONS

D. In respect of standards, the standardizing body shall accord treatment to products originating in the territory of any other Member of the WTO no less favourable than that accorded to like products of national origin and to like products originating in any other country.

E. The standardizing body shall ensure that standards are not prepared, adopted or applied with a view to, or with the effect of, creating unnecessary obstacles to international trade.

F. Where international standards exist or their completion is imminent, the standardizing body shall use them, or the relevant parts of them, as a basis for the standards it develops, except where such international standards or relevant parts would be ineffective or inappropriate, for instance, because of an insufficient level of protection or fundamental climatic or geographical factors or fundamental technological problems.

G. With a view to harmonizing standards on as wide a basis as possible, the standardizing body shall, in an appropriate way, play a full part, within the limits of its resources, in the preparation by relevant international standardizing bodies of international standards regarding subject matter for which it either has adopted, or expects to adopt, standards. For standardizing bodies within the territory of a Member, participation in a particular international standardization activity shall, whenever possible, take place through one delegation representing all standardizing bodies in the territory that have adopted, or expect to adopt, standards for the subject matter to which the international standardization activity relates.

H. The standardizing body within the territory of a Member shall make every effort to avoid duplication of, or overlap with, the work of other standardizing bodies in the national territory or with the work of relevant international or regional standardizing bodies. They shall also make every effort to achieve a national consensus on the standards they develop. Likewise the regional standardizing body shall make every effort to avoid duplication of, or overlap with, the work of relevant international standardizing bodies.

I.   Wherever appropriate, the standardizing body shall specify standards based on product requirements in terms of performance rather than design or descriptive characteristics.

J.   At least once every six months, the standardizing body shall publish a work programme containing its name and address, the standards it is currently preparing and the standards which it has adopted in the preceding period. A standard is under preparation from the moment a decision has been taken to develop a standard until that standard has been adopted. The titles of specific draft standards shall, upon request, be provided in English, French or Spanish. A notice of the existence of the work programme shall be published in a national or, as the case may be, regional publication of standardization activities.

The work programme shall for each standard indicate, in accordance with any ISONET rules, the classification relevant to the subject matter, the stage attained in the standard's development, and the references of any international standards taken as a basis. No later than at the time of publication of its work programme, the standardizing body shall notify the existence thereof to the ISO/IEC Information Centre in Geneva.

The notification shall contain the name and address of the standardizing body, the name and issue of the publication in which the work programme is published, the period to which the work programme applies, its price (if any), and how and where it can be obtained. The notification may be sent directly to the ISO/IEC Information Centre, or, preferably, through the relevant national member or international affiliate of ISONET, as appropriate.

K.   The national member of ISO/IEC shall make every effort to become a member of ISONET or to appoint another body to become a member as well as to acquire the most advanced membership type possible for the ISONET member. Other standardizing bodies shall make every effort to associate themselves with the ISONET member.

L.   Before adopting a standard, the standardizing body shall allow a period of at least 60 days for the submission of comments on the draft standard by interested parties within the territory of a Member of the WTO. This period may, however, be shortened in cases where urgent problems of safety, health or environment arise or threaten to arise. No later than at the start of the comment period, the standardizing body shall publish a notice announcing the period for commenting in the publication referred to in paragraph J. Such notification shall include, as far as practicable, whether the draft standard deviates from relevant international standards.

M.   On the request of any interested party within the territory of a Member of the WTO, the standardizing body shall promptly provide, or arrange to provide, a copy of a draft standard which it has submitted for comments. Any fees charged for this service shall, apart from the real cost of delivery, be the same for foreign and domestic parties.

N.   The standardizing body shall take into account, in the further processing of the standard, the comments received during the period for commenting. Comments received through standardizing bodies that have accepted this Code of Good Practice shall, if so requested, be replied to as promptly as possible. The reply shall include an explanation why a deviation from relevant international standards is necessary.

O. Once the standard has been adopted, it shall be promptly published.

P. On the request of any interested party within the territory of a Member of the WTO, the standardizing body shall promptly provide, or arrange to provide, a copy of its most recent work programme or of a standard which it produced. Any fees charged for this service shall, apart from the real cost of delivery, be the same for foreign and domestic parties.

Q. The standardizing body shall afford sympathetic consideration to, and adequate opportunity for, consultation regarding representations with respect to the operation of this Code presented by standardizing bodies that have accepted this Code of Good Practice. It shall make an objective effort to solve any complaints.

AGREEMENT ON TRADE–RELATED INVESTMENT MEASURES

Members,

Considering that Ministers agreed in the Punta del Este Declaration that "Following an examination of the operation of GATT Articles related to the trade restrictive and distorting effects of investment measures, negotiations should elaborate, as appropriate, further provisions that may be necessary to avoid such adverse effects on trade";

Desiring to promote the expansion and progressive liberalisation of world trade and to facilitate investment across international frontiers so as to increase the economic growth of all trading partners, particularly developing country Members, while ensuring free competition;

Taking into account the particular trade, development and financial needs of developing country Members, particularly those of the least-developed country Members;

Recognizing that certain investment measures can cause trade-restrictive and distorting effects;

Hereby *agree* as follows:

Article 1

Coverage

This Agreement applies to investment measures related to trade in goods only (referred to in this Agreement as "TRIMs").

Article 2

National Treatment and Quantitative Restrictions

1. Without prejudice to other rights and obligations under GATT 1994, no Member shall apply any TRIM that is inconsistent with the provisions of Article III or Article XI of GATT 1994.

2. An illustrative list of TRIMs that are inconsistent with the obligation of national treatment provided for in paragraph 4 of Article III of GATT 1994 and the obligation of general elimination of quantitative restrictions provided for in paragraph 1 of Article XI of GATT 1994 is contained in the Annex to this Agreement.

Article 3

Exceptions

All exceptions under GATT 1994 shall apply, as appropriate, to the provisions of this Agreement.

Article 4
Developing Country Members

A developing country Member shall be free to deviate temporarily from the provisions of Article 2 to the extent and in such a manner as Article XVIII of GATT 1994, the Understanding on the Balance-of-Payments Provisions of GATT 1994, and the Declaration on Trade Measures Taken for Balance-of-Payments Purposes adopted on 28 November 1979 (BISD 26S/205–209) permit the Member to deviate from the provisions of Articles III and XI of GATT 1994.

Article 5
Notification and Transitional Arrangements

1.　Members, within 90 days of the date of entry into force of the WTO Agreement, shall notify the Council for Trade in Goods of all TRIMs they are applying that are not in conformity with the provisions of this Agreement. Such TRIMs of general or specific application shall be notified, along with their principal features.[1]

2.　Each Member shall eliminate all TRIMs which are notified under paragraph 1 within two years of the date of entry into force of the WTO Agreement in the case of a developed country Member, within five years in the case of a developing country Member, and within seven years in the case of a least-developed country Member.

3.　On request, the Council for Trade in Goods may extend the transition period for the elimination of TRIMs notified under paragraph 1 for a developing country Member, including a least-developed country Member, which demonstrates particular difficulties in implementing the provisions of this Agreement.　In considering such a request, the Council for Trade in Goods shall take into account the individual development, financial and trade needs of the Member in question.

4.　During the transition period, a Member shall not modify the terms of any TRIM which it notifies under paragraph 1 from those prevailing at the date of entry into force of the WTO Agreement so as to increase the degree of inconsistency with the provisions of Article 2.　TRIMs introduced less than 180 days before the date of entry into force of the WTO Agreement shall not benefit from the transitional arrangements provided in paragraph 2.

5.　Notwithstanding the provisions of Article 2, a Member, in order not to disadvantage established enterprises which are subject to a TRIM notified under paragraph 1, may apply during the transition period the same TRIM to a new investment (*i*) where the products of such investment are like products to those of the established enterprises, and (*ii*) where necessary to avoid distorting the conditions of competition between the new investment and the established enterprises.　Any TRIM so applied to a new investment shall be notified to the Council for Trade in Goods.　The terms of such a TRIM shall be equivalent in their competitive effect to those applicable to the established enterprises, and it shall be terminated at the same time.

1.　In the case of TRIMs applied under discretionary authority, each specific application shall be notified.　Information that would prejudice the legitimate commercial interests of particular enterprises need not be disclosed.

Article 6

Transparency

1.   Members reaffirm, with respect to TRIMs, their commitment to obligations on transparency and notification in Article X of GATT 1994, in the undertaking on "Notification" contained in the Understanding Regarding Notification, Consultation, Dispute Settlement and Surveillance adopted on 28 November 1979 and in the Ministerial Decision on Notification Procedures adopted on 15 April 1994.

2.   Each Member shall notify the Secretariat of the publications in which TRIMs may be found, including those applied by regional and local governments and authorities within their territories.

3.   Each Member shall accord sympathetic consideration to requests for information, and afford adequate opportunity for consultation, on any matter arising from this Agreement raised by another Member. In conformity with Article X of GATT 1994 no Member is required to disclose information the disclosure of which would impede law enforcement or otherwise be contrary to the public interest or would prejudice the legitimate commercial interests of particular enterprises, public or private.

Article 7

Committee on Trade–Related Investment Measures

1.   A Committee on Trade–Related Investment Measures (referred to in this Agreement as the "Committee") is hereby established, and shall be open to all Members. The Committee shall elect its own Chairman and Vice–Chairman, and shall meet not less than once a year and otherwise at the request of any Member.

2.   The Committee shall carry out responsibilities assigned to it by the Council for Trade in Goods and shall afford Members the opportunity to consult on any matters relating to the operation and implementation of this Agreement.

3.   The Committee shall monitor the operation and implementation of this Agreement and shall report thereon annually to the Council for Trade in Goods.

Article 8

Consultation and Dispute Settlement

The provisions of Articles XXII and XXIII of GATT 1994, as elaborated and applied by the Dispute Settlement Understanding, shall apply to consultations and the settlement of disputes under this Agreement.

Article 9

Review by the Council for Trade in Goods

Not later than five years after the date of entry into force of the WTO Agreement, the Council for Trade in Goods shall review the operation of this Agreement and, as appropriate, propose to the Ministerial Conference amendments to its text. In the course of this review, the Council for Trade in Goods shall consider whether the Agreement should be complemented with provisions on investment policy and competition policy.

ANNEX

Illustrative List

1. TRIMs that are inconsistent with the obligation of national treatment provided for in paragraph 4 of Article III of GATT 1994 include those which are mandatory or enforceable under domestic law or under administrative rulings, or compliance with which is necessary to obtain an advantage, and which require:

(a) the purchase or use by an enterprise of products of domestic origin or from any domestic source, whether specified in terms of particular products, in terms of volume or value of products, or in terms of a proportion of volume or value of its local production; or

(b) that an enterprise's purchases or use of imported products be limited to an amount related to the volume or value of local products that it exports.

2. TRIMs that are inconsistent with the obligation of general elimination of quantitative restrictions provided for in paragraph 1 of Article XI of GATT 1994 include those which are mandatory or enforceable under domestic law or under administrative rulings, or compliance with which is necessary to obtain an advantage, and which restrict:

(a) the importation by an enterprise of products used in or related to its local production, generally or to an amount related to the volume or value of local production that it exports;

(b) the importation by an enterprise of products used in or related to its local production by restricting its access to foreign exchange to an amount related to the foreign exchange inflows attributable to the enterprise; or

(c) the exportation or sale for export by an enterprise of products, whether specified in terms of particular products, in terms of volume or value of products, or in terms of a proportion of volume or value of its local production.

Item 9

AGREEMENT ON IMPLEMENTATION OF ARTICLE VI OF THE GENERAL AGREEMENT ON TARIFFS AND TRADE 1994

Members hereby *agree* as follows:

PART I

Article 1

Principles

An anti-dumping measure shall be applied only under the circumstances provided for in Article VI of GATT 1994 and pursuant to investigations initiated [1] and conducted in accordance with the provisions of this Agreement. The following provisions govern the application of Article VI of GATT 1994 in so far as action is taken under anti-dumping legislation or regulations.

Article 2

Determination of Dumping

2.1 For the purpose of this Agreement, a product is to be considered as being dumped, i.e. introduced into the commerce of another country at less than its normal value, if the export price of the product exported from one country to another is less than the comparable price, in the ordinary course of trade, for the like product when destined for consumption in the exporting country.

2.2 When there are no sales of the like product in the ordinary course of trade in the domestic market of the exporting country or when, because of the particular market situation or the low volume of the sales in the domestic market of the exporting country [2], such sales do not permit a proper comparison, the margin of dumping shall be determined by comparison with a comparable price of the like product when exported to an appropriate third country, provided that this price is representative, or with the cost of production in the country of origin plus a reasonable amount for administrative, selling and general costs and for profits.

2.2.1 Sales of the like product in the domestic market of the exporting country or sales to a third country at prices below per unit (fixed and variable) costs of production plus administrative, selling and general costs may be treated as not being in the ordinary course of trade by reason of

---

1. The term "initiated" as used in this Agreement means the procedural action by which a Member formally commences an investigation as provided in Article 5.

2. Sales of the like product destined for consumption in the domestic market of the exporting country shall normally be considered a sufficient quantity for the determination of the normal value if such sales constitute 5 per cent or more of the sales of the product under consideration to the importing Member, provided that a lower ratio should be acceptable where the evidence demonstrates that domestic sales at such lower ratio are nonetheless of sufficient magnitude to provide for a proper comparison.

price and may be disregarded in determining normal value only if the authorities[3] determine that such sales are made within an extended period of time[4] in substantial quantities[5] and are at prices which do not provide for the recovery of all costs within a reasonable period of time. If prices which are below per unit costs at the time of sale are above weighted average per unit costs for the period of investigation, such prices shall be considered to provide for recovery of costs within a reasonable period of time.

2.2.1.1 For the purpose of paragraph 2, costs shall normally be calculated on the basis of records kept by the exporter or producer under investigation, provided that such records are in accordance with the generally accepted accounting principles of the exporting country and reasonably reflect the costs associated with the production and sale of the product under consideration. Authorities shall consider all available evidence on the proper allocation of costs, including that which is made available by the exporter or producer in the course of the investigation provided that such allocations have been historically utilized by the exporter or producer, in particular in relation to establishing appropriate amortization and depreciation periods and allowances for capital expenditures and other development costs. Unless already reflected in the cost allocations under this sub-paragraph, costs shall be adjusted appropriately for those non-recurring items of cost which benefit future and/or current production, or for circumstances in which costs during the period of investigation are affected by start-up operations.[6]

2.2.2 For the purpose of paragraph 2, the amounts for administrative, selling and general costs and for profits shall be based on actual data pertaining to production and sales in the ordinary course of trade of the like product by the exporter or producer under investigation. When such amounts cannot be determined on this basis, the amounts may be determined on the basis of:

(i) the actual amounts incurred and realized by the exporter or producer in question in respect of production and sales in the domestic market of the country of origin of the same general category of products;

(ii) the weighted average of the actual amounts incurred and realized by other exporters or producers subject to investigation in respect of production and sales of the like product in the domestic market of the country of origin;

3. When in this Agreement the term "authorities" is used, it shall be interpreted as meaning authorities at an appropriate senior level.

4. The extended period of time should normally be one year but shall in no case be less than six months.

5. Sales below per unit costs are made in substantial quantities when the authorities establish that the weighted average selling price of the transactions under consideration for the determination of the normal value is below the weighted average per unit costs, or that the volume of sales below per unit costs represents not less than 20 per cent of the volume sold in transactions under consideration for the determination of the normal value.

6. The adjustment made for start-up operations shall reflect the costs at the end of the start-up period or, if that period extends beyond the period of investigation, the most recent costs which can reasonably be taken into account by the authorities during the investigation.

(iii) any other reasonable method, provided that the amount for profit so established shall not exceed the profit normally realized by other exporters or producers on sales of products of the same general category in the domestic market of the country of origin.

2.3 In cases where there is no export price or where it appears to the authorities concerned that the export price is unreliable because of association or a compensatory arrangement between the exporter and the importer or a third party, the export price may be constructed on the basis of the price at which the imported products are first resold to an independent buyer, or if the products are not resold to an independent buyer, or not resold in the condition as imported, on such reasonable basis as the authorities may determine.

2.4 A fair comparison shall be made between the export price and the normal value. This comparison shall be made at the same level of trade, normally at the ex-factory level, and in respect of sales made at as nearly as possible the same time. Due allowance shall be made in each case, on its merits, for differences which affect price comparability, including differences in conditions and terms of sale, taxation, levels of trade, quantities, physical characteristics, and any other differences which are also demonstrated to affect price comparability.[7] In the cases referred to in paragraph 3, allowances for costs, including duties and taxes, incurred between importation and resale, and for profits accruing, should also be made. If in these cases price comparability has been affected, the authorities shall establish the normal value at a level of trade equivalent to the level of trade of the constructed export price, or shall make due allowance as warranted under this paragraph. The authorities shall indicate to the parties in question what information is necessary to ensure a fair comparison and shall not impose an unreasonable burden of proof on those parties.

2.4.1 When the comparison under paragraph 4 requires a conversion of currencies, such conversion should be made using the rate of exchange on the date of sale[8], provided that when a sale of foreign currency on forward markets is directly linked to the export sale involved, the rate of exchange in the forward sale shall be used. Fluctuations in exchange rates shall be ignored and in an investigation the authorities shall allow exporters at least 60 days to have adjusted their export prices to reflect sustained movements in exchange rates during the period of investigation.

2.4.2 Subject to the provisions governing fair comparison in paragraph 4, the existence of margins of dumping during the investigation phase shall normally be established on the basis of a comparison of a weighted average normal value with a weighted average of prices of all comparable export transactions or by a comparison of normal value and export prices on a transaction-to-transaction basis. A normal value established on a weighted average basis may be compared to prices of individual export transactions if the authorities find a pattern of export

7. It is understood that some of the above factors may overlap, and authorities shall ensure that they do not duplicate adjustments that have been already made under this provision.

8. Normally, the date of sale would be the date of contract, purchase order, order confirmation, or invoice, whichever establishes the material terms of sale.

prices which differ significantly among different purchasers, regions or time periods, and if an explanation is provided as to why such differences cannot be taken into account appropriately by the use of a weighted average-to-weighted average or transaction-to-transaction comparison.

2.5 In the case where products are not imported directly from the country of origin but are exported to the importing Member from an intermediate country, the price at which the products are sold from the country of export to the importing Member shall normally be compared with the comparable price in the country of export. However, comparison may be made with the price in the country of origin, if, for example, the products are merely transshipped through the country of export, or such products are not produced in the country of export, or there is no comparable price for them in the country of export.

2.6 Throughout this Agreement the term "like product" ("produit similaire") shall be interpreted to mean a product which is identical, i.e. alike in all respects to the product under consideration, or in the absence of such a product, another product which, although not alike in all respects, has characteristics closely resembling those of the product under consideration.

2.7 This Article is without prejudice to the second Supplementary Provision to paragraph 1 of Article VI in Annex I to GATT 1994.

Article 3

Determination of Injury[9]

3.1 A determination of injury for purposes of Article VI of GATT 1994 shall be based on positive evidence and involve an objective examination of both (a) the volume of the dumped imports and the effect of the dumped imports on prices in the domestic market for like products, and (b) the consequent impact of these imports on domestic producers of such products.

3.2 With regard to the volume of the dumped imports, the investigating authorities shall consider whether there has been a significant increase in dumped imports, either in absolute terms or relative to production or consumption in the importing Member. With regard to the effect of the dumped imports on prices, the investigating authorities shall consider whether there has been a significant price undercutting by the dumped imports as compared with the price of a like product of the importing Member, or whether the effect of such imports is otherwise to depress prices to a significant degree or prevent price increases, which otherwise would have occurred, to a significant degree. No one or several of these factors can necessarily give decisive guidance.

3.3 Where imports of a product from more than one country are simultaneously subject to anti-dumping investigations, the investigating authorities may cumulatively assess the effects of such imports only if they determine that (a) the margin of dumping established in relation to the imports from each country is more than *de minimis* as defined in paragraph 8 of Article 5 and the volume of imports from each country is not negligible and (b) a

---

9. Under this Agreement the term "injury" shall, unless otherwise specified, be taken to mean material injury to a domestic industry, threat of material injury to a domestic industry or material retardation of the establishment of such an industry and shall be interpreted in accordance with the provisions of this Article.

cumulative assessment of the effects of the imports is appropriate in light of the conditions of competition between the imported products and the conditions of competition between the imported products and the like domestic product.

3.4 The examination of the impact of the dumped imports on the domestic industry concerned shall include an evaluation of all relevant economic factors and indices having a bearing on the state of the industry, including actual and potential decline in sales, profits, output, market share, productivity, return on investments, or utilization of capacity; factors affecting domestic prices; the magnitude of the margin of dumping; actual and potential negative effects on cash flow, inventories, employment, wages, growth, ability to raise capital or investments. This list is not exhaustive, nor can one or several of these factors necessarily give decisive guidance.

3.5 It must be demonstrated that the dumped imports are, through the effects of dumping, as set forth in paragraphs 2 and 4, causing injury within the meaning of this Agreement. The demonstration of a causal relationship between the dumped imports and the injury to the domestic industry shall be based on an examination of all relevant evidence before the authorities. The authorities shall also examine any known factors other than the dumped imports which at the same time are injuring the domestic industry, and the injuries caused by these other factors must not be attributed to the dumped imports. Factors which may be relevant in this respect include, *inter alia*, the volume and prices of imports not sold at dumping prices, contraction in demand or changes in the patterns of consumption, trade restrictive practices of and competition between the foreign and domestic producers, developments in technology and the export performance and productivity of the domestic industry.

3.6 The effect of the dumped imports shall be assessed in relation to the domestic production of the like product when available data permit the separate identification of that production on the basis of such criteria as the production process, producers' sales and profits. If such separate identification of that production is not possible, the effects of the dumped imports shall be assessed by the examination of the production of the narrowest group or range of products, which includes the like product, for which the necessary information can be provided.

3.7 A determination of a threat of material injury shall be based on facts and not merely on allegation, conjecture or remote possibility. The change in circumstances which would create a situation in which the dumping would cause injury must be clearly foreseen and imminent.[10] In making a determination regarding the existence of a threat of material injury, the authorities should consider, *inter alia*, such factors as:

  (i) a significant rate of increase of dumped imports into the domestic market indicating the likelihood of substantially increased importation;

  (ii) sufficient freely disposable, or an imminent, substantial increase in, capacity of the exporter indicating the likelihood of substantially

---

10. One example, though not an exclusive one, is that there is convincing reason to believe that there will be, in the near future, substantially increased importation of the product at dumped prices.

increased dumped exports to the importing Member's market, taking into account the availability of other export markets to absorb any additional exports;

(iii) whether imports are entering at prices that will have a significant depressing or suppressing effect on domestic prices, and would likely increase demand for further imports; and

(iv) inventories of the product being investigated.

No one of these factors by itself can necessarily give decisive guidance but the totality of the factors considered must lead to the conclusion that further dumped exports are imminent and that, unless protective action is taken, material injury would occur.

3.8 With respect to cases where injury is threatened by dumped imports, the application of anti-dumping measures shall be considered and decided with special care.

Article 4
Definition of Domestic Industry

4.1 For the purposes of this Agreement, the term "domestic industry" shall be interpreted as referring to the domestic producers as a whole of the like products or to those of them whose collective output of the products constitutes a major proportion of the total domestic production of those products, except that:

(i) when producers are related [11] to the exporters or importers or are themselves importers of the allegedly dumped product, the term "domestic industry" may be interpreted as referring to the rest of the producers;

(ii) in exceptional circumstances the territory of a Member may, for the production in question, be divided into two or more competitive markets and the producers within each market may be regarded as a separate industry if (a) the producers within such market sell all or almost all of their production of the product in question in that market, and (b) the demand in that market is not to any substantial degree supplied by producers of the product in question located elsewhere in the territory. In such circumstances, injury may be found to exist even where a major portion of the total domestic industry is not injured, provided there is a concentration of dumped imports into such an isolated market and provided further that the dumped imports are causing injury to the producers of all or almost all of the production within such market.

4.2 When the domestic industry has been interpreted as referring to the producers in a certain area, i.e. a market as defined in paragraph 1(ii), anti-dumping duties shall be levied [12] only on the products in question consigned

11. For the purpose of this paragraph, producers shall be deemed to be related to exporters or importers only if (a) one of them directly or indirectly controls the other; or (b) both of them are directly or indirectly controlled by a third person; or (c) together they directly or indirectly control a third person, provided that there are grounds for believing or suspecting that the effect of the relationship is such as to cause the producer concerned to behave differently from non-related producers. For the purpose of this paragraph, one shall be deemed to control another when the former is legally or operationally in a position to exercise restraint or direction over the latter.

12. As used in this Agreement "levy" shall mean the definitive or final legal assessment or collection of a duty or tax.

for final consumption to that area. When the constitutional law of the importing Member does not permit the levying of anti-dumping duties on such a basis, the importing Member may levy the anti-dumping duties without limitation only if *(a)* the exporters shall have been given an opportunity to cease exporting at dumped prices to the area concerned or otherwise give assurances pursuant to Article 8 and adequate assurances in this regard have not been promptly given, and *(b)* such duties cannot be levied only on products of specific producers which supply the area in question.

4.3 Where two or more countries have reached under the provisions of paragraph 8(a) of Article XXIV of GATT 1994 such a level of integration that they have the characteristics of a single, unified market, the industry in the entire area of integration shall be taken to be the domestic industry referred to in paragraph 1.

4.4 The provisions of paragraph 6 of Article 3 shall be applicable to this Article.

Article 5
Initiation and Subsequent Investigation

5.1 Except as provided for in paragraph 6, an investigation to determine the existence, degree and effect of any alleged dumping shall be initiated upon a written application by or on behalf of the domestic industry.

5.2 An application under paragraph 1 shall include evidence of *(a)* dumping, *(b)* injury within the meaning of Article VI of GATT 1994 as interpreted by this Agreement and *(c)* a causal link between the dumped imports and the alleged injury. Simple assertion, unsubstantiated by relevant evidence, cannot be considered sufficient to meet the requirements of this paragraph. The application shall contain such information as is reasonably available to the applicant on the following:

(i) the identity of the applicant and a description of the volume and value of the domestic production of the like product by the applicant. Where a written application is made on behalf of the domestic industry, the application shall identify the industry on behalf of which the application is made by a list of all known domestic producers of the like product (or associations of domestic producers of the like product) and, to the extent possible, a description of the volume and value of domestic production of the like product accounted for by such producers;

(ii) a complete description of the allegedly dumped product, the names of the country or countries of origin or export in question, the identity of each known exporter or foreign producer and a list of known persons importing the product in question;

(iii) information on prices at which the product in question is sold when destined for consumption in the domestic markets of the country or countries of origin or export (or, where appropriate, information on the prices at which the product is sold from the country or countries of origin or export to a third country or countries, or on the constructed value of the product) and information on export prices or, where appropriate, on the prices at which the product is first resold to an independent buyer in the territory of the importing Member;

(iv) information on the evolution of the volume of the allegedly dumped imports, the effect of these imports on prices of the like product in the domestic market and the consequent impact of the imports on the domestic industry, as demonstrated by relevant factors and indices having a bearing on the state of the domestic industry, such as those listed in paragraphs 2 and 4 of Article 3.

5.3 The authorities shall examine the accuracy and adequacy of the evidence provided in the application to determine whether there is sufficient evidence to justify the initiation of an investigation.

5.4 An investigation shall not be initiated pursuant to paragraph 1 unless the authorities have determined, on the basis of an examination of the degree of support for, or opposition to, the application expressed [13] by domestic producers of the like product, that the application has been made by or on behalf of the domestic industry.[14] The application shall be considered to have been made "by or on behalf of the domestic industry" if it is supported by those domestic producers whose collective output constitutes more than 50 per cent of the total production of the like product produced by that portion of the domestic industry expressing either support for or opposition to the application. However, no investigation shall be initiated when domestic producers expressly supporting the application account for less than 25 per cent of total production of the like product produced by the domestic industry.

5.5 The authorities shall avoid, unless a decision has been made to initiate an investigation, any publicizing of the application for the initiation of an investigation. However, after receipt of a properly documented application and before proceeding to initiate an investigation, the authorities shall notify the government of the exporting Member concerned.

5.6 If, in special circumstances, the authorities concerned decide to initiate an investigation without having received a written application by or on behalf of a domestic industry for the initiation of such investigation, they shall proceed only if they have sufficient evidence of dumping, injury and a causal link, as described in paragraph 2, to justify the initiation of an investigation.

5.7 The evidence of both dumping and injury shall be considered simultaneously *(a)* in the decision whether or not to initiate an investigation, and *(b)* thereafter, during the course of the investigation, starting on a date not later than the earliest date on which in accordance with the provisions of this Agreement provisional measures may be applied.

5.8 An application under paragraph 1 shall be rejected and an investigation shall be terminated promptly as soon as the authorities concerned are satisfied that there is not sufficient evidence of either dumping or of injury to justify proceeding with the case. There shall be immediate termination in cases where the authorities determine that the margin of dumping is *de minimis*, or that the volume of dumped imports, actual or potential, or the

13. In the case of fragmented industries involving an exceptionally large number of producers, authorities may determine support and opposition by using statistically valid sampling techniques.

14. Members are aware that in the territory of certain Members employees of domestic producers of the like product or representatives of those employees may make or support an application for an investigation under paragraph 1.

injury, is negligible. The margin of dumping shall be considered to be *de minimis* if this margin is less than 2 per cent, expressed as a percentage of the export price. The volume of dumped imports shall normally be regarded as negligible if the volume of dumped imports from a particular country is found to account for less than 3 per cent of imports of the like product in the importing Member, unless countries which individually account for less than 3 per cent of the imports of the like product in the importing Member collectively account for more than 7 per cent of imports of the like product in the importing Member.

5.9 An anti-dumping proceeding shall not hinder the procedures of customs clearance.

5.10 Investigations shall, except in special circumstances, be concluded within one year, and in no case more than 18 months, after their initiation.

Article 6

Evidence

6.1 All interested parties in an anti-dumping investigation shall be given notice of the information which the authorities require and ample opportunity to present in writing all evidence which they consider relevant in respect of the investigation in question.

    6.1.1 Exporters or foreign producers receiving questionnaires used in an anti-dumping investigation shall be given at least 30 days for reply.[15] Due consideration should be given to any request for an extension of the 30–day period and, upon cause shown, such an extension should be granted whenever practicable.

    6.1.2 Subject to the requirement to protect confidential information, evidence presented in writing by one interested party shall be made available promptly to other interested parties participating in the investigation.

    6.1.3 As soon as an investigation has been initiated, the authorities shall provide the full text of the written application received under paragraph 1 of Article 5 to the known exporters [16] and to the authorities of the exporting Member and shall make it available, upon request, to other interested parties involved. Due regard shall be paid to the requirement for the protection of confidential information, as provided for in paragraph 5.

6.2 Throughout the anti-dumping investigation all interested parties shall have a full opportunity for the defence of their interests. To this end, the authorities shall, on request, provide opportunities for all interested parties to meet those parties with adverse interests, so that opposing views may be presented and rebuttal arguments offered. Provision of such opportunities

---

15. As a general rule, the time-limit for exporters shall be counted from the date of receipt of the questionnaire, which for this purpose shall be deemed to have been received one week from the date on which it was sent to the respondent or transmitted to the appropriate diplomatic representative of the exporting Member or, in the case of a separate customs territory Member of the WTO, an official representative of the exporting territory.

16. It being understood that, where the number of exporters involved is particularly high, the full text of the written application should instead be provided only to the authorities of the exporting Member or to the relevant trade association.

must take account of the need to preserve confidentiality and of the convenience to the parties. There shall be no obligation on any party to attend a meeting, and failure to do so shall not be prejudicial to that party's case. Interested parties shall also have the right, on justification, to present other information orally.

6.3 Oral information provided under paragraph 2 shall be taken into account by the authorities only in so far as it is subsequently reproduced in writing and made available to other interested parties, as provided for in subparagraph 1.2.

6.4 The authorities shall whenever practicable provide timely opportunities for all interested parties to see all information that is relevant to the presentation of their cases, that is not confidential as defined in paragraph 5, and that is used by the authorities in an anti-dumping investigation, and to prepare presentations on the basis of this information.

6.5 Any information which is by nature confidential (for example, because its disclosure would be of significant competitive advantage to a competitor or because its disclosure would have a significantly adverse effect upon a person supplying the information or upon a person from whom that person acquired the information), or which is provided on a confidential basis by parties to an investigation shall, upon good cause shown, be treated as such by the authorities. Such information shall not be disclosed without specific permission of the party submitting it.[17]

6.5.1 The authorities shall require interested parties providing confidential information to furnish non-confidential summaries thereof. These summaries shall be in sufficient detail to permit a reasonable understanding of the substance of the information submitted in confidence. In exceptional circumstances, such parties may indicate that such information is not susceptible of summary. In such exceptional circumstances, a statement of the reasons why summarization is not possible must be provided.

6.5.2 If the authorities find that a request for confidentiality is not warranted and if the supplier of the information is either unwilling to make the information public or to authorize its disclosure in generalized or summary form, the authorities may disregard such information unless it can be demonstrated to their satisfaction from appropriate sources that the information is correct.[18]

6.6 Except in circumstances provided for in paragraph 8, the authorities shall during the course of an investigation satisfy themselves as to the accuracy of the information supplied by interested parties upon which their findings are based.

6.7 In order to verify information provided or to obtain further details, the authorities may carry out investigations in the territory of other Members as required, provided they obtain the agreement of the firms concerned and notify the representatives of the government of the Member in question, and

---

17. Members are aware that in the territory of certain Members disclosure pursuant to a narrowly-drawn protective order may be required.

18. Members agree that requests for confidentiality should not be arbitrarily rejected.

unless that Member objects to the investigation. The procedures described in Annex I shall apply to investigations carried out in the territory of other Members. Subject to the requirement to protect confidential information, the authorities shall make the results of any such investigations available, or shall provide disclosure thereof pursuant to paragraph 9, to the firms to which they pertain and may make such results available to the applicants.

6.8 In cases in which any interested party refuses access to, or otherwise does not provide, necessary information within a reasonable period or significantly impedes the investigation, preliminary and final determinations, affirmative or negative, may be made on the basis of the facts available. The provisions of Annex II shall be observed in the application of this paragraph.

6.9 The authorities shall, before a final determination is made, inform all interested parties of the essential facts under consideration which form the basis for the decision whether to apply definitive measures. Such disclosure should take place in sufficient time for the parties to defend their interests.

6.10 The authorities shall, as a rule, determine an individual margin of dumping for each known exporter or producer concerned of the product under investigation. In cases where the number of exporters, producers, importers or types of products involved is so large as to make such a determination impracticable, the authorities may limit their examination either to a reasonable number of interested parties or products by using samples which are statistically valid on the basis of information available to the authorities at the time of the selection, or to the largest percentage of the volume of the exports from the country in question which can reasonably be investigated.

6.10.1 Any selection of exporters, producers, importers or types of products made under this paragraph shall preferably be chosen in consultation with and with the consent of the exporters, producers or importers concerned.

6.10.2 In cases where the authorities have limited their examination, as provided for in this paragraph, they shall nevertheless determine an individual margin of dumping for any exporter or producer not initially selected who submits the necessary information in time for that information to be considered during the course of the investigation, except where the number of exporters or producers is so large that individual examinations would be unduly burdensome to the authorities and prevent the timely completion of the investigation. Voluntary responses shall not be discouraged.

6.11 For the purposes of this Agreement, "interested parties" shall include:

(i) an exporter or foreign producer or the importer of a product subject to investigation, or a trade or business association a majority of the members of which are producers, exporters or importers of such product;

(ii) the government of the exporting Member; and

(iii) a producer of the like product in the importing Member or a trade and business association a majority of the members of which produce the like product in the territory of the importing Member.

This list shall not preclude Members from allowing domestic or foreign parties other than those mentioned above to be included as interested parties.

6.12 The authorities shall provide opportunities for industrial users of the product under investigation, and for representative consumer organizations in cases where the product is commonly sold at the retail level, to provide information which is relevant to the investigation regarding dumping, injury and causality.

6.13 The authorities shall take due account of any difficulties experienced by interested parties, in particular small companies, in supplying information requested, and shall provide any assistance practicable.

6.14 The procedures set out above are not intended to prevent the authorities of a Member from proceeding expeditiously with regard to initiating an investigation, reaching preliminary or final determinations, whether affirmative or negative, or from applying provisional or final measures, in accordance with relevant provisions of this Agreement.

Article 7

Provisional Measures

7.1 Provisional measures may be applied only if:

(i) an investigation has been initiated in accordance with the provisions of Article 5, a public notice has been given to that effect and interested parties have been given adequate opportunities to submit information and make comments;

(ii) a preliminary affirmative determination has been made of dumping and consequent injury to a domestic industry; and

(iii) the authorities concerned judge such measures necessary to prevent injury being caused during the investigation.

7.2 Provisional measures may take the form of a provisional duty or, preferably, a security—by cash deposit or bond—equal to the amount of the anti-dumping duty provisionally estimated, being not greater than the provisionally estimated margin of dumping. Withholding of appraisement is an appropriate provisional measure, provided that the normal duty and the estimated amount of the anti-dumping duty be indicated and as long as the withholding of appraisement is subject to the same conditions as other provisional measures.

7.3 Provisional measures shall not be applied sooner than 60 days from the date of initiation of the investigation.

7.4 The application of provisional measures shall be limited to as short a period as possible, not exceeding four months or, on decision of the authorities concerned, upon request by exporters representing a significant percentage of the trade involved, to a period not exceeding six months. When authorities, in the course of an investigation, examine whether a duty lower than the margin of dumping would be sufficient to remove injury, these periods may be six and nine months, respectively.

7.5 The relevant provisions of Article 9 shall be followed in the application of provisional measures.

Article 8
Price Undertakings

8.1 Proceedings may [19] be suspended or terminated without the imposition of provisional measures or anti-dumping duties upon receipt of satisfactory voluntary undertakings from any exporter to revise its prices or to cease exports to the area in question at dumped prices so that the authorities are satisfied that the injurious effect of the dumping is eliminated. Price increases under such undertakings shall not be higher than necessary to eliminate the margin of dumping. It is desirable that the price increases be less than the margin of dumping if such increases would be adequate to remove the injury to the domestic industry.

8.2 Price undertakings shall not be sought or accepted from exporters unless the authorities of the importing Member have made a preliminary affirmative determination of dumping and injury caused by such dumping.

8.3 Undertakings offered need not be accepted if the authorities consider their acceptance impractical, for example, if the number of actual or potential exporters is too great, or for other reasons, including reasons of general policy. Should the case arise and where practicable, the authorities shall provide to the exporter the reasons which have led them to consider acceptance of an undertaking as inappropriate, and shall, to the extent possible, give the exporter an opportunity to make comments thereon.

8.4 If an undertaking is accepted, the investigation of dumping and injury shall nevertheless be completed if the exporter so desires or the authorities so decide. In such a case, if a negative determination of dumping or injury is made, the undertaking shall automatically lapse, except in cases where such a determination is due in large part to the existence of a price undertaking. In such cases, the authorities may require that an undertaking be maintained for a reasonable period consistent with the provisions of this Agreement. In the event that an affirmative determination of dumping and injury is made, the undertaking shall continue consistent with its terms and the provisions of this Agreement.

8.5 Price undertakings may be suggested by the authorities of the importing Member, but no exporter shall be forced to enter into such undertakings. The fact that exporters do not offer such undertakings, or do not accept an invitation to do so, shall in no way prejudice the consideration of the case. However, the authorities are free to determine that a threat of injury is more likely to be realized if the dumped imports continue.

8.6 Authorities of an importing Member may require any exporter from whom an undertaking has been accepted to provide periodically information relevant to the fulfilment of such an undertaking and to permit verification of pertinent data. In case of violation of an undertaking, the authorities of the importing Member may take, under this Agreement in conformity with its provisions, expeditious actions which may constitute immediate application of provisional measures using the best information available. In such cases, definitive duties may be levied in accordance with this Agreement on products

---

19. The word "may" shall not be interpreted to allow the simultaneous continuation of proceedings with the implementation of price undertakings except as provided in paragraph 4.

entered for consumption not more than 90 days before the application of such provisional measures, except that any such retroactive assessment shall not apply to imports entered before the violation of the undertaking.

Article 9
Imposition and Collection of Anti–Dumping Duties

9.1 The decision whether or not to impose an anti-dumping duty in cases where all requirements for the imposition have been fulfilled, and the decision whether the amount of the anti-dumping duty to be imposed shall be the full margin of dumping or less, are decisions to be made by the authorities of the importing Member. It is desirable that the imposition be permissive in the territory of all Members, and that the duty be less than the margin if such lesser duty would be adequate to remove the injury to the domestic industry.

9.2 When an anti-dumping duty is imposed in respect of any product, such anti-dumping duty shall be collected in the appropriate amounts in each case, on a non-discriminatory basis on imports of such product from all sources found to be dumped and causing injury, except as to imports from those sources from which price undertakings under the terms of this Agreement have been accepted. The authorities shall name the supplier or suppliers of the product concerned. If, however, several suppliers from the same country are involved, and it is impracticable to name all these suppliers, the authorities may name the supplying country concerned. If several suppliers from more than one country are involved, the authorities may name either all the suppliers involved, or, if this is impracticable, all the supplying countries involved.

9.3 The amount of the anti-dumping duty shall not exceed the margin of dumping as established under Article 2.

9.3.1 When the amount of the anti-dumping duty is assessed on a retrospective basis, the determination of the final liability for payment of anti-dumping duties shall take place as soon as possible, normally within 12 months, and in no case more than 18 months, after the date on which a request for a final assessment of the amount of the anti-dumping duty has been made.[20] Any refund shall be made promptly and normally in not more than 90 days following the determination of final liability made pursuant to this sub-paragraph. In any case, where a refund is not made within 90 days, the authorities shall provide an explanation if so requested.

9.3.2 When the amount of the anti-dumping duty is assessed on a prospective basis, provision shall be made for a prompt refund, upon request, of any duty paid in excess of the margin of dumping. A refund of any such duty paid in excess of the actual margin of dumping shall normally take place within 12 months, and in no case more than 18 months, after the date on which a request for a refund, duly supported by evidence, has been made by an importer of the product subject to the anti-dumping duty. The refund authorized should normally be made within 90 days of the above-noted decision.

---

20. It is understood that the observance of the time-limits mentioned in this subparagraph and in subparagraph 3.2 may not be possible where the product in question is subject to judicial review proceedings.

9.3.3 In determining whether and to what extent a reimbursement should be made when the export price is constructed in accordance with paragraph 3 of Article 2, authorities should take account of any change in normal value, any change in costs incurred between importation and resale, and any movement in the resale price which is duly reflected in subsequent selling prices, and should calculate the export price with no deduction for the amount of anti-dumping duties paid when conclusive evidence of the above is provided.

9.4 When the authorities have limited their examination in accordance with the second sentence of paragraph 10 of Article 6, any anti-dumping duty applied to imports from exporters or producers not included in the examination shall not exceed:

(i) the weighted average margin of dumping established with respect to the selected exporters or producers or,

(ii) where the liability for payment of anti-dumping duties is calculated on the basis of a prospective normal value, the difference between the weighted average normal value of the selected exporters or producers and the export prices of exporters or producers not individually examined,

provided that the authorities shall disregard for the purpose of this paragraph any zero and *de minimis* margins and margins established under the circumstances referred to in paragraph 8 of Article 6. The authorities shall apply individual duties or normal values to imports from any exporter or producer not included in the examination who has provided the necessary information during the course of the investigation, as provided for in subparagraph 10.2 of Article 6.

9.5 If a product is subject to anti-dumping duties in an importing Member, the authorities shall promptly carry out a review for the purpose of determining individual margins of dumping for any exporters or producers in the exporting country in question who have not exported the product to the importing Member during the period of investigation, provided that these exporters or producers can show that they are not related to any of the exporters or producers in the exporting country who are subject to the anti-dumping duties on the product. Such a review shall be initiated and carried out on an accelerated basis, compared to normal duty assessment and review proceedings in the importing Member. No anti-dumping duties shall be levied on imports from such exporters or producers while the review is being carried out. The authorities may, however, withhold appraisement and/or request guarantees to ensure that, should such a review result in a determination of dumping in respect of such producers or exporters, anti-dumping duties can be levied retroactively to the date of the initiation of the review.

Article 10

Retroactivity

10.1 Provisional measures and anti-dumping duties shall only be applied to products which enter for consumption after the time when the decision taken under paragraph 1 of Article 7 and paragraph 1 of Article 9, respectively, enters into force, subject to the exceptions set out in this Article.

10.2 Where a final determination of injury (but not of a threat thereof or of a material retardation of the establishment of an industry) is made or, in the case of a final determination of a threat of injury, where the effect of the dumped imports would, in the absence of the provisional measures, have led to a determination of injury, anti-dumping duties may be levied retroactively for the period for which provisional measures, if any, have been applied.

10.3 If the definitive anti-dumping duty is higher than the provisional duty paid or payable, or the amount estimated for the purpose of the security, the difference shall not be collected. If the definitive duty is lower than the provisional duty paid or payable, or the amount estimated for the purpose of the security, the difference shall be reimbursed or the duty recalculated, as the case may be.

10.4 Except as provided in paragraph 2, where a determination of threat of injury or material retardation is made (but no injury has yet occurred) a definitive anti-dumping duty may be imposed only from the date of the determination of threat of injury or material retardation, and any cash deposit made during the period of the application of provisional measures shall be refunded and any bonds released in an expeditious manner.

10.5 Where a final determination is negative, any cash deposit made during the period of the application of provisional measures shall be refunded and any bonds released in an expeditious manner.

10.6 A definitive anti-dumping duty may be levied on products which were entered for consumption not more than 90 days prior to the date of application of provisional measures, when the authorities determine for the dumped product in question that:

(i) there is a history of dumping which caused injury or that the importer was, or should have been, aware that the exporter practises dumping and that such dumping would cause injury, and

(ii) the injury is caused by massive dumped imports of a product in a relatively short time which in light of the timing and the volume of the dumped imports and other circumstances (such as a rapid build-up of inventories of the imported product) is likely to seriously undermine the remedial effect of the definitive anti-dumping duty to be applied, provided that the importers concerned have been given an opportunity to comment.

10.7 The authorities may, after initiating an investigation, take such measures as the withholding of appraisement or assessment as may be necessary to collect anti-dumping duties retroactively, as provided for in paragraph 6, once they have sufficient evidence that the conditions set forth in that paragraph are satisfied.

10.8 No duties shall be levied retroactively pursuant to paragraph 6 on products entered for consumption prior to the date of initiation of the investigation.

Article 11
Duration and Review of Anti–Dumping Duties and Price Undertakings

11.1 An anti-dumping duty shall remain in force only as long as and to the extent necessary to counteract dumping which is causing injury.

11.2 The authorities shall review the need for the continued imposition of the duty, where warranted, on their own initiative or, provided that a reasonable period of time has elapsed since the imposition of the definitive anti-dumping duty, upon request by any interested party which submits positive information substantiating the need for a review.[21] Interested parties shall have the right to request the authorities to examine whether the continued imposition of the duty is necessary to offset dumping, whether the injury would be likely to continue or recur if the duty were removed or varied, or both. If, as a result of the review under this paragraph, the authorities determine that the anti-dumping duty is no longer warranted, it shall be terminated immediately.

11.3 Notwithstanding the provisions of paragraphs 1 and 2, any definitive anti-dumping duty shall be terminated on a date not later than five years from its imposition (or from the date of the most recent review under paragraph 2 if that review has covered both dumping and injury, or under this paragraph), unless the authorities determine, in a review initiated before that date on their own initiative or upon a duly substantiated request made by or on behalf of the domestic industry within a reasonable period of time prior to that date, that the expiry of the duty would be likely to lead to continuation or recurrence of dumping and injury.[22] The duty may remain in force pending the outcome of such a review.

11.4 The provisions of Article 6 regarding evidence and procedure shall apply to any review carried out under this Article. Any such review shall be carried out expeditiously and shall normally be concluded within 12 months of the date of initiation of the review.

11.5 The provisions of this Article shall apply *mutatis mutandis* to price undertakings accepted under Article 8.

Article 12

Public Notice and Explanation of Determinations

12.1 When the authorities are satisfied that there is sufficient evidence to justify the initiation of an anti-dumping investigation pursuant to Article 5, the Member or Members the products of which are subject to such investigation and other interested parties known to the investigating authorities to have an interest therein shall be notified and a public notice shall be given.

12.1.1 A public notice of the initiation of an investigation shall contain, or otherwise make available through a separate report [23], adequate information on the following:

(i) the name of the exporting country or countries and the product involved;

21. A determination of final liability for payment of anti-dumping duties, as provided for in paragraph 3 of Article 9, does not by itself constitute a review within the meaning of this Article.

22. When the amount of the anti-dumping duty is assessed on a retrospective basis, a finding in the most recent assessment proceeding under subparagraph 3.1 of Article 9 that no duty is to be levied shall not by itself require the authorities to terminate the definitive duty.

23. Where authorities provide information and explanations under the provisions of this Article in a separate report, they shall ensure that such report is readily available to the public.

(ii) the date of initiation of the investigation;

(iii) the basis on which dumping is alleged in the application;

(iv) a summary of the factors on which the allegation of injury is based;

(v) the address to which representations by interested parties should be directed;

(vi) the time-limits allowed to interested parties for making their views known.

12.2 Public notice shall be given of any preliminary or final determination, whether affirmative or negative, of any decision to accept an undertaking pursuant to Article 8, of the termination of such an undertaking, and of the termination of a definitive anti-dumping duty. Each such notice shall set forth, or otherwise make available through a separate report, in sufficient detail the findings and conclusions reached on all issues of fact and law considered material by the investigating authorities. All such notices and reports shall be forwarded to the Member or Members the products of which are subject to such determination or undertaking and to other interested parties known to have an interest therein.

12.2.1 A public notice of the imposition of provisional measures shall set forth, or otherwise make available through a separate report, sufficiently detailed explanations for the preliminary determinations on dumping and injury and shall refer to the matters of fact and law which have led to arguments being accepted or rejected. Such a notice or report shall, due regard being paid to the requirement for the protection of confidential information, contain in particular:

(i) the names of the suppliers, or when this is impracticable, the supplying countries involved;

(ii) a description of the product which is sufficient for customs purposes;

(iii) the margins of dumping established and a full explanation of the reasons for the methodology used in the establishment and comparison of the export price and the normal value under Article 2;

(iv) considerations relevant to the injury determination as set out in Article 3;

(v) the main reasons leading to the determination.

12.2.2 A public notice of conclusion or suspension of an investigation in the case of an affirmative determination providing for the imposition of a definitive duty or the acceptance of a price undertaking shall contain, or otherwise make available through a separate report, all relevant information on the matters of fact and law and reasons which have led to the imposition of final measures or the acceptance of a price undertaking, due regard being paid to the requirement for the protection of confidential information. In particular, the notice or report shall contain the information described in subparagraph 2.1, as well as the reasons for the acceptance or rejection of relevant arguments or claims made by the exporters and importers, and the basis for any decision made under subparagraph 10.2 of Article 6.

12.2.3 A public notice of the termination or suspension of an investigation following the acceptance of an undertaking pursuant to Article 8 shall include, or otherwise make available through a separate report, the non-confidential part of this undertaking.

12.3 The provisions of this Article shall apply *mutatis mutandis* to the initiation and completion of reviews pursuant to Article 11 and to decisions under Article 10 to apply duties retroactively.

Article 13

Judicial Review

Each Member whose national legislation contains provisions on anti-dumping measures shall maintain judicial, arbitral or administrative tribunals or procedures for the purpose, *inter alia*, of the prompt review of administrative actions relating to final determinations and reviews of determinations within the meaning of Article 11. Such tribunals or procedures shall be independent of the authorities responsible for the determination or review in question.

Article 14

Anti-Dumping Action on Behalf of a Third Country

14.1 An application for anti-dumping action on behalf of a third country shall be made by the authorities of the third country requesting action.

14.2 Such an application shall be supported by price information to show that the imports are being dumped and by detailed information to show that the alleged dumping is causing injury to the domestic industry concerned in the third country. The government of the third country shall afford all assistance to the authorities of the importing country to obtain any further information which the latter may require.

14.3 In considering such an application, the authorities of the importing country shall consider the effects of the alleged dumping on the industry concerned as a whole in the third country; that is to say, the injury shall not be assessed in relation only to the effect of the alleged dumping on the industry's exports to the importing country or even on the industry's total exports.

14.4 The decision whether or not to proceed with a case shall rest with the importing country. If the importing country decides that it is prepared to take action, the initiation of the approach to the Council for Trade in Goods seeking its approval for such action shall rest with the importing country.

Article 15

Developing Country Members

It is recognized that special regard must be given by developed country Members to the special situation of developing country Members when considering the application of anti-dumping measures under this Agreement. Possibilities of constructive remedies provided for by this Agreement shall be explored before applying anti-dumping duties where they would affect the essential interests of developing country Members.

PART II

Article 16

Committee on Anti–Dumping Practices

16.1 There is hereby established a Committee on Anti–Dumping Practices (referred to in this Agreement as the "Committee") composed of representatives from each of the Members. The Committee shall elect its own Chairman and shall meet not less than twice a year and otherwise as envisaged by relevant provisions of this Agreement at the request of any Member. The Committee shall carry out responsibilities as assigned to it under this Agreement or by the Members and it shall afford Members the opportunity of consulting on any matters relating to the operation of the Agreement or the furtherance of its objectives. The WTO Secretariat shall act as the secretariat to the Committee.

16.2 The Committee may set up subsidiary bodies as appropriate.

16.3 In carrying out their functions, the Committee and any subsidiary bodies may consult with and seek information from any source they deem appropriate. However, before the Committee or a subsidiary body seeks such information from a source within the jurisdiction of a Member, it shall inform the Member involved. It shall obtain the consent of the Member and any firm to be consulted.

16.4 Members shall report without delay to the Committee all preliminary or final anti-dumping actions taken. Such reports shall be available in the Secretariat for inspection by other Members. Members shall also submit, on a semi-annual basis, reports of any anti-dumping actions taken within the preceding six months. The semi-annual reports shall be submitted on an agreed standard form.

16.5 Each Member shall notify the Committee (a) which of its authorities are competent to initiate and conduct investigations referred to in Article 5 and (b) its domestic procedures governing the initiation and conduct of such investigations.

Article 17

Consultation and Dispute Settlement

17.1 Except as otherwise provided herein, the Dispute Settlement Understanding is applicable to consultations and the settlement of disputes under this Agreement.

17.2 Each Member shall afford sympathetic consideration to, and shall afford adequate opportunity for consultation regarding, representations made by another Member with respect to any matter affecting the operation of this Agreement.

17.3 If any Member considers that any benefit accruing to it, directly or indirectly, under this Agreement is being nullified or impaired, or that the achievement of any objective is being impeded, by another Member or Members, it may, with a view to reaching a mutually satisfactory resolution of the matter, request in writing consultations with the Member or Members in question. Each Member shall afford sympathetic consideration to any request from another Member for consultation.

17.4 If the Member that requested consultations considers that the consultations pursuant to paragraph 3 have failed to achieve a mutually agreed solution, and if final action has been taken by the administering authorities of the importing Member to levy definitive anti-dumping duties or to accept price undertakings, it may refer the matter to the Dispute Settlement Body ("DSB"). When a provisional measure has a significant impact and the Member that requested consultations considers that the measure was taken contrary to the provisions of paragraph 1 of Article 7, that Member may also refer such matter to the DSB.

17.5 The DSB shall, at the request of the complaining party, establish a panel to examine the matter based upon:

(i) a written statement of the Member making the request indicating how a benefit accruing to it, directly or indirectly, under this Agreement has been nullified or impaired, or that the achieving of the objectives of the Agreement is being impeded, and

(ii) the facts made available in conformity with appropriate domestic procedures to the authorities of the importing Member.

17.6 In examining the matter referred to in paragraph 5:

(i) in its assessment of the facts of the matter, the panel shall determine whether the authorities' establishment of the facts was proper and whether their evaluation of those facts was unbiased and objective. If the establishment of the facts was proper and the evaluation was unbiased and objective, even though the panel might have reached a different conclusion, the evaluation shall not be overturned;

(ii) the panel shall interpret the relevant provisions of the Agreement in accordance with customary rules of interpretation of public international law. Where the panel finds that a relevant provision of the Agreement admits of more than one permissible interpretation, the panel shall find the authorities' measure to be in conformity with the Agreement if it rests upon one of those permissible interpretations.

17.7 Confidential information provided to the panel shall not be disclosed without formal authorization from the person, body or authority providing such information. Where such information is requested from the panel but release of such information by the panel is not authorized, a non-confidential summary of the information, authorized by the person, body or authority providing the information, shall be provided.

PART III

Article 18

Final Provisions

18.1 No specific action against dumping of exports from another Member can be taken except in accordance with the provisions of GATT 1994, as interpreted by this Agreement.[24]

---

24. This is not intended to preclude action   as appropriate.
under other relevant provisions of GATT 1994,

18.2 Reservations may not be entered in respect of any of the provisions of this Agreement without the consent of the other Members.

18.3 Subject to subparagraphs 3.1 and 3.2, the provisions of this Agreement shall apply to investigations, and reviews of existing measures, initiated pursuant to applications which have been made on or after the date of entry into force for a Member of the WTO Agreement.

18.3.1 With respect to the calculation of margins of dumping in refund procedures under paragraph 3 of Article 9, the rules used in the most recent determination or review of dumping shall apply.

18.3.2 For the purposes of paragraph 3 of Article 11, existing antidumping measures shall be deemed to be imposed on a date not later than the date of entry into force for a Member of the WTO Agreement, except in cases in which the domestic legislation of a Member in force on that date already included a clause of the type provided for in that paragraph.

18.4 Each Member shall take all necessary steps, of a general or particular character, to ensure, not later than the date of entry into force of the WTO Agreement for it, the conformity of its laws, regulations and administrative procedures with the provisions of this Agreement as they may apply for the Member in question.

18.5 Each Member shall inform the Committee of any changes in its laws and regulations relevant to this Agreement and in the administration of such laws and regulations.

18.6 The Committee shall review annually the implementation and operation of this Agreement taking into account the objectives thereof. The Committee shall inform annually the Council for Trade in Goods of developments during the period covered by such reviews.

18.7 The Annexes to this Agreement constitute an integral part thereof.

ANNEX I

PROCEDURES FOR ON–THE–SPOT INVESTIGATIONS
PURSUANT TO PARAGRAPH 7 OF ARTICLE 6

1. Upon initiation of an investigation, the authorities of the exporting Member and the firms known to be concerned should be informed of the intention to carry out on-the-spot investigations.

2. If in exceptional circumstances it is intended to include non-governmental experts in the investigating team, the firms and the authorities of the exporting Member should be so informed. Such non-governmental experts should be subject to effective sanctions for breach of confidentiality requirements.

3. It should be standard practice to obtain explicit agreement of the firms concerned in the exporting Member before the visit is finally scheduled.

4. As soon as the agreement of the firms concerned has been obtained, the investigating authorities should notify the authorities of the exporting Member of the names and addresses of the firms to be visited and the dates agreed.

5.   Sufficient advance notice should be given to the firms in question before the visit is made.

6.   Visits to explain the questionnaire should only be made at the request of an exporting firm. Such a visit may only be made if *(a)* the authorities of the importing Member notify the representatives of the Member in question and *(b)* the latter do not object to the visit.

7.   As the main purpose of the on-the-spot investigation is to verify information provided or to obtain further details, it should be carried out after the response to the questionnaire has been received unless the firm agrees to the contrary and the government of the exporting Member is informed by the investigating authorities of the anticipated visit and does not object to it; further, it should be standard practice prior to the visit to advise the firms concerned of the general nature of the information to be verified and of any further information which needs to be provided, though this should not preclude requests to be made on the spot for further details to be provided in the light of information obtained.

8.   Enquiries or questions put by the authorities or firms of the exporting Members and essential to a successful on-the-spot investigation should, whenever possible, be answered before the visit is made.

ANNEX II
BEST INFORMATION AVAILABLE IN TERMS
OF PARAGRAPH 8 OF ARTICLE 6

1.   As soon as possible after the initiation of the investigation, the investigating authorities should specify in detail the information required from any interested party, and the manner in which that information should be structured by the interested party in its response. The authorities should also ensure that the party is aware that if information is not supplied within a reasonable time, the authorities will be free to make determinations on the basis of the facts available, including those contained in the application for the initiation of the investigation by the domestic industry.

2.   The authorities may also request that an interested party provide its response in a particular medium (e.g. computer tape) or computer language. Where such a request is made, the authorities should consider the reasonable ability of the interested party to respond in the preferred medium or computer language, and should not request the party to use for its response a computer system other than that used by the party. The authority should not maintain a request for a computerized response if the interested party does not maintain computerized accounts and if presenting the response as requested would result in an unreasonable extra burden on the interested party, e.g. it would entail unreasonable additional cost and trouble. The authorities should not maintain a request for a response in a particular medium or computer language if the interested party does not maintain its computerized accounts in such medium or computer language and if presenting the response as requested would result in an unreasonable extra burden on the interested party, e.g. it would entail unreasonable additional cost and trouble.

3.   All information which is verifiable, which is appropriately submitted so that it can be used in the investigation without undue difficulties, which is

supplied in a timely fashion, and, where applicable, which is supplied in a medium or computer language requested by the authorities, should be taken into account when determinations are made. If a party does not respond in the preferred medium or computer language but the authorities find that the circumstances set out in paragraph 2 have been satisfied, the failure to respond in the preferred medium or computer language should not be considered to significantly impede the investigation.

4. Where the authorities do not have the ability to process information if provided in a particular medium (e.g. computer tape), the information should be supplied in the form of written material or any other form acceptable to the authorities.

5. Even though the information provided may not be ideal in all respects, this should not justify the authorities from disregarding it, provided the interested party has acted to the best of its ability.

6. If evidence or information is not accepted, the supplying party should be informed forthwith of the reasons therefor, and should have an opportunity to provide further explanations within a reasonable period, due account being taken of the time-limits of the investigation. If the explanations are considered by the authorities as not being satisfactory, the reasons for the rejection of such evidence or information should be given in any published determinations.

7. If the authorities have to base their findings, including those with respect to normal value, on information from a secondary source, including the information supplied in the application for the initiation of the investigation, they should do so with special circumspection. In such cases, the authorities should, where practicable, check the information from other independent sources at their disposal, such as published price lists, official import statistics and customs returns, and from the information obtained from other interested parties during the investigation. It is clear, however, that if an interested party does not cooperate and thus relevant information is being withheld from the authorities, this situation could lead to a result which is less favourable to the party than if the party did cooperate.

Item 10

AGREEMENT ON IMPLEMENTATION OF ARTICLE VII OF THE GENERAL AGREEMENT ON TARIFFS AND TRADE 1994

GENERAL INTRODUCTORY COMMENTARY

1. The primary basis for customs value under this Agreement is "transaction value" as defined in Article 1. Article 1 is to be read together with Article 8 which provides, *inter alia*, for adjustments to the price actually paid or payable in cases where certain specific elements which are considered to form a part of the value for customs purposes are incurred by the buyer but are not included in the price actually paid or payable for the imported goods. Article 8 also provides for the inclusion in the transaction value of certain considerations which may pass from the buyer to the seller in the form of specified goods or services rather than in the form of money. Articles 2 through 7 provide methods of determining the customs value whenever it cannot be determined under the provisions of Article 1.

2. Where the customs value cannot be determined under the provisions of Article 1 there should normally be a process of consultation between the customs administration and importer with a view to arriving at a basis of value under the provisions of Article 2 or 3. It may occur, for example, that the importer has information about the customs value of identical or similar imported goods which is not immediately available to the customs administration in the port of importation. On the other hand, the customs administration may have information about the customs value of identical or similar imported goods which is not readily available to the importer. A process of consultation between the two parties will enable information to be exchanged, subject to the requirements of commercial confidentiality, with a view to determining a proper basis of value for customs purposes.

3. Articles 5 and 6 provide two bases for determining the customs value where it cannot be determined on the basis of the transaction value of the imported goods or of identical or similar imported goods. Under paragraph 1 of Article 5 the customs value is determined on the basis of the price at which the goods are sold in the condition as imported to an unrelated buyer in the country of importation. The importer also has the right to have goods which are further processed after importation valued under the provisions of Article 5 if the importer so requests. Under Article 6 the customs value is determined on the basis of the computed value. Both these methods present certain difficulties and because of this the importer is given the right, under the provisions of Article 4, to choose the order of application of the two methods.

4. Article 7 sets out how to determine the customs value in cases where it cannot be determined under the provisions of any of the preceding Articles.

Members,

Having regard to the Multilateral Trade Negotiations;

Desiring to further the objectives of GATT 1994 and to secure additional benefits for the international trade of developing countries;

Recognizing the importance of the provisions of Article VII of GATT 1994 and desiring to elaborate rules for their application in order to provide greater uniformity and certainty in their implementation;

Recognizing the need for a fair, uniform and neutral system for the valuation of goods for customs purposes that precludes the use of arbitrary or fictitious customs values;

Recognizing that the basis for valuation of goods for customs purposes should, to the greatest extent possible, be the transaction value of the goods being valued;

Recognizing that customs value should be based on simple and equitable criteria consistent with commercial practices and that valuation procedures should be of general application without distinction between sources of supply;

Recognizing that valuation procedures should not be used to combat dumping;

Hereby *agree* as follows:

PART I

RULES ON CUSTOMS VALUATION

Article 1

1. The customs value of imported goods shall be the transaction value, that is the price actually paid or payable for the goods when sold for export to the country of importation adjusted in accordance with the provisions of Article 8, provided:

(a) that there are no restrictions as to the disposition or use of the goods by the buyer other than restrictions which:

(i) are imposed or required by law or by the public authorities in the country of importation;

(ii) limit the geographical area in which the goods may be resold; or

(iii) do not substantially affect the value of the goods;

(b) that the sale or price is not subject to some condition or consideration for which a value cannot be determined with respect to the goods being valued;

(c) that no part of the proceeds of any subsequent resale, disposal or use of the goods by the buyer will accrue directly or indirectly to the seller, unless an appropriate adjustment can be made in accordance with the provisions of Article 8; and

(d) that the buyer and seller are not related, or where the buyer and seller are related, that the transaction value is acceptable for customs purposes under the provisions of paragraph 2.

2.   (a) In determining whether the transaction value is acceptable for the purposes of paragraph 1, the fact that the buyer and the seller are related within the meaning of Article 15 shall not in itself be grounds for regarding the transaction value as unacceptable.   In such case the circumstances surrounding the sale shall be examined and the transaction value shall be accepted provided that the relationship did not influence the price. If, in the light of information provided by the importer or otherwise, the customs administration has grounds for considering that the relationship influenced the price, it shall communicate its grounds to the importer and the importer shall be given a reasonable opportunity to respond. If the importer so requests, the communication of the grounds shall be in writing.

(b) In a sale between related persons, the transaction value shall be accepted and the goods valued in accordance with the provisions of paragraph 1 whenever the importer demonstrates that such value closely approximates to one of the following occurring at or about the same time:

(i) the transaction value in sales to unrelated buyers of identical or similar goods for export to the same country of importation;

(ii) the customs value of identical or similar goods as determined under the provisions of Article 5;

(iii) the customs value of identical or similar goods as determined under the provisions of Article 6;

In applying the foregoing tests, due account shall be taken of demonstrated differences in commercial levels, quantity levels, the elements enumerated in Article 8 and costs incurred by the seller in sales in which the seller and the buyer are not related that are not incurred by the seller in sales in which the seller and the buyer are related.

(c) The tests set forth in paragraph 2(b) are to be used at the initiative of the importer and only for comparison purposes. Substitute values may not be established under the provisions of paragraph 2(b).

Article 2

1.   (a) If the customs value of the imported goods cannot be determined under the provisions of Article 1, the customs value shall be the transaction value of identical goods sold for export to the same country of importation and exported at or about the same time as the goods being valued.

(b) In applying this Article, the transaction value of identical goods in a sale at the same commercial level and in substantially the same quantity as the goods being valued shall be used to determine the customs value. Where no such sale is found, the transaction value of identical goods sold at a different commercial level and/or in different quantities, adjusted to take account of differences attributable to commercial level and/or to quantity, shall be used, provided that such adjustments can be made on the basis of demonstrated evidence which clearly establishes the reasonableness and accuracy of the adjustment, whether the adjustment leads to an increase or a decrease in the value.

2.   Where the costs and charges referred to in paragraph 2 of Article 8 are included in the transaction value, an adjustment shall be made to take account of significant differences in such costs and charges between the

imported goods and the identical goods in question arising from differences in distances and modes of transport.

3. If, in applying this Article, more than one transaction value of identical goods is found, the lowest such value shall be used to determine the customs value of the imported goods.

Article 3

1. (a) If the customs value of the imported goods cannot be determined under the provisions of Articles 1 and 2, the customs value shall be the transaction value of similar goods sold for export to the same country of importation and exported at or about the same time as the goods being valued.

(b) In applying this Article, the transaction value of similar goods in a sale at the same commercial level and in substantially the same quantity as the goods being valued shall be used to determine the customs value. Where no such sale is found, the transaction value of similar goods sold at a different commercial level and/or in different quantities, adjusted to take account of differences attributable to commercial level and/or to quantity, shall be used, provided that such adjustments can be made on the basis of demonstrated evidence which clearly establishes the reasonableness and accuracy of the adjustment, whether the adjustment leads to an increase or a decrease in the value.

2. Where the costs and charges referred to in paragraph 2 of Article 8 are included in the transaction value, an adjustment shall be made to take account of significant differences in such costs and charges between the imported goods and the similar goods in question arising from differences in distances and modes of transport.

3. If, in applying this Article, more than one transaction value of similar goods is found, the lowest such value shall be used to determine the customs value of the imported goods.

Article 4

If the customs value of the imported goods cannot be determined under the provisions of Articles 1, 2 and 3, the customs value shall be determined under the provisions of Article 5 or, when the customs value cannot be determined under that Article, under the provisions of Article 6 except that, at the request of the importer, the order of application of Articles 5 and 6 shall be reversed.

Article 5

1. (a) If the imported goods or identical or similar imported goods are sold in the country of importation in the condition as imported, the customs value of the imported goods under the provisions of this Article shall be based on the unit price at which the imported goods or identical or similar imported goods are so sold in the greatest aggregate quantity, at or about the time of the importation of the goods being valued, to persons who are not related to the persons from whom they buy such goods, subject to deductions for the following:

(i) either the commissions usually paid or agreed to be paid or the additions usually made for profit and general expenses in connection with sales in such country of imported goods of the same class or kind;

(ii) the usual costs of transport and insurance and associated costs incurred within the country of importation;

(iii) where appropriate, the costs and charges referred to in paragraph 2 of Article 8; and

(iv) the customs duties and other national taxes payable in the country of importation by reason of the importation or sale of the goods.

(b) If neither the imported goods nor identical nor similar imported goods are sold at or about the time of importation of the goods being valued, the customs value shall, subject otherwise to the provisions of paragraph 1(a), be based on the unit price at which the imported goods or identical or similar imported goods are sold in the country of importation in the condition as imported at the earliest date after the importation of the goods being valued but before the expiration of 90 days after such importation.

2.   If neither the imported goods nor identical nor similar imported goods are sold in the country of importation in the condition as imported, then, if the importer so requests, the customs value shall be based on the unit price at which the imported goods, after further processing, are sold in the greatest aggregate quantity to persons in the country of importation who are not related to the persons from whom they buy such goods, due allowance being made for the value added by such processing and the deductions provided for in paragraph 1(a).

Article 6

1.   The customs value of imported goods under the provisions of this Article shall be based on a computed value. Computed value shall consist of the sum of:

(a) the cost or value of materials and fabrication or other processing employed in producing the imported goods;

(b) an amount for profit and general expenses equal to that usually reflected in sales of goods of the same class or kind as the goods being valued which are made by producers in the country of exportation for export to the country of importation;

(c) the cost or value of all other expenses necessary to reflect the valuation option chosen by the Member under paragraph 2 of Article 8.

2.   No Member may require or compel any person not resident in its own territory to produce for examination, or to allow access to, any account or other record for the purposes of determining a computed value. However, information supplied by the producer of the goods for the purposes of determining the customs value under the provisions of this Article may be verified in another country by the authorities of the country of importation with the agreement of the producer and provided they give sufficient advance notice to the government of the country in question and the latter does not object to the investigation.

Article 7

1. If the customs value of the imported goods cannot be determined under the provisions of Articles 1 through 6, inclusive, the customs value shall be determined using reasonable means consistent with the principles and general provisions of this Agreement and of Article VII of GATT 1994 and on the basis of data available in the country of importation.

2. No customs value shall be determined under the provisions of this Article on the basis of:

(a) the selling price in the country of importation of goods produced in such country;

(b) a system which provides for the acceptance for customs purposes of the higher of two alternative values;

(c) the price of goods on the domestic market of the country of exportation;

(d) the cost of production other than computed values which have been determined for identical or similar goods in accordance with the provisions of Article 6;

(e) the price of the goods for export to a country other than the country of importation;

(f) minimum customs values; or

(g) arbitrary or fictitious values.

3. If the importer so requests, the importer shall be informed in writing of the customs value determined under the provisions of this Article and the method used to determine such value.

Article 8

1. In determining the customs value under the provisions of Article 1, there shall be added to the price actually paid or payable for the imported goods:

(a) the following, to the extent that they are incurred by the buyer but are not included in the price actually paid or payable for the goods:

(i) commissions and brokerage, except buying commissions;

(ii) the cost of containers which are treated as being one for customs purposes with the goods in question;

(iii) the cost of packing whether for labour or materials;

(b) the value, apportioned as appropriate, of the following goods and services where supplied directly or indirectly by the buyer free of charge or at reduced cost for use in connection with the production and sale for export of the imported goods, to the extent that such value has not been included in the price actually paid or payable:

(i) materials, components, parts and similar items incorporated in the imported goods;

(ii) tools, dies, moulds and similar items used in the production of the imported goods;

(iii) materials consumed in the production of the imported goods;

(iv) engineering, development, artwork, design work, and plans and sketches undertaken elsewhere than in the country of importation and necessary for the production of the imported goods;

(c) royalties and licence fees related to the goods being valued that the buyer must pay, either directly or indirectly, as a condition of sale of the goods being valued, to the extent that such royalties and fees are not included in the price actually paid or payable;

(d) the value of any part of the proceeds of any subsequent resale, disposal or use of the imported goods that accrues directly or indirectly to the seller.

2. In framing its legislation, each Member shall provide for the inclusion in or the exclusion from the customs value, in whole or in part, of the following:

(a) the cost of transport of the imported goods to the port or place of importation;

(b) loading, unloading and handling charges associated with the transport of the imported goods to the port or place of importation; and

(c) the cost of insurance.

3. Additions to the price actually paid or payable shall be made under this Article only on the basis of objective and quantifiable data.

4. No additions shall be made to the price actually paid or payable in determining the customs value except as provided in this Article.

Article 9

1. Where the conversion of currency is necessary for the determination of the customs value, the rate of exchange to be used shall be that duly published by the competent authorities of the country of importation concerned and shall reflect as effectively as possible, in respect of the period covered by each such document of publication, the current value of such currency in commercial transactions in terms of the currency of the country of importation.

2. The conversion rate to be used shall be that in effect at the time of exportation or the time of importation, as provided by each Member.

Article 10

All information which is by nature confidential or which is provided on a confidential basis for the purposes of customs valuation shall be treated as strictly confidential by the authorities concerned who shall not disclose it without the specific permission of the person or government providing such information, except to the extent that it may be required to be disclosed in the context of judicial proceedings.

Article 11

1. The legislation of each Member shall provide in regard to a determination of customs value for the right of appeal, without penalty, by the importer or any other person liable for the payment of the duty.

2. An initial right of appeal without penalty may be to an authority within the customs administration or to an independent body, but the legislation of each Member shall provide for the right of appeal without penalty to a judicial authority.

3. Notice of the decision on appeal shall be given to the appellant and the reasons for such decision shall be provided in writing. The appellant shall also be informed of any rights of further appeal.

Article 12

Laws, regulations, judicial decisions and administrative rulings of general application giving effect to this Agreement shall be published in conformity with Article X of GATT 1994 by the country of importation concerned.

Article 13

If, in the course of determining the customs value of imported goods, it becomes necessary to delay the final determination of such customs value, the importer of the goods shall nevertheless be able to withdraw them from customs if, where so required, the importer provides sufficient guarantee in the form of a surety, a deposit or some other appropriate instrument, covering the ultimate payment of customs duties for which the goods may be liable. The legislation of each Member shall make provisions for such circumstances.

Article 14

The notes at Annex I to this Agreement form an integral part of this Agreement and the Articles of this Agreement are to be read and applied in conjunction with their respective notes. Annexes II and III also form an integral part of this Agreement.

Article 15

1. In this Agreement:

(a) "customs value of imported goods" means the value of goods for the purposes of levying ad valorem duties of customs on imported goods;

(b) "country of importation" means country or customs territory of importation; and

(c) "produced" includes grown, manufactured and mined.

2. In this Agreement:

(a) "identical goods" means goods which are the same in all respects, including physical characteristics, quality and reputation. Minor differences in appearance would not preclude goods otherwise conforming to the definition from being regarded as identical;

(b) "similar goods" means goods which, although not alike in all respects, have like characteristics and like component materials which enable them to perform the same functions and to be commercially interchangeable. The quality of the goods, their reputation and the existence of a trademark are among the factors to be considered in determining whether goods are similar;

(c) the terms "identical goods" and "similar goods" do not include, as the case may be, goods which incorporate or reflect engineering, development, artwork, design work, and plans and sketches for which no adjustment has been made under paragraph 1(b)(iv) of Article 8 because such elements were undertaken in the country of importation;

(d) goods shall not be regarded as "identical goods" or "similar goods" unless they were produced in the same country as the goods being valued;

(e) goods produced by a different person shall be taken into account only when there are no identical goods or similar goods, as the case may be, produced by the same person as the goods being valued.

3. In this Agreement "goods of the same class or kind" means goods which fall within a group or range of goods produced by a particular industry or industry sector, and includes identical or similar goods.

4. For the purposes of this Agreement, persons shall be deemed to be related only if:

(a) they are officers or directors of one another's businesses;

(b) they are legally recognized partners in business;

(c) they are employer and employee;

(d) any person directly or indirectly owns, controls or holds 5 per cent or more of the outstanding voting stock or shares of both of them;

(e) one of them directly or indirectly controls the other;

(f) both of them are directly or indirectly controlled by a third person;

(g) together they directly or indirectly control a third person; or

(h) they are members of the same family.

5. Persons who are associated in business with one another in that one is the sole agent, sole distributor or sole concessionaire, however described, of the other shall be deemed to be related for the purposes of this Agreement if they fall within the criteria of paragraph 4.

Article 16

Upon written request, the importer shall have the right to an explanation in writing from the customs administration of the country of importation as to how the customs value of the importer's goods was determined.

Article 17

Nothing in this Agreement shall be construed as restricting or calling into question the rights of customs administrations to satisfy themselves as to the truth or accuracy of any statement, document or declaration presented for customs valuation purposes.

PART II
ADMINISTRATION, CONSULTATIONS AND DISPUTE SETTLEMENT
Article 18
Institutions

1. There is hereby established a Committee on Customs Valuation (referred to in this Agreement as "the Committee") composed of representa-

tives from each of the Members. The Committee shall elect its own Chairman and shall normally meet once a year, or as is otherwise envisaged by the relevant provisions of this Agreement, for the purpose of affording Members the opportunity to consult on matters relating to the administration of the customs valuation system by any Member as it might affect the operation of this Agreement or the furtherance of its objectives and carrying out such other responsibilities as may be assigned to it by the Members. The WTO Secretariat shall act as the secretariat to the Committee.

2. There shall be established a Technical Committee on Customs Valuation (referred to in this Agreement as "the Technical Committee") under the auspices of the Customs Co-operation Council (referred to in this Agreement as "the CCC"), which shall carry out the responsibilities described in Annex II to this Agreement and shall operate in accordance with the rules of procedure contained therein.

Article 19

Consultations and Dispute Settlement

1. Except as otherwise provided herein, the Dispute Settlement Understanding is applicable to consultations and the settlement of disputes under this Agreement.

2. If any Member considers that any benefit accruing to it, directly or indirectly, under this Agreement is being nullified or impaired, or that the achievement of any objective of this Agreement is being impeded, as a result of the actions of another Member or of other Members, it may, with a view to reaching a mutually satisfactory solution of this matter, request consultations with the Member or Members in question. Each Member shall afford sympathetic consideration to any request from another Member for consultations.

3. The Technical Committee shall provide, upon request, advice and assistance to Members engaged in consultations.

4. At the request of a party to the dispute, or on its own initiative, a panel established to examine a dispute relating to the provisions of this Agreement may request the Technical Committee to carry out an examination of any questions requiring technical consideration. The panel shall determine the terms of reference of the Technical Committee for the particular dispute and set a time period for receipt of the report of the Technical Committee. The panel shall take into consideration the report of the Technical Committee. In the event that the Technical Committee is unable to reach consensus on a matter referred to it pursuant to this paragraph, the panel should afford the parties to the dispute an opportunity to present their views on the matter to the panel.

5. Confidential information provided to the panel shall not be disclosed without formal authorization from the person, body or authority providing such information. Where such information is requested from the panel but release of such information by the panel is not authorized, a non-confidential summary of this information, authorized by the person, body or authority providing the information, shall be provided.

PART III
SPECIAL AND DIFFERENTIAL TREATMENT
Article 20

1. Developing country Members not party to the Agreement on Implementation of Article VII of the General Agreement on Tariffs and Trade done on 12 April 1979 may delay application of the provisions of this Agreement for a period not exceeding five years from the date of entry into force of the WTO Agreement for such Members. Developing country Members who choose to delay application of this Agreement shall notify the Director–General of the WTO accordingly.

2. In addition to paragraph 1, developing country Members not party to the Agreement on Implementation of Article VII of the General Agreement on Tariffs and Trade done on 12 April 1979 may delay application of paragraph 2(b)(iii) of Article 1 and Article 6 for a period not exceeding three years following their application of all other provisions of this Agreement. Developing country Members that choose to delay application of the provisions specified in this paragraph shall notify the Director–General of the WTO accordingly.

3. Developed country Members shall furnish, on mutually agreed terms, technical assistance to developing country Members that so request. On this basis developed country Members shall draw up programmes of technical assistance which may include, *inter alia*, training of personnel, assistance in preparing implementation measures, access to sources of information regarding customs valuation methodology, and advice on the application of the provisions of this Agreement.

PART IV
FINAL PROVISIONS
Article 21
Reservations

Reservations may not be entered in respect of any of the provisions of this Agreement without the consent of the other Members.

Article 22
National Legislation

1. Each Member shall ensure, not later than the date of application of the provisions of this Agreement for it, the conformity of its laws, regulations and administrative procedures with the provisions of this Agreement.

2. Each Member shall inform the Committee of any changes in its laws and regulations relevant to this Agreement and in the administration of such laws and regulations.

Article 23
Review

The Committee shall review annually the implementation and operation of this Agreement taking into account the objectives thereof. The Committee shall annually inform the Council for Trade in Goods of developments during the period covered by such reviews.

Article 24
Secretariat

This Agreement shall be serviced by the WTO Secretariat except in regard to those responsibilities specifically assigned to the Technical Committee, which will be serviced by the CCC Secretariat.

ANNEX I
INTERPRETATIVE NOTES
General Note

Sequential Application of Valuation Methods

1. Articles 1 through 7 define how the customs value of imported goods is to be determined under the provisions of this Agreement. The methods of valuation are set out in a sequential order of application. The primary method for customs valuation is defined in Article 1 and imported goods are to be valued in accordance with the provisions of this Article whenever the conditions prescribed therein are fulfilled.

2. Where the customs value cannot be determined under the provisions of Article 1, it is to be determined by proceeding sequentially through the succeeding Articles to the first such Article under which the customs value can be determined. Except as provided in Article 4, it is only when the customs value cannot be determined under the provisions of a particular Article that the provisions of the next Article in the sequence can be used.

3. If the importer does not request that the order of Articles 5 and 6 be reversed, the normal order of the sequence is to be followed. If the importer does so request but it then proves impossible to determine the customs value under the provisions of Article 6, the customs value is to be determined under the provisions of Article 5, if it can be so determined.

4. Where the customs value cannot be determined under the provisions of Articles 1 through 6 it is to be determined under the provisions of Article 7.

Use of Generally Accepted Accounting Principles

1. "Generally accepted accounting principles" refers to the recognized consensus or substantial authoritative support within a country at a particular time as to which economic resources and obligations should be recorded as assets and liabilities, which changes in assets and liabilities should be recorded, how the assets and liabilities and changes in them should be measured, what information should be disclosed and how it should be disclosed, and which financial statements should be prepared. These standards may be broad guidelines of general application as well as detailed practices and procedures.

2. For the purposes of this Agreement, the customs administration of each Member shall utilize information prepared in a manner consistent with generally accepted accounting principles in the country which is appropriate for the Article in question. For example, the determination of usual profit and general expenses under the provisions of Article 5 would be carried out

utilizing information prepared in a manner consistent with generally accepted accounting principles of the country of importation. On the other hand, the determination of usual profit and general expenses under the provisions of Article 6 would be carried out utilizing information prepared in a manner consistent with generally accepted accounting principles of the country of production. As a further example, the determination of an element provided for in paragraph 1(b)(ii) of Article 8 undertaken in the country of importation would be carried out utilizing information in a manner consistent with the generally accepted accounting principles of that country.

Note to Article 1

Price Actually Paid or Payable

1. The price actually paid or payable is the total payment made or to be made by the buyer to or for the benefit of the seller for the imported goods. The payment need not necessarily take the form of a transfer of money. Payment may be made by way of letters of credit or negotiable instruments. Payment may be made directly or indirectly. An example of an indirect payment would be the settlement by the buyer, whether in whole or in part, of a debt owed by the seller.

2. Activities undertaken by the buyer on the buyer's own account, other than those for which an adjustment is provided in Article 8, are not considered to be an indirect payment to the seller, even though they might be regarded as of benefit to the seller. The costs of such activities shall not, therefore, be added to the price actually paid or payable in determining the customs value.

3. The customs value shall not include the following charges or costs, provided that they are distinguished from the price actually paid or payable for the imported goods:

(a) charges for construction, erection, assembly, maintenance or technical assistance, undertaken after importation on imported goods such as industrial plant, machinery or equipment;

(b) the cost of transport after importation;

(c) duties and taxes of the country of importation.

4. The price actually paid or payable refers to the price for the imported goods. Thus the flow of dividends or other payments from the buyer to the seller that do not relate to the imported goods are not part of the customs value.

Paragraph 1(a)(iii)

Among restrictions which would not render a price actually paid or payable unacceptable are restrictions which do not substantially affect the value of the goods. An example of such restrictions would be the case where a seller requires a buyer of automobiles not to sell or exhibit them prior to a fixed date which represents the beginning of a model year.

Paragraph 1(b)

1. If the sale or price is subject to some condition or consideration for which a value cannot be determined with respect to the goods being valued,

the transaction value shall not be acceptable for customs purposes. Some examples of this include:

(a) the seller establishes the price of the imported goods on condition that the buyer will also buy other goods in specified quantities;

(b) the price of the imported goods is dependent upon the price or prices at which the buyer of the imported goods sells other goods to the seller of the imported goods;

(c) the price is established on the basis of a form of payment extraneous to the imported goods, such as where the imported goods are semi-finished goods which have been provided by the seller on condition that the seller will receive a specified quantity of the finished goods.

2. However, conditions or considerations relating to the production or marketing of the imported goods shall not result in rejection of the transaction value. For example, the fact that the buyer furnishes the seller with engineering and plans undertaken in the country of importation shall not result in rejection of the transaction value for the purposes of Article 1. Likewise, if the buyer undertakes on the buyer's own account, even though by agreement with the seller, activities relating to the marketing of the imported goods, the value of these activities is not part of the customs value nor shall such activities result in rejection of the transaction value.

Paragraph 2

1. Paragraphs 2(a) and 2(b) provide different means of establishing the acceptability of a transaction value.

2. Paragraph 2(a) provides that where the buyer and the seller are related, the circumstances surrounding the sale shall be examined and the transaction value shall be accepted as the customs value provided that the relationship did not influence the price. It is not intended that there should be an examination of the circumstances in all cases where the buyer and the seller are related. Such examination will only be required where there are doubts about the acceptability of the price. Where the customs administration have no doubts about the acceptability of the price, it should be accepted without requesting further information from the importer. For example, the customs administration may have previously examined the relationship, or it may already have detailed information concerning the buyer and the seller, and may already be satisfied from such examination or information that the relationship did not influence the price.

3. Where the customs administration is unable to accept the transaction value without further inquiry, it should give the importer an opportunity to supply such further detailed information as may be necessary to enable it to examine the circumstances surrounding the sale. In this context, the customs administration should be prepared to examine relevant aspects of the transaction, including the way in which the buyer and seller organize their commercial relations and the way in which the price in question was arrived at, in order to determine whether the relationship influenced the price. Where it can be shown that the buyer and seller, although related under the provisions of Article 15, buy from and sell to each other as if they were not related, this would demonstrate that the price had not been influenced by the

relationship. As an example of this, if the price had been settled in a manner consistent with the normal pricing practices of the industry in question or with the way the seller settles prices for sales to buyers who are not related to the seller, this would demonstrate that the price had not been influenced by the relationship. As a further example, where it is shown that the price is adequate to ensure recovery of all costs plus a profit which is representative of the firm's overall profit realized over a representative period of time (e.g. on an annual basis) in sales of goods of the same class or kind, this would demonstrate that the price had not been influenced.

4. Paragraph 2(b) provides an opportunity for the importer to demonstrate that the transaction value closely approximates to a "test" value previously accepted by the customs administration and is therefore acceptable under the provisions of Article 1. Where a test under paragraph 2(b) is met, it is not necessary to examine the question of influence under paragraph 2(a). If the customs administration has already sufficient information to be satisfied, without further detailed inquiries, that one of the tests provided in paragraph 2(b) has been met, there is no reason for it to require the importer to demonstrate that the test can be met. In paragraph 2(b) the term "unrelated buyers" means buyers who are not related to the seller in any particular case.

Paragraph 2(b)

A number of factors must be taken into consideration in determining whether one value "closely approximates" to another value. These factors include the nature of the imported goods, the nature of the industry itself, the season in which the goods are imported, and, whether the difference in values is commercially significant. Since these factors may vary from case to case, it would be impossible to apply a uniform standard such as a fixed percentage, in each case. For example, a small difference in value in a case involving one type of goods could be unacceptable while a large difference in a case involving another type of goods might be acceptable in determining whether the transaction value closely approximates to the "test" values set forth in paragraph 2(b) of Article 1.

Note to Article 2

1. In applying Article 2, the customs administration shall, wherever possible, use a sale of identical goods at the same commercial level and in substantially the same quantities as the goods being valued. Where no such sale is found, a sale of identical goods that takes place under any one of the following three conditions may be used:

(a) a sale at the same commercial level but in different quantities;

(b) a sale at a different commercial level but in substantially the same quantities; or

(c) a sale at a different commercial level and in different quantities.

2. Having found a sale under any one of these three conditions adjustments will then be made, as the case may be, for:

(a) quantity factors only;

(b) commercial level factors only; or

(c) both commercial level and quantity factors.

3. The expression "and/or" allows the flexibility to use the sales and make the necessary adjustments in any one of the three conditions described above.

4. For the purposes of Article 2, the transaction value of identical imported goods means a customs value, adjusted as provided for in paragraphs 1(b) and 2, which has already been accepted under Article 1.

5. A condition for adjustment because of different commercial levels or different quantities is that such adjustment, whether it leads to an increase or a decrease in the value, be made only on the basis of demonstrated evidence that clearly establishes the reasonableness and accuracy of the adjustments, e.g. valid price lists containing prices referring to different levels or different quantities. As an example of this, if the imported goods being valued consist of a shipment of 10 units and the only identical imported goods for which a transaction value exists involved a sale of 500 units, and it is recognized that the seller grants quantity discounts, the required adjustment may be accomplished by resorting to the seller's price list and using that price applicable to a sale of 10 units. This does not require that a sale had to have been made in quantities of 10 as long as the price list has been established as being bona fide through sales at other quantities. In the absence of such an objective measure, however, the determination of a customs value under the provisions of Article 2 is not appropriate.

Note to Article 3

1. In applying Article 3, the customs administration shall, wherever possible, use a sale of similar goods at the same commercial level and in substantially the same quantities as the goods being valued. Where no such sale is found, a sale of similar goods that takes place under any one of the following three conditions may be used:

(a) a sale at the same commercial level but in different quantities;

(b) a sale at a different commercial level but in substantially the same quantities; or

(c) a sale at a different commercial level and in different quantities.

2. Having found a sale under any one of these three conditions adjustments will then be made, as the case may be, for:

(a) quantity factors only;

(b) commercial level factors only; or

(c) both commercial level and quantity factors.

3. The expression "and/or" allows the flexibility to use the sales and make the necessary adjustments in any one of the three conditions described above.

4. For the purpose of Article 3, the transaction value of similar imported goods means a customs value, adjusted as provided for in paragraphs 1(b) and 2, which has already been accepted under Article 1.

5. A condition for adjustment because of different commercial levels or different quantities is that such adjustment, whether it leads to an increase or

a decrease in the value, be made only on the basis of demonstrated evidence that clearly establishes the reasonableness and accuracy of the adjustment, e.g. valid price lists containing prices referring to different levels or different quantities. As an example of this, if the imported goods being valued consist of a shipment of 10 units and the only similar imported goods for which a transaction value exists involved a sale of 500 units, and it is recognized that the seller grants quantity discounts, the required adjustment may be accomplished by resorting to the seller's price list and using that price applicable to a sale of 10 units. This does not require that a sale had to have been made in quantities of 10 as long as the price list has been established as being bona fide through sales at other quantities. In the absence of such an objective measure, however, the determination of a customs value under the provisions of Article 3 is not appropriate.

Note to Article 5

1. The term "unit price at which ... goods are sold in the greatest aggregate quantity" means the price at which the greatest number of units is sold in sales to persons who are not related to the persons from whom they buy such goods at the first commercial level after importation at which such sales take place.

2. As an example of this, goods are sold from a price list which grants favourable unit prices for purchases made in larger quantities.

Sale quantity	Unit price	Number of sales	Total quantity sold at each price
1–10 units	100	10 sales of 5 units 5 sales of 3 units	65
11–25 units	95	5 sales of 11 units	55
over 25 units	90	1 sale of 30 units 1 sale of 50 units	80

The greatest number of units sold at a price is 80; therefore, the unit price in the greatest aggregate quantity is 90.

3. As another example of this, two sales occur. In the first sale 500 units are sold at a price of 95 currency units each. In the second sale 400 units are sold at a price of 90 currency units each. In this example, the greatest number of units sold at a particular price is 500; therefore, the unit price in the greatest aggregate quantity is 95.

4. A third example would be the following situation where various quantities are sold at various prices.

(a) Sales

Sale quantity	Unit price
40 units	100
30 units	90
15 units	100
50 units	95
25 units	105
35 units	90
5 units	100

(b) Totals

Total quantity sold	Unit price
65	90
50	95
60	100
25	105

In this example, the greatest number of units sold at a particular price is 65; therefore, the unit price in the greatest aggregate quantity is 90.

5. Any sale in the importing country, as described in paragraph 1 above, to a person who supplies directly or indirectly free of charge or at reduced cost for use in connection with the production and sale for export of the imported goods any of the elements specified in paragraph 1(b) of Article 8, should not be taken into account in establishing the unit price for the purposes of Article 5.

6. It should be noted that "profit and general expenses" referred to in paragraph 1 of Article 5 should be taken as a whole. The figure for the purposes of this deduction should be determined on the basis of information supplied by or on behalf of the importer unless the importer's figures are inconsistent with those obtained in sales in the country of importation of imported goods of the same class or kind. Where the importer's figures are inconsistent with such figures, the amount for profit and general expenses may be based upon relevant information other than that supplied by or on behalf of the importer.

7. The "general expenses" include the direct and indirect costs of marketing the goods in question.

8. Local taxes payable by reason of the sale of the goods for which a deduction is not made under the provisions of paragraph 1(a)(iv) of Article 5 shall be deducted under the provisions of paragraph 1(a)(i) of Article 5.

9. In determining either the commissions or the usual profits and general expenses under the provisions of paragraph 1 of Article 5, the question whether certain goods are "of the same class or kind" as other goods must be determined on a case-by-case basis by reference to the circumstances involved. Sales in the country of importation of the narrowest group or range of imported goods of the same class or kind, which includes the goods being valued, for which the necessary information can be provided, should be examined. For the purposes of Article 5, "goods of the same class or kind" includes goods imported from the same country as the goods being valued as well as goods imported from other countries.

10.   For the purposes of paragraph 1(b) of Article 5, the "earliest date" shall be the date by which sales of the imported goods or of identical or similar imported goods are made in sufficient quantity to establish the unit price.

11.   Where the method in paragraph 2 of Article 5 is used, deductions made for the value added by further processing shall be based on objective and quantifiable data relating to the cost of such work.   Accepted industry formulas, recipes, methods of construction, and other industry practices would form the basis of the calculations.

12.   It is recognized that the method of valuation provided for in paragraph 2 of Article 5 would normally not be applicable when, as a result of the further processing, the imported goods lose their identity.   However, there can be instances where, although the identity of the imported goods is lost, the value added by the processing can be determined accurately without unreasonable difficulty.   On the other hand, there can also be instances where the imported goods maintain their identity but form such a minor element in the goods sold in the country of importation that the use of this valuation method would be unjustified.   In view of the above, each situation of this type must be considered on a case-by-case basis.

Note to Article 6

1.   As a general rule, customs value is determined under this Agreement on the basis of information readily available in the country of importation.   In order to determine a computed value, however, it may be necessary to examine the costs of producing the goods being valued and other information which has to be obtained from outside the country of importation.   Furthermore, in most cases the producer of the goods will be outside the jurisdiction of the authorities of the country of importation.   The use of the computed value method will generally be limited to those cases where the buyer and seller are related, and the producer is prepared to supply to the authorities of the country of importation the necessary costings and to provide facilities for any subsequent verification which may be necessary.

2.   The "cost or value" referred to in paragraph 1(a) of Article 6 is to be determined on the basis of information relating to the production of the goods being valued supplied by or on behalf of the producer.   It is to be based upon the commercial accounts of the producer, provided that such accounts are consistent with the generally accepted accounting principles applied in the country where the goods are produced.

3.   The "cost or value" shall include the cost of elements specified in paragraphs 1(a)(ii) and (iii) of Article 8.   It shall also include the value, apportioned as appropriate under the provisions of the relevant note to Article 8, of any element specified in paragraph 1(b) of Article 8 which has been supplied directly or indirectly by the buyer for use in connection with the production of the imported goods.   The value of the elements specified in paragraph 1(b)(iv) of Article 8 which are undertaken in the country of importation shall be included only to the extent that such elements are charged to the producer.   It is to be understood that no cost or value of the elements referred to in this paragraph shall be counted twice in determining the computed value.

4. The "amount for profit and general expenses" referred to in paragraph 1(b) of Article 6 is to be determined on the basis of information supplied by or on behalf of the producer unless the producer's figures are inconsistent with those usually reflected in sales of goods of the same class or kind as the goods being valued which are made by producers in the country of exportation for export to the country of importation.

5. It should be noted in this context that the "amount for profit and general expenses" has to be taken as a whole. It follows that if, in any particular case, the producer's profit figure is low and the producer's general expenses are high, the producer's profit and general expenses taken together may nevertheless be consistent with that usually reflected in sales of goods of the same class or kind. Such a situation might occur, for example, if a product were being launched in the country of importation and the producer accepted a nil or low profit to offset high general expenses associated with the launch. Where the producer can demonstrate a low profit on sales of the imported goods because of particular commercial circumstances, the producer's actual profit figures should be taken into account provided that the producer has valid commercial reasons to justify them and the producer's pricing policy reflects usual pricing policies in the branch of industry concerned. Such a situation might occur, for example, where producers have been forced to lower prices temporarily because of an unforeseeable drop in demand, or where they sell goods to complement a range of goods being produced in the country of importation and accept a low profit to maintain competitivity. Where the producer's own figures for profit and general expenses are not consistent with those usually reflected in sales of goods of the same class or kind as the goods being valued which are made by producers in the country of exportation for export to the country of importation, the amount for profit and general expenses may be based upon relevant information other than that supplied by or on behalf of the producer of the goods.

6. Where information other than that supplied by or on behalf of the producer is used for the purposes of determining a computed value, the authorities of the importing country shall inform the importer, if the latter so requests, of the source of such information, the data used and the calculations based upon such data, subject to the provisions of Article 10.

7. The "general expenses" referred to in paragraph 1(b) of Article 6 covers the direct and indirect costs of producing and selling the goods for export which are not included under paragraph 1(a) of Article 6.

8. Whether certain goods are "of the same class or kind" as other goods must be determined on a case-by-case basis with reference to the circumstances involved. In determining the usual profits and general expenses under the provisions of Article 6, sales for export to the country of importation of the narrowest group or range of goods, which includes the goods being valued, for which the necessary information can be provided, should be examined. For the purposes of Article 6, "goods of the same class or kind" must be from the same country as the goods being valued.

Note to Article 7

1. Customs values determined under the provisions of Article 7 should, to the greatest extent possible, be based on previously determined customs values.

2.   The methods of valuation to be employed under Article 7 should be those laid down in Articles 1 through 6 but a reasonable flexibility in the application of such methods would be in conformity with the aims and provisions of Article 7.

3.   Some examples of reasonable flexibility are as follows:

(a) *Identical goods*—the requirement that the identical goods should be exported at or about the same time as the goods being valued could be flexibly interpreted; identical imported goods produced in a country other than the country of exportation of the goods being valued could be the basis for customs valuation; customs values of identical imported goods already determined under the provisions of Articles 5 and 6 could be used.

(b) *Similar goods*—the requirement that the similar goods should be exported at or about the same time as the goods being valued could be flexibly interpreted; similar imported goods produced in a country other than the country of exportation of the goods being valued could be the basis for customs valuation; customs values of similar imported goods already determined under the provisions of Articles 5 and 6 could be used.

(c) *Deductive method*—the requirement that the goods shall have been sold in the "condition as imported" in paragraph 1(a) of Article 5 could be flexibly interpreted; the "90 days" requirement could be administered flexibly.

Note to Article 8

Paragraph 1(a)(i)

The term "buying commissions" means fees paid by an importer to the importer's agent for the service of representing the importer abroad in the purchase of the goods being valued.

Paragraph 1(b)(ii)

1.   There are two factors involved in the apportionment of the elements specified in paragraph 1(b)(ii) of Article 8 to the imported goods—the value of the element itself and the way in which that value is to be apportioned to the imported goods. The apportionment of these elements should be made in a reasonable manner appropriate to the circumstances and in accordance with generally accepted accounting principles.

2.   Concerning the value of the element, if the importer acquires the element from a seller not related to the importer at a given cost, the value of the element is that cost. If the element was produced by the importer or by a person related to the importer, its value would be the cost of producing it. If the element had been previously used by the importer, regardless of whether it had been acquired or produced by such importer, the original cost of acquisition or production would have to be adjusted downward to reflect its use in order to arrive at the value of the element.

3.   Once a value has been determined for the element, it is necessary to apportion that value to the imported goods. Various possibilities exist. For example, the value might be apportioned to the first shipment if the importer wishes to pay duty on the entire value at one time. As another example, the importer may request that the value be apportioned over the number of units

produced up to the time of the first shipment. As a further example, the importer may request that the value be apportioned over the entire anticipated production where contracts or firm commitments exist for that production. The method of apportionment used will depend upon the documentation provided by the importer.

4. As an illustration of the above, an importer provides the producer with a mould to be used in the production of the imported goods and contracts with the producer to buy 10,000 units. By the time of arrival of the first shipment of 1,000 units, the producer has already produced 4,000 units. The importer may request the customs administration to apportion the value of the mould over 1,000 units, 4,000 units or 10,000 units.

Paragraph 1(b)(iv)

1. Additions for the elements specified in paragraph 1(b)(iv) of Article 8 should be based on objective and quantifiable data. In order to minimize the burden for both the importer and customs administration in determining the values to be added, data readily available in the buyer's commercial record system should be used in so far as possible.

2. For those elements supplied by the buyer which were purchased or leased by the buyer, the addition would be the cost of the purchase or the lease. No addition shall be made for those elements available in the public domain, other than the cost of obtaining copies of them.

3. The ease with which it may be possible to calculate the values to be added will depend on a particular firm's structure and management practice, as well as its accounting methods.

4. For example, it is possible that a firm which imports a variety of products from several countries maintains the records of its design centre outside the country of importation in such a way as to show accurately the costs attributable to a given product. In such cases, a direct adjustment may appropriately be made under the provisions of Article 8.

5. In another case, a firm may carry the cost of the design centre outside the country of importation as a general overhead expense without allocation to specific products. In this instance, an appropriate adjustment could be made under the provisions of Article 8 with respect to the imported goods by apportioning total design centre costs over total production benefiting from the design centre and adding such apportioned cost on a unit basis to imports.

6. Variations in the above circumstances will, of course, require different factors to be considered in determining the proper method of allocation.

7. In cases where the production of the element in question involves a number of countries and over a period of time, the adjustment should be limited to the value actually added to that element outside the country of importation.

Paragraph 1(c)

1. The royalties and licence fees referred to in paragraph 1(c) of Article 8 may include, among other things, payments in respect to patents, trade marks and copyrights. However, the charges for the right to reproduce the imported goods in the country of importation shall not be added to the price

actually paid or payable for the imported goods in determining the customs value.

2.   Payments made by the buyer for the right to distribute or resell the imported goods shall not be added to the price actually paid or payable for the imported goods if such payments are not a condition of the sale for export to the country of importation of the imported goods.

Paragraph 3

Where objective and quantifiable data do not exist with regard to the additions required to be made under the provisions of Article 8, the transaction value cannot be determined under the provisions of Article 1. As an illustration of this, a royalty is paid on the basis of the price in a sale in the importing country of a litre of a particular product that was imported by the kilogram and made up into a solution after importation. If the royalty is based partially on the imported goods and partially on other factors which have nothing to do with the imported goods (such as when the imported goods are mixed with domestic ingredients and are no longer separately identifiable, or when the royalty cannot be distinguished from special financial arrangements between the buyer and the seller), it would be inappropriate to attempt to make an addition for the royalty. However, if the amount of this royalty is based only on the imported goods and can be readily quantified, an addition to the price actually paid or payable can be made.

Note to Article 9

For the purposes of Article 9, "time of importation" may include the time of entry for customs purposes.

Note to Article 11

1.   Article 11 provides the importer with the right to appeal against a valuation determination made by the customs administration for the goods being valued. Appeal may first be to a higher level in the customs administration, but the importer shall have the right in the final instance to appeal to the judiciary.

2.   "Without penalty" means that the importer shall not be subject to a fine or threat of fine merely because the importer chose to exercise the right of appeal. Payment of normal court costs and lawyers' fees shall not be considered to be a fine.

3.   However, nothing in Article 11 shall prevent a Member from requiring full payment of assessed customs duties prior to an appeal.

Note to Article 15

Paragraph 4

For the purposes of Article 15, the term "persons" includes a legal person, where appropriate.

Paragraph 4(e)

For the purposes of this Agreement, one person shall be deemed to control another when the former is legally or operationally in a position to exercise restraint or direction over the latter.

ANNEX II
TECHNICAL COMMITTEE ON CUSTOMS VALUATION

1. In accordance with Article 18 of this Agreement, the Technical Committee shall be established under the auspices of the CCC with a view to ensuring, at the technical level, uniformity in interpretation and application of this Agreement.

2. The responsibilities of the Technical Committee shall include the following:

(a) to examine specific technical problems arising in the day-to-day administration of the customs valuation system of Members and to give advisory opinions on appropriate solutions based upon the facts presented;

(b) to study, as requested, valuation laws, procedures and practices as they relate to this Agreement and to prepare reports on the results of such studies;

(c) to prepare and circulate annual reports on the technical aspects of the operation and status of this Agreement;

(d) to furnish such information and advice on any matters concerning the valuation of imported goods for customs purposes as may be requested by any Member or the Committee. Such information and advice may take the form of advisory opinions, commentaries or explanatory notes;

(e) to facilitate, as requested, technical assistance to Members with a view to furthering the international acceptance of this Agreement;

(f) to carry out an examination of a matter referred to it by a panel under Article 19 of this Agreement; and

(g) to exercise such other responsibilities as the Committee may assign to it.

General

3. The Technical Committee shall attempt to conclude its work on specific matters, especially those referred to it by Members, the Committee or a panel, in a reasonably short period of time. As provided in paragraph 4 of Article 19, a panel shall set a specific time period for receipt of a report of the Technical Committee and the Technical Committee shall provide its report within that period.

4. The Technical Committee shall be assisted as appropriate in its activities by the CCC Secretariat.

Representation

5. Each Member shall have the right to be represented on the Technical Committee. Each Member may nominate one delegate and one or more alternates to be its representatives on the Technical Committee. Such a Member so represented on the Technical Committee is referred to in this Annex as a "member of the Technical Committee". Representatives of members of the Technical Committee may be assisted by advisers. The WTO Secretariat may also attend such meetings with observer status.

6. Members of the CCC which are not Members of the WTO may be represented at meetings of the Technical Committee by one delegate and one or more alternates. Such representatives shall attend meetings of the Technical Committee as observers.

7. Subject to the approval of the Chairman of the Technical Committee, the Secretary–General of the CCC (referred to in this Annex as "the Secretary–General") may invite representatives of governments which are neither Members of the WTO nor members of the CCC and representatives of international governmental and trade organizations to attend meetings of the Technical Committee as observers.

8. Nominations of delegates, alternates and advisers to meetings of the Technical Committee shall be made to the Secretary–General.

Technical Committee Meetings

9. The Technical Committee shall meet as necessary but at least two times a year. The date of each meeting shall be fixed by the Technical Committee at its preceding session. The date of the meeting may be varied either at the request of any member of the Technical Committee concurred in by a simple majority of the members of the Technical Committee or, in cases requiring urgent attention, at the request of the Chairman. Notwithstanding the provisions in sentence 1 of this paragraph, the Technical Committee shall meet as necessary to consider matters referred to it by a panel under the provisions of Article 19 of this Agreement.

10. The meetings of the Technical Committee shall be held at the headquarters of the CCC unless otherwise decided.

11. The Secretary–General shall inform all members of the Technical Committee and those included under paragraphs 6 and 7 at least 30 days in advance, except in urgent cases, of the opening date of each session of the Technical Committee.

Agenda

12. A provisional agenda for each session shall be drawn up by the Secretary–General and circulated to the members of the Technical Committee and to those included under paragraphs 6 and 7 at least 30 days in advance of the session, except in urgent cases. This agenda shall comprise all items whose inclusion has been approved by the Technical Committee during its preceding session, all items included by the Chairman on the Chairman's own initiative, and all items whose inclusion has been requested by the Secretary–General, by the Committee or by any member of the Technical Committee.

13. The Technical Committee shall determine its agenda at the opening of each session. During the session the agenda may be altered at any time by the Technical Committee.

Officers and Conduct of Business

14. The Technical Committee shall elect from among the delegates of its members a Chairman and one or more Vice–Chairmen. The Chairman and Vice–Chairmen shall each hold office for a period of one year. The retiring Chairman and Vice–Chairmen are eligible for re-election. The mandate of a

Chairman or Vice–Chairman who no longer represents a member of the Technical Committee shall terminate automatically.

15. If the Chairman is absent from any meeting or part thereof, a Vice–Chairman shall preside. In that event, the latter shall have the same powers and duties as the Chairman.

16. The Chairman of the meeting shall participate in the proceedings of the Technical Committee as such and not as the representative of a member of the Technical Committee.

17. In addition to exercising the other powers conferred upon the Chairman by these rules, the Chairman shall declare the opening and closing of each meeting, direct the discussion, accord the right to speak, and, pursuant to these rules, have control of the proceedings. The Chairman may also call a speaker to order if the speaker's remarks are not relevant.

18. During discussion of any matter a delegation may raise a point of order. In this event, the Chairman shall immediately state a ruling. If this ruling is challenged, the Chairman shall submit it to the meeting for decision and it shall stand unless overruled.

19. The Secretary–General, or officers of the CCC Secretariat designated by the Secretary–General, shall perform the secretarial work of meetings of the Technical Committee.

Quorum and Voting

20. Representatives of a simple majority of the members of the Technical Committee shall constitute a quorum.

21. Each member of the Technical Committee shall have one vote. A decision of the Technical Committee shall be taken by a majority comprising at least two thirds of the members present. Regardless of the outcome of the vote on a particular matter, the Technical Committee shall be free to make a full report to the Committee and to the CCC on that matter indicating the different views expressed in the relevant discussions. Notwithstanding the above provisions of this paragraph, on matters referred to it by a panel, the Technical Committee shall take decisions by consensus. Where no agreement is reached in the Technical Committee on the question referred to it by a panel, the Technical Committee shall provide a report detailing the facts of the matter and indicating the views of the members.

Languages and Records

22. The official languages of the Technical Committee shall be English, French and Spanish. Speeches or statements made in any of these three languages shall be immediately translated into the other official languages unless all delegations agree to dispense with translation. Speeches or statements made in any other language shall be translated into English, French and Spanish, subject to the same conditions, but in that event the delegation concerned shall provide the translation into English, French or Spanish. Only English, French and Spanish shall be used for the official documents of the Technical Committee. Memoranda and correspondence for the consideration of the Technical Committee must be presented in one of the official languages.

23.   The Technical Committee shall draw up a report of all its sessions and, if the Chairman considers it necessary, minutes or summary records of its meetings. The Chairman or a designee of the Chairman shall report on the work of the Technical Committee at each meeting of the Committee and at each meeting of the CCC.

ANNEX III

1.   The five-year delay in the application of the provisions of the Agreement by developing country Members provided for in paragraph 1 of Article 20 may, in practice, be insufficient for certain developing country Members. In such cases a developing country Member may request before the end of the period referred to in paragraph 1 of Article 20 an extension of such period, it being understood that the Members will give sympathetic consideration to such a request in cases where the developing country Member in question can show good cause.

2.   Developing countries which currently value goods on the basis of officially established minimum values may wish to make a reservation to enable them to retain such values on a limited and transitional basis under such terms and conditions as may be agreed to by the Members.

3.   Developing countries which consider that the reversal of the sequential order at the request of the importer provided for in Article 4 of the Agreement may give rise to real difficulties for them may wish to make a reservation to Article 4 in the following terms:

"The Government of _____ reserves the right to provide that the relevant provision of Article 4 of the Agreement shall apply only when the customs authorities agree to the request to reverse the order of Articles 5 and 6."

If developing countries make such a reservation, the Members shall consent to it under Article 21 of the Agreement.

4.   Developing countries may wish to make a reservation with respect to paragraph 2 of Article 5 of the Agreement in the following terms:

"The Government of _____ reserves the right to provide that paragraph 2 of Article 5 of the Agreement shall be applied in accordance with the provisions of the relevant note thereto whether or not the importer so requests."

If developing countries make such a reservation, the Members shall consent to it under Article 21 of the Agreement.

5.   Certain developing countries may have problems in the implementation of Article 1 of the Agreement insofar as it relates to importations into their countries by sole agents, sole distributors and sole concessionaires. If such problems arise in practice in developing country Members applying the Agreement, a study of this question shall be made, at the request of such Members, with a view to finding appropriate solutions.

6.   Article 17 recognizes that in applying the Agreement, customs administrations may need to make enquiries concerning the truth or accuracy of any statement, document or declaration presented to them for customs valuation purposes. The Article thus acknowledges that enquiries may be made which

are, for example, aimed at verifying that the elements of value declared or presented to customs in connection with a determination of customs value are complete and correct. Members, subject to their national laws and procedures, have the right to expect the full cooperation of importers in these enquiries.

7. The price actually paid or payable includes all payments actually made or to be made as a condition of sale of the imported goods, by the buyer to the seller, or by the buyer to a third party to satisfy an obligation of the seller.

Item 11

AGREEMENT ON PRESHIPMENT INSPECTION

Members,

Noting that Ministers on 20 September 1986 agreed that the Uruguay Round of Multilateral Trade Negotiations shall aim to "bring about further liberalization and expansion of world trade", "strengthen the role of GATT" and "increase the responsiveness of the GATT system to the evolving international economic environment";

Noting that a number of developing country Members have recourse to preshipment inspection;

Recognizing the need of developing countries to do so for as long and in so far as it is necessary to verify the quality, quantity or price of imported goods;

Mindful that such programmes must be carried out without giving rise to unnecessary delays or unequal treatment;

Noting that this inspection is by definition carried out on the territory of exporter Members;

Recognizing the need to establish an agreed international framework of rights and obligations of both user Members and exporter Members;

Recognizing that the principles and obligations of GATT 1994 apply to those activities of preshipment inspection entities that are mandated by governments that are Members of the WTO;

Recognizing that it is desirable to provide transparency of the operation of preshipment inspection entities and of laws and regulations relating to preshipment inspection;

Desiring to provide for the speedy, effective and equitable resolution of disputes between exporters and preshipment inspection entities arising under this Agreement;

Hereby *agree* as follows:

Article 1

Coverage—Definitions

1.   This Agreement shall apply to all preshipment inspection activities carried out on the territory of Members, whether such activities are contracted or mandated by the government, or any government body, of a Member.

2.   The term "user Member" means a Member of which the government or any government body contracts for or mandates the use of preshipment inspection activities.

3.   Preshipment inspection activities are all activities relating to the verification of the quality, the quantity, the price, including currency ex-

change rate and financial terms, and/or the customs classification of goods to be exported to the territory of the user Member.

4.   The term "preshipment inspection entity" is any entity contracted or mandated by a Member to carry out preshipment inspection activities.[1]

Article 2
Obligations of User Members

Non-discrimination

1.   User Members shall ensure that preshipment inspection activities are carried out in a non-discriminatory manner, and that the procedures and criteria employed in the conduct of these activities are objective and are applied on an equal basis to all exporters affected by such activities.   They shall ensure uniform performance of inspection by all the inspectors of the preshipment inspection entities contracted or mandated by them.

Governmental Requirements

2.   User Members shall ensure that in the course of preshipment inspection activities relating to their laws, regulations and requirements, the provisions of paragraph 4 of Article III of GATT 1994 are respected to the extent that these are relevant.

Site of Inspection

3.   User Members shall ensure that all preshipment inspection activities, including the issuance of a Clean Report of Findings or a note of non-issuance, are performed in the customs territory from which the goods are exported or, if the inspection cannot be carried out in that customs territory given the complex nature of the products involved, or if both parties agree, in the customs territory in which the goods are manufactured.

Standards

4.   User Members shall ensure that quantity and quality inspections are performed in accordance with the standards defined by the seller and the buyer in the purchase agreement and that, in the absence of such standards, relevant international standards [2] apply.

Transparency

5.   User Members shall ensure that preshipment inspection activities are conducted in a transparent manner.

6.   User Members shall ensure that, when initially contacted by exporters, preshipment inspection entities provide to the exporters a list of all the information which is necessary for the exporters to comply with inspection requirements.   The preshipment inspection entities shall provide the actual information when so requested by exporters.   This information shall include a reference to the laws and regulations of user Members relating to preship-

---

1. It is understood that this provision does not obligate Members to allow government entities of other Members to conduct preshipment inspection activities on their territory.

2. An international standard is a standard adopted by a governmental or non-governmental body whose membership is open to all Members, one of whose recognized activities is in the field of standardization.

ment inspection activities, and shall also include the procedures and criteria used for inspection and for price and currency exchange-rate verification purposes, the exporters' rights vis-à-vis the inspection entities, and the appeals procedures set up under paragraph 21. Additional procedural requirements or changes in existing procedures shall not be applied to a shipment unless the exporter concerned is informed of these changes at the time the inspection date is arranged. However, in emergency situations of the types addressed by Articles XX and XXI of GATT 1994, such additional requirements or changes may be applied to a shipment before the exporter has been informed. This assistance shall not, however, relieve exporters from their obligations in respect of compliance with the import regulations of the user Members.

7. User Members shall ensure that the information referred to in paragraph 6 is made available to exporters in a convenient manner, and that the preshipment inspection offices maintained by preshipment inspection entities serve as information points where this information is available.

8. User Members shall publish promptly all applicable laws and regulations relating to preshipment inspection activities in such a manner as to enable other governments and traders to become acquainted with them.

Protection of Confidential Business Information

9. User Members shall ensure that preshipment inspection entities treat all information received in the course of the preshipment inspection as business confidential to the extent that such information is not already published, generally available to third parties, or otherwise in the public domain. User Members shall ensure that preshipment inspection entities maintain procedures to this end.

10. User Members shall provide information to Members on request on the measures they are taking to give effect to paragraph 9. The provisions of this paragraph shall not require any Member to disclose confidential information the disclosure of which would jeopardize the effectiveness of the preshipment inspection programmes or would prejudice the legitimate commercial interest of particular enterprises, public or private.

11. User Members shall ensure that preshipment inspection entities do not divulge confidential business information to any third party, except that preshipment inspection entities may share this information with the government entities that have contracted or mandated them. User Members shall ensure that confidential business information which they receive from preshipment inspection entities contracted or mandated by them is adequately safeguarded. Preshipment inspection entities shall share confidential business information with the governments contracting or mandating them only to the extent that such information is customarily required for letters of credit or other forms of payment or for customs, import licensing or exchange control purposes.

12. User Members shall ensure that preshipment inspection entities do not request exporters to provide information regarding:

(a) manufacturing data related to patented, licensed or undisclosed processes, or to processes for which a patent is pending;

(b) unpublished technical data other than data necessary to demonstrate compliance with technical regulations or standards;

(c) internal pricing, including manufacturing costs;

(d) profit levels;

(e) the terms of contracts between exporters and their suppliers unless it is not otherwise possible for the entity to conduct the inspection in question. In such cases, the entity shall only request the information necessary for this purpose.

13. The information referred to in paragraph 12, which preshipment inspection entities shall not otherwise request, may be released voluntarily by the exporter to illustrate a specific case.

Conflicts of Interest

14. User Members shall ensure that preshipment inspection entities, bearing in mind also the provisions on protection of confidential business information in paragraphs 9 through 13, maintain procedures to avoid conflicts of interest:

(a) between preshipment inspection entities and any related entities of the preshipment inspection entities in question, including any entities in which the latter have a financial or commercial interest or any entities which have a financial interest in the preshipment inspection entities in question, and whose shipments the preshipment inspection entities are to inspect;

(b) between preshipment inspection entities and any other entities, including other entities subject to preshipment inspection, with the exception of the government entities contracting or mandating the inspections;

(c) with divisions of preshipment inspection entities engaged in activities other than those required to carry out the inspection process.

Delays

15. User Members shall ensure that preshipment inspection entities avoid unreasonable delays in inspection of shipments. User Members shall ensure that, once a preshipment inspection entity and an exporter agree on an inspection date, the preshipment inspection entity conducts the inspection on that date unless it is rescheduled on a mutually agreed basis between the exporter and the preshipment inspection entity, or the preshipment inspection entity is prevented from doing so by the exporter or by *force majeure.*[3]

16. User Members shall ensure that, following receipt of the final documents and completion of the inspection, preshipment inspection entities, within five working days, either issue a Clean Report of Findings or provide a detailed written explanation specifying the reasons for non-issuance. User Members shall ensure that, in the latter case, preshipment inspection entities give exporters the opportunity to present their views in writing and, if

---

3. It is understood that, for the purposes of this Agreement, *"force majeure"* shall mean "irresistible compulsion or coercion, unforeseeable course of events excusing from fulfilment of contract".

exporters so request, arrange for re-inspection at the earliest mutually convenient date.

17.   User Members shall ensure that, whenever so requested by the exporters, preshipment inspection entities undertake, prior to the date of physical inspection, a preliminary verification of price and, where applicable, of currency exchange rate, on the basis of the contract between exporter and importer, the *pro forma* invoice and, where applicable, the application for import authorization.   User Members shall ensure that a price or currency exchange rate that has been accepted by a preshipment inspection entity on the basis of such preliminary verification is not withdrawn, providing the goods conform to the import documentation and/or import licence.   They shall ensure that, after a preliminary verification has taken place, preshipment inspection entities immediately inform exporters in writing either of their acceptance or of their detailed reasons for non-acceptance of the price and/or currency exchange rate.

18.   User Members shall ensure that, in order to avoid delays in payment, preshipment inspection entities send to exporters or to designated representatives of the exporters a Clean Report of Findings as expeditiously as possible.

19.   User Members shall ensure that, in the event of a clerical error in the Clean Report of Findings, preshipment inspection entities correct the error and forward the corrected information to the appropriate parties as expeditiously as possible.

Price Verification

20.   User Members shall ensure that, in order to prevent over- and under-invoicing and fraud, preshipment inspection entities conduct price verification [4] according to the following guidelines:

(a) preshipment inspection entities shall only reject a contract price agreed between an exporter and an importer if they can demonstrate that their findings of an unsatisfactory price are based on a verification process which is in conformity with the criteria set out in subparagraphs (b) through (e);

(b) the preshipment inspection entity shall base its price comparison for the verification of the export price on the price(s) of identical or similar goods offered for export from the same country of exportation at or about the same time, under competitive and comparable conditions of sale, in conformity with customary commercial practices and net of any applicable standard discounts.   Such comparison shall be based on the following:

(i) only prices providing a valid basis of comparison shall be used, taking into account the relevant economic factors pertaining to the country of importation and a country or countries used for price comparison;

---

4.   The obligations of user Members with respect to the services of preshipment inspection entities in connection with customs valuation shall be the obligations which they have accepted in GATT 1994 and the other Multilateral Trade Agreements included in Annex 1A of the WTO Agreement.

(ii) the preshipment inspection entity shall not rely upon the price of goods offered for export to different countries of importation to arbitrarily impose the lowest price upon the shipment;

(iii) the preshipment inspection entity shall take into account the specific elements listed in subparagraph (c);

(iv) at any stage in the process described above, the preshipment inspection entity shall provide the exporter with an opportunity to explain the price;

(c) when conducting price verification, preshipment inspection entities shall make appropriate allowances for the terms of the sales contract and generally applicable adjusting factors pertaining to the transaction; these factors shall include but not be limited to the commercial level and quantity of the sale, delivery periods and conditions, price escalation clauses, quality specifications, special design features, special shipping or packing specifications, order size, spot sales, seasonal influences, licence or other intellectual property fees, and services rendered as part of the contract if these are not customarily invoiced separately; they shall also include certain elements relating to the exporter's price, such as the contractual relationship between the exporter and importer;

(d) the verification of transportation charges shall relate only to the agreed price of the mode of transport in the country of exportation as indicated in the sales contract;

(e) the following shall not be used for price verification purposes:

(i) the selling price in the country of importation of goods produced in such country;

(ii) the price of goods for export from a country other than the country of exportation;

(iii) the cost of production;

(iv) arbitrary or fictitious prices or values.

Appeals Procedures

21. User Members shall ensure that preshipment inspection entities establish procedures to receive, consider and render decisions concerning grievances raised by exporters, and that information concerning such procedures is made available to exporters in accordance with the provisions of paragraphs 6 and 7. User Members shall ensure that the procedures are developed and maintained in accordance with the following guidelines:

(a) preshipment inspection entities shall designate one or more officials who shall be available during normal business hours in each city or port in which they maintain a preshipment inspection administrative office to receive, consider and render decisions on exporters' appeals or grievances;

(b) exporters shall provide in writing to the designated official(s) the facts concerning the specific transaction in question, the nature of the grievance and a suggested solution;

(c) the designated official(s) shall afford sympathetic consideration to exporters' grievances and shall render a decision as soon as possible after receipt of the documentation referred to in subparagraph (b).

Derogation

22.　By derogation to the provisions of Article 2, user Members shall provide that, with the exception of part shipments, shipments whose value is less than a minimum value applicable to such shipments as defined by the user Member shall not be inspected, except in exceptional circumstances. This minimum value shall form part of the information furnished to exporters under the provisions of paragraph 6.

Article 3
Obligations of Exporter Members

Non-discrimination

1.　Exporter Members shall ensure that their laws and regulations relating to preshipment inspection activities are applied in a non-discriminatory manner.

Transparency

2.　Exporter Members shall publish promptly all applicable laws and regulations relating to preshipment inspection activities in such a manner as to enable other governments and traders to become acquainted with them.

Technical Assistance

3.　Exporter Members shall offer to provide to user Members, if requested, technical assistance directed towards the achievement of the objectives of this Agreement on mutually agreed terms.[5]

Article 4
Independent Review Procedures

Members shall encourage preshipment inspection entities and exporters mutually to resolve their disputes. However, two working days after submission of the grievance in accordance with the provisions of paragraph 21 of Article 2, either party may refer the dispute to independent review. Members shall take such reasonable measures as may be available to them to ensure that the following procedures are established and maintained to this end:

(a) these procedures shall be administered by an independent entity constituted jointly by an organization representing preshipment inspection entities and an organization representing exporters for the purposes of this Agreement;

(b) the independent entity referred to in subparagraph (a) shall establish a list of experts as follows:

(i) a section of members nominated by an organization representing preshipment inspection entities;

---

5. It is understood that such technical assistance may be given on a bilateral, plurilateral or multilateral basis.

(ii) a section of members nominated by an organization representing exporters;

(iii) a section of independent trade experts, nominated by the independent entity referred to in subparagraph (a).

The geographical distribution of the experts on this list shall be such as to enable any disputes raised under these procedures to be dealt with expeditiously. This list shall be drawn up within two months of the entry into force of the WTO Agreement and shall be updated annually. The list shall be publicly available. It shall be notified to the Secretariat and circulated to all Members;

(c) an exporter or preshipment inspection entity wishing to raise a dispute shall contact the independent entity referred to in subparagraph (a) and request the formation of a panel. The independent entity shall be responsible for establishing a panel. This panel shall consist of three members. The members of the panel shall be chosen so as to avoid unnecessary costs and delays. The first member shall be chosen from section (i) of the above list by the preshipment inspection entity concerned, provided that this member is not affiliated to that entity. The second member shall be chosen from section (ii) of the above list by the exporter concerned, provided that this member is not affiliated to that exporter. The third member shall be chosen from section (iii) of the above list by the independent entity referred to in subparagraph (a). No objections shall be made to any independent trade expert drawn from section (iii) of the above list;

(d) the independent trade expert drawn from section (iii) of the above list shall serve as the chairman of the panel. The independent trade expert shall take the necessary decisions to ensure an expeditious settlement of the dispute by the panel, for instance, whether the facts of the case require the panelists to meet and, if so, where such a meeting shall take place, taking into account the site of the inspection in question;

(e) if the parties to the dispute so agree, one independent trade expert could be selected from section (iii) of the above list by the independent entity referred to in subparagraph (a) to review the dispute in question. This expert shall take the necessary decisions to ensure an expeditious settlement of the dispute, for instance taking into account the site of the inspection in question;

(f) the object of the review shall be to establish whether, in the course of the inspection in dispute, the parties to the dispute have complied with the provisions of this Agreement. The procedures shall be expeditious and provide the opportunity for both parties to present their views in person or in writing;

(g) decisions by a three-member panel shall be taken by majority vote. The decision on the dispute shall be rendered within eight working days of the request for independent review and be communicated to the parties to the dispute. This time-limit could be extended upon agreement by the parties to the dispute. The panel or independent trade expert shall apportion the costs, based on the merits of the case;

(h) the decision of the panel shall be binding upon the preshipment inspection entity and the exporter which are parties to the dispute.

Article 5
Notification

Members shall submit to the Secretariat copies of the laws and regulations by which they put this Agreement into force, as well as copies of any other laws and regulations relating to preshipment inspection, when the WTO Agreement enters into force with respect to the Member concerned. No changes in the laws and regulations relating to preshipment inspection shall be enforced before such changes have been officially published. They shall be notified to the Secretariat immediately after their publication. The Secretariat shall inform the Members of the availability of this information.

Article 6
Review

At the end of the second year from the date of entry into force of the WTO Agreement and every three years thereafter, the Ministerial Conference shall review the provisions, implementation and operation of this Agreement, taking into account the objectives thereof and experience gained in its operation. As a result of such review, the Ministerial Conference may amend the provisions of the Agreement.

Article 7
Consultation

Members shall consult with other Members upon request with respect to any matter affecting the operation of this Agreement. In such cases, the provisions of Article XXII of GATT 1994, as elaborated and applied by the Dispute Settlement Understanding, are applicable to this Agreement.

Article 8
Dispute Settlement

Any disputes among Members regarding the operation of this Agreement shall be subject to the provisions of Article XXIII of GATT 1994, as elaborated and applied by the Dispute Settlement Understanding.

Article 9
Final Provisions

1. Members shall take the necessary measures for the implementation of the present Agreement.

2. Members shall ensure that their laws and regulations shall not be contrary to the provisions of this Agreement.

Item 12

AGREEMENT ON RULES OF ORIGIN

Members,

Noting that Ministers on 20 September 1986 agreed that the Uruguay Round of Multilateral Trade Negotiations shall aim to "bring about further liberalization and expansion of world trade", "strengthen the role of GATT" and "increase the responsiveness of the GATT system to the evolving international economic environment";

Desiring to further the objectives of GATT 1994;

Recognizing that clear and predictable rules of origin and their application facilitate the flow of international trade;

Desiring to ensure that rules of origin themselves do not create unnecessary obstacles to trade;

Desiring to ensure that rules of origin do not nullify or impair the rights of Members under GATT 1994;

Recognizing that it is desirable to provide transparency of laws, regulations, and practices regarding rules of origin;

Desiring to ensure that rules of origin are prepared and applied in an impartial, transparent, predictable, consistent and neutral manner;

Recognizing the availability of a consultation mechanism and procedures for the speedy, effective and equitable resolution of disputes arising under this Agreement;

Desiring to harmonize and clarify rules of origin;

Hereby *agree* as follows:

PART I

DEFINITIONS AND COVERAGE

Article 1

Rules of Origin

1. For the purposes of Parts I to IV of this Agreement, rules of origin shall be defined as those laws, regulations and administrative determinations of general application applied by any Member to determine the country of origin of goods provided such rules of origin are not related to contractual or autonomous trade regimes leading to the granting of tariff preferences going beyond the application of paragraph 1 of Article I of GATT 1994.

2. Rules of origin referred to in paragraph 1 shall include all rules of origin used in non-preferential commercial policy instruments, such as in the application of: most-favoured-nation treatment under Articles I, II, III, XI and XIII of GATT 1994; anti-dumping and countervailing duties under Article VI of GATT 1994; safeguard measures under Article XIX of GATT

1994; origin marking requirements under Article IX of GATT 1994; and any discriminatory quantitative restrictions or tariff quotas. They shall also include rules of origin used for government procurement and trade statistics.[1]

PART II
DISCIPLINES TO GOVERN THE APPLICATION OF RULES OF ORIGIN
Article 2
Disciplines During the Transition Period

Until the work programme for the harmonization of rules of origin set out in Part IV is completed, Members shall ensure that:

(a) when they issue administrative determinations of general application, the requirements to be fulfilled are clearly defined. In particular:

(i) in cases where the criterion of change of tariff classification is applied, such a rule of origin, and any exceptions to the rule, must clearly specify the subheadings or headings within the tariff nomenclature that are addressed by the rule;

(ii) in cases where the ad valorem percentage criterion is applied, the method for calculating this percentage shall also be indicated in the rules of origin;

(iii) in cases where the criterion of manufacturing or processing operation is prescribed, the operation that confers origin on the good concerned shall be precisely specified;

(b) notwithstanding the measure or instrument of commercial policy to which they are linked, their rules of origin are not used as instruments to pursue trade objectives directly or indirectly;

(c) rules of origin shall not themselves create restrictive, distorting, or disruptive effects on international trade. They shall not pose unduly strict requirements or require the fulfilment of a certain condition not related to manufacturing or processing, as a prerequisite for the determination of the country of origin. However, costs not directly related to manufacturing or processing may be included for the purposes of the application of an ad valorem percentage criterion consistent with subparagraph (a);

(d) the rules of origin that they apply to imports and exports are not more stringent than the rules of origin they apply to determine whether or not a good is domestic and shall not discriminate between other Members, irrespective of the affiliation of the manufacturers of the good concerned[2];

(e) their rules of origin are administered in a consistent, uniform, impartial and reasonable manner;

(f) their rules of origin are based on a positive standard. Rules of origin that state what does not confer origin (negative standard) are

---

1. It is understood that this provision is without prejudice to those determinations made for purposes of defining "domestic industry" or "like products of domestic industry" or similar terms wherever they apply.

2. With respect to rules of origin applied for the purposes of government procurement, this provision shall not create obligations additional to those already assumed by Members under GATT 1994.

permissible as part of a clarification of a positive standard or in individual cases where a positive determination of origin is not necessary;

(g) their laws, regulations, judicial decisions and administrative rulings of general application relating to rules of origin are published as if they were subject to, and in accordance with, the provisions of paragraph 1 of Article X of GATT 1994;

(h) upon the request of an exporter, importer or any person with a justifiable cause, assessments of the origin they would accord to a good are issued as soon as possible but no later than 150 days [3] after a request for such an assessment provided that all necessary elements have been submitted. Requests for such assessments shall be accepted before trade in the good concerned begins and may be accepted at any later point in time. Such assessments shall remain valid for three years provided that the facts and conditions, including the rules of origin, under which they have been made remain comparable. Provided that the parties concerned are informed in advance, such assessments will no longer be valid when a decision contrary to the assessment is made in a review as referred to in subparagraph (j). Such assessments shall be made publicly available subject to the provisions of subparagraph (k);

(i) when introducing changes to their rules of origin or new rules of origin, they shall not apply such changes retroactively as defined in, and without prejudice to, their laws or regulations;

(j) any administrative action which they take in relation to the determination of origin is reviewable promptly by judicial, arbitral or administrative tribunals or procedures, independent of the authority issuing the determination, which can effect the modification or reversal of the determination;

(k) all information that is by nature confidential or that is provided on a confidential basis for the purpose of the application of rules of origin is treated as strictly confidential by the authorities concerned, which shall not disclose it without the specific permission of the person or government providing such information, except to the extent that it may be required to be disclosed in the context of judicial proceedings.

Article 3

Disciplines After the Transition Period

Taking into account the aim of all Members to achieve, as a result of the harmonization work programme set out in Part IV, the establishment of harmonized rules of origin, Members shall ensure, upon the implementation of the results of the harmonization work programme, that:

(a) they apply rules of origin equally for all purposes as set out in Article 1;

(b) under their rules of origin, the country to be determined as the origin of a particular good is either the country where the good has been wholly obtained or, when more than one country is concerned in the

---

3. In respect of requests made during the first year from the date of entry into force of the WTO Agreement, Members shall only be required to issue these assessments as soon as possible.

production of the good, the country where the last substantial transformation has been carried out;

(c) the rules of origin that they apply to imports and exports are not more stringent than the rules of origin they apply to determine whether or not a good is domestic and shall not discriminate between other Members, irrespective of the affiliation of the manufacturers of the good concerned;

(d) the rules of origin are administered in a consistent, uniform, impartial and reasonable manner;

(e) their laws, regulations, judicial decisions and administrative rulings of general application relating to rules of origin are published as if they were subject to, and in accordance with, the provisions of paragraph 1 of Article X of GATT 1994;

(f) upon the request of an exporter, importer or any person with a justifiable cause, assessments of the origin they would accord to a good are issued as soon as possible but no later than 150 days after a request for such an assessment provided that all necessary elements have been submitted. Requests for such assessments shall be accepted before trade in the good concerned begins and may be accepted at any later point in time. Such assessments shall remain valid for three years provided that the facts and conditions, including the rules of origin, under which they have been made remain comparable. Provided that the parties concerned are informed in advance, such assessments will no longer be valid when a decision contrary to the assessment is made in a review as referred to in subparagraph (h). Such assessments shall be made publicly available subject to the provisions of subparagraph (i);

(g) when introducing changes to their rules of origin or new rules of origin, they shall not apply such changes retroactively as defined in, and without prejudice to, their laws or regulations;

(h) any administrative action which they take in relation to the determination of origin is reviewable promptly by judicial, arbitral or administrative tribunals or procedures, independent of the authority issuing the determination, which can effect the modification or reversal of the determination;

(i) all information which is by nature confidential or which is provided on a confidential basis for the purpose of the application of rules of origin is treated as strictly confidential by the authorities concerned, which shall not disclose it without the specific permission of the person or government providing such information, except to the extent that it may be required to be disclosed in the context of judicial proceedings.

PART III
PROCEDURAL ARRANGEMENTS ON NOTIFICATION, REVIEW, CONSULTATION AND DISPUTE SETTLEMENT

Article 4

Institutions

1. There is hereby established a Committee on Rules of Origin (referred to in this Agreement as "the Committee") composed of the representatives

from each of the Members. The Committee shall elect its own Chairman and shall meet as necessary, but not less than once a year, for the purpose of affording Members the opportunity to consult on matters relating to the operation of Parts I, II, III and IV or the furtherance of the objectives set out in these Parts and to carry out such other responsibilities assigned to it under this Agreement or by the Council for Trade in Goods. Where appropriate, the Committee shall request information and advice from the Technical Committee referred to in paragraph 2 on matters related to this Agreement. The Committee may also request such other work from the Technical Committee as it considers appropriate for the furtherance of the above-mentioned objectives of this Agreement. The WTO Secretariat shall act as the secretariat to the Committee.

2.   There shall be established a Technical Committee on Rules of Origin (referred to in this Agreement as "the Technical Committee") under the auspices of the Customs Co-operation Council (CCC) as set out in Annex I. The Technical Committee shall carry out the technical work called for in Part IV and prescribed in Annex I. Where appropriate, the Technical Committee shall request information and advice from the Committee on matters related to this Agreement. The Technical Committee may also request such other work from the Committee as it considers appropriate for the furtherance of the above-mentioned objectives of the Agreement. The CCC Secretariat shall act as the secretariat to the Technical Committee.

Article 5

Information and Procedures for Modification and Introduction of New Rules of Origin

1.   Each Member shall provide to the Secretariat, within 90 days after the date of entry into force of the WTO Agreement for it, its rules of origin, judicial decisions, and administrative rulings of general application relating to rules of origin in effect on that date. If by inadvertence a rule of origin has not been provided, the Member concerned shall provide it immediately after this fact becomes known. Lists of information received and available with the Secretariat shall be circulated to the Members by the Secretariat.

2.   During the period referred to in Article 2, Members introducing modifications, other than *de minimis* modifications, to their rules of origin or introducing new rules of origin, which, for the purpose of this Article, shall include any rule of origin referred to in paragraph 1 and not provided to the Secretariat, shall publish a notice to that effect at least 60 days before the entry into force of the modified or new rule in such a manner as to enable interested parties to become acquainted with the intention to modify a rule of origin or to introduce a new rule of origin, unless exceptional circumstances arise or threaten to arise for a Member. In these exceptional cases, the Member shall publish the modified or new rule as soon as possible.

Article 6

Review

1.   The Committee shall review annually the implementation and operation of Parts II and III of this Agreement having regard to its objectives. The

Committee shall annually inform the Council for Trade in Goods of developments during the period covered by such reviews.

2.   The Committee shall review the provisions of Parts I, II and III and propose amendments as necessary to reflect the results of the harmonization work programme.

3.   The Committee, in cooperation with the Technical Committee, shall set up a mechanism to consider and propose amendments to the results of the harmonization work programme, taking into account the objectives and principles set out in Article 9.   This may include instances where the rules need to be made more operational or need to be updated to take into account new production processes as affected by any technological change.

Article 7

Consultation

The provisions of Article XXII of GATT 1994, as elaborated and applied by the Dispute Settlement Understanding, are applicable to this Agreement.

Article 8

Dispute Settlement

The provisions of Article XXIII of GATT 1994, as elaborated and applied by the Dispute Settlement Understanding, are applicable to this Agreement.

PART IV

HARMONIZATION OF RULES OF ORIGIN

Article 9

Objectives and Principles

1.   With the objectives of harmonizing rules of origin and, *inter alia*, providing more certainty in the conduct of world trade, the Ministerial Conference shall undertake the work programme set out below in conjunction with the CCC, on the basis of the following principles:

(a) rules of origin should be applied equally for all purposes as set out in Article 1;

(b) rules of origin should provide for the country to be determined as the origin of a particular good to be either the country where the good has been wholly obtained or, when more than one country is concerned in the production of the good, the country where the last substantial transformation has been carried out;

(c) rules of origin should be objective, understandable and predictable;

(d) notwithstanding the measure or instrument to which they may be linked, rules of origin should not be used as instruments to pursue trade objectives directly or indirectly.   They should not themselves create restrictive, distorting or disruptive effects on international trade.   They should not pose unduly strict requirements or require the fulfilment of a certain condition not relating to manufacturing or processing as a prerequisite for the determination of the country of origin.   However, costs not directly related to manufacturing or processing may be included for purposes of the application of an ad valorem percentage criterion;

(e) rules of origin should be administrable in a consistent, uniform, impartial and reasonable manner;

(f) rules of origin should be coherent;

(g) rules of origin should be based on a positive standard. Negative standards may be used to clarify a positive standard.

Work Programme

2. (a) The work programme shall be initiated as soon after the entry into force of the WTO Agreement as possible and will be completed within three years of initiation.

(b) The Committee and the Technical Committee provided for in Article 4 shall be the appropriate bodies to conduct this work.

(c) To provide for detailed input by the CCC, the Committee shall request the Technical Committee to provide its interpretations and opinions resulting from the work described below on the basis of the principles listed in paragraph 1. To ensure timely completion of the work programme for harmonization, such work shall be conducted on a product sector basis, as represented by various chapters or sections of the Harmonized System (HS) nomenclature.

(i) *Wholly Obtained and Minimal Operations or Processes*

The Technical Committee shall develop harmonized definitions of:

— the goods that are to be considered as being wholly obtained in one country. This work shall be as detailed as possible;

— minimal operations or processes that do not by themselves confer origin to a good.

The results of this work shall be submitted to the Committee within three months of receipt of the request from the Committee.

(ii) *Substantial Transformation—Change in Tariff Classification*

— The Technical Committee shall consider and elaborate upon, on the basis of the criterion of substantial transformation, the use of change in tariff subheading or heading when developing rules of origin for particular products or a product sector and, if appropriate, the minimum change within the nomenclature that meets this criterion.

— The Technical Committee shall divide the above work on a product basis taking into account the chapters or sections of the HS nomenclature, so as to submit results of its work to the Committee at least on a quarterly basis. The Technical Committee shall complete the above work within one year and three months from receipt of the request of the Committee.

(iii) *Substantial Transformation—Supplementary Criteria*

Upon completion of the work under subparagraph (ii) for each product sector or individual product category where the exclusive use of the HS nomenclature does not allow for the expression of substantial transformation, the Technical Committee:

— shall consider and elaborate upon, on the basis of the criterion of substantial transformation, the use, in a supplementary or exclusive manner, of other requirements, including ad valorem percentages [4] and/or manufacturing or processing operations [5], when developing rules of origin for particular products or a product sector;

— may provide explanations for its proposals;

— shall divide the above work on a product basis taking into account the chapters or sections of the HS nomenclature, so as to submit results of its work to the Committee at least on a quarterly basis. The Technical Committee shall complete the above work within two years and three months of receipt of the request from the Committee.

Role of the Committee

3. On the basis of the principles listed in paragraph 1:

(a) the Committee shall consider the interpretations and opinions of the Technical Committee periodically in accordance with the time-frames provided in subparagraphs (i), (ii) and (iii) of paragraph 2(c) with a view to endorsing such interpretations and opinions. The Committee may request the Technical Committee to refine or elaborate its work and/or to develop new approaches. To assist the Technical Committee, the Committee should provide its reasons for requests for additional work and, as appropriate, suggest alternative approaches;

(b) upon completion of all the work identified in subparagraphs (i), (ii) and (iii) of paragraph 2(c), the Committee shall consider the results in terms of their overall coherence.

Results of the Harmonization Work Programme and Subsequent Work

4. The Ministerial Conference shall establish the results of the harmonization work programme in an annex as an integral part of this Agreement.[6] The Ministerial Conference shall establish a time-frame for the entry into force of this annex.

ANNEX I
TECHNICAL COMMITTEE ON RULES OF ORIGIN

Responsibilities

1. The ongoing responsibilities of the Technical Committee shall include the following:

4. If the ad valorem criterion is prescribed, the method for calculating this percentage shall also be indicated in the rules of origin.

5. If the criterion of manufacturing or processing operation is prescribed, the operation that confers origin on the product concerned shall be precisely specified.

6. At the same time, consideration shall be given to arrangements concerning the settlement of disputes relating to customs classification.

(a) at the request of any member of the Technical Committee, to examine specific technical problems arising in the day-to-day administration of the rules of origin of Members and to give advisory opinions on appropriate solutions based upon the facts presented;

(b) to furnish information and advice on any matters concerning the origin determination of goods as may be requested by any Member or the Committee;

(c) to prepare and circulate periodic reports on the technical aspects of the operation and status of this Agreement; and

(d) to review annually the technical aspects of the implementation and operation of Parts II and III.

2. The Technical Committee shall exercise such other responsibilities as the Committee may request of it.

3. The Technical Committee shall attempt to conclude its work on specific matters, especially those referred to it by Members or the Committee, in a reasonably short period of time.

Representation

4. Each Member shall have the right to be represented on the Technical Committee. Each Member may nominate one delegate and one or more alternates to be its representatives on the Technical Committee. Such a Member so represented on the Technical Committee is hereinafter referred to as a "member" of the Technical Committee. Representatives of members of the Technical Committee may be assisted by advisers at meetings of the Technical Committee. The WTO Secretariat may also attend such meetings with observer status.

5. Members of the CCC which are not Members of the WTO may be represented at meetings of the Technical Committee by one delegate and one or more alternates. Such representatives shall attend meetings of the Technical Committee as observers.

6. Subject to the approval of the Chairman of the Technical Committee, the Secretary–General of the CCC (referred to in this Annex as "the Secretary–General") may invite representatives of governments which are neither Members of the WTO nor members of the CCC and representatives of international governmental and trade organizations to attend meetings of the Technical Committee as observers.

7. Nominations of delegates, alternates and advisers to meetings of the Technical Committee shall be made to the Secretary–General.

Meetings

8. The Technical Committee shall meet as necessary, but not less than once a year.

Procedures

9. The Technical Committee shall elect its own Chairman and shall establish its own procedures.

ANNEX II
COMMON DECLARATION WITH REGARD TO
PREFERENTIAL RULES OF ORIGIN

1. Recognizing that some Members apply preferential rules of origin, distinct from non-preferential rules of origin, the Members hereby *agree* as follows.

2. For the purposes of this Common Declaration, preferential rules of origin shall be defined as those laws, regulations and administrative determinations of general application applied by any Member to determine whether goods qualify for preferential treatment under contractual or autonomous trade regimes leading to the granting of tariff preferences going beyond the application of paragraph 1 of Article I of GATT 1994.

3. The Members *agree* to ensure that:

(a) when they issue administrative determinations of general application, the requirements to be fulfilled are clearly defined. In particular:

(i) in cases where the criterion of change of tariff classification is applied, such a preferential rule of origin, and any exceptions to the rule, must clearly specify the subheadings or headings within the tariff nomenclature that are addressed by the rule;

(ii) in cases where the ad valorem percentage criterion is applied, the method for calculating this percentage shall also be indicated in the preferential rules of origin;

(iii) in cases where the criterion of manufacturing or processing operation is prescribed, the operation that confers preferential origin shall be precisely specified;

(b) their preferential rules of origin are based on a positive standard. Preferential rules of origin that state what does not confer preferential origin (negative standard) are permissible as part of a clarification of a positive standard or in individual cases where a positive determination of preferential origin is not necessary;

(c) their laws, regulations, judicial decisions and administrative rulings of general application relating to preferential rules of origin are published as if they were subject to, and in accordance with, the provisions of paragraph 1 of Article X of GATT 1994;

(d) upon request of an exporter, importer or any person with a justifiable cause, assessments of the preferential origin they would accord to a good are issued as soon as possible but no later than 150 days [7] after a request for such an assessment provided that all necessary elements have been submitted. Requests for such assessments shall be accepted before trade in the good concerned begins and may be accepted at any later point in time. Such assessments shall remain valid for three years provided that the facts and conditions, including the preferential rules of origin, under which they have been made remain comparable. Provided that the parties concerned are informed in advance, such assessments will no longer be valid when a decision contrary to the assessment is made in

---

7. In respect of requests made during the first year from entry into force of the WTO Agreement, Members shall only be required to issue these assessments as soon as possible.

a review as referred to in subparagraph (f). Such assessments shall be made publicly available subject to the provisions of subparagraph (g);

(e) when introducing changes to their preferential rules of origin or new preferential rules of origin, they shall not apply such changes retroactively as defined in, and without prejudice to, their laws or regulations;

(f) any administrative action which they take in relation to the determination of preferential origin is reviewable promptly by judicial, arbitral or administrative tribunals or procedures, independent of the authority issuing the determination, which can effect the modification or reversal of the determination;

(g) all information that is by nature confidential or that is provided on a confidential basis for the purpose of the application of preferential rules of origin is treated as strictly confidential by the authorities concerned, which shall not disclose it without the specific permission of the person or government providing such information, except to the extent that it may be required to be disclosed in the context of judicial proceedings.

4. Members *agree* to provide to the Secretariat promptly their preferential rules of origin, including a listing of the preferential arrangements to which they apply, judicial decisions, and administrative rulings of general application relating to their preferential rules of origin in effect on the date of entry into force of the WTO Agreement for the Member concerned. Furthermore, Members agree to provide any modifications to their preferential rules of origin or new preferential rules of origin as soon as possible to the Secretariat. Lists of information received and available with the Secretariat shall be circulated to the Members by the Secretariat.

Item 13

AGREEMENT ON IMPORT LICENSING PROCEDURES

Members,

Having regard to the Multilateral Trade Negotiations;

Desiring to further the objectives of GATT 1994;

Taking into account the particular trade, development and financial needs of developing country Members;

Recognizing the usefulness of automatic import licensing for certain purposes and that such licensing should not be used to restrict trade;

Recognizing that import licensing may be employed to administer measures such as those adopted pursuant to the relevant provisions of GATT 1994;

Recognizing the provisions of GATT 1994 as they apply to import licensing procedures;

Desiring to ensure that import licensing procedures are not utilized in a manner contrary to the principles and obligations of GATT 1994;

Recognizing that the flow of international trade could be impeded by the inappropriate use of import licensing procedures;

Convinced that import licensing, particularly non-automatic import licensing, should be implemented in a transparent and predictable manner;

Recognizing that non-automatic licensing procedures should be no more administratively burdensome than absolutely necessary to administer the relevant measure;

Desiring to simplify, and bring transparency to, the administrative procedures and practices used in international trade, and to ensure the fair and equitable application and administration of such procedures and practices;

Desiring to provide for a consultative mechanism and the speedy, effective and equitable resolution of disputes arising under this Agreement;

Hereby *agree* as follows:

Article 1

General Provisions

1. For the purpose of this Agreement, import licensing is defined as administrative procedures [1] used for the operation of import licensing regimes requiring the submission of an application or other documentation (other than that required for customs purposes) to the relevant administrative body

---

1. Those procedures referred to as "licens-ing" as well as other similar administrative procedures.

as a prior condition for importation into the customs territory of the importing Member.

2. Members shall ensure that the administrative procedures used to implement import licensing regimes are in conformity with the relevant provisions of GATT 1994 including its annexes and protocols, as interpreted by this Agreement, with a view to preventing trade distortions that may arise from an inappropriate operation of those procedures, taking into account the economic development purposes and financial and trade needs of developing country Members.[2]

3. The rules for import licensing procedures shall be neutral in application and administered in a fair and equitable manner.

4. (a) The rules and all information concerning procedures for the submission of applications, including the eligibility of persons, firms and institutions to make such applications, the administrative body(ies) to be approached, and the lists of products subject to the licensing requirement shall be published, in the sources notified to the Committee on Import Licensing provided for in Article 4 (referred to in this Agreement as "the Committee"), in such a manner as to enable governments[3] and traders to become acquainted with them. Such publication shall take place, whenever practicable, 21 days prior to the effective date of the requirement but in all events not later than such effective date. Any exception, derogations or changes in or from the rules concerning licensing procedures or the list of products subject to import licensing shall also be published in the same manner and within the same time periods as specified above. Copies of these publications shall also be made available to the Secretariat.

(b) Members which wish to make comments in writing shall be provided the opportunity to discuss these comments upon request. The concerned Member shall give due consideration to these comments and results of discussion.

5. Application forms and, where applicable, renewal forms shall be as simple as possible. Such documents and information as are considered strictly necessary for the proper functioning of the licensing regime may be required on application.

6. Application procedures and, where applicable, renewal procedures shall be as simple as possible. Applicants shall be allowed a reasonable period for the submission of licence applications. Where there is a closing date, this period should be at least 21 days with provision for extension in circumstances where insufficient applications have been received within this period. Applicants shall have to approach only one administrative body in connection with an application. Where it is strictly indispensable to approach more than one administrative body, applicants shall not need to approach more than three administrative bodies.

7. No application shall be refused for minor documentation errors which do not alter basic data contained therein. No penalty greater than necessary

---

2. Nothing in this Agreement shall be taken as implying that the basis, scope or duration of a measure being implemented by a licensing procedure is subject to question under this Agreement.

3. For the purpose of this Agreement, the term "governments" is deemed to include the competent authorities of the European Communities.

to serve merely as a warning shall be imposed in respect of any omission or mistake in documentation or procedures which is obviously made without fraudulent intent or gross negligence.

8. Licensed imports shall not be refused for minor variations in value, quantity or weight from the amount designated on the licence due to differences occurring during shipment, differences incidental to bulk loading and other minor differences consistent with normal commercial practice.

9. The foreign exchange necessary to pay for licensed imports shall be made available to licence holders on the same basis as to importers of goods not requiring import licences.

10. With regard to security exceptions, the provisions of Article XXI of GATT 1994 apply.

11. The provisions of this Agreement shall not require any Member to disclose confidential information which would impede law enforcement or otherwise be contrary to the public interest or would prejudice the legitimate commercial interests of particular enterprises, public or private.

Article 2

Automatic Import Licensing [4]

1. Automatic import licensing is defined as import licensing where approval of the application is granted in all cases, and which is in accordance with the requirements of paragraph 2(a).

2. The following provisions [5], in addition to those in paragraphs 1 through 11 of Article 1 and paragraph 1 of this Article, shall apply to automatic import licensing procedures:

(a) automatic licensing procedures shall not be administered in such a manner as to have restricting effects on imports subject to automatic licensing. Automatic licensing procedures shall be deemed to have trade-restricting effects unless, *inter alia*:

(i) any person, firm or institution which fulfils the legal requirements of the importing Member for engaging in import operations involving products subject to automatic licensing is equally eligible to apply for and to obtain import licences;

(ii) applications for licences may be submitted on any working day prior to the customs clearance of the goods;

(iii) applications for licences when submitted in appropriate and complete form are approved immediately on receipt, to the extent administratively feasible, but within a maximum of 10 working days;

(b) Members recognize that automatic import licensing may be necessary whenever other appropriate procedures are not available. Auto-

---

4. Those import licensing procedures requiring a security which have no restrictive effects on imports are to be considered as falling within the scope of paragraphs 1 and 2.

5. A developing country Member, other than a developing country Member which was a Party to the Agreement on Import Licensing Procedures done on 12 April 1979, which has specific difficulties with the requirements of subparagraphs (a)(ii) and (a)(iii) may, upon notification to the Committee, delay the application of these subparagraphs by not more than two years from the date of entry into force of the WTO Agreement for such Member.

matic import licensing may be maintained as long as the circumstances which gave rise to its introduction prevail and as long as its underlying administrative purposes cannot be achieved in a more appropriate way.

Article 3

Non-automatic Import Licensing

1. The following provisions, in addition to those in paragraphs 1 through 11 of Article 1, shall apply to non-automatic import licensing procedures. Non-automatic import licensing procedures are defined as import licensing not falling within the definition contained in paragraph 1 of Article 2.

2. Non-automatic licensing shall not have trade-restrictive or -distortive effects on imports additional to those caused by the imposition of the restriction. Non-automatic licensing procedures shall correspond in scope and duration to the measure they are used to implement, and shall be no more administratively burdensome than absolutely necessary to administer the measure.

3. In the case of licensing requirements for purposes other than the implementation of quantitative restrictions, Members shall publish sufficient information for other Members and traders to know the basis for granting and/or allocating licences.

4. Where a Member provides the possibility for persons, firms or institutions to request exceptions or derogations from a licensing requirement, it shall include this fact in the information published under paragraph 4 of Article 1 as well as information on how to make such a request and, to the extent possible, an indication of the circumstances under which requests would be considered.

5. (a) Members shall provide, upon the request of any Member having an interest in the trade in the product concerned, all relevant information concerning:

(i) the administration of the restrictions;

(ii) the import licences granted over a recent period;

(iii) the distribution of such licences among supplying countries;

(iv) where practicable, import statistics (i.e. value and/or volume) with respect to the products subject to import licensing. Developing country Members would not be expected to take additional administrative or financial burdens on this account;

(b) Members administering quotas by means of licensing shall publish the overall amount of quotas to be applied by quantity and/or value, the opening and closing dates of quotas, and any change thereof, within the time periods specified in paragraph 4 of Article 1 and in such a manner as to enable governments and traders to become acquainted with them;

(c) in the case of quotas allocated among supplying countries, the Member applying the restrictions shall promptly inform all other Members having an interest in supplying the product concerned of the shares in the quota currently allocated, by quantity or value, to the various supplying countries and shall publish this information within the time periods specified in paragraph 4 of Article 1 and in such a manner as to enable governments and traders to become acquainted with them;

(d) where situations arise which make it necessary to provide for an early opening date of quotas, the information referred to in paragraph 4 of Article 1 should be published within the time-periods specified in paragraph 4 of Article 1 and in such a manner as to enable governments and traders to become acquainted with them;

(e) any person, firm or institution which fulfils the legal and administrative requirements of the importing Member shall be equally eligible to apply and to be considered for a licence. If the licence application is not approved, the applicant shall, on request, be given the reason therefor and shall have a right of appeal or review in accordance with the domestic legislation or procedures of the importing Member;

(f) the period for processing applications shall, except when not possible for reasons outside the control of the Member, not be longer than 30 days if applications are considered as and when received, i.e. on a first-come first-served basis, and no longer than 60 days if all applications are considered simultaneously. In the latter case, the period for processing applications shall be considered to begin on the day following the closing date of the announced application period;

(g) the period of licence validity shall be of reasonable duration and not be so short as to preclude imports. The period of licence validity shall not preclude imports from distant sources, except in special cases where imports are necessary to meet unforeseen short-term requirements;

(h) when administering quotas, Members shall not prevent importation from being effected in accordance with the issued licences, and shall not discourage the full utilization of quotas;

(i) when issuing licences, Members shall take into account the desirability of issuing licences for products in economic quantities;

(j) in allocating licences, the Member should consider the import performance of the applicant. In this regard, consideration should be given as to whether licences issued to applicants in the past have been fully utilized during a recent representative period. In cases where licences have not been fully utilized, the Member shall examine the reasons for this and take these reasons into consideration when allocating new licences. Consideration shall also be given to ensuring a reasonable distribution of licences to new importers, taking into account the desirability of issuing licences for products in economic quantities. In this regard, special consideration should be given to those importers importing products originating in developing country Members and, in particular, the least-developed country Members;

(k) in the case of quotas administered through licences which are not allocated among supplying countries, licence holders [6] shall be free to choose the sources of imports. In the case of quotas allocated among supplying countries, the licence shall clearly stipulate the country or countries;

---

6. Sometimes referred to as "quota holders".

(*l*) in applying paragraph 8 of Article 1, compensating adjustments may be made in future licence allocations where imports exceeded a previous licence level.

Article 4

Institutions

There is hereby established a Committee on Import Licensing composed of representatives from each of the Members. The Committee shall elect its own Chairman and Vice–Chairman and shall meet as necessary for the purpose of affording Members the opportunity of consulting on any matters relating to the operation of this Agreement or the furtherance of its objectives.

Article 5

Notification

1. Members which institute licensing procedures or changes in these procedures shall notify the Committee of such within 60 days of publication.

2. Notifications of the institution of import licensing procedures shall include the following information:

(a) list of products subject to licensing procedures;

(b) contact point for information on eligibility;

(c) administrative body(ies) for submission of applications;

(d) date and name of publication where licensing procedures are published;

(e) indication of whether the licensing procedure is automatic or non-automatic according to definitions contained in Articles 2 and 3;

(f) in the case of automatic import licensing procedures, their administrative purpose;

(g) in the case of non-automatic import licensing procedures, indication of the measure being implemented through the licensing procedure; and

(h) expected duration of the licensing procedure if this can be estimated with some probability, and if not, reason why this information cannot be provided.

3. Notifications of changes in import licensing procedures shall indicate the elements mentioned above, if changes in such occur.

4. Members shall notify the Committee of the publication(s) in which the information required in paragraph 4 of Article 1 will be published.

5. Any interested Member which considers that another Member has not notified the institution of a licensing procedure or changes therein in accordance with the provisions of paragraphs 1 through 3 may bring the matter to the attention of such other Member. If notification is not made promptly thereafter, such Member may itself notify the licensing procedure or changes therein, including all relevant and available information.

Article 6

Consultation and Dispute Settlement

Consultations and the settlement of disputes with respect to any matter affecting the operation of this Agreement shall be subject to the provisions of Articles XXII and XXIII of GATT 1994, as elaborated and applied by the Dispute Settlement Understanding.

Article 7

Review

1.   The Committee shall review as necessary, but at least once every two years, the implementation and operation of this Agreement, taking into account the objectives thereof, and the rights and obligations contained therein.

2.   As a basis for the Committee review, the Secretariat shall prepare a factual report based on information provided under Article 5, responses to the annual questionnaire on import licensing procedures [7] and other relevant reliable information which is available to it.   This report shall provide a synopsis of the aforementioned information, in particular indicating any changes or developments during the period under review, and including any other information as agreed by the Committee.

3.   Members undertake to complete the annual questionnaire on import licensing procedures promptly and in full.

4.   The Committee shall inform the Council for Trade in Goods of developments during the period covered by such reviews.

Article 8

Final Provisions

Reservations

1.   Reservations may not be entered in respect of any of the provisions of this Agreement without the consent of the other Members.

Domestic Legislation

2.   (a) Each Member shall ensure, not later than the date of entry into force of the WTO Agreement for it, the conformity of its laws, regulations and administrative procedures with the provisions of this Agreement.

(b) Each Member shall inform the Committee of any changes in its laws and regulations relevant to this Agreement and in the administration of such laws and regulations.

---

7. Originally circulated as GATT 1947 document L/3515 of 23 March 1971.

Item 14

AGREEMENT ON SUBSIDIES AND COUNTERVAILING MEASURES

Members hereby *agree* as follows:

PART I: GENERAL PROVISIONS

Article 1

Definition of a Subsidy

1.1 For the purpose of this Agreement, a subsidy shall be deemed to exist if:

(a) (1) there is a financial contribution by a government or any public body within the territory of a Member (referred to in this Agreement as "government"), i.e. where:

(i) a government practice involves a direct transfer of funds (e.g. grants, loans, and equity infusion), potential direct transfers of funds or liabilities (e.g. loan guarantees);

(ii) government revenue that is otherwise due is foregone or not collected (e.g. fiscal incentives such as tax credits)[1];

(iii) a government provides goods or services other than general infrastructure, or purchases goods;

(iv) a government makes payments to a funding mechanism, or entrusts or directs a private body to carry out one or more of the type of functions illustrated in (i) to (iii) above which would normally be vested in the government and the practice, in no real sense, differs from practices normally followed by governments;

or

(a) (2) there is any form of income or price support in the sense of Article XVI of GATT 1994;

and

(b) a benefit is thereby conferred.

1.2 A subsidy as defined in paragraph 1 shall be subject to the provisions of Part II or shall be subject to the provisions of Part III or V only if such a subsidy is specific in accordance with the provisions of Article 2.

---

1. In accordance with the provisions of Article XVI of GATT 1994 (Note to Article XVI) and the provisions of Annexes I through III of this Agreement, the exemption of an exported product from duties or taxes borne by the like product when destined for domestic consumption, or the remission of such duties or taxes in amounts not in excess of those which have accrued, shall not be deemed to be a subsidy.

Article 2

Specificity

2.1   In order to determine whether a subsidy, as defined in paragraph 1 of Article 1, is specific to an enterprise or industry or group of enterprises or industries (referred to in this Agreement as "certain enterprises") within the jurisdiction of the granting authority, the following principles shall apply:

(a) Where the granting authority, or the legislation pursuant to which the granting authority operates, explicitly limits access to a subsidy to certain enterprises, such subsidy shall be specific.

(b) Where the granting authority, or the legislation pursuant to which the granting authority operates, establishes objective criteria or conditions[2] governing the eligibility for, and the amount of, a subsidy, specificity shall not exist, provided that the eligibility is automatic and that such criteria and conditions are strictly adhered to. The criteria or conditions must be clearly spelled out in law, regulation, or other official document, so as to be capable of verification.

(c) If, notwithstanding any appearance of non-specificity resulting from the application of the principles laid down in subparagraphs (a) and (b), there are reasons to believe that the subsidy may in fact be specific, other factors may be considered. Such factors are: use of a subsidy programme by a limited number of certain enterprises, predominant use by certain enterprises, the granting of disproportionately large amounts of subsidy to certain enterprises, and the manner in which discretion has been exercised by the granting authority in the decision to grant a subsidy.[3] In applying this subparagraph, account shall be taken of the extent of diversification of economic activities within the jurisdiction of the granting authority, as well as of the length of time during which the subsidy programme has been in operation.

2.2   A subsidy which is limited to certain enterprises located within a designated geographical region within the jurisdiction of the granting authority shall be specific. It is understood that the setting or change of generally applicable tax rates by all levels of government entitled to do so shall not be deemed to be a specific subsidy for the purposes of this Agreement.

2.3   Any subsidy falling under the provisions of Article 3 shall be deemed to be specific.

2.4   Any determination of specificity under the provisions of this Article shall be clearly substantiated on the basis of positive evidence.

PART II: PROHIBITED SUBSIDIES

Article 3

Prohibition

3.1   Except as provided in the Agreement on Agriculture, the following subsidies, within the meaning of Article 1, shall be prohibited:

2. Objective criteria or conditions, as used herein, mean criteria or conditions which are neutral, which do not favour certain enterprises over others, and which are economic in nature and horizontal in application, such as number of employees or size of enterprise.

3. In this regard, in particular, information on the frequency with which applications for a subsidy are refused or approved and the reasons for such decisions shall be considered.

(a) subsidies contingent, in law or in fact[4], whether solely or as one of several other conditions, upon export performance, including those illustrated in Annex I[5];

(b) subsidies contingent, whether solely or as one of several other conditions, upon the use of domestic over imported goods.

3.2   A Member shall neither grant nor maintain subsidies referred to in paragraph 1.

Article 4
Remedies

4.1   Whenever a Member has reason to believe that a prohibited subsidy is being granted or maintained by another Member, such Member may request consultations with such other Member.

4.2   A request for consultations under paragraph 1 shall include a statement of available evidence with regard to the existence and nature of the subsidy in question.

4.3   Upon request for consultations under paragraph 1, the Member believed to be granting or maintaining the subsidy in question shall enter into such consultations as quickly as possible. The purpose of the consultations shall be to clarify the facts of the situation and to arrive at a mutually agreed solution.

4.4   If no mutually agreed solution has been reached within 30 days[6] of the request for consultations, any Member party to such consultations may refer the matter to the Dispute Settlement Body ("DSB") for the immediate establishment of a panel, unless the DSB decides by consensus not to establish a panel.

4.5   Upon its establishment, the panel may request the assistance of the Permanent Group of Experts[7] (referred to in this Agreement as the "PGE") with regard to whether the measure in question is a prohibited subsidy. If so requested, the PGE shall immediately review the evidence with regard to the existence and nature of the measure in question and shall provide an opportunity for the Member applying or maintaining the measure to demonstrate that the measure in question is not a prohibited subsidy. The PGE shall report its conclusions to the panel within a time-limit determined by the panel. The PGE's conclusions on the issue of whether or not the measure in question is a prohibited subsidy shall be accepted by the panel without modification.

4.6   The panel shall submit its final report to the parties to the dispute. The report shall be circulated to all Members within 90 days of the date of the composition and the establishment of the panel's terms of reference.

4. This standard is met when the facts demonstrate that the granting of a subsidy, without having been made legally contingent upon export performance, is in fact tied to actual or anticipated exportation or export earnings. The mere fact that a subsidy is granted to enterprises which export shall not for that reason alone be considered to be an export subsidy within the meaning of this provision.

5. Measures referred to in Annex I as not constituting export subsidies shall not be prohibited under this or any other provision of this Agreement.

6. Any time-periods mentioned in this Article may be extended by mutual agreement.

7. As established in Article 24.

4.7   If the measure in question is found to be a prohibited subsidy, the panel shall recommend that the subsidizing Member withdraw the subsidy without delay. In this regard, the panel shall specify in its recommendation the time-period within which the measure must be withdrawn.

4.8   Within 30 days of the issuance of the panel's report to all Members, the report shall be adopted by the DSB unless one of the parties to the dispute formally notifies the DSB of its decision to appeal or the DSB decides by consensus not to adopt the report.

4.9   Where a panel report is appealed, the Appellate Body shall issue its decision within 30 days from the date when the party to the dispute formally notifies its intention to appeal. When the Appellate Body considers that it cannot provide its report within 30 days, it shall inform the DSB in writing of the reasons for the delay together with an estimate of the period within which it will submit its report. In no case shall the proceedings exceed 60 days. The appellate report shall be adopted by the DSB and unconditionally accepted by the parties to the dispute unless the DSB decides by consensus not to adopt the appellate report within 20 days following its issuance to the Members.[8]

4.10   In the event the recommendation of the DSB is not followed within the time-period specified by the panel, which shall commence from the date of adoption of the panel's report or the Appellate Body's report, the DSB shall grant authorization to the complaining Member to take appropriate[9] counter-measures, unless the DSB decides by consensus to reject the request.

4.11   In the event a party to the dispute requests arbitration under paragraph 6 of Article 22 of the Dispute Settlement Understanding ("DSU"), the arbitrator shall determine whether the countermeasures are appropriate.[10]

4.12   For purposes of disputes conducted pursuant to this Article, except for time-periods specifically prescribed in this Article, time-periods applicable under the DSU for the conduct of such disputes shall be half the time prescribed therein.

PART III: ACTIONABLE SUBSIDIES

Article 5

Adverse Effects

No Member should cause, through the use of any subsidy referred to in paragraphs 1 and 2 of Article 1, adverse effects to the interests of other Members, i.e.:

(a) injury to the domestic industry of another Member[11];

(b) nullification or impairment of benefits accruing directly or indirectly to other Members under GATT 1994 in particular the benefits of concessions bound under Article II of GATT 1994[12];

8.   If a meeting of the DSB is not scheduled during this period, such a meeting shall be held for this purpose.

9.   This expression is not meant to allow countermeasures that are disproportionate in light of the fact that the subsidies dealt with under these provisions are prohibited.

10.   This expression is not meant to allow countermeasures that are disproportionate in light of the fact that the subsidies dealt with under these provisions are prohibited.

11.   The term "injury to the domestic industry" is used here in the same sense as it is used in Part V.

12.   The term "nullification or impairment" is used in this Agreement in the same sense as it is used in the relevant provisions of GATT 1994, and the existence of such nullification or

(c) serious prejudice to the interests of another Member.[13]

This Article does not apply to subsidies maintained on agricultural products as provided in Article 13 of the Agreement on Agriculture.

Article 6 [Ed. Note: See Article 31]

Serious Prejudice

6.1 Serious prejudice in the sense of paragraph (c) of Article 5 shall be deemed to exist in the case of:

(a) the total ad valorem subsidization[14] of a product exceeding 5 per cent[15];

(b) subsidies to cover operating losses sustained by an industry;

(c) subsidies to cover operating losses sustained by an enterprise, other than one-time measures which are non-recurrent and cannot be repeated for that enterprise and which are given merely to provide time for the development of long-term solutions and to avoid acute social problems;

(d) direct forgiveness of debt, i.e. forgiveness of government-held debt, and grants to cover debt repayment.[16]

6.2 Notwithstanding the provisions of paragraph 1, serious prejudice shall not be found if the subsidizing Member demonstrates that the subsidy in question has not resulted in any of the effects enumerated in paragraph 3.

6.3 Serious prejudice in the sense of paragraph (c) of Article 5 may arise in any case where one or several of the following apply:

(a) the effect of the subsidy is to displace or impede the imports of a like product of another Member into the market of the subsidizing Member;

(b) the effect of the subsidy is to displace or impede the exports of a like product of another Member from a third country market;

(c) the effect of the subsidy is a significant price undercutting by the subsidized product as compared with the price of a like product of another Member in the same market or significant price suppression, price depression or lost sales in the same market;

(d) the effect of the subsidy is an increase in the world market share of the subsidizing Member in a particular subsidized primary product or commodity[17] as compared to the average share it had during the previous

---

impairment shall be established in accordance with the practice of application of these provisions.

13. The term "serious prejudice to the interests of another Member" is used in this Agreement in the same sense as it is used in paragraph 1 of Article XVI of GATT 1994, and includes threat of serious prejudice.

14. The total ad valorem subsidization shall be calculated in accordance with the provisions of Annex IV.

15. Since it is anticipated that civil aircraft will be subject to specific multilateral rules, the threshold in this subparagraph does not apply to civil aircraft.

16. Members recognize that where royalty-based financing for a civil aircraft programme is not being fully repaid due to the level of actual sales falling below the level of forecast sales, this does not in itself constitute serious prejudice for the purposes of this subparagraph.

17. Unless other multilaterally agreed specific rules apply to the trade in the product or commodity in question.

period of three years and this increase follows a consistent trend over a period when subsidies have been granted.

6.4   For the purpose of paragraph 3(b), the displacement or impeding of exports shall include any case in which, subject to the provisions of paragraph 7, it has been demonstrated that there has been a change in relative shares of the market to the disadvantage of the non-subsidized like product (over an appropriately representative period sufficient to demonstrate clear trends in the development of the market for the product concerned, which, in normal circumstances, shall be at least one year). "Change in relative shares of the market" shall include any of the following situations: *(a)* there is an increase in the market share of the subsidized product; *(b)* the market share of the subsidized product remains constant in circumstances in which, in the absence of the subsidy, it would have declined; *(c)* the market share of the subsidized product declines, but at a slower rate than would have been the case in the absence of the subsidy.

6.5   For the purpose of paragraph 3(c), price undercutting shall include any case in which such price undercutting has been demonstrated through a comparison of prices of the subsidized product with prices of a non-subsidized like product supplied to the same market. The comparison shall be made at the same level of trade and at comparable times, due account being taken of any other factor affecting price comparability. However, if such a direct comparison is not possible, the existence of price undercutting may be demonstrated on the basis of export unit values.

6.6   Each Member in the market of which serious prejudice is alleged to have arisen shall, subject to the provisions of paragraph 3 of Annex V, make available to the parties to a dispute arising under Article 7, and to the panel established pursuant to paragraph 4 of Article 7, all relevant information that can be obtained as to the changes in market shares of the parties to the dispute as well as concerning prices of the products involved.

6.7   Displacement or impediment resulting in serious prejudice shall not arise under paragraph 3 where any of the following circumstances exist[18] during the relevant period:

(a) prohibition or restriction on exports of the like product from the complaining Member or on imports from the complaining Member into the third country market concerned;

(b) decision by an importing government operating a monopoly of trade or state trading in the product concerned to shift, for non-commercial reasons, imports from the complaining Member to another country or countries;

(c) natural disasters, strikes, transport disruptions or other *force majeure* substantially affecting production, qualities, quantities or prices of the product available for export from the complaining Member;

(d) existence of arrangements limiting exports from the complaining Member;

---

18.   The fact that certain circumstances are referred to in this paragraph does not, in itself, confer upon them any legal status in terms of either GATT 1994 or this Agreement. These circumstances must not be isolated, sporadic or otherwise insignificant.

(e) voluntary decrease in the availability for export of the product concerned from the complaining Member (including, *inter alia*, a situation where firms in the complaining Member have been autonomously reallocating exports of this product to new markets);

(f) failure to conform to standards and other regulatory requirements in the importing country.

6.8 In the absence of circumstances referred to in paragraph 7, the existence of serious prejudice should be determined on the basis of the information submitted to or obtained by the panel, including information submitted in accordance with the provisions of Annex V.

6.9 This Article does not apply to subsidies maintained on agricultural products as provided in Article 13 of the Agreement on Agriculture.

Article 7

Remedies

7.1 Except as provided in Article 13 of the Agreement on Agriculture, whenever a Member has reason to believe that any subsidy referred to in Article 1, granted or maintained by another Member, results in injury to its domestic industry, nullification or impairment or serious prejudice, such Member may request consultations with such other Member.

7.2 A request for consultations under paragraph 1 shall include a statement of available evidence with regard to *(a)* the existence and nature of the subsidy in question, and *(b)* the injury caused to the domestic industry, or the nullification or impairment, or serious prejudice[19] caused to the interests of the Member requesting consultations.

7.3 Upon request for consultations under paragraph 1, the Member believed to be granting or maintaining the subsidy practice in question shall enter into such consultations as quickly as possible. The purpose of the consultations shall be to clarify the facts of the situation and to arrive at a mutually agreed solution.

7.4 If consultations do not result in a mutually agreed solution within 60 days[20], any Member party to such consultations may refer the matter to the DSB for the establishment of a panel, unless the DSB decides by consensus not to establish a panel. The composition of the panel and its terms of reference shall be established within 15 days from the date when it is established.

7.5 The panel shall review the matter and shall submit its final report to the parties to the dispute. The report shall be circulated to all Members within 120 days of the date of the composition and establishment of the panel's terms of reference.

7.6 Within 30 days of the issuance of the panel's report to all Members, the report shall be adopted by the DSB[21] unless one of the parties to the

19. In the event that the request relates to a subsidy deemed to result in serious prejudice in terms of paragraph 1 of Article 6, the available evidence of serious prejudice may be limited to the available evidence as to whether the conditions of paragraph 1 of Article 6 have been met or not.

20. Any time-periods mentioned in this Article may be extended by mutual agreement.

21. If a meeting of the DSB is not scheduled during this period, such a meeting shall be held for this purpose.

dispute formally notifies the DSB of its decision to appeal or the DSB decides by consensus not to adopt the report.

7.7   Where a panel report is appealed, the Appellate Body shall issue its decision within 60 days from the date when the party to the dispute formally notifies its intention to appeal. When the Appellate Body considers that it cannot provide its report within 60 days, it shall inform the DSB in writing of the reasons for the delay together with an estimate of the period within which it will submit its report. In no case shall the proceedings exceed 90 days. The appellate report shall be adopted by the DSB and unconditionally accepted by the parties to the dispute unless the DSB decides by consensus not to adopt the appellate report within 20 days following its issuance to the Members.[22]

7.8   Where a panel report or an Appellate Body report is adopted in which it is determined that any subsidy has resulted in adverse effects to the interests of another Member within the meaning of Article 5, the Member granting or maintaining such subsidy shall take appropriate steps to remove the adverse effects or shall withdraw the subsidy.

7.9   In the event the Member has not taken appropriate steps to remove the adverse effects of the subsidy or withdraw the subsidy within six months from the date when the DSB adopts the panel report or the Appellate Body report, and in the absence of agreement on compensation, the DSB shall grant authorization to the complaining Member to take countermeasures, commensurate with the degree and nature of the adverse effects determined to exist, unless the DSB decides by consensus to reject the request.

7.10   In the event that a party to the dispute requests arbitration under paragraph 6 of Article 22 of the DSU, the arbitrator shall determine whether the countermeasures are commensurate with the degree and nature of the adverse effects determined to exist.

PART IV: NON–ACTIONABLE SUBSIDIES

Article 8 [Ed. Note: See Article 31]

Identification of Non-actionable Subsidies

8.1   The following subsidies shall be considered as non-actionable[23]:

(a) subsidies which are not specific within the meaning of Article 2;

(b) subsidies which are specific within the meaning of Article 2 but which meet all of the conditions provided for in paragraphs 2(a), 2(b) or 2(c) below.

8.2   Notwithstanding the provisions of Parts III and V, the following subsidies shall be non-actionable:

22. If a meeting of the DSB is not scheduled during this period, such a meeting shall be held for this purpose.

23. It is recognized that government assistance for various purposes is widely provided by Members and that the mere fact that such assistance may not qualify for non-actionable treatment under the provisions of this Article does not in itself restrict the ability of Members to provide such assistance.

(a) assistance for research activities conducted by firms or by higher education or research establishments on a contract basis with firms if:[24,25,26]

the assistance covers[27] not more than 75 per cent of the costs of industrial research[28] or 50 per cent of the costs of pre-competitive development activity[29,30]; and provided that such assistance is limited exclusively to:

(i) costs of personnel (researchers, technicians and other supporting staff employed exclusively in the research activity);

(ii) costs of instruments, equipment, land and buildings used exclusively and permanently (except when disposed of on a commercial basis) for the research activity;

(iii) costs of consultancy and equivalent services used exclusively for the research activity, including bought-in research, technical knowledge, patents, etc.;

(iv) additional overhead costs incurred directly as a result of the research activity;

(v) other running costs (such as those of materials, supplies and the like), incurred directly as a result of the research activity.

(b) assistance to disadvantaged regions within the territory of a Member given pursuant to a general framework of regional development[31]

24. Since it is anticipated that civil aircraft will be subject to specific multilateral rules, the provisions of this subparagraph do not apply to that product.

25. Not later than 18 months after the date of entry into force of the WTO Agreement, the Committee on Subsidies and Countervailing Measures provided for in Article 24 (referred to in this Agreement as "the Committee") shall review the operation of the provisions of subparagraph 2(a) with a view to making all necessary modifications to improve the operation of these provisions. In its consideration of possible modifications, the Committee shall carefully review the definitions of the categories set forth in this subparagraph in the light of the experience of Members in the operation of research programmes and the work in other relevant international institutions.

26. The provisions of this Agreement do not apply to fundamental research activities independently conducted by higher education or research establishments. The term "fundamental research" means an enlargement of general scientific and technical knowledge not linked to industrial or commercial objectives.

27. The allowable levels of non-actionable assistance referred to in this subparagraph shall be established by reference to the total eligible costs incurred over the duration of an individual project.

28. The term "industrial research" means planned search or critical investigation aimed at discovery of new knowledge, with the objective that such knowledge may be useful in developing new products, processes or services, or in bringing about a significant improvement to existing products, processes or services.

29. The term "pre-competitive development activity" means the translation of industrial research findings into a plan, blueprint or design for new, modified or improved products, processes or services whether intended for sale or use, including the creation of a first prototype which would not be capable of commercial use. It may further include the conceptual formulation and design of products, processes or services alternatives and initial demonstration or pilot projects, provided that these same projects cannot be converted or used for industrial application or commercial exploitation. It does not include routine or periodic alterations to existing products, production lines, manufacturing processes, services, and other on-going operations even though those alterations may represent improvements.

30. In the case of programmes which span industrial research and pre-competitive development activity, the allowable level of non-actionable assistance shall not exceed the simple average of the allowable levels of non-actionable assistance applicable to the above two categories, calculated on the basis of all eligible costs as set forth in items (i) to (v) of this subparagraph.

31. A "general framework of regional development" means that regional subsidy programmes are part of an internally consistent and generally applicable regional development policy and that regional development subsidies are not granted in isolated geographical points having no, or virtually no, influence on the development of a region.

and non-specific (within the meaning of Article 2) within eligible regions provided that:

(i) each disadvantaged region must be a clearly designated contiguous geographical area with a definable economic and administrative identity;

(ii) the region is considered as disadvantaged on the basis of neutral and objective criteria[32], indicating that the region's difficulties arise out of more than temporary circumstances; such criteria must be clearly spelled out in law, regulation, or other official document, so as to be capable of verification;

(iii) the criteria shall include a measurement of economic development which shall be based on at least one of the following factors:

— one of either income per capita or household income per capita, or GDP per capita, which must not be above 85 per cent of the average for the territory concerned;

— unemployment rate, which must be at least 110 per cent of the average for the territory concerned;

as measured over a three-year period; such measurement, however, may be a composite one and may include other factors.

(c) assistance to promote adaptation of existing facilities[33] to new environmental requirements imposed by law and/or regulations which result in greater constraints and financial burden on firms, provided that the assistance:

(i) is a one-time non-recurring measure; and

(ii) is limited to 20 per cent of the cost of adaptation; and

(iii) does not cover the cost of replacing and operating the assisted investment, which must be fully borne by firms; and

(iv) is directly linked to and proportionate to a firm's planned reduction of nuisances and pollution, and does not cover any manufacturing cost savings which may be achieved; and

(v) is available to all firms which can adopt the new equipment and/or production processes.

8.3 A subsidy programme for which the provisions of paragraph 2 are invoked shall be notified in advance of its implementation to the Committee in accordance with the provisions of Part VII. Any such notification shall be sufficiently precise to enable other Members to evaluate the consistency of the programme with the conditions and criteria provided for in the relevant provisions of paragraph 2. Members shall also provide the Committee with yearly updates of such notifications, in particular by supplying information on

---

32. "Neutral and objective criteria" means criteria which do not favour certain regions beyond what is appropriate for the elimination or reduction of regional disparities within the framework of the regional development policy. In this regard, regional subsidy programmes shall include ceilings on the amount of assistance which can be granted to each subsidized project. Such ceilings must be differentiated according to the different levels of development of assisted regions and must be expressed in terms of investment costs or cost of job cre-ation. Within such ceilings, the distribution of assistance shall be sufficiently broad and even to avoid the predominant use of a subsidy by, or the granting of disproportionately large amounts of subsidy to, certain enterprises as provided for in Article 2.

33. The term "existing facilities" means facilities which have been in operation for at least two years at the time when new environmental requirements are imposed.

global expenditure for each programme, and on any modification of the programme. Other Members shall have the right to request information about individual cases of subsidization under a notified programme.[34]

8.4 Upon request of a Member, the Secretariat shall review a notification made pursuant to paragraph 3 and, where necessary, may require additional information from the subsidizing Member concerning the notified programme under review. The Secretariat shall report its findings to the Committee. The Committee shall, upon request, promptly review the findings of the Secretariat (or, if a review by the Secretariat has not been requested, the notification itself), with a view to determining whether the conditions and criteria laid down in paragraph 2 have not been met. The procedure provided for in this paragraph shall be completed at the latest at the first regular meeting of the Committee following the notification of a subsidy programme, provided that at least two months have elapsed between such notification and the regular meeting of the Committee. The review procedure described in this paragraph shall also apply, upon request, to substantial modifications of a programme notified in the yearly updates referred to in paragraph 3.

8.5 Upon the request of a Member, the determination by the Committee referred to in paragraph 4, or a failure by the Committee to make such a determination, as well as the violation, in individual cases, of the conditions set out in a notified programme, shall be submitted to binding arbitration. The arbitration body shall present its conclusions to the Members within 120 days from the date when the matter was referred to the arbitration body. Except as otherwise provided in this paragraph, the DSU shall apply to arbitrations conducted under this paragraph.

Article 9 [Ed. Note: See Article 31]
Consultations and Authorized Remedies

9.1 If, in the course of implementation of a programme referred to in paragraph 2 of Article 8, notwithstanding the fact that the programme is consistent with the criteria laid down in that paragraph, a Member has reasons to believe that this programme has resulted in serious adverse effects to the domestic industry of that Member, such as to cause damage which would be difficult to repair, such Member may request consultations with the Member granting or maintaining the subsidy.

9.2 Upon request for consultations under paragraph 1, the Member granting or maintaining the subsidy programme in question shall enter into such consultations as quickly as possible. The purpose of the consultations shall be to clarify the facts of the situation and to arrive at a mutually acceptable solution.

9.3 If no mutually acceptable solution has been reached in consultations under paragraph 2 within 60 days of the request for such consultations, the requesting Member may refer the matter to the Committee.

9.4 Where a matter is referred to the Committee, the Committee shall immediately review the facts involved and the evidence of the effects referred to in paragraph 1. If the Committee determines that such effects exist, it may

---

34. It is recognized that nothing in this notification provision requires the provision of confidential information, including confidential business information.

recommend to the subsidizing Member to modify this programme in such a way as to remove these effects. The Committee shall present its conclusions within 120 days from the date when the matter is referred to it under paragraph 3. In the event the recommendation is not followed within six months, the Committee shall authorize the requesting Member to take appropriate countermeasures commensurate with the nature and degree of the effects determined to exist.

PART V: COUNTERVAILING MEASURES

Article 10

Application of Article VI of GATT 1994[35]

Members shall take all necessary steps to ensure that the imposition of a countervailing duty[36] on any product of the territory of any Member imported into the territory of another Member is in accordance with the provisions of Article VI of GATT 1994 and the terms of this Agreement. Countervailing duties may only be imposed pursuant to investigations initiated[37] and conducted in accordance with the provisions of this Agreement and the Agreement on Agriculture.

Article 11

Initiation and Subsequent Investigation

11.1   Except as provided in paragraph 6, an investigation to determine the existence, degree and effect of any alleged subsidy shall be initiated upon a written application by or on behalf of the domestic industry.

11.2   An application under paragraph 1 shall include sufficient evidence of the existence of *(a)* a subsidy and, if possible, its amount, *(b)* injury within the meaning of Article VI of GATT 1994 as interpreted by this Agreement, and *(c)* a causal link between the subsidized imports and the alleged injury. Simple assertion, unsubstantiated by relevant evidence, cannot be considered sufficient to meet the requirements of this paragraph. The application shall contain such information as is reasonably available to the applicant on the following:

     (i) the identity of the applicant and a description of the volume and value of the domestic production of the like product by the applicant.

35.   The provisions of Part II or III may be invoked in parallel with the provisions of Part V; however, with regard to the effects of a particular subsidy in the domestic market of the importing Member, only one form of relief (either a countervailing duty, if the requirements of Part V are met, or a countermeasure under Articles 4 or 7) shall be available. The provisions of Parts III and V shall not be invoked regarding measures considered non-actionable in accordance with the provisions of Part IV. However, measures referred to in paragraph 1(a) of Article 8 may be investigated in order to determine whether or not they are specific within the meaning of Article 2. In addition, in the case of a subsidy referred to in paragraph 2 of Article 8 conferred pursuant to a programme which has not been notified in accordance with paragraph 3 of Article 8, the provisions of Part III or V may be invoked, but such subsidy shall be treated as non-actionable if it is found to conform to the standards set forth in paragraph 2 of Article 8.

36.   The term "countervailing duty" shall be understood to mean a special duty levied for the purpose of offsetting any subsidy bestowed directly or indirectly upon the manufacture, production or export of any merchandise, as provided for in paragraph 3 of Article VI of GATT 1994.

37.   The term "initiated" as used hereinafter means procedural action by which a Member formally commences an investigation as provided in Article 11.

Where a written application is made on behalf of the domestic industry, the application shall identify the industry on behalf of which the application is made by a list of all known domestic producers of the like product (or associations of domestic producers of the like product) and, to the extent possible, a description of the volume and value of domestic production of the like product accounted for by such producers;

(ii) a complete description of the allegedly subsidized product, the names of the country or countries of origin or export in question, the identity of each known exporter or foreign producer and a list of known persons importing the product in question;

(iii) evidence with regard to the existence, amount and nature of the subsidy in question;

(iv) evidence that alleged injury to a domestic industry is caused by subsidized imports through the effects of the subsidies; this evidence includes information on the evolution of the volume of the allegedly subsidized imports, the effect of these imports on prices of the like product in the domestic market and the consequent impact of the imports on the domestic industry, as demonstrated by relevant factors and indices having a bearing on the state of the domestic industry, such as those listed in paragraphs 2 and 4 of Article 15.

11.3   The authorities shall review the accuracy and adequacy of the evidence provided in the application to determine whether the evidence is sufficient to justify the initiation of an investigation.

11.4   An investigation shall not be initiated pursuant to paragraph 1 unless the authorities have determined, on the basis of an examination of the degree of support for, or opposition to, the application expressed[38] by domestic producers of the like product, that the application has been made by or on behalf of the domestic industry.[39] The application shall be considered to have been made "by or on behalf of the domestic industry" if it is supported by those domestic producers whose collective output constitutes more than 50 per cent of the total production of the like product produced by that portion of the domestic industry expressing either support for or opposition to the application. However, no investigation shall be initiated when domestic producers expressly supporting the application account for less than 25 per cent of total production of the like product produced by the domestic industry.

11.5   The authorities shall avoid, unless a decision has been made to initiate an investigation, any publicizing of the application for the initiation of an investigation.

11.6   If, in special circumstances, the authorities concerned decide to initiate an investigation without having received a written application by or on behalf of a domestic industry for the initiation of such investigation, they shall proceed only if they have sufficient evidence of the existence of a

38. In the case of fragmented industries involving an exceptionally large number of producers, authorities may determine support and opposition by using statistically valid sampling techniques.

39. Members are aware that in the territory of certain Members employees of domestic producers of the like product or representatives of those employees may make or support an application for an investigation under paragraph 1.

subsidy, injury and causal link, as described in paragraph 2, to justify the initiation of an investigation.

11.7 The evidence of both subsidy and injury shall be considered simultaneously *(a)* in the decision whether or not to initiate an investigation and *(b)* thereafter, during the course of the investigation, starting on a date not later than the earliest date on which in accordance with the provisions of this Agreement provisional measures may be applied.

11.8 In cases where products are not imported directly from the country of origin but are exported to the importing Member from an intermediate country, the provisions of this Agreement shall be fully applicable and the transaction or transactions shall, for the purposes of this Agreement, be regarded as having taken place between the country of origin and the importing Member.

11.9 An application under paragraph 1 shall be rejected and an investigation shall be terminated promptly as soon as the authorities concerned are satisfied that there is not sufficient evidence of either subsidization or of injury to justify proceeding with the case. There shall be immediate termination in cases where the amount of a subsidy is *de minimis*, or where the volume of subsidized imports, actual or potential, or the injury, is negligible. For the purpose of this paragraph, the amount of the subsidy shall be considered to be *de minimis* if the subsidy is less than 1 per cent ad valorem.

11.10 An investigation shall not hinder the procedures of customs clearance.

11.11 Investigations shall, except in special circumstances, be concluded within one year, and in no case more than 18 months, after their initiation.

Article 12
Evidence

12.1 Interested Members and all interested parties in a countervailing duty investigation shall be given notice of the information which the authorities require and ample opportunity to present in writing all evidence which they consider relevant in respect of the investigation in question.

12.1.1 Exporters, foreign producers or interested Members receiving questionnaires used in a countervailing duty investigation shall be given at least 30 days for reply.[40] Due consideration should be given to any request for an extension of the 30–day period and, upon cause shown, such an extension should be granted whenever practicable.

12.1.2 Subject to the requirement to protect confidential information, evidence presented in writing by one interested Member or interested party shall be made available promptly to other interested Members or interested parties participating in the investigation.

12.1.3 As soon as an investigation has been initiated, the authorities shall provide the full text of the written application received under

---

40. As a general rule, the time-limit for exporters shall be counted from the date of receipt of the questionnaire, which for this purpose shall be deemed to have been received one week from the date on which it was sent to the respondent or transmitted to the appropriate diplomatic representatives of the exporting Member or, in the case of a separate customs territory Member of the WTO, an official representative of the exporting territory.

paragraph 1 of Article 11 to the known exporters[41] and to the authorities of the exporting Member and shall make it available, upon request, to other interested parties involved. Due regard shall be paid to the protection of confidential information, as provided for in paragraph 4.

12.2 Interested Members and interested parties also shall have the right, upon justification, to present information orally. Where such information is provided orally, the interested Members and interested parties subsequently shall be required to reduce such submissions to writing. Any decision of the investigating authorities can only be based on such information and arguments as were on the written record of this authority and which were available to interested Members and interested parties participating in the investigation, due account having been given to the need to protect confidential information.

12.3 The authorities shall whenever practicable provide timely opportunities for all interested Members and interested parties to see all information that is relevant to the presentation of their cases, that is not confidential as defined in paragraph 4, and that is used by the authorities in a countervailing duty investigation, and to prepare presentations on the basis of this information.

12.4 Any information which is by nature confidential (for example, because its disclosure would be of significant competitive advantage to a competitor or because its disclosure would have a significantly adverse effect upon a person supplying the information or upon a person from whom the supplier acquired the information), or which is provided on a confidential basis by parties to an investigation shall, upon good cause shown, be treated as such by the authorities. Such information shall not be disclosed without specific permission of the party submitting it.[42]

12.4.1 The authorities shall require interested Members or interested parties providing confidential information to furnish non-confidential summaries thereof. These summaries shall be in sufficient detail to permit a reasonable understanding of the substance of the information submitted in confidence. In exceptional circumstances, such Members or parties may indicate that such information is not susceptible of summary. In such exceptional circumstances, a statement of the reasons why summarization is not possible must be provided.

12.4.2 If the authorities find that a request for confidentiality is not warranted and if the supplier of the information is either unwilling to make the information public or to authorize its disclosure in generalized or summary form, the authorities may disregard such information unless it can be demonstrated to their satisfaction from appropriate sources that the information is correct.[43]

---

41. It being understood that where the number of exporters involved is particularly high, the full text of the application should instead be provided only to the authorities of the exporting Member or to the relevant trade association who then should forward copies to the exporters concerned.

42. Members are aware that in the territory of certain Members disclosure pursuant to a narrowly-drawn protective order may be required.

43. Members agree that requests for confidentiality should not be arbitrarily rejected. Members further agree that the investigating authority may request the waiving of confidentiality only regarding information relevant to the proceedings.

12.5 Except in circumstances provided for in paragraph 7, the authorities shall during the course of an investigation satisfy themselves as to the accuracy of the information supplied by interested Members or interested parties upon which their findings are based.

12.6 The investigating authorities may carry out investigations in the territory of other Members as required, provided that they have notified in good time the Member in question and unless that Member objects to the investigation. Further, the investigating authorities may carry out investigations on the premises of a firm and may examine the records of a firm if *(a)* the firm so agrees and *(b)* the Member in question is notified and does not object. The procedures set forth in Annex VI shall apply to investigations on the premises of a firm. Subject to the requirement to protect confidential information, the authorities shall make the results of any such investigations available, or shall provide disclosure thereof pursuant to paragraph 8, to the firms to which they pertain and may make such results available to the applicants.

12.7 In cases in which any interested Member or interested party refuses access to, or otherwise does not provide, necessary information within a reasonable period or significantly impedes the investigation, preliminary and final determinations, affirmative or negative, may be made on the basis of the facts available.

12.8 The authorities shall, before a final determination is made, inform all interested Members and interested parties of the essential facts under consideration which form the basis for the decision whether to apply definitive measures. Such disclosure should take place in sufficient time for the parties to defend their interests.

12.9 For the purposes of this Agreement, "interested parties" shall include:

(i) an exporter or foreign producer or the importer of a product subject to investigation, or a trade or business association a majority of the members of which are producers, exporters or importers of such product; and

(ii) a producer of the like product in the importing Member or a trade and business association a majority of the members of which produce the like product in the territory of the importing Member.

This list shall not preclude Members from allowing domestic or foreign parties other than those mentioned above to be included as interested parties.

12.10 The authorities shall provide opportunities for industrial users of the product under investigation, and for representative consumer organizations in cases where the product is commonly sold at the retail level, to provide information which is relevant to the investigation regarding subsidization, injury and causality.

12.11 The authorities shall take due account of any difficulties experienced by interested parties, in particular small companies, in supplying information requested, and shall provide any assistance practicable.

12.12 The procedures set out above are not intended to prevent the authorities of a Member from proceeding expeditiously with regard to initiating an investigation, reaching preliminary or final determinations, whether affirmative or negative, or from applying provisional or final measures, in accordance with relevant provisions of this Agreement.

Article 13

Consultations

13.1   As soon as possible after an application under Article 11 is accepted, and in any event before the initiation of any investigation, Members the products of which may be subject to such investigation shall be invited for consultations with the aim of clarifying the situation as to the matters referred to in paragraph 2 of Article 11 and arriving at a mutually agreed solution.

13.2   Furthermore, throughout the period of investigation, Members the products of which are the subject of the investigation shall be afforded a reasonable opportunity to continue consultations, with a view to clarifying the factual situation and to arriving at a mutually agreed solution.[44]

13.3   Without prejudice to the obligation to afford reasonable opportunity for consultation, these provisions regarding consultations are not intended to prevent the authorities of a Member from proceeding expeditiously with regard to initiating the investigation, reaching preliminary or final determinations, whether affirmative or negative, or from applying provisional or final measures, in accordance with the provisions of this Agreement.

13.4   The Member which intends to initiate any investigation or is conducting such an investigation shall permit, upon request, the Member or Members the products of which are subject to such investigation access to non-confidential evidence, including the non-confidential summary of confidential data being used for initiating or conducting the investigation.

Article 14

Calculation of the Amount of a Subsidy in Terms of the Benefit to the Recipient

For the purpose of Part V, any method used by the investigating authority to calculate the benefit to the recipient conferred pursuant to paragraph 1 of Article 1 shall be provided for in the national legislation or implementing regulations of the Member concerned and its application to each particular case shall be transparent and adequately explained. Furthermore, any such method shall be consistent with the following guidelines:

(a) government provision of equity capital shall not be considered as conferring a benefit, unless the investment decision can be regarded as inconsistent with the usual investment practice (including for the provision of risk capital) of private investors in the territory of that Member;

(b) a loan by a government shall not be considered as conferring a benefit, unless there is a difference between the amount that the firm receiving the loan pays on the government loan and the amount the firm

---

44. It is particularly important, in accordance with the provisions of this paragraph, that no affirmative determination whether preliminary or final be made without reasonable opportunity for consultations having been given. Such consultations may establish the basis for proceeding under the provisions of Part II, III or X.

would pay on a comparable commercial loan which the firm could actually obtain on the market. In this case the benefit shall be the difference between these two amounts;

(c) a loan guarantee by a government shall not be considered as conferring a benefit, unless there is a difference between the amount that the firm receiving the guarantee pays on a loan guaranteed by the government and the amount that the firm would pay on a comparable commercial loan absent the government guarantee. In this case the benefit shall be the difference between these two amounts adjusted for any differences in fees;

(d) the provision of goods or services or purchase of goods by a government shall not be considered as conferring a benefit unless the provision is made for less than adequate remuneration, or the purchase is made for more than adequate remuneration. The adequacy of remuneration shall be determined in relation to prevailing market conditions for the good or service in question in the country of provision or purchase (including price, quality, availability, marketability, transportation and other conditions of purchase or sale).

Article 15

Determination of Injury[45]

15.1   A determination of injury for purposes of Article VI of GATT 1994 shall be based on positive evidence and involve an objective examination of both *(a)* the volume of the subsidized imports and the effect of the subsidized imports on prices in the domestic market for like products[46] and *(b)* the consequent impact of these imports on the domestic producers of such products.

15.2   With regard to the volume of the subsidized imports, the investigating authorities shall consider whether there has been a significant increase in subsidized imports, either in absolute terms or relative to production or consumption in the importing Member. With regard to the effect of the subsidized imports on prices, the investigating authorities shall consider whether there has been a significant price undercutting by the subsidized imports as compared with the price of a like product of the importing Member, or whether the effect of such imports is otherwise to depress prices to a significant degree or to prevent price increases, which otherwise would have occurred, to a significant degree. No one or several of these factors can necessarily give decisive guidance.

15.3   Where imports of a product from more than one country are simultaneously subject to countervailing duty investigations, the investigating authorities may cumulatively assess the effects of such imports only if they

---

45. Under this Agreement the term "injury" shall, unless otherwise specified, be taken to mean material injury to a domestic industry, threat of material injury to a domestic industry or material retardation of the establishment of such an industry and shall be interpreted in accordance with the provisions of this Article.

46. Throughout this Agreement the term "like product" ("produit similaire") shall be interpreted to mean a product which is identical, i.e. alike in all respects to the product under consideration, or in the absence of such a product, another product which, although not alike in all respects, has characteristics closely resembling those of the product under consideration.

determine that *(a)* the amount of subsidization established in relation to the imports from each country is more than *de minimis* as defined in paragraph 9 of Article 11 and the volume of imports from each country is not negligible and *(b)* a cumulative assessment of the effects of the imports is appropriate in light of the conditions of competition between the imported products and the conditions of competition between the imported products and the like domestic product.

15.4 The examination of the impact of the subsidized imports on the domestic industry shall include an evaluation of all relevant economic factors and indices having a bearing on the state of the industry, including actual and potential decline in output, sales, market share, profits, productivity, return on investments, or utilization of capacity; factors affecting domestic prices; actual and potential negative effects on cash flow, inventories, employment, wages, growth, ability to raise capital or investments and, in the case of agriculture, whether there has been an increased burden on government support programmes. This list is not exhaustive, nor can one or several of these factors necessarily give decisive guidance.

15.5 It must be demonstrated that the subsidized imports are, through the effects[47] of subsidies, causing injury within the meaning of this Agreement. The demonstration of a causal relationship between the subsidized imports and the injury to the domestic industry shall be based on an examination of all relevant evidence before the authorities. The authorities shall also examine any known factors other than the subsidized imports which at the same time are injuring the domestic industry, and the injuries caused by these other factors must not be attributed to the subsidized imports. Factors which may be relevant in this respect include, *inter alia*, the volumes and prices of non-subsidized imports of the product in question, contraction in demand or changes in the patterns of consumption, trade restrictive practices of and competition between the foreign and domestic producers, developments in technology and the export performance and productivity of the domestic industry.

15.6 The effect of the subsidized imports shall be assessed in relation to the domestic production of the like product when available data permit the separate identification of that production on the basis of such criteria as the production process, producers' sales and profits. If such separate identification of that production is not possible, the effects of the subsidized imports shall be assessed by the examination of the production of the narrowest group or range of products, which includes the like product, for which the necessary information can be provided.

15.7 A determination of a threat of material injury shall be based on facts and not merely on allegation, conjecture or remote possibility. The change in circumstances which would create a situation in which the subsidy would cause injury must be clearly foreseen and imminent. In making a determination regarding the existence of a threat of material injury, the investigating authorities should consider, *inter alia*, such factors as:

(i) nature of the subsidy or subsidies in question and the trade effects likely to arise therefrom;

47. As set forth in paragraphs 2 and 4.

(ii) a significant rate of increase of subsidized imports into the domestic market indicating the likelihood of substantially increased importation;

(iii) sufficient freely disposable, or an imminent, substantial increase in, capacity of the exporter indicating the likelihood of substantially increased subsidized exports to the importing Member's market, taking into account the availability of other export markets to absorb any additional exports;

(iv) whether imports are entering at prices that will have a significant depressing or suppressing effect on domestic prices, and would likely increase demand for further imports; and

(v) inventories of the product being investigated.

No one of these factors by itself can necessarily give decisive guidance but the totality of the factors considered must lead to the conclusion that further subsidized exports are imminent and that, unless protective action is taken, material injury would occur.

15.8 With respect to cases where injury is threatened by subsidized imports, the application of countervailing measures shall be considered and decided with special care.

Article 16

Definition of Domestic Industry

16.1 For the purposes of this Agreement, the term "domestic industry" shall, except as provided in paragraph 2, be interpreted as referring to the domestic producers as a whole of the like products or to those of them whose collective output of the products constitutes a major proportion of the total domestic production of those products, except that when producers are related[48] to the exporters or importers or are themselves importers of the allegedly subsidized product or a like product from other countries, the term "domestic industry" may be interpreted as referring to the rest of the producers.

16.2 In exceptional circumstances, the territory of a Member may, for the production in question, be divided into two or more competitive markets and the producers within each market may be regarded as a separate industry if (a) the producers within such market sell all or almost all of their production of the product in question in that market, and (b) the demand in that market is not to any substantial degree supplied by producers of the product in question located elsewhere in the territory. In such circumstances, injury may be found to exist even where a major portion of the total domestic

---

48. For the purpose of this paragraph, producers shall be deemed to be related to exporters or importers only if (a) one of them directly or indirectly controls the other; or (b) both of them are directly or indirectly controlled by a third person; or (c) together they directly or indirectly control a third person, provided that there are grounds for believing or suspecting that the effect of the relationship is such as to cause the producer concerned to behave differently from non-related producers. For the purpose of this paragraph, one shall be deemed to control another when the former is legally or operationally in a position to exercise restraint or direction over the latter.

industry is not injured, provided there is a concentration of subsidized imports into such an isolated market and provided further that the subsidized imports are causing injury to the producers of all or almost all of the production within such market.

16.3   When the domestic industry has been interpreted as referring to the producers in a certain area, i.e. a market as defined in paragraph 2, countervailing duties shall be levied only on the products in question consigned for final consumption to that area. When the constitutional law of the importing Member does not permit the levying of countervailing duties on such a basis, the importing Member may levy the countervailing duties without limitation only if *(a)* the exporters shall have been given an opportunity to cease exporting at subsidized prices to the area concerned or otherwise give assurances pursuant to Article 18, and adequate assurances in this regard have not been promptly given, and *(b)* such duties cannot be levied only on products of specific producers which supply the area in question.

16.4   Where two or more countries have reached under the provisions of paragraph 8(a) of Article XXIV of GATT 1994 such a level of integration that they have the characteristics of a single, unified market, the industry in the entire area of integration shall be taken to be the domestic industry referred to in paragraphs 1 and 2.

16.5   The provisions of paragraph 6 of Article 15 shall be applicable to this Article.

Article 17

Provisional Measures

17.1   Provisional measures may be applied only if:

(a) an investigation has been initiated in accordance with the provisions of Article 11, a public notice has been given to that effect and interested Members and interested parties have been given adequate opportunities to submit information and make comments;

(b) a preliminary affirmative determination has been made that a subsidy exists and that there is injury to a domestic industry caused by subsidized imports; and

(c) the authorities concerned judge such measures necessary to prevent injury being caused during the investigation.

17.2   Provisional measures may take the form of provisional countervailing duties guaranteed by cash deposits or bonds equal to the amount of the provisionally calculated amount of subsidization.

17.3   Provisional measures shall not be applied sooner than 60 days from the date of initiation of the investigation.

17.4   The application of provisional measures shall be limited to as short a period as possible, not exceeding four months.

17.5   The relevant provisions of Article 19 shall be followed in the application of provisional measures.

Article 18

Undertakings

18.1   Proceedings may[49] be suspended or terminated without the imposition of provisional measures or countervailing duties upon receipt of satisfactory voluntary undertakings under which:

(a) the government of the exporting Member agrees to eliminate or limit the subsidy or take other measures concerning its effects; or

(b) the exporter agrees to revise its prices so that the investigating authorities are satisfied that the injurious effect of the subsidy is eliminated. Price increases under such undertakings shall not be higher than necessary to eliminate the amount of the subsidy. It is desirable that the price increases be less than the amount of the subsidy if such increases would be adequate to remove the injury to the domestic industry.

18.2   Undertakings shall not be sought or accepted unless the authorities of the importing Member have made a preliminary affirmative determination of subsidization and injury caused by such subsidization and, in case of undertakings from exporters, have obtained the consent of the exporting Member.

18.3   Undertakings offered need not be accepted if the authorities of the importing Member consider their acceptance impractical, for example if the number of actual or potential exporters is too great, or for other reasons, including reasons of general policy. Should the case arise and where practicable, the authorities shall provide to the exporter the reasons which have led them to consider acceptance of an undertaking as inappropriate, and shall, to the extent possible, give the exporter an opportunity to make comments thereon.

18.4   If an undertaking is accepted, the investigation of subsidization and injury shall nevertheless be completed if the exporting Member so desires or the importing Member so decides. In such a case, if a negative determination of subsidization or injury is made, the undertaking shall automatically lapse, except in cases where such a determination is due in large part to the existence of an undertaking. In such cases, the authorities concerned may require that an undertaking be maintained for a reasonable period consistent with the provisions of this Agreement. In the event that an affirmative determination of subsidization and injury is made, the undertaking shall continue consistent with its terms and the provisions of this Agreement.

18.5   Price undertakings may be suggested by the authorities of the importing Member, but no exporter shall be forced to enter into such undertakings. The fact that governments or exporters do not offer such undertakings, or do not accept an invitation to do so, shall in no way prejudice the consideration of the case. However, the authorities are free to determine that a threat of injury is more likely to be realized if the subsidized imports continue.

18.6   Authorities of an importing Member may require any government or exporter from whom an undertaking has been accepted to provide periodi-

---

49. The word "may" shall not be interpreted to allow the simultaneous continuation of proceedings with the implementation of undertakings, except as provided in paragraph 4.

cally information relevant to the fulfilment of such an undertaking, and to permit verification of pertinent data. In case of violation of an undertaking, the authorities of the importing Member may take, under this Agreement in conformity with its provisions, expeditious actions which may constitute immediate application of provisional measures using the best information available. In such cases, definitive duties may be levied in accordance with this Agreement on products entered for consumption not more than 90 days before the application of such provisional measures, except that any such retroactive assessment shall not apply to imports entered before the violation of the undertaking.

Article 19

Imposition and Collection of Countervailing Duties

19.1   If, after reasonable efforts have been made to complete consultations, a Member makes a final determination of the existence and amount of the subsidy and that, through the effects of the subsidy, the subsidized imports are causing injury, it may impose a countervailing duty in accordance with the provisions of this Article unless the subsidy or subsidies are withdrawn.

19.2   The decision whether or not to impose a countervailing duty in cases where all requirements for the imposition have been fulfilled, and the decision whether the amount of the countervailing duty to be imposed shall be the full amount of the subsidy or less, are decisions to be made by the authorities of the importing Member. It is desirable that the imposition should be permissive in the territory of all Members, that the duty should be less than the total amount of the subsidy if such lesser duty would be adequate to remove the injury to the domestic industry, and that procedures should be established which would allow the authorities concerned to take due account of representations made by domestic interested parties[50] whose interests might be adversely affected by the imposition of a countervailing duty.

19.3   When a countervailing duty is imposed in respect of any product, such countervailing duty shall be levied, in the appropriate amounts in each case, on a non-discriminatory basis on imports of such product from all sources found to be subsidized and causing injury, except as to imports from those sources which have renounced any subsidies in question or from which undertakings under the terms of this Agreement have been accepted. Any exporter whose exports are subject to a definitive countervailing duty but who was not actually investigated for reasons other than a refusal to cooperate, shall be entitled to an expedited review in order that the investigating authorities promptly establish an individual countervailing duty rate for that exporter.

19.4   No countervailing duty shall be levied[51] on any imported product in excess of the amount of the subsidy found to exist, calculated in terms of subsidization per unit of the subsidized and exported product.

50. For the purpose of this paragraph, the term "domestic interested parties" shall include consumers and industrial users of the imported product subject to investigation.

51. As used in this Agreement "levy" shall mean the definitive or final legal assessment or collection of a duty or tax.

Article 20

Retroactivity

20.1 Provisional measures and countervailing duties shall only be applied to products which enter for consumption after the time when the decision under paragraph 1 of Article 17 and paragraph 1 of Article 19, respectively, enters into force, subject to the exceptions set out in this Article.

20.2 Where a final determination of injury (but not of a threat thereof or of a material retardation of the establishment of an industry) is made or, in the case of a final determination of a threat of injury, where the effect of the subsidized imports would, in the absence of the provisional measures, have led to a determination of injury, countervailing duties may be levied retroactively for the period for which provisional measures, if any, have been applied.

20.3 If the definitive countervailing duty is higher than the amount guaranteed by the cash deposit or bond, the difference shall not be collected. If the definitive duty is less than the amount guaranteed by the cash deposit or bond, the excess amount shall be reimbursed or the bond released in an expeditious manner.

20.4 Except as provided in paragraph 2, where a determination of threat of injury or material retardation is made (but no injury has yet occurred) a definitive countervailing duty may be imposed only from the date of the determination of threat of injury or material retardation, and any cash deposit made during the period of the application of provisional measures shall be refunded and any bonds released in an expeditious manner.

20.5 Where a final determination is negative, any cash deposit made during the period of the application of provisional measures shall be refunded and any bonds released in an expeditious manner.

20.6 In critical circumstances where for the subsidized product in question the authorities find that injury which is difficult to repair is caused by massive imports in a relatively short period of a product benefiting from subsidies paid or bestowed inconsistently with the provisions of GATT 1994 and of this Agreement and where it is deemed necessary, in order to preclude the recurrence of such injury, to assess countervailing duties retroactively on those imports, the definitive countervailing duties may be assessed on imports which were entered for consumption not more than 90 days prior to the date of application of provisional measures.

Article 21

Duration and Review of Countervailing Duties and Undertakings

21.1 A countervailing duty shall remain in force only as long as and to the extent necessary to counteract subsidization which is causing injury.

21.2 The authorities shall review the need for the continued imposition of the duty, where warranted, on their own initiative or, provided that a reasonable period of time has elapsed since the imposition of the definitive countervailing duty, upon request by any interested party which submits positive information substantiating the need for a review. Interested parties shall have the right to request the authorities to examine whether the continued imposition of the duty is necessary to offset subsidization, whether the injury would be likely to continue or recur if the duty were removed or varied, or both. If, as a result of the review under this paragraph, the authorities determine that the countervailing duty is no longer warranted, it shall be terminated immediately.

21.3   Notwithstanding the provisions of paragraphs 1 and 2, any definitive countervailing duty shall be terminated on a date not later than five years from its imposition (or from the date of the most recent review under paragraph 2 if that review has covered both subsidization and injury, or under this paragraph), unless the authorities determine, in a review initiated before that date on their own initiative or upon a duly substantiated request made by or on behalf of the domestic industry within a reasonable period of time prior to that date, that the expiry of the duty would be likely to lead to continuation or recurrence of subsidization and injury.[52] The duty may remain in force pending the outcome of such a review.

21.4   The provisions of Article 12 regarding evidence and procedure shall apply to any review carried out under this Article. Any such review shall be carried out expeditiously and shall normally be concluded within 12 months of the date of initiation of the review.

21.5   The provisions of this Article shall apply *mutatis mutandis* to undertakings accepted under Article 18.

Article 22

Public Notice and Explanation of Determinations

22.1   When the authorities are satisfied that there is sufficient evidence to justify the initiation of an investigation pursuant to Article 11, the Member or Members the products of which are subject to such investigation and other interested parties known to the investigating authorities to have an interest therein shall be notified and a public notice shall be given.

22.2   A public notice of the initiation of an investigation shall contain, or otherwise make available through a separate report[53], adequate information on the following:

(i) the name of the exporting country or countries and the product involved;

(ii) the date of initiation of the investigation;

(iii) a description of the subsidy practice or practices to be investigated;

(iv) a summary of the factors on which the allegation of injury is based;

(v) the address to which representations by interested Members and interested parties should be directed; and

(vi) the time-limits allowed to interested Members and interested parties for making their views known.

---

52. When the amount of the countervailing duty is assessed on a retrospective basis, a finding in the most recent assessment proceeding that no duty is to be levied shall not by itself require the authorities to terminate the definitive duty.

53. Where authorities provide information and explanations under the provisions of this Article in a separate report, they shall ensure that such report is readily available to the public.

22.3   Public notice shall be given of any preliminary or final determination, whether affirmative or negative, of any decision to accept an undertaking pursuant to Article 18, of the termination of such an undertaking, and of the termination of a definitive countervailing duty. Each such notice shall set forth, or otherwise make available through a separate report, in sufficient detail the findings and conclusions reached on all issues of fact and law considered material by the investigating authorities. All such notices and reports shall be forwarded to the Member or Members the products of which are subject to such determination or undertaking and to other interested parties known to have an interest therein.

22.4   A public notice of the imposition of provisional measures shall set forth, or otherwise make available through a separate report, sufficiently detailed explanations for the preliminary determinations on the existence of a subsidy and injury and shall refer to the matters of fact and law which have led to arguments being accepted or rejected. Such a notice or report shall, due regard being paid to the requirement for the protection of confidential information, contain in particular:

(i) the names of the suppliers or, when this is impracticable, the supplying countries involved;

(ii) a description of the product which is sufficient for customs purposes;

(iii) the amount of subsidy established and the basis on which the existence of a subsidy has been determined;

(iv) considerations relevant to the injury determination as set out in Article 15;

(v) the main reasons leading to the determination.

22.5   A public notice of conclusion or suspension of an investigation in the case of an affirmative determination providing for the imposition of a definitive duty or the acceptance of an undertaking shall contain, or otherwise make available through a separate report, all relevant information on the matters of fact and law and reasons which have led to the imposition of final measures or the acceptance of an undertaking, due regard being paid to the requirement for the protection of confidential information. In particular, the notice or report shall contain the information described in paragraph 4, as well as the reasons for the acceptance or rejection of relevant arguments or claims made by interested Members and by the exporters and importers.

22.6   A public notice of the termination or suspension of an investigation following the acceptance of an undertaking pursuant to Article 18 shall include, or otherwise make available through a separate report, the non-confidential part of this undertaking.

22.7   The provisions of this Article shall apply *mutatis mutandis* to the initiation and completion of reviews pursuant to Article 21 and to decisions under Article 20 to apply duties retroactively.

Article 23

Judicial Review

Each Member whose national legislation contains provisions on countervailing duty measures shall maintain judicial, arbitral or administrative tribunals or procedures for the purpose, *inter alia*, of the prompt review of administrative actions relating to final determinations and reviews of determinations within the meaning of Article 21. Such tribunals or procedures shall be independent of the authorities responsible for the determination or review in question, and shall provide all interested parties who participated in the administrative proceeding and are directly and individually affected by the administrative actions with access to review.

PART VI: INSTITUTIONS

Article 24

Committee on Subsidies and Countervailing Measures and Subsidiary Bodies

24.1   There is hereby established a Committee on Subsidies and Countervailing Measures composed of representatives from each of the Members. The Committee shall elect its own Chairman and shall meet not less than twice a year and otherwise as envisaged by relevant provisions of this Agreement at the request of any Member. The Committee shall carry out responsibilities as assigned to it under this Agreement or by the Members and it shall afford Members the opportunity of consulting on any matter relating to the operation of the Agreement or the furtherance of its objectives. The WTO Secretariat shall act as the secretariat to the Committee.

24.2   The Committee may set up subsidiary bodies as appropriate.

24.3   The Committee shall establish a Permanent Group of Experts composed of five independent persons, highly qualified in the fields of subsidies and trade relations. The experts will be elected by the Committee and one of them will be replaced every year. The PGE may be requested to assist a panel, as provided for in paragraph 5 of Article 4. The Committee may also seek an advisory opinion on the existence and nature of any subsidy.

24.4   The PGE may be consulted by any Member and may give advisory opinions on the nature of any subsidy proposed to be introduced or currently maintained by that Member. Such advisory opinions will be confidential and may not be invoked in proceedings under Article 7.

24.5   In carrying out their functions, the Committee and any subsidiary bodies may consult with and seek information from any source they deem appropriate. However, before the Committee or a subsidiary body seeks such information from a source within the jurisdiction of a Member, it shall inform the Member involved.

PART VII: NOTIFICATION AND SURVEILLANCE

Article 25

Notifications

25.1   Members agree that, without prejudice to the provisions of paragraph 1 of Article XVI of GATT 1994, their notifications of subsidies shall be submitted not later than 30 June of each year and shall conform to the provisions of paragraphs 2 through 6.

25.2   Members shall notify any subsidy as defined in paragraph 1 of Article 1, which is specific within the meaning of Article 2, granted or maintained within their territories.

25.3   The content of notifications should be sufficiently specific to enable other Members to evaluate the trade effects and to understand the operation of notified subsidy programmes. In this connection, and without prejudice to the contents and form of the questionnaire on subsidies[54], Members shall ensure that their notifications contain the following information:

(i) form of a subsidy (i.e. grant, loan, tax concession, etc.);

(ii) subsidy per unit or, in cases where this is not possible, the total amount or the annual amount budgeted for that subsidy (indicating, if possible, the average subsidy per unit in the previous year);

(iii) policy objective and/or purpose of a subsidy;

(iv) duration of a subsidy and/or any other time-limits attached to it;

(v) statistical data permitting an assessment of the trade effects of a subsidy.

25.4   Where specific points in paragraph 3 have not been addressed in a notification, an explanation shall be provided in the notification itself.

25.5   If subsidies are granted to specific products or sectors, the notifications should be organized by product or sector.

25.6   Members which consider that there are no measures in their territories requiring notification under paragraph 1 of Article XVI of GATT 1994 and this Agreement shall so inform the Secretariat in writing.

25.7   Members recognize that notification of a measure does not prejudge either its legal status under GATT 1994 and this Agreement, the effects under this Agreement, or the nature of the measure itself.

25.8   Any Member may, at any time, make a written request for information on the nature and extent of any subsidy granted or maintained by another Member (including any subsidy referred to in Part IV), or for an explanation of the reasons for which a specific measure has been considered as not subject to the requirement of notification.

25.9   Members so requested shall provide such information as quickly as possible and in a comprehensive manner, and shall be ready, upon request, to provide additional information to the requesting Member. In particular, they shall provide sufficient details to enable the other Member to assess their compliance with the terms of this Agreement. Any Member which considers that such information has not been provided may bring the matter to the attention of the Committee.

25.10   Any Member which considers that any measure of another Member having the effects of a subsidy has not been notified in accordance with the provisions of paragraph 1 of Article XVI of GATT 1994 and this Article may bring the matter to the attention of such other Member. If the alleged subsidy is not thereafter notified promptly, such Member may itself bring the alleged subsidy in question to the notice of the Committee.

---

54. The Committee shall establish a Working Party to review the contents and form of   the questionnaire as contained in BISD 9S/ 193–194.

25.11 Members shall report without delay to the Committee all preliminary or final actions taken with respect to countervailing duties. Such reports shall be available in the Secretariat for inspection by other Members. Members shall also submit, on a semi-annual basis, reports on any countervailing duty actions taken within the preceding six months. The semi-annual reports shall be submitted on an agreed standard form.

25.12 Each Member shall notify the Committee *(a)* which of its authorities are competent to initiate and conduct investigations referred to in Article 11 and *(b)* its domestic procedures governing the initiation and conduct of such investigations.

Article 26

Surveillance

26.1 The Committee shall examine new and full notifications submitted under paragraph 1 of Article XVI of GATT 1994 and paragraph 1 of Article 25 of this Agreement at special sessions held every third year. Notifications submitted in the intervening years (updating notifications) shall be examined at each regular meeting of the Committee.

26.2 The Committee shall examine reports submitted under paragraph 11 of Article 25 at each regular meeting of the Committee.

PART VIII: DEVELOPING COUNTRY MEMBERS

Article 27

Special and Differential Treatment of Developing Country Members

27.1 Members recognize that subsidies may play an important role in economic development programmes of developing country Members.

27.2 The prohibition of paragraph 1(a) of Article 3 shall not apply to:

(a) developing country Members referred to in Annex VII.

(b) other developing country Members for a period of eight years from the date of entry into force of the WTO Agreement, subject to compliance with the provisions in paragraph 4.

27.3 The prohibition of paragraph 1(b) of Article 3 shall not apply to developing country Members for a period of five years, and shall not apply to least developed country Members for a period of eight years, from the date of entry into force of the WTO Agreement.

27.4 Any developing country Member referred to in paragraph 2(b) shall phase out its export subsidies within the eight-year period, preferably in a progressive manner. However, a developing country Member shall not increase the level of its export subsidies[55], and shall eliminate them within a period shorter than that provided for in this paragraph when the use of such export subsidies is inconsistent with its development needs. If a developing country Member deems it necessary to apply such subsidies beyond the 8–year period, it shall not later than one year before the expiry of this period enter into consultation with the Committee, which will determine whether an

55. For a developing country Member not granting export subsidies as of the date of entry into force of the WTO Agreement, this paragraph shall apply on the basis of the level of export subsidies granted in 1986.

extension of this period is justified, after examining all the relevant economic, financial and development needs of the developing country Member in question. If the Committee determines that the extension is justified, the developing country Member concerned shall hold annual consultations with the Committee to determine the necessity of maintaining the subsidies. If no such determination is made by the Committee, the developing country Member shall phase out the remaining export subsidies within two years from the end of the last authorized period.

27.5   A developing country Member which has reached export competitiveness in any given product shall phase out its export subsidies for such product(s) over a period of two years. However, for a developing country Member which is referred to in Annex VII and which has reached export competitiveness in one or more products, export subsidies on such products shall be gradually phased out over a period of eight years.

27.6   Export competitiveness in a product exists if a developing country Member's exports of that product have reached a share of at least 3.25 per cent in world trade of that product for two consecutive calendar years. Export competitiveness shall exist either (a) on the basis of notification by the developing country Member having reached export competitiveness, or (b) on the basis of a computation undertaken by the Secretariat at the request of any Member. For the purpose of this paragraph, a product is defined as a section heading of the Harmonized System Nomenclature. The Committee shall review the operation of this provision five years from the date of the entry into force of the WTO Agreement.

27.7   The provisions of Article 4 shall not apply to a developing country Member in the case of export subsidies which are in conformity with the provisions of paragraphs 2 through 5. The relevant provisions in such a case shall be those of Article 7.

27.8   There shall be no presumption in terms of paragraph 1 of Article 6 that a subsidy granted by a developing country Member results in serious prejudice, as defined in this Agreement. Such serious prejudice, where applicable under the terms of paragraph 9, shall be demonstrated by positive evidence, in accordance with the provisions of paragraphs 3 through 8 of Article 6.

27.9   Regarding actionable subsidies granted or maintained by a developing country Member other than those referred to in paragraph 1 of Article 6, action may not be authorized or taken under Article 7 unless nullification or impairment of tariff concessions or other obligations under GATT 1994 is found to exist as a result of such a subsidy, in such a way as to displace or impede imports of a like product of another Member into the market of the subsidizing developing country Member or unless injury to a domestic industry in the market of an importing Member occurs.

27.10   Any countervailing duty investigation of a product originating in a developing country Member shall be terminated as soon as the authorities concerned determine that:

    (a) the overall level of subsidies granted upon the product in question does not exceed 2 per cent of its value calculated on a per unit basis; or

(b) the volume of the subsidized imports represents less than 4 per cent of the total imports of the like product in the importing Member, unless imports from developing country Members whose individual shares of total imports represent less than 4 per cent collectively account for more than 9 per cent of the total imports of the like product in the importing Member.

27.11   For those developing country Members within the scope of paragraph 2(b) which have eliminated export subsidies prior to the expiry of the period of eight years from the date of entry into force of the WTO Agreement, and for those developing country Members referred to in Annex VII, the number in paragraph 10(a) shall be 3 per cent rather than 2 per cent. This provision shall apply from the date that the elimination of export subsidies is notified to the Committee, and for so long as export subsidies are not granted by the notifying developing country Member. This provision shall expire eight years from the date of entry into force of the WTO Agreement.

27.12   The provisions of paragraphs 10 and 11 shall govern any determination of *de minimis* under paragraph 3 of Article 15.

27.13   The provisions of Part III shall not apply to direct forgiveness of debts, subsidies to cover social costs, in whatever form, including relinquishment of government revenue and other transfer of liabilities when such subsidies are granted within and directly linked to a privatization programme of a developing country Member, provided that both such programme and the subsidies involved are granted for a limited period and notified to the Committee and that the programme results in eventual privatization of the enterprise concerned.

27.14   The Committee shall, upon request by an interested Member, undertake a review of a specific export subsidy practice of a developing country Member to examine whether the practice is in conformity with its development needs.

27.15   The Committee shall, upon request by an interested developing country Member, undertake a review of a specific countervailing measure to examine whether it is consistent with the provisions of paragraphs 10 and 11 as applicable to the developing country Member in question.

PART IX: TRANSITIONAL ARRANGEMENTS

Article 28

Existing Programmes

28.1   Subsidy programmes which have been established within the territory of any Member before the date on which such a Member signed the WTO Agreement and which are inconsistent with the provisions of this Agreement shall be:

(a) notified to the Committee not later than 90 days after the date of entry into force of the WTO Agreement for such Member; and

(b) brought into conformity with the provisions of this Agreement within three years of the date of entry into force of the WTO Agreement for such Member and until then shall not be subject to Part II.

28.2 No Member shall extend the scope of any such programme, nor shall such a programme be renewed upon its expiry.

Article 29
Transformation into a Market Economy

29.1 Members in the process of transformation from a centrally-planned into a market, free-enterprise economy may apply programmes and measures necessary for such a transformation.

29.2 For such Members, subsidy programmes falling within the scope of Article 3, and notified according to paragraph 3, shall be phased out or brought into conformity with Article 3 within a period of seven years from the date of entry into force of the WTO Agreement. In such a case, Article 4 shall not apply. In addition during the same period:

(a) Subsidy programmes falling within the scope of paragraph 1(d) of Article 6 shall not be actionable under Article 7;

(b) With respect to other actionable subsidies, the provisions of paragraph 9 of Article 27 shall apply.

29.3 Subsidy programmes falling within the scope of Article 3 shall be notified to the Committee by the earliest practicable date after the date of entry into force of the WTO Agreement. Further notifications of such subsidies may be made up to two years after the date of entry into force of the WTO Agreement.

29.4 In exceptional circumstances Members referred to in paragraph 1 may be given departures from their notified programmes and measures and their time-frame by the Committee if such departures are deemed necessary for the process of transformation.

PART X: DISPUTE SETTLEMENT
Article 30

The provisions of Articles XXII and XXIII of GATT 1994 as elaborated and applied by the Dispute Settlement Understanding shall apply to consultations and the settlement of disputes under this Agreement, except as otherwise specifically provided herein.

PART XI: FINAL PROVISIONS
Article 31
Provisional Application

The provisions of paragraph 1 of Article 6 and the provisions of Article 8 and Article 9 shall apply for a period of five years, beginning with the date of entry into force of the WTO Agreement. Not later than 180 days before the end of this period, the Committee shall review the operation of those provisions, with a view to determining whether to extend their application, either as presently drafted or in a modified form, for a further period. [Editors' Note: No such decision had been taken as of July 2002.]

Article 32
Other Final Provisions

32.1 No specific action against a subsidy of another Member can be taken except in accordance with the provisions of GATT 1994, as interpreted by this Agreement.[56]

32.2   Reservations may not be entered in respect of any of the provisions of this Agreement without the consent of the other Members.

32.3   Subject to paragraph 4, the provisions of this Agreement shall apply to investigations, and reviews of existing measures, initiated pursuant to applications which have been made on or after the date of entry into force for a Member of the WTO Agreement.

32.4   For the purposes of paragraph 3 of Article 21, existing countervailing measures shall be deemed to be imposed on a date not later than the date of entry into force for a Member of the WTO Agreement, except in cases in which the domestic legislation of a Member in force at that date already included a clause of the type provided for in that paragraph.

32.5   Each Member shall take all necessary steps, of a general or particular character, to ensure, not later than the date of entry into force of the WTO Agreement for it, the conformity of its laws, regulations and administrative procedures with the provisions of this Agreement as they may apply to the Member in question.

32.6   Each Member shall inform the Committee of any changes in its laws and regulations relevant to this Agreement and in the administration of such laws and regulations.

32.7   The Committee shall review annually the implementation and operation of this Agreement, taking into account the objectives thereof. The Committee shall inform annually the Council for Trade in Goods of developments during the period covered by such reviews.

32.8   The Annexes to this Agreement constitute an integral part thereof.

ANNEX I

ILLUSTRATIVE LIST OF EXPORT SUBSIDIES

(a) The provision by governments of direct subsidies to a firm or an industry contingent upon export performance.

(b) Currency retention schemes or any similar practices which involve a bonus on exports.

(c) Internal transport and freight charges on export shipments, provided or mandated by governments, on terms more favourable than for domestic shipments.

(d) The provision by governments or their agencies either directly or indirectly through government-mandated schemes, of imported or domestic products or services for use in the production of exported goods, on terms or conditions more favourable than for provision of like or directly competitive products or services for use in the production of goods for domestic consumption, if (in the case of products) such terms or conditions are more favourable than those commercially available[57] on world markets to their exporters.

---

56. This paragraph is not intended to preclude action under other relevant provisions of GATT 1994, where appropriate.

57. The term "commercially available" means that the choice between domestic and imported products is unrestricted and depends only on commercial considerations.

(e) The full or partial exemption remission, or deferral specifically related to exports, of direct taxes[58] or social welfare charges paid or payable by industrial or commercial enterprises.[59]

(f) The allowance of special deductions directly related to exports or export performance, over and above those granted in respect to production for domestic consumption, in the calculation of the base on which direct taxes are charged.

(g) The exemption or remission, in respect of the production and distribution of exported products, of indirect taxes [58]in excess of those levied in respect of the production and distribution of like products when sold for domestic consumption.

(h) The exemption, remission or deferral of prior-stage cumulative indirect taxes [58]on goods or services used in the production of exported products in excess of the exemption, remission or deferral of like prior-stage cumulative indirect taxes on goods or services used in the production of like products when sold for domestic consumption; provided, however, that prior-stage cumulative indirect taxes may be exempted, remitted or deferred on exported products even when not exempted, remitted or deferred on like products when sold for domestic consumption, if the prior-stage cumulative indirect taxes are levied on inputs that are consumed in the production of the exported product (making normal allowance for waste).[60] This item shall be interpreted in accordance with the guidelines on consumption of inputs in the production process contained in Annex II.

58. For the purpose of this Agreement:

The term "direct taxes" shall mean taxes on wages, profits, interests, rents, royalties, and all other forms of income, and taxes on the ownership of real property;

The term "import charges" shall mean tariffs, duties, and other fiscal charges not elsewhere enumerated in this note that are levied on imports;

The term "indirect taxes" shall mean sales, excise, turnover, value added, franchise, stamp, transfer, inventory and equipment taxes, border taxes and all taxes other than direct taxes and import charges;

"Prior-stage" indirect taxes are those levied on goods or services used directly or indirectly in making the product;

"Cumulative" indirect taxes are multistaged taxes levied where there is no mechanism for subsequent crediting of the tax if the goods or services subject to tax at one stage of production are used in a succeeding stage of production;

"Remission" of taxes includes the refund or rebate of taxes;

"Remission or drawback" includes the full or partial exemption or deferral of import charges.

59. The Members recognize that deferral need not amount to an export subsidy where, for example, appropriate interest charges are collected. The Members reaffirm the principle that prices for goods in transactions between exporting enterprises and foreign buyers under their or under the same control should for tax purposes be the prices which would be charged between independent enterprises acting at arm's length. Any Member may draw the attention of another Member to administrative or other practices which may contravene this principle and which result in a significant saving of direct taxes in export transactions. In such circumstances the Members shall normally attempt to resolve their differences using the facilities of existing bilateral tax treaties or other specific international mechanisms, without prejudice to the rights and obligations of Members under GATT 1994, including the right of consultation created in the preceding sentence.

Paragraph (e) is not intended to limit a Member from taking measures to avoid the double taxation of foreign-source income earned by its enterprises or the enterprises of another Member.

60. Paragraph (h) does not apply to value-added tax systems and border-tax adjustment in lieu thereof; the problem of the excessive remission of value-added taxes is exclusively covered by paragraph (g).

(i) The remission or drawback of import charges [58]in excess of those levied on imported inputs that are consumed in the production of the exported product (making normal allowance for waste); provided, however, that in particular cases a firm may use a quantity of home market inputs equal to, and having the same quality and characteristics as, the imported inputs as a substitute for them in order to benefit from this provision if the import and the corresponding export operations both occur within a reasonable time period, not to exceed two years. This item shall be interpreted in accordance with the guidelines on consumption of inputs in the production process contained in Annex II and the guidelines in the determination of substitution drawback systems as export subsidies contained in Annex III.

(j) The provision by governments (or special institutions controlled by governments) of export credit guarantee or insurance programmes, of insurance or guarantee programmes against increases in the cost of exported products or of exchange risk programmes, at premium rates which are inadequate to cover the long-term operating costs and losses of the programmes.

(k) The grant by governments (or special institutions controlled by and/or acting under the authority of governments) of export credits at rates below those which they actually have to pay for the funds so employed (or would have to pay if they borrowed on international capital markets in order to obtain funds of the same maturity and other credit terms and denominated in the same currency as the export credit), or the payment by them of all or part of the costs incurred by exporters or financial institutions in obtaining credits, in so far as they are used to secure a material advantage in the field of export credit terms.

Provided, however, that if a Member is a party to an international undertaking on official export credits to which at least twelve original Members to this Agreement are parties as of 1 January 1979 (or a successor undertaking which has been adopted by those original Members), or if in practice a Member applies the interest rates provisions of the relevant undertaking, an export credit practice which is in conformity with those provisions shall not be considered an export subsidy prohibited by this Agreement.

(*l*) Any other charge on the public account constituting an export subsidy in the sense of Article XVI of GATT 1994.

ANNEX II

GUIDELINES ON CONSUMPTION OF INPUTS IN THE PRODUCTION PROCESS[61]

I

1. Indirect tax rebate schemes can allow for exemption, remission or deferral of prior-stage cumulative indirect taxes levied on inputs that are consumed in the production of the exported product (making normal allowance for waste). Similarly, drawback schemes can allow for the remission or

---

61. Inputs consumed in the production process are inputs physically incorporated, energy, fuels and oil used in the production process and catalysts which are consumed in the course of their use to obtain the exported product.

drawback of import charges levied on inputs that are consumed in the production of the exported product (making normal allowance for waste).

2.   The Illustrative List of Export Subsidies in Annex I of this Agreement makes reference to the term "inputs that are consumed in the production of the exported product" in paragraphs (h) and (i). Pursuant to paragraph (h), indirect tax rebate schemes can constitute an export subsidy to the extent that they result in exemption, remission or deferral of prior-stage cumulative indirect taxes in excess of the amount of such taxes actually levied on inputs that are consumed in the production of the exported product. Pursuant to paragraph (i), drawback schemes can constitute an export subsidy to the extent that they result in a remission or drawback of import charges in excess of those actually levied on inputs that are consumed in the production of the exported product. Both paragraphs stipulate that normal allowance for waste must be made in findings regarding consumption of inputs in the production of the exported product. Paragraph (i) also provides for substitution, where appropriate.

II

In examining whether inputs are consumed in the production of the exported product, as part of a countervailing duty investigation pursuant to this Agreement, investigating authorities should proceed on the following basis:

1.   Where it is alleged that an indirect tax rebate scheme, or a drawback scheme, conveys a subsidy by reason of over-rebate or excess drawback of indirect taxes or import charges on inputs consumed in the production of the exported product, the investigating authorities should first determine whether the government of the exporting Member has in place and applies a system or procedure to confirm which inputs are consumed in the production of the exported product and in what amounts. Where such a system or procedure is determined to be applied, the investigating authorities should then examine the system or procedure to see whether it is reasonable, effective for the purpose intended, and based on generally accepted commercial practices in the country of export. The investigating authorities may deem it necessary to carry out, in accordance with paragraph 6 of Article 12, certain practical tests in order to verify information or to satisfy themselves that the system or procedure is being effectively applied.

2.   Where there is no such system or procedure, where it is not reasonable, or where it is instituted and considered reasonable but is found not to be applied or not to be applied effectively, a further examination by the exporting Member based on the actual inputs involved would need to be carried out in the context of determining whether an excess payment occurred. If the investigating authorities deemed it necessary, a further examination would be carried out in accordance with paragraph 1.

3.   Investigating authorities should treat inputs as physically incorporated if such inputs are used in the production process and are physically present in the product exported. The Members note that an input need not be present in the final product in the same form in which it entered the production process.

4.   In determining the amount of a particular input that is consumed in the production of the exported product, a "normal allowance for waste" should be taken into account, and such waste should be treated as consumed in the production of the exported product. The term "waste" refers to that portion of a given input which does not serve an independent function in the production process, is not consumed in the production of the exported product (for reasons such as inefficiencies) and is not recovered, used or sold by the same manufacturer.

5.   The investigating authority's determination of whether the claimed allowance for waste is "normal" should take into account the production process, the average experience of the industry in the country of export, and other technical factors, as appropriate. The investigating authority should bear in mind that an important question is whether the authorities in the exporting Member have reasonably calculated the amount of waste, when such an amount is intended to be included in the tax or duty rebate or remission.

ANNEX III

GUIDELINES IN THE DETERMINATION OF SUBSTITUTION DRAWBACK SYSTEMS AS EXPORT SUBSIDIES

I

Drawback systems can allow for the refund or drawback of import charges on inputs which are consumed in the production process of another product and where the export of this latter product contains domestic inputs having the same quality and characteristics as those substituted for the imported inputs. Pursuant to paragraph (i) of the Illustrative List of Export Subsidies in Annex I, substitution drawback systems can constitute an export subsidy to the extent that they result in an excess drawback of the import charges levied initially on the imported inputs for which drawback is being claimed.

II

In examining any substitution drawback system as part of a countervailing duty investigation pursuant to this Agreement, investigating authorities should proceed on the following basis:

1.   Paragraph (i) of the Illustrative List stipulates that home market inputs may be substituted for imported inputs in the production of a product for export provided such inputs are equal in quantity to, and have the same quality and characteristics as, the imported inputs being substituted. The existence of a verification system or procedure is important because it enables the government of the exporting Member to ensure and demonstrate that the quantity of inputs for which drawback is claimed does not exceed the quantity of similar products exported, in whatever form, and that there is not drawback of import charges in excess of those originally levied on the imported inputs in question.

2.   Where it is alleged that a substitution drawback system conveys a subsidy, the investigating authorities should first proceed to determine whether the government of the exporting Member has in place and applies a verification system or procedure. Where such a system or procedure is

determined to be applied, the investigating authorities should then examine the verification procedures to see whether they are reasonable, effective for the purpose intended, and based on generally accepted commercial practices in the country of export. To the extent that the procedures are determined to meet this test and are effectively applied, no subsidy should be presumed to exist. It may be deemed necessary by the investigating authorities to carry out, in accordance with paragraph 6 of Article 12, certain practical tests in order to verify information or to satisfy themselves that the verification procedures are being effectively applied.

3. Where there are no verification procedures, where they are not reasonable, or where such procedures are instituted and considered reasonable but are found not to be actually applied or not applied effectively, there may be a subsidy. In such cases a further examination by the exporting Member based on the actual transactions involved would need to be carried out to determine whether an excess payment occurred. If the investigating authorities deemed it necessary, a further examination would be carried out in accordance with paragraph 2.

4. The existence of a substitution drawback provision under which exporters are allowed to select particular import shipments on which drawback is claimed should not of itself be considered to convey a subsidy.

5. An excess drawback of import charges in the sense of paragraph (i) would be deemed to exist where governments paid interest on any monies refunded under their drawback schemes, to the extent of the interest actually paid or payable.

ANNEX IV
CALCULATION OF THE TOTAL AD VALOREM SUBSIDIZATION (PARAGRAPH 1(A) OF ARTICLE 6)[62]

1. Any calculation of the amount of a subsidy for the purpose of paragraph 1(a) of Article 6 shall be done in terms of the cost to the granting government.

2. Except as provided in paragraphs 3 through 5, in determining whether the overall rate of subsidization exceeds 5 per cent of the value of the product, the value of the product shall be calculated as the total value of the recipient firm's[63] sales in the most recent 12–month period, for which sales data is available, preceding the period in which the subsidy is granted.[64]

3. Where the subsidy is tied to the production or sale of a given product, the value of the product shall be calculated as the total value of the recipient firm's sales of that product in the most recent 12–month period, for which sales data is available, preceding the period in which the subsidy is granted.

4. Where the recipient firm is in a start-up situation, serious prejudice shall be deemed to exist if the overall rate of subsidization exceeds 15 per cent

---

62. An understanding among Members should be developed, as necessary, on matters which are not specified in this Annex or which need further clarification for the purposes of paragraph 1(a) of Article 6.

63. The recipient firm is a firm in the territory of the subsidizing Member.

64. In the case of tax-related subsidies the value of the product shall be calculated as the total value of the recipient firm's sales in the fiscal year in which the tax-related measure was earned.

of the total funds invested. For purposes of this paragraph, a start-up period will not extend beyond the first year of production.[65]

5. Where the recipient firm is located in an inflationary economy country, the value of the product shall be calculated as the recipient firm's total sales (or sales of the relevant product, if the subsidy is tied) in the preceding calendar year indexed by the rate of inflation experienced in the 12 months preceding the month in which the subsidy is to be given.

6. In determining the overall rate of subsidization in a given year, subsidies given under different programmes and by different authorities in the territory of a Member shall be aggregated.

7. Subsidies granted prior to the date of entry into force of the WTO Agreement, the benefits of which are allocated to future production, shall be included in the overall rate of subsidization.

8. Subsidies which are non-actionable under relevant provisions of this Agreement shall not be included in the calculation of the amount of a subsidy for the purpose of paragraph 1(a) of Article 6.

ANNEX V
PROCEDURES FOR DEVELOPING INFORMATION CONCERNING SERIOUS PREJUDICE

1. Every Member shall cooperate in the development of evidence to be examined by a panel in procedures under paragraphs 4 through 6 of Article 7. The parties to the dispute and any third-country Member concerned shall notify to the DSB, as soon as the provisions of paragraph 4 of Article 7 have been invoked, the organization responsible for administration of this provision within its territory and the procedures to be used to comply with requests for information.

2. In cases where matters are referred to the DSB under paragraph 4 of Article 7, the DSB shall, upon request, initiate the procedure to obtain such information from the government of the subsidizing Member as necessary to establish the existence and amount of subsidization, the value of total sales of the subsidized firms, as well as information necessary to analyze the adverse effects caused by the subsidized product.[66] This process may include, where appropriate, presentation of questions to the government of the subsidizing Member and of the complaining Member to collect information, as well as to clarify and obtain elaboration of information available to the parties to a dispute through the notification procedures set forth in Part VII.[67]

3. In the case of effects in third-country markets, a party to a dispute may collect information, including through the use of questions to the government of the third-country Member, necessary to analyse adverse effects, which is not otherwise reasonably available from the complaining

---

65. Start-up situations include instances where financial commitments for product development or construction of facilities to manufacture products benefiting from the subsidy have been made, even though production has not begun.

66. In cases where the existence of serious prejudice has to be demonstrated.

67. The information-gathering process by the DSB shall take into account the need to protect information which is by nature confidential or which is provided on a confidential basis by any Member involved in this process.

Member or the subsidizing Member. This requirement should be administered in such a way as not to impose an unreasonable burden on the third-country Member. In particular, such a Member is not expected to make a market or price analysis specially for that purpose. The information to be supplied is that which is already available or can be readily obtained by this Member (e.g. most recent statistics which have already been gathered by relevant statistical services but which have not yet been published, customs data concerning imports and declared values of the products concerned, etc.). However, if a party to a dispute undertakes a detailed market analysis at its own expense, the task of the person or firm conducting such an analysis shall be facilitated by the authorities of the third-country Member and such a person or firm shall be given access to all information which is not normally maintained confidential by the government.

4. The DSB shall designate a representative to serve the function of facilitating the information-gathering process. The sole purpose of the representative shall be to ensure the timely development of the information necessary to facilitate expeditious subsequent multilateral review of the dispute. In particular, the representative may suggest ways to most efficiently solicit necessary information as well as encourage the cooperation of the parties.

5. The information-gathering process outlined in paragraphs 2 through 4 shall be completed within 60 days of the date on which the matter has been referred to the DSB under paragraph 4 of Article 7. The information obtained during this process shall be submitted to the panel established by the DSB in accordance with the provisions of Part X. This information should include, *inter alia*, data concerning the amount of the subsidy in question (and, where appropriate, the value of total sales of the subsidized firms), prices of the subsidized product, prices of the non-subsidized product, prices of other suppliers to the market, changes in the supply of the subsidized product to the market in question and changes in market shares. It should also include rebuttal evidence, as well as such supplemental information as the panel deems relevant in the course of reaching its conclusions.

6. If the subsidizing and/or third-country Member fail to cooperate in the information-gathering process, the complaining Member will present its case of serious prejudice, based on evidence available to it, together with facts and circumstances of the non-cooperation of the subsidizing and/or third-country Member. Where information is unavailable due to non-cooperation by the subsidizing and/or third-country Member, the panel may complete the record as necessary relying on best information otherwise available.

7. In making its determination, the panel should draw adverse inferences from instances of non-cooperation by any party involved in the information-gathering process.

8. In making a determination to use either best information available or adverse inferences, the panel shall consider the advice of the DSB representative nominated under paragraph 4 as to the reasonableness of any requests for information and the efforts made by parties to comply with these requests in a cooperative and timely manner.

9. Nothing in the information-gathering process shall limit the ability of the panel to seek such additional information it deems essential to a proper

resolution to the dispute, and which was not adequately sought or developed during that process. However, ordinarily the panel should not request additional information to complete the record where the information would support a particular party's position and the absence of that information in the record is the result of unreasonable non-cooperation by that party in the information-gathering process.

ANNEX VI

PROCEDURES FOR ON–THE–SPOT INVESTIGATIONS PURSUANT TO PARAGRAPH 6 OF ARTICLE 12

1. Upon initiation of an investigation, the authorities of the exporting Member and the firms known to be concerned should be informed of the intention to carry out on-the-spot investigations.

2. If in exceptional circumstances it is intended to include non-governmental experts in the investigating team, the firms and the authorities of the exporting Member should be so informed. Such non-governmental experts should be subject to effective sanctions for breach of confidentiality requirements.

3. It should be standard practice to obtain explicit agreement of the firms concerned in the exporting Member before the visit is finally scheduled.

4. As soon as the agreement of the firms concerned has been obtained, the investigating authorities should notify the authorities of the exporting Member of the names and addresses of the firms to be visited and the dates agreed.

5. Sufficient advance notice should be given to the firms in question before the visit is made.

6. Visits to explain the questionnaire should only be made at the request of an exporting firm. In case of such a request the investigating authorities may place themselves at the disposal of the firm; such a visit may only be made if *(a)* the authorities of the importing Member notify the representatives of the government of the Member in question and *(b)* the latter do not object to the visit.

7. As the main purpose of the on-the-spot investigation is to verify information provided or to obtain further details, it should be carried out after the response to the questionnaire has been received unless the firm agrees to the contrary and the government of the exporting Member is informed by the investigating authorities of the anticipated visit and does not object to it; further, it should be standard practice prior to the visit to advise the firms concerned of the general nature of the information to be verified and of any further information which needs to be provided, though this should not preclude requests to be made on the spot for further details to be provided in the light of information obtained.

8. Enquiries or questions put by the authorities or firms of the exporting Members and essential to a successful on-the-spot investigation should, whenever possible, be answered before the visit is made.

ANNEX VII
DEVELOPING COUNTRY MEMBERS REFERRED TO IN PARAGRAPH 2(A) OF ARTICLE 27

The developing country Members not subject to the provisions of paragraph 1(a) of Article 3 under the terms of paragraph 2(a) of Article 27 are:

(a) Least-developed countries designated as such by the United Nations which are Members of the WTO.

(b) Each of the following developing countries which are Members of the WTO shall be subject to the provisions which are applicable to other developing country Members according to paragraph 2(b) of Article 27 when GNP per capita has reached $1,000 per annum[68]: Bolivia, Cameroon, Congo, Côte d'Ivoire, Dominican Republic, Egypt, Ghana, Guatemala, Guyana, India, Indonesia, Kenya, Morocco, Nicaragua, Nigeria, Pakistan, Philippines, Senegal, Sri Lanka and Zimbabwe.

68. The inclusion of developing country Members in the list in paragraph (b) is based on the most recent data from the World Bank on GNP per capita.

Item 15

AGREEMENT ON SAFEGUARDS

Members,

Having in mind the overall objective of the Members to improve and strengthen the international trading system based on GATT 1994;

Recognizing the need to clarify and reinforce the disciplines of GATT 1994, and specifically those of its Article XIX (Emergency Action on Imports of Particular Products), to re-establish multilateral control over safeguards and eliminate measures that escape such control;

Recognizing the importance of structural adjustment and the need to enhance rather than limit competition in international markets; and

Recognizing further that, for these purposes, a comprehensive agreement, applicable to all Members and based on the basic principles of GATT 1994, is called for;

Hereby *agree* as follows:

Article 1

General Provision

This Agreement establishes rules for the application of safeguard measures which shall be understood to mean those measures provided for in Article XIX of GATT 1994.

Article 2

Conditions

1. A Member [1] may apply a safeguard measure to a product only if that Member has determined, pursuant to the provisions set out below, that such product is being imported into its territory in such increased quantities, absolute or relative to domestic production, and under such conditions as to cause or threaten to cause serious injury to the domestic industry that produces like or directly competitive products.

2. Safeguard measures shall be applied to a product being imported irrespective of its source.

---

1. A customs union may apply a safeguard measure as a single unit or on behalf of a member State. When a customs union applies a safeguard measure as a single unit, all the requirements for the determination of serious injury or threat thereof under this Agreement shall be based on the conditions existing in the customs union as a whole. When a safeguard measure is applied on behalf of a member State, all the requirements for the determination of serious injury or threat thereof shall be based on the conditions existing in that member State and the measure shall be limited to that member State. Nothing in this Agreement prejudges the interpretation of the relationship between Article XIX and paragraph 8 of Article XXIV of GATT 1994.

Article 3

Investigation

1.   A Member may apply a safeguard measure only following an investigation by the competent authorities of that Member pursuant to procedures previously established and made public in consonance with Article X of GATT 1994.   This investigation shall include reasonable public notice to all interested parties and public hearings or other appropriate means in which importers, exporters and other interested parties could present evidence and their views, including the opportunity to respond to the presentations of other parties and to submit their views, *inter alia*, as to whether or not the application of a safeguard measure would be in the public interest.   The competent authorities shall publish a report setting forth their findings and reasoned conclusions reached on all pertinent issues of fact and law.

2.   Any information which is by nature confidential or which is provided on a confidential basis shall, upon cause being shown, be treated as such by the competent authorities.   Such information shall not be disclosed without permission of the party submitting it.   Parties providing confidential information may be requested to furnish non-confidential summaries thereof or, if such parties indicate that such information cannot be summarized, the reasons why a summary cannot be provided.   However, if the competent authorities find that a request for confidentiality is not warranted and if the party concerned is either unwilling to make the information public or to authorize its disclosure in generalized or summary form, the authorities may disregard such information unless it can be demonstrated to their satisfaction from appropriate sources that the information is correct.

Article 4

Determination of Serious Injury or Threat Thereof

1.   For the purposes of this Agreement:

(a) "serious injury" shall be understood to mean a significant overall impairment in the position of a domestic industry;

(b) "threat of serious injury" shall be understood to mean serious injury that is clearly imminent, in accordance with the provisions of paragraph 2.   A determination of the existence of a threat of serious injury shall be based on facts and not merely on allegation, conjecture or remote possibility; and

(c) in determining injury or threat thereof, a "domestic industry" shall be understood to mean the producers as a whole of the like or directly competitive products operating within the territory of a Member, or those whose collective output of the like or directly competitive products constitutes a major proportion of the total domestic production of those products.

2.   (a) In the investigation to determine whether increased imports have caused or are threatening to cause serious injury to a domestic industry under the terms of this Agreement, the competent authorities shall evaluate all relevant factors of an objective and quantifiable nature having a bearing on the situation of that industry, in particular, the rate and amount of the

increase in imports of the product concerned in absolute and relative terms, the share of the domestic market taken by increased imports, changes in the level of sales, production, productivity, capacity utilization, profits and losses, and employment.

(b) The determination referred to in subparagraph (a) shall not be made unless this investigation demonstrates, on the basis of objective evidence, the existence of the causal link between increased imports of the product concerned and serious injury or threat thereof. When factors other than increased imports are causing injury to the domestic industry at the same time, such injury shall not be attributed to increased imports.

(c) The competent authorities shall publish promptly, in accordance with the provisions of Article 3, a detailed analysis of the case under investigation as well as a demonstration of the relevance of the factors examined.

Article 5

Application of Safeguard Measures

1. A Member shall apply safeguard measures only to the extent necessary to prevent or remedy serious injury and to facilitate adjustment. If a quantitative restriction is used, such a measure shall not reduce the quantity of imports below the level of a recent period which shall be the average of imports in the last three representative years for which statistics are available, unless clear justification is given that a different level is necessary to prevent or remedy serious injury. Members should choose measures most suitable for the achievement of these objectives.

2. (a) In cases in which a quota is allocated among supplying countries, the Member applying the restrictions may seek agreement with respect to the allocation of shares in the quota with all other Members having a substantial interest in supplying the product concerned. In cases in which this method is not reasonably practicable, the Member concerned shall allot to Members having a substantial interest in supplying the product shares based upon the proportions, supplied by such Members during a previous representative period, of the total quantity or value of imports of the product, due account being taken of any special factors which may have affected or may be affecting the trade in the product.

(b) A Member may depart from the provisions in subparagraph (a) provided that consultations under paragraph 3 of Article 12 are conducted under the auspices of the Committee on Safeguards provided for in paragraph 1 of Article 13 and that clear demonstration is provided to the Committee that (i) imports from certain Members have increased in disproportionate percentage in relation to the total increase of imports of the product concerned in the representative period, (ii) the reasons for the departure from the provisions in subparagraph (a) are justified, and (iii) the conditions of such departure are equitable to all suppliers of the product concerned. The duration of any such measure shall not be extended beyond the initial period under paragraph 1 of Article 7. The departure referred to above shall not be permitted in the case of threat of serious injury.

Article 6
Provisional Safeguard Measures

In critical circumstances where delay would cause damage which it would be difficult to repair, a Member may take a provisional safeguard measure pursuant to a preliminary determination that there is clear evidence that increased imports have caused or are threatening to cause serious injury. The duration of the provisional measure shall not exceed 200 days, during which period the pertinent requirements of Articles 2 through 7 and 12 shall be met. Such measures should take the form of tariff increases to be promptly refunded if the subsequent investigation referred to in paragraph 2 of Article 4 does not determine that increased imports have caused or threatened to cause serious injury to a domestic industry. The duration of any such provisional measure shall be counted as a part of the initial period and any extension referred to in paragraphs 1, 2 and 3 of Article 7.

Article 7
Duration and Review of Safeguard Measures

1. A Member shall apply safeguard measures only for such period of time as may be necessary to prevent or remedy serious injury and to facilitate adjustment. The period shall not exceed four years, unless it is extended under paragraph 2.

2. The period mentioned in paragraph 1 may be extended provided that the competent authorities of the importing Member have determined, in conformity with the procedures set out in Articles 2, 3, 4 and 5, that the safeguard measure continues to be necessary to prevent or remedy serious injury and that there is evidence that the industry is adjusting, and provided that the pertinent provisions of Articles 8 and 12 are observed.

3. The total period of application of a safeguard measure including the period of application of any provisional measure, the period of initial application and any extension thereof, shall not exceed eight years.

4. In order to facilitate adjustment in a situation where the expected duration of a safeguard measure as notified under the provisions of paragraph 1 of Article 12 is over one year, the Member applying the measure shall progressively liberalize it at regular intervals during the period of application. If the duration of the measure exceeds three years, the Member applying such a measure shall review the situation not later than the mid-term of the measure and, if appropriate, withdraw it or increase the pace of liberalization. A measure extended under paragraph 2 shall not be more restrictive than it was at the end of the initial period, and should continue to be liberalized.

5. No safeguard measure shall be applied again to the import of a product which has been subject to such a measure, taken after the date of entry into force of the WTO Agreement, for a period of time equal to that during which such measure had been previously applied, provided that the period of non-application is at least two years.

6. Notwithstanding the provisions of paragraph 5, a safeguard measure with a duration of 180 days or less may be applied again to the import of a product if:

(a) at least one year has elapsed since the date of introduction of a safeguard measure on the import of that product; and

(b) such a safeguard measure has not been applied on the same product more than twice in the five-year period immediately preceding the date of introduction of the measure.

Article 8

Level of Concessions and Other Obligations

1. A Member proposing to apply a safeguard measure or seeking an extension of a safeguard measure shall endeavour to maintain a substantially equivalent level of concessions and other obligations to that existing under GATT 1994 between it and the exporting Members which would be affected by such a measure, in accordance with the provisions of paragraph 3 of Article 12. To achieve this objective, the Members concerned may agree on any adequate means of trade compensation for the adverse effects of the measure on their trade.

2. If no agreement is reached within 30 days in the consultations under paragraph 3 of Article 12, then the affected exporting Members shall be free, not later than 90 days after the measure is applied, to suspend, upon the expiration of 30 days from the day on which written notice of such suspension is received by the Council for Trade in Goods, the application of substantially equivalent concessions or other obligations under GATT 1994, to the trade of the Member applying the safeguard measure, the suspension of which the Council for Trade in Goods does not disapprove.

3. The right of suspension referred to in paragraph 2 shall not be exercised for the first three years that a safeguard measure is in effect, provided that the safeguard measure has been taken as a result of an absolute increase in imports and that such a measure conforms to the provisions of this Agreement.

Article 9

Developing Country Members

1. Safeguard measures shall not be applied against a product originating in a developing country Member as long as its share of imports of the product concerned in the importing Member does not exceed 3 per cent, provided that developing country Members with less than 3 per cent import share collectively account for not more than 9 per cent of total imports of the product concerned.[2]

2. A developing country Member shall have the right to extend the period of application of a safeguard measure for a period of up to two years beyond the maximum period provided for in paragraph 3 of Article 7. Notwithstanding the provisions of paragraph 5 of Article 7, a developing country Member shall have the right to apply a safeguard measure again to the import of a product which has been subject to such a measure, taken after the date of entry into force of the WTO Agreement, after a period of time equal to half that during which such a measure has been previously applied, provided that the period of non-application is at least two years.

---

2. A Member shall immediately notify an action taken under paragraph 1 of Article 9 to the Committee on Safeguards.

Article 10
Pre-existing Article XIX Measures

Members shall terminate all safeguard measures taken pursuant to Article XIX of GATT 1947 that were in existence on the date of entry into force of the WTO Agreement not later than eight years after the date on which they were first applied or five years after the date of entry into force of the WTO Agreement, whichever comes later.

Article 11
Prohibition and Elimination of Certain Measures

1.   (a) A Member shall not take or seek any emergency action on imports of particular products as set forth in Article XIX of GATT 1994 unless such action conforms with the provisions of that Article applied in accordance with this Agreement.

(b) Furthermore, a Member shall not seek, take or maintain any voluntary export restraints, orderly marketing arrangements or any other similar measures on the export or the import side.[3, 4] These include actions taken by a single Member as well as actions under agreements, arrangements and understandings entered into by two or more Members. Any such measure in effect on the date of entry into force of the WTO Agreement shall be brought into conformity with this Agreement or phased out in accordance with paragraph 2.

(c) This Agreement does not apply to measures sought, taken or maintained by a Member pursuant to provisions of GATT 1994 other than Article XIX, and Multilateral Trade Agreements in Annex 1A other than this Agreement, or pursuant to protocols and agreements or arrangements concluded within the framework of GATT 1994.

2.   The phasing out of measures referred to in paragraph 1(b) shall be carried out according to timetables to be presented to the Committee on Safeguards by the Members concerned not later than 180 days after the date of entry into force of the WTO Agreement. These timetables shall provide for all measures referred to in paragraph 1 to be phased out or brought into conformity with this Agreement within a period not exceeding four years after the date of entry into force of the WTO Agreement, subject to not more than one specific measure per importing Member[5], the duration of which shall not extend beyond 31 December 1999. Any such exception must be mutually agreed between the Members directly concerned and notified to the Committee on Safeguards for its review and acceptance within 90 days of the entry into force of the WTO Agreement. The Annex to this Agreement indicates a measure which has been agreed as falling under this exception.

3.   Members shall not encourage or support the adoption or maintenance by public and private enterprises of non-governmental measures equivalent to those referred to in paragraph 1.

---

3. An import quota applied as a safeguard measure in conformity with the relevant provisions of GATT 1994 and this Agreement may, by mutual agreement, be administered by the exporting Member.

4. Examples of similar measures include export moderation, export-price or import-price monitoring systems, export or import surveil-lance, compulsory import cartels and discretionary export or import licensing schemes, any of which afford protection.

5. The only such exception to which the European Communities is entitled is indicated in the Annex to this Agreement.

Article 12

Notification and Consultation

1. A Member shall immediately notify the Committee on Safeguards upon:

> (a) initiating an investigatory process relating to serious injury or threat thereof and the reasons for it;

> (b) making a finding of serious injury or threat thereof caused by increased imports; and

> (c) taking a decision to apply or extend a safeguard measure.

2. In making the notifications referred to in paragraphs 1(b) and 1(c), the Member proposing to apply or extend a safeguard measure shall provide the Committee on Safeguards with all pertinent information, which shall include evidence of serious injury or threat thereof caused by increased imports, precise description of the product involved and the proposed measure, proposed date of introduction, expected duration and timetable for progressive liberalization. In the case of an extension of a measure, evidence that the industry concerned is adjusting shall also be provided. The Council for Trade in Goods or the Committee on Safeguards may request such additional information as they may consider necessary from the Member proposing to apply or extend the measure.

3. A Member proposing to apply or extend a safeguard measure shall provide adequate opportunity for prior consultations with those Members having a substantial interest as exporters of the product concerned, with a view to, *inter alia*, reviewing the information provided under paragraph 2, exchanging views on the measure and reaching an understanding on ways to achieve the objective set out in paragraph 1 of Article 8.

4. A Member shall make a notification to the Committee on Safeguards before taking a provisional safeguard measure referred to in Article 6. Consultations shall be initiated immediately after the measure is taken.

5. The results of the consultations referred to in this Article, as well as the results of mid-term reviews referred to in paragraph 4 of Article 7, any form of compensation referred to in paragraph 1 of Article 8, and proposed suspensions of concessions and other obligations referred to in paragraph 2 of Article 8, shall be notified immediately to the Council for Trade in Goods by the Members concerned.

6. Members shall notify promptly the Committee on Safeguards of their laws, regulations and administrative procedures relating to safeguard measures as well as any modifications made to them.

7. Members maintaining measures described in Article 10 and paragraph 1 of Article 11 which exist on the date of entry into force of the WTO Agreement shall notify such measures to the Committee on Safeguards not later than 60 days after the date of entry into force of the WTO Agreement.

8. Any Member may notify the Committee on Safeguards of all laws, regulations, administrative procedures and any measures or actions dealt with in this Agreement that have not been notified by other Members that are required by this Agreement to make such notifications.

9. Any Member may notify the Committee on Safeguards of any non-governmental measures referred to in paragraph 3 of Article 11.

10.   All notifications to the Council for Trade in Goods referred to in this Agreement shall normally be made through the Committee on Safeguards.

11.   The provisions on notification in this Agreement shall not require any Member to disclose confidential information the disclosure of which would impede law enforcement or otherwise be contrary to the public interest or would prejudice the legitimate commercial interests of particular enterprises, public or private.

Article 13

Surveillance

1.   A Committee on Safeguards is hereby established, under the authority of the Council for Trade in Goods, which shall be open to the participation of any Member indicating its wish to serve on it.   The Committee will have the following functions:

(a) to monitor, and report annually to the Council for Trade in Goods on, the general implementation of this Agreement and make recommendations towards its improvement;

(b) to find, upon request of an affected Member, whether or not the procedural requirements of this Agreement have been complied with in connection with a safeguard measure, and report its findings to the Council for Trade in Goods;

(c) to assist Members, if they so request, in their consultations under the provisions of this Agreement;

(d) to examine measures covered by Article 10 and paragraph 1 of Article 11, monitor the phase-out of such measures and report as appropriate to the Council for Trade in Goods;

(e) to review, at the request of the Member taking a safeguard measure, whether proposals to suspend concessions or other obligations are "substantially equivalent", and report as appropriate to the Council for Trade in Goods;

(f) to receive and review all notifications provided for in this Agreement and report as appropriate to the Council for Trade in Goods; and

(g) to perform any other function connected with this Agreement that the Council for Trade in Goods may determine.

2.   To assist the Committee in carrying out its surveillance function, the Secretariat shall prepare annually a factual report on the operation of this Agreement based on notifications and other reliable information available to it.

Article 14

Dispute Settlement

The provisions of Articles XXII and XXIII of GATT 1994 as elaborated and applied by the Dispute Settlement Understanding shall apply to consultations and the settlement of disputes arising under this Agreement.

ANNEX

EXCEPTION REFERRED TO IN PARAGRAPH 2 OF ARTICLE 11

Members concerned	Product	Termination
EC/Japan	Passenger cars, off road vehicles, light commercial vehicles, light trucks (up to 5 tonnes), and the same vehicles in wholly knocked-down form (CKD sets).	31 December 1999

Item 16

ANNEX 1B
GENERAL AGREEMENT ON TRADE IN SERVICES

Table of Contents

Annex on Article II Exemptions.
Annex on Movement of Natural Persons Supplying Services Under the Agreement.
Annex on Air Transport Services.
Annex on Financial Services.
Second Annex on Financial Services.
Annex on Negotiations on Maritime Transport Services.
Annex on Telecommunications.
Annex on Negotiations on Basic Telecommunications.

GENERAL AGREEMENT ON TRADE IN SERVICES

Members,

Recognizing the growing importance of trade in services for the growth and development of the world economy;

Wishing to establish a multilateral framework of principles and rules for trade in services with a view to the expansion of such trade under conditions of transparency and progressive liberalization and as a means of promoting the economic growth of all trading partners and the development of developing countries;

Desiring the early achievement of progressively higher levels of liberalization of trade in services through successive rounds of multilateral negotiations aimed at promoting the interests of all participants on a mutually advantageous basis and at securing an overall balance of rights and obligations, while giving due respect to national policy objectives;

Recognizing the right of Members to regulate, and to introduce new regulations, on the supply of services within their territories in order to meet national policy objectives and, given asymmetries existing with respect to the degree of development of services regulations in different countries, the particular need of developing countries to exercise this right;

Desiring to facilitate the increasing participation of developing countries in trade in services and the expansion of their service exports including, *inter alia*, through the strengthening of their domestic services capacity and its efficiency and competitiveness;

Taking particular account of the serious difficulty of the least-developed countries in view of their special economic situation and their development, trade and financial needs;

Hereby *agree* as follows:

PART I

SCOPE AND DEFINITION

Article I

Scope and Definition

1. This Agreement applies to measures by Members affecting trade in services.

2. For the purposes of this Agreement, trade in services is defined as the supply of a service:

    (a) from the territory of one Member into the territory of any other Member;

(b) in the territory of one Member to the service consumer of any other Member;

(c) by a service supplier of one Member, through commercial presence in the territory of any other Member;

(d) by a service supplier of one Member, through presence of natural persons of a Member in the territory of any other Member.

3. For the purposes of this Agreement:

(a) "measures by Members" means measures taken by:

(i) central, regional or local governments and authorities; and

(ii) non-governmental bodies in the exercise of powers delegated by central, regional or local governments or authorities;

In fulfilling its obligations and commitments under the Agreement, each Member shall take such reasonable measures as may be available to it to ensure their observance by regional and local governments and authorities and non-governmental bodies within its territory;

(b) "services" includes any service in any sector except services supplied in the exercise of governmental authority;

(c) "a service supplied in the exercise of governmental authority" means any service which is supplied neither on a commercial basis, nor in competition with one or more service suppliers.

PART II

GENERAL OBLIGATIONS AND DISCIPLINES

Article II

Most–Favoured–Nation Treatment

1. With respect to any measure covered by this Agreement, each Member shall accord immediately and unconditionally to services and service suppliers of any other Member treatment no less favourable than that it accords to like services and service suppliers of any other country.

2. A Member may maintain a measure inconsistent with paragraph 1 provided that such a measure is listed in, and meets the conditions of, the Annex on Article II Exemptions.

3. The provisions of this Agreement shall not be so construed as to prevent any Member from conferring or according advantages to adjacent countries in order to facilitate exchanges limited to contiguous frontier zones of services that are both locally produced and consumed.

Article III

Transparency

1. Each Member shall publish promptly and, except in emergency situations, at the latest by the time of their entry into force, all relevant measures of general application which pertain to or affect the operation of this Agreement. International agreements pertaining to or affecting trade in services to which a Member is a signatory shall also be published.

2. Where publication as referred to in paragraph 1 is not practicable, such information shall be made otherwise publicly available.

3. Each Member shall promptly and at least annually inform the Council for Trade in Services of the introduction of any new, or any changes to existing, laws, regulations or administrative guidelines which significantly affect trade in services covered by its specific commitments under this Agreement.

4. Each Member shall respond promptly to all requests by any other Member for specific information on any of its measures of general application or international agreements within the meaning of paragraph 1. Each Member shall also establish one or more enquiry points to provide specific information to other Members, upon request, on all such matters as well as those subject to the notification requirement in paragraph 3. Such enquiry points shall be established within two years from the date of entry into force of the Agreement Establishing the WTO (referred to in this Agreement as the "WTO Agreement"). Appropriate flexibility with respect to the time-limit within which such enquiry points are to be established may be agreed upon for individual developing country Members. Enquiry points need not be depositories of laws and regulations.

5. Any Member may notify to the Council for Trade in Services any measure, taken by any other Member, which it considers affects the operation of this Agreement.

Article III bis

Disclosure of Confidential Information

Nothing in this Agreement shall require any Member to provide confidential information, the disclosure of which would impede law enforcement, or otherwise be contrary to the public interest, or which would prejudice legitimate commercial interests of particular enterprises, public or private.

Article IV

Increasing Participation of Developing Countries

1. The increasing participation of developing country Members in world trade shall be facilitated through negotiated specific commitments, by different Members pursuant to Parts III and IV of this Agreement, relating to:

(a) the strengthening of their domestic services capacity and its efficiency and competitiveness, *inter alia* through access to technology on a commercial basis;

(b) the improvement of their access to distribution channels and information networks; and

(c) the liberalization of market access in sectors and modes of supply of export interest to them.

2. Developed country Members, and to the extent possible other Members, shall establish contact points within two years from the date of entry into force of the WTO Agreement to facilitate the access of developing country Members' service suppliers to information, related to their respective markets, concerning:

(a) commercial and technical aspects of the supply of services;

(b) registration, recognition and obtaining of professional qualifications; and

(c) the availability of services technology.

3.   Special priority shall be given to the least-developed country Members in the implementation of paragraphs 1 and 2. Particular account shall be taken of the serious difficulty of the least-developed countries in accepting negotiated specific commitments in view of their special economic situation and their development, trade and financial needs.

Article V

Economic Integration

1.   This Agreement shall not prevent any of its Members from being a party to or entering into an agreement liberalizing trade in services between or among the parties to such an agreement, provided that such an agreement:

(a) has substantial sectoral coverage [1], and

(b) provides for the absence or elimination of substantially all discrimination, in the sense of Article XVII, between or among the parties, in the sectors covered under subparagraph (a), through:

(i) elimination of existing discriminatory measures, and/or

(ii) prohibition of new or more discriminatory measures,

either at the entry into force of that agreement or on the basis of a reasonable time-frame, except for measures permitted under Articles XI, XII, XIV and XIV bis.

2.   In evaluating whether the conditions under paragraph 1(b) are met, consideration may be given to the relationship of the agreement to a wider process of economic integration or trade liberalization among the countries concerned.

3.   (a) Where developing countries are parties to an agreement of the type referred to in paragraph 1, flexibility shall be provided for regarding the conditions set out in paragraph 1, particularly with reference to subparagraph (b) thereof, in accordance with the level of development of the countries concerned, both overall and in individual sectors and subsectors.

(b) Notwithstanding paragraph 6, in the case of an agreement of the type referred to in paragraph 1 involving only developing countries, more favourable treatment may be granted to juridical persons owned or controlled by natural persons of the parties to such an agreement.

4.   Any agreement referred to in paragraph 1 shall be designed to facilitate trade between the parties to the agreement and shall not in respect of any Member outside the agreement raise the overall level of barriers to trade in services within the respective sectors or subsectors compared to the level applicable prior to such an agreement.

1. This condition is understood in terms of number of sectors, volume of trade affected and modes of supply. In order to meet this condition, agreements should not provide for the *a priori* exclusion of any mode of supply.

5. If, in the conclusion, enlargement or any significant modification of any agreement under paragraph 1, a Member intends to withdraw or modify a specific commitment inconsistently with the terms and conditions set out in its Schedule, it shall provide at least 90 days advance notice of such modification or withdrawal and the procedure set forth in paragraphs 2, 3 and 4 of Article XXI shall apply.

6. A service supplier of any other Member that is a juridical person constituted under the laws of a party to an agreement referred to in paragraph 1 shall be entitled to treatment granted under such agreement, provided that it engages in substantive business operations in the territory of the parties to such agreement.

7. (a) Members which are parties to any agreement referred to in paragraph 1 shall promptly notify any such agreement and any enlargement or any significant modification of that agreement to the Council for Trade in Services. They shall also make available to the Council such relevant information as may be requested by it. The Council may establish a working party to examine such an agreement or enlargement or modification of that agreement and to report to the Council on its consistency with this Article.

(b) Members which are parties to any agreement referred to in paragraph 1 which is implemented on the basis of a time-frame shall report periodically to the Council for Trade in Services on its implementation. The Council may establish a working party to examine such reports if it deems such a working party necessary.

(c) Based on the reports of the working parties referred to in subparagraphs (a) and (b), the Council may make recommendations to the parties as it deems appropriate.

8. A Member which is a party to any agreement referred to in paragraph 1 may not seek compensation for trade benefits that may accrue to any other Member from such agreement.

Article V bis

Labour Markets Integration Agreements

This Agreement shall not prevent any of its Members from being a party to an agreement establishing full integration[2] of the labour markets between or among the parties to such an agreement, provided that such an agreement:

(a) exempts citizens of parties to the agreement from requirements concerning residency and work permits;

(b) is notified to the Council for Trade in Services.

Article VI

Domestic Regulation

1. In sectors where specific commitments are undertaken, each Member shall ensure that all measures of general application affecting trade in services are administered in a reasonable, objective and impartial manner.

2. Typically, such integration provides citizens of the parties concerned with a right of free entry to the employment markets of the parties and includes measures concerning conditions of pay, other conditions of employment and social benefits.

2.   (a) Each Member shall maintain or institute as soon as practicable judicial, arbitral or administrative tribunals or procedures which provide, at the request of an affected service supplier, for the prompt review of, and where justified, appropriate remedies for, administrative decisions affecting trade in services. Where such procedures are not independent of the agency entrusted with the administrative decision concerned, the Member shall ensure that the procedures in fact provide for an objective and impartial review.

(b) The provisions of subparagraph (a) shall not be construed to require a Member to institute such tribunals or procedures where this would be inconsistent with its constitutional structure or the nature of its legal system.

3.   Where authorization is required for the supply of a service on which a specific commitment has been made, the competent authorities of a Member shall, within a reasonable period of time after the submission of an application considered complete under domestic laws and regulations, inform the applicant of the decision concerning the application. At the request of the applicant, the competent authorities of the Member shall provide, without undue delay, information concerning the status of the application.

4.   With a view to ensuring that measures relating to qualification requirements and procedures, technical standards and licensing requirements do not constitute unnecessary barriers to trade in services, the Council for Trade in Services shall, through appropriate bodies it may establish, develop any necessary disciplines. Such disciplines shall aim to ensure that such requirements are, *inter alia*:

(a) based on objective and transparent criteria, such as competence and the ability to supply the service;

(b) not more burdensome than necessary to ensure the quality of the service;

(c) in the case of licensing procedures, not in themselves a restriction on the supply of the service.

5.   (a) In sectors in which a Member has undertaken specific commitments, pending the entry into force of disciplines developed in these sectors pursuant to paragraph 4, the Member shall not apply licensing and qualification requirements and technical standards that nullify or impair such specific commitments in a manner which:

(i) does not comply with the criteria outlined in subparagraphs 4(a), (b) or (c); and

(ii) could not reasonably have been expected of that Member at the time the specific commitments in those sectors were made.

(b) In determining whether a Member is in conformity with the obligation under paragraph 5(a), account shall be taken of international standards of relevant international organizations [3] applied by that Member.

6.   In sectors where specific commitments regarding professional services are undertaken, each Member shall provide for adequate procedures to verify the competence of professionals of any other Member.

---

3. The term "relevant international organizations" refers to international bodies whose membership is open to the relevant bodies of at least all Members of the WTO.

Article VII

Recognition

1. For the purposes of the fulfilment, in whole or in part, of its standards or criteria for the authorization, licensing or certification of services suppliers, and subject to the requirements of paragraph 3, a Member may recognize the education or experience obtained, requirements met, or licenses or certifications granted in a particular country. Such recognition, which may be achieved through harmonization or otherwise, may be based upon an agreement or arrangement with the country concerned or may be accorded autonomously.

2. A Member that is a party to an agreement or arrangement of the type referred to in paragraph 1, whether existing or future, shall afford adequate opportunity for other interested Members to negotiate their accession to such an agreement or arrangement or to negotiate comparable ones with it. Where a Member accords recognition autonomously, it shall afford adequate opportunity for any other Member to demonstrate that education, experience, licenses, or certifications obtained or requirements met in that other Member's territory should be recognized.

3. A Member shall not accord recognition in a manner which would constitute a means of discrimination between countries in the application of its standards or criteria for the authorization, licensing or certification of services suppliers, or a disguised restriction on trade in services.

4. Each Member shall:

(a) within 12 months from the date on which the WTO Agreement takes effect for it, inform the Council for Trade in Services of its existing recognition measures and state whether such measures are based on agreements or arrangements of the type referred to in paragraph 1;

(b) promptly inform the Council for Trade in Services as far in advance as possible of the opening of negotiations on an agreement or arrangement of the type referred to in paragraph 1 in order to provide adequate opportunity to any other Member to indicate their interest in participating in the negotiations before they enter a substantive phase;

(c) promptly inform the Council for Trade in Services when it adopts new recognition measures or significantly modifies existing ones and state whether the measures are based on an agreement or arrangement of the type referred to in paragraph 1.

5. Wherever appropriate, recognition should be based on multilaterally agreed criteria. In appropriate cases, Members shall work in cooperation with relevant intergovernmental and non-governmental organizations towards the establishment and adoption of common international standards and criteria for recognition and common international standards for the practice of relevant services trades and professions.

Article VIII

Monopolies and Exclusive Service Suppliers

1. Each Member shall ensure that any monopoly supplier of a service in its territory does not, in the supply of the monopoly service in the relevant

market, act in a manner inconsistent with that Member's obligations under Article II and specific commitments.

2. Where a Member's monopoly supplier competes, either directly or through an affiliated company, in the supply of a service outside the scope of its monopoly rights and which is subject to that Member's specific commitments, the Member shall ensure that such a supplier does not abuse its monopoly position to act in its territory in a manner inconsistent with such commitments.

3. The Council for Trade in Services may, at the request of a Member which has a reason to believe that a monopoly supplier of a service of any other Member is acting in a manner inconsistent with paragraph 1 or 2, request the Member establishing, maintaining or authorizing such supplier to provide specific information concerning the relevant operations.

4. If, after the date of entry into force of the WTO Agreement, a Member grants monopoly rights regarding the supply of a service covered by its specific commitments, that Member shall notify the Council for Trade in Services no later than three months before the intended implementation of the grant of monopoly rights and the provisions of paragraphs 2, 3 and 4 of Article XXI shall apply.

5. The provisions of this Article shall also apply to cases of exclusive service suppliers, where a Member, formally or in effect, (a) authorizes or establishes a small number of service suppliers and (b) substantially prevents competition among those suppliers in its territory.

Article IX

Business Practices

1. Members recognize that certain business practices of service suppliers, other than those falling under Article VIII, may restrain competition and thereby restrict trade in services.

2. Each Member shall, at the request of any other Member, enter into consultations with a view to eliminating practices referred to in paragraph 1. The Member addressed shall accord full and sympathetic consideration to such a request and shall cooperate through the supply of publicly available non-confidential information of relevance to the matter in question. The Member addressed shall also provide other information available to the requesting Member, subject to its domestic law and to the conclusion of satisfactory agreement concerning the safeguarding of its confidentiality by the requesting Member.

Article X

Emergency Safeguard Measures

1. There shall be multilateral negotiations on the question of emergency safeguard measures based on the principle of non-discrimination. The results of such negotiations shall enter into effect on a date not later than three years from the date of entry into force of the WTO Agreement.

2. In the period before the entry into effect of the results of the negotiations referred to in paragraph 1, any Member may, notwithstanding the provisions of paragraph 1 of Article XXI, notify the Council on Trade in

Services of its intention to modify or withdraw a specific commitment after a period of one year from the date on which the commitment enters into force; provided that the Member shows cause to the Council that the modification or withdrawal cannot await the lapse of the three-year period provided for in paragraph 1 of Article XXI.

3. The provisions of paragraph 2 shall cease to apply three years after the date of entry into force of the WTO Agreement.

Article XI

Payments and Transfers

1. Except under the circumstances envisaged in Article XII, a Member shall not apply restrictions on international transfers and payments for current transactions relating to its specific commitments.

2. Nothing in this Agreement shall affect the rights and obligations of the members of the International Monetary Fund under the Articles of Agreement of the Fund, including the use of exchange actions which are in conformity with the Articles of Agreement, provided that a Member shall not impose restrictions on any capital transactions inconsistently with its specific commitments regarding such transactions, except under Article XII or at the request of the Fund.

Article XII

Restrictions to Safeguard the Balance of Payments

1. In the event of serious balance-of-payments and external financial difficulties or threat thereof, a Member may adopt or maintain restrictions on trade in services on which it has undertaken specific commitments, including on payments or transfers for transactions related to such commitments. It is recognized that particular pressures on the balance of payments of a Member in the process of economic development or economic transition may necessitate the use of restrictions to ensure, *inter alia,* the maintenance of a level of financial reserves adequate for the implementation of its programme of economic development or economic transition.

2. The restrictions referred to in paragraph 1:

    (a) shall not discriminate among Members;

    (b) shall be consistent with the Articles of Agreement of the International Monetary Fund;

    (c) shall avoid unnecessary damage to the commercial, economic and financial interests of any other Member;

    (d) shall not exceed those necessary to deal with the circumstances described in paragraph 1;

    (e) shall be temporary and be phased out progressively as the situation specified in paragraph 1 improves.

3. In determining the incidence of such restrictions, Members may give priority to the supply of services which are more essential to their economic or development programmes. However, such restrictions shall not be adopted or maintained for the purpose of protecting a particular service sector.

4.   Any restrictions adopted or maintained under paragraph 1, or any changes therein, shall be promptly notified to the General Council.

5.   (a) Members applying the provisions of this Article shall consult promptly with the Committee on Balance-of-Payments Restrictions on restrictions adopted under this Article.

(b) The Ministerial Conference shall establish procedures [4] for periodic consultations with the objective of enabling such recommendations to be made to the Member concerned as it may deem appropriate.

(c) Such consultations shall assess the balance-of-payment situation of the Member concerned and the restrictions adopted or maintained under this Article, taking into account, *inter alia,* such factors as:

(i) the nature and extent of the balance-of-payments and the external financial difficulties;

(ii) the external economic and trading environment of the consulting Member;

(iii) alternative corrective measures which may be available.

(d) The consultations shall address the compliance of any restrictions with paragraph 2, in particular the progressive phaseout of restrictions in accordance with paragraph 2(e).

(e) In such consultations, all findings of statistical and other facts presented by the International Monetary Fund relating to foreign exchange, monetary reserves and balance of payments, shall be accepted and conclusions shall be based on the assessment by the Fund of the balance-of-payments and the external financial situation of the consulting Member.

6.   If a Member which is not a member of the International Monetary Fund wishes to apply the provisions of this Article, the Ministerial Conference shall establish a review procedure and any other procedures necessary.

Article XIII
Government Procurement

1.   Articles II, XVI and XVII shall not apply to laws, regulations or requirements governing the procurement by governmental agencies of services purchased for governmental purposes and not with a view to commercial resale or with a view to use in the supply of services for commercial sale.

2.   There shall be multilateral negotiations on government procurement in services under this Agreement within two years from the date of entry into force of the WTO Agreement.

Article XIV
General Exceptions

Subject to the requirement that such measures are not applied in a manner which would constitute a means of arbitrary or unjustifiable discrimination between countries where like conditions prevail, or a disguised restric-

---

4. It is understood that the procedures under paragraph 5 shall be the same as the   GATT 1994 procedures.

tion on trade in services, nothing in this Agreement shall be construed to prevent the adoption or enforcement by any Member of measures:

(a) necessary to protect public morals or to maintain public order; [5]

(b) necessary to protect human, animal or plant life or health;

(c) necessary to secure compliance with laws or regulations which are not inconsistent with the provisions of this Agreement including those relating to:

(i) the prevention of deceptive and fraudulent practices or to deal with the effects of a default on services contracts;

(ii) the protection of the privacy of individuals in relation to the processing and dissemination of personal data and the protection of confidentiality of individual records and accounts;

(iii) safety;

(d) inconsistent with Article XVII, provided that the difference in treatment is aimed at ensuring the equitable or effective [6] imposition or collection of direct taxes in respect of services or service suppliers of other Members;

(e) inconsistent with Article II, provided that the difference in treatment is the result of an agreement on the avoidance of double taxation or provisions on the avoidance of double taxation in any other international agreement or arrangement by which the Member is bound.

Article XIV bis

Security Exceptions

1.   Nothing in this Agreement shall be construed:

(a) to require any Member to furnish any information, the disclosure of which it considers contrary to its essential security interests; or

(b) to prevent any Member from taking any action which it considers necessary for the protection of its essential security interests:

5. The public order exception may be invoked only where a genuine and sufficiently serious threat is posed to one of the fundamental interests of society.

6. Measures that are aimed at ensuring the equitable or effective imposition or collection of direct taxes include measures taken by a Member under its taxation system which:

(i) apply to non-resident service suppliers in recognition of the fact that the tax obligation of non-residents is determined with respect to taxable items sourced or located in the Member's territory; or

(ii) apply to non-residents in order to ensure the imposition or collection of taxes in the Member's territory; or

(iii) apply to non-residents or residents in order to prevent the avoidance or evasion of taxes, including compliance measures; or

(iv) apply to consumers of services supplied in or from the territory of another

Member in order to ensure the imposition or collection of taxes on such consumers derived from sources in the Member's territory; or

(v) distinguish service suppliers subject to tax on worldwide taxable items from other service suppliers, in recognition of the difference in the nature of the tax base between them; or

(vi) determine, allocate or apportion income, profit, gain, loss, deduction or credit of resident persons or branches, or between related persons or branches of the same person, in order to safeguard the Member's tax base.

Tax terms or concepts in paragraph (d) of Article XIV and in this footnote are determined according to tax definitions and concepts, or equivalent or similar definitions and concepts, under the domestic law of the Member taking the measure.

(i) relating to the supply of services as carried out directly or indirectly for the purpose of provisioning a military establishment;

(ii) relating to fissionable and fusionable materials or the materials from which they are derived;

(iii) taken in time of war or other emergency in international relations; or

(c) to prevent any Member from taking any action in pursuance of its obligations under the United Nations Charter for the maintenance of international peace and security.

2. The Council for Trade in Services shall be informed to the fullest extent possible of measures taken under paragraphs 1(b) and (c) and of their termination.

Article XV
Subsidies

1. Members recognize that, in certain circumstances, subsidies may have distortive effects on trade in services. Members shall enter into negotiations with a view to developing the necessary multilateral disciplines to avoid such trade-distortive effects.[7] The negotiations shall also address the appropriateness of countervailing procedures. Such negotiations shall recognize the role of subsidies in relation to the development programmes of developing countries and take into account the needs of Members, particularly developing country Members, for flexibility in this area. For the purpose of such negotiations, Members shall exchange information concerning all subsidies related to trade in services that they provide to their domestic service suppliers.

2. Any Member which considers that it is adversely affected by a subsidy of another Member may request consultations with that Member on such matters. Such requests shall be accorded sympathetic consideration.

PART III
SPECIFIC COMMITMENTS
Article XVI
Market Access

1. With respect to market access through the modes of supply identified in Article I, each Member shall accord services and service suppliers of any other Member treatment no less favourable than that provided for under the terms, limitations and conditions agreed and specified in its Schedule.[8]

2. In sectors where market-access commitments are undertaken, the measures which a Member shall not maintain or adopt either on the basis of a

7. A future work programme shall determine how, and in what time-frame, negotiations on such multilateral disciplines will be conducted.

8. If a Member undertakes a market-access commitment in relation to the supply of a service through the mode of supply referred to in subparagraph 2(a) of Article I and if the cross-border movement of capital is an essential part of the service itself, that Member is thereby committed to allow such movement of capital. If a Member undertakes a market-access commitment in relation to the supply of a service through the mode of supply referred to in subparagraph 2(c) of Article I, it is thereby committed to allow related transfers of capital into its territory.

regional subdivision or on the basis of its entire territory, unless otherwise specified in its Schedule, are defined as:

    (a) limitations on the number of service suppliers whether in the form of numerical quotas, monopolies, exclusive service suppliers or the requirements of an economic needs test;

    (b) limitations on the total value of service transactions or assets in the form of numerical quotas or the requirement of an economic needs test;

    (c) limitations on the total number of service operations or on the total quantity of service output expressed in terms of designated numerical units in the form of quotas or the requirement of an economic needs test; [9]

    (d) limitations on the total number of natural persons that may be employed in a particular service sector or that a service supplier may employ and who are necessary for, and directly related to, the supply of a specific service in the form of numerical quotas or the requirement of an economic needs test;

    (e) measures which restrict or require specific types of legal entity or joint venture through which a service supplier may supply a service; and

    (f) limitations on the participation of foreign capital in terms of maximum percentage limit on foreign shareholding or the total value of individual or aggregate foreign investment.

Article XVII
National Treatment

1.   In the sectors inscribed in its Schedule, and subject to any conditions and qualifications set out therein, each Member shall accord to services and service suppliers of any other Member, in respect of all measures affecting the supply of services, treatment no less favourable than that it accords to its own like services and service suppliers.[10]

2.   A Member may meet the requirement of paragraph 1 by according to services and service suppliers of any other Member, either formally identical treatment or formally different treatment to that it accords to its own like services and service suppliers.

3.   Formally identical or formally different treatment shall be considered to be less favourable if it modifies the conditions of competition in favour of services or service suppliers of the Member compared to like services or service suppliers of any other Member.

Article XVIII
Additional Commitments

Members may negotiate commitments with respect to measures affecting trade in services not subject to scheduling under Articles XVI or XVII,

---

9. Subparagraph 2(c) does not cover measures of a Member which limit inputs for the supply of services.

10. Specific commitments assumed under this Article shall not be construed to require any Member to compensate for any inherent competitive disadvantages which result from the foreign character of the relevant services or service suppliers.

including those regarding qualifications, standards or licensing matters. Such commitments shall be inscribed in a Member's Schedule.

PART IV

PROGRESSIVE LIBERALIZATION

Article XIX

Negotiation of Specific Commitments

1.   In pursuance of the objectives of this Agreement, Members shall enter into successive rounds of negotiations, beginning not later than five years from the date of entry into force of the WTO Agreement and periodically thereafter, with a view to achieving a progressively higher level of liberalization. Such negotiations shall be directed to the reduction or elimination of the adverse effects on trade in services of measures as a means of providing effective market access. This process shall take place with a view to promoting the interests of all participants on a mutually advantageous basis and to securing an overall balance of rights and obligations.

2.   The process of liberalization shall take place with due respect for national policy objectives and the level of development of individual Members, both overall and in individual sectors. There shall be appropriate flexibility for individual developing country Members for opening fewer sectors, liberalizing fewer types of transactions, progressively extending market access in line with their development situation and, when making access to their markets available to foreign service suppliers, attaching to such access conditions aimed at achieving the objectives referred to in Article IV.

3.   For each round, negotiating guidelines and procedures shall be established. For the purposes of establishing such guidelines, the Council for Trade in Services shall carry out an assessment of trade in services in overall terms and on a sectoral basis with reference to the objectives of this Agreement, including those set out in paragraph 1 of Article IV. Negotiating guidelines shall establish modalities for the treatment of liberalization undertaken autonomously by Members since previous negotiations, as well as for the special treatment for least-developed country Members under the provisions of paragraph 3 of Article IV.

4.   The process of progressive liberalization shall be advanced in each such round through bilateral, plurilateral or multilateral negotiations directed towards increasing the general level of specific commitments undertaken by Members under this Agreement.

Article XX

Schedules of Specific Commitments

1.   Each Member shall set out in a schedule the specific commitments it undertakes under Part III of this Agreement. With respect to sectors where such commitments are undertaken, each Schedule shall specify:

(a) terms, limitations and conditions on market access;

(b) conditions and qualifications on national treatment;

(c) undertakings relating to additional commitments;

(d) where appropriate the time-frame for implementation of such commitments; and

(e) the date of entry into force of such commitments.

2.   Measures inconsistent with both Articles XVI and XVII shall be inscribed in the column relating to Article XVI. In this case the inscription will be considered to provide a condition or qualification to Article XVII as well.

3.   Schedules of specific commitments shall be annexed to this Agreement and shall form an integral part thereof.

Article XXI
Modification of Schedules

1.   (a) A Member (referred to in this Article as the "modifying Member") may modify or withdraw any commitment in its Schedule, at any time after three years have elapsed from the date on which that commitment entered into force, in accordance with the provisions of this Article.

(b) A modifying Member shall notify its intent to modify or withdraw a commitment pursuant to this Article to the Council for Trade in Services no later than three months before the intended date of implementation of the modification or withdrawal.

2.   (a) At the request of any Member the benefits of which under this Agreement may be affected (referred to in this Article as an "affected Member") by a proposed modification or withdrawal notified under subparagraph 1(b), the modifying Member shall enter into negotiations with a view to reaching agreement on any necessary compensatory adjustment. In such negotiations and agreement, the Members concerned shall endeavour to maintain a general level of mutually advantageous commitments not less favourable to trade than that provided for in Schedules of specific commitments prior to such negotiations.

(b) Compensatory adjustments shall be made on a most-favoured-nation basis.

3.   (a) If agreement is not reached between the modifying Member and any affected Member before the end of the period provided for negotiations, such affected Member may refer the matter to arbitration. Any affected Member that wishes to enforce a right that it may have to compensation must participate in the arbitration.

(b) If no affected Member has requested arbitration, the modifying Member shall be free to implement the proposed modification or withdrawal.

4.   (a) The modifying Member may not modify or withdraw its commitment until it has made compensatory adjustments in conformity with the findings of the arbitration.

(b) If the modifying Member implements its proposed modification or withdrawal and does not comply with the findings of the arbitration, any affected Member that participated in the arbitration may modify or withdraw substantially equivalent benefits in conformity with those findings. Notwithstanding Article II, such a modification or withdrawal may be implemented solely with respect to the modifying Member.

5. The Council for Trade in Services shall establish procedures for rectification or modification of Schedules. Any Member which has modified or withdrawn scheduled commitments under this Article shall modify its Schedule according to such procedures.

PART V

INSTITUTIONAL PROVISIONS

Article XXII

Consultation

1. Each Member shall accord sympathetic consideration to, and shall afford adequate opportunity for, consultation regarding such representations as may be made by any other Member with respect to any matter affecting the operation of this Agreement. The Dispute Settlement Understanding (DSU) shall apply to such consultations.

2. The Council for Trade in Services or the Dispute Settlement Body (DSB) may, at the request of a Member, consult with any Member or Members in respect of any matter for which it has not been possible to find a satisfactory solution through consultation under paragraph 1.

3. A Member may not invoke Article XVII, either under this Article or Article XXIII, with respect to a measure of another Member that falls within the scope of an international agreement between them relating to the avoidance of double taxation. In case of disagreement between Members as to whether a measure falls within the scope of such an agreement between them, it shall be open to either Member to bring this matter before the Council for Trade in Services.[11] The Council shall refer the matter to arbitration. The decision of the arbitrator shall be final and binding on the Members.

Article XXIII

Dispute Settlement and Enforcement

1. If any Member should consider that any other Member fails to carry out its obligations or specific commitments under this Agreement, it may with a view to reaching a mutually satisfactory resolution of the matter have recourse to the DSU.

2. If the DSB considers that the circumstances are serious enough to justify such action, it may authorize a Member or Members to suspend the application to any other Member or Members of obligations and specific commitments in accordance with Article 22 of the DSU.

3. If any Member considers that any benefit it could reasonably have expected to accrue to it under a specific commitment of another Member under Part III of this Agreement is being nullified or impaired as a result of the application of any measure which does not conflict with the provisions of this Agreement, it may have recourse to the DSU. If the measure is determined by the DSB to have nullified or impaired such a benefit, the Member affected shall be entitled to a mutually satisfactory adjustment on the basis of paragraph 2 of Article XXI, which may include the modification or

11. With respect to agreements on the avoidance of double taxation which exist on the date of entry into force of the WTO Agreement, such a matter may be brought before the Council for Trade in Services only with the consent of both parties to such an agreement.

withdrawal of the measure. In the event an agreement cannot be reached between the Members concerned, Article 22 of the DSU shall apply.

Article XXIV
Council for Trade in Services

1. The Council for Trade in Services shall carry out such functions as may be assigned to it to facilitate the operation of this Agreement and further its objectives. The Council may establish such subsidiary bodies as it considers appropriate for the effective discharge of its functions.

2. The Council and, unless the Council decides otherwise, its subsidiary bodies shall be open to participation by representatives of all Members.

3. The Chairman of the Council shall be elected by the Members.

Article XXV
Technical Cooperation

1. Service suppliers of Members which are in need of such assistance shall have access to the services of contact points referred to in paragraph 2 of Article IV.

2. Technical assistance to developing countries shall be provided at the multilateral level by the Secretariat and shall be decided upon by the Council for Trade in Services.

Article XXVI
Relationship With Other International Organizations

The General Council shall make appropriate arrangements for consultation and cooperation with the United Nations and its specialized agencies as well as with other intergovernmental organizations concerned with services.

PART VI
FINAL PROVISIONS
Article XXVII
Denial of Benefits

A Member may deny the benefits of this Agreement:

(a) to the supply of a service, if it establishes that the service is supplied from or in the territory of a non-Member or of a Member to which the denying Member does not apply the WTO Agreement;

(b) in the case of the supply of a maritime transport service, if it establishes that the service is supplied:

(i) by a vessel registered under the laws of a non-Member or of a Member to which the denying Member does not apply the WTO Agreement, and

(ii) by a person which operates and/or uses the vessel in whole or in part but which is of a non-Member or of a Member to which the denying Member does not apply the WTO Agreement;

(c) to a service supplier that is a juridical person, if it establishes that it is not a service supplier of another Member, or that it is a service supplier of a Member to which the denying Member does not apply the WTO Agreement.

Article XXVIII

Definitions

For the purpose of this Agreement:

(a) "measure" means any measure by a Member, whether in the form of a law, regulation, rule, procedure, decision, administrative action, or any other form;

(b) "supply of a service" includes the production, distribution, marketing, sale and delivery of a service;

(c) "measures by Members affecting trade in services" include measures in respect of

(i) the purchase, payment or use of a service;

(ii) the access to and use of, in connection with the supply of a service, services which are required by those Members to be offered to the public generally;

(iii) the presence, including commercial presence, of persons of a Member for the supply of a service in the territory of another Member;

(d) "commercial presence" means any type of business or professional establishment, including through

(i) the constitution, acquisition or maintenance of a juridical person, or

(ii) the creation or maintenance of a branch or a representative office,

within the territory of a Member for the purpose of supplying a service;

(e) "sector" of a service means,

(i) with reference to a specific commitment, one or more, or all, subsectors of that service, as specified in a Member's Schedule,

(ii) otherwise, the whole of that service sector, including all of its subsectors;

(f) "service of another Member" means a service which is supplied,

(i) from or in the territory of that other Member, or in the case of maritime transport, by a vessel registered under the laws of that other Member, or by a person of that other Member which supplies the service through the operation of a vessel and/or its use in whole or in part; or

(ii) in the case of the supply of a service through commercial presence or through the presence of natural persons, by a service supplier of that other Member;

(g) "service supplier" means any person that supplies a service; [12]

---

12. Where the service is not supplied directly by a juridical person but through other forms of commercial presence such as a branch or a representative office, the service supplier

(h) "monopoly supplier of a service" means any person, public or private, which in the relevant market of the territory of a Member is authorized or established formally or in effect by that Member as the sole supplier of that service;

(i) "service consumer" means any person that receives or uses a service;

(j) "person" means either a natural person or a juridical person;

(k) "natural person of another Member" means a natural person who resides in the territory of that other Member or any other Member, and who under the law of that other Member:

(i) is a national of that other Member; or

(ii) has the right of permanent residence in that other Member, in the case of a Member which:

1. does not have nationals; or

2. accords substantially the same treatment to its permanent residents as it does to its nationals in respect of measures affecting trade in services, as notified in its acceptance of or accession to the WTO Agreement, provided that no Member is obligated to accord to such permanent residents treatment more favourable than would be accorded by that other Member to such permanent residents. Such notification shall include the assurance to assume, with respect to those permanent residents, in accordance with its laws and regulations, the same responsibilities that other Member bears with respect to its nationals;

(l) "juridical person" means any legal entity duly constituted or otherwise organized under applicable law, whether for profit or otherwise, and whether privately-owned or governmentally-owned, including any corporation, trust, partnership, joint venture, sole proprietorship or association;

(m) "juridical person of another Member" means a juridical person which is either:

(i) constituted or otherwise organized under the law of that other Member, and is engaged in substantive business operations in the territory of that Member or any other Member; or

(ii) in the case of the supply of a service through commercial presence, owned or controlled by:

1. natural persons of that Member; or

2. juridical persons of that other Member identified under subparagraph (i);

(n) a juridical person is:

(i.e. the juridical person) shall, nonetheless, through such presence be accorded the treatment provided for service suppliers under the Agreement. Such treatment shall be extended to the presence through which the service is supplied and need not be extended to any other parts of the supplier located outside the territory where the service is supplied.

(i) "owned" by persons of a Member if more than 50 per cent of the equity interest in it is beneficially owned by persons of that Member;

(ii) "controlled" by persons of a Member if such persons have the power to name a majority of its directors or otherwise to legally direct its actions;

(iii) "affiliated" with another person when it controls, or is controlled by, that other person; or when it and the other person are both controlled by the same person;

(*o*) "direct taxes" comprise all taxes on total income, on total capital or on elements of income or of capital, including taxes on gains from the alienation of property, taxes on estates, inheritances and gifts, and taxes on the total amounts of wages or salaries paid by enterprises, as well as taxes on capital appreciation.

Article XXIX

Annexes

The Annexes to this Agreement are an integral part of this Agreement.

ANNEX ON ARTICLE II EXEMPTIONS

Scope

1. This Annex specifies the conditions under which a Member, at the entry into force of this Agreement, is exempted from its obligations under paragraph 1 of Article II.

2. Any new exemptions applied for after the date of entry into force of the WTO Agreement shall be dealt with under paragraph 3 of Article IX of that Agreement.

Review

3. The Council for Trade in Services shall review all exemptions granted for a period of more than 5 years. The first such review shall take place no more than 5 years after the entry into force of the WTO Agreement.

4. The Council for Trade in Services in a review shall:

(a) examine whether the conditions which created the need for the exemption still prevail; and

(b) determine the date of any further review.

Termination

5. The exemption of a Member from its obligations under paragraph 1 of Article II of the Agreement with respect to a particular measure terminates on the date provided for in the exemption.

6. In principle, such exemptions should not exceed a period of 10 years. In any event, they shall be subject to negotiation in subsequent trade liberalizing rounds.

7. A Member shall notify the Council for Trade in Services at the termination of the exemption period that the inconsistent measure has been brought into conformity with paragraph 1 of Article II of the Agreement.

Lists of Article II Exemptions

[The agreed lists of exemptions under paragraph 2 of Article II will be annexed here in the treaty copy of the WTO Agreement.]

ANNEX ON MOVEMENT OF NATURAL PERSONS SUPPLYING SERVICES UNDER THE AGREEMENT

1. This Annex applies to measures affecting natural persons who are service suppliers of a Member, and natural persons of a Member who are employed by a service supplier of a Member, in respect of the supply of a service.

2. The Agreement shall not apply to measures affecting natural persons seeking access to the employment market of a Member, nor shall it apply to measures regarding citizenship, residence or employment on a permanent basis.

3. In accordance with Parts III and IV of the Agreement, Members may negotiate specific commitments applying to the movement of all categories of natural persons supplying services under the Agreement. Natural persons covered by a specific commitment shall be allowed to supply the service in accordance with the terms of that commitment.

4. The Agreement shall not prevent a Member from applying measures to regulate the entry of natural persons into, or their temporary stay in, its territory, including those measures necessary to protect the integrity of, and to ensure the orderly movement of natural persons across, its borders, provided that such measures are not applied in such a manner as to nullify or impair the benefits accruing to any Member under the terms of a specific commitment.[1]

ANNEX ON AIR TRANSPORT SERVICES

1. This Annex applies to measures affecting trade in air transport services, whether scheduled or non-scheduled, and ancillary services. It is confirmed that any specific commitment or obligation assumed under this Agreement shall not reduce or affect a Member's obligations under bilateral or multilateral agreements that are in effect on the date of entry into force of the WTO Agreement.

2. The Agreement, including its dispute settlement procedures, shall not apply to measures affecting:

(a) traffic rights, however granted; or

(b) services directly related to the exercise of traffic rights,

except as provided in paragraph 3 of this Annex.

3. The Agreement shall apply to measures affecting:

---

1. The sole fact of requiring a visa for natural persons of certain Members and not for those of others shall not be regarded as nullifying or impairing benefits under a specific commitment.

(a) aircraft repair and maintenance services;

(b) the selling and marketing of air transport services;

(c) computer reservation system (CRS) services.

4.   The dispute settlement procedures of the Agreement may be invoked only where obligations or specific commitments have been assumed by the concerned Members and where dispute settlement procedures in bilateral and other multilateral agreements or arrangements have been exhausted.

5.   The Council for Trade in Services shall review periodically, and at least every five years, developments in the air transport sector and the operation of this Annex with a view to considering the possible further application of the Agreement in this sector.

6.   Definitions:

(a) "Aircraft repair and maintenance services" mean such activities when undertaken on an aircraft or a part thereof while it is withdrawn from service and do not include so-called line maintenance.

(b) "Selling and marketing of air transport services" mean opportunities for the air carrier concerned to sell and market freely its air transport services including all aspects of marketing such as market research, advertising and distribution. These activities do not include the pricing of air transport services nor the applicable conditions.

(c) "Computer reservation system (CRS) services" mean services provided by computerised systems that contain information about air carriers' schedules, availability, fares and fare rules, through which reservations can be made or tickets may be issued.

(d) "Traffic rights" mean the right for scheduled and non-scheduled services to operate and/or to carry passengers, cargo and mail for remuneration or hire from, to, within, or over the territory of a Member, including points to be served, routes to be operated, types of traffic to be carried, capacity to be provided, tariffs to be charged and their conditions, and criteria for designation of airlines, including such criteria as number, ownership, and control.

ANNEX ON FINANCIAL SERVICES

1.   *Scope and Definition*

(a) This Annex applies to measures affecting the supply of financial services. Reference to the supply of a financial service in this Annex shall mean the supply of a service as defined in paragraph 2 of Article I of the Agreement.

(b) For the purposes of subparagraph 3(b) of Article I of the Agreement, "services supplied in the exercise of governmental authority" means the following:

(i) activities conducted by a central bank or monetary authority or by any other public entity in pursuit of monetary or exchange rate policies;

(ii) activities forming part of a statutory system of social security or public retirement plans; and

(iii) other activities conducted by a public entity for the account or with the guarantee or using the financial resources of the Government.

(c) For the purposes of subparagraph 3(b) of Article I of the Agreement, if a Member allows any of the activities referred to in subparagraphs (b)(ii) or (b)(iii) of this paragraph to be conducted by its financial service suppliers in competition with a public entity or a financial service supplier, "services" shall include such activities.

(d) Subparagraph 3(c) of Article I of the Agreement shall not apply to services covered by this Annex.

2. *Domestic Regulation*

(a) Notwithstanding any other provisions of the Agreement, a Member shall not be prevented from taking measures for prudential reasons, including for the protection of investors, depositors, policy holders or persons to whom a fiduciary duty is owed by a financial service supplier, or to ensure the integrity and stability of the financial system. Where such measures do not conform with the provisions of the Agreement, they shall not be used as a means of avoiding the Member's commitments or obligations under the Agreement.

(b) Nothing in the Agreement shall be construed to require a Member to disclose information relating to the affairs and accounts of individual customers or any confidential or proprietary information in the possession of public entities.

3. *Recognition*

(a) A Member may recognize prudential measures of any other country in determining how the Member's measures relating to financial services shall be applied. Such recognition, which may be achieved through harmonization or otherwise, may be based upon an agreement or arrangement with the country concerned or may be accorded autonomously.

(b) A Member that is a party to such an agreement or arrangement referred to in subparagraph (a), whether future or existing, shall afford adequate opportunity for other interested Members to negotiate their accession to such agreements or arrangements, or to negotiate comparable ones with it, under circumstances in which there would be equivalent regulation, oversight, implementation of such regulation, and, if appropriate, procedures concerning the sharing of information between the parties to the agreement or arrangement. Where a Member accords recognition autonomously, it shall afford adequate opportunity for any other Member to demonstrate that such circumstances exist.

(c) Where a Member is contemplating according recognition to prudential measures of any other country, paragraph 4(b) of Article VII shall not apply.

4. *Dispute Settlement*

Panels for disputes on prudential issues and other financial matters shall have the necessary expertise relevant to the specific financial service under dispute.

5. *Definitions*

For the purposes of this Annex:

(a) A financial service is any service of a financial nature offered by a financial service supplier of a Member. Financial services include all insurance and insurance-related services, and all banking and other financial services (excluding insurance). Financial services include the following activities:

Insurance and insurance-related services

    (i) Direct insurance (including co-insurance):

        (A) life

        (B) non-life

    (ii) Reinsurance and retrocession;

    (iii) Insurance intermediation, such as brokerage and agency;

    (iv) Services auxiliary to insurance, such as consultancy, actuarial, risk assessment and claim settlement services.

Banking and other financial services (excluding insurance)

    (v) Acceptance of deposits and other repayable funds from the public;

    (vi) Lending of all types, including consumer credit, mortgage credit, factoring and financing of commercial transaction;

    (vii) Financial leasing;

    (viii) All payment and money transmission services, including credit, charge and debit cards, travellers cheques and bankers drafts;

    (ix) Guarantees and commitments;

    (x) Trading for own account or for account of customers, whether on an exchange, in an over-the-counter market or otherwise, the following:

        (A) money market instruments (including cheques, bills, certificates of deposits);

        (B) foreign exchange;

        (C) derivative products including, but not limited to, futures and options;

        (D) exchange rate and interest rate instruments, including products such as swaps, forward rate agreements;

        (E) transferable securities;

        (F) other negotiable instruments and financial assets, including bullion.

    (xi) Participation in issues of all kinds of securities, including underwriting and placement as agent (whether publicly or privately) and provision of services related to such issues;

    (xii) Money broking;

    (xiii) Asset management, such as cash or portfolio management, all forms of collective investment management, pension fund management, custodial, depository and trust services;

(xiv) Settlement and clearing services for financial assets, including securities, derivative products, and other negotiable instruments;

(xv) Provision and transfer of financial information, and financial data processing and related software by suppliers of other financial services;

(xvi) Advisory, intermediation and other auxiliary financial services on all the activities listed in subparagraphs (v) through (xv), including credit reference and analysis, investment and portfolio research and advice, advice on acquisitions and on corporate restructuring and strategy.

(b) A financial service supplier means any natural or juridical person of a Member wishing to supply or supplying financial services but the term "financial service supplier" does not include a public entity.

(c) "Public entity" means:

(i) a government, a central bank or a monetary authority, of a Member, or an entity owned or controlled by a Member, that is principally engaged in carrying out governmental functions or activities for governmental purposes, not including an entity principally engaged in supplying financial services on commercial terms; or

(ii) a private entity, performing functions normally performed by a central bank or monetary authority, when exercising those functions.

SECOND ANNEX ON FINANCIAL SERVICES

1. Notwithstanding Article II of the Agreement and paragraphs 1 and 2 of the Annex on Article II Exemptions, a Member may, during a period of 60 days beginning four months after the date of entry into force of the WTO Agreement, list in that Annex measures relating to financial services which are inconsistent with paragraph 1 of Article II of the Agreement.

2. Notwithstanding Article XXI of the Agreement, a Member may, during a period of 60 days beginning four months after the date of entry into force of the WTO Agreement, improve, modify or withdraw all or part of the specific commitments on financial services inscribed in its Schedule.

3. The Council for Trade in Services shall establish any procedures necessary for the application of paragraphs 1 and 2.

ANNEX ON NEGOTIATIONS ON MARITIME TRANSPORT SERVICES

1. Article II and the Annex on Article II Exemptions, including the requirement to list in the Annex any measure inconsistent with most-favoured-nation treatment that a Member will maintain, shall enter into force for international shipping, auxiliary services and access to and use of port facilities only on:

(a) the implementation date to be determined under paragraph 4 of the Ministerial Decision on Negotiations on Maritime Transport Services; or,

(b) should the negotiations not succeed, the date of the final report of the Negotiating Group on Maritime Transport Services provided for in that Decision.

2. Paragraph 1 shall not apply to any specific commitment on maritime transport services which is inscribed in a Member's Schedule.

3. From the conclusion of the negotiations referred to in paragraph 1, and before the implementation date, a Member may improve, modify or withdraw all or part of its specific commitments in this sector without offering compensation, notwithstanding the provisions of Article XXI.

ANNEX ON TELECOMMUNICATIONS

1. *Objectives*

Recognizing the specificities of the telecommunications services sector and, in particular, its dual role as a distinct sector of economic activity and as the underlying transport means for other economic activities, the Members have agreed to the following Annex with the objective of elaborating upon the provisions of the Agreement with respect to measures affecting access to and use of public telecommunications transport networks and services. Accordingly, this Annex provides notes and supplementary provisions to the Agreement.

2. *Scope*

(a) This Annex shall apply to all measures of a Member that affect access to and use of public telecommunications transport networks and services.[1]

(b) This Annex shall not apply to measures affecting the cable or broadcast distribution of radio or television programming.

(c) Nothing in this Annex shall be construed:

(i) to require a Member to authorize a service supplier of any other Member to establish, construct, acquire, lease, operate, or supply telecommunications transport networks or services, other than as provided for in its Schedule; or

(ii) to require a Member (or to require a Member to oblige service suppliers under its jurisdiction) to establish, construct, acquire, lease, operate or supply telecommunications transport networks or services not offered to the public generally.

3. *Definitions*

For the purposes of this Annex:

(a) "Telecommunications" means the transmission and reception of signals by any electromagnetic means.

(b) "Public telecommunications transport service" means any telecommunications transport service required, explicitly or in effect, by a Member to be offered to the public generally. Such services may include, *inter alia*, telegraph, telephone, telex, and data transmission typically involving the real-time transmission of customer-supplied information between two or more points without any end-to-end change in the form or content of the customer's information.

---

1. This paragraph is understood to mean that each Member shall ensure that the obligations of this Annex are applied with respect to suppliers of public telecommunications transport networks and services by whatever measures are necessary.

(c) "Public telecommunications transport network" means the public telecommunications infrastructure which permits telecommunications between and among defined network termination points.

(d) "Intra-corporate communications" means telecommunications through which a company communicates within the company or with or among its subsidiaries, branches and, subject to a Member's domestic laws and regulations, affiliates. For these purposes, "subsidiaries", "branches" and, where applicable, "affiliates" shall be as defined by each Member. "Intra-corporate communications" in this Annex excludes commercial or non-commercial services that are supplied to companies that are not related subsidiaries, branches or affiliates, or that are offered to customers or potential customers.

(e) Any reference to a paragraph or subparagraph of this Annex includes all subdivisions thereof.

4. *Transparency*

In the application of Article III of the Agreement, each Member shall ensure that relevant information on conditions affecting access to and use of public telecommunications transport networks and services is publicly available, including: tariffs and other terms and conditions of service; specifications of technical interfaces with such networks and services; information on bodies responsible for the preparation and adoption of standards affecting such access and use; conditions applying to attachment of terminal or other equipment; and notifications, registration or licensing requirements, if any.

5. *Access to and use of Public Telecommunications Transport Networks and Services*

(a) Each Member shall ensure that any service supplier of any other Member is accorded access to and use of public telecommunications transport networks and services on reasonable and non-discriminatory terms and conditions, for the supply of a service included in its Schedule. This obligation shall be applied, *inter alia*, through paragraphs (b) through (f).[2]

(b) Each Member shall ensure that service suppliers of any other Member have access to and use of any public telecommunications transport network or service offered within or across the border of that Member, including private leased circuits, and to this end shall ensure, subject to paragraphs (e) and (f), that such suppliers are permitted:

(i) to purchase or lease and attach terminal or other equipment which interfaces with the network and which is necessary to supply a supplier's services;

(ii) to interconnect private leased or owned circuits with public telecommunications transport networks and services or with circuits leased or owned by another service supplier; and

---

2. The term "non-discriminatory" is understood to refer to most-favoured-nation and national treatment as defined in the Agreement, as well as to reflect sector-specific usage of the term to mean "terms and conditions no less favourable than those accorded to any other user of like public telecommunications transport networks or services under like circumstances".

(iii) to use operating protocols of the service supplier's choice in the supply of any service, other than as necessary to ensure the availability of telecommunications transport networks and services to the public generally.

(c) Each Member shall ensure that service suppliers of any other Member may use public telecommunications transport networks and services for the movement of information within and across borders, including for intra-corporate communications of such service suppliers, and for access to information contained in data bases or otherwise stored in machine-readable form in the territory of any Member. Any new or amended measures of a Member significantly affecting such use shall be notified and shall be subject to consultation, in accordance with relevant provisions of the Agreement.

(d) Notwithstanding the preceding paragraph, a Member may take such measures as are necessary to ensure the security and confidentiality of messages, subject to the requirement that such measures are not applied in a manner which would constitute a means of arbitrary or unjustifiable discrimination or a disguised restriction on trade in services.

(e) Each Member shall ensure that no condition is imposed on access to and use of public telecommunications transport networks and services other than as necessary:

(i) to safeguard the public service responsibilities of suppliers of public telecommunications transport networks and services, in particular their ability to make their networks or services available to the public generally;

(ii) to protect the technical integrity of public telecommunications transport networks or services; or

(iii) to ensure that service suppliers of any other Member do not supply services unless permitted pursuant to commitments in the Member's Schedule.

(f) Provided that they satisfy the criteria set out in paragraph (e), conditions for access to and use of public telecommunications transport networks and services may include:

(i) restrictions on resale or shared use of such services;

(ii) a requirement to use specified technical interfaces, including interface protocols, for inter-connection with such networks and services;

(iii) requirements, where necessary, for the inter-operability of such services and to encourage the achievement of the goals set out in paragraph 7(a);

(iv) type approval of terminal or other equipment which interfaces with the network and technical requirements relating to the attachment of such equipment to such networks;

(v) restrictions on inter-connection of private leased or owned circuits with such networks or services or with circuits leased or owned by another service supplier; or

(vi) notification, registration and licensing.

(g) Notwithstanding the preceding paragraphs of this section, a developing country Member may, consistent with its level of development, place reasonable conditions on access to and use of public telecommunications transport networks and services necessary to strengthen its domestic telecommunications infrastructure and service capacity and to increase its participation in international trade in telecommunications services. Such conditions shall be specified in the Member's Schedule.

6. *Technical Cooperation*

(a) Members recognize that an efficient, advanced telecommunications infrastructure in countries, particularly developing countries, is essential to the expansion of their trade in services. To this end, Members endorse and encourage the participation, to the fullest extent practicable, of developed and developing countries and their suppliers of public telecommunications transport networks and services and other entities in the development programmes of international and regional organizations, including the International Telecommunication Union, the United Nations Development Programme, and the International Bank for Reconstruction and Development.

(b) Members shall encourage and support telecommunications cooperation among developing countries at the international, regional and subregional levels.

(c) In cooperation with relevant international organizations, Members shall make available, where practicable, to developing countries information with respect to telecommunications services and developments in telecommunications and information technology to assist in strengthening their domestic telecommunications services sector.

(d) Members shall give special consideration to opportunities for the least-developed countries to encourage foreign suppliers of telecommunications services to assist in the transfer of technology, training and other activities that support the development of their telecommunications infrastructure and expansion of their telecommunications services trade.

7. *Relation to International Organizations and Agreements*

(a) Members recognize the importance of international standards for global compatibility and inter-operability of telecommunication networks and services and undertake to promote such standards through the work of relevant international bodies, including the International Telecommunication Union and the International Organization for Standardization.

(b) Members recognize the role played by intergovernmental and non-governmental organizations and agreements in ensuring the efficient operation of domestic and global telecommunications services, in particular the International Telecommunication Union. Members shall make appropriate arrangements, where relevant, for consultation with such organizations on matters arising from the implementation of this Annex.

ANNEX ON NEGOTIATIONS ON BASIC TELECOMMUNICATIONS

1. Article II and the Annex on Article II Exemptions, including the requirement to list in the Annex any measure inconsistent with most-

favoured-nation treatment that a Member will maintain, shall enter into force for basic telecommunications only on:

(a) the implementation date to be determined under paragraph 5 of the Ministerial Decision on Negotiations on Basic Telecommunications; or,

(b) should the negotiations not succeed, the date of the final report of the Negotiating Group on Basic Telecommunications provided for in that Decision.

2. Paragraph 1 shall not apply to any specific commitment on basic telecommunications which is inscribed in a Member's Schedule.

Item 17

ANNEX 1C
AGREEMENT ON TRADE–RELATED ASPECTS OF INTELLECTUAL PROPERTY RIGHTS

Table of Contents

AGREEMENT ON TRADE–RELATED ASPECTS OF INTELLECTUAL PROPERTY RIGHTS

Members,

Desiring to reduce distortions and impediments to international trade, and taking into account the need to promote effective and adequate protection of intellectual property rights, and to ensure that measures and procedures to enforce intellectual property rights do not themselves become barriers to legitimate trade;

Recognizing, to this end, the need for new rules and disciplines concerning:

(a) the applicability of the basic principles of GATT 1994 and of relevant international intellectual property agreements or conventions;

(b) the provision of adequate standards and principles concerning the availability, scope and use of trade-related intellectual property rights;

(c) the provision of effective and appropriate means for the enforcement of trade-related intellectual property rights, taking into account differences in national legal systems;

(d) the provision of effective and expeditious procedures for the multilateral prevention and settlement of disputes between governments; and

(e) transitional arrangements aiming at the fullest participation in the results of the negotiations;

Recognizing the need for a multilateral framework of principles, rules and disciplines dealing with international trade in counterfeit goods;

Recognizing that intellectual property rights are private rights;

Recognizing the underlying public policy objectives of national systems for the protection of intellectual property, including developmental and technological objectives;

Recognizing also the special needs of the least-developed country Members in respect of maximum flexibility in the domestic implementation of laws and regulations in order to enable them to create a sound and viable technological base;

Emphasizing the importance of reducing tensions by reaching strengthened commitments to resolve disputes on trade-related intellectual property issues through multilateral procedures;

Desiring to establish a mutually supportive relationship between the WTO and the World Intellectual Property Organization (referred to in this Agreement as "WIPO") as well as other relevant international organizations;

Hereby agree as follows:

PART I

GENERAL PROVISIONS AND BASIC PRINCIPLES

Article 1

Nature and Scope of Obligations

1.　Members shall give effect to the provisions of this Agreement. Members may, but shall not be obliged to, implement in their law more extensive protection than is required by this Agreement, provided that such protection does not contravene the provisions of this Agreement. Members shall be free to determine the appropriate method of implementing the provisions of this Agreement within their own legal system and practice.

2.　For the purposes of this Agreement, the term "intellectual property" refers to all categories of intellectual property that are the subject of Sections 1 through 7 of Part II.

3.　Members shall accord the treatment provided for in this Agreement to the nationals of other Members.[1] In respect of the relevant intellectual

---

1. When "nationals" are referred to in this Agreement, they shall be deemed, in the case of a separate customs territory Member of the WTO, to mean persons, natural or legal, who

property right, the nationals of other Members shall be understood as those natural or legal persons that would meet the criteria for eligibility for protection provided for in the Paris Convention (1967), the Berne Convention (1971), the Rome Convention and the Treaty on Intellectual Property in Respect of Integrated Circuits, were all Members of the WTO members of those conventions.[2] Any Member availing itself of the possibilities provided in paragraph 3 of Article 5 or paragraph 2 of Article 6 of the Rome Convention shall make a notification as foreseen in those provisions to the Council for Trade–Related Aspects of Intellectual Property Rights (the "Council for TRIPS").

Article 2

Intellectual Property Conventions

1. In respect of Parts II, III and IV of this Agreement, Members shall comply with Articles 1 through 12, and Article 19, of the Paris Convention (1967).

2. Nothing in Parts I to IV of this Agreement shall derogate from existing obligations that Members may have to each other under the Paris Convention, the Berne Convention, the Rome Convention and the Treaty on Intellectual Property in Respect of Integrated Circuits.

Article 3

National Treatment

1. Each Member shall accord to the nationals of other Members treatment no less favourable than that it accords to its own nationals with regard to the protection[3] of intellectual property, subject to the exceptions already provided in, respectively, the Paris Convention (1967), the Berne Convention (1971), the Rome Convention or the Treaty on Intellectual Property in Respect of Integrated Circuits. In respect of performers, producers of phonograms and broadcasting organizations, this obligation only applies in respect of the rights provided under this Agreement. Any Member availing itself of the possibilities provided in Article 6 of the Berne Convention (1971) or paragraph 1(b) of Article 16 of the Rome Convention shall make a notification as foreseen in those provisions to the Council for TRIPS.

2. Members may avail themselves of the exceptions permitted under paragraph 1 in relation to judicial and administrative procedures, including

---

are domiciled or who have a real and effective industrial or commercial establishment in that customs territory.

2. In this Agreement, "Paris Convention" refers to the Paris Convention for the Protection of Industrial Property; "Paris Convention (1967)" refers to the Stockholm Act of this Convention of 14 July 1967. "Berne Convention" refers to the Berne Convention for the Protection of Literary and Artistic Works; "Berne Convention (1971)" refers to the Paris Act of this Convention of 24 July 1971. "Rome Convention" refers to the International Convention for the Protection of Performers, Producers of Phonograms and Broadcasting Organizations, adopted at Rome on 26 October

1961. "Treaty on Intellectual Property in Respect of Integrated Circuits" (IPIC Treaty) refers to the Treaty on Intellectual Property in Respect of Integrated Circuits, adopted at Washington on 26 May 1989. "WTO Agreement" refers to the Agreement Establishing the WTO.

3. For the purposes of Articles 3 and 4, "protection" shall include matters affecting the availability, acquisition, scope, maintenance and enforcement of intellectual property rights as well as those matters affecting the use of intellectual property rights specifically addressed in this Agreement.

the designation of an address for service or the appointment of an agent within the jurisdiction of a Member, only where such exceptions are necessary to secure compliance with laws and regulations which are not inconsistent with the provisions of this Agreement and where such practices are not applied in a manner which would constitute a disguised restriction on trade.

Article 4

Most–Favoured–Nation Treatment

With regard to the protection of intellectual property, any advantage, favour, privilege or immunity granted by a Member to the nationals of any other country shall be accorded immediately and unconditionally to the nationals of all other Members. Exempted from this obligation are any advantage, favour, privilege or immunity accorded by a Member:

(a) deriving from international agreements on judicial assistance or law enforcement of a general nature and not particularly confined to the protection of intellectual property;

(b) granted in accordance with the provisions of the Berne Convention (1971) or the Rome Convention authorizing that the treatment accorded be a function not of national treatment but of the treatment accorded in another country;

(c) in respect of the rights of performers, producers of phonograms and broadcasting organizations not provided under this Agreement;

(d) deriving from international agreements related to the protection of intellectual property which entered into force prior to the entry into force of the WTO Agreement, provided that such agreements are notified to the Council for TRIPS and do not constitute an arbitrary or unjustifiable discrimination against nationals of other Members.

Article 5

Multilateral Agreements on Acquisition or Maintenance of Protection

The obligations under Articles 3 and 4 do not apply to procedures provided in multilateral agreements concluded under the auspices of WIPO relating to the acquisition or maintenance of intellectual property rights.

Article 6

Exhaustion

For the purposes of dispute settlement under this Agreement, subject to the provisions of Articles 3 and 4 nothing in this Agreement shall be used to address the issue of the exhaustion of intellectual property rights.

Article 7

Objectives

The protection and enforcement of intellectual property rights should contribute to the promotion of technological innovation and to the transfer and dissemination of technology, to the mutual advantage of producers and users of technological knowledge and in a manner conducive to social and economic welfare, and to a balance of rights and obligations.

Article 8

Principles

1. Members may, in formulating or amending their laws and regulations, adopt measures necessary to protect public health and nutrition, and to promote the public interest in sectors of vital importance to their socioeconomic and technological development, provided that such measures are consistent with the provisions of this Agreement.

2. Appropriate measures, provided that they are consistent with the provisions of this Agreement, may be needed to prevent the abuse of intellectual property rights by right holders or the resort to practices which unreasonably restrain trade or adversely affect the international transfer of technology.

PART II

STANDARDS CONCERNING THE AVAILABILITY, SCOPE AND USE OF INTELLECTUAL PROPERTY RIGHTS

SECTION 1: COPYRIGHT AND RELATED RIGHTS

Article 9

Relation to the Berne Convention

1. Members shall comply with Articles 1 through 21 of the Berne Convention (1971) and the Appendix thereto. However, Members shall not have rights or obligations under this Agreement in respect of the rights conferred under Article 6 *bis* of that Convention or of the rights derived therefrom.

2. Copyright protection shall extend to expressions and not to ideas, procedures, methods of operation or mathematical concepts as such.

Article 10

Computer Programs and Compilations of Data

1. Computer programs, whether in source or object code, shall be protected as literary works under the Berne Convention (1971).

2. Compilations of data or other material, whether in machine readable or other form, which by reason of the selection or arrangement of their contents constitute intellectual creations shall be protected as such. Such protection, which shall not extend to the data or material itself, shall be without prejudice to any copyright subsisting in the data or material itself.

Article 11

Rental Rights

In respect of at least computer programs and cinematographic works, a Member shall provide authors and their successors in title the right to authorize or to prohibit the commercial rental to the public of originals or copies of their copyright works. A Member shall be excepted from this obligation in respect of cinematographic works unless such rental has led to widespread copying of such works which is materially impairing the exclusive right of reproduction conferred in that Member on authors and their successors in title. In respect of computer programs, this obligation does not apply to rentals where the program itself is not the essential object of the rental.

Article 12

Term of Protection

Whenever the term of protection of a work, other than a photographic work or a work of applied art, is calculated on a basis other than the life of a natural person, such term shall be no less than 50 years from the end of the calendar year of authorized publication, or, failing such authorized publication within 50 years from the making of the work, 50 years from the end of the calendar year of making.

Article 13

Limitations and Exceptions

Members shall confine limitations or exceptions to exclusive rights to certain special cases which do not conflict with a normal exploitation of the work and do not unreasonably prejudice the legitimate interests of the right holder.

Article 14

Protection of Performers, Producers of Phonograms (Sound Recordings) and Broadcasting Organizations

1.   In respect of a fixation of their performance on a phonogram, performers shall have the possibility of preventing the following acts when undertaken without their authorization: the fixation of their unfixed performance and the reproduction of such fixation. Performers shall also have the possibility of preventing the following acts when undertaken without their authorization: the broadcasting by wireless means and the communication to the public of their live performance.

2.   Producers of phonograms shall enjoy the right to authorize or prohibit the direct or indirect reproduction of their phonograms.

3.   Broadcasting organizations shall have the right to prohibit the following acts when undertaken without their authorization: the fixation, the reproduction of fixations, and the rebroadcasting by wireless means of broadcasts, as well as the communication to the public of television broadcasts of the same. Where Members do not grant such rights to broadcasting organizations, they shall provide owners of copyright in the subject matter of broadcasts with the possibility of preventing the above acts, subject to the provisions of the Berne Convention (1971).

4.   The provisions of Article 11 in respect of computer programs shall apply *mutatis mutandis* to producers of phonograms and any other right holders in phonograms as determined in a Member's law. If on 15 April 1994 a Member has in force a system of equitable remuneration of right holders in respect of the rental of phonograms, it may maintain such system provided that the commercial rental of phonograms is not giving rise to the material impairment of the exclusive rights of reproduction of right holders.

5.   The term of the protection available under this Agreement to performers and producers of phonograms shall last at least until the end of a

period of 50 years computed from the end of the calendar year in which the fixation was made or the performance took place. The term of protection granted pursuant to paragraph 3 shall last for at least 20 years from the end of the calendar year in which the broadcast took place.

6. Any Member may, in relation to the rights conferred under paragraphs 1, 2 and 3, provide for conditions, limitations, exceptions and reservations to the extent permitted by the Rome Convention. However, the provisions of Article 18 of the Berne Convention (1971) shall also apply, *mutatis mutandis*, to the rights of performers and producers of phonograms in phonograms.

SECTION 2: TRADEMARKS

Article 15

Protectable Subject Matter

1. Any sign, or any combination of signs, capable of distinguishing the goods or services of one undertaking from those of other undertakings, shall be capable of constituting a trademark. Such signs, in particular words including personal names, letters, numerals, figurative elements and combinations of colours as well as any combination of such signs, shall be eligible for registration as trademarks. Where signs are not inherently capable of distinguishing the relevant goods or services, Members may make registrability depend on distinctiveness acquired through use. Members may require, as a condition of registration, that signs be visually perceptible.

2. Paragraph 1 shall not be understood to prevent a Member from denying registration of a trademark on other grounds, provided that they do not derogate from the provisions of the Paris Convention (1967).

3. Members may make registrability depend on use. However, actual use of a trademark shall not be a condition for filing an application for registration. An application shall not be refused solely on the ground that intended use has not taken place before the expiry of a period of three years from the date of application.

4. The nature of the goods or services to which a trademark is to be applied shall in no case form an obstacle to registration of the trademark.

5. Members shall publish each trademark either before it is registered or promptly after it is registered and shall afford a reasonable opportunity for petitions to cancel the registration. In addition, Members may afford an opportunity for the registration of a trademark to be opposed.

Article 16

Rights Conferred

1. The owner of a registered trademark shall have the exclusive right to prevent all third parties not having the owner's consent from using in the course of trade identical or similar signs for goods or services which are identical or similar to those in respect of which the trademark is registered where such use would result in a likelihood of confusion. In case of the use of an identical sign for identical goods or services, a likelihood of confusion shall be presumed. The rights described above shall not prejudice any existing prior

rights, nor shall they affect the possibility of Members making rights available on the basis of use.

2. Article 6 *bis* of the Paris Convention (1967) shall apply, *mutatis mutandis*, to services. In determining whether a trademark is well-known, Members shall take account of the knowledge of the trademark in the relevant sector of the public, including knowledge in the Member concerned which has been obtained as a result of the promotion of the trademark.

3. Article 6 *bis* of the Paris Convention (1967) shall apply, *mutatis mutandis*, to goods or services which are not similar to those in respect of which a trademark is registered, provided that use of that trademark in relation to those goods or services would indicate a connection between those goods or services and the owner of the registered trademark and provided that the interests of the owner of the registered trademark are likely to be damaged by such use.

Article 17
Exceptions

Members may provide limited exceptions to the rights conferred by a trademark, such as fair use of descriptive terms, provided that such exceptions take account of the legitimate interests of the owner of the trademark and of third parties.

Article 18
Term of Protection

Initial registration, and each renewal of registration, of a trademark shall be for a term of no less than seven years. The registration of a trademark shall be renewable indefinitely.

Article 19
Requirement of Use

1. If use is required to maintain a registration, the registration may be cancelled only after an uninterrupted period of at least three years of non-use, unless valid reasons based on the existence of obstacles to such use are shown by the trademark owner. Circumstances arising independently of the will of the owner of the trademark which constitute an obstacle to the use of the trademark, such as import restrictions on or other government requirements for goods or services protected by the trademark, shall be recognized as valid reasons for non-use.

2. When subject to the control of its owner, use of a trademark by another person shall be recognized as use of the trademark for the purpose of maintaining the registration.

Article 20
Other Requirements

The use of a trademark in the course of trade shall not be unjustifiably encumbered by special requirements, such as use with another trademark, use in a special form or use in a manner detrimental to its capability to distinguish the goods or services of one undertaking from those of other undertakings. This will not preclude a requirement prescribing the use of the trademark identifying the undertaking producing the goods or services along with, but without linking it to, the trademark distinguishing the specific goods or services in question of that undertaking.

Article 21

Licensing and Assignment

Members may determine conditions on the licensing and assignment of trademarks, it being understood that the compulsory licensing of trademarks shall not be permitted and that the owner of a registered trademark shall have the right to assign the trademark with or without the transfer of the business to which the trademark belongs.

SECTION 3: GEOGRAPHICAL INDICATIONS

Article 22

Protection of Geographical Indications

1. Geographical indications are, for the purposes of this Agreement, indications which identify a good as originating in the territory of a Member, or a region or locality in that territory, where a given quality, reputation or other characteristic of the good is essentially attributable to its geographical origin.

2. In respect of geographical indications, Members shall provide the legal means for interested parties to prevent:

(a) the use of any means in the designation or presentation of a good that indicates or suggests that the good in question originates in a geographical area other than the true place of origin in a manner which misleads the public as to the geographical origin of the good;

(b) any use which constitutes an act of unfair competition within the meaning of Article 10 *bis* of the Paris Convention (1967).

3. A Member shall, *ex officio* if its legislation so permits or at the request of an interested party, refuse or invalidate the registration of a trademark which contains or consists of a geographical indication with respect to goods not originating in the territory indicated, if use of the indication in the trademark for such goods in that Member is of such a nature as to mislead the public as to the true place of origin.

4. The protection under paragraphs 1, 2 and 3 shall be applicable against a geographical indication which, although literally true as to the territory, region or locality in which the goods originate, falsely represents to the public that the goods originate in another territory.

Article 23

Additional Protection for Geographical Indications for Wines and Spirits

1. Each Member shall provide the legal means for interested parties to prevent use of a geographical indication identifying wines for wines not originating in the place indicated by the geographical indication in question or identifying spirits for spirits not originating in the place indicated by the geographical indication in question, even where the true origin of the goods is

indicated or the geographical indication is used in translation or accompanied by expressions such as "kind", "type", "style", "imitation" or the like.[4]

2.   The registration of a trademark for wines which contains or consists of a geographical indication identifying wines or for spirits which contains or consists of a geographical indication identifying spirits shall be refused or invalidated, *ex officio* if a Member's legislation so permits or at the request of an interested party, with respect to such wines or spirits not having this origin.

3.   In the case of homonymous geographical indications for wines, protection shall be accorded to each indication, subject to the provisions of paragraph 4 of Article 22. Each Member shall determine the practical conditions under which the homonymous indications in question will be differentiated from each other, taking into account the need to ensure equitable treatment of the producers concerned and that consumers are not misled.

4.   In order to facilitate the protection of geographical indications for wines, negotiations shall be undertaken in the Council for TRIPS concerning the establishment of a multilateral system of notification and registration of geographical indications for wines eligible for protection in those Members participating in the system.

Article 24
International Negotiations; Exceptions

1.   Members agree to enter into negotiations aimed at increasing the protection of individual geographical indications under Article 23. The provisions of paragraphs 4 through 8 below shall not be used by a Member to refuse to conduct negotiations or to conclude bilateral or multilateral agreements. In the context of such negotiations, Members shall be willing to consider the continued applicability of these provisions to individual geographical indications whose use was the subject of such negotiations.

2.   The Council for TRIPS shall keep under review the application of the provisions of this Section; the first such review shall take place within two years of the entry into force of the WTO Agreement. Any matter affecting the compliance with the obligations under these provisions may be drawn to the attention of the Council, which, at the request of a Member, shall consult with any Member or Members in respect of such matter in respect of which it has not been possible to find a satisfactory solution through bilateral or plurilateral consultations between the Members concerned. The Council shall take such action as may be agreed to facilitate the operation and further the objectives of this Section.

3.   In implementing this Section, a Member shall not diminish the protection of geographical indications that existed in that Member immediately prior to the date of entry into force of the WTO Agreement.

4.   Nothing in this Section shall require a Member to prevent continued and similar use of a particular geographical indication of another Member identifying wines or spirits in connection with goods or services by any of its nationals or domiciliaries who have used that geographical indication in a

---

4. Notwithstanding the first sentence of Article 42, Members may, with respect to these obligations, instead provide for enforcement by administrative action.

continuous manner with regard to the same or related goods or services in the territory of that Member either (a) for at least 10 years preceding 15 April 1994 or (b) in good faith preceding that date.

5. Where a trademark has been applied for or registered in good faith, or where rights to a trademark have been acquired through use in good faith either:

> (a) before the date of application of these provisions in that Member as defined in Part VI; or

> (b) before the geographical indication is protected in its country of origin;

measures adopted to implement this Section shall not prejudice eligibility for or the validity of the registration of a trademark, or the right to use a trademark, on the basis that such a trademark is identical with, or similar to, a geographical indication.

6. Nothing in this Section shall require a Member to apply its provisions in respect of a geographical indication of any other Member with respect to goods or services for which the relevant indication is identical with the term customary in common language as the common name for such goods or services in the territory of that Member. Nothing in this Section shall require a Member to apply its provisions in respect of a geographical indication of any other Member with respect to products of the vine for which the relevant indication is identical with the customary name of a grape variety existing in the territory of that Member as of the date of entry into force of the WTO Agreement.

7. A Member may provide that any request made under this Section in connection with the use or registration of a trademark must be presented within five years after the adverse use of the protected indication has become generally known in that Member or after the date of registration of the trademark in that Member provided that the trademark has been published by that date, if such date is earlier than the date on which the adverse use became generally known in that Member, provided that the geographical indication is not used or registered in bad faith.

8. The provisions of this Section shall in no way prejudice the right of any person to use, in the course of trade, that person's name or the name of that person's predecessor in business, except where such name is used in such a manner as to mislead the public.

9. There shall be no obligation under this Agreement to protect geographical indications which are not or cease to be protected in their country of origin, or which have fallen into disuse in that country.

SECTION 4: INDUSTRIAL DESIGNS

Article 25

Requirements for Protection

1. Members shall provide for the protection of independently created industrial designs that are new or original. Members may provide that designs are not new or original if they do not significantly differ from known designs or combinations of known design features. Members may provide that such

protection shall not extend to designs dictated essentially by technical or functional considerations.

2. Each Member shall ensure that requirements for securing protection for textile designs, in particular in regard to any cost, examination or publication, do not unreasonably impair the opportunity to seek and obtain such protection. Members shall be free to meet this obligation through industrial design law or through copyright law.

Article 26
Protection

1. The owner of a protected industrial design shall have the right to prevent third parties not having the owner's consent from making, selling or importing articles bearing or embodying a design which is a copy, or substantially a copy, of the protected design, when such acts are undertaken for commercial purposes.

2. Members may provide limited exceptions to the protection of industrial designs, provided that such exceptions do not unreasonably conflict with the normal exploitation of protected industrial designs and do not unreasonably prejudice the legitimate interests of the owner of the protected design, taking account of the legitimate interests of third parties.

3. The duration of protection available shall amount to at least 10 years.

SECTION 5: PATENTS
Article 27
Patentable Subject Matter

1. Subject to the provisions of paragraphs 2 and 3, patents shall be available for any inventions, whether products or processes, in all fields of technology, provided that they are new, involve an inventive step and are capable of industrial application.[5] Subject to paragraph 4 of Article 65, paragraph 8 of Article 70 and paragraph 3 of this Article, patents shall be available and patent rights enjoyable without discrimination as to the place of invention, the field of technology and whether products are imported or locally produced.

2. Members may exclude from patentability inventions, the prevention within their territory of the commercial exploitation of which is necessary to protect *ordre public* or morality, including to protect human, animal or plant life or health or to avoid serious prejudice to the environment, provided that such exclusion is not made merely because the exploitation is prohibited by their law.

3. Members may also exclude from patentability:

(a) diagnostic, therapeutic and surgical methods for the treatment of humans or animals;

(b) plants and animals other than micro-organisms, and essentially biological processes for the production of plants or animals other than

---

5. For the purposes of this Article, the terms "inventive step" and "capable of industrial application" may be deemed by a Member to be synonymous with the terms "non-obvious" and "useful" respectively.

non-biological and microbiological processes. However, Members shall provide for the protection of plant varieties either by patents or by an effective *sui generis* system or by any combination thereof. The provisions of this subparagraph shall be reviewed four years after the date of entry into force of the WTO Agreement.

Article 28

Rights Conferred

1. A patent shall confer on its owner the following exclusive rights:

    (a) where the subject matter of a patent is a product, to prevent third parties not having the owner's consent from the acts of: making, using, offering for sale, selling, or importing[6] for these purposes that product;

    (b) where the subject matter of a patent is a process, to prevent third parties not having the owner's consent from the act of using the process, and from the acts of: using, offering for sale, selling, or importing for these purposes at least the product obtained directly by that process.

2. Patent owners shall also have the right to assign, or transfer by succession, the patent and to conclude licensing contracts.

Article 29

Conditions on Patent Applicants

1. Members shall require that an applicant for a patent shall disclose the invention in a manner sufficiently clear and complete for the invention to be carried out by a person skilled in the art and may require the applicant to indicate the best mode for carrying out the invention known to the inventor at the filing date or, where priority is claimed, at the priority date of the application.

2. Members may require an applicant for a patent to provide information concerning the applicant's corresponding foreign applications and grants.

Article 30

Exceptions to Rights Conferred

Members may provide limited exceptions to the exclusive rights conferred by a patent, provided that such exceptions do not unreasonably conflict with a normal exploitation of the patent and do not unreasonably prejudice the legitimate interests of the patent owner, taking account of the legitimate interests of third parties.

Article 31

Other Use Without Authorization of the Right Holder

Where the law of a Member allows for other use[7] of the subject matter of a patent without the authorization of the right holder, including use by the

---

6. This right, like all other rights conferred under this Agreement in respect of the use, sale, importation or other distribution of goods, is subject to the provisions of Article 6.

7. "Other use" refers to use other than that allowed under Article 30.

government or third parties authorized by the government, the following provisions shall be respected:

(a) authorization of such use shall be considered on its individual merits;

(b) such use may only be permitted if, prior to such use, the proposed user has made efforts to obtain authorization from the right holder on reasonable commercial terms and conditions and that such efforts have not been successful within a reasonable period of time. This requirement may be waived by a Member in the case of a national emergency or other circumstances of extreme urgency or in cases of public non-commercial use. In situations of national emergency or other circumstances of extreme urgency, the right holder shall, nevertheless, be notified as soon as reasonably practicable. In the case of public non-commercial use, where the government or contractor, without making a patent search, knows or has demonstrable grounds to know that a valid patent is or will be used by or for the government, the right holder shall be informed promptly;

(c) the scope and duration of such use shall be limited to the purpose for which it was authorized, and in the case of semi-conductor technology shall only be for public non-commercial use or to remedy a practice determined after judicial or administrative process to be anti-competitive;

(d) such use shall be non-exclusive;

(e) such use shall be non-assignable, except with that part of the enterprise or goodwill which enjoys such use;

(f) any such use shall be authorized predominantly for the supply of the domestic market of the Member authorizing such use;

(g) authorization for such use shall be liable, subject to adequate protection of the legitimate interests of the persons so authorized, to be terminated if and when the circumstances which led to it cease to exist and are unlikely to recur. The competent authority shall have the authority to review, upon motivated request, the continued existence of these circumstances;

(h) the right holder shall be paid adequate remuneration in the circumstances of each case, taking into account the economic value of the authorization;

(i) the legal validity of any decision relating to the authorization of such use shall be subject to judicial review or other independent review by a distinct higher authority in that Member;

(j) any decision relating to the remuneration provided in respect of such use shall be subject to judicial review or other independent review by a distinct higher authority in that Member;

(k) Members are not obliged to apply the conditions set forth in subparagraphs (b) and (f) where such use is permitted to remedy a practice determined after judicial or administrative process to be anti-competitive. The need to correct anti-competitive practices may be taken into account in determining the amount of remuneration in such cases. Competent authorities shall have the authority to refuse termination of authorization if and when the conditions which led to such authorization are likely to recur;

(*l*) where such use is authorized to permit the exploitation of a patent ("the second patent") which cannot be exploited without infringing another patent ("the first patent"), the following additional conditions shall apply:

(i) the invention claimed in the second patent shall involve an important technical advance of considerable economic significance in relation to the invention claimed in the first patent;

(ii) the owner of the first patent shall be entitled to a cross-licence on reasonable terms to use the invention claimed in the second patent; and

(iii) the use authorized in respect of the first patent shall be non-assignable except with the assignment of the second patent.

Article 32
Revocation/Forfeiture

An opportunity for judicial review of any decision to revoke or forfeit a patent shall be available.

Article 33
Term of Protection

The term of protection available shall not end before the expiration of a period of twenty years counted from the filing date.[8]

Article 34
Process Patents: Burden of Proof

1. For the purposes of civil proceedings in respect of the infringement of the rights of the owner referred to in paragraph 1(b) of Article 28, if the subject matter of a patent is a process for obtaining a product, the judicial authorities shall have the authority to order the defendant to prove that the process to obtain an identical product is different from the patented process. Therefore, Members shall provide, in at least one of the following circumstances, that any identical product when produced without the consent of the patent owner shall, in the absence of proof to the contrary, be deemed to have been obtained by the patented process:

(a) if the product obtained by the patented process is new;

(b) if there is a substantial likelihood that the identical product was made by the process and the owner of the patent has been unable through reasonable efforts to determine the process actually used.

2. Any Member shall be free to provide that the burden of proof indicated in paragraph 1 shall be on the alleged infringer only if the condition referred to in subparagraph (a) is fulfilled or only if the condition referred to in subparagraph (b) is fulfilled.

3. In the adduction of proof to the contrary, the legitimate interests of defendants in protecting their manufacturing and business secrets shall be taken into account.

---

8. It is understood that those Members which do not have a system of original grant may provide that the term of protection shall be computed from the filing date in the system of original grant.

SECTION 6: LAYOUT–DESIGNS (TOPOGRAPHIES) OF INTEGRATED CIRCUITS

Article 35

Relation to the IPIC Treaty

Members agree to provide protection to the layout-designs (topographies) of integrated circuits (referred to in this Agreement as "layout-designs") in accordance with Articles 2 through 7 (other than paragraph 3 of Article 6), Article 12 and paragraph 3 of Article 16 of the Treaty on Intellectual Property in Respect of Integrated Circuits and, in addition, to comply with the following provisions.

Article 36

Scope of the Protection

Subject to the provisions of paragraph 1 of Article 37, Members shall consider unlawful the following acts if performed without the authorization of the right holder:[9] importing, selling, or otherwise distributing for commercial purposes a protected layout-design, an integrated circuit in which a protected layout-design is incorporated, or an article incorporating such an integrated circuit only in so far as it continues to contain an unlawfully reproduced layout-design.

Article 37

Acts Not Requiring the Authorization of the Right Holder

1. Notwithstanding Article 36, no Member shall consider unlawful the performance of any of the acts referred to in that Article in respect of an integrated circuit incorporating an unlawfully reproduced layout-design or any article incorporating such an integrated circuit where the person performing or ordering such acts did not know and had no reasonable ground to know, when acquiring the integrated circuit or article incorporating such an integrated circuit, that it incorporated an unlawfully reproduced layout-design. Members shall provide that, after the time that such person has received sufficient notice that the layout-design was unlawfully reproduced, that person may perform any of the acts with respect to the stock on hand or ordered before such time, but shall be liable to pay to the right holder a sum equivalent to a reasonable royalty such as would be payable under a freely negotiated licence in respect of such a layout-design.

2. The conditions set out in subparagraphs (a) through (k) of Article 31 shall apply *mutatis mutandis* in the event of any non-voluntary licensing of a layout-design or of its use by or for the government without the authorization of the right holder.

Article 38

Term of Protection

1. In Members requiring registration as a condition of protection, the term of protection of layout-designs shall not end before the expiration of a

---

9. The term "right holder" in this Section shall be understood as having the same meaning as the term "holder of the right" in the IPIC Treaty.

period of 10 years counted from the date of filing an application for registration or from the first commercial exploitation wherever in the world it occurs.

2.   In Members not requiring registration as a condition for protection, layout-designs shall be protected for a term of no less than 10 years from the date of the first commercial exploitation wherever in the world it occurs.

3.   Notwithstanding paragraphs 1 and 2, a Member may provide that protection shall lapse 15 years after the creation of the layout-design.

SECTION 7:   PROTECTION OF UNDISCLOSED INFORMATION

Article 39

1.   In the course of ensuring effective protection against unfair competition as provided in Article 10 *bis* of the Paris Convention (1967), Members shall protect undisclosed information in accordance with paragraph 2 and data submitted to governments or governmental agencies in accordance with paragraph 3.

2.   Natural and legal persons shall have the possibility of preventing information lawfully within their control from being disclosed to, acquired by, or used by others without their consent in a manner contrary to honest commercial practices[10] so long as such information:

> (a) is secret in the sense that it is not, as a body or in the precise configuration and assembly of its components, generally known among or readily accessible to persons within the circles that normally deal with the kind of information in question;

> (b) has commercial value because it is secret; and

> (c) has been subject to reasonable steps under the circumstances, by the person lawfully in control of the information, to keep it secret.

3.   Members, when requiring, as a condition of approving the marketing of pharmaceutical or of agricultural chemical products which utilize new chemical entities, the submission of undisclosed test or other data, the origination of which involves a considerable effort, shall protect such data against unfair commercial use. In addition, Members shall protect such data against disclosure, except where necessary to protect the public, or unless steps are taken to ensure that the data are protected against unfair commercial use.

SECTION 8:   CONTROL OF ANTI–COMPETITIVE
PRACTICES IN CONTRACTUAL LICENCES

Article 40

1.   Members agree that some licensing practices or conditions pertaining to intellectual property rights which restrain competition may have adverse effects on trade and may impede the transfer and dissemination of technology.

---

10. For the purpose of this provision, "a manner contrary to honest commercial practices" shall mean at least practices such as breach of contract, breach of confidence and inducement to breach, and includes the acquisition of undisclosed information by third parties who knew, or were grossly negligent in failing to know, that such practices were involved in the acquisition.

2.   Nothing in this Agreement shall prevent Members from specifying in their legislation licensing practices or conditions that may in particular cases constitute an abuse of intellectual property rights having an adverse effect on competition in the relevant market. As provided above, a Member may adopt, consistently with the other provisions of this Agreement, appropriate measures to prevent or control such practices, which may include for example exclusive grantback conditions, conditions preventing challenges to validity and coercive package licensing, in the light of the relevant laws and regulations of that Member.

3.   Each Member shall enter, upon request, into consultations with any other Member which has cause to believe that an intellectual property right owner that is a national or domiciliary of the Member to which the request for consultations has been addressed is undertaking practices in violation of the requesting Member's laws and regulations on the subject matter of this Section, and which wishes to secure compliance with such legislation, without prejudice to any action under the law and to the full freedom of an ultimate decision of either Member. The Member addressed shall accord full and sympathetic consideration to, and shall afford adequate opportunity for, consultations with the requesting Member, and shall cooperate through supply of publicly available non-confidential information of relevance to the matter in question and of other information available to the Member, subject to domestic law and to the conclusion of mutually satisfactory agreements concerning the safeguarding of its confidentiality by the requesting Member.

4.   A Member whose nationals or domiciliaries are subject to proceedings in another Member concerning alleged violation of that other Member's laws and regulations on the subject matter of this Section shall, upon request, be granted an opportunity for consultations by the other Member under the same conditions as those foreseen in paragraph 3.

PART III
ENFORCEMENT OF INTELLECTUAL PROPERTY RIGHTS
SECTION 1:   GENERAL OBLIGATIONS
Article 41

1.   Members shall ensure that enforcement procedures as specified in this Part are available under their law so as to permit effective action against any act of infringement of intellectual property rights covered by this Agreement, including expeditious remedies to prevent infringements and remedies which constitute a deterrent to further infringements. These procedures shall be applied in such a manner as to avoid the creation of barriers to legitimate trade and to provide for safeguards against their abuse.

2.   Procedures concerning the enforcement of intellectual property rights shall be fair and equitable. They shall not be unnecessarily complicated or costly, or entail unreasonable time-limits or unwarranted delays.

3.   Decisions on the merits of a case shall preferably be in writing and reasoned. They shall be made available at least to the parties to the proceeding without undue delay. Decisions on the merits of a case shall be based only on evidence in respect of which parties were offered the opportunity to be heard.

4. Parties to a proceeding shall have an opportunity for review by a judicial authority of final administrative decisions and, subject to jurisdictional provisions in a Member's law concerning the importance of a case, of at least the legal aspects of initial judicial decisions on the merits of a case. However, there shall be no obligation to provide an opportunity for review of acquittals in criminal cases.

5. It is understood that this Part does not create any obligation to put in place a judicial system for the enforcement of intellectual property rights distinct from that for the enforcement of law in general, nor does it affect the capacity of Members to enforce their law in general. Nothing in this Part creates any obligation with respect to the distribution of resources as between enforcement of intellectual property rights and the enforcement of law in general.

SECTION 2: CIVIL AND ADMINISTRATIVE PROCEDURES AND REMEDIES

Article 42

Fair and Equitable Procedures

Members shall make available to right holders[11] civil judicial procedures concerning the enforcement of any intellectual property right covered by this Agreement. Defendants shall have the right to written notice which is timely and contains sufficient detail, including the basis of the claims. Parties shall be allowed to be represented by independent legal counsel, and procedures shall not impose overly burdensome requirements concerning mandatory personal appearances. All parties to such procedures shall be duly entitled to substantiate their claims and to present all relevant evidence. The procedure shall provide a means to identify and protect confidential information, unless this would be contrary to existing constitutional requirements.

Article 43

Evidence

1. The judicial authorities shall have the authority, where a party has presented reasonably available evidence sufficient to support its claims and has specified evidence relevant to substantiation of its claims which lies in the control of the opposing party, to order that this evidence be produced by the opposing party, subject in appropriate cases to conditions which ensure the protection of confidential information.

2. In cases in which a party to a proceeding voluntarily and without good reason refuses access to, or otherwise does not provide necessary information within a reasonable period, or significantly impedes a procedure relating to an enforcement action, a Member may accord judicial authorities the authority to make preliminary and final determinations, affirmative or negative, on the basis of the information presented to them, including the complaint or the allegation presented by the party adversely affected by the denial of access to information, subject to providing the parties an opportunity to be heard on the allegations or evidence.

11. For the purpose of this Part, the term "right holder" includes federations and associations having legal standing to assert such rights.

Article 44

Injunctions

1.   The judicial authorities shall have the authority to order a party to desist from an infringement, *inter alia* to prevent the entry into the channels of commerce in their jurisdiction of imported goods that involve the infringement of an intellectual property right, immediately after customs clearance of such goods. Members are not obliged to accord such authority in respect of protected subject matter acquired or ordered by a person prior to knowing or having reasonable grounds to know that dealing in such subject matter would entail the infringement of an intellectual property right.

2.   Notwithstanding the other provisions of this Part and provided that the provisions of Part II specifically addressing use by governments, or by third parties authorized by a government, without the authorization of the right holder are complied with, Members may limit the remedies available against such use to payment of remuneration in accordance with subparagraph (h) of Article 31. In other cases, the remedies under this Part shall apply or, where these remedies are inconsistent with a Member's law, declaratory judgments and adequate compensation shall be available.

Article 45

Damages

1.   The judicial authorities shall have the authority to order the infringer to pay the right holder damages adequate to compensate for the injury the right holder has suffered because of an infringement of that person's intellectual property right by an infringer who knowingly, or with reasonable grounds to know, engaged in infringing activity.

2.   The judicial authorities shall also have the authority to order the infringer to pay the right holder expenses, which may include appropriate attorney's fees. In appropriate cases, Members may authorize the judicial authorities to order recovery of profits and/or payment of pre-established damages even where the infringer did not knowingly, or with reasonable grounds to know, engage in infringing activity.

Article 46

Other Remedies

In order to create an effective deterrent to infringement, the judicial authorities shall have the authority to order that goods that they have found to be infringing be, without compensation of any sort, disposed of outside the channels of commerce in such a manner as to avoid any harm caused to the right holder, or, unless this would be contrary to existing constitutional requirements, destroyed. The judicial authorities shall also have the authority to order that materials and implements the predominant use of which has been in the creation of the infringing goods be, without compensation of any sort, disposed of outside the channels of commerce in such a manner as to minimize the risks of further infringements. In considering such requests, the need for proportionality between the seriousness of the infringement and the remedies ordered as well as the interests of third parties shall be taken into account. In regard to counterfeit trademark goods, the simple removal of the trademark unlawfully affixed shall not be sufficient, other than in exceptional cases, to permit release of the goods into the channels of commerce.

Article 47

Right of Information

Members may provide that the judicial authorities shall have the authority, unless this would be out of proportion to the seriousness of the infringement, to order the infringer to inform the right holder of the identity of third persons involved in the production and distribution of the infringing goods or services and of their channels of distribution.

Article 48

Indemnification of the Defendant

1.   The judicial authorities shall have the authority to order a party at whose request measures were taken and who has abused enforcement procedures to provide to a party wrongfully enjoined or restrained adequate compensation for the injury suffered because of such abuse. The judicial authorities shall also have the authority to order the applicant to pay the defendant expenses, which may include appropriate attorney's fees.

2.   In respect of the administration of any law pertaining to the protection or enforcement of intellectual property rights, Members shall only exempt both public authorities and officials from liability to appropriate remedial measures where actions are taken or intended in good faith in the course of the administration of that law.

Article 49

Administrative Procedures

To the extent that any civil remedy can be ordered as a result of administrative procedures on the merits of a case, such procedures shall conform to principles equivalent in substance to those set forth in this Section.

SECTION 3:   PROVISIONAL MEASURES

Article 50

1.   The judicial authorities shall have the authority to order prompt and effective provisional measures:

(a) to prevent an infringement of any intellectual property right from occurring, and in particular to prevent the entry into the channels of commerce in their jurisdiction of goods, including imported goods immediately after customs clearance;

(b) to preserve relevant evidence in regard to the alleged infringement.

2.   The judicial authorities shall have the authority to adopt provisional measures *inaudita altera parte* where appropriate, in particular where any delay is likely to cause irreparable harm to the right holder, or where there is a demonstrable risk of evidence being destroyed.

3. The judicial authorities shall have the authority to require the applicant to provide any reasonably available evidence in order to satisfy themselves with a sufficient degree of certainty that the applicant is the right holder and that the applicant's right is being infringed or that such infringement is imminent, and to order the applicant to provide a security or equivalent assurance sufficient to protect the defendant and to prevent abuse.

4. Where provisional measures have been adopted *inaudita altera parte*, the parties affected shall be given notice, without delay after the execution of the measures at the latest. A review, including a right to be heard, shall take place upon request of the defendant with a view to deciding, within a reasonable period after the notification of the measures, whether these measures shall be modified, revoked or confirmed.

5. The applicant may be required to supply other information necessary for the identification of the goods concerned by the authority that will execute the provisional measures.

6. Without prejudice to paragraph 4, provisional measures taken on the basis of paragraphs 1 and 2 shall, upon request by the defendant, be revoked or otherwise cease to have effect, if proceedings leading to a decision on the merits of the case are not initiated within a reasonable period, to be determined by the judicial authority ordering the measures where a Member's law so permits or, in the absence of such a determination, not to exceed 20 working days or 31 calendar days, whichever is the longer.

7. Where the provisional measures are revoked or where they lapse due to any act or omission by the applicant, or where it is subsequently found that there has been no infringement or threat of infringement of an intellectual property right, the judicial authorities shall have the authority to order the applicant, upon request of the defendant, to provide the defendant appropriate compensation for any injury caused by these measures.

8. To the extent that any provisional measure can be ordered as a result of administrative procedures, such procedures shall conform to principles equivalent in substance to those set forth in this Section.

SECTION 4: SPECIAL REQUIREMENTS RELATED TO BORDER MEASURES[12]

Article 51

Suspension of Release by Customs Authorities

Members shall, in conformity with the provisions set out below, adopt procedures[13] to enable a right holder, who has valid grounds for suspecting that the importation of counterfeit trademark or pirated copyright goods[14] may take place, to lodge an application in writing with competent authorities,

---

12. Where a Member has dismantled substantially all controls over movement of goods across its border with another Member with which it forms part of a customs union, it shall not be required to apply the provisions of this Section at that border.

13. It is understood that there shall be no obligation to apply such procedures to imports of goods put on the market in another country by or with the consent of the right holder, or to goods in transit.

14. For the purposes of this Agreement:

(a) "counterfeit trademark goods" shall mean any goods, including packaging, bearing without authorization a trademark which is identical to the trademark validly registered in respect of such goods, or which cannot be distinguished in its essential aspects from such a trademark, and which

administrative or judicial, for the suspension by the customs authorities of the release into free circulation of such goods. Members may enable such an application to be made in respect of goods which involve other infringements of intellectual property rights, provided that the requirements of this Section are met. Members may also provide for corresponding procedures concerning the suspension by the customs authorities of the release of infringing goods destined for exportation from their territories.

Article 52
Application

Any right holder initiating the procedures under Article 51 shall be required to provide adequate evidence to satisfy the competent authorities that, under the laws of the country of importation, there is *prima facie* an infringement of the right holder's intellectual property right and to supply a sufficiently detailed description of the goods to make them readily recognizable by the customs authorities. The competent authorities shall inform the applicant within a reasonable period whether they have accepted the application and, where determined by the competent authorities, the period for which the customs authorities will take action.

Article 53
Security or Equivalent Assurance

1. The competent authorities shall have the authority to require an applicant to provide a security or equivalent assurance sufficient to protect the defendant and the competent authorities and to prevent abuse. Such security or equivalent assurance shall not unreasonably deter recourse to these procedures.

2. Where pursuant to an application under this Section the release of goods involving industrial designs, patents, layout-designs or undisclosed information into free circulation has been suspended by customs authorities on the basis of a decision other than by a judicial or other independent authority, and the period provided for in Article 55 has expired without the granting of provisional relief by the duly empowered authority, and provided that all other conditions for importation have been complied with, the owner, importer, or consignee of such goods shall be entitled to their release on the posting of a security in an amount sufficient to protect the right holder for any infringement. Payment of such security shall not prejudice any other remedy available to the right holder, it being understood that the security shall be released if the right holder fails to pursue the right of action within a reasonable period of time.

Article 54
Notice of Suspension

The importer and the applicant shall be promptly notified of the suspension of the release of goods according to Article 51.

thereby infringes the rights of the owner of the trademark in question under the law of the country of importation;

(b) "pirated copyright goods" shall mean any goods which are copies made without the consent of the right holder or person duly authorized by the right holder in the country of production and which are made directly or indirectly from an article where the making of that copy would have constituted an infringement of a copyright or a related right under the law of the country of importation.

Article 55
Duration of Suspension

If, within a period not exceeding 10 working days after the applicant has been served notice of the suspension, the customs authorities have not been informed that proceedings leading to a decision on the merits of the case have been initiated by a party other than the defendant, or that the duly empowered authority has taken provisional measures prolonging the suspension of the release of the goods, the goods shall be released, provided that all other conditions for importation or exportation have been complied with; in appropriate cases, this time-limit may be extended by another 10 working days. If proceedings leading to a decision on the merits of the case have been initiated, a review, including a right to be heard, shall take place upon request of the defendant with a view to deciding, within a reasonable period, whether these measures shall be modified, revoked or confirmed. Notwithstanding the above, where the suspension of the release of goods is carried out or continued in accordance with a provisional judicial measure, the provisions of paragraph 6 of Article 50 shall apply.

Article 56
Indemnification of the Importer and of the Owner of the Goods

Relevant authorities shall have the authority to order the applicant to pay the importer, the consignee and the owner of the goods appropriate compensation for any injury caused to them through the wrongful detention of goods or through the detention of goods released pursuant to Article 55.

Article 57
Right of Inspection and Information

Without prejudice to the protection of confidential information, Members shall provide the competent authorities the authority to give the right holder sufficient opportunity to have any goods detained by the customs authorities inspected in order to substantiate the right holder's claims. The competent authorities shall also have authority to give the importer an equivalent opportunity to have any such goods inspected. Where a positive determination has been made on the merits of a case, Members may provide the competent authorities the authority to inform the right holder of the names and addresses of the consignor, the importer and the consignee and of the quantity of the goods in question.

Article 58
Ex Officio Action

Where Members require competent authorities to act upon their own initiative and to suspend the release of goods in respect of which they have acquired *prima facie* evidence that an intellectual property right is being infringed:

    (a) the competent authorities may at any time seek from the right holder any information that may assist them to exercise these powers;

    (b) the importer and the right holder shall be promptly notified of the suspension. Where the importer has lodged an appeal against the suspension with the competent authorities, the suspension shall be subject to the conditions, *mutatis mutandis*, set out at Article 55;

(c) Members shall only exempt both public authorities and officials from liability to appropriate remedial measures where actions are taken or intended in good faith.

Article 59

Remedies

Without prejudice to other rights of action open to the right holder and subject to the right of the defendant to seek review by a judicial authority, competent authorities shall have the authority to order the destruction or disposal of infringing goods in accordance with the principles set out in Article 46. In regard to counterfeit trademark goods, the authorities shall not allow the re-exportation of the infringing goods in an unaltered state or subject them to a different customs procedure, other than in exceptional circumstances.

Article 60

De Minimis Imports

Members may exclude from the application of the above provisions small quantities of goods of a non-commercial nature contained in travellers' personal luggage or sent in small consignments.

SECTION 5: CRIMINAL PROCEDURES

Article 61

Members shall provide for criminal procedures and penalties to be applied at least in cases of wilful trademark counterfeiting or copyright piracy on a commercial scale. Remedies available shall include imprisonment and/or monetary fines sufficient to provide a deterrent, consistently with the level of penalties applied for crimes of a corresponding gravity. In appropriate cases, remedies available shall also include the seizure, forfeiture and destruction of the infringing goods and of any materials and implements the predominant use of which has been in the commission of the offence. Members may provide for criminal procedures and penalties to be applied in other cases of infringement of intellectual property rights, in particular where they are committed wilfully and on a commercial scale.

PART IV

ACQUISITION AND MAINTENANCE OF INTELLECTUAL PROPERTY RIGHTS AND RELATED INTER–PARTES PROCEDURES

Article 62

1. Members may require, as a condition of the acquisition or maintenance of the intellectual property rights provided for under Sections 2 through 6 of Part II, compliance with reasonable procedures and formalities. Such procedures and formalities shall be consistent with the provisions of this Agreement.

2. Where the acquisition of an intellectual property right is subject to the right being granted or registered, Members shall ensure that the proce-

dures for grant or registration, subject to compliance with the substantive conditions for acquisition of the right, permit the granting or registration of the right within a reasonable period of time so as to avoid unwarranted curtailment of the period of protection.

3.   Article 4 of the Paris Convention (1967) shall apply *mutatis mutandis* to service marks.

4.   Procedures concerning the acquisition or maintenance of intellectual property rights and, where a Member's law provides for such procedures, administrative revocation and *inter partes* procedures such as opposition, revocation and cancellation, shall be governed by the general principles set out in paragraphs 2 and 3 of Article 41.

5.   Final administrative decisions in any of the procedures referred to under paragraph 4 shall be subject to review by a judicial or quasi-judicial authority. However, there shall be no obligation to provide an opportunity for such review of decisions in cases of unsuccessful opposition or administrative revocation, provided that the grounds for such procedures can be the subject of invalidation procedures.

PART V
DISPUTE PREVENTION AND SETTLEMENT

Article 63

Transparency

1.   Laws and regulations, and final judicial decisions and administrative rulings of general application, made effective by a Member pertaining to the subject matter of this Agreement (the availability, scope, acquisition, enforcement and prevention of the abuse of intellectual property rights) shall be published, or where such publication is not practicable made publicly available, in a national language, in such a manner as to enable governments and right holders to become acquainted with them. Agreements concerning the subject matter of this Agreement which are in force between the government or a governmental agency of a Member and the government or a governmental agency of another Member shall also be published.

2.   Members shall notify the laws and regulations referred to in paragraph 1 to the Council for TRIPS in order to assist that Council in its review of the operation of this Agreement. The Council shall attempt to minimize the burden on Members in carrying out this obligation and may decide to waive the obligation to notify such laws and regulations directly to the Council if consultations with WIPO on the establishment of a common register containing these laws and regulations are successful. The Council shall also consider in this connection any action required regarding notifications pursuant to the obligations under this Agreement stemming from the provisions of Article 6 *ter* of the Paris Convention (1967).

3.   Each Member shall be prepared to supply, in response to a written request from another Member, information of the sort referred to in paragraph 1. A Member, having reason to believe that a specific judicial decision or administrative ruling or bilateral agreement in the area of intellectual property rights affects its rights under this Agreement, may also request in writing

to be given access to or be informed in sufficient detail of such specific judicial decisions or administrative rulings or bilateral agreements.

4.   Nothing in paragraphs 1, 2 and 3 shall require Members to disclose confidential information which would impede law enforcement or otherwise be contrary to the public interest or would prejudice the legitimate commercial interests of particular enterprises, public or private.

Article 64
Dispute Settlement

1.   The provisions of Articles XXII and XXIII of GATT 1994 as elaborated and applied by the Dispute Settlement Understanding shall apply to consultations and the settlement of disputes under this Agreement except as otherwise specifically provided herein.

2.   Subparagraphs 1(b) and 1(c) of Article XXIII of GATT 1994 shall not apply to the settlement of disputes under this Agreement for a period of five years from the date of entry into force of the WTO Agreement.

3.   During the time period referred to in paragraph 2, the Council for TRIPS shall examine the scope and modalities for complaints of the type provided for under subparagraphs 1(b) and 1(c) of Article XXIII of GATT 1994 made pursuant to this Agreement, and submit its recommendations to the Ministerial Conference for approval. Any decision of the Ministerial Conference to approve such recommendations or to extend the period in paragraph 2 shall be made only by consensus, and approved recommendations shall be effective for all Members without further formal acceptance process. [Editors' Note: No such decision had been taken as of July 2002.]

PART VI
TRANSITIONAL ARRANGEMENTS
Article 65
Transitional Arrangements

1.   Subject to the provisions of paragraphs 2, 3 and 4, no Member shall be obliged to apply the provisions of this Agreement before the expiry of a general period of one year following the date of entry into force of the WTO Agreement.

2.   A developing country Member is entitled to delay for a further period of four years the date of application, as defined in paragraph 1, of the provisions of this Agreement other than Articles 3, 4 and 5.

3.   Any other Member which is in the process of transformation from a centrally-planned into a market, free-enterprise economy and which is undertaking structural reform of its intellectual property system and facing special problems in the preparation and implementation of intellectual property laws and regulations, may also benefit from a period of delay as foreseen in paragraph 2.

4.   To the extent that a developing country Member is obliged by this Agreement to extend product patent protection to areas of technology not so protectable in its territory on the general date of application of this Agreement for that Member, as defined in paragraph 2, it may delay the application

of the provisions on product patents of Section 5 of Part II to such areas of technology for an additional period of five years.

5. A Member availing itself of a transitional period under paragraphs 1, 2, 3 or 4 shall ensure that any changes in its laws, regulations and practice made during that period do not result in a lesser degree of consistency with the provisions of this Agreement.

Article 66

Least–Developed Country Members

1. In view of the special needs and requirements of least-developed country Members, their economic, financial and administrative constraints, and their need for flexibility to create a viable technological base, such Members shall not be required to apply the provisions of this Agreement, other than Articles 3, 4 and 5, for a period of 10 years from the date of application as defined under paragraph 1 of Article 65. The Council for TRIPS shall, upon duly motivated request by a least-developed country Member, accord extensions of this period.

2. Developed country Members shall provide incentives to enterprises and institutions in their territories for the purpose of promoting and encouraging technology transfer to least-developed country Members in order to enable them to create a sound and viable technological base.

Article 67

Technical Cooperation

In order to facilitate the implementation of this Agreement, developed country Members shall provide, on request and on mutually agreed terms and conditions, technical and financial cooperation in favour of developing and least-developed country Members. Such cooperation shall include assistance in the preparation of laws and regulations on the protection and enforcement of intellectual property rights as well as on the prevention of their abuse, and shall include support regarding the establishment or reinforcement of domestic offices and agencies relevant to these matters, including the training of personnel.

PART VII

INSTITUTIONAL ARRANGEMENTS; FINAL PROVISIONS

Article 68

Council for Trade–Related Aspects of Intellectual Property Rights

The Council for TRIPS shall monitor the operation of this Agreement and, in particular, Members' compliance with their obligations hereunder, and shall afford Members the opportunity of consulting on matters relating to the trade-related aspects of intellectual property rights. It shall carry out such other responsibilities as assigned to it by the Members, and it shall, in particular, provide any assistance requested by them in the context of dispute settlement procedures. In carrying out its functions, the Council for TRIPS may consult with and seek information from any source it deems appropriate. In consultation with WIPO, the Council shall seek to establish, within one year of its first meeting, appropriate arrangements for cooperation with bodies of that Organization.

Article 69

International Cooperation

Members agree to cooperate with each other with a view to eliminating international trade in goods infringing intellectual property rights. For this purpose, they shall establish and notify contact points in their administrations and be ready to exchange information on trade in infringing goods. They shall, in particular, promote the exchange of information and cooperation between customs authorities with regard to trade in counterfeit trademark goods and pirated copyright goods.

Article 70

Protection of Existing Subject Matter

1.   This Agreement does not give rise to obligations in respect of acts which occurred before the date of application of the Agreement for the Member in question.

2.   Except as otherwise provided for in this Agreement, this Agreement gives rise to obligations in respect of all subject matter existing at the date of application of this Agreement for the Member in question, and which is protected in that Member on the said date, or which meets or comes subsequently to meet the criteria for protection under the terms of this Agreement. In respect of this paragraph and paragraphs 3 and 4, copyright obligations with respect to existing works shall be solely determined under Article 18 of the Berne Convention (1971), and obligations with respect to the rights of producers of phonograms and performers in existing phonograms shall be determined solely under Article 18 of the Berne Convention (1971) as made applicable under paragraph 6 of Article 14 of this Agreement.

3.   There shall be no obligation to restore protection to subject matter which on the date of application of this Agreement for the Member in question has fallen into the public domain.

4.   In respect of any acts in respect of specific objects embodying protected subject matter which become infringing under the terms of legislation in conformity with this Agreement, and which were commenced, or in respect of which a significant investment was made, before the date of acceptance of the WTO Agreement by that Member, any Member may provide for a limitation of the remedies available to the right holder as to the continued performance of such acts after the date of application of this Agreement for that Member. In such cases the Member shall, however, at least provide for the payment of equitable remuneration.

5.   A Member is not obliged to apply the provisions of Article 11 and of paragraph 4 of Article 14 with respect to originals or copies purchased prior to the date of application of this Agreement for that Member.

6.   Members shall not be required to apply Article 31, or the requirement in paragraph 1 of Article 27 that patent rights shall be enjoyable without discrimination as to the field of technology, to use without the authorization

of the right holder where authorization for such use was granted by the government before the date this Agreement became known.

7.   In the case of intellectual property rights for which protection is conditional upon registration, applications for protection which are pending on the date of application of this Agreement for the Member in question shall be permitted to be amended to claim any enhanced protection provided under the provisions of this Agreement. Such amendments shall not include new matter.

8.   Where a Member does not make available as of the date of entry into force of the WTO Agreement patent protection for pharmaceutical and agricultural chemical products commensurate with its obligations under Article 27, that Member shall:

(a) notwithstanding the provisions of Part VI, provide as from the date of entry into force of the WTO Agreement a means by which applications for patents for such inventions can be filed;

(b) apply to these applications, as of the date of application of this Agreement, the criteria for patentability as laid down in this Agreement as if those criteria were being applied on the date of filing in that Member or, where priority is available and claimed, the priority date of the application; and

(c) provide patent protection in accordance with this Agreement as from the grant of the patent and for the remainder of the patent term, counted from the filing date in accordance with Article 33 of this Agreement, for those of these applications that meet the criteria for protection referred to in subparagraph (b).

9.   Where a product is the subject of a patent application in a Member in accordance with paragraph 8(a), exclusive marketing rights shall be granted, notwithstanding the provisions of Part VI, for a period of five years after obtaining marketing approval in that Member or until a product patent is granted or rejected in that Member, whichever period is shorter, provided that, subsequent to the entry into force of the WTO Agreement, a patent application has been filed and a patent granted for that product in another Member and marketing approval obtained in such other Member.

Article 71

Review and Amendment

1.   The Council for TRIPS shall review the implementation of this Agreement after the expiration of the transitional period referred to in paragraph 2 of Article 65. The Council shall, having regard to the experience gained in its implementation, review it two years after that date, and at identical intervals thereafter. The Council may also undertake reviews in the light of any relevant new developments which might warrant modification or amendment of this Agreement.

2.   Amendments merely serving the purpose of adjusting to higher levels of protection of intellectual property rights achieved, and in force, in other multilateral agreements and accepted under those agreements by all Members of the WTO may be referred to the Ministerial Conference for action in

accordance with paragraph 6 of Article X of the WTO Agreement on the basis of a consensus proposal from the Council for TRIPS.

Article 72

Reservations

Reservations may not be entered in respect of any of the provisions of this Agreement without the consent of the other Members.

Article 73

Security Exceptions

Nothing in this Agreement shall be construed:

(a) to require a Member to furnish any information the disclosure of which it considers contrary to its essential security interests; or

(b) to prevent a Member from taking any action which it considers necessary for the protection of its essential security interests;

    (i) relating to fissionable materials or the materials from which they are derived;

    (ii) relating to the traffic in arms, ammunition and implements of war and to such traffic in other goods and materials as is carried on directly or indirectly for the purpose of supplying a military establishment;

    (iii) taken in time of war or other emergency in international relations; or

(c) to prevent a Member from taking any action in pursuance of its obligations under the United Nations Charter for the maintenance of international peace and security.

Item 18

ANNEX 2
UNDERSTANDING ON RULES AND PROCEDURES GOVERNING THE SETTLEMENT OF DISPUTES

Members hereby *agree* as follows:

Article 1

Coverage and Application

1. The rules and procedures of this Understanding shall apply to disputes brought pursuant to the consultation and dispute settlement provisions of the agreements listed in Appendix 1 to this Understanding (referred to in this Understanding as the "covered agreements"). The rules and procedures of this Understanding shall also apply to consultations and the settlement of disputes between Members concerning their rights and obligations under the provisions of the Agreement Establishing the World Trade Organization (referred to in this Understanding as the "WTO Agreement") and of this Understanding taken in isolation or in combination with any other covered agreement.

2. The rules and procedures of this Understanding shall apply subject to such special or additional rules and procedures on dispute settlement contained in the covered agreements as are identified in Appendix 2 to this Understanding. To the extent that there is a difference between the rules and procedures of this Understanding and the special or additional rules and procedures set forth in Appendix 2, the special or additional rules and procedures in Appendix 2 shall prevail. In disputes involving rules and procedures under more than one covered agreement, if there is a conflict between special or additional rules and procedures of such agreements under review, and where the parties to the dispute cannot agree on rules and procedures within 20 days of the establishment of the panel, the Chairman of the Dispute Settlement Body provided for in paragraph 1 of Article 2 (referred to in this Understanding as the "DSB"), in consultation with the parties to the dispute, shall determine the rules and procedures to be followed within 10 days after a request by either Member. The Chairman shall be guided by the principle that special or additional rules and procedures should be used where possible, and the rules and procedures set out in this Understanding should be used to the extent necessary to avoid conflict.

Article 2

Administration

1. The Dispute Settlement Body is hereby established to administer these rules and procedures and, except as otherwise provided in a covered agreement, the consultation and dispute settlement provisions of the covered agreements. Accordingly, the DSB shall have the authority to establish

panels, adopt panel and Appellate Body reports, maintain surveillance of implementation of rulings and recommendations, and authorize suspension of concessions and other obligations under the covered agreements. With respect to disputes arising under a covered agreement which is a Plurilateral Trade Agreement, the term "Member" as used herein shall refer only to those Members that are parties to the relevant Plurilateral Trade Agreement. Where the DSB administers the dispute settlement provisions of a Plurilateral Trade Agreement, only those Members that are parties to that Agreement may participate in decisions or actions taken by the DSB with respect to that dispute.

2.   The DSB shall inform the relevant WTO Councils and Committees of any developments in disputes related to provisions of the respective covered agreements.

3.   The DSB shall meet as often as necessary to carry out its functions within the time-frames provided in this Understanding.

4.   Where the rules and procedures of this Understanding provide for the DSB to take a decision, it shall do so by consensus.[1]

Article 3
General Provisions

1.   Members affirm their adherence to the principles for the management of disputes heretofore applied under Articles XXII and XXIII of GATT 1947, and the rules and procedures as further elaborated and modified herein.

2.   The dispute settlement system of the WTO is a central element in providing security and predictability to the multilateral trading system. The Members recognize that it serves to preserve the rights and obligations of Members under the covered agreements, and to clarify the existing provisions of those agreements in accordance with customary rules of interpretation of public international law. Recommendations and rulings of the DSB cannot add to or diminish the rights and obligations provided in the covered agreements.

3.   The prompt settlement of situations in which a Member considers that any benefits accruing to it directly or indirectly under the covered agreements are being impaired by measures taken by another Member is essential to the effective functioning of the WTO and the maintenance of a proper balance between the rights and obligations of Members.

4.   Recommendations or rulings made by the DSB shall be aimed at achieving a satisfactory settlement of the matter in accordance with the rights and obligations under this Understanding and under the covered agreements.

5.   All solutions to matters formally raised under the consultation and dispute settlement provisions of the covered agreements, including arbitration awards, shall be consistent with those agreements and shall not nullify or impair benefits accruing to any Member under those agreements, nor impede the attainment of any objective of those agreements.

---

1. The DSB shall be deemed to have decided by consensus on a matter submitted for its consideration, if no Member, present at the meeting of the DSB when the decision is taken, formally objects to the proposed decision.

6. Mutually agreed solutions to matters formally raised under the consultation and dispute settlement provisions of the covered agreements shall be notified to the DSB and the relevant Councils and Committees, where any Member may raise any point relating thereto.

7. Before bringing a case, a Member shall exercise its judgment as to whether action under these procedures would be fruitful. The aim of the dispute settlement mechanism is to secure a positive solution to a dispute. A solution mutually acceptable to the parties to a dispute and consistent with the covered agreements is clearly to be preferred. In the absence of a mutually agreed solution, the first objective of the dispute settlement mechanism is usually to secure the withdrawal of the measures concerned if these are found to be inconsistent with the provisions of any of the covered agreements. The provision of compensation should be resorted to only if the immediate withdrawal of the measure is impracticable and as a temporary measure pending the withdrawal of the measure which is inconsistent with a covered agreement. The last resort which this Understanding provides to the Member invoking the dispute settlement procedures is the possibility of suspending the application of concessions or other obligations under the covered agreements on a discriminatory basis vis-á-vis the other Member, subject to authorization by the DSB of such measures.

8. In cases where there is an infringement of the obligations assumed under a covered agreement, the action is considered *prima facie* to constitute a case of nullification or impairment. This means that there is normally a presumption that a breach of the rules has an adverse impact on other Members parties to that covered agreement, and in such cases, it shall be up to the Member against whom the complaint has been brought to rebut the charge.

9. The provisions of this Understanding are without prejudice to the rights of Members to seek authoritative interpretation of provisions of a covered agreement through decision-making under the WTO Agreement or a covered agreement which is a Plurilateral Trade Agreement.

10. It is understood that requests for conciliation and the use of the dispute settlement procedures should not be intended or considered as contentious acts and that, if a dispute arises, all Members will engage in these procedures in good faith in an effort to resolve the dispute. It is also understood that complaints and counter-complaints in regard to distinct matters should not be linked.

11. This Understanding shall be applied only with respect to new requests for consultations under the consultation provisions of the covered agreements made on or after the date of entry into force of the WTO Agreement. With respect to disputes for which the request for consultations was made under GATT 1947 or under any other predecessor agreement to the covered agreements before the date of entry into force of the WTO Agreement, the relevant dispute settlement rules and procedures in effect immediately prior to the date of entry into force of the WTO Agreement shall continue to apply.[2]

---

2. This paragraph shall also be applied to disputes on which panel reports have not been adopted or fully implemented.

12. Notwithstanding paragraph 11, if a complaint based on any of the covered agreements is brought by a developing country Member against a developed country Member, the complaining party shall have the right to invoke, as an alternative to the provisions contained in Articles 4, 5, 6 and 12 of this Understanding, the corresponding provisions of the Decision of 5 April 1966 (BISD 14S/18), except that where the Panel considers that the time-frame provided for in paragraph 7 of that Decision is insufficient to provide its report and with the agreement of the complaining party, that time-frame may be extended. To the extent that there is a difference between the rules and procedures of Articles 4, 5, 6 and 12 and the corresponding rules and procedures of the Decision, the latter shall prevail.

Article 4
Consultations

1. Members affirm their resolve to strengthen and improve the effectiveness of the consultation procedures employed by Members.

2. Each Member undertakes to accord sympathetic consideration to and afford adequate opportunity for consultation regarding any representations made by another Member concerning measures affecting the operation of any covered agreement taken within the territory of the former.[3]

3. If a request for consultations is made pursuant to a covered agreement, the Member to which the request is made shall, unless otherwise mutually agreed, reply to the request within 10 days after the date of its receipt and shall enter into consultations in good faith within a period of no more than 30 days after the date of receipt of the request, with a view to reaching a mutually satisfactory solution. If the Member does not respond within 10 days after the date of receipt of the request, or does not enter into consultations within a period of no more than 30 days, or a period otherwise mutually agreed, after the date of receipt of the request, then the Member that requested the holding of consultations may proceed directly to request the establishment of a panel.

4. All such requests for consultations shall be notified to the DSB and the relevant Councils and Committees by the Member which requests consultations. Any request for consultations shall be submitted in writing and shall give the reasons for the request, including identification of the measures at issue and an indication of the legal basis for the complaint.

5. In the course of consultations in accordance with the provisions of a covered agreement, before resorting to further action under this Understanding, Members should attempt to obtain satisfactory adjustment of the matter.

6. Consultations shall be confidential, and without prejudice to the rights of any Member in any further proceedings.

7. If the consultations fail to settle a dispute within 60 days after the date of receipt of the request for consultations, the complaining party may request the establishment of a panel. The complaining party may request a

---

3. Where the provisions of any other covered agreement concerning measures taken by regional or local governments or authorities within the territory of a Member contain provisions different from the provisions of this paragraph, the provisions of such other covered agreement shall prevail.

panel during the 60–day period if the consulting parties jointly consider that consultations have failed to settle the dispute.

8.   In cases of urgency, including those which concern perishable goods, Members shall enter into consultations within a period of no more than 10 days after the date of receipt of the request. If the consultations have failed to settle the dispute within a period of 20 days after the date of receipt of the request, the complaining party may request the establishment of a panel.

9.   In cases of urgency, including those which concern perishable goods, the parties to the dispute, panels and the Appellate Body shall make every effort to accelerate the proceedings to the greatest extent possible.

10.   During consultations Members should give special attention to the particular problems and interests of developing country Members.

11.   Whenever a Member other than the consulting Members considers that it has a substantial trade interest in consultations being held pursuant to paragraph 1 of Article XXII of GATT 1994, paragraph 1 of Article XXII of GATS, or the corresponding provisions in other covered agreements [4], such Member may notify the consulting Members and the DSB, within 10 days after the date of the circulation of the request for consultations under said Article, of its desire to be joined in the consultations. Such Member shall be joined in the consultations, provided that the Member to which the request for consultations was addressed agrees that the claim of substantial interest is well-founded. In that event they shall so inform the DSB. If the request to be joined in the consultations is not accepted, the applicant Member shall be free to request consultations under paragraph 1 of Article XXII or paragraph 1 of Article XXIII of GATT 1994, paragraph 1 of Article XXII or paragraph 1 of Article XXIII of GATS, or the corresponding provisions in other covered agreements.

Article 5
Good Offices, Conciliation and Mediation

1.   Good offices, conciliation and mediation are procedures that are undertaken voluntarily if the parties to the dispute so agree.

2.   Proceedings involving good offices, conciliation and mediation, and in particular positions taken by the parties to the dispute during these proceedings, shall be confidential, and without prejudice to the rights of either party in any further proceedings under these procedures.

3.   Good offices, conciliation or mediation may be requested at any time by any party to a dispute. They may begin at any time and be terminated at

---

4.   The corresponding consultation provisions in the covered agreements are listed hereunder: Agreement on Agriculture, Article 19; Agreement on the Application of Sanitary and Phytosanitary Measures, paragraph 1 of Article 11; Agreement on Textiles and Clothing, paragraph 4 of Article 8; Agreement on Technical Barriers to Trade, paragraph 1 of Article 14; Agreement on Trade–Related Investment Measures, Article 8; Agreement on Implementation of Article VI of GATT 1994, paragraph 2 of Article 17; Agreement on Implementation of Article VII of GATT 1994, paragraph 2 of Article 19; Agreement on Preshipment Inspection, Article 7; Agreement on Rules of Origin, Article 7; Agreement on Import Licensing Procedures, Article 6; Agreement on Subsidies and Countervailing Measures, Article 30; Agreement on Safeguards, Article 14; Agreement on Trade–Related Aspects of Intellectual Property Rights, Article 64.1; and any corresponding consultation provisions in Plurilateral Trade Agreements as determined by the competent bodies of each Agreement and as notified to the DSB.

any time. Once procedures for good offices, conciliation or mediation are terminated, a complaining party may then proceed with a request for the establishment of a panel.

4. When good offices, conciliation or mediation are entered into within 60 days after the date of receipt of a request for consultations, the complaining party must allow a period of 60 days after the date of receipt of the request for consultations before requesting the establishment of a panel. The complaining party may request the establishment of a panel during the 60–day period if the parties to the dispute jointly consider that the good offices, conciliation or mediation process has failed to settle the dispute.

5. If the parties to a dispute agree, procedures for good offices, conciliation or mediation may continue while the panel process proceeds.

6. The Director–General may, acting in an *ex officio* capacity, offer good offices, conciliation or mediation with the view to assisting Members to settle a dispute.

Article 6
Establishment of Panels

1. If the complaining party so requests, a panel shall be established at the latest at the DSB meeting following that at which the request first appears as an item on the DSB's agenda, unless at that meeting the DSB decides by consensus not to establish a panel.[5]

2. The request for the establishment of a panel shall be made in writing. It shall indicate whether consultations were held, identify the specific measures at issue and provide a brief summary of the legal basis of the complaint sufficient to present the problem clearly. In case the applicant requests the establishment of a panel with other than standard terms of reference, the written request shall include the proposed text of special terms of reference.

Article 7
Terms of Reference of Panels

1. Panels shall have the following terms of reference unless the parties to the dispute agree otherwise within 20 days from the establishment of the panel:

> "To examine, in the light of the relevant provisions in (name of the covered agreement(s) cited by the parties to the dispute), the matter referred to the DSB by (name of party) in document ... and to make such findings as will assist the DSB in making the recommendations or in giving the rulings provided for in that/those agreement(s)."

2. Panels shall address the relevant provisions in any covered agreement or agreements cited by the parties to the dispute.

3. In establishing a panel, the DSB may authorize its Chairman to draw up the terms of reference of the panel in consultation with the parties to the dispute, subject to the provisions of paragraph 1. The terms of reference thus

---

5. If the complaining party so requests, a meeting of the DSB shall be convened for this purpose within 15 days of the request, provid-ed that at least 10 days' advance notice of the meeting is given.

drawn up shall be circulated to all Members. If other than standard terms of reference are agreed upon, any Member may raise any point relating thereto in the DSB.

Article 8

Composition of Panels

1.   Panels shall be composed of well-qualified governmental and/or non-governmental individuals, including persons who have served on or presented a case to a panel, served as a representative of a Member or of a contracting party to GATT 1947 or as a representative to the Council or Committee of any covered agreement or its predecessor agreement, or in the Secretariat, taught or published on international trade law or policy, or served as a senior trade policy official of a Member.

2.   Panel members should be selected with a view to ensuring the independence of the members, a sufficiently diverse background and a wide spectrum of experience.

3.   Citizens of Members whose governments [6] are parties to the dispute or third parties as defined in paragraph 2 of Article 10 shall not serve on a panel concerned with that dispute, unless the parties to the dispute agree otherwise.

4.   To assist in the selection of panelists, the Secretariat shall maintain an indicative list of governmental and non-governmental individuals possessing the qualifications outlined in paragraph 1, from which panelists may be drawn as appropriate. That list shall include the roster of non-governmental panelists established on 30 November 1984 (BISD 31S/9), and other rosters and indicative lists established under any of the covered agreements, and shall retain the names of persons on those rosters and indicative lists at the time of entry into force of the WTO Agreement. Members may periodically suggest names of governmental and non-governmental individuals for inclusion on the indicative list, providing relevant information on their knowledge of international trade and of the sectors or subject matter of the covered agreements, and those names shall be added to the list upon approval by the DSB. For each of the individuals on the list, the list shall indicate specific areas of experience or expertise of the individuals in the sectors or subject matter of the covered agreements.

5.   Panels shall be composed of three panelists unless the parties to the dispute agree, within 10 days from the establishment of the panel, to a panel composed of five panelists. Members shall be informed promptly of the composition of the panel.

6.   The Secretariat shall propose nominations for the panel to the parties to the dispute. The parties to the dispute shall not oppose nominations except for compelling reasons.

7.   If there is no agreement on the panelists within 20 days after the date of the establishment of a panel, at the request of either party, the Director–General, in consultation with the Chairman of the DSB and the Chairman of

---

6. In the case where customs unions or common markets are parties to a dispute, this provision applies to citizens of all member countries of the customs unions or common markets.

the relevant Council or Committee, shall determine the composition of the panel by appointing the panelists whom the Director–General considers most appropriate in accordance with any relevant special or additional rules or procedures of the covered agreement or covered agreements which are at issue in the dispute, after consulting with the parties to the dispute. The Chairman of the DSB shall inform the Members of the composition of the panel thus formed no later than 10 days after the date the Chairman receives such a request.

8. Members shall undertake, as a general rule, to permit their officials to serve as panelists.

9. Panelists shall serve in their individual capacities and not as government representatives, nor as representatives of any organization. Members shall therefore not give them instructions nor seek to influence them as individuals with regard to matters before a panel.

10. When a dispute is between a developing country Member and a developed country Member the panel shall, if the developing country Member so requests, include at least one panelist from a developing country Member.

11. Panelists' expenses, including travel and subsistence allowance, shall be met from the WTO budget in accordance with criteria to be adopted by the General Council, based on recommendations of the Committee on Budget, Finance and Administration.

Article 9

Procedures for Multiple Complainants

1. Where more than one Member requests the establishment of a panel related to the same matter, a single panel may be established to examine these complaints taking into account the rights of all Members concerned. A single panel should be established to examine such complaints whenever feasible.

2. The single panel shall organize its examination and present its findings to the DSB in such a manner that the rights which the parties to the dispute would have enjoyed had separate panels examined the complaints are in no way impaired. If one of the parties to the dispute so requests, the panel shall submit separate reports on the dispute concerned. The written submissions by each of the complainants shall be made available to the other complainants, and each complainant shall have the right to be present when any one of the other complainants presents its views to the panel.

3. If more than one panel is established to examine the complaints related to the same manner, to the greatest extent possible the same persons shall serve as panelists on each of the separate panels and the timetable for the panel process in such disputes shall be harmonized.

Article 10

Third Parties

1. The interests of the parties to a dispute and those of other Members under a covered agreement at issue in the dispute shall be fully taken into account during the panel process.

2. Any Member having a substantial interest in a matter before a panel and having notified its interest to the DSB (referred to in this Understanding as a "third party") shall have an opportunity to be heard by the panel and to make written submissions to the panel. These submissions shall also be given to the parties to the dispute and shall be reflected in the panel report.

3. Third parties shall receive the submissions of the parties to the dispute [at] the first meeting of the panel.

4. If a third party considers that a measure already the subject of a panel proceeding nullifies or impairs benefits accruing to it under any covered agreement, that Member may have recourse to normal dispute settlement procedures under this Understanding. Such a dispute shall be referred to the original panel wherever possible.

Article 11

Function of Panels

The function of panels is to assist the DSB in discharging its responsibilities under this Understanding and the covered agreements. Accordingly, a panel should make an objective assessment of the matter before it, including an objective assessment of the facts of the case and the applicability of and conformity with the relevant covered agreements, and make such other findings as will assist the DSB in making the recommendations or in giving the rulings provided for in the covered agreements. Panels should consult regularly with the parties to the dispute and give them adequate opportunity to develop a mutually satisfactory solution.

Article 12

Panel Procedures

1. Panels shall follow the Working Procedures in Appendix 3 unless the panel decides otherwise after consulting the parties to the dispute.

2. Panel procedures should provide sufficient flexibility so as to ensure high-quality panel reports, while not unduly delaying the panel process.

3. After consulting the parties to the dispute, the panelists shall, as soon as practicable and whenever possible within one week after the composition and terms of reference of the panel have been agreed upon, fix the timetable for the panel process, taking into account the provisions of paragraph 9 of Article 4, if relevant.

4. In determining the timetable for the panel process, the panel shall provide sufficient time for the parties to the dispute to prepare their submissions.

5. Panels should set precise deadlines for written submissions by the parties and the parties should respect those deadlines.

6. Each party to the dispute shall deposit its written submissions with the Secretariat for immediate transmission to the panel and to the other party or parties to the dispute. The complaining party shall submit its first submission in advance of the responding party's first submission unless the panel decides, in fixing the timetable referred to in paragraph 3 and after consultations with the parties to the dispute, that the parties should submit

their first submissions simultaneously. When there are sequential arrangements for the deposit of first submissions, the panel shall establish a firm time-period for receipt of the responding party's submission. Any subsequent written submissions shall be submitted simultaneously.

7. Where the parties to the dispute have failed to develop a mutually satisfactory solution, the panel shall submit its findings in the form of a written report to the DSB. In such cases, the report of a panel shall set out the findings of fact, the applicability of relevant provisions and the basic rationale behind any findings and recommendations that it makes. Where a settlement of the matter among the parties to the dispute has been found, the report of the panel shall be confined to a brief description of the case and to reporting that a solution has been reached.

8. In order to make the procedures more efficient, the period in which the panel shall conduct its examination, from the date that the composition and terms of reference of the panel have been agreed upon until the date the final report is issued to the parties to the dispute, shall, as a general rule, not exceed six months. In cases of urgency, including those relating to perishable goods, the panel shall aim to issue its report to the parties to the dispute within three months.

9. When the panel considers that it cannot issue its report within six months, or within three months in cases of urgency, it shall inform the DSB in writing of the reasons for the delay together with an estimate of the period within which it will issue its report. In no case should the period from the establishment of the panel to the circulation of the report to the Members exceed nine months.

10. In the context of consultations involving a measure taken by a developing country Member, the parties may agree to extend the periods established in paragraphs 7 and 8 of Article 4. If, after the relevant period has elapsed, the consulting parties cannot agree that the consultations have concluded, the Chairman of the DSB shall decide, after consultation with the parties, whether to extend the relevant period and, if so, for how long. In addition, in examining a complaint against a developing country Member, the panel shall accord sufficient time for the developing country Member to prepare and present its argumentation. The provisions of paragraph 1 of Article 20 and paragraph 4 of Article 21 are not affected by any action pursuant to this paragraph.

11. Where one or more of the parties is a developing country Member, the panel's report shall explicitly indicate the form in which account has been taken of relevant provisions on differential and more-favourable treatment for developing country Members that form part of the covered agreements which have been raised by the developing country Member in the course of the dispute settlement procedures.

12. The panel may suspend its work at any time at the request of the complaining party for a period not to exceed 12 months. In the event of such a suspension, the time-frames set out in paragraphs 8 and 9 of this Article, paragraph 1 of Article 20, and paragraph 4 of Article 21 shall be extended by the amount of time that the work was suspended. If the work of the panel has been suspended for more than 12 months, the authority for establishment of the panel shall lapse.

Article 13

Right to Seek Information

1. Each panel shall have the right to seek information and technical advice from any individual or body which it deems appropriate. However, before a panel seeks such information or advice from any individual or body within the jurisdiction of a Member it shall inform the authorities of that Member. A Member should respond promptly and fully to any request by a panel for such information as the panel considers necessary and appropriate. Confidential information which is provided shall not be revealed without formal authorization from the individual, body, or authorities of the Member providing the information.

2. Panels may seek information from any relevant source and may consult experts to obtain their opinion on certain aspects of the matter. With respect to a factual issue concerning a scientific or other technical matter raised by a party to a dispute, a panel may request an advisory report in writing from an expert review group. Rules for the establishment of such a group and its procedures are set forth in Appendix 4.

Article 14

Confidentiality

1. Panel deliberations shall be confidential.

2. The reports of panels shall be drafted without the presence of the parties to the dispute in the light of the information provided and the statements made.

3. Opinions expressed in the panel report by individual panelists shall be anonymous.

Article 15

Interim Review Stage

1. Following the consideration of rebuttal submissions and oral arguments, the panel shall issue the descriptive (factual and argument) sections of its draft report to the parties to the dispute. Within a period of time set by the panel, the parties shall submit their comments in writing.

2. Following the expiration of the set period of time for receipt of comments from the parties to the dispute, the panel shall issue an interim report to the parties, including both the descriptive sections and the panel's findings and conclusions. Within a period of time set by the panel, a party may submit a written request for the panel to review precise aspects of the interim report prior to circulation of the final report to the Members. At the request of a party, the panel shall hold a further meeting with the parties on the issues identified in the written comments. If no comments are received from any party within the comment period, the interim report shall be considered the final panel report and circulated promptly to the Members.

3. The findings of the final panel report shall include a discussion of the arguments made at the interim review stage. The interim review stage shall be conducted within the time-period set out in paragraph 8 of Article 12.

Article 16
Adoption of Panel Reports

1. In order to provide sufficient time for the Members to consider panel reports, the reports shall not be considered for adoption by the DSB until 20 days after the date they have been circulated to the Members.

2. Members having objections to a panel report shall give written reasons to explain their objections for circulation at least 10 days prior to the DSB meeting at which the panel report will be considered.

3. The parties to a dispute shall have the right to participate fully in the consideration of the panel report by the DSB, and their views shall be fully recorded.

4. Within 60 days after the date of circulation of a panel report to the Members, the report shall be adopted at a DSB meeting [7] unless a party to the dispute formally notifies the DSB of its decision to appeal or the DSB decides by consensus not to adopt the report. If a party has notified its decision to appeal, the report by the panel shall not be considered for adoption by the DSB until after completion of the appeal. This adoption procedure is without prejudice to the right of Members to express their views on a panel report.

Article 17
Appellate Review

Standing Appellate Body

1. A standing Appellate Body shall be established by the DSB. The Appellate Body shall hear appeals from panel cases. It shall be composed of seven persons, three of whom shall serve on any one case. Persons serving on the Appellate Body shall serve in rotation. Such rotation shall be determined in the working procedures of the Appellate Body.

2. The DSB shall appoint persons to serve on the Appellate Body for a four-year term, and each person may be reappointed once. However, the terms of three of the seven persons appointed immediately after the entry into force of the WTO Agreement shall expire at the end of two years, to be determined by lot. Vacancies shall be filled as they arise. A person appointed to replace a person whose term of office has not expired shall hold office for the remainder of the predecessor's term.

3. The Appellate Body shall comprise persons of recognized authority, with demonstrated expertise in law, international trade and the subject matter of the covered agreements generally. They shall be unaffiliated with any government. The Appellate Body membership shall be broadly representative of membership in the WTO. All persons serving on the Appellate Body shall be available at all times and on short notice, and shall stay abreast of dispute settlement activities and other relevant activities of the WTO. They shall not participate in the consideration of any disputes that would create a direct or indirect conflict of interest.

4. Only parties to the dispute, not third parties, may appeal a panel report. Third parties which have notified the DSB of a substantial interest in

---

7. If a meeting of the DSB is not scheduled within this period at a time that enables the requirements of paragraphs 1 and 4 of Article 16 to be met, a meeting of the DSB shall be held for this purpose.

the matter pursuant to paragraph 2 of Article 10 may make written submissions to, and be given an opportunity to be heard by, the Appellate Body.

5.   As a general rule, the proceedings shall not exceed 60 days from the date a party to the dispute formally notifies its decision to appeal to the date the Appellate Body circulates its report. In fixing its timetable the Appellate Body shall take into account the provisions of paragraph 9 of Article 4, if relevant. When the Appellate Body considers that it cannot provide its report within 60 days, it shall inform the DSB in writing of the reasons for the delay together with an estimate of the period within which it will submit its report. In no case shall the proceedings exceed 90 days.

6.   An appeal shall be limited to issues of law covered in the panel report and legal interpretations developed by the panel.

7.   The Appellate Body shall be provided with appropriate administrative and legal support as it requires.

8.   The expenses of persons serving on the Appellate Body, including travel and subsistence allowance, shall be met from the WTO budget in accordance with criteria to be adopted by the General Council, based on recommendations of the Committee on Budget, Finance and Administration.

Procedures for Appellate Review

9.   Working procedures shall be drawn up by the Appellate Body in consultation with the Chairman of the DSB and the Director–General, and communicated to the Members for their information.

10.   The proceedings of the Appellate Body shall be confidential. The reports of the Appellate Body shall be drafted without the presence of the parties to the dispute and in the light of the information provided and the statements made.

11.   Opinions expressed in the Appellate Body report by individuals serving on the Appellate Body shall be anonymous.

12.   The Appellate Body shall address each of the issues raised in accordance with paragraph 6 during the appellate proceeding.

13.   The Appellate Body may uphold, modify or reverse the legal findings and conclusions of the panel.

Adoption of Appellate Body Reports

14.   An Appellate Body report shall be adopted by the DSB and unconditionally accepted by the parties to the dispute unless the DSB decides by consensus not to adopt the Appellate Body report within 30 days following its circulation to the Members.[8] This adoption procedure is without prejudice to the right of Members to express their views on an Appellate Body report.

Article 18

Communications With the Panel or Appellate Body

1.   There shall be no *ex parte* communications with the panel or Appellate Body concerning matters under consideration by the panel or Appellate Body.

---

8. If a meeting of the DSB is not scheduled during this period, such a meeting of the DSB   shall be held for this purpose.

2. Written submissions to the panel or the Appellate Body shall be treated as confidential, but shall be made available to the parties to the dispute. Nothing in this Understanding shall preclude a party to a dispute from disclosing statements of its own positions to the public. Members shall treat as confidential information submitted by another Member to the panel or the Appellate Body which that Member has designated as confidential. A party to a dispute shall also, upon request of a Member, provide a non-confidential summary of the information contained in its written submissions that could be disclosed to the public.

Article 19

Panel and Appellate Body Recommendations

1. Where a panel or the Appellate Body concludes that a measure is inconsistent with a covered agreement, it shall recommend that the Member concerned [9] bring the measure into conformity with that agreement.[10] In addition to its recommendations, the panel or Appellate Body may suggest ways in which the Member concerned could implement the recommendations.

2. In accordance with paragraph 2 of Article 3, in their findings and recommendations, the panel and Appellate Body cannot add to or diminish the rights and obligations provided in the covered agreements.

Article 20

Time-frame for DSB Decisions

Unless otherwise agreed to by the parties to the dispute, the period from the date of establishment of the panel by the DSB until the date the DSB considers the panel or appellate report for adoption shall as a general rule not exceed nine months where the panel report is not appealed or 12 months where the report is appealed. Where either the panel or the Appellate Body has acted, pursuant to paragraph 9 of Article 12 or paragraph 5 of Article 17, to extend the time for providing its report, the additional time taken shall be added to the above periods.

Article 21

Surveillance of Implementation of Recommendations and Rulings

1. Prompt compliance with recommendations or rulings of the DSB is essential in order to ensure effective resolution of disputes to the benefit of all Members.

2. Particular attention should be paid to matters affecting the interests of developing country Members with respect to measures which have been subject to dispute settlement.

3. At a DSB meeting held within 30 days [11] after the date of adoption of the panel or Appellate Body report, the Member concerned shall inform the DSB of its intentions in respect of implementation of the recommendations

9. The "Member concerned" is the party to the dispute to which the panel or Appellate Body recommendations are directed.

10. With respect to recommendations in cases not involving a violation of GATT 1994 or any other covered agreement, see Article 26.

11. If a meeting of the DSB is not scheduled during this period, such a meeting of the DSB shall be held for this purpose.

and rulings of the DSB. If it is impracticable to comply immediately with the recommendations and rulings, the Member concerned shall have a reasonable period of time in which to do so. The reasonable period of time shall be:

(a) the period of time proposed by the Member concerned, provided that such period is approved by the DSB; or, in the absence of such approval,

(b) a period of time mutually agreed by the parties to the dispute within 45 days after the date of adoption of the recommendations and rulings; or, in the absence of such agreement,

(c) a period of time determined through binding arbitration within 90 days after the date of adoption of the recommendations and rulings.[12] In such arbitration, a guideline for the arbitrator [13] should be that the reasonable period of time to implement panel or Appellate Body recommendations should not exceed 15 months from the date of adoption of a panel or Appellate Body report. However, that time may be shorter or longer, depending upon the particular circumstances.

4.   Except where the panel or the Appellate Body has extended, pursuant to paragraph 9 of Article 12 or paragraph 5 of Article 17, the time of providing its report, the period from the date of establishment of the panel by the DSB until the date of determination of the reasonable period of time shall not exceed 15 months unless the parties to the dispute agree otherwise. Where either the panel or the Appellate Body has acted to extend the time of providing its report, the additional time taken shall be added to the 15–month period; provided that unless the parties to the dispute agree that there are exceptional circumstances, the total time shall not exceed 18 months.

5.   Where there is disagreement as to the existence or consistency with a covered agreement of measures taken to comply with the recommendations and rulings such dispute shall be decided through recourse to these dispute settlement procedures, including wherever possible resort to the original panel. The panel shall circulate its report within 90 days after the date of referral of the matter to it. When the panel considers that it cannot provide its report within this time frame, it shall inform the DSB in writing of the reasons for the delay together with an estimate of the period within which it will submit its report.

6.   The DSB shall keep under surveillance the implementation of adopted recommendations or rulings. The issue of implementation of the recommendations or rulings may be raised at the DSB by any Member at any time following their adoption. Unless the DSB decides otherwise, the issue of implementation of the recommendations or rulings shall be placed on the agenda of the DSB meeting after six months following the date of establishment of the reasonable period of time pursuant to paragraph 3 and shall remain on the DSB's agenda until the issue is resolved. At least 10 days prior to each such DSB meeting, the Member concerned shall provide the DSB with

12. If the parties cannot agree on an arbitrator within ten days after referring the matter to arbitration, the arbitrator shall be appointed by the Director–General within ten days, after consulting the parties.

13. The expression "arbitrator" shall be interpreted as referring either to an individual or a group.

a status report in writing of its progress in the implementation of the recommendations or rulings.

7.   If the matter is one which has been raised by a developing country Member, the DSB shall consider what further action it might take which would be appropriate to the circumstances.

8.   If the case is one brought by a developing country Member, in considering what appropriate action might be taken, the DSB shall take into account not only the trade coverage of measures complained of, but also their impact on the economy of developing country Members concerned.

Article 22

Compensation and the Suspension of Concessions

1.   Compensation and the suspension of concessions or other obligations are temporary measures available in the event that the recommendations and rulings are not implemented within a reasonable period of time.   However, neither compensation nor the suspension of concessions or other obligations is preferred to full implementation of a recommendation to bring a measure into conformity with the covered agreements.   Compensation is voluntary and, if granted, shall be consistent with the covered agreements.

2.   If the Member concerned fails to bring the measure found to be inconsistent with a covered agreement into compliance therewith or otherwise comply with the recommendations and rulings within the reasonable period of time determined pursuant to paragraph 3 of Article 21, such Member shall, if so requested, and no later than the expiry of the reasonable period of time, enter into negotiations with any party having invoked the dispute settlement procedures, with a view to developing mutually acceptable compensation.   If no satisfactory compensation has been agreed within 20 days after the date of expiry of the reasonable period of time, any party having invoked the dispute settlement procedures may request authorization from the DSB to suspend the application to the Member concerned of concessions or other obligations under the covered agreements.

3.   In considering what concessions or other obligations to suspend, the complaining party shall apply the following principles and procedures:

(a) the general principle is that the complaining party should first seek to suspend concessions or other obligations with respect to the same sector(s) as that in which the panel or Appellate Body has found a violation or other nullification or impairment;

(b) if that party considers that it is not practicable or effective to suspend concessions or other obligations with respect to the same sector(s), it may seek to suspend concessions or other obligations in other sectors under the same agreement;

(c) if that party considers that it is not practicable or effective to suspend concessions or other obligations with respect to other sectors under the same agreement, and that the circumstances are serious enough, it may seek to suspend concessions or other obligations under another covered agreement;

(d) in applying the above principles, that party shall take into account:

(i) the trade in the sector or under the agreement under which the panel or Appellate Body has found a violation or other nullification or impairment, and the importance of such trade to that party;

(ii) the broader economic elements related to the nullification or impairment and the broader economic consequences of the suspension of concessions or other obligations;

(e) if that party decides to request authorization to suspend concessions or other obligations pursuant to subparagraphs (b) or (c), it shall state the reasons therefor in its request. At the same time as the request is forwarded to the DSB, it also shall be forwarded to the relevant Councils and also, in the case of a request pursuant to subparagraph (b), the relevant sectoral bodies;

(f) for purposes of this paragraph, "sector" means:

(i) with respect to goods, all goods;

(ii) with respect to services, a principal sector as identified in the current "Services Sectoral Classification List" which identifies such sectors,[14]

(iii) with respect to trade-related intellectual property rights, each of the categories of intellectual property rights covered in Section 1, or Section 2, or Section 3, or Section 4, or Section 5, or Section 6, or Section 7 of Part II, or the obligations under Part III, or Part IV of the Agreement on TRIPS;

(g) for purposes of this paragraph, "agreement" means:

(i) with respect to goods, the agreements listed in Annex 1A of the WTO Agreement, taken as a whole as well as the Plurilateral Trade Agreements in so far as the relevant parties to the dispute are parties to these agreements;

(ii) with respect to services, the GATS;

(iii) with respect to intellectual property rights, the Agreement on TRIPS.

4.   The level of the suspension of concessions or other obligations authorized by the DSB shall be equivalent to the level of the nullification or impairment.

5.   The DSB shall not authorize suspension of concessions or other obligations if a covered agreement prohibits such suspension.

6.   When the situation described in paragraph 2 occurs, the DSB, upon request, shall grant authorization to suspend concessions or other obligations within 30 days of the expiry of the reasonable period of time unless the DSB decides by consensus to reject the request. However, if the Member concerned objects to the level of suspension proposed, or claims that the principles and procedures set forth in paragraph 3 have not been followed where a complaining party has requested authorization to suspend concessions or other obligations pursuant to paragraph 3(b) or (c), the matter shall be

14.   The list in document MTN.GNS/W/120 identifies eleven sectors.

referred to arbitration. Such arbitration shall be carried out by the original panel, if members are available, or by an arbitrator [15] appointed by the Director–General and shall be completed within 60 days after the date of expiry of the reasonable period of time. Concessions or other obligations shall not be suspended during the course of the arbitration.

7. The arbitrator [16] acting pursuant to paragraph 6 shall not examine the nature of the concessions or other obligations to be suspended but shall determine whether the level of such suspension is equivalent to the level of nullification or impairment. The arbitrator may also determine if the proposed suspension of concessions or other obligations is allowed under the covered agreement. However, if the matter referred to arbitration includes a claim that the principles and procedures set forth in paragraph 3 have not been followed, the arbitrator shall examine that claim. In the event the arbitrator determines that those principles and procedures have not been followed, the complaining party shall apply them consistent with paragraph 3. The parties shall accept the arbitrator's decision as final and the parties concerned shall not seek a second arbitration. The DSB shall be informed promptly of the decision of the arbitrator and shall upon request, grant authorization to suspend concessions or other obligations where the request is consistent with the decision of the arbitrator, unless the DSB decides by consensus to reject the request.

8. The suspension of concessions or other obligations shall be temporary and shall only be applied until such time as the measure found to be inconsistent with a covered agreement has been removed, or the Member that must implement recommendations or rulings provides a solution to the nullification or impairment of benefits, or a mutually satisfactory solution is reached. In accordance with paragraph 6 of Article 21, the DSB shall continue to keep under surveillance the implementation of adopted recommendations or rulings, including those cases where compensation has been provided or concessions or other obligations have been suspended but the recommendations to bring a measure into conformity with the covered agreements have not been implemented.

9. The dispute settlement provisions of the covered agreements may be invoked in respect of measures affecting their observance taken by regional or local governments or authorities within the territory of a Member. When the DSB has ruled that a provision of a covered agreement has not been observed, the responsible Member shall take such reasonable measures as may be available to it to ensure its observance. The provisions of the covered agreements and this Understanding relating to compensation and suspension of concessions or other obligations apply in cases where it has not been possible to secure such observance. [17]

15. The expression "arbitrator" shall be interpreted as referring either to an individual or a group.

16. The expression "arbitrator" shall be interpreted as referring either to an individual or a group or to the members of the original panel when serving in the capacity of arbitrator.

17. Where the provisions of any covered agreement concerning measures taken by regional or local governments or authorities within the territory of a Member contain provisions different from the provisions of this paragraph, the provisions of such covered agreement shall prevail.

Article 23

Strengthening of the Multilateral System

1. When Members seek the redress of a violation of obligations or other nullification or impairment of benefits under the covered agreements or an impediment to the attainment of any objective of the covered agreements, they shall have recourse to, and abide by, the rules and procedures of this Understanding.

2. In such cases, Members shall:

(a) not make a determination to the effect that a violation has occurred, that benefits have been nullified or impaired or that the attainment of any objective of the covered agreements has been impeded, except through recourse to dispute settlement in accordance with the rules and procedures of this Understanding, and shall make any such determination consistent with the findings contained in the panel or Appellate Body report adopted by the DSB or an arbitration award rendered under this Understanding;

(b) follow the procedures set forth in Article 21 to determine the reasonable period of time for the Member concerned to implement the recommendations and rulings; and

(c) follow the procedures set forth in Article 22 to determine the level of suspension of concessions or other obligations and obtain DSB authorization in accordance with those procedures before suspending concessions or other obligations under the covered agreements in response to the failure of the Member concerned to implement the recommendations and rulings within that reasonable period of time.

Article 24

Special Procedures Involving Least–Developed Country Members

1. At all stages of the determination of the causes of a dispute and of dispute settlement procedures involving a least-developed country Member, particular consideration shall be given to the special situation of least-developed country Members. In this regard, Members shall exercise due restraint in raising matters under these procedures involving a least-developed country Member. If nullification or impairment is found to result from a measure taken by a least-developed country Member, complaining parties shall exercise due restraint in asking for compensation or seeking authorization to suspend the application of concessions or other obligations pursuant to these procedures.

2. In dispute settlement cases involving a least-developed country Member, where a satisfactory solution has not been found in the course of consultations the Director–General or the Chairman of the DSB shall, upon request by a least-developed country Member offer their good offices, conciliation and mediation with a view to assisting the parties to settle the dispute, before a request for a panel is made. The Director–General or the Chairman of the DSB, in providing the above assistance, may consult any source which either deems appropriate.

Article 25

Arbitration

1.   Expeditious arbitration within the WTO as an alternative means of dispute settlement can facilitate the solution of certain disputes that concern issues that are clearly defined by both parties.

2.   Except as otherwise provided in this Understanding, resort to arbitration shall be subject to mutual agreement of the parties which shall agree on the procedures to be followed.   Agreements to resort to arbitration shall be notified to all Members sufficiently in advance of the actual commencement of the arbitration process.

3.   Other Members may become party to an arbitration proceeding only upon the agreement of the parties which have agreed to have recourse to arbitration.   The parties to the proceeding shall agree to abide by the arbitration award.   Arbitration awards shall be notified to the DSB and the Council or Committee of any relevant agreement where any Member may raise any point relating thereto.

4.   Articles 21 and 22 of this Understanding shall apply *mutatis mutandis* to arbitration awards.

Article 26

1. *Non–Violation Complaints of the Type Described in Paragraph 1(b) of Article XXIII of GATT 1994*

Where the provisions of paragraph 1(b) of Article XXIII of GATT 1994 are applicable to a covered agreement, a panel or the Appellate Body may only make rulings and recommendations where a party to the dispute considers that any benefit accruing to it directly or indirectly under the relevant covered agreement is being nullified or impaired or the attainment of any objective of that Agreement is being impeded as a result of the application by a Member of any measure, whether or not it conflicts with the provisions of that Agreement.   Where and to the extent that such party considers and a panel or the Appellate Body determines that a case concerns a measure that does not conflict with the provisions of a covered agreement to which the provisions of paragraph 1(b) of Article XXIII of GATT 1994 are applicable, the procedures in this Understanding shall apply, subject to the following:

(a) the complaining party shall present a detailed justification in support of any complaint relating to a measure which does not conflict with the relevant covered agreement;

(b) where a measure has been found to nullify or impair benefits under, or impede the attainment of objectives, of the relevant covered agreement without violation thereof, there is no obligation to withdraw the measure.   However, in such cases, the panel or the Appellate Body shall recommend that the Member concerned make a mutually satisfactory adjustment;

(c) notwithstanding the provisions of Article 21, the arbitration provided for in paragraph 3 of Article 21, upon request of either party, may include a determination of the level of benefits which have been nullified or impaired, and may also suggest ways and means of reaching a mutually satisfactory adjustment; such suggestions shall not be binding upon the parties to the dispute;

(d) notwithstanding the provisions of paragraph 1 of Article 22, compensation may be part of a mutually satisfactory adjustment as final settlement of the dispute.

2. *Complaints of the Type Described in Paragraph 1(c) of Article XXIII of GATT 1994*

Where the provisions of paragraph 1(c) of Article XXIII of GATT 1994 are applicable to a covered agreement, a panel may only make rulings and recommendations where a party considers that any benefit accruing to it directly or indirectly under the relevant covered agreement is being nullified or impaired or the attainment of any objective of that Agreement is being impeded as a result of the existence of any situation other than those to which the provisions of paragraphs 1(a) and 1(b) of Article XXIII of GATT 1994 are applicable.   Where and to the extent that such party considers and a panel determines that the matter is covered by this paragraph, the procedures of this Understanding shall apply only up to and including the point in the proceedings where the panel report has been circulated to the Members.   The dispute settlement rules and procedures contained in the Decision of 12 April 1989 (BISD 36S/61–67) shall apply to consideration for adoption, and surveillance and implementation of recommendations and rulings.   The following shall also apply:

(a) the complaining party shall present a detailed justification in support of any argument made with respect to issues covered under this paragraph;

(b) in cases involving matters covered by this paragraph, if a panel finds that cases also involve dispute settlement matters other than those covered by this paragraph, the panel shall circulate a report to the DSB addressing any such matters and a separate report on matters falling under this paragraph.

Article 27

Responsibilities of the Secretariat

1.   The Secretariat shall have the responsibility of assisting panels, especially on the legal, historical and procedural aspects of the matters dealt with, and of providing secretarial and technical support.

2.   While the Secretariat assists Members in respect of dispute settlement at their request, there may also be a need to provide additional legal advice and assistance in respect of dispute settlement to developing country Members.   To this end, the Secretariat shall make available a qualified legal expert from the WTO technical cooperation services to any developing country Member which so requests.   This expert shall assist the developing country Member in a manner ensuring the continued impartiality of the Secretariat.

3.   The Secretariat shall conduct special training courses for interested Members concerning these dispute settlement procedures and practices so as to enable Members' experts to be better informed in this regard.

APPENDIX 1
AGREEMENTS COVERED BY THE UNDERSTANDING

(A) Agreement Establishing the World Trade Organization

(B) Multilateral Trade Agreements

    Annex 1A: Multilateral Agreements on Trade in Goods

    Annex 1B: General Agreement on Trade in Services

    Annex 1C: Agreement on Trade–Related Aspects of Intellectual Property Rights

    Annex 2: Understanding on Rules and Procedures Governing the Settlement of Disputes

(C) Plurilateral Trade Agreements

    Annex 4: Agreement on Trade in Civil Aircraft

              Agreement on Government Procurement

              International Dairy Agreement

              International Bovine Meat Agreement

The applicability of this Understanding to the Plurilateral Trade Agreements shall be subject to the adoption of a decision by the parties to each agreement setting out the terms for the application of the Understanding to the individual agreement, including any special or additional rules or procedures for inclusion in Appendix 2, as notified to the DSB.

APPENDIX 2
SPECIAL OR ADDITIONAL RULES AND PROCEDURES CONTAINED IN THE COVERED AGREEMENTS

Agreement	*Rules and Procedures*
Agreement on the Application of Sanitary and Phytosanitary Measures	11.2
Agreement on Textiles and Clothing	2.14, 2.21, 4.4, 5.2, 5.4, 5.6, 6.9, 6.10, 6.11, 8.1 through 8.12
Agreement on Technical Barriers to Trade	14.2 through 14.4, Annex 2
Agreement on Implementation of Article VI of GATT 1994	17.4 through 17.7
Agreement on Implementation of Article VII of GATT 1994	19.3 through 19.5, Annex II.2(f), 3, 9, 21
Agreement on Subsidies and Countervailing Measures	4.2 through 4.12, 6.6, 7.2 through 7.10, 8.5, footnote 35, 24.4, 27.7, Annex V
General Agreement on Trade in Services	XXII:3, XXIII:3
Annex on Financial Services	4
Annex on Air Transport Services	4
Decision on Certain Dispute Settlement Procedures for the GATS	1 through 5

The list of rules and procedures in this Appendix includes provisions where only a part of the provision may be relevant in this context.

Any special or additional rules or procedures in the Plurilateral Trade Agreements as determined by the competent bodies of each agreement and as notified to the DSB.

APPENDIX 3
WORKING PROCEDURES

1. In its proceedings the panel shall follow the relevant provisions of this Understanding. In addition, the following working procedures shall apply.

2. The panel shall meet in closed session. The parties to the dispute, and interested parties, shall be present at the meetings only when invited by the panel to appear before it.

3. The deliberations of the panel and the documents submitted to it shall be kept confidential. Nothing in this Understanding shall preclude a party to a dispute from disclosing statements of its own positions to the public. Members shall treat as confidential information submitted by another Member to the panel which that Member has designated as confidential. Where a party to a dispute submits a confidential version of its written submissions to the panel, it shall also, upon request of a Member, provide a non-confidential summary of the information contained in its submissions that could be disclosed to the public.

4. Before the first substantive meeting of the panel with the parties, the parties to the dispute shall transmit to the panel written submissions in which they present the facts of the case and their arguments.

5. At its first substantive meeting with the parties, the panel shall ask the party which has brought the complaint to present its case. Subsequently, and still at the same meeting, the party against which the complaint has been brought shall be asked to present its point of view.

6. All third parties which have notified their interest in the dispute to the DSB shall be invited in writing to present their views during a session of the first substantive meeting of the panel set aside for that purpose. All such third parties may be present during the entirety of this session.

7. Formal rebuttals shall be made at a second substantive meeting of the panel. The party complained against shall have the right to take the floor first to be followed by the complaining party. The parties shall submit, prior to that meeting, written rebuttals to the panel.

8. The panel may at any time put questions to the parties and ask them for explanations either in the course of a meeting with the parties or in writing.

9. The parties to the dispute and any third party invited to present its views in accordance with Article 10 shall make available to the panel a written version of their oral statements.

10. In the interest of full transparency, the presentations, rebuttals and statements referred to in paragraphs 5 to 9 shall be made in the presence of the parties. Moreover, each party's written submissions, including any comments on the descriptive part of the report and responses to questions put by the panel, shall be made available to the other party or parties.

11. Any additional procedures specific to the panel.

12. Proposed timetable for panel work:

(a) Receipt of first written submissions of the parties:
     (1) complaining Party: ____ 3–6 weeks

(2) Party complained against:	____ 2–3 weeks
(b) Date, time and place of first substantive meeting with the parties; third party session:	____ 1–2 weeks
(c) Receipt of written rebuttals of the parties:	____ 2–3 weeks
(d) Date, time and place of second substantive meeting with the parties:	____ 1–2 weeks
(e) Issuance of descriptive part of the report to the parties:	____ 2–4 weeks
(f) Receipt of comments by the parties on the descriptive part of the report:	____ 2 weeks
(g) Issuance of the interim report, including the findings and conclusions, to the parties:	____ 2–4 weeks
(h) Deadline for party to request review of part(s) of report:	____ 1 week
(i) Period of review by panel, including possible additional meeting with parties:	____ 2 weeks
(j) Issuance of final report to parties to dispute:	____ 2 weeks
(k) Circulation of the final report to the Members:	____ 3 weeks

The above calendar may be changed in the light of unforeseen developments. Additional meetings with the parties shall be scheduled if required.

APPENDIX 4

EXPERT REVIEW GROUPS

The following rules and procedures shall apply to expert review groups established in accordance with the provisions of paragraph 2 of Article 13.

1. Expert review groups are under the panel's authority. Their terms of reference and detailed working procedures shall be decided by the panel, and they shall report to the panel.

2. Participation in expert review groups shall be restricted to persons of professional standing and experience in the field in question.

3. Citizens of parties to the dispute shall not serve on an expert review group without the joint agreement of the parties to the dispute, except in exceptional circumstances when the panel considers that the need for specialized scientific expertise cannot be fulfilled otherwise. Government officials of parties to the dispute shall not serve on an expert review group. Members of expert review groups shall serve in their individual capacities and not as government representatives, nor as representatives of any organization. Governments or organizations shall therefore not give them instructions with regard to matters before an expert review group.

4. Expert review groups may consult and seek information and technical advice from any source they deem appropriate. Before an expert review group seeks such information or advice from a source within the jurisdiction of a Member, it shall inform the government of that Member. Any Member shall respond promptly and fully to any request by an expert review group for such information as the expert review group considers necessary and appropriate.

5.   The parties to a dispute shall have access to all relevant information provided to an expert review group, unless it is of a confidential nature. Confidential information provided to the expert review group shall not be released without formal authorization from the government, organization or person providing the information.   Where such information is requested from the expert review group but release of such information by the expert review group is not authorized, a non-confidential summary of the information will be provided by the government, organization or person supplying the information.

6.   The expert review group shall submit a draft report to the parties to the dispute with a view to obtaining their comments, and taking them into account, as appropriate, in the final report, which shall also be issued to the parties to the dispute when it is submitted to the panel.   The final report of the expert review group shall be advisory only.

Item 19

ANNEX 3
TRADE POLICY REVIEW MECHANISM

Members hereby *agree* as follows:

A. *Objectives*

(i) The purpose of the Trade Policy Review Mechanism ("TPRM") is to contribute to improved adherence by all Members to rules, disciplines and commitments made under the Multilateral Trade Agreements and, where applicable, the Plurilateral Trade Agreements, and hence to the smoother functioning of the multilateral trading system, by achieving greater transparency in, and understanding of, the trade policies and practices of Members. Accordingly, the review mechanism enables the regular collective appreciation and evaluation of the full range of individual Members' trade policies and practices and their impact on the functioning of the multilateral trading system. It is not, however, intended to serve as a basis for the enforcement of specific obligations under the Agreements or for dispute settlement procedures, or to impose new policy commitments on Members.

(ii) The assessment carried out under the review mechanism takes place, to the extent relevant, against the background of the wider economic and developmental needs, policies and objectives of the Member concerned, as well as of its external environment. However, the function of the review mechanism is to examine the impact of a Member's trade policies and practices on the multilateral trading system.

B. *Domestic Transparency*

Members recognize the inherent value of domestic transparency of government decision-making on trade policy matters for both Members' economies and the multilateral trading system, and agree to encourage and promote greater transparency within their own systems, acknowledging that the implementation of domestic transparency must be on a voluntary basis and take account of each Member's legal and political systems.

C. *Procedures for Review*

(i) The Trade Policy Review Body (referred to herein as the "TPRB") is hereby established to carry out trade policy reviews.

(ii) The trade policies and practices of all Members shall be subject to periodic review. The impact of individual Members on the functioning of the multilateral trading system, defined in terms of their share of world trade in a recent representative period, will be the determining factor in deciding on the frequency of reviews. The first four trading entities so identified (counting the European Communities as one) shall be subject to review every two years. The next 16 shall be reviewed every four years. Other Members shall be reviewed every six years, except that a longer period may be fixed for least-developed country Members. It is understood that the review of entities having a common external policy covering more than one Member shall cover all components of policy affecting trade including relevant policies and practices of the individual Members. Exceptionally, in the event of changes in a Member's trade policies or practices that may have a significant impact on its trading partners, the Member concerned may be requested by the TPRB, after consultation, to bring forward its next review.

(iii) Discussions in the meetings of the TPRB shall be governed by the objectives set forth in paragraph A. The focus of these discussions shall be on the Member's trade policies and practices, which are the subject of the assessment under the review mechanism.

(iv) The TPRB shall establish a basic plan for the conduct of the reviews. It may also discuss and take note of update reports from Members. The TPRB shall establish a programme of reviews for each year in consultation with the Members directly concerned. In consultation with the Member or Members under review, the Chairman may choose discussants who, acting in their personal capacity, shall introduce the discussions in the TPRB.

(v) The TPRB shall base its work on the following documentation:

(a) a full report, referred to in paragraph D, supplied by the Member or Members under review;

(b) a report, to be drawn up by the Secretariat on its own responsibility, based on the information available to it and that provided by the Member or Members concerned. The Secretariat should seek clarification from the Member or Members concerned of their trade policies and practices.

(vi) The reports by the Member under review and by the Secretariat, together with the minutes of the respective meeting of the TPRB, shall be published promptly after the review.

(vii) These documents will be forwarded to the Ministerial Conference, which shall take note of them.

D. *Reporting*

In order to achieve the fullest possible degree of transparency, each Member shall report regularly to the TPRB. Full reports shall describe the trade policies and practices pursued by the Member or Members concerned, based on an agreed format to be decided upon by the TPRB. This format shall initially be based on the Outline Format for Country Reports established by the Decision of 19 July 1989 (BISD 36S/406–409), amended as necessary to extend the coverage of reports to all aspects of trade policies covered by the Multilateral Trade Agreements in Annex 1 and, where applicable, the Plurilateral Trade Agreements. This format may be revised by the TPRB in the light of experience. Between reviews, Members shall provide brief reports when there are any significant changes in their trade policies; an annual update of statistical information will be provided according to the agreed format. Particular account shall be taken of difficulties presented to least-developed country Members in compiling their reports. The Secretariat shall make available technical assistance on request to developing country Members, and in particular to the least-developed country Members. Information contained in reports should to the greatest extent possible be coordinated with notifications made under provisions of the Multilateral Trade Agreements and, where applicable, the Plurilateral Trade Agreements.

E. *Relationship With the Balance-of-Payments Provisions of GATT 1994 and GATS*

Members recognize the need to minimize the burden for governments also subject to full consultations under the balance-of-payments provisions of GATT 1994 or GATS. To this end, the Chairman of the TPRB shall, in consultation with the Member or Members concerned, and with the Chairman of the Committee on Balance-of-Payments Restrictions, devise administrative arrangements that harmonize the normal rhythm of the trade policy reviews with the timetable for balance-of-payments consultations but do not postpone the trade policy review by more than 12 months.

F. *Appraisal of the Mechanism*

The TPRB shall undertake an appraisal of the operation of the TPRM not more than five years after the entry into force of the Agreement Establishing the WTO. The results of the appraisal will be presented to the Ministerial Conference. It may subsequently undertake appraisals of the TPRM at intervals to be determined by it or as requested by the Ministerial Conference.

G. *Overview of Developments in the International Trading Environment*

An annual overview of developments in the international trading environment which are having an impact on the multilateral trading system shall also be undertaken by the TPRB. The overview is to be assisted by an annual report by the Director–General setting out major activities of the WTO and highlighting significant policy issues affecting the trading system.

Item 20

ANNEX 4
PLURILATERAL TRADE AGREEMENTS

AGREEMENT ON TRADE IN CIVIL AIRCRAFT

The Agreement on Trade in Civil Aircraft, done at Geneva on 12 April 1979 (BISD 26S/162), as subsequently modified, rectified or amended. [OMITTED]

AGREEMENT ON GOVERNMENT PROCUREMENT

The Agreement on Government Procurement done at Marrakesh on 15 April 1994.

INTERNATIONAL DAIRY AGREEMENT

The International Dairy Agreement done at Marrakesh on 15 April 1994. [OMITTED]

INTERNATIONAL BOVINE MEAT AGREEMENT

The International Bovine Meat Agreement done at Marrakesh on 15 April 1994. [OMITTED]

[Editors' Note: The Dairy and Bovine Meat Agreements were terminated in 1997.]

Item 21

AGREEMENT ON GOVERNMENT PROCUREMENT

Parties to this Agreement (hereinafter referred to as "Parties"),

Recognizing the need for an effective multilateral framework of rights and obligations with respect to laws, regulations, procedures and practices regarding government procurement with a view to achieving greater liberalization and expansion of world trade and improving the international framework for the conduct of world trade;

Recognizing that laws, regulations, procedures and practices regarding government procurement should not be prepared, adopted or applied to foreign or domestic products and services and to foreign or domestic suppliers so as to afford protection to domestic products or services or domestic suppliers and should not discriminate among foreign products or services or among foreign suppliers;

Recognizing that it is desirable to provide transparency of laws, regulations, procedures and practices regarding government procurement;

Recognizing the need to establish international procedures on notification, consultation, surveillance and dispute settlement with a view to ensuring a fair, prompt and effective enforcement of the international provisions on government procurement and to maintain the balance of rights and obligations at the highest possible level;

Recognizing the need to take into account the development, financial and trade needs of developing countries, in particular the least-developed countries;

Desiring, in accordance with paragraph 6(b) of Article IX of the Agreement on Government Procurement done on 12 April 1979, as amended on 2 February 1987, to broaden and improve the Agreement on the basis of mutual reciprocity and to expand the coverage of the Agreement to include service contracts;

Desiring to encourage acceptance of and accession to this Agreement by governments not party to it;

Having undertaken further negotiations in pursuance of these objectives;

Hereby *agree* as follows:

Article I

Scope and Coverage

1. This Agreement applies to any law, regulation, procedure or practice regarding any procurement by entities covered by this Agreement, as specified in Appendix I.[1]

---

1. For each party, Appendix I is divided into five Annexes:

— Annex 1 contains central government entities.

2.   This Agreement applies to procurement by any contractual means, including through such methods as purchase or as lease, rental or hire purchase, with or without an option to buy, including any combination of products and services.

3.   Where entities, in the context of procurement covered under this Agreement, require enterprises not included in Appendix I to award contracts in accordance with particular requirements, Article III shall apply mutatis mutandis to such requirements.

4.   This agreement applies to any procurement contract of a value of not less than the relevant threshold specified in Appendix I.

Article II

Valuation of Contracts

1.   The following provisions shall apply in determining the value of contracts[2] for purposes of implementing this Agreement.

2.   Valuation shall take into account all forms of remuneration, including any premiums, fees, commissions and interest receivable.

3.   The selection of the valuation method by the entity shall not be used, nor shall any procurement requirement be divided, with the intention of avoiding the application of this Agreement.

4.   If an individual requirement for a procurement results in the award of more than one contract, or in contracts being awarded in separate parts, the basis for valuation shall be either:

(a) the actual value of similar recurring contracts concluded over the previous fiscal year or 12 months adjusted, where possible, for anticipated changes in quantity and value over the subsequent 12 months; or

(b) the estimated value of recurring contracts in the fiscal year or 12 months subsequent to the initial contract.

5.   In cases of contracts for the lease, rental or hire purchase of products or services, or in the case of contracts which do not specify a total price, the basis for valuation shall be:

(a) in the case of fixed term contracts, where their term is 12 months or less, the total contract value for their duration, or, where their term exceeds 12 months, their total value including the estimated residual value;

(b) in the case of contracts for an indefinite period, the monthly instalment multiplied by 48.

— Annex 2 contains sub-central government entities.

— Annex 3 contains all other entities that procure in accordance with the provisions of this Agreement.

— Annex 4 specifies services, whether listed positively or negatively, covered by this Agreement.

— Annex 5 specifies covered construction services.

Relevant thresholds are specified in each Party's Annexes.

2.   This Agreement shall apply to any procurement contract for which the contract value is estimated to equal or exceed the threshold at the time of publication of the notice in accordance with Article IX.

If there is any doubt, the second basis for valuation, namely (b), is to be used.

6.   In cases where an intended procurement specifies the need for option clauses, the basis for valuation shall be the total value of the maximum permissible procurement, inclusive of optional purchases.

Article III
National Treatment and Non-discrimination

1.   With respect to all laws, regulations, procedures and practices regarding government procurement covered by this Agreement, each Party shall provide immediately and unconditionally to the products, services and suppliers of other Parties offering products or services of the Parties, treatment no less favourable than:

   (a) that accorded to domestic products, services and suppliers; and

   (b) that accorded to products, services and suppliers of any other Party.

2.   With respect to all laws, regulations, procedures and practices regarding government procurement covered by this Agreement, each Party shall ensure:

   (a) that its entities shall not treat a locally-established supplier less favourably than another locally established supplier on the basis of degree of foreign affiliation or ownership; and

   (b) that its entities shall not discriminate against locally-established suppliers on the basis of the country of production of the good or service being supplied, provided that the country of production is a Party to the Agreement in accordance with the provisions of Article IV.

3.   The provisions of paragraphs 1 and 2 shall not apply to customs duties and charges of any kind imposed on or in connection with importation, the method of levying such duties and charges, other import regulations and formalities, and measures affecting trade in services other than laws, regulations, procedures and practices regarding government procurement covered by this Agreement.

Article IV
Rules of Origin

1.   A Party shall not apply rules of origin to products or services imported or supplied for purposes of government procurement covered by this Agreement from other Parties, which are different from the rules of origin applied in the normal course of trade and at the time of the transaction in question to imports or supplies of the same products or services from the same Parties.

2.   Following the conclusion of the work programme for the harmonization of rules of origin for goods to be undertaken under the Agreement on Rules of Origin in Annex 1A of the Agreement Establishing the World Trade Organization (herein referred to as "WTO Agreement") and negotiations regarding trade in services, Parties shall take the results of that work programme and those negotiations into account in amending paragraph 1 as appropriate.

Article V

Special and Differential Treatment for Developing Countries Objectives

1.   Parties shall, in the implementation and administration of this Agreement, through the provisions set out in this Article, duly take into account the development, financial and trade needs of developing countries, in particular least-developed countries, in their need to:

(a) safeguard their balance-of-payments position and ensure a level of reserves adequate for the implementation of programmes of economic development;

(b) promote the establishment or development of domestic industries including the development of small-scale and cottage industries in rural or backward areas; and economic development of other sectors of the economy;

(c) support industrial units so long as they are wholly or substantially dependent on government procurement; and

(d) encourage their economic development through regional or global arrangements among developing countries presented to the Ministerial Conference of the World Trade Organization (hereinafter referred to as the "WTO") and not disapproved by it.

2.   Consistently with the provisions of this Agreement, each Party shall, in the preparation and application of laws, regulations and procedures affecting government procurement, facilitate increased imports from developing countries, bearing in mind the special problems of least-developed countries and of those countries at low stages of economic development.

Coverage

3.   With a view to ensuring that developing countries are able to adhere to this Agreement on terms consistent with their development, financial and trade needs, the objectives listed in paragraph 1 shall be duly taken into account in the course of negotiations with respect to the procurement of developing countries to be covered by the provisions of this Agreement. Developed countries, in the preparation of their coverage lists under the provisions of this Agreement, shall endeavour to include entities procuring products and services of export interest to developing countries.

Agreed Exclusions

4.   A developing country may negotiate with other participants in negotiations under this Agreement mutually acceptable exclusions from the rules on national treatment with respect to certain entities, products or services that are included in its coverage lists, having regard to the particular circumstances of each case. In such negotiations, the considerations mentioned in subparagraphs 1(a) through 1(c) shall be duly taken into account. A developing country participating in regional or global arrangements among developing countries referred to in subparagraph 1(d) may also negotiate exclusions to its lists, having regard to the particular circumstances of each case, taking into account, *inter alia*, the provisions on government procurement provided for in the regional or global arrangements concerned and, in particular,

products or services which may be subject to common industrial development programmes.

5.   After entry into force of this Agreement, a developing country Party may modify its coverage lists in accordance with the provisions for modification of such lists contained in paragraph 6 of Article XXIV, having regard to its development, financial and trade needs, or may request the Committee on Government Procurement (hereinafter referred to as "the Committee") to grant exclusions from the rules on national treatment for certain entities, products or services that are included in its coverage lists, having regard to the particular circumstances of each case and taking duly into account the provisions of subparagraphs 1(a) through 1(c).   After entry into force of this Agreement, a developing country Party may also request the Committee to grant exclusions for certain entities, products or services that are included in its coverage lists in the light of its participation in regional or global arrangements among developing countries, having regard to the particular circumstances of each case and taking duly into account the provisions of subparagraph 1(d).   Each request to the Committee by a developing country Party relating to modification of a list shall be accompanied by documentation relevant to the request or by such information as may be necessary for consideration of the matter.

6.   Paragraphs 4 and 5 shall apply *mutatis mutandis* to developing countries acceding to this Agreement after its entry into force.

7.   Such agreed exclusions as mentioned in paragraphs 4, 5 and 6 shall be subject to review in accordance with the provisions of paragraph 14 below.

Technical Assistance for Developing Country Parties

8.   Each developed country Party shall, upon request, provide all technical assistance which it may deem appropriate to developing country Parties in resolving their problems in the field of government procurement.

9.   This assistance, which shall be provided on the basis of non-discrimination among developing country Parties, shall relate, *inter alia*, to:

— the solution of particular technical problems relating to the award of a specific contract; and

— any other problem which the Party making the request and another Party agree to deal with in the context of this assistance.

10.   Technical assistance referred to in paragraphs 8 and 9 would include translation of qualification documentation and tenders made by suppliers of developing country Parties into an official language of the WTO designated by the entity, unless developed country Parties deem translation to be burdensome, and in that case explanation shall be given to developing country Parties upon their request addressed either to the developed country Parties or to their entities.

Information Centres

11.   Developed country Parties shall establish, individually or jointly, information centres to respond to reasonable requests from developing country Parties for information relating to, *inter alia*, laws, regulations, procedures and practices regarding government procurement, notices about intend-

ed procurements which have been published, addresses of the entities covered by this Agreement, and the nature and volume of products or services procured or to be procured, including available information about future tenders. The Committee may also set up an information centre.

Special Treatment for Least–Developed Countries

12.   Having regard to paragraph 6 of the Decision of the CONTRACT-ING PARTIES to GATT 1947 of 28 November 1979 on Differential and More Favourable Treatment, Reciprocity and Fuller Participation of Developing Countries (BISD 26S/203–205), special treatment shall be granted to least-developed country Parties and to the suppliers in those Parties with respect to products or services originating in those Parties, in the context of any general or specific measures in favour of developing country Parties. A Party may also grant the benefits of this Agreement to suppliers in least-developed countries which are not Parties, with respect to products or services originating in those countries.

13.   Each developed country Party shall, upon request, provide assistance which it may deem appropriate to potential tenders in least-developed countries in submitting their tenders and selecting the products or services which are likely to be of interest to its entities as well as to suppliers in least-developed countries, and likewise assist them to comply with technical regulations and standards relating to products or services which are the subject of the intended procurement.

Review

14.   The Committee shall review annually the operation and effectiveness of this Article and, after each three years of its operation on the basis of reports to be submitted by Parties, shall carry out a major review in order to evaluate its effects. As part of the three-yearly reviews and with a view to achieving the maximum implementation of the provisions of this Agreement, including in particular Article III, and having regard to the development, financial and trade situation of the developing countries concerned, the Committee shall examine whether exclusions provided for in accordance with the provisions of paragraphs 4 through 6 of this Article shall be modified or extended.

15.   In the course of further rounds of negotiations in accordance with the provisions of paragraph 7 of Article XXIV, each developing country Party shall give consideration to the possibility of enlarging its coverage lists, having regard to its economic, financial and trade situation.

Article VI

Technical Specifications

1.   Technical specifications laying down the characteristics of the products or services to be procured, such as quality, performance, safety and dimensions, symbols, terminology, packaging, marking and labelling, or the processes and methods for their production and requirements relating to conformity assessment procedures prescribed by procuring entities, shall not be prepared, adopted or applied with a view to, or with the effect of, creating unnecessary obstacles to international trade.

2.   Technical specifications prescribed by procuring entities shall, where appropriate:

(a) be in terms of performance rather than design or descriptive characteristics; and

(b) be based on international standards, where such exist; otherwise, on national technical regulations,[3] recognized national standards,[4] or building codes.

3. There shall be no requirement or reference to a particular trademark or trade name, patent, design or type, specific origin, producer or supplier, unless there is no sufficiently precise or intelligible way of describing the procurement requirements and provided that words such as "or equivalent" are included in the tender documentation.

4. Entities shall not seek or accept, in a manner which would have the effect of precluding competition, advice which may be used in the preparation of specifications for a specific procurement from a firm that may have a commercial interest in the procurement.

Article VII
Tendering Procedures

1. Each Party shall ensure that the tendering procedures of its entities are applied in a non-discriminatory manner and are consistent with the provisions contained in Articles VII through XVI.

2. Entities shall not provide to any supplier information with regard to a specific procurement in a manner which would have the effect of precluding competition.

3. For the purposes of this Agreement:

(a) Open tendering procedures are those procedures under which all interested suppliers may submit a tender.

(b) Selective tendering procedures are those procedures under which, consistent with paragraph 3 of Article X and other relevant provisions of this Agreement, those suppliers invited to do so by the entity may submit a tender.

(c) Limited tendering procedures are those procedures where the entity contacts suppliers individually, only under the conditions specified in Article XV.

Article VIII
Qualification of Suppliers

In the process of qualifying suppliers, entities shall not discriminate among suppliers of other Parties or between domestic suppliers and suppliers

---

3. For the purpose of this Agreement, a technical regulation is a document which lays down characteristics of a product or a service or their related processes and production methods, including the applicable administrative provisions, with which compliance is mandatory. It may also include or deal exclusively with terminology, symbols, packaging, marking or labelling requirements as they apply to a product, service, process or production method.

4. For the purpose of this Agreement, a standard is a document approved by a recognized body, that provides, for common and repeated use, rules, guidelines or characteristics for products or services or related processes and production methods, with which compliance is not mandatory. It may also include or deal exclusively with terminology, symbols, packaging, marking or labelling requirements as they apply to a product, service, process or production method.

of other Parties. Qualification procedures shall be consistent with the following:

(a) any conditions for participation in tendering procedures shall be published in adequate time to enable interested suppliers to initiate and, to the extent that it is compatible with efficient operation of the procurement process, complete the qualification procedures;

(b) any conditions for participation in tendering procedures shall be limited to those which are essential to ensure the firm's capability to fulfil the contract in question. Any conditions for participation required from suppliers, including financial guarantees, technical qualifications and information necessary for establishing the financial, commercial and technical capacity of suppliers, as well as the verification of qualifications, shall be no less favourable to suppliers of other Parties than to domestic suppliers and shall not discriminate among suppliers of other Parties. The financial, commercial and technical capacity of a supplier shall be judged on the basis both of that supplier's global business activity as well as of its activity in the territory of the procuring entity, taking due account of the legal relationship between the supply organizations;

(c) the process of, and the time required for, qualifying suppliers shall not be used in order to keep suppliers of other Parties off a suppliers' list or from being considered for a particular intended procurement. Entities shall recognize as qualified suppliers such domestic suppliers or suppliers of other Parties who meet the conditions for participation in a particular intended procurement. Suppliers requesting to participate in a particular intended procurement who may not yet be qualified shall also be considered, provided there is sufficient time to complete the qualification procedure;

(d) entities maintaining permanent lists of qualified suppliers shall ensure that suppliers may apply for qualification at any time; and that all qualified suppliers so requesting are included in the lists within a reasonably short time;

(e) if, after publication of the notice under paragraph 1 of Article IX, a supplier not yet qualified requests to participate in an intended procurement, the entity shall promptly start procedures for qualification;

(f) any supplier having requested to become a qualified supplier shall be advised by the entities concerned of the decision in this regard. Qualified suppliers included on permanent lists by entities shall also be notified of the termination of any such lists or of their removal from them;

(g) each Party shall ensure that:

(i) each entity and its constituent parts follow a single qualification procedure, except in cases of duly substantiated need for a different procedure; and

(ii) efforts be made to minimize differences in qualification procedures between entities.

(h) nothing in subparagraphs (a) through (g) shall preclude the exclusion of any supplier on grounds such as bankruptcy or false declarations, provided that such an action is consistent with the national treatment and non-discrimination provisions of this Agreement.

Article IX

Invitation to Participate Regarding Intended Procurement

1. In accordance with paragraphs 2 and 3, entities shall publish an invitation to participate for all cases of intended procurement, except as otherwise provided for in Article XV (limiting tendering). The notice shall be published in the appropriate publication listed in Appendix II.

2. The invitation to participate may take the form of a notice of proposed procurement, as provided for in paragraph 6.

3. Entities in Annexes 2 and 3 may use a notice of planned procurement, as provided for in paragraph 7, or a notice regarding a qualification system, as provided for in paragraph 9, as an invitation to participate.

4. Entities which use a notice of planned procurement as an invitation to participate shall subsequently invite all suppliers who have expressed an interest to confirm their interest on the basis of information which shall include at least the information referred to in paragraph 6.

5. Entities which use a notice regarding a qualification system as an invitation to participate shall provide, subject to the considerations referred to in paragraph 4 of Article XVIII and in a timely manner, information which allows all those who have expressed an interest to have a meaningful opportunity to assess their interest in participating in the procurement. This information shall include the information contained in the notices referred to in paragraphs 6 and 8, to the extent such information is available. Information provided to one interested supplier shall be provided in a non-discriminatory manner to the other interested suppliers.

6. Each notice of proposed procurement, referred to in paragraph 2, shall contain the following information:

(a) the nature and quantity, including any options for further procurement and, if possible, an estimate of the timing when such options may be exercised; in the case of recurring contracts the nature and quantity and, if possible, an estimate of the timing of the subsequent tender notices for the products or services to be procured;

(b) whether the procedure is open or selective or will involve negotiation;

(c) any date for starting delivery or completion of delivery of goods or services;

(d) the address and final date for submitting an application to be invited to tender or for qualifying for the suppliers' lists, or for receiving tenders, as well as the languages in which they must be submitted;

(e) the address of the entity awarding the contract and providing any information necessary for obtaining specifications and other documents;

(f) any economic and technical requirements, financial guarantees and information required from suppliers;

(g) the amount and terms of payment of any sum payable for the tender documentation; and

(h) whether the entity is inviting offers for purchase, lease, rental or hire purchase, or more than one of these methods.

7. Each notice of planned procurement referred to in paragraph 3 shall contain as much of the information referred to in paragraph 6 as is available. It shall in any case include the information referred to in paragraph 8 and:

(a) a statement that interested suppliers should express their interest in the procurement to the entity;

(b) a contact point with the entity from which further information may be obtained.

8. For each case of intended procurement, the entity shall publish a summary notice in one of the official languages of the WTO. The notice shall contain at least the following information:

(a) the subject matter of the contract;

(b) the time-limits set for the submission of tenders or an application to be invited to tender; and

(c) the addresses from which documents relating to the contracts may be requested.

9. In the case of selective tendering procedures, entities maintaining permanent lists of qualified suppliers shall publish annually in one of the publications listed in Appendix III a notice of the following:

(a) the enumeration of the lists maintained, including their headings, in relation to the products or services or categories of products or services or categories of products or services to be procured through the lists;

(b) the conditions to be fulfilled by suppliers with a view to their inscription on those lists and the methods according to which each of those conditions will be verified by the entity concerned; and

(c) the period of validity of the lists, and the formalities for their renewal.

When such a notice is used as an invitation to participate in accordance with paragraph 3, the notice shall, in addition, include the following information:

(d) the nature of the products or services concerned;

(e) a statement that the notice constitutes an invitation to participate.

However, when the duration of the qualification system is three years or less, and if the duration of the system is made clear in the notice and it is also made clear that further notices will not be published, it shall be sufficient to publish the notice once only, at the beginning of the system. Such a system shall not be used in a manner which circumvents the provisions of this Agreement.

10. If, after publication of an invitation to participate in any case of intended procurement, but before the time set for opening or receipt of tenders as specified in the notices or the tender documentation, it becomes

necessary to amend or re-issue the notice, the amendment or the re-issued notice shall be given the same circulation as the original documents upon which the amendment is based. Any significant information given to one supplier with respect to a particular intended procurement shall be given simultaneously to all other suppliers concerned in adequate time to permit the suppliers to consider such information and to respond to it.

11. Entities shall make clear, in the notices referred to in this Article or in the publication in which the notices appear, that the procurement is covered by the Agreement.

Article X
Selection Procedures

1. To ensure optimum effective international competition under selective tendering procedures, entities shall, for each intended procurement, invite tenders from the maximum number of domestic suppliers and suppliers of other Parties, consistent with the efficient operation of the procurement system. They shall select the suppliers to participate in the procedure in a fair and non-discriminatory manner.

2. Entities maintaining permanent lists of qualified suppliers may select suppliers to be invited to tender from among those listed. Any selection shall allow for equitable opportunities for suppliers on the lists.

3. Suppliers requesting to participate in a particular intended procurement shall be permitted to submit a tender and be considered, provided, in the case of those not yet qualified, there is sufficient time to complete the qualification procedure under Articles VIII and IX. The number of additional suppliers permitted to participate shall be limited only by the efficient operation of the procurement system.

4. Requests to participate in selective tendering procedures may be submitted by telex, telegram or facsimile.

Article XI
Time-Limits for Tendering and Delivery

General

1. (a) Any prescribed time-limit shall be adequate to allow suppliers of other Parties as well as domestic suppliers to prepare and submit tenders before the closing of the tendering procedures. In determining any such time-limit, entities shall, consistent with their own reasonable needs, take into account such factors as the complexity of the intended procurement, the extent of subcontracting anticipated and the normal time for transmitting tenders by mail from foreign as well as domestic points.

(b) Each Party shall ensure that its entities shall take due account of publication delays when setting the final date for receipt of tenders or of applications to be invited to tender.

Deadlines

2. Except in so far as provided in paragraph 3,

(a) in open procedures, the period for the receipt of tenders shall not be less than 40 days from the date of publication referred to in paragraph 1 of Article IX;

(b) in selective procedures not involving the use of a permanent list of qualified suppliers, the period for submitting an application to be invited to tender shall not be less than 25 days from the date of publication referred to in paragraph 1 of Article IX; the period for receipt of tenders shall in no case be less than 40 days from the date of issuance of the invitation to tender;

(c) in selective procedures involving the use of a permanent list of qualified suppliers, the period for receipt of tenders shall not be less than 40 days from the date of the initial issuance of invitations to tender, whether or not the date of the initial issuance of invitations to tender coincides with the date of the publication referred to in paragraph 1 of Article IX.

3.   The periods referred to in paragraph 2 may be reduced in the circumstances set out below:

(a) if a separate notice has been published 40 days and not more than 12 months in advance and the notice contains at least:

(i) as much of the information referred to in paragraph 6 of Article IX as is available;

(ii) the information referred to in paragraph 8 of Article IX;

(iii) a statement that interested suppliers should express their interest in the procurement to the entity; and

(iv) a contact point with the entity from which further information may be obtained,

the 40–day limit for receipt of tenders may be replaced by a period sufficiently long to enable responsive tendering, which, as a general rule, shall not be less than 24 days, but in any case not less than 10 days;

(b) in the case of the second or subsequent publications dealing with contracts of a recurring nature within the meaning of paragraph 6 of Article IX, the 40–day limit for receipt of tenders may be reduced to not less than 24 days;

(c) where a state of urgency duly substantiated by the entity renders impracticable the periods in question, the periods specified in paragraph 2 may be reduced but shall in no case be less than 10 days from the date of the publication referred to in paragraph 1 of Article IX; or

(d) the period referred to in paragraph 2(c) may, for procurements by entities listed in Annexes 2 and 3, be fixed by mutual agreement between the entity and the selected suppliers. In the absence of agreement, the entity may fix periods which shall be sufficiently long to enable responsive tendering and shall in any case not be less than 10 days.

4.   Consistent with the entity's own reasonable needs, any delivery date shall take into account such factors as the complexity of the intended procurement, the extent of subcontracting anticipated and the realistic time

required for production, de-stocking and transport of goods from the points of supply or for supply of services.

Article XII
Tender Documentation

1. If, in tendering procedures, an entity allows tenderers to be submitted in several languages, one of these languages shall be one of the official languages of the WTO.

2. Tender documentation provided to suppliers shall contain all information necessary to permit them to submit responsive tenders, including information required to be published in the notice of intended procurement, except for paragraph 6(g) of Article IX, and the following:

   (a) the address of the entity to which tenders should be sent;

   (b) the address where requests for supplementary information should be sent;

   (c) the language or languages in which tenders and tendering documents must be submitted;

   (d) the closing date and time for receipt of tenders and the length of time during which any tender should be open for acceptance;

   (e) the persons authorized to be present at the opening of tenders and the date, time and place of this opening;

   (f) any economic and technical requirement, financial guarantees and information or documents required from suppliers;

   (g) a complete description of the products or services required or of any requirements including technical specifications, conformity certification to be fulfilled, necessary plans, drawings and instructional materials;

   (h) the criteria for awarding the contract, including any factors other than price that are to be considered in the evaluation of tenders and the cost elements to be included in evaluating tender prices, such as transport, insurance and inspection costs, and in the case of products or services of other Parties, customs duties and other import charges, taxes and currency of payment;

   (i) the terms of payment;

   (j) any other terms or conditions;

   (k) in accordance with Article XVII the terms and conditions, if any, under which tenders from countries not Parties to this Agreement, but which apply the procedures of that Article, will be entertained.

Forwarding of Tender Documentation by the Entities

3. (a) In open procedures, entities shall forward the tender documentation at the request of any supplier participating in the procedure, and shall reply promptly to any reasonable request for explanations relating thereto.

   (b) In selective procedures, entities shall forward the tender documentation at the request of any supplier requesting to participate, and shall reply promptly to any reasonable request for explanations relating thereto.

(c) Entities shall reply promptly to any reasonable request for relevant information submitted by a supplier participating in the tendering procedure, on condition that such information does not give that supplier an advantage over its competitors in the procedure for the award of the contract.

Article XIII

Submission, Receipt and Opening of Tenders and Awarding of Contracts

1. The submission, receipt and opening of tenders and awarding of contracts shall be consistent with the following:

(a) tenders shall normally be submitted in writing directly or by mail. If tenders by telex, telegram or facsimile are permitted, the tender made thereby must include all the information necessary for the evaluation of the tender, in particular the definitive price proposed by the tenderer and a statement that the tenderer agrees to all the terms, conditions and provisions of the invitation to tender. The tender must be confirmed promptly by letter or by the despatch of a signed copy of the telex, telegram or facsimile. Tenders presented by telephone shall not be permitted. The content of the telex, telegram or facsimile shall prevail where there is a difference or conflict between that content and any documentation received after the time-limit; and

(b) the opportunities that may be given to tenderers to correct unintentional errors of form between the opening of tenders and the awarding of the contract shall not be permitted to give rise to any discriminatory practice.

Receipt of Tenders

2. A supplier shall not be penalized if a tender is received in the office designated in the tender documentation after the time specified because of delay due solely to mishandling on the part of the entity. Tenders may also be considered in other exceptional circumstances if the procedures of the entity concerned so provide.

Opening of Tenders

3. All tenders solicited under open or selective procedures by entities shall be received and opened under procedures and conditions guaranteeing the regularity of the openings. The receipt and opening of tenders shall also be consistent with the national treatment and non-discrimination provisions of this Agreement. Information on the opening of tenders shall remain with the entity concerned at the disposal of the government authorities responsible for the entity in order that it may be used if required under the procedures of Articles XVIII, XIX, XX and XXII.

Award of Contracts

4. (a) To be considered for award, a tender must, at the time of opening, conform to the essential requirements of the notices or tender documentation and be from a supplier which complies with the conditions for participation. If an entity has received a tender abnormally lower than other tenders submitted, it may enquire with the tenderer to ensure that it can comply with

the conditions of participation and be capable of fulfilling the terms of the contract.

(b) Unless in the public interest an entity decides not to issue the contract, the entity shall make the award to the tenderer who has been determined to be fully capable of undertaking the contract and whose tender, whether for domestic products or services, or products or services of other Parties, is either the lowest tender or the tender which in terms of the specific evaluation criteria set forth in the notices or tender documentation is determined to be the most advantageous.

(c) Awards shall be made in accordance with the criteria and essential requirements specified in the tender documentation.

Option Clauses

5. Option clauses shall not be used in a manner which circumvents the provisions of the Agreement.

Article XIV

Negotiation

1. A Party may provide for entities to conduct negotiations:

(a) in the context of procurements in which they have indicated such intent, namely in the notice referred to in paragraph 2 of Article IX (the invitation to suppliers to participate in the procedure for the proposed procurement); or

(b) when it appears from evaluation that no one tender is obviously the most advantageous in terms of the specific evaluation criteria set forth in the notices or tender documentation.

2. Negotiations shall primarily be used to identify the strengths and weaknesses in tenders.

3. Entities shall treat tenders in confidence. In particular, they shall not provide information intended to assist particular participants to bring their tenders up to the level of other participants.

4. Entities shall not, in the course of negotiations, discriminate between different suppliers. In particular, they shall ensure that:

(a) any elimination of participants is carried out in accordance with the criteria set forth in the notices and tender documentation;

(b) all modifications to the criteria and to the technical requirements are transmitted in writing to all remaining participants in the negotiations;

(c) all remaining participants are afforded an opportunity to submit new or amended submissions on the basis of the revised requirements; and

(d) when negotiations are concluded, all participants remaining in the negotiations shall be permitted to submit final tenders in accordance with a common deadline.

Article XV

Limited Tendering

1. The provisions of Articles VII through XIV governing open and selective tendering procedures need not apply in the following conditions, provided that limited tendering is not used with a view to avoiding maximum possible competition or in a manner which would constitute a means of discrimination among suppliers of other Parties or protection to domestic producers or suppliers:

(a) in the absence of tenders in response to an open or selective tender, or when the tenders submitted have been collusive, or not in conformity with the essential requirements in the tender, or from suppliers who do not comply with the conditions for participation provided for in accordance with this Agreement, on condition, however, that the requirements of the initial tender are not substantially modified in the contract as awarded;

(b) when, for works of art or for reasons connected with protection of exclusive rights, such as patents or copyrights, or in the absence of competition for technical reasons, the products or services can be supplied only by a particular supplier and no reasonable alternative or substitute exists;

(c) in so far as is strictly necessary when, for reasons of extreme urgency brought about by events unforeseeable by the entity, the products or services could not be obtained in time by means of open or selective tendering procedures;

(d) for additional deliveries by the original supplier which are intended either as parts replacement for existing supplies, or installations, or as the extension of existing supplies, services, or installations where a change of supplier would compel the entity to procure equipment or services not meeting requirements of interchangeability with already existing equipment or services;[5]

(e) when an entity procures prototypes or a first product or service which are developed at its request in the course of, and for, a particular contract for research, experiment, study or original development. When such contracts have been fulfilled, subsequent procurements of products or services shall be subject to Articles VII through XIV;[6]

(f) when additional construction services which were not included in the initial contract but which were within the objectives of the original tender documentation have, through unforeseeable circumstances, become necessary to complete the construction services described therein, and the entity needs to award contracts for the additional construction services to the contractor carrying out the construction services concerned since the separation of the additional construction services from

5. It is the understanding that "existing equipment" includes software to the extent that the initial procurement of the software was covered by the Agreement.

6. Original development of a first product or service may include limited production or supply in order to incorporate the results of field testing and to demonstrate that the product or service is suitable for production or supply in quantity to acceptable quality standards. It does not extend to quantity production or supply to establish commercial viability or to recover research and development costs.

the initial contract would be difficult for technical or economic reasons and cause significant inconvenience to the entity. However, the total value of contracts awarded for the additional construction services may not exceed 50 per cent of the amount of the main contract;

(g) for new construction services consisting of the repetition of similar construction services which conform to a basic project for which an initial contract was awarded in accordance with Articles VII through XIV and for which the entity has indicated in the notice of intended procurement concerning the initial construction service, that limited tendering procedures might be used in awarding contracts for such new construction services;

(h) for products purchased on a commodity market;

(i) for purchases made under exceptionally advantageous conditions which only arise in the very short term. This provision is intended to cover unusual disposals by firms which are not normally suppliers, or disposal of assets of businesses in liquidation or receivership. It is not intended to cover routine purchases from regular suppliers;

(j) in the case of contracts awarded to the winner of a design contest provided that the contest has been organized in a manner which is consistent with the principles of this Agreement, notably as regards the publication, in the sense of Article IX, of an invitation to suitably qualified suppliers, to participate in such a contest which shall be judged by an independent jury with a view to design contracts being awarded to the winners.

2. Entities shall prepare a report in writing on each contract awarded under the provisions of paragraph 1. Each report shall contain the name of the procuring entity, value and kind of goods or services procured, country of origin, and a statement of the conditions in this Article which prevailed. This report shall remain with the entities concerned at the disposal of the government authorities responsible for the entity in order that it may be used if required under the procedures of Articles XVIII, XIX, XX and XXII.

Article XVI

Offsets

1. Entities shall not, in the qualification and selection of suppliers, products, or services, or in the evaluation of tenders and award of contract, impose, seek or consider offsets.[7]

2. Nevertheless, having regard to general policy considerations, including those relating to development, a developing country may at the time of accession negotiate conditions for the use of offsets, such as requirements for the incorporation of domestic content. Such requirements shall be used only for qualification to participate in the procurement process and not as criteria for awarding contracts. Conditions shall be objective, clearly defined and non-discriminatory. They shall be set forth in the country's Appendix I and may include precise limitations on the imposition of offsets in any contract

---

7. Offsets in government procurement are measures used to encourage local development or improve the balance-of-payments accounts by means of domestic content, licensing of technology, investment requirements, countertrade or similar requirements.

subject to this Agreement. the existence of such conditions shall be notified to the Committee and included in the notice of intended procurement and other documentation.

Article XVII

Transparency

1.   Each Party shall encourage entities to indicate the terms and conditions, including any deviations from competitive tendering procedures or access to challenge procedures, under which tenders will be entertained from suppliers situated in countries not Parties to this Agreement but which, with a view to creating transparency in their own contract awards, nevertheless:

(a) specify their contracts in accordance with Article VI (technical specifications);

(b) publish the procurement notices referred to in Article IX, including, in the version of the notice referred to in paragraph 8 of Article IX (summary of the notice of intended procurement) which is published in an official language of the WTO, an indication of the terms and conditions under which tenders shall be entertained from suppliers situated in countries Parties to this Agreement;

(c) are willing to ensure that their procurement regulations shall not normally change during a procurement and, in the event that such change proves unavoidable, to ensure the availability of a satisfactory means of redress.

2.   Governments not Parties to the Agreement which comply with the conditions specified in paragraphs 1(a) through 1(c), shall be entitled if they so inform the Parties to participate in the Committee as observers.

Article XVIII

Information and Review as Regards Obligations of Entities

1.   Entities shall publish a notice in the appropriate publication listed in Appendix II not later than 72 days after the award of each contract under Articles XIII through XV. These notices shall contain:

(a) the nature and quantity of products or services in the contract award;

(b) the name and address of the entity awarding the contract;

(c) the date of award;

(d) the name and address of winning tenderer;

(e) the value of the winning award or the highest and lowest offer taken into account in the award of the contract;

(f) where appropriate, means of identifying the notice issued under paragraph 1 of Article IX or justification according to Article XV for the use of such procedure; and

(g) the type of procedure used.

2.   Each entity shall, on request from a supplier of a Party, promptly provide;

(a) an explanation of its procurement practices and procedures;

(b) pertinent information concerning the reasons why the supplier's application to qualify was rejected, why its existing qualification was brought to an end and why it was not selected; and

(c) to an unsuccessful tenderer, pertinent information concerning the reasons why its tender was not selected and on the characteristics and relative advantages of the tender selected as well as the name of the winning tenderer.

3.   Entities shall promptly inform participating suppliers of decisions on contract awards and, upon request, in writing.

4.   However, entities may decide that certain information on the contract award, contained in paragraphs 1 and 2(c), be withheld where release of such information would impede law enforcement or otherwise be contrary to the public interest or would prejudice the legitimate commercial interest of particular enterprises, public or private, or might prejudice fair competition between suppliers.

Article XIX
Information and Review as Regards Obligations of Parties

1.   Each Party shall promptly publish any law, regulation, judicial decision, administrative ruling of general application, and any procedure (including standard contract clauses) regarding government procurement covered by this Agreement, in the appropriate publications listed in Appendix IV and in such a manner as to enable other Parties and suppliers to become acquainted with them.   Each Party shall be prepared, upon request, to explain to any other Party its government procurement procedures.

2.   The government of an unsuccessful tenderer which is a Party to this Agreement may seek, without prejudice to the provisions under Article XXII, such additional information on the contract award as may be necessary to ensure that the procurement was made fairly and impartially.   To this end, the procuring government shall provide information on both the characteristics and relative advantages of the winning tender and the contract price. Normally this latter information may be disclosed by the government of the unsuccessful tenderer provided it exercises this right with discretion.   In cases where release of this information would prejudice competition in future tenders, this information shall not be disclosed except after consultation with and agreement of the Party which gave the information to the government of the unsuccessful tenderer.

3.   Available information concerning procurement by covered entities and their individual contract awards shall be provided, upon request, to any other Party.

4.   Confidential information provided to any Party which would impede law enforcement or otherwise be contrary to the public interest or would prejudice the legitimate commercial interest of particular enterprises, public or private, or might prejudice fair competition between suppliers shall not be revealed without formal authorization from the party providing the information.

5.   Each Party shall collect and provide to the Committee on an annual basis statistics on its procurements covered by this Agreement. Such reports shall contain the following information with respect to contracts awarded by all procurement entities covered under this Agreement:

(a) for entities in Annex 1, statistics on the estimated value of contracts awarded, both above and below the threshold value, on a global basis and broken down by entities; for entities in Annexes 2 and 3, statistics on the estimated value of contracts awarded above the threshold value on a global basis and broken down by categories of entities;

(b) for entities in Annex 1, statistics on the number and total value of contracts awarded above the threshold value, broken down by entities and categories of products and services according to uniform classification systems; for entities in Annexes 2 and 3, statistics on the estimated value of contracts awarded above the threshold value broken down by categories of entities and categories of products and services;

(c) for entities in Annex 1, statistics, broken down by entity and by categories of products and services, on the number and total value of contracts awarded under each of the cases of Article XV; for categories of entities in Annexes 2 and 3, statistics on the total value of contracts awarded above the threshold value under each of the cases of Article XV; and

(d) for entities in Annex 1, statistics, broken down by entities, on the number and total value of contracts awarded under derogations to the Agreement contained in the relevant Annexes; for categories of entities in Annexes 2 and 3, statistics on the total value of contracts awarded under derogations to the Agreement contained in the relevant Annexes.

To the extent that such information is available, each Party shall provide statistics on the country of origin of products and services purchased by its entities. With a view to ensuring that such statistics are comparable, the Committee shall provide guidance on methods to be used. With a view to ensuring effective monitoring of procurement covered by this Agreement, the Committee may decide unanimously to modify the requirements of subparagraphs (a) through (d) as regards the nature and the extent of statistical information to be provided and the breakdowns and classifications to be used.

Article XX
Challenge Procedures

Consultations

1.   In the event of a complaint by a supplier that there has been a breach of this Agreement in the context of a procurement, each Party shall encourage the supplier to seek resolution of its complaint in consultation with the procuring entity. In such instances the procuring entity shall accord impartial and timely consideration to any such complaint, in a manner that is not prejudicial to obtaining corrective measures under the challenge system.

Challenge

2.   Each Party shall provide non-discriminatory, timely, transparent and effective procedures enabling suppliers to challenge alleged breaches of the

Agreement arising in the context of procurements in which they have, or have had, an interest.

3. Each Party shall provide its challenge procedures in writing and make them generally available.

4. Each Party shall ensure that documentation relating to all aspects of the process concerning procurements covered by this Agreement shall be retained for three years.

5. The interested supplier may be required to initiate a challenge procedure and notify the procuring entity within specified time-limits from the time when the basis of the complaint is known or reasonably should have been known, but in no case within a period of less than 10 days.

6. Challenges shall be heard by a court or by an impartial and independent review body with no interest in the outcome of the procurement and the members of which are secure from external influence during the term of appointment. A review body which is not a court shall either be subject to judicial review or shall have procedures which provide that:

(a) participants can be heard before an opinion is given or a decision is reached;

(b) participants can be represented and accompanied;

(c) participants shall have access to all proceedings;

(d) proceedings can take place in public;

(e) opinions or decisions are given in writing with a statement describing the basis for the opinions or decisions;

(f) witnesses can be presented;

(g) documents are disclosed to the review body.

7. Challenge procedures shall provide for:

(a) rapid interim measures to correct breaches of the Agreement and to preserve commercial opportunities. Such action may result in suspension of the procurement process. However, procedures may provide that overriding adverse consequences for the interests concerned, including the public interest, may be taken into account in deciding whether such measures should be applied. In such circumstances, just cause for not acting shall be provided in writing;

(b) an assessment and a possibility for a decision on the justification of the challenge;

(c) correction of the breach of the Agreement or compensation for the loss or damages suffered, which may be limited to costs for tender preparation or protest.

8. With a view to the preservation of the commercial and other interests involved, the challenge procedure shall normally be completed in a timely fashion.

Article XXI

Institutions

1. A Committee on Government Procurement composed of representatives from each of the Parties shall be established. This Committee shall

elect its own Chairman and Vice–Chairman and shall meet as necessary but not less than once a year for the purpose of affording Parties the opportunity to consult on any matters relating to the operation of this Agreement or the furtherance of its objectives, and to carry out such other responsibilities as may be assigned to it by the Parties.

2. The Committee may establish working parties or other subsidiary bodies which shall carry out such functions as may be given to them by the Committee.

Article XXII

Consultations and Dispute Settlement

1. The provisions of the Understanding on Rules and Procedures Governing the Settlement of Disputes under the WTO Agreement (hereinafter referred to as the "Dispute Settlement Understanding") shall be applicable except as otherwise specifically provided below.

2. If any Party considers that any benefit accruing to it, directly or indirectly, under this Agreement is being nullified or impaired, or that the attainment of any objective of this Agreement is being impeded as the result of the failure of another Party or Parties to carry out its obligations under this Agreement, or the application by another Party or Parties of any measure, whether or not it conflicts with the provisions of this Agreement, it may with a view to reaching a mutually satisfactory resolution of the matter, make written representations or proposals to the other Party or Parties which it considers be concerned. Such action shall be promptly notified to the Dispute Settlement Body established under the Dispute Settlement Understanding (hereinafter referred to as "DSB"), as specified below. Any Party thus approached shall give sympathetic consideration to the representations or proposals made to it.

3. The DSB shall have the authority to establish panels, adopt panel and Appellate Body reports, make recommendations or give rulings on the matter, maintain surveillance of implementation of rulings and recommendations, and authorize suspension of concessions and other obligations under this Agreement or consultations regarding remedies when withdrawal of measures found to be in contravention of the Agreement is not possible, provided that only Members of the WTO Party to this Agreement shall participate in decisions or actions taken by the DAB with respect to disputes under this Agreement.

4. Panels shall have the following terms of reference unless the parties to the dispute agree otherwise within 20 days of the establishment of the panel:

> "To examine, in the light of the relevant provisions of this Agreement and of (name of any other covered Agreement cited by the parties to the dispute), the matter referred to the DSB by (name of party) in document . . . and to make such findings as will assist the DSB in making the recommendations or in giving the rulings provided for in this Agreement."

In the case of a dispute in which provisions both of this Agreement and of one or more other Agreements listed in Appendix 1 of the Dispute Settlement

Understanding are invoked by one of the parties to the dispute, paragraph 3 shall apply only to those parts of the panel report concerning the interpretation and application of this Agreement.

5. Panels established by the DSB to examine disputes under this Agreement shall include persons qualified in the area of government procurement.

6. Every effort shall be made to accelerate the proceedings to the greatest extent possible. Notwithstanding the provisions of paragraphs 8 and 9 of Article 12 of the Dispute Settlement Understanding, the panel shall attempt to provide its final report to the parties to the dispute not later than four months, and in case of delay not later than seven months, after the date on which the composition and terms of reference of the panel are agreed. Consequently, every effort shall be made to reduce also the periods foreseen in paragraph 1 of Article 20 and paragraph 4 of Article 21 of the Dispute Settlement Understanding by two months. Moreover, notwithstanding the provisions of paragraph 5 of Article 21 of the Dispute Settlement Understanding, the panel shall attempt to issue its decision, in case of a disagreement as to the existence or consistency with a covered Agreement of measures taken to comply with the recommendations and rulings, within 60 days.

7. Notwithstanding paragraph 2 of Article 22 of the Dispute Settlement Understanding, any dispute arising under any Agreement listed in Appendix 1 to the Dispute Settlement Understanding other than this Agreement shall not result in the suspension of concessions or other obligations under this Agreement, and any dispute arising under this Agreement shall not result in the suspension of concessions or other obligations under any other Agreement listed in the said Appendix 1.

Article XXIII

Exceptions to the Agreement

1. Nothing in this Agreement shall be construed to prevent any Party from taking any action or not disclosing any information which it considers necessary for the protection of its essential security interests relating to the procurement of arms, ammunition or war materials, or to procurement indispensable for national security or for national defense purposes.

2. Subject to the requirement that such measures are not applied in a manner which would constitute a means of arbitrary or unjustifiable discrimination between countries where the same conditions prevail or a disguised restriction on international trade, nothing in this Agreement shall be construed to prevent any Party from imposing or enforcing measures: necessary to protect public morals, order or safety, human, animal or plant life or health or intellectual property; or relating to the products or services of handicapped persons, of philanthropic institutions or of prison labour.

Article XXIV

Final Provisions

1. *Acceptance and Entry into Force*

This Agreement shall enter force on 1 January 1996 for those governments[8] whose agreed coverage is contained in Annexes 1 through 5 of Appendix I of this Agreement and which have, by signature, accepted the Agreement on 15 April 1994 or have, by that date, signed the Agreement subject to ratification and subsequently ratified the Agreement before 1 January 1996.

2. *Accession*

Any government which is a Member of the WTO, or prior to the date of entry into force of the WTO Agreement which is a contracting party to GATT 1947, and which is not a Party to this Agreement may accede to this Agreement on terms to be agreed between that government and the Parties. Accession shall take place by deposit with the Director–General of the WTO of an instrument of accession which states the terms so agreed. The Agreement shall enter into force for an acceding government on the 30th day following the date of its accession to the Agreement.

3. *Transitional Arrangements*

(a) Hong Kong and Korea may delay application of the provisions of this Agreement, except Articles XXI and XXII, to a date not later than 1 January 1997. The commencement date of their application of the provisions, if prior to 1 January 1997, shall be notified to the Director–General of the WTO 30 days in advance.

(b) During the period between the date of entry into force of this Agreement and the date of its application by Hong King, the rights and obligations between Hong Kong and all other Parties to this Agreement which were on 15 April 1994 Parties to the Agreement on Government Procurement done at Geneva on 12 April 1979 as amended on 2 February 1987 (the "1988 Agreement") shall be governed by the substantive[9] provisions of the 1988 Agreement, including its Annexes as modified or rectified, which provisions are incorporated herein by reference for that purpose and shall remain in force until 31 December 1996.

(c) Between parties to this Agreement which are also Parties to the 1988 Agreement, the rights and obligations of this Agreement shall supersede those under the 1988 Agreement.

(d) Article XXII shall not enter into force until the date of entry into force of the WTO Agreement. Until such time, the provisions of Article VII of the 1988 Agreement shall apply to consultations and dispute settlement under this agreement, which provisions are hereby incorporated in the Agreement by reference for that purpose. These provisions shall be applied under the auspices of the Committee under this Agreement.

(e) Prior to the date of entry into force of the WTO Agreement, references to WTO bodies shall be construed as referring to the corresponding GATT body and references to the Director–General of the WTO and to the WTO Secretariat shall be construed as references to, respec-

---

8. For the purpose of this Agreement, the term "government" is deemed to include the competent authorities of the European Communities.

9. All provisions of the 1988 Agreement except the Preamble, Article VII and Article IX other than paragraphs 5(a) and (b) and paragraph 10.

tively, the Director–General to the CONTRACTING PARTIES to GATT 1947 and to the GATT Secretariat.

4. *Reservations*

Reservations may not be entered in respect of any of the provisions of this Agreement.

5. *National Legislation*

(a) Each government accepting or acceding to this Agreement shall ensure, not later than the date of entry into force of this Agreement for it, the conformity of its laws, regulations and administrative procedures, and the rules, procedures and practices applied by the entities contained in its lists annexed hereto, with the provisions of this Agreement.

(b) Each Party shall inform the Committee of any changes in its laws and regulations relevant to this Agreement and in the administration of such laws and regulations.

6. *Rectifications or Modifications*

(a) Rectifications, transfers of an entity from one Annex to another or, in exceptional cases, other modifications relating to Appendixes I through IV shall be notified to the Committee, along with information as to the likely consequences of the change for the mutually agreed coverage provided in this Agreement. If the rectifications, transfers or other modifications are of a purely formal or minor nature, they shall become effective provided there is no objection within 30 days. In other cases, the Chairman of the Committee shall promptly convene a meeting of the Committee. The Committee shall consider the proposal and any claim for compensatory adjustments, with a view to maintaining a balance of rights and obligations and a comparable level of mutually agreed coverage provided in this Agreement prior to such notification. In the event of agreement not being reached, the matter may be pursued in accordance with the provisions contained in Article XXII.

(b) Where a Party wishes, in exercise of its rights, to withdraw an entity from Appendix I on the grounds that government control or influence over it has been effectively eliminated, that Party shall notify the Committee. Such modification shall become effective the day after the end of the following meeting of the Committee, provided that the meeting is no sooner than 30 days from the date of notification and no objection has been made. In the event of an objection, the matter may be pursued in accordance with the procedures on consultations and dispute settlement contained in Article XXII. In considering the proposed modification to Appendix I and any consequential compensatory adjustment, allowance shall be made for the market-opening effects of the removal of government control or influence.

7. *Reviews, Negotiations and Future Work*

(a) The Committee shall review annually the implementation and operation of this Agreement taking into account the objectives thereof.

The Committee shall annually inform the General Council of the WTO of developments during the periods covered by such reviews.

(b) Not later than the end of the third year from the date of entry into force of the Agreement and periodically thereafter, the Parties thereto shall undertake further negotiations, with a view to improving this Agreement and achieving the greatest possible extension of its coverage among all Parties on the basis of mutual reciprocity, having regard to the provisions of Article V relating to developing countries.

(c) parties shall seek to avoid introducing or prolonging discriminatory measures and practices which distort open procurement and shall, in the context of negotiations under subparagraph (b), seek to eliminate those which remain on the date of entry into force of this Agreement.

8. *Information Technology*

With a view to ensuring that the Agreement does not constitute an unnecessary obstacle to technical progress, Parties shall consult regularly in the Committee regarding developments in the use of information technology in government procurement and shall, if necessary, negotiate modifications to the Agreement. These consultations shall in particular aim to ensure that the use of information technology promotes the aims of open, non-discriminatory and efficient government procurement through transparent procedures, that contracts covered under the Agreement are clearly identified and that all available information relating to a particular contract can be identified. When a Party intends to innovate, it shall endeavour to take into account the views expressed by other Parties regarding any potential problems.

9. *Amendments*

Parties may amend this Agreement having regard, *inter alia*, to the experience gained in its implementation. Such an amendment, once the Parties have concurred in accordance with the procedures established by the Committee, shall not enter into force for any Party until it has been accepted by such Party.

10. *Withdrawal*

(a) Any party may withdraw from this Agreement. The withdrawal shall take effect upon the expiration of 60 days from the date on which written notice of withdrawal is received by the Director–General of the WTO. Any Party may upon such notification request an immediate meeting of the Committee.

(b) If a party to this Agreement does not become a Member of the WTO within one year of the date of entry into force of the WTO Agreement or ceases to be a Member of the WTO, it shall cease to be a Party to this Agreement with effect from the same date.

11. *Non-application of This Agreement Between Particular Parties*

This Agreement shall not apply as between any two Parties if either of the Parties, at the time either accepts or accedes to this Agreement, does not consent to such application.

12. *Notes, Appendices and Annexes*

The Notes, Appendices and Annexes to this Agreement constitute an integral part thereof.

13. *Secretariat*

This Agreement shall be serviced by the WTO Secretariat.

14. *Deposit*

This Agreement shall be deposited with the Director–General of the WTO, who shall promptly furnish to each party a certified true copy of this Agreement, of each rectification or modification thereto pursuant to paragraph 6 and of each amendment thereto pursuant to paragraph 9, and a notification of each acceptance thereof or accession thereto pursuant to paragraphs 1 and 2 and of each withdrawal therefrom pursuant to paragraph 10 of this Article.

15. *Registration*

This Agreement shall be registered in accordance with the provisions of Article 102 of the Charter of the United Nations.

Done at Marrakesh this fifteenth day of April one thousand nine hundred and ninety-four in a single copy, in the English, French and Spanish languages, each text being authentic, except as otherwise specified with respect to the Appendices hereto.

NOTES

The terms "country" or "countries" as used in this Agreement, including the Appendices, are to be understood to include any separate customs territory Party to this Agreement.

In the case of a separate customs territory Party to this Agreement, where an expression in this Agreement is qualified by the term "national", such expression shall be read as pertaining to that customs territory, unless otherwise specified.

Article 1, paragraph 1

Having regard to general policy considerations relating to tied aid, including the objective of developing countries with respect to the untying of such aid, this Agreement does not apply to procurement made in furtherance of tied aid to developing countries so long as it is practised by Parties.

Item 22

DECISION ON MEASURES IN FAVOUR OF LEAST–DEVELOPED COUNTRIES

Ministers,

Recognizing the plight of the least-developed countries and the need to ensure their effective participation in the world trading system, and to take further measures to improve their trading opportunities;

Recognizing the specific needs of the least-developed countries in the area of market access where continued preferential access remains an essential means for improving their trading opportunities;

Reaffirming their commitment to implement fully the provisions concerning the least-developed countries contained in paragraphs 2(*d.*), 6 and 8 of the Decision of 28 November 1979 on Differential and More Favourable Treatment, Reciprocity and Fuller Participation of Developing Countries;

Having regard to the commitment of the participants as set out in Section B (vii) of Part I of the Punta del Este Ministerial Declaration;

1. *Decide* that, if not already provided for in the instruments negotiated in the course of the Uruguay Round, notwithstanding their acceptance of these instruments, the least-developed countries, and for so long as they remain in that category, while complying with the general rules set out in the aforesaid instruments, will only be required to undertake commitments and concessions to the extent consistent with their individual development, financial and trade needs, or their administrative and institutional capabilities. The least-developed countries shall be given additional time of one year from 15 April 1994 to submit their schedules as required in Article XI of the Agreement Establishing the World Trade Organization.

2. *Agree* that:

(i) Expeditious implementation of all special and differential measures taken in favour of least-developed countries including those taken within the context of the Uruguay Round shall be ensured through, *inter alia*, regular reviews.

(ii) To the extent possible, MFN concessions on tariff and non-tariff measures agreed in the Uruguay Round on products of export interest to the least-developed countries may be implemented autonomously, in advance and without staging. Consideration shall be given to further improve GSP and other schemes for products of particular export interest to least-developed countries.

(iii) The rules set out in the various agreements and instruments and the transitional provisions in the Uruguay Round should be applied in a flexible and supportive manner for the least-developed countries. To this effect, sympathetic consideration shall be given to specific and

422

motivated concerns raised by the least-developed countries in the appropriate Councils and Committees.

(iv) In the application of import relief measures and other measures referred to in paragraph 3(c) of Article XXXVII of GATT 1947 and the corresponding provision of GATT 1994, special consideration shall be given to the export interests of least-developed countries.

(v) Least-developed countries shall be accorded substantially increased technical assistance in the development, strengthening and diversification of their production and export bases including those of services, as well as in trade promotion, to enable them to maximize the benefits from liberalized access to markets.

3. *Agree* to keep under review the specific needs of the least-developed countries and to continue to seek the adoption of positive measures which facilitate the expansion of trading opportunities in favour of these countries.

Item 23

DECLARATION ON THE CONTRIBUTION OF THE WORLD TRADE ORGANIZATION TO ACHIEVING GREATER COHERENCE IN GLOBAL ECONOMIC POLICYMAKING

1. *Ministers recognize* that the globalization of the world economy has led to ever-growing interactions between the economic policies pursued by individual countries, including interactions between the structural, macroeconomic, trade, financial and development aspects of economic policymaking. The task of achieving harmony between these policies falls primarily on governments at the national level, but their coherence internationally is an important and valuable element in increasing the effectiveness of these policies at national level. The Agreements reached in the Uruguay Round show that all the participating governments recognize the contribution that liberal trading policies can make to the healthy growth and development of their own economies and of the world economy as a whole.

2. Successful cooperation in each area of economic policy contributes to progress in other areas. Greater exchange rate stability, based on more orderly underlying economic and financial conditions, should contribute towards the expansion of trade, sustainable growth and development, and the correction of external imbalances. There is also a need for an adequate and timely flow of concessional and non-concessional financial and real investment resources to developing countries and for further efforts to address debt problems, to help ensure economic growth and development. Trade liberalization forms an increasingly important component in the success of the adjustment programmes that many countries are undertaking, often involving significant transitional social costs. In this connection, Ministers note the role of the World Bank and the IMF in supporting adjustment to trade liberalization, including support to net food-importing developing countries facing short-term costs arising from agricultural trade reforms.

3. The positive outcome of the Uruguay Round is a major contribution towards more coherent and complementary international economic policies. The results of the Uruguay Round ensure an expansion of market access to the benefit of all countries, as well as a framework of strengthened multilateral disciplines for trade. They also guarantee that trade policy will be conducted in a more transparent manner and with greater awareness of the benefits for domestic competitiveness of an open trading environment. The strengthened multilateral trading system emerging from the Uruguay Round has the capacity to provide an improved forum for liberalization, to contribute to more effective surveillance, and to ensure strict observance of multilaterally agreed rules and disciplines. These improvements mean that trade policy can in the future play a more substantial role in ensuring the coherence of global economic policymaking.

4. *Ministers recognize*, however, that difficulties the origins of which lie outside the trade field cannot be redressed through measures taken in the trade field alone. This underscores the importance of efforts to improve other elements of global economic policymaking to complement the effective implementation of the results achieved in the Uruguay Round.

5. The interlinkages between the different aspects of economic policy require that the international institutions with responsibilities in each of these areas follow consistent and mutually supportive policies. The World Trade Organization should therefore pursue and develop cooperation with the international organizations responsible for monetary and financial matters, while respecting the mandate, the confidentiality requirements and the necessary autonomy in decision-making procedures of each institution, and avoiding the imposition on governments of cross-conditionality or additional conditions. Ministers further invite the Director–General of the WTO to review with the Managing Director of the International Monetary Fund and the President of the World Bank, the implications of the WTO's responsibilities for its cooperation with the Bretton Woods institutions, as well as the forms such cooperation might take, with a view to achieving greater coherence in global economic policymaking.

Item 24

DECISION ON NOTIFICATION PROCEDURES

Ministers decide to recommend adoption by the Ministerial Conference of the decision on improvement and review of notification procedures set out below.

Members,

Desiring to improve the operation of notification procedures under the Agreement Establishing the World Trade Organization (hereinafter referred to as the "WTO Agreement"), and thereby to contribute to the transparency of Members' trade policies and to the effectiveness of surveillance arrangements established to that end;

Recalling obligations under the WTO Agreement to publish and notify, including obligations assumed under the terms of specific protocols of accession, waivers, and other agreements entered into by Members;

Agree as follows:

I. *General obligation to notify*

Members affirm their commitment to obligations under the Multilateral Trade Agreements and, where applicable, the Plurilateral Trade Agreements, regarding publication and notification.

Members recall their undertakings set out in the Understanding Regarding Notification, Consultation, Dispute Settlement and Surveillance adopted on 28 November 1979 (BISD 26S/210). With regard to their undertaking therein to notify, to the maximum extent possible, their adoption of trade measures affecting the operation of GATT 1994, such notification itself being without prejudice to views on the consistency of measures with or their relevance to rights and obligations under the Multilateral Trade Agreements and, where applicable, the Plurilateral Trade Agreements, Members agree to be guided, as appropriate, by the annexed list of measures. Members therefore agree that the introduction or modification of such measures is subject to the notification requirements of the 1979 Understanding.

II. *Central registry of notifications*

A central registry of notifications shall be established under the responsibility of the Secretariat. While Members will continue to follow existing notification procedures, the Secretariat shall ensure that the central registry records such elements of the information provided on the measure by the Member concerned as its purpose, its trade coverage, and the requirement under which it has been notified. The central registry shall cross-reference its records of notifications by Member and obligation.

The central registry shall inform each Member annually of the regular notification obligations to which that Member will be expected to respond in the course of the following year.

The central registry shall draw the attention of individual Members to regular notification requirements which remain unfulfilled.

Information in the central registry regarding individual notifications shall be made available on request to any Member entitled to receive the notification concerned.

III. *Review of notification obligations and procedures*

The Council for Trade in Goods will undertake a review of notification obligations and procedures under the Agreements in Annex 1A of the WTO Agreement. The review will be carried out by a working group, membership in which will be open to all Members. The group will be established immediately after the date of entry into force of the WTO Agreement.

The terms of reference of the working group will be:

— to undertake a thorough review of all existing notification obligations of Members established under the Agreements in Annex 1A of the WTO Agreement, with a view to simplifying, standardizing and consolidating these obligations to the greatest extent practicable, as well as to improving compliance with these obligations, bearing in mind the overall objective of improving the transparency of the trade policies of Members and the effectiveness of surveillance arrangements established to this end, and also bearing in mind the possible need of some developing country Members for assistance in meeting their notification obligations;

— to make recommendations to the Council for Trade in Goods not later than two years after the entry into force of the WTO Agreement.

ANNEX
INDICATIVE LIST [1] OF NOTIFIABLE MEASURES

Tariffs (including range and scope of bindings, GSP provisions, rates applied to members of free-trade areas/customs unions, other preferences)

Tariff quotas and surcharges

Quantitative restrictions, including voluntary export restraints and orderly marketing arrangements affecting imports

Other non-tariff measures such as licensing and mixing requirements; variable levies

Customs valuation

Rules of origin

Government procurement

Technical barriers

Safeguard actions

Anti-dumping actions

Countervailing actions

1. This list does not alter existing notification requirements in the Multilateral Trade Agreements in Annex 1A to the WTO Agreement or, where applicable, the Plurilateral Trade Agreements in Annex 4 of the WTO Agreement.

Export taxes

Export subsidies, tax exemptions and concessionary export financing

Free-trade zones, including in-bond manufacturing

Export restrictions, including voluntary export restraints and orderly marketing arrangements

Other government assistance, including subsidies, tax exemptions

Role of state-trading enterprises

Foreign exchange controls related to imports and exports

Government-mandated countertrade

Any other measure covered by the Multilateral Trade Agreements in Annex
1A to the WTO Agreement

Item 25

DECLARATION ON THE RELATIONSHIP OF THE WORLD TRADE ORGANIZATION WITH THE INTERNATIONAL MONETARY FUND

Ministers,

Noting the close relationship between the CONTRACTING PARTIES to the GATT 1947 and the International Monetary Fund, and the provisions of the GATT 1947 governing that relationship, in particular Article XV of the GATT 1947;

Recognizing the desire of participants to base the relationship of the World Trade Organization with the International Monetary Fund, with regard to the areas covered by the Multilateral Trade Agreements in Annex 1A of the WTO Agreement, on the provisions that have governed the relationship of the CONTRACTING PARTIES to the GATT 1947 with the International Monetary Fund;

Hereby *reaffirm* that, unless otherwise provided for in the Final Act, the relationship of the WTO with the International Monetary Fund, with regard to the areas covered by the Multilateral Trade Agreements in Annex 1A of the WTO Agreement, will be based on the provisions that have governed the relationship of the CONTRACTING PARTIES to the GATT 1947 with the International Monetary Fund.

Item 26

DECISION ON MEASURES CONCERNING THE POSSIBLE NEGATIVE EFFECTS OF THE REFORM PROGRAMME ON LEAST-DEVELOPED AND NET FOOD-IMPORTING DEVELOPING COUNTRIES

1. *Ministers recognize* that the progressive implementation of the results of the Uruguay Round as a whole will generate increasing opportunities for trade expansion and economic growth to the benefit of all participants.

2. *Ministers recognize* that during the reform programme leading to greater liberalization of trade in agriculture least-developed and net food-importing developing countries may experience negative effects in terms of the availability of adequate supplies of basic foodstuffs from external sources on reasonable terms and conditions, including short-term difficulties in financing normal levels of commercial imports of basic foodstuffs.

3. *Ministers* accordingly *agree* to establish appropriate mechanisms to ensure that the implementation of the results of the Uruguay Round on trade in agriculture does not adversely affect the availability of food aid at a level which is sufficient to continue to provide assistance in meeting the food needs of developing countries, especially least-developed and net food-importing developing countries. To this end *Ministers agree*:

(i) to review the level of food aid established periodically by the Committee on Food Aid under the Food Aid Convention 1986 and to initiate negotiations in the appropriate forum to establish a level of food aid commitments sufficient to meet the legitimate needs of developing countries during the reform programme;

(ii) to adopt guidelines to ensure that an increasing proportion of basic foodstuffs is provided to least-developed and net food-importing developing countries in fully grant form and/or on appropriate concessional terms in line with Article IV of the Food Aid Convention 1986;

(iii) to give full consideration in the context of their aid programmes to requests for the provision of technical and financial assistance to least-developed and net food-importing developing countries to improve their agricultural productivity and infrastructure.

4. *Ministers* further *agree* to ensure that any agreement relating to agricultural export credits makes appropriate provision for differential treatment in favour of least-developed and net food-importing developing countries.

5. *Ministers recognize* that as a result of the Uruguay Round certain developing countries may experience short-term difficulties in financing normal levels of commercial imports and that these countries may be eligible to draw on the resources of international financial institutions under existing

430

facilities, or such facilities as may be established, in the context of adjustment programmes, in order to address such financing difficulties. In this regard Ministers take note of paragraph 37 of the report of the Director–General to the CONTRACTING PARTIES to GATT 1947 on his consultations with the Managing Director of the International Monetary Fund and the President of the World Bank (MTN.GNG/NG 14/W/35).

6. The provisions of this Decision will be subject to regular review by the Ministerial Conference, and the follow-up to this Decision shall be monitored, as appropriate, by the Committee on Agriculture.

Item 27

DECISION ON NOTIFICATION OF FIRST INTE-GRATION UNDER ARTICLE 2.6 OF THE AGREE-MENT ON TEXTILES AND CLOTHING

Ministers agree that the participants maintaining restrictions falling under paragraph 1 of Article 2 of the Agreement on Textiles and Clothing shall notify full details of the actions to be taken pursuant to paragraph 6 of Article 2 of that Agreement to the GATT Secretariat not later than 1 October 1994. The GATT Secretariat shall promptly circulate these notifications to the other participants for information. These notifications will be made available to the Textiles Monitoring Body, when established, for the purposes of paragraph 21 of Article 2 of the Agreement on Textiles and Clothing.

Item 28

DECISIONS RELATING TO THE AGREEMENT ON TECHNICAL BARRIERS TO TRADE

DECISION ON PROPOSED UNDERSTANDING ON WTO–ISO STANDARDS INFORMATION SYSTEM

Ministers decide to recommend that the Secretariat of the World Trade Organization reach an understanding with the International Organization for Standardization ("ISO") to establish an information system under which:

1. ISONET members shall transmit to the ISO/IEC Information Centre in Geneva the notifications referred to in paragraphs C and J of the Code of Good Practice for the Preparation, Adoption and Application of Standards in Annex 3 to the Agreement on Technical Barriers to Trade, in the manner indicated there;

2. the following (alpha)numeric classification systems shall be used in the work programmes referred to in paragraph J:

    (a) *a standards classification system* which would allow standardizing bodies to give for each standard mentioned in the work programme an (alpha)numeric indication of the subject matter;

    (b) *a stage code system* which would allow standardizing bodies to give for each standard mentioned in the work programme an (alpha)numeric indication of the stage of development of the standard; for this purpose, at least five stages of development should be distinguished: (*1*) the stage at which the decision to develop a standard has been taken, but technical work has not yet begun; (*2*) the stage at which technical work has begun, but the period for the submission of comments has not yet started; (*3*) the stage at which the period for the submission of comments has started, but has not yet been completed; (*4*) the stage at which the period for the submission of comments has been completed, but the standard has not yet been adopted; and (*5*) the stage at which the standard has been adopted;

    (c) *an identification system* covering all international standards which would allow standardizing bodies to give for each standard mentioned in the work programme an (alpha)numeric indication of the international standard(s) used as a basis;

3. the ISO/IEC Information Centre shall promptly convey to the Secretariat copies of any notifications referred to in paragraph C of the Code of Good Practice;

4. the ISO/IEC Information Centre shall regularly publish the information received in the notifications made to it under paragraphs C and J of the Code of Good Practice; this publication, for which a reasonable fee

may be charged, shall be available to ISONET members and through the Secretariat to the Members of the WTO.

DECISION ON REVIEW OF THE ISO/IEC INFORMATION CENTRE PUBLICATION

Ministers decide that in conformity with paragraph 1 of Article 13 of the Agreement on Technical Barriers to Trade in Annex 1A of the Agreement Establishing the World Trade Organization, the Committee on Technical Barriers to Trade established thereunder shall, without prejudice to provisions on consultation and dispute settlement, at least once a year review the publication provided by the ISO/IEC Information Centre on information received according to the Code of Good Practice for the Preparation, Adoption and Application of Standards in Annex 3 of the Agreement, for the purpose of affording Members opportunity of discussing any matters relating to the operation of that Code.

In order to facilitate this discussion, the Secretariat shall provide a list by Member of all standardizing bodies that have accepted the Code, as well as a list of those standardizing bodies that have accepted or withdrawn from the Code since the previous review.

The Secretariat shall also distribute promptly to the Members copies of the notifications it receives from the ISO/IEC Information Centre.

Item 29

DECISIONS AND DECLARATIONS RELATING TO THE AGREEMENT ON IMPLEMENTATION OF ARTICLE VI OF THE GENERAL AGREEMENT ON TARIFFS AND TRADE 1994

DECISION ON ANTI–CIRCUMVENTION

Ministers,

Noting that while the problem of circumvention of anti-dumping duty measures formed part of the negotiations which preceded the Agreement on Implementation of Article VI of GATT 1994, negotiators were unable to agree on specific text,

Mindful of the desirability of the applicability of uniform rules in this area as soon as possible,

Decide to refer this matter to the Committee on Anti–Dumping Practices established under that Agreement for resolution.

DECISION ON REVIEW OF ARTICLE 17.6 OF THE AGREEMENT ON IMPLEMENTATION OF ARTICLE VI OF THE GENERAL AGREEMENT ON TARIFFS AND TRADE 1994

Ministers decide as follows:

The standard of review in paragraph 6 of Article 17 of the Agreement on Implementation of Article VI of GATT 1994 shall be reviewed after a period of three years with a view to considering the question of whether it is capable of general application.

Ed. Note: This issue was raised in the DSV review. See Item 33. No action was taken.

DECLARATION ON DISPUTE SETTLEMENT PURSUANT TO THE AGREEMENT ON IMPLEMENTATION OF ARTICLE VI OF THE GENERAL AGREEMENT ON TARIFFS AND TRADE 1994 OR PART V OF THE AGREEMENT ON SUBSIDIES AND COUNTERVAILING MEASURES

Ministers recognize, with respect to dispute settlement pursuant to the Agreement on Implementation of Article VI of GATT 1994 or Part V of the Agreement on Subsidies and Countervailing Measures, the need for the consistent resolution of disputes arising from anti-dumping and countervailing duty measures.

Item 30

DECISIONS RELATING TO THE AGREEMENT ON IMPLEMENTATION OF ARTICLE VII OF THE GENERAL AGREEMENT ON TARIFFS AND TRADE 1994

DECISION REGARDING CASES WHERE CUSTOMS ADMINISTRATIONS HAVE REASONS TO DOUBT THE TRUTH OR ACCURACY OF THE DECLARED VALUE

Ministers invite the Committee on Customs Valuation established under the Agreement on Implementation of Article VII of GATT 1994 to take the following decision:

The Committee on Customs Valuation,

Reaffirming that the transaction value is the primary basis of valuation under the Agreement on Implementation of Article VII of GATT 1994 (hereinafter referred to as the "Agreement");

Recognizing that the customs administration may have to address cases where it has reason to doubt the truth or accuracy of the particulars or of documents produced by traders in support of a declared value;

Emphasizing that in so doing the customs administration should not prejudice the legitimate commercial interests of traders;

Taking into account Article 17 of the Agreement, paragraph 6 of Annex III to the Agreement, and the relevant decisions of the Technical Committee on Customs Valuation;

Decides as follows:

1. When a declaration has been presented and where the customs administration has reason to doubt the truth or accuracy of the particulars or of documents produced in support of this declaration, the customs administration may ask the importer to provide further explanation, including documents or other evidence, that the declared value represents the total amount actually paid or payable for the imported goods, adjusted in accordance with the provisions of Article 8. If, after receiving further information, or in the absence of a response, the customs administration still has reasonable doubts about the truth or accuracy of the declared value, it may, bearing in mind the provisions of Article 11, be deemed that the customs value of the imported goods cannot be determined under the provisions of Article 1. Before taking a final decision, the customs administration shall communicate to the importer, in writing if requested, its grounds for doubting the truth or accuracy of the particulars or documents produced and the importer shall be given a reasonable opportunity to respond. When a final decision is made, the customs administration shall communicate to the importer in writing its decision and the grounds therefor.

2. It is entirely appropriate in applying the Agreement for one Member to assist another Member on mutually agreed terms.

DECISION ON TEXTS RELATING TO MINIMUM VALUES AND IMPORTS BY SOLE AGENTS, SOLE DISTRIBUTORS AND SOLE CONCESSIONAIRES

Ministers decide to refer the following texts to the Committee on Customs Valuation established under the Agreement on Implementation of Article VII of GATT 1994, for adoption.

I

Where a developing country makes a reservation to retain officially established minimum values within the terms of paragraph 2 of Annex III and shows good cause, the Committee shall give the request for the reservation sympathetic consideration.

Where a reservation is consented to, the terms and conditions referred to in paragraph 2 of Annex III shall take full account of the development, financial and trade needs of the developing country concerned.

II

1. A number of developing countries have a concern that problems may exist in the valuation of imports by sole agents, sole distributors and sole concessionaires. Under paragraph 1 of Article 20, developing country Members have a period of delay of up to five years prior to the application of the Agreement. In this context, developing country Members availing themselves of this provision could use the period to conduct appropriate studies and to take such other actions as are necessary to facilitate application.

2. In consideration of this, the Committee recommends that the Customs Co-operation Council assist developing country Members, in accordance with the provisions of Annex II, to formulate and conduct studies in areas identified as being of potential concern, including those relating to importations by sole agents, sole distributors and sole concessionaires.

Item 31

DECISIONS RELATING TO THE
GENERAL AGREEMENT ON
TRADE IN SERVICES

DECISION ON INSTITUTIONAL ARRANGEMENTS FOR THE
GENERAL AGREEMENT ON TRADE IN SERVICES

Ministers decide to recommend that the Council for Trade in Services at its first meeting adopt the decision on subsidiary bodies set out below.

The Council for Trade in Services,

Acting pursuant to Article XXIV with a view to facilitating the operation and furthering the objectives of the General Agreement on Trade in Services,

Decides as follows:

1. Any subsidiary bodies that the Council may establish shall report to the Council annually or more often as necessary. Each such body shall establish its own rules of procedure, and may set up its own subsidiary bodies as appropriate.

2. Any sectoral committee shall carry out responsibilities as assigned to it by the Council, and shall afford Members the opportunity to consult on any matters relating to trade in services in the sector concerned and the operation of the sectoral annex to which it may pertain. Such responsibilities shall include:

(a) to keep under continuous review and surveillance the application of the Agreement with respect to the sector concerned;

(b) to formulate proposals or recommendations for consideration by the Council in connection with any matter relating to trade in the sector concerned;

(c) if there is an annex pertaining to the sector, to consider proposals for amendment of that sectoral annex, and to make appropriate recommendations to the Council;

(d) to provide a forum for technical discussions, to conduct studies on measures of Members and to conduct examinations of any other technical matters affecting trade in services in the sector concerned;

(e) to provide technical assistance to developing country Members and developing countries negotiating accession to the Agreement Establishing the World Trade Organization in respect of the application of obligations or other matters affecting trade in services in the sector concerned; and

(f) to cooperate with any other subsidiary bodies established under the General Agreement on Trade in Services or any international organizations active in any sector concerned.

3. There is hereby established a Committee on Trade in Financial Services which will have the responsibilities listed in paragraph 2.

DECISION ON CERTAIN DISPUTE SETTLEMENT PROCEDURES FOR THE GENERAL AGREEMENT ON TRADE IN SERVICES

Ministers decide to recommend that the Council for Trade in Services at its first meeting adopt the decision set out below.

The Council for Trade in Services,

Taking into account the specific nature of the obligations and specific commitments of the Agreement, and of trade in services, with respect to dispute settlement under Articles XXII and XXIII,

Decides as follows:

1. A roster of panelists shall be established to assist in the selection of panelists.

2. To this end, Members may suggest names of individuals possessing the qualifications referred to in paragraph 3 for inclusion on the roster, and shall provide a curriculum vitae of their qualifications including, if applicable, indication of sector-specific expertise.

3. Panels shall be composed of well-qualified governmental and/or nongovernmental individuals who have experience in issues related to the General Agreement on Trade in Services and/or trade in services, including associated regulatory matters. Panelists shall serve in their individual capacities and not as representatives of any government or organisation.

4. Panels for disputes regarding sectoral matters shall have the necessary expertise relevant to the specific services sectors which the dispute concerns.

5. The Secretariat shall maintain the roster and shall develop procedures for its administration in consultation with the Chairman of the Council.

DECISION ON TRADE IN SERVICES AND THE ENVIRONMENT

Ministers decide to recommend that the Council for Trade in Services at its first meeting adopt the decision set out below.

The Council for Trade in Services,

Acknowledging that measures necessary to protect the environment may conflict with the provisions of the Agreement; and

Noting that since measures necessary to protect the environment typically have as their objective the protection of human, animal or plant life or health, it is not clear that there is a need to provide for more than is contained in paragraph (b) of Article XIV;

Decides as follows:

1. In order to determine whether any modification of Article XIV of the Agreement is required to take account of such measures, to request the Committee on Trade and Environment to examine and report, with recommendations if any, on the relationship between services trade and the environment including the issue of sustainable development. The Committee

shall also examine the relevance of inter-governmental agreements on the environment and their relationship to the Agreement.

2. The Committee shall report the results of its work to the first biennial meeting of the Ministerial Conference after the entry into force of the Agreement Establishing the World Trade Organization.

DECISION ON NEGOTIATIONS ON MOVEMENT OF NATURAL PERSONS

Ministers,

Noting the commitments resulting from the Uruguay Round negotiations on the movement of natural persons for the purpose of supplying services;

Mindful of the objectives of the General Agreement on Trade in Services, including the increasing participation of developing countries in trade in services and the expansion of their service exports;

Recognizing the importance of achieving higher levels of commitments on the movement of natural persons, in order to provide for a balance of benefits under the General Agreement on Trade in Services;

Decide as follows:

1. Negotiations on further liberalization of movement of natural persons for the purpose of supplying services shall continue beyond the conclusion of the Uruguay Round, with a view to allowing the achievement of higher levels of commitments by participants under the General Agreement on Trade in Services.

2. A Negotiating Group on Movement of Natural Persons is established to carry out the negotiations. The group shall establish its own procedures and shall report periodically to the Council on Trade in Services.

3. The negotiating group shall hold its first negotiating session no later than 16 May 1994. It shall conclude these negotiations and produce a final report no later than six months after the entry into force of the Agreement Establishing the World Trade Organization.

4. Commitments resulting from these negotiations shall be inscribed in Members' Schedules of specific commitments.

DECISION ON FINANCIAL SERVICES

Ministers,

Noting that commitments scheduled by participants on financial services at the conclusion of the Uruguay Round shall enter into force on an MFN basis at the same time as the Agreement Establishing the World Trade Organization (hereinafter referred to as the "WTO Agreement"),

Decide as follows:

1. At the conclusion of a period ending no later than six months after the date of entry into force of the WTO Agreement, Members shall be free to improve, modify or withdraw all or part of their commitments in this sector without offering compensation, notwithstanding the provisions of Article XXI of the General Agreement on Trade in Services. At the same time Members shall finalize their positions relating to MFN exemptions in this sector,

notwithstanding the provisions of the Annex on Article II Exemptions. From the date of entry into force of the WTO Agreement and until the end of the period referred to above, exemptions listed in the Annex on Article II Exemptions which are conditional upon the level of commitments undertaken by other participants or upon exemptions by other participants will not be applied.

2. The Committee on Trade in Financial Services shall monitor the progress of any negotiations undertaken under the terms of this Decision and shall report thereon to the Council for Trade in Services no later than four months after the date of entry into force of the WTO Agreement.

DECISION ON NEGOTIATIONS ON MARITIME TRANSPORT SERVICES

Ministers,

Noting that commitments scheduled by participants on maritime transport services at the conclusion of the Uruguay Round shall enter into force on an MFN basis at the same time as the Agreement Establishing the World Trade Organization (hereinafter referred to as the "WTO Agreement"),

Decide as follows:

1. Negotiations shall be entered into on a voluntary basis in the sector of maritime transport services within the framework of the General Agreement on Trade in Services. The negotiations shall be comprehensive in scope, aiming at commitments in international shipping, auxiliary services and access to and use of port facilities, leading to the elimination of restrictions within a fixed time scale.

2. A Negotiating Group on Maritime Transport Services (hereinafter referred to as the "NGMTS") is established to carry out this mandate. The NGMTS shall report periodically on the progress of these negotiations.

3. The negotiations in the NGMTS shall be open to all governments and the European Communities which announce their intention to participate. To date, the following have announced their intention to take part in the negotiations:

Argentina, Canada, European Communities and their member States, Finland, Hong Kong, Iceland, Indonesia, Korea, Malaysia, Mexico, New Zealand, Norway, Philippines, Poland, Romania, Singapore, Sweden, Switzerland, Thailand, Turkey, United States.

Further notifications of intention to participate shall be addressed to the depositary of the WTO Agreement.

4. The NGMTS shall hold its first negotiating session no later than 16 May 1994. It shall conclude these negotiations and make a final report no later than June 1996. The final report of the NGMTS shall include a date for the implementation of results of these negotiations.

5. Until the conclusion of the negotiations Article II and paragraphs 1 and 2 of the Annex on Article II Exemptions are suspended in their application to this sector, and it is not necessary to list MFN exemptions. At the conclusion of the negotiations, Members shall be free to improve, modify or withdraw any commitments made in this sector during the Uruguay Round

without offering compensation, notwithstanding the provisions of Article XXI of the Agreement. At the same time Members shall finalize their positions relating to MFN exemptions in this sector, notwithstanding the provisions of the Annex on Article II Exemptions. Should negotiations not succeed, the Council for Trade in Services shall decide whether to continue the negotiations in accordance with this mandate.

6. Any commitments resulting from the negotiations, including the date of their entry into force, shall be inscribed in the Schedules annexed to the General Agreement on Trade in Services and be subject to all the provisions of the Agreement.

7. Commencing immediately and continuing until the implementation date to be determined under paragraph 4, it is understood that participants shall not apply any measure affecting trade in maritime transport services except in response to measures applied by other countries and with a view to maintaining or improving the freedom of provision of maritime transport services, nor in such a manner as would improve their negotiating position and leverage.

8. The implementation of paragraph 7 shall be subject to surveillance in the NGMTS. Any participant may bring to the attention of the NGMTS any action or omission which it believes to be relevant to the fulfilment of paragraph 7. Such notifications shall be deemed to have been submitted to the NGMTS upon their receipt by the Secretariat.

DECISION ON NEGOTIATIONS ON BASIC TELECOMMUNICATIONS

Ministers decide as follows:

1. Negotiations shall be entered into on a voluntary basis with a view to the progressive liberalization of trade in telecommunications transport networks and services (hereinafter referred to as "basic telecommunications") within the framework of the General Agreement on Trade in Services.

2. Without prejudice to their outcome, the negotiations shall be comprehensive in scope, with no basic telecommunications excluded *a priori*.

3. A Negotiating Group on Basic Telecommunications (hereinafter referred to as the "NGBT") is established to carry out this mandate. The NGBT shall report periodically on the progress of these negotiations.

4. The negotiations in the NGBT shall be open to all governments and the European Communities which announce their intention to participate. To date, the following have announced their intention to take part in the negotiations:

> Australia, Austria, Canada, Chile, Cyprus, European Communities and their member States, Finland, Hong Kong, Hungary, Japan, Korea, Mexico, New Zealand, Norway, Slovak Republic, Sweden, Switzerland, Turkey, United States.

Further notifications of intention to participate shall be addressed to the depositary of the Agreement Establishing the World Trade Organization.

5. The NGBT shall hold its first negotiating session no later than 16 May 1994. It shall conclude these negotiations and make a final report no

later than 30 April 1996. The final report of the NGBT shall include a date for the implementation of results of these negotiations.

6. Any commitments resulting from the negotiations, including the date of their entry into force, shall be inscribed in the Schedules annexed to the General Agreement on Trade in Services and shall be subject to all the provisions of the Agreement.

7. Commencing immediately and continuing until the implementation date to be determined under paragraph 5, it is understood that no participant shall apply any measure affecting trade in basic telecommunications in such a manner as would improve its negotiating position and leverage. It is understood that this provision shall not prevent the pursuit of commercial and governmental arrangements regarding the provision of basic telecommunications services.

8. The implementation of paragraph 7 shall be subject to surveillance in the NGBT. Any participant may bring to the attention of the NGBT any action or omission which it believes to be relevant to the fulfilment of paragraph 7. Such notifications shall be deemed to have been submitted to the NGBT upon their receipt by the Secretariat.

DECISION ON PROFESSIONAL SERVICES

Ministers decide to recommend that the Council for Trade in Services at its first meeting adopt the decision set out below.

The Council for Trade in Services,

Recognizing the impact of regulatory measures relating to professional qualifications, technical standards and licensing on the expansion of trade in professional services;

Desiring to establish multilateral disciplines with a view to ensuring that, when specific commitments are undertaken, such regulatory measures do not constitute unnecessary barriers to the supply of professional services;

Decides as follows:

1. The work programme foreseen in paragraph 4 of Article VI on Domestic Regulation should be put into effect immediately. To this end, a Working Party on Professional Services shall be established to examine and report, with recommendations, on the disciplines necessary to ensure that measures relating to qualification requirements and procedures, technical standards and licensing requirements in the field of professional services do not constitute unnecessary barriers to trade.

2. As a matter of priority, the Working Party shall make recommendations for the elaboration of multilateral disciplines in the accountancy sector, so as to give operational effect to specific commitments. In making these recommendations, the Working Party shall concentrate on:

    (a) developing multilateral disciplines relating to market access so as to ensure that domestic regulatory requirements are: (*i*) based on objective and transparent criteria, such as competence and the ability to supply the service; (*ii*) not more burdensome than necessary to ensure the quality of the service, thereby facilitating the effective liberalization of accountancy services;

(b) the use of international standards and, in doing so, it shall encourage the cooperation with the relevant international organizations as defined under paragraph 5(b) of Article VI, so as to give full effect to paragraph 5 of Article VII;

(c) facilitating the effective application of paragraph 6 of Article VI of the Agreement by establishing guidelines for the recognition of qualifications.

In elaborating these disciplines, the Working Party shall take account of the importance of the governmental and non-governmental bodies regulating professional services.

Item 32

DECISION ON ACCESSION TO THE AGREEMENT ON GOVERNMENT PROCUREMENT

1. *Ministers invite* the Committee on Government Procurement established under the Agreement on Government Procurement in Annex 4(b) of the Agreement Establishing the World Trade Organization to clarify that:

(a) a Member interested in accession according to paragraph 2 of Article XXIV of the Agreement on Government Procurement would communicate its interest to the Director–General of the WTO, submitting relevant information, including a coverage offer for incorporation in Appendix I having regard to the relevant provisions of the Agreement, in particular Article I and, where appropriate, Article V;

(b) the communication would be circulated to Parties to the Agreement;

(c) the Member interested in accession would hold consultations with the Parties on the terms for its accession to the Agreement;

(d) with a view to facilitating accession, the Committee would establish a working party if the Member in question, or any of the Parties to the Agreement, so requests. The working party should examine: (*i*) the coverage offer made by the applicant Member; and (*ii*) relevant information pertaining to export opportunities in the markets of the Parties, taking into account the existing and potential export capabilities of the applicant Member and export opportunities for the Parties in the market of the applicant Member;

(e) upon a decision by the Committee agreeing to the terms of accession including the coverage lists of the acceding Member, the acceding Member would deposit with the Director–General of the WTO an instrument of accession which states the terms so agreed. The acceding Member's coverage lists in English, French and Spanish would be appended to the Agreement;

(f) prior to the date of entry into force of the WTO Agreement, the above procedures would apply *mutatis mutandis* to contracting parties to the GATT 1947 interested in accession, and the tasks assigned to the Director–General of the WTO would be carried out by the Director–General to the CONTRACTING PARTIES to the GATT 1947.

2. It is noted that Committee decisions are arrived at on the basis of consensus. It is also noted that the non-application clause of paragraph 11 of Article XXIV is available to any Party.

Item 33

DECISION ON THE APPLICATION AND REVIEW OF THE UNDERSTANDING ON RULES AND PROCEDURES GOVERNING THE SETTLEMENT OF DISPUTES

Ministers,

Recalling the Decision of 22 February 1994 that existing rules and procedures of GATT 1947 in the field of dispute settlement shall remain in effect until the date of entry into force of the Agreement Establishing the World Trade Organization,

Invite the relevant Councils and Committees to decide that they shall remain in operation for the purpose of dealing with any dispute for which the request for consultation was made before that date;

Invite the Ministerial Conference to complete a full review of dispute settlement rules and procedures under the World Trade Organization within four years after the entry into force of the Agreement Establishing the World Trade Organization, and to take a decision on the occasion of its first meeting after the completion of the review, whether to continue, modify or terminate such dispute settlement rules and procedures.

Ed. Note: The review ended in July 1999, and no action was taken.

Item 34

UNDERSTANDING ON COMMITMENTS IN FINANCIAL SERVICES

Participants in the Uruguay Round have been enabled to take on specific commitments with respect to financial services under the General Agreement on Trade in Services (hereinafter referred to as the "Agreement") on the basis of an alternative approach to that covered by the provisions of Part III of the Agreement. It was agreed that this approach could be applied subject to the following understanding:

(i) it does not conflict with the provisions of the Agreement;

(ii) it does not prejudice the right of any Member to schedule its specific commitments in accordance with the approach under Part III of the Agreement;

(iii) resulting specific commitments shall apply on a most-favoured-nation basis;

(iv) no presumption has been created as to the degree of liberalization to which a Member is committing itself under the Agreement.

Interested Members, on the basis of negotiations, and subject to conditions and qualifications where specified, have inscribed in their schedule specific commitments conforming to the approach set out below.

A. *Standstill*

Any conditions, limitations and qualifications to the commitments noted below shall be limited to existing non-conforming measures.

B. *Market Access*

Monopoly Rights

1. In addition to Article VIII of the Agreement, the following shall apply:

Each Member shall list in its schedule pertaining to financial services existing monopoly rights and shall endeavour to eliminate them or reduce their scope. Notwithstanding subparagraph 1(b) of the Annex on Financial Services, this paragraph applies to the activities referred to in subparagraph 1(b)(iii) of the Annex.

Financial Services Purchased by Public Entities

2. Notwithstanding Article XIII of the Agreement, each Member shall ensure that financial service suppliers of any other Member established in its territory are accorded most-favoured-nation treatment and national treatment as regards the purchase or acquisition of financial services by public entities of the Member in its territory.

Cross–Border Trade

3. Each Member shall permit non-resident suppliers of financial services to supply, as a principal, through an intermediary or as an intermediary, and under terms and conditions that accord national treatment, the following services:

(a) insurance of risks relating to:

(i) maritime shipping and commercial aviation and space launching and freight (including satellites), with such insurance to cover any or all of the following: the goods being transported, the vehicle transporting the goods and any liability arising therefrom; and

(ii) goods in international transit;

(b) reinsurance and retrocession and the services auxiliary to insurance as referred to in subparagraph 5(a)(iv) of the Annex;

(c) provision and transfer of financial information and financial data processing as referred to in subparagraph 5(a)(xv) of the Annex and advisory and other auxiliary services, excluding intermediation, relating to banking and other financial services as referred to in subparagraph 5(a)(xvi) of the Annex.

4. Each Member shall permit its residents to purchase in the territory of any other Member the financial services indicated in:

(a) subparagraph 3(a);

(b) subparagraph 3(b); and

(c) subparagraphs 5(a)(v) to (xvi) of the Annex.

Commercial Presence

5. Each Member shall grant financial service suppliers of any other Member the right to establish or expand within its territory, including through the acquisition of existing enterprises, a commercial presence.

6. A Member may impose terms, conditions and procedures for authorization of the establishment and expansion of a commercial presence in so far as they do not circumvent the Member's obligation under paragraph 5 and they are consistent with the other obligations of the Agreement.

New Financial Services

7. A Member shall permit financial service suppliers of any other Member established in its territory to offer in its territory any new financial service.

Transfers of Information and Processing of Information

8. No Member shall take measures that prevent transfers of information or the processing of financial information, including transfers of data by electronic means, or that, subject to importation rules consistent with international agreements, prevent transfers of equipment, where such transfers of information, processing of financial information or transfers of equipment are necessary for the conduct of the ordinary business of a financial service supplier. Nothing in this paragraph restricts the right of a Member to protect personal data, personal privacy and the confidentiality of individual

records and accounts so long as such right is not used to circumvent the provisions of the Agreement.

Temporary Entry of Personnel

9. (a) Each Member shall permit temporary entry into its territory of the following personnel of a financial service supplier of any other Member that is establishing or has established a commercial presence in the territory of the Member:

(i) senior managerial personnel possessing proprietary information essential to the establishment, control and operation of the services of the financial service supplier; and

(ii) specialists in the operation of the financial service supplier.

(b) Each Member shall permit, subject to the availability of qualified personnel in its territory, temporary entry into its territory of the following personnel associated with a commercial presence of a financial service supplier of any other Member:

(i) specialists in computer services, telecommunication services and accounts of the financial service supplier; and

(ii) actuarial and legal specialists.

Non-discriminatory Measures

10. Each Member shall endeavour to remove or to limit any significant adverse effects on financial service suppliers of any other Member of:

(a) non-discriminatory measures that prevent financial service suppliers from offering in the Member's territory, in the form determined by the Member, all the financial services permitted by the Member;

(b) non-discriminatory measures that limit the expansion of the activities of financial service suppliers into the entire territory of the Member;

(c) measures of a Member, when such a Member applies the same measures to the supply of both banking and securities services, and a financial service supplier of any other Member concentrates its activities in the provision of securities services; and

(d) other measures that, although respecting the provisions of the Agreement, affect adversely the ability of financial service suppliers of any other Member to operate, compete or enter the Member's market;

provided that any action taken under this paragraph would not unfairly discriminate against financial service suppliers of the Member taking such action.

11. With respect to the non-discriminatory measures referred to in subparagraphs 10(a) and (b), a Member shall endeavour not to limit or restrict the present degree of market opportunities nor the benefits already enjoyed by financial service suppliers of all other Members as a class in the territory of the Member, provided that this commitment does not result in unfair discrimination against financial service suppliers of the Member applying such measures.

C. *National Treatment*

1. Under terms and conditions that accord national treatment, each Member shall grant to financial service suppliers of any other Member established in its territory access to payment and clearing systems operated by public entities, and to official funding and refinancing facilities available in the normal course of ordinary business. This paragraph is not intended to confer access to the Member's lender of last resort facilities.

2. When membership or participation in, or access to, any self-regulatory body, securities or futures exchange or market, clearing agency, or any other organization or association, is required by a Member in order for financial service suppliers of any other Member to supply financial services on an equal basis with financial service suppliers of the Member, or when the Member provides directly or indirectly such entities, privileges or advantages in supplying financial services, the Member shall ensure that such entities accord national treatment to financial service suppliers of any other Member resident in the territory of the Member.

D. *Definitions*

For the purposes of this approach:

1. A non-resident supplier of financial services is a financial service supplier of a Member which supplies a financial service into the territory of another Member from an establishment located in the territory of another Member, regardless of whether such a financial service supplier has or has not a commercial presence in the territory of the Member in which the financial service is supplied.

2. "Commercial presence" means an enterprise within a Member's territory for the supply of financial services and includes wholly- or partly-owned subsidiaries, joint ventures, partnerships, sole proprietorships, franchising operations, branches, agencies, representative offices or other organizations.

3. A new financial service is a service of a financial nature, including services related to existing and new products or the manner in which a product is delivered, that is not supplied by any financial service supplier in the territory of a particular Member but which is supplied in the territory of another Member.

Item 35

SINGAPORE MINISTERIAL DECLARATION

Adopted December 13, 1996, at Singapore

Purpose

1. We, the Ministers, have met in Singapore from 9 to 13 December 1996 for the first regular biennial meeting of the WTO at Ministerial level, as called for in Article IV of the Agreement Establishing the World Trade Organization, to further strengthen the WTO as a forum for negotiation, the continuing liberalization of trade within a rule-based system, and the multilateral review and assessment of trade policies, and in particular to:

- assess the implementation of our commitments under the WTO Agreements and decisions;
- review the ongoing negotiations and Work Programme;
- examine developments in world trade; and
- address the challenges of an evolving world economy.

Trade and Economic Growth

2. For nearly 50 years Members have sought to fulfil, first in the GATT and now in the WTO, the objectives reflected in the preamble to the WTO Agreement of conducting our trade relations with a view to raising standards of living worldwide. The rise in global trade facilitated by trade liberalization within the rules-based system has created more and better-paid jobs in many countries. The achievements of the WTO during its first two years bear witness to our desire to work together to make the most of the possibilities that the multilateral system provides to promote sustainable growth and development while contributing to a more stable and secure climate in international relations.

Integration of Economies; Opportunities and Challenges

3. We believe that the scope and pace of change in the international economy, including the growth in trade in services and direct investment, and the increasing integration of economies offer unprecedented opportunities for improved growth, job creation, and development. These developments require adjustment by economies and societies. They also pose challenges to the trading system. We commit ourselves to address these challenges.

Core Labour Standards

4. We renew our commitment to the observance of internationally recognized core labour standards. The International Labour Organization (ILO) is the competent body to set and deal with these standards, and we affirm our support for its work in promoting them. We believe that economic growth and development fostered by increased trade and further trade liberal-

ization contribute to the promotion of these standards. We reject the use of labour standards for protectionist purposes, and agree that the comparative advantage of countries, particularly low-wage developing countries, must in no way be put into question. In this regard, we note that the WTO and ILO Secretariats will continue their existing collaboration.

Marginalization

5. We commit ourselves to address the problem of marginalization for least-developed countries, and the risk of it for certain developing countries. We will also continue to work for greater coherence in international economic policy-making and for improved coordination between the WTO and other agencies in providing technical assistance.

Role of WTO

6. In pursuit of the goal of sustainable growth and development for the common good, we envisage a world where trade flows freely. To this end we renew our commitment to:

- a fair, equitable and more open rule-based system;
- progressive liberalization and elimination of tariff and non-tariff barriers to trade in goods;
- progressive liberalization of trade in services;
- rejection of all forms of protectionism;
- elimination of discriminatory treatment in international trade relations;
- integration of developing and least-developed countries and economies in transition into the multilateral system; and
- the maximum possible level of transparency.

Regional Agreements

7. We note that trade relations of WTO Members are being increasingly influenced by regional trade agreements, which have expanded vastly in number, scope and coverage. Such initiatives can promote further liberalization and may assist least-developed, developing and transition economies in integrating into the international trading system. In this context, we note the importance of existing regional arrangements involving developing and least-developed countries. The expansion and extent of regional trade agreements make it important to analyse whether the system of WTO rights and obligations as it relates to regional trade agreements needs to be further clarified. We reaffirm the primacy of the multilateral trading system, which includes a framework for the development of regional trade agreements, and we renew our commitment to ensure that regional trade agreements are complementary to it and consistent with its rules. In this regard, we welcome the establishment and endorse the work of the new Committee on Regional Trade Agreements. We shall continue to work through progressive liberalization in the WTO as we are committed in the WTO Agreement and Decisions adopted at Marrakesh, and in so doing facilitate mutually supportive processes of global and regional trade liberalization.

Accessions

8. It is important that the 28 applicants now negotiating accession contribute to completing the accession process by accepting the WTO rules and by offering meaningful market access commitments. We will work to bring these applicants expeditiously into the WTO system.

Dispute Settlement

9. The Dispute Settlement Understanding (DSU) offers a means for the settlement of disputes among Members that is unique in international agreements. We consider its impartial and transparent operation to be of fundamental importance in assuring the resolution of trade disputes, and in fostering the implementation and application of the WTO agreements. The Understanding, with its predictable procedures, including the possibility of appeal of panel decisions to an Appellate Body and provisions on implementation of recommendations, has improved Members' means of resolving their differences. We believe that the DSU has worked effectively during its first two years. We also note the role that several WTO bodies have played in helping to avoid disputes. We renew our determination to abide by the rules and procedures of the DSU and other WTO agreements in the conduct of our trade relations and the settlement of disputes. We are confident that longer experience with the DSU, including the implementation of panel and appellate recommendations, will further enhance the effectiveness and credibility of the dispute settlement system.

Implementation

10. We attach high priority to full and effective implementation of the WTO Agreement in a manner consistent with the goal of trade liberalization. Implementation thus far has been generally satisfactory, although some Members have expressed dissatisfaction with certain aspects. It is clear that further effort in this area is required, as indicated by the relevant WTO bodies in their reports. Implementation of the specific commitments scheduled by Members with respect to market access in industrial goods and trade in services appears to be proceeding smoothly. With respect to industrial market access, monitoring of implementation would be enhanced by the timely availability of trade and tariff data. Progress has been made also in advancing the WTO reform programme in agriculture, including in implementation of agreed market access concessions and domestic subsidy and export subsidy commitments.

Legislation and Notifications

11. Compliance with notification requirements has not been fully satisfactory. Because the WTO system relies on mutual monitoring as a means to assess implementation, those Members which have not submitted notifications in a timely manner, or whose notifications are not complete, should renew their efforts. At the same time, the relevant bodies should take appropriate steps to promote full compliance while considering practical proposals for simplifying the notification process.

12. Where legislation is needed to implement WTO rules, Members are mindful of their obligations to complete their domestic legislative process

without further delay. Those Members entitled to transition periods are urged to take steps as they deem necessary to ensure timely implementation of obligations as they come into effect. Each Member should carefully review all its existing or proposed legislation, programmes and measures to ensure their full compatibility with the WTO obligations, and should carefully consider points made during review in the relevant WTO bodies regarding the WTO consistency of legislation, programmes and measures, and make appropriate changes where necessary.

Developing Countries

13. The integration of developing countries in the multilateral trading system is important for their economic development and for global trade expansion. In this connection, we recall that the WTO Agreement embodies provisions conferring differential and more favourable treatment for developing countries, including special attention to the particular situation of least-developed countries. We acknowledge the fact that developing country Members have undertaken significant new commitments, both substantive and procedural, and we recognize the range and complexity of the efforts that they are making to comply with them. In order to assist them in these efforts, including those with respect to notification and legislative requirements, we will improve the availability of technical assistance under the agreed guidelines. We have also agreed to recommendations relative to the decision we took at Marrakesh concerning the possible negative effects of the agricultural reform programme on least-developed and net food-importing developing countries.

Least-Developed Countries

14. We remain concerned by the problems of the least-developed countries and have agreed to:

- a Plan of Action, including provision for taking positive measures, for example duty-free access, on an autonomous basis, aimed at improving their overall capacity to respond to the opportunities offered by the trading system;

- seek to give operational content to the Plan of Action, for example, by enhancing conditions for investment and providing predictable and favourable market access conditions for LLDCs' products, to foster the expansion and diversification of their exports to the markets of all developed countries; and in the case of relevant developing countries in the context of the Global System of Trade Preferences; and

- organize a meeting with UNCTAD and the International Trade Centre as soon as possible in 1997, with the participation of aid agencies, multilateral financial institutions and least-developed countries to foster an integrated approach to assisting these countries in enhancing their trading opportunities.

Textiles and Clothing

15. We confirm our commitment to full and faithful implementation of the provisions of the Agreement on Textiles and Clothing (ATC). We stress the importance of the integration of textile products, as provided for in the

ATC, into GATT 1994 under its strengthened rules and disciplines because of its systemic significance for the rule-based, non-discriminatory trading system and its contribution to the increase in export earnings of developing countries. We attach importance to the implementation of this Agreement so as to ensure an effective transition to GATT 1994 by way of integration which is progressive in character. The use of safeguard measures in accordance with ATC provisions should be as sparing as possible. We note concerns regarding the use of other trade distortive measures and circumvention. We reiterate the importance of fully implementing the provisions of the ATC relating to small suppliers, new entrants and least-developed country Members, as well as those relating to cotton-producing exporting Members. We recognize the importance of wool products for some developing country Members. We reaffirm that as part of the integration process and with reference to the specific commitments undertaken by the Members as a result of the Uruguay Round, all Members shall take such action as may be necessary to abide by GATT 1994 rules and disciplines so as to achieve improved market access for textiles and clothing products. We agree that, keeping in view its quasi-judicial nature, the Textiles Monitoring Body (TMB) should achieve transparency in providing rationale for its findings and recommendations. We expect that the TMB shall make findings and recommendations whenever called upon to do so under the Agreement. We emphasize the responsibility of the Goods Council in overseeing, in accordance with Article IV:5 of the WTO Agreement and Article 8 of the ATC, the functioning of the ATC, whose implementation is being supervised by the TMB.

Trade and Environment

16.   The Committee on Trade and Environment has made an important contribution towards fulfilling its Work Programme. The Committee has been examining and will continue to examine, *inter alia*, the scope of the complementarities between trade liberalization, economic development and environmental protection. Full implementation of the WTO Agreements will make an important contribution to achieving the objectives of sustainable development. The work of the Committee has underlined the importance of policy coordination at the national level in the area of trade and environment. In this connection, the work of the Committee has been enriched by the participation of environmental as well as trade experts from Member governments and the further participation of such experts in the Committee's deliberations would be welcomed. The breadth and complexity of the issues covered by the Committee's Work Programme shows that further work needs to be undertaken on all items of its agenda, as contained in its report. We intend to build on the work accomplished thus far, and therefore direct the Committee to carry out its work, reporting to the General Council, under its existing terms of reference.

Services Negotiations

17.   The fulfilment of the objectives agreed at Marrakesh for negotiations on the improvement of market access in services—in financial services, movement of natural persons, maritime transport services and basic telecommunications—has proved to be difficult. The results have been below expectations. In three areas, it has been necessary to prolong negotiations beyond the

original deadlines. We are determined to obtain a progressively higher level of liberalization in services on a mutually advantageous basis with appropriate flexibility for individual developing country Members, as envisaged in the Agreement, in the continuing negotiations and those scheduled to begin no later than 1 January 2000. In this context, we look forward to full MFN agreements based on improved market access commitments and national treatment. Accordingly, we will:

- achieve a successful conclusion to the negotiations on basic telecommunications in February 1997; and

- resume financial services negotiations in April 1997 with the aim of achieving significantly improved market access commitments with a broader level of participation in the agreed time frame.

With the same broad objectives in mind, we also look forward to a successful conclusion of the negotiations on Maritime Transport Services in the next round of negotiations on services liberalization.

In professional services, we shall aim at completing the work on the accountancy sector by the end of 1997, and will continue to develop multilateral disciplines and guidelines. In this connection, we encourage the successful completion of international standards in the accountancy sector by IFAC, IASC, and IOSCO. With respect to GATS rules, we shall undertake the necessary work with a view to completing the negotiations on safeguards by the end of 1997. We also note that more analytical work will be needed on emergency safeguards measures, government procurement in services and subsidies.

ITA and Pharmaceuticals

18.   Taking note that a number of Members have agreed on a Declaration on Trade in Information Technology Products, we welcome the initiative taken by a number of WTO Members and other States or separate customs territories which have applied to accede to the WTO, who have agreed to tariff elimination for trade in information technology products on an MFN basis as well as the addition by a number of Members of over 400 products to their lists of tariff-free products in pharmaceuticals.

Work Programme and Built-in Agenda

19.   Bearing in mind that an important aspect of WTO activities is a continuous overseeing of the implementation of various agreements, a periodic examination and updating of the WTO Work Programme is a key to enable the WTO to fulfil its objectives. In this context, we endorse the reports of the various WTO bodies. A major share of the Work Programme stems from the WTO Agreement and decisions adopted at Marrakesh. As part of these Agreements and decisions we agreed to a number of provisions calling for future negotiations on Agriculture, Services and aspects of TRIPS, or reviews and other work on Anti–Dumping, Customs Valuation, Dispute Settlement Understanding, Import Licensing, Preshipment Inspection, Rules of Origin, Sanitary and Phyto–Sanitary Measures, Safeguards, Subsidies and Countervailing Measures, Technical Barriers to Trade, Textiles and Clothing, Trade Policy Review Mechanism, Trade–Related Aspects of Intellectual Property Rights and Trade–Related Investment Measures. We agree to a process of

analysis and exchange of information, where provided for in the conclusions and recommendations of the relevant WTO bodies, on the Built-in Agenda issues, to allow Members to better understand the issues involved and identify their interests before undertaking the agreed negotiations and reviews. We agree that:

- the time frames established in the Agreements will be respected in each case;

- the work undertaken shall not prejudge the scope of future negotiations where such negotiations are called for; and

- the work undertaken shall not prejudice the nature of the activity agreed upon (i.e. negotiation or review).

Investment and Competition

20.   Having regard to the existing WTO provisions on matters related to investment and competition policy and the built-in agenda in these areas, including under the TRIMs Agreement, and on the understanding that the work undertaken shall not prejudge whether negotiations will be initiated in the future, we also agree to:

- establish a working group to examine the relationship between trade and investment; and

- establish a working group to study issues raised by Members relating to the interaction between trade and competition policy, including anti-competitive practices, in order to identify any areas that may merit further consideration in the WTO framework.

These groups shall draw upon each other's work if necessary and also draw upon and be without prejudice to the work in UNCTAD and other appropriate intergovernmental fora. As regards UNCTAD, we welcome the work under way as provided for in the Midrand Declaration and the contribution it can make to the understanding of issues. In the conduct of the work of the working groups, we encourage cooperation with the above organizations to make the best use of available resources and to ensure that the development dimension is taken fully into account. The General Council will keep the work of each body under review, and will determine after two years how the work of each body should proceed. It is clearly understood that future negotiations, if any, regarding multilateral disciplines in these areas, will take place only after an explicit consensus decision is taken among WTO Members regarding such negotiations.

Transparency in Government Procurement
Trade Facilitation

21.   We further agree to:

- establish a working group to conduct a study on transparency in government procurement practices, taking into account national policies, and, based on this study, to develop elements for inclusion in an appropriate agreement; and

- direct the Council for Trade in Goods to undertake exploratory and analytical work, drawing on the work of other relevant international organizations, on the simplification of trade procedures in order to assess the scope for WTO rules in this area.

22.   In the organization of the work referred to in paragraphs 20 and 21, careful attention will be given to minimizing the burdens on delegations, especially those with more limited resources, and to coordinating meetings with those of relevant UNCTAD bodies. The technical cooperation programme of the Secretariat will be available to developing and, in particular, least-developed country Members to facilitate their participation in this work.

23.   Noting that the 50th anniversary of the multilateral trading system will occur early in 1998, we instruct the General Council to consider how this historic event can best be commemorated.

* * * * *

Finally, we express our warmest thanks to the Chairman of the Ministerial Conference, Mr. Yeo Cheow Tong, for his personal contribution to the success of this Ministerial Conference. We also want to express our sincere gratitude to Prime Minister Goh Chok Tong, his colleagues in the Government of Singapore and the people of Singapore for their warm hospitality and the excellent organization they have provided. The fact that this first Ministerial Conference of the WTO has been held at Singapore is an additional manifestation of Singapore's commitment to an open world trading system.

Item 36

DOHA MINISTERIAL DECLARATION

Adopted on 14 November 2001, at Doha

1. The multilateral trading system embodied in the World Trade Organization has contributed significantly to economic growth, development and employment throughout the past fifty years. We are determined, particularly in the light of the global economic slowdown, to maintain the process of reform and liberalization of trade policies, thus ensuring that the system plays its full part in promoting recovery, growth and development. We therefore strongly reaffirm the principles and objectives set out in the Marrakesh Agreement Establishing the World Trade Organization, and pledge to reject the use of protectionism.

2. International trade can play a major role in the promotion of economic development and the alleviation of poverty. We recognize the need for all our peoples to benefit from the increased opportunities and welfare gains that the multilateral trading system generates. The majority of WTO Members are developing countries. We seek to place their needs and interests at the heart of the Work Programme adopted in this Declaration. Recalling the Preamble to the Marrakesh Agreement, we shall continue to make positive efforts designed to ensure that developing countries, and especially the least-developed among them, secure a share in the growth of world trade commensurate with the needs of their economic development. In this context, enhanced market access, balanced rules, and well targeted, sustainably financed technical assistance and capacity-building programmes have important roles to play.

3. We recognize the particular vulnerability of the least-developed countries and the special structural difficulties they face in the global economy. We are committed to addressing the marginalization of least-developed countries in international trade and to improving their effective participation in the multilateral trading system. We recall the commitments made by Ministers at our meetings in Marrakesh, Singapore and Geneva, and by the international community at the Third UN Conference on Least–Developed Countries in Brussels, to help least-developed countries secure beneficial and meaningful integration into the multilateral trading system and the global economy. We are determined that the WTO will play its part in building effectively on these commitments under the Work Programme we are establishing.

4. We stress our commitment to the WTO as the unique forum for global trade rule-making and liberalization, while also recognizing that regional trade agreements can play an important role in promoting the liberalization and expansion of trade and in fostering development.

5. We are aware that the challenges Members face in a rapidly changing international environment cannot be addressed through measures taken in the trade field alone. We shall continue to work with the Bretton Woods institutions for greater coherence in global economic policy-making.

6. We strongly reaffirm our commitment to the objective of sustainable development, as stated in the Preamble to the Marrakesh Agreement. We are convinced that the aims of upholding and safeguarding an open and non-discriminatory multilateral trading system, and acting for the protection of the environment and the promotion of sustainable development can and must be mutually supportive. We take note of the efforts by Members to conduct national environmental assessments of trade policies on a voluntary basis. We recognize that under WTO rules no country should be prevented from taking measures for the protection of human, animal or plant life or health, or of the environment at the levels it considers appropriate, subject to the requirement that they are not applied in a manner which would constitute a means of arbitrary or unjustifiable discrimination between countries where the same conditions prevail, or a disguised restriction on international trade, and are otherwise in accordance with the provisions of the WTO Agreements. We welcome the WTO's continued cooperation with UNEP and other inter-governmental environmental organizations. We encourage efforts to promote cooperation between the WTO and relevant international environmental and developmental organizations, especially in the lead-up to the World Summit on Sustainable Development to be held in Johannesburg, South Africa, in September 2002.

7. We reaffirm the right of Members under the General Agreement on Trade in Services to regulate, and to introduce new regulations on, the supply of services.

8. We reaffirm our declaration made at the Singapore Ministerial Conference regarding internationally recognized core labour standards. We take note of work under way in the International Labour Organization (ILO) on the social dimension of globalization.

9. We note with particular satisfaction that this Conference has completed the WTO accession procedures for China and Chinese Taipei. We also welcome the accession as new Members, since our last Session, of Albania, Croatia, Georgia, Jordan, Lithuania, Moldova and Oman, and note the extensive market-access commitments already made by these countries on accession. These accessions will greatly strengthen the multilateral trading system, as will those of the 28 countries now negotiating their accession. We therefore attach great importance to concluding accession proceedings as quickly as possible. In particular, we are committed to accelerating the accession of least-developed countries.

10. Recognizing the challenges posed by an expanding WTO membership, we confirm our collective responsibility to ensure internal transparency and the effective participation of all Members. While emphasizing the inter-governmental character of the organization, we are committed to making the WTO's operations more transparent, including through more effective and prompt dissemination of information, and to improve dialogue with the public. We shall therefore at the national and multilateral levels continue to promote a better public understanding of the WTO and to communicate the benefits of a liberal, rules-based multilateral trading system.

11. In view of these considerations, we hereby agree to undertake the broad and balanced Work Programme set out below. This incorporates both

an expanded negotiating agenda and other important decisions and activities necessary to address the challenges facing the multilateral trading system.

WORK PROGRAMME

IMPLEMENTATION-RELATED ISSUES AND CONCERNS

12. We attach the utmost importance to the implementation-related issues and concerns raised by Members and are determined to find appropriate solutions to them. In this connection, and having regard to the General Council Decisions of 3 May and 15 December 2000, we further adopt the Decision on Implementation–Related Issues and Concerns in document WT/MIN(01)/17 to address a number of implementation problems faced by Members. We agree that negotiations on outstanding implementation issues shall be an integral part of the Work Programme we are establishing, and that agreements reached at an early stage in these negotiations shall be treated in accordance with the provisions of paragraph 47 below. In this regard, we shall proceed as follows: (a) where we provide a specific negotiating mandate in this Declaration, the relevant implementation issues shall be addressed under that mandate; (b) the other outstanding implementation issues shall be addressed as a matter of priority by the relevant WTO bodies, which shall report to the Trade Negotiations Committee, established under paragraph 46 below, by the end of 2002 for appropriate action.

AGRICULTURE

13. We recognize the work already undertaken in the negotiations initiated in early 2000 under Article 20 of the Agreement on Agriculture, including the large number of negotiating proposals submitted on behalf of a total of 121 Members. We recall the long-term objective referred to in the Agreement to establish a fair and market-oriented trading system through a programme of fundamental reform encompassing strengthened rules and specific commitments on support and protection in order to correct and prevent restrictions and distortions in world agricultural markets. We reconfirm our commitment to this programme. Building on the work carried out to date and without prejudging the outcome of the negotiations we commit ourselves to comprehensive negotiations aimed at: substantial improvements in market access; reductions of, with a view to phasing out, all forms of export subsidies; and substantial reductions in trade-distorting domestic support. We agree that special and differential treatment for developing countries shall be an integral part of all elements of the negotiations and shall be embodied in the Schedules of concessions and commitments and as appropriate in the rules and disciplines to be negotiated, so as to be operationally effective and to enable developing countries to effectively take account of their development needs, including food security and rural development. We take note of the non-trade concerns reflected in the negotiating proposals submitted by Members and confirm that non-trade concerns will be taken into account in the negotiations as provided for in the Agreement on Agriculture.

14. Modalities for the further commitments, including provisions for special and differential treatment, shall be established no later than 31 March 2003. Participants shall submit their comprehensive draft Schedules based on these modalities no later than the date of the Fifth Session of the Ministerial Conference. The negotiations, including with respect to rules and disciplines

and related legal texts, shall be concluded as part and at the date of conclusion of the negotiating agenda as a whole.

SERVICES

15.   The negotiations on trade in services shall be conducted with a view to promoting the economic growth of all trading partners and the development of developing and least-developed countries. We recognize the work already undertaken in the negotiations, initiated in January 2000 under Article XIX of the General Agreement on Trade in Services, and the large number of proposals submitted by Members on a wide range of sectors and several horizontal issues, as well as on movement of natural persons. We reaffirm the Guidelines and Procedures for the Negotiations adopted by the Council for Trade in Services on 28 March 2001 as the basis for continuing the negotiations, with a view to achieving the objectives of the General Agreement on Trade in Services, as stipulated in the Preamble, Article IV and Article XIX of that Agreement. Participants shall submit initial requests for specific commitments by 30 June 2002 and initial offers by 31 March 2003.

MARKET ACCESS FOR NON-AGRICULTURAL PRODUCTS

16.   We agree to negotiations which shall aim, by modalities to be agreed, to reduce or as appropriate eliminate tariffs, including the reduction or elimination of tariff peaks, high tariffs, and tariff escalation, as well as non-tariff barriers, in particular on products of export interest to developing countries. Product coverage shall be comprehensive and without *a priori* exclusions. The negotiations shall take fully into account the special needs and interests of developing and least-developed country participants, including through less than full reciprocity in reduction commitments, in accordance with the relevant provisions of Article XXVIII *bis* of GATT 1994 and the provisions cited in paragraph 50 below. To this end, the modalities to be agreed will include appropriate studies and capacity-building measures to assist least-developed countries to participate effectively in the negotiations.

TRADE-RELATED ASPECTS OF INTELLECTUAL PROPERTY RIGHTS

17.   We stress the importance we attach to implementation and interpretation of the Agreement on Trade–Related Aspects of Intellectual Property Rights (TRIPS Agreement) in a manner supportive of public health, by promoting both access to existing medicines and research and development into new medicines and, in this connection, are adopting a separate Declaration.

18.   With a view to completing the work started in the Council for Trade–Related Aspects of Intellectual Property Rights (Council for TRIPS) on the implementation of Article 23.4, we agree to negotiate the establishment of a multilateral system of notification and registration of geographical indications for wines and spirits by the Fifth Session of the Ministerial Conference. We note that issues related to the extension of the protection of geographical indications provided for in Article 23 to products other than wines and spirits will be addressed in the Council for TRIPS pursuant to paragraph 12 of this Declaration.

19.   We instruct the Council for TRIPS, in pursuing its work programme including under the review of Article 27.3(b), the review of the implementation of the TRIPS Agreement under Article 71.1 and the work foreseen

pursuant to paragraph 12 of this Declaration, to examine, *inter alia*, the relationship between the TRIPS Agreement and the Convention on Biological Diversity, the protection of traditional knowledge and folklore, and other relevant new developments raised by Members pursuant to Article 71.1. In undertaking this work, the TRIPS Council shall be guided by the objectives and principles set out in Articles 7 and 8 of the TRIPS Agreement and shall take fully into account the development dimension.

RELATIONSHIP BETWEEN TRADE AND INVESTMENT

20. Recognizing the case for a multilateral framework to secure transparent, stable and predictable conditions for long-term cross-border investment, particularly foreign direct investment, that will contribute to the expansion of trade, and the need for enhanced technical assistance and capacity-building in this area as referred to in paragraph 21, we agree that negotiations will take place after the Fifth Session of the Ministerial Conference on the basis of a decision to be taken, by explicit consensus, at that Session on modalities of negotiations.

21. We recognize the needs of developing and least-developed countries for enhanced support for technical assistance and capacity building in this area, including policy analysis and development so that they may better evaluate the implications of closer multilateral cooperation for their development policies and objectives, and human and institutional development. To this end, we shall work in cooperation with other relevant intergovernmental organisations, including UNCTAD, and through appropriate regional and bilateral channels, to provide strengthened and adequately resourced assistance to respond to these needs.

22. In the period until the Fifth Session, further work in the Working Group on the Relationship Between Trade and Investment will focus on the clarification of: scope and definition; transparency; non-discrimination; modalities for pre-establishment commitments based on a GATS-type, positive list approach; development provisions; exceptions and balance-of-payments safeguards; consultation and the settlement of disputes between Members. Any framework should reflect in a balanced manner the interests of home and host countries, and take due account of the development policies and objectives of host governments as well as their right to regulate in the public interest. The special development, trade and financial needs of developing and least-developed countries should be taken into account as an integral part of any framework, which should enable Members to undertake obligations and commitments commensurate with their individual needs and circumstances. Due regard should be paid to other relevant WTO provisions. Account should be taken, as appropriate, of existing bilateral and regional arrangements on investment.

INTERACTION BETWEEN TRADE AND COMPETITION POLICY

23. Recognizing the case for a multilateral framework to enhance the contribution of competition policy to international trade and development, and the need for enhanced technical assistance and capacity-building in this area as referred to in paragraph 24, we agree that negotiations will take place after the Fifth Session of the Ministerial Conference on the basis of a decision to be taken, by explicit consensus, at that Session on modalities of negotiations.

24.   We recognize the needs of developing and least-developed countries for enhanced support for technical assistance and capacity building in this area, including policy analysis and development so that they may better evaluate the implications of closer multilateral cooperation for their development policies and objectives, and human and institutional development. To this end, we shall work in cooperation with other relevant intergovernmental organisations, including UNCTAD, and through appropriate regional and bilateral channels, to provide strengthened and adequately resourced assistance to respond to these needs.

25.   In the period until the Fifth Session, further work in the Working Group on the Interaction between Trade and Competition Policy will focus on the clarification of: core principles, including transparency, non-discrimination and procedural fairness, and provisions on hardcore cartels; modalities for voluntary cooperation; and support for progressive reinforcement of competition institutions in developing countries through capacity building. Full account shall be taken of the needs of developing and least-developed country participants and appropriate flexibility provided to address them.

TRANSPARENCY IN GOVERNMENT PROCUREMENT

26.   Recognizing the case for a multilateral agreement on transparency in government procurement and the need for enhanced technical assistance and capacity building in this area, we agree that negotiations will take place after the Fifth Session of the Ministerial Conference on the basis of a decision to be taken, by explicit consensus, at that Session on modalities of negotiations. These negotiations will build on the progress made in the Working Group on Transparency in Government Procurement by that time and take into account participants' development priorities, especially those of least-developed country participants. Negotiations shall be limited to the transparency aspects and therefore will not restrict the scope for countries to give preferences to domestic supplies and suppliers. We commit ourselves to ensuring adequate technical assistance and support for capacity building both during the negotiations and after their conclusion.

TRADE FACILITATION

27.   Recognizing the case for further expediting the movement, release and clearance of goods, including goods in transit, and the need for enhanced technical assistance and capacity building in this area, we agree that negotiations will take place after the Fifth Session of the Ministerial Conference on the basis of a decision to be taken, by explicit consensus, at that Session on modalities of negotiations. In the period until the Fifth Session, the Council for Trade in Goods shall review and as appropriate, clarify and improve relevant aspects of Articles V, VIII and X of the GATT 1994 and identify the trade facilitation needs and priorities of Members, in particular developing and least-developed countries. We commit ourselves to ensuring adequate technical assistance and support for capacity building in this area.

WTO RULES

28.   In the light of experience and of the increasing application of these instruments by Members, we agree to negotiations aimed at clarifying and improving disciplines under the Agreements on Implementation of Article VI of the GATT 1994 and on Subsidies and Countervailing Measures, while

preserving the basic concepts, principles and effectiveness of these Agreements and their instruments and objectives, and taking into account the needs of developing and least-developed participants. In the initial phase of the negotiations, participants will indicate the provisions, including disciplines on trade distorting practices, that they seek to clarify and improve in the subsequent phase. In the context of these negotiations, participants shall also aim to clarify and improve WTO disciplines on fisheries subsidies, taking into account the importance of this sector to developing countries. We note that fisheries subsidies are also referred to in paragraph 31.

29.   We also agree to negotiations aimed at clarifying and improving disciplines and procedures under the existing WTO provisions applying to regional trade agreements. The negotiations shall take into account the developmental aspects of regional trade agreements.

DISPUTE SETTLEMENT UNDERSTANDING

30.   We agree to negotiations on improvements and clarifications of the Dispute Settlement Understanding. The negotiations should be based on the work done thus far as well as any additional proposals by Members, and aim to agree on improvements and clarifications not later than May 2003, at which time we will take steps to ensure that the results enter into force as soon as possible thereafter.

TRADE AND ENVIRONMENT

31.   With a view to enhancing the mutual supportiveness of trade and environment, we agree to negotiations, without prejudging their outcome, on:

(i) the relationship between existing WTO rules and specific trade obligations set out in multilateral environmental agreements (MEAs). The negotiations shall be limited in scope to the applicability of such existing WTO rules as among parties to the MEA in question. The negotiations shall not prejudice the WTO rights of any Member that is not a party to the MEA in question;

(ii) procedures for regular information exchange between MEA Secretariats and the relevant WTO committees, and the criteria for the granting of observer status;

(iii) the reduction or, as appropriate, elimination of tariff and non-tariff barriers to environmental goods and services.

We note that fisheries subsidies form part of the negotiations provided for in paragraph 28.

32.   We instruct the Committee on Trade and Environment, in pursuing work on all items on its agenda within its current terms of reference, to give particular attention to:

(i) the effect of environmental measures on market access, especially in relation to developing countries, in particular the least-developed among them, and those situations in which the elimination or reduction of trade restrictions and distortions would benefit trade, the environment and development;

(ii) the relevant provisions of the Agreement on Trade–Related Aspects of Intellectual Property Rights; and

(iii) labelling requirements for environmental purposes.

Work on these issues should include the identification of any need to clarify relevant WTO rules. The Committee shall report to the Fifth Session of the Ministerial Conference, and make recommendations, where appropriate, with respect to future action, including the desirability of negotiations. The outcome of this work as well as the negotiations carried out under paragraph 31(i) and (ii) shall be compatible with the open and non-discriminatory nature of the multilateral trading system, shall not add to or diminish the rights and obligations of Members under existing WTO agreements, in particular the Agreement on the Application of Sanitary and Phytosanitary Measures, nor alter the balance of these rights and obligations, and will take into account the needs of developing and least-developed countries.

33.   We recognize the importance of technical assistance and capacity building in the field of trade and environment to developing countries, in particular the least-developed among them. We also encourage that expertise and experience be shared with Members wishing to perform environmental reviews at the national level. A report shall be prepared on these activities for the Fifth Session.

ELECTRONIC COMMERCE

34.   We take note of the work which has been done in the General Council and other relevant bodies since the Ministerial Declaration of 20 May 1998 and agree to continue the Work Programme on Electronic Commerce. The work to date demonstrates that electronic commerce creates new challenges and opportunities for trade for Members at all stages of development, and we recognize the importance of creating and maintaining an environment which is favourable to the future development of electronic commerce. We instruct the General Council to consider the most appropriate institutional arrangements for handling the Work Programme, and to report on further progress to the Fifth Session of the Ministerial Conference. We declare that Members will maintain their current practice of not imposing customs duties on electronic transmissions until the Fifth Session.

SMALL ECONOMIES

35.   We agree to a work programme, under the auspices of the General Council, to examine issues relating to the trade of small economies. The objective of this work is to frame responses to the trade-related issues identified for the fuller integration of small, vulnerable economies into the multilateral trading system, and not to create a sub-category of WTO Members. The General Council shall review the work programme and make recommendations for action to the Fifth Session of the Ministerial Conference.

TRADE, DEBT AND FINANCE

36.   We agree to an examination, in a Working Group under the auspices of the General Council, of the relationship between trade, debt and finance, and of any possible recommendations on steps that might be taken within the mandate and competence of the WTO to enhance the capacity of the multilateral trading system to contribute to a durable solution to the problem of external indebtedness of developing and least-developed countries, and to strengthen the coherence of international trade and financial policies, with a

view to safeguarding the multilateral trading system from the effects of financial and monetary instability. The General Council shall report to the Fifth Session of the Ministerial Conference on progress in the examination.

TRADE AND TRANSFER OF TECHNOLOGY

37. We agree to an examination, in a Working Group under the auspices of the General Council, of the relationship between trade and transfer of technology, and of any possible recommendations on steps that might be taken within the mandate of the WTO to increase flows of technology to developing countries. The General Council shall report to the Fifth Session of the Ministerial Conference on progress in the examination.

TECHNICAL COOPERATION AND CAPACITY BUILDING

38. We confirm that technical cooperation and capacity building are core elements of the development dimension of the multilateral trading system, and we welcome and endorse the New Strategy for WTO Technical Cooperation for Capacity Building, Growth and Integration. We instruct the Secretariat, in coordination with other relevant agencies, to support domestic efforts for mainstreaming trade into national plans for economic development and strategies for poverty reduction. The delivery of WTO technical assistance shall be designed to assist developing and least-developed countries and low-income countries in transition to adjust to WTO rules and disciplines, implement obligations and exercise the rights of membership, including drawing on the benefits of an open, rules-based multilateral trading system. Priority shall also be accorded to small, vulnerable, and transition economies, as well as to Members and Observers without representation in Geneva. We reaffirm our support for the valuable work of the International Trade Centre, which should be enhanced.

39. We underscore the urgent necessity for the effective coordinated delivery of technical assistance with bilateral donors, in the OECD Development Assistance Committee and relevant international and regional intergovernmental institutions, within a coherent policy framework and timetable. In the coordinated delivery of technical assistance, we instruct the Director–General to consult with the relevant agencies, bilateral donors and beneficiaries, to identify ways of enhancing and rationalizing the Integrated Framework for Trade–Related Technical Assistance to Least–Developed Countries and the Joint Integrated Technical Assistance Programme (JITAP).

40. We agree that there is a need for technical assistance to benefit from secure and predictable funding. We therefore instruct the Committee on Budget, Finance and Administration to develop a plan for adoption by the General Council in December 2001 that will ensure long-term funding for WTO technical assistance at an overall level no lower than that of the current year and commensurate with the activities outlined above.

41. We have established firm commitments on technical cooperation and capacity building in various paragraphs in this Ministerial Declaration. We reaffirm these specific commitments contained in paragraphs 16, 21, 24, 26, 27, 33, 38–40, 42 and 43, and also reaffirm the understanding in paragraph 2 on the important role of sustainably financed technical assistance and capacity-building programmes. We instruct the Director–General to report to the Fifth Session of the Ministerial Conference, with an interim report to the

General Council in December 2002 on the implementation and adequacy of these commitments in the identified paragraphs.

LEAST-DEVELOPED COUNTRIES

42.   We acknowledge the seriousness of the concerns expressed by the least-developed countries (LDCs) in the Zanzibar Declaration adopted by their Ministers in July 2001. We recognize that the integration of the LDCs into the multilateral trading system requires meaningful market access, support for the diversification of their production and export base, and trade-related technical assistance and capacity building. We agree that the meaningful integration of LDCs into the trading system and the global economy will involve efforts by all WTO Members. We commit ourselves to the objective of duty-free, quota-free market access for products originating from LDCs. In this regard, we welcome the significant market access improvements by WTO Members in advance of the Third UN Conference on LDCs (LDC–III), in Brussels, May 2001. We further commit ourselves to consider additional measures for progressive improvements in market access for LDCs. Accession of LDCs remains a priority for the Membership. We agree to work to facilitate and accelerate negotiations with acceding LDCs. We instruct the Secretariat to reflect the priority we attach to LDCs' accessions in the annual plans for technical assistance. We reaffirm the commitments we undertook at LDC–III, and agree that the WTO should take into account, in designing its work programme for LDCs, the trade-related elements of the Brussels Declaration and Programme of Action, consistent with the WTO's mandate, adopted at LDC–III. We instruct the Sub–Committee for Least–Developed Countries to design such a work programme and to report on the agreed work programme to the General Council at its first meeting in 2002.

43.   We endorse the Integrated Framework for Trade–Related Technical Assistance to Least–Developed Countries (IF) as a viable model for LDCs' trade development. We urge development partners to significantly increase contributions to the IF Trust Fund and WTO extra-budgetary trust funds in favour of LDCs. We urge the core agencies, in coordination with development partners, to explore the enhancement of the IF with a view to addressing the supply-side constraints of LDCs and the extension of the model to all LDCs, following the review of the IF and the appraisal of the ongoing Pilot Scheme in selected LDCs. We request the Director–General, following coordination with heads of the other agencies, to provide an interim report to the General Council in December 2002 and a full report to the Fifth Session of the Ministerial Conference on all issues affecting LDCs.

SPECIAL AND DIFFERENTIAL TREATMENT

44.   We reaffirm that provisions for special and differential treatment are an integral part of the WTO Agreements. We note the concerns expressed regarding their operation in addressing specific constraints faced by developing countries, particularly least-developed countries. In that connection, we also note that some Members have proposed a Framework Agreement on Special and Differential Treatment (WT/GC/W/442). We therefore agree that all special and differential treatment provisions shall be reviewed with a view to strengthening them and making them more precise, effective and operational. In this connection, we endorse the work programme on special and differential treatment set out in the Decision on Implementation–Related Issues and Concerns.

ORGANIZATION AND MANAGEMENT OF THE WORK PRO-GRAMME

45.   The negotiations to be pursued under the terms of this Declaration shall be concluded not later than 1 January 2005. The Fifth Session of the Ministerial Conference will take stock of progress in the negotiations, provide any necessary political guidance, and take decisions as necessary. When the results of the negotiations in all areas have been established, a Special Session of the Ministerial Conference will be held to take decisions regarding the adoption and implementation of those results.

46.   The overall conduct of the negotiations shall be supervised by a Trade Negotiations Committee under the authority of the General Council. The Trade Negotiations Committee shall hold its first meeting not later than 31 January 2002. It shall establish appropriate negotiating mechanisms as required and supervise the progress of the negotiations.

47.   With the exception of the improvements and clarifications of the Dispute Settlement Understanding, the conduct, conclusion and entry into force of the outcome of the negotiations shall be treated as parts of a single undertaking. However, agreements reached at an early stage may be implemented on a provisional or a definitive basis. Early agreements shall be taken into account in assessing the overall balance of the negotiations.

48.   Negotiations shall be open to:

(i) all Members of the WTO; and

(ii) States and separate customs territories currently in the process of accession and those that inform Members, at a regular meeting of the General Council, of their intention to negotiate the terms of their membership and for whom an accession working party is established.

Decisions on the outcomes of the negotiations shall be taken only by WTO Members.

49.   The negotiations shall be conducted in a transparent manner among participants, in order to facilitate the effective participation of all. They shall be conducted with a view to ensuring benefits to all participants and to achieving an overall balance in the outcome of the negotiations.

50.   The negotiations and the other aspects of the Work Programme shall take fully into account the principle of special and differential treatment for developing and least-developed countries embodied in: Part IV of the GATT 1994; the Decision of 28 November 1979 on Differential and More Favourable Treatment, Reciprocity and Fuller Participation of Developing Countries; the Uruguay Round Decision on Measures in Favour of Least-Developed Countries; and all other relevant WTO provisions.

51.   The Committee on Trade and Development and the Committee on Trade and Environment shall, within their respective mandates, each act as a forum to identify and debate developmental and environmental aspects of the negotiations, in order to help achieve the objective of having sustainable development appropriately reflected.

52.   Those elements of the Work Programme which do not involve negotiations are also accorded a high priority. They shall be pursued under the overall supervision of the General Council, which shall report on progress to the Fifth Session of the Ministerial Conference.

Item 37

DOHA DECLARATION ON THE
TRIPS AGREEMENT AND
PUBLIC HEALTH

Adopted on 14 November 2001 at Doha

1.   We recognize the gravity of the public health problems afflicting many developing and least-developed countries, especially those resulting from HIV/AIDS, tuberculosis, malaria and other epidemics.

2.   We stress the need for the WTO Agreement on Trade–Related Aspects of Intellectual Property Rights (TRIPS Agreement) to be part of the wider national and international action to address these problems.

3.   We recognize that intellectual property protection is important for the development of new medicines. We also recognize the concerns about its effects on prices.

4.   We agree that the TRIPS Agreement does not and should not prevent Members from taking measures to protect public health. Accordingly, while reiterating our commitment to the TRIPS Agreement, we affirm that the Agreement can and should be interpreted and implemented in a manner supportive of WTO Members' right to protect public health and, in particular, to promote access to medicines for all.

In this connection, we reaffirm the right of WTO Members to use, to the full, the provisions in the TRIPS Agreement, which provide flexibility for this purpose.

5.   Accordingly and in the light of paragraph 4 above, while maintaining our commitments in the TRIPS Agreement, we recognize that these flexibilities include:

(a) In applying the customary rules of interpretation of public international law, each provision of the TRIPS Agreement shall be read in the light of the object and purpose of the Agreement as expressed, in particular, in its objectives and principles.

(b) Each Member has the right to grant compulsory licences and the freedom to determine the grounds upon which such licences are granted.

(c) Each Member has the right to determine what constitutes a national emergency or other circumstances of extreme urgency, it being understood that public health crises, including those relating to HIV/AIDS, tuberculosis, malaria and other epidemics, can represent a national emergency or other circumstances of extreme urgency.

(d) The effect of the provisions in the TRIPS Agreement that are relevant to the exhaustion of intellectual property rights is to leave each Member free to establish its own regime for such exhaustion without challenge, subject to the MFN and national treatment provisions of Articles 3 and 4.

6.   We recognize that WTO Members with insufficient or no manufacturing capacities in the pharmaceutical sector could face difficulties in making effective use of compulsory licensing under the TRIPS Agreement. We instruct the Council for TRIPS to find an expeditious solution to this problem and to report to the General Council before the end of 2002.

7.   We reaffirm the commitment of developed-country Members to provide incentives to their enterprises and institutions to promote and encourage technology transfer to least-developed country Members pursuant to Article 66.2. We also agree that the least-developed country Members will not be obliged, with respect to pharmaceutical products, to implement or apply Sections 5 and 7 of Part II of the TRIPS Agreement or to enforce rights provided for under these Sections until 1 January 2016, without prejudice to the right of least-developed country Members to seek other extensions of the transition periods as provided for in Article 66.1 of the TRIPS Agreement. We instruct the Council for TRIPS to take the necessary action to give effect to this pursuant to Article 66.1 of the TRIPS Agreement.

GATS TELECOMMUNICATIONS REFERENCE PAPER

As explained by the WTO Secretariat, during the negotiations that led to the GATS Fourth Protocol, in which a significant number of WTO Members added specific market access commitments in the telecommunications sector to their GATS schedules, there was concern that the regulatory environment applicable to telecommunications in individual Members should not hinder, but rather should be conducive to market entry. This concern led to proposals that Members should undertake additional commitments in their schedules so as to safeguard the value of the market access commitments. Such additional commitments were agreed in a document referred to as the Reference Paper. The Reference Paper essentially contains a set of principles covering matters such as competition safeguards, interconnection guarantees, transparent licensing processes and the independence of regulators. Over 50 Members incorporated the Reference Paper in whole or part in their GATS telecommunications schedule.

Definitions

Users mean service consumers and service suppliers.

Essential facilities mean facilities of a public telecommunications transport network or service that

(a) are exclusively or predominantly provided by a single or limited number of suppliers; and

(b) cannot feasibly be economically or technically substituted in order to provide a service.

A *major supplier* is a supplier which has the ability to materially affect the terms of participation (having regard to price and supply) in the relevant market for basic telecommunications services as a result of:

(a) control over essential facilities; or

(b) use of its position in the market.

1. Competitive safeguards

1.1 Prevention of anti-competitive practices in telecommunications

Appropriate measures shall be maintained for the purpose of preventing suppliers who, alone or together, are a major supplier from engaging in or continuing anti-competitive practices.

1.2   Safeguards

The anti-competitive practices referred to above shall include in particular:

(a) engaging in anti-competitive cross-subsidization;

(b) using information obtained from competitors with anti-competitive results; and

(c) not making available to other services suppliers on a timely basis technical information about essential facilities and commercially relevant information which are necessary for them to provide services.

2.   Interconnection

2.1   This section applies to linking with suppliers providing public telecommunications transport networks or services in order to allow the users of one supplier to communicate with users of another supplier and to access services provided by another supplier, where specific commitments are undertaken.

2.2   Interconnection to be ensured

Interconnection with a major supplier will be ensured at any technically feasible point in the network. Such interconnection is provided

(a) under non-discriminatory terms, conditions (including technical standards and specifications) and rates and of a quality no less favourable than that provided for its own like services or for like services of non-affiliated service suppliers or for its subsidiaries or other affiliates;

(b) in a timely fashion, on terms, conditions (including technical standards and specifications) and cost-oriented rates that are transparent, reasonable, having regard to economic feasibility, and sufficiently unbundled so that the supplier need not pay for network components or facilities that it does not require for the service to be provided; and

(c) upon request, at points in addition to the network termination points offered to the majority of users, subject to charges that reflect the cost of construction of necessary additional facilities.

2.3   Public availability of the procedures for interconnection negotiations

The procedures applicable for interconnection to a major supplier will be made publicly available.

2.4   Transparency of interconnection arrangements

It is ensured that a major supplier will make publicly available either its interconnection agreements or a reference interconnection offer.

2.5   Interconnection: dispute settlement

A service supplier requesting interconnection with a major supplier will have recourse, either:

(a) at any time or

(b) after a reasonable period of time which has been made publicly known

to an independent domestic body, which may be a regulatory body as referred to in paragraph 5 below, to resolve disputes regarding appropriate terms, conditions and rates for interconnection within a reasonable period of time, to the extent that these have not been established previously.

3. Universal Service

Any Member has the right to define the kind of universal service obligation it wishes to maintain. Such obligations will not be regarded as anti-competitive per se, provided they are administered in a transparent, non-discriminatory and competitively neutral manner and are not more burdensome than necessary for the kind of universal service defined by the Member.

4. Public availability of licensing criteria

Where a licence is required, the following will be made publicly available:

(a) all the licensing criteria and the period of time normally required to reach a decision concerning an application for a licence and

(b) the terms and conditions of individual licences.

The reasons for the denial of a licence will be made known to the applicant upon request.

5. Independent regulators

The regulatory body is separate from, and not accountable to, any supplier of basic telecommunications services. The decisions of and the procedures used by regulators shall be impartial with respect to all market participants.

6. Allocation and use of scarce resources

Any procedures for the allocation and use of scarce resources, including frequencies, numbers and rights of way, will be carried out in an objective, timely, transparent and non-discriminatory manner. The current state of allocated frequency bands will be made publicly available, but detailed identification of frequencies allocated for specific government uses is not required.

Part II

THE INTERNATIONAL MONETARY FUND

Item 39

THE ARTICLES OF AGREEMENT OF THE INTERNATIONAL MONETARY FUND (AS AMENDED)

List of Articles and Sections

475

Schedules [omitted]

INTRODUCTORY ARTICLE

(i) The International Monetary Fund is established and shall operate in accordance with the provisions of this Agreement as originally adopted and subsequently amended.

(ii) To enable the Fund to conduct its operations and transactions, the Fund shall maintain a General Department and a Special Drawing Rights Department. Membership in the Fund shall give the right to participation in the Special Drawing Rights Department.

(iii) Operations and transactions authorized by this Agreement shall be conducted through the General Department, consisting in accordance with the provisions of this Agreement of the General Resources Account, the Special Disbursement Account, and the Investment Account; except that operations and transactions involving special drawing rights shall be conducted through the Special Drawing Rights Department.

Article I

Purposes

The purposes of the International Monetary Fund are:

(i) To promote international monetary cooperation through a permanent institution which provides the machinery for consultation and collaboration on international monetary problems.

(ii) To facilitate the expansion and balanced growth of international trade, and to contribute thereby to the promotion and maintenance of high levels of employment and real income and to the development of the productive resources of all members as primary objectives of economic policy.

(iii) To promote exchange stability, to maintain orderly exchange arrangements among members, and to avoid competitive exchange depreciation.

(iv) To assist in the establishment of a multilateral system of payments in respect of current transactions between members and in the elimination of foreign exchange restrictions which hamper the growth of world trade.

(v) To give confidence to members by making the general resources of the Fund temporarily available to them under adequate safeguards, thus providing them with opportunity to correct maladjustments in their balance of payments without resorting to measures destructive of national or international prosperity.

(vi) In accordance with the above, to shorten the duration and lessen the degree of disequilibrium in the international balances of payments of members.

The Fund shall be guided in all its policies and decisions by the purposes set forth in this Article.

Article II
Membership

Section 1. Original members

The original members of the Fund shall be those of the countries represented at the United Nations Monetary and Financial Conference whose governments accept membership before December 31, 1945.

Section 2. Other members

Membership shall be open to other countries at such times and in accordance with such terms as may be prescribed by the Board of Governors. These terms, including the terms for subscriptions, shall be based on principles consistent with those applied to other countries that are already members.

Article III
Quotas and Subscriptions

Section 1. Quotas and payment of subscriptions

Each member shall be assigned a quota expressed in special drawing rights. The quotas of the members represented at the United Nations Monetary and Financial Conference which accept membership before December 31, 1945 shall be those set forth in Schedule A. The quotas of other members shall be determined by the Board of Governors. The subscription of each member shall be equal to its quota and shall be paid in full to the Fund at the appropriate depository.

Section 2. Adjustment of quotas

(a) The Board of Governors shall at intervals of not more than five years conduct a general review, and if it deems it appropriate propose an adjustment, of the quotas of the members. It may also, if it thinks fit, consider at any other time the adjustment of any particular quota at the request of the member concerned.

(*b*) The Fund may at any time propose an increase in the quotas of those members of the Fund that were members on August 31, 1975 in proportion to their quotas on that date in a cumulative amount not in excess of amounts transferred under Article V, Section 12(*f*), (*i*) and (*j*) from the Special Disbursement Account to the General Resources Account.

(*c*) An eighty-five percent majority of the total voting power shall be required for any change in quotas.

(*d*) The quota of a member shall not be changed until the member has consented and until payment has been made unless payment is deemed to have been made in accordance with Section 3(*b*) of this Article.

Section 3. *Payments when quotas are changed*

(*a*) Each member which consents to an increase in its quota under Section 2(*a*) of this Article shall, within a period determined by the Fund, pay to the Fund twenty-five percent of the increase in special drawing rights, but the Board of Governors may prescribe that this payment may be made, on the same basis for all members, in whole or in part in the currencies of other members specified, with their concurrence, by the Fund, or in the member's own currency. A non-participant shall pay in the currencies of other members specified by the Fund, with their concurrence, a proportion of the increase corresponding to the proportion to be paid in special drawing rights by participants. The balance of the increase shall be paid by the member in its own currency. The Fund's holdings of a member's currency shall not be increased above the level at which they would be subject to charges under Article V, Section 8(*b*)(ii), as a result of payments by other members under this provision.

(*b*) Each member which consents to an increase in its quota under Section 2(*b*) of this Article shall be deemed to have paid to the Fund an amount of subscription equal to such increase.

(*c*) If a member consents to a reduction in its quota, the Fund shall, within sixty days, pay to the member an amount equal to the reduction. The payment shall be made in the member's currency and in such amount of special drawing rights or the currencies of other members specified, with their concurrence, by the Fund as is necessary to prevent the reduction of the Fund's holdings of the currency below the new quota, provided that in exceptional circumstances the Fund may reduce its holdings of the currency below the new quota by payment to the member in its own currency.

(*d*) A seventy percent majority of the total voting power shall be required for any decision under (*a*) above, except for the determination of a period and the specification of currencies under that provision.

Section 4. *Substitution of securities for currency*

The Fund shall accept from any member, in place of any part of the member's currency in the General Resources Account which in the judgment of the Fund is not needed for its operations and transactions, notes or similar obligations issued by the member or the depository designated by the member under Article XIII, Section 2, which shall be non-negotiable, non-interest bearing and payable at their face value on demand by crediting the account of the Fund in the designated depository. This Section shall apply not only to currency subscribed by members but also to any currency otherwise due to, or acquired by, the Fund and to be placed in the General Resources Account.

Article IV

Obligations Regarding Exchange Arrangements

Section 1.   General obligations of members

Recognizing that the essential purpose of the international monetary system is to provide a framework that facilitates the exchange of goods, services, and capital among countries, and that sustains sound economic growth, and that a principal objective is the continuing development of the orderly underlying conditions that are necessary for financial and economic stability, each member undertakes to collaborate with the Fund and other members to assure orderly exchange arrangements and to promote a stable system of exchange rates.   In particular, each member shall:

(i) endeavor to direct its economic and financial policies toward the objective of fostering orderly economic growth with reasonable price stability, with due regard to its circumstances;

(ii) seek to promote stability by fostering orderly underlying economic and financial conditions and a monetary system that does not tend to produce erratic disruptions;

(iii) avoid manipulating exchange rates or the international monetary system in order to prevent effective balance of payments adjustment or to gain an unfair competitive advantage over other members; and

(iv) follow exchange policies compatible with the undertakings under this Section.

Section 2.   General exchange arrangements

(a) Each member shall notify the Fund, within thirty days after the date of the second amendment of this Agreement, of the exchange arrangements it intends to apply in fulfillment of its obligations under Section 1 of this Article, and shall notify the Fund promptly of any changes in its exchange arrangements.

(b) Under an international monetary system of the kind prevailing on January 1, 1976, exchange arrangements may include (i) the maintenance by a member of a value for its currency in terms of the special drawing right or another denominator, other than gold, selected by the member, or (ii) cooperative arrangements by which members maintain the value of their currencies in relation to the value of the currency or currencies of other members, or (iii) other exchange arrangements of a member's choice.

(c) To accord with the development of the international monetary system, the Fund, by an eighty-five percent majority of the total voting power, may make provision for general exchange arrangements without limiting the right of members to have exchange arrangements of their choice consistent with the purposes of the Fund and the obligations under Section 1 of this Article.

Section 3.   Surveillance over exchange arrangements

(a) The Fund shall oversee the international monetary system in order to ensure its effective operation, and shall oversee the compliance of each member with its obligations under Section 1 of this Article.

(*b*) In order to fulfill its functions under (*a*) above, the Fund shall exercise firm surveillance over the exchange rate policies of members, and shall adopt specific principles for the guidance of all members with respect to those policies. Each member shall provide the Fund with the information necessary for such surveillance, and, when requested by the Fund, shall consult with it on the member's exchange rate policies. The principles adopted by the Fund shall be consistent with cooperative arrangements by which members maintain the value of their currencies in relation to the value of the currency or currencies of other members, as well as with other exchange arrangements of a member's choice consistent with the purposes of the Fund and Section 1 of this Article. These principles shall respect the domestic social and political policies of members, and in applying these principles the Fund shall pay due regard to the circumstances of members.

Section 4.   *Par values*

The Fund may determine, by an eighty-five percent majority of the total voting power, that international economic conditions permit the introduction of a widespread system of exchange arrangements based on stable but adjustable par values. The Fund shall make the determination on the basis of the underlying stability of the world economy, and for this purpose shall take into account price movements and rates of expansion in the economies of members. The determination shall be made in light of the evolution of the international monetary system, with particular reference to sources of liquidity, and, in order to ensure the effective operation of a system of par values, to arrangements under which both members in surplus and members in deficit in their balances of payments take prompt, effective, and symmetrical action to achieve adjustment, as well as to arrangements for intervention and the treatment of imbalances. Upon making such determination, the Fund shall notify members that the provisions of Schedule C apply.

Section 5.   *Separate currencies within a member's territories*

(*a*) Action by a member with respect to its currency under this Article shall be deemed to apply to the separate currencies of all territories in respect of which the member has accepted this Agreement under Article XXXI, Section 2(*g*) unless the member declares that its action relates either to the metropolitan currency alone, or only to one or more specified separate currencies, or to the metropolitan currency and one or more specified separate currencies.

(*b*) Action by the Fund under this Article shall be deemed to relate to all currencies of a member referred to in (*a*) above unless the Fund declares otherwise.

Article V

Operations and Transactions of the Fund

Section 1.   *Agencies dealing with the Fund*

Each member shall deal with the Fund only through its Treasury, central bank, stabilization fund, or other similar fiscal agency, and the Fund shall deal only with or through the same agencies.

Section 2. Limitation on the Fund's operations and transactions

(a) Except as otherwise provided in this Agreement, transactions on the account of the Fund shall be limited to transactions for the purpose of supplying a member, on the initiative of such member, with special drawing rights or the currencies of other members from the general resources of the Fund, which shall be held in the General Resources Account, in exchange for the currency of the member desiring to make the purchase.

(b) If requested, the Fund may decide to perform financial and technical services, including the administration of resources contributed by members, that are consistent with the purposes of the Fund. Operations involved in the performance of such financial services shall not be on the account of the Fund. Services under this subsection shall not impose any obligation on a member without its consent.

Section 3. Conditions governing use of the Fund's general resources

(a) The Fund shall adopt policies on the use of its general resources, including policies on stand-by or similar arrangements, and may adopt special policies for special balance of payments problems, that will assist members to solve their balance of payments problems in a manner consistent with the provisions of this Agreement and that will establish adequate safeguards for the temporary use of the general resources of the Fund.

(b) A member shall be entitled to purchase the currencies of other members from the Fund in exchange for an equivalent amount of its own currency subject to the following conditions:

(i) the member's use of the general resources of the Fund would be in accordance with the provisions of this Agreement and the policies adopted under them;

(ii) the member represents that it has a need to make the purchase because of its balance of payments or its reserve position or developments in its reserves;

(iii) the proposed purchase would be a reserve tranche purchase, or would not cause the Fund's holdings of the purchasing member's currency to exceed two hundred percent of its quota;

(iv) the Fund has not previously declared under Section 5 of this Article, Article VI, Section 1, or Article XXVI, Section 2(a) that the member desiring to purchase is ineligible to use the general resources of the Fund.

(c) The Fund shall examine a request for a purchase to determine whether the proposed purchase would be consistent with the provisions of this Agreement and the policies adopted under them, provided that requests for reserve tranche purchases shall not be subject to challenge.

(d) The Fund shall adopt policies and procedures on the selection of currencies to be sold that take into account, in consultation with members, the balance of payments and reserve position of members and developments in the exchange markets, as well as the desirability of promoting over time balanced positions in the Fund, provided that if a member represents that it is proposing to purchase the currency of another member because the purchasing member wishes to obtain an equivalent amount of its own currency offered by the other member, it shall be entitled to purchase the currency of the other member unless the Fund has given notice under Article VII, Section 3 that its holdings of the currency have become scarce.

(*e*) (i) Each member shall ensure that balances of its currency purchased from the Fund are balances of a freely usable currency or can be exchanged at the time of purchase for a freely usable currency of its choice at an exchange rate between the two currencies equivalent to the exchange rate between them on the basis of Article XIX, Section 7(*a*).

(ii) Each member whose currency is purchased from the Fund or is obtained in exchange for currency purchased from the Fund shall collaborate with the Fund and other members to enable such balances of its currency to be exchanged, at the time of purchase, for the freely usable currencies of other members.

(iii) An exchange under (i) above of a currency that is not freely usable shall be made by the member whose currency is purchased unless that member and the purchasing member agree on another procedure.

(iv) A member purchasing from the Fund the freely usable currency of another member and wishing to exchange it at the time of purchase for another freely usable currency shall make the exchange with the other member if requested by that member. The exchange shall be made for a freely usable currency selected by the other member at the rate of exchange referred to in (i) above.

(*f*) Under policies and procedures which it shall adopt, the Fund may agree to provide a participant making a purchase in accordance with this Section with special drawing rights instead of the currencies of other members.

Section 4. Waiver of conditions

The Fund may in its discretion, and on terms which safeguard its interests, waive any of the conditions prescribed in Section 3(*b*)(iii) and (iv) of this Article, especially in the case of members with a record of avoiding large or continuous use of the Fund's general resources. In making a waiver it shall take into consideration periodic or exceptional requirements of the member requesting the waiver. The Fund shall also take into consideration a member's willingness to pledge as collateral security acceptable assets having a value sufficient in the opinion of the Fund to protect its interests and may require as a condition of waiver the pledge of such collateral security.

Section 5. Ineligibility to use the Fund's general resources

Whenever the Fund is of the opinion that any member is using the general resources of the Fund in a manner contrary to the purposes of the Fund, it shall present to the member a report setting forth the views of the Fund and prescribing a suitable time for reply. After presenting such a report to a member, the Fund may limit the use of its general resources by the member. If no reply to the report is received from the member within the prescribed time, or if the reply received is unsatisfactory, the Fund may continue to limit the member's use of the general resources of the Fund or may, after giving reasonable notice to the member, declare it ineligible to use the general resources of the Fund.

Section 6.   Other purchases and sales of special drawing rights by the Fund

(*a*) The Fund may accept special drawing rights offered by a participant in exchange for an equivalent amount of the currencies of other members.

(*b*) The Fund may provide a participant, at its request, with special drawing rights for an equivalent amount of the currencies of other members. The Fund's holdings of a member's currency shall not be increased as a result of these transactions above the level at which the holdings would be subject to charges under Section 8(*b*)(ii) of this Article.

(*c*) The currencies provided or accepted by the Fund under this Section shall be selected in accordance with policies that take into account the principles of Section 3(*d*) or 7(i) of this Article. The Fund may enter into transactions under this Section only if a member whose currency is provided or accepted by the Fund concurs in that use of its currency.

Section 7.   Repurchase by a member of its currency held by the Fund

(*a*) A member shall be entitled to repurchase at any time the Fund's holdings of its currency that are subject to charges under Section 8(*b*) of this Article.

(*b*) A member that has made a purchase under Section 3 of this Article will be expected normally, as its balance of payments and reserve position improves, to repurchase the Fund's holdings of its currency that result from the purchase and are subject to charges under Section 8(*b*) of this Article. A member shall repurchase these holdings if, in accordance with policies on repurchase that the Fund shall adopt and after consultation with the member, the Fund represents to the member that it should repurchase because of an improvement in its balance of payments and reserve position.

(*c*) A member that has made a purchase under Section 3 of this Article shall repurchase the Fund's holdings of its currency that result from the purchase and are subject to charges under Section 8(*b*) of this Article not later than five years after the date on which the purchase was made. The Fund may prescribe that repurchase shall be made by a member in installments during the period beginning three years and ending five years after the date of a purchase. The Fund, by an eighty-five percent majority of the total voting power, may change the periods for repurchase under this subsection, and any period so adopted shall apply to all members.

(*d*) The Fund, by an eighty-five percent majority of the total voting power, may adopt periods other than those that apply in accordance with (c) above, which shall be the same for all members, for the repurchase of holdings of currency acquired by the Fund pursuant to a special policy on the use of its general resources.

(*e*) A member shall repurchase, in accordance with policies that the Fund shall adopt by a seventy percent majority of the total voting power, the Fund's holdings of its currency that are not acquired as a result of purchases and are subject to charges under Section 8(*b*)(ii) of this Article.

(*f*) A decision prescribing that under a policy on the use of the general resources of the Fund the period for repurchase under (*c*) or (*d*) above shall be shorter than the one in effect under the policy shall apply only to holdings acquired by the Fund subsequent to the effective date of the decision.

(*g*) The Fund, on the request of a member, may postpone the date of discharge of a repurchase obligation, but not beyond the maximum period under (*c*) or (*d*) above or under policies adopted by the Fund under (*e*) above, unless the Fund determines, by a seventy percent majority of the total voting power, that a longer period for repurchase which is consistent with the temporary use of the general resources of the Fund is justified because discharge on the due date would result in exceptional hardship for the member.

(*h*) The Fund's policies under Section 3(*d*) of this Article may be supplemented by policies under which the Fund may decide after consultation with a member to sell under Section 3(*b*) of this Article its holdings of the member's currency that have not been repurchased in accordance with this Section 7, without prejudice to any action that the Fund may be authorized to take under any other provision of this Agreement.

(*i*) All repurchases under this Section shall be made with special drawing rights or with the currencies of other members specified by the Fund. The Fund shall adopt policies and procedures with regard to the currencies to be used by members in making repurchases that take into account the principles in Section 3(*d*) of this Article. The Fund's holdings of a member's currency that is used in repurchase shall not be increased by the repurchase above the level at which they would be subject to charges under Section 8(*b*)(ii) of this Article.

(*j*) (i) If a member's currency specified by the Fund under (i) above is not a freely usable currency, the member shall ensure that the repurchasing member can obtain it at the time of the repurchase in exchange for a freely usable currency selected by the member whose currency has been specified. An exchange of currency under this provision shall take place at an exchange rate between the two currencies equivalent to the exchange rate between them on the basis of Article XIX, Section 7(*a*).

(ii) Each member whose currency is specified by the Fund for repurchase shall collaborate with the Fund and other members to enable repurchasing members, at the time of the repurchase, to obtain the specified currency in exchange for the freely usable currencies of other members.

(iii) An exchange under (*j*)(i) above shall be made with the member whose currency is specified unless that member and the repurchasing member agree on another procedure.

(iv) If a repurchasing member wishes to obtain, at the time of the repurchase, the freely usable currency of another member specified by the Fund under (i) above, it shall, if requested by the other member, obtain the currency from the other member in exchange for a freely usable currency at the rate of exchange referred to in (*j*)(i) above. The Fund may adopt regulations on the freely usable currency to be provided in an exchange.

Section 8.   Charges

(*a*) (i) The Fund shall levy a service charge on the purchase by a member of special drawing rights or the currency of another member held in the General Resources Account in exchange for its own currency, provided that the Fund may levy a lower service charge on reserve tranche purchases than on other purchases. The service charge on reserve tranche purchases shall not exceed one-half of one percent.

(ii) The Fund may levy a charge for stand-by or similar arrangements. The Fund may decide that the charge for an arrangement shall be offset against the service charge levied under (i) above on purchases under the arrangement.

(*b*) The Fund shall levy charges on its average daily balances of a member's currency held in the General Resources Account to the extent that they

(i) have been acquired under a policy that has been the subject of an exclusion under Article XXX(*c*), or

(ii) exceed the amount of the member's quota after excluding any balances referred to in (i) above.

The rates of charge normally shall rise at intervals during the period in which balances are held.

(*c*) If a member fails to make a repurchase required under Section 7 of this Article, the Fund, after consultation with the member on the reduction of the Fund's holdings of its currency, may impose such charges as the Fund deems appropriate on its holdings of the member's currency that should have been repurchased.

(*d*) A seventy percent majority of the total voting power shall be required for the determination of the rates of charge under (*a*) and (*b*) above, which shall be uniform for all members, and under (*c*) above.

(*e*) A member shall pay all charges in special drawing rights, provided that in exceptional circumstances the Fund may permit a member to pay charges in the currencies of other members specified by the Fund, after consultation with them, or in its own currency. The Fund's holdings of a member's currency shall not be increased as a result of payments by other members under this provision above the level at which they would be subject to charges under (*b*) (ii) above.

Section 9.   Remuneration

(*a*) The Fund shall pay remuneration on the amount by which the percentage of quota prescribed under (*b*) or (*c*) below exceeds the Fund's average daily balances of a member's currency held in the General Resources Account other than balances acquired under a policy that has been the subject of an exclusion under Article XXX(*c*). The rate of remuneration, which shall be determined by the Fund by a seventy percent majority of the total voting power, shall be the same for all members and shall be not more than, nor less than four-fifths of, the rate of interest under Article XX, Section 3. In establishing the rate of remuneration, the Fund shall take into account the rates of charge under Article V, Section 8(*b*).

(*b*) The percentage of quota applying for the purposes of (*a*) above shall be:

(i) for each member that became a member before the second amendment of this Agreement, a percentage of quota corresponding to seventy-five percent of its quota on the date of the second amendment of this Agreement, and for each member that became a member after the date of the second amendment of this Agreement, a percentage of quota calculated by dividing the total of the amounts corresponding to the percentages of quota that apply to the other members on the date on which the member became a member by the total of the quotas of the other members on the same date; plus

(ii) the amounts it has paid to the Fund in currency or special drawing rights under Article III, Section 3(*a*) since the date applicable under (*b*)(i) above; and minus

(iii) the amounts it has received from the Fund in currency or special drawing rights under Article III, Section 3(*c*) since the date applicable under (*b*)(i) above.

(*c*) The Fund, by a seventy percent majority of the total voting power, may raise the latest percentage of quota applying for the purposes of (*a*) above to each member to:

(i) a percentage, not in excess of one hundred percent, that shall be determined for each member on the basis of the same criteria for all members, or

(ii) one hundred percent for all members.

(*d*) Remuneration shall be paid in special drawing rights, provided that either the Fund or the member may decide that the payment to the member shall be made in its own currency.

Section 10.   Computations

(*a*) The value of the Fund's assets held in the accounts of the General Department shall be expressed in terms of the special drawing right.

(*b*) All computations relating to currencies of members for the purpose of applying the provisions of this Agreement, except Article IV and Schedule C, shall be at the rates at which the Fund accounts for these currencies in accordance with Section 11 of this Article.

(*c*) Computations for the determination of amounts of currency in relation to quota for the purpose of applying the provisions of this Agreement shall not include currency held in the Special Disbursement Account or in the Investment Account.

Section 11.   Maintenance of value

(*a*) The value of the currencies of members held in the General Resources Account shall be maintained in terms of the special drawing right in accordance with exchange rates under Article XIX, Section 7(*a*).

(*b*) An adjustment in the Fund's holdings of a member's currency pursuant to this Section shall be made on the occasion of the use of that currency in an operation or transaction between the Fund and another member and at such other times as the Fund may decide or the member may request. Payments to or by the Fund in respect of an adjustment shall be made within a reasonable time, as determined by the Fund, after the date of adjustment, and at any other time requested by the member.

Section 12. Other operations and transactions

(*a*) The Fund shall be guided in all its policies and decisions under this Section by the objectives set forth in Article VIII, Section 7 and by the objective of avoiding the management of the price, or the establishment of a fixed price, in the gold market.

(*b*) Decisions of the Fund to engage in operations or transactions under (*c*), (*d*), and (*e*) below shall be made by an eighty-five percent majority of the total voting power.

(*c*) The Fund may sell gold for the currency of any member after consulting the member for whose currency the gold is sold, provided that the Fund's holdings of a member's currency held in the General Resources Account shall not be increased by the sale above the level at which they would be subject to charges under Section 8(*b*)(ii) of this Article without the concurrence of the member, and provided that, at the request of the member, the Fund at the time of sale shall exchange for the currency of another member such part of the currency received as would prevent such an increase. The exchange of a currency for the currency of another member shall be made after consultation with that member, and shall not increase the Fund's holdings of that member's currency above the level at which they would be subject to charges under Section 8(*b*)(ii) of this Article. The Fund shall adopt policies and procedures with regard to exchanges that take into account the principles applied under Section 7(*i*) of this Article. Sales under this provision to a member shall be at a price agreed for each transaction on the basis of prices in the market.

(*d*) The Fund may accept payments from a member in gold instead of special drawing rights or currency in any operations or transactions under this Agreement. Payments to the Fund under this provision shall be at a price agreed for each operation or transaction on the basis of prices in the market.

(*e*) The Fund may sell gold held by it on the date of the second amendment of this Agreement to those members that were members on August 31, 1975 and that agree to buy it, in proportion to their quotas on that date. If the Fund intends to sell gold under (*c*) above for the purpose of (*f*)(ii) below, it may sell to each developing member that agrees to buy it that portion of the gold which, if sold under (*c*) above, would have produced the excess that could have been distributed to it under (*f*)(iii) below. The gold that would be sold under this provision to a member that has been declared ineligible to use the general resources of the Fund under Section 5 of this Article shall be sold to it when the ineligibility ceases, unless the Fund decides to make the sale sooner. The sale of gold to a member under this subsection (*e*) shall be made in exchange for its currency and at a price equivalent at the time of sale to one special drawing right per 0.888 671 gram of fine gold.

(*f*) Whenever under (*c*) above the Fund sells gold held by it on the date of the second amendment of this Agreement, an amount of the proceeds equivalent at the time of sale to one special drawing right per 0.888 671 gram of fine gold shall be placed in the General Resources Account and, except as the Fund may decide otherwise under (*g*) below, any excess shall be held in the Special Disbursement Account. The assets held in the Special Disbursement Account shall be held separately from the other accounts of the General Department, and may be used at any time:

    (i) to make transfers to the General Resources Account for immediate use in operations and transactions authorized by provisions of this Agreement other than this Section;

    (ii) for operations and transactions that are not authorized by other provisions of this Agreement but are consistent with the purposes of the Fund. Under this subsection (*f*)(ii) balance of payments assistance may be made available on special terms to developing members in difficult circumstances, and for this purpose the Fund shall take into account the level of per capita income;

    (iii) for distribution to those developing members that were members on August 31, 1975, in proportion to their quotas on that date, of such part of the assets that the Fund decides to use for the purposes of (ii) above as corresponds to the proportion of the quotas of these members on the date of distribution to the total of the quotas of all members on the same date, provided that the distribution under this provision to a member that has been declared ineligible to use the general resources of the Fund under Section 5 of this Article shall be made when the ineligibility ceases, unless the Fund decides to make the distribution sooner.

Decisions to use assets pursuant to (i) above shall be taken by a seventy percent majority of the total voting power, and decisions pursuant to (ii) and (iii) above shall be taken by an eighty-five percent majority of the total voting power.

    (*g*) The Fund may decide, by an eighty-five percent majority of the total voting power, to transfer a part of the excess referred to in (*f*) above to the Investment Account for use pursuant to the provisions of Article XII, Section 6(*f*).

    (*h*) Pending uses specified under (*f*) above, the Fund may invest a member's currency held in the Special Disbursement Account in marketable obligations of that member or in marketable obligations of international financial organizations. The income of investment and interest received under (*f*)(ii) above shall be placed in the Special Disbursement Account. No investment shall be made without the concurrence of the member whose currency is used to make the investment. The Fund shall invest only in obligations denominated in special drawing rights or in the currency used for investment.

    (*i*) The General Resources Account shall be reimbursed from time to time in respect of the expenses of administration of the Special Disbursement Account paid from the General Resources Account by transfers from the Special Disbursement Account on the basis of a reasonable estimate of such expenses.

(*j*) The Special Disbursement Account shall be terminated in the event of the liquidation of the Fund and may be terminated prior to liquidation of the Fund by a seventy percent majority of the total voting power. Upon termination of the account because of the liquidation of the Fund, any assets in this account shall be distributed in accordance with the provisions of Schedule K. Upon termination prior to liquidation of the Fund, any assets in this account shall be transferred to the General Resources Account for immediate use in operations and transactions. The Fund, by a seventy percent majority of the total voting power, shall adopt rules and regulations for the administration of the Special Disbursement Account.

Article VI

Capital Transfers

Section 1.   Use of the Fund's general resources for capital transfers

(*a*) A member may not use the Fund's general resources to meet a large or sustained outflow of capital except as provided in Section 2 of this Article, and the Fund may request a member to exercise controls to prevent such use of the general resources of the Fund. If, after receiving such a request, a member fails to exercise appropriate controls, the Fund may declare the member ineligible to use the general resources of the Fund.

(*b*) Nothing in this Section shall be deemed:

(i) to prevent the use of the general resources of the Fund for capital transactions of reasonable amount required for the expansion of exports or in the ordinary course of trade, banking, or other business; or

(ii) to affect capital movements which are met out of a member's own resources, but members undertake that such capital movements will be in accordance with the purposes of the Fund.

Section 2.   Special provisions for capital transfers

A member shall be entitled to make reserve tranche purchases to meet capital transfers.

Section 3.   Controls of capital transfers

Members may exercise such controls as are necessary to regulate international capital movements, but no member may exercise these controls in a manner which will restrict payments for current transactions or which will unduly delay transfers of funds in settlement of commitments, except as provided in Article VII, Section 3(*b*) and in Article XIV, Section 2.

Article VII

Replenishment and Scarce Currencies

Section 1.   Measures to replenish the Fund's holdings of currencies

The Fund may, if it deems such action appropriate to replenish its holdings of any member's currency in the General Resources Account needed in connection with its transactions, take either or both of the following steps:

(i) propose to the member that, on terms and conditions agreed between the Fund and the member, the latter lend its currency to the

Fund or that, with the concurrence of the member, the Fund borrow such currency from some other source either within or outside the territories of the member, but no member shall be under any obligation to make such loans to the Fund or to concur in the borrowing of its currency by the Fund from any other source;

(ii) require the member, if it is a participant, to sell its currency to the Fund for special drawing rights held in the General Resources Account, subject to Article XIX, Section 4. In replenishing with special drawing rights, the Fund shall pay due regard to the principles of designation under Article XIX, Section 5.

Section 2.   *General scarcity of currency*

If the Fund finds that a general scarcity of a particular currency is developing, the Fund may so inform members and may issue a report setting forth the causes of the scarcity and containing recommendations designed to bring it to an end. A representative of the member whose currency is involved shall participate in the preparation of the report.

Section 3.   *Scarcity of the Fund's holdings*

(a) If it becomes evident to the Fund that the demand for a member's currency seriously threatens the Fund's ability to supply that currency, the Fund, whether or not it has issued a report under Section 2 of this Article, shall formally declare such currency scarce and shall thenceforth apportion its existing and accruing supply of the scarce currency with due regard to the relative needs of members, the general international economic situation, and any other pertinent considerations. The Fund shall also issue a report concerning its action.

(b) A formal declaration under (a) above shall operate as an authorization to any member, after consultation with the Fund, temporarily to impose limitations on the freedom of exchange operations in the scarce currency. Subject to the provisions of Article IV and Schedule C, the member shall have complete jurisdiction in determining the nature of such limitations, but they shall be no more restrictive than is necessary to limit the demand for the scarce currency to the supply held by, or accruing to, the member in question, and they shall be relaxed and removed as rapidly as conditions permit.

(c) The authorization under (b) above shall expire whenever the Fund formally declares the currency in question to be no longer scarce.

Section 4.   *Administration of restrictions*

Any member imposing restrictions in respect of the currency of any other member pursuant to the provisions of Section 3(b) of this Article shall give sympathetic consideration to any representations by the other member regarding the administration of such restrictions.

Section 5.   *Effect of other international agreements on restrictions*

Members agree not to invoke the obligations of any engagements entered into with other members prior to this Agreement in such a manner as will prevent the operation of the provisions of this Article.

Article VIII

General Obligations of Members

Section 1. Introduction

In addition to the obligations assumed under other articles of this Agreement, each member undertakes the obligations set out in this Article.

Section 2. Avoidance of restrictions on current payments

(*a*) Subject to the provisions of Article VII, Section 3(*b*) and Article XIV, Section 2, no member shall, without the approval of the Fund, impose restrictions on the making of payments and transfers for current international transactions.

(*b*) Exchange contracts which involve the currency of any member and which are contrary to the exchange control regulations of that member maintained or imposed consistently with this Agreement shall be unenforceable in the territories of any member. In addition, members may, by mutual accord, cooperate in measures for the purpose of making the exchange control regulations of either member more effective, provided that such measures and regulations are consistent with this Agreement.

Section 3. Avoidance of discriminatory currency practices

No member shall engage in, or permit any of its fiscal agencies referred to in Article V, Section 1 to engage in, any discriminatory currency arrangements or multiple currency practices, whether within or outside margins under Article IV or prescribed by or under Schedule C, except as authorized under this Agreement or approved by the Fund. If such arrangements and practices are engaged in at the date when this Agreement enters into force, the member concerned shall consult with the Fund as to their progressive removal unless they are maintained or imposed under Article XIV, Section 2, in which case the provisions of Section 3 of that Article shall apply.

Section 4. Convertibility of foreign-held balances

(*a*) Each member shall buy balances of its currency held by another member if the latter, in requesting the purchase, represents:

(i) that the balances to be bought have been recently acquired as a result of current transactions; or

(ii) that their conversion is needed for making payments for current transactions.

The buying member shall have the option to pay either in special drawing rights, subject to Article XIX, Section 4, or in the currency of the member making the request.

(*b*) The obligation in (*a*) above shall not apply when:

(i) the convertibility of the balances has been restricted consistently with Section 2 of this Article or Article VI, Section 3;

(ii) the balances have accumulated as a result of transactions effected before the removal by a member of restrictions maintained or imposed under Article XIV, Section 2;

(iii) the balances have been acquired contrary to the exchange regulations of the member which is asked to buy them;

(iv) the currency of the member requesting the purchase has been declared scarce under Article VII, Section 3(*a*); or

(v) the member requested to make the purchase is for any reason not entitled to buy currencies of other members from the Fund for its own currency.

Section 5. Furnishing of information

(*a*) The Fund may require members to furnish it with such information as it deems necessary for its activities, including, as the minimum necessary for the effective discharge of the Fund's duties, national data on the following matters:

(i) official holdings at home and abroad of (1) gold, (2) foreign exchange;

(ii) holdings at home and abroad by banking and financial agencies, other than official agencies, of (1) gold, (2) foreign exchange;

(iii) production of gold;

(iv) gold exports and imports according to countries of destination and origin;

(v) total exports and imports of merchandise, in terms of local currency values, according to countries of destination and origin;

(vi) international balance of payments, including (1) trade in goods and services, (2) gold transactions, (3) known capital transactions, and (4) other items;

(vii) international investment position, i.e., investments within the territories of the member owned abroad and investments abroad owned by persons in its territories so far as it is possible to furnish this information;

(viii) national income;

(ix) price indices, i.e., indices of commodity prices in wholesale and retail markets and of export and import prices;

(x) buying and selling rates for foreign currencies;

(xi) exchange controls, i.e., a comprehensive statement of exchange controls in effect at the time of assuming membership in the Fund and details of subsequent changes as they occur; and

(xii) where official clearing arrangements exist, details of amounts awaiting clearance in respect of commercial and financial transactions, and of the length of time during which such arrears have been outstanding.

(*b*) In requesting information the Fund shall take into consideration the varying ability of members to furnish the data requested. Members shall be under no obligation to furnish information in such detail that the affairs of individuals or corporations are disclosed. Members undertake, however, to furnish the desired information in as detailed and accurate a manner as is practicable and, so far as possible, to avoid mere estimates.

(c) The Fund may arrange to obtain further information by agreement with members. It shall act as a centre for the collection and exchange of information on monetary and financial problems, thus facilitating the preparation of studies designed to assist members in developing policies which further the purposes of the Fund.

Section 6. Consultation between members regarding existing international agreements

Where under this Agreement a member is authorized in the special or temporary circumstances specified in the Agreement to maintain or establish restrictions on exchange transactions, and there are other engagements between members entered into prior to this Agreement which conflict with the application of such restrictions, the parties to such engagements shall consult with one another with a view to making such mutually acceptable adjustments as may be necessary. The provisions of this Article shall be without prejudice to the operation of Article VII, Section 5.

Section 7. Obligation to collaborate regarding policies on reserve assets

Each member undertakes to collaborate with the Fund and with other members in order to ensure that the policies of the member with respect to reserve assets shall be consistent with the objectives of promoting better international surveillance of international liquidity and making the special drawing right the principal reserve asset in the international monetary system.

Article IX

Status, Immunities, and Privileges

Section 1. Purposes of Article

To enable the Fund to fulfill the functions with which it is entrusted, the status, immunities, and privileges set forth in this Article shall be accorded to the Fund in the territories of each member.

Section 2. Status of the Fund

The Fund shall possess full juridical personality, and in particular, the capacity:

> (i) to contract;

> (ii) to acquire and dispose of immovable and movable property; and

> (iii) to institute legal proceedings.

Section 3. Immunity from judicial process

The Fund, its property and its assets, wherever located and by whomsoever held, shall enjoy immunity from every form of judicial process except to the extent that it expressly waives its immunity for the purpose of any proceedings or by the terms of any contract.

Section 4.   Immunity from other action

Property and assets of the Fund, wherever located and by whomsoever held, shall be immune from search, requisition, confiscation, expropriation, or any other form of seizure by executive or legislative action.

Section 5.   Immunity of archives

The archives of the Fund shall be inviolable.

Section 6.   Freedom of assets from restrictions

To the extent necessary to carry out the activities provided for in this Agreement, all property and assets of the Fund shall be free from restrictions, regulations, controls, and moratoria of any nature.

Section 7.   Privilege for communications

The official communications of the Fund shall be accorded by members the same treatment as the official communications of other members.

Section 8.   Immunities and privileges of officers and employees

All Governors, Executive Directors, Alternates, members of committees, representatives appointed under Article XII, Section 3(*j*), advisors of any of the foregoing persons, officers, and employees of the Fund:

> (i) shall be immune from legal process with respect to acts performed by them in their official capacity except when the Fund waives this immunity;

> (ii) not being local nationals, shall be granted the same immunities from immigration restrictions, alien registration requirements, and national service obligations and the same facilities as regards exchange restrictions as are accorded by members to the representatives, officials, and employees of comparable rank of other members; and

> (iii) shall be granted the same treatment in respect of traveling facilities as is accorded by members to representatives, officials, and employees of comparable rank of other members.

Section 9.   Immunities from taxation

(*a*) The Fund, its assets, property, income, and its operations and transactions authorized by this Agreement shall be immune from all taxation and from all customs duties. The Fund shall also be immune from liability for the collection or payment of any tax or duty.

(*b*) No tax shall be levied on or in respect of salaries and emoluments paid by the Fund to Executive Directors, Alternates, officers, or employees of the Fund who are not local citizens, local subjects, or other local nationals.

(*c*) No taxation of any kind shall be levied on any obligation or security issued by the Fund, including any dividend or interest thereon, by whomsoever held:

> (i) which discriminates against such obligation or security solely because of its origin; or

(ii) if the sole jurisdictional basis for such taxation is the place or currency in which it is issued, made payable or paid, or the location of any office or place of business maintained by the Fund.

Section 10. *Application of Article*

Each member shall take such action as is necessary in its own territories for the purpose of making effective in terms of its own law the principles set forth in this Article and shall inform the Fund of the detailed action which it has taken.

Article X

Relations With Other International Organizations

The Fund shall cooperate within the terms of this Agreement with any general international organization and with public international organizations having specialized responsibilities in related fields. Any arrangements for such cooperation which would involve a modification of any provision of this Agreement may be effected only after amendment to this Agreement under Article XXVIII.

Article XI

Relations With Non-member Countries

Section 1. *Undertakings regarding relations with non-member countries*

Each member undertakes:

(i) not to engage in, nor to permit any of its fiscal agencies referred to in Article V, Section 1 to engage in, any transactions with a non-member or with persons in a non-member's territories which would be contrary to the provisions of this Agreement or the purposes of the Fund;

(ii) not to cooperate with a non-member or with persons in a non-member's territories in practices which would be contrary to the provisions of this Agreement or the purposes of the Fund; and

(iii) to cooperate with the Fund with a view to the application in its territories of appropriate measures to prevent transactions with non-members or with persons in their territories which would be contrary to the provisions of this Agreement or the purposes of the Fund.

Section 2. *Restrictions on transactions with non-member countries*

Nothing in this Agreement shall affect the right of any member to impose restrictions on exchange transactions with non-members or with persons in their territories unless the Fund finds that such restrictions prejudice the interests of members and are contrary to the purposes of the Fund.

Article XII

Organization and Management

Section 1. *Structure of the Fund*

The Fund shall have a Board of Governors, an Executive Board, a Managing Director, and a staff, and a Council if the Board of Governors decides, by an eighty-five percent majority of the total voting power, that the provisions of Schedule D shall be applied.

Section 2.   *Board of Governors*

(*a*) All powers under this Agreement not conferred directly on the Board of Governors, the Executive Board, or the Managing Director shall be vested in the Board of Governors.   The Board of Governors shall consist of one Governor and one Alternate appointed by each member in such manner as it may determine.   Each Governor and each Alternate shall serve until a new appointment is made.   No Alternate may vote except in the absence of his principal.   The Board of Governors shall select one of the Governors as chairman.

(*b*) The Board of Governors may delegate to the Executive Board authority to exercise any powers of the Board of Governors, except the powers conferred directly by this Agreement on the Board of Governors.

(*c*) The Board of Governors shall hold such meetings as may be provided for by the Board of Governors or called by the Executive Board.   Meetings of the Board of Governors shall be called whenever requested by fifteen members or by members having one-quarter of the total voting power.

(*d*) A quorum for any meeting of the Board of Governors shall be a majority of the Governors having not less than two-thirds of the total voting power.

(*e*) Each Governor shall be entitled to cast the number of votes allotted under Section 5 of this Article to the member appointing him.

(*f*) The Board of Governors may by regulation establish a procedure whereby the Executive Board, when it deems such action to be in the best interests of the Fund, may obtain a vote of the Governors on a specific question without calling a meeting of the Board of Governors.

(*g*) The Board of Governors, and the Executive Board to the extent authorized, may adopt such rules and regulations as may be necessary or appropriate to conduct the business of the Fund.

(*h*) Governors and Alternates shall serve as such without compensation from the Fund, but the Fund may pay them reasonable expenses incurred in attending meetings.

(*i*) The Board of Governors shall determine the remuneration to be paid to the Executive Directors and their Alternates and the salary and terms of the contract of service of the Managing Director.

(*j*) The Board of Governors and the Executive Board may appoint such committees as they deem advisable.   Membership of committees need not be limited to Governors or Executive Directors or their Alternates.

Section 3.   *Executive Board*

(*a*) The Executive Board shall be responsible for conducting the business of the Fund, and for this purpose shall exercise all the powers delegated to it by the Board of Governors.

(*b*) The Executive Board shall consist of Executive Directors with the Managing Director as chairman.   Of the Executive Directors:

(i) five shall be appointed by the five members having the largest quotas; and

(ii) fifteen shall be elected by the other members.

For the purpose of each regular election of Executive Directors, the Board of Governors, by an eighty-five percent majority of the total voting power, may increase or decrease the number of Executive Directors in (ii) above. The number of Executive Directors in (ii) above shall be reduced by one or two, as the case may be, if Executive Directors are appointed under (c) below, unless the Board of Governors decides, by an eighty-five percent majority of the total voting power, that this reduction would hinder the effective discharge of the functions of the Executive Board or of Executive Directors or would threaten to upset a desirable balance in the Executive Board.

(c) If, at the second regular election of Executive Directors and thereafter, the members entitled to appoint Executive Directors under (b)(i) above do not include the two members, the holdings of whose currencies by the Fund in the General Resources Account have been, on the average over the preceding two years, reduced below their quotas by the largest absolute amounts in terms of the special drawing right, either one or both of such members, as the case may be, may appoint an Executive Director.

(d) Elections of elective Executive Directors shall be conducted at intervals of two years in accordance with the provisions of Schedule E, supplemented by such regulations as the Fund deems appropriate. For each regular election of Executive Directors, the Board of Governors may issue regulations making changes in the proportion of votes required to elect Executive Directors under the provision of Schedule E.

(e) Each Executive Director shall appoint an Alternate with full power to act for him when he is not present. When the Executive Directors appointing them are present, Alternates may participate in meetings but may not vote.

(f) Executive Directors shall continue in office until their successors are appointed or elected. If the office of an elected Executive Director becomes vacant more than ninety days before the end of his term, another Executive Director shall be elected for the remainder of the term by the members that elected the former Executive Director. A majority of the votes cast shall be required for election. While the office remains vacant, the Alternate of the former Executive Director shall exercise his powers, except that of appointing an Alternate.

(g) The Executive Board shall function in continuous session at the principal office of the Fund and shall meet as often as the business of the Fund may require.

(h) A quorum for any meeting of the Executive Board shall be a majority of the Executive Directors having not less than one-half of the total voting power.

(i) (i) Each appointed Executive Director shall be entitled to cast the number of votes allotted under Section 5 of this Article to the member appointing him.

(ii) If the votes allotted to a member that appoints an Executive Director under (c) above were cast by an Executive Director together with the votes allotted to other members as a result of the last regular election of Executive Directors, the member may agree with each of the other members that the number of votes allotted to it shall be cast by the appointed Executive Director. A member making such an agreement shall not participate in the election of Executive Directors.

(iii) Each elected Executive Director shall be entitled to cast the number of votes which counted towards his election.

(iv) When the provisions of Section 5(b) of this Article are applicable, the votes which an Executive Director would otherwise be entitled to cast shall be increased or decreased correspondingly. All the votes which an Executive Director is entitled to cast shall be cast as a unit.

(j) The Board of Governors shall adopt regulations under which a member not entitled to appoint an Executive Director under (b) above may send a representative to attend any meeting of the Executive Board when a request made by, or a matter particularly affecting, that member is under consideration.

Section 4. Managing Director and staff

(a) The Executive Board shall select a Managing Director who shall not be a Governor or an Executive Director. The Managing Director shall be chairman of the Executive Board, but shall have no vote except a deciding vote in case of an equal division. He may participate in meetings of the Board of Governors, but shall not vote at such meetings. The Managing Director shall cease to hold office when the Executive Board so decides.

(b) The Managing Director shall be chief of the operating staff of the Fund and shall conduct, under the direction of the Executive Board, the ordinary business of the Fund. Subject to the general control of the Executive Board, he shall be responsible for the organization, appointment, and dismissal of the staff of the Fund.

(c) The Managing Director and the staff of the Fund, in the discharge of their functions, shall owe their duty entirely to the Fund and to no other authority. Each member of the Fund shall respect the international character of this duty and shall refrain from all attempts to influence any of the staff in the discharge of these functions.

(d) In appointing the staff the Managing Director shall, subject to the paramount importance of securing the highest standards of efficiency and of technical competence, pay due regard to the importance of recruiting personnel on as wide a geographical basis as possible.

Section 5. Voting

(a) Each member shall have two hundred fifty votes plus one additional vote for each part of its quota equivalent to one hundred thousand special drawing rights.

(b) Whenever voting is required under Article V, Section 4 or 5, each member shall have the number of votes to which it is entitled under (a) above adjusted

(i) by the addition of one vote for the equivalent of each four hundred thousand special drawing rights of net sales of its currency from the general resources of the Fund up to the date when the vote is taken, or

(ii) by the subtraction of one vote for the equivalent of each four hundred thousand special drawing rights of its net purchases under Article V, Section 3(*b*) and (*f*) up to the date when the vote is taken,

provided that neither net purchases nor net sales shall be deemed at any time to exceed an amount equal to the quota of the member involved.

(*c*) Except as otherwise specifically provided, all decisions of the Fund shall be made by a majority of the votes cast.

Section 6.   Reserves, distribution of net income, and investment

(*a*) The Fund shall determine annually what part of its net income shall be placed to general reserve or special reserve, and what part, if any, shall be distributed.

(*b*) The Fund may use the special reserve for any purpose for which it may use the general reserve, except distribution.

(*c*) If any distribution is made of the net income of any year, it shall be made to all members in proportion to their quotas.

(*d*) The Fund, by a seventy percent majority of the total voting power, may decide at any time to distribute any part of the general reserve. Any such distribution shall be made to all members in proportion to their quotas.

(*e*) Payments under (*c*) and (*d*) above shall be made in special drawing rights, provided that either the Fund or the member may decide that the payment to the member shall be made in its own currency.

(*f*) (i) The Fund may establish an Investment Account for the purposes of this subsection (*f*). The assets of the Investment Account shall be held separately from the other accounts of the General Department.

(ii) The Fund may decide to transfer to the Investment Account a part of the proceeds of the sale of gold in accordance with Article V, Section 12(*g*) and, by a seventy percent majority of the total voting power, may decide to transfer to the Investment Account, for immediate investment, currencies held in the General Resources Account. The amount of these transfers shall not exceed the total amount of the general reserve and the special reserve at the time of the decision.

(iii) The Fund may invest a member's currency held in the Investment Account in marketable obligations of that member or in marketable obligations of international financial organizations. No investment shall be made without the concurrence of the member whose currency is used to make the investment. The Fund shall invest only in obligations denominated in special drawing rights or in the currency used for investment.

(iv) The income of investment may be invested in accordance with the provisions of this subsection (*f*). Income not invested shall be held in the Investment Account or may be used for meeting the expenses of conducting the business of the Fund.

(v) The Fund may use a member's currency held in the Investment Account to obtain the currencies needed to meet the expenses of conducting the business of the Fund.

(vi) The Investment Account shall be terminated in the event of liquidation of the Fund and may be terminated, or the amount of the investment may be reduced, prior to liquidation of the Fund by a seventy percent majority of the total voting power. The Fund, by a seventy percent majority of the total voting power, shall adopt rules and regulations regarding administration of the Investment Account, which shall be consistent with (vii), (viii), and (ix) below.

(vii) Upon termination of the Investment Account because of liquidation of the Fund, any assets in this account shall be distributed in accordance with the provisions of Schedule K, provided that a portion of these assets corresponding to the proportion of the assets transferred to this account under Article V, Section 12(g) to the total of the assets transferred to this account shall be deemed to be assets held in the Special Disbursement Account and shall be distributed in accordance with Schedule K, paragraph 2(a)(ii).

(viii) Upon termination of the Investment Account prior to liquidation of the Fund, a portion of the assets held in this account corresponding to the proportion of the assets transferred to this account under Article V, Section 12(g) to the total of the assets transferred to the account shall be transferred to the Special Disbursement Account if it has not been terminated, and the balance of the assets held in the Investment Account shall be transferred to the General Resources Account for immediate use in operations and transactions.

(ix) On a reduction of the amount of the investment by the Fund, a portion of the reduction corresponding to the proportion of the assets transferred to the Investment Account under Article V, Section 12(g) to the total of the assets transferred to this account shall be transferred to the Special Disbursement Account if it has not been terminated, and the balance of the reduction shall be transferred to the General Resources Account for immediate use in operations and transactions.

Section 7.   *Publication of reports*

(a) The Fund shall publish an annual report containing an audited statement of its accounts, and shall issue, at intervals of three months or less, a summary statement of its operations and transactions and its holdings of special drawing rights, gold, and currencies of members.

(b) The Fund may publish such other reports as it deems desirable for carrying out its purposes.

Section 8.   *Communication of views to members*

The Fund shall at all times have the right to communicate its views informally to any member on any matter arising under this Agreement. The Fund may, by a seventy percent majority of the total voting power, decide to publish a report made to a member regarding its monetary or economic conditions and developments which directly tend to produce a serious disequilibrium in the international balance of payments of members. If the member is not entitled to appoint an Executive Director, it shall be entitled to representation in accordance with Section 3(*j*) of this Article. The Fund shall not publish a report involving changes in the fundamental structure of the economic organization of members.

Article XIII

Offices and Depositories

Section 1. Location of offices

The principal office of the Fund shall be located in the territory of the member having the largest quota, and agencies or branch offices may be established in the territories of other members.

Section 2. Depositories

(*a*) Each member shall designate its central bank as a depository for all the Fund's holdings of its currency, or if it has no central bank it shall designate such other institution as may be acceptable to the Fund.

(*b*) The Fund may hold other assets, including gold, in the depositories designated by the five members having the largest quotas and in such other designated depositories as the Fund may select. Initially, at least one-half of the holdings of the Fund shall be held in the depository designated by the member in whose territories the Fund has its principal office and at least forty percent shall be held in the depositories designated by the remaining four members referred to above. However, all transfers of gold by the Fund shall be made with due regard to the costs of transport and anticipated requirements of the Fund. In an emergency the Executive Board may transfer all or any part of the Fund's gold holdings to any place where they can be adequately protected.

Section 3. Guarantee of the Fund's assets

Each member guarantees all assets of the Fund against loss resulting from failure or default on the part of the depository designated by it.

* * *

Article XV

Special Drawing Rights

Section 1. Authority to allocate special drawing rights

To meet the need, as and when it arises, for a supplement to existing reserve assets, the Fund is authorized to allocate special drawing rights to members that are participants in the Special Drawing Rights Department.

Section 2. Valuation of the special drawing right

The method of valuation of the special drawing right shall be determined by the Fund by a seventy percent majority of the total voting power, provided, however, that an eighty-five percent majority of the total voting power shall be required for a change in the principle of valuation or a fundamental change in the application of the principle in effect.

* * *

Article XXII

General Obligations of Participants

In addition to the obligations assumed with respect to special drawing rights under other articles of this Agreement, each participant undertakes to collaborate with the Fund and with other participants in order to facilitate the effective functioning of the Special Drawing Rights Department and the proper use of special drawing rights in accordance with this Agreement and with the objective of making the special drawing right the principal reserve asset in the international monetary system.

Article XXIII

Suspension of Operations and Transactions in Special Drawing Rights

Section 1. Emergency provisions

In the event of an emergency or the development of unforeseen circumstances threatening the activities of the Fund with respect to the Special Drawing Rights Department, the Executive Board, by an eighty-five percent majority of the total voting power, may suspend for a period of not more than one year the operation of any of the provisions relating to operations and transactions in special drawing rights, and the provisions of Article XXVII, Section 1(*b*), (*c*), and (*d*) shall then apply.

Section 2. Failure to fulfill obligations

(*a*) If the Fund finds that a participant has failed to fulfill its obligations under Article XIX, Section 4, the right of the participant to use its special drawing rights shall be suspended unless the Fund otherwise decides.

(*b*) If the Fund finds that a participant has failed to fulfill any other obligation with respect to special drawing rights, the Fund may suspend the right of the participant to use special drawing rights it acquires after the suspension.

(*c*) Regulations shall be adopted to ensure that before action is taken against any participant under (*a*) or (*b*) above, the participant shall be informed immediately of the complaint against it and given an adequate opportunity for stating its case, both orally and in writing. Whenever the participant is thus informed of a complaint relating to (*a*) above, it shall not use special drawing rights pending the disposition of the complaint.

(*d*) Suspension under (*a*) or (*b*) above or limitation under (*c*) above shall not affect a participant's obligation to provide currency in accordance with Article XIX, Section 4.

(*e*) The Fund may at any time terminate a suspension under (*a*) or (*b*) above, provided that a suspension imposed on a participant under (*b*) above for failure to fulfill the obligations under Article XIX, Section 6(*a*) shall not be terminated until one hundred eighty days after the end of the first calendar quarter during which the participant complies with the rules for reconstitution.

(*f*) The right of a participant to use its special drawing rights shall not be suspended because it has become ineligible to use the Fund's general resources under Article V, Section 5, Article VI, Section 1, or Article XXVI,

Section 2(*a*). Article XXVI, Section 2 shall not apply because a participant has failed to fulfill any obligations with respect to special drawing rights.

Article XXIV

Termination of Participation

Section 1. Right to terminate participation

(*a*) Any participant may terminate its participation in the Special Drawing Rights Department at any time by transmitting a notice in writing to the Fund at its principal office. Termination shall become effective on the date the notice is received.

(*b*) A participant that withdraws from membership in the Fund shall be deemed to have simultaneously terminated its participation in the Special Drawing Rights Department.

Section 2. Settlement on termination

(*a*) When a participant terminates its participation in the Special Drawing Rights Department, all operations and transactions by the terminating participant in special drawing rights shall cease except as otherwise permitted under an agreement made pursuant to (*c*) below in order to facilitate a settlement or as provided in Sections 3, 5, and 6 of this Article or in Schedule H. Interest and charges that accrued to the date of termination and assessments levied before that date but not paid shall be paid in special drawing rights.

(*b*) The Fund shall be obligated to redeem all special drawing rights held by the terminating participant, and the terminating participant shall be obligated to pay to the Fund an amount equal to its net cumulative allocation and any other amounts that may be due and payable because of its participation in the Special Drawing Rights Department. These obligations shall be set off against each other and the amount of special drawing rights held by the terminating participant that is used in the setoff to extinguish its obligation to the Fund shall be cancelled.

(*c*) A settlement shall be made with reasonable despatch by agreement between the terminating participant and the Fund with respect to any obligation of the terminating participant or the Fund after the setoff in (*b*) above. If agreement on a settlement is not reached promptly the provisions of Schedule H shall apply.

Section 3. Interest and charges

After the date of termination the Fund shall pay interest on any outstanding balance of special drawing rights held by a terminating participant, and the terminating participant shall pay charges on any outstanding obligation owed to the Fund at the times and rates prescribed under Article XX. Payment shall be made in special drawing rights. A terminating participant shall be entitled to obtain special drawing rights with a freely usable currency to pay charges or assessments in a transaction with a participant specified by the Fund or by agreement from any other holder, or to dispose of special drawing rights received as interest in a transaction with any participant designated under Article XIX, Section 5 or by agreement with any other holder.

Section 4.   Settlement of obligation to the Fund

Currency received by the Fund from a terminating participant shall be used by the Fund to redeem special drawing rights held by participants in proportion to the amount by which each participant's holdings of special drawing rights exceed its net cumulative allocation at the time the currency is received by the Fund.   Special drawing rights so redeemed and special drawing rights obtained by a terminating participant under the provisions of this Agreement to meet any installment due under an agreement on settlement or under Schedule H and set off against that installment shall be cancelled.

Section 5.   Settlement of obligation to a terminating participant

Whenever the Fund is required to redeem special drawing rights held by a terminating participant, redemption shall be made with currency provided by participants specified by the Fund.   These participants shall be specified in accordance with the principles in Article XIX, Section 5.   Each specified participant shall provide at its option the currency of the terminating participant or a freely usable currency to the Fund and shall receive an equivalent amount of special drawing rights.   However, a terminating participant may use its special drawing rights to obtain its own currency, a freely usable currency, or any other asset from any holder, if the Fund so permits.

Section 6.   General Resources Account transactions

In order to facilitate settlement with a terminating participant, the Fund may decide that a terminating participant shall

(i) use any special drawing rights held by it after the setoff in Section 2(*b*) of this Article, when they are to be redeemed, in a transaction with the Fund conducted through the General Resources Account to obtain its own currency or a freely usable currency at the option of the Fund, or

(ii) obtain special drawing rights in a transaction with the Fund conducted through the General Resources Account for a currency acceptable to the Fund to meet any charges or installment due under an agreement or the provisions of Schedule H.

Article XXV

Liquidation of the Special Drawing Rights Department

(*a*) The Special Drawing Rights Department may not be liquidated except by decision of the Board of Governors.   In an emergency, if the Executive Board decides that liquidation of the Special Drawing Rights Department may be necessary, it may temporarily suspend allocations or cancellations and all operations and transactions in special drawing rights pending decision by the Board of Governors.   A decision by the Board of Governors to liquidate the Fund shall be a decision to liquidate both the General Department and the Special Drawing Rights Department.

(*b*) If the Board of Governors decides to liquidate the Special Drawing Rights Department, all allocations or cancellations and all operations and transactions in special drawing rights and the activities of the Fund with respect to the Special Drawing Rights Department shall cease except those incidental to the orderly discharge of the obligations of participants and of the

Fund with respect to special drawing rights, and all obligations of the Fund and of participants under this Agreement with respect to special drawing rights shall cease except those set out in this Article, Article XX, Article XXI(*d*), Article XXIV, Article XXIX(*c*), and Schedule H, or any agreement reached under Article XXIV subject to paragraph 4 of Schedule H, and Schedule I.

(*c*) Upon liquidation of the Special Drawing Rights Department, interest and charges that accrued to the date of liquidation and assessments levied before that date but not paid shall be paid in special drawing rights. The Fund shall be obligated to redeem all special drawing rights held by holders, and each participant shall be obligated to pay the Fund an amount equal to its net cumulative allocation of special drawing rights and such other amounts as may be due and payable because of its participation in the Special Drawing Rights Department.

(*d*) Liquidation of the Special Drawing Rights Department shall be administered in accordance with the provisions of Schedule I.

Article XXVI

Withdrawal From Membership

Section 1. Right of members to withdraw

Any member may withdraw from the Fund at any time by transmitting a notice in writing to the Fund at its principal office. Withdrawal shall become effective on the date such notice is received.

Section 2. Compulsory withdrawal

(*a*) If a member fails to fulfill any of its obligations under this Agreement, the Fund may declare the member ineligible to use the general resources of the Fund. Nothing in this Section shall be deemed to limit the provisions of Article V, Section 5 or Article VI, Section 1.

(*b*) If, after the expiration of a reasonable period the member persists in its failure to fulfill any of its obligations under this Agreement, the Fund may, by a seventy percent majority of the total voting power, suspend the voting rights of the member. During the period of suspension, the provisions of Schedule L shall apply. The Fund may, by a seventy percent majority of the total voting power, terminate the suspension at any time.

(*c*) If, after the expiration of a reasonable period following a decision of suspension under (*b*) above, the member persists in its failure to fulfill any of its obligations under this Agreement, that member may be required to withdraw from membership in the Fund by a decision of the Board of Governors carried by a majority of the Governors having eighty-five percent of the total voting power.

(*d*) Regulations shall be adopted to ensure that before action is taken against any member under (*a*), (*b*) or (*c*) above, the member shall be informed in reasonable time of the complaint against it and given an adequate opportunity for stating its case, both orally and in writing.

Section 3.   Settlement of accounts with members withdrawing

When a member withdraws from the Fund, normal operations and transactions of the Fund in its currency shall cease and settlement of all accounts between it and the Fund shall be made with reasonable despatch by agreement between it and the Fund. If agreement is not reached promptly, the provisions of Schedule J shall apply to the settlement of accounts.

Article XXVII

Emergency Provisions

Section 1.   Temporary suspension

(*a*) In the event of an emergency or the development of unforeseen circumstances threatening the activities of the Fund, the Executive Board, by an eighty-five percent majority of the total voting power, may suspend for a period of not more than one year the operation of any of the following provisions:

  (i) Article V, Sections 2, 3, 7, 8(*a*)(i) and (*e*);

  (ii) Article VI, Section 2;

  (iii) Article XI, Section 1;

  (iv) Schedule C, paragraph 5.

(*b*) A suspension of the operation of a provision under (*a*) above may not be extended beyond one year except by the Board of Governors which, by an eighty-five percent majority of the total voting power, may extend a suspension for an additional period of not more than two years if it finds that the emergency or unforeseen circumstances referred to in (*a*) above continue to exist.

(*c*) The Executive Board may, by a majority of the total voting power, terminate such suspension at any time.

(*d*) The Fund may adopt rules with respect to the subject matter of a provision during the period in which its operation is suspended.

Section 2.   Liquidation of the Fund

(*a*) The Fund may not be liquidated except by decision of the Board of Governors. In an emergency, if the Executive Board decides that liquidation of the Fund may be necessary, it may temporarily suspend all operations and transactions, pending decision by the Board of Governors.

(*b*) If the Board of Governors decides to liquidate the Fund, the Fund shall forthwith cease to engage in any activities except those incidental to the orderly collection and liquidation of its assets and the settlement of its liabilities, and all obligations of members under this Agreement shall cease except those set out in this Article, in Article XXIX(*c*), in Schedule J, paragraph 7, and in Schedule K.

(*c*) Liquidation shall be administered in accordance with the provisions of Schedule K.

Article XXVIII

Amendments

(*a*) Any proposal to introduce modifications in this Agreement, whether emanating from a member, a Governor, or the Executive Board, shall be communicated to the chairman of the Board of Governors who shall bring the proposal before the Board of Governors. If the proposed amendment is approved by the Board of Governors, the Fund shall, by circular letter or telegram, ask all members whether they accept the proposed amendment. When three-fifths of the members, having eighty-five percent of the total voting power, have accepted the proposed amendment, the Fund shall certify the fact by a formal communication addressed to all members.

(*b*) Notwithstanding (*a*) above, acceptance by all members is required in the case of any amendment modifying:

(i) the right to withdraw from the Fund (Article XXVI, Section 1);

(ii) the provision that no change in a member's quota shall be made without its consent (Article III, Section 2(*d*)); and

(iii) the provision that no change may be made in the par value of a member's currency except on the proposal of that member (Schedule C, paragraph 6).

(*c*) Amendments shall enter into force for all members three months after the date of the formal communication unless a shorter period is specified in the circular letter or telegram.

Article XXIX

Interpretation

(*a*) Any question of interpretation of the provisions of this Agreement arising between any member and the Fund or between any members of the Fund shall be submitted to the Executive Board for its decision. If the question particularly affects any member not entitled to appoint an Executive Director, it shall be entitled to representation in accordance with Article XII, Section 3(*j*).

(*b*) In any case where the Executive Board has given a decision under (*a*) above, any member may require, within three months from the date of the decision, that the question be referred to the Board of Governors, whose decision shall be final. Any question referred to the Board of Governors shall be considered by a Committee on Interpretation of the Board of Governors. Each Committee member shall have one vote. The Board of Governors shall establish the membership, procedures, and voting majorities of the Committee. A decision of the Committee shall be the decision of the Board of Governors unless the Board of Governors, by an eighty-five percent majority of the total voting power, decides otherwise. Pending the result of the reference to the Board of Governors the Fund may, so far as it deems necessary, act on the basis of the decision of the Executive Board.

(*c*) Whenever a disagreement arises between the Fund and a member which has withdrawn, or between the Fund and any member during liquidation of the Fund, such disagreement shall be submitted to arbitration by a tribunal of three arbitrators, one appointed by the Fund, another by the member or withdrawing member, and an umpire who, unless the parties otherwise agree, shall be appointed by the President of the International Court of Justice or such other authority as may have been prescribed by regulation adopted by the Fund. The umpire shall have full power to settle all questions of procedure in any case where the parties are in disagreement with respect thereto.

Article XXX

Explanation of Terms

In interpreting the provisions of this Agreement the Fund and its members shall be guided by the following provisions:

(*a*) The Fund's holdings of a member's currency in the General Resources Account shall include any securities accepted by the Fund under Article III, Section 4.

(*b*) Stand-by arrangement means a decision of the Fund by which a member is assured that it will be able to make purchases from the General Resources Account in accordance with the terms of the decision during a specified period and up to a specified amount.

(*c*) Reserve tranche purchase means a purchase by a member of special drawing rights or the currency of another member in exchange for its own currency which does not cause the Fund's holdings of the member's currency in the General Resources Account to exceed its quota, provided that for the purposes of this definition the Fund may exclude purchases and holdings under:

(i) policies on the use of its general resources for compensatory financing of export fluctuations;

(ii) policies on the use of its general resources in connection with the financing of contributions to international buffer stocks of primary products; and

(iii) other policies on the use of its general resources in respect of which the Fund decides, by an eighty-five percent majority of the total voting power, that an exclusion shall be made.

(*d*) Payments for current transactions means payments which are not for the purpose of transferring capital, and includes, without limitation:

(1) all payments due in connection with foreign trade, other current business, including services, and normal short-term banking and credit facilities;

(2) payments due as interest on loans and as net income from other investments;

(3) payments of moderate amount for amortization of loans or for depreciation of direct investments; and

(4) moderate remittances for family living expenses.

The Fund may, after consultation with the members concerned, determine whether certain specific transactions are to be considered current transactions or capital transactions.

(*e*) Net cumulative allocation of special drawing rights means the total amount of special drawing rights allocated to a participant less its share of special drawing rights that have been cancelled under Article XVIII, Section 2(*a*).

(*f*) A freely usable currency means a member's currency that the Fund determines (i) is, in fact, widely used to make payments for international transactions, and (ii) is widely traded in the principal exchange markets.

(*g*) Members that were members on August 31, 1975, shall be deemed to include a member that accepted membership after that date pursuant to a resolution of the Board of Governors adopted before that date.

(*h*) Transactions of the Fund means exchanges of monetary assets by the Fund for other monetary assets. Operations of the Fund means other uses or receipts of monetary assets by the Fund.

(*i*) Transactions in special drawing rights means exchanges of special drawing rights for other monetary assets. Operations in special drawing rights means other uses of special drawing rights.

Article XXXI

Final Provisions

Section 1. Entry into force

This Agreement shall enter into force when it has been signed on behalf of governments having sixty-five percent of the total of the quotas set forth in Schedule A and when the instruments referred to in Section 2(*a*) of this Article have been deposited on their behalf, but in no event shall this Agreement enter into force before May 1, 1945.

Section 2. Signature

(*a*) Each government on whose behalf this Agreement is signed shall deposit with the Government of the United States of America an instrument setting forth that it has accepted this Agreement in accordance with its law and has taken all steps necessary to enable it to carry out all of its obligations under this Agreement.

(*b*) Each country shall become a member of the Fund as from the date of the deposit on its behalf of the instrument referred to in (*a*) above, except that no country shall become a member before this Agreement enters into force under Section 1 of this Article.

(*c*) The Government of the United States of America shall inform the governments of all countries whose names are set forth in Schedule A, and the governments of all countries whose membership is approved in accordance with Article II, Section 2, of all signatures of this Agreement and of the deposit of all instruments referred to in (*a*) above.

(*d*) At the time this Agreement is signed on its behalf, each government shall transmit to the Government of the United States of America one one-hundredth of one percent of its total subscription in gold or United States dollars for the purpose of meeting administrative expenses of the Fund. The Government of the United States of America shall hold such funds in a special deposit account and shall transmit them to the Board of Governors of the

Fund when the initial meeting has been called. If this Agreement has not come into force by December 31, 1945, the Government of the United States of America shall return such funds to the governments that transmitted them.

(*e*) This Agreement shall remain open for signature at Washington on behalf of the governments of the countries whose names are set forth in Schedule A until December 31, 1945.

(*f*) After December 31, 1945, this Agreement shall be open for signature on behalf of the Government of any country whose membership has been approved in accordance with Article II, Section 2.

(*g*) By their signature of this Agreement, all governments accept it both on their own behalf and in respect of all their colonies, overseas territories, all territories under their protection, suzerainty, or authority, and all territories in respect of which they exercise a mandate.

(*h*) Subsection (*d*) above shall come into force with regard to each signatory government as from the date of its signature.

[The signature and depositary clause reproduced below followed the text of Article XX in the original Articles of Agreement]

Done at Washington, in a single copy which shall remain deposited in the archives of the Government of the United States of America, which shall transmit certified copies to all governments whose names are set forth in Schedule A and to all governments whose membership is approved in accordance with Article II, Section 2.

Part III

THE NORTH AMERICAN FREE TRADE AGREEMENT

Introduction to Part III

Part III contains the North American Free Trade Agreement and the related side agreements on the environment, labor and safeguards (emergency action).

Because of space considerations, we did not include certain product lists in the agreement itself nor the schedules and many of the annexes.

Table of Contents

Item 40

NORTH AMERICAN FREE TRADE AGREEMENT BE-TWEEN THE GOVERNMENT OF THE UNITED STATES OF AMERICA, THE GOVERNMENT OF CANADA AND THE GOVERNMENT OF THE UNITED MEXICAN STATES

Table of Contents

PART EIGHT: OTHER PROVISIONS

Chapter Twenty–One: Exceptions
Chapter Twenty–Two: Final Provisions
Notes

PREAMBLE

The Government of the United States of America, the Government of Canada and the Government of the United Mexican States, resolved to: STRENGTHEN the special bonds of friendship and cooperation among their nations; CONTRIBUTE to the harmonious development and expansion of world trade and provide a catalyst to broader international cooperation; CREATE an expanded and secure market for the goods and services produced in their territories; REDUCE distortions to trade; ESTABLISH clear and mutually advantageous rules governing their trade; ENSURE a predictable commercial framework for business planning and investment; BUILD on their respective rights and obligations under the General Agreement on Tariffs and Trade and other multilateral and bilateral instruments of cooperation; ENHANCE the competitiveness of their firms in global markets; FOSTER creativity and innovation, and promote trade in goods and services that are the subject of intellectual property rights; CREATE new employment opportunities and improve working conditions and living standards in their respective territories; UNDERTAKE each of the preceding in a manner consistent with environmental protection and conservation; PRESERVE their flexibility to safeguard the public welfare; PROMOTE sustainable development; STRENGTHEN the development and enforcement of environmental laws and regulations; and PROTECT, enhance and enforce basic workers' rights;

HAVE AGREED as follows:

PART ONE

GENERAL

CHAPTER ONE: OBJECTIVES

Article 101

Establishment of the Free Trade Area

The Parties to this Agreement, consistent with Article XXIV of the General Agreement on Tariffs and Trade, hereby establish a free trade area.

Article 102

Objectives

1. The objectives of this Agreement, as elaborated more specifically through its principles and rules, including national treatment, most-favored-nation treatment and transparency, are to:

(a) eliminate barriers to trade in, and facilitate the cross-border movement of, goods and services between the territories of the Parties;

(b) promote conditions of fair competition in the free trade area;

(c) increase substantially investment opportunities in the territories of the Parties;

(d) provide adequate and effective protection and enforcement of intellectual property rights in each Party's territory;

(e) create effective procedures for the implementation and application of this Agreement, for its joint administration and for the resolution of disputes; and

(f) establish a framework for further trilateral, regional and multilateral cooperation to expand and enhance the benefits of this Agreement.

2. The Parties shall interpret and apply the provisions of this Agreement in the light of its objectives set out in paragraph 1 and in accordance with applicable rules of international law.

Article 103
Relation to Other Agreements

1. The Parties affirm their existing rights and obligations with respect to each other under the General Agreement on Tariffs and Trade and other agreements to which such Parties are party.

2. In the event of any inconsistency between this Agreement and such other agreements, this Agreement shall prevail to the extent of the inconsistency, except as otherwise provided in this Agreement.

Article 104
Relation to Environmental and Conservation Agreements

1. In the event of any inconsistency between this Agreement and the specific trade obligations set out in:

(a) the Convention on International Trade in Endangered Species of Wild Fauna and Flora, done at Washington, March 3, 1973, as amended June 22, 1979,

(b) the Montreal Protocol on Substances that Deplete the Ozone Layer, done at Montreal, September 16, 1987, as amended June 29, 1990,

(c) the Basel Convention on the Control of Transboundary Movements of Hazardous Wastes and Their Disposal, done at Basel, March 22, 1989, on its entry into force for Canada, Mexico and the United States, or

(d) the agreements set out in Annex 104.1,

such obligations shall prevail to the extent of the inconsistency, provided that where a Party has a choice among equally effective and reasonably available means of complying with such obligations, the Party chooses the alternative that is the least inconsistent with the other provisions of this Agreement.

2. The Parties may agree in writing to modify Annex 104.1 to include any amendment to an agreement referred to in paragraph 1, and any other environmental or conservation agreement.

Annex 104.1
Bilateral and Other Environmental and Conservation Agreements

1. The Agreement Between the Government of Canada and the Government of the United States of America Concerning the Transboundary Movement of Hazardous Waste, signed at Ottawa, October 28, 1986.

2. The Agreement Between the United States of America and the United Mexican States on Cooperation for the Protection and Improvement of the Environment in the Border Area, signed at La Paz, Baja California Sur, August 14, 1983.

Article 105
Extent of Obligations

The Parties shall ensure that all necessary measures are taken in order to give effect to the provisions of this Agreement, including their observance, except as otherwise provided in this Agreement, by state and provincial governments.

CHAPTER TWO: GENERAL DEFINITIONS

Article 201: Definitions of General Application

1. For purposes of this Agreement, unless otherwise specified:

Commission means the Free Trade Commission established under Article 2001(1) (The Free Trade Commission);

Customs Valuation Code means the Agreement on Implementation of Article VII of the General Agreement on Tariffs and Trade, including its interpretative notes;

days means calendar days, including weekends and holidays;

enterprise means any entity constituted or organized under applicable law, whether or not for profit, and whether privately-owned or governmentally-owned, including any corporation, trust, partnership, sole proprietorship, joint venture or other association;

enterprise of a Party means an enterprise constituted or organized under the law of a Party;

existing means in effect on the date of entry into force of this Agreement;

Generally Accepted Accounting Principles means the recognized consensus or substantial authoritative support in the territory of a Party with respect to the recording of revenues, expenses, costs, assets and liabilities, disclosure of information and preparation of financial statements. These standards may be broad guidelines of general application as well as detailed standards, practices and procedures;

goods of a Party means domestic products as these are understood in the General Agreement on Tariffs and Trade or such goods as the Parties may agree, and includes originating goods of that Party;

Harmonized System (HS) means the Harmonized Commodity Description and Coding System, and its legal notes and rules, as adopted and implemented by the Parties in their respective tariff laws;

measure includes any law, regulation, procedure, requirement or practice;

national means a natural person who is a citizen or permanent resident of a Party and any other natural person referred to in Annex 201.1;

originating means qualifying under the rules of origin set out in Chapter Four (Rules of Origin);

person means a natural person or an enterprise;

person of a Party means a national, or an enterprise of a Party;

Secretariat means the Secretariat established under Article 2002(1) (The Secretariat);

state enterprise means an enterprise that is owned, or controlled through ownership interests, by a Party; and

territory means for a Party the territory of that Party as set out in Annex 201.1.

2. For purposes of this Agreement, unless otherwise specified, a reference to a state or province includes local governments of that state or province.

Annex 201.1
Country–Specific Definitions

For purposes of this Agreement, unless otherwise specified:

national also includes: (a) with respect to Mexico, a national or a citizen according to Articles 30 and 34, respectively, of the Mexican Constitution; and (b) with respect to the United States, "national of the United States" as defined in the existing provisions of the Immigration and Nationality Act;

territory means: (a) with respect to Canada, the territory to which its customs laws apply, including any areas beyond the territorial seas of Canada within which, in accordance with international law and its domestic law, Canada may exercise rights with respect to the seabed and subsoil and their natural resources; (b) with respect to Mexico, (i) the states of the Federation and the Federal District, (ii) the islands, including the reefs and keys, in adjacent seas, (iii) the islands of Guadalupe and Revillagigedo situated in the Pacific Ocean, (iv) the continental shelf and the submarine shelf of such islands, keys and reefs, (v) the waters of the territorial seas, in accordance with international law, and its interior maritime waters, (vi) the space located above the national territory, in accordance with international law, and (vii) any areas beyond the territorial seas of Mexico within which, in accordance with international law, including the United Nations Convention on the Law of the Sea, and its domestic law, Mexico may exercise rights with respect to the seabed and subsoil and their natural resources; and (c) with respect to the United States, (i) the customs territory of the United States, which includes the 50 states, the District of Columbia and Puerto Rico, (ii) the foreign trade zones located in the United States and Puerto Rico, and (iii) any areas beyond the territorial seas of the United States within which, in accordance with international law and its domestic law, the United States may exercise rights with respect to the seabed and subsoil and their natural resources.

PART TWO
TRADE IN GOODS
CHAPTER THREE: NATIONAL TREATMENT AND MARKET ACCESS FOR GOODS
Article 300
Scope and Coverage

This Chapter applies to trade in goods of a Party, including: (a) goods covered by Annex 300–A (Trade and Investment in the Automotive Sector),

(b) goods covered by Annex 300–B (Textile and Apparel Goods), and (c) goods covered by another Chapter in this Part, except as provided in such Annex or Chapter.

Section A—National Treatment
Article 301
National Treatment

1.   Each Party shall accord national treatment to the goods of another Party in accordance with Article III of the General Agreement on Tariffs and Trade (GATT), including its interpretative notes, and to this end Article III of the GATT and its interpretative notes, or any equivalent provision of a successor agreement to which all Parties are party, are incorporated into and made part of this Agreement.

2.   The provisions of paragraph 1 regarding national treatment shall mean, with respect to a state or province, treatment no less favorable than the most favorable treatment accorded by such state or province to any like, directly competitive or substitutable goods, as the case may be, of the Party of which it forms a part.

3.   Paragraphs 1 and 2 do not apply to the measures set out in Annex 301.3.

Annex 301.3
Exceptions to Articles 301 and 309
Section A—Canadian Measures

1.   Articles 301 and 309 shall not apply to controls by Canada on the export of logs of all species.

2.   Articles 301 and 309 shall not apply to controls by Canada on the export of unprocessed fish pursuant to the following existing statutes, as amended as of August 12, 1992: (a) New Brunswick Fish Processing Act, R.S.N.B. c. F–18.01 (1982), and Fisheries Development Act, S.N.B. c. F–15.1 (1977); (b) Newfoundland Fish Inspection Act, R.S.N.1990, c. F–12; (c) Nova Scotia Fisheries Act, S.N.S.1977, c. 9; (d) Prince Edward Island Fish Inspection Act, R.S.P.E.I.1988, c. F–13; and (e) Quebec Marine Products Processing Act, No. 38, S.Q.1987, c. 51.

3.   Articles 301 and 309 shall not apply to: (a) except as provided in Annex 300–A, Appendix 300–A.1, paragraph 4, measures by Canada respecting the importation of any goods enumerated or referred to in Schedule VII of the Customs Tariff, R.S.C.1985, c. 41 (3rd Supp.), as amended, (b) measures by Canada respecting the exportation of liquor for delivery into any country into which the importation of liquor is prohibited by law under the existing provisions of the Export Act, R.S.C.1985, c. E–18, as amended, (c) measures by Canada respecting preferential rates for certain freight traffic under the existing provisions of the Maritime Freight Rate Act, R.S.C.1985, c. M–1, as amended, (d) Canadian excise duties on absolute alcohol used in manufacturing under the existing provisions of the Excise Act, R.S.C.1985, c. E–14, as amended, and (e) measures by Canada prohibiting the use of foreign or non-duty paid ships in the coasting trade of Canada unless granted a license under the Coasting Trade Act, S.C.1992, c. 31, to the extent that such provisions

were mandatory legislation at the time of Canada's accession to the GATT and have not been amended so as to decrease their conformity with the GATT.

4.　Articles 301 and 309 shall not apply to quantitative import restrictions on goods that originate in the territory of the United States, considering operations performed in, or materials obtained from, Mexico as if they were performed in, or obtained from, a non-Party, and that are indicated by asterisks in Chapter 89 in Annex 401.2 (Tariff Schedule of Canada) of the Canada–United States Free Trade Agreement for as long as the measures taken under the Merchant Marine Act of 1920, 46 App. U.S.C. § 883, and the Merchant Marine Act of 1936, 46 App. U.S.C. §§ 1171, 1176, 1241 and 1241o, apply with quantitative effect to comparable Canadian origin goods sold or offered for sale into the U.S. market.

5.　Articles 301 and 309 shall not apply to: (a) the continuation or prompt renewal of a non-conforming provision of any statute referred to in paragraph 2 or 3; and (b) the amendment to a non-conforming provision of any statute referred to in paragraph 2 or 3 to the extent that the amendment does not decrease the conformity of the provision with Articles 301 and 309.

Section B—Mexican Measures

1.　Articles 301 and 309 shall not apply to controls by Mexico on the export of logs of all species.

2.　Articles 301 and 309 shall not apply to: (a) measures under the existing provisions of Articles 192 through 194 of the General Ways of Communication Act ("Ley de Vias Generales de Communicacion") reserving exclusively to Mexican vessels all services and operations not authorized for foreign vessels and empowering the Mexican Ministry of Communications and Transportation to deny foreign vessels the right to perform authorized services if their country of origin does not grant reciprocal rights to Mexican vessels; and (b) export permit measures applied to goods for exportation to another Party that are subject to quantitative restrictions or tariff rate quotas adopted or maintained by that other Party.

3.　Articles 301 and 309 shall not apply to: (a) the continuation or prompt renewal of a non-conforming provision of the statute referred to in paragraph 2(a); and (b) the amendment to a non-conforming provision of the statute referred to in paragraph 2(a) to the extent that the amendment does not decrease the conformity of the provision with Articles 301 and 309.

4.　(a) Notwithstanding Article 309, for the first 10 years after the date of entry into force of this Agreement, Mexico may adopt or maintain prohibitions or restrictions on the importation of used goods provided for in the items, as of August 12, 1992, in the Tariff Schedule of the General Import Duty Act (Tarifa de la "Ley del Impuesto General de Importacion") set out below: * * *

(b) Notwithstanding subparagraph (a), Mexico shall not prohibit or restrict the importation, on a temporary basis, of used goods provided for in the items set out in subparagraph (c) for the provision of a cross-border service subject to Chapter Twelve (Cross–Border Trade in Services) or the performance of a contract subject to Chapter Ten (Government Procurement), provided that the imported goods (i) are necessary to the provision of the cross-border service or the performance of the contract awarded to a supplier of another Party, (ii) are used solely by or under the supervision of the service provider or the supplier performing the contract, (iii) are not sold, leased or loaned while in the territory of Mexico, (iv) are imported in no greater quantity than is necessary for the provision of the service or the performance of the contract, (v) are re-exported promptly on completion of the service or the contract, and (vi) comply with other applicable requirements on the importation of such goods to the extent they are not inconsistent with this Agreement.

(c) Subparagraph (b) applies to used goods provided for in the following items: * * *

Section C—U.S. Measures

1. Articles 301 and 309 shall not apply to controls by the United States on the export of logs of all species.

2. Articles 301 and 309 shall not apply to: (a) taxes on imported perfume containing distilled spirits under existing provisions of sections 5001(a)(3) and 5007(b)(2) of the Internal Revenue Code of 1986, 26 U.S.C. §§ 5001(a)(3) and 5007(b)(2), and (b) measures under existing provisions of the Merchant Marine Act of 1920, 46 App.U.S.C. § 883; the Passenger Vessel Act, 46 App.U.S.C. §§ 289, 292 and 316; and 46 U.S.C. § 12108, to the extent that such measures were mandatory legislation at the time of the United States' accession to the GATT and have not been amended so as to decrease their conformity with the GATT.

3. Articles 301 and 309 shall not apply to: (a) the continuation or prompt renewal of a non-conforming provision of any statute referred to in paragraph 2; and (b) the amendment to a non-conforming provision of any statute referred to in paragraph 2 to the extent that the amendment does not decrease the conformity of the provision with Articles 301 and 309.

Section B—Tariffs
Article 302
Tariff Elimination

1. Except as otherwise provided in this Agreement, no Party may increase any existing customs duty, or adopt any customs duty, on an originating good.

2. Except as otherwise provided in this Agreement, each Party shall progressively eliminate its customs duties on originating goods in accordance with its Schedule to Annex 302.2.

3. On the request of any Party, the Parties shall consult to consider accelerating the elimination of customs duties set out in their Schedules. An agreement between two or more Parties to accelerate the elimination of a customs duty on a good shall supersede any duty rate or staging category determined pursuant to their Schedules for such good when approved by each such Party in accordance with its applicable legal procedures.

4. Each Party may adopt or maintain import measures to allocate in-quota imports made pursuant to a tariff rate quota set out in Annex 302.2,

provided that such measures do not have trade restrictive effects on imports additional to those caused by the imposition of the tariff rate quota.

5.   On written request of any Party, a Party applying or intending to apply measures pursuant to paragraph 4 shall consult to review the administration of those measures.

Annex 302.2
Tariff Elimination

1.   Except as otherwise provided in a Party's Schedule attached to this Annex, the following staging categories apply to the elimination of customs duties by each Party pursuant to Article 302(2): (a) duties on goods provided for in the items in staging category A in a Party's Schedule shall be eliminated entirely and such goods shall be duty-free, effective January 1, 1994; (b) duties on goods provided for in the items in staging category B in a Party's Schedule shall be removed in five equal annual stages beginning on January 1, 1994, and such goods shall be duty-free, effective January 1, 1998; (c) duties on goods provided for in the items in staging category C in a Party's Schedule shall be removed in 10 equal annual stages beginning on January 1, 1994, and such goods shall be duty-free, effective January 1, 2003; (d) duties on goods provided for in the items in staging category C+ in a Party's Schedule shall be removed in 15 equal annual stages beginning on January 1, 1994, and such goods shall be duty-free, effective January 1, 2008; and (e) goods provided for in the items in staging category D in a Party's Schedule shall continue to receive duty-free treatment.

2.   The base rate of customs duty and staging category for determining the interim rate of customs duty at each stage of reduction for an item are indicated for the item in each Party's Schedule attached to this Annex. These rates generally reflect the rate of duty in effect on July 1, 1991, including rates under the U.S. Generalized System of Preferences and the General Preferential Tariff of Canada.

3.   For the purpose of the elimination of customs duties in accordance with Article 302, interim staged rates shall be rounded down, except as set out in each Party's Schedule attached to this Annex, at least to the nearest tenth of a percentage point or, if the rate of duty is expressed in monetary units, at least to the nearest .001 of the official monetary unit of the Party.

4.   Canada shall apply a rate of customs duty no higher than the rate applicable under the staging category set out for an item in Annex 401.2, as amended, of the Canada–United States Free Trade Agreement, which Annex is hereby incorporated into and made a part of this Agreement, to an originating good provided that: (a) notwithstanding any provision in Chapter Four, in determining whether such good is an originating good, operations performed in or materials obtained from Mexico are considered as if they were performed in or obtained from a non-Party; and (b) any processing that occurs in Mexico after the good would qualify as an originating good in accordance with subparagraph (a) does not increase the transaction value of the good by greater than seven percent.

5.   Canada shall apply a rate of customs duty no higher than the rate applicable under the staging category set out for an item in Column I of its Schedule to this Annex to an originating good provided that: (a) notwith-

standing any provision in Chapter Four, in determining whether such good is an originating good, operations performed in or materials obtained from the United States are considered as if they were performed in or obtained from a non-Party; and (b) any processing that occurs in the United States after the good would qualify as an originating good in accordance with subparagraph (a) does not increase the transaction value of the good by greater than seven percent.

6. Canada shall apply to an originating good to which neither paragraph 4 nor 5 applies a rate of customs duty no higher than the rate indicated for its corresponding item in Column II of its Schedule to this Annex. The rate of customs duty in Column II for such good shall be: (a) in each year of the staging category indicated in Column I, the higher of (i) the rate of customs duty under the staging category set out for the item in Annex 401.2, as amended, of the Canada–United States Free Trade Agreement, and (ii) the General Preferential Tariff rate of customs duty for the item applied on July 1, 1991, reduced in accordance with the applicable staging category set out for the item in Column I of its Schedule to this Annex; or (b) where specified in Column II of its Schedule to this Annex, the most-favored-nation rate of customs duty for the item applied on July 1, 1991, reduced in accordance with the applicable staging category set out for the item in Column I of its Schedule to this Annex, or reduced in accordance with the applicable staging category otherwise indicated.

7. Paragraphs 4 through 6 and 10 through 13 shall not apply to textile and apparel goods identified in Appendix 1.1 of Annex 300–B (Textiles and Apparel Goods).

8. Paragraphs 4, 5 and 6 shall not apply to agricultural goods as defined in Article 708. For these goods, Canada shall apply the rate applicable under the staging category set out for an item in Annex 401.2, as amended, of the Canada–United States Free Trade Agreement to an originating good when the good qualifies to be marked as a good of the United States pursuant to Annex 311, without regard to whether the good is marked. When an originating good qualifies to be marked as a good of Mexico, pursuant to Annex 311, whether or not the good is marked, Canada shall apply the rate applicable under the staging category set out for an item in Column I of its Schedule to this Annex.

9. As between the United States and Canada, Article 401(7) and (8) of the Canada–United States Free Trade Agreement is hereby incorporated and made a part of this Annex. The term "goods originating in the territory of the United States of America" in Article 401(7) of that agreement shall be determined in accordance with paragraph 4 of this Annex. The term "goods originating in the territory of Canada" in Article 401(8) of that agreement shall be determined in accordance with paragraph 12 of this Annex.

10. Mexico shall apply a rate of customs duty no higher than the rate applicable under the staging category set out for an item in Column I of its Schedule to this Annex to an originating good when the good qualifies to be marked as a good of the United States, pursuant to Annex 311, without regard to whether the good is marked.

11. Mexico shall apply a rate of customs duty no higher than the rate applicable under the staging category set out for an item in Column II of its

Schedule to this Annex to an originating good when the good qualifies to be marked as a good of Canada, pursuant to Annex 311, without regard to whether the good is marked.

12.   The United States shall apply a rate of customs duty no higher than the rate applicable under the staging category set out for an item in Annex 401.2, as amended, of the Canada–United States Free Trade Agreement to an originating good when the good qualifies to be marked as a good of Canada pursuant to Annex 311, without regard to whether the good is marked.

13.   The United States shall apply a rate of customs duty no higher than the rate applicable under the staging category set out for an item in its Schedule to this Annex to an originating good when the good qualifies to be marked as a good of Mexico pursuant to Annex 311, whether or not the good is marked.

Schedule of Canada

* * *

Schedule of Mexico

* * *

Schedule of the United States

* * *

Article 303

Restriction on Drawback and Duty Deferral Programs

1.   Except as otherwise provided in this Article, no Party may refund the amount of customs duties paid, or waive or reduce the amount of customs duties owed, on a good imported into its territory, on condition that the good is: (a) subsequently exported to the territory of another Party, (b) used as a material in the production of another good that is subsequently exported to the territory of another Party, or (c) substituted by an identical or similar good used as a material in the production of another good that is subsequently exported to the territory of another Party, in an amount that exceeds the lesser of the total amount of customs duties paid or owed on the good on importation into its territory and the total amount of customs duties paid to another Party on the good that has been subsequently exported to the territory of that other Party.

2.   No Party may, on condition of export, refund, waive or reduce: (a) an antidumping or countervailing duty that is applied pursuant to a Party's domestic law and that is not applied inconsistently with Chapter Nineteen (Review and Dispute Settlement in Antidumping and Countervailing Duty Matters); (b) a premium offered or collected on an imported good arising out of any tendering system in respect of the administration of quantitative import restrictions, tariff rate quotas or tariff preference levels; (c) a fee applied pursuant to section 22 of the U.S. Agricultural Adjustment Act, subject to Chapter Seven (Agriculture and Sanitary and Phytosanitary Measures); or (d) customs duties paid or owed on a good imported into its

territory and substituted by an identical or similar good that is subsequently exported to the territory of another Party.

3.   Where a good is imported into the territory of a Party pursuant to a duty deferral program and is subsequently exported to the territory of another Party, or is used as a material in the production of another good that is subsequently exported to the territory of another Party, or is substituted by an identical or similar good used as a material in the production of another good that is subsequently exported to the territory of another Party, the Party from whose territory the good is exported: (a) shall assess the customs duties as if the exported good had been withdrawn for domestic consumption; and (b) may waive or reduce such customs duties to the extent permitted under paragraph 1.

4.   In determining the amount of customs duties that may be refunded, waived or reduced pursuant to paragraph 1 on a good imported into its territory, each Party shall require presentation of satisfactory evidence of the amount of customs duties paid to another Party on the good that has been subsequently exported to the territory of that other Party.

5.   Where satisfactory evidence of the customs duties paid to the Party to which a good is subsequently exported under a duty deferral program described in paragraph 3 is not presented within 60 days after the date of exportation, the Party from whose territory the good was exported: (a) shall collect customs duties as if the exported good had been withdrawn for domestic consumption; and (b) may refund such customs duties to the extent permitted under paragraph 1 on the timely presentation of such evidence under its laws and regulations.

6.   This Article does not apply to: (a) a good entered under bond for transportation and exportation to the territory of another Party; (b) a good exported to the territory of another Party in the same condition as when imported into the territory of the Party from which the good was exported (processes such as testing, cleaning, repacking or inspecting the good, or preserving it in its same condition, shall not be considered to change a good's condition). Except as provided in Annex 703.2, Section A, paragraph 12, where such a good has been commingled with fungible goods and exported in the same condition, its origin for purposes of this subparagraph may be determined on the basis of the inventory methods provided for in the Uniform Regulations established under Article 511 (Uniform Regulations); (c) a good imported into the territory of a Party that is deemed to be exported from its territory, or used as a material in the production of another good that is deemed to be exported to the territory of another Party, or is substituted by an identical or similar good used as a material in the production of another good that is deemed to be exported to the territory of another Party, by reason of (i) delivery to a duty-free shop, (ii) delivery for ship's stores or supplies for ships or aircraft, or (iii) delivery for use in joint undertakings of two or more of the Parties and that will subsequently become the property of the Party into whose territory the good was deemed to be exported; (d) a refund of customs duties by a Party on a particular good imported into its territory and subsequently exported to the territory of another Party, where that refund is granted by reason of the failure of such good to conform to sample or specification, or by reason of the shipment of such good without the

consent of the consignee; (e) an originating good that is imported into the territory of a Party and is subsequently exported to the territory of another Party, or used as a material in the production of another good that is subsequently exported to the territory of another Party, or is substituted by an identical or similar good used as a material in the production of another good that is subsequently exported to the territory of another Party; or (f) a good set out in Annex 303.6.

7. Except for paragraph 2(d), this Article shall apply as of the date set out in each Party's Section of Annex 303.7.

8. Notwithstanding any other provision of this Article and except as specifically provided in Annex 303.8, no Party may refund the amount of customs duties paid, or waive or reduce the amount of customs duties owed, on a non-originating good provided for in item 8540.11.aa (color cathode-ray television picture tubes, including video monitor tubes, with a diagonal exceeding 14 inches) or 8540.11.cc (color cathode-ray television picture tubes for high definition television, with a diagonal exceeding 14 inches) that is imported into the Party's territory and subsequently exported to the territory of another Party, or is used as a material in the production of another good that is subsequently exported to the territory of another Party, or is substituted by an identical or similar good used as a material in the production of another good that is subsequently exported to the territory of another Party.

9. For purposes of this Article:

customs duties are the customs duties that would be applicable to a good entered for consumption in the customs territory of a Party if the good were not exported to the territory of another party;

identical or similar goods means "identical or similar goods" as defined in Article 415 (Rules of Origin—Definitions);

material means "material" as defined in Article 415; and

used means "used" as defined in Article 415.

10. For purposes of this Article:

Where a good referred to by a tariff item number in this Article is described in parentheses following the tariff item number, the description is provided for purposes of reference only.

Annex 303.6
Goods Not Subject to Article 303

1. For exports from the territory of the United States to the territory of Canada or Mexico, a good provided for in U.S. tariff item 1701.11.02 that is imported into the territory of the United States and used as a material in the production of, or substituted by an identical or similar good used as a material in the production of, a good provided for in Canadian tariff item 1701.99.00 or Mexican tariff items 1701.99.01 and 1701.99.99 (refined sugar) is not subject to Article 303.

2. For trade between Canada and the United States the following are not subject to Article 303: (a) imported citrus products; (b) an imported good used as a material in the production of, or substituted by an identical or similar good used as a material in the production of, a good provided for in

U.S. items 5811.00.20 (quilted cotton piece goods), 5811.00.30 (quilted man-made piece goods) or 6307.90.99 (furniture moving pads), or Canadian items 5811.00.10 (quilted cotton piece goods), 5811.00.20 (quilted man-made piece goods) or 6307.90.30 (furniture moving pads), that are subject to the most-favored-nation rate of duty when exported to the territory of the other Party; and (c) an imported good used as a material in the production of, or substituted by an identical or similar good used as a material in the production of, apparel that is subject to the most-favored-nation rate of duty when exported to the territory of the other Party.

Annex 303.7

Effective Dates for the Application of Article 303

Section A—Canada

For Canada, Article 303 shall apply to a good imported into the territory of Canada that is: (a) subsequently exported to the territory of the United States on or after January 1, 1996, or subsequently exported to the territory of Mexico on or after January 1, 2001; (b) used as a material in the production of another good that is subsequently exported to the territory of the United States on or after January 1, 1996, or used as a material in the production of another good that is subsequently exported to the territory of Mexico on or after January 1, 2001; or (c) substituted by an identical or similar good used as a material in the production of another good that is subsequently exported to the territory of the United States on or after January 1, 1996, or substituted by an identical or similar good used as a material in the production of another good that is subsequently exported to the territory of Mexico on or after January 1, 2001.

Section B—Mexico

For Mexico, Article 303 shall apply to a good imported into the territory of Mexico that is: (a) subsequently exported to the territory of another Party on or after January 1, 2001; (b) used as a material in the production of another good that is subsequently exported to the territory of another Party on or after January 1, 2001; or (c) substituted by an identical or similar good used as a material in the production of another good that is subsequently exported to the territory of another Party on or after January 1, 2001.

Section C—United States

For the United States, Article 303 shall apply to a good imported into the territory of the United States that is: (a) subsequently exported to the territory of Canada on or after January 1, 1996, or subsequently exported to the territory of Mexico on or after January 1, 2001; (b) used as a material in the production of another good that is subsequently exported to the territory of Canada on or after January 1, 1996, or used as a material in the production of another good that is subsequently exported to the territory of Mexico on or after January 1, 2001; or (c) substituted by an identical or similar good used as a material in the production of another good subsequently exported to the territory of Canada on or after January 1, 1996, or substituted by an identical or similar good used as a material in the production of another good subsequently exported to the territory of Mexico on or after January 1, 2001.

Annex 303.8

Exception to Article 303(8) for Certain Color Cathode–
Ray Television Picture Tubes—Mexico * * *

Article 304

Waiver of Customs Duties

1.   Except as set out in Annex 304.1, no Party may adopt any new waiver of customs duties, or expand with respect to existing recipients or extend to any new recipient the application of an existing waiver of customs duties, where the waiver is conditioned, explicitly or implicitly, on the fulfillment of a performance requirement.

2.   Except as set out in Annex 304.2, no Party may, explicitly or implicitly, condition on the fulfillment of a performance requirement the continuation of any existing waiver of customs duties.

3.   If a waiver or a combination of waivers of customs duties granted by a Party with respect to goods for commercial use by a designated person can be shown by another Party to have an adverse impact on the commercial interests of a person of that Party, or of a person owned or controlled by a person of that Party that is located in the territory of the Party granting the waiver, or on the other Party's economy, the Party granting the waiver shall either cease to grant it or make it generally available to any importer.

4.   This Article shall not apply to measures subject to Article 303.

Annex 304.1

Exceptions for Existing Waiver Measures

Article 304(1) shall not apply in respect of existing Mexican waivers of customs duties, except that Mexico shall not: (a) increase the ratio of customs duties waived to customs duties owed relative to the performance required under any such waiver; or (b) add any type of imported good to those qualifying on July 1, 1991, in respect of any waiver of customs duties in effect on that date.

Annex 304.2

Continuation of Existing Waivers of Customs Duties

For purposes of Article 304(2): (a) as between Canada and Mexico, Canada may condition on the fulfillment of a performance requirement the waiver of customs duties under any measure in effect on or before January 1, 1989, on any goods entered or withdrawn from warehouse for consumption before January 1, 1998; (b) as between Canada and the United States, Article 405 of the Canada–United States Free Trade Agreement is hereby incorporated and made a part of this Annex solely with respect to measures adopted by Canada or the United States prior to the date of entry into force of this Agreement; (c) Mexico may condition on the fulfillment of a performance requirement the waiver of customs duties under any measure in effect on July 1, 1991, on any goods entered or withdrawn from warehouse for consumption before January 1, 2001; and (d) Canada may grant waivers of customs duties as set out in Annex 300–A (Trade and Investment in the Automotive Sector).

Article 305

Temporary Admission of Goods

1. Each Party shall grant duty-free temporary admission for: (a) professional equipment necessary for carrying out the business activity, trade or profession of a business person who qualifies for temporary entry pursuant to Chapter Sixteen (Temporary Entry for Business Persons), (b) equipment for the press or for sound or television broadcasting and cinematographic equipment, (c) goods imported for sports purposes and goods intended for display or demonstration, and (d) commercial samples and advertising films, imported from the territory of another Party, regardless of their origin and regardless of whether like, directly competitive or substitutable goods are available in the territory of the Party.

2. Except as otherwise provided in this Agreement, no Party may condition the duty-free temporary admission of a good referred to in paragraph 1(a), (b) or (c), other than to require that such good: (a) be imported by a national or resident of another Party who seeks temporary entry; (b) be used solely by or under the personal supervision of such person in the exercise of the business activity, trade or profession of that person; (c) not be sold or leased while in its territory; (d) be accompanied by a bond in an amount no greater than 110 percent of the charges that would otherwise be owed on entry or final importation, or by another form of security, releasable on exportation of the good, except that a bond for customs duties shall not be required for an originating good; (e) be capable of identification when exported; (f) be exported on the departure of that person or within such other period of time as is reasonably related to the purpose of the temporary admission; and (g) be imported in no greater quantity than is reasonable for its intended use.

3. Except as otherwise provided in this Agreement, no Party may condition the duty-free temporary admission of a good referred to in paragraph 1(d), other than to require that such good: (a) be imported solely for the solicitation of orders for goods, or services provided from the territory, of another Party or non-Party; (b) not be sold, leased or put to any use other than exhibition or demonstration while in its territory; (c) be capable of identification when exported; (d) be exported within such period as is reasonably related to the purpose of the temporary admission; and (e) be imported in no greater quantity than is reasonable for its intended use.

4. A Party may impose the customs duty and any other charge on a good temporarily admitted duty-free under paragraph 1 that would be owed on entry or final importation of such good if any condition that the Party imposes under paragraph 2 or 3 has not been fulfilled.

5. Subject to Chapters Eleven (Investment) and Twelve (Cross–Border Trade in Services): (a) each Party shall allow a vehicle or container used in international traffic that enters its territory from the territory of another Party to exit its territory on any route that is reasonably related to the economic and prompt departure of such vehicle or container; (b) no Party may require any bond or impose any penalty or charge solely by reason of any difference between the port of entry and the port of departure of a vehicle or container; (c) no Party may condition the release of any obligation, including any bond, that it imposes in respect of the entry of a vehicle or container into

its territory on its exit through any particular port of departure; and (d) no Party may require that the vehicle or carrier bringing a container from the territory of another Party into its territory be the same vehicle or carrier that takes such container to the territory of another Party.

6. For purposes of paragraph 5, "vehicle" means a truck, a truck tractor, tractor, trailer unit or trailer, a locomotive, or a railway car or other railroad equipment.

Article 306
Duty–Free Entry of Certain Commercial Samples and Printed Advertising Materials

Each Party shall grant duty-free entry to commercial samples of negligible value, and to printed advertising materials, imported from the territory of another Party, regardless of their origin, but may require that: (a) such samples be imported solely for the solicitation of orders for goods, or services provided from the territory, of another Party or non-Party; or (b) such advertising materials be imported in packets that each contain no more than one copy of each such material and that neither such materials nor packets form part of a larger consignment.

Article 307
Goods Re–Entered After Repair or Alteration

1. Except as set out in Annex 307.1, no Party may apply a customs duty to a good, regardless of its origin, that re-enters its territory after that good has been exported from its territory to the territory of another Party for repair or alteration, regardless of whether such repair or alteration could be performed in its territory.

2. Notwithstanding Article 303, no Party may apply a customs duty to a good, regardless of its origin, imported temporarily from the territory of another Party for repair or alteration.

3. Annex 307.3 applies to the Parties specified in that Annex respecting the repair and rebuilding of vessels.

Annex 307.1
Goods Re-entered After Repair or Alteration
Section A—Canada

Canada may impose customs duties on goods, regardless of their origin, that re-enter its territory after such goods have been exported from its territory to the territory of another Party for repair or alteration as follows: (a) for goods set out in Section D that re-enter its territory from the territory of Mexico, Canada shall apply to the value of the repair or alteration of such goods the rate of customs duty for such goods applicable under its Schedule to Annex 302.2; (b) for goods other than those set out in Section D that re-enter its territory from the territory of the United States or Mexico, other than goods repaired or altered pursuant to a warranty, Canada shall apply to the value of the repair or alteration of such goods the rate of customs duty for such goods applicable under the Tariff Schedule of Canada attached to Annex 401.2 of the Canada–United States Free Trade Agreement, as incorporated into Annex 302.2 of this Agreement; and (c) for goods set out in Section D that re-enter its territory from the territory of the United States, Canada shall apply to the value of the repair or alteration of such goods the rate of customs duty for such goods applicable under its Schedule attached to Annex 401.2 of the Canada–United States Free Trade Agreement, as incorporated into Annex 302.2 of this Agreement.

Section B—Mexico

Mexico may impose customs duties on goods set out in Section D, regardless of their origin, that re-enter its territory after such goods have been exported from its territory to the territory of another Party for repair or alteration, by applying to the value of the repair or alteration of those goods the rate of customs duty for such goods that would apply if such goods were included in staging category B in Mexico's Schedule to Annex 302.2.

Section C—United States

1. The United States may impose customs duties on: (a) goods set out in Section D, or (b) goods that are not set out in Section D and that are not repaired or altered pursuant to a warranty, regardless of their origin, that re-enter its territory after such goods have been exported from its territory to the territory of Canada for repair or alteration, by applying to the value of the repair or alteration of such goods the rate of customs duty applicable under the Canada–United States Free Trade Agreement, as incorporated into Annex 302.2 of this Agreement.

2. The United States may impose customs duties on goods set out in Section D, regardless of their origin, that re-enter its territory after such goods have been exported from its territory to the territory of Mexico for repair or alteration, by applying to the value of the repair or alteration of such goods a rate of customs duty of 50 percent reduced in five equal annual stages beginning on January 1, 1994, and the value of such repair or alteration shall be duty-free on January 1, 1998.

Section D—List of Goods

Any vessel, including the following goods, documented by a Party under its law to engage in foreign or coastwise trade, or a vessel intended to be employed in such trade: (a) cruise ships, excursion boats, ferry-boats, cargo ships, barges and similar vessels for the transport of persons or goods, including (i) tankers, (ii) refrigerated vessels, other than tankers, and (iii) other vessels for the transport of goods and other vessels for the transport of both persons and goods, including open vessels; (b) fishing vessels, including factory ships and other vessels for processing or preserving fishery products of a registered length not exceeding 30.5m; (c) light-vessels, fire-floats, dredgers, floating cranes, and other vessels the navigability of which is subsidiary to their main function, floating docks, floating or submersible drilling or production platforms; and drilling ships, drilling barges and floating drilling rigs; and (d) tugboats.

Annex 307.3
Repair and Rebuilding of Vessels
United States

For the purpose of increasing transparency regarding the types of repairs that may be performed in shipyards outside the territory of the United States that do not result in any loss of privileges for such vessel to: (a) remain eligible to engage in coastwise trade or to access U.S. fisheries, (b) transport U.S. government cargo, or (c) participate in U.S. assistance programs, including the "operating difference subsidy," the United States shall, (d) provide written clarification no later than July 1, 1993, to the other Parties of current U.S. Customs and Coast Guard practices that constitute, and differentiate between, the repair and the rebuilding of vessels, including clarifications with respect to "jumboizing", vessel conversions and casualty repairs, and (e) begin a process, no later than the date of entry into force of this Agreement, to define the terms "repairs" and "rebuilding" under U.S. maritime law, including the Merchant Marine Act of 1920, 46 App.U.S.C. § 883, and the Merchant Marine Act of 1936, 46 App.U.S.C. §§ 1171, 1176, 1241 and 1241o.

Article 308
Most–Favored–Nation Rates of Duty on Certain Goods

1.   Annex 308.1 applies to certain automatic data processing goods and their parts.

2.   Annex 308.2 applies to certain color television tubes.

3.   Each Party shall accord most-favored-nation duty-free treatment to any local area network apparatus imported into its territory, and shall consult in accordance with Annex 308.3.

Annex 308.1
Most–Favored–Nation Rates of Duty on Certain Automatic Data Processing Goods and Their Parts
Section A—General Provisions

1.   Each Party shall reduce its most-favored-nation rate of duty applicable to a good provided for under the tariff provisions set out in Tables 308.1.1 and 308.1.2 in Section B to the rate set out therein, to the lowest rate agreed by any Party in the Uruguay Round of Multilateral Trade Negotiations, or to such reduced rate as the Parties may agree, in accordance with the schedule set out in Section B, or with such accelerated schedule as the Parties may agree.

2.   Notwithstanding Chapter Four (Rules of Origin), when the most-favored-nation rate of duty applicable to a good provided for under the tariff provisions set out in Table 308.1.1 in Section B conforms with the rate established under paragraph 1, each Party shall consider the good, when imported into its territory from the territory of another Party, to be an originating good.

3.   A Party may reduce in advance of the schedule set out in Table 308.1.1 or Table 308.1.2 in Section B, or of such accelerated schedule as the Parties may agree, its most-favored-nation rate of duty applicable to any good provided for under the tariff provisions set out therein, to the lowest rate agreed by any Party in the Uruguay Round of Multilateral Trade Negotiations, or the rate set out in Table 308.1.1 or 308.1.2, or to such reduced rate as the Parties may agree.

4.   For greater certainty, most-favored-nation rate of duty does not include any other concessionary rate of duty.

Section B—Rates of Duty and Schedule for Reduction

* * *

Annex 308.2
Most–Favored–Nation Rates of Duty on Certain Color Cathode–Ray Television Picture Tubes

1.   Any Party considering the reduction of its most-favored-nation rate of customs duty for goods provided for in item 8540.11.aa (color cathode-ray television picture tubes, including video monitor cathode-ray tubes, with a diagonal exceeding 14 inches) or 8540.11.cc (color cathode-ray television picture tubes for high definition television, with a diagonal exceeding 14 inches) during the first 10 years after the date of entry into force of this Agreement shall consult with the other Parties in advance of such reduction.

2.   If any other Party objects in writing to such reduction, other than a reduction in the Uruguay Round of Multilateral Trade Negotiations, and the Party proceeds with the reduction, any objecting Party may raise its applicable rate of duty on originating goods provided for in the corresponding tariff item set out in its Schedule to Annex 302.2, up to the applicable rate of duty as if such good had been placed in staging category C for purpose of tariff elimination.

Annex 308.3
Most–Favored–Nation Duty–Free Treatment of Local Area Network Apparatus

To facilitate the operation of Article 308(3), the Parties shall consult regarding the tariff classification of local area network apparatus and shall endeavor to agree, no later than January 1, 1994, on the classification of such goods in each Party's tariff schedule.

Section C—Non–Tariff Measures
Article 309
Import and Export Restrictions

1.   Except as otherwise provided in this Agreement, no Party may adopt or maintain any prohibition or restriction on the importation of any good of another Party or on the exportation or sale for export of any good destined for the territory of another Party, except in accordance with Article XI of the GATT, including its interpretative notes, and to this end Article XI of the GATT and its interpretative notes, or any equivalent provision of a successor agreement to which all Parties are party, are incorporated into and made a part of this Agreement.

2.   The Parties understand that the GATT rights and obligations incorporated by paragraph 1 prohibit, in any circumstances in which any other form of restriction is prohibited, export price requirements and, except as permitted in enforcement of countervailing and antidumping orders and undertakings, import price requirements.

3.   In the event that a Party adopts or maintains a prohibition or restriction on the importation from or exportation to a non-Party of a good,

nothing in this Agreement shall be construed to prevent the Party from: (a) limiting or prohibiting the importation from the territory of another Party of such good of that non-Party; or (b) requiring as a condition of export of such good of the Party to the territory of another Party, that the good not be re-exported to the non-Party, directly or indirectly, without being consumed in the territory of the other Party.

4. In the event that a Party adopts or maintains a prohibition or restriction on the importation of a good from a non-Party, the Parties, on request of any Party, shall consult with a view to avoiding undue interference with or distortion of pricing, marketing and distribution arrangements in another Party.

5. Paragraphs 1 through 4 shall not apply to the measures set out in Annex 301.3.

Article 310
Customs User Fees

1. No Party may adopt any customs user fee of the type referred to in Annex 310.1 for originating goods.

2. The Parties specified in Annex 310.1 may maintain existing such fees in accordance with that Annex.

Annex 310.1
Existing Customs User Fees
Section A—Mexico

Mexico shall not increase its customs processing fee ("derechos de tramite aduanero") on originating goods, and shall eliminate such fee on originating goods by June 30, 1999.

Section B—United States

1. The United States shall not increase its merchandise processing fee and shall eliminate such fee according to the schedule set out in Article 403 of the Canada–United States Free Trade Agreement on originating goods where those goods qualify to be marked as goods of Canada pursuant to Annex 311, without regard to whether the goods are marked.

2. The United States shall not increase its merchandise processing fee and shall eliminate such fee by June 30, 1999, on originating goods where those goods qualify to be marked as goods of Mexico pursuant to Annex 311, without regard to whether the goods are marked.

Article 311
Country of Origin Marking

Annex 311 applies to measures relating to country of origin marking.

Annex 311
Country of Origin Marking

1. The Parties shall establish by January 1, 1994, rules for determining whether a good is a good of a Party ("Marking Rules") for purposes of this

Annex, Annex 300–B and Annex 302.2, and for such other purposes as the Parties may agree.

2.   Each Party may require that a good of another Party, as determined in accordance with the Marking Rules, bear a country of origin marking, when imported into its territory, that indicates to the ultimate purchaser of that good the name of its country of origin.

3.   Each Party shall permit the country of origin marking of a good of another Party to be indicated in English, French or Spanish, except that a Party may, as part of its general consumer information measures, require that an imported good be marked with its country of origin in the same manner as prescribed for goods of that Party.

4.   Each Party shall, in adopting, maintaining and applying any measure relating to country of origin marking, minimize the difficulties, costs and inconveniences that the measure may cause to the commerce and industry of the other Parties.

5.   Each Party shall: (a) accept any reasonable method of marking of a good of another Party, including the use of stickers, labels, tags or paint, that ensures that the marking is conspicuous, legible and sufficiently permanent; (b) exempt from a country of origin marking requirement a good of another Party that (i) is incapable of being marked, (ii) cannot be marked prior to exportation to the territory of another Party without causing injury to the goods, (iii) cannot be marked except at a cost that is substantial in relation to its customs value so as to discourage its exportation to the territory of the Party, (iv) cannot be marked without materially impairing its function or substantially detracting from its appearance, (v) is in a container that is marked in a manner that will reasonably indicate the good's origin to the ultimate purchaser, (vi) is a crude substance, (vii) is imported for use by the importer and is not intended for sale in the form in which it was imported, (viii) is to undergo production in the territory of the importing Party by the importer, or on its behalf, in a manner that would result in the good becoming a good of the importing Party under the Marking Rules, (ix) by reason of its character, or the circumstances of its importation, the ultimate purchaser would reasonably know its country of origin even though it is not marked, (x) was produced more than 20 years prior to its importation, (xi) was imported without the required marking and cannot be marked after its importation except at a cost that would be substantial in relation to its customs value, provided that the failure to mark the good before importation was not for the purpose of avoiding compliance with the requirement, (xii) for purposes of temporary duty-free admission, is in transit or in bond or otherwise under customs administration control, (xiii) is an original work of art, or (xiv) is provided for in subheading 6904.10, or heading 8541 or 8542.

6.   Except for a good described in subparagraphs 5(b)(vi), (vii), (viii), (ix), (x), (xii), (xiii) and (xiv), a Party may provide that, wherever a good is exempted under subparagraph 5(b), its outermost usual container shall be marked so as to indicate the country of origin of the good it contains.

7.   Each Party shall provide that: (a) a usual container imported empty, whether or not disposable, shall not be required to be marked with its own country of origin, but the container in which it is imported may be required to be marked with the country of origin of its contents; and (b) a usual

container imported filled, whether or not disposable, (i) shall not be required to be marked with its own country of origin, but (ii) may be required to be marked with the country of origin of its contents, unless the contents are marked with their country of origin and the container can be readily opened for inspection of the contents, or the marking of the contents is clearly visible through the container.

8.   Each Party shall, wherever administratively practicable, permit an importer to mark a good of a Party subsequent to importation but prior to release of the good from customs control or custody, unless there have been repeated violations of the country of origin marking requirements of the Party by the same importer and that importer has been previously notified in writing that such good is required to be marked prior to importation.

9.   Each Party shall provide that, except with respect to importers that have been notified under paragraph 8, no special duty or penalty shall be imposed for failure to comply with country of origin marking requirements of that Party, unless the good is removed from customs custody or control without being properly marked, or a deceptive marking has been used.

10.   The Parties shall cooperate and consult on matters related to this Annex, including additional exemptions from a country of origin marking requirement, in accordance with Article 513 (Customs Procedures—Working Group and Customs Subgroup).

11.   For purposes of this Annex:

conspicuous means capable of being easily seen with normal handling of the good or container;

customs value means the value of a good for purposes of levying duties of customs on an imported good;

legible means capable of being easily read;

sufficiently permanent means capable of remaining in place until the good reaches the ultimate purchaser, unless deliberately removed;

the form in which it was imported means the condition of the good before it has undergone one of the changes in tariff classification described in the Marking Rules;

ultimate purchaser means the last person in the territory of an importing Party that purchases the good in the form in which it was imported; such purchaser need not be the last person that will use the good; and

usual container means the container in which a good will ordinarily reach its ultimate purchaser.

Article 312
Wine and Distilled Spirits

1.   No Party may adopt or maintain any measure requiring that distilled spirits imported from the territory of another Party for bottling be blended with any distilled spirits of the Party.

2.   Annex 312.2 applies to other measures relating to wine and distilled spirits.

Annex 312.2

Wine and Distilled Spirits

Section A—Canada and the United States

As between Canada and the United States, any measure related to the internal sale and distribution of wine and distilled spirits, other than a measure covered by Article 312(1) or 313, shall be governed under this Agreement exclusively in accordance with the relevant provisions of the Canada–United States Free Trade Agreement, which for this purpose are hereby incorporated into and made a part of this Agreement.

Section B—Canada and Mexico

As between Canada and Mexico:

1. Except as provided in paragraphs 3 through 6, in respect of any measure related to the internal sale and distribution of wine and distilled spirits, Article 301 shall not apply to: (a) a non-conforming provision of any existing measure; (b) the continuation or prompt renewal of a non-conforming provision of any existing measure; or (c) an amendment to a non-conforming provision of any existing measure to the extent that the amendment does not decrease its conformity with Article 301.

2. The Party asserting that paragraph 1 applies to one of its measures shall have the burden of establishing the validity of such assertion.

3. (a) Any measure related to the listing of wine and distilled spirits of the other Party shall: (i) conform with Article 301, (ii) be transparent, non-discriminatory and provide for prompt decision on any listing application, prompt written notification of such decision to the applicant and, in the case of a negative decision, provide for a statement of the reason for refusal, (iii) establish administrative appeal procedures for listing decisions that provide for prompt, fair and objective rulings, (iv) be based on normal commercial considerations, (v) not create disguised barriers to trade, and (vi) be published and made generally available to persons of the other Party. (b) Notwithstanding paragraph 3(a) and Article 301, and provided that listing measures of British Columbia otherwise conform with paragraph 3(a) and Article 301, automatic listing measures in the province of British Columbia may be maintained provided they apply only to existing estate wineries producing less than 30,000 gallons of wine annually and meeting the existing content rule.

4. (a) Where the distributor is a public entity, the entity may charge the actual cost-of-service differential between wine or distilled spirits of the other Party and domestic wine or distilled spirits. Any such differential shall not exceed the actual amount by which the audited cost of service for the wine or distilled spirits of the exporting Party exceeds the audited cost of service for the wine or distilled spirits of the importing Party. (b) Notwithstanding Article 301, Article I (Definitions) except for the definition of "distilled spirits", Article IV.3 (Wine), and Annexes A, B, and C, of the Agreement between Canada and the European Economic Community concerning Trade and Commerce in Alcoholic Beverages, dated February 28, 1989, shall apply with such changes as the circumstances may require. (c) All discriminatory mark-ups on distilled spirits shall be eliminated immediately on the date of entry into force of this Agreement. Cost-of-service differential mark-ups as

described in subparagraph (a) shall be permitted. (d) Any other discriminatory pricing measure shall be eliminated on the date of entry into force of this Agreement.

5. (a) Any measure related to distribution of wine or distilled spirits of the other Party shall conform with Article 301. (b) Notwithstanding subparagraph (a), and provided that distribution measures otherwise ensure conformity with Article 301, a Party may (i) maintain or introduce a measure limiting on-premise sales by a winery or distillery to those wines or distilled spirits produced on its premises, and (ii) maintain a measure requiring existing private wine store outlets in the provinces of Ontario and British Columbia to discriminate in favor of wine of those provinces to a degree no greater than the discrimination required by such existing measure. (c) Nothing in this Agreement shall prohibit the Province of Quebec from requiring that any wine sold in grocery stores in Quebec be bottled in Quebec, provided that alternative outlets are provided in Quebec for the sale of wine of the other Party, whether or not such wine is bottled in Quebec.

6. Unless otherwise specifically provided in this Annex, the Parties retain their rights and obligations under the GATT and agreements negotiated under the GATT.

7. For purposes of this Annex:

wine includes wine and wine-containing beverages.

Article 313
Distinctive Products

Annex 313 applies to standards and labelling of the distinctive products set out in that Annex.

Annex 313
Distinctive Products

1. Canada and Mexico shall recognize Bourbon Whiskey and Tennessee Whiskey, which is a straight Bourbon Whiskey authorized to be produced only in the State of Tennessee, as distinctive products of the United States. Accordingly, Canada and Mexico shall not permit the sale of any product as Bourbon Whiskey or Tennessee Whiskey, unless it has been manufactured in the United States in accordance with the laws and regulations of the United States governing the manufacture of Bourbon Whiskey and Tennessee Whiskey.

2. Mexico and the United States shall recognize Canadian Whisky as a distinctive product of Canada. Accordingly, Mexico and the United States shall not permit the sale of any product as Canadian Whisky, unless it has been manufactured in Canada in accordance with the laws and regulations of Canada governing the manufacture of Canadian Whisky for consumption in Canada.

3. Canada and the United States shall recognize Tequila and Mezcal as distinctive products of Mexico. Accordingly, Canada and the United States shall not permit the sale of any product as Tequila or Mezcal, unless it has been manufactured in Mexico in accordance with the laws and regulations of Mexico governing the manufacture of Tequila and Mezcal. This provision

shall apply to Mezcal, either on the date of entry into force of this Agreement, or 90 days after the date when the official standard for this product is made obligatory by the Government of Mexico, whichever is later.

Article 314

Export Taxes

Except as set out in Annex 314, no Party may adopt or maintain any duty, tax or other charge on the export of any good to the territory of another Party, unless such duty, tax or charge is adopted or maintained on: (a) exports of any such good to the territory of all other Parties; and (b) any such good when destined for domestic consumption.

Annex 314

Export Taxes

Mexico

1.   Mexico may adopt or maintain a duty, tax or other charge on the export of those basic foodstuffs set out in paragraph 4, on their ingredients or on the goods from which such foodstuffs are derived, if such duty, tax or other charge is adopted or maintained on the export of such goods to the territory of all other Parties, and is used: (a) to limit to domestic consumers the benefits of a domestic food assistance program with respect to such foodstuff; or (b) to ensure the availability of sufficient quantities of such foodstuff to domestic consumers or of sufficient quantities of its ingredients, or of the goods from which such foodstuffs are derived, to a domestic processing industry, when the domestic price of such foodstuff is held below the world price as part of a governmental stabilization plan, provided that such duty, tax, or other charge (i) does not operate to increase the protection afforded to such domestic industry, and (ii) is maintained only for such period of time as is necessary to maintain the integrity of the stabilization plan.

2.   Notwithstanding paragraph 1, Mexico may adopt or maintain a duty, tax or other charge on the export of any foodstuff to the territory of another Party if such duty, tax or other charge is temporarily applied to relieve critical shortages of that foodstuff. For purposes of this paragraph, "temporarily" means up to one year, or such longer period as the Parties may agree.

3.   Mexico may maintain its existing tax on the export of goods provided for under tariff item 4001.30.02 of the Tariff Schedule of the General Export Duty Act ("Tarifa de la Ley del Impuesto General de Exportacion") for up to 10 years after the date of entry into force of this Agreement.

4.   For purposes of paragraph 1, "basic foodstuffs" means: * * *

Article 315

Other Export Measures

1.   Except as set out in Annex 315, a Party may adopt or maintain a restriction otherwise justified under Articles XI:2(a) or XX(g), (i) or (j) of the GATT with respect to the export of a good of the Party to the territory of another Party, only if: (a) the restriction does not reduce the proportion of the total export shipments of the specific good made available to that other Party relative to the total supply of that good of the Party maintaining the

restriction as compared to the proportion prevailing in the most recent 36–month period for which data are available prior to the imposition of the measure, or in such other representative period on which the Parties may agree; (b) the Party does not impose a higher price for exports of a good to that other Party than the price charged for such good when consumed domestically, by means of any measure, such as licenses, fees, taxation and minimum price requirements. The foregoing provision does not apply to a higher price that may result from a measure taken pursuant to subparagraph (a) that only restricts the volume of exports; and (c) the restriction does not require the disruption of normal channels of supply to that other Party or normal proportions among specific goods or categories of goods supplied to that other Party.

2. The Parties shall cooperate in the maintenance and development of effective controls on the export of each other's goods to a non-Party in implementing this Article.

Annex 315

Other Export Measures

Article 315 shall not apply as between Mexico and the other Parties.

Section D—Consultations

Article 316

Consultations and Committee on Trade in Goods

1. The Parties hereby establish a Committee on Trade in Goods, comprising representatives of each Party.

2. The Committee shall meet on the request of any Party or the Commission to consider any matter arising under this Chapter.

3. The Parties shall convene at least once each year a meeting of their officials responsible for customs, immigration, inspection of food and agricultural products, border inspection facilities, and regulation of transportation for the purpose of addressing issues related to movement of goods through the Parties' ports of entry.

Article 317

Third–Country Dumping

1. The Parties affirm the importance of cooperation with respect to actions under Article 12 of the Agreement on Implementation of Article VI of the General Agreement on Tariffs and Trade.

2. Where a Party presents an application to another Party requesting antidumping action on its behalf, those Parties shall consult within 30 days respecting the factual basis of the request, and the requested Party shall give full consideration to the request.

Section E—Definitions

Article 318

Definitions

For purposes of this Chapter:

advertising films means recorded visual media, with or without sound-tracks, consisting essentially of images showing the nature or operation of goods or services offered for sale or lease by a person established or resident in the territory of any Party, provided that the films are of a kind suitable for exhibition to prospective customers but not for broadcast to the general public, and provided that they are imported in packets that each contain no more than one copy of each film and that do not form part of a larger consignment;

commercial samples of negligible value means commercial samples having a value, individually or in the aggregate as shipped, of not more than one U.S. dollar, or the equivalent amount in the currency of another Party, or so marked, torn, perforated or otherwise treated that they are unsuitable for sale or for use except as commercial samples;

consumed means: (a) actually consumed; or (b) further processed or manufactured so as to result in a substantial change in value, form or use of the good or in the production of another good;

customs duty includes any customs or import duty and a charge of any kind imposed in connection with the importation of a good, including any form of surtax or surcharge in connection with such importation, but does not include any: (a) charge equivalent to an internal tax imposed consistently with Article III:2 of the GATT, or any equivalent provision of a successor agreement to which all Parties are party, in respect of like, directly competitive or substitutable goods of the Party, or in respect of goods from which the imported good has been manufactured or produced in whole or in part; (b) antidumping or countervailing duty that is applied pursuant to a Party's domestic law and not applied inconsistently with Chapter Nineteen (Review and Dispute Settlement in Antidumping and Countervailing Duty Matters); (c) fee or other charge in connection with importation commensurate with the cost of services rendered; (d) premium offered or collected on an imported good arising out of any tendering system in respect of the administration of quantitative import restrictions, tariff rate quotas or tariff preference levels; and (e) fee applied pursuant to section 22 of the U.S. Agricultural Adjustment Act, subject to Chapter Seven (Agriculture and Sanitary and Phytosanitary Measures);

distilled spirits include distilled spirits and distilled spirit-containing beverages;

duty deferral program includes measures such as those governing foreign-trade zones, temporary importations under bond, bonded warehouses, "maquiladoras" and inward processing programs;

duty-free means free of customs duty;

goods imported for sports purposes means sports requisites for use in sports contests, demonstrations or training in the territory of the Party into whose territory such goods are imported;

goods intended for display or demonstration includes their component parts, ancillary apparatus and accessories;

item means a tariff classification item at the eight- or 10–digit level set out in a Party's tariff schedule;

local area network apparatus means a good dedicated for use solely or principally to permit the interconnection of automatic data processing machines and units thereof for a network that is used primarily for the sharing of resources such as central processor units, data storage devices and input or output units, including in-line repeaters, converters, concentrators, bridges and routers, and printed circuit assemblies for physical incorporation into automatic data processing machines and units thereof suitable for use solely or principally with a private network, and providing for the transmission, receipt, error-checking, control, signal conversion or correction functions for non-voice data to move through a local area network;

performance requirement means a requirement that: (a) a given level or percentage of goods or services be exported; (b) domestic goods or services of the Party granting a waiver of customs duties be substituted for imported goods or services; (c) a person benefitting from a waiver of customs duties purchase other goods or services in the territory of the Party granting the waiver or accord a preference to domestically produced goods or services; (d) a person benefitting from a waiver of customs duties produce goods or provide services, in the territory of the Party granting the waiver, with a given level or percentage of domestic content; or (e) relates in any way the volume or value of imports to the volume or value of exports or to the amount of foreign exchange inflows;

printed advertising materials means those goods classified in Chapter 49 of the Harmonized System, including brochures, pamphlets, leaflets, trade catalogues, yearbooks published by trade associations, tourist promotional materials and posters, that are used to promote, publicize or advertise a good or service, are essentially intended to advertise a good or service, and are supplied free of charge;

repair or alteration does not include an operation or process that either destroys the essential characteristics of a good or creates a new or commercially different good;

satisfactory evidence means: (a) a receipt, or a copy of a receipt, evidencing payment of customs duties on a particular entry; (b) a copy of the entry document with evidence that it was received by a customs administration; (c) a copy of a final customs duty determination by a customs administration respecting the relevant entry; or (d) any other evidence of payment of customs duties acceptable under the Uniform Regulations established in accordance with Chapter Five (Customs Procedures);

total export shipments means all shipments from total supply to users located in the territory of another Party;

total supply means all shipments, whether intended for domestic or foreign users, from: (a) domestic production; (b) domestic inventory; and (c) other imports as appropriate; and

waiver of customs duties means a measure that waives otherwise applicable customs duties on any good imported from any country, including the territory of another Party.

CHAPTER FOUR: RULES OF ORIGIN
Article 401
Originating Goods

Except as otherwise provided in this Chapter, a good shall originate in the territory of a Party where:

(a) the good is wholly obtained or produced entirely in the territory of one or more of the Parties, as defined in Article 415;

(b) each of the non-originating materials used in the production of the good undergoes an applicable change in tariff classification set out in Annex 401 as a result of production occurring entirely in the territory of one or more of the Parties, or the good otherwise satisfies the applicable requirements of that Annex where no change in tariff classification is required, and the good satisfies all other applicable requirements of this Chapter;

(c) the good is produced entirely in the territory of one or more of the Parties exclusively from originating materials; or

(d) except for a good provided for in Chapters 61 through 63 of the Harmonized System, the good is produced entirely in the territory of one or more of the Parties but one or more of the non-originating materials provided for as parts under the Harmonized System that are used in the production of the good does not undergo a change in tariff classification because (i) the good was imported into the territory of a Party in an unassembled or a disassembled form but was classified as an assembled good pursuant to General Rule of Interpretation 2(a) of the Harmonized System, or (ii) the heading for the good provides for and specifically describes both the good itself and its parts and is not further subdivided into subheadings, or the subheading for the good provides for and specifically describes both the good itself and its parts, provided that the regional value content of the good, determined in accordance with Article 402, is not less than 60 percent where the transaction value method is used, or is not less than 50 percent where the net cost method is used, and that the good satisfies all other applicable requirements of this Chapter.

Article 402

Regional Value Content

1.   Except as provided in paragraph 5, each Party shall provide that the regional value content of a good shall be calculated, at the choice of the exporter or producer of the good, on the basis of either the transaction value method set out in paragraph 2 or the net cost method set out in paragraph 3.

2.   Each Party shall provide that an exporter or producer may calculate the regional value content of a good on the basis of the following transaction value method: $RVC = TV-VNM / TV \times 100$ where RVC is the regional value content, expressed as a percentage; TV is the transaction value of the good adjusted to a F.O.B. basis; and VNM is the value of non-originating materials used by the producer in the production of the good.

3.   Each Party shall provide that an exporter or producer may calculate the regional value content of a good on the basis of the following net cost method: $RVC = NC-VNM / NC \times 100$ where RVC is the regional value content, expressed as a percentage; NC is the net cost of the good; and VNM is the value of non-originating materials used by the producer in the production of the good.

4.   Except as provided in Article 403(1) and for a motor vehicle identified in Article 403(2) or a component identified in Annex 403.2, the value of non-originating materials used by the producer in the production of a good shall

not, for purposes of calculating the regional value content of the good under paragraph 2 or 3, include the value of non-originating materials used to produce originating materials that are subsequently used in the production of the good.

5. Each Party shall provide that an exporter or producer shall calculate the regional value content of a good solely on the basis of the net cost method set out in paragraph 3 where: (a) there is no transaction value for the good; (b) the transaction value of the good is unacceptable under Article 1 of the Customs Valuation Code; (c) the good is sold by the producer to a related person and the volume, by units of quantity, of sales of identical or similar goods to related persons during the six-month period immediately preceding the month in which the good is sold exceeds 85 percent of the producer's total sales of such goods during that period; (d) the good is (i) a motor vehicle provided for in heading 87.01 or 87.02, subheading 8703.21 through 8703.90, or heading 87.04, 87.05 or 87.06, (ii) identified in Annex 403.1 or 403.2 and is for use in a motor vehicle provided for in heading 87.01 or 87.02, subheading 8703.21 through 8703.90, or heading 87.04, 87.05 or 87.06, (iii) provided for in subheading 6401.10 through 6406.10, or (iv) provided for in tariff item 8469.10.aa (word processing machines); (e) the exporter or producer chooses to accumulate the regional value content of the good in accordance with Article 404; or (f) the good is designated as an intermediate material under paragraph 10 and is subject to a regional value-content requirement.

6. If an exporter or producer of a good calculates the regional value content of the good on the basis of the transaction value method set out in paragraph 2 and a Party subsequently notifies the exporter or producer, during the course of a verification pursuant to Chapter Five (Customs Procedures), that the transaction value of the good, or the value of any material used in the production of the good, is required to be adjusted or is unacceptable under Article 1 of the Customs Valuation Code, the exporter or producer may then also calculate the regional value content of the good on the basis of the net cost method set out in paragraph 3.

7. Nothing in paragraph 6 shall be construed to prevent any review or appeal available under Article 510 (Review and Appeal) of an adjustment to or a rejection of: (a) the transaction value of a good; or (b) the value of any material used in the production of a good.

8. For purposes of calculating the net cost of a good under paragraph 3, the producer of the good may: (a) calculate the total cost incurred with respect to all goods produced by that producer, subtract any sales promotion, marketing and after-sales service costs, royalties, shipping and packing costs, and non-allowable interest costs that are included in the total cost of all such goods, and then reasonably allocate the resulting net cost of those goods to the good, (b) calculate the total cost incurred with respect to all goods produced by that producer, reasonably allocate the total cost to the good, and then subtract any sales promotion, marketing and after-sales service costs, royalties, shipping and packing costs and non-allowable interest costs that are included in the portion of the total cost allocated to the good, or (c) reasonably allocate each cost that forms part of the total cost incurred with respect to the good so that the aggregate of these costs does not include any sales promotion, marketing and after-sales service costs, royalties, shipping and packing costs,

and non-allowable interest costs, provided that the allocation of all such costs is consistent with the provisions regarding the reasonable allocation of costs set out in the Uniform Regulations, established under Article 511 (Customs Procedures—Uniform Regulations).

9. Except as provided in paragraph 11, the value of a material used in the production of a good shall: (a) be the transaction value of the material determined in accordance with Article 1 of the Customs Valuation Code; or (b) in the event that there is no transaction value or the transaction value of the material is unacceptable under Article 1 of the Customs Valuation Code, be determined in accordance with Articles 2 through 7 of the Customs Valuation Code; and (c) where not included under subparagraph (a) or (b), include (i) freight, insurance, packing and all other costs incurred in transporting the material to the location of the producer, (ii) duties, taxes and customs brokerage fees on the material paid in the territory of one or more of the Parties, and (iii) the cost of waste and spoilage resulting from the use of the material in the production of the good, less the value of renewable scrap or by-product.

10. Except as provided in Article 403(1), any self-produced material, other than a component identified in Annex 403.2, that is used in the production of a good may be designated by the producer of the good as an intermediate material for the purpose of calculating the regional value content of the good under paragraph 2 or 3, provided that where the intermediate material is subject to a regional value-content requirement, no other self-produced material subject to a regional value-content requirement used in the production of that intermediate material may itself be designated by the producer as an intermediate material.

11. The value of an intermediate material shall be: (a) the total cost incurred with respect to all goods produced by the producer of the good that can be reasonably allocated to that intermediate material; or (b) the aggregate of each cost that forms part of the total cost incurred with respect to that intermediate material that can be reasonably allocated to that intermediate material.

12. The value of an indirect material shall be based on the Generally Accepted Accounting Principles applicable in the territory of the Party in which the good is produced.

Article 403
Automotive Goods

1. For purposes of calculating the regional value content under the net cost method set out in Article 402(3) for: (a) a good that is a motor vehicle provided for in tariff item 8702.10.bb or 8702.90.bb (vehicles for the transport of 15 or fewer persons), or subheading 8703.21 through 8703.90, 8704.21 or 8704.31, or (b) a good provided for in the tariff provisions listed in Annex 403.1 where the good is subject to a regional value-content requirement and is for use as original equipment in the production of a good provided for in tariff item 8702.10.bb or 8702.90.bb (vehicles for the transport of 15 or fewer persons), or subheading 8703.21 through 8703.90, 8704.21 or 8704.31, the value of non-originating materials used by the producer in the production of the good shall be the sum of the values of non-originating materials, deter-

mined in accordance with Article 402(9) at the time the non-originating materials are received by the first person in the territory of a Party who takes title to them, that are imported from outside the territories of the Parties under the tariff provisions listed in Annex 403.1 and that are used in the production of the good or that are used in the production of any material used in the production of the good.

2.   For purposes of calculating the regional value content under the net cost method set out in Article 402(3) for a good that is a motor vehicle provided for in heading 87.01, tariff item 8702.10.aa or 8702.90.aa (vehicles for the transport of 16 or more persons), subheading 8704.10, 8704.22, 8704.23, 8704.32 or 8704.90, or heading 87.05 or 87.06, or for a component identified in Annex 403.2 for use as original equipment in the production of the motor vehicle, the value of non-originating materials used by the producer in the production of the good shall be the sum of: (a) for each material used by the producer listed in Annex 403.2, whether or not produced by the producer, at the choice of the producer and determined in accordance with Article 402, either (i) the value of such material that is non-originating, or (ii) the value of non-originating materials used in the production of such material; and (b) the value of any other non-originating material used by the producer that is not listed in Annex 403.2, determined in accordance with Article 402.

3.   For purposes of calculating the regional value content of a motor vehicle identified in paragraph 1 or 2, the producer may average its calculation over its fiscal year, using any one of the following categories, on the basis of either all motor vehicles in the category or only those motor vehicles in the category that are exported to the territory of one or more of the other Parties: (a) the same model line of motor vehicles in the same class of vehicles produced in the same plant in the territory of a Party; (b) the same class of motor vehicles produced in the same plant in the territory of a Party; (c) the same model line of motor vehicles produced in the territory of a Party; or (d) if applicable, the basis set out in Annex 403.3.

4.   For purposes of calculating the regional value content for any or all goods provided for in a tariff provision listed in Annex 403.1, or a component or material identified in Annex 403.2, produced in the same plant, the producer of the good may: (a) average its calculation (i) over the fiscal year of the motor vehicle producer to whom the good is sold, (ii) over any quarter or month, or (iii) over its fiscal year, if the good is sold as an aftermarket part; (b) calculate the average referred to in subparagraph (a) separately for any or all goods sold to one or more motor vehicle producers; or (c) with respect to any calculation under this paragraph, calculate separately for those goods that are exported to the territory of one or more of the Parties.

5.   Notwithstanding Annex 401, and except as provided in paragraph 6, the regional value-content requirement shall be: (a) for a producer's fiscal year beginning on the day closest to January 1, 1998 and thereafter, 56 percent under the net cost method, and for a producer's fiscal year beginning on the day closest to January 1, 2002 and thereafter, 62.5 percent under the net cost method, for (i) a good that is a motor vehicle provided for in tariff item 8702.10.bb or 8702.90.bb (vehicles for the transport of 15 or fewer persons), or subheading 8703.21 through 8703.90, 8704.21 or 8704.31, and (ii) a good provided for in heading 84.07 or 84.08, or subheading 8708.40, that is

for use in a motor vehicle identified in subparagraph (a)(i); and (b) for a producer's fiscal year beginning on the day closest to January 1, 1998 and thereafter, 55 percent under the net cost method, and for a producer's fiscal year beginning on the day closest to January 1, 2002 and thereafter, 60 percent under the net cost method, for (i) a good that is a motor vehicle provided for in heading 87.01, tariff item 8702.10.aa or 8702.90.aa (vehicles for the transport of 16 or more persons), 8704.10, 8704.22, 8704.23, 8704.32 or 8704.90, or heading 87.05 or 87.06, (ii) a good provided for in heading 84.07 or 84.08 or subheading 8708.40 that is for use in a motor vehicle identified in subparagraph (b)(i), and (iii) except for a good identified in subparagraph (a)(ii) or provided for in subheading 8482.10 through 8482.80, 8483.20 or 8483.30, a good identified in Annex 403.1 that is subject to a regional value content requirement and that is for use in a motor vehicle identified in subparagraph (a)(i) or (b)(i).

6. The regional value-content requirement for a motor vehicle identified in Article 403(1) or (2) shall be: (a) 50 percent for five years after the date on which the first motor vehicle prototype is produced in a plant by a motor vehicle assembler, if (i) it is a motor vehicle of a class, or marque, or, except for a motor vehicle identified in Article 403(2), size category and underbody, not previously produced by the motor vehicle assembler in the territory of any of the Parties, (ii) the plant consists of a new building in which the motor vehicle is assembled, and (iii) the plant contains substantially all new machinery that is used in the assembly of the motor vehicle; or (b) 50 percent for two years after the date on which the first motor vehicle prototype is produced at a plant following a refit, if it is a different motor vehicle of a class, or marque, or, except for a motor vehicle identified in Article 403(2), size category and underbody, than was assembled by the motor vehicle assembler in the plant before the refit.

Article 404

Accumulation

1. For purposes of determining whether a good is an originating good, the production of the good in the territory of one or more of the Parties by one or more producers shall, at the choice of the exporter or producer of the good for which preferential tariff treatment is claimed, be considered to have been performed in the territory of any of the Parties by that exporter or producer, provided that: (a) all non-originating materials used in the production of the good undergo an applicable tariff classification change set out in Annex 401, and the good satisfies any applicable regional value-content requirement, entirely in the territory of one or more of the Parties; and (b) the good satisfies all other applicable requirements of this Chapter.

2. For purposes of Article 402(10), the production of a producer that chooses to accumulate its production with that of other producers under paragraph 1 shall be considered to be the production of a single producer.

Article 405

De Minimis

1. Except as provided in paragraphs 3 through 6, a good shall be considered to be an originating good if the value of all non-originating

materials used in the production of the good that do not undergo an applicable change in tariff classification set out in Annex 401 is not more than seven percent of the transaction value of the good, adjusted to a F.O.B. basis, or, if the transaction value of the good is unacceptable under Article 1 of the Customs Valuation Code, the value of all such non-originating materials is not more than seven percent of the total cost of the good, provided that: (a) if the good is subject to a regional value-content requirement, the value of such non-originating materials shall be taken into account in calculating the regional value content of the good; and (b) the good satisfies all other applicable requirements of this Chapter.

2. A good that is otherwise subject to a regional value-content requirement shall not be required to satisfy such requirement if the value of all non-originating materials used in the production of the good is not more than seven percent of the transaction value of the good, adjusted to a F.O.B. basis, or, if the transaction value of the good is unacceptable under Article 1 of the Customs Valuation Code, the value of all non-originating materials is not more than seven percent of the total cost of the good, provided that the good satisfies all other applicable requirements of this Chapter.

3. Paragraph 1 does not apply to: (a) a non-originating material provided for in Chapter 4 of the Harmonized System or tariff item 1901.90.aa (dairy preparations containing over 10 percent by weight of milk solids) that is used in the production of a good provided for in Chapter 4 of the Harmonized System; (b) a non-originating material provided for in Chapter 4 of the Harmonized System or tariff item 1901.90.aa (dairy preparations containing over 10 percent by weight of milk solids) that is used in the production of a good provided for in tariff item 1901.10.aa (infant preparations containing over 10 percent by weight of milk solids), 1901.20.aa (mixes and doughs, containing over 25 percent by weight of butterfat, not put up for retail sale), 1901.90.aa (dairy preparations containing over 10 percent by weight of milk solids), heading 21.05, or tariff item 2106.90.dd (preparations containing over 10 percent by weight of milk solids), 2202.90.cc (beverages containing milk) or 2309.90.aa (animal feeds containing over 10 percent by weight of milk solids); (c) a non-originating material provided for in heading 08.05 or subheading 2009.11 through 2009.30 that is used in the production of a good provided for in subheading 2009.11 through 2009.30 or tariff item 2106.90.bb (concentrated fruit or vegetable juice of any single fruit or vegetable, fortified with minerals or vitamins) or 2202.90.aa (fruit or vegetable juice of any single fruit or vegetable, fortified with minerals or vitamins); (d) a non-originating material provided for in Chapter 9 of the Harmonized System that is used in the production of a good provided for in tariff item 2101.10.aa (instant coffee, not flavored); (e) a non-originating material provided for in Chapter 15 of the Harmonized System that is used in the production of a good provided for in heading 15.01 through 15.08, 15.12, 15.14 or 15.15; (f) a non-originating material provided for in heading 17.01 that is used in the production of a good provided for in heading 17.01 through 17.03; (g) a non-originating material provided for in Chapter 17 of the Harmonized System or heading 18.05 that is used in the production of a good provided for in subheading 1806.10; (h) a non-originating material provided for in heading 22.03 through 22.08 that is used in the production of a good provided for in heading 22.07 through 22.08; (i) a non-originating material used in the production of a good provided for in

tariff item 7321.11.aa (gas stove or range), subheading 8415.10, 8415.81 through 8415.83, 8418.10 through 8418.21, 8418.29 through 8418.40, 8421.12, 8422.11, 8450.11 through 8450.20 or 8451.21 through 8451.29, Mexican tariff item 8479.82.aa (trash compactors) or Canadian or U.S. tariff item 8479.89.aa (trash compactors), or tariff item 8516.60.aa (electric stove or range); and (j) a printed circuit assembly that is a non-originating material used in the production of a good where the applicable change in tariff classification for the good, as set out in Annex 401, places restrictions on the use of such non-originating material.

4. Paragraph 1 does not apply to a non-originating single juice ingredient provided for in heading 20.09 that is used in the production of a good provided for in subheading 2009.90, or tariff item 2106.90.cc (concentrated mixtures of fruit or vegetable juice, fortified with minerals or vitamins) or 2202.90.bb (mixtures of fruit or vegetable juices, fortified with minerals or vitamins).

5. Paragraph 1 does not apply to a non-originating material used in the production of a good provided for in Chapter 1 through 27 of the Harmonized System unless the non-originating material is provided for in a different subheading than the good for which origin is being determined under this Article.

6. A good provided for in Chapter 50 through 63 of the Harmonized System that does not originate because certain fibers or yarns used in the production of the component of the good that determines the tariff classification of the good do not undergo an applicable change in tariff classification set out in Annex 401, shall nonetheless be considered to originate if the total weight of all such fibers or yarns in that component is not more than seven percent of the total weight of that component.

Article 406
Fungible Goods and Materials

For purposes of determining whether a good is an originating good: (a) where originating and non-originating fungible materials are used in the production of a good, the determination of whether the materials are originating need not be made through the identification of any specific fungible material, but may be determined on the basis of any of the inventory management methods set out in the Uniform Regulations; and (b) where originating and non-originating fungible goods are commingled and exported in the same form, the determination may be made on the basis of any of the inventory management methods set out in the Uniform Regulations.

Article 407
Accessories, Spare Parts and Tools

Accessories, spare parts or tools delivered with the good that form part of the good's standard accessories, spare parts, or tools, shall be considered as originating if the good originates and shall be disregarded in determining whether all the non-originating materials used in the production of the good undergo the applicable change in tariff classification set out in Annex 401, provided that: (a) the accessories, spare parts or tools are not invoiced separately from the good; (b) the quantities and value of the accessories, spare parts or tools are customary for the good; and (c) if the good is subject to a regional value-content requirement, the value of the accessories, spare parts or tools shall be taken into account as originating or non-originating materials, as the case may be, in calculating the regional value content of the good.

Article 408

Indirect Materials

An indirect material shall be considered to be an originating material without regard to where it is produced.

Article 409

Packaging Materials and Containers for Retail Sale

Packaging materials and containers in which a good is packaged for retail sale shall, if classified with the good, be disregarded in determining whether all the non-originating materials used in the production of the good undergo the applicable change in tariff classification set out in Annex 401, and, if the good is subject to a regional value-content requirement, the value of such packaging materials and containers shall be taken into account as originating or non-originating materials, as the case may be, in calculating the regional value content of the good.

Article 410

Packing Materials and Containers for Shipment

Packing materials and containers in which a good is packed for shipment shall be disregarded in determining whether: (a) the non-originating materials used in the production of the good undergo an applicable change in tariff classification set out in Annex 401; and (b) the good satisfies a regional value-content requirement.

Article 411

Transshipment

A good shall not be considered to be an originating good by reason of having undergone production that satisfies the requirements of Article 401 if, subsequent to that production, the good undergoes further production or any other operation outside the territories of the Parties, other than unloading, reloading or any other operation necessary to preserve it in good condition or to transport the good to the territory of a Party.

Article 412

Non–Qualifying Operations

A good shall not be considered to be an originating good merely by reason of: (a) mere dilution with water or another substance that does not materially alter the characteristics of the good; or (b) any production or pricing practice in respect of which it may be demonstrated, on the basis of a preponderance of evidence, that the object was to circumvent this Chapter.

Article 413

Interpretation and Application

For purposes of this Chapter: (a) the basis for tariff classification in this Chapter is the Harmonized System; (b) where a good referred to by a tariff item number is described in parentheses following the tariff item number, the description is provided for purposes of reference only; (c) where applying Article 401(d), the determination of whether a heading or subheading under the Harmonized System provides for and specifically describes both a good and its parts shall be made on the basis of the nomenclature of the heading or subheading, or the General Rules of Interpretation, the Chapter Notes or the Section Notes of the Harmonized System; (d) in applying the Customs Valuation Code under this Chapter, (i) the principles of the Customs Valuation Code shall apply to domestic transactions, with such modifications as may be required by the circumstances, as would apply to international transactions, (ii) the provisions of this Chapter shall take precedence over the Customs Valuation Code to the extent of any difference, and (iii) the definitions in Article 415 shall take precedence over the definitions in the Customs Valuation Code to the extent of any difference; and (e) all costs referred to in this Chapter shall be recorded and maintained in accordance with the Generally Accepted Accounting Principles applicable in the territory of the Party in which the good is produced.

Article 414

Consultation and Modifications

1. The Parties shall consult regularly to ensure that this Chapter is administered effectively, uniformly and consistently with the spirit and objectives of this Agreement, and shall cooperate in the administration of this Chapter in accordance with Chapter Five.

2. Any Party that considers that this Chapter requires modification to take into account developments in production processes or other matters may submit a proposed modification along with supporting rationale and any studies to the other Parties for consideration and any appropriate action under Chapter Five.

Article 415

Definitions

For purposes of this Chapter:

class of motor vehicles means any one of the following categories of motor vehicles: (a) motor vehicles provided for in subheading 8701.20, tariff item 8702.10.aa or 8702.90.aa (vehicles for the transport of 16 or more persons), subheading 8704.10, 8704.22, 8704.23, 8704.32 or 8704.90, or heading 87.05 or 87.06; (b) motor vehicles provided for in subheading 8701.10 or 8701.30 through 8701.90; (c) motor vehicles provided for in tariff item 8702.10.bb or 8702.90.bb (vehicles for the transport of 15 or fewer persons), or subheading 8704.21 or 8704.31; or (d) motor vehicles provided for in subheading 8703.21 through 8703.90;

F.O.B. means free on board, regardless of the mode of transportation, at the point of direct shipment by the seller to the buyer;

fungible goods or fungible materials means goods or materials that are interchangeable for commercial purposes and whose properties are essentially identical;

goods wholly obtained or produced entirely in the territory of one or more of the Parties means: (a) mineral goods extracted in the territory of one or more of the Parties; (b) vegetable goods, as such goods are defined in the Harmonized System, harvested in the territory of one or more of the Parties; (c) live animals born and raised in the territory of one or more of the Parties; (d) goods obtained from hunting, trapping or fishing in the territory of one or more of the Parties; (e) goods (fish, shellfish and other marine life) taken from the sea by vessels registered or recorded with a Party and flying its flag; (f) goods produced on board factory ships from the goods referred to in subparagraph (e) provided such factory ships are registered or recorded with that Party and fly its flag; (g) goods taken by a Party or a person of a Party from the seabed or beneath the seabed outside territorial waters, provided that a Party has rights to exploit such seabed; (h) goods taken from outer space, provided they are obtained by a Party or a person of a Party and not processed in a non-Party; (i) waste and scrap derived from (i) production in the territory of one or more of the Parties, or (ii) used goods collected in the territory of one or more of the Parties, provided such goods are fit only for the recovery of raw materials; and (j) goods produced in the territory of one or more of the Parties exclusively from goods referred to in subparagraphs (a) through (i), or from their derivatives, at any stage of production;

identical or similar goods means "identical goods" and "similar goods", respectively, as defined in the Customs Valuation Code;

indirect material means a good used in the production, testing or inspection of a good but not physically incorporated into the good, or a good used in the maintenance of buildings or the operation of equipment associated with the production of a good, including: (a) fuel and energy; (b) tools, dies and molds; (c) spare parts and materials used in the maintenance of equipment and buildings; (d) lubricants, greases, compounding materials and other materials used in production or used to operate equipment and buildings; (e) gloves, glasses, footwear, clothing, safety equipment and supplies; (f) equipment, devices, and supplies used for testing or inspecting the goods; (g) catalysts and solvents; and (h) any other goods that are not incorporated into the good but whose use in the production of the good can reasonably be demonstrated to be a part of that production;

intermediate material means a material that is self-produced and used in the production of a good, and designated pursuant to Article 402(10);

marque means the trade name used by a separate marketing division of a motor vehicle assembler;

material means a good that is used in the production of another good, and includes a part or an ingredient;

model line means a group of motor vehicles having the same platform or model name;

motor vehicle assembler means a producer of motor vehicles and any related persons or joint ventures in which the producer participates;

new building means a new construction, including at least the pouring or construction of new foundation and floor, the erection of a new structure and roof, and installation of new plumbing, electrical and other utilities to house a complete vehicle assembly process;

net cost means total cost minus sales promotion, marketing and after-sales service costs, royalties, shipping and packing costs, and non-allowable interest costs that are included in the total cost;

net cost of a good means the net cost that can be reasonably allocated to a good using one of the methods set out in Article 402(8);

non-allowable interest costs means interest costs incurred by a producer that exceed 700 basis points above the applicable federal government interest rate identified in the Uniform Regulations for comparable maturities;

non-originating good or non-originating material means a good or material that does not qualify as originating under this Chapter;

producer means a person who grows, mines, harvests, fishes, traps, hunts, manufactures, processes or assembles a good;

production means growing, mining, harvesting, fishing, trapping, hunting, manufacturing, processing or assembling a good;

reasonably allocate means to apportion in a manner appropriate to the circumstances;

refit means a plant closure, for purposes of plant conversion or retooling, that lasts at least three months;

related person means a person related to another person on the basis that: (a) they are officers or directors of one another's businesses; (b) they are legally recognized partners in business; (c) they are employer and employee; (d) any person directly or indirectly owns, controls or holds 25 percent or more of the outstanding voting stock or shares of each of them; (e) one of them directly or indirectly controls the other; (f) both of them are directly or indirectly controlled by a third person; or (g) they are members of the same family (members of the same family are natural or adoptive children, brothers, sisters, parents, grandparents, or spouses);

royalties means payments of any kind, including payments under technical assistance or similar agreements, made as consideration for the use or right to use any copyright, literary, artistic, or scientific work, patent, trademark, design, model, plan, secret formula or process, excluding those payments under technical assistance or similar agreements that can be related to specific services such as: (a) personnel training, without regard to where performed; and (b) if performed in the territory of one or more of the Parties, engineering, tooling, die-setting, software design and similar computer services, or other services;

sales promotion, marketing and after-sales service costs means the following costs related to sales promotion, marketing and after-sales service: (a) sales and marketing promotion; media advertising; advertising and market research; promotional and demonstration materials; exhibits; sales conferences, trade shows and conventions; banners; marketing displays; free samples; sales, marketing and after-sales service literature (product brochures, catalogs, technical literature, price lists, service manuals, sales aid information); establishment and protection of logos and trademarks; sponsorships; wholesale and retail restocking charges; entertainment; (b) sales and marketing incentives; consumer, retailer or wholesaler rebates; merchandise incentives; (c) salaries and wages, sales commissions, bonuses, benefits (for example, medical, insurance, pension), travelling and living expenses, membership and professional fees, for sales promotion, marketing and after-sales service personnel; (d) recruiting and training of sales promotion, marketing and after-sales service personnel, and after-sales training of customers' employees, where such costs are identified separately for sales promotion, marketing and after-sales service of goods on the financial statements or cost accounts of the producer; (e) product liability insurance; (f) office supplies for sales promotion, marketing and after-sales service of goods, where such costs are identified separately for sales promotion, marketing and after-sales service of goods on the financial statements or cost accounts of the producer; (g) telephone, mail and other communications, where such costs are identified separately for sales promotion, marketing and after-sales service of goods on the financial statements or cost accounts of the producer; (h) rent and depreciation of sales promotion, marketing and after-sales service offices and distribution centers; (i) property insurance premiums, taxes, cost of utilities, and repair and maintenance of sales promotion, marketing and after-sales service offices and distribution centers, where such costs are identified separately for sales promotion, marketing and after-sales service of goods on the financial statements or cost accounts of the producer; and (j) payments by the producer to other persons for warranty repairs;

self-produced material means a material that is produced by the producer of a good and used in the production of that good;

shipping and packing costs means the costs incurred in packing a good for shipment and shipping the good from the point of direct shipment to the buyer, excluding costs of preparing and packaging the good for retail sale;

size category means for a motor vehicle identified in Article 403(1)(a): (a) 85 or less cubic feet of passenger and luggage interior volume, (b) between 85 and 100 cubic feet of passenger and luggage interior volume, (c) 100 to 110 cubic feet of passenger and luggage interior volume, (d) between 110 and 120 cubic feet of passenger and luggage interior volume, and (e) 120 and more cubic feet of passenger and luggage interior volume;

total cost means all product costs, period costs and other costs incurred in the territory of one or more of the Parties;

transaction value means the price actually paid or payable for a good or material with respect to a transaction of, except for the application of Article 403(1) or 403(2)(a), the producer of the good, adjusted in accordance with the principles of paragraphs 1, 3 and 4 of Article 8 of the Customs Valuation Code, regardless of whether the good or material is sold for export;

used means used or consumed in the production of goods; and

underbody means the floor pan of a motor vehicle.

CHAPTER FIVE: CUSTOMS PROCEDURES
Section A—Certification of Origin
Article 501

Certificate of Origin

1.　The Parties shall establish by January 1, 1994 a Certificate of Origin for the purpose of certifying that a good being exported from the territory of a

Party into the territory of another Party qualifies as an originating good, and may thereafter revise the Certificate by agreement.

2.   Each Party may require that a Certificate of Origin for a good imported into its territory be completed in a language required under its law.

3.   Each Party shall: (a) require an exporter in its territory to complete and sign a Certificate of Origin for any exportation of a good for which an importer may claim preferential tariff treatment on importation of the good into the territory of another Party; and (b) provide that where an exporter in its territory is not the producer of the good, the exporter may complete and sign a Certificate on the basis of (i) its knowledge of whether the good qualifies as an originating good, (ii) its reasonable reliance on the producer's written representation that the good qualifies as an originating good, or (iii) a completed and signed Certificate for the good voluntarily provided to the exporter by the producer.

4.   Nothing in paragraph 3 shall be construed to require a producer to provide a Certificate of Origin to an exporter.

5.   Each Party shall provide that a Certificate of Origin that has been completed and signed by an exporter or a producer in the territory of another Party that is applicable to: (a) a single importation of a good into the Party's territory, or (b) multiple importations of identical goods into the Party's territory that occur within a specified period, not exceeding 12 months, set out therein by the exporter or producer, shall be accepted by its customs administration for four years after the date on which the Certificate was signed.

Article 502
Obligations Regarding Importations

1.   Except as otherwise provided in this Chapter, each Party shall require an importer in its territory that claims preferential tariff treatment for a good imported into its territory from the territory of another Party to: (a) make a written declaration, based on a valid Certificate of Origin, that the good qualifies as an originating good; (b) have the Certificate in its possession at the time the declaration is made; (c) provide, on the request of that Party's customs administration, a copy of the Certificate; and (d) promptly make a corrected declaration and pay any duties owing where the importer has reason to believe that a Certificate on which a declaration was based contains information that is not correct.

2.   Each Party shall provide that, where an importer in its territory claims preferential tariff treatment for a good imported into its territory from the territory of another Party: (a) the Party may deny preferential tariff treatment to the good if the importer fails to comply with any requirement under this Chapter; and (b) the importer shall not be subject to penalties for the making of an incorrect declaration, if it voluntarily makes a corrected declaration pursuant to paragraph 1(d).

3.   Each Party shall provide that, where a good would have qualified as an originating good when it was imported into the territory of that Party but no claim for preferential tariff treatment was made at that time, the importer of the good may, no later than one year after the date on which the good was imported, apply for a refund of any excess duties paid as the result of the good not having been accorded preferential tariff treatment, on presentation of: (a)

a written declaration that the good qualified as an originating good at the time of importation; (b) a copy of the Certificate of Origin; and (c) such other documentation relating to the importation of the good as that Party may require.

Article 503
Exceptions

Each Party shall provide that a Certificate of Origin shall not be required for: (a) a commercial importation of a good whose value does not exceed US $1,000 or its equivalent amount in the Party's currency, or such higher amount as it may establish, except that it may require that the invoice accompanying the importation include a statement certifying that the good qualifies as an originating good, (b) a non-commercial importation of a good whose value does not exceed US $1,000 or its equivalent amount in the Party's currency, or such higher amount as it may establish, or (c) an importation of a good for which the Party into whose territory the good is imported has waived the requirement for a Certificate of Origin, provided that the importation does not form part of a series of importations that may reasonably be considered to have been undertaken or arranged for the purpose of avoiding the certification requirements of Articles 501 and 502.

Article 504
Obligations Regarding Exportations

1. Each Party shall provide that: (a) an exporter in its territory, or a producer in its territory that has provided a copy of a Certificate of Origin to that exporter pursuant to Article 501(3)(b)(iii), shall provide a copy of the Certificate to its customs administration on request; and (b) an exporter or a producer in its territory that has completed and signed a Certificate of Origin, and that has reason to believe that the Certificate contains information that is not correct, shall promptly notify in writing all persons to whom the Certificate was given by the exporter or producer of any change that could affect the accuracy or validity of the Certificate.

2. Each Party: (a) shall provide that a false certification by an exporter or a producer in its territory that a good to be exported to the territory of another Party qualifies as an originating good shall have the same legal consequences, with appropriate modifications, as would apply to an importer in its territory for a contravention of its customs laws and regulations regarding the making of a false statement or representation; and (b) may apply such measures as the circumstances may warrant where an exporter or a producer in its territory fails to comply with any requirement of this Chapter.

3. No Party may impose penalties on an exporter or a producer in its territory that voluntarily provides written notification pursuant to paragraph (1)(b) with respect to the making of an incorrect certification.

Section B—Administration and Enforcement
Article 505
Records

Each Party shall provide that: (a) an exporter or a producer in its territory that completes and signs a Certificate of Origin shall maintain in its territory, for five years after the date on which the Certificate was signed or for such longer period as the Party may specify, all records relating to the origin of a good for which preferential tariff treatment was claimed in the territory of another Party, including records associated with (i) the purchase of, cost of, value of, and payment for, the good that is exported from its territory, (ii) the purchase of, cost of, value of, and payment for, all materials, including indirect materials, used in the production of the good that is exported from its territory, and (iii) the production of the good in the form in which the good is exported from its territory; and (b) an importer claiming preferential tariff treatment for a good imported into the Party's territory shall maintain in that territory, for five years after the date of importation of the good or for such longer period as the Party may specify, such documentation, including a copy of the Certificate, as the Party may require relating to the importation of the good.

Article 506
Origin Verifications

1. For purposes of determining whether a good imported into its territory from the territory of another Party qualifies as an originating good, a Party may, through its customs administration, conduct a verification solely by means of: (a) written questionnaires to an exporter or a producer in the territory of another Party; (b) visits to the premises of an exporter or a producer in the territory of another Party to review the records referred to in Article 505(a) and observe the facilities used in the production of the good; or (c) such other procedure as the Parties may agree.

2. Prior to conducting a verification visit pursuant to paragraph (1)(b), a Party shall, through its customs administration: (a) deliver a written notification of its intention to conduct the visit to (i) the exporter or producer whose premises are to be visited, (ii) the customs administration of the Party in whose territory the visit is to occur, and (iii) if requested by the Party in whose territory the visit is to occur, the embassy of that Party in the territory of the Party proposing to conduct the visit; and (b) obtain the written consent of the exporter or producer whose premises are to be visited.

3. The notification referred to in paragraph 2 shall include: (a) the identity of the customs administration issuing the notification; (b) the name of the exporter or producer whose premises are to be visited; (c) the date and place of the proposed verification visit; (d) the object and scope of the proposed verification visit, including specific reference to the good that is the subject of the verification; (e) the names and titles of the officials performing the verification visit; and (f) the legal authority for the verification visit.

4. Where an exporter or a producer has not given its written consent to a proposed verification visit within 30 days of receipt of notification pursuant to paragraph 2, the notifying Party may deny preferential tariff treatment to the good that would have been the subject of the visit.

5. Each Party shall provide that, where its customs administration receives notification pursuant to paragraph 2, the customs administration may, within 15 days of receipt of the notification, postpone the proposed verification visit for a period not exceeding 60 days from the date of such receipt, or for such longer period as the Parties may agree.

6. A Party shall not deny preferential tariff treatment to a good based solely on the postponement of a verification visit pursuant to paragraph 5.

7. Each Party shall permit an exporter or a producer whose good is the subject of a verification visit by another Party to designate two observers to be present during the visit, provided that: (a) the observers do not participate in a manner other than as observers; and (b) the failure of the exporter or producer to designate observers shall not result in the postponement of the visit.

8. Each Party shall, through its customs administration, conduct a verification of a regional value-content requirement in accordance with the Generally Accepted Accounting Principles applied in the territory of the Party from which the good was exported.

9. The Party conducting a verification shall provide the exporter or producer whose good is the subject of the verification with a written determination of whether the good qualifies as an originating good, including findings of fact and the legal basis for the determination.

10. Where verifications by a Party indicate a pattern of conduct by an exporter or a producer of false or unsupported representations that a good imported into its territory qualifies as an originating good, the Party may withhold preferential tariff treatment to identical goods exported or produced by such person until that person establishes compliance with Chapter Four (Rules of Origin).

11. Each Party shall provide that where it determines that a certain good imported into its territory does not qualify as an originating good based on a tariff classification or a value applied by the Party to one or more materials used in the production of the good, which differs from the tariff classification or value applied to the materials by the Party from whose territory the good was exported, the Party's determination shall not become effective until it notifies in writing both the importer of the good and the person that completed and signed the Certificate of Origin for the good of its determination.

12. A Party shall not apply a determination made under paragraph 11 to an importation made before the effective date of the determination where: (a) the customs administration of the Party from whose territory the good was exported has issued an advance ruling under Article 509 or any other ruling on the tariff classification or on the value of such materials, or has given consistent treatment to the entry of the materials under the tariff classification or value at issue, on which a person is entitled to rely; and (b) the advance ruling, other ruling or consistent treatment was given prior to notification of the determination.

13. If a Party denies preferential tariff treatment to a good pursuant to a determination made under paragraph 11, it shall postpone the effective date of the denial for a period not exceeding 90 days where the importer of the good, or the person who completed and signed the Certificate of Origin for the good, demonstrates that it has relied in good faith to its detriment on the tariff classification or value applied to such materials by the customs administration of the Party from whose territory the good was exported.

Article 507

Confidentiality

1.   Each Party shall maintain, in accordance with its law, the confidentiality of confidential business information collected pursuant to this Chapter and shall protect that information from disclosure that could prejudice the competitive position of the persons providing the information.

2.   The confidential business information collected pursuant to this Chapter may only be disclosed to those authorities responsible for the administration and enforcement of determinations of origin, and of customs and revenue matters.

Article 508

Penalties

1.   Each Party shall maintain measures imposing criminal, civil or administrative penalties for violations of its laws and regulations relating to this Chapter.

2.   Nothing in Article 502(2), 504(3) or 506(6) shall be construed to prevent a Party from applying such measures as the circumstances may warrant.

Section C—Advance Rulings

Article 509

Advance Rulings

1.   Each Party shall, through its customs administration, provide for the expeditious issuance of written advance rulings, prior to the importation of a good into its territory, to an importer in its territory or an exporter or a producer in the territory of another Party, on the basis of the facts and circumstances presented by such importer, exporter or producer of the good, concerning: (a) whether materials imported from a non-Party used in the production of a good undergo an applicable change in tariff classification set out in Annex 401 as a result of production occurring entirely in the territory of one or more of the Parties; (b) whether a good satisfies a regional value-content requirement under either the transaction value method or the net cost method set out in Chapter Four (Rules of Origin); (c) for the purpose of determining whether a good satisfies a regional value-content requirement under Chapter Four, the appropriate basis or method for value to be applied by an exporter or a producer in the territory of another Party, in accordance with the principles of the Customs Valuation Code, for calculating the transaction value of the good or of the materials used in the production of the good; (d) for the purpose of determining whether a good satisfies a regional value-content requirement under Chapter Four, the appropriate basis or method for reasonably allocating costs, in accordance with the allocation methods set out in the Uniform Regulations, for calculating the net cost of the good or the value of an intermediate material; (e) whether a good qualifies as an originating good under Chapter Four; (f) whether a good that re-enters its territory after the good has been exported from its territory to the territory of another Party for repair or alteration qualifies for duty-free treatment in accordance with Article 307 (Goods Re–Entered after Repair or Alteration);

(g) whether the proposed or actual marking of a good satisfies country of origin marking requirements under Article 311 (Country of Origin Marking); (h) whether an originating good qualifies as a good of a Party under Annex 300–B (Textile and Apparel Goods), Annex 302.2 (Tariff Elimination) or Chapter Seven (Agriculture and Sanitary and Phytosanitary Measures); (i) whether a good is a qualifying good under Chapter Seven; or (j) such other matters as the Parties may agree.

2.   Each Party shall adopt or maintain procedures for the issuance of advance rulings, including a detailed description of the information reasonably required to process an application for a ruling.

3.   Each Party shall provide that its customs administration: (a) may, at any time during the course of an evaluation of an application for an advance ruling, request supplemental information from the person requesting the ruling; (b) shall, after it has obtained all necessary information from the person requesting an advance ruling, issue the ruling within the periods specified in the Uniform Regulations; and (c) shall, where the advance ruling is unfavorable to the person requesting it, provide to that person a full explanation of the reasons for the ruling.

4.   Subject to paragraph 6, each Party shall apply an advance ruling to importations into its territory of the good for which the ruling was requested, beginning on the date of its issuance or such later date as may be specified in the ruling.

5.   Each Party shall provide to any person requesting an advance ruling the same treatment, including the same interpretation and application of provisions of Chapter Four regarding a determination of origin, as it provided to any other person to whom it issued an advance ruling, provided that the facts and circumstances are identical in all material respects.

6.   The issuing Party may modify or revoke an advance ruling: (a) if the ruling is based on an error (i) of fact, (ii) in the tariff classification of a good or a material that is the subject of the ruling, (iii) in the application of a regional value-content requirement under Chapter Four, (iv) in the application of the rules for determining whether a good qualifies as a good of a Party under Annex 300–B, Annex 302.2 or Chapter Seven, (v) in the application of the rules for determining whether a good is a qualifying good under Chapter Seven, or (vi) in the application of the rules for determining whether a good that re-enters its territory after the good has been exported from its territory to the territory of another Party for repair or alteration qualifies for duty-free treatment under Article 307; (b) if the ruling is not in accordance with an interpretation agreed by the Parties regarding Chapter Three (National Treatment and Market Access for Goods) or Chapter Four; (c) if there is a change in the material facts or circumstances on which the ruling is based; (d) to conform with a modification of Chapter Three, Chapter Four, this Chapter, Chapter Seven, the Marking Rules or the Uniform Regulations; or (e) to conform with a judicial decision or a change in its domestic law.

7.   Each Party shall provide that any modification or revocation of an advance ruling shall be effective on the date on which the modification or revocation is issued, or on such later date as may be specified therein, and shall not be applied to importations of a good that have occurred prior to that

date, unless the person to whom the advance ruling was issued has not acted in accordance with its terms and conditions.

8. Notwithstanding paragraph 7, the issuing Party shall postpone the effective date of such modification or revocation for a period not exceeding 90 days where the person to whom the advance ruling was issued demonstrates that it has relied in good faith to its detriment on that ruling.

9. Each Party shall provide that where its customs administration examines the regional value content of a good for which it has issued an advance ruling pursuant to subparagraph 1(c), (d) or (f), it shall evaluate whether: (a) the exporter or producer has complied with the terms and conditions of the advance ruling; (b) the exporter's or producer's operations are consistent with the material facts and circumstances on which the advance ruling is based; and (c) the supporting data and computations used in applying the basis or method for calculating value or allocating cost were correct in all material respects.

10. Each Party shall provide that where its customs administration determines that any requirement in paragraph 9 has not been satisfied, it may modify or revoke the advance ruling as the circumstances may warrant.

11. Each Party shall provide that, where the person to whom an advance ruling was issued demonstrates that it used reasonable care and acted in good faith in presenting the facts and circumstances on which the ruling was based, and where the customs administration of a Party determines that the ruling was based on incorrect information, the person to whom the ruling was issued shall not be subject to penalties.

12. Each Party shall provide that where it issues an advance ruling to a person that has misrepresented or omitted material facts or circumstances on which the ruling is based or has failed to act in accordance with the terms and conditions of the ruling, the Party may apply such measures as the circumstances may warrant.

Section D—Review and Appeal of Origin Determinations and Advance Rulings

Article 510

Review and Appeal

1. Each Party shall grant substantially the same rights of review and appeal of marking determinations of origin, country of origin determinations and advance rulings by its customs administration as it provides to importers in its territory to any person: (a) who completes and signs a Certificate of Origin for a good that has been the subject of a determination of origin; (b) whose good has been the subject of a country of origin marking determination pursuant to Article 311 (Country of Origin Marking); or (c) who has received an advance ruling pursuant to Article 509(1).

2. Further to Articles 1804 (Administrative Proceedings) and 1805 (Review and Appeal), each Party shall provide that the rights of review and appeal referred to in paragraph 1 shall include access to: (a) at least one level of administrative review independent of the official or office responsible for the determination under review; and (b) in accordance with its domestic law,

judicial or quasi-judicial review of the determination or decision taken at the final level of administrative review.

Section E—Uniform Regulations
Article 511
Uniform Regulations

1. The Parties shall establish, and implement through their respective laws or regulations by January 1, 1994, Uniform Regulations regarding the interpretation, application and administration of Chapter Four, this Chapter and other matters as may be agreed by the Parties.

2. Each Party shall implement any modification of or addition to the Uniform Regulations no later than 180 days after the Parties agree on such modification or addition, or such other period as the Parties may agree.

Section F—Cooperation
Article 512
Cooperation

1. Each Party shall notify the other Parties of the following determinations, measures and rulings, including to the greatest extent practicable those that are prospective in application: (a) a determination of origin issued as the result of a verification conducted pursuant to Article 506(1); (b) a determination of origin that the Party is aware is contrary to (i) a ruling issued by the customs administration of another Party with respect to the tariff classification or value of a good, or of materials used in the production of a good, or the reasonable allocation of costs where calculating the net cost of a good, that is the subject of a determination of origin, or (ii) consistent treatment given by the customs administration of another Party with respect to the tariff classification or value of a good, or of materials used in the production of a good, or the reasonable allocation of costs where calculating the net cost of a good, that is the subject of a determination of origin; (c) a measure establishing or significantly modifying an administrative policy that is likely to affect future determinations of origin, country of origin marking requirements or determinations as to whether a good qualifies as a good of a Party under the Marking Rules; and (d) an advance ruling, or a ruling modifying or revoking an advance ruling, pursuant to Article 509.

2. The Parties shall cooperate: (a) in the enforcement of their respective customs-related laws or regulations implementing this Agreement, and under any customs mutual assistance agreement or other customs-related agreement to which they are party; (b) for purposes of the detection and prevention of unlawful transshipments of textile and apparel goods of a non-Party, in the enforcement of prohibitions or quantitative restrictions, including the verification by a Party, in accordance with the procedures set out in this Chapter, of the capacity for production of goods by an exporter or a producer in the territory of another Party, provided that the customs administration of the Party proposing to conduct the verification, prior to conducting the verification (i) obtains the consent of the Party in whose territory the verification is to occur, and (ii) provides notification to the exporter or producer whose premises are to be visited, except that procedures for notifying the exporter or producer whose premises are to be visited shall be in accordance with such

other procedures as the Parties may agree; (c) to the extent practicable and for purposes of facilitating the flow of trade between them, in such customs-related matters as the collection and exchange of statistics regarding the importation and exportation of goods, the harmonization of documentation used in trade, the standardization of data elements, the acceptance of an international data syntax and the exchange of information; and (d) to the extent practicable, in the storage and transmission of customs-related documentation.

Article 513
Working Group and Customs Subgroup

1. The Parties hereby establish a Working Group on Rules of Origin, comprising representatives of each Party, to ensure: (a) the effective implementation and administration of Articles 303 (Restriction on Drawback and Duty Deferral Programs), 308 (Most–Favored–Nation Rates of Duty on Certain Goods) and 311, Chapter Four, this Chapter, the Marking Rules and the Uniform Regulations; and (b) the effective administration of the customs-related aspects of Chapter Three.

2. The Working Group shall meet at least four times each year and on the request of any Party.

3. The Working Group shall: (a) monitor the implementation and administration by the customs administrations of the Parties of Articles 303, 308 and 311, Chapter Four, this Chapter, the Marking Rules and the Uniform Regulations to ensure their uniform interpretation; (b) endeavor to agree, on the request of any Party, on any proposed modification of or addition to Article 303, 308 or 311, Chapter Four, this Chapter, the Marking Rules or the Uniform Regulations; (c) notify the Commission of any agreed modification of or addition to the Uniform Regulations; (d) propose to the Commission any modification of or addition to Article 303, 308 or 311, Chapter Four, this Chapter, the Marking Rules, the Uniform Regulations or any other provision of this Agreement as may be required to conform with any change to the Harmonized System; and (e) consider any other matter referred to it by a Party or by the Customs Subgroup established under paragraph 6.

4. Each Party shall, to the greatest extent practicable, take all necessary measures to implement any modification of or addition to this Agreement within 180 days of the date on which the Commission agrees on the modification or addition.

5. If the Working Group fails to resolve a matter referred to it pursuant to paragraph 3(e) within 30 days of such referral, any Party may request a meeting of the Commission under Article 2007 (Commission—Good Offices, Conciliation and Mediation).

6. The Working Group shall establish, and monitor the work of, a Customs Subgroup, comprising representatives of each Party. The Subgroup shall meet at least four times each year and on the request of any Party and shall: (a) endeavor to agree on (i) the uniform interpretation, application and administration of Articles 303, 308 and 311, Chapter Four, this Chapter, the Marking Rules and the Uniform Regulations, (ii) tariff classification and valuation matters relating to determinations of origin, (iii) equivalent procedures and criteria for the request, approval, modification, revocation and

implementation of advance rulings, (iv) revisions to the Certificate of Origin, (v) any other matter referred to it by a Party, the Working Group or the Committee on Trade in Goods established under Article 316, and (vi) any other customs-related matter arising under this Agreement; (b) consider (i) the harmonization of customs-related automation requirements and documentation, and (ii) proposed customs-related administrative and operational changes that may affect the flow of trade between the Parties' territories; (c) report periodically to the Working Group and notify it of any agreement reached under this paragraph; and (d) refer to the Working Group any matter on which it has been unable to reach agreement within 60 days of referral of the matter to it pursuant to subparagraph (a)(v).

7.   Nothing in this Chapter shall be construed to prevent a Party from issuing a determination of origin or an advance ruling relating to a matter under consideration by the Working Group or the Customs Subgroup or from taking such other action as it considers necessary, pending a resolution of the matter under this Agreement.

Article 514

Definitions

For purposes of this Chapter:

commercial importation means the importation of a good into the territory of any Party for the purpose of sale, or any commercial, industrial or other like use;

customs administration means the competent authority that is responsible under the law of a Party for the administration of customs laws and regulations;

determination of origin means a determination as to whether a good qualifies as an originating good in accordance with Chapter Four;

exporter in the territory of a Party means an exporter located in the territory of a Party and an exporter required under this Chapter to maintain records in the territory of that Party regarding exportations of a good;

identical goods means goods that are the same in all respects, including physical characteristics, quality and reputation, irrespective of minor differences in appearance that are not relevant to a determination of origin of those goods under Chapter Four;

importer in the territory of a Party means an importer located in the territory of a Party and an importer required under this Chapter to maintain records in the territory of that Party regarding importations of a good;

intermediate material means "intermediate material" as defined in Article 415;

Marking Rules means "Marking Rules" established under Annex 311;

material means "material" as defined in Article 415;

net cost of a good means "net cost of a good" as defined in Article 415;

preferential tariff treatment means the duty rate applicable to an originating good;

producer means "producer" as defined in Article 415;

production means "production" as defined in Article 415;

transaction value means "transaction value" as defined in Article 415;

Uniform Regulations means "Uniform Regulations" established under Article 511;

used means "used" as defined in Article 415; and

value means value of a good or material for purposes of calculating customs duties or for purposes of applying Chapter Four.

CHAPTER SIX: ENERGY AND BASIC PETROCHEMICALS

Article 601

Principles

1.   The Parties confirm their full respect for their Constitutions.

2.   The Parties recognize that it is desirable to strengthen the important role that trade in energy and basic petrochemical goods plays in the free trade area and to enhance this role through sustained and gradual liberalization.

3.   The Parties recognize the importance of having viable and internationally competitive energy and petrochemical sectors to further their individual national interests.

Article 602

Scope and Coverage

1.   This Chapter applies to measures relating to energy and basic petrochemical goods originating in the territories of the Parties and to measures relating to investment and to the cross-border trade in services associated with such goods, as set forth in this Chapter.

2.   For purposes of this Chapter, energy and basic petrochemical goods refer to those goods classified under the Harmonized System as: (a) subheading 2612.10; (b) headings 27.01 through 27.06; (c) subheading 2707.50; (d) subheading 2707.99 (only with respect to solvent naphtha, rubber extender oils and carbon black feedstocks); (e) headings 27.08 and 27.09; (f) heading 27.10 (except for normal paraffin mixtures in the range of C sub9 to C sub15); (g) heading 27.11 (except for ethylene, propylene, butylene and butadiene in purities over 50 percent); (h) headings 27.12 through 27.16; (i) subheadings 2844.10 through 2844.50 (only with respect to uranium compounds classified under those subheadings); (j) subheading 2845.10; and (k) subheading 2901.10 (only with respect to ethane, butanes, pentanes, hexanes, and heptanes).

3.   Except as specified in Annex 602.3, energy and petrochemical goods and activities shall be governed by the provisions of this Agreement.

Annex 602.3

Reservations and Special Provisions

Reservations

1.   The Mexican State reserves to itself the following strategic activities, including investment in such activities and the provision of services in such activities: (a) exploration and exploitation of crude oil and natural gas;

refining or processing of crude oil and natural gas; and production of artificial gas, basic petrochemicals and their feedstocks and pipelines; (b) foreign trade; transportation, storage and distribution, up to and including the first hand sales of the following goods: (i) crude oil, (ii) natural and artificial gas, (iii) goods covered by this Chapter obtained from the refining or processing of crude oil and natural gas, and (iv) basic petrochemicals; (c) the supply of electricity as a public service in Mexico, including, except as provided in paragraph 5, the generation, transmission, transformation, distribution and sale of electricity; and (d) exploration, exploitation and processing of radioactive minerals, the nuclear fuel cycle, the generation of nuclear energy, the transportation and storage of nuclear waste, the use and reprocessing of nuclear fuel and the regulation of their applications for other purposes and the production of heavy water. In the event of an inconsistency between this paragraph and another provision of this Agreement, this paragraph shall prevail to the extent of that inconsistency.

2. Pursuant to Article 1101(2) (Investment—Scope and Coverage), private investment is not permitted in the activities listed in paragraph 1. Chapter Twelve (Cross–Border Trade in Services) shall only apply to activities involving the provision of services covered in paragraph 1 when Mexico permits a contract to be granted in respect of such activities and only to the extent of that contract.

Trade in Natural Gas and Basic Petrochemicals

3. Where end-users and suppliers of natural gas or basic petrochemical goods consider that cross-border trade in such goods may be in their interests, each Party shall permit such end-users and suppliers, and any state enterprise of that Party as may be required under its domestic law, to negotiate supply contracts.

Each Party shall leave the modalities of the implementation of any such contract to the end-users, suppliers, and any state enterprise of the Party as may be required under its domestic law, which may take the form of individual contracts between the state enterprise and each of the other entities. Such contracts may be subject to regulatory approval.

Performance Clauses

4. Each Party shall allow its state enterprises to negotiate performance clauses in their service contracts.

Activities and Investment in Electricity Generation Facilities

5. (a) Production for Own Use. An enterprise of another Party may acquire, establish, and/or operate an electrical generating facility in Mexico to meet the enterprise's own supply needs. Electricity generated in excess of such needs must be sold to the Federal Electricity Commission (Comision Federal de Electricidad) (CFE) and CFE shall purchase such electricity under terms and conditions agreed to by CFE and the enterprise. (b) Co-generation. An enterprise of another Party may acquire, establish, and/or operate a co-generation facility in Mexico that generates electricity using heat, steam or other energy sources associated with an industrial process. Owners of the industrial facility need not be the owners of the co-generating facility. Elec-

tricity generated in excess of the industrial facility's supply requirements must be sold to CFE and CFE shall purchase such electricity under terms and conditions agreed to by CFE and the enterprise. (c) Independent Power Production. An enterprise of another Party may acquire, establish, and/or operate an electricity generating facility for independent power production (IPP) in Mexico. Electricity generated by such a facility for sale in Mexico shall be sold to CFE and CFE shall purchase such electricity under terms and conditions agreed to by CFE and the enterprise. Where an IPP located in Mexico and an electric utility of another Party consider that cross-border trade in electricity may be in their interests, each relevant Party shall permit these entities and CFE to negotiate terms and conditions of power purchase and power sale contracts. The modalities of implementing such supply contracts are left to the end users, suppliers and CFE and may take the form of individual contracts between CFE and each of the other entities. Each relevant Party shall determine whether such contracts are subject to regulatory approval.

Article 603

Import and Export Restrictions

1. Subject to the further rights and obligations of this Agreement, the Parties incorporate the provisions of the General Agreement on Tariffs and Trade (GATT), with respect to prohibitions or restrictions on trade in energy and basic petrochemical goods. The Parties agree that this language does not incorporate their respective protocols of provisional application to the GATT.

2. The Parties understand that the provisions of the GATT incorporated in paragraph 1 prohibit, in any circumstances in which any other form of quantitative restriction is prohibited, minimum or maximum export-price requirements and, except as permitted in enforcement of countervailing and antidumping orders and undertakings, minimum or maximum import-price requirements.

3. In circumstances where a Party adopts or maintains a restriction on importation from or exportation to a non-Party of an energy or basic petrochemical good, nothing in this Agreement shall be construed to prevent the Party from: (a) limiting or prohibiting the importation from the territory of any Party of such energy or basic petrochemical good of the non-Party; or (b) requiring as a condition of export of such energy or basic petrochemical good of the Party to the territory of any other Party that the good be consumed within the territory of the other Party.

4. In the event that a Party adopts or maintains a restriction on imports of an energy or basic petrochemical good from non-Party countries, the Parties, on request of any Party, shall consult with a view to avoiding undue interference with or distortion of pricing, marketing and distribution arrangements in another Party.

5. Each Party may administer a system of import and export licensing for energy or basic petrochemical goods provided that such system is operated in a manner consistent with the provisions of this Agreement, including paragraph 1 and Article 1502 (Monopolies and State Enterprises).

6. This Article is subject to the reservations set out in Annex 603.6.

Annex 603.6

Exception to Article 603

For only those goods listed below, Mexico may restrict the granting of import and export licenses for the sole purpose of reserving foreign trade in these goods to itself.

2707.50 Other aromatic hydrocarbon mixtures of which 65 percent or more by volume (including losses) distills at 250 degrees C by the ASTM D 86 method.

2707.99 Rubber extender oils, solvent naphtha and carbon black feedstocks only.

27.09 Petroleum oils and oils obtained from bituminous minerals, crude.

27.10 Aviation gasoline; gasoline and motor fuel blending stocks (except aviation gasoline) and reformates when used as motor fuel blending stocks; kerosene; gas oil and diesel oil; petroleum ether; fuel oil; paraffinic oils other than for lubricating purposes; pentanes; carbon black feedstocks; hexanes; heptanes and naphthas.

27.11 Petroleum gases and other gaseous hydrocarbons other than: ethylene, propylene, butylene and butadiene, in purities over 50 percent.

2712.90 Only paraffin wax containing by weight more than 0.75 percent of oil, in bulk (Mexico classifies these goods under HS 2712.90.02) and only when imported to be used for further refining.

2713.11 Petroleum coke not calcined.

2713.20 Petroleum bitumen (except when used for road surfacing purposes under HS 2713.20.01).

2713.90 Other residues of petroleum oils or of oils obtained from bituminous minerals.

27.14 Bitumen and asphalt, natural; bituminous or oil shale and tar sands, asphaltites and asphaltic rocks (except when used for road surfacing purposes under HS 2714.90.01).

2901.10 Ethane, butanes, pentanes, hexanes, and heptanes only.

Article 604

Export Taxes

No Party may adopt or maintain any duty, tax or other charge on the export of any energy or basic petrochemical good to the territory of another Party, unless such duty, tax or charge is adopted or maintained on: (a) exports of any such good to the territory of all other Parties; and (b) any such good when destined for domestic consumption.

Article 605

Other Export Measures

Subject to Annex 605, a Party may adopt or maintain a restriction otherwise justified under Article XI:2(a) or XX(g), (i) or (j) of the GATT with respect to the export of an energy or basic petrochemical good to the territory of another Party, only if: (a) the restriction does not reduce the proportion of the total export shipments of the specific energy or basic petrochemical good made available to that other Party relative to the total supply of that good of the Party maintaining the restriction as compared to the proportion prevailing in the most recent 36–month period for which data are available prior to the imposition of the measure, or in such other representative period on which the Parties may agree; (b) the Party does not impose a higher price for exports of an energy or basic petrochemical good to that other Party than the price charged for such good when consumed domestically, by means of any measure such as licenses, fees, taxation and minimum price requirements. The foregoing provision does not apply to a higher price that may result from a measure taken pursuant to subparagraph (a) that only restricts the volume of exports; and (c) the restriction does not require the disruption of normal channels of supply to that other Party or normal proportions among specific energy or basic petrochemical goods supplied to that other Party, such as, for example, between crude oil and refined products and among different categories of crude oil and of refined products.

Annex 605
Exception to Article 605

Notwithstanding any other provision of this Chapter, the provisions of Article 605 shall not apply as between the other Parties and Mexico.

Article 606
Energy Regulatory Measures

1.   The Parties recognize that energy regulatory measures are subject to the disciplines of: (a) national treatment, as provided in Article 301; (b) import and export restrictions, as provided in Article 603; and (c) export taxes, as provided in Article 604.

2.   Each Party shall seek to ensure that in the application of any energy regulatory measure, energy regulatory bodies within its territory avoid disruption of contractual relationships to the maximum extent practicable, and provide for orderly and equitable implementation appropriate to such measures.

Article 607
National Security Measures

Subject to Annex 607, no Party may adopt or maintain a measure restricting imports of an energy or basic petrochemical good from, or exports of an energy or basic petrochemical good to, another Party under Article XXI of the GATT or under Article 2102 (National Security), except to the extent necessary to: (a) supply a military establishment of a Party or enable fulfillment of a critical defense contract of a Party; (b) respond to a situation of armed conflict involving the Party taking the measure; (c) implement national policies or international agreements relating to the non-proliferation of nuclear weapons or other nuclear explosive devices; or (d) respond to direct threats of disruption in the supply of nuclear materials for defense purposes.

Annex 607
National Security

1.   Article 607 shall impose no obligations and confer no rights on Mexico.

2.   Article 2102 (National Security) shall apply as between Mexico and the other Parties.

Article 608

Miscellaneous Provisions

1.   The Parties agree to allow existing or future incentives for oil and gas exploration, development and related activities in order to maintain the reserve base for these energy resources.

2.   Annex 608.2 applies only to the Parties specified in that Annex with respect to other agreements relating to trade in energy goods.

Annex 608.2

Other Agreements

1.   Canada and the United States shall act in accordance with the terms of Annexes 902.5 and 905.2 of the Canada–United States Free Trade Agreement, which are hereby incorporated into and made a part of this Agreement for such purpose.   This paragraph shall impose no obligations and confer no rights on Mexico.

2.   Canada and the United States intend no inconsistency between this Chapter and the Agreement on an International Energy Program (IEP).   In the event of any inconsistency between the IEP and this Chapter, the IEP shall prevail as between Canada and the United States to the extent of that inconsistency.

Article 609

Definitions

For purposes of this Chapter:

consumed means transformed so as to qualify under the rules of origin set out in Chapter Four (Rules of Origin), or actually consumed;

cross-border trade in services means "cross-border trade in services" as defined in Article 1213 (Cross–Border Trade in Services—Definitions);

energy regulatory measure means any measure by federal or sub-federal entities that directly affects the transportation, transmission or distribution, purchase or sale, of an energy or basic petrochemical good;

enterprise means "enterprise" as defined in Article 1139 (Investment—Definitions);

enterprise of a Party means "enterprise of a Party" as defined in Article 1139;

facility for independent power production means a facility that is used for the generation of electric energy exclusively for sale to an electric utility for further resale;

first hand sale refers to the first commercial transaction affecting the good in question;

investment means investment as defined in Article 1139;

restriction means any limitation, whether made effective through quotas, licenses, permits, minimum or maximum price requirements or any other means;

total export shipments means the total shipments from total supply to users located in the territory of the other Party; and

total supply means shipments to domestic users and foreign users from: (a) domestic production; (b) domestic inventory; and (c) other imports, as appropriate.

CHAPTER SEVEN: AGRICULTURE AND SANITARY AND PHYTOSANITARY MEASURES

Section A—Agriculture

Article 701

Scope and Coverage

1.   This Section applies to measures adopted or maintained by a Party relating to agricultural trade.

2.   In the event of any inconsistency between this Section and another provision of this Agreement, this Section shall prevail to the extent of the inconsistency.

Article 702

International Obligations

1.   Annex 702.1 applies to the Parties specified in that Annex with respect to agricultural trade under certain agreements between them.

2.   Prior to adopting pursuant to an intergovernmental commodity agreement, a measure that may affect trade in an agricultural good between the Parties, the Party proposing to adopt the measure shall consult with the other Parties with a view to avoiding nullification or impairment of a concession granted by that Party in its Schedule to Annex 302.2.

3.   Annex 702.3 applies to the Parties specified in that Annex with respect to measures adopted or maintained pursuant to an intergovernmental coffee agreement.

Article 703

Market Access

1.   The Parties shall work together to improve access to their respective markets through the reduction or elimination of import barriers to trade between them in agricultural goods.

Customs Duties, Quantitative Restrictions, and Agricultural Grading and Marketing Standards

2.   Annex 703.2 applies to the Parties specified in that Annex with respect to customs duties and quantitative restrictions, trade in sugar and syrup goods, and agricultural grading and marketing standards.

Special Safeguard Provisions

3. Each Party may, in accordance with its Schedule to Annex 302.2, adopt or maintain a special safeguard in the form of a tariff rate quota on an agricultural good listed in its Section of Annex 703.3. Notwithstanding Article 302(2), a Party may not apply an over-quota tariff rate under a special safeguard that exceeds the lesser of: (a) the most-favored-nation (MFN) rate as of July 1, 1991; and (b) the prevailing MFN rate.

4. No Party may, with respect to the same good and the same country, at the same time: (a) apply an over-quota tariff rate under paragraph 3; and (b) take an emergency action covered by Chapter Eight (Emergency Action).

Article 704

Domestic Support

The Parties recognize that domestic support measures can be of crucial importance to their agricultural sectors but may also have trade distorting and production effects and that domestic support reduction commitments may result from agricultural multilateral trade negotiations under the General Agreement on Tariffs and Trade (GATT). Accordingly, where a Party supports its agricultural producers, that Party should endeavor to work toward domestic support measures that: (a) have minimal or no trade distorting or production effects; or (b) are exempt from any applicable domestic support reduction commitments that may be negotiated under the GATT. The Parties further recognize that a Party may change its domestic support measures, including those that may be subject to reduction commitments, at the Party's discretion, subject to its rights and obligations under the GATT.

Article 705

Export Subsidies

1. The Parties share the objective of the multilateral elimination of export subsidies for agricultural goods and shall cooperate in an effort to achieve an agreement under the GATT to eliminate those subsidies.

2. The Parties recognize that export subsidies for agricultural goods may prejudice the interests of importing and exporting Parties and, in particular, may disrupt the markets of importing Parties. Accordingly, in addition to the rights and obligations of the Parties specified in Annex 702.1, the Parties affirm that it is inappropriate for a Party to provide an export subsidy for an agricultural good exported to the territory of another Party where there are no other subsidized imports of that good into the territory of that other Party.

3. Except as provided in Annex 702.1, where an exporting Party considers that a non-Party is exporting an agricultural good to the territory of another Party with the benefit of export subsidies, the importing Party shall, on written request of the exporting Party, consult with the exporting Party with a view to agreeing on specific measures that the importing Party may adopt to counter the effect of any such subsidized imports. If the importing Party adopts the agreed-upon measures, the exporting Party shall refrain from applying, or immediately cease to apply, any export subsidy to exports of such good to the territory of the importing Party.

4. Except as provided in Annex 702.1, an exporting Party shall deliver written notice to the importing Party at least three days, excluding weekends, prior to adopting an export subsidy measure on an agricultural good exported to the territory of another Party. The exporting Party shall consult with the importing Party within 72 hours of receipt of the importing Party's written request, with a view to eliminating the subsidy or minimizing any adverse impact on the market of the importing Party for that good. The importing Party shall, when requesting consultations with the exporting Party, at the same time, deliver written notice to a third Party of the request. A third Party may request to participate in such consultations.

5. Each Party shall take into account the interests of the other Parties in the use of any export subsidy on an agricultural good, recognizing that such subsidies may have prejudicial effects on the interests of the other Parties.

6. The Parties hereby establish a Working Group on Agricultural Subsidies, comprising representatives of each Party, which shall meet at least semi-annually or as the Parties may otherwise agree, to work toward elimination of all export subsidies affecting agricultural trade between the Parties. The functions of the Working Group shall include: (a) monitoring the volume and price of imports into the territory of any Party of agricultural goods that have benefitted from export subsidies; (b) providing a forum for the Parties to develop mutually acceptable criteria and procedures for reaching agreement on the limitation or elimination of export subsidies for imports of agricultural goods into the territories of the Parties; and (c) reporting annually to the Committee on Agricultural Trade, established under Article 706, on the implementation of this Article.

7. Notwithstanding any other provision of this Article: (a) if the importing and exporting Parties agree to an export subsidy for an agricultural good exported to the territory of the importing Party, the exporting Party or Parties may adopt or maintain such subsidy; and (b) each Party retains its rights to apply countervailing duties to subsidized imports of agricultural goods from the territory of a Party or non-Party.

Article 706

Committee on Agricultural Trade

1. The Parties hereby establish a Committee on Agricultural Trade, comprising representatives of each Party.

2. The Committee's functions shall include: (a) monitoring and promoting cooperation on the implementation and administration of this Section; (b) providing a forum for the Parties to consult on issues related to this Section at least semi-annually and as the Parties may otherwise agree; and (c) reporting annually to the Commission on the implementation of this Section.

Article 707

Advisory Committee on Private Commercial
Disputes regarding Agricultural Goods

The Committee shall establish an Advisory Committee on Private Commercial Disputes regarding Agricultural Goods, comprising persons with expertise or experience in the resolution of private commercial disputes in agricultural trade. The Advisory Committee shall report and provide recommendations to the Committee for the development of systems in the territory of each Party to achieve the prompt and effective resolution of such disputes, taking into account any special circumstance, including the perishability of certain agricultural goods.

Article 708

Definitions

For purposes of this Section:

agricultural good means a good provided for in any of the following:

(a) Harmonized System (HS) Chapters 1 through 24 (other than a fish or fish product); or

(b) [HS subheadings 2905.43–.44, 33.01, 35.01–.05, 3809.10, 3823.60, 41.01–.03, 43.01, 50.01–.03, 51.01–.03, 52.01–.03, 53.01, 53.02]

customs duty means "customs duty" as defined in Article 318 (National Treatment and Market Access for Goods—Definitions);

duty-free means "duty-free" as defined in Article 318;

fish or fish product means a fish or crustacean, mollusc or other aquatic invertebrate, marine mammal, or a product thereof provided for in any of the following: [HS Chapter 03; HS heading 05.07, 05.08, 05.09, 05.11; dead animals of Chapter 3; HS heading 15.04, 16.03, 16.04, 16.05, HS subheading 2301.20]

material means "material" as defined in Article 415 (Rules of Origin—Definitions);

over-quota tariff rate means the rate of customs duty to be applied to quantities in excess of the quantity specified under a tariff rate quota;

sugar or syrup good means "sugar or syrup good" as defined in Annex 703.2;

tariff item means a "tariff item" as defined in Annex 401; and

tariff rate quota means a mechanism that provides for the application of a customs duty at a certain rate to imports of a particular good up to a specified quantity (in-quota quantity), and at a different rate to imports of that good that exceed that quantity.

[Note: Annexes to Chapter 7A have been omitted.]

Section B—Sanitary and Phytosanitary Measures

Article 709

Scope and Coverage

In order to establish a framework of rules and disciplines to guide the development, adoption and enforcement of sanitary and phytosanitary measures, this Section applies to any such measure of a Party that may, directly or indirectly, affect trade between the Parties.

Article 710

Relation to Other Chapters

Articles 301 (National Treatment) and 309 (Import and Export Restrictions), and the provisions of Article XX(b) of the GATT as incorporated into Article 2101(1) (General Exceptions), do not apply to any sanitary or phytosanitary measure.

Article 711

Reliance on Non-governmental Entities

Each Party shall ensure that any non-governmental entity on which it relies in applying a sanitary or phytosanitary measure acts in a manner consistent with this Section.

Article 712

Basic Rights and Obligations

Right to Take Sanitary and Phytosanitary Measures

1.   Each Party may, in accordance with this Section, adopt, maintain or apply any sanitary or phytosanitary measure necessary for the protection of human, animal or plant life or health in its territory, including a measure more stringent than an international standard, guideline or recommendation.

Right to Establish Level of Protection

2.   Notwithstanding any other provision of this Section, each Party may, in protecting human, animal or plant life or health, establish its appropriate levels of protection in accordance with Article 715.

Scientific Principles

3.   Each Party shall ensure that any sanitary or phytosanitary measure that it adopts, maintains or applies is: (a) based on scientific principles, taking into account relevant factors including, where appropriate, different geographic conditions; (b) not maintained where there is no longer a scientific basis for it; and (c) based on a risk assessment, as appropriate to the circumstances.

Non-discriminatory Treatment

4.   Each Party shall ensure that a sanitary or phytosanitary measure that it adopts, maintains or applies does not arbitrarily or unjustifiably discriminate between its goods and like goods of another Party, or between goods of another Party and like goods of any other country, where identical or similar conditions prevail.

Unnecessary Obstacles

5.   Each Party shall ensure that any sanitary or phytosanitary measure that it adopts, maintains or applies is applied only to the extent necessary to achieve its appropriate level of protection, taking into account technical and economic feasibility.

Disguised Restrictions

6. No Party may adopt, maintain or apply any sanitary or phytosanitary measure with a view to, or with the effect of, creating a disguised restriction on trade between the Parties.

Article 713
International Standards and Standardizing Organizations

1. Without reducing the level of protection of human, animal or plant life or health, each Party shall use, as a basis for its sanitary and phytosanitary measures, relevant international standards, guidelines or recommendations with the objective, among others, of making its sanitary and phytosanitary measures equivalent or, where appropriate, identical to those of the other Parties.

2. A Party's sanitary or phytosanitary measure that conforms to a relevant international standard, guideline or recommendation shall be presumed to be consistent with Article 712. A measure that results in a level of sanitary or phytosanitary protection different from that which would be achieved by a measure based on a relevant international standard, guideline or recommendation shall not for that reason alone be presumed to be inconsistent with this Section.

3. Nothing in Paragraph 1 shall be construed to prevent a Party from adopting, maintaining or applying, in accordance with the other provisions of this Section, a sanitary or phytosanitary measure that is more stringent than the relevant international standard, guideline or recommendation.

4. Where a Party has reason to believe that a sanitary or phytosanitary measure of another Party is adversely affecting or may adversely affect its exports and the measure is not based on a relevant international standard, guideline or recommendation, it may request, and the other Party shall provide in writing, the reasons for the measure.

5. Each Party shall, to the greatest extent practicable, participate in relevant international and North American standardizing organizations, including the Codex Alimentarius Commission, the International Office of Epizootics, the International Plant Protection Convention, and the North American Plant Protection Organization, with a view to promoting the development and periodic review of international standards, guidelines and recommendations.

Article 714
Equivalence

1. Without reducing the level of protection of human, animal or plant life or health, the Parties shall, to the greatest extent practicable and in accordance with this Section, pursue equivalence of their respective sanitary and phytosanitary measures.

2. Each importing Party: (a) shall treat a sanitary or phytosanitary measure adopted or maintained by an exporting Party as equivalent to its own where the exporting Party, in cooperation with the importing Party, provides to the importing Party scientific evidence or other information, in accordance with risk assessment methodologies agreed on by those Parties, to

demonstrate objectively, subject to subparagraph (b), that the exporting Party's measure achieves the importing Party's appropriate level of protection; (b) may, where it has a scientific basis, determine that the exporting Party's measure does not achieve the importing Party's appropriate level of protection; and (c) shall provide to the exporting Party, on request, its reasons in writing for a determination under subparagraph (b).

3.   For purposes of establishing equivalence, each exporting Party shall, on the request of an importing Party, take such reasonable measures as may be available to it to facilitate access in its territory for inspection, testing and other relevant procedures.

4.   Each Party should, in the development of a sanitary or phytosanitary measure, consider relevant actual or proposed sanitary or phytosanitary measures of the other Parties.

Article 715
Risk Assessment and Appropriate Level of Protection

1.   In conducting a risk assessment, each Party shall take into account: (a) relevant risk assessment techniques and methodologies developed by international or North American standardizing organizations; (b) relevant scientific evidence; (c) relevant processes and production methods; (d) relevant inspection, sampling and testing methods; (e) the prevalence of relevant diseases or pests, including the existence of pest-free or disease-free areas or areas of low pest or disease prevalence; (f) relevant ecological and other environmental conditions; and (g) relevant treatments, such as quarantines.

2.   Further to paragraph 1, each Party shall, in establishing its appropriate level of protection regarding the risk associated with the introduction, establishment or spread of an animal or plant pest or disease, and in assessing the risk, also take into account the following economic factors, where relevant: (a) loss of production or sales that may result from the pest or disease; (b) costs of control or eradication of the pest or disease in its territory; and (c) the relative cost-effectiveness of alternative approaches to limiting risks.

3.   Each Party, in establishing its appropriate level of protection: (a) should take into account the objective of minimizing negative trade effects; and (b) shall, with the objective of achieving consistency in such levels, avoid arbitrary or unjustifiable distinctions in such levels in different circumstances, where such distinctions result in arbitrary or unjustifiable discrimination against a good of another Party or constitute a disguised restriction on trade between the Parties.

4.   Notwithstanding paragraphs (1) through (3) and Article 712(3)(c), where a Party conducting a risk assessment determines that available relevant scientific evidence or other information is insufficient to complete the assessment, it may adopt a provisional sanitary or phytosanitary measure on the basis of available relevant information, including from international or North American standardizing organizations and from sanitary or phytosanitary measures of other Parties. The Party shall, within a reasonable period after information sufficient to complete the assessment is presented to it, complete its assessment, review and, where appropriate, revise the provisional measure in the light of the assessment.

5. Where a Party is able to achieve its appropriate level of protection through the phased application of a sanitary or phytosanitary measure, it may, on the request of another Party and in accordance with this Section, allow for such a phased application, or grant specified exceptions for limited periods from the measure, taking into account the requesting Party's export interests.

Article 716
Adaptation to Regional Conditions

1. Each Party shall adapt any of its sanitary or phytosanitary measures relating to the introduction, establishment or spread of an animal or plant pest or disease, to the sanitary or phytosanitary characteristics of the area where a good subject to such a measure is produced and the area in its territory to which the good is destined, taking into account any relevant conditions, including those relating to transportation and handling, between those areas. In assessing such characteristics of an area, including whether an area is, and is likely to remain, a pest-free or disease-free area or an area of low pest or disease prevalence, each Party shall take into account, among other factors: (a) the prevalence of relevant pests or diseases in that area; (b) the existence of eradication or control programs in that area; and (c) any relevant international standard, guideline or recommendation.

2. Further to paragraph 1, each Party shall, in determining whether an area is a pest-free or disease-free area or an area of low pest or disease prevalence, base its determination on factors such as geography, ecosystems, epidemiological surveillance and the effectiveness of sanitary or phytosanitary controls in that area.

3. Each importing Party shall recognize that an area in the territory of the exporting Party is, and is likely to remain, a pest-free or disease-free area or an area of low pest or disease prevalence, where the exporting Party provides to the importing Party scientific evidence or other information sufficient to so demonstrate to the satisfaction of the importing Party. For this purpose, each exporting Party shall provide reasonable access in its territory to the importing Party for inspection, testing and other relevant procedures.

4. Each Party may, in accordance with this Section: (a) adopt, maintain or apply a different risk assessment procedure for a pest-free or disease-free area than for an area of low pest or disease prevalence, or (b) make a different final determination for the disposition of a good produced in a pest-free or disease-free area than for a good produced in an area of low pest or disease prevalence, taking into account any relevant conditions, including those relating to transportation and handling.

5. Each Party shall, in adopting, maintaining or applying a sanitary or phytosanitary measure relating to the introduction, establishment or spread of an animal or plant pest or disease, accord a good produced in a pest-free or disease-free area in the territory of another Party no less favorable treatment than it accords a good produced in a pest-free or disease-free area, in another country, that poses the same level of risk. The Party shall use equivalent risk assessment techniques to evaluate relevant conditions and controls in the pest-free or disease-free area and in the area surrounding that area and take

into account any relevant conditions, including those relating to transportation and handling.

6. Each importing Party shall pursue an agreement with an exporting Party, on request, on specific requirements the fulfillment of which allows a good produced in an area of low pest or disease prevalence in the territory of an exporting Party to be imported into the territory of the importing Party and achieves the importing Party's appropriate level of protection.

Article 717
Control, Inspection and Approval Procedures

1. Each Party, with respect to any control or inspection procedure that it conducts: (a) shall initiate and complete the procedure as expeditiously as possible and in no less favorable manner for a good of another Party than for a like good of the Party or of any other country; (b) shall publish the normal processing period for the procedure or communicate the anticipated processing period to the applicant on request; (c) shall ensure that the competent body (i) on receipt of an application, promptly examines the completeness of the documentation and informs the applicant in a precise and complete manner of any deficiency, (ii) transmits to the applicant as soon as possible the results of the procedure in a form that is precise and complete so that the applicant may take any necessary corrective action, (iii) where the application is deficient, proceeds as far as practicable with the procedure if the applicant so requests, and (iv) informs the applicant, on request, of the status of the application and the reasons for any delay; (d) shall limit the information the applicant is required to supply to that necessary for conducting the procedure; (e) shall accord confidential or proprietary information arising from, or supplied in connection with, the procedure conducted for a good of another Party (i) treatment no less favorable than for a good of the Party, and (ii) in any event, treatment that protects the applicant's legitimate commercial interests, to the extent provided under the Party's law; (f) shall limit any requirement regarding individual specimens or samples of a good to that which is reasonable and necessary; (g) should not impose a fee for conducting the procedure that is higher for a good of another Party than is equitable in relation to any such fee it imposes for its like goods or for like goods of any other country, taking into account communication, transportation and other related costs; (h) should use criteria for selecting the location of facilities at which the procedure is conducted that do not cause unnecessary inconvenience to an applicant or its agent; (i) shall provide a mechanism to review complaints concerning the operation of the procedure and to take corrective action when a complaint is justified; (j) should use criteria for selecting samples of goods that do not cause unnecessary inconvenience to an applicant or its agent; and (k) shall limit the procedure, for a good modified subsequent to a determination that the good fulfills the requirements of the applicable sanitary or phytosanitary measure, to that necessary to determine that the good continues to fulfill the requirements of that measure.

2. Each Party shall apply, with such modifications as may be necessary, paragraphs 1(a) through (i) to its approval procedures.

3. Where an importing Party's sanitary or phytosanitary measure requires the conduct of a control or inspection procedure at the level of

production, an exporting Party shall, on the request of the importing Party, take such reasonable measures as may be available to it to facilitate access in its territory and to provide assistance necessary to facilitate the conduct of the importing Party's control or inspection procedure.

4. A Party maintaining an approval procedure may require its approval for the use of an additive, or its establishment of a tolerance for a contaminant, in a food, beverage or feedstuff, under that procedure prior to granting access to its domestic market for a food, beverage or feedstuff containing that additive or contaminant. Where such Party so requires, it shall consider using a relevant international standard, guideline or recommendation as the basis for granting access until it completes the procedure.

Article 718
Notification, Publication and Provision of Information

1. Further to Articles 1802 (Publication) and 1803 (Notification and Provision of Information), each Party proposing to adopt or modify a sanitary or phytosanitary measure of general application at the federal level shall: (a) at least 60 days prior to the adoption or modification of the measure, other than a law, publish a notice and notify in writing the other Parties of the proposed measure and provide to the other Parties and publish the full text of the proposed measure, in such a manner as to enable interested persons to become acquainted with the proposed measure; (b) identify in the notice and notification the good to which the measure would apply, and provide a brief description of the objective and reasons for the measure; (c) provide a copy of the proposed measure to any Party or interested person that so requests and, wherever possible, identify any provision that deviates in substance from relevant international standards, guidelines or recommendations; and (d) without discrimination, allow other Parties and interested persons to make comments in writing and shall, on request, discuss the comments and take the comments and the results of the discussions into account.

2. Each Party shall seek, through appropriate measures, to ensure, with respect to a sanitary or phytosanitary measure of a state or provincial government: (a) that, at an early appropriate stage, a notice and notification of the type referred to in paragraph 1(a) and (b) are made prior to their adoption; and (b) observance of paragraph 1(c) and (d).

3. Where a Party considers it necessary to address an urgent problem relating to sanitary or phytosanitary protection, it may omit any step set out in paragraph 1 or 2, provided that, on adoption of a sanitary or phytosanitary measure, it shall: (a) immediately provide to the other Parties a notification of the type referred to in paragraph 1(b), including a brief description of the urgent problem; (b) provide a copy of the measure to any Party or interested person that so requests; and (c) without discrimination, allow other Parties and interested persons to make comments in writing and shall, on request, discuss the comments and take the comments and the results of the discussions into account.

4. Each Party shall, except where necessary to address an urgent problem referred to in paragraph 3, allow a reasonable period between the publication of a sanitary or phytosanitary measure of general application and

the date that it becomes effective to allow time for interested persons to adapt to the measure.

5.　Each Party shall designate a government authority responsible for the implementation at the federal level of the notification provisions of this Article, and shall notify the other Parties thereof.　Where a Party designates two or more government authorities for this purpose, it shall provide to the other Parties complete and unambiguous information on the scope of responsibility of each such authority.

6.　Where an importing Party denies entry into its territory of a good of another Party because it does not comply with a sanitary or phytosanitary measure, the importing Party shall provide a written explanation to the exporting Party, on request, that identifies the applicable measure and the reasons that the good is not in compliance.

Article 719
Inquiry Points

1.　Each Party shall ensure that there is one inquiry point that is able to answer all reasonable inquiries from other Parties and interested persons, and to provide relevant documents, regarding:　(a) any sanitary or phytosanitary measure of general application, including any control or inspection procedure or approval procedure, proposed, adopted or maintained in its territory at the federal, state or provincial government level;　(b) the Party's risk assessment procedures and factors it considers in conducting the assessment and in establishing its appropriate levels of protection;　(c) the membership and participation of the Party, or its relevant federal, state or provincial government authorities in international and regional sanitary and phytosanitary organizations and systems, and in bilateral and multilateral arrangements within the scope of this Section, and the provisions of those systems and arrangements;　and (d) the location of notices published pursuant to this Section or where such information can be obtained.

2.　Each Party shall ensure that where copies of documents are requested by another Party or by interested persons in accordance with this Section, they are supplied at the same price, apart from the actual cost of delivery, as the price for domestic purchase.

Article 720
Technical Cooperation

1.　Each Party shall, on the request of another Party, facilitate the provision of technical advice, information and assistance, on mutually agreed terms and conditions, to enhance that Party's sanitary and phytosanitary measures and related activities, including research, processing technologies, infrastructure and the establishment of national regulatory bodies.　Such assistance may include credits, donations and grants for the acquisition of technical expertise, training and equipment that will facilitate the Party's adjustment to and compliance with a Party's sanitary or phytosanitary measure.

2.　Each Party shall, on the request of another Party:　(a) provide to that Party information on its technical cooperation programs regarding sanitary or phytosanitary measures relating to specific areas of interest; and (b) consult with the other Party during the development of, or prior to the adoption or change in the application of, any sanitary or phytosanitary measure.

Article 721

Limitations on the Provision of Information

Nothing in this Section shall be construed to require a Party to: (a) communicate, publish texts or provide particulars or copies of documents other than in an official language of the Party; or (b) furnish any information the disclosure of which would impede law enforcement or otherwise be contrary to the public interest or would prejudice the legitimate commercial interests of particular enterprises.

Article 722

Committee on Sanitary and Phytosanitary Measures

1. The Parties hereby establish a Committee on Sanitary and Phytosanitary Measures, comprising representatives of each Party who have responsibility for sanitary and phytosanitary matters.

2. The Committee should facilitate: (a) the enhancement of food safety and improvement of sanitary and phytosanitary conditions in the territories of the Parties; (b) activities of the Parties pursuant to Articles 713 and 714; (c) technical cooperation between the Parties, including cooperation in the development, application and enforcement of sanitary or phytosanitary measures; and (d) consultations on specific matters relating to sanitary or phytosanitary measures.

3. The Committee: (a) shall, to the extent possible, in carrying out its functions, seek the assistance of relevant international and North American standardizing organizations to obtain available scientific and technical advice and minimize duplication of effort; (b) may draw on such experts and expert bodies as it considers appropriate; (c) shall report annually to the Commission on the implementation of this Section; (d) shall meet on the request of any Party and, unless the Parties otherwise agree, at least once each year; and (e) may, as it considers appropriate, establish and determine the scope and mandate of working groups.

Article 723

Technical Consultations

1. A Party may request consultations with another Party on any matter covered by this Section.

2. Each Party should use the good offices of relevant international and North American standardizing organizations, including those referred to in Article 713(5), for advice and assistance on sanitary and phytosanitary matters within their respective mandates.

3. Where a Party requests consultations regarding the application of this Section to a Party's sanitary or phytosanitary measure, and so notifies the Committee, the Committee may facilitate the consultations, if it does not consider the matter itself, by referring the matter for non-binding technical

advice or recommendations to a working group, including an ad hoc working group, or to another forum.

4. The Committee should consider any matter referred to it under paragraph 3 as expeditiously as possible, particularly regarding perishable goods, and promptly forward to the Parties any technical advice or recommendations that it develops or receives concerning the matter. Each Party involved shall provide a written response to the Committee concerning the technical advice or recommendations within such time as the Committee may request.

5. Where the involved Parties have had recourse to consultations facilitated by the Committee under paragraph 3, the consultations shall, on the agreement of the Parties involved, constitute consultations under Article 2006 (Consultations).

6. The Parties confirm that a Party asserting that a sanitary or phytosanitary measure of another Party is inconsistent with this Section shall have the burden of establishing the inconsistency.

Article 724
Definitions

For purposes of this Section:

animal includes fish and wild fauna;

appropriate level of protection means the level of protection of human, animal or plant life or health in the territory of a Party that the Party considers appropriate;

approval procedure means any registration, notification or other mandatory administrative procedure for: (a) approving the use of an additive for a stated purpose or under stated conditions, or (b) establishing a tolerance for a stated purpose or under stated conditions for a contaminant, in a food, beverage or feedstuff prior to permitting the use of the additive or the marketing of a food, beverage or feedstuff containing the additive or contaminant;

area means a country, part of a country or all or parts of several countries;

area of low pest or disease prevalence means an area in which a specific pest or disease occurs at low levels;

contaminant includes pesticide and veterinary drug residues and extraneous matter;

control or inspection procedure means any procedure used, directly or indirectly, to determine that a sanitary or phytosanitary measure is fulfilled, including sampling, testing, inspection, evaluation, verification, monitoring, auditing, assurance of conformity, accreditation, registration, certification or other procedure involving the physical examination of a good, of the packaging of a good, or of the equipment or facilities directly related to production, marketing or use of a good, but does not mean an approval procedure;

international standard, guideline or recommendation means a standard, guideline or recommendation: (a) regarding food safety, adopted by the Codex Alimentarius Commission, including one regarding decomposition elaborated by the Codex Committee on Fish and Fishery Products, food additives, contaminants, hygienic practice, and methods of analysis and sampling; (b) regarding animal health and zoonoses, developed under the auspices of the International Office of Epizootics; (c) regarding plant health, developed under the auspices of the Secretariat of the International Plant Protection Convention in cooperation with the North American Plant Protection Organization; or (d) established by or developed under any other international organization agreed on by the Parties;

pest includes a weed;

pest-free or disease-free area means an area in which a specific pest or disease does not occur;

plant includes wild flora;

risk assessment means an evaluation of: (a) the potential for the introduction, establishment or spread of a pest or disease and associated biological and economic consequences; or (b) the potential for adverse effects on human or animal life or health arising from the presence of an additive, contaminant, toxin or disease-causing organism in a food, beverage or feedstuff;

sanitary or phytosanitary measure means a measure that a Party adopts, maintains or applies to: (a) protect animal or plant life or health in its territory from risks arising from the introduction, establishment or spread of a pest or disease, (b) protect human or animal life or health in its territory from risks arising from the presence of an additive, contaminant, toxin or disease- causing organism in a food, beverage or feedstuff, (c) protect human life or health in its territory from risks arising from a disease-causing organism or pest carried by an animal or plant, or a product thereof, or (d) prevent or limit other damage in its territory arising from the introduction, establishment or spread of a pest, including end product criteria; a product-related processing or production method; a testing, inspection, certification or approval procedure; a relevant statistical method; a sampling procedure; a method of risk assessment; a packaging and labelling requirement directly related to food safety; and a quarantine treatment, such as a relevant requirement associated with the transportation of animals or plants or with material necessary for their survival during transportation; and

scientific basis means a reason based on data or information derived using scientific methods.

CHAPTER EIGHT: EMERGENCY ACTION

Article 801

Bilateral Actions

1. Subject to paragraphs 2 through 4 and Annex 801.1, and during the transition period only, if a good originating in the territory of a Party, as a result of the reduction or elimination of a duty provided for in this Agreement, is being imported into the territory of another Party in such increased quantities, in absolute terms, and under such conditions that the imports of the good from that Party alone constitute a substantial cause of serious injury, or threat thereof, to a domestic industry producing a like or directly

competitive good, the Party into whose territory the good is being imported may, to the minimum extent necessary to remedy or prevent the injury: (a) suspend the further reduction of any rate of duty provided for under this Agreement on the good; (b) increase the rate of duty on the good to a level not to exceed the lesser of (i) the most-favored-nation (MFN) applied rate of duty in effect at the time the action is taken, and (ii) the MFN applied rate of duty in effect on the day immediately preceding the date of entry into force of this Agreement; or (c) in the case of a duty applied to a good on a seasonal basis, increase the rate of duty to a level not to exceed the MFN applied rate of duty that was in effect on the good for the corresponding season immediately preceding the date of entry into force of this Agreement.

2. The following conditions and limitations shall apply to a proceeding that may result in emergency action under paragraph 1: (a) a Party shall, without delay, deliver to any Party that may be affected written notice of, and a request for consultations regarding, the institution of a proceeding that could result in emergency action against a good originating in the territory of a Party; (b) any such action shall be initiated no later than one year after the date of institution of the proceeding; (c) no action may be maintained (i) for a period exceeding three years, except where the good against which the action is taken is provided for in the items in staging category C+ of the Schedule to Annex 302.2 of the Party taking the action and that Party determines that the affected industry has undertaken adjustment and requires an extension of the period of relief, in which case the period of relief may be extended for one year provided that the duty applied during the initial period of relief is substantially reduced at the beginning of the extension period, or (ii) beyond the expiration of the transition period, except with the consent of the Party against whose good the action is taken; (d) no action may be taken by a Party against any particular good originating in the territory of another Party more than once during the transition period; and (e) on the termination of the action, the rate of duty shall be the rate that, according to the Party's Schedule to Annex 302.2 for the staged elimination of the tariff, would have been in effect one year after the initiation of the action, and beginning January 1 of the year following the termination of the action, at the option of the Party that has taken the action (i) the rate of duty shall conform to the applicable rate set out in its Schedule to Annex 302.2, or (ii) the tariff shall be eliminated in equal annual stages ending on the date set out in its Schedule to Annex 302.2 for the elimination of the tariff.

3. A Party may take a bilateral emergency action after the expiration of the transition period to deal with cases of serious injury, or threat thereof, to a domestic industry arising from the operation of this Agreement only with the consent of the Party against whose good the action would be taken.

4. The Party taking an action under this Article shall provide to the Party against whose good the action is taken mutually agreed trade liberalizing compensation in the form of concessions having substantially equivalent trade effects or equivalent to the value of the additional duties expected to result from the action. If the Parties concerned are unable to agree on compensation, the Party against whose good the action is taken may take tariff action having trade effects substantially equivalent to the action taken under this Article. The Party taking the tariff action shall apply the action

only for the minimum period necessary to achieve the substantially equivalent effects.

5.   This Article does not apply to emergency actions respecting goods covered by Annex 300–B (Textile and Apparel Goods).

Annex 801.1
Bilateral Actions

1.   Notwithstanding Article 801, bilateral emergency actions between Canada and the United States on goods originating in the territory of either Party, other than goods covered by Annex 300–B (Textile and Apparel Goods), shall be governed in accordance with the terms of Article 1101 of the Canada–United States Free Trade Agreement, which is hereby incorporated into and made a part of this Agreement for such purpose.

2.   For such purposes, "good originating in the territory of one Party" means "good originating in the territory of a Party" as defined in Article 805.

Article 802
Global Actions

1.   Each Party retains its rights and obligations under Article XIX of the GATT or any safeguard agreement pursuant thereto except those regarding compensation or retaliation and exclusion from an action to the extent that such rights or obligations are inconsistent with this Article.   Any Party taking an emergency action under Article XIX or any such agreement shall exclude imports of a good from each other Party from the action unless: (a) imports from a Party, considered individually, account for a substantial share of total imports; and (b) imports from a Party, considered individually, or in exceptional circumstances imports from Parties considered collectively, contribute importantly to the serious injury, or threat thereof, caused by imports.

2.   In determining whether: (a) imports from a Party, considered individually, account for a substantial share of total imports, those imports normally shall not be considered to account for a substantial share of total imports if that Party is not among the top five suppliers of the good subject to the proceeding, measured in terms of import share during the most recent three-year period; and (b) imports from a Party or Parties contribute importantly to the serious injury, or threat thereof, the competent investigating authority shall consider such factors as the change in the import share of each Party, and the level and change in the level of imports of each Party.   In this regard, imports from a Party normally shall not be deemed to contribute importantly to serious injury, or the threat thereof, if the growth rate of imports from a Party during the period in which the injurious surge in imports occurred is appreciably lower than the growth rate of total imports from all sources over the same period.

3.   A Party taking such action, from which a good from another Party or Parties is initially excluded pursuant to paragraph 1, shall have the right subsequently to include that good from the other Party or Parties in the action in the event that the competent investigating authority determines that a surge in imports of such good from the other Party or Parties undermines the effectiveness of the action.

4. A Party shall, without delay, deliver written notice to the other Parties of the institution of a proceeding that may result in emergency action under paragraph 1 or 3.

5. No Party may impose restrictions on a good in an action under paragraph 1 or 3: (a) without delivery of prior written notice to the Commission, and without adequate opportunity for consultation with the Party or Parties against whose good the action is proposed to be taken, as far in advance of taking the action is practicable; and (b) that would have the effect of reducing imports of such good from a Party below the trend of imports of the good from that Party over a recent representative base period with allowance for reasonable growth.

6. The Party taking an action pursuant to this Article shall provide to the Party or Parties against whose good the action is taken mutually agreed trade liberalizing compensation in the form of concessions having substantially equivalent trade effects or equivalent to the value of the additional duties expected to result from the action. If the Parties concerned are unable to agree on compensation, the Party against whose good the action is taken may take action having trade effects substantially equivalent to the action taken under paragraph 1 or 3.

Article 803
Administration of Emergency Action Proceedings

1. Each Party shall ensure the consistent, impartial and reasonable administration of its laws, regulations, decisions and rulings governing all emergency action proceedings.

2. Each Party shall entrust determinations of serious injury, or threat thereof, in emergency action proceedings to a competent investigating authority, subject to review by judicial or administrative tribunals, to the extent provided by domestic law. Negative injury determinations shall not be subject to modification, except by such review. The competent investigating authority empowered under domestic law to conduct such proceedings should be provided with the necessary resources to enable it to fulfill its duties.

3. Each Party shall adopt or maintain equitable, timely, transparent and effective procedures for emergency action proceedings, in accordance with the requirements set out in Annex 803.3.

4. This Article does not apply to emergency actions taken under Annex 300–B (Textile and Apparel Goods).

Annex 803.3
Administration of Emergency Action Proceedings
Institution of a Proceeding

1. An emergency action proceeding may be instituted by a petition or complaint by entities specified in domestic law. The entity filing the petition or complaint shall demonstrate that it is representative of the domestic industry producing a good like or directly competitive with the imported good.

2. A Party may institute a proceeding on its own motion or request the competent investigating authority to conduct a proceeding.

Contents of a Petition or Complaint

3.   Where the basis for an investigation is a petition or complaint filed by an entity representative of a domestic industry, the petitioning entity shall, in its petition or complaint, provide the following information to the extent that such information is publicly available from governmental or other sources, or best estimates and the basis therefor if such information is not available: (a) product description—the name and description of the imported good concerned, the tariff subheading under which that good is classified, its current tariff treatment and the name and description of the like or directly competitive domestic good concerned; (b) representativeness—(i) the names and addresses of the entities filing the petition or complaint, and the locations of the establishments in which they produce the domestic good, (ii) the percentage of domestic production of the like or directly competitive good that such entities account for and the basis for claiming that they are representative of an industry, and (iii) the names and locations of all other domestic establishments in which the like or directly competitive good is produced; (c) import data—import data for each of the five most recent full years that form the basis of the claim that the good concerned is being imported in increased quantities, either in absolute terms or relative to domestic production as appropriate; (d) domestic production data—data on total domestic production of the like or directly competitive good for each of the five most recent full years; (e) data showing injury—quantitative and objective data indicating the nature and extent of injury to the concerned industry, such as data showing changes in the level of sales, prices, production, productivity, capacity utilization, market share, profits and losses, and employment; (f) cause of injury— an enumeration and description of the alleged causes of the injury, or threat thereof, and a summary of the basis for the assertion that increased imports, either actual or relative to domestic production, of the imported good are causing or threatening to cause serious injury, supported by pertinent data; and (g) criteria for inclusion—quantitative and objective data indicating the share of imports accounted for by imports from the territory of each other Party and the petitioner's views on the extent to which such imports are contributing importantly to the serious injury, or threat thereof, caused by imports of that good.

4.   Petitions or complaints, except to the extent that they contain confidential business information, shall promptly be made available for public inspection on being filed.

Notice Requirement

5.   On instituting an emergency action proceeding, the competent investigating authority shall publish notice of the institution of the proceeding in the official journal of the Party. The notice shall identify the petitioner or other requester, the imported good that is the subject of the proceeding and its tariff subheading, the nature and timing of the determination to be made, the time and place of the public hearing, dates of deadlines for filing briefs, statements and other documents, the place at which the petition and any other documents filed in the course of the proceeding may be inspected, and the name, address and telephone number of the office to be contacted for more information.

6. With respect to an emergency action proceeding instituted on the basis of a petition or complaint filed by an entity asserting that it is representative of the domestic industry, the competent investigating authority shall not publish the notice required by paragraph 5 without first assessing carefully that the petition or complaint meets the requirements of paragraph 3, including representativeness.

Public Hearing

7. In the course of each proceeding, the competent investigating authority shall: (a) hold a public hearing, after providing reasonable notice, to allow all interested parties, and any association whose purpose is to represent the interests of consumers in the territory of the Party instituting the proceeding, to appear in person or by counsel, to present evidence and to be heard on the questions of serious injury, or threat thereof, and the appropriate remedy; and (b) provide an opportunity to all interested parties and any such association appearing at the hearing to cross-question interested parties making presentations at that hearing.

Confidential Information

8. The competent investigating authority shall adopt or maintain procedures for the treatment of confidential information, protected under domestic law, that is provided in the course of a proceeding, including a requirement that interested parties and consumer associations providing such information furnish non-confidential written summaries thereof, or where they indicate that the information cannot be summarized, the reasons why a summary cannot be provided.

Evidence of Injury and Causation

9. In conducting its proceeding the competent investigating authority shall gather, to the best of its ability, all relevant information appropriate to the determination it must make. It shall evaluate all relevant factors of an objective and quantifiable nature having a bearing on the situation of that industry, including the rate and amount of the increase in imports of the good concerned, in absolute and relative terms as appropriate, the share of the domestic market taken by increased imports, and changes in the level of sales, production, productivity, capacity utilization, profits and losses, and employment. In making its determination, the competent investigating authority may also consider other economic factors, such as changes in prices and inventories, and the ability of firms in the industry to generate capital.

10. The competent investigating authority shall not make an affirmative injury determination unless its investigation demonstrates, on the basis of objective evidence, the existence of a clear causal link between increased imports of the good concerned and serious injury, or threat thereof. Where factors other than increased imports are causing injury to the domestic industry at the same time, such injury shall not be attributed to increased imports.

Deliberation and Report

11. Except in critical circumstances and in global actions involving perishable agricultural goods, the competent investigating authority, before

making an affirmative determination in an emergency action proceeding, shall allow sufficient time to gather and consider the relevant information, hold a public hearing and provide an opportunity for all interested parties and consumer associations to prepare and submit their views.

12. The competent investigating authority shall publish promptly a report, including a summary thereof in the official journal of the Party, setting out its findings and reasoned conclusions on all pertinent issues of law and fact. The report shall describe the imported good and its tariff item number, the standard applied and the finding made. The statement of reasons shall set out the basis for the determination, including a description of: (a) the domestic industry seriously injured or threatened with serious injury; (b) information supporting a finding that imports are increasing, the domestic industry is seriously injured or threatened with serious injury, and increasing imports are causing or threatening serious injury; and (c) if provided for by domestic law, any finding or recommendation regarding the appropriate remedy and the basis therefor.

13. In its report, the competent investigating authority shall not disclose any confidential information provided pursuant to any undertaking concerning confidential information that may have been made in the course of the proceedings.

Article 804

Dispute Settlement in Emergency Action Matters

No Party may request the establishment of an arbitral panel under Article 2008 (Request for an Arbitral Panel) regarding any proposed emergency action.

Article 805

Definitions

For purposes of this Chapter:

competent investigating authority means the "competent investigating authority" of a Party as defined in Annex 805;

contribute importantly means an important cause, but not necessarily the most important cause;

critical circumstances means circumstances where delay would cause damage that would be difficult to repair;

domestic industry means the producers as a whole of the like or directly competitive good operating in the territory of a Party;

emergency action does not include any emergency action pursuant to a proceeding instituted prior to January 1, 1994;

good originating in the territory of a Party means an originating good, except that in determining the Party in whose territory that good originates, the relevant rules of Annex 302.2 shall apply;

serious injury means a significant overall impairment of a domestic industry;

surge means a significant increase in imports over the trend for a recent representative base period;

threat of serious injury means serious injury that, on the basis of facts and not merely on allegation, conjecture or remote possibility, is clearly imminent; and

transition period means the 10–year period beginning on January 1, 1994, except where the good against which the action is taken is provided for in the items in staging category C+ of the Schedule to Annex 302.2 of the Party taking the action, in which case the transition period shall be the period of staged tariff elimination for that good.

Annex 805
Country–Specific Definitions

For purposes of this Chapter: **competent investigating authority** means: (a) in the case of Canada, the Canadian International Trade Tribunal, or its successor; (b) in the case of Mexico, the designated authority within the Ministry of Trade and Industrial Development ("Secretaria de Comercio y Fomento Industrial"), or its successor; and (c) in the case of the United States, the U.S. International Trade Commission, or its successor.

PART THREE
TECHNICAL BARRIERS TO TRADE
CHAPTER NINE: STANDARDS–RELATED MEASURES
Article 901
Scope and Coverage

1.   This Chapter applies to standards-related measures of a Party, other than those covered by Section B of Chapter Seven (Sanitary and Phytosanitary Measures), that may, directly or indirectly, affect trade in goods or services between the Parties, and to measures of the Parties relating to such measures.

2.   Technical specifications prepared by governmental bodies for production or consumption requirements of such bodies shall be governed exclusively by Chapter Ten (Government Procurement).

Article 902
Extent of Obligations

1.   Article 105 (Extent of Obligations) does not apply to this Chapter.

2.   Each Party shall seek, through appropriate measures, to ensure observance of Articles 904 through 908 by state or provincial governments and by non-governmental standardizing bodies in its territory.

Article 903
Affirmation of Agreement on Technical Barriers
to Trade and Other Agreements

Further to Article 103 (Relation to Other Agreements), the Parties affirm with respect to each other their existing rights and obligations relating to standards-related measures under the GATT Agreement on Technical Barriers to Trade and all other international agreements, including environmental and conservation agreements, to which those Parties are party.

Article 904
Basic Rights and Obligations

Right to Take Standards–Related Measures

1.   Each Party may, in accordance with this Agreement, adopt, maintain or apply any standards-related measure, including any such measure relating to safety, the protection of human, animal or plant life or health, the environment or consumers, and any measure to ensure its enforcement or implementation.   Such measures include those to prohibit the importation of a good of another Party or the provision of a service by a service provider of another Party that fails to comply with the applicable requirements of those measures or to complete the Party's approval procedures.

Right to Establish Level of Protection

2.   Notwithstanding any other provision of this Chapter, each Party may, in pursuing its legitimate objectives of safety or the protection of human, animal or plant life or health, the environment or consumers, establish the levels of protection that it considers appropriate in accordance with Article 907(2).

Non-discriminatory Treatment

3.   Each Party shall, in respect of its standards-related measures, accord to goods and service providers of another Party: (a) national treatment in accordance with Article 301 (Market Access) or Article 1202 (Cross–Border Trade in Services); and (b) treatment no less favorable than that it accords to like goods, or in like circumstances to service providers, of any other country.

Unnecessary Obstacles

4.   No Party may prepare, adopt, maintain or apply any standards-related measure with a view to or with the effect of creating an unnecessary obstacle to trade between the Parties.   An unnecessary obstacle to trade shall not be deemed to be created where: (a) the demonstrable purpose of the measure is to achieve a legitimate objective; and (b) the measure does not operate to exclude goods of another Party that meet that legitimate objective.

Article 905
Use of International Standards

1.   Each Party shall use, as a basis for its standards-related measures, relevant international standards or international standards whose completion is imminent, except where such standards would be an ineffective or inappropriate means to fulfill its legitimate objectives, for example because of fundamental climatic, geographical, technological or infrastructural factors, scientific justification or the level of protection that the Party considers appropriate.

2.   A Party's standards-related measure that conforms to an international standard shall be presumed to be consistent with Article 904(3) and (4).

3.   Nothing in paragraph 1 shall be construed to prevent a Party, in pursuing its legitimate objectives, from adopting, maintaining or applying any

standards-related measure that results in a higher level of protection than would be achieved if the measure were based on the relevant international standard.

Article 906
Compatibility and Equivalence

1.   Recognizing the crucial role of standards-related measures in achieving legitimate objectives, the Parties shall, in accordance with this Chapter, work jointly to enhance the level of safety and of protection of human, animal and plant life and health, the environment and consumers.

2.   Without reducing the level of safety or of protection of human, animal or plant life or health, the environment or consumers, without prejudice to the rights of any Party under this Chapter, and taking into account international standardization activities, the Parties shall, to the greatest extent practicable, make compatible their respective standards-related measures, so as to facilitate trade in a good or service between the Parties.

3.   Further to Articles 902 and 905, a Party shall, on request of another Party, seek, through appropriate measures, to promote the compatibility of a specific standard or conformity assessment procedure that is maintained in its territory with the standards or conformity assessment procedures maintained in the territory of the other Party.

4.   Each importing Party shall treat a technical regulation adopted or maintained by an exporting Party as equivalent to its own where the exporting Party, in cooperation with the importing Party, demonstrates to the satisfaction of the importing Party that its technical regulation adequately fulfills the importing Party's legitimate objectives.

5.   The importing Party shall provide to the exporting Party, on request, its reasons in writing for not treating a technical regulation as equivalent under paragraph 4.

6.   Each Party shall, wherever possible, accept the results of a conformity assessment procedure conducted in the territory of another Party, provided that it is satisfied that the procedure offers an assurance, equivalent to that provided by a procedure it conducts or a procedure conducted in its territory the results of which it accepts, that the relevant good or service complies with the applicable technical regulation or standard adopted or maintained in the Party's territory.

7.   Prior to accepting the results of a conformity assessment procedure pursuant to paragraph 6, and to enhance confidence in the continued reliability of each other's conformity assessment results, the Parties may consult on such matters as the technical competence of the conformity assessment bodies involved, including verified compliance with relevant international standards through such means as accreditation.

Article 907
Assessment of Risk

1.   A Party may, in pursuing its legitimate objectives, conduct an assessment of risk. In conducting an assessment, a Party may take into account, among other factors relating to a good or service: (a) available scientific

evidence or technical information; (b) intended end uses; (c) processes or production, operating, inspection, sampling or testing methods; or (d) environmental conditions.

2. Where pursuant to Article 904(2) a Party establishes a level of protection that it considers appropriate and conducts an assessment of risk, it should avoid arbitrary or unjustifiable distinctions between similar goods or services in the level of protection it considers appropriate, where the distinctions: (a) result in arbitrary or unjustifiable discrimination against goods or service providers of another Party; (b) constitute a disguised restriction on trade between the Parties; or (c) discriminate between similar goods or services for the same use under the same conditions that pose the same level of risk and provide similar benefits.

3. Where a Party conducting an assessment of risk determines that available scientific evidence or other information is insufficient to complete the assessment, it may adopt a provisional technical regulation on the basis of available relevant information. The Party shall, within a reasonable period after information sufficient to complete the assessment of risk is presented to it, complete its assessment, review and, where appropriate, revise the provisional technical regulation in the light of that assessment.

Article 908
Conformity Assessment

1. The Parties shall, further to Article 906 and recognizing the existence of substantial differences in the structure, organization and operation of conformity assessment procedures in their respective territories, make compatible those procedures to the greatest extent practicable.

2. Recognizing that it should be to the mutual advantage of the Parties concerned and except as set out in Annex 908.2, each Party shall accredit, approve, license or otherwise recognize conformity assessment bodies in the territory of another Party on terms no less favorable than those accorded to conformity assessment bodies in its territory.

3. Each Party shall, with respect to its conformity assessment procedures: (a) not adopt or maintain any such procedure that is stricter, nor apply the procedure more strictly, than necessary to give it confidence that a good or a service conforms with an applicable technical regulation or standard, taking into account the risks that non-conformity would create; (b) initiate and complete the procedure as expeditiously as possible; (c) in accordance with Article 904(3), undertake processing of applications in non-discriminatory order; (d) publish the normal processing period for each such procedure or communicate the anticipated processing period to an applicant on request; (e) ensure that the competent body (i) on receipt of an application, promptly examines the completeness of the documentation and informs the applicant in a precise and complete manner of any deficiency, (ii) transmits to the applicant as soon as possible the results of the conformity assessment procedure in a form that is precise and complete so that the applicant may take any necessary corrective action, (iii) where the application is deficient, proceeds as far as practicable with the procedure where the applicant so requests, and (iv) informs the applicant, on request, of the status of the application and the reasons for any delay; (f) limit the information the applicant is required to

supply to that necessary to conduct the procedure and to determine appropriate fees; (g) accord confidential or proprietary information arising from, or supplied in connection with, the conduct of the procedure for a good of another Party or for a service provided by a person of another Party (i) the same treatment as that for a good of the Party or a service provided by a person of the Party, and (ii) in any event, treatment that protects an applicant's legitimate commercial interests to the extent provided under the Party's law; (h) ensure that any fee it imposes for conducting the procedure is no higher for a good of another Party or a service provider of another Party than is equitable in relation to any such fee imposed for its like goods or service providers or for like goods or service providers of any other country, taking into account communication, transportation and other related costs; (i) ensure that the location of facilities at which a conformity assessment procedure is conducted does not cause unnecessary inconvenience to an applicant or its agent; (j) limit the procedure, for a good or service modified subsequent to a determination that the good or service conforms to the applicable technical regulation or standard, to that necessary to determine that the good or service continues to conform to the technical regulation or standard; and (k) limit any requirement regarding samples of a good to that which is reasonable, and ensure that the selection of samples does not cause unnecessary inconvenience to an applicant or its agent.

4. Each Party shall apply, with such modifications as may be necessary, the relevant provisions of paragraph 3 to its approval procedures.

5. Each Party shall, on request of another Party, take such reasonable measures as may be available to it to facilitate access in its territory for conformity assessment activities.

6. Each Party shall give sympathetic consideration to a request by another Party to negotiate agreements for the mutual recognition of the results of that other Party's conformity assessment procedures.

Annex 908.2

Transitional Rules for Conformity Assessment Procedures

1. Except in respect of governmental conformity assessment bodies, Article 908(2) shall impose no obligation and confer no right on Mexico until four years after the date of entry into force of this Agreement.

2. Where a Party charges a reasonable fee, limited in amount to the approximate cost of the service rendered, to accredit, approve, license or otherwise recognize a conformity assessment body in the territory of another Party, it need not, prior to December 31, 1998 or such earlier date as the Parties may agree, charge such a fee to a conformity assessment body in its territory.

Article 909

Notification, Publication, and Provision of Information

1. Further to Articles 1802 (Publication) and 1803 (Notification and Provision of Information), each Party proposing to adopt or modify a technical regulation shall: (a) at least 60 days prior to the adoption or modification of the measure, other than a law, publish a notice and notify in writing the other

Parties of the proposed measure in such a manner as to enable interested persons to become acquainted with the proposed measure, except that in the case of any such measure relating to perishable goods, each Party shall, to the greatest extent practicable, publish the notice and provide the notification at least 30 days prior to the adoption or modification of the measure, but no later than when notification is provided to domestic producers; (b) identify in the notice and notification the good or service to which the measure would apply, and shall provide a brief description of the objective of, and reasons for the measure; (c) provide a copy of the proposed measure to any Party or interested person that so requests, and shall, wherever possible, identify any provision that deviates in substance from relevant international standards; and (d) without discrimination, allow other Parties and interested persons to make comments in writing and shall, on request, discuss the comments and take the comments and the results of the discussions into account.

2.   Each Party proposing to adopt or modify a standard or any conformity assessment procedure not otherwise considered to be a technical regulation shall, where an international standard relevant to the proposed measure does not exist or such measure is not substantially the same as an international standard, and where the measure may have a significant effect on the trade of the other Parties: (a) at an early appropriate stage, publish a notice and provide a notification of the type required in paragraph 1(a) and (b); and (b) observe paragraph 1(c) and (d).

3.   Each Party shall seek, through appropriate measures, to ensure, with respect to a technical regulation of a state or provincial government other than a local government: (a) that, at an early appropriate stage, a notice and notification of the type required under paragraph 1(a) and (b) are made prior to their adoption; and (b) observance of paragraph 1(c) and (d).

4.   Where a Party considers it necessary to address an urgent problem relating to safety or to protection of human, animal or plant life or health, the environment or consumers, it may omit any step set out in paragraph 1 or 3, provided that on adoption of a standards-related measure it shall: (a) immediately provide to the other Parties a notification of the type required under paragraph 1(b), including a brief description of the urgent problem; (b) provide a copy of the measure to any Party or interested person that so requests; and (c) without discrimination, allow other Parties and interested persons to make comments in writing, and shall, on request, discuss the comments and take the comments and the results of the discussions into account.

5.   Each Party shall, except where necessary to address an urgent problem referred to in paragraph 4, allow a reasonable period between the publication of a standards-related measure and the date that it becomes effective to allow time for interested persons to adapt to the measure.

6.   Where a Party allows non-governmental persons in its territory to be present during the process of development of standards-related measures, it shall also allow non-governmental persons from the territories of the other Parties to be present.

7.   Each Party shall notify the other Parties of the development of, amendment to, or change in the application of its standards-related measures

no later than the time at which it notifies non-governmental persons in general or the relevant sector in its territory.

8.   Each Party shall seek, through appropriate measures, to ensure the observance of paragraphs 6 and 7 by a state or provincial government, and by non-governmental standardizing bodies in its territory.

9.   Each Party shall designate by January 1, 1994 a government authority responsible for the implementation at the federal level of the notification provisions of this Article, and shall notify the other Parties thereof.   Where a Party designates two or more government authorities for that purpose, it shall provide to the other Parties complete and unambiguous information on the scope of responsibility of each such authority.

Article 910

Inquiry Points

1.   Each Party shall ensure that there is an inquiry point that is able to answer all reasonable inquiries from other Parties and interested persons, and to provide relevant documents regarding: (a) any standards-related measure proposed, adopted or maintained in its territory at the federal, state or provincial government level; (b) the membership and participation of the Party, or its relevant federal, state or provincial government authorities, in international and regional standardizing bodies and conformity assessment systems, and in bilateral and multilateral arrangements regarding standards-related measures, and the provisions of those systems and arrangements; (c) the location of notices published pursuant to Article 909, or where the information can be obtained; (d) the location of the inquiry points referred to in paragraph 3; and (e) the Party's procedures for assessment of risk, and factors it considers in conducting the assessment and in establishing, pursuant to Article 904(2), the levels of protection that it considers appropriate.

2.   Where a Party designates more than one inquiry point, it shall: (a) provide to the other Parties complete and unambiguous information on the scope of responsibility of each inquiry point; and (b) ensure that any inquiry addressed to an incorrect inquiry point is promptly conveyed to the correct inquiry point.

3.   Each Party shall take such reasonable measures as may be available to it to ensure that there is at least one inquiry point that is able to answer all reasonable inquiries from other Parties and interested persons and to provide relevant documents or information as to where they can be obtained regarding: (a) any standard or conformity assessment procedure proposed, adopted or maintained by non-governmental standardizing bodies in its territory; and (b) the membership and participation of relevant non-governmental bodies in its territory in international and regional standardizing bodies and conformity assessment systems.

4.   Each Party shall ensure that where copies of documents are requested by another Party or by interested persons in accordance with this Chapter, they are supplied at the same price, apart from the actual cost of delivery, as the price for domestic purchase.

Article 911

Technical Cooperation

1.   Each Party shall, on request of another Party: (a) provide to that Party technical advice, information and assistance on mutually agreed terms and conditions to enhance that Party's standards-related measures, and related activities, processes and systems; (b) provide to that Party information on its technical cooperation programs regarding standards-related measures relating to specific areas of interest; and (c) consult with that Party during the development of, or prior to the adoption or change in the application of, any standards-related measure.

2.   Each Party shall encourage standardizing bodies in its territory to cooperate with the standardizing bodies in the territories of the other Parties in their participation, as appropriate, in standardizing activities, such as through membership in international standardizing bodies.

Article 912

Limitations on the Provision of Information

Nothing in this Chapter shall be construed to require a Party to: (a) communicate, publish texts, or provide particulars or copies of documents other than in an official language of the Party; or (b) furnish any information the disclosure of which would impede law enforcement or otherwise be contrary to the public interest, or would prejudice the legitimate commercial interests of particular enterprises.

Article 913

Committee on Standards–Related Measures

1.   The Parties hereby establish a Committee on Standards–Related Measures, comprising representatives of each Party.

2.   The Committee's functions shall include: (a) monitoring the implementation and administration of this Chapter, including the progress of the subcommittees and working groups established under paragraph 4, and the operation of the inquiry points established under Article 910; (b) facilitating the process by which the Parties make compatible their standards-related measures; (c) providing a forum for the Parties to consult on issues relating to standards-related measures, including the provision of technical advice and recommendations under Article 914; (d) enhancing cooperation on the development, application and enforcement of standards-related measures; and (e) considering non-governmental, regional and multilateral developments regarding standards-related measures, including under the GATT.

3.   The Committee shall: (a) meet on request of any Party and, unless the Parties otherwise agree, at least once each year; and (b) report annually to the Commission on the implementation of this Chapter.

4.   The Committee may, as it considers appropriate, establish and determine the scope and mandate of subcommittees or working groups, comprising representatives of each Party. Each subcommittee or working group may: (a) as it considers necessary or desirable, include or consult with (i) representatives of non-governmental bodies, including standardizing bodies, (ii) scien-

tists, and (iii) technical experts; and (b) determine its work program, taking into account relevant international activities.

5. Further to paragraph 4, the Committee shall establish: (a) the following subcommittees (i) Land Transportation Standards Subcommittee, in accordance with Annex 913.5.a–1, (ii) Telecommunications Standards Subcommittee, in accordance with Annex 913.5.a–2, (iii) Automotive Standards Council, in accordance with Annex 913.5.a–3, and (iv) Subcommittee on Labelling of Textile and Apparel Goods, in accordance with Annex 913.5.a–4; and (b) such other subcommittees or working groups as it considers appropriate to address any topic, including (i) identification and nomenclature for goods subject to standards-related measures, (ii) quality and identity standards and technical regulations, (iii) packaging, labelling and presentation of consumer information, including languages, measurement systems, ingredients, sizes, terminology, symbols and related matters, (iv) product approval and post-market surveillance programs, (v) principles for the accreditation and recognition of conformity assessment bodies, procedures and systems, (vi) development and implementation of a uniform chemical hazard classification and communication system, (vii) enforcement programs, including training and inspections by regulatory, analytical and enforcement personnel, (viii) promotion and implementation of good laboratory practices, (ix) promotion and implementation of good manufacturing practices, (x) criteria for assessment of potential environmental hazards of goods, (xi) methodologies for assessment of risk, (xii) guidelines for testing of chemicals, including industrial and agricultural chemicals, pharmaceuticals and biologicals, (xiii) methods by which consumer protection, including matters relating to consumer redress, can be facilitated, and (xiv) extension of the application of this Chapter to other services.

6. Each Party shall, on request of another Party, take such reasonable measures as may be available to it to provide for the participation in the activities of the Committee, where and as appropriate, of representatives of state or provincial governments.

7. A Party requesting technical advice, information or assistance pursuant to Article 911 shall notify the Committee which shall facilitate any such request.

Annex 913.5.a–1

Land Transportation Standards Subcommittee

1. The Land Transportation Standards Subcommittee, established under Article 913(5)(a)(i), shall comprise representatives of each Party.

2. The Subcommittee shall implement the following work program for making compatible the Parties' relevant standards-related measures for: (a) bus and truck operations (i) no later than one and one-half years after the date of entry into force of this Agreement, for non-medical standards-related measures respecting drivers, including measures relating to the age of and language used by drivers, (ii) no later than two and one-half years after the date of entry into force of this Agreement, for medical standards-related measures respecting drivers, (iii) no later than three years after the date of entry into force of this Agreement, for standards-related measures respecting vehicles, including measures relating to weights and dimensions, tires, brakes,

parts and accessories, securement of cargo, maintenance and repair, inspections, and emissions and environmental pollution levels not covered by the Automotive Standards Council's work program established under Annex 913.5.a–3, (iv) no later than three years after the date of entry into force of this Agreement, for standards-related measures respecting each Party's supervision of motor carriers' safety compliance, and (v) no later than three years after the date of entry into force of this Agreement, for standards-related measures respecting road signs; (b) rail operations (i) no later than one year after the date of entry into force of this Agreement, for standards-related measures respecting operating personnel that are relevant to cross-border operations, and (ii) no later than one year after the date of entry into force of this Agreement, for standards-related measures respecting locomotives and other rail equipment; and (c) transportation of dangerous goods, no later than six years after the date of entry into force of this Agreement, using as their basis the United Nations Recommendations on the Transport of Dangerous Goods, or such other standards as the Parties may agree.

3. The Subcommittee may address other related standards-related measures as it considers appropriate.

Annex 913.5.a–2
Telecommunications Standards Subcommittee

1. The Telecommunications Standards Subcommittee, established under Article 913(5)(a)(ii), shall comprise representatives of each Party.

2. The Subcommittee shall, within six months of the date of entry into force of this Agreement, develop a work program, including a timetable, for making compatible, to the greatest extent practicable, the standards-related measures of the Parties for authorized equipment as defined in Chapter Thirteen (Telecommunications).

3. The Subcommittee may address other appropriate standards-related matters respecting telecommunications equipment or services and such other matters as it considers appropriate.

4. The Subcommittee shall take into account relevant work carried out by the Parties in other forums, and that of non-governmental standardizing bodies.

Annex 913.5.a–3
Automotive Standards Council

1. The Automotive Standards Council, established under Article 913.5(a)(iii), shall comprise representatives of each Party.

2. The purpose of the Council shall be, to the extent practicable, to facilitate the attainment of compatibility among, and review the implementation of, national standards-related measures of the Parties that apply to automotive goods, and to address other related matters.

3. To facilitate its objectives, the Council may establish subgroups, consultation procedures and other appropriate operational mechanisms. On the agreement of the Parties, the Council may include state and provincial government or private sector representatives in its subgroups.

4. Any recommendation of the Council shall require agreement of the Parties. Where the adoption of a law is not required for a Party, the Council's recommendations shall be implemented by the Party within a reasonable time in accordance with the legal and procedural requirements and international obligations of the Party. Where the adoption of a law is required for a Party, the Party shall use its best efforts to secure the adoption of the law and shall implement any such law within a reasonable time.

5. Recognizing the existing disparity in standards-related measures of the Parties, the Council shall develop a work program for making compatible the national standards-related measures that apply to automotive goods and other related matters based on the following criteria: (a) the impact on industry integration; (b) the extent of the barriers to trade; (c) the level of trade affected; and (d) the extent of the disparity. In developing its work program, the Council may address other related matters, including emissions from on-road and non-road mobile sources.

6. Each Party shall take such reasonable measures as may be available to it to promote the objectives of this Annex with respect to standards-related measures that are maintained by state and provincial government authorities and private sector organizations. The Council shall make every effort to assist these entities with such activities, especially the identification of priorities and the establishment of work schedules.

Annex 913.5.a–4

Subcommittee on Labelling of Textile and Apparel Goods

1. The Subcommittee on Labelling of Textile and Apparel Goods, established under Article 913(5)(a)(iv), shall comprise representatives of each Party.

2. The Subcommittee shall include, and consult with, technical experts as well as a broadly representative group from the manufacturing and retailing sectors in the territory of each Party.

3. The Subcommittee shall develop and pursue a work program on the harmonization of labelling requirements to facilitate trade in textile and apparel goods between the Parties through the adoption of uniform labelling provisions. The work program should include the following matters: (a) pictograms and symbols to replace, where possible, required written information, as well as other methods to reduce the need for labels on textile and apparel goods in multiple languages; (b) care instructions for textile and apparel goods; (c) fiber content information for textile and apparel goods; (d) uniform methods acceptable for the attachment of required information to textile and apparel goods; and (e) use in the territory of the other Parties of each Party's national registration numbers for manufacturers or importers of textile and apparel goods.

Article 914

Technical Consultations

1. Where a Party requests consultations regarding the application of this Chapter to a standards-related measure, and so notifies the Committee, the Committee may facilitate the consultations, if it does not consider the

matter itself, by referring the matter for non-binding technical advice or recommendations to a subcommittee or working group, including an ad hoc subcommittee or working group, or to another forum.

2. The Committee should consider any matter referred to it under paragraph 1 as expeditiously as possible and promptly forward to the Parties any technical advice or recommendations that it develops or receives concerning the matter. The Parties involved shall provide a written response to the Committee concerning the technical advice or recommendations within such time as the Committee may request.

3. Where the involved Parties have had recourse to consultations facilitated by the Committee under paragraph 1, the consultations shall, on the agreement of the Parties involved, constitute consultations under Article 2006 (Consultations).

4. The Parties confirm that a Party asserting that a standards-related measure of another Party is inconsistent with this Chapter shall have the burden of establishing the inconsistency.

Article 915

Definitions

1. For purposes of this Chapter:

approval procedure means any registration, notification or other mandatory administrative procedure for granting permission for a good or service to be produced, marketed or used for a stated purpose or under stated conditions;

assessment of risk means evaluation of the potential for adverse effects;

conformity assessment procedure means any procedure used, directly or indirectly, to determine that a technical regulation or standard is fulfilled, including sampling, testing, inspection, evaluation, verification, monitoring, auditing, assurance of conformity, accreditation, registration or approval used for such a purpose, but does not mean an approval procedure;

international standard means a standards-related measure, or other guide or recommendation, adopted by an international standardizing body and made available to the public;

international standardizing body means a standardizing body whose membership is open to the relevant bodies of at least all the parties to the GATT Agreement on Technical Barriers to Trade, including the International Organization for Standardization (ISO), the International Electrotechnical Commission (IEC), Codex Alimentarius Commission, the World Health Organization (WHO), the Food and Agriculture Organization (FAO), the International Telecommunication Union (ITU); or any other body that the Parties designate;

land transportation service means a transportation service provided by means of motor carrier or rail;

legitimate objective includes an objective such as: (a) safety, (b) protection of human, animal or plant life or health, the environment or consumers, including matters relating to quality and identifiability of goods or services, and (c) sustainable development, considering, among other things, where appropriate, fundamental climatic or other geographical factors, technological or infrastructure factors, or scientific justification but does not include the protection of domestic production;

make compatible means bring different standards-related measures of the same scope approved by different standardizing bodies to a level such that they are either identical, equivalent or have the effect of permitting goods or services to be used in place of one another or fulfill the same purpose;

services means land transportation services and telecommunications services;

standard means a document, approved by a recognized body, that provides, for common and repeated use, rules, guidelines or characteristics for goods or related processes and production methods, or for services or related operating methods, with which compliance is not mandatory. It may also include or deal exclusively with terminology, symbols, packaging, marking or labelling requirements as they apply to a good, process, or production or operating method;

standardizing body means a body having recognized activities in standardization; standards-related measure means a standard, technical regulation or conformity assessment procedure;

technical regulation means a document which lays down goods' characteristics or their related processes and production methods, or services' characteristics or their related operating methods, including the applicable administrative provisions, with which compliance is mandatory. It may also include or deal exclusively with terminology, symbols, packaging, marking or labelling requirements as they apply to a good, process, or production or operating method; and

telecommunications service means a service provided by means of the transmission and reception of signals by any electromagnetic means, but does not mean the cable, broadcast or other electromagnetic distribution of radio or television programming to the public generally.

2. Except as they are otherwise defined in this Agreement, other terms in this Chapter shall be interpreted in accordance with their ordinary meaning in context and in the light of the objectives of this Agreement, and where appropriate by reference to the terms presented in the sixth edition of the ISO/IEC Guide 2: 1991, General Terms and Their Definitions Concerning Standardization and Related Activities.

PART FOUR

GOVERNMENT PROCUREMENT

CHAPTER TEN: GOVERNMENT PROCUREMENT

Section A—Scope and Coverage and National Treatment

Article 1001

Scope and Coverage

1. This Chapter applies to measures adopted or maintained by a Party relating to procurement: (a) by a federal government entity set out in Annex 1001.1a–1, a government enterprise set out in Annex 1001.1a–2, or a state or provincial government entity set out in Annex 1001.1a–3 in accordance with

Article 1024; (b) of goods in accordance with Annex 1001.1b–1, services in accordance with Annex 1001.1b–2, or construction services in accordance with Annex 1001.1b–3; and (c) where the value of the contract to be awarded is estimated to be equal to or greater than a threshold, calculated and adjusted according to the U.S. inflation rate as set out in Annex 1001.1c, of (i) for federal government entities, US$50,000 for contracts for goods, services or any combination thereof, and US$6.5 million for contracts for construction services, (ii) for government enterprises, US$250,000 for contracts for goods, services or any combination thereof, and US$8.0 million for contracts for construction services, and (iii) for state and provincial government entities, the applicable threshold, as set out in Annex 1001.1a–3 in accordance with Article 1024.

2.   Paragraph 1 is subject to: (a) the transitional provisions set out in Annex 1001.2a; (b) the General Notes set out in Annex 1001.2b; and (c) Annex 1001.2c, for the Parties specified therein.

3.   Subject to paragraph 4, where a contract to be awarded by an entity is not covered by this Chapter, this Chapter shall not be construed to cover any good or service component of that contract.

4.   No Party may prepare, design or otherwise structure any procurement contract in order to avoid the obligations of this Chapter.

5.   Procurement includes procurement by such methods as purchase, lease or rental, with or without an option to buy. Procurement does not include: (a) non-contractual agreements or any form of government assistance, including cooperative agreements, grants, loans, equity infusions, guarantees, fiscal incentives, and government provision of goods and services to persons or state, provincial and regional governments; and (b) the acquisition of fiscal agency or depository services, liquidation and management services for regulated financial institutions and sale and distribution services for government debt.

Article 1002
Valuation of Contracts

1.   Each Party shall ensure that its entities, in determining whether a contract is covered by this Chapter, apply paragraphs 2 through 7 in calculating the value of that contract.

2.   The value of a contract shall be estimated as at the time of publication of a notice in accordance with Article 1010.

3.   In calculating the value of a contract, an entity shall take into account all forms of remuneration, including premiums, fees, commissions and interest.

4.   Further to Article 1001(4), an entity may not select a valuation method, or divide procurement requirements into separate contracts, to avoid the obligations of this Chapter.

5.   Where an individual requirement for a procurement results in the award of more than one contract, or in contracts being awarded in separate parts, the basis for valuation shall be either: (a) the actual value of similar recurring contracts concluded over the prior fiscal year or 12 months adjusted, where possible, for anticipated changes in quantity and value over the

subsequent 12 months; or (b) the estimated value of recurring contracts in the fiscal year or 12 months subsequent to the initial contract.

6.   In the case of a contract for lease or rental, with or without an option to buy, or in the case of a contract that does not specify a total price, the basis for valuation shall be: (a) in the case of a fixed-term contract, where the term is 12 months or less, the total contract value, for its duration or, where the term exceeds 12 months, the total contract value, including the estimated residual value; or (b) in the case of a contract for an indefinite period, the estimated monthly installment multiplied by 48.   If the entity is uncertain as to whether a contract is for a fixed or an indefinite term, the entity shall calculate the value of the contract using the method set out in subparagraph (b).

7.   Where tender documentation requires option clauses, the basis for valuation shall be the total value of the maximum permissible procurement, including all possible optional purchases.

Article 1003

National Treatment and Non-discrimination

1.   With respect to measures covered by this Chapter, each Party shall accord to goods of another Party, to the suppliers of such goods and to service suppliers of another Party, treatment no less favorable than the most favorable treatment that the Party accords to: (a) its own goods and suppliers; and (b) goods and suppliers of another Party.

2.   With respect to measures covered by this Chapter, no Party may: (a) treat a locally established supplier less favorably than another locally established supplier on the basis of degree of foreign affiliation or ownership; or (b) discriminate against a locally established supplier on the basis that the goods or services offered by that supplier for the particular procurement are goods or services of another Party.

3.   Paragraph 1 does not apply to measures respecting customs duties or other charges of any kind imposed on or in connection with importation, the method of levying such duties or charges or other import regulations, including restrictions and formalities.

Article 1004

Rules of Origin

No Party may apply rules of origin to goods imported from another Party for purposes of government procurement covered by this Chapter that are different from or inconsistent with the rules of origin the Party applies in the normal course of trade, which may be the Marking Rules established under Annex 311 if they become the rules of origin applied by that Party in the normal course of its trade.

Article 1005

Denial of Benefits

1.   Subject to prior notification and consultation in accordance with Articles 1803 (Notification and Provision of Information) and 2006 (Consultations), a Party may deny the benefits of this Chapter to a service supplier of

another Party where the Party establishes that the service is being provided by an enterprise that is owned or controlled by persons of a non-Party and that has no substantial business activities in the territory of any Party.

2.   A Party may deny to an enterprise of another Party the benefits of this Chapter if nationals of a non-Party own or control the enterprise and: (a) the circumstance set out in Article 1113(1)(a) (Denial of Benefits) is met; or (b) the denying Party adopts or maintains measures with respect to the non-Party that prohibit transactions with the enterprise or that would be violated or circumvented if the benefits of this Chapter were accorded to the enterprise.

Article 1006
Prohibition of Offsets

Each Party shall ensure that its entities do not, in the qualification and selection of suppliers, goods or services, in the evaluation of bids or the award of contracts, consider, seek or impose offsets. For purposes of this Article, offsets means conditions imposed or considered by an entity prior to or in the course of its procurement process that encourage local development or improve its Party's balance of payments accounts, by means of requirements of local content, licensing of technology, investment, counter-trade or similar requirements.

Article 1007
Technical Specifications

1.   Each Party shall ensure that its entities do not prepare, adopt or apply any technical specification with the purpose or the effect of creating unnecessary obstacles to trade.

2.   Each Party shall ensure that any technical specification prescribed by its entities is, where appropriate: (a) specified in terms of performance criteria rather than design or descriptive characteristics; and (b) based on international standards, national technical regulations, recognized national standards, or building codes.

3.   Each Party shall ensure that the technical specifications prescribed by its entities do not require or refer to a particular trademark or name, patent, design or type, specific origin or producer or supplier unless there is no sufficiently precise or intelligible way of otherwise describing the procurement requirements and provided that, in such cases, words such as "or equivalent" are included in the tender documentation.

4.   Each Party shall ensure that its entities do not seek or accept, in a manner that would have the effect of precluding competition, advice that may be used in the preparation or adoption of any technical specification for a specific procurement from a person that may have a commercial interest in that procurement.

Section B—Tendering Procedures
Article 1008
Tendering Procedures

1.   Each Party shall ensure that the tendering procedures of its entities are: (a) applied in a non-discriminatory manner; and (b) consistent with this Article and Articles 1009 through 1016.

2. In this regard, each Party shall ensure that its entities: (a) do not provide to any supplier information with regard to a specific procurement in a manner that would have the effect of precluding competition; and (b) provide all suppliers equal access to information with respect to a procurement during the period prior to the issuance of any notice or tender documentation.

Article 1009

Qualification of Suppliers

1. Further to Article 1003, no entity of a Party may, in the process of qualifying suppliers in a tendering procedure, discriminate between suppliers of the other Parties or between domestic suppliers and suppliers of the other Parties.

2. The qualification procedures followed by an entity shall be consistent with the following: (a) conditions for participation by suppliers in tendering procedures shall be published sufficiently in advance so as to provide the suppliers adequate time to initiate and, to the extent that it is compatible with efficient operation of the procurement process, to complete the qualification procedures; (b) conditions for participation by suppliers in tendering procedures, including financial guarantees, technical qualifications and information necessary for establishing the financial, commercial and technical capacity of suppliers, as well as the verification of whether a supplier meets those conditions, shall be limited to those that are essential to ensure the fulfillment of the contract in question; (c) the financial, commercial and technical capacity of a supplier shall be judged both on the basis of that supplier's global business activity, including its activity in the territory of the Party of the supplier, and its activity, if any, in the territory of the Party of the procuring entity; (d) an entity shall not misuse the process of, including the time required for, qualification in order to exclude suppliers of another Party from a suppliers' list or from being considered for a particular procurement; (e) an entity shall recognize as qualified suppliers those suppliers of another Party that meet the conditions for participation in a particular procurement; (f) an entity shall consider for a particular procurement those suppliers of another Party that request to participate in the procurement and that are not yet qualified, provided there is sufficient time to complete the qualification procedure; (g) an entity that maintains a permanent list of qualified suppliers shall ensure that suppliers may apply for qualification at any time, that all qualified suppliers so requesting are included in the list within a reasonably short period of time and that all qualified suppliers included in the list are notified of the termination of the list or of their removal from it; (h) where, after publication of a notice in accordance with Article 1010, a supplier that is not yet qualified requests to participate in a particular procurement, the entity shall promptly start the qualification procedure; (i) an entity shall advise any supplier that requests to become a qualified supplier of its decision as to whether that supplier has become qualified; and (j) where an entity rejects a supplier's application to qualify or ceases to recognize a supplier as qualified, the entity shall, on request of the supplier, promptly provide pertinent information concerning the entity's reasons for doing so.

3. Each Party shall: (a) ensure that each of its entities uses a single qualification procedure, except that an entity may use additional qualification

procedures where the entity determines the need for a different procedure and is prepared, on request of another Party, to demonstrate that need; and (b) endeavor to minimize differences in the qualification procedures of its entities.

4. Nothing in paragraphs 2 and 3 shall prevent an entity from excluding a supplier on grounds such as bankruptcy or false declarations.

Article 1010

Invitation to Participate

1. Except as otherwise provided in Article 1016, an entity shall publish an invitation to participate for all procurements in accordance with paragraphs 2, 3 and 5, in the appropriate publication referred to in Annex 1010.1.

2. The invitation to participate shall take the form of a notice of proposed procurement that shall contain the following information: (a) a description of the nature and quantity of the goods or services to be procured, including any options for further procurement and, if possible, (i) an estimate of when such options may be exercised, and (ii) in the case of recurring contracts, an estimate of when the subsequent notices will be issued; (b) a statement as to whether the procedure is open or selective and whether it will involve negotiation; (c) any date for starting or completion of delivery of the goods or services to be procured; (d) the address to which an application to be invited to tender or to qualify for the suppliers' lists must be submitted, the final date for receiving the application and the language or languages in which it may be submitted; (e) the address to which tenders must be submitted, the final date for receiving tenders and the language or languages in which tenders may be submitted; (f) the address of the entity that will award the contract and that will provide any information necessary for obtaining specifications and other documents; (g) a statement of any economic or technical requirements and of any financial guarantees, information and documents required from suppliers; (h) the amount and terms of payment of any sum payable for the tender documentation; and (i) a statement as to whether the entity is inviting offers for purchase, lease or rental, with or without an option to buy.

3. Notwithstanding paragraph 2, an entity listed in Annex 1001.1a–2 or 1001.1a–3 may use as an invitation to participate a notice of planned procurement that shall contain as much of the information referred to in paragraph 2 as is available to the entity, but that shall include, at a minimum, the following information: (a) a description of the subject matter of the procurement; (b) the time limits set for the receipt of tenders or applications to be invited to tender; (c) the address to which requests for documents relating to the procurement should be submitted; (d) a statement that interested suppliers should express their interest in the procurement to the entity; and (e) the identification of a contact point within the entity from which further information may be obtained.

4. An entity that uses a notice of planned procurement as an invitation to participate shall subsequently invite suppliers that have expressed an interest in the procurement to confirm their interest on the basis of information provided by the entity, which shall include at least the information referred to in paragraph 2.

5.   Notwithstanding paragraph 2, an entity listed in Annex 1001.1a–2 or 1001.1a–3 may use as an invitation to participate a notice regarding a qualification system.   An entity that uses such a notice shall, subject to the considerations referred to Article 1015(8), provide in a timely manner information that allows all suppliers that have expressed an interest in participating in the procurement to have a meaningful opportunity to assess their interest.   The information shall normally include the information required for notices referred to in paragraph 2.   Information provided to any interested supplier shall be provided in a non-discriminatory manner to all other interested suppliers.

6.   In the case of selective tendering procedures, an entity that maintains a permanent list of qualified suppliers shall publish annually in the appropriate publication referred to in Annex 1010.1 a notice containing the following information: (a) an enumeration of any such lists maintained, including their headings, in relation to the goods or services or categories of goods or services to be procured through the lists;   (b) the conditions to be fulfilled by suppliers in view of their inscription on the lists and the methods according to which each of those conditions will be verified by the entity concerned;   and (c) the period of validity of the lists and the formalities for their renewal.

7.   Where, after publication of an invitation to participate, but before the time set for the opening or receipt of tenders as specified in the notices or the tender documentation, an entity finds that it has become necessary to amend or reissue the notice or tender documentation, the entity shall ensure that the amended or reissued notice or tender documentation is given the same circulation as the original.   Any significant information given by an entity to a supplier with respect to a particular procurement shall be given simultaneously to all other interested suppliers and sufficiently in advance so as to provide all suppliers concerned adequate time to consider the information and to respond.

8.   An entity shall indicate in the notices referred to in this Article that the procurement is covered by this Chapter.

Article 1011

Selective Tendering Procedures

1.   To ensure optimum effective competition between the suppliers of the Parties under selective tendering procedures, an entity shall, for each procurement, invite tenders from the maximum number of domestic suppliers and suppliers of the other Parties, consistent with the efficient operation of the procurement system.

2.   Subject to paragraph 3, an entity that maintains a permanent list of qualified suppliers may select suppliers to be invited to tender for a particular procurement from among those listed.   In the process of making a selection, the entity shall provide for equitable opportunities for suppliers on the list.

3.   Subject to Article 1009(2)(f), an entity shall allow a supplier that requests to participate in a particular procurement to submit a tender and shall consider the tender.   The number of additional suppliers permitted to participate shall be limited only by the efficient operation of the procurement system.

4.   Where an entity does not invite or admit a supplier to tender, the entity shall, on request of the supplier, promptly provide pertinent information concerning its reasons for not doing so.

Article 1012

Time Limits for Tendering and Delivery

1.   An entity shall: (a) in prescribing a time limit, provide adequate time to allow suppliers of another Party to prepare and submit tenders before the closing of the tendering procedures; (b) in determining a time limit, consistent with its own reasonable needs, take into account such factors as the complexity of the procurement, the extent of subcontracting anticipated, and the time normally required for transmitting tenders by mail from foreign as well as domestic points; and (c) take due account of publication delays when setting the final date for receipt of tenders or applications to be invited to tender.

2.   Subject to paragraph 3, an entity shall provide that: (a) in open tendering procedures, the period for the receipt of tenders is no less than 40 days from the date of publication of a notice in accordance with Article 1010; (b) in selective tendering procedures not involving the use of a permanent list of qualified suppliers, the period for submitting an application to be invited to tender is no less than 25 days from the date of publication of a notice in accordance with Article 1010, and the period for receipt of tenders is no less than 40 days from the date of issuance of the invitation to tender; and (c) in selective tendering procedures involving the use of a permanent list of qualified suppliers, the period for receipt of tenders is no less than 40 days from the date of the initial issuance of invitations to tender, but where the date of initial issuance of invitations to tender does not coincide with the date of publication of a notice in accordance with Article 1010, there shall not be less than 40 days between those two dates.

3.   An entity may reduce the periods referred to in paragraph 2 in accordance with the following: (a) where a notice referred to in Article 1010(3) or (5) has been published for a period of no less than 40 days and no more than 12 months, the 40-day limit for receipt of tenders may be reduced to no less than 24 days; (b) in the case of the second or subsequent publications dealing with recurring contracts within the meaning of Article 1010(2)(a), the 40-day limit for receipt of tenders may be reduced to no less than 24 days; (c) where a state of urgency duly substantiated by the entity renders impracticable the periods in question, the periods may be reduced to no less than 10 days from the date of publication of a notice in accordance with Article 1010; or (d) where an entity listed in Annex 1001.1a-2 or 1001.1a-3 is using as an invitation to participate a notice referred to in Article 1010(5), the periods may be fixed by mutual agreement between the entity and all selected suppliers but, in the absence of agreement, the entity may fix periods that shall be sufficiently long to allow for responsive bidding and in any event shall be no less than 10 days.

4.   An entity shall, in establishing a delivery date for goods or services and consistent with its own reasonable needs, take into account such factors as the complexity of the procurement, the extent of subcontracting anticipated

and the time realistically required for production, destocking and transport of goods from the points of supply.

Article 1013
Tender Documentation

1. Where an entity provides tender documentation to suppliers, the documentation shall contain all information necessary to permit suppliers to submit responsive tenders, including information required to be published in the notice referred to in Article 1010(2), except for the information required under Article 1010(2)(h). The documentation shall also include: (a) the address of the entity to which tenders should be submitted; (b) the address to which requests for supplementary information should be submitted; (c) the language or languages in which tenders and tendering documents may be submitted; (d) the closing date and time for receipt of tenders and the length of time during which tenders should be open for acceptance; (e) the persons authorized to be present at the opening of tenders and the date, time and place of the opening; (f) a statement of any economic or technical requirements and of any financial guarantees, information and documents required from suppliers; (g) a complete description of the goods or services to be procured and any other requirements, including technical specifications, conformity certification and necessary plans, drawings and instructional materials; (h) the criteria for awarding the contract, including any factors other than price that are to be considered in the evaluation of tenders and the cost elements to be included in evaluating tender prices, such as transportation, insurance and inspection costs, and in the case of goods or services of another Party, customs duties and other import charges, taxes and the currency of payment; (i) the terms of payment; and (j) any other terms or conditions.

2. An entity shall: (a) forward tender documentation on the request of a supplier that is participating in open tendering procedures or has requested to participate in selective tendering procedures, and reply promptly to any reasonable request for explanations relating thereto; and (b) reply promptly to any reasonable request for relevant information made by a supplier participating in the tendering procedure, on condition that such information does not give that supplier an advantage over its competitors in the procedure for the award of the contract.

Article 1014
Negotiation Disciplines

1. An entity may conduct negotiations only: (a) in the context of procurement in which the entity has, in a notice published in accordance with Article 1010, indicated its intent to negotiate; or (b) where it appears to the entity from the evaluation of the tenders that no one tender is obviously the most advantageous in terms of the specific evaluation criteria set out in the notices or tender documentation.

2. An entity shall use negotiations primarily to identify the strengths and weaknesses in the tenders.

3. An entity shall treat all tenders in confidence. In particular, no entity may provide to any person information intended to assist any supplier to bring its tender up to the level of any other tender.

4. No entity may, in the course of negotiations, discriminate between suppliers. In particular, an entity shall: (a) carry out any elimination of suppliers in accordance with the criteria set out in the notices and tender documentation; (b) provide in writing all modifications to the criteria or technical requirements to all suppliers remaining in the negotiations; (c) permit all remaining suppliers to submit new or amended tenders on the basis of the modified criteria or requirements; and (d) when negotiations are concluded, permit all remaining suppliers to submit final tenders in accordance with a common deadline.

Article 1015

Submission, Receipt and Opening of Tenders and Awarding of Contracts

1. An entity shall use procedures for the submission, receipt and opening of tenders and the awarding of contracts that are consistent with the following: (a) tenders shall normally be submitted in writing directly or by mail; (b) where tenders by telex, telegram, telecopy or other means of electronic transmission are permitted, the tender made thereby must include all the information necessary for the evaluation of the tender, in particular the definitive price proposed by the supplier and a statement that the supplier agrees to all the terms and conditions of the invitation to tender; (c) a tender made by telex, telegram, telecopy or other means of electronic transmission must be confirmed promptly by letter or by the dispatch of a signed copy of the telex, telegram, telecopy or electronic message; (d) the content of the telex, telegram, telecopy or electronic message shall prevail where there is a difference or conflict between that content and the content of any documentation received after the time limit for submission of tenders; (e) tenders presented by telephone shall not be permitted; (f) requests to participate in selective tendering procedures may be submitted by telex, telegram or telecopy and if permitted, may be submitted by other means of electronic transmission; and (g) the opportunities that may be given to suppliers to correct unintentional errors of form between the opening of tenders and the awarding of the contract shall not be administered in a manner that would result in discrimination between suppliers. In this paragraph, "means of electronic transmission" consists of means capable of producing for the recipient at the destination of the transmission a printed copy of the tender.

2. No entity may penalize a supplier whose tender is received in the office designated in the tender documentation after the time specified for receiving tenders if the delay is due solely to mishandling on the part of the entity. An entity may also consider, in exceptional circumstances, tenders received after the time specified for receiving tenders if the entity's procedures so provide.

3. All tenders solicited by an entity under open or selective tendering procedures shall be received and opened under procedures and conditions guaranteeing the regularity of the opening of tenders. The entity shall retain the information on the opening of tenders. The information shall remain at the disposal of the competent authorities of the Party for use, if required, under Article 1017, Article 1019 or Chapter Twenty (Institutional Arrangements and Dispute Settlement Procedures).

4.   An entity shall award contracts in accordance with the following: (a) to be considered for award, a tender must, at the time of opening, conform to the essential requirements of the notices or tender documentation and have been submitted by a supplier that complies with the conditions for participation; (b) if the entity has received a tender that is abnormally lower in price than other tenders submitted, the entity may inquire of the supplier to ensure that it can comply with the conditions of participation and is or will be capable of fulfilling the terms of the contract; (c) unless the entity decides in the public interest not to award the contract, the entity shall make the award to the supplier that has been determined to be fully capable of undertaking the contract and whose tender is either the lowest-priced tender or the tender determined to be the most advantageous in terms of the specific evaluation criteria set out in the notices or tender documentation; (d) awards shall be made in accordance with the criteria and essential requirements specified in the tender documentation; and (e) option clauses shall not be used in a manner that circumvents this Chapter.

5.   No entity of a Party may make it a condition of the awarding of a contract that the supplier has previously been awarded one or more contracts by an entity of that Party or that the supplier has prior work experience in the territory of that Party.

6.   An entity shall: (a) on request, promptly inform suppliers participating in tendering procedures of decisions on contract awards and, if so requested, inform them in writing; and (b) on request of a supplier whose tender was not selected for award, provide pertinent information to that supplier concerning the reasons for not selecting its tender, the relevant characteristics and advantages of the tender selected and the name of the winning supplier.

7.   No later than 72 days after the award of a contract, an entity shall publish a notice in the appropriate publication referred to in Annex 1010.1 that shall contain the following information: (a) a description of the nature and quantity of goods or services included in the contract; (b) the name and address of the entity awarding the contract; (c) the date of the award; (d) the name and address of each winning supplier; (e) the value of the contract, or the highest-priced and lowest-priced tenders considered in the process of awarding the contract; and (f) the tendering procedure used.

8.   Notwithstanding paragraphs 1 through 7, an entity may withhold certain information on the award of a contract where disclosure of the information: (a) would impede law enforcement or otherwise be contrary to the public interest; (b) would prejudice the legitimate commercial interest of a particular person; or (c) might prejudice fair competition between suppliers.

Article 1016

Limited Tendering Procedures

1.   An entity of a Party may, in the circumstances and subject to the conditions set out in paragraph 2, use limited tendering procedures and thus derogate from Articles 1008 through 1015, provided that such limited tendering procedures are not used with a view to avoiding maximum possible competition or in a manner that would constitute a means of discrimination between suppliers of the other Parties or protection of domestic suppliers.

2. An entity may use limited tendering procedures in the following circumstances and subject to the following conditions, as applicable: (a) in the absence of tenders in response to an open or selective call for tenders, or where the tenders submitted either have resulted from collusion or do not conform to the essential requirements of the tender documentation, or where the tenders submitted come from suppliers that do not comply with the conditions for participation provided for in accordance with this Chapter, on condition that the requirements of the initial procurement are not substantially modified in the contract as awarded; (b) where, for works of art, or for reasons connected with the protection of patents, copyrights or other exclusive rights, or proprietary information or where there is an absence of competition for technical reasons, the goods or services can be supplied only by a particular supplier and no reasonable alternative or substitute exists; (c) in so far as is strictly necessary where, for reasons of extreme urgency brought about by events unforeseeable by the entity, the goods or services could not be obtained in time by means of open or selective tendering procedures; (d) for additional deliveries by the original supplier that are intended either as replacement parts or continuing services for existing supplies, services or installations, or as the extension of existing supplies, services or installations, where a change of supplier would compel the entity to procure equipment or services not meeting requirements of interchangeability with already existing equipment or services, including software to the extent that the initial procurement of the software was covered by this Chapter; (e) where an entity procures a prototype or a first good or service that is developed at its request in the course of and for a particular contract for research, experiment, study or original development. Where such contracts have been fulfilled, subsequent procurement of goods or services shall be subject to Articles 1008 through 1015. Original development of a first good may include limited production in order to incorporate the results of field testing and to demonstrate that the good is suitable for production in quantity to acceptable quality standards, but does not include quantity production to establish commercial viability or to recover research and development costs; (f) for goods purchased on a commodity market; (g) for purchases made under exceptionally advantageous conditions that only arise in the very short term, such as unusual disposals by enterprises that are not normally suppliers or disposal of assets of businesses in liquidation or receivership, but not routine purchases from regular suppliers; (h) for a contract to be awarded to the winner of an architectural design contest, on condition that the contest is (i) organized in a manner consistent with the principles of this Chapter, including regarding publication of an invitation to suitably qualified suppliers to participate in the contest, (ii) organized with a view to awarding the design contract to the winner, and (iii) to be judged by an independent jury; and (i) where an entity needs to procure consulting services regarding matters of a confidential nature, the disclosure of which could reasonably be expected to compromise government confidences, cause economic disruption or similarly be contrary to the public interest.

3. An entity shall prepare a report in writing on each contract awarded by it under paragraph 2. Each report shall contain the name of the procuring entity, indicate the value and kind of goods or services procured, the name of the country of origin, and a statement indicating the circumstances and

conditions described in paragraph 2 that justified the use of limited tendering. The entity shall retain each report. They shall remain at the disposal of the competent authorities of the Party for use, if required, under Article 1017, Article 1019 or Chapter Twenty (Institutional Arrangements and Dispute Settlement Procedures).

Section C—Bid Challenge

Article 1017

Bid Challenge

1. In order to promote fair, open and impartial procurement procedures, each Party shall adopt and maintain bid challenge procedures for procurement covered by this Chapter in accordance with the following: (a) each Party shall allow suppliers to submit bid challenges concerning any aspect of the procurement process, which for the purposes of this Article begins after an entity has decided on its procurement requirement and continues through the contract award; (b) a Party may encourage a supplier to seek a resolution of any complaint with the entity concerned prior to initiating a bid challenge; (c) each Party shall ensure that its entities accord fair and timely consideration to any complaint regarding procurement covered by this Chapter; (d) whether or not a supplier has attempted to resolve its complaint with the entity, or following an unsuccessful attempt at such a resolution, no Party may prevent the supplier from initiating a bid challenge or seeking any other relief; (e) a Party may require a supplier to notify the entity on initiation of a bid challenge; (f) a Party may limit the period within which a supplier may initiate a bid challenge, but in no case shall the period be less than 10 working days from the time when the basis of the complaint became known or reasonably should have become known to the supplier; (g) each Party shall establish or designate a reviewing authority with no substantial interest in the outcome of procurements to receive bid challenges and make findings and recommendations concerning them; (h) on receipt of a bid challenge, the reviewing authority shall expeditiously investigate the challenge; (i) a Party may require its reviewing authority to limit its considerations to the challenge itself; (j) in investigating the challenge, the reviewing authority may delay the awarding of the proposed contract pending resolution of the challenge, except in cases of urgency or where the delay would be contrary to the public interest; (k) the reviewing authority shall issue a recommendation to resolve the challenge, which may include directing the entity to re-evaluate offers, terminate or re-compete the contract in question; (*l*) entities normally shall follow the recommendations of the reviewing authority; (m) each Party should authorize its reviewing authority, following the conclusion of a bid challenge procedure, to make additional recommendations in writing to an entity respecting any facet of the entity's procurement process that is identified as problematic during the investigation of the challenge, including recommendations for changes in the procurement procedures of the entity to bring them into conformity with this Chapter; (n) the reviewing authority shall provide its findings and recommendations respecting bid challenges in writing and in a timely manner, and shall make them available to the Parties and interested persons; (o) each Party shall specify in writing and shall make generally available all its bid challenge procedures; and (p) each Party shall ensure that each of its entities maintains complete documentation regarding

each of its procurements, including a written record of all communications substantially affecting each procurement, for at least three years from the date the contract was awarded, to allow verification that the procurement process was carried out in accordance with this Chapter.

2. A Party may require that a bid challenge be initiated only after the notice of procurement has been published or, where a notice is not published, after tender documentation has been made available. Where a Party imposes such a requirement, the 10–working day period described in paragraph 1(f) shall begin no earlier than the date that the notice is published or the tender documentation is made available.

Section D—General Provisions
Article 1018
Exceptions

1. Nothing in this Chapter shall be construed to prevent a Party from taking any action or not disclosing any information which it considers necessary for the protection of its essential security interests relating to the procurement of arms, ammunition or war materials, or to procurement indispensable for national security or for national defense purposes.

2. Provided that such measures are not applied in a manner that would constitute a means of arbitrary or unjustifiable discrimination between Parties where the same conditions prevail or a disguised restriction on trade between the Parties, nothing in this Chapter shall be construed to prevent any Party from adopting or maintaining measures: (a) necessary to protect public morals, order or safety; (b) necessary to protect human, animal or plant life or health; (c) necessary to protect intellectual property; or (d) relating to goods or services of handicapped persons, of philanthropic institutions or of prison labor.

Article 1019
Provision of Information

1. Further to Article 1802(1) (Publication), each Party shall promptly publish any law, regulation, precedential judicial decision, administrative ruling of general application and any procedure, including standard contract clauses, regarding government procurement covered by this Chapter in the appropriate publications referred to in Annex 1010.1.

2. Each Party shall: (a) on request, explain to another Party its government procurement procedures; (b) ensure that its entities, on request from a supplier, promptly explain their procurement practices and procedures; and (c) designate by January 1, 1994 one or more contact points to (i) facilitate communication between the Parties, and (ii) answer all reasonable inquiries from other Parties to provide relevant information on matters covered by this Chapter.

3. A Party may seek such additional information on the award of the contract as may be necessary to determine whether the procurement was made fairly and impartially, in particular with respect to unsuccessful tenders. To this end, the Party of the procuring entity shall provide information on the characteristics and relative advantages of the winning tender and the

contract price. Where release of this information would prejudice competition in future tenders, the information shall not be released by the requesting Party except after consultation with and agreement of the Party that provided the information.

4.   On request, each Party shall provide to another Party information available to that Party and its entities concerning covered procurement of its entities and the individual contracts awarded by its entities.

5.   No Party may disclose confidential information the disclosure of which would prejudice the legitimate commercial interests of a particular person or might prejudice fair competition between suppliers, without the formal authorization of the person that provided the information to that Party.

6.   Nothing in this Chapter shall be construed as requiring any Party to disclose confidential information the disclosure of which would impede law enforcement or otherwise be contrary to the public interest.

7.   With a view to ensuring effective monitoring of procurement covered by this Chapter, each Party shall collect statistics and provide to the other Parties an annual report in accordance with the following reporting requirements, unless the Parties otherwise agree: (a) statistics on the estimated value of all contracts awarded, both above and below the applicable threshold values, broken down by entities; (b) statistics on the number and total value of contracts above the applicable threshold values, broken down by entities, by categories of goods and services established in accordance with classification systems developed under this Chapter and by the country of origin of the goods and services procured; (c) statistics on the number and total value of contracts awarded under each use of the procedures referred to in Article 1016, broken down by entities, by categories of goods and services, and by country of origin of the goods and services procured; and (d) statistics on the number and total value of contracts awarded under derogations to this Chapter set out in Annexes 1001.2a and 1001.2b, broken down by entities.

8.   Each Party may organize by state or province any portion of a report referred to in paragraph 7 that pertains to entities listed in Annex 1001.1a–3.

Article 1020
Technical Cooperation

1.   The Parties shall cooperate, on mutually agreed terms, to increase understanding of their respective government procurement systems, with a view to maximizing access to government procurement opportunities for the suppliers of all Parties.

2.   Each Party shall provide to the other Parties and to the suppliers of such Parties, on a cost recovery basis, information concerning training and orientation programs regarding its government procurement system, and access on a non-discriminatory basis to any program it conducts.

3.   The training and orientation programs referred to in paragraph 2 include: (a) training of government personnel directly involved in government procurement procedures; (b) training of suppliers interested in pursuing government procurement opportunities; (c) an explanation and description of specific elements of each Party's government procurement system, such as its

bid challenge mechanism; and (d) information about government procurement market opportunities.

4. Each Party shall establish by January 1, 1994 at least one contact point to provide information on the training and orientation programs referred to in this Article.

Article 1021
Joint Programs for Small Business

1. The Parties shall establish, within 12 months after the date of entry into force of this Agreement, the Committee on Small Business, comprising representatives of the Parties. The Committee shall meet as mutually agreed, but not less than once each year, and shall report annually to the Commission on the efforts of the Parties to promote government procurement opportunities for their small businesses.

2. The Committee shall work to facilitate the following activities of the Parties: (a) identification of available opportunities for the training of small business personnel in government procurement procedures; (b) identification of small businesses interested in becoming trading partners of small businesses in the territory of another Party; (c) development of data bases of small businesses in the territory of each Party for use by entities of another Party wishing to procure from small businesses; (d) consultations regarding the factors that each Party uses in establishing its criteria for eligibility for any small business programs; and (e) activities to address any related matter.

Article 1022
Rectifications or Modifications

1. A Party may modify its coverage under this Chapter only in exceptional circumstances.

2. Where a Party modifies its coverage under this Chapter, the Party shall: (a) notify the other Parties and its Section of the Secretariat of the modification; (b) reflect the change in the appropriate Annex; and (c) propose to the other Parties appropriate compensatory adjustments to its coverage in order to maintain a level of coverage comparable to that existing prior to the modification.

3. Notwithstanding paragraphs 1 and 2, a Party may make rectifications of a purely formal nature and minor amendments to its Schedules to Annexes 1001.1a–1 through 1001.1b–3 and Annexes 1001.2a and 1001.2b, provided that it notifies such rectifications to the other Parties and its Section of the Secretariat, and another Party does not object to such proposed rectification within 30 days. In such cases, compensation need not be proposed.

4. Notwithstanding any other provision of this Chapter, a Party may undertake reorganizations of its government procurement entities covered by this Chapter, including programs through which the procurement of such entities is decentralized or the corresponding government functions cease to be performed by any government entity, whether or not subject to this Chapter. In such cases, compensation need not be proposed. No Party may undertake such reorganizations or programs to avoid the obligations of this Chapter.

5. Where a Party considers that: (a) an adjustment proposed under paragraph (2)(c) is not adequate to maintain a comparable level of mutually agreed coverage, or (b) a rectification or a minor amendment under paragraph 3 or a reorganization under paragraph 4 does not meet the applicable requirements of those paragraphs and should require compensation, the Party may have recourse to dispute settlement procedures under Chapter Twenty (Institutional Arrangements and Dispute Settlement Procedures).

Article 1023
Divestiture of Entities

1. Nothing in this Chapter shall be construed to prevent a Party from divesting an entity covered by this Chapter.

2. If, on the public offering of shares of an entity listed in Annex 1001.1a- 2, or through other methods, the entity is no longer subject to federal government control, the Party may delete the entity from its Schedule to that Annex, and withdraw the entity from the coverage of this Chapter, on notification to the other Parties and its Section of the Secretariat.

3. Where a Party objects to the withdrawal on the grounds that the entity remains subject to federal government control, that Party may have recourse to dispute settlement procedures under Chapter Twenty.

Article 1024
Further Negotiations

1. The Parties shall commence further negotiations no later than December 31, 1998, with a view to the further liberalization of their respective government procurement markets.

2. In such negotiations, the Parties shall review all aspects of their government procurement practices for purposes of: (a) assessing the functioning of their government procurement systems; (b) seeking to expand the coverage of this Chapter, including by adding (i) other government enterprises, and (ii) procurement otherwise subject to legislated or administrative exceptions; and (c) reviewing thresholds.

3. Prior to such review, the Parties shall endeavor to consult with their state and provincial governments with a view to obtaining commitments, on a voluntary and reciprocal basis, to include within this Chapter procurement by state and provincial government entities and enterprises.

4. If the negotiations pursuant to Article IX:6(b) of the GATT Agreement on Government Procurement ("the Code") are completed prior to such review, the Parties shall: (a) immediately begin consultations with their state and provincial governments with a view to obtaining commitments, on a voluntary and reciprocal basis, to include within this Chapter procurement by state and provincial government entities and enterprises; and (b) increase the obligations and coverage of this Chapter to a level at least commensurate with that of the Code.

5. The Parties shall undertake further negotiations, to commence no later than one year after the date of entry into force of this Agreement, on the subject of electronic transmission.

Article 1025

Definitions

For purposes of this Chapter:

construction services contract means a contract for the realization by any means of civil or building works listed in Appendix 1001.1b–3–A;

entity means an entity listed in Annex 1001.1a–1, 1001.1a–2 or 1001.1a–3;

goods of another Party means goods originating in the territory of another Party, determined in accordance with Article 1004;

international standard means "international standard", as defined in Article 915 (Standards–Related Measures—Definitions);

limited tendering procedures means procedures where an entity contacts suppliers individually, only in the circumstances and under the conditions specified in Article 1016;

locally established supplier includes a natural person resident in the territory of the Party, an enterprise organized or established under the Party's law, and a branch or representative office located in the Party's territory;

open tendering procedures means those procedures under which all interested suppliers may submit a tender;

selective tendering procedures means procedures under which, consistent with Article 1011, those suppliers invited to do so by an entity may submit a tender;

services includes construction services contracts, unless otherwise specified;

standard means "standard", as defined in Article 915;

supplier means a person that has provided or could provide goods or services in response to an entity's call for tender;

technical regulation means "technical regulation", as defined in Article 915;

technical specification means a specification which lays down goods characteristics or their related processes and production methods, or services characteristics or their related operating methods, including the applicable administrative provisions. It may also include or deal exclusively with terminology, symbols, packaging, marking or labelling requirements as they apply to a good, process, or production or operating method; and

tendering procedures means open tendering procedures, selective tendering procedures and limited tendering procedures.

PART FIVE
INVESTMENT, SERVICES AND RELATED MATTERS
CHAPTER ELEVEN: INVESTMENT
Section A—Investment

Article 1101

Scope and Coverage

1. This Chapter applies to measures adopted or maintained by a Party relating to: (a) investors of another Party; (b) investments of investors of

another Party in the territory of the Party; and (c) with respect to Articles 1106 and 1114, all investments in the territory of the Party.

2. A Party has the right to perform exclusively the economic activities set out in Annex III and to refuse to permit the establishment of investment in such activities.

3. This Chapter does not apply to measures adopted or maintained by a Party to the extent that they are covered by Chapter Fourteen (Financial Services).

4. Nothing in this Chapter shall be construed to prevent a Party from providing a service or performing a function such as law enforcement, correctional services, income security or insurance, social security or insurance, social welfare, public education, public training, health, and child care, in a manner that is not inconsistent with this Chapter.

Article 1102

National Treatment

1. Each Party shall accord to investors of another Party treatment no less favorable than that it accords, in like circumstances, to its own investors with respect to the establishment, acquisition, expansion, management, conduct, operation, and sale or other disposition of investments.

2. Each Party shall accord to investments of investors of another Party treatment no less favorable than that it accords, in like circumstances, to investments of its own investors with respect to the establishment, acquisition, expansion, management, conduct, operation, and sale or other disposition of investments.

3. The treatment accorded by a Party under paragraphs 1 and 2 means, with respect to a state or province, treatment no less favorable than the most favorable treatment accorded, in like circumstances, by that state or province to investors, and to investments of investors, of the Party of which it forms a part.

4. For greater certainty, no Party may: (a) impose on an investor of another Party a requirement that a minimum level of equity in an enterprise in the territory of the Party be held by its nationals, other than nominal qualifying shares for directors or incorporators of corporations; or (b) require an investor of another Party, by reason of its nationality, to sell or otherwise dispose of an investment in the territory of the Party.

Article 1103

Most–Favored–Nation Treatment

1. Each Party shall accord to investors of another Party treatment no less favorable than that it accords, in like circumstances, to investors of any other Party or of a non-Party with respect to the establishment, acquisition, expansion, management, conduct, operation, and sale or other disposition of investments.

2. Each Party shall accord to investments of investors of another Party treatment no less favorable than that it accords, in like circumstances, to investments of investors of any other Party or of a non-Party with respect to

the establishment, acquisition, expansion, management, conduct, operation, and sale or other disposition of investments.

Article 1104
Standard of Treatment

Each Party shall accord to investors of another Party and to investments of investors of another Party the better of the treatment required by Articles 1102 and 1103.

Article 1105
Minimum Standard of Treatment

1. Each Party shall accord to investments of investors of another Party treatment in accordance with international law, including fair and equitable treatment and full protection and security.

2. Without prejudice to paragraph 1 and notwithstanding Article 1108(7)(b), each Party shall accord to investors of another Party, and to investments of investors of another Party, non-discriminatory treatment with respect to measures it adopts or maintains relating to losses suffered by investments in its territory owing to armed conflict or civil strife.

3. Paragraph 2 does not apply to existing measures relating to subsidies or grants that would be inconsistent with Article 1102 but for Article 1108(7)(b).

Article 1106
Performance Requirements

1. No Party may impose or enforce any of the following requirements, or enforce any commitment or undertaking, in connection with the establishment, acquisition, expansion, management, conduct or operation of an investment of an investor of a Party or of a non-Party in its territory: (a) to export a given level or percentage of goods or services; (b) to achieve a given level or percentage of domestic content; (c) to purchase, use or accord a preference to goods produced or services provided in its territory, or to purchase goods or services from persons in its territory; (d) to relate in any way the volume or value of imports to the volume or value of exports or to the amount of foreign exchange inflows associated with such investment; (e) to restrict sales of goods or services in its territory that such investment produces or provides by relating such sales in any way to the volume or value of its exports or foreign exchange earnings; (f) to transfer technology, a production process or other proprietary knowledge to a person in its territory, except when the requirement is imposed or the commitment or undertaking is enforced by a court, administrative tribunal or competition authority to remedy an alleged violation of competition laws or to act in a manner not inconsistent with other provisions of this Agreement; or (g) to act as the exclusive supplier of the goods it produces or services it provides to a specific region or world market.

2. A measure that requires an investment to use a technology to meet generally applicable health, safety or environmental requirements shall not be construed to be inconsistent with paragraph 1(f). For greater certainty, Articles 1102 and 1103 apply to the measure.

3. No Party may condition the receipt or continued receipt of an advantage, in connection with an investment in its territory of an investor of a Party or of a non-Party, on compliance with any of the following requirements: (a) to achieve a given level or percentage of domestic content; (b) to purchase, use or accord a preference to goods produced in its territory, or to purchase goods from producers in its territory; (c) to relate in any way the volume or value of imports to the volume or value of exports or to the amount of foreign exchange inflows associated with such investment; or (d) to restrict sales of goods or services in its territory that such investment produces or provides by relating such sales in any way to the volume or value of its exports or foreign exchange earnings.

4. Nothing in paragraph 3 shall be construed to prevent a Party from conditioning the receipt or continued receipt of an advantage, in connection with an investment in its territory of an investor of a Party or of a non-Party, on compliance with a requirement to locate production, provide a service, train or employ workers, construct or expand particular facilities, or carry out research and development, in its territory.

5. Paragraphs 1 and 3 do not apply to any requirement other than the requirements set out in those paragraphs.

6. Provided that such measures are not applied in an arbitrary or unjustifiable manner, or do not constitute a disguised restriction on international trade or investment, nothing in paragraph 1(b) or (c) or 3(a) or (b) shall be construed to prevent any Party from adopting or maintaining measures, including environmental measures: (a) necessary to secure compliance with laws and regulations that are not inconsistent with the provisions of this Agreement; (b) necessary to protect human, animal or plant life or health; or (c) necessary for the conservation of living or non-living exhaustible natural resources.

Article 1107

Senior Management and Boards of Directors

1. No Party may require that an enterprise of that Party that is an investment of an investor of another Party appoint to senior management positions individuals of any particular nationality.

2. A Party may require that a majority of the board of directors, or any committee thereof, of an enterprise of that Party that is an investment of an investor of another Party, be of a particular nationality, or resident in the territory of the Party, provided that the requirement does not materially impair the ability of the investor to exercise control over its investment.

Article 1108

Reservations and Exceptions

1. Articles 1102, 1103, 1106 and 1107 do not apply to: (a) any existing non-conforming measure that is maintained by (i) a Party at the federal level, as set out in its Schedule to Annex I or III, (ii) a state or province, for two years after the date of entry into force of this Agreement, and thereafter as set out by a Party in its Schedule to Annex I in accordance with paragraph 2, or (iii) a local government; (b) the continuation or prompt renewal of any

non-conforming measure referred to in subparagraph (a); or (c) an amendment to any non-conforming measure referred to in subparagraph (a) to the extent that the amendment does not decrease the conformity of the measure, as it existed immediately before the amendment, with Articles 1102, 1103, 1106 and 1107.

2. Each Party may set out in its Schedule to Annex I, within two years of the date of entry into force of this Agreement, any existing non-conforming measure maintained by a state or province, not including a local government.

3. Articles 1102, 1103, 1106 and 1107 do not apply to any measure that a Party adopts or maintains with respect to sectors, subsectors or activities, as set out in its Schedule to Annex II.

4. No Party may, under any measure adopted after the date of entry into force of this Agreement and covered by its Schedule to Annex II, require an investor of another Party, by reason of its nationality, to sell or otherwise dispose of an investment existing at the time the measure becomes effective.

5. Articles 1102 and 1103 do not apply to any measure that is an exception to, or derogation from, the obligations under Article 1703 (Intellectual Property—National Treatment) as specifically provided for in that Article.

6. Article 1103 does not apply to treatment accorded by a Party pursuant to agreements, or with respect to sectors, set out in its Schedule to Annex IV.

7. Articles 1102, 1103 and 1107 do not apply to: (a) procurement by a Party or a state enterprise; or (b) subsidies or grants provided by a Party or a state enterprise, including government-supported loans, guarantees and insurance.

8. The provisions of: (a) Article 1106(1)(a), (b) and (c), and (3)(a) and (b) do not apply to qualification requirements for goods or services with respect to export promotion and foreign aid programs; (b) Article 1106(1)(b), (c), (f) and (g), and (3)(a) and (b) do not apply to procurement by a Party or a state enterprise; and (c) Article 1106(3)(a) and (b) do not apply to requirements imposed by an importing Party relating to the content of goods necessary to qualify for preferential tariffs or preferential quotas.

Article 1109

Transfers

1. Each Party shall permit all transfers relating to an investment of an investor of another Party in the territory of the Party to be made freely and without delay. Such transfers include: (a) profits, dividends, interest, capital gains, royalty payments, management fees, technical assistance and other fees, returns in kind and other amounts derived from the investment; (b) proceeds from the sale of all or any part of the investment or from the partial or complete liquidation of the investment; (c) payments made under a contract entered into by the investor, or its investment, including payments made pursuant to a loan agreement; (d) payments made pursuant to Article 1110; and (e) payments arising under Section B.

2. Each Party shall permit transfers to be made in a freely usable currency at the market rate of exchange prevailing on the date of transfer with respect to spot transactions in the currency to be transferred.

3. No Party may require its investors to transfer, or penalize its investors that fail to transfer, the income, earnings, profits or other amounts derived from, or attributable to, investments in the territory of another Party.

4. Notwithstanding paragraphs 1 and 2, a Party may prevent a transfer through the equitable, non-discriminatory and good faith application of its laws relating to: (a) bankruptcy, insolvency or the protection of the rights of creditors; (b) issuing, trading or dealing in securities; (c) criminal or penal offenses; (d) reports of transfers of currency or other monetary instruments; or (e) ensuring the satisfaction of judgments in adjudicatory proceedings.

5. Paragraph 3 shall not be construed to prevent a Party from imposing any measure through the equitable, non-discriminatory and good faith application of its laws relating to the matters set out in subparagraphs (a) through (e) of paragraph 4.

6. Notwithstanding paragraph 1, a Party may restrict transfers of returns in kind in circumstances where it could otherwise restrict such transfers under this Agreement, including as set out in paragraph 4.

Article 1110

Expropriation and Compensation

1. No Party may directly or indirectly nationalize or expropriate an investment of an investor of another Party in its territory or take a measure tantamount to nationalization or expropriation of such an investment ("expropriation"), except: (a) for a public purpose; (b) on a non-discriminatory basis; (c) in accordance with due process of law and Article 1105(1); and (d) on payment of compensation in accordance with paragraphs 2 through 6.

2. Compensation shall be equivalent to the fair market value of the expropriated investment immediately before the expropriation took place ("date of expropriation"), and shall not reflect any change in value occurring because the intended expropriation had become known earlier. Valuation criteria shall include going concern value, asset value including declared tax value of tangible property, and other criteria, as appropriate, to determine fair market value.

3. Compensation shall be paid without delay and be fully realizable.

4. If payment is made in a G7 currency, compensation shall include interest at a commercially reasonable rate for that currency from the date of expropriation until the date of actual payment.

5. If a Party elects to pay in a currency other than a G7 currency, the amount paid on the date of payment, if converted into a G7 currency at the market rate of exchange prevailing on that date, shall be no less than if the amount of compensation owed on the date of expropriation had been converted into that G7 currency at the market rate of exchange prevailing on that date, and interest had accrued at a commercially reasonable rate for that G7 currency from the date of expropriation until the date of payment.

6. On payment, compensation shall be freely transferable as provided in Article 1109.

7. This Article does not apply to the issuance of compulsory licenses granted in relation to intellectual property rights, or to the revocation, limitation or creation of intellectual property rights, to the extent that such issuance, revocation, limitation or creation is consistent with Chapter Seventeen (Intellectual Property).

8. For purposes of this Article and for greater certainty, a non-discriminatory measure of general application shall not be considered a measure tantamount to an expropriation of a debt security or loan covered by this Chapter solely on the ground that the measure imposes costs on the debtor that cause it to default on the debt.

Article 1111
Special Formalities and Information Requirements

1. Nothing in Article 1102 shall be construed to prevent a Party from adopting or maintaining a measure that prescribes special formalities in connection with the establishment of investments by investors of another Party, such as a requirement that investors be residents of the Party or that investments be legally constituted under the laws or regulations of the Party, provided that such formalities do not materially impair the protections afforded by a Party to investors of another Party and investments of investors of another Party pursuant to this Chapter.

2. Notwithstanding Articles 1102 or 1103, a Party may require an investor of another Party, or its investment in its territory, to provide routine information concerning that investment solely for informational or statistical purposes. The Party shall protect such business information that is confidential from any disclosure that would prejudice the competitive position of the investor or the investment. Nothing in this paragraph shall be construed to prevent a Party from otherwise obtaining or disclosing information in connection with the equitable and good faith application of its law.

Article 1112
Relation to Other Chapters

1. In the event of any inconsistency between this Chapter and another Chapter, the other Chapter shall prevail to the extent of the inconsistency.

2. A requirement by a Party that a service provider of another Party post a bond or other form of financial security as a condition of providing a service into its territory does not of itself make this Chapter applicable to the provision of that cross-border service. This Chapter applies to that Party's treatment of the posted bond or financial security.

Article 1113
Denial of Benefits

1. A Party may deny the benefits of this Chapter to an investor of another Party that is an enterprise of such Party and to investments of such investor if investors of a non-Party own or control the enterprise and the denying Party: (a) does not maintain diplomatic relations with the non-Party;

or (b) adopts or maintains measures with respect to the non-Party that prohibit transactions with the enterprise or that would be violated or circumvented if the benefits of this Chapter were accorded to the enterprise or to its investments.

2. Subject to prior notification and consultation in accordance with Articles 1803 (Notification and Provision of Information) and 2006 (Consultations), a Party may deny the benefits of this Chapter to an investor of another Party that is an enterprise of such Party and to investments of such investors if investors of a non-Party own or control the enterprise and the enterprise has no substantial business activities in the territory of the Party under whose law it is constituted or organized.

Article 1114

Environmental Measures

1. Nothing in this Chapter shall be construed to prevent a Party from adopting, maintaining or enforcing any measure otherwise consistent with this Chapter that it considers appropriate to ensure that investment activity in its territory is undertaken in a manner sensitive to environmental concerns.

2. The Parties recognize that it is inappropriate to encourage investment by relaxing domestic health, safety or environmental measures. Accordingly, a Party should not waive or otherwise derogate from, or offer to waive or otherwise derogate from, such measures as an encouragement for the establishment, acquisition, expansion or retention in its territory of an investment of an investor. If a Party considers that another Party has offered such an encouragement, it may request consultations with the other Party and the two Parties shall consult with a view to avoiding any such encouragement.

Section B—Settlement of Disputes Between a Party and an Investor of Another Party

Article 1115

Purpose

Without prejudice to the rights and obligations of the Parties under Chapter Twenty (Institutional Arrangements and Dispute Settlement Procedures), this Section establishes a mechanism for the settlement of investment disputes that assures both equal treatment among investors of the Parties in accordance with the principle of international reciprocity and due process before an impartial tribunal.

Article 1116

Claim by an Investor of a Party on Its Own Behalf

1. An investor of a Party may submit to arbitration under this Section a claim that another Party has breached an obligation under: (a) Section A or Article 1503(2) (State Enterprises), or (b) Article 1502(3)(a) (Monopolies and State Enterprises) where the monopoly has acted in a manner inconsistent with the Party's obligations under Section A, and that the investor has incurred loss or damage by reason of, or arising out of, that breach.

2.   An investor may not make a claim if more than three years have elapsed from the date on which the investor first acquired, or should have first acquired, knowledge of the alleged breach and knowledge that the investor has incurred loss or damage.

Article 1117

Claim by an Investor of a Party on Behalf of an Enterprise

1.   An investor of a Party, on behalf of an enterprise of another Party that is a juridical person that the investor owns or controls directly or indirectly, may submit to arbitration under this Section a claim that the other Party has breached an obligation under: (a) Section A or Article 1503(2) (State Enterprises), or (b) Article 1502(3)(a) (Monopolies and State Enterprises) where the monopoly has acted in a manner inconsistent with the Party's obligations under Section A, and that the enterprise has incurred loss or damage by reason of, or arising out of, that breach.

2.   An investor may not make a claim on behalf of an enterprise described in paragraph 1 if more than three years have elapsed from the date on which the enterprise first acquired, or should have first acquired, knowledge of the alleged breach and knowledge that the enterprise has incurred loss or damage.

3.   Where an investor makes a claim under this Article and the investor or a non-controlling investor in the enterprise makes a claim under Article 1116 arising out of the same events that gave rise to the claim under this Article, and two or more of the claims are submitted to arbitration under Article 1120, the claims should be heard together by a Tribunal established under Article 1126, unless the Tribunal finds that the interests of a disputing party would be prejudiced thereby.

4.   An investment may not make a claim under this Section.

Article 1118

Settlement of a Claim Through Consultation and Negotiation

The disputing parties should first attempt to settle a claim through consultation or negotiation.

Article 1119

Notice of Intent to Submit a Claim to Arbitration

The disputing investor shall deliver to the disputing Party written notice of its intention to submit a claim to arbitration at least 90 days before the claim is submitted, which notice shall specify: (a) the name and address of the disputing investor and, where a claim is made under Article 1117, the name and address of the enterprise; (b) the provisions of this Agreement alleged to have been breached and any other relevant provisions; (c) the issues and the factual basis for the claim; and (d) the relief sought and the approximate amount of damages claimed.

Article 1120

Submission of a Claim to Arbitration

1.   Except as provided in Annex 1120.1, and provided that six months have elapsed since the events giving rise to a claim, a disputing investor may

submit the claim to arbitration under: (a) the ICSID Convention, provided that both the disputing Party and the Party of the investor are parties to the Convention; (b) the Additional Facility Rules of ICSID, provided that either the disputing Party or the Party of the investor, but not both, is a party to the ICSID Convention; or (c) the UNCITRAL Arbitration Rules.

2. The applicable arbitration rules shall govern the arbitration except to the extent modified by this Section.

Annex 1120.1

Submission of a Claim to Arbitration

Mexico

With respect to the submission of a claim to arbitration: (a) an investor of another Party may not allege that Mexico has breached an obligation under: (i) Section A or Article 1503(2) (State Enterprises), or (ii) Article 1502(3)(a) (Monopolies and State Enterprises) where the monopoly has acted in a manner inconsistent with the Party's obligations under Section A, both in an arbitration under this Section and in proceedings before a Mexican court or administrative tribunal; and (b) where an enterprise of Mexico that is a juridical person that an investor of another Party owns or controls directly or indirectly alleges in proceedings before a Mexican court or administrative tribunal that Mexico has breached an obligation under: (i) Section A or Article 1503(2) (State Enterprises), or (ii) Article 1502(3)(a) (Monopolies and State Enterprises) where the monopoly has acted in a manner inconsistent with the Party's obligations under Section A, the investor may not allege the breach in an arbitration under this Section.

Article 1121

Conditions Precedent to Submission of a Claim to Arbitration

1. A disputing investor may submit a claim under Article 1116 to arbitration only if: (a) the investor consents to arbitration in accordance with the procedures set out in this Agreement; and (b) the investor and, where the claim is for loss or damage to an interest in an enterprise of another Party that is a juridical person that the investor owns or controls directly or indirectly, the enterprise, waive their right to initiate or continue before any administrative tribunal or court under the law of any Party, or other dispute settlement procedures, any proceedings with respect to the measure of the disputing Party that is alleged to be a breach referred to in Article 1116, except for proceedings for injunctive, declaratory or other extraordinary relief, not involving the payment of damages, before an administrative tribunal or court under the law of the disputing Party.

2. A disputing investor may submit a claim under Article 1117 to arbitration only if both the investor and the enterprise: (a) consent to arbitration in accordance with the procedures set out in this Agreement; and (b) waive their right to initiate or continue before any administrative tribunal or court under the law of any Party, or other dispute settlement procedures, any proceedings with respect to the measure of the disputing Party that is alleged to be a breach referred to in Article 1117, except for proceedings for injunctive, declaratory or other extraordinary relief, not involving the pay-

ment of damages, before an administrative tribunal or court under the law of the disputing Party.

3. A consent and waiver required by this Article shall be in writing, shall be delivered to the disputing Party and shall be included in the submission of a claim to arbitration.

4. Only where a disputing Party has deprived a disputing investor of control of an enterprise: (a) a waiver from the enterprise under paragraph 1(b) or 2(b) shall not be required; and (b) Annex 1120.1(b) shall not apply.

Article 1122

Consent to Arbitration

1. Each Party consents to the submission of a claim to arbitration in accordance with the procedures set out in this Agreement.

2. The consent given by paragraph 1 and the submission by a disputing investor of a claim to arbitration shall satisfy the requirement of: (a) Chapter II of the ICSID Convention (Jurisdiction of the Centre) and the Additional Facility Rules for written consent of the parties; (b) Article II of the New York Convention for an agreement in writing; and (c) Article I of the Inter–American Convention for an agreement.

Article 1123

Number of Arbitrators and Method of Appointment

Except in respect of a Tribunal established under Article 1126, and unless the disputing parties otherwise agree, the Tribunal shall comprise three arbitrators, one arbitrator appointed by each of the disputing parties and the third, who shall be the presiding arbitrator, appointed by agreement of the disputing parties.

Article 1124

Constitution of a Tribunal When a Party Fails to Appoint an Arbitrator or the Disputing Parties Are Unable to Agree on a Presiding Arbitrator

1. The Secretary–General shall serve as appointing authority for an arbitration under this Section.

2. If a Tribunal, other than a Tribunal established under Article 1126, has not been constituted within 90 days from the date that a claim is submitted to arbitration, the Secretary–General, on the request of either disputing party, shall appoint, in his discretion, the arbitrator or arbitrators not yet appointed, except that the presiding arbitrator shall be appointed in accordance with paragraph 3.

3. The Secretary–General shall appoint the presiding arbitrator from the roster of presiding arbitrators referred to in paragraph 4, provided that the presiding arbitrator shall not be a national of the disputing Party or a national of the Party of the disputing investor. In the event that no such presiding arbitrator is available to serve, the Secretary–General shall appoint, from the ICSID Panel of Arbitrators, a presiding arbitrator who is not a national of any of the Parties.

4.   On the date of entry into force of this Agreement, the Parties shall establish, and thereafter maintain, a roster of 45 presiding arbitrators meeting the qualifications of the Convention and rules referred to in Article 1120 and experienced in international law and investment matters. The roster members shall be appointed by consensus and without regard to nationality.

Article 1125

Agreement to Appointment of Arbitrators

For purposes of Article 39 of the ICSID Convention and Article 7 of Schedule C to the ICSID Additional Facility Rules, and without prejudice to an objection to an arbitrator based on Article 1124(3) or on a ground other than nationality: (a) the disputing Party agrees to the appointment of each individual member of a Tribunal established under the ICSID Convention or the ICSID Additional Facility Rules; (b) a disputing investor referred to in Article 1116 may submit a claim to arbitration, or continue a claim, under the ICSID Convention or the ICSID Additional Facility Rules, only on condition that the disputing investor agrees in writing to the appointment of each individual member of the Tribunal; and (c) a disputing investor referred to in Article 1117(1) may submit a claim to arbitration, or continue a claim, under the ICSID Convention or the ICSID Additional Facility Rules, only on condition that the disputing investor and the enterprise agree in writing to the appointment of each individual member of the Tribunal.

Article 1126

Consolidation

1.   A Tribunal established under this Article shall be established under the UNCITRAL Arbitration Rules and shall conduct its proceedings in accordance with those Rules, except as modified by this Section.

2.   Where a Tribunal established under this Article is satisfied that claims have been submitted to arbitration under Article 1120 that have a question of law or fact in common, the Tribunal may, in the interests of fair and efficient resolution of the claims, and after hearing the disputing parties, by order: (a) assume jurisdiction over, and hear and determine together, all or part of the claims; or (b) assume jurisdiction over, and hear and determine one or more of the claims, the determination of which it believes would assist in the resolution of the others.

3.   A disputing party that seeks an order under paragraph 2 shall request the Secretary–General to establish a Tribunal and shall specify in the request: (a) the name of the disputing Party or disputing investors against which the order is sought; (b) the nature of the order sought; and (c) the grounds on which the order is sought.

4.   The disputing party shall deliver to the disputing Party or disputing investors against which the order is sought a copy of the request.

5.   Within 60 days of receipt of the request, the Secretary–General shall establish a Tribunal comprising three arbitrators. The Secretary–General shall appoint the presiding arbitrator from the roster referred to in Article 1124(4). In the event that no such presiding arbitrator is available to serve, the Secretary–General shall appoint, from the ICSID Panel of Arbitrators, a

presiding arbitrator who is not a national of any of the Parties. The Secretary–General shall appoint the two other members from the roster referred to in Article 1124(4), and to the extent not available from that roster, from the ICSID Panel of Arbitrators, and to the extent not available from that Panel, in the discretion of the Secretary–General. One member shall be a national of the disputing Party and one member shall be a national of a Party of the disputing investors.

6. Where a Tribunal has been established under this Article, a disputing investor that has submitted a claim to arbitration under Article 1116 or 1117 and that has not been named in a request made under paragraph 3 may make a written request to the Tribunal that it be included in an order made under paragraph 2, and shall specify in the request: (a) the name and address of the disputing investor; (b) the nature of the order sought; and (c) the grounds on which the order is sought.

7. A disputing investor referred to in paragraph 6 shall deliver a copy of its request to the disputing parties named in a request made under paragraph 3.

8. A Tribunal established under Article 1120 shall not have jurisdiction to decide a claim, or a part of a claim, over which a Tribunal established under this Article has assumed jurisdiction.

9. On application of a disputing party, a Tribunal established under this Article, pending its decision under paragraph 2, may order that the proceedings of a Tribunal established under Article 1120 be stayed, unless the latter Tribunal has already adjourned its proceedings.

10. A disputing Party shall deliver to the Secretariat, within 15 days of receipt by the disputing Party, a copy of: (a) a request for arbitration made under paragraph (1) of Article 36 of the ICSID Convention; (b) a notice of arbitration made under Article 2 of Schedule C of the ICSID Additional Facility Rules; or (c) a notice of arbitration given under the UNCITRAL Arbitration Rules.

11. A disputing Party shall deliver to the Secretariat a copy of a request made under paragraph 3: (a) within 15 days of receipt of the request, in the case of a request made by a disputing investor; (b) within 15 days of making the request, in the case of a request made by the disputing Party.

12. A disputing Party shall deliver to the Secretariat a copy of a request made under paragraph 6 within 15 days of receipt of the request.

13. The Secretariat shall maintain a public register of the documents referred to in paragraphs 10, 11 and 12.

Article 1127

Notice

A disputing Party shall deliver to the other Parties: (a) written notice of a claim that has been submitted to arbitration no later than 30 days after the date that the claim is submitted; and (b) copies of all pleadings filed in the arbitration.

Article 1128
Participation by a Party

On written notice to the disputing parties, a Party may make submissions to a Tribunal on a question of interpretation of this Agreement.

Article 1129
Documents

1.   A Party shall be entitled to receive from the disputing Party, at the cost of the requesting Party a copy of: (a) the evidence that has been tendered to the Tribunal; and (b) the written argument of the disputing parties.

2.   A Party receiving information pursuant to paragraph 1 shall treat the information as if it were a disputing Party.

Article 1130
Place of Arbitration

Unless the disputing parties agree otherwise, a Tribunal shall hold an arbitration in the territory of a Party that is a party to the New York Convention, selected in accordance with: (a) the ICSID Additional Facility Rules if the arbitration is under those Rules or the ICSID Convention; or (b) the UNCITRAL Arbitration Rules if the arbitration is under those Rules.

Article 1131
Governing Law

1.   A Tribunal established under this Section shall decide the issues in dispute in accordance with this Agreement and applicable rules of international law.

2.   An interpretation by the Commission of a provision of this Agreement shall be binding on a Tribunal established under this Section.

Article 1132
Interpretation of Annexes

1.   Where a disputing Party asserts as a defense that the measure alleged to be a breach is within the scope of a reservation or exception set out in Annex I, Annex II, Annex III or Annex IV, on request of the disputing Party, the Tribunal shall request the interpretation of the Commission on the issue. The Commission, within 60 days of delivery of the request, shall submit in writing its interpretation to the Tribunal.

2.   Further to Article 1131(2), a Commission interpretation submitted under paragraph 1 shall be binding on the Tribunal. If the Commission fails to submit an interpretation within 60 days, the Tribunal shall decide the issue.

Article 1133
Expert Reports

Without prejudice to the appointment of other kinds of experts where authorized by the applicable arbitration rules, a Tribunal, at the request of a disputing party or, unless the disputing parties disapprove, on its own initiative, may appoint one or more experts to report to it in writing on any factual issue concerning environmental, health, safety or other scientific matters raised by a disputing party in a proceeding, subject to such terms and conditions as the disputing parties may agree.

Article 1134
Interim Measures of Protection

A Tribunal may order an interim measure of protection to preserve the rights of a disputing party, or to ensure that the Tribunal's jurisdiction is made fully effective, including an order to preserve evidence in the possession or control of a disputing party or to protect the Tribunal's jurisdiction. A Tribunal may not order attachment or enjoin the application of the measure alleged to constitute a breach referred to in Article 1116 or 1117. For purposes of this paragraph, an order includes a recommendation.

Article 1135
Final Award

1. Where a Tribunal makes a final award against a Party, the Tribunal may award, separately or in combination, only: (a) monetary damages and any applicable interest; (b) restitution of property, in which case the award shall provide that the disputing Party may pay monetary damages and any applicable interest in lieu of restitution.

A tribunal may also award costs in accordance with the applicable arbitration rules.

2. Subject to paragraph 1, where a claim is made under Article 1117(1): (a) an award of restitution of property shall provide that restitution be made to the enterprise; (b) an award of monetary damages and any applicable interest shall provide that the sum be paid to the enterprise; and (c) the award shall provide that it is made without prejudice to any right that any person may have in the relief under applicable domestic law.

3. A Tribunal may not order a Party to pay punitive damages.

Article 1136
Finality and Enforcement of an Award

1. An award made by a Tribunal shall have no binding force except between the disputing parties and in respect of the particular case.

2. Subject to paragraph 3 and the applicable review procedure for an interim award, a disputing party shall abide by and comply with an award without delay.

3. A disputing party may not seek enforcement of a final award until: (a) in the case of a final award made under the ICSID Convention (i) 120 days have elapsed from the date the award was rendered and no disputing party has requested revision or annulment of the award, or (ii) revision or annulment proceedings have been completed; and (b) in the case of a final award under the ICSID Additional Facility Rules or the UNCITRAL Arbitration Rules (i) three months have elapsed from the date the award was rendered and no disputing party has commenced a proceeding to revise, set aside or

annul the award, or (ii) a court has dismissed or allowed an application to revise, set aside or annul the award and there is no further appeal.

4. Each Party shall provide for the enforcement of an award in its territory.

5. If a disputing Party fails to abide by or comply with a final award, the Commission, on delivery of a request by a Party whose investor was a party to the arbitration, shall establish a panel under Article 2008 (Request for an Arbitral Panel). The requesting Party may seek in such proceedings: (a) a determination that the failure to abide by or comply with the final award is inconsistent with the obligations of this Agreement; and (b) a recommendation that the Party abide by or comply with the final award.

6. A disputing investor may seek enforcement of an arbitration award under the ICSID Convention, the New York Convention or the Inter–American Convention regardless of whether proceedings have been taken under paragraph 5.

7. A claim that is submitted to arbitration under this Section shall be considered to arise out of a commercial relationship or transaction for purposes of Article I of the New York Convention and Article I of the Inter–American Convention.

Article 1137

General

Time When a Claim Is Submitted to Arbitration

1. A claim is submitted to arbitration under this Section when: (a) the request for arbitration under paragraph (1) of Article 36 of the ICSID Convention has been received by the Secretary–General; (b) the notice of arbitration under Article 2 of Schedule C of the ICSID Additional Facility Rules has been received by the Secretary–General; or (c) the notice of arbitration given under the UNCITRAL Arbitration Rules is received by the disputing Party.

Service of Documents

2. Delivery of notice and other documents on a Party shall be made to the place named for that Party in Annex 1137.2.

Receipts Under Insurance or Guarantee Contracts

3. In an arbitration under this Section, a Party shall not assert, as a defense, counterclaim, right of setoff or otherwise, that the disputing investor has received or will receive, pursuant to an insurance or guarantee contract, indemnification or other compensation for all or part of its alleged damages.

Publication of an Award

4. Annex 1137.4 applies to the Parties specified in that Annex with respect to publication of an award.

Annex 1137.2

Service of Documents on a Party Under Section B

Each Party shall set out in this Annex and publish in its official journal by January 1, 1994, the place for delivery of notice and other documents under this Section.

Annex 1137.4

Publication of an Award

Canada

Where Canada is the disputing Party, either Canada or a disputing investor that is a party to the arbitration may make an award public.

Mexico

Where Mexico is the disputing Party, the applicable arbitration rules apply to the publication of an award.

United States

Where the United States is the disputing Party, either the United States or a disputing investor that is a party to the arbitration may make an award public.

Article 1138

Exclusions

1. Without prejudice to the applicability or non-applicability of the dispute settlement provisions of this Section or of Chapter Twenty (Institutional Arrangements and Dispute Settlement Procedures) to other actions taken by a Party pursuant to Article 2102 (National Security), a decision by a Party to prohibit or restrict the acquisition of an investment in its territory by an investor of another Party, or its investment, pursuant to that Article shall not be subject to such provisions.

2. The dispute settlement provisions of this Section and of Chapter Twenty shall not apply to the matters referred to in Annex 1138.2.

Annex 1138.2

Exclusions From Dispute Settlement

Canada

A decision by Canada following a review under the Investment Canada Act, with respect to whether or not to permit an acquisition that is subject to review, shall not be subject to the dispute settlement provisions of Section B or of Chapter Twenty (Institutional Arrangements and Dispute Settlement Procedures).

Mexico

A decision by the National Commission on Foreign Investment ("Comision Nacional de Inversiones Extranjeras") following a review pursuant to Annex I, page I–M–4, with respect to whether or not to permit an acquisition that is subject to review, shall not be subject to the dispute settlement provisions of Section B or of Chapter Twenty.

Section C—Definitions

Article 1139

Definitions

For purposes of this Chapter:

disputing investor means an investor that makes a claim under Section B;

disputing parties means the disputing investor and the disputing Party;

disputing party means the disputing investor or the disputing Party;

disputing Party means a Party against which a claim is made under Section B;

enterprise means an "enterprise" as defined in Article 201 (Definitions of General Application), and a branch of an enterprise;

enterprise of a Party means an enterprise constituted or organized under the law of a Party, and a branch located in the territory of a Party and carrying out business activities there.

equity or debt securities includes voting and non-voting shares, bonds, convertible debentures, stock options and warrants;

G7 Currency means the currency of Canada, France, Germany, Italy, Japan, the United Kingdom of Great Britain and Northern Ireland or the United States;

ICSID means the International Centre for Settlement of Investment Disputes;

ICSID Convention means the Convention on the Settlement of Investment Disputes between States and Nationals of other States, done at Washington, March 18, 1965;

Inter–American Convention means the Inter–American Convention on International Commercial Arbitration, done at Panama, January 30, 1975;

investment means: (a) an enterprise; (b) an equity security of an enterprise; (c) a debt security of an enterprise (i) where the enterprise is an affiliate of the investor, or (ii) where the original maturity of the debt security is at least three years, but does not include a debt security, regardless of original maturity, of a state enterprise; (d) a loan to an enterprise (i) where the enterprise is an affiliate of the investor, or (ii) where the original maturity of the loan is at least three years, but does not include a loan, regardless of original maturity, to a state enterprise; (e) an interest in an enterprise that entitles the owner to share in income or profits of the enterprise; (f) an interest in an enterprise that entitles the owner to share in the assets of that enterprise on dissolution, other than a debt security or a loan excluded from subparagraph (c) or (d); (g) real estate or other property, tangible or intangible, acquired in the expectation or used for the purpose of economic benefit or other business purposes; and (h) interests arising from the commitment of capital or other resources in the territory of a Party to economic activity in such territory, such as under (i) contracts involving the presence of an investor's property in the territory of the Party, including turnkey or construction contracts, or concessions, or (ii) contracts where remuneration depends substantially on the production, revenues or profits of an enterprise; but investment does not mean, (i) claims to money that arise solely from (i) commercial contracts for the sale of goods or services by a national or enterprise in the territory of a Party to an enterprise in the territory of another Party, or (ii) the extension of credit in connection with a commercial transaction, such as trade financing, other than a loan covered by subparagraph (d); or (j) any other claims to money, that do not involve the kinds of interests set out in subparagraphs (a) through (h);

investment of an investor of a Party means an investment owned or controlled directly or indirectly by an investor of such Party;

investor of a Party means a Party or state enterprise thereof, or a national or an enterprise of such Party, that seeks to make, is making or has made an investment;

investor of a non-Party means an investor other than an investor of a Party, that seeks to make, is making or has made an investment;

New York Convention means the United Nations Convention on the Recognition and Enforcement of Foreign Arbitral Awards, done at New York, June 10, 1958;

Secretary–General means the Secretary–General of ICSID;

transfers means transfers and international payments;

Tribunal means an arbitration tribunal established under Article 1120 or 1126; and

UNCITRAL Arbitration Rules means the arbitration rules of the United Nations Commission on International Trade Law, approved by the United Nations General Assembly on December 15, 1976.

CHAPTER TWELVE: CROSS–BORDER TRADE IN SERVICES
Article 1201
Scope and Coverage

1. This Chapter applies to measures adopted or maintained by a Party relating to cross-border trade in services by service providers of another Party, including measures respecting: (a) the production, distribution, marketing, sale and delivery of a service; (b) the purchase or use of, or payment for, a service; (c) the access to and use of distribution and transportation systems in connection with the provision of a service; (d) the presence in its territory of a service provider of another Party; and (e) the provision of a bond or other form of financial security as a condition for the provision of a service.

2. This Chapter does not apply to: (a) financial services, as defined in Chapter Fourteen (Financial Services); (b) air services, including domestic and international air transportation services, whether scheduled or non-scheduled, and related services in support of air services, other than (i) aircraft repair and maintenance services during which an aircraft is withdrawn from service, and (ii) specialty air services; (c) procurement by a Party or a state enterprise; or (d) subsidies or grants provided by a Party or a state enterprise, including government-supported loans, guarantees and insurance.

3. Nothing in this Chapter shall be construed to: (a) impose any obligation on a Party with respect to a national of another Party seeking access to its employment market, or employed on a permanent basis in its territory, or to confer any right on that national with respect to that access or employment; or (b) prevent a Party from providing a service or performing a function such as law enforcement, correctional services, income security or insurance, social security or insurance, social welfare, public education, public

training, health, and child care, in a manner that is not inconsistent with this Chapter.

Article 1202

National Treatment

1.   Each Party shall accord to service providers of another Party treatment no less favorable than that it accords, in like circumstances, to its own service providers.

2.   The treatment accorded by a Party under paragraph 1 means, with respect to a state or province, treatment no less favorable than the most favorable treatment accorded, in like circumstances, by that state or province to service providers of the Party of which it forms a part.

Article 1203

Most–Favored–Nation Treatment

Each Party shall accord to service providers of another Party treatment no less favorable than that it accords, in like circumstances, to service providers of any other Party or of a non-Party.

Article 1204

Standard of Treatment

Each Party shall accord to service providers of any other Party the better of the treatment required by Articles 1202 and 1203.

Article 1205

Local Presence

No Party may require a service provider of another Party to establish or maintain a representative office or any form of enterprise, or to be resident, in its territory as a condition for the cross-border provision of a service.

Article 1206

Reservations

1.   Articles 1202, 1203 and 1205 do not apply to: (a) any existing non-conforming measure that is maintained by (i) a Party at the federal level, as set out in its Schedule to Annex I, (ii) a state or province, for two years after the date of entry into force of this Agreement, and thereafter as set out by a Party in its Schedule to Annex I in accordance with paragraph 2, or (iii) a local government; (b) the continuation or prompt renewal of any non-conforming measure referred to in subparagraph (a); or (c) an amendment to any non-conforming measure referred to in subparagraph (a) to the extent that the amendment does not decrease the conformity of the measure, as it existed immediately before the amendment, with Articles 1202, 1203 and 1205.

2.   Each Party may set out in its Schedule to Annex I, within two years of the date of entry into force of this Agreement, any existing non-conforming measure maintained by a state or province, not including a local government.

3.   Articles 1202, 1203 and 1205 do not apply to any measure that a Party adopts or maintains with respect to sectors, subsectors or activities, as set out in its Schedule to Annex II.

Article 1207
Quantitative Restrictions

1.   Each Party shall set out in its Schedule to Annex V any quantitative restriction that it maintains at the federal level.

2.   Within one year of the date of entry into force of this Agreement, each Party shall set out in its Schedule to Annex V any quantitative restriction maintained by a state or province, not including a local government.

3.   Each Party shall notify the other Parties of any quantitative restriction that it adopts, other than at the local government level, after the date of entry into force of this Agreement and shall set out the restriction in its Schedule to Annex V.

4.   The Parties shall periodically, but in any event at least every two years, endeavor to negotiate the liberalization or removal of the quantitative restrictions set out in Annex V pursuant to paragraphs 1 through 3.

Article 1208
Liberalization of Non-discriminatory Measures

Each Party shall set out in its Schedule to Annex VI its commitments to liberalize quantitative restrictions, licensing requirements, performance requirements or other non-discriminatory measures.

Article 1209
Procedures

The Commission shall establish procedures for: (a) a Party to notify and include in its relevant Schedule (i) state or provincial measures in accordance with Article 1206(2), (ii) quantitative restrictions in accordance with Article 1207(2) and (3), (iii) commitments pursuant to Article 1208, and (iv) amendments of measures referred to in Article 1206(1)(c); and (b) consultations on reservations, quantitative restrictions or commitments with a view to further liberalization.

Article 1210
Licensing and Certification

1.   With a view to ensuring that any measure adopted or maintained by a Party relating to the licensing or certification of nationals of another Party does not constitute an unnecessary barrier to trade, each Party shall endeavor to ensure that any such measure: (a) is based on objective and transparent criteria, such as competence and the ability to provide a service; (b) is not more burdensome than necessary to ensure the quality of a service; and (c) does not constitute a disguised restriction on the cross-border provision of a service.

2.   Where a Party recognizes, unilaterally or by agreement, education, experience, licenses or certifications obtained in the territory of another Party or of a non-Party: (a) nothing in Article 1203 shall be construed to require

the Party to accord such recognition to education, experience, licenses or certifications obtained in the territory of another Party; and (b) the Party shall afford another Party an adequate opportunity to demonstrate that education, experience, licenses or certifications obtained in that other Party's territory should also be recognized or to conclude an agreement or arrangement of comparable effect.

3. Each Party shall, within two years of the date of entry into force of this Agreement, eliminate any citizenship or permanent residency requirement set out in its Schedule to Annex I that it maintains for the licensing or certification of professional service providers of another Party. Where a Party does not comply with this obligation with respect to a particular sector, any other Party may, in the same sector and for such period as the non-complying Party maintains its requirement, solely have recourse to maintaining an equivalent requirement set out in its Schedule to Annex I or reinstating: (a) any such requirement at the federal level that it eliminated pursuant to this Article; or (b) on notification to the non-complying Party, any such requirement at the state or provincial level existing on the date of entry into force of this Agreement.

4. The Parties shall consult periodically with a view to determining the feasibility of removing any remaining citizenship or permanent residency requirement for the licensing or certification of each other's service providers.

5. Annex 1210.5 applies to measures adopted or maintained by a Party relating to the licensing or certification of professional service providers.

Annex 1210.5

Professional Services

Section A—General Provisions

Processing of Applications for Licenses and Certifications

1. Each Party shall ensure that its competent authorities, within a reasonable time after the submission by a national of another Party of an application for a license or certification: (a) where the application is complete, make a determination on the application and inform the applicant of that determination; or (b) where the application is not complete, inform the applicant without undue delay of the status of the application and the additional information that is required under the Party's law.

Development of Professional Standards

2. The Parties shall encourage the relevant bodies in their respective territories to develop mutually acceptable standards and criteria for licensing and certification of professional service providers and to provide recommendations on mutual recognition to the Commission.

3. The standards and criteria referred to in paragraph 2 may be developed with regard to the following matters: (a) education—accreditation of schools or academic programs; (b) examinations—qualifying examinations for licensing, including alternative methods of assessment such as oral examinations and interviews; (c) experience—length and nature of experience required for licensing; (d) conduct and ethics—standards of professional conduct and the nature of disciplinary action for non-conformity with those

standards; (e) professional development and re-certification—continuing education and ongoing requirements to maintain professional certification; (f) scope of practice—extent of, or limitations on, permissible activities; (g) local knowledge—requirements for knowledge of such matters as local laws, regulations, language, geography or climate; and (h) consumer protection—alternatives to residency requirements, including bonding, professional liability insurance and client restitution funds, to provide for the protection of consumers.

4. On receipt of a recommendation referred to in paragraph 2, the Commission shall review the recommendation within a reasonable time to determine whether it is consistent with this Agreement.   Based on the Commission's review, each Party shall encourage its respective competent authorities, where appropriate, to implement the recommendation within a mutually agreed time.

Temporary Licensing

5. Where the Parties agree, each Party shall encourage the relevant bodies in its territory to develop procedures for the temporary licensing of professional service providers of another Party.

Review

6. The Commission shall periodically, and at least once every three years, review the implementation of this Section.

Section B—Foreign Legal Consultants

1. Each Party shall, in implementing its obligations and commitments regarding foreign legal consultants as set out in its relevant Schedules and subject to any reservations therein, ensure that a national of another Party is permitted to practice or advise on the law of any country in which that national is authorized to practice as a lawyer.

Consultations With Professional Bodies

2. Each Party shall consult with its relevant professional bodies to obtain their recommendations on: (a) the form of association or partnership between lawyers authorized to practice in its territory and foreign legal consultants; (b) the development of standards and criteria for the authorization of foreign legal consultants in conformity with Article 1210; and (c) other matters relating to the provision of foreign legal consultancy services.

3. Prior to initiation of consultations under paragraph 7, each Party shall encourage its relevant professional bodies to consult with the relevant professional bodies designated by each of the other Parties regarding the development of joint recommendations on the matters referred to in paragraph 2.

Future Liberalization

4. Each Party shall establish a work program to develop common procedures throughout its territory for the authorization of foreign legal consultants.

5. Each Party shall promptly review any recommendation referred to in paragraphs 2 and 3 to ensure its consistency with this Agreement. If the recommendation is consistent with this Agreement, each Party shall encourage its competent authorities to implement the recommendation within one year.

6. Each Party shall report to the Commission within one year of the date of entry into force of this Agreement, and each year thereafter, on its progress in implementing the work program referred to in paragraph 4.

7. The Parties shall meet within one year of the date of entry into force of this Agreement with a view to: (a) assessing the implementation of paragraphs 2 through 5; (b) amending or removing, where appropriate, reservations on foreign legal consultancy services; and (c) assessing further work that may be appropriate regarding foreign legal consultancy services.

Section C—Temporary Licensing of Engineers

1. The Parties shall meet within one year of the date of entry into force of this Agreement to establish a work program to be undertaken by each Party, in conjunction with its relevant professional bodies, to provide for the temporary licensing in its territory of nationals of another Party who are licensed as engineers in the territory of that other Party.

2. To this end, each Party shall consult with its relevant professional bodies to obtain their recommendations on: (a) the development of procedures for the temporary licensing of such engineers to permit them to practice their engineering specialties in each jurisdiction in its territory; (b) the development of model procedures for adoption by the competent authorities throughout its territory to facilitate the temporary licensing of such engineers; (c) the engineering specialties to which priority should be given in developing temporary licensing procedures; and (d) other matters relating to the temporary licensing of engineers identified by the Party in such consultations.

3. Each Party shall request its relevant professional bodies to make recommendations on the matters referred to in paragraph 2 within two years of the date of entry into force of this Agreement.

4. Each Party shall encourage its relevant professional bodies to meet at the earliest opportunity with the relevant professional bodies of the other Parties with a view to cooperating in the development of joint recommendations on the matters referred to in paragraph 2 within two years of the date of entry into force of this Agreement. Each Party shall request an annual report from its relevant professional bodies on the progress achieved in developing those recommendations.

5. The Parties shall promptly review any recommendation referred to in paragraph 3 or 4 to ensure its consistency with this Agreement. If the recommendation is consistent with this Agreement, each Party shall encourage its competent authorities to implement the recommendation within one year.

6. The Commission shall review the implementation of this Section within two years of the date of entry into force of this Section.

7. Appendix 1210.5–C applies to the Parties specified therein.

Appendix 1210.5–C
Civil Engineers

The rights and obligations of Section C of Annex 1210.5 apply to Mexico with respect to civil engineers ("ingenieros civiles") and to such other engineering specialties that Mexico may designate.

Article 1211
Denial of Benefits

1. A Party may deny the benefits of this Chapter to a service provider of another Party where the Party establishes that: (a) the service is being provided by an enterprise owned or controlled by nationals of a non-Party, and (i) the denying Party does not maintain diplomatic relations with the non-Party, or (ii) the denying Party adopts or maintains measures with respect to the non-Party that prohibit transactions with the enterprise or that would be violated or circumvented if the benefits of this Chapter were accorded to the enterprise; or (b) the cross-border provision of a transportation service covered by this Chapter is provided using equipment not registered by any Party.

2. Subject to prior notification and consultation in accordance with Articles 1803 (Notification and Provision of Information) and 2006 (Consultations), a Party may deny the benefits of this Chapter to a service provider of another Party where the Party establishes that the service is being provided by an enterprise that is owned or controlled by persons of a non-Party and that has no substantial business activities in the territory of any Party.

Article 1212
Sectoral Annex

Annex 1212 applies to specific sectors.

Annex 1212
Land Transportation

Contact Points

1. Further to Article 1801 (Contact Points), each Party shall designate by January 1, 1994 contact points to provide information published by that Party relating to land transportation services regarding operating authority, safety requirements, taxation, data, studies and technology, and to provide assistance in contacting its relevant government agencies.

Review Process

2. The Commission shall, during the fifth year after the date of entry into force of this Agreement and during every second year thereafter until the liberalization for bus and truck transportation set out in the Parties' Schedules to Annex I is complete, receive and consider a report from the Parties that assesses progress respecting liberalization, including: (a) the effectiveness of the liberalization; (b) specific problems for, or unanticipated effects on, each Party's bus and truck transportation industries arising from liberalization; and (c) modifications to the period for liberalization. The Commis-

sion shall endeavor to resolve any matter arising from its consideration of a report.

3.   The Parties shall consult, no later than seven years after the date of entry into force of this Agreement, to consider further liberalization commitments.

Article 1213
Definitions

1.   For purposes of this Chapter, a reference to a federal, state or provincial government includes any non-governmental body in the exercise of any regulatory, administrative or other governmental authority delegated to it by that government.

2.   For purposes of this Chapter:

cross-border provision of a service or cross-border trade in services means the provision of a service: (a) from the territory of a Party into the territory of another Party, (b) in the territory of a Party by a person of that Party to a person of another Party, or (c) by a national of a Party in the territory of another Party, but does not include the provision of a service in the territory of a Party by an investment, as defined in Article 1139 (Investment—Definitions), in that territory;

enterprise means an "enterprise" as defined in Article 201 (Definitions of General Application), and a branch of an enterprise;

enterprise of a Party means an enterprise constituted or organized under the law of a Party, and a branch located in the territory of a Party and carrying out business activities there;

professional services means services, the provision of which requires specialized post-secondary education, or equivalent training or experience, and for which the right to practice is granted or restricted by a Party, but does not include services provided by trades-persons or vessel and aircraft crew members;

quantitative restriction means a non-discriminatory measure that imposes limitations on: (a) the number of service providers, whether in the form of a quota, a monopoly or an economic needs test, or by any other quantitative means; or (b) the operations of any service provider, whether in the form of a quota or an economic needs test, or by any other quantitative means;

service provider of a Party means a person of a Party that seeks to provide or provides a service; and

specialty air services means aerial mapping, aerial surveying, aerial photography, forest fire management, fire fighting, aerial advertising, glider towing, parachute jumping, aerial construction, heli-logging, aerial sightseeing, flight training, aerial inspection and surveillance, and aerial spraying services.

CHAPTER THIRTEEN: TELECOMMUNICATIONS
Article 1301
Scope and Coverage

1.   This Chapter applies to: (a) measures adopted or maintained by a Party relating to access to and use of public telecommunications transport

networks or services by persons of another Party, including access and use by such persons operating private networks; (b) measures adopted or maintained by a Party relating to the provision of enhanced or value-added services by persons of another Party in the territory, or across the borders, of a Party; and (c) standards-related measures relating to attachment of terminal or other equipment to public telecommunications transport networks.

2.   Except to ensure that persons operating broadcast stations and cable systems have continued access to and use of public telecommunications transport networks and services, this Chapter does not apply to any measure adopted or maintained by a Party relating to broadcast or cable distribution of radio or television programming.

3.   Nothing in this Chapter shall be construed to: (a) require a Party to authorize a person of another Party to establish, construct, acquire, lease, operate or provide telecommunications transport networks or telecommunications transport services; (b) require a Party, or require a Party to compel any person, to establish, construct, acquire, lease, operate or provide telecommunications transport networks or telecommunications transport services not offered to the public generally; (c) prevent a Party from prohibiting persons operating private networks from using their networks to provide public telecommunications transport networks or services to third persons; or (d) require a Party to compel any person engaged in the broadcast or cable distribution of radio or television programming to make available its cable or broadcast facilities as a public telecommunications transport network.

Article 1302
Access to and Use of Public Telecommunications Transport Networks and Services

1.   Each Party shall ensure that persons of another Party have access to and use of any public telecommunications transport network or service, including private leased circuits, offered in its territory or across its borders for the conduct of their business, on reasonable and non-discriminatory terms and conditions, including as set out in paragraphs 2 through 8.

2.   Subject to paragraphs 6 and 7, each Party shall ensure that such persons are permitted to: (a) purchase or lease, and attach terminal or other equipment that interfaces with the public telecommunications transport network; (b) interconnect private leased or owned circuits with public telecommunications transport networks in the territory, or across the borders, of that Party, including for use in providing dial-up access to and from their customers or users, or with circuits leased or owned by another person on terms and conditions mutually agreed by those persons; (c) perform switching, signalling and processing functions; and (d) use operating protocols of their choice.

3.   Each Party shall ensure that: (a) the pricing of public telecommunications transport services reflects economic costs directly related to providing the services; and (b) private leased circuits are available on a flat-rate pricing basis. Nothing in this paragraph shall be construed to prevent cross-subsidization between public telecommunications transport services.

4.   Each Party shall ensure that persons of another Party may use public telecommunications transport networks or services for the movement of information in its territory or across its borders, including for intracorporate

communications, and for access to information contained in data bases or otherwise stored in machine-readable form in the territory of any Party.

5. Further to Article 2101 (General Exceptions), nothing in this Chapter shall be construed to prevent a Party from adopting or enforcing any measure necessary to: (a) ensure the security and confidentiality of messages; or (b) protect the privacy of subscribers to public telecommunications transport networks or services.

6. Each Party shall ensure that no condition is imposed on access to and use of public telecommunications transport networks or services, other than that necessary to: (a) safeguard the public service responsibilities of providers of public telecommunications transport networks or services, in particular their ability to make their networks or services available to the public generally; or (b) protect the technical integrity of public telecommunications transport networks or services.

7. Provided that conditions for access to and use of public telecommunications transport networks or services satisfy the criteria set out in paragraph 6, such conditions may include: (a) a restriction on resale or shared use of such services; (b) a requirement to use specified technical interfaces, including interface protocols, for interconnection with such networks or services; (c) a restriction on interconnection of private leased or owned circuits with such networks or services or with circuits leased or owned by another person, where the circuits are used in the provision of public telecommunications transport networks or services; and (d) a licensing, permit, registration or notification procedure which, if adopted or maintained, is transparent and applications filed thereunder are processed expeditiously.

8. For purposes of this Article, "non-discriminatory" means on terms and conditions no less favorable than those accorded to any other customer or user of like public telecommunications transport networks or services in like circumstances.

Article 1303

Conditions for the Provision of Enhanced or Value–Added Services

1. Each Party shall ensure that: (a) any licensing, permit, registration or notification procedure that it adopts or maintains relating to the provision of enhanced or value-added services is transparent and non-discriminatory, and that applications filed thereunder are processed expeditiously; and (b) information required under such procedures is limited to that necessary to demonstrate that the applicant has the financial solvency to begin providing services or to assess conformity of the applicant's terminal or other equipment with the Party's applicable standards or technical regulations.

2. No Party may require a person providing enhanced or value-added services to: (a) provide those services to the public generally; (b) cost-justify its rates; (c) file a tariff; (d) interconnect its networks with any particular customer or network; or (e) conform with any particular standard or technical regulation for interconnection other than for interconnection to a public telecommunications transport network.

3. Notwithstanding paragraph 2(c), a Party may require the filing of a tariff by: (a) such provider to remedy a practice of that provider that the

Party has found in a particular case to be anticompetitive under its law; or (b) a monopoly to which Article 1305 applies.

Article 1304

Standards–Related Measures

1. Further to Article 904(4) (Unnecessary Obstacles), each Party shall ensure that its standards-related measures relating to the attachment of terminal or other equipment to the public telecommunications transport networks, including those measures relating to the use of testing and measuring equipment for conformity assessment procedures, are adopted or maintained only to the extent necessary to: (a) prevent technical damage to public telecommunications transport networks; (b) prevent technical interference with, or degradation of, public telecommunications transport services; (c) prevent electromagnetic interference, and ensure compatibility, with other uses of the electromagnetic spectrum; (d) prevent billing equipment malfunction; or (e) ensure users' safety and access to public telecommunications transport networks or services.

2. A Party may require approval for the attachment to the public telecommunications transport network of terminal or other equipment that is not authorized, provided that the criteria for that approval are consistent with paragraph 1.

3. Each Party shall ensure that the network termination points for its public telecommunications transport networks are defined on a reasonable and transparent basis.

4. No Party may require separate authorization for equipment that is connected on the customer's side of authorized equipment that serves as a protective device fulfilling the criteria of paragraph 1.

5. Further to Article 904(3) (Non–Discriminatory Treatment), each Party shall: (a) ensure that its conformity assessment procedures are transparent and non-discriminatory and that applications filed thereunder are processed expeditiously; (b) permit any technically qualified entity to perform the testing required under the Party's conformity assessment procedures for terminal or other equipment to be attached to the public telecommunications transport network, subject to the Party's right to review the accuracy and completeness of the test results; and (c) ensure that any measure that it adopts or maintains requiring persons to be authorized to act as agents for suppliers of telecommunications equipment before the Party's relevant conformity assessment bodies is non-discriminatory.

6. No later than one year after the date of entry into force of this Agreement, each Party shall adopt, as part of its conformity assessment procedures, provisions necessary to accept the test results from laboratories or testing facilities in the territory of another Party for tests performed in accordance with the accepting Party's standards-related measures and procedures.

7. The Telecommunications Standards Subcommittee established under Article 913(5) (Committee on Standards–Related Measures) shall perform the functions set out in Annex 913.5.a–2.

Article 1305
Monopolies

1. Where a Party maintains or designates a monopoly to provide public telecommunications transport networks or services, and the monopoly, directly or through an affiliate, competes in the provision of enhanced or value-added services or other telecommunications-related services or telecommunications-related goods, the Party shall ensure that the monopoly does not use its monopoly position to engage in anticompetitive conduct in those markets, either directly or through its dealings with its affiliates, in such a manner as to affect adversely a person of another Party. Such conduct may include cross-subsidization, predatory conduct and the discriminatory provision of access to public telecommunications transport networks or services.

2. To prevent such anticompetitive conduct, each Party shall adopt or maintain effective measures, such as: (a) accounting requirements; (b) requirements for structural separation; (c) rules to ensure that the monopoly accords its competitors access to and use of its public telecommunications transport networks or services on terms and conditions no less favorable than those it accords to itself or its affiliates; or (d) rules to ensure the timely disclosure of technical changes to public telecommunications transport networks and their interfaces.

Article 1306
Transparency

Further to Article 1802 (Publication), each Party shall make publicly available its measures relating to access to and use of public telecommunications transport networks or services, including measures relating to: (a) tariffs and other terms and conditions of service; (b) specifications of technical interfaces with the networks or services; (c) information on bodies responsible for the preparation and adoption of standards-related measures affecting such access and use; (d) conditions applying to attachment of terminal or other equipment to the networks; and (e) notification, permit, registration or licensing requirements.

Article 1307
Relation to Other Chapters

In the event of any inconsistency between this Chapter and another Chapter, this Chapter shall prevail to the extent of the inconsistency.

Article 1308
Relation to International Organizations and Agreements

The Parties recognize the importance of international standards for global compatibility and interoperability of telecommunication networks or services and undertake to promote those standards through the work of relevant international bodies, including the International Telecommunication Union and the International Organization for Standardization.

Article 1309
Technical Cooperation and Other Consultations

1. To encourage the development of interoperable telecommunications transport services infrastructure, the Parties shall cooperate in the exchange

of technical information, the development of government-to-government training programs and other related activities. In implementing this obligation, the Parties shall give special emphasis to existing exchange programs.

2. The Parties shall consult with a view to determining the feasibility of further liberalizing trade in all telecommunications services, including public telecommunications transport networks and services.

Article 1310
Definitions

For purposes of this Chapter:

authorized equipment means terminal or other equipment that has been approved for attachment to the public telecommunications transport network in accordance with a Party's conformity assessment procedures;

conformity assessment procedure means "conformity assessment procedure" as defined in Article 915 (Standards–Related Measures—Definitions), and includes the procedures referred to in Annex 1310;

enhanced or value-added services means those telecommunications services employing computer processing applications that: (a) act on the format, content, code, protocol or similar aspects of a customer's transmitted information; (b) provide a customer with additional, different or restructured information; or (c) involve customer interaction with stored information;

flat-rate pricing basis means pricing on the basis of a fixed charge per period of time regardless of the amount of use;

intracorporate communications means telecommunications through which an enterprise communicates: (a) internally or with or among its subsidiaries, branches or affiliates, as defined by each Party, or (b) on a noncommercial basis with other persons that are fundamental to the economic activity of the enterprise and that have a continuing contractual relationship with it, but does not include telecommunications services provided to persons other than those described herein;

network termination point means the final demarcation of the public telecommunications transport network at the customer's premises;

private network means a telecommunications transport network that is used exclusively for intracorporate communications;

protocol means a set of rules and formats that govern the exchange of information between two peer entities for purposes of transferring signaling or data information;

public telecommunications transport network means public telecommunications infrastructure that permits telecommunications between defined network termination points;

public telecommunications transport networks or services means public telecommunications transport networks or public telecommunications transport services;

public telecommunications transport service means any telecommunications transport service required by a Party, explicitly or in effect, to be offered to the public generally, including telegraph, telephone, telex and data transmission, that typically involves the real-time transmission of customer-supplied information between two or more points without any end-to-end change in the form or content of the customer's information;

standards-related measure means a "standards-related measure" as defined in Article 915;

telecommunications means the transmission and reception of signals by any electromagnetic means; and

terminal equipment means any digital or analog device capable of processing, receiving, switching, signaling or transmitting signals by electromagnetic means and that is connected by radio or wire to a public telecommunications transport network at a termination point.

Annex 1310

Conformity Assessment Procedures

For Canada:

Department of Communications, Terminal Attachment Program Certification Procedures (CP–01) Department of Communications Act, R.S.C.1985, c. C–35 Railway Act, R.S.C.1985, c. R–3 Radiocommunication Act, R.S.C.1985, c. R–2, as amended by S.C.1989, c. 17 Telecommunications Act (Bill C–62)

For Mexico:

Secretaria de Comunicaciones y Transportes

Subsecretaria de Comunicaciones y Desarrollo Tecnologico Reglamento de Telecomunicaciones, Capitulo X

For the United States:

Part 15 and Part 68 of the Federal Communications Commission's Rules, Title 47 of the Code of Federal Regulations

CHAPTER FOURTEEN: FINANCIAL SERVICES

Article 1401

Scope and Coverage

1. This Chapter applies to measures adopted or maintained by a Party relating to: (a) financial institutions of another Party; (b) investors of another Party, and investments of such investors, in financial institutions in the Party's territory; and (c) cross-border trade in financial services.

2. Articles 1109 through 1111, 1113, 1114 and 1211 are hereby incorporated into and made a part of this Chapter. Articles 1115 through 1138 are hereby incorporated into and made a part of this Chapter solely for breaches by a Party of Articles 1109 through 1111, 1113 and 1114, as incorporated into this Chapter.

3. Nothing in this Chapter shall be construed to prevent a Party, including its public entities, from exclusively conducting or providing in its territory: (a) activities or services forming part of a public retirement plan or statutory system of social security; or (b) activities or services for the account or with the guarantee or using the financial resources of the Party, including its public entities.

4. Annex 1401.4 applies to the Parties specified in that Annex.

Annex 1401.4

Country–Specific Commitments

For Canada and the United States, Article 1702(1) and (2) of the Canada–United States Free Trade Agreement is hereby incorporated into and made a part of this Agreement.

Article 1402

Self–Regulatory Organizations

Where a Party requires a financial institution or a cross-border financial service provider of another Party to be a member of, participate in, or have access to, a self-regulatory organization to provide a financial service in or into the territory of that Party, the Party shall ensure observance of the obligations of this Chapter by such self-regulatory organization.

Article 1403

Establishment of Financial Institutions

1. The Parties recognize the principle that an investor of another Party should be permitted to establish a financial institution in the territory of a Party in the juridical form chosen by such investor.

2. The Parties also recognize the principle that an investor of another Party should be permitted to participate widely in a Party's market through the ability of such investor to: (a) provide in that Party's territory a range of financial services through separate financial institutions as may be required by that Party; (b) expand geographically in that Party's territory; and (c) own financial institutions in that Party's territory without being subject to ownership requirements specific to foreign financial institutions.

3. Subject to Annex 1403.3, at such time as the United States permits commercial banks of another Party located in its territory to expand through subsidiaries or direct branches into substantially all of the United States market, the Parties shall review and assess market access provided by each Party in relation to the principles in paragraphs 1 and 2 with a view to adopting arrangements permitting investors of another Party to choose the juridical form of establishment of commercial banks.

4. Each Party shall permit an investor of another Party that does not own or control a financial institution in the Party's territory to establish a financial institution in that territory. A Party may: (a) require an investor of another Party to incorporate under the Party's law any financial institution it establishes in the Party's territory; or (b) impose terms and conditions on establishment that are consistent with Article 1405.

5. For purposes of this Article, "investor of another Party" means an investor of another Party engaged in the business of providing financial services in the territory of that Party.

Annex 1403.3

Review of Market Access

The review of market access referred to in Article 1403(3) shall not include the market access limitations specified in Section B of the Schedule of Mexico to Annex VII.

Article 1404
Cross–Border Trade

1. No Party may adopt any measure restricting any type of cross-border trade in financial services by cross-border financial service providers of another Party that the Party permits on the date of entry into force of this Agreement, except to the extent set out in Section B of the Party's Schedule to Annex VII.

2. Each Party shall permit persons located in its territory, and its nationals wherever located, to purchase financial services from cross-border financial service providers of another Party located in the territory of that other Party or of another Party. This obligation does not require a Party to permit such providers to do business or solicit in its territory. Subject to paragraph 1, each Party may define "doing business" and "solicitation" for purposes of this obligation.

3. Without prejudice to other means of prudential regulation of cross-border trade in financial services, a Party may require the registration of cross-border financial service providers of another Party and of financial instruments.

4. The Parties shall consult on future liberalization of cross-border trade in financial services as set out in Annex 1404.4.

Annex 1404.4
Consultations on Liberalization of Cross–Border Trade

No later than January 1, 2000, the Parties shall consult on further liberalization of cross-border trade in financial services. In such consultations the Parties shall, with respect to insurance: (a) consider the possibility of allowing a wider range of insurance services to be provided on a cross-border basis in or into their respective territories; and (b) determine whether the limitations on cross-border insurance services specified in Section A of the Schedule of Mexico to Annex VII shall be maintained, modified or eliminated.

Article 1405
National Treatment

1. Each Party shall accord to investors of another Party treatment no less favorable than that it accords to its own investors, in like circumstances, with respect to the establishment, acquisition, expansion, management, conduct, operation, and sale or other disposition of financial institutions and investments in financial institutions in its territory.

2. Each Party shall accord to financial institutions of another Party and to investments of investors of another Party in financial institutions treatment no less favorable than that it accords to its own financial institutions and to investments of its own investors in financial institutions, in like circumstances, with respect to the establishment, acquisition, expansion, management, conduct, operation, and sale or other disposition of financial institutions and investments.

3. Subject to Article 1404, where a Party permits the cross-border provision of a financial service it shall accord to the cross-border financial service providers of another Party treatment no less favorable than that it

accords to its own financial service providers, in like circumstances, with respect to the provision of such service.

4.   The treatment that a Party is required to accord under paragraphs 1, 2 and 3 means, with respect to a measure of any state or province: (a) in the case of an investor of another Party with an investment in a financial institution, an investment of such investor in a financial institution, or a financial institution of such investor, located in a state or province, treatment no less favorable than the treatment accorded to an investor of the Party in a financial institution, an investment of such investor in a financial institution, or a financial institution of such investor, located in that state or province, in like circumstances; and (b) in any other case, treatment no less favorable than the most favorable treatment accorded to an investor of the Party in a financial institution, its financial institution or its investment in a financial institution, in like circumstances. For greater certainty, in the case of an investor of another Party with investments in financial institutions or financial institutions of such investor, located in more than one state or province, the treatment required under subparagraph (a) means: (c) treatment of the investor that is no less favorable than the most favorable treatment accorded to an investor of the Party with an investment located in such states or provinces, in like circumstances; and (d) with respect to an investment of the investor in a financial institution or a financial institution of such investor, located in a state or province, treatment no less favorable than that accorded to an investment of an investor of the Party, or a financial institution of such investor, located in that state or province, in like circumstances.

5.   A Party's treatment of financial institutions and cross-border financial service providers of another Party, whether different or identical to that accorded to its own institutions or providers in like circumstances, is consistent with paragraphs 1 through 3 if the treatment affords equal competitive opportunities.

6.   A Party's treatment affords equal competitive opportunities if it does not disadvantage financial institutions and cross-border financial services providers of another Party in their ability to provide financial services as compared with the ability of the Party's own financial institutions and financial services providers to provide such services, in like circumstances.

7.   Differences in market share, profitability or size do not in themselves establish a denial of equal competitive opportunities, but such differences may be used as evidence regarding whether a Party's treatment affords equal competitive opportunities.

Article 1406

Most–Favored–Nation Treatment

1.   Each Party shall accord to investors of another Party, financial institutions of another Party, investments of investors in financial institutions and cross-border financial service providers of another Party treatment no less favorable than that it accords to the investors, financial institutions, investments of investors in financial institutions and cross-border financial service providers of any other Party or of a non-Party, in like circumstances.

2.   A Party may recognize prudential measures of another Party or of a non-Party in the application of measures covered by this Chapter. Such

recognition may be: (a) accorded unilaterally; (b) achieved through harmonization or other means; or (c) based upon an agreement or arrangement with the other Party or non-Party.

3. A Party according recognition of prudential measures under paragraph 2 shall provide adequate opportunity to another Party to demonstrate that circumstances exist in which there are or would be equivalent regulation, oversight, implementation of regulation, and if appropriate, procedures concerning the sharing of information between the Parties.

4. Where a Party accords recognition of prudential measures under paragraph 2(c) and the circumstances set out in paragraph 3 exist, the Party shall provide adequate opportunity to another Party to negotiate accession to the agreement or arrangement, or to negotiate a comparable agreement or arrangement.

Article 1407
New Financial Services and Data Processing

1. Each Party shall permit a financial institution of another Party to provide any new financial service of a type similar to those services that the Party permits its own financial institutions, in like circumstances, to provide under its domestic law. A Party may determine the institutional and juridical form through which the service may be provided and may require authorization for the provision of the service. Where such authorization is required, a decision shall be made within a reasonable time and the authorization may only be refused for prudential reasons.

2. Each Party shall permit a financial institution of another Party to transfer information in electronic or other form, into and out of the Party's territory, for data processing where such processing is required in the ordinary course of business of such institution.

Article 1408
Senior Management and Boards of Directors

1. No Party may require financial institutions of another Party to engage individuals of any particular nationality as senior managerial or other essential personnel.

2. No Party may require that more than a simple majority of the board of directors of a financial institution of another Party be composed of nationals of the Party, persons residing in the territory of the Party, or a combination thereof.

Article 1409
Reservations and Specific Commitments

1. Articles 1403 through 1408 do not apply to: (a) any existing nonconforming measure that is maintained by (i) a Party at the federal level, as set out in Section A of its Schedule to Annex VII, (ii) a state or province, for the period ending on the date specified in Annex 1409.1 for that state or province, and thereafter as described by the Party in Section A of its Schedule to Annex VII in accordance with Annex 1409.1, or (iii) a local government; (b) the continuation or prompt renewal of any non-conforming measure referred

to in subparagraph (a); or (c) an amendment to any non-conforming measure referred to in subparagraph (a) to the extent that the amendment does not decrease the conformity of the measure, as it existed immediately before the amendment, with Articles 1403 through 1408.

2. Articles 1403 through 1408 do not apply to any non-conforming measure that a Party adopts or maintains in accordance with Section B of its Schedule to Annex VII.

3. Section C of each Party's Schedule to Annex VII sets out certain specific commitments by that Party.

4. Where a Party has set out a reservation to Article 1102, 1103, 1202 or 1203 in its Schedule to Annex I, II, III or IV, the reservation shall be deemed to constitute a reservation to Article 1405 or 1406, as the case may be, to the extent that the measure, sector, subsector or activity set out in the reservation is covered by this Chapter.

Annex 1409.1
Provincial and State Reservations

1. Canada may set out in Section A of its Schedule to Annex VII by the date of entry into force of this Agreement any existing non-conforming measure maintained at the provincial level.

2. The United States may set out in Section A of its Schedule to Annex VII by the date of entry into force of this Agreement any existing non-conforming measures maintained by California, Florida, Illinois, New York, Ohio and Texas. Existing non-conforming state measures of all other states may be set out by January 1, 1995.

Article 1410
Exceptions

1. Nothing in this Part shall be construed to prevent a Party from adopting or maintaining reasonable measures for prudential reasons, such as: (a) the protection of investors, depositors, financial market participants, policy-holders, policy-claimants, or persons to whom a fiduciary duty is owed by a financial institution or cross-border financial service provider; (b) the maintenance of the safety, soundness, integrity or financial responsibility of financial institutions or cross-border financial service providers; and (c) ensuring the integrity and stability of a Party's financial system.

2. Nothing in this Part applies to non-discriminatory measures of general application taken by any public entity in pursuit of monetary and related credit policies or exchange rate policies. This paragraph shall not affect a Party's obligations under Article 1106 (Performance Requirements) with respect to measures covered by Chapter Eleven (Investment) or Article 1109 (Transfers).

3. Article 1405 shall not apply to the granting by a Party to a financial institution of an exclusive right to provide a financial service referred to in Article 1401(3)(a).

4. Notwithstanding Article 1109(1), (2) and (3), as incorporated into this Chapter, and without limiting the applicability of Article 1109(4), as incorpo-

rated into this Chapter, a Party may prevent or limit transfers by a financial institution or cross-border financial services provider to, or for the benefit of, an affiliate of or person related to such institution or provider, through the equitable, non-discriminatory and good faith application of measures relating to maintenance of the safety, soundness, integrity or financial responsibility of financial institutions or cross-border financial service providers. This paragraph does not prejudice any other provision of this Agreement that permits a Party to restrict transfers.

Article 1411

Transparency

1. In lieu of Article 1802(2) (Publication), each Party shall, to the extent practicable, provide in advance to all interested persons any measure of general application that the Party proposes to adopt in order to allow an opportunity for such persons to comment on the measure. Such measure shall be provided: (a) by means of official publication; (b) in other written form; or (c) in such other form as permits an interested person to make informed comments on the proposed measure.

2. Each Party's regulatory authorities shall make available to interested persons their requirements for completing applications relating to the provision of financial services.

3. On the request of an applicant, the regulatory authority shall inform the applicant of the status of its application. If such authority requires additional information from the applicant, it shall notify the applicant without undue delay.

4. A regulatory authority shall make an administrative decision on a completed application of an investor in a financial institution, a financial institution or a cross-border financial service provider of another Party relating to the provision of a financial service within 120 days, and shall promptly notify the applicant of the decision. An application shall not be considered complete until all relevant hearings are held and all necessary information is received. Where it is not practicable for a decision to be made within 120 days, the regulatory authority shall notify the applicant without undue delay and shall endeavor to make the decision within a reasonable time thereafter.

5. Nothing in this Chapter requires a Party to furnish or allow access to: (a) information related to the financial affairs and accounts of individual customers of financial institutions or cross-border financial service providers; or (b) any confidential information, the disclosure of which would impede law enforcement or otherwise be contrary to the public interest or prejudice legitimate commercial interests of particular enterprises.

6. Each Party shall maintain or establish one or more inquiry points no later than 180 days after the date of entry into force of this Agreement, to respond in writing as soon as practicable, to all reasonable inquiries from interested persons regarding measures of general application covered by this Chapter.

Article 1412

Financial Services Committee

1. The Parties hereby establish the Financial Services Committee. The principal representative of each Party shall be an official of the Party's authority responsible for financial services set out in Annex 1412.1.

2. Subject to Article 2001(2)(d) (Free Trade Commission), the Committee shall: (a) supervise the implementation of this Chapter and its further elaboration; (b) consider issues regarding financial services that are referred to it by a Party; and (c) participate in the dispute settlement procedures in accordance with Article 1415.

3. The Committee shall meet annually to assess the functioning of this Agreement as it applies to financial services. The Committee shall inform the Commission of the results of each annual meeting.

Annex 1412.1

Authorities Responsible for Financial Services

The authority of each Party responsible for financial services shall be: (a) for Canada, the Department of Finance of Canada; (b) for Mexico, the Secretaria de Hacienda y Credito Publico; and (c) for the United States, the Department of the Treasury for banking and other financial services and the Department of Commerce for insurance services.

Article 1413

Consultations

1. A Party may request consultations with another Party regarding any matter arising under this Agreement that affects financial services. The other Party shall give sympathetic consideration to the request. The consulting Parties shall report the results of their consultations to the Committee at its annual meeting.

2. Consultations under this Article shall include officials of the authorities specified in Annex 1412.1.

3. A Party may request that regulatory authorities of another Party participate in consultations under this Article regarding that other Party's measures of general application which may affect the operations of financial institutions or cross-border financial service providers in the requesting Party's territory.

4. Nothing in this Article shall be construed to require regulatory authorities participating in consultations under paragraph 3 to disclose information or take any action that would interfere with individual regulatory, supervisory, administrative or enforcement matters.

5. Where a Party requires information for supervisory purposes concerning a financial institution in another Party's territory or a cross-border financial service provider in another Party's territory, the Party may approach the competent regulatory authority in the other Party's territory to seek the information.

6. Annex 1413.6 shall apply to further consultations and arrangements.

Annex 1413.6

Further Consultations and Arrangements

Section A—Limited Scope Financial Institutions

Three years after the date of entry into force of this Agreement, the Parties shall consult on the aggregate limit on limited scope financial institutions described in paragraph 8 of Section B of the Schedule of Mexico to Annex VII.

Section B—Payments System Protection

1. If the sum of the authorized capital of foreign commercial bank affiliates (as such term is defined in the Schedule of Mexico to Annex VII), measured as a percentage of the aggregate capital of all commercial banks in Mexico, reaches 25 percent, Mexico may request consultations with the other Parties on the potential adverse effects arising from the presence of commercial banks of the other Parties in the Mexican market and the possible need for remedial action, including further temporary limitations on market participation. The consultations shall be completed expeditiously.

2. In considering the potential adverse effects, the Parties shall take into account: (a) the threat that the Mexican payments system may be controlled by non-Mexican persons; (b) the effects foreign commercial banks established in Mexico may have on Mexico's ability to conduct monetary and exchange-rate policy effectively; and (c) the adequacy of this Chapter in protecting the Mexican payments system.

3. If no consensus is reached on the matters referred to in paragraph 1, any Party may request the establishment of an arbitral panel under Article 1414 or Article 2008 (Request for an Arbitral Panel). The panel proceedings shall be conducted in accordance with the Model Rules of Procedure established under Article 2012 (Rules of Procedure). The Panel shall present its determination within 60 days after the last panelist is selected or such other period as the Parties to the proceeding may agree. Article 2018 (Implementation of Final Report) and 2019 (Non–Implementation—Suspension of Benefits) shall not apply in such proceedings.

Article 1414

Dispute Settlement

1. Section B of Chapter Twenty (Institutional Arrangements and Dispute Settlement Procedures) applies as modified by this Article to the settlement of disputes arising under this Chapter.

2. The Parties shall establish by January 1, 1994 and maintain a roster of up to 15 individuals who are willing and able to serve as financial services panelists. Financial services roster members shall be appointed by consensus for terms of three years, and may be reappointed.

3. Financial services roster members shall: (a) have expertise or experience in financial services law or practice, which may include the regulation of financial institutions; (b) be chosen strictly on the basis of objectivity, reliability and sound judgment; and (c) meet the qualifications set out in Article 2009(2)(b) and (c) (Roster).

4.   Where a Party claims that a dispute arises under this Chapter, Article 2011 (Panel Selection) shall apply, except that: (a) where the disputing Parties so agree, the panel shall be composed entirely of panelists meeting the qualifications in paragraph 3; and (b) in any other case, (i) each disputing Party may select panelists meeting the qualifications set out in paragraph 3 or in Article 2010(1) (Qualifications of Panelists), and (ii) if the Party complained against invokes Article 1410, the chair of the panel shall meet the qualifications set out in paragraph 3.

5.   In any dispute where a panel finds a measure to be inconsistent with the obligations of this Agreement and the measure affects: (a) only the financial services sector, the complaining Party may suspend benefits only in the financial services sector; (b) the financial services sector and any other sector, the complaining Party may suspend benefits in the financial services sector that have an effect equivalent to the effect of the measure in the Party's financial services sector; or (c) only a sector other than the financial services sector, the complaining Party may not suspend benefits in the financial services sector.

Article 1415

Investment Disputes in Financial Services

1.   Where an investor of another Party submits a claim under Article 1116 or 1117 to arbitration under Section B of Chapter Eleven (Investment—Settlement of Disputes between a Party and an Investor of Another Party) against a Party and the disputing Party invokes Article 1410, on request of the disputing Party, the Tribunal shall refer the matter in writing to the Committee for a decision.   The Tribunal may not proceed pending receipt of a decision or report under this Article.

2.   In a referral pursuant to paragraph 1, the Committee shall decide the issue of whether and to what extent Article 1410 is a valid defense to the claim of the investor.   The Committee shall transmit a copy of its decision to the Tribunal and to the Commission.   The decision shall be binding on the Tribunal.

3.   Where the Committee has not decided the issue within 60 days of the receipt of the referral under paragraph 1, the disputing Party or the Party of the disputing investor may request the establishment of an arbitral panel under Article 2008 (Request for an Arbitral Panel).   The panel shall be constituted in accordance with Article 1414.   Further to Article 2017 (Final Report), the panel shall transmit its final report to the Committee and to the Tribunal.   The report shall be binding on the Tribunal.

4.   Where no request for the establishment of a panel pursuant to paragraph 3 has been made within 10 days of the expiration of the 60-day period referred to in paragraph 3, the Tribunal may proceed to decide the matter.

Article 1416

Definitions

For purposes of this Chapter:

cross-border financial service provider of a Party means a person of a Party that is engaged in the business of providing a financial service within the territory of the Party and that seeks to provide or provides financial services through the cross-border provision of such services;

cross-border provision of a financial service or cross-border trade in financial services means the provision of a financial service: (a) from the territory of a Party into the territory of another Party, (b) in the territory of a Party by a person of that Party to a person of another Party, or (c) by a national of a Party in the territory of another Party, but does not include the provision of a service in the territory of a Party by an investment in that territory;

financial institution means any financial intermediary or other enterprise that is authorized to do business and regulated or supervised as a financial institution under the law of the Party in whose territory it is located;

financial institution of another Party means a financial institution, including a branch, located in the territory of a Party that is controlled by persons of another Party;

financial service means a service of a financial nature, including insurance, and a service incidental or auxiliary to a service of a financial nature;

financial service provider of a Party means a person of a Party that is engaged in the business of providing a financial service within the territory of that Party;

investment means "investment" as defined in Article 1139 (Investment—Definitions), except that, with respect to "loans" and "debt securities" referred to in that Article: (a) a loan to or debt security issued by a financial institution is an investment only where it is treated as regulatory capital by the Party in whose territory the financial institution is located; and (b) a loan granted by or debt security owned by a financial institution, other than a loan to or debt security of a financial institution referred to in subparagraph (a), is not an investment; for greater certainty: (c) a loan to, or debt security issued by, a Party or a state enterprise thereof is not an investment; and (d) a loan granted by or debt security owned by a cross-border financial service provider, other than a loan to or debt security issued by a financial institution, is an investment if such loan or debt security meets the criteria for investments set out in Article 1139;

investor of a Party means a Party or state enterprise thereof, or a person of that Party, that seeks to make, makes, or has made an investment;

new financial service means a financial service not provided in the Party's territory that is provided within the territory of another Party, and includes any new form of delivery of a financial service or the sale of a financial product that is not sold in the Party's territory;

person of a Party means "person of a Party" as defined in Chapter Two (General Definitions) and, for greater certainty, does not include a branch of an enterprise of a non-Party;

public entity means a central bank or monetary authority of a Party, or any financial institution owned or controlled by a Party; and

self-regulatory organization means any non-governmental body, including any securities or futures exchange or market, clearing agency, or other organization or association, that exercises its own or delegated regulatory or supervisory authority over financial service providers or financial institutions.

CHAPTER FIFTEEN: COMPETITION POLICY, MONOPOLIES AND STATE ENTERPRISES

Article 1501

Competition Law

1. Each Party shall adopt or maintain measures to proscribe anti-competitive business conduct and take appropriate action with respect thereto, recognizing that such measures will enhance the fulfillment of the objectives of this Agreement. To this end the Parties shall consult from time to time about the effectiveness of measures undertaken by each Party.

2. Each Party recognizes the importance of cooperation and coordination among their authorities to further effective competition law enforcement in the free trade area. The Parties shall cooperate on issues of competition law enforcement policy, including mutual legal assistance, notification, consultation and exchange of information relating to the enforcement of competition laws and policies in the free trade area.

3. No Party may have recourse to dispute settlement under this Agreement for any matter arising under this Article.

Article 1502

Monopolies and State Enterprises

1. Nothing in this Agreement shall be construed to prevent a Party from designating a monopoly.

2. Where a Party intends to designate a monopoly and the designation may affect the interests of persons of another Party, the Party shall: (a) wherever possible, provide prior written notification to the other Party of the designation; and (b) endeavor to introduce at the time of the designation such conditions on the operation of the monopoly as will minimize or eliminate any nullification or impairment of benefits in the sense of Annex 2004 (Nullification and Impairment).

3. Each Party shall ensure, through regulatory control, administrative supervision or the application of other measures, that any privately-owned monopoly that it designates and any government monopoly that it maintains or designates: (a) acts in a manner that is not inconsistent with the Party's obligations under this Agreement wherever such a monopoly exercises any regulatory, administrative or other governmental authority that the Party has delegated to it in connection with the monopoly good or service, such as the power to grant import or export licenses, approve commercial transactions or impose quotas, fees or other charges; (b) except to comply with any terms of its designation that are not inconsistent with subparagraph (c) or (d), acts solely in accordance with commercial considerations in its purchase or sale of the monopoly good or service in the relevant market, including with regard to price, quality, availability, marketability, transportation and other terms and

conditions of purchase or sale; (c) provides non-discriminatory treatment to investments of investors, to goods and to service providers of another Party in its purchase or sale of the monopoly good or service in the relevant market; and (d) does not use its monopoly position to engage, either directly or indirectly, including through its dealings with its parent, its subsidiary or other enterprise with common ownership, in anticompetitive practices in a non-monopolized market in its territory that adversely affect an investment of an investor of another Party, including through the discriminatory provision of the monopoly good or service, cross-subsidization or predatory conduct.

4.   Paragraph 3 does not apply to procurement by governmental agencies of goods or services for governmental purposes and not with a view to commercial resale or with a view to use in the production of goods or the provision of services for commercial sale.

5.   For purposes of this Article "maintain" means designate prior to the date of entry into force of this Agreement and existing on January 1, 1994.

Article 1503
State Enterprises

1.   Nothing in this Agreement shall be construed to prevent a Party from maintaining or establishing a state enterprise.

2.   Each Party shall ensure, through regulatory control, administrative supervision or the application of other measures, that any state enterprise that it maintains or establishes acts in a manner that is not inconsistent with the Party's obligations under Chapters Eleven (Investment) and Fourteen (Financial Services) wherever such enterprise exercises any regulatory, administrative or other governmental authority that the Party has delegated to it, such as the power to expropriate, grant licenses, approve commercial transactions or impose quotas, fees or other charges.

3.   Each Party shall ensure that any state enterprise that it maintains or establishes accords non-discriminatory treatment in the sale of its goods or services to investments in the Party's territory of investors of another Party.

Article 1504
Working Group on Trade and Competition

The Commission shall establish a Working Group on Trade and Competition, comprising representatives of each Party, to report, and to make recommendations on further work as appropriate, to the Commission within five years of the date of entry into force of this Agreement on relevant issues concerning the relationship between competition laws and policies and trade in the free trade area.

Article 1505
Definitions

For purposes of this Chapter:

designate means to establish, designate or authorize, or to expand the scope of a monopoly to cover an additional good or service, after the date of entry into force of this Agreement;

discriminatory provision includes treating: (a) a parent, a subsidiary or other enterprise with common ownership more favorably than an unaffiliated enterprise, or (b) one class of enterprises more favorably than another, in like circumstances;

government monopoly means a monopoly that is owned, or controlled through ownership interests, by the federal government of a Party or by another such monopoly;

in accordance with commercial considerations means consistent with normal business practices of privately-held enterprises in the relevant business or industry;

market means the geographic and commercial market for a good or service;

monopoly means an entity, including a consortium or government agency, that in any relevant market in the territory of a Party is designated as the sole provider or purchaser of a good or service, but does not include an entity that has been granted an exclusive intellectual property right solely by reason of such grant;

non-discriminatory treatment means the better of national treatment and most-favored-nation treatment, as set out in the relevant provisions of this Agreement; and

state enterprise means, except as set out in Annex 1505, an enterprise owned, or controlled through ownership interests, by a Party.

Annex 1505
Country—Specific Definitions of State Enterprises

For purposes of Article 1503(3), "**state enterprise**": (a) with respect to Canada, means a Crown corporation within the meaning of the Financial Administration Act (Canada), a Crown corporation within the meaning of any comparable provincial law or equivalent entity that is incorporated under other applicable provincial law; and (b) with respect to Mexico, does not include, the Compania Nacional de Subsistencias Populares (National Company for Basic Commodities) and its existing affiliates, or any successor enterprise or its affiliates, for purposes of sales of maize, beans and powdered milk.

CHAPTER SIXTEEN: TEMPORARY ENTRY FOR BUSINESS PERSONS
Article 1601
General Principles

Further to Article 102 (Objectives), this Chapter reflects the preferential trading relationship between the Parties, the desirability of facilitating temporary entry on a reciprocal basis and of establishing transparent criteria and procedures for temporary entry, and the need to ensure border security and to protect the domestic labor force and permanent employment in their respective territories.

Article 1602
General Obligations

1. Each Party shall apply its measures relating to the provisions of this Chapter in accordance with Article 1601 and, in particular, shall apply

expeditiously those measures so as to avoid unduly impairing or delaying trade in goods or services or conduct of investment activities under this Agreement.

2. The Parties shall endeavor to develop and adopt common criteria, definitions and interpretations for the implementation of this Chapter.

Article 1603
Grant of Temporary Entry

1. Each Party shall grant temporary entry to business persons who are otherwise qualified for entry under applicable measures relating to public health and safety and national security, in accordance with this Chapter, including the provisions of Annex 1603.

2. A Party may refuse to issue an immigration document authorizing employment to a business person where the temporary entry of that person might affect adversely: (a) the settlement of any labor dispute that is in progress at the place or intended place of employment; or (b) the employment of any person who is involved in such dispute.

3. When a Party refuses pursuant to paragraph 2 to issue an immigration document authorizing employment, it shall: (a) inform in writing the business person of the reasons for the refusal; and (b) promptly notify in writing the Party whose business person has been refused entry of the reasons for the refusal.

4. Each Party shall limit any fees for processing applications for temporary entry of business persons to the approximate cost of services rendered.

Annex 1603
Temporary Entry for Business Persons
Section A—Business Visitors

1. Each Party shall grant temporary entry to a business person seeking to engage in a business activity set out in Appendix 1603.A.1, without requiring that person to obtain an employment authorization, provided that the business person otherwise complies with existing immigration measures applicable to temporary entry, on presentation of: (a) proof of citizenship of a Party; (b) documentation demonstrating that the business person will be so engaged and describing the purpose of entry; and (c) evidence demonstrating that the proposed business activity is international in scope and that the business person is not seeking to enter the local labor market.

2. Each Party shall provide that a business person may satisfy the requirements of paragraph 1(c) by demonstrating that: (a) the primary source of remuneration for the proposed business activity is outside the territory of the Party granting temporary entry; and (b) the business person's principal place of business and the actual place of accrual of profits, at least predominantly, remain outside such territory. A Party shall normally accept an oral declaration as to the principal place of business and the actual place of accrual of profits. Where the Party requires further proof, it shall normally consider a letter from the employer attesting to these matters as sufficient proof.

3. Each Party shall grant temporary entry to a business person seeking to engage in a business activity other than those set out in Appendix 1603.A.1,

without requiring that person to obtain an employment authorization, on a basis no less favorable than that provided under the existing provisions of the measures set out in Appendix 1603.A.3, provided that the business person otherwise complies with existing immigration measures applicable to temporary entry.

4. No Party may: (a) as a condition for temporary entry under paragraph 1 or 3, require prior approval procedures, petitions, labor certification tests or other procedures of similar effect; or (b) impose or maintain any numerical restriction relating to temporary entry under paragraph 1 or 3.

5. Notwithstanding paragraph 4, a Party may require a business person seeking temporary entry under this Section to obtain a visa or its equivalent prior to entry. Before imposing a visa requirement, the Party shall consult with a Party whose business persons would be affected with a view to avoiding the imposition of the requirement. With respect to an existing visa requirement, a Party shall consult, on request, with a Party whose business persons are subject to the requirement with a view to its removal.

Section B—Traders and Investors

1. Each Party shall grant temporary entry and provide confirming documentation to a business person seeking to: (a) carry on substantial trade in goods or services principally between the territory of the Party of which the business person is a citizen and the territory of the Party into which entry is sought, or (b) establish, develop, administer or provide advice or key technical services to the operation of an investment to which the business person or the business person's enterprise has committed, or is in the process of committing, a substantial amount of capital, in a capacity that is supervisory, executive or involves essential skills, provided that the business person otherwise complies with existing immigration measures applicable to temporary entry.

2. No Party may: (a) as a condition for temporary entry under paragraph 1, require labor certification tests or other procedures of similar effect; or (b) impose or maintain any numerical restriction relating to temporary entry under paragraph 1.

3. Notwithstanding paragraph 2, a Party may require a business person seeking temporary entry under this Section to obtain a visa or its equivalent prior to entry.

Section C—Intra–Company Transferees

1. Each Party shall grant temporary entry and provide confirming documentation to a business person employed by an enterprise who seeks to render services to that enterprise or a subsidiary or affiliate thereof, in a capacity that is managerial, executive or involves specialized knowledge, provided that the business person otherwise complies with existing immigration measures applicable to temporary entry. A Party may require the business person to have been employed continuously by the enterprise for one year within the three-year period immediately preceding the date of the application for admission.

2. No Party may: (a) as a condition for temporary entry under paragraph 1, require labor certification tests or other procedures of similar effect;

or (b) impose or maintain any numerical restriction relating to temporary entry under paragraph 1.

3. Notwithstanding paragraph 2, a Party may require a business person seeking temporary entry under this Section to obtain a visa or its equivalent prior to entry. Before imposing a visa requirement, the Party shall consult with a Party whose business persons would be affected with a view to avoiding the imposition of the requirement. With respect to an existing visa requirement, a Party shall consult, on request, with a Party whose business persons are subject to the requirement with a view to its removal.

Section D—Professionals

1. Each Party shall grant temporary entry and provide confirming documentation to a business person seeking to engage in a business activity at a professional level in a profession set out in Appendix 1603.D.1, if the business person otherwise complies with existing immigration measures applicable to temporary entry, on presentation of: (a) proof of citizenship of a Party; and (b) documentation demonstrating that the business person will be so engaged and describing the purpose of entry.

2. No Party may: (a) as a condition for temporary entry under paragraph 1, require prior approval procedures, petitions, labor certification tests or other procedures of similar effect; or (b) impose or maintain any numerical restriction relating to temporary entry under paragraph 1.

3. Notwithstanding paragraph 2, a Party may require a business person seeking temporary entry under this Section to obtain a visa or its equivalent prior to entry. Before imposing a visa requirement, the Party shall consult with a Party whose business persons would be affected with a view to avoiding the imposition of the requirement. With respect to an existing visa requirement, a Party shall consult, on request, with a Party whose business persons are subject to the requirement with a view to its removal.

4. Notwithstanding paragraphs 1 and 2, a Party may establish an annual numerical limit, which shall be set out in Appendix 1603.D.4, regarding temporary entry of business persons of another Party seeking to engage in business activities at a professional level in a profession set out in Appendix 1603.D.1, if the Parties concerned have not agreed otherwise prior to the date of entry into force of this Agreement for those Parties. In establishing such a limit, the Party shall consult with the other Party concerned.

5. A Party establishing a numerical limit pursuant to paragraph 4, unless the Parties concerned agree otherwise: (a) shall, for each year after the first year after the date of entry into force of this Agreement, consider increasing the numerical limit set out in Appendix 1603.D.4 by an amount to be established in consultation with the other Party concerned, taking into account the demand for temporary entry under this Section; (b) shall not apply its procedures established pursuant to paragraph 1 to the temporary entry of a business person subject to the numerical limit, but may require the business person to comply with its other procedures applicable to the temporary entry of professionals; and (c) may, in consultation with the other Party concerned, grant temporary entry under paragraph 1 to a business person who practices in a profession where accreditation, licensing, and certification requirements are mutually recognized by those Parties.

6. Nothing in paragraph 4 or 5 shall be construed to limit the ability of a business person to seek temporary entry under a Party's applicable immigration measures relating to the entry of professionals other than those adopted or maintained pursuant to paragraph 1.

7. Three years after a Party establishes a numerical limit pursuant to paragraph 4, it shall consult with the other Party concerned with a view to determining a date after which the limit shall cease to apply.

Appendix 1603.A.1

Business Visitors

Research and Design

—Technical, scientific and statistical researchers conducting independent research or research for an enterprise located in the territory of another Party.

Growth, Manufacture and Production

—Harvester owner supervising a harvesting crew admitted under applicable law.

—Purchasing and production management personnel conducting commercial transactions for an enterprise located in the territory of another Party.

Marketing

—Market researchers and analysts conducting independent research or analysis or research or analysis for an enterprise located in the territory of another Party.

—Trade fair and promotional personnel attending a trade convention.

Sales

—Sales representatives and agents taking orders or negotiating contracts for goods or services for an enterprise located in the territory of another Party but not delivering goods or providing services.

—Buyers purchasing for an enterprise located in the territory of another Party.

Distribution

—Transportation operators transporting goods or passengers to the territory of a Party from the territory of another Party or loading and transporting goods or passengers from the territory of a Party, with no unloading in that territory, to the territory of another Party.

—With respect to temporary entry into the territory of the United States, Canadian customs brokers performing brokerage duties relating to the export of goods from the territory of the United States to or through the territory of Canada.

—With respect to temporary entry into the territory of Canada, United States customs brokers performing brokerage duties relating to the export of goods from the territory of Canada to or through the territory of the United States.

—Customs brokers providing consulting services regarding the facilitation of the import or export of goods.

After–Sales Service

—Installers, repair and maintenance personnel, and supervisors, possessing specialized knowledge essential to a seller's contractual obligation, performing services or training workers to perform services, pursuant to a warranty or other service contract incidental to the sale of commercial or industrial equipment or machinery, including computer software, purchased from an enterprise located outside the territory of the Party into which temporary entry is sought, during the life of the warranty or service agreement.

General Service

—Professionals engaging in a business activity at a professional level in a profession set out in Appendix 1603.D.1.

—Management and supervisory personnel engaging in a commercial transaction for an enterprise located in the territory of another Party.

—Financial services personnel (insurers, bankers or investment brokers) engaging in commercial transactions for an enterprise located in the territory of another Party.

—Public relations and advertising personnel consulting with business associates, or attending or participating in conventions.

—Tourism personnel (tour and travel agents, tour guides or tour operators) attending or participating in conventions or conducting a tour that has begun in the territory of another Party.

—Tour bus operators entering the territory of a Party: (a) with a group of passengers on a bus tour that has begun in, and will return to, the territory of another Party; (b) to meet a group of passengers on a bus tour that will end, and the predominant portion of which will take place, in the territory of another Party; or (c) with a group of passengers on a bus tour to be unloaded in the territory of the Party into which temporary entry is sought, and returning with no passengers or reloading with the group for transportation to the territory of another Party.

—Translators or interpreters performing services as employees of an enterprise located in the territory of another Party.

Definitions

For purposes of this Appendix:

territory of another Party means the territory of a Party other than the territory of the Party into which temporary entry is sought;

tour bus operator means a natural person, including relief personnel accompanying or following to join, necessary for the operation of a tour bus for the duration of a trip; and

transportation operator means a natural person, other than a tour bus operator, including relief personnel accompanying or following to join, necessary for the operation of a vehicle for the duration of a trip.

Appendix 1603.A.3

Existing Immigration Measures

1.   In the case of Canada, subsection 19(1) of the Immigration Regulations, 1978, SOR/78–172, as amended, made under the Immigration Act, R.S.C. 1985, c. I–2, as amended.

2.   In the case of the United States, section 101(a)(15)(B) of the Immigration and Nationality Act, 1952, as amended.

3.   In the case of Mexico, Chapter III of the General Demography Law ("Ley General de Poblacion"), 1974, as amended.

* * *

Appendix 1603.D.4

United States

1.   Beginning on the date of entry into force of this Agreement as between the United States and Mexico, the United States shall annually approve as many as 5,500 initial petitions of business persons of Mexico seeking temporary entry under Section D of Annex 1603 to engage in a business activity at a professional level in a profession set out in Appendix 1603.D.1.

2.   For purposes of paragraph 1, the United States shall not take into account: (a) the renewal of a period of temporary entry; (b) the entry of a spouse or children accompanying or following to join the principal business person; (c) an admission under section 101(a)(15)(H)(i)(b) of the Immigration and Nationality Act, 1952, as may be amended, including the worldwide numerical limit established by section 214(g)(1)(A) of that Act; or (d) an admission under any other provision of section 101(a)(15) of that Act relating to the entry of professionals.

3.   Paragraphs 4 and 5 of Section D of Annex 1603 shall apply as between the United States and Mexico for no longer than: (a) the period that such paragraphs or similar provisions may apply as between the United States and any other Party other than Canada or any non-Party; or (b) 10 years after the date of entry into force of this Agreement as between such Parties, whichever period is shorter.

Article 1604

Provision of Information

1.   Further to Article 1802 (Publication), each Party shall: (a) provide to the other Parties such materials as will enable them to become acquainted with its measures relating to this Chapter; and (b) no later than one year after the date of entry into force of this Agreement, prepare, publish and make available in its own territory, and in the territories of the other Parties, explanatory material in a consolidated document regarding the requirements for temporary entry under this Chapter in such a manner as will enable business persons of the other Parties to become acquainted with them.

2.   Subject to Annex 1604.2, each Party shall collect and maintain, and make available to the other Parties in accordance with its domestic law, data respecting the granting of temporary entry under this Chapter to business

persons of the other Parties who have been issued immigration documentation, including data specific to each occupation, profession or activity.

Annex 1604.2
Provision of Information

The obligations under Article 1604(2) shall take effect with respect to Mexico one year after the date of entry into force of this Agreement.

Article 1605
Working Group

1. The Parties hereby establish a Temporary Entry Working Group, comprising representatives of each Party, including immigration officials.

2. The Working Group shall meet at least once each year to consider: (a) the implementation and administration of this Chapter; (b) the development of measures to further facilitate temporary entry of business persons on a reciprocal basis; (c) the waiving of labor certification tests or procedures of similar effect for spouses of business persons who have been granted temporary entry for more than one year under Section B, C or D of Annex 1603; and (d) proposed modifications of or additions to this Chapter.

Article 1606
Dispute Settlement

1. A Party may not initiate proceedings under Article 2007 (Commission—Good Offices, Conciliation and Mediation) regarding a refusal to grant temporary entry under this Chapter or a particular case arising under Article 1602(1) unless: (a) the matter involves a pattern of practice; and (b) the business person has exhausted the available administrative remedies regarding the particular matter.

2. The remedies referred to in paragraph (1)(b) shall be deemed to be exhausted if a final determination in the matter has not been issued by the competent authority within one year of the institution of an administrative proceeding, and the failure to issue a determination is not attributable to delay caused by the business person.

Article 1607
Relation to Other Chapters

Except for this Chapter, Chapters One (Objectives), Two (General Definitions), Twenty (Institutional Arrangements and Dispute Settlement Procedures) and Twenty–Two (Final Provisions) and Articles 1801 (Contact Points), 1802 (Publication), 1803 (Notification and Provision of Information) and 1804 (Administrative Proceedings), no provision of this Agreement shall impose any obligation on a Party regarding its immigration measures.

Article 1608
Definitions

For purposes of this Chapter:

business person means a citizen of a Party who is engaged in trade in goods, the provision of services or the conduct of investment activities;

citizen means "citizen" as defined in Annex 1608 for the Parties specified in that Annex;

existing means "existing" as defined in Annex 1608 for the Parties specified in that Annex; and

temporary entry means entry into the territory of a Party by a business person of another Party without the intent to establish permanent residence.

Annex 1608
Country—Specific Definitions

For purposes of this Chapter:

citizen means, with respect to Mexico, a national or a citizen according to the existing provisions of Articles 30 and 34, respectively, of the Mexican Constitution; and

existing means, as between: (a) Canada and Mexico, and Mexico and the United States, in effect on the date of entry into force of this Agreement; and (b) Canada and the United States, in effect on January 1, 1989.

PART SIX
INTELLECTUAL PROPERTY
CHAPTER SEVENTEEN: INTELLECTUAL PROPERTY
Article 1701
Nature and Scope of Obligations

1. Each Party shall provide in its territory to the nationals of another Party adequate and effective protection and enforcement of intellectual property rights, while ensuring that measures to enforce intellectual property rights do not themselves become barriers to legitimate trade.

2. To provide adequate and effective protection and enforcement of intellectual property rights, each Party shall, at a minimum, give effect to this Chapter and to the substantive provisions of: (a) the Geneva Convention for the Protection of Producers of Phonograms Against Unauthorized Duplication of their Phonograms, 1971 (Geneva Convention); (b) the Berne Convention for the Protection of Literary and Artistic Works, 1971 (Berne Convention); (c) the Paris Convention for the Protection of Industrial Property, 1967 (Paris Convention); and (d) the International Convention for the Protection of New Varieties of Plants, 1978 (UPOV Convention), or the International Convention for the Protection of New Varieties of Plants, 1991 (UPOV Convention). If a Party has not acceded to the specified text of any such Conventions on or before the date of entry into force of this Agreement, it shall make every effort to accede.

3. Annex 1701.3 applies to the Parties specified in that Annex.

Annex 1701.3
Intellectual Property Conventions

1. Mexico shall: (a) make every effort to comply with the substantive provisions of the 1978 or 1991 UPOV Convention as soon as possible and shall do so no later than two years after the date of signature of this Agreement; and (b) accept from the date of entry into force of this Agreement applications

from plant breeders for varieties in all plant genera and species and grant protection, in accordance with such substantive provisions, promptly after complying with subparagraph (a).

2.   Notwithstanding Article 1701(2)(b), this Agreement confers no rights and imposes no obligations on the United States with respect to Article 6bis of the Berne Convention, or the rights derived from that Article.

Article 1702

More Extensive Protection

A Party may implement in its domestic law more extensive protection of intellectual property rights than is required under this Agreement, provided that such protection is not inconsistent with this Agreement.

Article 1703

National Treatment

1.   Each Party shall accord to nationals of another Party treatment no less favorable than that it accords to its own nationals with regard to the protection and enforcement of all intellectual property rights.   In respect of sound recordings, each Party shall provide such treatment to producers and performers of another Party, except that a Party may limit rights of performers of another Party in respect of secondary uses of sound recordings to those rights its nationals are accorded in the territory of such other Party.

2.   No Party may, as a condition of according national treatment under this Article, require right holders to comply with any formalities or conditions in order to acquire rights in respect of copyright and related rights.

3.   A Party may derogate from paragraph 1 in relation to its judicial and administrative procedures for the protection or enforcement of intellectual property rights, including any procedure requiring a national of another Party to designate for service of process an address in the Party's territory or to appoint an agent in the Party's territory, if the derogation is consistent with the relevant Convention listed in Article 1701(2), provided that such derogation: (a) is necessary to secure compliance with measures that are not inconsistent with this Chapter; and (b) is not applied in a manner that would constitute a disguised restriction on trade.

4.   No Party shall have any obligation under this Article with respect to procedures provided in multilateral agreements concluded under the auspices of the World Intellectual Property Organization relating to the acquisition or maintenance of intellectual property rights.

Article 1704

Control of Abusive or Anticompetitive Practices or Conditions

Nothing in this Chapter shall prevent a Party from specifying in its domestic law licensing practices or conditions that may in particular cases constitute an abuse of intellectual property rights having an adverse effect on competition in the relevant market.   A Party may adopt or maintain, consistent with the other provisions of this Agreement, appropriate measures to prevent or control such practices or conditions.

Article 1705

Copyright

1. Each Party shall protect the works covered by Article 2 of the Berne Convention, including any other works that embody original expression within the meaning of that Convention. In particular: (a) all types of computer programs are literary works within the meaning of the Berne Convention and each Party shall protect them as such; and (b) compilations of data or other material, whether in machine readable or other form, which by reason of the selection or arrangement of their contents constitute intellectual creations, shall be protected as such. The protection a Party provides under subparagraph (b) shall not extend to the data or material itself, or prejudice any copyright subsisting in that data or material.

2. Each Party shall provide to authors and their successors in interest those rights enumerated in the Berne Convention in respect of works covered by paragraph 1, including the right to authorize or prohibit: (a) the importation into the Party's territory of copies of the work made without the right holder's authorization; (b) the first public distribution of the original and each copy of the work by sale, rental or otherwise; (c) the communication of a work to the public; and (d) the commercial rental of the original or a copy of a computer program. Subparagraph (d) shall not apply where the copy of the computer program is not itself an essential object of the rental. Each Party shall provide that putting the original or a copy of a computer program on the market with the right holder's consent shall not exhaust the rental right.

3. Each Party shall provide that for copyright and related rights: (a) any person acquiring or holding economic rights may freely and separately transfer such rights by contract for purposes of their exploitation and enjoyment by the transferee; and (b) any person acquiring or holding such economic rights by virtue of a contract, including contracts of employment underlying the creation of works and sound recordings, shall be able to exercise those rights in its own name and enjoy fully the benefits derived from those rights.

4. Each Party shall provide that, where the term of protection of a work, other than a photographic work or a work of applied art, is to be calculated on a basis other than the life of a natural person, the term shall be not less than 50 years from the end of the calendar year of the first authorized publication of the work or, failing such authorized publication within 50 years from the making of the work, 50 years from the end of the calendar year of making.

5. Each Party shall confine limitations or exceptions to the rights provided for in this Article to certain special cases that do not conflict with a normal exploitation of the work and do not unreasonably prejudice the legitimate interests of the right holder.

6. No Party may grant translation and reproduction licenses permitted under the Appendix to the Berne Convention where legitimate needs in that Party's territory for copies or translations of the work could be met by the right holder's voluntary actions but for obstacles created by the Party's measures.

7. Annex 1705.7 applies to the Parties specified in that Annex.

Annex 1705.7

Copyright

The United States shall provide protection to motion pictures produced in another Party's territory that have been declared to be in the public domain pursuant to 17 U.S.C. section 405. This obligation shall apply to the extent that it is consistent with the Constitution of the United States, and is subject to budgetary considerations.

Article 1706

Sound Recordings

1. Each Party shall provide to the producer of a sound recording the right to authorize or prohibit: (a) the direct or indirect reproduction of the sound recording; (b) the importation into the Party's territory of copies of the sound recording made without the producer's authorization; (c) the first public distribution of the original and each copy of the sound recording by sale, rental or otherwise; and (d) the commercial rental of the original or a copy of the sound recording, except where expressly otherwise provided in a contract between the producer of the sound recording and the authors of the works fixed therein. Each Party shall provide that putting the original or a copy of a sound recording on the market with the right holder's consent shall not exhaust the rental right.

2. Each Party shall provide a term of protection for sound recordings of at least 50 years from the end of the calendar year in which the fixation was made.

3. Each Party shall confine limitations or exceptions to the rights provided for in this Article to certain special cases that do not conflict with a normal exploitation of the sound recording and do not unreasonably prejudice the legitimate interests of the right holder.

Article 1707

Protection of Encrypted Program–Carrying Satellite Signals

Within one year from the date of entry into force of this Agreement, each Party shall make it: (a) a criminal offense to manufacture, import, sell, lease or otherwise make available a device or system that is primarily of assistance in decoding an encrypted program-carrying satellite signal without the authorization of the lawful distributor of such signal; and (b) a civil offense to receive, in connection with commercial activities, or further distribute, an encrypted program-carrying satellite signal that has been decoded without the authorization of the lawful distributor of the signal or to engage in any activity prohibited under subparagraph (a). Each Party shall provide that any civil offense established under subparagraph (b) shall be actionable by any person that holds an interest in the content of such signal.

Article 1708

Trademarks

1. For purposes of this Agreement, a trademark consists of any sign, or any combination of signs, capable of distinguishing the goods or services of one person from those of another, including personal names, designs, letters,

numerals, colors, figurative elements, or the shape of goods or of their packaging. Trademarks shall include service marks and collective marks, and may include certification marks. A Party may require, as a condition for registration, that a sign be visually perceptible.

2. Each Party shall provide to the owner of a registered trademark the right to prevent all persons not having the owner's consent from using in commerce identical or similar signs for goods or services that are identical or similar to those goods or services in respect of which the owner's trademark is registered, where such use would result in a likelihood of confusion. In the case of the use of an identical sign for identical goods or services, a likelihood of confusion shall be presumed. The rights described above shall not prejudice any prior rights, nor shall they affect the possibility of a Party making rights available on the basis of use.

3. A Party may make registrability depend on use. However, actual use of a trademark shall not be a condition for filing an application for registration. No Party may refuse an application solely on the ground that intended use has not taken place before the expiry of a period of three years from the date of application for registration.

4. Each Party shall provide a system for the registration of trademarks, which shall include: (a) examination of applications; (b) notice to be given to an applicant of the reasons for the refusal to register a trademark; (c) a reasonable opportunity for the applicant to respond to the notice; (d) publication of each trademark either before or promptly after it is registered; and (e) a reasonable opportunity for interested persons to petition to cancel the registration of a trademark. A Party may provide for a reasonable opportunity for interested persons to oppose the registration of a trademark.

5. The nature of the goods or services to which a trademark is to be applied shall in no case form an obstacle to the registration of the trademark.

6. Article 6bis of the Paris Convention shall apply, with such modifications as may be necessary, to services. In determining whether a trademark is well-known, account shall be taken of the knowledge of the trademark in the relevant sector of the public, including knowledge in the Party's territory obtained as a result of the promotion of the trademark. No Party may require that the reputation of the trademark extend beyond the sector of the public that normally deals with the relevant goods or services.

7. Each Party shall provide that the initial registration of a trademark be for a term of at least 10 years and that the registration be indefinitely renewable for terms of not less than 10 years when conditions for renewal have been met.

8. Each Party shall require the use of a trademark to maintain a registration. The registration may be canceled for the reason of non-use only after an uninterrupted period of at least two years of non-use, unless valid reasons based on the existence of obstacles to such use are shown by the trademark owner. Each Party shall recognize, as valid reasons for non-use, circumstances arising independently of the will of the trademark owner that constitute an obstacle to the use of the trademark, such as import restrictions on, or other government requirements for, goods or services identified by the trademark.

9. Each Party shall recognize use of a trademark by a person other than the trademark owner, where such use is subject to the owner's control, as use of the trademark for purposes of maintaining the registration.

10. No Party may encumber the use of a trademark in commerce by special requirements, such as a use that reduces the trademark's function as an indication of source or a use with another trademark.

11. A Party may determine conditions on the licensing and assignment of trademarks, it being understood that the compulsory licensing of trademarks shall not be permitted and that the owner of a registered trademark shall have the right to assign its trademark with or without the transfer of the business to which the trademark belongs.

12. A Party may provide limited exceptions to the rights conferred by a trademark, such as fair use of descriptive terms, provided that such exceptions take into account the legitimate interests of the trademark owner and of other persons.

13. Each Party shall prohibit the registration as a trademark of words, at least in English, French or Spanish, that generically designate goods or services or types of goods or services to which the trademark applies.

14. Each Party shall refuse to register trademarks that consist of or comprise immoral, deceptive or scandalous matter, or matter that may disparage or falsely suggest a connection with persons, living or dead, institutions, beliefs or any Party's national symbols, or bring them into contempt or disrepute.

Article 1709
Patents

1. Subject to paragraphs 2 and 3, each Party shall make patents available for any inventions, whether products or processes, in all fields of technology, provided that such inventions are new, result from an inventive step and are capable of industrial application. For purposes of this Article, a Party may deem the terms "inventive step" and "capable of industrial application" to be synonymous with the terms "non-obvious" and "useful", respectively.

2. A Party may exclude from patentability inventions if preventing in its territory the commercial exploitation of the inventions is necessary to protect ordre public or morality, including to protect human, animal or plant life or health or to avoid serious prejudice to nature or the environment, provided that the exclusion is not based solely on the ground that the Party prohibits commercial exploitation in its territory of the subject matter of the patent.

3. A Party may also exclude from patentability: (a) diagnostic, therapeutic and surgical methods for the treatment of humans or animals; (b) plants and animals other than microorganisms; and (c) essentially biological processes for the production of plants or animals, other than non-biological and microbiological processes for such production. Notwithstanding subparagraph (b), each Party shall provide for the protection of plant varieties through patents, an effective scheme of sui generis protection, or both.

4. If a Party has not made available product patent protection for pharmaceutical or agricultural chemicals commensurate with paragraph 1:

(a) as of January 1, 1992, for subject matter that relates to naturally occurring substances prepared or produced by, or significantly derived from, microbiological processes and intended for food or medicine, and (b) as of July 1, 1991, for any other subject matter, that Party shall provide to the inventor of any such product or its assignee the means to obtain product patent protection for such product for the unexpired term of the patent for such product granted in another Party, as long as the product has not been marketed in the Party providing protection under this paragraph and the person seeking such protection makes a timely request.

5. Each Party shall provide that: (a) where the subject matter of a patent is a product, the patent shall confer on the patent owner the right to prevent other persons from making, using or selling the subject matter of the patent, without the patent owner's consent; and (b) where the subject matter of a patent is a process, the patent shall confer on the patent owner the right to prevent other persons from using that process and from using, selling, or importing at least the product obtained directly by that process, without the patent owner's consent.

6. A Party may provide limited exceptions to the exclusive rights conferred by a patent, provided that such exceptions do not unreasonably conflict with a normal exploitation of the patent and do not unreasonably prejudice the legitimate interests of the patent owner, taking into account the legitimate interests of other persons.

7. Subject to paragraphs 2 and 3, patents shall be available and patent rights enjoyable without discrimination as to the field of technology, the territory of the Party where the invention was made and whether products are imported or locally produced.

8. A Party may revoke a patent only when: (a) grounds exist that would have justified a refusal to grant the patent; or (b) the grant of a compulsory license has not remedied the lack of exploitation of the patent.

9. Each Party shall permit patent owners to assign and transfer by succession their patents, and to conclude licensing contracts.

10. Where the law of a Party allows for use of the subject matter of a patent, other than that use allowed under paragraph 6, without the authorization of the right holder, including use by the government or other persons authorized by the government, the Party shall respect the following provisions: (a) authorization of such use shall be considered on its individual merits; (b) such use may only be permitted if, prior to such use, the proposed user has made efforts to obtain authorization from the right holder on reasonable commercial terms and conditions and such efforts have not been successful within a reasonable period of time. The requirement to make such efforts may be waived by a Party in the case of a national emergency or other circumstances of extreme urgency or in cases of public non-commercial use. In situations of national emergency or other circumstances of extreme urgency, the right holder shall, nevertheless, be notified as soon as reasonably practicable. In the case of public non-commercial use, where the government or contractor, without making a patent search, knows or has demonstrable grounds to know that a valid patent is or will be used by or for the government, the right holder shall be informed promptly; (c) the scope and duration of such use shall be limited to the purpose for which it was

authorized; (d) such use shall be non-exclusive; (e) such use shall be non-assignable, except with that part of the enterprise or goodwill that enjoys such use; (f) any such use shall be authorized predominantly for the supply of the Party's domestic market; (g) authorization for such use shall be liable, subject to adequate protection of the legitimate interests of the persons so authorized, to be terminated if and when the circumstances that led to it cease to exist and are unlikely to recur. The competent authority shall have the authority to review, on motivated request, the continued existence of these circumstances; (h) the right holder shall be paid adequate remuneration in the circumstances of each case, taking into account the economic value of the authorization; (i) the legal validity of any decision relating to the authorization shall be subject to judicial or other independent review by a distinct higher authority; (j) any decision relating to the remuneration provided in respect of such use shall be subject to judicial or other independent review by a distinct higher authority; (k) the Party shall not be obliged to apply the conditions set out in subparagraphs (b) and (f) where such use is permitted to remedy a practice determined after judicial or administrative process to be anticompetitive. The need to correct anticompetitive practices may be taken into account in determining the amount of remuneration in such cases. Competent authorities shall have the authority to refuse termination of authorization if and when the conditions that led to such authorization are likely to recur; (l) the Party shall not authorize the use of the subject matter of a patent to permit the exploitation of another patent except as a remedy for an adjudicated violation of domestic laws regarding anticompetitive practices.

11. Where the subject matter of a patent is a process for obtaining a product, each Party shall, in any infringement proceeding, place on the defendant the burden of establishing that the allegedly infringing product was made by a process other than the patented process in one of the following situations: (a) the product obtained by the patented process is new; or (b) a substantial likelihood exists that the allegedly infringing product was made by the process and the patent owner has been unable through reasonable efforts to determine the process actually used. In the gathering and evaluation of evidence, the legitimate interests of the defendant in protecting its trade secrets shall be taken into account.

12. Each Party shall provide a term of protection for patents of at least 20 years from the date of filing or 17 years from the date of grant. A Party may extend the term of patent protection, in appropriate cases, to compensate for delays caused by regulatory approval processes.

Article 1710

Layout Designs of Semiconductor Integrated Circuits

1. Each Party shall protect layout designs (topographies) of integrated circuits ("layout designs") in accordance with Articles 2 through 7, 12 and 16(3), other than Article 6(3), of the Treaty on Intellectual Property in Respect of Integrated Circuits as opened for signature on May 26, 1989.

2. Subject to paragraph 3, each Party shall make it unlawful for any person without the right holder's authorization to import, sell or otherwise distribute for commercial purposes any of the following: (a) a protected layout design; (b) an integrated circuit in which a protected layout design is

incorporated; or (c) an article incorporating such an integrated circuit, only insofar as it continues to contain an unlawfully reproduced layout design.

3. No Party may make unlawful any of the acts referred to in paragraph 2 performed in respect of an integrated circuit that incorporates an unlawfully reproduced layout design, or any article that incorporates such an integrated circuit, where the person performing those acts or ordering those acts to be done did not know and had no reasonable ground to know, when it acquired the integrated circuit or article incorporating such an integrated circuit, that it incorporated an unlawfully reproduced layout design.

4. Each Party shall provide that, after the person referred to in paragraph 3 has received sufficient notice that the layout design was unlawfully reproduced, such person may perform any of the acts with respect to the stock on hand or ordered before such notice, but shall be liable to pay the right holder for doing so an amount equivalent to a reasonable royalty such as would be payable under a freely negotiated license in respect of such a layout design.

5. No Party may permit the compulsory licensing of layout designs of integrated circuits.

6. Any Party that requires registration as a condition for protection of a layout design shall provide that the term of protection shall not end before the expiration of a period of 10 years counted from the date of: (a) filing of the application for registration; or (b) the first commercial exploitation of the layout design, wherever in the world it occurs.

7. Where a Party does not require registration as a condition for protection of a layout design, the Party shall provide a term of protection of not less than 10 years from the date of the first commercial exploitation of the layout design, wherever in the world it occurs.

8. Notwithstanding paragraphs 6 and 7, a Party may provide that the protection shall lapse 15 years after the creation of the layout design.

9. Annex 1710.9 applies to the Parties specified in that Annex.

Annex 1710.9

Layout Designs

Mexico shall make every effort to implement the requirements of Article 1710 as soon as possible, and shall do so no later than four years after the date of entry into force of this Agreement.

Article 1711

Trade Secrets

1. Each Party shall provide the legal means for any person to prevent trade secrets from being disclosed to, acquired by, or used by others without the consent of the person lawfully in control of the information in a manner contrary to honest commercial practices, in so far as: (a) the information is secret in the sense that it is not, as a body or in the precise configuration and assembly of its components, generally known among or readily accessible to persons that normally deal with the kind of information in question; (b) the information has actual or potential commercial value because it is secret; and

(c) the person lawfully in control of the information has taken reasonable steps under the circumstances to keep it secret.

2.   A Party may require that to qualify for protection a trade secret must be evidenced in documents, electronic or magnetic means, optical discs, microfilms, films or other similar instruments.

3.   No Party may limit the duration of protection for trade secrets, so long as the conditions in paragraph 1 exist.

4.   No Party may discourage or impede the voluntary licensing of trade secrets by imposing excessive or discriminatory conditions on such licenses or conditions that dilute the value of the trade secrets.

5.   If a Party requires, as a condition for approving the marketing of pharmaceutical or agricultural chemical products that utilize new chemical entities, the submission of undisclosed test or other data necessary to determine whether the use of such products is safe and effective, the Party shall protect against disclosure of the data of persons making such submissions, where the origination of such data involves considerable effort, except where the disclosure is necessary to protect the public or unless steps are taken to ensure that the data is protected against unfair commercial use.

6.   Each Party shall provide that for data subject to paragraph 5 that are submitted to the Party after the date of entry into force of this Agreement, no person other than the person that submitted them may, without the latter's permission, rely on such data in support of an application for product approval during a reasonable period of time after their submission. For this purpose, a reasonable period shall normally mean not less than five years from the date on which the Party granted approval to the person that produced the data for approval to market its product, taking account of the nature of the data and the person's efforts and expenditures in producing them. Subject to this provision, there shall be no limitation on any Party to implement abbreviated approval procedures for such products on the basis of bioequivalence and bioavailability studies.

7.   Where a Party relies on a marketing approval granted by another Party, the reasonable period of exclusive use of the data submitted in connection with obtaining the approval relied on shall begin with the date of the first marketing approval relied on.

Article 1712
Geographical Indications

1.   Each Party shall provide, in respect of geographical indications, the legal means for interested persons to prevent: (a) the use of any means in the designation or presentation of a good that indicates or suggests that the good in question originates in a territory, region or locality other than the true place of origin, in a manner that misleads the public as to the geographical origin of the good; (b) any use that constitutes an act of unfair competition within the meaning of Article 10bis of the Paris Convention.

2.   Each Party shall, on its own initiative if its domestic law so permits or at the request of an interested person, refuse to register, or invalidate the registration of, a trademark containing or consisting of a geographical indication with respect to goods that do not originate in the indicated territory,

region or locality, if use of the indication in the trademark for such goods is of such a nature as to mislead the public as to the geographical origin of the good.

3. Each Party shall also apply paragraphs 1 and 2 to a geographical indication that, although correctly indicating the territory, region or locality in which the goods originate, falsely represents to the public that the goods originate in another territory, region or locality.

4. Nothing in this Article shall be construed to require a Party to prevent continued and similar use of a particular geographical indication of another Party in connection with goods or services by any of its nationals or domiciliaries who have used that geographical indication in a continuous manner with regard to the same or related goods or services in that Party's territory, either: (a) for at least 10 years, or (b) in good faith, before the date of signature of this Agreement.

5. Where a trademark has been applied for or registered in good faith, or where rights to a trademark have been acquired through use in good faith, either: (a) before the date of application of these provisions in that Party, or (b) before the geographical indication is protected in its Party of origin, no Party may adopt any measure to implement this Article that prejudices eligibility for, or the validity of, the registration of a trademark, or the right to use a trademark, on the basis that such a trademark is identical with, or similar to, a geographical indication.

6. No Party shall be required to apply this Article to a geographical indication if it is identical to the customary term in common language in that Party's territory for the goods or services to which the indication applies.

7. A Party may provide that any request made under this Article in connection with the use or registration of a trademark must be presented within five years after the adverse use of the protected indication has become generally known in that Party or after the date of registration of the trademark in that Party, provided that the trademark has been published by that date, if such date is earlier than the date on which the adverse use became generally known in that Party, provided that the geographical indication is not used or registered in bad faith.

8. No Party shall adopt any measure implementing this Article that would prejudice any person's right to use, in the course of trade, its name or the name of its predecessor in business, except where such name forms all or part of a valid trademark in existence before the geographical indication became protected and with which there is a likelihood of confusion, or such name is used in such a manner as to mislead the public.

9. Nothing in this Chapter shall be construed to require a Party to protect a geographical indication that is not protected, or has fallen into disuse, in the Party of origin.

Article 1713
Industrial Designs

1. Each Party shall provide for the protection of independently created industrial designs that are new or original. A Party may provide that: (a) designs are not new or original if they do not significantly differ from known

designs or combinations of known design features; and (b) such protection shall not extend to designs dictated essentially by technical or functional considerations.

2. Each Party shall ensure that the requirements for securing protection for textile designs, in particular in regard to any cost, examination or publication, do not unreasonably impair a person's opportunity to seek and obtain such protection. A Party may comply with this obligation through industrial design law or copyright law.

3. Each Party shall provide the owner of a protected industrial design the right to prevent other persons not having the owner's consent from making or selling articles bearing or embodying a design that is a copy, or substantially a copy, of the protected design, when such acts are undertaken for commercial purposes.

4. A Party may provide limited exceptions to the protection of industrial designs, provided that such exceptions do not unreasonably conflict with the normal exploitation of protected industrial designs and do not unreasonably prejudice the legitimate interests of the owner of the protected design, taking into account the legitimate interests of other persons.

5. Each Party shall provide a term of protection for industrial designs of at least 10 years.

Article 1714

Enforcement of Intellectual Property Rights: General Provisions

1. Each Party shall ensure that enforcement procedures, as specified in this Article and Articles 1715 through 1718, are available under its domestic law so as to permit effective action to be taken against any act of infringement of intellectual property rights covered by this Chapter, including expeditious remedies to prevent infringements and remedies to deter further infringements. Such enforcement procedures shall be applied so as to avoid the creation of barriers to legitimate trade and to provide for safeguards against abuse of the procedures.

2. Each Party shall ensure that its procedures for the enforcement of intellectual property rights are fair and equitable, are not unnecessarily complicated or costly, and do not entail unreasonable time-limits or unwarranted delays.

3. Each Party shall provide that decisions on the merits of a case in judicial and administrative enforcement proceedings shall: (a) preferably be in writing and preferably state the reasons on which the decisions are based; (b) be made available at least to the parties in a proceeding without undue delay; and (c) be based only on evidence in respect of which such parties were offered the opportunity to be heard.

4. Each Party shall ensure that parties in a proceeding have an opportunity to have final administrative decisions reviewed by a judicial authority of that Party and, subject to jurisdictional provisions in its domestic laws concerning the importance of a case, to have reviewed at least the legal aspects of initial judicial decisions on the merits of a case. Notwithstanding the above, no Party shall be required to provide for judicial review of acquittals in criminal cases.

5. Nothing in this Article or Articles 1715 through 1718 shall be construed to require a Party to establish a judicial system for the enforcement of intellectual property rights distinct from that Party's system for the enforcement of laws in general.

6. For the purposes of Articles 1715 through 1718, the term "right holder" includes federations and associations having legal standing to assert such rights.

Article 1715
Specific Procedural and Remedial Aspects of
Civil and Administrative Procedures

1. Each Party shall make available to right holders civil judicial procedures for the enforcement of any intellectual property right provided in this Chapter. Each Party shall provide that: (a) defendants have the right to written notice that is timely and contains sufficient detail, including the basis of the claims; (b) parties in a proceeding are allowed to be represented by independent legal counsel; (c) the procedures do not include imposition of overly burdensome requirements concerning mandatory personal appearances; (d) all parties in a proceeding are duly entitled to substantiate their claims and to present relevant evidence; and (e) the procedures include a means to identify and protect confidential information.

2. Each Party shall provide that its judicial authorities shall have the authority: (a) where a party in a proceeding has presented reasonably available evidence sufficient to support its claims and has specified evidence relevant to the substantiation of its claims that is within the control of the opposing party, to order the opposing party to produce such evidence, subject in appropriate cases to conditions that ensure the protection of confidential information; (b) where a party in a proceeding voluntarily and without good reason refuses access to, or otherwise does not provide relevant evidence under that party's control within a reasonable period, or significantly impedes a proceeding relating to an enforcement action, to make preliminary and final determinations, affirmative or negative, on the basis of the evidence presented, including the complaint or the allegation presented by the party adversely affected by the denial of access to evidence, subject to providing the parties an opportunity to be heard on the allegations or evidence; (c) to order a party in a proceeding to desist from an infringement, including to prevent the entry into the channels of commerce in their jurisdiction of imported goods that involve the infringement of an intellectual property right, which order shall be enforceable at least immediately after customs clearance of such goods; (d) to order the infringer of an intellectual property right to pay the right holder damages adequate to compensate for the injury the right holder has suffered because of the infringement where the infringer knew or had reasonable grounds to know that it was engaged in an infringing activity; (e) to order an infringer of an intellectual property right to pay the right holder's expenses, which may include appropriate attorney's fees; and (f) to order a party in a proceeding at whose request measures were taken and who has abused enforcement procedures to provide adequate compensation to any party wrongfully enjoined or restrained in the proceeding for the injury suffered because of such abuse and to pay that party's expenses, which may include appropriate attorney's fees.

3. With respect to the authority referred to in subparagraph 2(c), no Party shall be obliged to provide such authority in respect of protected subject matter that is acquired or ordered by a person before that person knew or had reasonable grounds to know that dealing in that subject matter would entail the infringement of an intellectual property right.

4. With respect to the authority referred to in subparagraph 2(d), a Party may, at least with respect to copyrighted works and sound recordings, authorize the judicial authorities to order recovery of profits or payment of pre-established damages, or both, even where the infringer did not know or had no reasonable grounds to know that it was engaged in an infringing activity.

5. Each Party shall provide that, in order to create an effective deterrent to infringement, its judicial authorities shall have the authority to order that: (a) goods that they have found to be infringing be, without compensation of any sort, disposed of outside the channels of commerce in such a manner as to avoid any injury caused to the right holder or, unless this would be contrary to existing constitutional requirements, destroyed; and (b) materials and implements the predominant use of which has been in the creation of the infringing goods be, without compensation of any sort, disposed of outside the channels of commerce in such a manner as to minimize the risks of further infringements. In considering whether to issue such an order, judicial authorities shall take into account the need for proportionality between the seriousness of the infringement and the remedies ordered as well as the interests of other persons. In regard to counterfeit goods, the simple removal of the trademark unlawfully affixed shall not be sufficient, other than in exceptional cases, to permit release of the goods into the channels of commerce.

6. In respect of the administration of any law pertaining to the protection or enforcement of intellectual property rights, each Party shall only exempt both public authorities and officials from liability to appropriate remedial measures where actions are taken or intended in good faith in the course of the administration of such laws.

7. Notwithstanding the other provisions of Articles 1714 through 1718, where a Party is sued with respect to an infringement of an intellectual property right as a result of its use of that right or use on its behalf, that Party may limit the remedies available against it to the payment to the right holder of adequate remuneration in the circumstances of each case, taking into account the economic value of the use.

8. Each Party shall provide that, where a civil remedy can be ordered as a result of administrative procedures on the merits of a case, such procedures shall conform to principles equivalent in substance to those set out in this Article.

Article 1716

Provisional Measures

1. Each Party shall provide that its judicial authorities shall have the authority to order prompt and effective provisional measures: (a) to prevent an infringement of any intellectual property right, and in particular to prevent the entry into the channels of commerce in their jurisdiction of

allegedly infringing goods, including measures to prevent the entry of imported goods at least immediately after customs clearance; and (b) to preserve relevant evidence in regard to the alleged infringement.

2. Each Party shall provide that its judicial authorities shall have the authority to require any applicant for provisional measures to provide to the judicial authorities any evidence reasonably available to that applicant that the judicial authorities consider necessary to enable them to determine with a sufficient degree of certainty whether: (a) the applicant is the right holder; (b) the applicant's right is being infringed or such infringement is imminent; and (c) any delay in the issuance of such measures is likely to cause irreparable harm to the right holder, or there is a demonstrable risk of evidence being destroyed. Each Party shall provide that its judicial authorities shall have the authority to require the applicant to provide a security or equivalent assurance sufficient to protect the interests of the defendant and to prevent abuse.

3. Each Party shall provide that its judicial authorities shall have the authority to require an applicant for provisional measures to provide other information necessary for the identification of the relevant goods by the authority that will execute the provisional measures.

4. Each Party shall provide that its judicial authorities shall have the authority to order provisional measures on an ex parte basis, in particular where any delay is likely to cause irreparable harm to the right holder, or where there is a demonstrable risk of evidence being destroyed.

5. Each Party shall provide that where provisional measures are adopted by that Party's judicial authorities on an ex parte basis: (a) a person affected shall be given notice of those measures without delay but in any event no later than immediately after the execution of the measures; (b) a defendant shall, on request, have those measures reviewed by that Party's judicial authorities for the purpose of deciding, within a reasonable period after notice of those measures is given, whether the measures shall be modified, revoked or confirmed, and shall be given an opportunity to be heard in the review proceedings.

6. Without prejudice to paragraph 5, each Party shall provide that, on the request of the defendant, the Party's judicial authorities shall revoke or otherwise cease to apply the provisional measures taken on the basis of paragraphs 1 and 4 if proceedings leading to a decision on the merits are not initiated: (a) within a reasonable period as determined by the judicial authority ordering the measures where the Party's domestic law so permits; or (b) in the absence of such a determination, within a period of no more than 20 working days or 31 calendar days, whichever is longer.

7. Each Party shall provide that, where the provisional measures are revoked or where they lapse due to any act or omission by the applicant, or where the judicial authorities subsequently find that there has been no infringement or threat of infringement of an intellectual property right, the judicial authorities shall have the authority to order the applicant, on request of the defendant, to provide the defendant appropriate compensation for any injury caused by these measures.

8. Each Party shall provide that, where a provisional measure can be ordered as a result of administrative procedures, such procedures shall conform to principles equivalent in substance to those set out in this Article.

Article 1717
Criminal Procedures and Penalties

1. Each Party shall provide criminal procedures and penalties to be applied at least in cases of willful trademark counterfeiting or copyright piracy on a commercial scale. Each Party shall provide that penalties available include imprisonment or monetary fines, or both, sufficient to provide a deterrent, consistent with the level of penalties applied for crimes of a corresponding gravity.

2. Each Party shall provide that, in appropriate cases, its judicial authorities may order the seizure, forfeiture and destruction of infringing goods and of any materials and implements the predominant use of which has been in the commission of the offense.

3. A Party may provide criminal procedures and penalties to be applied in cases of infringement of intellectual property rights, other than those in paragraph 1, where they are committed wilfully and on a commercial scale.

Article 1718
Enforcement of Intellectual Property Rights at the Border

1. Each Party shall, in conformity with this Article, adopt procedures to enable a right holder, who has valid grounds for suspecting that the importation of counterfeit trademark goods or pirated copyright goods may take place, to lodge an application in writing with its competent authorities, whether administrative or judicial, for the suspension by the customs administration of the release of such goods into free circulation. No Party shall be obligated to apply such procedures to goods in transit. A Party may permit such an application to be made in respect of goods that involve other infringements of intellectual property rights, provided that the requirements of this Article are met. A Party may also provide for corresponding procedures concerning the suspension by the customs administration of the release of infringing goods destined for exportation from its territory.

2. Each Party shall require any applicant who initiates procedures under paragraph 1 to provide adequate evidence: (a) to satisfy that Party's competent authorities that, under the domestic laws of the country of importation, there is prima facie an infringement of its intellectual property right; and (b) to supply a sufficiently detailed description of the goods to make them readily recognizable by the customs administration. The competent authorities shall inform the applicant within a reasonable period whether they have accepted the application and, if so, the period for which the customs administration will take action.

3. Each Party shall provide that its competent authorities shall have the authority to require an applicant under paragraph 1 to provide a security or equivalent assurance sufficient to protect the defendant and the competent authorities and to prevent abuse. Such security or equivalent assurance shall not unreasonably deter recourse to these procedures.

4. Each Party shall provide that, where pursuant to an application under procedures adopted pursuant to this Article, its customs administration suspends the release of goods involving industrial designs, patents, integrated circuits or trade secrets into free circulation on the basis of a decision other than by a judicial or other independent authority, and the period provided for in paragraphs 6 through 8 has expired without the granting of provisional relief by the duly empowered authority, and provided that all other conditions for importation have been complied with, the owner, importer or consignee of such goods shall be entitled to their release on the posting of a security in an amount sufficient to protect the right holder against any infringement. Payment of such security shall not prejudice any other remedy available to the right holder, it being understood that the security shall be released if the right holder fails to pursue its right of action within a reasonable period of time.

5. Each Party shall provide that its customs administration shall promptly notify the importer and the applicant when the customs administration suspends the release of goods pursuant to paragraph 1.

6. Each Party shall provide that its customs administration shall release goods from suspension if, within a period not exceeding 10 working days after the applicant under paragraph 1 has been served notice of the suspension, the customs administration has not been informed that: (a) a party other than the defendant has initiated proceedings leading to a decision on the merits of the case, or (b) a competent authority has taken provisional measures prolonging the suspension, provided that all other conditions for importation or exportation have been met. Each Party shall provide that, in appropriate cases, the customs administration may extend the suspension by another 10 working days.

7. Each Party shall provide that if proceedings leading to a decision on the merits of the case have been initiated, a review, including a right to be heard, shall take place on request of the defendant with a view to deciding, within a reasonable period, whether these measures shall be modified, revoked or confirmed.

8. Notwithstanding paragraphs 6 and 7, where the suspension of the release of goods is carried out or continued in accordance with a provisional judicial measure, Article 1716(6) shall apply.

9. Each Party shall provide that its competent authorities shall have the authority to order the applicant under paragraph 1 to pay the importer, the consignee and the owner of the goods appropriate compensation for any injury caused to them through the wrongful detention of goods or through the detention of goods released pursuant to paragraph 6.

10. Without prejudice to the protection of confidential information, each Party shall provide that its competent authorities shall have the authority to give the right holder sufficient opportunity to have any goods detained by the customs administration inspected in order to substantiate the right holder's claims. Each Party shall also provide that its competent authorities have the authority to give the importer an equivalent opportunity to have any such goods inspected. Where the competent authorities have made a positive determination on the merits of a case, a Party may provide the competent authorities the authority to inform the right holder of the names and

addresses of the consignor, the importer and the consignee, and of the quantity of the goods in question.

11.   Where a Party requires its competent authorities to act on their own initiative and to suspend the release of goods in respect of which they have acquired prima facie evidence that an intellectual property right is being infringed: (a) the competent authorities may at any time seek from the right holder any information that may assist them to exercise these powers; (b) the importer and the right holder shall be promptly notified of the suspension by the Party's competent authorities, and where the importer lodges an appeal against the suspension with competent authorities, the suspension shall be subject to the conditions, with such modifications as may be necessary, set out in paragraphs 6 through 8; and (c) the Party shall only exempt both public authorities and officials from liability to appropriate remedial measures where actions are taken or intended in good faith.

12.   Without prejudice to other rights of action open to the right holder and subject to the defendant's right to seek judicial review, each Party shall provide that its competent authorities shall have the authority to order the destruction or disposal of infringing goods in accordance with the principles set out in Article 1715(5).   In regard to counterfeit goods, the authorities shall not allow the re-exportation of the infringing goods in an unaltered state or subject them to a different customs procedure, other than in exceptional circumstances.

13.   A Party may exclude from the application of paragraphs 1 through 12 small quantities of goods of a non-commercial nature contained in travellers' personal luggage or sent in small consignments that are not repetitive.

14.   Annex 1718.14 applies to the Parties specified in that Annex.

Annex 1718.14
Enforcement of Intellectual Property Rights

Mexico shall make every effort to comply with the requirements of Article 1718 as soon as possible and shall do so no later than three years after the date of signature of this Agreement.

Article 1719
Cooperation and Technical Assistance

1.   The Parties shall provide each other on mutually agreed terms with technical assistance and shall promote cooperation between their competent authorities.   Such cooperation shall include the training of personnel.

2.   The Parties shall cooperate with a view to eliminating trade in goods that infringe intellectual property rights.   For this purpose, each Party shall establish and notify the other Parties by January 1, 1994 of contact points in its federal government and shall exchange information concerning trade in infringing goods.

Article 1720
Protection of Existing Subject Matter

1.   Except as required under Article 1705(7), this Agreement does not give rise to obligations in respect of acts that occurred before the date of application of the relevant provisions of this Agreement for the Party in question.

2.   Except as otherwise provided for in this Agreement, each Party shall apply this Agreement to all subject matter existing on the date of application of the relevant provisions of this Agreement for the Party in question and that is protected in a Party on such date, or that meets or subsequently meets the criteria for protection under the terms of this Chapter. In respect of this paragraph and paragraphs 3 and 4, a Party's obligations with respect to existing works shall be solely determined under Article 18 of the Berne Convention and with respect to the rights of producers of sound recordings in existing sound recordings shall be determined solely under Article 18 of that Convention, as made applicable under this Agreement.

3.   Except as required under Article 1705(7), and notwithstanding the first sentence of paragraph 2, no Party may be required to restore protection to subject matter that, on the date of application of the relevant provisions of this Agreement for the Party in question, has fallen into the public domain in its territory.

4.   In respect of any acts relating to specific objects embodying protected subject matter that become infringing under the terms of laws in conformity with this Agreement, and that were begun or in respect of which a significant investment was made, before the date of entry into force of this Agreement for that Party, any Party may provide for a limitation of the remedies available to the right holder as to the continued performance of such acts after the date of application of this Agreement for that Party. In such cases, the Party shall, however, at least provide for payment of equitable remuneration.

5.   No Party shall be obliged to apply Article 1705(2)(d) or 1706(1)(d) with respect to originals or copies purchased prior to the date of application of the relevant provisions of this Agreement for that Party.

6.   No Party shall be required to apply Article 1709(10), or the requirement in Article 1709(7) that patent rights shall be enjoyable without discrimination as to the field of technology, to use without the authorization of the right holder where authorization for such use was granted by the government before the text of the Draft Final Act Embodying the Results of the Uruguay Round of Multilateral Trade Negotiations became known.

7.   In the case of intellectual property rights for which protection is conditional on registration, applications for protection that are pending on the date of application of the relevant provisions of this Agreement for the Party in question shall be permitted to be amended to claim any enhanced protection provided under this Agreement. Such amendments shall not include new matter.

Article 1721

Definitions

1.   For purposes of this Chapter:

confidential information includes trade secrets, privileged information and other materials exempted from disclosure under the Party's domestic law.

2.   For purposes of this Agreement:

encrypted program-carrying satellite signal means a program-carrying satellite signal that is transmitted in a form whereby the aural or visual characteristics, or both, are modified or altered for the purpose of preventing the unauthorized reception, by persons without the authorized equipment that is designed to eliminate the effects of such modification or alteration, of a program carried in that signal;

geographical indication means any indication that identifies a good as originating in the territory of a Party, or a region or locality in that territory, where a particular quality, reputation or other characteristic of the good is essentially attributable to its geographical origin;

in a manner contrary to honest commercial practices means at least practices such as breach of contract, breach of confidence and inducement to breach, and includes the acquisition of undisclosed information by other persons who knew, or were grossly negligent in failing to know, that such practices were involved in the acquisition;

intellectual property rights refers to copyright and related rights, trademark rights, patent rights, rights in layout designs of semiconductor integrated circuits, trade secret rights, plant breeders' rights, rights in geographical indications and industrial design rights;

nationals of another Party means, in respect of the relevant intellectual property right, persons who would meet the criteria for eligibility for protection provided for in the Paris Convention (1967), the Berne Convention (1971), the Geneva Convention (1971), the International Convention for the Protection of Performers, Producers of Phonograms and Broadcasting Organizations (1961), the UPOV Convention (1978), the UPOV Convention (1991) or the Treaty on Intellectual Property in Respect of Integrated Circuits, as if each Party were a party to those Conventions, and with respect to intellectual property rights that are not the subject of these Conventions, "nationals of another Party" shall be understood to be at least individuals who are citizens or permanent residents of that Party and also includes any other natural person referred to in Annex 201.1 (Country–Specific Definitions);

public includes, with respect to rights of communication and performance of works provided for under Articles 11, 11bis(1) and 14(1)(ii) of the Berne Convention, with respect to dramatic, dramatico-musical, musical and cinematographic works, at least, any aggregation of individuals intended to be the object of, and capable of perceiving, communications or performances of works, regardless of whether they can do so at the same or different times or in the same or different places, provided that such an aggregation is larger than a family and its immediate circle of acquaintances or is not a group comprising a limited number of individuals having similarly close ties that has not been formed for the principal purpose of receiving such performances and communications of works; and

secondary uses of sound recordings means the use directly for broadcasting or for any other public communication of a sound recording.

PART SEVEN
ADMINISTRATIVE AND INSTITUTIONAL PROVISIONS
CHAPTER EIGHTEEN: PUBLICATION, NOTIFICATION AND ADMINISTRATION OF LAWS

Article 1801

Contact Points

Each Party shall designate a contact point to facilitate communications between the Parties on any matter covered by this Agreement. On the request of another Party, the contact point shall identify the office or official responsible for the matter and assist, as necessary, in facilitating communication with the requesting Party.

Article 1802
Publication

1. Each Party shall ensure that its laws, regulations, procedures and administrative rulings of general application respecting any matter covered by this Agreement are promptly published or otherwise made available in such a manner as to enable interested persons and Parties to become acquainted with them.

2. To the extent possible, each Party shall: (a) publish in advance any such measure that it proposes to adopt; and (b) provide interested persons and Parties a reasonable opportunity to comment on such proposed measures.

Article 1803
Notification and Provision of Information

1. To the maximum extent possible, each Party shall notify any other Party with an interest in the matter of any proposed or actual measure that the Party considers might materially affect the operation of this Agreement or otherwise substantially affect that other Party's interests under this Agreement.

2. On request of another Party, a Party shall promptly provide information and respond to questions pertaining to any actual or proposed measure, whether or not that other Party has been previously notified of that measure.

3. Any notification or information provided under this Article shall be without prejudice as to whether the measure is consistent with this Agreement.

Article 1804
Administrative Proceedings

With a view to administering in a consistent, impartial and reasonable manner all measures of general application affecting matters covered by this Agreement, each Party shall ensure that in its administrative proceedings applying measures referred to in Article 1802 to particular persons, goods or services of another Party in specific cases that: (a) wherever possible, persons of another Party that are directly affected by a proceeding are provided reasonable notice, in accordance with domestic procedures, when a proceeding is initiated, including a description of the nature of the proceeding, a statement of the legal authority under which the proceeding is initiated and a general description of any issues in controversy; (b) such persons are afforded a reasonable opportunity to present facts and arguments in support of their positions prior to any final administrative action, when time, the nature of the proceeding and the public interest permit; and (c) its procedures are in accordance with domestic law.

Article 1805
Review and Appeal

1. Each Party shall establish or maintain judicial, quasi-judicial or administrative tribunals or procedures for the purpose of the prompt review

and, where warranted, correction of final administrative actions regarding matters covered by this Agreement. Such tribunals shall be impartial and independent of the office or authority entrusted with administrative enforcement and shall not have any substantial interest in the outcome of the matter.

2. Each Party shall ensure that, in any such tribunals or procedures, the parties to the proceeding are provided with the right to: (a) a reasonable opportunity to support or defend their respective positions; and (b) a decision based on the evidence and submissions of record or, where required by domestic law, the record compiled by the administrative authority.

3. Each Party shall ensure, subject to appeal or further review as provided in its domestic law, that such decisions shall be implemented by, and shall govern the practice of, the offices or authorities with respect to the administrative action at issue.

Article 1806
Definitions

For purposes of this Chapter:

administrative ruling of general application means an administrative ruling or interpretation that applies to all persons and fact situations that fall generally within its ambit and that establishes a norm of conduct but does not include: (a) a determination or ruling made in an administrative or quasi-judicial proceeding that applies to a particular person, good or service of another Party in a specific case; or (b) a ruling that adjudicates with respect to a particular act or practice.

CHAPTER NINETEEN: REVIEW AND DISPUTE SETTLEMENT IN ANTIDUMPING AND COUNTERVAILING DUTY MATTERS
Article 1901
General Provisions

1. Article 1904 applies only with respect to goods that the competent investigating authority of the importing Party, applying the importing Party's antidumping or countervailing duty law to the facts of a specific case, determines are goods of another Party.

2. For purposes of Articles 1903 and 1904, panels shall be established in accordance with Annex 1901.2.

3. Except for Article 2203 (Entry into Force), no provision of any other Chapter of this Agreement shall be construed as imposing obligations on a Party with respect to the Party's antidumping law or countervailing duty law.

Annex 1901.2
Establishment of Binational Panels

1. On the date of entry into force of this Agreement, the Parties shall establish and thereafter maintain a roster of individuals to serve as panelists in disputes under this Chapter. The roster shall include judges or former judges to the fullest extent practicable. The Parties shall consult in developing the roster, which shall include at least 75 candidates. Each Party shall

select at least 25 candidates, and all candidates shall be citizens of Canada, Mexico or the United States. Candidates shall be of good character, high standing and repute, and shall be chosen strictly on the basis of objectivity, reliability, sound judgment and general familiarity with international trade law. Candidates shall not be affiliated with a Party, and in no event shall a candidate take instructions from a Party. The Parties shall maintain the roster, and may amend it, when necessary, after consultations.

2. A majority of the panelists on each panel shall be lawyers in good standing. Within 30 days of a request for a panel, each involved Party shall appoint two panelists, in consultation with the other involved Party. The involved Parties normally shall appoint panelists from the roster. If a panelist is not selected from the roster, the panelist shall be chosen in accordance with and be subject to the criteria of paragraph 1. Each involved Party shall have the right to exercise four peremptory challenges, to be exercised simultaneously and in confidence, disqualifying from appointment to the panel up to four candidates proposed by the other involved Party. Peremptory challenges and the selection of alternative panelists shall occur within 45 days of the request for the panel. If an involved Party fails to appoint its members to a panel within 30 days or if a panelist is struck and no alternative panelist is selected within 45 days, such panelist shall be selected by lot on the 31st or 46th day, as the case may be, from that Party's candidates on the roster.

3. Within 55 days of the request for a panel, the involved Parties shall agree on the selection of a fifth panelist. If the involved Parties are unable to agree, they shall decide by lot which of them shall select, by the 61st day, the fifth panelist from the roster, excluding candidates eliminated by peremptory challenges.

4. On appointment of the fifth panelist, the panelists shall promptly appoint a chair from among the lawyers on the panel by majority vote of the panelists. If there is no majority vote, the chair shall be appointed by lot from among the lawyers on the panel.

5. Decisions of the panel shall be by majority vote and based on the votes of all members of the panel. The panel shall issue a written decision with reasons, together with any dissenting or concurring opinions of panelists.

6. Panelists shall be subject to the code of conduct established pursuant to Article 1909. If an involved Party believes that a panelist is in violation of the code of conduct, the involved Parties shall consult and if they agree, the panelist shall be removed and a new panelist shall be selected in accordance with the procedures of this Annex.

7. When a panel is convened pursuant to Article 1904 each panelist shall be required to sign: (a) an application for a protective order for information supplied by the United States or its persons covering business proprietary and other privileged information; (b) an undertaking for information supplied by Canada or its persons covering confidential, personal, business proprietary and other privileged information; or (c) an undertaking for information supplied by Mexico or its persons covering confidential, business proprietary and other privileged information.

8. On a panelist's acceptance of the obligations and terms of an application for a protective order or disclosure undertaking, the importing Party shall grant access to the information covered by such order or disclosure undertaking. Each Party shall establish appropriate sanctions for violations of protective orders or disclosure undertakings issued by or given to any Party. Each Party shall enforce such sanctions with respect to any person within its jurisdiction. Failure by a panelist to sign an application for a protective order or disclosure undertaking shall result in disqualification of the panelist.

9. If a panelist becomes unable to fulfill panel duties or is disqualified, proceedings of the panel shall be suspended pending the selection of a substitute panelist in accordance with the procedures of this Annex.

10. Subject to the code of conduct established pursuant to Article 1909, and provided that it does not interfere with the performance of the duties of such panelist, a panelist may engage in other business during the term of the panel.

11. While acting as a panelist, a panelist may not appear as counsel before another panel.

12. With the exception of violations of protective orders or disclosure undertakings, signed pursuant to paragraph 7, panelists shall be immune from suit and legal process relating to acts performed by them in their official capacity.

Article 1902
Retention of Domestic Antidumping Law and Countervailing Duty Law

1. Each Party reserves the right to apply its antidumping law and countervailing duty law to goods imported from the territory of any other Party. Antidumping law and countervailing duty law include, as appropriate for each Party, relevant statutes, legislative history, regulations, administrative practice and judicial precedents.

2. Each Party reserves the right to change or modify its antidumping law or countervailing duty law, provided that in the case of an amendment to a Party's antidumping or countervailing duty statute: (a) such amendment shall apply to goods from another Party only if the amending statute specifies that it applies to goods from that Party or from the Parties to this Agreement; (b) the amending Party notifies in writing the Parties to which the amendment applies of the amending statute as far in advance as possible of the date of enactment of such statute; (c) following notification, the amending Party, on request of any Party to which the amendment applies, consults with that Party prior to the enactment of the amending statute; and (d) such amendment, as applicable to that other Party, is not inconsistent with (i) the General Agreement on Tariffs and Trade (GATT), the Agreement on Implementation of Article VI of the General Agreement on Tariffs and Trade (the Antidumping Code) or the Agreement on the Interpretation and Application of Articles VI, XVI and XXIII of the General Agreement on Tariffs and Trade (the Subsidies Code), or any successor agreement to which all the original signatories to this Agreement are party, or (ii) the object and purpose of this Agreement and this Chapter, which is to establish fair and predictable conditions for the progressive liberalization of trade between the Parties to

this Agreement while maintaining effective and fair disciplines on unfair trade practices, such object and purpose to be ascertained from the provisions of this Agreement, its preamble and objectives, and the practices of the Parties.

Article 1903

Review of Statutory Amendments

1. A Party to which an amendment of another Party's antidumping or countervailing duty statute applies may request in writing that such amendment be referred to a binational panel for a declaratory opinion as to whether: (a) the amendment does not conform to Article 1902(2)(d)(i) or (ii); or (b) such amendment has the function and effect of overturning a prior decision of a panel made pursuant to Article 1904 and does not conform to Article 1902(2)(d)(i) or (ii). Such declaratory opinion shall have force or effect only as provided in this Article.

2. The panel shall conduct its review in accordance with the procedures of Annex 1903.2.

3. In the event that the panel recommends modifications to the amending statute to remedy a non-conformity that it has identified in its opinion: (a) the two Parties shall immediately begin consultations and shall seek to achieve a mutually satisfactory solution to the matter within 90 days of the issuance of the panel's final declaratory opinion. Such solution may include seeking corrective legislation with respect to the statute of the amending Party; (b) if corrective legislation is not enacted within nine months from the end of the 90–day consultation period referred to in subparagraph (a) and no other mutually satisfactory solution has been reached, the Party that requested the panel may (i) take comparable legislative or equivalent executive action, or (ii) terminate this Agreement with regard to the amending Party on 60–day written notice to that Party.

Annex 1903.2

Panel Procedures Under Article 1903

1. The panel shall establish its own rules of procedure unless the Parties otherwise agree prior to the establishment of that panel. The procedures shall ensure a right to at least one hearing before the panel, as well as the opportunity to provide written submissions and rebuttal arguments. The proceedings of the panel shall be confidential, unless the two Parties otherwise agree. The panel shall base its decisions solely on the arguments and submissions of the two Parties.

2. Unless the Parties to the dispute otherwise agree, the panel shall, within 90 days after its chair is appointed, present to the two Parties an initial written declaratory opinion containing findings of fact and its determination pursuant to Article 1903.

3. If the findings of the panel are affirmative, the panel may include in its report its recommendations as to the means by which the amending statute could be brought into conformity with Article 1902(2)(d). In determining what, if any, recommendations are appropriate, the panel shall consider the extent to which the amending statute affects interests under this

Agreement. Individual panelists may provide separate opinions on matters not unanimously agreed. The initial opinion of the panel shall become the final declaratory opinion, unless a Party to the dispute requests a reconsideration of the initial opinion pursuant to paragraph 4.

4. Within 14 days of the issuance of the initial declaratory opinion, a Party to the dispute disagreeing in whole or in part with the opinion may present a written statement of its objections and the reasons for those objections to the panel. In such event, the panel shall request the views of both Parties and shall reconsider its initial opinion. The panel shall conduct any further examination that it deems appropriate, and shall issue a final written opinion, together with dissenting or concurring views of individual panelists, within 30 days of the request for reconsideration.

5. Unless the Parties to the dispute otherwise agree, the final declaratory opinion of the panel shall be made public, along with any separate opinions of individual panelists and any written views that either Party may wish to be published.

6. Unless the Parties to the dispute otherwise agree, meetings and hearings of the panel shall take place at the office of the amending Party's Section of the Secretariat.

Article 1904
Review of Final Antidumping and Countervailing Duty Determinations

1. As provided in this Article, each Party shall replace judicial review of final antidumping and countervailing duty determinations with binational panel review.

2. An involved Party may request that a panel review, based on the administrative record, a final antidumping or countervailing duty determination of a competent investigating authority of an importing Party to determine whether such determination was in accordance with the antidumping or countervailing duty law of the importing Party. For this purpose, the antidumping or countervailing duty law consists of the relevant statutes, legislative history, regulations, administrative practice and judicial precedents to the extent that a court of the importing Party would rely on such materials in reviewing a final determination of the competent investigating authority. Solely for purposes of the panel review provided for in this Article, the antidumping and countervailing duty statutes of the Parties, as those statutes may be amended from time to time, are incorporated into and made a part of this Agreement.

3. The panel shall apply the standard of review set out in Annex 1911 and the general legal principles that a court of the importing Party otherwise would apply to a review of a determination of the competent investigating authority.

4. A request for a panel shall be made in writing to the other involved Party within 30 days following the date of publication of the final determination in question in the official journal of the importing Party. In the case of final determinations that are not published in the official journal of the importing Party, the importing Party shall immediately notify the other involved Party of such final determination where it involves goods from the

other involved Party, and the other involved Party may request a panel within 30 days of receipt of such notice. Where the competent investigating authority of the importing Party has imposed provisional measures in an investigation, the other involved Party may provide notice of its intention to request a panel under this Article, and the Parties shall begin to establish a panel at that time. Failure to request a panel within the time specified in this paragraph shall preclude review by a panel.

5. An involved Party on its own initiative may request review of a final determination by a panel and shall, on request of a person who would otherwise be entitled under the law of the importing Party to commence domestic procedures for judicial review of that final determination, request such review.

6. The panel shall conduct its review in accordance with the procedures established by the Parties pursuant to paragraph 14. Where both involved Parties request a panel to review a final determination, a single panel shall review that determination.

7. The competent investigating authority that issued the final determination in question shall have the right to appear and be represented by counsel before the panel. Each Party shall provide that other persons who, pursuant to the law of the importing Party, otherwise would have had the right to appear and be represented in a domestic judicial review proceeding concerning the determination of the competent investigating authority, shall have the right to appear and be represented by counsel before the panel.

8. The panel may uphold a final determination, or remand it for action not inconsistent with the panel's decision. Where the panel remands a final determination, the panel shall establish as brief a time as is reasonable for compliance with the remand, taking into account the complexity of the factual and legal issues involved and the nature of the panel's decision. In no event shall the time permitted for compliance with a remand exceed an amount of time equal to the maximum amount of time (counted from the date of the filing of a petition, complaint or application) permitted by statute for the competent investigating authority in question to make a final determination in an investigation. If review of the action taken by the competent investigating authority on remand is needed, such review shall be before the same panel, which shall normally issue a final decision within 90 days of the date on which such remand action is submitted to it.

9. The decision of a panel under this Article shall be binding on the involved Parties with respect to the particular matter between the Parties that is before the panel.

10. This Agreement shall not affect: (a) the judicial review procedures of any Party, or (b) cases appealed under those procedures, with respect to determinations other than final determinations.

11. A final determination shall not be reviewed under any judicial review procedures of the importing Party if an involved Party requests a panel with respect to that determination within the time limits set out in this Article. No Party may provide in its domestic legislation for an appeal from a panel decision to its domestic courts.

12.   This Article shall not apply where: (a) neither involved Party seeks panel review of a final determination; (b) a revised final determination is issued as a direct result of judicial review of the original final determination by a court of the importing Party in cases where neither involved Party sought panel review of that original final determination; or (c) a final determination is issued as a direct result of judicial review that was commenced in a court of the importing Party before the date of entry into force of this Agreement.

13.   Where, within a reasonable time after the panel decision is issued, an involved Party alleges that: (a) (i) a member of the panel was guilty of gross misconduct, bias, or a serious conflict of interest, or otherwise materially violated the rules of conduct, (ii) the panel seriously departed from a fundamental rule of procedure, or (iii) the panel manifestly exceeded its powers, authority or jurisdiction set out in this Article, for example by failing to apply the appropriate standard of review, and (b) any of the actions set out in subparagraph (a) has materially affected the panel's decision and threatens the integrity of the binational panel review process, that Party may avail itself of the extraordinary challenge procedure set out in Annex 1904.13.

14.   To implement this Article, the Parties shall adopt rules of procedure by January 1, 1994.   Such rules shall be based, where appropriate, on judicial rules of appellate procedure, and shall include rules concerning: the content and service of requests for panels; a requirement that the competent investigating authority transmit to the panel the administrative record of the proceeding; the protection of business proprietary, government classified, and other privileged information (including sanctions against persons participating before panels for improper release of such information); participation by private persons; limitations on panel review to errors alleged by the Parties or private persons; filing and service; computation and extensions of time; the form and content of briefs and other papers; pre- and post-hearing conferences; motions; oral argument; requests for rehearing; and voluntary terminations of panel reviews.   The rules shall be designed to result in final decisions within 315 days of the date on which a request for a panel is made, and shall allow: (a) 30 days for the filing of the complaint; (b) 30 days for designation or certification of the administrative record and its filing with the panel; (c) 60 days for the complainant to file its brief; (d) 60 days for the respondent to file its brief; (e) 15 days for the filing of reply briefs; (f) 15 to 30 days for the panel to convene and hear oral argument; and (g) 90 days for the panel to issue its written decision.

15.   In order to achieve the objectives of this Article, the Parties shall amend their antidumping and countervailing duty statutes and regulations with respect to antidumping or countervailing duty proceedings involving goods of the other Parties, and other statutes and regulations to the extent that they apply to the operation of the antidumping and countervailing duty laws.   In particular, without limiting the generality of the foregoing, each Party shall: (a) amend its statutes or regulations to ensure that existing procedures concerning the refund, with interest, of antidumping or countervailing duties operate to give effect to a final panel decision that a refund is due; (b) amend its statutes or regulations to ensure that its courts shall give full force and effect, with respect to any person within its jurisdiction, to all sanctions imposed pursuant to the laws of the other Parties to enforce

provisions of any protective order or undertaking that such other Party has promulgated or accepted in order to permit access for purposes of panel review or of the extraordinary challenge procedure to confidential, personal, business proprietary or other privileged information; (c) amend its statutes or regulations to ensure that (i) domestic procedures for judicial review of a final determination may not be commenced until the time for requesting a panel under paragraph 4 has expired, and (ii) as a prerequisite to commencing domestic judicial review procedures to review a final determination, a Party or other person intending to commence such procedures shall provide notice of such intent to the Parties concerned and to other persons entitled to commence such review procedures of the same final determination no later than 10 days prior to the latest date on which a panel may be requested; and (d) make the further amendments set out in its Schedule to Annex 1904.15.

Annex 1904.13
Extraordinary Challenge Procedure

1.   The involved Parties shall establish an extraordinary challenge committee, comprising three members, within 15 days of a request pursuant to Article 1904(13). The members shall be selected from a 15–person roster comprised of judges or former judges of a federal judicial court of the United States or a judicial court of superior jurisdiction of Canada, or a federal judicial court of Mexico. Each Party shall name five persons to this roster. Each involved Party shall select one member from this roster and the involved Parties shall decide by lot which of them shall select the third member from the roster.

2.   The Parties shall establish by the date of entry into force of the Agreement rules of procedure for committees. The rules shall provide for a decision of a committee within 90 days of its establishment.

3.   Committee decisions shall be binding on the Parties with respect to the particular matter between the Parties that was before the panel. After examination of the legal and factual analysis underlying the findings and conclusions of the panel's decision in order to determine whether one of the grounds set out in Article 1904(13) has been established, and on finding that one of those grounds has been established, the committee shall vacate the original panel decision or remand it to the original panel for action not inconsistent with the committee's decision; if the grounds are not established, it shall deny the challenge and, therefore, the original panel decision shall stand affirmed. If the original decision is vacated, a new panel shall be established pursuant to Annex 1901.2.

Annex 1904.15
Amendments to Domestic Laws
Schedule of Canada

1.   Canada shall amend sections 56 and 58 of the Special Import Measures Act, as amended, to allow the United States with respect to goods of the United States or Mexico with respect to goods of Mexico or a United States or a Mexican manufacturer, producer, or exporter, without regard to payment of duties, to make a written request for a redetermination; and section 59 to require the Deputy Minister to make a ruling on a request for a redetermina-

tion within one year of a request to a designated officer or other customs officer.

2.   Canada shall amend section 18.3(1) of the Federal Court Act, as amended, to render that section inapplicable to the United States and to Mexico; and shall provide in its statutes or regulations that persons (including producers of goods subject to an investigation) have standing to ask Canada to request a panel review where such persons would be entitled to commence domestic procedures for judicial review if the final determination were reviewable by the Federal Court pursuant to section 18.1(4).

3.   Canada shall amend the Special Import Measures Act, as amended, and any other relevant provisions of law, to provide that the following actions of the Deputy Minister shall be deemed for the purposes of this Article to be final determinations subject to judicial review: (a) a determination by the Deputy Minister pursuant to section 41; (b) a re-determination by the Deputy Minister pursuant to section 59; and (c) a review by the Deputy Minister of an undertaking pursuant to section 53(1).

4.   Canada shall amend Part II of the Special Import Measures Act, as amended, to provide for binational panel review respecting goods of Mexico and the United States.

5.   Canada shall amend Part II of the Special Import Measures Act, as amended, to provide for definitions related to this Chapter, as may be required.

6.   Canada shall amend Part II of the Special Import Measures Act, as amended, to permit the governments of Mexico and the United States to request binational panel review of final determinations respecting goods of Mexico and the United States.

7.   Canada shall amend Part II of the Special Import Measures Act, as amended, to provide for the establishment of binational panels requested to review final determinations in respect of goods of Mexico and the United States.

8.   Canada shall amend Part II of the Special Import Measures Act, as amended, to provide that binational panel review of a final determination shall be conducted in accordance with this Chapter.

9.   Canada shall amend Part II of the Special Import Measures Act, as amended, to provide that an extraordinary challenge proceeding shall be requested and conducted in accordance with Article 1904 and Annex 1904.13.

10.   Canada shall amend Part II of the Special Import Measures Act, as amended, to provide for a code of conduct, immunity for anything done or omitted to be done during the course of panel proceedings, the signing of and compliance with disclosure undertakings respecting confidential information, and remuneration for members of panels and committees established pursuant to this Chapter.

11.   Canada shall make such amendments as are necessary to establish a Canadian Secretariat for this Agreement and generally to facilitate the operation of this Chapter and the work of the binational panels, extraordinary challenge committees and special committees convened under this Chapter.

Schedule of Mexico

Mexico shall amend its antidumping and countervailing duty statutes and regulations, and other statutes and regulations to the extent that they apply to the operation of the antidumping and countervailing duty laws, to provide the following:

(a) elimination of the possibility of imposing duties within the five-day period after the acceptance of a petition;

(b) substitution of the term Initial Resolution ("Resolucion de Inicio") for the term Provisional Resolution ("Resolucion Provisional") and the term Provisional Resolution ("Resolucion Provisional") for the term Resolution Reviewing the Provisional Resolution ("Resolucion que revisa a la Resolucion Provisional");

(c) full participation in the administrative process for interested parties, as well as the right to administrative appeal and judicial review of final determinations of investigations, reviews, product coverage or other final decisions affecting them;

(d) elimination of the possibility of imposing provisional duties before the issuance of a preliminary determination;

(e) the right to immediate access to review of final determinations by binational panels for interested parties, without the need to exhaust first the administrative appeal;

(f) explicit and adequate timetables for determinations of the competent investigating authority and for the submission of questionnaires, evidence and comments by interested parties, as well as an opportunity for them to present facts and arguments in support of their positions prior to any final determination, to the extent time permits, including an opportunity to be adequately informed in a timely manner of and to comment on all aspects of preliminary determinations of dumping or subsidization;

(g) written notice to interested parties of any of the actions or resolutions rendered by the competent investigating authority, including initiation of an administrative review as well as its conclusion;

(h) disclosure meetings with interested parties by the competent investigating authority conducting its investigations and reviews, within seven calendar days after the date of publication in the Federal Official Journal ("Diario Oficial de la Federacion") of preliminary and final determinations, to explain the margins of dumping and the amount of subsidies calculations and to provide the interested parties with copies of sample calculations and, if used, computer programs;

(i) timely access by eligible counsel of interested parties during the course of the proceeding (including disclosure meetings) and on appeal, either before a national tribunal or a panel, to all information contained in the administrative record of the proceeding, including confidential information, excepting proprietary information of such a high degree of sensitivity that its release would lead to substantial and irreversible harm to the owner as well as government classified information, subject to an undertaking for confidentiality that strictly forbids use of the information for personal benefit and its disclosure to persons who are not authorized to receive such information; and for sanctions that are specific to violations of undertakings in proceedings before national tribunals or panels;

(j) timely access by interested parties during the course of the proceeding, to all non-confidential information contained in the administrative record and access to such information by interested parties or their representatives in any proceeding after 90 days following the issuance of the final determination;

(k) a mechanism requiring that any person submitting documents to the competent investigating authority shall simultaneously serve on interested persons, including foreign interests, any submissions after the complaint;

(l) preparation of summaries of ex parte meetings held between the competent investigating authority and any interested party and the inclusion in the administrative record of such summaries, which shall be made available to parties to the proceeding; if such summaries contain business proprietary information, the documents must be disclosed to a party's representative under an undertaking to ensure confidentiality;

(m) maintenance by the competent investigating authority of an administrative record as defined in this Chapter and a requirement that the final determination be based solely on the administrative record;

(n) informing interested parties in writing of all data and information the administering authority requires them to submit for the investigation, review, product coverage proceeding, or other antidumping or countervailing duty proceeding;

(o) the right to an annual individual review on request by the interested parties through which they can obtain their own dumping margin or countervailing duty rate, or can change the margin or rate they received in the investigation or a previous review, reserving to the competent investigating authority the ability to initiate a review, at any time, on its own motion and requiring that the competent investigating authority issue a notice of initiation within a reasonable period of time after the request;

(p) application of determinations issued as a result of judicial, administrative, or panel review, to the extent they are relevant to interested parties in addition to the plaintiff, so that all interested parties will benefit;

(q) issuance of binding decisions by the competent investigating authority if an interested party seeks clarification outside the context of an antidumping or countervailing duty investigation or review with respect to whether a particular product is covered by an antidumping or countervailing duty order;

(r) a detailed statement of reasons and the legal basis for final determinations in a manner sufficient to permit interested parties to make an informed decision as to whether to seek judicial or panel review, including an explanation of methodological or policy issues raised in the calculation of dumping or subsidization;

(s) written notice to interested parties and publication in the Federal Official Journal ("Diario Oficial de la Federacion") of initiation of investigations setting forth the nature of the proceeding, the legal authority under which the proceeding is initiated, and a description of the product at issue;

(t) documentation in writing of all advisory bodies' decisions or recommendations, including the basis for the decisions, and release of such written decisions to parties to the proceeding; all decisions or recommendations of any advisory body shall be placed in the administrative record and made available to parties to the proceeding; and

(u) a standard of review to be applied by binational panels as set out in subparagraph (c) of the definition of "standard of review" in Annex 1911.

Schedule of the United States

1. The United States shall amend section 301 of the Customs Courts Act of 1980, as amended, and any other relevant provisions of law, to eliminate the authority to issue declaratory judgments in any civil action involving an antidumping or countervailing duty proceeding regarding a class or kind of Canadian or Mexican merchandise.

2. The United States shall amend section 405(a) of the United States–Canada Free–Trade Agreement Implementation Act of 1988, to provide that the interagency group established under section 242 of the Trade Expansion Act of 1962 shall prepare a list of individuals qualified to serve as members of binational panels, extraordinary challenge committees and special committees convened under this Chapter.

3. The United States shall amend section 405(b) of the United States–Canada Free–Trade Agreement Implementation Act of 1988, to provide that panelists selected to serve on panels or committees convened pursuant to this Chapter, and individuals designated to assist such appointed individuals, shall not be considered employees of the United States.

4. The United States shall amend section 405(c) of the United States–Canada Free–Trade Agreement Implementation Act of 1988, to provide that panelists selected to serve on panels or committees convened pursuant to this Chapter, and individuals designated to assist the individuals serving on such panels or committees, shall be immune from suit and legal process relating to acts performed by such individuals in their official capacity and within the scope of their functions as such panelists or committee members, except with respect to the violation of protective orders described in section 777f(d)(3) of the Tariff Act of 1930, as amended.

5. The United States shall amend section 405(d) of the United States–Canada Free–Trade Agreement Implementation Act of 1988, to establish a United States Secretariat to facilitate the operation of this Chapter and the work of the binational panels, extraordinary challenge committees and special committees convened under this Chapter.

6. The United States shall amend section 407 of the United States–Canada Free–Trade Agreement Implementation Act of 1988, to provide that an extraordinary challenge committee convened pursuant to Article 1904 and Annex 1904.13 shall have authority to obtain information in the event of an allegation that a member of a binational panel was guilty of gross misconduct, bias, or a serious conflict of interest, or otherwise materially violated the rules of conduct, and for the committee to summon the attendance of witnesses, order the taking of depositions and obtain the assistance of any district or territorial court of the United States in aid of the committee's investigation.

7. The United States shall amend section 408 of the United States–Canada Free–Trade Agreement Implementation Act of 1988, to provide that,

in the case of a final determination of a competent investigating authority of Mexico, as well as Canada, the filing with the United States Secretary of a request for binational panel review by a person described in Article 1904(5) shall be deemed, on receipt of the request by the Secretary, to be a request for binational panel review within the meaning of Article 1904(4).

8.　The United States shall amend section 516A of the Tariff Act of 1930, as amended, to provide that judicial review of antidumping or countervailing duty cases regarding Mexican, as well as Canadian, merchandise shall not be commenced in the Court of International Trade if binational panel review is requested.

9.　The United States shall amend section 516A(a) of the Tariff Act of 1930, as amended, to provide that the time limits for commencing an action in the Court of International Trade with regard to antidumping or countervailing duty proceedings involving Mexican or Canadian merchandise shall not begin to run until the 31st day after the date of publication in the Federal Register of notice of the final determination or the antidumping duty order.

10.　The United States shall amend section 516A(g) of the Tariff Act of 1930, as amended, to provide, in accordance with the terms of this Chapter, for binational panel review of antidumping and countervailing duty cases involving Mexican or Canadian merchandise.　Such amendment shall provide that if binational panel review is requested such review will be exclusive.

11.　The United States shall amend section 516A(g) of the Tariff Act of 1930, as amended, to provide that the competent investigating authority shall, within the period specified by any panel formed to review a final determination regarding Mexican or Canadian merchandise, take action not inconsistent with the decision of the panel or committee.

12.　The United States shall amend section 777 of the Tariff Act of 1930, as amended, to provide for the disclosure to authorized persons under protective order of proprietary information in the administrative record, if binational panel review of a final determination regarding Mexican or Canadian merchandise is requested.

13.　The United States shall amend section 777 of the Tariff Act of 1930, as amended, to provide for the imposition of sanctions on any person who the competent investigating authority finds to have violated a protective order issued by the competent investigating authority of the United States or disclosure undertakings entered into with an authorized agency of Mexico or with a competent investigating authority of Canada to protect proprietary material during binational panel review.

Article 1905
Safeguarding the Panel Review System

1.　Where a Party alleges that the application of another Party's domestic law: (a) has prevented the establishment of a panel requested by the complaining Party; (b) has prevented a panel requested by the complaining Party from rendering a final decision; (c) has prevented the implementation of the decision of a panel requested by the complaining Party or denied it binding force and effect with respect to the particular matter that was before the panel; or (d) has resulted in a failure to provide opportunity for review of a final determination by a panel or court of competent jurisdiction that is independent of the competent investigating authorities, that examines the basis for the competent investigating authority's determination and whether the competent investigating authority properly applied domestic antidumping and countervailing duty law in reaching the challenged determination, and that employs the relevant standard of review identified in Article 1911, the Party may request in writing consultations with the other Party regarding the allegations. The consultations shall begin within 15 days of the date of the request.

2. If the matter has not been resolved within 45 days of the request for consultations, or such other period as the consulting Parties may agree, the complaining Party may request the establishment of a special committee.

3. Unless otherwise agreed by the disputing Parties, the special committee shall be established within 15 days of a request and perform its functions in a manner consistent with this Chapter.

4. The roster for special committees shall be that established under Annex 1904.13.

5. The special committee shall comprise three members selected in accordance with the procedures set out in Annex 1904.13.

6. The Parties shall establish rules of procedure in accordance with the principles set out in Annex 1905.6.

7. Where the special committee makes an affirmative finding with respect to one of the grounds specified in paragraph 1, the complaining Party and the Party complained against shall begin consultations within 10 days thereafter and shall seek to achieve a mutually satisfactory solution within 60 days of the issuance of the committee's report.

8. If, within the 60-day period, the Parties are unable to reach a mutually satisfactory solution to the matter, or the Party complained against has not demonstrated to the satisfaction of the special committee that it has corrected the problem or problems with respect to which the committee has made an affirmative finding, the complaining Party may suspend: (a) the operation of Article 1904 with respect to the Party complained against; or (b) the application to the Party complained against of such benefits under this Agreement as may be appropriate under the circumstances. If the complaining Party decides to take action under this paragraph, it shall do so within 30 days after the end of the 60-day consultation period.

9. In the event that a complaining Party suspends the operation of Article 1904 with respect to the Party complained against, the latter Party may reciprocally suspend the operation of Article 1904 within 30 days after the suspension of the operation of Article 1904 by the complaining Party. If either Party decides to suspend the operation of Article 1904, it shall provide written notice of such suspension to the other Party.

10. On the request of the Party complained against, the special committee shall reconvene to determine whether: (a) the suspension of benefits by the complaining Party pursuant to paragraph 8(b) is manifestly excessive; or (b) the Party complained against has corrected the problem or problems with respect to which the committee has made an affirmative finding. The special committee shall, within 45 days of the request, present a report to both

Parties containing its determination. Where the special committee determines that the Party complained against has corrected the problem or problems, any suspension effected by the complaining Party or the Party complained against, or both, pursuant to paragraph 8 or 9 shall be terminated.

11.   If the special committee makes an affirmative finding with respect to one of the grounds specified in paragraph 1, then effective as of the day following the date of issuance of the special committee's report: (a) binational panel or extraordinary challenge committee review under Article 1904 shall be stayed (i) in the case of review of any final determination of the complaining Party requested by the Party complained against, if such review was requested after the date on which consultations were requested pursuant to paragraph 1, and in no case more than 150 days prior to an affirmative finding by the special committee, or (ii) in the case of review of any final determination of the Party complained against requested by the complaining Party, on the request of the complaining Party; and (b) the time set out in Article 1904(4) or Annex 1904.13 for requesting panel or committee review shall not run unless and until resumed in accordance with paragraph 12.

12.   If either Party suspends the operation of Article 1904 pursuant to paragraph 8(a), the panel or committee review stayed under paragraph 11(a) shall be terminated and the challenge to the final determination shall be irrevocably referred to the appropriate domestic court for decision, as provided below: (a) in the case of review of any final determination of the complaining Party requested by the Party complained against, on the request of either Party, or of a party to the panel review under Article 1904; or (b) in the case of review of any final determination of the Party complained against requested by the complaining Party, on the request of the complaining Party, or of a person of the complaining Party that is a party to the panel review under Article 1904. If either Party suspends the operation of Article 1904 pursuant to paragraph 8(a), any running of time suspended under paragraph 11(b) shall resume.

If the suspension of the operation of Article 1904 does not become effective, panel or committee review stayed under paragraph 11(a), and any running of time suspended under paragraph 11(b), shall resume.

13.   If the complaining Party suspends the application to the Party complained against of such benefits under the Agreement as may be appropriate under the circumstances pursuant to paragraph 8(b), panel or committee review stayed under paragraph 11(a), and any running of time suspended under paragraph 11(b), shall resume.

14.   Each Party shall provide in its domestic law that, in the event of an affirmative finding by the special committee, the time for requesting judicial review of a final antidumping or countervailing duty determination shall not run unless and until the Parties concerned have negotiated a mutually satisfactory solution under paragraph 7, or have suspended the operation of Article 1904 or the application of other benefits under paragraph 8.

Annex 1905.6

Special Committee Procedures

The Parties shall establish rules of procedure by the date of entry into force of this Agreement in accordance with the following principles: (a) the procedures shall assure a right to at least one hearing before the special committee as well as the opportunity to provide initial and rebuttal written submissions; (b) the procedures shall assure that the special committee shall prepare an initial report typically within 60 days of the appointment of the last member, and shall afford the Parties 14 days to comment on that report prior to issuing a final report 30 days after presentation of the initial report; (c) the special committee's hearings, deliberations and initial report, and all written submissions to, and communications with, the special committee shall be confidential; (d) unless the Parties to the dispute otherwise agree, the decision of the special committee shall be published 10 days after it is transmitted to the disputing Parties, along with any separate opinions of individual members and any written views that either Party may wish to be published; and (e) unless the Parties to the dispute otherwise agree, meetings and hearings of the special committee shall take place at the office of the Section of the Secretariat of the Party complained against.

Article 1906

Prospective Application

This Chapter shall apply only prospectively to: (a) final determinations of a competent investigating authority made after the date of entry into force of this Agreement; and (b) with respect to declaratory opinions under Article 1903, amendments to antidumping or countervailing duty statutes enacted after the date of entry into force of this Agreement.

Article 1907

Consultations

1. The Parties shall consult annually, or on the request of any Party, to consider any problems that may arise with respect to the implementation or operation of this Chapter and recommend solutions, where appropriate. The Parties shall each designate one or more officials, including officials of the competent investigating authorities, to be responsible for ensuring that consultations occur, when required, so that the provisions of this Chapter are carried out expeditiously.

2. The Parties further agree to consult on: (a) the potential to develop more effective rules and disciplines concerning the use of government subsidies; and (b) the potential for reliance on a substitute system of rules for dealing with unfair transborder pricing practices and government subsidization.

3. The competent investigating authorities of the Parties shall consult annually, or on the request of any Party, and may submit reports to the Commission, where appropriate. In the context of these consultations, the Parties agree that it is desirable in the administration of antidumping and countervailing duty laws to: (a) publish notice of initiation of investigations in the importing Party's official journal, setting forth the nature of the proceeding, the legal authority under which the proceeding is initiated, and a description of the goods at issue; (b) provide notice of the times for submissions of information and for decisions that the competent investigating authorities are expressly required by statute or regulations to make; (c) provide explicit written notice and instructions as to the information required

from interested parties and reasonable time to respond to requests for information; (d) accord reasonable access to information, noting that in this context (i) "reasonable access" means access during the course of the investigation, to the extent practicable, so as to permit an opportunity to present facts and arguments as set out in subparagraph (e); when it is not practicable to provide access to information during the investigation in such time as to permit an opportunity to present facts and arguments, reasonable access shall mean in time to permit the adversely affected party to make an informed decision as to whether to seek judicial or panel review, and (ii) "access to information" means access to representatives determined by the competent investigating authority to be qualified to have access to information received by that competent investigating authority, including access to confidential (business proprietary) information, but does not include information of such high degree of sensitivity that its release would lead to substantial and irreversible harm to the owner or which is required to be kept confidential in accordance with domestic law of a Party; any privileges arising under the domestic law of the importing Party relating to communications between the competent investigating authorities and a lawyer in the employ of, or providing advice to, those authorities may be maintained; (e) provide an opportunity for interested parties to present facts and arguments, to the extent time permits, including an opportunity to comment on the preliminary determination of dumping or of subsidization; (f) protect confidential (business proprietary) information received by the competent investigating authority to ensure that there is no disclosure except to representatives determined by the competent investigating authority to be qualified; (g) prepare administrative records, including recommendations of official advisory bodies that may be required to be kept, and any record of ex parte meetings that may be required to be kept; (h) provide disclosure of relevant information, including an explanation of the calculation or the methodology used to determine the margin of dumping or the amount of the subsidy, on which any preliminary or final determination of dumping or of subsidization is based, within a reasonable time after a request by interested parties; (i) provide a statement of reasons concerning the final determination of dumping or subsidization; and (j) provide a statement of reasons for final determinations concerning material injury to a domestic industry, threat of material injury to a domestic industry or material retardation of the establishment of such an industry. Inclusion of an item in subparagraphs (a) through (j) is not intended to serve as guidance to a binational panel reviewing a final antidumping or countervailing duty determination pursuant to Article 1904 in determining whether such determination was in accordance with the antidumping or countervailing duty law of the importing Party.

Article 1908
Special Secretariat Provisions

1. Each Party shall establish a division within its section of the Secretariat established pursuant to Article 2002 to facilitate the operation of this Chapter, including the work of panels or committees that may be convened pursuant to this Chapter.

2. The Secretaries of the Secretariat shall act jointly to provide administrative assistance to all panels or committees established pursuant to this

Chapter. The Secretary for the Section of the Party in which a panel or committee proceeding is held shall prepare a record thereof and shall preserve an authentic copy of the same in that Party's Section office. Such Secretary shall, on request, provide to the Secretary for the Section of any other Party a copy of such portion of the record as is requested, except that only public portions of the record shall be provided to the Secretary for the Section of any Party that is not an involved Party.

3. Each Secretary shall receive and file all requests, briefs and other papers properly presented to a panel or committee in any proceeding before it that is instituted pursuant to this Chapter and shall number in numerical order all requests for a panel or committee. The number given to a request shall be the file number for briefs and other papers relating to such request.

4. The Secretary for the Section of the Party in which a panel or committee proceeding is held shall forward to the Secretary for the Section of the other involved Party copies of all official letters, documents or other papers received or filed with that Party's Section office pertaining to any proceeding before a panel or committee, except for the administrative record, which shall be handled in accordance with paragraph 2. The Secretary for the Section of an involved Party shall provide on request to the Secretary for the Section of a Party that is not an involved Party in the proceeding a copy of such public documents as are requested.

Article 1909

Code of Conduct

The Parties shall, by the date of entry into force of this Agreement, exchange letters establishing a code of conduct for panelists and members of committees established pursuant to Articles 1903, 1904 and 1905.

Article 1910

Miscellaneous

On request of another Party, the competent investigating authority of a Party shall provide to the other Party copies of all public information submitted to it for purposes of an antidumping or countervailing duty investigation with respect to goods of that other Party.

Article 1911

Definitions

For purposes of this Chapter:

administrative record means, unless otherwise agreed by the Parties and the other persons appearing before a panel: (a) all documentary or other information presented to or obtained by the competent investigating authority in the course of the administrative proceeding, including any governmental memoranda pertaining to the case, and including any record of ex parte meetings as may be required to be kept; (b) a copy of the final determination of the competent investigating authority, including reasons for the determination; (c) all transcripts or records of conferences or hearings before the competent investigating authority; and (d) all notices published in the official journal of the importing Party in connection with the administrative proceeding;

antidumping statute as referred to in Articles 1902 and 1903 means "antidumping statute" of a Party as defined in Annex 1911;

competent investigating authority means "competent investigating authority" of a Party as defined in Annex 1911;

countervailing duty statute as referred to in Articles 1902 and 1903 means "countervailing duty statute" of a Party as defined in Annex 1911;

domestic law for purposes of Article 1905(1) means a Party's constitution, statutes, regulations and judicial decisions to the extent they are relevant to the antidumping and countervailing duty laws;

final determination means "final determination" of a Party as defined in Annex 1911;

foreign interests includes exporters or producers of the Party whose goods are the subject of the proceeding or, in the case of a countervailing duty proceeding, the government of the Party whose goods are the subject of the proceeding;

general legal principles includes principles such as standing, due process, rules of statutory construction, mootness and exhaustion of administrative remedies;

goods of a Party means domestic products as these are understood in the General Agreement on Tariffs and Trade;

importing Party means the Party that issued the final determination;

interested parties includes foreign interests;

involved Party means: (a) the importing Party; or (b) a Party whose goods are the subject of the final determination;

remand means a referral back for a determination not inconsistent with the panel or committee decision; and

standard of review means the "standard of review" for each Party as defined in Annex 1911.

Annex 1911
Country–Specific Definitions

For purposes of this Chapter:

antidumping statute means:

(a) in the case of Canada, the relevant provisions of the Special Import Measures Act, as amended, and any successor statutes;

(b) in the case of the United States, the relevant provisions of Title VII of the Tariff Act of 1930, as amended, and any successor statutes;

(c) in the case of Mexico, the relevant provisions of the Foreign Trade Act Implementing Article 131 of the Constitution of the United Mexican States ("Ley Reglamentaria del Articulo 131 de la Constitucion Politica de los Estados Unidos Mexicanos en Materia de Comercio Exterior"), as amended, and any successor statutes; and

(d) the provisions of any other statute that provides for judicial review of final determinations under subparagraph (a), (b) or (c), or indicates the standard of review to be applied to such determinations;

competent investigating authority means:

(a) in the case of Canada, (i) the Canadian International Trade Tribunal, or its successor, or (ii) the Deputy Minister of National Revenue for Customs and Excise as defined in the Special Import Measures Act, as amended, or the Deputy Minister's successor;

(b) in the case of the United States, (i) the International Trade Administration of the U.S. Department of Commerce, or its successor, or (ii) the U.S. International Trade Commission, or its successor; and

(c) in the case of Mexico, the designated authority within the Secretariat of Trade and Industrial Development ("Secretaria de Comercio y Fomento Industrial"), or its successor;

countervailing duty statute means:

(a) in the case of Canada, the relevant provisions of the Special Import Measures Act, as amended, and any successor statutes;

(b) in the case of the United States, section 303 and the relevant provisions of Title VII of the Tariff Act of 1930, as amended, and any successor statutes;

(c) in the case of Mexico, the relevant provisions of the Foreign Trade Act Implementing Article 131 of the Constitution of the United Mexican States ("Ley Reglamentaria del Articulo 131 de la Constitucion Politica de los Estados Unidos Mexicanos en Materia de Comercio Exterior"), as amended, and any successor statutes; and

(d) the provisions of any other statute that provides for judicial review of final determinations under subparagraph (a), (b) or (c), or indicates the standard of review to be applied to such determinations;

final determination means:

(a) in the case of Canada, (i) an order or finding of the Canadian International Trade Tribunal under subsection 43(1) of the Special Import Measures Act, (ii) an order by the Canadian International Trade Tribunal under subsection 76(4) of the Special Import Measures Act, as amended, continuing an order or finding made under subsection 43(1) of the Act with or without amendment, (iii) a determination by the Deputy Minister of National Revenue for Customs and Excise pursuant to section 41 of the Special Import Measures Act, as amended, (iv) a re-determination by the Deputy Minister pursuant to section 59 of the Special Import Measures Act, as amended, (v) a decision by the Canadian International Trade Tribunal pursuant to subsection 76(3) of the Special Import Measures Act, as amended, not to initiate a review, (vi) a reconsideration by the Canadian International Trade Tribunal pursuant to subsection 91(3) of the Special Import Measures Act, as amended, and (vii) a review by the Deputy Minister of an undertaking pursuant to subsection 53(1) of the Special Import Measures Act, as amended,

(b) in the case of the United States, (i) a final affirmative determination by the International Trade Administration of the U.S. Department of Commerce or by the U.S. International Trade Commission under section 705 or

735 of the Tariff Act of 1930, as amended, including any negative part of such a determination, (ii) a final negative determination by the International Trade Administration of the U.S. Department of Commerce or by the U.S. International Trade Commission under section 705 or 735 of the Tariff Act of 1930, as amended, including any affirmative part of such a determination, (iii) a final determination, other than a determination in (iv), under section 751 of the Tariff Act of 1930, as amended, (iv) a determination by the U.S. International Trade Commission under section 751(b) of the Tariff Act of 1930, as amended, not to review a determination based on changed circumstances, and (v) a final determination by the International Trade Administration of the U.S. Department of Commerce as to whether a particular type of merchandise is within the class or kind of merchandise described in an existing finding of dumping or antidumping or countervailing duty order; and

(c) in the case of Mexico, (i) a final resolution regarding antidumping or countervailing duties investigations by the Secretariat of Trade and Industrial Development ("Secretaria de Comercio y Fomento Industrial"), pursuant to Article 13 of the Foreign Trade Act Implementing Article 131 of the Constitution of the United Mexican States ("Ley Reglamentaria del Articulo 131 de la Constitucion Politica de los Estados Unidos Mexicanos en Materia de Comercio Exterior"), as amended, (ii) a final resolution regarding an annual administrative review of antidumping or countervailing duties by the Secretariat of Trade and Industrial Development ("Secretaria de Comercio y Fomento Industrial"), as described in paragraph (o) of its Schedule to Annex 1904.15, and (iii) a final resolution by the Secretariat of Trade and Industrial Development ("Secretaria de Comercio y Fomento Industrial") as to whether a particular type of merchandise is within the class or kind of merchandise described in an existing antidumping or countervailing duty resolution; and

standard of review means the following standards, as may be amended from time to time by the relevant Party:

(a) in the case of Canada, the grounds set out in subsection 18.1(4) of the Federal Court Act, as amended, with respect to all final determinations;

(b) in the case of the United States, (i) the standard set out in section 516A(b)(1)(B) of the Tariff Act of 1930, as amended, with the exception of a determination referred to in (ii), and (ii) the standard set out in section 516A(b)(1)(A) of the Tariff Act of 1930, as amended, with respect to a determination by the U.S. International Trade Commission not to initiate a review pursuant to section 751(b) of the Tariff Act of 1930, as amended; and

(c) in the case of Mexico, the standard set out in Article 238 of the Federal Fiscal Code ("Codigo Fiscal de la Federacion"), or any successor statutes, based solely on the administrative record.

CHAPTER TWENTY: INSTITUTIONAL ARRANGEMENTS AND DISPUTE SETTLEMENT PROCEDURES

Section A—Institutions

Article 2001

The Free Trade Commission

1. The Parties hereby establish the Free Trade Commission, comprising cabinet-level representatives of the Parties or their designees.

2.   The Commission shall: (a) supervise the implementation of this Agreement; (b) oversee its further elaboration; (c) resolve disputes that may arise regarding its interpretation or application; (d) supervise the work of all committees and working groups established under this Agreement, referred to in Annex 2001.2; and (e) consider any other matter that may affect the operation of this Agreement.

3.   The Commission may: (a) establish, and delegate responsibilities to, ad hoc or standing committees, working groups or expert groups; (b) seek the advice of non-governmental persons or groups; and (c) take such other action in the exercise of its functions as the Parties may agree.

4.   The Commission shall establish its rules and procedures. All decisions of the Commission shall be taken by consensus, except as the Commission may otherwise agree.

5.   The Commission shall convene at least once a year in regular session. Regular sessions of the Commission shall be chaired successively by each Party.

Annex 2001.2
Committees and Working Groups

A.   Committees:

1.   Committee on Trade in Goods (Article 316)

2.   Committee on Trade in Worn Clothing (Annex 300–B, Section 9.1)

3.   Committee on Agricultural Trade (Article 706)—Advisory Committee on Private Commercial Disputes Regarding Agricultural Goods (Article 707)

4.   Committee on Sanitary and Phytosanitary Measures (Article 722)

5.   Committee on Standards–Related Measures (Article 913)—Land Transportation Standards Subcommittee (Article 913(5))—Telecommunications Standards Subcommittee (Article 913(5))—Automotive Standards Council (Article 913(5))—Subcommittee on Labelling of Textile and Apparel Goods (Article 913(5))

6.   Committee on Small Business (Article 1021)

7.   Financial Services Committee (Article 1412)

8.   Advisory Committee on Private Commercial Disputes (Article 2022(4))

B.   Working Groups:

1.   Working Group on Rules of Origin (Article 513)—Customs Subgroup (Article 513(6))

2.   Working Group on Agricultural Subsidies (Article 705(6))

3.   Bilateral Working Group (Mexico—United States) (Annex 703.2(A)(25))

4.   Bilateral Working Group (Canada—Mexico) (Annex 703.2(B)(13))

5.   Working Group on Trade and Competition (Article 1504)

6.   Temporary Entry Working Group (Article 1605)

C. Other Committees and Working Groups Established under this Agreement

Article 2002
The Secretariat

1. The Commission shall establish and oversee a Secretariat comprising national Sections.

2. Each Party shall: (a) establish a permanent office of its Section; (b) be responsible for (i) the operation and costs of its Section, and (ii) the remuneration and payment of expenses of panelists and members of committees and scientific review boards established under this Agreement, as set out in Annex 2002.2; (c) designate an individual to serve as Secretary for its Section, who shall be responsible for its administration and management; and (d) notify the Commission of the location of its Section's office.

3. The Secretariat shall: (a) provide assistance to the Commission; (b) provide administrative assistance to (i) panels and committees established under Chapter Nineteen (Review and Dispute Settlement in Antidumping and Countervailing Duty Matters), in accordance with the procedures established pursuant to Article 1908, and (ii) panels established under this Chapter, in accordance with procedures established pursuant to Article 2012; and (c) as the Commission may direct (i) support the work of other committees and groups established under this Agreement, and (ii) otherwise facilitate the operation of this Agreement.

Annex 2002.2
Remuneration and Payment of Expenses

1. The Commission shall establish the amounts of remuneration and expenses that will be paid to the panelists, committee members and members of scientific review boards.

2. The remuneration of panelists or committee members and their assistants, members of scientific review boards, their travel and lodging expenses, and all general expenses of panels, committees or scientific review boards shall be borne equally by: (a) in the case of panels or committees established under Chapter Nineteen (Review and Dispute Settlement in Antidumping and Countervailing Duty Matters), the involved Parties, as they are defined in Article 1911; or (b) in the case of panels and scientific review boards established under this Chapter, the disputing Parties.

3. Each panelist or committee member shall keep a record and render a final account of the person's time and expenses, and the panel, committee or scientific review board shall keep a record and render a final account of all general expenses.

Section B—Dispute Settlement
Article 2003
Cooperation

The Parties shall at all times endeavor to agree on the interpretation and application of this Agreement, and shall make every attempt through cooperation and consultations to arrive at a mutually satisfactory resolution of any matter that might affect its operation.

Article 2004

Recourse to Dispute Settlement Procedures

Except for the matters covered in Chapter Nineteen (Review and Dispute Settlement in Antidumping and Countervailing Duty Matters) and as otherwise provided in this Agreement, the dispute settlement provisions of this Chapter shall apply with respect to the avoidance or settlement of all disputes between the Parties regarding the interpretation or application of this Agreement or wherever a Party considers that an actual or proposed measure of another Party is or would be inconsistent with the obligations of this Agreement or cause nullification or impairment in the sense of Annex 2004.

Annex 2004

Nullification and Impairment

1. If any Party considers that any benefit it could reasonably have expected to accrue to it under any provision of: (a) Part Two (Trade in Goods), except for those provisions of Annex 300–A (Automotive Sector) or Chapter Six (Energy) relating to investment, (b) Part Three (Technical Barriers to Trade), (c) Chapter Twelve (Cross–Border Trade in Services), or (d) Part Six (Intellectual Property), is being nullified or impaired as a result of the application of any measure that is not inconsistent with this Agreement, the Party may have recourse to dispute settlement under this Chapter.

2. A Party may not invoke: (a) paragraph 1(a) or (b), to the extent that the benefit arises from any cross-border trade in services provision of Part Two or Three, or (b) paragraph 1(c) or (d), with respect to any measure subject to an exception under Article 2101 (General Exceptions).

Article 2005

GATT Dispute Settlement

1. Subject to paragraphs 2, 3 and 4, disputes regarding any matter arising under both this Agreement and the General Agreement on Tariffs and Trade, any agreement negotiated thereunder, or any successor agreement (GATT), may be settled in either forum at the discretion of the complaining Party.

2. Before a Party initiates a dispute settlement proceeding in the GATT against another Party on grounds that are substantially equivalent to those available to that Party under this Agreement, that Party shall notify any third Party of its intention. If a third Party wishes to have recourse to dispute settlement procedures under this Agreement regarding the matter, it shall inform promptly the notifying Party and those Parties shall consult with a view to agreement on a single forum. If those Parties cannot agree, the dispute normally shall be settled under this Agreement.

3. In any dispute referred to in paragraph 1 where the responding Party claims that its action is subject to Article 104 (Relation to Environmental and Conservation Agreements) and requests in writing that the matter be considered under this Agreement, the complaining Party may, in respect of that

matter, thereafter have recourse to dispute settlement procedures solely under this Agreement.

4. In any dispute referred to in paragraph 1 that arises under Section B of Chapter Seven (Sanitary and Phytosanitary Measures) or Chapter Nine (Standards-Related Measures): (a) concerning a measure adopted or maintained by a Party to protect its human, animal or plant life or health, or to protect its environment, and (b) that raises factual issues concerning the environment, health, safety or conservation, including directly related scientific matters, where the responding Party requests in writing that the matter be considered under this Agreement, the complaining Party may, in respect of that matter, thereafter have recourse to dispute settlement procedures solely under this Agreement.

5. The responding Party shall deliver a copy of a request made pursuant to paragraph 3 or 4 to the other Parties and to its Section of the Secretariat. Where the complaining Party has initiated dispute settlement proceedings regarding any matter subject to paragraph 3 or 4, the responding Party shall deliver its request no later than 15 days thereafter. On receipt of such request, the complaining Party shall promptly withdraw from participation in those proceedings and may initiate dispute settlement procedures under Article 2007.

6. Once dispute settlement procedures have been initiated under Article 2007 or dispute settlement proceedings have been initiated under the GATT, the forum selected shall be used to the exclusion of the other, unless a Party makes a request pursuant to paragraph 3 or 4.

7. For purposes of this Article, dispute settlement proceedings under the GATT are deemed to be initiated by a Party's request for a panel, such as under Article XXIII:2 of the General Agreement on Tariffs and Trade 1947, or for a committee investigation, such as under Article 20.1 of the Customs Valuation Code.

Consultations
Article 2006
Consultations

1. Any Party may request in writing consultations with any other Party regarding any actual or proposed measure or any other matter that it considers might affect the operation of this Agreement.

2. The requesting Party shall deliver the request to the other Parties and to its Section of the Secretariat.

3. Unless the Commission otherwise provides in its rules and procedures established under Article 2001(4), a third Party that considers it has a substantial interest in the matter shall be entitled to participate in the consultations on delivery of written notice to the other Parties and to its Section of the Secretariat.

4. Consultations on matters regarding perishable agricultural goods shall commence within 15 days of the date of delivery of the request.

5. The consulting Parties shall make every attempt to arrive at a mutually satisfactory resolution of any matter through consultations under

this Article or other consultative provisions of this Agreement. To this end, the consulting Parties shall: (a) provide sufficient information to enable a full examination of how the actual or proposed measure or other matter might affect the operation of this Agreement; (b) treat any confidential or proprietary information exchanged in the course of consultations on the same basis as the Party providing the information; and (c) seek to avoid any resolution that adversely affects the interests under this Agreement of any other Party.

Initiation of Procedures
Article 2007
Commission—Good Offices, Conciliation and Mediation

1. If the consulting Parties fail to resolve a matter pursuant to Article 2006 within: (a) 30 days of delivery of a request for consultations, (b) 45 days of delivery of such request if any other Party has subsequently requested or has participated in consultations regarding the same matter, (c) 15 days of delivery of a request for consultations in matters regarding perishable agricultural goods, or (d) such other period as they may agree, any such Party may request in writing a meeting of the Commission.

2. A Party may also request in writing a meeting of the Commission where: (a) it has initiated dispute settlement proceedings under the GATT regarding any matter subject to Article 2005(3) or (4), and has received a request pursuant to Article 2005(5) for recourse to dispute settlement procedures under this Chapter; or (b) consultations have been held pursuant to Article 513 (Working Group on Rules of Origin), Article 723 (Sanitary and Phytosanitary Measures—Technical Consultations) and Article 914 (Standards–Related Measures—Technical Consultations).

3. The requesting Party shall state in the request the measure or other matter complained of and indicate the provisions of this Agreement that it considers relevant, and shall deliver the request to the other Parties and to its Section of the Secretariat.

4. Unless it decides otherwise, the Commission shall convene within 10 days of delivery of the request and shall endeavor to resolve the dispute promptly.

5. The Commission may: (a) call on such technical advisers or create such working groups or expert groups as it deems necessary, (b) have recourse to good offices, conciliation, mediation or such other dispute resolution procedures, or (c) make recommendations, as may assist the consulting Parties to reach a mutually satisfactory resolution of the dispute.

6. Unless it decides otherwise, the Commission shall consolidate two or more proceedings before it pursuant to this Article regarding the same measure. The Commission may consolidate two or more proceedings regarding other matters before it pursuant to this Article that it determines are appropriate to be considered jointly.

Panel Proceedings
Article 2008
Request for an Arbitral Panel

1. If the Commission has convened pursuant to Article 2007(4), and the matter has not been resolved within: (a) 30 days thereafter, (b) 30 days after

the Commission has convened in respect of the matter most recently referred to it, where proceedings have been consolidated pursuant to Article 2007(6), or (c) such other period as the consulting Parties may agree, any consulting Party may request in writing the establishment of an arbitral panel. The requesting Party shall deliver the request to the other Parties and to its Section of the Secretariat.

2.   On delivery of the request, the Commission shall establish an arbitral panel.

3.   A third Party that considers it has a substantial interest in the matter shall be entitled to join as a complaining Party on delivery of written notice of its intention to participate to the disputing Parties and its Section of the Secretariat. The notice shall be delivered at the earliest possible time, and in any event no later than seven days after the date of delivery of a request by a Party for the establishment of a panel.

4.   If a third Party does not join as a complaining Party in accordance with paragraph 3, it normally shall refrain thereafter from initiating or continuing: (a) a dispute settlement procedure under this Agreement, or (b) a dispute settlement proceeding in the GATT on grounds that are substantially equivalent to those available to that Party under this Agreement, regarding the same matter in the absence of a significant change in economic or commercial circumstances.

5.   Unless otherwise agreed by the disputing Parties, the panel shall be established and perform its functions in a manner consistent with the provisions of this Chapter.

Article 2009
Roster

1.   The Parties shall establish by January 1, 1994 and maintain a roster of up to 30 individuals who are willing and able to serve as panelists. The roster members shall be appointed by consensus for terms of three years, and may be reappointed.

2.   Roster members shall: (a) have expertise or experience in law, international trade, other matters covered by this Agreement or the resolution of disputes arising under international trade agreements, and shall be chosen strictly on the basis of objectivity, reliability and sound judgment; (b) be independent of, and not be affiliated with or take instructions from, any Party; and (c) comply with a code of conduct to be established by the Commission.

Article 2010
Qualifications of Panelists

1.   All panelists shall meet the qualifications set out in Article 2009(2).

2.   Individuals may not serve as panelists for a dispute in which they have participated pursuant to Article 2007(5).

Article 2011
Panel Selection

1.   Where there are two disputing Parties, the following procedures shall apply: (a) The panel shall comprise five members. (b) The disputing Parties

shall endeavor to agree on the chair of the panel within 15 days of the delivery of the request for the establishment of the panel. If the disputing Parties are unable to agree on the chair within this period, the disputing Party chosen by lot shall select within five days as chair an individual who is not a citizen of that Party. (c) Within 15 days of selection of the chair, each disputing Party shall select two panelists who are citizens of the other disputing Party. (d) If a disputing Party fails to select its panelists within such period, such panelists shall be selected by lot from among the roster members who are citizens of the other disputing Party.

2. Where there are more than two disputing Parties, the following procedures shall apply: (a) The panel shall comprise five members. (b) The disputing Parties shall endeavor to agree on the chair of the panel within 15 days of the delivery of the request for the establishment of the panel. If the disputing Parties are unable to agree on the chair within this period, the Party or Parties on the side of the dispute chosen by lot shall select within 10 days a chair who is not a citizen of such Party or Parties. (c) Within 15 days of selection of the chair, the Party complained against shall select two panelists, one of whom is a citizen of a complaining Party, and the other of whom is a citizen of another complaining Party. The complaining Parties shall select two panelists who are citizens of the Party complained against. (d) If any disputing Party fails to select a panelist within such period, such panelist shall be selected by lot in accordance with the citizenship criteria of subparagraph (c).

3. Panelists shall normally be selected from the roster. Any disputing Party may exercise a peremptory challenge against any individual not on the roster who is proposed as a panelist by a disputing Party within 15 days after the individual has been proposed.

4. If a disputing Party believes that a panelist is in violation of the code of conduct, the disputing Parties shall consult and if they agree, the panelist shall be removed and a new panelist shall be selected in accordance with this Article.

Article 2012

Rules of Procedure

1. The Commission shall establish by January 1, 1994, Model Rules of Procedure, in accordance with the following principles: (a) the procedures shall assure a right to at least one hearing before the panel as well as the opportunity to provide initial and rebuttal written submissions; and (b) the panel's hearings, deliberations and initial report, and all written submissions to and communications with the panel shall be confidential.

2. Unless the disputing Parties otherwise agree, the panel shall conduct its proceedings in accordance with the Model Rules of Procedure.

3. Unless the disputing Parties otherwise agree within 20 days from the date of the delivery of the request for the establishment of the panel, the terms of reference shall be: "To examine, in the light of the relevant provisions of the Agreement, the matter referred to the Commission (as set out in the request for a Commission meeting) and to make findings, determinations and recommendations as provided in Article 2016(2)."

4.   If a complaining Party wishes to argue that a matter has nullified or impaired benefits, the terms of reference shall so indicate.

5.   If a disputing Party wishes the panel to make findings as to the degree of adverse trade effects on any Party of any measure found not to conform with the obligations of the Agreement or to have caused nullification or impairment in the sense of Annex 2004, the terms of reference shall so indicate.

Article 2013

Third Party Participation

A Party that is not a disputing Party, on delivery of a written notice to the disputing Parties and to its Section of the Secretariat, shall be entitled to attend all hearings, to make written and oral submissions to the panel and to receive written submissions of the disputing Parties.

Article 2014

Role of Experts

On request of a disputing Party, or on its own initiative, the panel may seek information and technical advice from any person or body that it deems appropriate, provided that the disputing Parties so agree and subject to such terms and conditions as such Parties may agree.

Article 2015

Scientific Review Boards

1.   On request of a disputing Party or, unless the disputing Parties disapprove, on its own initiative, the panel may request a written report of a scientific review board on any factual issue concerning environmental, health, safety or other scientific matters raised by a disputing Party in a proceeding, subject to such terms and conditions as such Parties may agree.

2.   The board shall be selected by the panel from among highly qualified, independent experts in the scientific matters, after consultations with the disputing Parties and the scientific bodies set out in the Model Rules of Procedure established pursuant to Article 2012(1).

3.   The participating Parties shall be provided: (a) advance notice of, and an opportunity to provide comments to the panel on, the proposed factual issues to be referred to the board; and (b) a copy of the board's report and an opportunity to provide comments on the report to the panel.

4.   The panel shall take the board's report and any comments by the Parties on the report into account in the preparation of its report.

Article 2016

Initial Report

1.   Unless the disputing Parties otherwise agree, the panel shall base its report on the submissions and arguments of the Parties and on any information before it pursuant to Article 2014 or 2015.

2.   Unless the disputing Parties otherwise agree, the panel shall, within 90 days after the last panelist is selected or such other period as the Model

Rules of Procedure established pursuant to Article 2012(1) may provide, present to the disputing Parties an initial report containing: (a) findings of fact, including any findings pursuant to a request under Article 2012(5); (b) its determination as to whether the measure at issue is or would be inconsistent with the obligations of this Agreement or cause nullification or impairment in the sense of Annex 2004, or any other determination requested in the terms of reference; and (c) its recommendations, if any, for resolution of the dispute.

3. Panelists may furnish separate opinions on matters not unanimously agreed.

4. A disputing Party may submit written comments to the panel on its initial report within 14 days of presentation of the report.

5. In such an event, and after considering such written comments, the panel, on its own initiative or on the request of any disputing Party, may: (a) request the views of any participating Party; (b) reconsider its report; and (c) make any further examination that it considers appropriate.

Article 2017

Final Report

1. The panel shall present to the disputing Parties a final report, including any separate opinions on matters not unanimously agreed, within 30 days of presentation of the initial report, unless the disputing Parties otherwise agree.

2. No panel may, either in its initial report or its final report, disclose which panelists are associated with majority or minority opinions.

3. The disputing Parties shall transmit to the Commission the final report of the panel, including any report of a scientific review board established under Article 2015, as well as any written views that a disputing Party desires to be appended, on a confidential basis within a reasonable period of time after it is presented to them.

4. Unless the Commission decides otherwise, the final report of the panel shall be published 15 days after it is transmitted to the Commission.

Implementation of Panel Reports

Article 2018

Implementation of Final Report

1. On receipt of the final report of a panel, the disputing Parties shall agree on the resolution of the dispute, which normally shall conform with the determinations and recommendations of the panel, and shall notify their Sections of the Secretariat of any agreed resolution of any dispute.

2. Wherever possible, the resolution shall be non-implementation or removal of a measure not conforming with this Agreement or causing nullification or impairment in the sense of Annex 2004 or, failing such a resolution, compensation.

Article 2019
Non–implementation—Suspension of Benefits

1. If in its final report a panel has determined that a measure is inconsistent with the obligations of this Agreement or causes nullification or impairment in the sense of Annex 2004 and the Party complained against has not reached agreement with any complaining Party on a mutually satisfactory resolution pursuant to Article 2018(1) within 30 days of receiving the final report, such complaining Party may suspend the application to the Party complained against of benefits of equivalent effect until such time as they have reached agreement on a resolution of the dispute.

2. In considering what benefits to suspend pursuant to paragraph 1: (a) a complaining Party should first seek to suspend benefits in the same sector or sectors as that affected by the measure or other matter that the panel has found to be inconsistent with the obligations of this Agreement or to have caused nullification or impairment in the sense of Annex 2004; and (b) a complaining Party that considers it is not practicable or effective to suspend benefits in the same sector or sectors may suspend benefits in other sectors.

3. On the written request of any disputing Party delivered to the other Parties and its Section of the Secretariat, the Commission shall establish a panel to determine whether the level of benefits suspended by a Party pursuant to paragraph 1 is manifestly excessive.

4. The panel proceedings shall be conducted in accordance with the Model Rules of Procedure. The panel shall present its determination within 60 days after the last panelist is selected or such other period as the disputing Parties may agree.

Section C—Domestic Proceedings and Private Commercial Dispute Settlement
Article 2020
Referrals of Matters from Judicial or Administrative Proceedings

1. If an issue of interpretation or application of this Agreement arises in any domestic judicial or administrative proceeding of a Party that any Party considers would merit its intervention, or if a court or administrative body solicits the views of a Party, that Party shall notify the other Parties and its Section of the Secretariat. The Commission shall endeavor to agree on an appropriate response as expeditiously as possible.

2. The Party in whose territory the court or administrative body is located shall submit any agreed interpretation of the Commission to the court or administrative body in accordance with the rules of that forum.

3. If the Commission is unable to agree, any Party may submit its own views to the court or administrative body in accordance with the rules of that forum.

Article 2021
Private Rights

No Party may provide for a right of action under its domestic law against any other Party on the ground that a measure of another Party is inconsistent with this Agreement.

Article 2022

Alternative Dispute Resolution

1. Each Party shall, to the maximum extent possible, encourage and facilitate the use of arbitration and other means of alternative dispute resolution for the settlement of international commercial disputes between private parties in the free trade area.

2. To this end, each Party shall provide appropriate procedures to ensure observance of agreements to arbitrate and for the recognition and enforcement of arbitral awards in such disputes.

3. A Party shall be deemed to be in compliance with paragraph 2 if it is a party to and is in compliance with the 1958 United Nations Convention on the Recognition and Enforcement of Foreign Arbitral Awards or the 1975 Inter-American Convention on International Commercial Arbitration.

4. The Commission shall establish an Advisory Committee on Private Commercial Disputes comprising persons with expertise or experience in the resolution of private international commercial disputes. The Committee shall report and provide recommendations to the Commission on general issues referred to it by the Commission respecting the availability, use and effectiveness of arbitration and other procedures for the resolution of such disputes in the free trade area.

PART EIGHT
OTHER PROVISIONS
CHAPTER TWENTY–ONE: EXCEPTIONS

Article 2101

General Exceptions

1. For purposes of: (a) Part Two (Trade in Goods), except to the extent that a provision of that Part applies to services or investment, and (b) Part Three (Technical Barriers to Trade), except to the extent that a provision of that Part applies to services, GATT Article XX and its interpretative notes, or any equivalent provision of a successor agreement to which all Parties are party, are incorporated into and made part of this Agreement. The Parties understand that the measures referred to in GATT Article XX(b) include environmental measures necessary to protect human, animal or plant life or health, and that GATT Article XX(g) applies to measures relating to the conservation of living and non-living exhaustible natural resources.

2. Provided that such measures are not applied in a manner that would constitute a means of arbitrary or unjustifiable discrimination between countries where the same conditions prevail or a disguised restriction on trade between the Parties, nothing in: (a) Part Two (Trade in Goods), to the extent that a provision of that Part applies to services, (b) Part Three (Technical Barriers to Trade), to the extent that a provision of that Part applies to services, (c) Chapter Twelve (Cross–Border Trade in Services), and (d) Chapter Thirteen (Telecommunications), shall be construed to prevent the adoption or enforcement by any Party of measures necessary to secure compliance with laws or regulations that are not inconsistent with the provisions of this Agreement, including those relating to health and safety and consumer protection.

Article 2102

National Security

1.   Subject to Articles 607 (Energy—National Security Measures) and 1018 (Government Procurement—Exceptions), nothing in this Agreement shall be construed: (a) to require any Party to furnish or allow access to any information the disclosure of which it determines to be contrary to its essential security interests; (b) to prevent any Party from taking any actions that it considers necessary for the protection of its essential security interests (i) relating to the traffic in arms, ammunition and implements of war and to such traffic and transactions in other goods, materials, services and technology undertaken directly or indirectly for the purpose of supplying a military or other security establishment, (ii) taken in time of war or other emergency in international relations, or (iii) relating to the implementation of national policies or international agreements respecting the non-proliferation of nuclear weapons or other nuclear explosive devices; or (c) to prevent any Party from taking action in pursuance of its obligations under the United Nations Charter for the maintenance of international peace and security.

Article 2103

Taxation

1.   Except as set out in this Article, nothing in this Agreement shall apply to taxation measures.

2.   Nothing in this Agreement shall affect the rights and obligations of any Party under any tax convention.   In the event of any inconsistency between this Agreement and any such convention, that convention shall prevail to the extent of the inconsistency.

3.   Notwithstanding paragraph 2: (a) Article 301 (Market Access—National Treatment) and such other provisions of this Agreement as are necessary to give effect to that Article shall apply to taxation measures to the same extent as does Article III of the GATT; and (b) Article 314 (Market Access—Export Taxes) and Article 604 (Energy—Export Taxes) shall apply to taxation measures.

4.   Subject to paragraph 2: (a) Article 1202 (Cross–Border Trade in Services—National Treatment) and Article 1405 (Financial Services—National Treatment) shall apply to taxation measures on income, capital gains or the taxable capital of corporations, and to those taxes listed in paragraph 1 of Annex 2103.4, that relate to the purchase or consumption of particular services, and (b) Articles 1102 and 1103 (Investment—National Treatment and Most–Favored Nation Treatment), Articles 1202 and 1203 (Cross–Border Trade in Services—National Treatment and Most–Favored–Nation Treatment) and Articles 1405 and 1406 (Financial Services—National Treatment and Most–Favored–Nation Treatment) shall apply to all taxation measures, other than those on income, capital gains or on the taxable capital of corporations, taxes on estates, inheritances, gifts and generation-skipping transfers and those taxes listed in paragraph 1 of Annex 2103.4, except that nothing in those Articles shall apply (c) any most-favored-nation obligation with respect to an advantage accorded by a Party pursuant to a tax convention, (d) to a non-conforming provision of any existing taxation measure, (e) to the continuation or prompt renewal of a non-conforming provision of any

existing taxation measure, (f) to an amendment to a non-conforming provision of any existing taxation measure to the extent that the amendment does not decrease its conformity, at the time of the amendment, with any of those Articles, (g) to any new taxation measure aimed at ensuring the equitable and effective imposition or collection of taxes and that does not arbitrarily discriminate between persons, goods or services of the Parties or arbitrarily nullify or impair benefits accorded under those Articles, in the sense of Annex 2004, or (h) to the measures listed in paragraph 2 of Annex 2103.4.

5. Subject to paragraph 2 and without prejudice to the rights and obligations of the Parties under paragraph 3, Article 1106(3), (4) and (5) (Performance Requirements) shall apply to taxation measures.

6. Article 1110 (Expropriation and Compensation) shall apply to taxation measures except that no investor may invoke that Article as the basis for a claim under Article 1116 (Claim by an Investor of a Party on its Own Behalf) or 1117 (Claim by an Investor of a Party on Behalf of an Enterprise), where it has been determined pursuant to this paragraph that the measure is not an expropriation. The investor shall refer the issue of whether the measure is not an expropriation for a determination to the appropriate competent authorities set out in Annex 2103.6 at the time that it gives notice under Article 1119 (Notice of Intent to Submit a Claim to Arbitration). If the competent authorities do not agree to consider the issue or, having agreed to consider it, fail to agree that the measure is not an expropriation within a period of six months of such referral, the investor may submit its claim to arbitration under Article 1120 (Submission of a Claim to Arbitration).

Annex 2103.4

Specific Taxation Measures

1. For purposes of Article 2103(4)(a) and (b), the listed tax is the asset tax under the Asset Tax Law ("Ley del Impuesto al Activo") of Mexico.

2. For purposes of Article 2103(4)(h), the listed tax is any excise tax on insurance premiums adopted by Mexico to the extent that such tax would, if levied by Canada or the United States, be covered by Article 2103(4)(d), (e) or (f).

Annex 2103.6

Competent Authorities

For purposes of this Chapter:

competent authority means (a) in the case of Canada, the Assistant Deputy Minister for Tax Policy, Department of Finance; (b) in the case of Mexico, the Deputy Minister of Revenue of the Ministry of Finance and Public Credit ("Secretaria de Hacienda y Credito Publico"); and (c) in the case of the United States, the Assistant Secretary of the Treasury (Tax Policy), Department of the Treasury.

Article 2104

Balance of Payments

1. Nothing in this Agreement shall be construed to prevent a Party from adopting or maintaining measures that restrict transfers where the Party

experiences serious balance of payments difficulties, or the threat thereof, and such restrictions are consistent with paragraphs 2 through 4 and are: (a) consistent with paragraph 5 to the extent they are imposed on transfers other than cross-border trade in financial services; or (b) consistent with paragraphs 6 and 7 to the extent they are imposed on cross-border trade in financial services.

General Rules

2. As soon as practicable after a Party imposes a measure under this Article, the Party shall: (a) submit any current account exchange restrictions to the IMF for review under Article VIII of the Articles of Agreement of the IMF; (b) enter into good faith consultations with the IMF on economic adjustment measures to address the fundamental underlying economic problems causing the difficulties; and (c) adopt or maintain economic policies consistent with such consultations.

3. A measure adopted or maintained under this Article shall: (a) avoid unnecessary damage to the commercial, economic or financial interests of another Party; (b) not be more burdensome than necessary to deal with the balance of payments difficulties or threat thereof; (c) be temporary and be phased out progressively as the balance of payments situation improves; (d) be consistent with paragraph 2(c) and with the Articles of Agreement of the IMF; and (e) be applied on a national treatment or most-favored-nation treatment basis, whichever is better.

4. A Party may adopt or maintain a measure under this Article that gives priority to services that are essential to its economic program, provided that a Party may not impose a measure for the purpose of protecting a specific industry or sector unless the measure is consistent with paragraph 2(c) and with Article VIII(3) of the Articles of Agreement of the IMF.

Restrictions on Transfers Other Than Cross–Border Trade in Financial Services

5. Restrictions imposed on transfers, other than on cross-border trade in financial services: (a) where imposed on payments for current international transactions, shall be consistent with Article VIII(3) of the Articles of Agreement of the IMF; (b) where imposed on international capital transactions, shall be consistent with Article VI of the Articles of Agreement of the IMF and be imposed only in conjunction with measures imposed on current international transactions under paragraph 2(a); (c) where imposed on transfers covered by Article 1109 (Investment—Transfers) and transfers related to trade in goods, may not substantially impede transfers from being made in a freely usable currency at a market rate of exchange; and (d) may not take the form of tariff surcharges, quotas, licenses or similar measures.

Restrictions on Cross–Border Trade in Financial Services

6. A Party imposing a restriction on cross-border trade in financial services: (a) may not impose more than one measure on any transfer, unless consistent with paragraph 2(c) and with Article VIII(3) of the Articles of Agreement of the IMF; and (b) shall promptly notify and consult with the other Parties to assess the balance of payments situation of the Party and the

measures it has adopted, taking into account among other elements (i) the nature and extent of the balance of payments difficulties of the Party, (ii) the external economic and trading environment of the Party, and (iii) alternative corrective measures that may be available.

7.   In consultations under paragraph 6(b), the Parties shall: (a) consider if measures adopted under this Article comply with paragraph 3, in particular paragraph 3(c); and (b) accept all findings of statistical and other facts presented by the IMF relating to foreign exchange, monetary reserves and balance of payments, and shall base their conclusions on the assessment by the IMF of the balance of payments situation of the Party adopting the measures.

Article 2105
Disclosure of Information

Nothing in this Agreement shall be construed to require a Party to furnish or allow access to information the disclosure of which would impede law enforcement or would be contrary to the Party's law protecting personal privacy or the financial affairs and accounts of individual customers of financial institutions.

Article 2106
Cultural Industries

Annex 2106 applies to the Parties specified in that Annex with respect to cultural industries.

Annex 2106
Cultural Industries

Notwithstanding any other provision of this Agreement, as between Canada and the United States, any measure adopted or maintained with respect to cultural industries, except as specifically provided in Article 302 (Market Access—Tariff Elimination), and any measure of equivalent commercial effect taken in response, shall be governed under this Agreement exclusively in accordance with the provisions of the Canada–United States Free Trade Agreement. The rights and obligations between Canada and any other Party with respect to such measures shall be identical to those applying between Canada and the United States.

Article 2107
Definitions

For purposes of this Chapter:

cultural industries means persons engaged in any of the following activities: (a) the publication, distribution, or sale of books, magazines, periodicals or newspapers in print or machine readable form but not including the sole activity of printing or typesetting any of the foregoing; (b) the production, distribution, sale or exhibition of film or video recordings; (c) the production, distribution, sale or exhibition of audio or video music recordings; (d) the publication, distribution or sale of music in print or machine readable form; or (e) radiocommunications in which the transmissions are intended for direct reception by the general public, and all radio, television and cable broadcasting undertakings and all satellite programming and broadcast network services;

international capital transactions means "international capital transactions" as defined under the Articles of Agreement of the IMF;

IMF means the International Monetary Fund;

payments for current international transactions means "payments for current international transactions" as defined under the Articles of Agreement of the IMF;

tax convention means a convention for the avoidance of double taxation or other international taxation agreement or arrangement;

taxes and taxation measures do not include: (a) a "customs duty" as defined in Article 318 (Market Access—Definitions); or (b) the measures listed in exceptions (b), (c), (d) and (e) of that definition; and

transfers means international transactions and related international transfers and payments.

CHAPTER TWENTY–TWO: FINAL PROVISIONS

Article 2201

Annexes

The Annexes to this Agreement constitute an integral part of this Agreement.

Article 2202

Amendments

1. The Parties may agree on any modification of or addition to this Agreement.

2. When so agreed, and approved in accordance with the applicable legal procedures of each Party, a modification or addition shall constitute an integral part of this Agreement.

Article 2203

Entry into Force

This Agreement shall enter into force on January 1, 1994, on an exchange of written notifications certifying the completion of necessary legal procedures.

Article 2204

Accession

1. Any country or group of countries may accede to this Agreement subject to such terms and conditions as may be agreed between such country or countries and the Commission and following approval in accordance with the applicable legal procedures of each country.

2. This Agreement shall not apply as between any Party and any acceding country or group of countries if, at the time of accession, either does not consent to such application.

Article 2205

Withdrawal

A Party may withdraw from this Agreement six months after it provides written notice of withdrawal to the other Parties. If a Party withdraws, the Agreement shall remain in force for the remaining Parties.

Article 2206

Authentic Texts

The English, French and Spanish texts of this Agreement are equally authentic.

IN WITNESS WHEREOF, the undersigned, being duly authorized by their respective Governments, have signed this Agreement.

DONE in triplicate at

Ottawa, on the 11th day and the 17th day of December 1992,

Mexico, D.F., on the 14th day and the 17th day of December 1992,

Washington, D.C., on the 8th day and the 17th day of December 1992.

FOR THE GOVERNMENT OF CANADA
FOR THE GOVERNMENT OF THE UNITED MEXICAN STATES
FOR THE GOVERNMENT OF THE UNITED STATES OF AMERICA

Notes

1. Article 201 (Definitions of General Application): A good of a Party may include materials of other countries.

2. Article 301 (Market Access—National Treatment): "goods of the Party" as used in paragraph 2 includes goods produced in the state or province of that Party.

3. Article 302(1) (Tariff Elimination): this paragraph is not intended to prevent any Party from modifying its non-NAFTA tariffs on originating goods for which no NAFTA tariff preference is claimed.

4. Article 302(1): this paragraph does not prohibit a Party from raising a tariff back to an agreed level in accordance with the NAFTA's phase-out schedule following a unilateral reduction.

5. Article 302(1) and (2): paragraphs 1 and 2 are not intended to prevent a Party from maintaining or increasing a customs duty as may be authorized by any dispute settlement provision of the GATT or any agreement negotiated under the GATT.

6. Article 303 (Restriction on Drawback and Duty Deferral): in applying the definition of "used" in Article 415 to this Article, the definition of "consumed" in Article 318 shall not apply.

7. Article 305(2)(d) (Temporary Admission of Goods): where another form of monetary security is used, it shall not be more burdensome than the bonding requirement referred to in this subparagraph. Where a Party uses a non-monetary form of security, it shall not be more burdensome than existing forms of security used by that Party.

8. Article 307(1) (Goods Re-entered After Repair or Alteration): this paragraph does not cover goods imported in bond, into foreign-trade zones or in similar status, that are exported for repairs and are not re-imported in bond, into foreign-trade zones or in similar status.

9. Article 307(1): for purposes of this paragraph, alteration includes laundering used textile and apparel goods and sterilizing previously sterilized textile and apparel goods.

10. Article 318 (Market Access—Definitions): 10–digit items set out in the Tariff Schedule of Canada are included for statistical purposes only.

11. Article 318: with respect to the definition of "repair or alteration", an operation or process that is part of the production or assembly of an unfinished good into a finished good is not a repair or alteration of the unfinished good; a component of a good is a good that may be subject to repair or alteration.

12. Annex 300–A (Trade and Investment in the Automotive Sector), Appendix 300–A.1—Canada: paragraphs 1 and 2 shall not be construed to modify the rights and obligations set out in Chapter Ten of the Canada–United States Free Trade Agreement, except that the NAFTA rules of origin shall replace the Canada–United States Free Trade Agreement rules of origin for purposes of Article 1005(1).

13. Annex 300–A, Appendix 300–A.2—Mexico: citations to the Auto Decree and the Auto Decree Implementing Regulations included in parentheses are provided for purposes of reference only.

14. Annex 300–B (Textile and Apparel Goods), Section 1 (Scope and Coverage): the general provisions of Chapter Two (Definitions), Chapter Three (Market Access), Chapter Four (Rules of Origin) and Chapter Eight (Emergency Action) are subject to the specific rules for textiles and apparel goods set out in the Annex.

15. Annex 300–B, Section 2 (Tariff Elimination): with respect to paragraph 1, "as otherwise provided in this Agreement" refers to such provisions as Section 4, Article 802 (Global Actions) and Chapter 22 (General Exceptions).

16. Annex 300–B, Sections 4 (Bilateral Emergency Actions (Tariff Actions)) and 5 (Bilateral Emergency Actions (Quantitative Restrictions)): for purposes of Sections 4 and 5: (a) "increased quantities" is intended to be interpreted more broadly than the standard provided in Article 801(1), which considers imports "in absolute terms" only. For purposes of these Sections, "increased quantities" is intended to be interpreted in the same manner as this standard is interpreted in the draft Agreement on Textiles and Clothing, contained in the Draft Final Act Embodying the Results of the Uruguay Round of Multilateral Trade Negotiations (GATT document MTN.TNC/W/FA) issued by the Director–General of the GATT on December 20, 1991 ("Draft Uruguay Round Agreement on Textiles and Clothing"); and (b) "serious damage" is intended as a less stringent standard than "serious injury" under Article 801(1). The "serious damage" standard is drawn from the Draft Uruguay Round Agreement on Textiles and Clothing. The factors to be considered in determining whether the standard has been met are set out in Section 4.2 and are also drawn from that Draft. "Serious damage" is to be

interpreted in the light of its meaning in Annex A of the Multifiber Arrangement or any successor agreement.

17. Annex 300–B, Section 5: in paragraph 5(c), the term "equitable treatment" is intended to have the same meaning as it has in customary practice under the Multifiber Arrangement.

18. Annex 300–B, Section 7, paragraph 1(c) (Review and Revision of Rules of Origin): for subheading 6212.10, the rule and paragraph 1 shall not be applied if the Parties agree, prior to entry into force of this Agreement, on measures to ease the administrative burden and reduce costs associated with the application of the rule for headings 62.06 through 62.11 to the apparel in subheading 6212.10.

19. Annex 300–B, Section 7, paragraph (2)(d)(ii): with respect to provisions (a) through (i) of the rule for subheadings 6205.20 through 6205.30, prior to the entry into force of this Agreement the Parties will extend cooperation as necessary in an effort to encourage production in the free trade area of shirting fabrics specifically identified in the rule.

20. Annex 300–B, Appendix 3.1, paragraph 17 (Administration of Import and Export Prohibitions, Restrictions and Consultation Levels): for purposes of applying paragraph 17, the determination of the component that determines the tariff classification of the good shall be based on GRI 3(b) of the Harmonized System, and if the component cannot be determined on the basis of GRI 3(b), then the determination will be based on GRI 3(c) or, if GRI 3(c) is inapplicable, GRI 4. When the component that determines the tariff classification is a blend of two or more yarns or fibers, all yarns and, where applicable, fibers, in that component are to be considered.

21. Annex 300–B, Schedule 3.1.3. (Conversion Factors): the conversion factors in this Schedule are those used for imports into the United States. Canada and Mexico may by mutual agreement develop their own conversion factors for trade between them.

22. Article 401 (Originating Goods): the phrase "specifically describes" is intended solely to prevent Article 401(d) from being used to qualify a part of another part, where the heading or subheading covers the final good, the part made from the other part and the other part.

23. Article 402 (Regional Value Content): (a) Article 402(4) applies to intermediate materials, and VNM in paragraphs 2 and 3 does not include (i) the value of any non-originating materials used by another producer to produce an originating material that is subsequently acquired and used in the production of the good by the producer of the good, and (ii) the value of non-originating materials used by the producer to produce an originating self-produced material that is designated by the producer as an intermediate material pursuant to Article 402(10); (b) with respect to paragraph 4, where an originating intermediate material is subsequently used by the producer with non-originating materials (whether or not produced by the producer) to produce the good, the value of such non-originating materials shall be included in the VNM of the good; (c) with respect to paragraph 8, sales promotion, marketing and after-sales service costs, royalties, shipping and packing costs, and non-allowable interest costs included in the value of materials used in the production of the good are not subtracted out of the net cost in the calculation

under Article 402(3); (d) with respect to paragraph 10, an intermediate material used by another producer in the production of a material that is subsequently acquired and used by the producer of the good shall not be taken into account in applying the proviso set out in that paragraph, except where two or more producers accumulate their production under Article 404; (e) with respect to paragraph 10, if a producer designates a self-produced material as an originating intermediate material and the Customs Administration of the importing Party subsequently determines that the intermediate material is not originating, the producer may rescind the designation and recalculate the value content of the good accordingly; in such a case, the producer shall retain its rights of appeal or review with regard to the determination of the origin of the intermediate material; and (f) under paragraph 4, with respect to any self-produced material that is not designated as an intermediate material, only the value of non-originating materials used to produce the self-produced material shall be included in VNM of the good.

24. Article 403 (Automotive Goods): (a) for purposes of paragraph 1, "first person in the territory of a Party" means the first person who uses the imported good in production or resells the imported good; and (b) for purposes of paragraph 2, (i) a producer may not designate as an intermediate material any assembly, including a component identified in Annex 403.2, containing one or more of the materials listed in Annex 403.2, and (ii) a producer of a material listed in Annex 403.2 may designate a self-produced material used in the production of that material as an intermediate material, in accordance with the provisions of Article 402(10).

25. Article 405(6) (De Minimis): for purposes of applying paragraph 6, the determination of the component that determines the tariff classification of the good shall be based on GRI 3(b) of the Harmonized System. If the component cannot be determined on the basis of GRI 3(b), then the determination will be based on GRI 3(c) or, if GRI 3(c) is inapplicable, GRI 4. When the component that determines the tariff classification is a blend of two or more yarns or fibers, all yarns and, where applicable, fibers, in that component are to be taken into account.

26. Article 413 (Interpretation and Application): the rules of origin under Chapter Four are based on the 1992 Harmonized System, amended by the new tariff items created for rules of origin purposes.

27. Article 415 (Rules of Origin—Definitions): the phrase "except for the application of Article 403(1) or 403(2)(a)" in the definition of "transaction value" is intended solely to ensure that the determination of transaction value in the context of Article 403(1) or (2)(a) shall not be limited to the transaction of the producer of the good.

28. Article 514 (Customs Procedures—Definitions): the Uniform Regulations will clarify that "determination of origin" includes a denial of preferential tariff treatment under Article 506(4), and that such denial is subject to review and appeal.

29. Article 603, paragraphs 1 through 5 (Energy—Import and Export Restrictions): these paragraphs shall be interpreted consistently with Article 309 (Import and Export Restrictions).

30.   Article 703 (Agriculture—Market Access): the most-favored-nation rate as of July 1, 1991 is the over-quota tariff rate specified in Annex 302.2.

31.   Annex 703.2, Section A (Mexico and the United States): this quota replaces Mexico's current access under the "first tier" of the U.S. tariff rate quota as described in Additional Note 3(b)(i) of Chapter 17 of the Harmonized Tariff Schedule of the United States prior to the date of entry into force of this Agreement.

32.   Annex 703.2, Section A (Mexico and the United States): the United States operates a re-export program under Additional U.S. Note 3 to Chapter 17 of the U.S. Harmonized Tariff Schedule and under 7 C.F.R. Part 1530 (subparts A and B).

33.   Annex 703.2, Section B (Canada and Mexico): the incorporation in paragraph 6 is not intended to override the exceptions to Articles 301 and 309 set out in Canada's and Mexico's respective Schedules to Annex 301.3.

34.   Article 906(4) and (6) (Compatibility and Equivalence): these paragraphs are not intended to restrict the right of the importing Party to revise its measures.

35.   Article 908(2) (Conformity Assessment): this paragraph does not treat the issue of membership in the Parties' respective conformity assessment bodies.

36.   Article 915 (Standards–Related Measures—Definitions): the definition of "standard" shall be interpreted to mean—(a) characteristics for a good or a service, (b) characteristics, rules or guidelines for (i) processes or production methods relating to such good, or (ii) operating methods relating to such service, and (c) provisions specifying terminology, symbols, packaging, marking or labelling for (i) a good or its related process or production method, or (ii) a service or its related operating method, for common and repeated use, including explanatory and other related provisions, set out in a document approved by a standardizing body, with which compliance is not mandatory.

37.   Article 915: the definition of "technical regulation" shall be interpreted to mean—(a) characteristics or their related processes and production methods for a good, (b) characteristics for a service or its related operating methods, or (c) provisions specifying terminology, symbols, packaging, marking, or labelling for (i) a good or its related process or production method, or (ii) a service or its related operating method, set out in a document, including applicable administrative, explanatory and other related provisions, with which compliance is mandatory.

38.   Annex 1001.2c (Country Specific Thresholds): Canada and the United States will consult regarding this Annex before the entry into force of this Agreement.

39.   Article 1101 (Investment—Scope and Coverage): this Chapter covers investments existing on the date of entry into force of this Agreement as well as investments made or acquired thereafter.

40.   Article 1101(2) and Annex 602.3: to the extent that a Party allows an investment to be made in an activity set out in Annex III or Annex 602.3, the investment shall be entitled to the protection of Chapter Eleven (Investment).

41. Article 1106 (Performance Requirements): Article 1106 does not preclude enforcement of any commitment, undertaking or requirement between private parties.

42. Article 1305 (Monopolies): for purposes of this Article, "monopoly" means an entity, including a consortium or government agency, that in any relevant market in the territory of a Party is maintained or designated as the sole provider of public telecommunications transport networks or services.

43. Article 1501 (Competition Law): no investor may have recourse to investor-state arbitration under the Investment Chapter for any matter arising under this Article.

44. Article 1502 (Monopolies and State Enterprises): nothing in this Article shall be construed to prevent a monopoly from charging different prices in different geographic markets, where such differences are based on normal commercial considerations, such as taking account of supply and demand conditions in those markets.

45. Article 1502(3): a "delegation" includes a legislative grant, and a government order, directive or other act transferring to the monopoly, or authorizing the exercise by the monopoly of, governmental authority.

46. Article 1502(3)(b): differences in pricing between classes of customers, between affiliated and non-affiliated firms, and cross-subsidization are not in themselves inconsistent with this provision; rather, they are subject to this subparagraph when they are used as instruments of anticompetitive behavior by the monopoly firm.

47. Article 2005(2) (GATT Dispute Settlement): this obligation is not intended to be subject to dispute settlement under this Chapter.

Item 41

NORTH AMERICAN AGREEMENT ON ENVIRONMENTAL COOPERATION

PREAMBLE

The Government of the United States of America, the Government of Canada and the Government of the United Mexican States:

CONVINCED of the importance of the conservation, protection and enhancement of the environment in their territories and the essential role of cooperation in these areas in achieving sustainable development for the well-being of present and future generations;

REAFFIRMING the sovereign right of States to exploit their own resources pursuant to their own environmental and development policies and their responsibility to ensure that activities within their jurisdiction or control do not cause damage to the environment of other States or of areas beyond the limits of national jurisdiction;

RECOGNIZING the interrelationship of their environments;

ACKNOWLEDGING the growing economic and social links between them, including the North American Free Trade Agreement (NAFTA);

RECONFIRMING the importance of the environmental goals and objectives of the NAFTA, including enhanced levels of environmental protection;

EMPHASIZING the importance of public participation in conserving, protecting and enhancing the environment;

NOTING the existence of differences in their respective natural endowments, climatic and geographical conditions, and economic, technological and infrastructural capabilities;

REAFFIRMING the Stockholm Declaration on the Human Environment of 1972 and the Rio Declaration on Environment and Development of 1992;

RECALLING their tradition of environmental cooperation and expressing their desire to support and build on international environmental agreements and existing policies and laws, in order to promote cooperation between them; and

CONVINCED of the benefits to be derived from a framework, including a Commission, to facilitate effective cooperation on the conservation, protection and enhancement of the environment in their territories;

HAVE AGREED AS FOLLOWS:

PART ONE
OBJECTIVES

Article 1: Objectives

The objectives of this Agreement are to: (a) foster the protection and improvement of the environment in the territories of the Parties for the well-being of present and future generations; (b) promote sustainable development based on cooperation and mutually supportive environmental and economic policies; (c) increase cooperation between the Parties to better conserve, protect, and enhance the environment, including wild flora and fauna; (d) support the environmental goals and objectives of the NAFTA; (e) avoid creating trade distortions or new trade barriers; (f) strengthen cooperation on the development and improvement of environmental laws, regulations, procedures, policies and practices; (g) enhance compliance with, and enforcement of, environmental laws and regulations; (h) promote transparency and public participation in the development of environmental laws, regulations and policies; (i) promote economically efficient and effective environmental measures; and (j) promote pollution prevention policies and practices.

PART TWO

OBLIGATIONS

Article 2: General Commitments

1. Each Party shall, with respect to its territory: (a) periodically prepare and make publicly available reports on the state of the environment; (b) develop and review environmental emergency preparedness measures; (c) promote education in environmental matters, including environmental law; (d) further scientific research and technology development in respect of environmental matters; (e) assess, as appropriate, environmental impacts; and (f) promote the use of economic instruments for the efficient achievement of environmental goals.

2. Each Party shall consider implementing in its law any recommendation developed by the Council under Article 10(5)(b).

3. Each Party shall consider prohibiting the export to the territories of the other Parties of a pesticide or toxic substance whose use is prohibited within the Party's territory. When a Party adopts a measure prohibiting or severely restricting the use of a pesticide or toxic substance in its territory, it shall notify the other Parties of the measure, either directly or through an appropriate international organization.

Article 3: Levels of Protection

Recognizing the right of each Party to establish its own levels of domestic environmental protection and environmental development policies and priorities, and to adopt or modify accordingly its environmental laws and regulations, each Party shall ensure that its laws and regulations provide for high levels of environmental protection and shall strive to continue to improve those laws and regulations.

Article 4: Publication

1. Each Party shall ensure that its laws, regulations, procedures and administrative rulings of general application respecting any matter covered by this Agreement are promptly published or otherwise made available in such a manner as to enable interested persons and Parties to become acquainted with them.

2. To the extent possible, each Party shall: (a) publish in advance any such measure that it proposes to adopt; and (b) provide interested persons and Parties a reasonable opportunity to comment on such proposed measures.

Article 5: Government Enforcement Action

1. With the aim of achieving high levels of environmental protection and compliance with its environmental laws and regulations, each Party shall effectively enforce its environmental laws and regulations through appropriate governmental action, subject to Article 37, such as: (a) appointing and training inspectors; (b) monitoring compliance and investigating suspected violations, including through on-site inspections; (c) seeking assurances of voluntary compliance and compliance agreements; (d) publicly releasing non-compliance information; (e) issuing bulletins or other periodic statements on enforcement procedures; (f) promoting environmental audits; (g) requiring record keeping and reporting; (h) providing or encouraging mediation and arbitration services; (i) using licenses, permits or authorizations; (j) initiating, in a timely manner, judicial, quasi-judicial or administrative proceedings to seek appropriate sanctions or remedies for violations of its environmental laws and regulations; (k) providing for search, seizure or detention; or (l) issuing administrative orders, including orders of a preventative, curative or emergency nature.

2. Each Party shall ensure that judicial, quasi-judicial or administrative enforcement proceedings are available under its law to sanction or remedy violations of its environmental laws and regulations.

3. Sanctions and remedies provided for a violation of a Party's environmental laws and regulations shall, as appropriate: (a) take into consideration the nature and gravity of the violation, any economic benefit derived from the violation by the violator, the economic condition of the violator, and other relevant factors; and (b) include compliance agreements, fines, imprisonment, injunctions, the closure of facilities, and the cost of containing or cleaning up pollution.

Article 6: Private Access to Remedies

1. Each Party shall ensure that interested persons may request the Party's competent authorities to investigate alleged violations of its environmental laws and regulations and shall give such requests due consideration in accordance with law.

2. Each Party shall ensure that persons with a legally recognized interest under its law in a particular matter have appropriate access to administrative, quasi-judicial or judicial proceedings for the enforcement of the Party's environmental laws and regulations.

3. Private access to remedies shall include rights, in accordance with the Party's law, such as: (a) to sue another person under that Party's jurisdiction for damages; (b) to seek sanctions or remedies such as monetary penalties, emergency closures or orders to mitigate the consequences of violations of its environmental laws and regulations; (c) to request the competent authorities to take appropriate action to enforce that Party's environmental laws and regulations in order to protect the environment or to avoid environmental harm; or (d) to seek injunctions where a person suffers, or may suffer, loss,

damage or injury as a result of conduct by another person under that Party's jurisdiction contrary to that Party's environmental laws and regulations or from tortious conduct.

Article 7: Procedural Guarantees

1. Each Party shall ensure that its administrative, quasi-judicial and judicial proceedings referred to in Articles 5(2) and 6(2) are fair, open and equitable, and to this end shall provide that such proceedings: (a) comply with due process of law; (b) are open to the public, except where the administration of justice otherwise requires; (c) entitle the parties to the proceedings to support or defend their respective positions and to present information or evidence; and (d) are not unnecessarily complicated and do not entail unreasonable charges or time limits or unwarranted delays.

2. Each Party shall provide that final decisions on the merits of the case in such proceedings are: (a) in writing and preferably state the reasons on which the decisions are based; (b) made available without undue delay to the parties to the proceedings and, consistent with its law, to the public; and (c) based on information or evidence in respect of which the parties were offered the opportunity to be heard.

3. Each Party shall provide, as appropriate, that parties to such proceedings have the right, in accordance with its law, to seek review and, where warranted, correction of final decisions issued in such proceedings.

4. Each Party shall ensure that tribunals that conduct or review such proceedings are impartial and independent and do not have any substantial interest in the outcome of the matter.

PART THREE
COMMISSION FOR ENVIRONMENTAL COOPERATION

Article 8: The Commission

1. The Parties hereby establish the Commission for Environmental Cooperation.

2. The Commission shall comprise a Council, a Secretariat and a Joint Public Advisory Committee.

Section A: The Council
Article 9: Council Structure and Procedures

1. The Council shall comprise cabinet-level or equivalent representatives of the Parties, or their designees.

2. The Council shall establish its rules and procedures.

3. The Council shall convene: (a) at least once a year in regular session; and (b) in special session at the request of any Party. Regular sessions shall be chaired successively by each Party.

4. The Council shall hold public meetings in the course of all regular sessions. Other meetings held in the course of regular or special sessions shall be public where the Council so decides.

5. The Council may: (a) establish, and assign responsibilities to, ad hoc or standing committees, working groups or expert groups; (b) seek the advice

of non-governmental organizations or persons, including independent experts; and (c) take such other action in the exercise of its functions as the Parties may agree.

6. All decisions and recommendations of the Council shall be taken by consensus, except as the Council may otherwise decide or as otherwise provided in this Agreement.

7. All decisions and recommendations of the Council shall be made public, except as the Council may otherwise decide or as otherwise provided in this Agreement.

Article 10: Council Functions

1. The Council shall be the governing body of the Commission and shall: (a) serve as a forum for the discussion of environmental matters within the scope of this Agreement; (b) oversee the implementation and develop recommendations on the further elaboration of this Agreement and, to this end, the Council shall, within four years after the date of entry into force of this Agreement, review its operation and effectiveness in the light of experience; (c) oversee the Secretariat; (d) address questions and differences that may arise between the Parties regarding the interpretation or application of this Agreement; (e) approve the annual program and budget of the Commission; and (f) promote and facilitate cooperation between the Parties with respect to environmental matters.

2. The Council may consider, and develop recommendations regarding: (a) comparability of techniques and methodologies for data gathering and analysis, data management and electronic data communications on matters covered by this Agreement; (b) pollution prevention techniques and strategies; (c) approaches and common indicators for reporting on the state of the environment; (d) the use of economic instruments for the pursuit of domestic and internationally agreed environmental objectives; (e) scientific research and technology development in respect of environmental matters; (f) promotion of public awareness regarding the environment; (g) transboundary and border environmental issues, such as the long-range transport of air and marine pollutants; (h) exotic species that may be harmful; (i) the conservation and protection of wild flora and fauna and their habitat, and specially protected natural areas; (j) the protection of endangered and threatened species; (k) environmental emergency preparedness and response activities; (l) environmental matters as they relate to economic development; (m) the environmental implications of goods throughout their life cycles; (n) human resource training and development in the environmental field; (o) the exchange of environmental scientists and officials; (p) approaches to environmental compliance and enforcement; (q) ecologically sensitive national accounts; (r) eco-labelling; and (s) other matters as it may decide.

3. The Council shall strengthen cooperation on the development and continuing improvement of environmental laws and regulations, including by: (a) promoting the exchange of information on criteria and methodologies used in establishing domestic environmental standards; and (b) without reducing levels of environmental protection, establishing a process for developing recommendations on greater compatibility of environmental technical regula-

tions, standards and conformity assessment procedures in a manner consistent with the NAFTA.

4. The Council shall encourage: (a) effective enforcement by each Party of its environmental laws and regulations; (b) compliance with those laws and regulations; and (c) technical cooperation between the Parties.

5. The Council shall promote and, as appropriate, develop recommendations regarding: (a) public access to information concerning the environment that is held by public authorities of each Party, including information on hazardous materials and activities in its communities, and opportunity to participate in decision-making processes related to such public access; and (b) appropriate limits for specific pollutants, taking into account differences in ecosystems.

6. The Council shall cooperate with the NAFTA Free Trade Commission to achieve the environmental goals and objectives of the NAFTA by: (a) acting as a point of inquiry and receipt for comments from non-governmental organizations and persons concerning those goals and objectives; (b) providing assistance in consultations under Article 1114 of the NAFTA where a Party considers that another Party is waiving or derogating from, or offering to waive or otherwise derogate from, an environmental measure as an encouragement to establish, acquire, expand or retain an investment of an investor, with a view to avoiding any such encouragement; (c) contributing to the prevention or resolution of environment-related trade disputes by: (i) seeking to avoid disputes between the Parties, (ii) making recommendations to the Free Trade Commission with respect to the avoidance of such disputes, and (iii) identifying experts able to provide information or technical advice to NAFTA committees, working groups and other NAFTA bodies; (d) considering on an ongoing basis the environmental effects of the NAFTA; and (e) otherwise assisting the Free Trade Commission in environment-related matters.

7. Recognizing the significant bilateral nature of many transboundary environmental issues, the Council shall, with a view to agreement between the Parties pursuant to this Article within three years on obligations, consider and develop recommendations with respect to: (a) assessing the environmental impact of proposed projects subject to decisions by a competent government authority and likely to cause significant adverse transboundary effects, including a full evaluation of comments provided by other Parties and persons of other Parties; (b) notification, provision of relevant information and consultation between Parties with respect to such projects; and (c) mitigation of the potential adverse effects of such projects.

8. The Council shall encourage the establishment by each Party of appropriate administrative procedures pursuant to its environmental laws to permit another Party to seek the reduction, elimination or mitigation of transboundary pollution on a reciprocal basis.

9. The Council shall consider and, as appropriate, develop recommendations on the provision by a Party, on a reciprocal basis, of access to and rights and remedies before its courts and administrative agencies for persons in another Party's territory who have suffered or are likely to suffer damage or injury caused by pollution originating in its territory as if the damage or injury were suffered in its territory.

Section B: The Secretariat

Article 11: Secretariat Structure and Procedures

1. The Secretariat shall be headed by an Executive Director, who shall be chosen by the Council for a three-year term, which may be renewed by the Council for one additional three-year term. The position of Executive Director shall rotate consecutively between nationals of each Party. The Council may remove the Executive Director solely for cause.

2. The Executive Director shall appoint and supervise the staff of the Secretariat, regulate their powers and duties and fix their remuneration in accordance with general standards to be established by the Council. The general standards shall provide that: (a) staff shall be appointed and retained, and their conditions of employment shall be determined, strictly on the basis of efficiency, competence and integrity; (b) in appointing staff, the Executive Director shall take into account lists of candidates prepared by the Parties and by the Joint Public Advisory Committee; (c) due regard shall be paid to the importance of recruiting an equitable proportion of the professional staff from among the nationals of each Party; and (d) the Executive Director shall inform the Council of all appointments.

3. The Council may decide, by a two-thirds vote, to reject any appointment that does not meet the general standards. Any such decision shall be made and held in confidence.

4. In the performance of their duties, the Executive Director and the staff shall not seek or receive instructions from any government or any other authority external to the Council. Each Party shall respect the international character of the responsibilities of the Executive Director and the staff and shall not seek to influence them in the discharge of their responsibilities.

5. The Secretariat shall provide technical, administrative and operational support to the Council and to committees and groups established by the Council, and such other support as the Council may direct.

6. The Executive Director shall submit for the approval of the Council the annual program and budget of the Commission, including provision for proposed cooperative activities and for the Secretariat to respond to contingencies.

7. The Secretariat shall, as appropriate, provide the Parties and the public information on where they may receive technical advice and expertise with respect to environmental matters.

8. The Secretariat shall safeguard: (a) from disclosure information it receives that could identify a non-governmental organization or person making a submission if the person or organization so requests or the Secretariat otherwise considers it appropriate; and (b) from public disclosure any information it receives from any non-governmental organization or person where the information is designated by that non-governmental organization or person as confidential or proprietary.

Article 12: Annual Report of the Commission

1. The Secretariat shall prepare an annual report of the Commission in accordance with instructions from the Council. The Secretariat shall submit

a draft of the report for review by the Council. The final report shall be released publicly.

2. The report shall cover: (a) activities and expenses of the Commission during the previous year; (b) the approved program and budget of the Commission for the subsequent year; (c) the actions taken by each Party in connection with its obligations under this Agreement, including data on the Party's environmental enforcement activities; (d) relevant views and information submitted by non-governmental organizations and persons, including summary data regarding submissions, and any other relevant information the Council deems appropriate; (e) recommendations made on any matter within the scope of this Agreement; and (f) any other matter that the Council instructs the Secretariat to include.

3. The report shall periodically address the state of the environment in the territories of the Parties.

Article 13: Secretariat Reports

1. The Secretariat may prepare a report for the Council on any matter within the scope of the annual program. Should the Secretariat wish to prepare a report on any other environmental matter related to the cooperative functions of this Agreement, it shall notify the Council and may proceed unless, within 30 days of such notification, the Council objects by a two-thirds vote to the preparation of the report. Such other environmental matters shall not include issues related to whether a Party has failed to enforce its environmental laws and regulations. Where the Secretariat does not have specific expertise in the matter under review, it shall obtain the assistance of one or more independent experts of recognized experience in the matter to assist in the preparation of the report.

2. In preparing such a report, the Secretariat may draw upon any relevant technical, scientific or other information, including information: (a) that is publicly available; (b) submitted by interested non-governmental organizations and persons; (c) submitted by the Joint Public Advisory Committee; (d) furnished by a Party; (e) gathered through public consultations, such as conferences, seminars and symposia; or (f) developed by the Secretariat, or by independent experts engaged pursuant to paragraph 1.

3. The Secretariat shall submit its report to the Council, which shall make it publicly available, normally within 60 days following its submission, unless the Council otherwise decides.

Article 14: Submissions on Enforcement Matters

1. The Secretariat may consider a submission from any non-governmental organization or person asserting that a Party is failing to effectively enforce its environmental law, if the Secretariat finds that the submission: (a) is in writing in a language designated by that Party in a notification to the Secretariat; (b) clearly identifies the person or organization making the submission; (c) provides sufficient information to allow the Secretariat to review the submission, including any documentary evidence on which the submission may be based; (d) appears to be aimed at promoting enforcement rather than at harassing industry; (e) indicates that the matter has been communicated in writing to the relevant authorities of the Party and indicates

the Party's response, if any; and (f) is filed by a person or organization residing or established in the territory of a Party.

2. Where the Secretariat determines that a submission meets the criteria set out in paragraph 1, the Secretariat shall determine whether the submission merits requesting a response from the Party. In deciding whether to request a response, the Secretariat shall be guided by whether: (a) the submission alleges harm to the person or organization making the submission; (b) the submission, alone or in combination with other submissions, raises matters whose further study in this process would advance the goals of this Agreement; (c) private remedies available under the Party's law have been pursued; and (d) the submission is drawn exclusively from mass media reports. Where the Secretariat makes such a request, it shall forward to the Party a copy of the submission and any supporting information provided with the submission.

3. The Party shall advise the Secretariat within 30 days or, in exceptional circumstances and on notification to the Secretariat, within 60 days of delivery of the request: (a) whether the matter is the subject of a pending judicial or administrative proceeding, in which case the Secretariat shall proceed no further; and (b) of any other information that the Party wishes to submit, such as (i) whether the matter was previously the subject of a judicial or administrative proceeding, and (ii) whether private remedies in connection with the matter are available to the person or organization making the submission and whether they have been pursued.

Article 15: Factual Record

1. If the Secretariat considers that the submission, in the light of any response provided by the Party, warrants developing a factual record, the Secretariat shall so inform the Council and provide its reasons.

2. The Secretariat shall prepare a factual record if the Council, by a two-thirds vote, instructs it to do so.

3. The preparation of a factual record by the Secretariat pursuant to this Article shall be without prejudice to any further steps that may be taken with respect to any submission.

4. In preparing a factual record, the Secretariat shall consider any information furnished by a Party and may consider any relevant technical, scientific or other information: (a) that is publicly available; (b) submitted by interested non-governmental organizations or persons; (c) submitted by the Joint Public Advisory Committee; or (d) developed by the Secretariat or by independent experts.

5. The Secretariat shall submit a draft factual record to the Council. Any Party may provide comments on the accuracy of the draft within 45 days thereafter.

6. The Secretariat shall incorporate, as appropriate, any such comments in the final factual record and submit it to the Council.

7. The Council may, by a two-thirds vote, make the final factual record publicly available, normally within 60 days following its submission.

Section C: Advisory Committees

Article 16: Joint Public Advisory Committee

1. The Joint Public Advisory Committee shall comprise 15 members, unless the Council otherwise decides. Each Party or, if the Party so decides, its National Advisory Committee convened under Article 17, shall appoint an equal number of members.

2. The Council shall establish the rules of procedure for the Joint Public Advisory Committee, which shall choose its own chair.

3. The Joint Public Advisory Committee shall convene at least once a year at the time of the regular session of the Council and at such other times as the Council, or the Committee's chair with the consent of a majority of its members, may decide.

4. The Joint Public Advisory Committee may provide advice to the Council on any matter within the scope of this Agreement, including on any documents provided to it under paragraph 6, and on the implementation and further elaboration of this Agreement, and may perform such other functions as the Council may direct.

5. The Joint Public Advisory Committee may provide relevant technical, scientific or other information to the Secretariat, including for purposes of developing a factual record under Article 15. The Secretariat shall forward to the Council copies of any such information.

6. The Secretariat shall provide to the Joint Public Advisory Committee at the time they are submitted to the Council copies of the proposed annual program and budget of the Commission, the draft annual report, and any report the Secretariat prepares pursuant to Article 13.

7. The Council may, by a two-thirds vote, make a factual record available to the Joint Public Advisory Committee.

Article 17: National Advisory Committees

Each Party may convene a national advisory committee, comprising members of its public, including representatives of non-governmental organizations and persons, to advise it on the implementation and further elaboration of this Agreement.

Article 18: Governmental Committees

Each Party may convene a governmental committee, which may comprise or include representatives of federal and state or provincial governments, to advise it on the implementation and further elaboration of this Agreement.

Section D: Official Languages

Article 19: Official Languages

The official languages of the Commission shall be English, French and Spanish. All annual reports under Article 12, reports submitted to the Council under Article 13, factual records submitted to the Council under Article 15(6) and panel reports under Part Five shall be available in each official language at the time they are made public. The Council shall establish rules and procedures regarding interpretation and translation.

PART FOUR
COOPERATION AND PROVISION OF INFORMATION

Article 20: Cooperation

1. The Parties shall at all times endeavor to agree on the interpretation and application of this Agreement, and shall make every attempt through cooperation and consultations to resolve any matter that might affect its operation.

2. To the maximum extent possible, each Party shall notify any other Party with an interest in the matter of any proposed or actual environmental measure that the Party considers might materially affect the operation of this Agreement or otherwise substantially affect that other Party's interests under this Agreement.

3. On request of any other Party, a Party shall promptly provide information and respond to questions pertaining to any such actual or proposed environmental measure, whether or not that other Party has been previously notified of that measure.

4. Any Party may notify any other Party of, and provide to that Party, any credible information regarding possible violations of its environmental law, specific and sufficient to allow the other Party to inquire into the matter. The notified Party shall take appropriate steps in accordance with its law to so inquire and to respond to the other Party.

Article 21: Provision of Information

1. On request of the Council or the Secretariat, each Party shall, in accordance with its law, provide such information as the Council or the Secretariat may require, including: (a) promptly making available any information in its possession required for the preparation of a report or factual record, including compliance and enforcement data; and (b) taking all reasonable steps to make available any other such information requested.

2. If a Party considers that a request for information from the Secretariat is excessive or otherwise unduly burdensome, it may so notify the Council. The Secretariat shall revise the scope of its request to comply with any limitations established by the Council by a two-thirds vote.

3. If a Party does not make available information requested by the Secretariat, as may be limited pursuant to paragraph 2, it shall promptly advise the Secretariat of its reasons in writing.

PART FIVE
CONSULTATION AND RESOLUTION OF DISPUTES

Article 22: Consultations

1. Any Party may request in writing consultations with any other Party regarding whether there has been a persistent pattern of failure by that other Party to effectively enforce its environmental law.

2. The requesting Party shall deliver the request to the other Parties and to the Secretariat.

3. Unless the Council otherwise provides in its rules and procedures established under Article 9(2), a third Party that considers it has a substantial interest in the matter shall be entitled to participate in the consultations on delivery of written notice to the other Parties and to the Secretariat.

4. The consulting Parties shall make every attempt to arrive at a mutually satisfactory resolution of the matter through consultations under this Article.

Article 23: Initiation of Procedures

1. If the consulting Parties fail to resolve the matter pursuant to Article 22 within 60 days of delivery of a request for consultations, or such other period as the consulting Parties may agree, any such Party may request in writing a special session of the Council.

2. The requesting Party shall state in the request the matter complained of and shall deliver the request to the other Parties and to the Secretariat.

3. Unless it decides otherwise, the Council shall convene within 20 days of delivery of the request and shall endeavor to resolve the dispute promptly.

4. The Council may: (a) call on such technical advisers or create such working groups or expert groups as it deems necessary, (b) have recourse to good offices, conciliation, mediation or such other dispute resolution procedures, or (c) make recommendations, as may assist the consulting Parties to reach a mutually satisfactory resolution of the dispute. Any such recommendations shall be made public if the Council, by a two-thirds vote, so decides.

5. Where the Council decides that a matter is more properly covered by another agreement or arrangement to which the consulting Parties are party, it shall refer the matter to those Parties for appropriate action in accordance with such other agreement or arrangement.

Article 24: Request for an Arbitral Panel

1. If the matter has not been resolved within 60 days after the Council has convened pursuant to Article 23, the Council shall, on the written request of any consulting Party and by a two-thirds vote, convene an arbitral panel to consider the matter where the alleged persistent pattern of failure by the Party complained against to effectively enforce its environmental law relates to a situation involving workplaces, firms, companies or sectors that produce goods or provide services: (a) traded between the territories of the Parties; or (b) that compete, in the territory of the Party complained against, with goods or services produced or provided by persons of another Party.

2. A third Party that considers it has a substantial interest in the matter shall be entitled to join as a complaining Party on delivery of written notice of its intention to participate to the disputing Parties and the Secretariat. The notice shall be delivered at the earliest possible time, and in any event no later than seven days after the date of the vote of the Council to convene a panel.

3. Unless otherwise agreed by the disputing Parties, the panel shall be established and perform its functions in a manner consistent with the provisions of this Part.

Article 25: Roster

1. The Council shall establish and maintain a roster of up to 45 individuals who are willing and able to serve as panelists. The roster members shall be appointed by consensus for terms of three years, and may be reappointed.

2. Roster members shall: (a) have expertise or experience in environmental law or its enforcement, or in the resolution of disputes arising under international agreements, or other relevant scientific, technical or professional expertise or experience; (b) be chosen strictly on the basis of objectivity, reliability and sound judgment; (c) be independent of, and not be affiliated with or take instructions from, any Party, the Secretariat or the Joint Public Advisory Committee; and (d) comply with a code of conduct to be established by the Council.

Article 26: Qualifications of Panelists

1. All panelists shall meet the qualifications set out in Article 25(2).

2. Individuals may not serve as panelists for a dispute in which: (a) they have participated pursuant to Article 23(4); or (b) they have, or a person or organization with which they are affiliated has, an interest, as set out in the code of conduct established under Article 25(2)(d).

Article 27: Panel Selection

1. Where there are two disputing Parties, the following procedures shall apply: (a) The panel shall comprise five members. (b) The disputing Parties shall endeavor to agree on the chair of the panel within 15 days after the Council votes to convene the panel. If the disputing Parties are unable to agree on the chair within this period, the disputing Party chosen by lot shall select within five days a chair who is not a citizen of that Party. (c) Within 15 days of selection of the chair, each disputing Party shall select two panelists who are citizens of the other disputing Party. (d) If a disputing Party fails to select its panelists within such period, such panelists shall be selected by lot from among the roster members who are citizens of the other disputing Party.

2. Where there are more than two disputing Parties, the following procedures shall apply: (a) The panel shall comprise five members. (b) The disputing Parties shall endeavor to agree on the chair of the panel within 15 days after the Council votes to convene the panel. If the disputing Parties are unable to agree on the chair within this period, the Party or Parties on the side of the dispute chosen by lot shall select within 10 days a chair who is not a citizen of such Party or Parties. (c) Within 30 days of selection of the chair, the Party complained against shall select two panelists, one of whom is a citizen of a complaining Party, and the other of whom is a citizen of another complaining Party. The complaining Parties shall select two panelists who are citizens of the Party complained against. (d) If any disputing Party fails to select a panelist within such period, such panelist shall be selected by lot in accordance with the citizenship criteria of subparagraph (c).

3. Panelists shall normally be selected from the roster. Any disputing Party may exercise a peremptory challenge against any individual not on the

roster who is proposed as a panelist by a disputing Party within 30 days after the individual has been proposed.

4. If a disputing Party believes that a panelist is in violation of the code of conduct, the disputing Parties shall consult and, if they agree, the panelist shall be removed and a new panelist shall be selected in accordance with this Article.

Article 28: Rules of Procedure

1. The Council shall establish Model Rules of Procedure. The procedures shall provide: (a) a right to at least one hearing before the panel; (b) the opportunity to make initial and rebuttal written submissions; and (c) that no panel may disclose which panelists are associated with majority or minority opinions.

2. Unless the disputing Parties otherwise agree, panels convened under this Part shall be established and conduct their proceedings in accordance with the Model Rules of Procedure.

3. Unless the disputing Parties otherwise agree within 20 days after the Council votes to convene the panel, the terms of reference shall be: "To examine, in light of the relevant provisions of the Agreement, including those contained in Part Five, whether there has been a persistent pattern of failure by the Party complained against to effectively enforce its environmental law, and to make findings, determinations and recommendations in accordance with Article 31(2)."

Article 29: Third Party Participation

A Party that is not a disputing Party, on delivery of a written notice to the disputing Parties and to the Secretariat, shall be entitled to attend all hearings, to make written and oral submissions to the panel and to receive written submissions of the disputing Parties.

Article 30: Role of Experts

On request of a disputing Party, or on its own initiative, the panel may seek information and technical advice from any person or body that it deems appropriate, provided that the disputing Parties so agree and subject to such terms and conditions as such Parties may agree.

Article 31: Initial Report

1. Unless the disputing Parties otherwise agree, the panel shall base its report on the submissions and arguments of the Parties and on any information before it pursuant to Article 30.

2. Unless the disputing Parties otherwise agree, the panel shall, within 180 days after the last panelist is selected, present to the disputing Parties an initial report containing: (a) findings of fact; (b) its determination as to whether there has been a persistent pattern of failure by the Party complained against to effectively enforce its environmental law, or any other determination requested in the terms of reference; and (c) in the event the panel makes an affirmative determination under subparagraph (b), its recommendations, if any, for the resolution of the dispute, which normally shall be

that the Party complained against adopt and implement an action plan sufficient to remedy the pattern of non-enforcement.

3. Panelists may furnish separate opinions on matters not unanimously agreed.

4. A disputing Party may submit written comments to the panel on its initial report within 30 days of presentation of the report.

5. In such an event, and after considering such written comments, the panel, on its own initiative or on the request of any disputing Party, may: (a) request the views of any participating Party; (b) reconsider its report; and (c) make any further examination that it considers appropriate.

Article 32: Final Report

1. The panel shall present to the disputing Parties a final report, including any separate opinions on matters not unanimously agreed, within 60 days of presentation of the initial report, unless the disputing Parties otherwise agree.

2. The disputing Parties shall transmit to the Council the final report of the panel, as well as any written views that a disputing Party desires to be appended, on a confidential basis within 15 days after it is presented to them.

3. The final report of the panel shall be published five days after it is transmitted to the Council.

Article 33: Implementation of Final Report

If, in its final report, a panel determines that there has been a persistent pattern of failure by the Party complained against to effectively enforce its environmental law, the disputing Parties may agree on a mutually satisfactory action plan, which normally shall conform with the determinations and recommendations of the panel. The disputing Parties shall promptly notify the Secretariat and the Council of any agreed resolution of the dispute.

Article 34: Review of Implementation

1. If, in its final report, a panel determines that there has been a persistent pattern of failure by the Party complained against to effectively enforce its environmental law, and: (a) the disputing Parties have not agreed on an action plan under Article 33 within 60 days of the date of the final report, or (b) the disputing Parties cannot agree on whether the Party complained against is fully implementing (i) an action plan agreed under Article 33, (ii) an action plan deemed to have been established by a panel under paragraph 2, or (iii) an action plan approved or established by a panel under paragraph 4, any disputing Party may request that the panel be reconvened. The requesting Party shall deliver the request in writing to the other Parties and to the Secretariat. The Council shall reconvene the panel on delivery of the request to the Secretariat.

2. No Party may make a request under paragraph 1(a) earlier than 60 days, or later than 120 days, after the date of the final report. If the disputing Parties have not agreed to an action plan and if no request was made under paragraph 1(a), the last action plan, if any, submitted by the Party complained against to the complaining Party or Parties within 60 days

of the date of the final report, or such other period as the disputing Parties may agree, shall be deemed to have been established by the panel 120 days after the date of the final report.

3. A request under paragraph 1(b) may be made no earlier than 180 days after an action plan has been: (a) agreed under Article 33; (b) deemed to have been established by a panel under paragraph 2; or (c) approved or established by a panel under paragraph 4; and only during the term of any such action plan.

4. Where a panel has been reconvened under paragraph 1(a), it: (a) shall determine whether any action plan proposed by the Party complained against is sufficient to remedy the pattern of non-enforcement and (i) if so, shall approve the plan, or (ii) if not, shall establish such a plan consistent with the law of the Party complained against, and (b) may, where warranted, impose a monetary enforcement assessment in accordance with Annex 34, within 90 days after the panel has been reconvened or such other period as the disputing Parties may agree.

5. Where a panel has been reconvened under paragraph 1(b), it shall determine either that: (a) the Party complained against is fully implementing the action plan, in which case the panel may not impose a monetary enforcement assessment, or (b) the Party complained against is not fully implementing the action plan, in which case the panel shall impose a monetary enforcement assessment in accordance with Annex 34, within 60 days after it has been reconvened or such other period as the disputing Parties may agree.

6. A panel reconvened under this Article shall provide that the Party complained against shall fully implement any action plan referred to in paragraph 4(a)(ii) or 5(b), and pay any monetary enforcement assessment imposed under paragraph 4(b) or 5(b), and any such provision shall be final.

Article 35: Further Proceeding

A complaining Party may, at any time beginning 180 days after a panel determination under Article 34(5)(b), request in writing that a panel be reconvened to determine whether the Party complained against is fully implementing the action plan. On delivery of the request to the other Parties and the Secretariat, the Council shall reconvene the panel. The panel shall make the determination within 60 days after it has been reconvened or such other period as the disputing Parties may agree.

Article 36: Suspension of Benefits

1. Subject to Annex 36A, where a Party fails to pay a monetary enforcement assessment within 180 days after it is imposed by a panel: (a) under Article 34(4)(b), or (b) under Article 34(5)(b), except where benefits may be suspended under paragraph 2(a), any complaining Party or Parties may suspend, in accordance with Annex 36B, the application to the Party complained against of NAFTA benefits in an amount no greater than that sufficient to collect the monetary enforcement assessment.

2. Subject to Annex 36A, where a panel has made a determination under Article 34(5)(b) and the panel: (a) has previously imposed a monetary enforcement assessment under Article 34(4)(b) or established an action plan under Article 34(4)(a)(ii); or (b) has subsequently determined under Article

35 that a Party is not fully implementing an action plan; the complaining Party or Parties may, in accordance with Annex 36B, suspend annually the application to the Party complained against of NAFTA benefits in an amount no greater than the monetary enforcement assessment imposed by the panel under Article 34(5)(b).

3. Where more than one complaining Party suspends benefits under paragraph 1 or 2, the combined suspension shall be no greater than the amount of the monetary enforcement assessment.

4. Where a Party has suspended benefits under paragraph 1 or 2, the Council shall, on the delivery of a written request by the Party complained against to the other Parties and the Secretariat, reconvene the panel to determine whether the monetary enforcement assessment has been paid or collected, or whether the Party complained against is fully implementing the action plan, as the case may be. The panel shall submit its report within 45 days after it has been reconvened. If the panel determines that the assessment has been paid or collected, or that the Party complained against is fully implementing the action plan, the suspension of benefits under paragraph 1 or 2, as the case may be, shall be terminated.

5. On the written request of the Party complained against, delivered to the other Parties and the Secretariat, the Council shall reconvene the panel to determine whether the suspension of benefits by the complaining Party or Parties pursuant to paragraph 1 or 2 is manifestly excessive. Within 45 days of the request, the panel shall present a report to the disputing Parties containing its determination.

PART SIX

GENERAL PROVISIONS

Article 37: Enforcement Principle

Nothing in this Agreement shall be construed to empower a Party's authorities to undertake environmental law enforcement activities in the territory of another Party.

Article 38: Private Rights

No Party may provide for a right of action under its law against any other Party on the ground that another Party has acted in a manner inconsistent with this Agreement.

Article 39: Protection of Information

1. Nothing in this Agreement shall be construed to require a Party to make available or allow access to information: (a) the disclosure of which would impede its environmental law enforcement; or (b) that is protected from disclosure by its law governing business or proprietary information, personal privacy or the confidentiality of governmental decision making.

2. If a Party provides confidential or proprietary information to another Party, the Council, the Secretariat or the Joint Public Advisory Committee, the recipient shall treat the information on the same basis as the Party providing the information.

3. Confidential or proprietary information provided by a Party to a panel under this Agreement shall be treated in accordance with the rules of procedure established under Article 28.

Article 40: Relation to Other Environmental Agreements

Nothing in this Agreement shall be construed to affect the existing rights and obligations of the Parties under other international environmental agreements, including conservation agreements, to which such Parties are party.

Article 41: Extent of Obligations

Annex 41 applies to the Parties specified in that Annex.

Article 42: National Security

Nothing in this Agreement shall be construed: (a) to require any Party to make available or provide access to information the disclosure of which it determines to be contrary to its essential security interests; or (b) to prevent any Party from taking any actions that it considers necessary for the protection of its essential security interests relating to (i) arms, ammunition and implements of war, or (ii) the implementation of national policies or international agreements respecting the non-proliferation of nuclear weapons or other nuclear explosive devices.

Article 43: Funding of the Commission

Each Party shall contribute an equal share of the annual budget of the Commission, subject to the availability of appropriated funds in accordance with the Party's legal procedures. No Party shall be obligated to pay more than any other Party in respect of an annual budget.

Article 44: Privileges and Immunities

The Executive Director and staff of the Secretariat shall enjoy in the territory of each Party such privileges and immunities as are necessary for the exercise of their functions.

Article 45: Definitions

1. For purposes of this Agreement:

A Party has not failed to "effectively enforce its environmental law" or to comply with Article 5(1) in a particular case where the action or inaction in question by agencies or officials of that Party: (a) reflects a reasonable exercise of their discretion in respect of investigatory, prosecutorial, regulatory or compliance matters; or (b) results from bona fide decisions to allocate resources to enforcement in respect of other environmental matters determined to have higher priorities;

"non-governmental organization" means any scientific, professional, business, non-profit, or public interest organization or association which is neither affiliated with, nor under the direction of, a government;

"persistent pattern" means a sustained or recurring course of action or inaction beginning after the date of entry into force of this Agreement;

"province" means a province of Canada, and includes the Yukon Territory and the Northwest Territories and their successors; and

"territory" means for a Party the territory of that Party as set out in Annex 45.

2. For purposes of Article 14(1) and Part Five: (a) "environmental law" means any statute or regulation of a Party, or provision thereof, the primary purpose of which is the protection of the environment, or the prevention of a danger to human life or health, through (i) the prevention, abatement or control of the release, discharge, or emission of pollutants or environmental contaminants, (ii) the control of environmentally hazardous or toxic chemicals, substances, materials and wastes, and the dissemination of information related thereto, or (iii) the protection of wild flora or fauna, including endangered species, their habitat, and specially protected natural areas in the Party's territory, but does not include any statute or regulation, or provision thereof, directly related to worker safety or health. (b) For greater certainty, the term "environmental law" does not include any statute or regulation, or provision thereof, the primary purpose of which is managing the commercial harvest or exploitation, or subsistence or aboriginal harvesting, of natural resources. (c) The primary purpose of a particular statutory or regulatory provision for purposes of subparagraphs (a) and (b) shall be determined by reference to its primary purpose, rather than to the primary purpose of the statute or regulation of which it is part.

3. For purposes of Article 14(3), "judicial or administrative proceeding" means: (a) a domestic judicial, quasi-judicial or administrative action pursued by the Party in a timely fashion and in accordance with its law. Such actions comprise: mediation; arbitration; the process of issuing a license, permit, or authorization; seeking an assurance of voluntary compliance or a compliance agreement; seeking sanctions or remedies in an administrative or judicial forum; and the process of issuing an administrative order; and (b) an international dispute resolution proceeding to which the Party is party.

PART SEVEN
FINAL PROVISIONS

Article 46: Annexes

The Annexes to this Agreement constitute an integral part of the Agreement.

Article 47: Entry into Force

This Agreement shall enter into force on January 1, 1994, immediately after entry into force of the NAFTA, on an exchange of written notifications certifying the completion of necessary legal procedures.

Article 48: Amendments

1. The Parties may agree on any modification of or addition to this Agreement.

2. When so agreed, and approved in accordance with the applicable legal procedures of each Party, a modification or addition shall constitute an integral part of this Agreement.

Article 49: Accession

Any country or group of countries may accede to this Agreement subject to such terms and conditions as may be agreed between such country or countries and the Council and following approval in accordance with the applicable legal procedures of each country.

Article 50: Withdrawal

A Party may withdraw from this Agreement six months after it provides written notice of withdrawal to the other Parties. If a Party withdraws, the Agreement shall remain in force for the remaining Parties.

Article 51: Authentic Texts

The English, French, and Spanish texts of this Agreement are equally authentic.

IN WITNESS WHEREOF, the undersigned, being duly authorized by the respective Governments, have signed this Agreement.

ANNEX 34
MONETARY ENFORCEMENT ASSESSMENTS

1. For the first year after the date of entry into force of this Agreement, any monetary enforcement assessment shall be no greater than 20 million dollars (U.S.) or its equivalent in the currency of the Party complained against. Thereafter, any monetary enforcement assessment shall be no greater than .007 percent of total trade in goods between the Parties during the most recent year for which data are available.

2. In determining the amount of the assessment, the panel shall take into account: (a) the pervasiveness and duration of the Party's persistent pattern of failure to effectively enforce its environmental law; (b) the level of enforcement that could reasonably be expected of a Party given its resource constraints; (c) the reasons, if any, provided by the Party for not fully implementing an action plan; (d) efforts made by the Party to begin remedying the pattern of non-enforcement after the final report of the panel; and (e) any other relevant factors.

3. All monetary enforcement assessments shall be paid in the currency of the Party complained against into a fund established in the name of the Commission by the Council and shall be expended at the direction of the Council to improve or enhance the environment or environmental law enforcement in the Party complained against, consistent with its law.

ANNEX 36A
CANADIAN DOMESTIC ENFORCEMENT AND COLLECTION

1. For the purposes of this Annex, "panel determination" means: (a) a determination by a panel under Article 34(4)(b) or 5(b) that provides that Canada shall pay a monetary enforcement assessment; and (b) a determination by a panel under Article 34(5)(b) that provides that Canada shall fully implement an action plan where the panel: (i) has previously established an action plan under Article 34(4)(a)(ii) or imposed a monetary enforcement

assessment under Article 34(4)(b); or (ii) has subsequently determined under Article 35 that Canada is not fully implementing an action plan.

2.   Canada shall adopt and maintain procedures that provide that: (a) subject to subparagraph (b), the Commission, at the request of a complaining Party, may in its own name file in a court of competent jurisdiction a certified copy of a panel determination; (b) the Commission may file in court a panel determination that is a panel determination described in paragraph 1(a) only if Canada has failed to comply with the determination within 180 days of when the determination was made; (c) when filed, the panel determination, for purposes of enforcement, shall become an order of the court; (d) the Commission may take proceedings for enforcement of a panel determination that is made an order of the court, in that court, against the person against whom the panel determination is addressed in accordance with paragraph 6 of Annex 41; (e) proceedings to enforce a panel determination that has been made an order of the court shall be conducted by way of summary proceedings; (f) in proceedings to enforce a panel determination that is a panel determination described in paragraph 1(b) and that has been made an order of the court, the court shall promptly refer any question of fact or any question of interpretation of the panel determination to the panel that made the panel determination, and the decision of the panel shall be binding on the court; (g) a panel determination that has been made an order of the court shall not be subject to domestic review or appeal; and (h) an order made by the court in proceedings to enforce a panel determination that has been made an order of the court shall not be subject to review or appeal.

3.   Where Canada is the Party complained against, the procedures adopted and maintained by Canada under this Annex shall apply and the procedures set out in Article 36 shall not apply.

4.   Any change by Canada to the procedures adopted and maintained by Canada under this Annex that have the effect of undermining the provisions of this Annex shall be considered a breach of this Agreement.

ANNEX 36B
SUSPENSION OF BENEFITS

1.   Where a complaining Party suspends NAFTA tariff benefits in accordance with this Agreement, the Party may increase the rates of duty on originating goods of the Party complained against to levels not to exceed the lesser of: (a) the rate that was applicable to those goods immediately prior to the date of entry into force of the NAFTA, and (b) the Most–Favored–Nation rate applicable to those goods on the date the Party suspends such benefits, and such increase may be applied only for such time as is necessary to collect, through such increase, the monetary enforcement assessment.

2.   In considering what tariff or other benefits to suspend pursuant to Article 36(1) or (2): (a) a complaining Party shall first seek to suspend benefits in the same sector or sectors as that in respect of which there has been a persistent pattern of failure by the Party complained against to effectively enforce its environmental law; and (b) a complaining Party that considers it is not practicable or effective to suspend benefits in the same sector or sectors may suspend benefits in other sectors.

ANNEX 41
EXTENT OF OBLIGATIONS

1.   On the date of signature of this Agreement, or of the exchange of written notifications under Article 47, Canada shall set out in a declaration a list of any provinces for which Canada is to be bound in respect of matters within their jurisdiction.   The declaration shall be effective on delivery to the other Parties, and shall carry no implication as to the internal distribution of powers within Canada.   Canada shall notify the other Parties six months in advance of any modification to its declaration.

2.   When considering whether to instruct the Secretariat to prepare a factual record pursuant to Article 15, the Council shall take into account whether the submission was made by a non-governmental organization or enterprise incorporated or otherwise organized under the laws of a province included in the declaration made under paragraph 1.

3.   Canada may not request consultations under Article 22 or a Council meeting under Article 23 or request the establishment of a panel or join as a complaining Party under Article 24 against another Party at the instance, or primarily for the benefit, of any government of a province not included in the declaration made under paragraph 1.

4.   Canada may not request a Council meeting under Article 23, or request the establishment of a panel or join as a complaining Party under Article 24 concerning whether there has been a persistent pattern of failure by another Party to effectively enforce its environmental law, unless Canada states in writing that the matter would be under federal jurisdiction if it were to arise within the territory of Canada, or: (a) Canada states in writing that the matter would be under provincial jurisdiction if it were to arise within the territory of Canada; and (b) the provinces included in the declaration account for at least 55 percent of Canada's Gross Domestic Product (GDP) for the most recent year in which data are available, and (c) where the matter concerns a specific industry or sector, at least 55 percent of total Canadian production in that industry or sector is accounted for by the provinces included in the declaration for the most recent year in which data are available.

5.   No other Party may request a Council meeting under Article 23 or request the establishment of a panel or join as a complaining Party under Article 24 concerning whether there has been a persistent failure to effectively enforce an environmental law of a province unless that province is included in the declaration made under paragraph 1 and the requirements of subparagraphs 4(b) and (c) have been met.

6.   Canada shall, no later than the date on which an arbitral panel is convened pursuant to Article 24 respecting a matter within the scope of paragraph 5 of this Annex, notify in writing the complaining Parties and the Secretariat of whether any monetary enforcement assessment or action plan imposed by a panel under Article 34(4) or 34(5) against Canada shall be addressed to Her Majesty in right of Canada or Her Majesty in right of the province concerned.

7.   Canada shall use its best efforts to make this Agreement applicable to as many of its provinces as possible.

8. Two years after the date of entry into force of this Agreement, the Council shall review the operation of this Annex and, in particular, shall consider whether the Parties should amend the thresholds established in paragraph 4.

ANNEX 45

COUNTRY–SPECIFIC DEFINITIONS

For purposes of this Agreement:

"territory" means: (a) with respect to Canada, the territory to which its customs laws apply, including any areas beyond the territorial seas of Canada within which, in accordance with international law and its domestic law, Canada may exercise rights with respect to the seabed and subsoil and their natural resources; (b) with respect to Mexico, (i) the states of the Federation and the Federal District, (ii) the islands, including the reefs and keys, in adjacent seas, (iii) the islands of Guadalupe and Revillagigedo situated in the Pacific Ocean, (iv) the continental shelf and the submarine shelf of such islands, keys and reefs, (v) the waters of the territorial seas, in accordance with international law, and its interior maritime waters, (vi) the space located above the national territory, in accordance with international law, and (vii) any areas beyond the territorial seas of Mexico within which, in accordance with international law, including the United Nations Convention on the Law of the Sea, and its domestic law, Mexico may exercise rights with respect to the seabed and subsoil and their natural resources; and (c) with respect to the United States, (i) the customs territory of the United States, which includes the 50 states, the District of Columbia and Puerto Rico, (ii) the foreign trade zones located in the United States and Puerto Rico, and (iii) any areas beyond the territorial seas of the United States within which, in accordance with international law and its domestic law, the United States may exercise rights with respect to the seabed and subsoil and their natural resources.

Item 42

NORTH AMERICAN AGREEMENT
ON LABOR COOPERATION

PREAMBLE

The Government of the United States of America, the Government of Canada and the Government of the United Mexican States:

RECALLING their resolve in the North American Free Trade Agreement (NAFTA) to:—create an expanded and secure market for the goods and services produced in their territories,—enhance the competitiveness of their firms in global markets,—create new employment opportunities and improve working conditions and living standards in their respective territories, and—protect, enhance and enforce basic workers' rights;

AFFIRMING their continuing respect for each Party's constitution and law;

DESIRING to build on their respective international commitments and to strengthen their cooperation on labor matters;

RECOGNIZING that their mutual prosperity depends on the promotion of competition based on innovation and rising levels of productivity and quality;

SEEKING to complement the economic opportunities created by the NAFTA with the human resource development, labor-management cooperation and continuous learning that characterize high-productivity economies;

ACKNOWLEDGING that protecting basic workers' rights will encourage firms to adopt high-productivity competitive strategies;

RESOLVED to promote, in accordance with their respective laws, high-skill, high-productivity economic development in North America by:—investing in continuous human resource development, including for entry into the workforce and during periods of unemployment;—promoting employment security and career opportunities for all workers through referral and other employment services;—strengthening labor-management cooperation to promote greater dialogue between worker organizations and employers and to foster creativity and productivity in the workplace;—promoting higher living standards as productivity increases;—encouraging consultation and dialogue between labor, business and government both in each country and in North America;—fostering investment with due regard for the importance of labor laws and principles;—encouraging employers and employees in each country to comply with labor laws and to work together in maintaining a progressive, fair, safe and healthy working environment;

BUILDING on existing institutions and mechanisms in Canada, Mexico and the United States to achieve the preceding economic and social goals; and

CONVINCED of the benefits to be gained from further cooperation between them on labor matters;

HAVE AGREED as follows:

PART ONE
OBJECTIVES

Article 1: Objectives

The objectives of this Agreement are to: (a) improve working conditions and living standards in each Party's territory; (b) promote, to the maximum extent possible, the labor principles set out in Annex 1; (c) encourage cooperation to promote innovation and rising levels of productivity and quality; (d) encourage publication and exchange of information, data development and coordination, and joint studies to enhance mutually beneficial understanding of the laws and institutions governing labor in each Party's territory; (e) pursue cooperative labor-related activities on the basis of mutual benefit; (f) promote compliance with, and effective enforcement by each Party of, its labor law; and (g) foster transparency in the administration of labor law.

PART TWO
OBLIGATIONS

Article 2: Levels of Protection

Affirming full respect for each Party's constitution, and recognizing the right of each Party to establish its own domestic labor standards, and to adopt or modify accordingly its labor laws and regulations, each Party shall ensure that its labor laws and regulations provide for high labor standards, consistent with high quality and productivity workplaces, and shall continue to strive to improve those standards in that light.

Article 3: Government Enforcement Action

1. Each Party shall promote compliance with and effectively enforce its labor law through appropriate government action, subject to Article 42, such as: (a) appointing and training inspectors; (b) monitoring compliance and investigating suspected violations, including through on-site inspections; (c) seeking assurances of voluntary compliance; (d) requiring record keeping and reporting; (e) encouraging the establishment of worker-management committees to address labor regulation of the workplace; (f) providing or encouraging mediation, conciliation and arbitration services; or (g) initiating, in a timely manner, proceedings to seek appropriate sanctions or remedies for violations of its labor law.

2. Each Party shall ensure that its competent authorities give due consideration in accordance with its law to any request by an employer, employee or their representatives, or other interested person, for an investigation of an alleged violation of the Party's labor law.

Article 4: Private Action

1. Each Party shall ensure that persons with a legally recognized interest under its law in a particular matter have appropriate access to

administrative, quasi-judicial, judicial or labor tribunals for the enforcement of the Party's labor law.

2. Each Party's law shall ensure that such persons may have recourse to, as appropriate, procedures by which rights arising under: (a) its labor law, including in respect of occupational safety and health, employment standards, industrial relations and migrant workers, and (b) collective agreements, can be enforced.

Article 5: Procedural Guarantees

1. Each Party shall ensure that its administrative, quasi-judicial, judicial and labor tribunal proceedings for the enforcement of its labor law are fair, equitable and transparent and, to this end, each Party shall provide that: (a) such proceedings comply with due process of law; (b) any hearings in such proceedings are open to the public, except where the administration of justice otherwise requires; (c) the parties to such proceedings are entitled to support or defend their respective positions and to present information or evidence; and (d) such proceedings are not unnecessarily complicated and do not entail unreasonable charges or time limits or unwarranted delays.

2. Each Party shall provide that final decisions on the merits of the case in such proceedings are: (a) in writing and preferably state the reasons on which the decisions are based; (b) made available without undue delay to the parties to the proceedings and, consistent with its law, to the public; and (c) based on information or evidence in respect of which the parties were offered the opportunity to be heard.

3. Each Party shall provide, as appropriate, that parties to such proceedings have the right, in accordance with its law, to seek review and, where warranted, correction of final decisions issued in such proceedings.

4. Each Party shall ensure that tribunals that conduct or review such proceedings are impartial and independent and do not have any substantial interest in the outcome of the matter.

5. Each Party shall provide that the parties to administrative, quasi-judicial, judicial or labor tribunal proceedings may seek remedies to ensure the enforcement of their labor rights. Such remedies may include, as appropriate, orders, compliance agreements, fines, penalties, imprisonment, injunctions or emergency workplace closures.

6. Each Party may, as appropriate, adopt or maintain labor defense offices to represent or advise workers or their organizations.

7. Nothing in this Article shall be construed to require a Party to establish, or to prevent a Party from establishing, a judicial system for the enforcement of its labor law distinct from its system for the enforcement of laws in general.

8. For greater certainty, decisions by each Party's administrative, quasi-judicial, judicial or labor tribunals, or pending decisions, as well as related proceedings shall not be subject to revision or reopened under the provisions of this Agreement.

Article 6: Publication

1. Each Party shall ensure that its laws, regulations, procedures and administrative rulings of general application respecting any matter covered by this Agreement are promptly published or otherwise made available in such a manner as to enable interested persons and Parties to become acquainted with them.

2. When so established by its law, each Party shall: (a) publish in advance any such measure that it proposes to adopt; and (b) provide interested persons a reasonable opportunity to comment on such proposed measures.

Article 7: Public Information and Awareness

Each Party shall promote public awareness of its labor law, including by: (a) ensuring that public information is available related to its labor law and enforcement and compliance procedures; and (b) promoting public education regarding its labor law.

PART THREE

COMMISSION FOR LABOR COOPERATION

Article 8: The Commission

1. The Parties hereby establish the Commission for Labor Cooperation.

2. The Commission shall comprise a ministerial Council and a Secretariat. The Commission shall be assisted by the National Administrative Office of each Party.

Section A: The Council

Article 9: Council Structure and Procedures

1. The Council shall comprise labor ministers of the Parties or their designees.

2. The Council shall establish its rules and procedures.

3. The Council shall convene: (a) at least once a year in regular session, and (b) in special session at the request of any Party. Regular sessions shall be chaired successively by each Party.

4. The Council may hold public sessions to report on appropriate matters.

5. The Council may: (a) establish, and assign responsibilities to, committees, working groups or expert groups; and (b) seek the advice of independent experts.

6. All decisions and recommendations of the Council shall be taken by consensus, except as the Council may otherwise decide or as otherwise provided in this Agreement.

Article 10: Council Functions

1. The Council shall be the governing body of the Commission and shall: (a) oversee the implementation and develop recommendations on the further elaboration of this Agreement and, to this end, the Council shall, within four years after the date of entry into force of this Agreement, review its operation

and effectiveness in the light of experience; (b) direct the work and activities of the Secretariat and of any committees or working groups convened by the Council; (c) establish priorities for cooperative action and, as appropriate, develop technical assistance programs on the matters set out in Article 11; (d) approve the annual plan of activities and budget of the Commission; (e) approve for publication, subject to such terms or conditions as it may impose, reports and studies prepared by the Secretariat, independent experts or working groups; (f) facilitate Party-to-Party consultations, including through the exchange of information; (g) address questions and differences that may arise between the Parties regarding the interpretation or application of this Agreement; and (h) promote the collection and publication of comparable data on enforcement, labor standards and labor market indicators.

2.   The Council may consider any other matter within the scope of this Agreement and take such other action in the exercise of its functions as the Parties may agree.

Article 11: Cooperative Activities

1.   The Council shall promote cooperative activities between the Parties, as appropriate, regarding: (a) occupational safety and health; (b) child labor; (c) migrant workers of the Parties; (d) human resource development; (e) labor statistics; (f) work benefits; (g) social programs for workers and their families; (h) programs, methodologies and experiences regarding productivity improvement; (i) labor-management relations and collective bargaining procedures; (j) employment standards and their implementation; (k) compensation for work-related injury or illness; (l) legislation relating to the formation and operation of unions, collective bargaining and the resolution of labor disputes, and its implementation; (m) the equality of women and men in the workplace; (n) forms of cooperation among workers, management and government; (o) the provision of technical assistance, at the request of a Party, for the development of its labor standards; and (p) such other matters as the Parties may agree.

2.   In carrying out the activities referred to in paragraph 1, the Parties may, commensurate with the availability of resources in each Party, cooperate through: (a) seminars, training sessions, working groups and conferences; (b) joint research projects, including sectoral studies; (c) technical assistance; and (d) such other means as the Parties may agree.

3.   The Parties shall carry out the cooperative activities referred to in paragraph 1 with due regard for the economic, social, cultural and legislative differences between them.

Section B: The Secretariat
Article 12: Secretariat Structure and Procedures

1.   The Secretariat shall be headed by an Executive Director, who shall be chosen by the Council for a three-year term, which may be renewed by the Council for one additional three-year term. The position of Executive Director shall rotate consecutively between nationals of each Party. The Council may remove the Executive Director solely for cause.

2.   The Executive Director shall appoint and supervise the staff of the Secretariat, regulate their powers and duties and fix their remuneration in

accordance with general standards to be established by the Council. The general standards shall provide that: (a) staff shall be appointed and retained, and their conditions of employment shall be determined, strictly on the basis of efficiency, competence and integrity; (b) in appointing staff, the Executive Director shall take into account lists of candidates prepared by the Parties; (c) due regard shall be paid to the importance of recruiting an equitable proportion of the professional staff from among the nationals of each Party; and (d) the Executive Director shall inform the Council of all appointments.

3. The number of staff positions shall initially be set at 15 and may be changed thereafter by the Council.

4. The Council may decide, by a two-thirds vote, to reject any appointment that does not meet the general standards. Any such decision shall be made and held in confidence.

5. In the performance of their duties, the Executive Director and the staff shall not seek or receive instructions from any government or any other authority external to the Council. Each Party shall respect the international character of the responsibilities of the Executive Director and the staff and shall not seek to influence them in the discharge of their responsibilities.

6. The Secretariat shall safeguard: (a) from disclosure information it receives that could identify an organization or person if the person or organization so requests or the Secretariat otherwise considers it appropriate; and (b) from public disclosure any information it receives from any organization or person where the information is designated by that organization or person as confidential or proprietary.

7. The Secretariat shall act under the direction of the Council in accordance with Article 10(1)(b).

Article 13: Secretariat Functions

1. The Secretariat shall assist the Council in exercising its functions and shall provide such other support as the Council may direct.

2. The Executive Director shall submit for the approval of the Council the annual plan of activities and budget for the Commission, including provision for contingencies and proposed cooperative activities.

3. The Secretariat shall report to the Council annually on its activities and expenditures.

4. The Secretariat shall periodically publish a list of matters resolved under Part Four or referred to Evaluation Committees of Experts.

Article 14: Secretariat Reports and Studies

1. The Secretariat shall periodically prepare background reports setting out publicly available information supplied by each Party on: (a) labor law and administrative procedures; (b) trends and administrative strategies related to the implementation and enforcement of labor law; (c) labor market conditions such as employment rates, average wages and labor productivity; and (d) human resource development issues such as training and adjustment programs.

2. The Secretariat shall prepare a study on any matter as the Council may request. The Secretariat shall prepare any such study in accordance with terms of reference established by the Council, and may (a) consider any relevant information; (b) where it does not have specific expertise in the matter, engage one or more independent experts of recognized experience; and (c) include proposals on the matter.

3. The Secretariat shall submit a draft of any report or study that it prepares pursuant to paragraph 1 or 2 to the Council. If the Council considers that a report or study is materially inaccurate or otherwise deficient, the Council may remand it to the Secretariat for reconsideration or other disposition.

4. Secretariat reports and studies shall be made public 45 days after their approval by the Council, unless the Council otherwise decides.

Section C: National Administrative Offices

Article 15: National Administrative Office Structure

1. Each Party shall establish a National Administrative Office (NAO) at the federal government level and notify the Secretariat and the other Parties of its location.

2. Each Party shall designate a Secretary for its NAO, who shall be responsible for its administration and management.

3. Each Party shall be responsible for the operation and costs of its NAO.

Article 16: NAO Functions

1. Each NAO shall serve as a point of contact with: (a) governmental agencies of that Party; (b) NAOs of the other Parties; and (c) the Secretariat.

2. Each NAO shall promptly provide publicly available information requested by: (a) the Secretariat for reports under Article 14(1); (b) the Secretariat for studies under Article 14(2); (c) a NAO of another Party; and (d) an ECE.

3. Each NAO shall provide for the submission and receipt, and periodically publish a list, of public communications on labor law matters arising in the territory of another Party. Each NAO shall review such matters, as appropriate, in accordance with domestic procedures.

Section D: National Committees

Article 17: National Advisory Committee

Each Party may convene a national advisory committee, comprising members of its public, including representatives of its labor and business organizations and other persons, to advise it on the implementation and further elaboration of this Agreement.

Article 18: Governmental Committee

Each Party may convene a governmental committee, which may comprise or include representatives of federal and state or provincial governments, to advise it on the implementation and further elaboration of this Agreement.

Section E: Official Languages

Article 19: Official Languages

The official languages of the Commission shall be English, French and Spanish. The Council shall establish rules and procedures regarding interpretation and translation.

PART FOUR
COOPERATIVE CONSULTATIONS AND EVALUATIONS

Article 20: Cooperation

The Parties shall at all times endeavor to agree on the interpretation and application of this Agreement, and shall make every attempt through cooperation and consultations to resolve any matter that might affect its operation.

Section A: Cooperative Consultations

Article 21: Consultations Between NAOs

1. A NAO may request consultations, to be conducted in accordance with the procedures set out in paragraph 2, with another NAO in relation to the other Party's labor law, its administration, or labor market conditions in its territory. The requesting NAO shall notify the NAOs of the other Parties and the Secretariat of its request.

2. In such consultations, the requested NAO shall promptly provide such publicly available data or information, including: (a) descriptions of its laws, regulations, procedures, policies or practices, (b) proposed changes to such procedures, policies or practices, and (c) such clarifications and explanations related to such matters, as may assist the consulting NAOs to better understand and respond to the issues raised.

3. Any other NAO shall be entitled to participate in the consultations on notice to the other NAOs and the Secretariat.

Article 22: Ministerial Consultations

1. Any Party may request in writing consultations with another Party at the ministerial level regarding any matter within the scope of this Agreement. The requesting Party shall provide specific and sufficient information to allow the requested Party to respond.

2. The requesting Party shall promptly notify the other Parties of the request. A third Party that considers it has a substantial interest in the matter shall be entitled to participate in the consultations on notice to the other Parties.

3. The consulting Parties shall make every attempt to resolve the matter through consultations under this Article, including through the exchange of sufficient publicly available information to enable a full examination of the matter.

Section B: Evaluations

Article 23: Evaluation Committee of Experts

1. If a matter has not been resolved after ministerial consultations pursuant to Article 22, any consulting Party may request in writing the

establishment of an Evaluation Committee of Experts (ECE). The requesting Party shall deliver the request to the other Parties and to the Secretariat. Subject to paragraphs 3 and 4, the Council shall establish an ECE on delivery of the request.

2. The ECE shall analyze, in the light of the objectives of this Agreement and in a non-adversarial manner, patterns of practice by each Party in the enforcement of its occupational safety and health or other technical labor standards as they apply to the particular matter considered by the Parties under Article 22.

3. No ECE may be convened if a Party obtains a ruling under Annex 23 that the matter: (a) is not trade-related; or (b) is not covered by mutually recognized labor laws.

4. No ECE may be convened regarding any matter that was previously the subject of an ECE report in the absence of such new information as would warrant a further report.

Article 24: Rules of Procedure

1. The Council shall establish rules of procedure for ECEs, which shall apply unless the Council otherwise decides. The rules of procedure shall provide that: (a) an ECE shall normally comprise three members; (b) the chair shall be selected by the Council from a roster of experts developed in consultation with the ILO pursuant to Article 45 and, where possible, other members shall be selected from a roster developed by the Parties; (c) ECE members shall (i) have expertise or experience in labor matters or other appropriate disciplines, (ii) be chosen strictly on the basis of objectivity, reliability and sound judgment, (iii) be independent of, and not be affiliated with or take instructions from, any Party or the Secretariat, and (iv) comply with a code of conduct to be established by the Council; (d) an ECE may invite written submissions from the Parties and the public; (e) an ECE may consider, in preparing its report, any information provided by (i) the Secretariat, (ii) the NAO of each Party, (iii) organizations, institutions and persons with relevant expertise, and (iv) the public; and (f) each Party shall have a reasonable opportunity to review and comment on information that the ECE receives and to make written submissions to the ECE.

2. The Secretariat and the NAOs shall provide appropriate administrative assistance to an ECE, in accordance with the rules of procedure established by the Council under paragraph 1.

Article 25: Draft Evaluation Reports

1. Within 120 days after it is established, or such other period as the Council may decide, the ECE shall present a draft report for consideration by the Council, which shall contain: (a) a comparative assessment of the matter under consideration; (b) its conclusions; and (c) where appropriate, practical recommendations that may assist the Parties in respect of the matter.

2. Each Party may submit written views to the ECE on its draft report. The ECE shall take such views into account in preparing its final report.

Article 26: Final Evaluation Reports

1. The ECE shall present a final report to the Council within 60 days after presentation of the draft report, unless the Council otherwise decides.

2. The final report shall be published within 30 days after its presentation to the Council, unless the Council otherwise decides.

3. The Parties shall provide to each other and the Secretariat written responses to the recommendations contained in the ECE report within 90 days of its publication.

4. The final report and such written responses shall be tabled for consideration at the next regular session of the Council. The Council may keep the matter under review.

PART FIVE

RESOLUTION OF DISPUTES

Article 27: Consultations

1. Following presentation to the Council under Article 26(1) of an ECE final report that addresses the enforcement of a Party's occupational safety and health, child labor or minimum wage technical labor standards, any Party may request in writing consultations with any other Party regarding whether there has been a persistent pattern of failure by that other Party to effectively enforce such standards in respect of the general subject matter addressed in the report.

2. The requesting Party shall deliver the request to the other Parties and to the Secretariat.

3. Unless the Council otherwise provides in its rules and procedures established under Article 9(2), a third Party that considers it has a substantial interest in the matter shall be entitled to participate in the consultations on delivery of written notice to the other Parties and to the Secretariat.

4. The consulting Parties shall make every attempt to arrive at a mutually satisfactory resolution of the matter through consultations under this Article.

Article 28: Initiation of Procedures

1. If the consulting Parties fail to resolve the matter pursuant to Article 27 within 60 days of delivery of a request for consultations, or such other period as the consulting Parties may agree, any such Party may request in writing a special session of the Council.

2. The requesting Party shall state in the request the matter complained of and shall deliver the request to the other Parties and to the Secretariat.

3. Unless it decides otherwise, the Council shall convene within 20 days of delivery of the request and shall endeavor to resolve the dispute promptly.

4. The Council may: (a) call on such technical advisers or create such working groups or expert groups as it deems necessary, (b) have recourse to good offices, conciliation, mediation or such other dispute resolution procedures, or (c) make recommendations, as may assist the consulting Parties to

reach a mutually satisfactory resolution of the dispute. Any such recommendations shall be made public if the Council, by a two-thirds vote, so decides.

5. Where the Council decides that a matter is more properly covered by another agreement or arrangement to which the consulting Parties are party, it shall refer the matter to those Parties for appropriate action in accordance with such other agreement or arrangement.

Article 29: Request for an Arbitral Panel

1. If the matter has not been resolved within 60 days after the Council has convened pursuant to Article 28, the Council shall, on the written request of any consulting Party and by a two-thirds vote, convene an arbitral panel to consider the matter where the alleged persistent pattern of failure by the Party complained against to effectively enforce its occupational safety and health, child labor or minimum wage technical labor standards is: (a) trade-related; and (b) covered by mutually recognized labor laws.

2. A third Party that considers it has a substantial interest in the matter shall be entitled to join as a complaining Party on delivery of written notice of its intention to participate to the disputing Parties and the Secretariat. The notice shall be delivered at the earliest possible time, and in any event no later than seven days after the date of the vote of the Council to convene a panel.

3. Unless otherwise agreed by the disputing Parties, the panel shall be established and perform its functions in a manner consistent with the provisions of this Part.

Article 30: Roster

1. The Council shall establish and maintain a roster of up to 45 individuals who are willing and able to serve as panelists. The roster members shall be appointed by consensus for terms of three years, and may be reappointed.

2. Roster members shall: (a) have expertise or experience in labor law or its enforcement, or in the resolution of disputes arising under international agreements, or other relevant scientific, technical or professional expertise or experience; (b) be chosen strictly on the basis of objectivity, reliability and sound judgment; (c) be independent of, and not be affiliated with or take instructions from, any Party or the Secretariat; and (d) comply with a code of conduct to be established by the Council.

Article 31: Qualifications of Panelists

1. All panelists shall meet the qualifications set out in Article 30.

2. Individuals may not serve as panelists for a dispute where: (a) they have participated pursuant to Article 28(4) or participated as members of an ECE that addressed the matter; or (b) they have, or a person or organization with which they are affiliated has, an interest in the matter, as set out in the code of conduct established under Article 30(2)(d).

Article 32: Panel Selection

1. Where there are two disputing Parties, the following procedures shall apply: (a) The panel shall comprise five members. (b) The disputing Parties

shall endeavor to agree on the chair of the panel within 15 days after the Council votes to convene the panel. If the disputing Parties are unable to agree on the chair within this period, the disputing Party chosen by lot shall select within five days a chair who is not a citizen of that Party. (c) Within 15 days of selection of the chair, each disputing Party shall select two panelists who are citizens of the other disputing Party. (d) If a disputing Party fails to select its panelists within such period, such panelists shall be selected by lot from among the roster members who are citizens of the other disputing Party.

2. Where there are more than two disputing Parties, the following procedures shall apply: (a) The panel shall comprise five members. (b) The disputing Parties shall endeavor to agree on the chair of the panel within 15 days after the Council votes to convene the panel. If the disputing Parties are unable to agree on the chair within this period, the Party or Parties on the side of the dispute chosen by lot shall select within 10 days a chair who is not a citizen of such Party or Parties. (c) Within 30 days of selection of the chair, the Party complained against shall select two panelists, one of whom is a citizen of a complaining Party, and the other of whom is a citizen of another complaining Party. The complaining Parties shall select two panelists who are citizens of the Party complained against. (d) If any disputing Party fails to select a panelist within such period, such panelist shall be selected by lot in accordance with the citizenship criteria of subparagraph (c).

3. Panelists shall normally be selected from the roster. Any disputing Party may exercise a peremptory challenge against any individual not on the roster who is proposed as a panelist by a disputing Party within 30 days after the individual has been proposed.

4. If a disputing Party believes that a panelist is in violation of the code of conduct, the disputing Parties shall consult and, if they agree, the panelist shall be removed and a new panelist shall be selected in accordance with this Article.

Article 33: Rules of Procedure

1. The Council shall establish Model Rules of Procedure. The procedures shall provide: (a) a right to at least one hearing before the panel; (b) the opportunity to make initial and rebuttal written submissions; and (c) that no panel may disclose which panelists are associated with majority or minority opinions.

2. Unless the disputing Parties otherwise agree, panels convened under this Part shall be established and conduct their proceedings in accordance with the Model Rules of Procedure.

3. Unless the disputing Parties otherwise agree within 20 days after the Council votes to convene the panel, the terms of reference shall be: "To examine, in light of the relevant provisions of the Agreement, including those contained in Part Five, whether there has been a persistent pattern of failure by the Party complained against to effectively enforce its occupational safety and health, child labor or minimum wage technical labor standards, and to make findings, determinations and recommendations in accordance with Article 36(2)."

Article 34: Third Party Participation

A Party that is not a disputing Party, on delivery of a written notice to the disputing Parties and the Secretariat, shall be entitled to attend all hearings, to make written and oral submissions to the panel and to receive written submissions of the disputing Parties.

Article 35: Role of Experts

On request of a disputing Party, or on its own initiative, the panel may seek information and technical advice from any person or body that it deems appropriate, provided that the disputing Parties so agree and subject to such terms and conditions as such Parties may agree.

Article 36: Initial Report

1. Unless the disputing Parties otherwise agree, the panel shall base its report on the submissions and arguments of the disputing Parties and on any information before it pursuant to Article 35.

2. Unless the disputing Parties otherwise agree, the panel shall, within 180 days after the last panelist is selected, present to the disputing Parties an initial report containing: (a) findings of fact; (b) its determination as to whether there has been a persistent pattern of failure by the Party complained against to effectively enforce its occupational safety and health, child labor or minimum wage technical labor standards in a matter that is trade-related and covered by mutually recognized labor laws, or any other determination requested in the terms of reference; and (c) in the event the panel makes an affirmative determination under subparagraph (b), its recommendations, if any, for the resolution of the dispute, which normally shall be that the Party complained against adopt and implement an action plan sufficient to remedy the pattern of non-enforcement.

3. Panelists may furnish separate opinions on matters not unanimously agreed.

4. A disputing Party may submit written comments to the panel on its initial report within 30 days of presentation of the report.

5. In such an event, and after considering such written comments, the panel, on its own initiative or on the request of any disputing Party, may: (a) request the views of any participating Party; (b) reconsider its report; and (c) make any further examination that it considers appropriate.

Article 37: Final Report

1. The panel shall present to the disputing Parties a final report, including any separate opinions on matters not unanimously agreed, within 60 days of presentation of the initial report, unless the disputing Parties otherwise agree.

2. The disputing Parties shall transmit to the Council the final report of the panel, as well as any written views that a disputing Party desires to be appended, on a confidential basis within 15 days after it is presented to them.

3. The final report of the panel shall be published five days after it is transmitted to the Council.

Article 38: Implementation of Final Report

If, in its final report, a panel determines that there has been a persistent pattern of failure by the Party complained against to effectively enforce its occupational safety and health, child labor or minimum wage technical labor standards, the disputing Parties may agree on a mutually satisfactory action plan, which normally shall conform with the determinations and recommendations of the panel. The disputing Parties shall promptly notify the Secretariat and the Council of any agreed resolution of the dispute.

Article 39: Review of Implementation

1. If, in its final report, a panel determines that there has been a persistent pattern of failure by the Party complained against to effectively enforce its occupational safety and health, child labor or minimum wage technical labor standards, and: (a) the disputing Parties have not agreed on an action plan under Article 38 within 60 days of the date of the final report, or (b) the disputing Parties cannot agree on whether the Party complained against is fully implementing (i) an action plan agreed under Article 38, (ii) an action plan deemed to have been established by a panel under paragraph 2, or (iii) an action plan approved or established by a panel under paragraph 4, any disputing Party may request that the panel be reconvened. The requesting Party shall deliver the request in writing to the other Parties and to the Secretariat. The Council shall reconvene the panel on delivery of the request to the Secretariat.

2. No Party may make a request under paragraph 1(a) earlier than 60 days, or later than 120 days, after the date of the final report. If the disputing Parties have not agreed to an action plan and if no request was made under paragraph 1(a), the last action plan, if any, submitted by the Party complained against to the complaining Party or Parties within 60 days of the date of the final report, or such other period as the disputing Parties may agree, shall be deemed to have been established by the panel 120 days after the date of the final report.

3. A request under paragraph 1(b) may be made no earlier than 180 days after an action plan has been: (a) agreed under Article 38, (b) deemed to have been established by a panel under paragraph 2, or (c) approved or established by a panel under paragraph 4, and only during the term of any such action plan.

4. Where a panel has been reconvened under paragraph 1(a), it: (a) shall determine whether any action plan proposed by the Party complained against is sufficient to remedy the pattern of non-enforcement and (i) if so, shall approve the plan, or (ii) if not, shall establish such a plan consistent with the law of the Party complained against, and (b) may, where warranted, impose a monetary enforcement assessment in accordance with Annex 39, within 90 days after the panel has been reconvened or such other period as the disputing Parties may agree.

5. Where a panel has been reconvened under paragraph 1(b), it shall determine either that: (a) the Party complained against is fully implementing the action plan, in which case the panel may not impose a monetary enforcement assessment, or (b) the Party complained against is not fully implementing the action plan, in which case the panel shall impose a monetary

enforcement assessment in accordance with Annex 39, within 60 days after it has been reconvened or such other period as the disputing Parties may agree.

6.   A panel reconvened under this Article shall provide that the Party complained against shall fully implement any action plan referred to in paragraph 4(a)(ii) or 5(b), and pay any monetary enforcement assessment imposed under paragraph 4(b) or 5(b), and any such provision shall be final.

Article 40: Further Proceeding

A complaining Party may, at any time beginning 180 days after a panel determination under Article 39(5)(b), request in writing that a panel be reconvened to determine whether the Party complained against is fully implementing the action plan. On delivery of the request to the other Parties and the Secretariat, the Council shall reconvene the panel. The panel shall make the determination within 60 days after it has been reconvened or such other period as the disputing Parties may agree.

Article 41: Suspension of Benefits

1.   Subject to Annex 41A, where a Party fails to pay a monetary enforcement assessment within 180 days after it is imposed by a panel: (a) under Article 39(4)(b), or (b) under Article 39(5)(b), except where benefits may be suspended under paragraph 2(a), any complaining Party or Parties may suspend, in accordance with Annex 41B, the application to the Party complained against of NAFTA benefits in an amount no greater than that sufficient to collect the monetary enforcement assessment.

2.   Subject to Annex 41A, where a panel has made a determination under Article 39(5)(b) and the panel: (a) has previously imposed a monetary enforcement assessment under Article 39(4)(b) or established an action plan under Article 39(4)(a)(ii), or (b) has subsequently determined under Article 40 that a Party is not fully implementing an action plan, the complaining Party or Parties may, in accordance with Annex 41B, suspend annually the application to the Party complained against of NAFTA benefits in an amount no greater than the monetary enforcement assessment imposed by the panel under Article 39(5)(b).

3.   Where more than one complaining Party suspends benefits under paragraph 1 or 2, the combined suspension shall be no greater than the amount of the monetary enforcement assessment.

4.   Where a Party has suspended benefits under paragraph 1 or 2, the Council shall, on the delivery of a written request by the Party complained against to the other Parties and the Secretariat, reconvene the panel to determine whether the monetary enforcement assessment has been paid or collected, or whether the Party complained against is fully implementing the action plan, as the case may be. The panel shall submit its report within 45 days after it has been reconvened. If the panel determines that the assessment has been paid or collected, or that the Party complained against is fully implementing the action plan, the suspension of benefits under paragraph 1 or 2, as the case may be, shall be terminated.

5.   On the written request of the Party complained against, delivered to the other Parties and the Secretariat, the Council shall reconvene the panel to determine whether the suspension of benefits by the complaining Party or

Parties pursuant to paragraph 1 or 2 is manifestly excessive. Within 45 days of the request, the panel shall present a report to the disputing Parties containing its determination.

PART SIX
GENERAL PROVISIONS

Article 42: Enforcement Principle

Nothing in this Agreement shall be construed to empower a Party's authorities to undertake labor law enforcement activities in the territory of another Party.

Article 43: Private Rights

No Party may provide for a right of action under its domestic law against any other Party on the ground that another Party has acted in a manner inconsistent with this Agreement.

Article 44: Protection of Information

1. If a Party provides confidential or proprietary information to another Party, including its NAO, the Council or the Secretariat, the recipient shall treat the information on the same basis as the Party providing the information.

2. Confidential or proprietary information provided by a Party to an ECE or a panel under this Agreement shall be treated in accordance with the rules of procedure established under Articles 24 and 33.

Article 45: Cooperation with the ILO

The Parties shall seek to establish cooperative arrangements with the ILO to enable the Council and Parties to draw on the expertise and experience of the ILO for purposes of implementing Article 24(1).

Article 46: Extent of Obligations

Annex 46 applies to the Parties specified in that Annex.

Article 47: Funding of the Commission

Each Party shall contribute an equal share of the annual budget of the Commission, subject to the availability of appropriated funds in accordance with the Party's legal procedures. No Party shall be obligated to pay more than any other Party in respect of an annual budget.

Article 48: Privileges and Immunities

The Executive Director and staff of the Secretariat shall enjoy in the territory of each of the Parties such privileges and immunities as are necessary for the exercise of their functions.

Article 49: Definitions

1. For purposes of this Agreement:

A Party has not failed to "effectively enforce its occupational safety and health, child labor or minimum wage technical labor standards" or comply with Article 3(1) in a particular case where the action or inaction by agencies or officials of that Party: (a) reflects a reasonable exercise of the agency's or the official's discretion with respect to investigatory, prosecutorial, regulatory or compliance matters; or (b) results from bona fide decisions to allocate resources to enforcement in respect of other labor matters determined to have higher priorities;

"labor law" means laws and regulations, or provisions thereof, that are directly related to: (a) freedom of association and protection of the right to organize; (b) the right to bargain collectively; (c) the right to strike; (d) prohibition of forced labor; (e) labor protections for children and young persons; (f) minimum employment standards, such as minimum wages and overtime pay, covering wage earners, including those not covered by collective agreements; (g) elimination of employment discrimination on the basis of grounds such as race, religion, age, sex, or other grounds as determined by each Party's domestic laws; (h) equal pay for men and women; (i) prevention of occupational injuries and illnesses; (j) compensation in cases of occupational injuries and illnesses; (k) protection of migrant workers;

"mutually recognized labor laws" means laws of both a requesting Party and the Party whose laws were the subject of ministerial consultations under Article 22 that address the same general subject matter in a manner that provides enforceable rights, protections or standards;

"pattern of practice" means a course of action or inaction beginning after the date of entry into force of the Agreement, and does not include a single instance or case;

"persistent pattern" means a sustained or recurring pattern of practice;

"province" means a province of Canada, and includes the Yukon Territory and the Northwest Territories and their successors;

"publicly available information" means information to which the public has a legal right under the statutory laws of the Party;

"technical labor standards" means laws and regulations, or specific provisions thereof, that are directly related to subparagraphs (d) through (k) of the definition of labor law. For greater certainty and consistent with the provisions of this Agreement, the setting of all standards and levels in respect of minimum wages and labor protections for children and young persons by each Party shall not be subject to obligations under this Agreement. Each Party's obligations under this Agreement pertain to enforcing the level of the general minimum wage and child labor age limits established by that Party;

"territory" means for a Party the territory of that Party as set out in Annex 49; and

"trade-related" means related to a situation involving workplaces, firms, companies or sectors that produce goods or provide services: (a) traded between the territories of the Parties; or (b) that compete, in the territory of the Party whose labor law was the subject of ministerial consultations under Article 22, with goods or services produced or provided by persons of another Party.

PART SEVEN
FINAL PROVISIONS

Article 50: Annexes

The Annexes to this Agreement constitute an integral part of the Agreement.

Article 51: Entry into Force

This Agreement shall enter into force on January 1, 1994, immediately after entry into force of the NAFTA, on an exchange of written notifications certifying the completion of necessary legal procedures.

Article 52: Amendments

1. The Parties may agree on any modification of or addition to this Agreement.

2. When so agreed, and approved in accordance with the applicable legal procedures of each Party, a modification or addition shall constitute an integral part of this Agreement.

Article 53: Accession

Any country or group of countries may accede to this Agreement subject to such terms and conditions as may be agreed between such country or countries and the Council and following approval in accordance with the applicable legal procedures of each country.

Article 54: Withdrawal

A Party may withdraw from this Agreement six months after it provides written notice of withdrawal to the other Parties. If a Party withdraws, the Agreement shall remain in force for the remaining Parties.

Article 55: Authentic Texts

The English, French and Spanish texts of this Agreement are equally authentic.

IN WITNESS WHEREOF, the undersigned, being duly authorized by the respective Governments, have signed this Agreement.

ANNEX 1
LABOR PRINCIPLES

The following are guiding principles that the Parties are committed to promote, subject to each Party's domestic law, but do not establish common minimum standards for their domestic law. They indicate broad areas of concern where the Parties have developed, each in its own way, laws, regulations, procedures and practices that protect the rights and interests of their respective workforces.

1. Freedom of association and protection of the right to organize

The right of workers exercised freely and without impediment to establish and join organizations of their own choosing to further and defend their interests.

2.   The right to bargain collectively

The protection of the right of organized workers to freely engage in collective bargaining on matters concerning the terms and conditions of employment.

3.   The right to strike

The protection of the right of workers to strike in order to defend their collective interests.

4.   Prohibition of forced labor

The prohibition and suppression of all forms of forced or compulsory labor, except for types of compulsory work generally considered acceptable by the Parties, such as compulsory military service, certain civic obligations, prison labor not for private purposes and work exacted in cases of emergency.

5.   Labor protections for children and young persons

The establishment of restrictions on the employment of children and young persons that may vary taking into consideration relevant factors likely to jeopardize the full physical, mental and moral development of young persons, including schooling and safety requirements.

6.   Minimum employment standards

The establishment of minimum employment standards, such as minimum wages and overtime pay, for wage earners, including those not covered by collective agreements.

7.   Elimination of employment discrimination

Elimination of employment discrimination on such grounds as race, religion, age, sex or other grounds, subject to certain reasonable exceptions, such as, where applicable, bona fide occupational requirements or qualifications and established practices or rules governing retirement ages, and special measures of protection or assistance for particular groups designed to take into account the effects of discrimination.

8.   Equal pay for women and men

Equal wages for women and men by applying the principle of equal pay for equal work in the same establishment.

9.   Prevention of occupational injuries and illnesses

Prescribing and implementing standards to minimize the causes of occupational injuries and illnesses.

10.   Compensation in cases of occupational injuries and illnesses

The establishment of a system providing benefits and compensation to workers or their dependents in cases of occupational injuries, accidents or fatalities arising out of, linked with or occurring in the course of employment.

11.   Protection of migrant workers

Providing migrant workers in a Party's territory with the same legal protection as the Party's nationals in respect of working conditions.

ANNEX 23
INTERPRETIVE RULING

1. Where a Party has requested the Council to convene an ECE, the Council shall, on the written request of any other Party, select an independent expert to make a ruling concerning whether the matter is: (a) trade-related; or (b) covered by mutually recognized labor laws.

2. The Council shall establish rules of procedure for the selection of the expert and for submissions by the Parties. Unless the Council decides otherwise, the expert shall present a ruling within 15 days after the expert is selected.

ANNEX 39
MONETARY ENFORCEMENT ASSESSMENTS

1. For the first year after the date of entry into force of this Agreement, any monetary enforcement assessment shall be no greater than 20 million dollars (U.S.) or its equivalent in the currency of the Party complained against. Thereafter, any monetary enforcement assessment shall be no greater than .007 percent of total trade in goods between the Parties during the most recent year for which data are available.

2. In determining the amount of the assessment, the panel shall take into account: (a) the pervasiveness and duration of the Party's persistent pattern of failure to effectively enforce its occupational safety and health, child labor or minimum wage technical labor standards; (b) the level of enforcement that could reasonably be expected of a Party given its resource constraints; (c) the reasons, if any, provided by the Party for not fully implementing an action plan; (d) efforts made by the Party to begin remedying the pattern of non-enforcement after the final report of the panel; and (e) any other relevant factors.

3. All monetary enforcement assessments shall be paid in the currency of the Party complained against into a fund established in the name of the Commission by the Council and shall be expended at the direction of the Council to improve or enhance the labor law enforcement in the Party complained against, consistent with its law.

ANNEX 41A
CANADIAN DOMESTIC ENFORCEMENT AND COLLECTION

1. For the purposes of this Annex, "panel determination" means: (a) a determination by a panel under Article 39(4)(b) or 5(b) that provides that Canada shall pay a monetary enforcement assessment; and (b) a determination by a panel under Article 39(5)(b) that provides that Canada shall fully implement an action plan where the panel: (i) has previously established an action plan under Article 39(4)(a)(ii) or imposed a monetary enforcement assessment under Article 39(4)(b); or (ii) has subsequently determined under Article 40 that Canada is not fully implementing an action plan.

2. Canada shall adopt and maintain procedures that provide that: (a) subject to subparagraph (b), the Commission, at the request of a complaining Party, may in its own name file in a court of competent jurisdiction a certified copy of a panel determination; (b) the Commission may file in court a panel

determination that is a panel determination described in paragraph 1(a) only if Canada has failed to comply with the determination within 180 days of when the determination was made; (c) when filed, the panel determination, for purposes of enforcement, shall become an order of the court; (d) the Commission may take proceedings for enforcement of a panel determination that is made an order of the court, in that court, against the person against whom the panel determination is addressed in accordance with paragraph 6 of Annex 46; (e) proceedings to enforce a panel determination that has been made an order of the court shall be conducted by way of summary proceedings; (f) in proceedings to enforce a panel determination that is a panel determination described in paragraph 1(b) and that has been made an order of the court, the court shall promptly refer any question of fact or any question of interpretation of the panel determination to the panel that made the panel determination, and the decision of the panel shall be binding on the court; (g) a panel determination that has been made an order of the court shall not be subject to domestic review or appeal; and (h) an order made by the court in proceedings to enforce a panel determination that has been made an order of the court shall not be subject to review or appeal.

3. Where Canada is the Party complained against, the procedures adopted and maintained by Canada under this Annex shall apply and the procedures set out in Article 41 shall not apply.

4. Any change by Canada to the procedures adopted and maintained by Canada under this Annex that have the effect of undermining the provisions of this Annex shall be considered a breach of this Agreement.

ANNEX 41B
SUSPENSION OF BENEFITS

1. Where a complaining Party suspends NAFTA tariff benefits in accordance with this Agreement, the Party may increase the rates of duty on originating goods of the Party complained against to levels not to exceed the lesser of: (a) the rate that was applicable to those goods immediately prior to the date of entry into force of the NAFTA, and (b) the Most–Favored–Nation rate applicable to those goods on the date the Party suspends such benefits, and such increase may be applied only for such time as is necessary to collect, through such increase, the monetary enforcement assessment.

2. In considering what tariff or other benefits to suspend pursuant to Article 41(1) or (2): (a) a complaining Party shall first seek to suspend benefits in the same sector or sectors as that in respect of which there has been a persistent pattern of failure by the Party complained against to effectively enforce its occupational safety and health, child labor or minimum wage technical labor standards; and (b) a complaining Party that considers it is not practicable or effective to suspend benefits in the same sector or sectors may suspend benefits in other sectors.

ANNEX 46
EXTENT OF OBLIGATIONS

1. On the date of signature of this Agreement, or of the exchange of written notifications under Article 51, Canada shall set out in a declaration a list of any provinces for which Canada is to be bound in respect of matters

within their jurisdiction. The declaration shall be effective on delivery to the other Parties, and shall carry no implication as to the internal distribution of powers within Canada. Canada shall notify the other Parties six months in advance of any modification to its declaration.

2. Unless a communication relates to a matter that would be under federal jurisdiction if it were to arise within the territory of Canada, the Canadian NAO shall identify the province of residence or establishment of the author of any communication regarding the labor law of another Party that it forwards to the NAO of another Party. That NAO may choose not to respond if that province is not included in the declaration made under paragraph 1.

3. Canada may not request consultations under Article 22, the establishment of an Evaluation Committee of Experts under Article 23, consultations under Article 27, the initiation of procedures under Article 28 or the establishment of a panel or join as a complaining Party under Article 29 at the instance, or primarily for the benefit, of any government of a province not included in the declaration made under paragraph 1.

4. Canada may not request consultations under Article 22, the establishment of an Evaluation Committee of Experts under Article 23, consultations under Article 27, the initiation of procedures under Article 28 or the establishment of a panel or join as a complaining Party under Article 29, unless Canada states in writing that the matter would be under federal jurisdiction if it were to arise within the territory of Canada, or: (a) Canada states in writing that the matter would be under provincial jurisdiction if it were to arise within the territory of Canada; and (b) the federal government and the provinces included in the declaration account for at least 35 percent of Canada's labor force for the most recent year in which data are available, and (c) where the matter concerns a specific industry or sector, at least 55 percent of the workers concerned are employed in provinces included in Canada's declaration under paragraph 1.

5. No other Party may request consultations under Article 22, the establishment of an Evaluation Committee of Experts under Article 23, consultations under Article 27, the initiation of procedures under Article 28 or the establishment of a panel or join as a complaining Party under Article 29, concerning a matter related to a labor law of a province unless that province is included in the declaration made under paragraph 1 and the requirements of subparagraphs 4(b) and (c) have been met.

6. Canada shall, no later than the date on which an arbitral panel is convened pursuant to Article 29 respecting a matter within the scope of paragraph 5 of this Annex, notify in writing the complaining Parties and the Secretariat of whether any monetary enforcement assessment or action plan imposed by a panel under Article 39(4) or (5) against Canada shall be addressed to Her Majesty in right of Canada or Her Majesty in right of the province concerned.

7. Canada shall use its best efforts to make the Agreement applicable to as many of its provinces as possible.

8. Two years after the date of entry into force of this Agreement, the Council shall review the operation of this Annex and, in particular, shall

consider whether the Parties should amend the thresholds established in paragraph 4.

ANNEX 49
COUNTRY–SPECIFIC DEFINITIONS

For purposes of this Agreement:

"territory" means: (a) with respect to Canada, the territory to which its customs laws apply, including any areas beyond the territorial seas of Canada within which, in accordance with international law and its domestic law, Canada may exercise rights with respect to the seabed and subsoil and their natural resources; (b) with respect to Mexico, (i) the states of the Federation and the Federal District, (ii) the islands, including the reefs and keys, in adjacent seas, (iii) the islands of Guadalupe and Revillagigedo situated in the Pacific Ocean, (iv) the continental shelf and the submarine shelf of such islands, keys and reefs, (v) the waters of the territorial seas, in accordance with international law, and its interior maritime waters, (vi) the space located above the national territory, in accordance with international law, and (vii) any areas beyond the territorial seas of Mexico within which, in accordance with international law, including the United Nations Convention on the Law of the Sea, and its domestic law, Mexico may exercise rights with respect to the seabed and subsoil and their natural resources; and (c) with respect to the United States, (i) the customs territory of the United States, which includes the 50 states, the District of Columbia and Puerto Rico, (ii) the foreign trade zones located in the United States and Puerto Rico, and (iii) any areas beyond the territorial seas of the United States within which, in accordance with international law and its domestic law, the United States may exercise rights with respect to the seabed and subsoil and their natural resources.

Item 43

UNDERSTANDING BETWEEN THE PARTIES TO THE NORTH AMERICAN FREE TRADE AGREEMENT CONCERNING CHAPTER EIGHT—EMERGENCY ACTION

Article 1: Objectives

The objectives of this Understanding are to establish additional procedures to facilitate the effective use of Chapter Eight of the North American Free Trade Agreement (NAFTA).

Article 2: Working Group on Emergency Action

1. The Parties hereby establish a Working Group on Emergency Action comprising one representative of each Party to the NAFTA. The Working Group shall be deemed to be a working group established under Article 2001(2)(d) of the NAFTA.

2. The Working Group shall report to the Free Trade Commission established under the NAFTA, and shall be subject to the supervision of the Commission.

3. The NAFTA Secretariat shall provide technical support to the Working Group.

4. The Working Group shall meet at least annually, unless the Parties otherwise agree, and on request of any Party.

5. The Working Group may call on the assistance of such experts and advisers as it deems appropriate.

6. All decisions of the Working Group shall be taken by consensus, except as otherwise agreed or provided for in this Understanding.

Article 3: Functions of the Working Group

1. The Working Group shall consider any issue related to recourse to Chapter Eight of the NAFTA and may make recommendations to the Commission.

2. The Working Group shall consider any recourse to Article XIX of the General Agreement on Tariffs and Trade by any Party to the NAFTA, and, at the request of any Party, may serve as a forum for consultations before or during any such use of Article XIX.

3. The Parties may consult in the Working Group on the request of a Party where a Party considers that: (a) in accordance with Article 801 or 802, goods originating in the territory of another Party are being imported in such increased quantities as to constitute a substantial cause of, or contribute importantly to, serious injury, or threat thereof, to its domestic industry, as evidenced by the factors set out in Annex 803.3(9) of the NAFTA, including

781

trade, productivity, and employment; or (b) another Party is contemplating having recourse to Chapter Eight.

Any consultations under this paragraph shall be without prejudice as to whether any subsequent emergency action proceeding is consistent with the NAFTA.

4. The Parties may agree that consultations under paragraph C [should be 3?] shall constitute consultations under Article 801(2) or 802(5) of the NAFTA.

5. Subject to the rights and obligations of the Parties under the NAFTA, the Working Group shall serve as a forum for examining, at the request of any Party and with the agreement of two-thirds of the Parties, trade, productivity, employment and other economic factors with respect to any good, provided that such discussions shall not serve as a justification for restricting or prohibiting trade in any manner inconsistent with Chapter Eight.

6. The Working Group may make recommendations to the Commission for any improvements to Chapter Eight of the NAFTA that the Working Group deems appropriate, consistent with the objectives of the NAFTA and of this Understanding.

Article 4: Definitions

Unless otherwise specified, all terms of this Understanding shall have the meaning assigned to them in the NAFTA.

Part IV

U.S. STATUTES

Introduction to Part IV

Part IV contains the principal U.S. statutes dealing with international trade. We have generally arranged these statutes by Act, since many provisions are best known as section such-and-such of the so-and-so Act (e.g., section 301 of the 1974 Act). By and large, the order of the sections of the principal Acts is the same as the codified order of title 19 of the United States Code. We give both the Act's section number and the U.S.C. cite for each section.

Among the more important topics covered by these statutes and their position in the U.S. trade acts are:

Dumping	Tariff Act of 1930 (item 45), §§ 731–783; Antidumping Act of 1916 (item 44), DOC Regulations (item 55)
Countervail	Tariff Act of 1930 (item 45), §§ 701–782, DOC Regulations (item 55)
Escape Clause	Trade Act of 1974 (item 47), §§ 201–204
Section 301	Trade Act of 1974 (item 47), §§ 301–310; see also Trade Act of 1974, §§ 181–182
Section 337	Tariff Act of 1930 (item 45), § 337
Technical Barriers	Trade Agreements Act of 1979 (item 48), §§ 401–73

We also note that at this writing, the Generalized System of Preferences (see item 47) and the Export Administration Act (item 54) are expired but will likely be renewed soon.

783

Item 44

ANTIDUMPING ACT OF 1916

15 USC 72

§ 72. Importation or Sale of Articles at Less Than Market Value or Wholesale Price

It shall be unlawful for any person importing or assisting in importing any articles from any foreign country into the United States, commonly and systematically to import, sell or cause to be imported or sold such articles within the United States at a price substantially less than the actual market value or wholesale price of such articles, at the time of exportation to the United States, in the principal markets of the country of their production, or of other foreign countries to which they are commonly exported after adding to such market value or wholesale price, freight, duty, and other charges and expenses necessarily incident to the importation and sale thereof in the United States: Provided, That such act or acts be done with the intent of destroying or injuring an industry in the United States, or of preventing the establishment of an industry in the United States, or of restraining or monopolizing any part of trade and commerce in such articles in the United States.

Any person who violates or combines or conspires with any other person to violate this section is guilty of a misdemeanor, and, on conviction thereof, shall be punished by a fine not exceeding $5,000, or imprisonment not exceeding one year, or both, in the discretion of the court.

Any person injured in his business or property by reason of any violation of, or combination or conspiracy to violate, this section, may sue therefor in the district court of the United States for the district in which the defendant resides or is found or has an agent, without respect to the amount in controversy, and shall recover threefold the damages sustained, and the cost of the suit, including a reasonable attorney's fee.

The foregoing provisions shall not be construed to deprive the proper State courts of jurisdiction in actions for damages thereunder.

Item 45

UNITED STATES: TARIFF ACT OF 1930

(Selected provisions, as amended)

Act of June 17, 1930, ch. 497, 46 Stat. 685

Table of Contents

SUBTITLE D.   GENERAL PROVISIONS

---

19 USC 1330

Sec. 330.   Organization of Commission

(a) **Membership.** The United States International Trade Commission (referred to in this subtitle as the "Commission") shall be composed of six commissioners who shall be appointed by the President, by and with the advice and consent of the Senate. No person shall be eligible for appointment as a commissioner unless he is a citizen of the United States, and, in the judgment of the President, is possessed of qualifications requisite for developing expert knowledge of international trade problems and efficiency in administering the duties and functions of the Commission. A person who has served as a commissioner for more than 5 years (excluding service as a commissioner before January 3, 1975) shall not be eligible for reappointment as a commissioner. Not more than three of the commissioners shall be members of the same political party, and in making appointments members of different political parties shall be appointed alternately as nearly as may be practicable.

(b) **Terms of office.** * * * The term of office of each commissioner appointed after [January 3, 1975] shall expire 9 years from the date of the expiration of the term for which his predecessor was appointed, except that—

(1) any commissioner appointed to fill a vacancy occurring prior to the expiration of the term for which his predecessor was appointed shall be appointed for the remainder of such term, and

(2) any commissioner may continue to serve as a commissioner after an expiration of his term of office until his successor is appointed and qualified.

* * *

(d) Effect of divided vote in certain cases.

(1) In a proceeding in which the Commission is required to determine—

(A) under section 202 of the Trade Act of 1974, whether increased imports of an article are a substantial cause of serious injury, or the threat thereof, as described in subsection (b)(1) of that section (hereafter in this subsection referred to as "serious injury"), or

(B) under section 406 of the Trade Act of 1974, whether market disruption exists,

and the commissioners voting are equally divided with respect to such determination, then the determination agreed upon by either group of commissioners may be considered by the President as the determination of the Commission.

(2) If under section 202(b) or 406 of the Trade Act of 1974 there is an affirmative determination of the Commission, or a determination of the Commission which the President may consider an affirmative determination under paragraph (1), that serious injury or market disruption exists, respectively, and a majority of the commissioners voting are unable to agree on a finding or recommendation described in section 202(e)(1) of the Trade Act of 1974 or the finding described in section 406(a)(3) of the Trade Act of 1974, as the case may be (hereafter in this subsection referred to as a "remedy finding"), then—

(A) if a plurality of not less than three commissioners so voting agree on a remedy finding, such remedy finding shall, for purposes of section 203 of the Trade Act of 1974, be treated as the remedy finding of the Commission, or

(B) if two groups, both of which include not less than 3 commissioners, each agree upon a remedy finding and the President reports under section 204(a) of the Trade Act of 1974 that—

(i) he is taking the action agreed upon by one such group, then the remedy finding agreed upon by the other group shall, for purposes of section 203 of the Trade Act of 1974, be treated as the remedy finding of the Commission, or

(ii) he is taking action which differs from the action agreed upon by both such groups, or that he will not take any action, then the remedy finding agreed upon by either such group may be considered by the Congress as the remedy finding of the Commission and shall, for purposes of section 203 of the Trade Act of 1974, be treated as the remedy finding of the Commission.

(3) In any proceeding to which paragraph (1) applies in which the commissioners voting are equally divided on a determination that serious injury exists, or that market disruption exists, the Commission shall report to the President the determination of each group of commissioners. In any proceeding to which paragraph (2) applies, the Commission shall report to the President the remedy finding of each group of commissioners voting.

(4) In a case to which paragraph (2)(B)(ii) applies, for purposes of section 203(a) of the Trade Act of 1974, notwithstanding section 152(a)(1)(A) thereof, the second blank space in the joint resolution described in such section 152(a)(1)(A) shall be filled with the appropriate date and the following: "The action which shall take effect under section 203(a) of the Trade Act of 1974 is the finding or recommendation agreed upon by Commissioners _____,

_____, and _____." The three blank spaces shall be filled with the names of the appropriate Commissioners.

* * *

19 USC 1337

Sec. 337. Unfair Practices in Import Trade

(a) Unfair methods of competition declared unlawful.

(1) Subject to paragraph (2), the following are unlawful, and when found by the Commission to exist shall be dealt with, in addition to any other provision of law, as provided in this section:

(A) Unfair methods of competition and unfair acts in the importation of articles (other than articles provided for in subparagraphs (B), (C), (D), and (E)) into the United States, or in the sale of such articles by the owner, importer, or consignee, the threat or effect of which is—

(i) to destroy or substantially injure an industry in the United States;

(ii) to prevent the establishment of such an industry; or

(iii) to restrain or monopolize trade and commerce in the United States.

(B) The importation into the United States, the sale for importation, or the sale within the United States after importation by the owner, importer, or consignee, of articles that—

(i) infringe a valid and enforceable United States patent or a valid and enforceable United States copyright registered under title 17, United States Code; or

(ii) are made, produced, processed, or mined under, or by means of, a process covered by the claims of a valid and enforceable United States patent.

(C) The importation into the United States, the sale for importation, or the sale within the United States after importation by the owner, importer, or consignee, of articles that infringe a valid and enforceable United States trademark registered under the Trademark Act of 1946.

(D) The importation into the United States, the sale for importation, or the sale within the United States after importation by the owner, importer, or consignee, of a semiconductor chip product in a manner that constitutes infringement of a mask work registered under chapter 9 of title 17, United States Code.

(E) The importation into the United States, the sale for importation, or the sale within the United States after importation by the owner, importer, or consigner, of an article that constitutes infringement of the exclusive rights in a design protected under chapter 13 of title 17, United States Code.

(2) Subparagraphs (B), (C), and (D) of paragraph (1) apply only if an industry in the United States, relating to the articles protected by the patent,

copyright, trademark, mask work, or design concerned, exists or is in the process of being established.

(3) For purposes of paragraph (2), an industry in the United States shall be considered to exist if there is in the United States, with respect to the articles protected by the patent, copyright, trademark, mask work, or design concerned—

(A) significant investment in plant and equipment;

(B) significant employment of labor or capital; or

(C) substantial investment in its exploitation, including engineering, research and development, or licensing.

(4) For the purposes of this section, the phrase "owner, importer, or consignee" includes any agent of the owner, importer, or consignee.

(b) Investigation of violations by Commission.

(1) The Commission shall investigate any alleged violation of this section on complaint under oath or upon its initiative. Upon commencing any such investigation, the Commission shall publish notice thereof in the Federal Register. The Commission shall conclude any such investigation and make its determination under this section at the earliest practicable time after the date of publication of notice of such investigation. To promote expeditious adjudication, the Commission shall, within 45 days after an investigation is initiated, establish a target date for its final determination.

(2) During the course of each investigation under this section, the Commission shall consult with, and seek advice and information from, the Department of Health and Human Services, the Department of Justice, the Federal Trade Commission, and such other departments and agencies as it considers appropriate.

(3) Whenever, in the course of an investigation under this section, the Commission has reason to believe, based on information before it, that a matter, in whole or in part, may come within the purview of subtitle B of title VII of this Act, it shall promptly notify the Secretary of Commerce so that such action may be taken as is otherwise authorized by such subtitle. If the Commission has reason to believe that the matter before it (A) is based solely on alleged acts and effects which are within the purview of section 701 or 731, or (B) relates to an alleged copyright infringement with respect to which action is prohibited by section 1008 of title 17, United States Code, the Commission shall terminate, or not institute, any investigation into the matter. If the Commission has reason to believe the matter before it is based in part on alleged acts and effects which are within the purview of section 701 or 731 of this Act, and in part on alleged acts and effects which may, independently from or in conjunction with those within the purview of such section, establish a basis for relief under this section, then it may institute or continue an investigation into the matter. If the Commission notifies the Secretary or the administering authority (as defined in section 771(1) of this Act) with respect to a matter under this paragraph, the Commission may suspend its investigation during the time the matter is before the Secretary or administering authority for final decision. Any final decision by the administering authority under section 701 or 731 of this Act with respect to the

matter within such section 701 or 731 of which the Commission has notified the Secretary or administering authority shall be conclusive upon the Commission with respect to the issue of less-than-fair-value sales or subsidization and the matters necessary for such decision.

(c) **Determinations; review.** The Commission shall determine, with respect to each investigation conducted by it under this section, whether or not there is a violation of this section, except that the Commission may, by issuing a consent order or on the basis of an agreement between the private parties to the investigation, including an agreement to present the matter for arbitration, terminate any such investigation, in whole or in part, without making such a determination. Each determination under subsection (d) or (e) shall be made on the record after notice and opportunity for a hearing in conformity with the provisions of subchapter II of chapter 5 of title 5, United States Code. All legal and equitable defenses may be presented in all cases. A respondent may raise any counterclaim in a manner prescribed by the Commission. Immediately after a counterclaim is received by the Commission, the respondent raising such counterclaim shall file a notice of removal with a United States district court in which venue for any of the counterclaims raised by the party would exist under section 1391 of title 28, United States Code. Any counterclaim raised pursuant to this section shall relate back to the date of the original complaint in the proceeding before the Commission. Action on such counterclaim shall not delay or affect the proceeding under this section, including the legal and equitable defenses that may be raised under this subsection. Any person adversely affected by a final determination of the Commission under subsection (d), (e), (f), or (g) may appeal such determination, within 60 days after the determination becomes final, to the United States Court of Appeals for the Federal Circuit for review in accordance with chapter 7 of title 5, United States Code. Notwithstanding the foregoing provisions of this subsection, Commission determinations under subsections (d), (e), (f), and (g) with respect to its findings on the public health and welfare, competitive conditions in the United States economy, the production of like or directly competitive articles in the United States, and United States consumers, the amount and nature of bond, or the appropriate remedy shall be reviewable in accordance with section 706 of title 5, United States Code. Determinations by the Commission under subsections (e), (f), and (j) with respect to forfeiture of bonds and under subsection (h) with respect to the imposition of sanctions for abuse of discovery or abuse of process shall also be reviewable in accordance with section 706 of title 5, United States Code.

(d) **Exclusion of articles from entry.**

(1) If the Commission determines, as a result of an investigation under this section, that there is a violation of this section, it shall direct that the articles concerned, imported by any person violating the provision of this section, be excluded from entry into the United States, unless, after considering the effect of such exclusion upon the public health and welfare, competitive conditions in the United States economy, the production of like or directly competitive articles in the United States, and United States consumers, it finds that such articles should not be excluded from entry. The Commission shall notify the Secretary of the Treasury of its action under this subsection

directing such exclusion from entry, and upon receipt of such notice, the Secretary shall, through the proper officers, refuse such entry.

(2) The authority of the Commission to order an exclusion from entry of articles shall be limited to persons determined by the Commission to be violating this section unless the Commission determines that—

(A) a general exclusion from entry of articles is necessary to prevent circumvention of an exclusion order limited to products of named persons; or

(B) there is a pattern of violation of this section and it is difficult to identify the source of infringing products.

(e) Exclusion of articles from entry during investigation except under bond.

(1) If, during the course of an investigation under this section, the Commission determines that there is reason to believe that there is a violation of this section, it may direct that the articles concerned, imported by any person with respect to whom there is reason to believe that such person is violating this section, be excluded from entry into the United States, unless, after considering the effect of such exclusion upon the public health and welfare, competitive conditions in the United States economy, the production of like or directly competitive articles in the United States, and United States consumers, it finds that such articles should not be excluded from entry. The Commission shall notify the Secretary of the Treasury of its action under this subsection directing such exclusion from entry, and upon receipt of such notice, the Secretary shall, through the proper officers, refuse such entry, except that such articles shall be entitled to entry under bond prescribed by the Secretary in an amount determined by the Commission to be sufficient to protect the complainant from any injury. If the Commission later determines that the respondent has violated the provisions of this section, the bond may be forfeited to the complainant.

(2) A complainant may petition the Commission for the issuance of an order under this subsection. The Commission shall make a determination with regard to such petition by no later than the 90th day after the date on which the Commission's notice of investigation is published in the Federal Register. The Commission may extend the 90–day period for an additional 60 days in a case it designates as a more complicated case. The Commission shall publish in the Federal Register its reasons why it designated the case as being more complicated. The Commission may require the complainant to post a bond as a prerequisite to the issuance of an order under this subsection. If the Commission later determines that the respondent has not violated the provisions of this section, the bond may be forfeited to the respondent.

(3) The Commission may grant preliminary relief under this subsection or subsection (f) to the same extent as preliminary injunctions and temporary restraining orders may be granted under the Federal Rules of Civil Procedure.

(4) The Commission shall prescribe the terms and conditions under which bonds may be forfeited under paragraphs (1) and (2).

(f) Cease and desist orders; civil penalty for violation of orders.

(1) In addition to, or in lieu of taking action under subsection (d) or (e), the Commission may issue and cause to be served on any person violating this section, or believed to be violating this section, as the case may be, an order directing such person to cease and desist from engaging in the unfair methods or acts involved, unless after considering the effect of such order upon the public health and welfare, competitive conditions in the United States economy, the production of like or directly competitive articles in the United States, and United States consumers, it finds that such order should not be issued. The Commission may at any time, upon such notice and in such manner as it deems proper, modify or revoke any such order, and, in the case of a revocation, may take action under subsection (d) or (e), as the case may be. If a temporary cease and desist order is issued in addition to, or in lieu of, an exclusion order under subsection (e), the Commission may require the complainant to post a bond, in an amount determined by the Commission to be sufficient to protect the respondent from any injury, as a prerequisite to the issuance of an order under this subsection. If the Commission later determines that the respondent has not violated the provisions of this section, the bond may be forfeited to the respondent. The Commission shall prescribe the terms and conditions under which the bonds may be forfeited under this paragraph.

(2) Any person who violates an order issued by the Commission under paragraph (1) after it has become final shall forfeit and pay to the United States a civil penalty for each day on which an importation of articles, or their sale, occurs in violation of the order of not more than the greater of $100,000 or twice the domestic value of the articles entered or sold on such day in violation of the order. Such penalty shall accrue to the United States and may be recovered for the United States in a civil action brought by the Commission in the Federal District Court for the District of Columbia or for the district in which the violation occurs. In such actions, the United States district courts may issue mandatory injunctions incorporating the relief sought by the Commission as they deem appropriate in the enforcement of such final orders of the Commission.

(g) Filing of complaint; exclusion.

(1) If—

(A) a complaint is filed against a person under this section;

(B) the complaint and a notice of investigation are served on the person;

(C) the person fails to respond to the complaint and notice or otherwise fails to appear to answer the complaint and notice;

(D) the person fails to show good cause why the person should not be found in default; and

(E) the complainant seeks relief limited solely to that person; the Commission shall presume the facts alleged in the complaint to be true and shall, upon request, issue an exclusion from entry or a cease and desist order, or both, limited to that person unless, after considering the effect of such exclusion or order upon the public health and welfare, competitive conditions in the United States economy, the production of like or directly competitive articles in the United States, and United States consumers, the Commission finds that such exclusion or order should not be issued.

(2) In addition to the authority of the Commission to issue a general exclusion from entry of articles when a respondent appears to contest an investigation concerning a violation of the provisions of this section, a general exclusion from entry of articles, regardless of the source or importer of the articles, may be issued if—

(A) no person appears to contest an investigation concerning a violation of the provisions of this section,

(B) such a violation is established by substantial, reliable, and probative evidence, and

(C) the requirements of subsection (d)(2) are met.

(h) Sanctions for abuse of discovery and abuse of process. The Commission may by rule prescribe sanctions for abuse of discovery and abuse of process to the extent authorized by Rule 11 and Rule 37 of the Federal Rules of Civil Procedure.

(i) Forfeiture.

(1) In addition to taking action under subsection (d), the Commission may issue an order providing that any article imported in violation of the provisions of this section be seized and forfeited to the United States if—

(A) the owner, importer, or consignee of the article previously attempted to import the article into the United States;

(B) the article was previously denied entry into the United States by reason of an order issued under subsection (d); and

(C) upon such previous denial of entry, the Secretary of the Treasury provided the owner, importer, or consignee of the article written notice of—

(i) such order, and

(ii) the seizure and forfeiture that would result from any further attempt to import the article into the United States.

(2) The Commission shall notify the Secretary of the Treasury of any order issued under this subsection and, upon receipt of such notice, the Secretary of the Treasury shall enforce such order in accordance with the provisions of this section.

(3) Upon the attempted entry of articles subject to an order issued under this subsection, the Secretary of the Treasury shall immediately notify all ports of entry of the attempted importation and shall identify the persons notified under paragraph (1)(C).

(4) The Secretary of the Treasury shall provide—

(A) the written notice described in paragraph (1)(C) to the owner, importer, or consignee of any article that is denied entry into the United States by reason of an order issued under subsection (d); and

(B) a copy of such written notice to the Commission.

(j) Referral to President.

(1) If the Commission determines that there is a violation of this section, or that, for purposes of subsection (e), there is reason to believe that there is such a violation, it shall—

(A) publish such determination in the Federal Register, and

(B) transmit to the President a copy of such determination and the action taken under subsection (d), (e), (f), (g), or (i), with respect thereto, together with the record upon which such determination is based.

(2) If, before the close of the 60–day period beginning on the day after the day on which he receives a copy of such determination, the President, for policy reasons, disapproves such determination and notifies the Commission of his disapproval, then, effective on the date of such notice, such determination and the action taken under subsection (d), (e), (f), (g), or (i) with respect thereto shall have no force or effect.

(3) Subject to the provisions of paragraph (2), such determination shall, except for purposes of subsection (c), be effective upon publication thereof in the Federal Register, and the action taken under subsection (d), (e), (f), (g), or (i) with respect thereto shall be effective as provided in such subsections, except that articles directed to be excluded from entry under subsection (d) or subject to a cease and desist order under subsection (f) shall, until such determination becomes final, be entitled to entry under bond prescribed by the Secretary in an amount determined by the Commission to be sufficient to protect the complainant from any injury. If the determination becomes final, the bond may be forfeited to the complainant. The Commission shall prescribe the terms and conditions under which bonds may be forfeited under this paragraph.

(4) If the President does not disapprove such determination within such 60–day period, or if he notifies the Commission before the close of such period that he approves such determination, then, for purposes of paragraph (3) and subsection (c) such determination shall become final on the day after the close of such period or the day on which the President notifies the Commission of his approval, as the case may be.

(k) Period of effectiveness; termination of violation or modification or rescission of exclusion or order.

(1) Except as provided in subsections (f) and (j), any exclusion from entry or order under this section shall continue in effect until the Commission finds, and in the case of exclusion from entry notifies the Secretary of the Treasury, that the conditions which led to such exclusion from entry or order no longer exist.

(2) If any person who has previously been found by the Commission to be in violation of this section petitions the Commission for a determination that the petitioner is no longer in violation of this section or for a modification or rescission of an exclusion from entry or order under subsection (d), (e), (f), (g), or (i)—

(A) the burden of proof in any proceeding before the Commission regarding such petition shall be on the petitioner; and

(B) relief may be granted by the Commission with respect to such petition—

(i) on the basis of new evidence or evidence that could not have been presented at the prior proceeding, or

(ii) on grounds which would permit relief from a judgment or order under the Federal Rules of Civil Procedure.

(*l*) **Importations by or for United States.** Any exclusion from entry or order under subsection (d), (e), (f), (g), or (i) in cases based on a proceeding involving a patent copyright, mask work, or design under subsection (a)(1), shall not apply to any articles imported by and for the use of the United States, or imported for, and to be used for, the United States with the authorization or consent of the Government. Whenever any article would have been excluded from entry or would not have been entered pursuant to the provisions of such subsections but for the operation of this subsection, an owner of the patent, copyright, mask work, or design adversely affected shall be entitled to reasonable and entire compensation in an action before the United States Court of Federal Claims pursuant to the procedures of section 1498 of title 28, United States Code.

(m) **Definition of United States.** For purposes of this section and sections 338 and 340, the term "United States" means the customs territory of the United States as defined in general note 2 of the Harmonized Tariff Schedule of the United States.

(n) **Disclosure.**

(1) Information submitted to the Commission or exchanged among the parties in connection with proceedings under this section which is properly designated as confidential pursuant to Commission rules may not be disclosed (except under a protective order issued under regulations of the Commission which authorizes limited disclosure of such information) to any person (other than a person described in paragraph (2)) without the consent of the person submitting it.

(2) Notwithstanding the prohibition contained in paragraph (1), information referred to in that paragraph may be disclosed to—

(A) an officer or employee of the Commission who is directly concerned with—

(i) carrying out the investigation or related proceeding in connection with which the information is submitted,

(ii) the administration of a bond posted pursuant to subsection (e), (f), or (j),

(iii) the administration or enforcement of an exclusion order issued pursuant to subsection (d), (e), or (g), a cease and desist order issued pursuant to subsection (f), or a consent order issued pursuant to subsection (c),

(iv) proceedings for the modification or rescission of a temporary or permanent order issued under subsection (d), (e), (f), (g), or (i), or a consent order issued under this section, or

(v) maintaining the administrative record of the investigation or related proceeding,

(B) an officer or employee of the United States Government who is directly involved in the review under subsection (j), or

(C) an officer or employee of the United States Customs Service who is directly involved in administering an exclusion from entry under subsection (d), (e), or (g) resulting from the investigation or related proceeding in connection with which the information is submitted.

19 USC 1401a

Sec. 402. Value

(a) In general. (1) Except as otherwise specifically provided for in this Act, imported merchandise shall be appraised, for the purposes of this Act, on the basis of the following:

(A) The transaction value provided for under subsection (b).

(B) The transaction value of identical merchandise provided for under subsection (c), if the value referred to in subparagraph (A) cannot be determined, or can be determined but cannot be used by reason of subsection (b)(2).

(C) The transaction value of similar merchandise provided for under subsection (c), if the value referred to in subparagraph (B) cannot be determined.

(D) The deductive value provided for under subsection (d), if the value referred to in subparagraph (C) cannot be determined and if the importer does not request alternative valuation under paragraph (2).

(E) The computed value provided for under subsection (e), if the value referred to in subparagraph (D) cannot be determined.

(F) The value provided for under subsection (f), if the value referred to in subparagraph (E) cannot be determined.

(2) If the value referred to in paragraph (1)(C) cannot be determined with respect to imported merchandise, the merchandise shall be appraised on the basis of the computed value provided for under paragraph (1)(E), rather than the deductive value provided for under paragraph (1)(D), if the importer makes a request to that effect to the customs officer concerned within such time as the Secretary shall prescribe. If the computed value of the merchandise cannot subsequently be determined, the merchandise may not be appraised on the basis of the value referred to in paragraph (1)(F) unless the deductive value of the merchandise cannot be determined under paragraph (1)(D).

(3) Upon written request therefor by the importer of merchandise, and subject to provisions of law regarding the disclosure of information, the customs officer concerned shall provide the importer with a written explanation of how the value of that merchandise was determined under this section.

(b) Transaction value of imported merchandise. (1) The transaction value of imported merchandise is the price actually paid or payable for the merchandise when sold for exportation to the United States, plus amounts equal to—

(A) the packing costs incurred by the buyer with respect to the imported merchandise;

(B) any selling commission incurred by the buyer with respect to the imported merchandise;

(C) the value, apportioned as appropriate, of any assist;

(D) any royalty or license fee related to the imported merchandise that the buyer is required to pay, directly or indirectly, as a condition of the sale of the imported merchandise for exportation to the United States; and

(E) the proceeds of any subsequent resale, disposal, or use of the imported merchandise that accrue, directly or indirectly, to the seller.

The price actually paid or payable for imported merchandise shall be increased by the amounts attributable to the items (and no others) described in subparagraphs (A) through (E) only to the extent that each such amount (i) is not otherwise included within the price actually paid or payable; and (ii) is based on sufficient information. If sufficient information is not available, for any reason, with respect to any amount referred to in the preceding sentence, the transaction value of the imported merchandise concerned shall be treated, for purposes of this section, as one that cannot be determined.

(2)(A) The transaction value of imported merchandise determined under paragraph (1) shall be the appraised value of that merchandise for the purposes of this Act only if—

(i) there are no restrictions on the disposition or use of the imported merchandise by the buyer other than restrictions that—

(I) are imposed or required by law,

(II) limit the geographical area in which the merchandise may be resold, or

(III) do not substantially affect the value of the merchandise;

(ii) the sale of, or the price actually paid or payable for, the imported merchandise is not subject to any condition or consideration for which a value cannot be determined with respect to the imported merchandise;

(iii) no part of the proceeds of any subsequent resale, disposal, or use of the imported merchandise by the buyer will accrue directly or indirectly to the seller, unless an appropriate adjustment therefor can be made under paragraph (1)(E); and

(iv) the buyer and seller are not related, or the buyer and seller are related but the transaction value is acceptable, for purposes of this subsection, under subparagraph (B).

(B) The transaction value between a related buyer and seller is acceptable for the purposes of this subsection if an examination of the circumstances of the sale of the imported merchandise indicates that the relationship between such buyer and seller did not influence the price actually paid or payable; or if the transaction value of the imported merchandise closely approximates—

(i) the transaction value of identical merchandise, or of similar merchandise, in sales to unrelated buyers in the United States;

(ii) the deductive value or computed value for identical merchandise or similar merchandise;

but only if each value referred to in clause (i) or (ii) that is used for comparison relates to merchandise that was exported to the United States at or about the same time as the imported merchandise.

(C) In applying the values used for comparison purposes under subparagraph (B), there shall be taken into account differences with respect to the sales involved (if such differences are based on sufficient information whether supplied by the buyer or otherwise available to the customs officer concerned) in—

(i) commercial levels;

(ii) quantity levels;

(iii) the costs, commissions, values, fees, and proceeds described in paragraph (1); and

(iv) the costs incurred by the seller in sales in which he and the buyer are not related that are not incurred by the seller in sales in which he and the buyer are related.

(3) The transaction value of imported merchandise does not include any of the following, if identified separately from the price actually paid or payable and from any cost or other item referred to in paragraph (1):

(A) Any reasonable cost or charge that is incurred for—

(i) the construction, erection, assembly, or maintenance of, or the technical assistance provided with respect to, the merchandise after its importation into the United States; or

(ii) the transportation of the merchandise after such importation.

(B) The customs duties and other Federal taxes currently payable on the imported merchandise by reason of its importation, and any Federal excise tax on, or measured by the value of, such merchandise for which vendors in the United States are ordinarily liable.

(4) For purposes of this subsection—

(A) The term "price actually paid or payable" means the total payment (whether direct or indirect, and exclusive of any costs, charges, or expenses incurred for transportation, insurance, and related services incident to the international shipment of the merchandise from the country of exportation to the place of importation in the United States) made, or to be made, for imported merchandise by the buyer to, or for the benefit of, the seller.

(B) Any rebate of, or other decrease in, the price actually paid or payable that is made or otherwise effected between the buyer and seller after the date of the importation of the merchandise into the United

States shall be disregarded in determining the transaction value under paragraph (1).

(c) Transaction value of identical merchandise and similar merchandise. (1) The transaction value of identical merchandise, or of similar merchandise, is the transaction value (acceptable as the appraised value for purposes of this Act under subsection (b) but adjusted under paragraph (2) of this subsection) of imported merchandise that is—

(A) with respect to the merchandise being appraised, either identical merchandise or similar merchandise, as the case may be; and

(B) exported to the United States at or about the time that the merchandise being appraised is exported to the United States.

(2) Transaction values determined under this subsection shall be based on sales of identical merchandise or similar merchandise, as the case may be, at the same commercial level and in substantially the same quantity as the sales of the merchandise being appraised. If no such sale is found, sales of identical merchandise or similar merchandise at either a different commercial level or in different quantities, or both, shall be used, but adjusted to take account of any such difference. Any adjustment made under this paragraph shall be based on sufficient information. If in applying this paragraph with respect to any imported merchandise, two or more transaction values for identical merchandise, or for similar merchandise, are determined, such imported merchandise shall be appraised on the basis of the lower or lowest of such values.

(d) Deductive value. (1) For purposes of this subsection, the term "merchandise concerned" means the merchandise being appraised, identical merchandise, or similar merchandise.

(2)(A) The deductive value of the merchandise being appraised is whichever of the following prices (as adjusted under paragraph (3)) is appropriate depending upon when and in what condition the merchandise concerned is sold in the United States:

(i) If the merchandise concerned is sold in the condition as imported at or about the date of importation of the merchandise being appraised, the price is the unit price at which the merchandise concerned is sold in the greatest aggregate quantity at or about such date.

(ii) If the merchandise concerned is sold in the condition as imported but not sold at or about the date of importation of the merchandise being appraised, the price is the unit price at which the merchandise concerned is sold in the greatest aggregate quantity after the date of importation of the merchandise being appraised but before the close of the 90th day after the date of such importation.

(iii) If the merchandise concerned was not sold in the condition as imported and not sold before the close of the 90th day after the date of importation of the merchandise being appraised, the price is the unit price at which the merchandise being appraised, after further processing, is sold in the greatest aggregate quantity before the 180th day after the date of such importation. This clause shall apply to appraisement of merchandise only if the importer so elects and notifies the customs officer concerned of that election within such time as shall be prescribed by the Secretary.

(B) For purposes of subparagraph (A), the unit price at which merchandise is sold in the greatest aggregate quantity is the unit price at which such merchandise is sold to unrelated persons, at the first commercial level after importation (in cases to which subparagraph (A) (i) or (ii) applies) or after further processing (in cases to which subparagraph (A)(iii) applies) at which such sales take place, in a total volume that is (i) greater than the total volume sold at any other unit price, and (ii) sufficient to establish the unit price.

(3)(A) The price determined under paragraph (2) shall be reduced by an amount equal to—

(i) any commission usually paid or agreed to be paid, or the addition usually made for profit and general expenses, in connection with sales in the United States of imported merchandise that is of the same class or kind, regardless of the country of exportation, as the merchandise concerned;

(ii) the actual costs and associated costs of transportation and insurance incurred with respect to international shipments of the merchandise concerned from the country of exportation to the United States;

(iii) the usual costs and associated costs of transportation and insurance incurred with respect to shipments of such merchandise from the place of importation to the place of delivery in the United States, if such costs are not included as a general expense under clause (i);

(iv) the customs duties and other Federal taxes currently payable on the merchandise concerned by reason of its importation, and any Federal excise tax on, or measured by the value of, such merchandise for which vendors in the United States are ordinarily liable; and

(v) (but only in the case of a price determined under paragraph (2)(A)(iii)) the value added by the processing of the merchandise after importation to the extent that the value is based on sufficient information relating to cost of such processing.

(B) For purposes of applying paragraph (A)—

(i) the deduction made for profits and general expenses shall be based upon the importer's profits and general expenses, unless such profits and general expenses are inconsistent with those reflected in sales in the United States of imported merchandise of the same class or kind, in which case the deduction shall be based on the usual profit and general expenses reflected in such sales, as determined from sufficient information; and

(ii) any State or local tax imposed on the importer with respect to the sale of imported merchandise shall be treated as a general expense.

(C) The price determined under paragraph (2) shall be increased (but only to the extent that such costs are not otherwise included) by an amount equal to the packing costs incurred by the importer or the buyer, as the case may be, with respect to the merchandise concerned.

(D) For purposes of determining the deductive value of imported merchandise, any sale to a person who supplies any assist for use in connection with the production or sale for export of the merchandise concerned shall be disregarded.

(e) Computed value. (1) The computed value of imported merchandise is the sum of—

(A) the cost or value of the materials and the fabrication and other processing of any kind employed in the production of the imported merchandise;

(B) an amount for profit and general expenses equal to that usually reflected in sales of merchandise of the same class or kind as the imported merchandise that are made by the producers in the country of exportation for export to the United States;

(C) any assist, if its value is not included under subparagraph (A) or (B); and

(D) the packing costs.

(2) For purposes of paragraph (1)—

(A) the cost or value of materials under paragraph (1)(A) shall not include the amount of any internal tax imposed by the country of exportation that is directly applicable to the materials or their disposition if the tax is remitted or refunded upon the exportation of the merchandise in the production of which the materials were used; and

(B) the amount for profit and general expenses under paragraph (1)(B) shall be based upon the producer's profits and expenses, unless the producer's profits and expenses are inconsistent with those usually reflected in sales of merchandise of the same class or kind as the imported merchandise that are made by producers in the country of exportation for export to the United States, in which case the amount under paragraph (1)(B) shall be based on the usual profit and general expenses of such producers in such sales, as determined from sufficient information.

(f) Value if other values cannot be determined or used. (1) If the value of imported merchandise cannot be determined, or otherwise used for the purposes of this Act, under subsections (b) through (e), the merchandise shall be appraised for the purposes of this Act on the basis of a value that is derived from the methods set forth in such subsections, with such methods being reasonably adjusted to the extent necessary to arrive at a value.

(2) Imported merchandise may not be appraised, for the purposes of this Act, on the basis of—

(A) the selling price in the United States of merchandise produced in the United States;

(B) a system that provides for the appraisement of imported merchandise at the higher of two alternative values;

(C) the price of merchandise in the domestic market of the country of exportation;

(D) a cost of production, other than a value determined under subsection (e) for merchandise that is identical merchandise or similar merchandise to the merchandise being appraised;

(E) the price of merchandise for export to a country other than the United States;

(F) minimum values for appraisement; or

(G) arbitrary or fictitious values.

This paragraph shall not apply with respect to the ascertainment, determination, or estimation of foreign market value or United States price under title VII.

(g) Special rules. (1) For purposes of this section, the persons specified in any of the following subparagraphs shall be treated as persons who are related:

(A) Members of the same family, including brothers and sisters (whether by whole or half blood), spouse, ancestors, and lineal descendants.

(B) Any officer or director of an organization and such organization.

(C) An officer or director of an organization and an officer or director of another organization, if each such individual is also an officer or director in the other organization.

(D) Partners.

(E) Employer and employee.

(F) Any person directly or indirectly owning, controlling, or holding with power to vote, 5 percent or more of the outstanding voting stock or shares of any organization and such organization.

(G) Two or more persons directly or indirectly controlling, controlled by, or under common control with, any person.

(2) For purposes of this section, merchandise (including, but not limited to, identical merchandise and similar merchandise) shall be treated as being of the same class or kind as other merchandise if it is within a group or range of merchandise produced by a particular industry or industry sector.

(3) For purposes of this section, information that is submitted by an importer, buyer, or producer in regard to the appraisement of merchandise may not be rejected by the customs officer concerned on the basis of the accounting method by which that information was prepared, if the preparation was in accordance with generally accepted accounting principles. The term "generally accepted accounting principles" refers to any generally recognized consensus or substantial authoritative support regarding—

(A) which economic resources and obligations should be recorded as assets and liabilities;

(B) which changes in assets and liabilities should be recorded;

(C) how the assets and liabilities and changes in them should be measured;

(D) what information should be disclosed and how it should be disclosed; and

(E) which financial statements should be prepared.

The applicability of a particular set of generally accepted accounting principles will depend upon the basis on which the value of the merchandise is sought to be established.

(h) Definitions. As used in this section—

(1)(A) The term "assist" means any of the following if supplied directly or indirectly, and free of charge or at reduced cost, by the buyer of imported merchandise for use in connection with the production or the sale for export to the United States of the merchandise:

(i) Materials, components, parts, and similar items incorporated in the imported merchandise.

(ii) Tools, dies, molds, and similar items used in the production of the imported merchandise.

(iii) Merchandise consumed in the production of the imported merchandise.

(iv) Engineering, development, artwork, design work, and plans and sketches that are undertaken elsewhere than in the United States and are necessary for the production of the imported merchandise.

(B) No service or work to which subparagraph (A)(iv) applies shall be treated as an assist for purposes of this section if such service or work—

(i) is performed by an individual who is domiciled within the United States;

(ii) is performed by that individual while he is acting as an employee or agent of the buyer of the imported merchandise; and

(iii) is incidental to other engineering, development, artwork, design work, or plans or sketches that are undertaken within the United States.

(C) For purposes of this section, the following apply in determining the value of assists described in subparagraph (A)(iv):

(i) The value of an assist that is available in the public domain is the cost of obtaining copies of the assist.

(ii) If the production of an assist occurred in the United States and one or more foreign countries, the value of the assist is the value thereof that is added outside the United States.

(2) The term "identical merchandise" means—

(A) merchandise that is identical in all respects to, and was produced in the same country and by the same person as, the merchandise being appraised; or

(B) if merchandise meeting the requirements under subparagraph (A) cannot be found (or for purposes of applying subsection (b)(2)(B)(i), regardless of whether merchandise meeting such requirements can be found), merchandise that is identical in all respects to, and was produced in the same country as, but not produced by the same person as, the merchandise being appraised.

Such term does not include merchandise that incorporates or reflects any engineering, development, artwork, design work, or plan or sketch that—

(I) was supplied free or at reduced cost by the buyer of the merchandise for use in connection with the production or the sale for export to the United States of the merchandise; and

(II) is not an assist because undertaken within the United States.

(3) The term "packing costs" means the cost of all containers and coverings of whatever nature and of packing, whether for labor or materials, used in placing merchandise in condition, packed ready for shipment to the United States.

(4) The term "similar merchandise" means—

(A) merchandise that—

(i) was produced in the same country and by the same person as the merchandise being appraised,

(ii) is like the merchandise being appraised in characteristics and component material, and

(iii) is commercially interchangeable with the merchandise being appraised; or

(B) if merchandise meeting the requirements under subparagraph (A) cannot be found (or for purposes of applying subsection (b)(2)(B)(i), regardless of whether merchandise meeting such requirements can be found), merchandise that—

(i) was produced in the same country as, but not produced by the same person as, the merchandise being appraised, and

(ii) meets the requirement set forth in subparagraph (A)(ii) and (iii).

Such term does not include merchandise that incorporates or reflects any engineering, development, artwork, design work, or plan or sketch that—

(I) was supplied free or at reduced cost by the buyer of the merchandise for use in connection with the production or the sale for export to the United States of the merchandise; and

(II) is not an assist because undertaken within the United States.

(5) The term "sufficient information", when required under this section for determining—

(A) any amount—

(i) added under subsection (b)(1) to the price actually paid or payable,

(ii) deducted under subsection (d)(3) as profit or general expense or value from further processing, or

(iii) added under subsection (e)(2) as profit or general expense;

(B) any difference taken into account for purposes of subsection (b)(2)(C); or

(C) any adjustment made under subsection (c)(2);

means information that establishes the accuracy of such amount, difference, or adjustment.

19 USC 1516a

Sec. 516a.   Judicial Review in Countervailing Duty and Antidumping Duty Proceedings

(a) Review of determination.

(1) Review of certain determinations. Within 30 days after the date of publication in the Federal Register of—

(A) a determination by the administering authority, under [section] 702(c) or 732(c) of this Act, not to initiate an investigation,

(B) a determination by the Commission, under section 751(b) of this Act, not to review a determination based upon changed circumstances,

(C) a negative determination by the Commission, under section 703(a) or 733(a) of this Act, as to whether there is reasonable indication of material injury, threat of material injury, or material retardation, or

(D) a final determination by the administering authority or the Commission under section 751(c)(3),

an interested party who is a party to the proceeding in connection with which the matter arises may commence an action in the United States Court of International Trade by filing concurrently a summons and complaint, each with the content and in the form, manner, and style prescribed by the rules of that court, contesting any factual findings or legal conclusions upon which the determination is based.

(2) Review of determinations on record.

(A) In general. Within thirty days after—

(i) the date of publication in the Federal Register of—

(I) notice of any determination described in clause (ii), (iii), (iv), (v), or (viii) of subparagraph (B),

(II) an antidumping or countervailing duty order based upon any determination described in clause (i) of subparagraph (B), or

(III) notice of the implementation of any determination described in clause (vii) of subparagraph (B), or

(ii) the date of mailing of a determination described in clause (vi) of subparagraph (B),

an interested party who is a party to the proceeding in connection with which the matter arises may commence an action in the United States Court of International Trade by filing a summons, and within thirty days thereafter a complaint, each with the content and in the form, manner, and style prescribed by the rules of that court, contesting any factual findings or legal conclusions upon which the determination is based.

(B) Reviewable determinations. The determinations which may be contested under subparagraph (A) are as follows:

(i) Final affirmative determinations by the administering authority and by the Commission under section 705 or 735 of this Act, including any negative part of such a determination (other than a part referred to in clause (ii)).

(ii) A final negative determination by the administering authority or the Commission under section 705 or 735 of this Act, including, at the option of the appellant, any part of a final affirmative determination which specifically excludes any company or product.

(iii) A final determination, other than a determination reviewable under paragraph (1), by the administering authority or the Commission under section 751 of this Act.

(iv) A determination by the administering authority, under section 704 or 734 of this Act, to suspend an antidumping duty or a countervailing duty investigation, including any final determination resulting from a continued investigation which changes the size of the dumping margin or net countervailable subsidy calculated, or the reasoning underlying such calculations, at the time the suspension agreement was concluded.

(v) An injurious effect determination by the Commission under section 704(h) or 734(h) of this Act.

(vi) A determination by the administering authority as to whether a particular type of merchandise is within the class of kind of merchandise described in an existing finding of dumping or antidumping or countervailing duty order.

(vii) A determination by the administering authority or the Commission under section 129 of the Uruguay Round Agreements Act concerning a determination under title VII of the Tariff Act of 1930.

(viii) A determination by the Commission under section 753(a)(1).

(3) Exception. Notwithstanding the limitation imposed by paragraph (2)(A)(i)(II) of this subsection, a final affirmative determination by the administering authority under section 705 or 735 of this Act may be contested by commencing an action, in accordance with the provisions of paragraph (2)(A), within thirty days after the date of publication in the Federal Register of a final negative determination by the Commission under section 705 or 735 of this Act.

(4) Procedures and fees. The procedures and fees set forth in chapter 169, of title 28, United States Code, apply to an action under this section.

(5) Time limits in cases involving merchandise from free trade area countries. Notwithstanding any other provision of this subsection, in the case of a determination to which the provisions of subsection (g) apply, an action under this subsection may not be commenced, and the time limits for commencing an action under this subsection shall not begin to run, until the day specified in whichever of the following subparagraphs applies:

(A) For a determination described in paragraph (1)(B) or clause (i), (ii) or (iii) of paragraph (2)(B), the 31st day after the date on which notice of the determination is published in the Federal Register.

(B) For a determination described in clause (vi) of paragraph (2)(B), the 31st day after the date on which the government of the relevant FTA country receives notice of the determination.

(C) For a determination with respect to which binational panel review has commenced in accordance with subsection (g)(8), the day after the date as of which—

(i) the binational panel has dismissed binational panel review of the determination for lack of jurisdiction, and

(ii) any interested party seeking review of the determination under paragraph (1), (2), or (3) of this subsection has provided timely notice under subsection (g)(3)(B).

If such an interested party files a summons and complaint under this subsection after dismissal by the binational panel, and if a request for an extraordinary challenge committee is made with respect to the decision by the binational panel to dismiss—

(I) judicial review under this subsection shall be stayed during consideration by the committee of the request, and

(II) the United States Court of International Trade shall dismiss the action if the committee vacates or remands the binational panel decision to dismiss.

(D) For a determination for which review by the United States Court of International Trade is provided for—

(i) under subsection (g)(12)(B), the day after the date of publication in the Federal Register of notice that article 1904 of the NAFTA has been suspended, or

(ii) under subsection (g)(12)(D), the day after the date that notice of settlement is published in the Federal Register.

(E) For a determination described in clause (vii) of paragraph (2)(B), the 31st day after the date on which notice of the implementation of the determination is published in the Federal Register.

(b) Standards of review.

(1) Remedy. The court shall hold unlawful any determination, finding, or conclusion found—

(A) in an action brought under subparagraph (A), (B), or (C) of subsection (a)(1), to be arbitrary, capricious, an abuse of discretion, or otherwise not in accordance with law, or

(B) (i) in an action brought under paragraph (2) of subsection (a), to be unsupported by substantial evidence on the record, or otherwise not in accordance with law, or

(ii) in an action brought under paragraph (1)(D) of subsection (a), to be arbitrary, capricious, an abuse of discretion, or otherwise not in accordance with law.

(2) Record for review.

(A) In general. For the purposes of this subsection, the record, unless otherwise stipulated by the parties, shall consist of—

(i) a copy of all information presented to or obtained by the Secretary, the administering authority, or the Commission during the course of the administrative proceeding, including all governmental memoranda pertaining to the case and the record of ex parte meetings required to be kept by section 777(a)(3); and

(ii) a copy of the determination, all transcripts or records of conferences or hearings, and all notices published in the Federal Register.

(B) Confidential or privileged material. The confidential or privileged status accorded to any documents, comments, or information shall be preserved in any action under this section. Notwithstanding the preceding sentence, the court may examine, in camera, the confidential or privileged material, and may disclose such material under such terms and conditions as it may order.

(3) Effect of decisions by NAFTA or United States–Canada binational panels. In making a decision in any action brought under subsection (a), a court of the United States is not bound by, but may take into consideration, a final decision of a binational panel or extraordinary challenge committee convened pursuant to article 1904 of the NAFTA or of the Agreement.

(c) Liquidation of entries.

(1) Liquidation in accordance with determination. Unless such liquidation is enjoined by the court under paragraph (2) of this subsection, entries of merchandise of the character covered by a determination of the Secretary, the administering authority, or the Commission contested under subsection (a) shall be liquidated in accordance with the determination of the Secretary, the administering authority, or the Commission, if they are entered, or withdrawn from warehouse, for consumption on or before the date of publication in the Federal Register by the Secretary or the administering authority of a notice of a decision of the United States Court of International Trade, or of the United States Court of Appeals for the Federal Circuit, not in harmony with that determination. Such notice of a decision shall be published within ten days from the date of the issuance of the court decision.

(2) Injunctive relief. In the case of a determination described in paragraph (2) of subsection (a) by the Secretary, the administering authority, or the Commission, the United States Court of International Trade may enjoin the liquidation of some or all entries of merchandise covered by a determination of the Secretary, the administering authority, or the Commission, upon a request by an interested party for such relief and a proper showing that the requested relief should be granted under the circumstances.

(3) Remand for final disposition. If the final disposition of an action brought under this section is not in harmony with the published determination of the Secretary, the administering authority, or the Commission, the matter shall be remanded to the Secretary, the administering authority, or

the Commission, as appropriate, for disposition consistent with the final disposition of the court.

(d) Standing. Any interested party who was a party to the proceeding under section 303 of this Act or title VII of this Act shall have the right to appear and be heard as a party in interest before the United States Court of International Trade. The party filing the action shall notify all such interested parties of the filing of an action under this section, in the form, manner, style, and within the time prescribed by rules of the court.

(e) Liquidation in accordance with final decision. If the cause of action is sustained in whole or in part by a decision of the United States Court of International Trade or of the United States Court of Appeals for the Federal Circuit—

(1) entries of merchandise of the character covered by the published determination of the Secretary, the administering authority, or the Commission, which is entered, or withdrawn from warehouse, for consumption after the date of publication in the Federal Register by the Secretary or the administering authority of a notice of the court decision, and

(2) entries, the liquidation of which was enjoined under subsection (c)(2),

shall be liquidated in accordance with the final court decision in the action. Such notice of the court decision shall be published within ten days from the date of the issuance of the court decision.

(f) Definitions. For purposes of this section—

(1) Administering authority. The term "administering authority" means the administering authority described in section 771(1) of this Act.

(2) Commission. The term "Commission" means the United States International Trade Commission.

(3) Interested party. The term "interested party" means any person described in section 771(9) of this Act.

(4) Secretary. The term "Secretary" means the Secretary of the Treasury.

(5) Agreement. The term "Agreement" means the United States–Canada Free–Trade Agreement.

(6) United States Secretary. The term "United States Secretary" means—

(A) the secretary for the United States Section referred to in article 1908 of the NAFTA, and

(B) the secretary of the United States Section provided for in article 1909 of the Agreement.

(7) Relevant FTA Secretary. The term "relevant FTA Secretary" means the Secretary—

(A) referred to in article 1908 of the NAFTA, or

(B) provided for in paragraph 5 of article 1909 of the Agreement, of the relevant FTA country.

(8) NAFTA. The term "NAFTA" means the North American Free Trade Agreement.

(9) Relevant FTA country. The term "relevant FTA country" means the free trade area country to which an antidumping or countervailing duty proceeding pertains.

(10) Free trade area country. The term "free trade area country" means the following:

(A) Canada for such time as the NAFTA is in force with respect to, and the United States applies the NAFTA to, Canada.

(B) Mexico for such time as the NAFTA is in force with respect to, and the United States applies the NAFTA to, Mexico.

(C) Canada for such time as—

(i) it is not a free trade area country under subparagraph (A); and

(ii) the Agreement is in force with respect to, and the United States applies the Agreement to, Canada.

(g) Review of countervailing duty and antidumping duty determinations involving free trade area country merchandise.

(1) Definition of determination. For purposes of this subsection, the term "determination" means a determination described in—

(A) paragraph (1)(B) of subsection (a), or

(B) clause (i), (ii), (iii), or (vi) of paragraph (2)(B) of subsection (a), if made in connection with a proceeding regarding a class or kind of free trade area country merchandise, as determined by the administering authority.

(2) Exclusive review of determination by binational panels. If binational panel review of a determination is requested pursuant to article 1904 of the NAFTA or of the Agreement, then, except as provided in paragraphs (3) and (4)—

(A) the determination is not reviewable under subsection (a), and

(B) no court of the United States has power or jurisdiction to review the determination on any question of law or fact by an action in the nature of mandamus or otherwise.

(3) Exception to exclusive binational panel review.

(A) In general. A determination is reviewable under subsection (a) if the determination sought to be reviewed is—

(i) a determination as to which neither the United States nor the relevant FTA country requested review by a binational panel pursuant to article 1904 of the NAFTA or of the Agreement,

(ii) a revised determination issued as a direct result of judicial review, commenced pursuant to subsection (a), if neither the United States nor the relevant FTA country requested review of the original determination,

(iii) a determination issued as a direct result of judicial review that was commenced pursuant to subsection (a) prior to the entry into force of the NAFTA or of the Agreement,

(iv) a determination which a binational panel has determined is not reviewable by the binational panel,

(v) a determination as to which binational panel review has terminated pursuant to paragraph 12 of article 1905 of the NAFTA, or

(vi) a determination as to which extraordinary challenge committee review has terminated pursuant to paragraph 12 of article 1905 of the NAFTA.

(B) Special rule. A determination described in subparagraph (A)(i) or (iv) is reviewable under subsection (a) only if the party seeking to commence review has provided timely notice of its intent to commence such review to—

(i) the United States Secretary and the relevant FTA Secretary;

(ii) all interested parties who were parties to the proceeding in connection with which the matter arises; and

(iii) the administering authority or the Commission, as appropriate.

Such notice is timely provided if the notice is delivered no later than the date that is 20 days after the date described in subparagraph (A) or (B) of subsection (a)(5) that is applicable to such determination, except that, if the time for requesting binational panel review is suspended under paragraph (8)(A)(ii) of this subsection, any unexpired time for providing notice of intent to commence judicial review shall, during the pendency of any such suspension, also be suspended. Such notice shall contain such information, and be in such form, manner, and style, as the administering authority, in consultation with the Commission, shall prescribe by regulations.

(4) Exception to exclusive binational panel review for constitutional issues.

(A) Constitutionality of binational panel review system. An action for declaratory judgment or injunctive relief, or both, regarding a determination on the grounds that any provision of, or amendment made by, the North American Free Trade Agreement Implementation Act implementing the binational dispute settlement system under chapter 19 of the NAFTA, or the United States–Canada Free–Trade Agreement Implementation Act of 1988 implementing the binational panel dispute settlement system under chapter 19 of the Agreement, violates the Constitution may be brought only in the United States Court of Appeals for the District of Columbia Circuit, which shall have jurisdiction of such action.

(B) Other constitutional review. Review is available under subsection (a) with respect to a determination solely concerning a constitutional issue (other than an issue to which subparagraph (A) applies) arising under any law of the United States as enacted or applied. An action for review under this subparagraph shall be assigned to a 3–judge panel of the United States Court of International Trade.

(C) Commencement of review. Notwithstanding the time limits in subsection (a), within 30 days after the date of publication in the Federal Register of notice that binational panel review has been completed, an interested party who is a party to the proceeding in connection with which the matter arises may commence an action under subparagraph (A) or (B) by filing an action in accordance with the rules of the court.

(D) Transfer of actions to appropriate court. Whenever an action is filed in a court under subparagraph (A) or (B) and that court finds that the action should have been filed in the other court, the court in which the action was filed shall transfer the action to the other court and the action shall proceed as if it had been filed in the court to which it is transferred on the date upon which it was actually filed in the court from which it is transferred.

(E) Frivolous claims. Frivolous claims brought under subparagraph (A) or (B) are subject to dismissal and sanctions as provided under section 1927 of title 28, United States Code, and the Federal Rules of Civil Procedure.

(F) Security.

(i) Subparagraph (A) Actions. The security requirements of rule 65(c) of the Federal Rules of Civil Procedure apply with respect to actions commenced under subparagraph (A).

(ii) Subparagraph (B) Actions. No claim shall be heard, and no temporary restraining order or temporary or permanent injunction shall be issued, under an action commenced under subparagraph (B), unless the party seeking review first files an undertaking with adequate security in an amount to be fixed by the court sufficient to recompense parties affected for any loss, expense, or damage caused by the improvident or erroneous issuance of such order or injunction. If a court upholds the constitutionality of the determination in question in such action, the court shall award to a prevailing party fees and expenses, in addition to any costs incurred by that party, unless the court finds that the position of the other party was substantially justified or that special circumstances make an award unjust.

(G) Panel record. The record of proceedings before the binational panel shall not be considered part of the record for review pursuant to subparagraph (A) or (B).

(H) Appeal to Supreme Court of court orders issued in subparagraph (A) Actions. Notwithstanding any other provision of law, any final judgment of the United States Court of Appeals for the District of Columbia Circuit which is issued pursuant to an action brought under subparagraph (A) shall be reviewable by appeal directly to the Supreme Court of the United States. Any such appeal shall be taken by a notice of appeal filed within 10 days after such order is entered; and the jurisdictional statement shall be filed within 30 days after such order is entered. No stay of an order issued pursuant to an action brought under subparagraph (A) may be issued by a single Justice of the Supreme Court.

(5) Liquidation of entries.

(A) Application. In the case of a determination for which binational panel review is requested pursuant to article 1904 of the NAFTA or of the Agreement, the rules provided in this paragraph shall apply, notwithstanding the provisions of subsection (c).

(B) General rule. In the case of a determination for which binational panel review is requested pursuant to article 1904 of the NAFTA or of the Agreement, entries of merchandise covered by such determination shall be liquidated in accordance with the determination of the administering authority or the Commission, if they are entered, or withdrawn from warehouse, for consumption on or before the date of publication in the Federal Register by the administering authority of notice of a final decision of a binational panel, or of an extraordinary challenge committee, not in harmony with that determination. Such notice of a decision shall be published within 10 days of the date of the issuance of the panel or committee decision.

(C) Suspension of liquidation.

(i) In general. Notwithstanding the provisions of subparagraph (B), in the case of a determination described in clause (iii) or (vi) of subsection (a)(2)(B) for which binational panel review is requested pursuant to article 1904 of the NAFTA or of the Agreement, the administering authority, upon request of an interested party who was a party to the proceeding in connection with which the matter arises and who is a participant in the binational panel review, shall order the continued suspension of liquidation of those entries of merchandise covered by the determination that are involved in the review pending the final disposition of the review.

(ii) Notice. At the same time as the interested party makes its request to the administering authority under clause (i), that party shall serve a copy of its request on the United States Secretary, the relevant FTA Secretary, and all interested parties who were parties to the proceeding in connection with which the matter arises.

(iii) Application of suspension. If the interested party requesting continued suspension of liquidation under clause (i) is a foreign manufacturer, producer, or exporter, or a United States importer, the continued suspension of liquidation shall apply only to entries of merchandise manufactured, produced, exported, or imported by that particular manufacturer, producer, exporter, or importer. If the interested party requesting the continued suspension of liquidation under clause (i) is an interested party described in subparagraph (C), (D), (E), or (F) of section 771(9), the continued suspension of liquidation shall apply only to entries which could be affected by a decision of the binational panel convened under chapter 19 of the NAFTA or of the Agreement.

(iv) Judicial review. Any action taken by the administering authority or the United States Customs Service under this subparagraph shall not be subject to judicial review, and no court of the United States shall have power or jurisdiction to review such action on any question of law or fact by an action in the nature of mandamus or otherwise.

(6) *Injunctive relief.* Except for cases under paragraph (4)(B), in the case of a determination for which binational panel review is requested pursuant to article 1904 of the NAFTA or of the Agreement, the provisions of subsection (c)(2) shall not apply.

(7) Implementation of international obligations under article 1904 of the NAFTA or the Agreement.

(A) Action upon remand. If a determination is referred to a binational panel or extraordinary challenge committee under the NAFTA or the Agreement and the panel or committee makes a decision remanding the determination to the administering authority or the Commission, the administering authority or the Commission shall, within the period specified by the panel or committee, take action not inconsistent with the decision of the panel or committee. Any action taken by the administering authority or the Commission under this paragraph shall not be subject to judicial review, and no court of the United States shall have power or jurisdiction to review such action on any question of law or fact by an action in the nature of mandamus or otherwise.

(B) Application if subparagraph (A) held unconstitutional. In the event that the provisions of subparagraph (A) are held unconstitutional under the provisions of subparagraphs (A) and (H) of paragraph (4), the provisions of this subparagraph shall take effect. In such event, the President is authorized on behalf of the United States to accept, as a whole, the decision of a binational panel or extraordinary challenge committee remanding the determination to the administering authority or the Commission within the period specified by the panel or committee. Upon acceptance by the President of such a decision, the administering authority or the Commission shall, within the period specified by the panel or committee, take action not inconsistent with such decision. Any action taken by the President, the administering authority, or the Commission under this subparagraph shall not be subject to judicial review, and no court of the United States shall have power or jurisdiction to review such action on any question of law or fact by an action in the nature of mandamus or otherwise.

(8) Requests for binational panel review.

(A) Interested party requests for binational panel review.

(i) General rule. An interested party who was a party to the proceeding in which a determination is made may request binational panel review of such determination by filing a request with the United States Secretary by no later than the date that is 30 days after the date described in subparagraph (A), (B), or (E) of subsection (a)(5) that is applicable to such determination. Receipt of such request by the United States Secretary shall be deemed to be a request for binational panel review within the meaning of article 1904(4) of the NAFTA or of the Agreement. Such request shall contain such information and be in such form, manner, and style as the administering authority, in consultation with the Commission, shall prescribe by regulations.

(ii) Suspension of time to request binational panel review under the NAFTA. Notwithstanding clause (i), the time for requesting binational panel review shall be suspended during the pendency of any stay of binational panel review that is issued pursuant to paragraph 11(a) of article 1905 of the NAFTA.

(B) Service of request for binational panel review.

(i) Service by interested party. If a request for binational panel review of a determination is filed under subparagraph (A), the party making the request shall serve a copy, by mail or personal service, on any other interested party who was a party to the proceeding in connection with which the matter arises, and on the administering authority or the Commission, as appropriate.

(ii) Service by United States Secretary. If an interested party to the proceeding requests binational panel review of a determination by filing a request with the relevant FTA Secretary, the United States Secretary shall serve a copy of the request by mail on any other interested party who was a party to the proceeding in connection with which the matter arises, and on the administering authority or the Commission, as appropriate.

(C) Limitation on request for binational panel review. Absent a request by an interested party under subparagraph (A), the United States may not request binational panel review of a determination under article 1904 of the NAFTA or the Agreement.

(9) Representation in panel proceedings. In the case of binational panel proceedings convened under chapter 19 of the NAFTA or of the Agreement, the administering authority and the Commission shall be represented by attorneys who are employees of the administering authority or the Commission, respectively. Interested parties who were parties to the proceeding in connection with which the matter arises shall have the right to appear and be represented by counsel before the binational panel.

(10) Notification of class or kind rulings. In the case of a determination which is described in paragraph (2)(B)(vi) of subsection (a) and which is subject to the provisions of paragraph (2), the administering authority, upon request, shall inform any interested person of the date on which the Government of the relevant FTA country received notice of the determination under paragraph 4 of article 1904 of the NAFTA or the Agreement.

(11) Suspension and termination of suspension of article 1904 of the NAFTA.

(A) Suspension of article 1904. If a special committee established under article 1905 of the NAFTA issues an affirmative finding, the Trade Representative may, in accordance with paragraph 8(a) or 9, as appropriate, of article 1905 of the NAFTA, suspend the operation of article 1904 of the NAFTA.

(B) Termination of suspension of article 1904. If a special committee is reconvened and makes an affirmative determination described in paragraph 10(b) of article 1905 of the NAFTA, any suspension of the operation of article 1904 of the NAFTA shall terminate.

(12) Judicial review upon termination of binational panel or committee review under the NAFTA.

(A) Notice of suspension or termination of suspension of article 1904.

(i) Upon notification by the Trade Representative or the Government of a country described in subsection (f)(10) (A) or (B) that the operation of article 1904 of the NAFTA has been suspended in accordance with paragraph 8(a) or 9 of article 1905 of the NAFTA, the United States Secretary shall publish in the Federal Register a notice of suspension of article 1904 of the NAFTA.

(ii) Upon notification by the Trade Representative or the Government of a country described in subsection (f)(10) (A) or (B) that the suspension of the operation of article 1904 of the NAFTA is terminated in accordance with paragraph 10 of article 1905 of the NAFTA, the United States Secretary shall publish in the Federal Register a notice of termination of suspension of article 1904 of the NAFTA.

(B) Transfer of final determinations for judicial review upon suspension of article 1904. If the operation of article 1904 of the NAFTA is suspended in accordance with paragraph 8(a) or 9 of article 1905 of the NAFTA—

(i) upon the request of an authorized person described in subparagraph (C), any final determination that is the subject of a binational panel review or an extraordinary challenge committee review shall be transferred to the United States Court of International Trade (in accordance with rules issued by the Court) for review under subsection (a); or

(ii) in a case in which—

(I) a binational panel review was completed fewer than 30 days before the suspension, and

(II) extraordinary challenge committee review has not been requested,

upon the request of an authorized person described in subparagraph (C) which is made within 60 days after the completion of the binational panel review, the final determination that was the subject of the binational panel review shall be transferred to the United States Court of International Trade (in accordance with rules issued by the Court) for review under subsection (a).

(C) Persons authorized to request transfer of final determinations for judicial review. A request that a final determination be transferred to the Court of International Trade under subparagraph (B) may be made by—

(i) if the United States made an allegation under paragraph 1 of article 1905 of the NAFTA and the operation of article 1904 of the NAFTA was suspended pursuant to paragraph 8(a) of article 1905 of the NAFTA—

(I) the government of the relevant country described in subsection (f)(10) (A) or (B),

(II) an interested party that was a party to the panel or committee review, or

(III) an interested party that was a party to the proceeding in connection with which panel review was requested, but only if the time period for filing notices of appearance in the panel review has not expired, or

(ii) if a country described in subsection (f)(10) (A) or (B) made an allegation under paragraph 1 of article 1905 of the NAFTA and the operation of article 1904 of the NAFTA was suspended pursuant to paragraph 9 of article 1905 of the NAFTA—

(I) the government of that country,

(II) an interested party that is a person of that country and that was a party to the panel or committee review, or

(III) an interested party that is a person of that country and that was a party to the proceeding in connection with which panel review was requested, but only if the time period for filing notices of appearance in the panel review has not expired.

(D) Transfer for judicial review upon settlement.

(i) If the Trade Representative achieves a settlement with the government of a country described in subsection (f)(10) (A) or (B) pursuant to paragraph 7 of article 1905 of the NAFTA, and referral for judicial review is among the terms of such settlement, any final determination that is the subject of a binational panel review or an extraordinary challenge committee review shall, upon a request described in clause (ii), be transferred to the United States Court of International Trade (in accordance with rules issued by the Court) for review under subsection (a).

(ii) A request referred to in clause (i) is a request made by—

(I) the country referred to in clause (i),

(II) an interested party that was a party to the panel or committee review, or

(III) an interested party that was a party to the proceeding in connection with which panel review was requested, but only if the time for filing notices of appearance in the panel review has not expired.

TITLE VII

COUNTERVAILING AND ANTIDUMPING DUTIES

Subtitle A

Imposition of Countervailing Duties

19 USC 1671

Sec. 701. Countervailing Duties Imposed

(a) General Rule. If—

(1) the administering authority determines that the government of a country or any public entity within the territory of a country is providing, directly or indirectly, a countervailable subsidy with respect to the manufacture, production, or export of a class or kind of merchandise imported, or sold (or likely to be sold) for importation, into the United States, and

(2) in the case of merchandise imported from a Subsidies Agreement country, the Commission determines that—

(A) an industry in the United States—

    (i) is materially injured, or

    (ii) is threatened with material injury, or

(B) the establishment of an industry in the United States is materially retarded, by reason of imports of that merchandise or by reason of sales (or the likelihood of sales) of that merchandise for importation, then there shall be imposed upon such merchandise a countervailing duty, in addition to any other duty imposed, equal to the amount of the net countervailable subsidy. For purposes of this subsection and section 705(b)(1), a reference to the sale of merchandise includes the entering into of any leasing arrangement regarding the merchandise that is equivalent to the sale of the merchandise.

(b) Subsidies Agreement Country. For purposes of this title, the term "Subsidies Agreement country" means—

(1) a WTO member country,

(2) a country which the President has determined has assumed obligations with respect to the United States which are substantially equivalent to the obligations under the Subsidies Agreement, or

(3) a country with respect to which the President determines that—

(A) there is an agreement in effect between the United States and that country which—

    (i) was in force on the date of the enactment of the Uruguay Round Agreements Act, and

    (ii) requires unconditional most-favored-nation treatment with respect to articles imported into the United States, and

(B) the agreement described in subparagraph (A) does not expressly permit—

    (i) actions required or permitted by the GATT 1947 or GATT 1994, as defined in section 2(1) of the Uruguay Round Agreements Act, or required by the Congress, or

    (ii) nondiscriminatory prohibitions or restrictions on importation which are designed to prevent deceptive or unfair practices.

(c) Countervailing Duty Investigations Involving Imports Not Entitled to a Material Injury Determination. In the case of any article or merchandise imported from a country which is not a Subsidies Agreement country—

(1) no determination by the Commission under section 703(a), 704, or 705(b) shall be required,

(2) an investigation may not be suspended under section 704(c) or 704(*l*),

(3) no determination as to the presence of critical circumstances shall be made under section 703(e) or 705(a)(2),

(4) section 706(c) shall not apply,

(5) any reference to a determination described in paragraph (1) or (3), or to the suspension of an investigation under section 704(c) or 704(*l*), shall be disregarded, and

(6) section 751(c) shall not apply.

(d) Treatment of international consortia. For purposes of this subtitle, if the members (or other participating entities) of an international consortium that is engaged in the production of subject merchandise receive countervailable subsidies from their respective home countries to assist, permit, or otherwise enable their participation in that consortium through production or manufacturing operations in their respective home countries, then the administering authority shall cumulate all such countervailable subsidies, as well as countervailable subsidies provided directly to the international consortium, in determining any countervailing duty upon such merchandise.

(e) Upstream subsidy. Whenever the administering authority has reasonable grounds to believe or suspect that an upstream subsidy, as defined in section 771A(a)(1), is being paid or bestowed, the administering authority shall investigate whether an upstream subsidy has in fact been paid or bestowed, and if so, shall include the amount of the upstream subsidy as provided in section 771A(a)(3).

19 USC 1671a

Sec. 702.   Procedures for Initiating a Countervailing Duty Investigation

(a) Initiation by administering authority. A countervailing duty investigation shall be initiated whenever the administering authority determines, from information available to it, that a formal investigation is warranted into the question of whether the elements necessary for the imposition of a duty under section 701(a) exist.

(b) Initiation by petition.

(1) Petition requirements. A countervailing duty proceeding shall be initiated whenever an interested party described in subparagraph (C), (D), (E), (F), or (G) of section 771(9) files a petition with the administering authority, on behalf of an industry, which alleges the elements necessary for the imposition of the duty imposed by section 701(a), and which is accompanied by information reasonably available to the petitioner supporting those allegations. The petition may be amended at such time, and upon such conditions, as the administering authority and the Commission may permit.

(2) Simultaneous filing with Commission. The petitioner shall file a copy of the petition with the Commission on the same day as it is filed with the administering authority.

(3) Petition based upon a derogation of an international undertaking on official export credits. If the sole basis of a petition filed under paragraph (1) is the derogation of an international undertaking on official export credits, the Administering Authority shall immediately notify the Secretary of the Treasury who shall, in consultation with the Administering Authority, within 5 days after the date on which the administering authority initiates an investi-

gation under subsection (c), determine the existence and estimated value of the derogation, if any, and shall publish such determination in the Federal Register.

(4) Action with respect to petitions.

(A) Notification of governments. Upon receipt of a petition filed under paragraph (1), the administering authority shall—

(i) notify the government of any exporting country named in the petition by delivering a public version of the petition to an appropriate representative of such country; and

(ii) provide the government of any exporting country named in the petition that is a Subsidies Agreement country an opportunity for consultations with respect to the petition.

(B) Acceptance of communications. The administering authority shall not accept any unsolicited oral or written communication from any person other than an interested party described in section 771(9) (C), (D), (E), (F), or (G) before the administering authority makes its decision whether to initiate an investigation, except as provided in subparagraph (A)(ii) and subsection (c)(4)(D), and except for inquiries regarding the status of the administering authority's consideration of the petition.

(C) Nondisclosure of certain information. The administering authority and the Commission shall not disclose information with regard to any draft petition submitted for review and comment before it is filed under paragraph (1).

(c) Petition determination.

(1) In general.

(A) Time for initial determination. Except as provided in subparagraph (B), within 20 days after the date on which a petition is filed under subsection (b), the administering authority shall—

(i) after examining, on the basis of sources readily available to the administering authority, the accuracy and adequacy of the evidence provided in the petition, determine whether the petition alleges the elements necessary for the imposition of a duty under section 701(a) and contains information reasonably available to the petitioner supporting the allegations, and

(ii) determine if the petition has been filed by or on behalf of the industry.

(B) Extension of time. In any case in which the administering authority is required to poll or otherwise determine support for the petition by the industry under paragraph (4)(D), the administering authority may, in exceptional circumstances, apply subparagraph (A) by substituting "a maximum of 40 days" for "20 days".

(C) Time limits where petition involves same merchandise as an order that has been revoked. If a petition is filed under this section with respect to merchandise that was the subject merchandise of—

(i) a countervailing duty order that was revoked under section 751(d)] in the 24 months preceding the date the petition is filed, or

(ii) a suspended investigation that was terminated under section 751(d) in the 24 months preceding the date the petition is filed, the administering authority and the Commission shall, to the maximum extent practicable, expedite any investigation initiated under this section with respect to the petition.

(2) Affirmative determinations. If the determinations under clauses (i) and (ii) of paragraph (1)(A) are affirmative, the administering authority shall initiate an investigation to determine whether a countervailable subsidy is being provided with respect to the subject merchandise.

(3) Negative determinations. If the determination under clause (i) or (ii) of paragraph (1)(A) is negative, the administering authority shall dismiss the petition, terminate the proceeding, and notify the petitioner in writing of the reasons for the determination.

(4) Determination of industry support.

(A) General rule. For purposes of this subsection, the administering authority shall determine that the petition has been filed by or on behalf of the industry, if—

(i) the domestic producers or workers who support the petition account for at least 25 percent of the total production of the domestic like product, and

(ii) the domestic producers or workers who support the petition account for more than 50 percent of the production of the domestic like product produced by that portion of the industry expressing support for or opposition to the petition.

(B) Certain positions disregarded.

(i) Producers related to foreign producers. In determining industry support under subparagraph (A), the administering authority shall disregard the position of domestic producers who oppose the petition, if such producers are related to foreign producers, as defined in section 771(4)(B)(ii), unless such domestic producers demonstrate that their interests as domestic producers would be adversely affected by the imposition of a countervailing duty order.

(ii) Producers who are importers. The administering authority may disregard the position of domestic producers of a domestic like product who are importers of the subject merchandise.

(C) Special rule for regional industries. If the petition alleges that the industry is a regional industry, the administering authority shall determine whether the petition has been filed by or on behalf of the industry by applying subparagraph (A) on the basis of production in the region.

(D) Polling the industry. If the petition does not establish support of domestic producers or workers accounting for more than 50 percent of the total production of the domestic like product, the administering authority shall—

(i) poll the industry or rely on other information in order to determine if there is support for the petition as required by subparagraph (A), or

(ii) if there is a large number of producers in the industry, the administering authority may determine industry support for the petition by using any statistically valid sampling method to poll the industry.

(E) Comments by interested parties. Before the administering authority makes a determination with respect to initiating an investigation, any person who would qualify as an interested party under section 771(9) if an investigation were initiated, may submit comments or information on the issue of industry support. After the administering authority makes a determination with respect to initiating an investigation, the determination regarding industry support shall not be reconsidered.

(5) Definition of domestic producers or workers. For purposes of this subsection, the term "domestic producers or workers" means those interested parties who are eligible to file a petition under subsection (b)(1).

(d) Notification to Commission of determination. The administering authority shall—

(1) notify the Commission immediately of any determination it makes under subsection (a) or (c), and

(2) if the determination is affirmative, make available to the Commission such information as it may have relating to the matter under investigation, under such procedures as the administering authority and the Commission may establish to prevent disclosure, other than with the consent of the party providing it or under protective order, of any information to which confidential treatment has been given by the administering authority.

(e) Information regarding critical circumstances. If, at any time after the initiation of an investigation under this subtitle, the administering authority finds a reasonable basis to suspect that the alleged countervailable subsidy is inconsistent with the Subsidies Agreement, the administering authority may request the Commissioner of Customs to compile information on an expedited basis regarding entries of the subject merchandise. Upon receiving such request, the Commissioner of Customs shall collect information regarding the volume and value of entries of the subject merchandise and shall transmit such information to the administering authority at such times as the administering authority shall direct (at least once every 30 days), until a final determination is made under section 705(a), the investigation is terminated, or the administering authority withdraws the request.

19 USC 1671b

Sec. 703. Preliminary Determinations

(a) Determination by Commission of Reasonable Indication of Injury.

(1) General rule. Except in the case of a petition dismissed by the administering authority under section 702(c)(3), the Commission, within the time specified in paragraph (2), shall determine, based on the information

available to it at the time of the determination, whether there is a reasonable indication

that—

(A) an industry in the United States

(i) is materially injured, or

(ii) is threatened with material injury, or

(B) the establishment of an industry in the United States is materially retarded, by reason of imports of the subject merchandise and that imports of the subject merchandise are not negligible. If the Commission finds that imports of the subject merchandise are negligible or otherwise makes a negative determination under this paragraph, the investigation shall be terminated.

(2) Time for commission determination. The Commission shall make the determination described in paragraph (1)—

(A) in the case of a petition filed under section 702(b)

(i) within 45 days after the date on which the petition is filed, or

(ii) if the time has been extended pursuant to section 702(c)(1)(B), within 25 days after the date on which the Commission receives notice from the administering authority of initiation of the investigation, and

(B) in the case of an investigation initiated under section 702(a), within 45 days after the date on which the Commission receives notice from the administering authority that an investigation has been initiated under such section.

(b) Preliminary determination by administering authority; expedited determinations; waiver of verification. (1) Within 65 days after the date on which the administering authority initiates an investigation under section 702(c), or an investigation is initiated under section 702(a), but not before an affirmative determination by the Commission under subsection (a) of this section, the administering authority shall make a determination, based upon the information available to it at the time of the determination, of whether there is a reasonable basis to believe or suspect that a countervailable subsidy is being provided with respect to the subject merchandise.

(2) Notwithstanding paragraph (1), when the petition is one subject to section 702(b)(3) of this Act, the administering authority shall, taking into account the nature of the countervailable subsidy concerned, make the determination required by paragraph (1) on an expedited basis and within 65 days after the date on which the administering authority initiates an investigation under section 702(c) unless the provisions of subsection (c) of this section apply.

(3) Preliminary determination under waiver of verification. Within 55 days after the initiation of an investigation the administering authority shall cause an official designated for such purpose to review the information concerning the case received during the first 50 days of the investigation, and, if there appears to be sufficient information available upon which the determination can reasonably be based, to disclose to the petitioner and any interested party, then a party to the proceedings that requests such disclosure, all available nonconfidential information and all other information which is disclosed pursuant to section 777. Within 3 days (not counting Saturdays, Sundays, or legal public holidays) after such disclosure, the petitioner and

each party which is an interested party described in subparagraph (C), (D), (E), (F), or (G) of section 771(9) to whom such disclosure was made may furnish to the administering authority an irrevocable written waiver of verification of the information received by the authority, and an agreement that it is willing to have a determination made on the basis of the record then available to the authority. If a timely waiver and agreement have been received from the petitioner and each party which is an interested party described in subparagraph (C), (D), (E), (F), or (G) of section 771(9) to whom the disclosure was made, and the authority finds that sufficient information is then available upon which the preliminary determination can reasonably be based, a preliminary determination shall be made on an expedited basis on the basis of the record established during the first 50 days after the investigation was initiated.

(4) De minimis countervailable subsidy.

(A) General rule. In making a determination under this subsection, the administering authority shall disregard any de minimis countervailable subsidy. For purposes of the preceding sentence, a countervailable subsidy is de minimis if the administering authority determines that the aggregate of the net countervailable subsidies is less than 1 percent ad valorem or the equivalent specific rate for the subject merchandise.

(B) Exception for developing countries. In the case of subject merchandise imported from a Subsidies Agreement country (other than a country to which subparagraph (C) applies) designated by the Trade Representative as a developing country in accordance with section 771(36), a countervailable subsidy is de minimis if the administering authority determines that the aggregate of the net countervailable subsidies does not exceed 2 percent ad valorem or the equivalent specific rate for the subject merchandise.

(C) Certain other developing countries. In the case of subject merchandise imported from a Subsidies Agreement country that is—

(i) a least developed country, as determined by the Trade Representative in accordance with section 771(36), or

(ii) a developing country with respect to which the Trade Representative has notified the administering authority that the country has eliminated its export subsidies on an expedited basis within the meaning of Article 27.11 of the Subsidies Agreement,

subparagraph (B) shall be applied by substituting "3 percent" for "2 percent".

(D) Limitations on application of subparagraph (c).

(i) In general. In the case of a country described in subparagraph (C)(i), the provisions of subparagraph (C) shall not apply after the date that is 8 years after the date the WTO Agreement enters into force.

(ii) Special rule for subparagraph (C)(ii) countries. In the case of a country described in subparagraph (C)(ii), the provisions of subparagraph (C) shall not apply after the earlier of—

(I) the date that is 8 years after the date the WTO Agreement enters into force, or

(II) the date on which the Trade Representative notifies the administering authority that such country is providing an export subsidy.

(5) Notification of article 8 violation. If the only subsidy under investigation is a subsidy with respect to which the administering authority received notice from the Trade Representative of a violation of Article 8 of the Subsidies Agreement, paragraph (1) shall be applied by substituting "60 days" for "65 days."

(c) Extension of period in extraordinarily complicated cases.

(1) In general. If—

(A) the petitioner makes a timely request for an extension of the period within which the determination must be made under subsection (b), or

(B) the administering authority concludes that the parties concerned are cooperating and determines that—

(i) the case is extraordinarily complicated by reason of—

(I) the number and complexity of the alleged countervailable subsidy practices;

(II) the novelty of the issues presented;

(III) the need to determine the extent to which particular countervailable subsidies are used by individual manufacturers, producers, and exporters; or

(IV) the number of firms whose activities must be investigated; and

(ii) additional time is necessary to make the preliminary determination,

then the administering authority may postpone making the preliminary determination under subsection (b) until not later than the 130th day after the date on which the administering authority initiates an investigation under section 702(c), or an investigation is initiated under section 702(a).

(2) Notice of postponement. The administering authority shall notify the parties to the investigation, not later than 20 days before the date on which the preliminary determination would otherwise be required under subsection (b), if it intends to postpone making the preliminary determination under paragraph (1). The notification shall include an explanation of the reasons for the postponement. Notice of the postponement shall be published in the Federal Register.

(d) Effect of determination by the administering authority. If the preliminary determination of the administering authority under subsection (b) is affirmative, the administering authority—

(1)(A) shall

(i) determine an estimated individual countervailable subsidy rate for each exporter and producer individually investigated, and, in accordance with section 705(c)(5), an estimated all-others rate for all exporters and producers not individually investigated and for new exporters and producers within the meaning of section 751(a)(2)(B), or

(ii) if section 777A(e)(2)(B) applies, determine a single estimated country-wide subsidy rate, applicable to all exporters and producers, and

(B) shall order the posting of a cash deposit, bond, or other security, as the administering authority deems appropriate, for each entry of the subject merchandise in an amount based on the estimated individual countervailable subsidy rate, the estimated all-others rate, or the estimated country-wide subsidy rate, whichever is applicable,

(2) shall order the suspension of liquidation of all entries of merchandise subject to the determination which are entered, or withdrawn from warehouse, for consumption on or after the later of

(A) the date on which notice of the determination is published in the Federal Register, or

(B) the date that is 60 days after the date on which notice of the determination to initiate the investigation is published in the Federal Register, and

(3) shall make available to the Commission all information upon which its determination was based and which the Commission considers relevant to its injury determination, under such procedures as the administering authority and the Commission may establish to prevent disclosure, other than with the consent of the party providing it or under protective order, of any information to which confidential treatment has been given by the administering authority.

The instructions of the administering authority under paragraphs (1) and (2) may not remain in effect for more than 4 months.

(e) Critical circumstances determinations.

(1) In general. If a petitioner alleges critical circumstances in its original petition, or by amendment at any time more than 20 days before the date of a final determination by the administering authority, then the administering authority shall promptly (at any time after the initiation of the investigation under this subtitle) determine, on the basis of the information available to it at that time, whether there is a reasonable basis to believe or suspect that—

(A) the alleged countervailable subsidy is inconsistent with the Subsidies Agreement, and

(B) there have been massive imports of the subject merchandise over a relatively short period.

(2) Suspension of liquidation. If the determination of the administering authority under paragraph (1) is affirmative, then any suspension of liquidation ordered under subsection (d)(2) shall apply, or, if notice of such suspension of liquidation is already published, be amended to apply, to unliquidated entries of merchandise entered, or withdrawn from warehouse, for consumption on or after the later of

(A) the date which is 90 days before the date on which the suspension of liquidation was first ordered, or

(B) the date on which notice of the determination to initiate the investigation is published in the Federal Register.

(f) Notice of Determination. Whenever the Commission or the administering authority makes a determination under this section, the Commission or the administering authority, as the case may be, shall notify the petitioner, and other parties to the investigation, and the Commission or the administering authority (whichever is appropriate) of its determination. The administering authority shall include with such notification the facts and conclusions on which its determination is based. Not later than 5 days after the date on which the determination is required to be made under subsection (a)(2), the Commission shall transmit to the administering authority the facts and conclusions on which its determination is based.

(g) Time period where upstream subsidization involved.

(1) In general. Whenever the administering authority concludes prior to a preliminary determination under section 703(b), that there is a reasonable basis to believe or suspect that an upstream subsidy is being bestowed, the time period within which a preliminary determination must be made shall be extended to 250 days after the filing of a petition under section 702(b) or initiation of an investigation under section 702(a) (310 days in cases declared extraordinarily complicated under section 703(c)), if the administering authority concludes that such additional time is necessary to make the required determination concerning upstream subsidization.

(2) Exceptions. Whenever the administering authority concludes, after a preliminary determination under section 703(b), that there is a reasonable basis to believe or suspect that an upstream subsidy is being bestowed—

(A) in cases in which the preliminary determination was negative, the time period within which a final determination must be made shall be extended to 165 days or 225 days, as appropriate, under section 705(a)(1); or

(B) in cases in which the preliminary determination is affirmative, the determination concerning upstream subsidization—

(i) need not be made until the conclusion of the first annual review under section 751 of any eventual Countervailing Duty Order, or, at the option of the petitioner, or

(ii) will be made in the investigation and the time period within which a final determination must be made shall be extended to 165 or 225 days, as appropriate, under section 705(a)(1), except that the suspension of liquidation ordered in the preliminary determination shall terminate at the end of 120 days from the date of publication of that determination and not be resumed unless and until the publication of a Countervailing Duty Order under section 706(a).

There may be an extension of time for the making of a final determination under this subsection only if the administering authority determines that such additional time is necessary to make the required determination concerning upstream subsidization.

19 USC 1671c

Sec. 704. Termination or Suspension of Investigation

(a) Termination of investigation upon withdrawal of petition.

(1) In general.

(A) Withdrawal of petition. Except as provided in paragraphs (2) and (3), an investigation under this subtitle may be terminated by either the administering authority or the Commission, after notice to all parties to the investigation, upon withdrawal of the petition by the petitioner or by the administering authority if the investigation was initiated under section 702(a).

(B) Refiling of petition. If, within 3 months after the withdrawal of a petition under subparagraph (A), a new petition is filed seeking the imposition of duties on both the subject merchandise of the withdrawn petition and the subject merchandise from another country, the administering authority and the Commission may use in the investigation initiated pursuant to the new petition any records compiled in an investigation conducted pursuant to the withdrawn petition. This subparagraph applies only with respect to the first withdrawal of a petition.

(2) Special rules for quantitative restriction agreements.

(A) In general. Subject to subparagraphs (B) and (C), the administering authority may not terminate an investigation under paragraph (1) by accepting, with the government of the country in which the countervailable subsidy practice is alleged to occur, an understanding or other kind of agreement to limit the volume of imports into the United States of the subject merchandise unless the administering authority is satisfied that termination on the basis of that agreement is in the public interest.

(B) Public interest factors. In making a decision under subparagraph (A) regarding the public interest, the administering authority shall take into account—

(i) whether, based upon the relative impact on consumer prices and the availability of supplies of the merchandise, the agreement would have a greater adverse impact on United States consumers than the imposition of countervailing duties;

(ii) the relative impact on the international economic interests of the United States; and

(iii) the relative impact on the competitiveness of the domestic industry producing the like merchandise, including any such impact on employment and investment in that industry.

(C) Prior consultations. Before making a decision under subparagraph (A) regarding the public interest, the administering authority shall, to the extent practicable, consult with—

(i) potentially affected consuming industries; and

(ii) potentially affected producers and workers in the domestic industry producing the like merchandise, including producers and workers not party to the investigation.

(3) Limitation on termination by commission. The Commission may not terminate an investigation under paragraph (1) before a preliminary determination is made by the administering authority under section 703(b).

(b) Agreements to eliminate or offset completely a countervailable subsidy or to cease exports of subject merchandise. The administering authority may suspend an investigation if the government of the country in which the countervailable subsidy practice is alleged to occur agrees, or exporters who account for substantially all of the imports of the subject merchandise agree—

(1) to eliminate the countervailable subsidy completely or to offset completely the amount of the net countervailable subsidy, with respect to that merchandise exported directly or indirectly to the United States, within 6 months after the date on which the investigation is suspended, or

(2) to cease exports of that merchandise to the United States within 6 months after the date on which the investigation is suspended.

(c) Agreements eliminating injurious effect.

(1) General rule. If the administering authority determines that extraordinary circumstances are present in a case, it may suspend an investigation upon the acceptance of an agreement from a government described in subsection (b), or from exporters described in subsection (b), if the agreement will eliminate completely the injurious effect of exports to the United States of the subject merchandise.

(2) Certain additional requirements. Except in the case of an agreement by a foreign government to restrict the volume of imports of the subject merchandise into the United States, the administering authority may not accept an agreement under this subsection unless—

(A) the suppression or undercutting of price levels of domestic products by imports of that merchandise will be prevented, and

(B) at least 85 percent of the net countervailable subsidy will be offset.

(3) Quantitative restrictions agreements. The administering authority may accept an agreement with a foreign government under this subsection to restrict the volume of imports of subject merchandise into the United States, but it may not accept such an agreement with exporters.

(4) Definition of extraordinary circumstances.

(A) Extraordinary circumstances. For purposes of this subsection, the term "extraordinary circumstances" means circumstances in which—

(i) suspension of an investigation will be more beneficial to the domestic industry than continuation of the investigation, and

(ii) the investigation is complex.

(B) Complex. For purposes of this paragraph, the term "complex" means—

(i) there are a large number of alleged countervailable subsidy practices and the practices are complicated,

(ii) the issues raised are novel, or

(iii) the number of exporters involved is large.

(d) Additional rules and conditions.

(1) Public interest; monitoring. The administering authority shall not accept an agreement under subsection (b) or (c) unless—

(A) it is satisfied that suspension of the investigation is in the public interest, and

(B) effective monitoring of the agreement by the United States is practicable.

Where practicable, the administering authority shall provide to the exporters who would have been subject to the agreement the reasons for not accepting the agreement and, to the extent possible, an opportunity to submit comments thereon. In applying subparagraph (A) with respect to any quantitative restriction agreement under subsection (c), the administering authority shall take into account, in addition to such other factors as are considered necessary or appropriate, the factors set forth in subsection (a)(2)(B)(i), (ii), and (iii) as they apply to the proposed suspension and agreement, after consulting with the appropriate consuming industries, producers, and workers referred to in subsection (a)(2)(C)(i) and (ii).

(2) Exports of merchandise to United States not to increase during interim period. The administering authority may not accept any agreement under subsection (b) unless that agreement provides a means of ensuring that the quantity of the merchandise covered by that agreement exported to the United States during the period provided for elimination or offset of the countervailable subsidy or cessation of exports does not exceed the quantity of such merchandise exported to the United States during the most recent representative period determined by the administering authority.

(3) Regulations governing entry or withdrawals. In order to carry out an agreement concluded under subsection (b) or (c), the administering authority is authorized to prescribe regulations governing the entry, or withdrawal from warehouse, for consumption of merchandise covered by such agreement.

(e) Suspension of investigation procedure.
Before an investigation may be suspended under subsection (b) or (c) the administering authority shall—

(1) notify the petitioner of, and consult with the petitioner concerning, its intention to suspend the investigation, and notify other parties to the investigation and the Commission not less than 30 days before the date on which it suspends the investigation,

(2) provide a copy of the proposed agreement to the petitioner at the time of the notification, together with an explanation of how the agreement will be carried out and enforced (including any action required of foreign governments), and of how the agreement will meet the requirements of subsections (b) and (d) or (c) and (d), and

(3) permit all interested parties described in section 771(9) to submit comments and information for the record before the date on which notice of suspension of the investigation is published under subsection (f)(1)(A).

(f) Effects of suspension of investigation.

(1) In general. If the administering authority determines to suspend an investigation upon acceptance of an agreement described in subsection (b) or (c), then—

(A) it shall suspend the investigation, publish notice of suspension of the investigation, and issue an affirmative preliminary determination under section 703(b) with respect to the subject merchandise, unless it has previously issued such a determination in the same investigation,

(B) the Commission shall suspend any investigation it is conducting with respect to that merchandise, and

(C) the suspension of investigation shall take effect on the day on which such notice is published.

(2) Liquidation of entries.

(A) Cessation of exports; complete elimination of net countervailable subsidy. If the agreement accepted by the administering authority is an agreement described in subsection (b), then—

(i) notwithstanding the affirmative preliminary determination required under paragraph (1)(A), the liquidation of entries of subject merchandise shall not be suspended under section 703(d)(2),

(ii) if the liquidation of entries of such merchandise was suspended pursuant to a previous affirmative preliminary determination in the same case with respect to such merchandise, that suspension of liquidation shall terminate, and

(iii) the administering authority shall refund any cash deposit and release any bond or other security deposited under section 703(d)(1)(B).

(B) Other agreements. If the agreement accepted by the administering authority is an agreement described in subsection (c), then the liquidation of entries of the subject merchandise shall be suspended under section 703(d)(2), or, if the liquidation of entries of such merchandise was suspended pursuant to a previous affirmative preliminary determination in the same case, that suspension of liquidation shall continue in effect, subject to subsection (h)(3), but the security required under section 703(d)(1)(B) may be adjusted to reflect the effect of the agreement.

(3) Where investigation is continued. If, pursuant to subsection (g), the administering authority and the Commission continue an investigation in which an agreement has been accepted under subsection (b) or (c), then—

(A) if the final determination by the administering authority or the Commission under section 705 is negative, the agreement shall have no force or effect and the investigation shall be terminated, or

(B) if the final determinations by the administering authority and the Commission under such section are affirmative, the agreement shall remain in force, but the administering authority shall not issue a countervailing duty order in the case so long as—

(i) the agreement remains in force,

(ii) the agreement continues to meet the requirements of subsections (b) and (d) or (c) and (d), and

(iii) the parties to the agreement carry out their obligations under the agreement in accordance with its terms.

(g) Investigation to be continued upon request. If the administering authority, within 20 days after the date of publication of the notice of suspension of an investigation, receives a request for the continuation of the investigation from—

(1) the government of the country in which the countervailable subsidy practice is alleged to occur, or

(2) an interested party described in subparagraph (C), (D), (E), (F), or (G) of section 771(9) which is a party to the investigation,

then the administering authority and the Commission shall continue the investigation.

(h) Review of suspension.

(1) In general. Within 20 days after the suspension of an investigation under subsection (c), an interested party which is a party to the investigation and which is described in subparagraph (C), (D), (E), (F) or (G) of section 771(9) may, by petition filed with the Commission and with notice to the administering authority, ask for a review of the suspension.

(2) Commission investigation. Upon receipt of a review petition under paragraph (1), the Commission shall, within 75 days after the date on which the petition is filed with it, determine whether the injurious effect of imports of the subject merchandise is eliminated completely by the agreement. If the Commission's determination under this subsection is negative, the investigation shall be resumed on the date of publication of notice of such determination as if the affirmative preliminary determination under section 703(b) had been made on that date.

(3) Suspension of liquidation to continue during review period. The suspension of liquidation of entries of the subject merchandise shall terminate at the close of the 20-day period beginning on the day after the date on which notice of suspension of the investigation is published in the Federal Register, or, if a review petition is filed under paragraph (1) with respect to the suspension of the investigation, in the case of an affirmative determination by the Commission under paragraph (2), the date on which notice of the affirmative determination by the Commission is published. If the determination of the Commission under paragraph (2) is affirmative, then the administering authority shall—

(A) terminate the suspension of liquidation under section 703(d)(2), and

(B) release any bond or other security, and refund any cash deposit, required under section 703(d)(1)(B).

(i) Violation of agreement.

(1) In general. If the administering authority determines that an agreement accepted under subsection (b) or (c) is being, or has been, violated, or no longer meets the requirements of such subsection (other than the requirement, under subsection (c)(1), of elimination of injury) and subsection (d), then, on the date of publication of its determination, it shall—

(A) suspend liquidation under section 703(d)(2) of unliquidated entries of the merchandise made on or after the later of—

(i) the date which is 90 days before the date of publication of the notice of suspension of liquidation, or

(ii) the date on which the merchandise, the sale or export to the United States of which was in violation of the agreement, or under an agreement which no longer meets the requirements of subsections (b) and (d) or (c) and (d), was first entered, or withdrawn from warehouse, for consumption,

(B) if the investigation was not completed, resume the investigation as if its affirmative preliminary determination under section 703(b) were made on the date of its determination under this paragraph,

(C) if the investigation was completed under subsection (g), issue a countervailing duty order under section 706(a) effective with respect to entries of merchandise the liquidation of which was suspended,

(D) if it considers the violation to be intentional, notify the Commissioner of Customs who shall take appropriate action under paragraph (2), and

(E) notify the petitioner, interested parties who are or were parties to the investigation, and the Commission of its action under this paragraph.

(2) Intentional violation to be punished by civil penalty. Any person who intentionally violates an agreement accepted by the administering authority under subsection (b) or (c) shall be subject to a civil penalty assessed in the same amount, in the same manner, and under the same procedure, as the penalty imposed for a fraudulent violation of section 592(a) of this Act.

(j) Determination not to take agreement into account. In making a final determination under section 705, or in conducting a review under section 751, in a case in which the administering authority has terminated a suspension of investigation under subsection (i)(1), or continued an investigation under subsection (g), the Commission and the administering authority shall consider all of the subject merchandise, without regard to the effect of any agreement under subsection (b) or (c).

(k) Termination of investigations initiated by administering authority. The administering authority may terminate any investigation initiated by the administering authority under section 702(a) after providing notice of such termination to all parties to the investigation.

(*l*) Special Rule for Regional Industry Investigations.

(1) Suspension agreements. If the Commission makes a regional industry determination under section 771(4)(C), the administering authority shall offer exporters of the subject merchandise who account for substantially all exports of that merchandise for sale in the region concerned the opportunity to enter into an agreement described in subsection (b) or (c).

(2) Requirements for suspension agreements. Any agreement described in paragraph (1) shall be subject to all the requirements imposed under this section for other agreements under subsection (b) or (c), except that if the Commission makes a regional industry determination described in paragraph (1) in the final affirmative determination under section 705(b) but not in the

preliminary affirmative determination under section 703(a), any agreement described in paragraph (1) may be accepted within 60 days after the countervailing duty order is published under section 706.

(3) Effect of suspension agreement on countervailing duty order. If an agreement described in paragraph (1) is accepted after the countervailing duty order is published, the administering authority shall rescind the order, refund any cash deposit and release any bond or other security deposited under section 703(d)(1)(B), and instruct the Customs Service that entries of the subject merchandise that were made during the period that the order was in effect shall be liquidated without regard to countervailing duties.

19 USC 1671d

Sec. 705.　Final Determinations

(a) Final determination by administering authority.

(1) In general. Within 75 days after the date of the preliminary determination under section 703(b), the administering authority shall make a final determination of whether or not a countervailable subsidy is being provided with respect to the subject merchandise; except that when an investigation under this subtitle is initiated simultaneously with an investigation under subtitle B, which involves imports of the same class or kind of merchandise from the same or other countries, the administering authority, if requested by the petitioner, shall extend the date of the final determination under this paragraph to the date of the final determination of the administering authority in such investigation initiated under subtitle B.

(2) Critical circumstances determinations. If the final determination of the administering authority is affirmative, then that determination, in any investigation in which the presence of critical circumstances has been alleged under section 703(e), shall also contain a finding as to whether—

> (A) the countervailable subsidy is inconsistent with the Subsidies Agreement, and

> (B) there have been massive imports of the subject merchandise over a relatively short period.

Such findings may be affirmative even though the preliminary determination under section 703(e)(1) was negative.

(3) De minimis countervailable subsidy. In making a determination under this subsection, the administering authority shall disregard any countervailable subsidy that is de minimis as defined in section 703(b)(4).

(b) Final determination by Commission.

(1) In general. The Commission shall make a final determination of whether

> (A) an industry in the United States—

>> (i) is materially injured, or

>> (ii) is threatened with material injury, or

> (B) the establishment of an industry in the United States is materially retarded,

by reason of imports, or sales (or the likelihood of sales) for importation, of the merchandise with respect to which the administering authority has made an affirmative determination under subsection (a). If the Commission determines that imports of the subject merchandise are negligible, the investigation shall be terminated.

(2) Period for injury determination following affirmative preliminary determination by administering authority. If the preliminary determination by the administering authority under section 703(b) is affirmative, then the Commission shall make the determination required by paragraph (1) before the later of—

(A) the 120th day after the day on which the administering authority makes its affirmative preliminary determination under section 703(b), or

(B) the 45th day after the day on which the administering authority makes its affirmative final determination under subsection (a).

(3) Period for injury determination following negative preliminary determination by administering authority. If the preliminary determination by the administering authority under section 703(b) is negative, and its final determination under subsection (a) is affirmative, then the final determination by the Commission under this subsection shall be made within 75 days after the date of that affirmative final determination.

(4) Certain additional findings.

(A) Commission standard for retroactive application.

(i) In general. If the finding of the administering authority under subsection (a)(2) is affirmative, then the final determination of the Commission shall include a finding as to whether the imports subject to the affirmative determination under subsection (a)(2) are likely to undermine seriously the remedial effect of the countervailing duty order to be issued under section 706.

(ii) Factors to consider. In making the evaluation under clause (i), the Commission shall consider, among other factors it considers relevant—

(I) the timing and the volume of the imports,

(II) any rapid increase in inventories of the imports, and

(III) any other circumstances indicating that the remedial effect of the countervailing duty order will be seriously undermined.

(B) If the final determination of the Commission is that there is no material injury but that there is threat of material injury, then its determination shall also include a finding as to whether material injury by reason of imports of the merchandise with respect to which the administering authority has made an affirmative determination under subsection (a) would have been found but for any suspension of liquidation of entries of that merchandise.

(c) Effect of final determinations.

(1) Effect of affirmative determination by the administering authority. If the determination of the administering authority under subsection (a) is affirmative, then—

(A) the administering authority shall make available to the Commission all information upon which such determination was based and which the Commission considers relevant to its determination, under such procedures as the administering authority and the Commission may establish to prevent disclosure, other than with the consent of the party providing it or under protective order, of any information to which confidential treatment has been given by the administering authority,

(B) (i) the administering authority shall—

(I) determine an estimated individual countervailable subsidy rate for each exporter and producer individually investigated, and, in accordance with paragraph (5), an estimated all-others rate for all exporters and producers not individually investigated and for new exporters and producers within the meaning of section 751(a)(2)(B), or

(II) if section 777A(e)(2)(B) applies, determine a single estimated country-wide subsidy rate, applicable to all exporters and producers,

(ii) shall order the posting of a cash deposit, bond, or other security, as the administering authority deems appropriate, for each entry of the subject merchandise in an amount based on the estimated individual countervailable subsidy rate, the estimated all-others rate, or the estimated country-wide subsidy rate, whichever is applicable, and

(C) in cases where the preliminary determination by the administering authority under section 703(b) was negative, the administering authority shall order under the suspension of liquidation under paragraph (2) of section 703(d).

(2) Issuance of order; effect of negative determination. If the determinations of the administering authority and the Commission under subsections (a)(1) and (b)(1) are affirmative, then the administering authority shall issue a countervailing duty order under section 706(a). If either of such determinations is negative, the investigation shall be terminated upon the publication of notice of that negative determination and the administering authority shall—

(A) terminate the suspension of liquidation under section 703(d)(2), and

(B) release any bond or other security and refund any cash deposit required under section 703(d)(1)(B).

(3) Effect of negative determinations under subsections (a)(2) and (b)(4)(A). If the determination of the administering authority or the Commission under subsection (a)(2) and (b)(4)(A), respectively, is negative, then the administering authority shall—

(A) terminate any retroactive suspension of liquidation required under paragraph (4) or section 703(e)(2), and

(B) release any bond or other security, and refund any cash deposit required, under section 703(b)(1)(B) with respect to entries of the merchandise the liquidation of which was suspended retroactively under section 703(e)(2).

(4) Effect of affirmative determination under subsection (a)(2). If the determination of the administering authority under subsection (a)(2) is affirmative, then the administering authority shall—

(A) in cases where the preliminary determinations by the administering authority under sections 703(b) and 703(e)(1) were both affirmative, continue the retroactive suspension of liquidation and the posting of a cash deposit, bond, or other security previously ordered under section 703(e)(2);

(B) in cases where the preliminary determination by the administering authority under section 703(b) was affirmative, but the preliminary determination under section 703(e)(1) was negative, shall modify any suspension of liquidation and security requirement previously ordered under section 703(d) to apply to unliquidated entries of merchandise entered, or withdrawn from warehouse, for consumption on or after the date which is 90 days before the date on which suspension of liquidation was first ordered; or

(C) in cases where the preliminary determination by the administering authority under section 703(b) was negative, shall apply any suspension of liquidation and security requirement ordered under subsection 705(c)(1)(B) [subsec. (c)(1)(B) of this section] to unliquidated entries of merchandise entered, or withdrawn from warehouse, for consumption on or after the date which is 90 days before the date on which suspension of liquidation is first ordered.

(5) Method for determining the all-others rate and the country-wide subsidy rate.

(A) All-others rate.

(i) General rule. For purposes of this subsection and section 703(d), the all-others rate shall be an amount equal to the weighted average countervailable subsidy rates established for exporters and producers individually investigated, excluding any zero and de minimis countervailable subsidy rates, and any rates determined entirely under section 776.

(ii) Exception. If the countervailable subsidy rates established for all exporters and producers individually investigated are zero or de minimis rates, or are determined entirely under section 776, the administering authority may use any reasonable method to establish an all-others rate for exporters and producers not individually investigated, including averaging the weighted average countervailable subsidy rates determined for the exporters and producers individually investigated.

(B) Country-wide subsidy rate. The administering authority may calculate a single country-wide subsidy rate, applicable to all exporters and producers, if the administering authority limits its examination pursuant to section 777A(e)(2)(B). The estimated country-wide rate determined under section 703(d)(1)(A)(ii) or paragraph (1)(B)(i)(II) of this subsection shall be based on industry-wide data regarding the use of subsidies determined to be countervailable.

(d) Publication of notice of determinations. Whenever the administering authority or the Commission makes a determination under this section, it shall notify the petitioner, other parties to the investigation, and the other agency of its determination and of the facts and conclusions of law upon which the determination is based, and it shall publish notice of its determination in the Federal Register.

(e) Correction of ministerial errors. The administering authority shall establish procedures for the correction of ministerial errors in final determinations within a reasonable time after the determinations are issued under this section. Such procedures shall ensure opportunity for interested parties to present their views regarding any such errors. As used in this subsection, the term "ministerial error" includes errors in addition, subtraction, or other arithmetic function, clerical errors resulting from inaccurate copying, duplication, or the like, and any other type of unintentional error which the administering authority considers ministerial.

19 USC 1671e

Sec. 706.   Assessment of Duty

(a) Publication of countervailing duty order. Within 7 days after being notified by the Commission of an affirmative determination under section 705(b), the administering authority shall publish a countervailing duty order which—

(1) directs customs officers to assess a countervailing duty equal to the amount of the net countervailable subsidy determined or estimated to exist, within 6 months after the date on which the administering authority receives satisfactory information upon which the assessment may be based, but in no event later than 12 months after the end of the annual accounting period of the manufacturer or exporter within which the merchandise is entered, or withdrawn from warehouse, for consumption,

(2) includes a description of the subject merchandise, in such detail as the administering authority deems necessary, and

(3) requires the deposit of estimated countervailing duties pending liquidation of entries of merchandise at the same time as estimated normal customs duties on that merchandise are deposited.

(b) Imposition of duties.

(1) General rule. If the Commission, in its final determination under section 705(b), finds material injury or threat of material injury which, but for the suspension of liquidation under section 703(d)(2), would have led to a finding of material injury, then entries of the merchandise subject to the countervailing duty order, the liquidation of which has been suspended under section 703(d)(2), shall be subject to the imposition of countervailing duties under section 701(a).

(2) Special rule. If the Commission, in its final determination under section 705(b), finds threat of material injury, other than threat of material injury described in paragraph (1), or material retardation of the establishment of an industry in the United States, then merchandise subject to a countervailing duty order which is entered, or withdrawn from warehouse, for

consumption on or after the date of publication of notice of an affirmative determination of the Commission under section 705(b) shall be subject to the imposition of countervailing duties under section 701(a), and the administering authority shall release any bond or other security, and refund any cash deposit made, to secure the payment of countervailing duties with respect to entries of the merchandise entered, or withdrawn from warehouse, for consumption before that date.

(c) Special Rule for Regional Industries.

(1) In general. In an investigation under this subtitle in which the Commission makes a regional industry determination under section 771(4)(C), the administering authority shall, to the maximum extent possible, direct that duties be assessed only on the subject merchandise of the specific exporters or producers that exported the subject merchandise for sale in the region concerned during the period of investigation.

(2) Exception for new exporters and producers. After publication of the countervailing duty order, if the administering authority finds that a new exporter or producer is exporting the subject merchandise for sale in the region concerned, the administering authority shall direct that duties be assessed on the subject merchandise of the new exporter or producer consistent with the provisions of section 751(a)(2)(B).

19 USC 1671f

Sec. 707. Treatment of Difference Between Deposit of Estimated Countervailing Duty and Final Assessed Duty Under Countervailing Duty Order

(a) Deposit of estimated countervailing duty under section 703(d)(1)(B). If the amount of a cash deposit, or the amount of any bond or other security, required as security for an estimated countervailing duty under section 703(d)(1)(B) is different from the amount of the countervailing duty determined under a countervailing duty order issued under section 706, then the difference for entries of merchandise entered, or withdrawn from warehouse, for consumption before notice of the affirmative determination of the Commission under section 705(b) is published shall be—

(1) disregarded, to the extent that the cash deposit, bond, or other security is lower than the duty under the order, or

(2) refunded or released, to the extent that the cash deposit, bond, or other security is higher than the duty under the order.

(b) Deposit of estimated countervailing duty under section 706(a)(3). If the amount of an estimated countervailing duty deposited under section 706(a)(3) is different from the amount of the countervailing duty determined under a countervailing duty order issued under section 706, then the difference for entries of merchandise entered, or withdrawn from warehouse, for consumption after notice of the affirmative determination of the Commission under section 705(b) is published shall be—

(1) collected, to the extent that the deposit under section 706(a)(3) is lower than the duty determined under the order, or

(2) refunded, to the extent that the deposit under section 706(a)(3) is higher than the duty determined under the order,

together with interest as provided by section 778.

19 USC 1671g

Sec. 708.   Effect of Derogation of Export-Import Bank Financing

Nothing in this subtitle shall be interpreted as superseding the provisions of section 635a-3 of Title 12, except that in the event of an assessment of duty based on a derogation under section 706 or action under section 703(d)(1)(B), the Secretary of the Treasury shall not authorize the Bank to provide guarantees, insurance and credits to competing United States sellers pursuant to section 635a-3 of Title 12.

19 USC 1671h

Sec. 709.   Conditional Payment of Countervailing Duty

(a) In general. For all entries, or withdrawals from warehouse, for consumption of merchandise subject to a countervailing duty order on or after the date of publication of such order, no customs officer may deliver merchandise of that class or kind to the person by whom or for whose account it was imported unless that person complies with the requirement of subsection (b) and deposits with the appropriate customs officer an estimated countervailing duty in an amount determined by the administering authority.

(b) Importer requirements. In order to meet the requirements of this subsection, a person shall—

(1) furnish, or arrange to have furnished, to the appropriate customs officer such information as the administering authority deems necessary for ascertaining any countervailing duty to be imposed under this subtitle,

(2) maintain and furnish to the customs officer such records concerning such merchandise as the administering authority, by regulation, requires, and

(3) pay, or agree to pay on demand, to the customs officer the amount of countervailing duty imposed under this subtitle on that merchandise.

Subtitle B

Imposition of Antidumping Duties

19 USC 1673

Sec. 731.   Antidumping Duties Imposed

If—

(1) the administering authority determines that a class or kind of foreign merchandise is being, or is likely to be, sold in the United States at less than its fair value, and

(2) the Commission determines that—

(A) an industry in the United States—

(i) is materially injured, or

(ii) is threatened with material injury, or

(B) the establishment of an industry in the United States is materially retarded,

by reason of imports of that merchandise or by reason of sales (or the likelihood of sales) of that merchandise for importation, then there shall be imposed upon such merchandise an antidumping duty, in addition to any other duty imposed, in an amount equal to the amount by which the normal value exceeds the export price (or the constructed export price) for the merchandise.

For purposes of this section and section 735(b)(1), a reference to the sale of foreign merchandise includes the entering into of any leasing arrangement regarding the merchandise that is equivalent to the sale of the merchandise.

19 USC 1673a

Sec. 732. Procedures for Initiating an Antidumping Duty Investigation

(a) Initiation by administering authority.

(1) In general. An antidumping duty investigation shall be initiated whenever the administering authority determines, from information available to it, that a formal investigation is warranted into the question of whether the elements necessary for the imposition of a duty under section 731 exists.

(2) Cases involving persistent dumping.

(A) Monitoring. The administering authority may establish a monitoring program with respect to imports of a class or kind of merchandise from any additional supplier country for a period not to exceed one year if—

(i) more than one antidumping order is in effect with respect to that class or kind of merchandise;

(ii) in the judgment of the administering authority there is reason to believe or suspect an extraordinary pattern of persistent injurious dumping from one or more additional supplier countries; and

(iii) in the judgment of the administering authority this extraordinary pattern is causing a serious commercial problem for the domestic industry.

(B) If during the period of monitoring referred to in subparagraph (A), the administering authority determines that there is sufficient information to initiate a formal investigation under this subsection regarding an additional supplier country, the administering authority shall immediately initiate such an investigation.

(C) Definition. For purposes of this paragraph, the term "additional supplier country" means a country regarding which no antidumping investigation is currently pending, and no antidumping duty order is currently in effect, with respect to imports of the class or kind of merchandise covered by subparagraph (A).

(D) Expeditious action. The administering authority and the Commission, to the extent practicable, shall expedite proceedings under this subtitle as a result of a formal investigation initiated under subparagraph (B).

(b) Initiation by petition.

(1) Petition requirements. An antidumping proceeding shall be initiated whenever an interested party described in subparagraph (C), (D), (E), (F), or (G) of section 771(9) files a petition with the administering authority, on behalf of an industry, which alleges the elements necessary for the imposition of the duty imposed by section 731, and which is accompanied by information reasonably available to the petitioner supporting those allegations. The petition may be amended at such time, and upon such conditions, as the administering authority and the Commission may permit.

(2) Simultaneous filing with Commission. The petitioner shall file a copy of the petition with the Commission on the same day as it is filed with the administering authority.

(3) Action with respect to petitions.

(A) Notification of governments. Upon receipt of a petition filed under paragraph (1), the administering authority shall notify the government of any exporting country named in the petition by delivering a public version of the petition to an appropriate representative of such country.

(B) Acceptance of communications. The administering authority shall not accept any unsolicited oral or written communication from any person other than an interested party described in section 771(9) (C), (D), (E), (F), or (G) before the administering authority makes its decision whether to initiate an investigation, except as provided in subsection (c)(4)(D), and except for inquiries regarding the status of the administering authority's consideration of the petition.

(C) Nondisclosure of certain information. The administering authority and the Commission shall not disclose information with regard to any draft petition submitted for review and comment before it is filed under paragraph (1).

(c) Petition determination.

(1) In general.

(A) Time for initial determination. Except as provided in subparagraph (B), within 20 days after the date on which a petition is filed under subsection (b), the administering authority shall—

    (i) after examining, on the basis of sources readily available to the administering authority, the accuracy and adequacy of the evidence provided in the petition, determine whether the petition alleges the elements necessary for the imposition of a duty under section 731 and contains information reasonably available to the petitioner supporting the allegations, and

    (ii) determine if the petition has been filed by or on behalf of the industry.

(B) Extension of time. In any case in which the administering authority is required to poll or otherwise determine support for the petition by the industry under paragraph (4)(D), the administering authority may, in exceptional circumstances, apply subparagraph (A) by substituting "a maximum of 40 days" for "20 days".

(C) Time limits where petition involves same merchandise as an order that has been revoked. If a petition is filed under this section with respect to merchandise that was the subject merchandise of—

(i) an antidumping duty order or finding that was revoked under section 751(d) in the 24 months preceding the date the petition is filed, or

(ii) a suspended investigation that was terminated under section 751(d) in the 24 months preceding the date the petition is filed,

the administering authority and the Commission shall, to the maximum extent practicable, expedite any investigation initiated under this section with respect to the petition.

(2) Affirmative determinations. If the determinations under clauses (i) and (ii) of paragraph (1)(A) are affirmative, the administering authority shall initiate an investigation to determine whether the subject merchandise is being, or is likely to be, sold in the United States at less than its fair value.

(3) Negative determinations. If the determination under clause (i) or (ii) of paragraph (1)(A) is negative, the administering authority shall dismiss the petition, terminate the proceeding, and notify the petitioner in writing of the reasons for the determination.

(4) Determination of industry support.

(A) General rule. For purposes of this subsection, the administering authority shall determine that the petition has been filed by or on behalf of the industry, if—

(i) the domestic producers or workers who support the petition account for at least 25 percent of the total production of the domestic like product, and

(ii) the domestic producers or workers who support the petition account for more than 50 percent of the production of the domestic like product produced by that portion of the industry expressing support for or opposition to the petition.

(B) Certain positions disregarded.

(i) Producers related to foreign producers. In determining industry support under subparagraph (A), the administering authority shall disregard the position of domestic producers who oppose the petition, if such producers are related to foreign producers, as defined in section 771(4)(B)(ii), unless such domestic producers demonstrate that their interests as domestic producers would be adversely affected by the imposition of an antidumping duty order.

(ii) Producers who are importers. The administering authority may disregard the position of domestic producers of a domestic like product who are importers of the subject merchandise.

(C) Special rule for regional industries. If the petition alleges the industry is a regional industry, the administering authority shall determine whether the petition has been filed by or on behalf of the industry by applying subparagraph (A) on the basis of production in the region.

(D) Polling the industry. If the petition does not establish support of domestic producers or workers accounting for more than 50 percent of the total production of the domestic like product, the administering authority shall—

(i) poll the industry or rely on other information in order to determine if there is support for the petition as required by subparagraph (A), or

(ii) if there is a large number of producers in the industry, the administering authority may determine industry support for the petition by using any statistically valid sampling method to poll the industry.

(E) Comments by interested parties. Before the administering authority makes a determination with respect to initiating an investigation, any person who would qualify as an interested party under section 771(9) if an investigation were initiated, may submit comments or information on the issue of industry support. After the administering authority makes a determination with respect to initiating an investigation, the determination regarding industry support shall not be reconsidered.

(5) *Definition of domestic producers or workers.* For purposes of this subsection, the term "domestic producers or workers" means those interested parties who are eligible to file a petition under subsection (b)(1).

(d) **Notification to Commission of determination.** The administering authority shall—

(1) notify the Commission immediately of any determination it makes under subsection (a) or (c), and

(2) if the determination is affirmative, make available to the Commission such information as it may have relating to the matter under investigation, under such procedures as the administering authority and the Commission may establish to prevent disclosure, other than with the consent of the party providing it or under protective order, of any information to which confidential treatment has been given by the administering authority.

(e) **Information regarding critical circumstances.** If, at any time after the initiation of an investigation under this subtitle, the administering authority finds a reasonable basis to suspect that—

(1) there is a history of dumping in the United States or elsewhere of the subject merchandise, or

(2) the person by whom, or for whose account, the merchandise was imported knew, or should have known, that the exporter was selling the subject merchandise at less than its fair value,

the administering authority may request the Commissioner of Customs to compile information on an expedited basis regarding entries of the subject merchandise. Upon receiving such request, the Commissioner of Customs shall collect information regarding the volume and value of entries of the subject merchandise and shall transmit such information to the administering authority at such times as the administering authority shall direct (at least once every 30 days), until a final determination is made under section 735(a), the investigation is terminated, or the administering authority withdraws the request.

19 USC 1673b

Sec. 733. Preliminary Determinations

(a) Determination by Commission of Reasonable Indication of Injury.

(1) General rule. Except in the case of a petition dismissed by the administering authority under section 732(c)(3), the Commission, within the time specified in paragraph (2), shall determine, based on the information available to it at the time of the determination, whether there is a reasonable indication that—

(A) an industry in the United States—

(i) is materially injured, or

(ii) is threatened with material injury, or

(B) the establishment of an industry in the United States is materially retarded, by reason of imports of the subject merchandise and that imports of the subject merchandise are not negligible. If the Commission finds that imports of the subject merchandise are negligible or otherwise makes a negative determination under this paragraph, the investigation shall be terminated.

(2) Time for commission determination. The Commission shall make the determination described in paragraph (1)

(A) in the case of a petition filed under section 732(b)—

(i) within 45 days after the date on which the petition is filed, or

(ii) if the time has been extended pursuant to section 732(c)(1)(B), within 25 days after the date on which the Commission receives notice from the administering authority of initiation of the investigation, and

(B) in the case of an investigation initiated under section 732(a), within 45 days after the date on which the Commission receives notice from the administering authority that an investigation has been initiated under such section.

(b) Preliminary determination by administering authority.

(1) Period of antidumping duty investigation.

(A) In general. Except as provided in subparagraph (B), within 140 days after the date on which the administering authority initiates an investigation under section 732(c), or an investigation is initiated under section 732(a), but not before an affirmative determination by the Commission under subsection (a) of this section, the administering authority shall make a determination, based upon the information available to it at the time of the determination, of whether there is a reasonable basis to believe or suspect that the merchandise is being sold, or is likely to be sold, at less than fair value.

(B) If certain short life cycle merchandise involved. If a petition filed under section 732(b), or an investigation initiated under section 732(a), concerns short life cycle merchandise that is included in a product category established under section 739(a), subparagraph (A) shall be applied—

(i) by substituting "100 days" for "140 days" if manufacturers that are second offenders account for a significant proportion of the merchandise under investigation, and

(ii) by substituting "80 days" for "140 days" if manufacturers that are multiple offenders account for a significant proportion of the merchandise under investigation.

(C) Definitions of offenders. For purposes of subparagraph (B)—

(i) The term "second offender" means a manufacturer that is specified in 2 affirmative dumping determinations (within the meaning of section 739) as the manufacturer of short life cycle merchandise that is—

(I) specified in both such determinations, and

(II) within the scope of the product category referred to in subparagraph (B).

(ii) The term "multiple offender" means a manufacturer that is specified in 3 or more affirmative dumping determinations (within the meaning of section 739) as the manufacturer of short life cycle merchandise that is—

(I) specified in each of such determinations, and

(II) within the scope of the product category referred to in subparagraph (B).

(2) *Preliminary determination under waiver of verification.* Within 75 days after the initiation of an investigation, the administering authority shall cause an official designated for such purpose to review the information concerning the case received during the first 60 days of the investigation, and, if there appears to be sufficient information available upon which the preliminary determination can reasonably be based, to disclose to the petitioner and any interested party, then a party to the proceedings that requests such disclosure, all available nonconfidential information and all other information which is disclosed pursuant to section 777. Within 3 days (not counting Saturdays, Sundays, or legal public holidays) after such disclosure, the petitioner and each party which is an interested party described in subparagraph (C), (D), (E), (F), or (G) of section 771(9) to whom such disclosure was made may furnish to the administering authority an irrevocable written waiver of verification of the information received by the authority, and an agreement that it is willing to have a preliminary determination made on the basis of the record then available to the authority. If a timely waiver and agreement have been received from the petitioner and each party which is an interested party described in subparagraph (C), (D), (E), (F), or (G) of section 771(9) to whom the disclosure was made, and the authority finds that sufficient information is

then available upon which the preliminary determination can reasonably be based, a preliminary determination shall be made within 90 days after the initiation of the investigation on the basis of the record established during the first 60 days after the investigation was initiated.

(3) De minimis dumping margin. In making a determination under this subsection, the administering authority shall disregard any weighted average dumping margin that is de minimis. For purposes of the preceding sentence, a weighted average dumping margin is de minimis if the administering authority determines that it is less than 2 percent ad valorem or the equivalent specific rate for the subject merchandise.

(c) Extension of period in extraordinarily complicated cases.

(1) In general. If—

(A) the petitioner makes a timely request for an extension of the period within which the determination must be made under subsection (b)(1), or

(B) the administering authority concludes that the parties concerned are cooperating and determines that—

(i) the case is extraordinarily complicated by reason of—

(I) the number and complexity of the transactions to be investigated or adjustments to be considered,

(II) the novelty of the issues presented, or

(III) the number of firms whose activities must be investigated, and

(ii) additional time is necessary to make the preliminary determination,

then the administering authority may postpone making the preliminary determination under subsection (b)(1) until not later than the 190th day after the date on which the administering authority initiates an investigation under section 732(c), or an investigation is initiated under section 732(a). No extension of a determination date may be made under this paragraph for any investigation in which a determination date provided for in subsection (b)(1)(B) applies unless the petitioner submits written notice to the administering authority of its consent to the extension.

(2) Notice of postponement. The administering authority shall notify the parties to the investigation, not later than 20 days before the date on which the preliminary determination would otherwise be required under subsection (b)(1), if it intends to postpone making the preliminary determination under paragraph (1). The notification shall include an explanation of the reasons for the postponement, and notice of the postponement shall be published in the Federal Register.

(d) Effect of determination by the administering authority. If the preliminary determination of the administering authority under subsection (b) is affirmative, the administering authority—

(1)(A) shall

(i) determine an estimated weighted average dumping margin for each exporter and producer individually investigated, and

(ii) determine, in accordance with section 735(c)(5), an estimated all-others rate for all exporters and producers not individually investigated, and

(B) shall order the posting of a cash deposit, bond, or other security, as the administering authority deems appropriate, for each entry of the subject merchandise in an amount based on the estimated weighted average dumping margin or the estimated all-others rate, whichever is applicable,

(2) shall order the suspension of liquidation of all entries of merchandise subject to the determination which are entered, or withdrawn from warehouse, for consumption on or after the later of

(A) the date on which notice of the determination is published in the Federal Register, or

(B) the date that is 60 days after the date on which notice of the determination to initiate the investigation is published in the Federal Register, and

(3) shall make available to the Commission all information upon which such determination was based and which the Commission considers relevant to its injury determination, under such procedures as the administering authority and the Commission may establish to prevent disclosure, other than with the consent of the party providing it or under protective order, of any information to which confidential treatment has been given by the administering authority.

The instructions of the administering authority under paragraphs (1) and (2) may not remain in effect for more than 4 months, except that the administering authority may, at the request of exporters representing a significant proportion of exports of the subject merchandise, extend that 4-month period to not more than 6 months.

(e) Critical circumstances determinations.

(1) In general. If a petitioner alleges critical circumstances in its original petition, or by amendment at any time more than 20 days before the date of a final determination by the administering authority, then the administering authority shall promptly (at any time after the initiation of the investigation under this subtitle) determine, on the basis of the information available to it at that time, whether there is a reasonable basis to believe or suspect that—

(A)(i) there is a history of dumping and material injury by reason of dumped imports in the United States or elsewhere of the subject merchandise, or

(ii) the person by whom, or for whose account, the merchandise was imported knew or should have known that the exporter was selling the subject merchandise at less than its fair value and that there was likely to be material injury by reason of such sales, and

(B) there have been massive imports of the subject merchandise over a relatively short period.

The administering authority shall be treated as having made an affirmative determination under subparagraph (A) in any investigation to which subsection (b)(1)(B) is applied.

(2) Suspension of liquidation. If the determination of the administering authority under paragraph (1) is affirmative, then any suspension of liquidation ordered under subsection (d)(2) shall apply, or, if notice of such suspension of liquidation is already published, be amended to apply, to unliquidated entries of merchandise entered, or withdrawn from warehouse, for consumption on or after the later of

(A) the date which is 90 days before the date on which the suspension of liquidation was first ordered, or

(B) the date on which notice of the determination to initiate the investigation is published in the Federal Register.

(f) Notice of Determination. Whenever the Commission or the administering authority makes a determination under this section, the Commission or the administering authority, as the case may be, shall notify the petitioner, and other parties to the investigation, and the Commission or the administering authority (whichever is appropriate) of its determination. The administering authority shall include with such notification the facts and conclusions on which its determination is based. Not later than 5 days after the date on which the determination is required to be made under subsection (a)(2), the Commission shall transmit to the administering authority the facts and conclusions on which its determination is based.

19 USC 1673c

Sec. 734. Termination or Suspension of Investigation

(a) Termination of investigation upon withdrawal of petition.

(1) In general.

(A) Withdrawal of petition. Except as provided in paragraphs (2) and (3), an investigation under this subtitle may be terminated by either the administering authority or the Commission, after notice to all parties to the investigation, upon withdrawal of the petition by the petitioner or by the administering authority if the investigation was initiated under section 732(a).

(B) Refiling of petition. If, within 3 months after the withdrawal of a petition under subparagraph (A), a new petition is filed seeking the imposition of duties on both the subject merchandise of the withdrawn petition and the subject merchandise from another country, the administering authority and the Commission may use in the investigation initiated pursuant to the new petition any records compiled in an investigation conducted pursuant to the withdrawn petition. This subparagraph applies only with respect to the first withdrawal of a petition.

(2) Special rules for quantitative restriction agreements.

(A) In general. Subject to subparagraphs (B) and (C), the administering authority may not terminate an investigation under paragraph (1) by accepting an understanding or other kind of agreement to limit the volume of imports into the United States of the subject merchandise unless the administering authority is satisfied that termination on the basis of that agreement is in the public interest.

(B) Public interest factors. In making a decision under subparagraph (A) regarding the public interest the administering authority shall take into account—

(i) whether, based upon the relative impact on consumer prices and the availability of supplies of the merchandise, the agreement would have a greater adverse impact on United States consumers than the imposition of antidumping duties;

(ii) the relative impact on the international economic interests of the United States; and

(iii) the relative impact on the competitiveness of the domestic industry producing the like merchandise, including any such impact on employment and investment in that industry.

(C) Prior consultations. Before making a decision under subparagraph (A) regarding the public interest, the administering authority shall, to the extent practicable, consult with—

(i) potentially affected consuming industries; and

(ii) potentially affected producers and workers in the domestic industry producing the like merchandise, including producers and workers not party to the investigation.

(3) Limitation on termination by commission. The Commission may not terminate an investigation under paragraph (1) before a preliminary determination is made by the administering authority under section 733(b).

(b) Agreements to eliminate completely sales at less than fair value or to cease exports of merchandise. The administering authority may suspend an investigation if the exporters of the subject merchandise who account for substantially all of the imports of that merchandise agree—

(1) to cease exports of the merchandise to the United States within 6 months after the date on which the investigation is suspended, or

(2) to revise their prices to eliminate completely any amount by which the normal value of the subject merchandise exceeds the export price (or the constructed export price) of that merchandise.

(c) Agreements eliminating injurious effect.

(1) General rule. If the administering authority determines that extraordinary circumstances are present in a case, it may suspend an investigation upon the acceptance of an agreement to revise prices from exporters of the subject merchandise who account for substantially all of the imports of that merchandise into the United States, if the agreement will eliminate completely the injurious effect of exports to the United States of that merchandise and if—

(A) the suppression or undercutting of price levels of domestic products by imports of that merchandise will be prevented, and

(B) for each entry of each exporter the amount by which the estimated normal value exceeds the export price (or the constructed export price) will not exceed 15 percent of the weighted average amount by which the estimated normal value exceeded the export price (or the constructed export price) for all less-than-fair-value entries of the exporter examined during the course of the investigation.

(2) Definition of extraordinary circumstances.

(A) Extraordinary circumstances. For purposes of this subsection, the term "extraordinary circumstances" means circumstances in which—

(i) suspension of an investigation will be more beneficial to the domestic industry than continuation of the investigation, and

(ii) the investigation is complex.

(B) Complex. For purposes of this paragraph, the term "complex" means—

(i) there are a large number of transactions to be investigated or adjustments to be considered,

(ii) the issues raised are novel, or

(iii) the number of firms involved is large.

(d) Additional rules and conditions. The administering authority may not accept an agreement under subsection (b) or (c) unless—

(1) it is satisfied that suspension of the investigation is in the public interest, and

(2) effective monitoring of the agreement by the United States is practicable.

Where practicable the administering authority shall provide to the exporters who would have been subject to the agreement the reasons for not accepting the agreement and, to the extent possible, an opportunity to submit comments thereon.

(e) Suspension of investigation procedure. Before an investigation may be suspended under subsection (b) or (c) the administering authority shall—

(1) notify the petitioner of, and consult with the petitioner concerning, its intention to suspend the investigation, and notify other parties to the investigation and the Commission not less than 30 days before the date on which it suspends the investigation,

(2) provide a copy of the proposed agreement to the petitioner at the time of the notification, together with an explanation of how the agreement will be carried out and enforced, and of how the agreement will meet the requirements of subsections (b) and (d) or (c) and (d), and

(3) permit all interested parties described in section 771(9) to submit comments and information for the record before the date on which notice of suspension of the investigation is published under subsection (f)(1)(A).

(f) Effects of suspension of investigation.

(1) In general. If the administering authority determines to suspend an investigation upon acceptance of an agreement described in subsection (b) or (c), then—

(A) it shall suspend the investigation, publish notice of suspension of the investigation, and issue an affirmative preliminary determination under section 733(b) with respect to the subject merchandise, unless it has previously issued such a determination in the same investigation.

(B) the Commission shall suspend any investigation it is conducting with respect to that merchandise, and

(C) the suspension of investigation shall take effect on the day on which such notice is published.

(2) Liquidation of entries.

(A) Cessation of exports; complete elimination of dumping margin. If the agreement accepted by the administering authority is an agreement described in subsection (b), then—

(i) notwithstanding the affirmative preliminary determination required under paragraph (1)(A), the liquidation of entries of subject merchandise shall not be suspended under section 733(d)(2),

(ii) if the liquidation of entries of such merchandise was suspended pursuant to a previous affirmative preliminary determination in the same case with respect to such merchandise, that suspension of liquidation shall terminate, and

(iii) the administering authority shall refund any cash deposit and release any bond or other security deposited under section 733(d)(1)(B).

(B) Other agreements. If the agreement accepted by the administering authority is an agreement described in subsection (c), the liquidation of entries of the subject merchandise shall be suspended under section 733(d)(2), or, if the liquidation of entries of such merchandise was suspended pursuant to a previous affirmative preliminary determination in the same case, that suspension of liquidation shall continue in effect, subject to subsection (h)(3), but the security required under section 733(d)(1)(B) may be adjusted to reflect the effect of the agreement.

(3) Where investigation is continued. If, pursuant to subsection (g), the administering authority and the Commission continue an investigation in which an agreement has been accepted under subsection (b) or (c), then—

(A) if the final determination by the administering authority or the Commission under section 735 is negative, the agreement shall have no force or effect and the investigation shall be terminated, or

(B) if the final determinations by the administering authority and the Commission under such section are affirmative, the agreement shall remain in force, but the administering authority shall not issue an antidumping duty order in the case so long as—

(i) the agreement remains in force,

(ii) the agreement continues to meet the requirements of subsections (b) and (d), or (c) and (d), and

(iii) the parties to the agreement carry out their obligations under the agreement in accordance with its terms.

(g) Investigation to be continued upon request. If the administering authority, within 20 days after the date of publication of the notice of suspension of an investigation, receives a request for the continuation of the investigation from—

(1) an exporter or exporters accounting for a significant proportion of exports to the United States of the subject merchandise, or

(2) an interested party described in subparagraph (C), (D), (E), (F), or (G) of section 771(9) which is a party to the investigation,

then the administering authority and the Commission shall continue the investigation.

(h) Review of suspension.

(1) In general. Within 20 days after the suspension of an investigation under subsection (c), an interested party which is a party to the investigation and which is described in subparagraph (C), (D), (E), (F), or (G) of section 771(9) may, by petition filed with the Commission and with notice to the administering authority, ask for a review of the suspension.

(2) Commission investigation. Upon receipt of a review petition under paragraph (1), the Commission shall, within 75 days after the date on which the petition is filed with it, determine whether the injurious effect of imports of the subject merchandise is eliminated completely by the agreement. If the Commission's determination under this subsection is negative, the investigation shall be resumed on the date of publication of notice of such determination as if the affirmative preliminary determination under section 733(b) had been made on that date.

(3) Suspension of liquidation to continue during review period. The suspension of liquidation of entries of the subject merchandise shall terminate at the close of the 20-day period beginning on the day after the date on which notice of suspension of the investigation is published in the Federal Register, or, if a review petition is filed under paragraph (1) with respect to the suspension of the investigation, in the case of an affirmative determination by the Commission under paragraph (2), the date on which notice of an affirmative determination by the Commission is published. If the determination of the Commission under paragraph (2) is affirmative, then the administering authority shall—

(A) terminate the suspension of liquidation under section 733(d)(2), and

(B) release any bond or other security, and refund any cash deposit, required under section 733(d)(1)(B).

(i) Violation of agreement.

(1) In general. If the administering authority determines that an agreement accepted under subsection (b) or (c) is being, or has been, violated, or no longer meets the requirements of such subsection (other than the requirement, under subsection (c)(1), of elimination of injury) and subsection (d), then, on the date of publication of its determination, it shall—

(A) suspend liquidation under section 733(d)(2) of unliquidated entries of the merchandise made on the later of—

(i) the date which is 90 days before the date of publication of the notice of suspension of liquidation, or

(ii) the date on which the merchandise, the sale or export to the United States of which was in violation of the agreement, or under an agreement which no longer meets the requirements of subsections (b) and (d), or (c) and (d), was first entered, or withdrawn from warehouse, for consumption,

(B) if the investigation was not completed, resume the investigation as if its affirmative preliminary determination were made on the date of its determination under this paragraph,

(C) if the investigation was completed under subsection (g), issue an antidumping duty order under section 736(a) effective with respect to entries of merchandise liquidation of which was suspended,

(D) if it considers the violation to be intentional, notify the Commissioner of Customs who shall take appropriate action under paragraph (2), and

(E) notify the petitioner, interested parties who are or were parties to the investigation, and the Commission of its action under this paragraph.

(2) Intentional violation to be punished by civil penalty. Any person who intentionally violates an agreement accepted by the administering authority under subsection (b) or (c) shall be subject to a civil penalty assessed in the same amount, in the same manner, and under the same procedures, as the penalty imposed for a fraudulent violation of section 592(a) of this Act.

(j) Determination not to take agreement into account. In making a final determination under section 735, or in conducting a review under section 751, in a case in which the administering authority has terminated a suspension of investigation under subsection (i)(1), or continued an investigation under subsection (g), the Commission and the administering authority shall consider all of the subject merchandise without regard to the effect of any agreement under subsection (b) or (c).

(k) Termination of investigation initiated by administering authority. The administering authority may terminate any investigation initiated by the administering authority under section 732(a) after providing notice of such termination to all parties to the investigation.

(*l*) Special rule for nonmarket economy countries.

(1) In general. The administering authority may suspend an investigation under this subtitle upon acceptance of an agreement with a nonmarket economy country to restrict the volume of imports into the United States of the merchandise under investigation only if the administering authority determines that—

(A) such agreement satisfies the requirements of subsection (d), and

(B) will prevent the suppression or undercutting of price levels of domestic products by imports of the merchandise under investigation.

(2) Failure of agreements. If the administering authority determines that an agreement accepted under this subsection no longer prevents the suppression or undercutting of domestic prices of merchandise manufactured in the United States, the provisions of subsection (i) shall apply.

(m) Special Rule for Regional Industry Investigations.

(1) Suspension agreements. If the Commission makes a regional industry determination under section 771(4)(C), the administering authority shall offer exporters of the subject merchandise who account for substantially all exports of that merchandise for sale in the region concerned the opportunity to enter into an agreement described in subsection (b), (c), or (*l*).

(2) Requirements for suspension agreements. Any agreement described in paragraph (1) shall be subject to all the requirements imposed under this section for other agreements under subsection (b), (c), or (*l*), except that if the Commission makes a regional industry determination described in paragraph (1) in the final affirmative determination under section 735(b) but not in the preliminary affirmative determination under section 733(a), any agreement described in paragraph (1) may be accepted within 60 days after the antidumping order is published under section 736.

(3) Effect of suspension agreement on antidumping duty order. If an agreement described in paragraph (1) is accepted after the antidumping duty order is published, the administering authority shall rescind the order, refund any cash deposit and release any bond or other security deposited under section 733(d)(1)(B), and instruct the Customs Service that entries of the subject merchandise that were made during the period that the order was in effect shall be liquidated without regard to antidumping duties.

19 USC 1673d

Sec. 735. Final Determinations

(a) Final determination by administering authority.

(1) General rule. Within 75 days after the date of its preliminary determination under section 733(b), the administering authority shall make a final determination of whether the subject merchandise is being, or is likely to be, sold in the United States at less than its fair value.

(2) Extension of period for determination. The administering authority may postpone making the final determination under paragraph (1) until not later than the 135th day after the date on which it published notice of its preliminary determination under section 733(b) if a request in writing for such a postponement is made by—

> (A) exporters who account for a significant proportion of exports of the merchandise which is the subject of the investigation, in a proceeding in which the preliminary determination by the administering authority under section 733(b) was affirmative, or

> (B) the petitioner, in a proceeding in which the preliminary determination by the administering authority under section 733(b) was negative.

(3) Critical circumstances determinations. If the final determination of the administering authority is affirmative, then that determination, in any investigation in which the presence of critical circumstances has been alleged under section 733(e), shall also contain a finding of whether—

> (A)(i) there is a history of dumping and material injury by reason of dumped imports in the United States or elsewhere of the subject merchandise, or

(ii) the person by whom, or for whose account, the merchandise was imported knew or should have known that the exporter was selling the subject merchandise at less than its fair value and that there would be material injury by reason of such sales, and

(B) there have been massive imports of the subject merchandise over a relatively short period.

Such findings may be affirmative even though the preliminary determination under section 733(e)(1) was negative.

(4) De minimis dumping margin. In making a determination under this subsection, the administering authority shall disregard any weighted average dumping margin that is de minimis as defined in section 733(b)(3).

(b) Final determination by commission.

(1) In general. The Commission shall make a final determination of whether—

(A) an industry in the United States—

(i) is materially injured, or

(ii) is threatened with material injury, or

(B) the establishment of an industry in the United States is materially retarded,

by reason of imports or sales (or the likelihood of sales) for importation of the merchandise with respect to which the administering authority has made an affirmative determination under subsection (a)(1). If the Commission determines that imports of the subject merchandise are negligible, the investigation shall be terminated.

(2) Period for injury determination following affirmative preliminary determination by administering authority. If the preliminary determination by the administering authority under section 733(b) is affirmative, then the Commission shall make the determination required by paragraph (1) before the later of—

(A) the 120th day after the day on which the administering authority makes its affirmative preliminary determination under section 733(b), or

(B) the 45th day after the day on which the administering authority makes its affirmative final determination under subsection (a).

(3) Period for injury determination following negative preliminary determination by administering authority. If the preliminary determination by the administering authority under section 733(b) is negative, and its final determination under subsection (a) is affirmative, then the final determination by the Commission under this subsection shall be made within 75 days after the date of that affirmative final determination.

(4) Certain additional findings.

(A) Commission standard for retroactive application.

(i) In general. If the finding of the administering authority under subsection (a)(3) is affirmative, then the final determination of the Commission shall include a finding as to whether the imports subject to the affirmative determination under subsection (a)(3) are likely to undermine seriously the remedial effect of the antidumping duty order to be issued under section 736.

(ii) Factors to consider. In making the evaluation under clause (i), the Commission shall consider, among other factors it considers relevant—

(I) the timing and the volume of the imports,

(II) a rapid increase in inventories of the imports, and

(III) any other circumstances indicating that the remedial effect of the antidumping order will be seriously undermined.

(A) Retroactive application.

(i) In general. If the finding of the administering authority under subsection (a)(3) is affirmative, then the final determination of the Commission shall include a finding as to whether retroactive imposition of antidumping duties on the merchandise appears necessary to prevent recurrence of material injury that was caused by massive imports of the merchandise over a relatively short period of time.

(ii) Prevention of recurrence. For purposes of making its finding under clause (i), the Commission shall make an evaluation as to whether the effectiveness of the antidumping duty order would be materially impaired if such imposition did not occur.

(iii) Evaluation of effectiveness. In making the evaluation under clause (ii), the Commission shall consider, among other factors it considers relevant—

(I) the condition of the domestic industry,

(II) whether massive imports of the merchandise in a relatively short period of time can be accounted for by efforts to avoid the potential imposition of antidumping duties,

(III) whether foreign economic conditions led to the massive imports of the merchandise, and

(IV) whether the impact of the massive imports of the merchandise is likely to continue for some period after issuance of the antidumping duty order under this subtitle.

(B) If the final determination of the Commission is that there is no material injury but that there is threat of material injury, then its determination shall also include a finding as to whether material injury by reason of the imports of the merchandise with respect to which the administering authority has made an affirmative determination under subsection (a) would have been found but for any suspension of liquidation of entries of the merchandise.

(c) Effect of final determinations.

(1) Effect of affirmative determination by the administering authority. If the determination of the administering authority under subsection (a) is affirmative, then—

(A) the administering authority shall make available to the Commission all information upon which such determination was based and which the Commission considers relevant to its determination, under such procedures as the administering authority and the Commission may establish to prevent disclosure, other than with the consent of the party providing it or under protective order, of any information as to which confidential treatment has been given by the administering authority,

(B) (i) the administering authority shall

(I) determine the estimated weighted average dumping margin for each exporter and producer individually investigated, and

(II) determine, accordance with paragraph (5), the estimated all-others rate for all exporters and producers not individually investigated, and

(ii) the administering authority shall order the posting of a cash deposit, bond, or other security as the administering authority deems appropriate, for each entry of the subject merchandise in an amount based on the estimated weighted average dumping margin or the estimated all-others rate, whichever is applicable, and

(C) in cases where the preliminary determination by the administering authority under section 733(b) was negative, the administering authority shall order the suspension of liquidation under section 733(d)(2).

(2) Issuance of order; effect of negative determination. If the determinations of the administering authority and the Commission under subsections (a)(1) and (b)(1) are affirmative, then the administering authority shall issue an antidumping duty order under section 736(a). If either of such determinations is negative, the investigation shall be terminated upon the publication of notice of that negative determination and the administering authority shall—

(A) terminate the suspension of liquidation under section 733(d)(2), and

(B) release any bond or other security, and refund any cash deposit, required under section 733(d)(1)(B).

(3) Effect of negative determinations under subsections (a)(3) and (b)(4)(A). If the determination of the administering authority or the Commission under subsection (a)(3) or (b)(4)(A), respectively, is negative, then the administering authority shall—

(A) terminate any retroactive suspension of liquidation required under paragraph (4) or section 733(e)(2), and

(B) release any bond or other security, and refund any cash deposit required, under section 733(d)(1)(B) with respect to entries of the merchandise the liquidation of which was suspended retroactively under section 733(e)(2).

(4) Effect of affirmative determination under subsection (a)(3). If the determination of the administering authority under subsection (a)(3) is affirmative, then the administering authority shall—

(A) in cases where the preliminary determinations by the administering authority under sections 733(b) and 733(e)(1) were both affirmative, continue the retroactive suspension of liquidation and the posting of a cash deposit, bond, or other security previously ordered under section 733(e)(2);

(B) in cases where the preliminary determination by the administering authority under section 733(b) was affirmative, but the preliminary determination under section 733(e)(1) was negative, shall modify any suspension of liquidation and security requirement previously ordered under section 733(d) to apply to unliquidated entries of merchandise entered, or withdrawn from warehouse, for consumption on or after the date which is 90 days before the date on which suspension of liquidation was first ordered; or

(C) in cases where the preliminary determination by the administering authority under section 733(b) was negative, shall apply any suspension of liquidation and security requirement ordered under subsection 735(c)(1)(B) to unliquidated entries of merchandise entered, or withdrawn from warehouse, for consumption on or after the date which is 90 days before the date on which suspension of liquidation is first ordered.

(5) Method for determining estimated all-others rate.

(A) General rule. For purposes of this subsection and section 733(d), the estimated all-others rate shall be an amount equal to the weighted average of the estimated weighted average dumping margins established for exporters and producers individually investigated, excluding any zero and de minimis margins, and any margins determined entirely under section 776.

(B) Exception. If the estimated weighted average dumping margins established for all exporters and producers individually investigated are zero or de minimis margins, or are determined entirely under section 776, the administering authority may use any reasonable method to establish the estimated all-others rate for exporters and producers not individually investigated, including averaging the estimated weighted average dumping margins determined for the exporters and producers individually investigated.

(d) Publication of Notice of Determinations. Whenever the administering authority or the Commission makes a determination under this section, it shall notify the petitioner, other parties to the investigation, and the other agency of its determination and of the facts and conclusions of law upon which the determination is based, and it shall publish notice of its determination in the Federal Register.

(e) Correction of Ministerial Errors. The administering authority shall establish procedures for the correction of ministerial errors in final determinations within a reasonable time after the determinations are issued under this section. Such procedures shall ensure opportunity for interested parties to present their views regarding any such errors. As used in this subsection, the term "ministerial error" includes errors in addition, subtraction, or other arithmetic function, clerical errors resulting from inaccurate copying, duplication, or the like, and any other type of unintentional error which the administering authority considers ministerial.

19 USC 1673e

Sec. 736. Assessment of Duty

(a) **Publication of antidumping duty order.** Within 7 days after being notified by the Commission of an affirmative determination under section 735(b), the administering authority shall publish an antidumping duty order which—

(1) directs customs officers to assess an antidumping duty equal to the amount by which the normal value of the merchandise exceeds the export price (or the constructed export price) of the merchandise, within 6 months after the date on which the administering authority receives satisfactory information upon which the assessment may be based, but in no event later than—

(A) 12 months after the end of the annual accounting period of the manufacturer or exporter within which the merchandise is entered, or withdrawn from warehouse, for consumption, or

(B) in the case of merchandise not sold prior to its importation into the United States, 12 months after the end of the annual accounting period of the manufacturer or exporter within which it is sold in the United States to a person who is not the exporter of that merchandise,

(2) includes a description of the subject merchandise, in such detail as the administering authority deems necessary, and

(3) requires the deposit of estimated antidumping duties pending liquidation of entries of merchandise at the same time as estimated normal customs duties on that merchandise are deposited.

(b) **Imposition of duty.**

(1) General rule. If the Commission, in its final determination under section 735(b), finds material injury or threat of material injury which, but for the suspension of liquidation under section 733(d)(2) would have led to a finding of material injury, then entries of the subject merchandise, the liquidation of which has been suspended under section 733(d)(2), shall be subject to the imposition of antidumping duties under section 731.

(2) Special rule. If the Commission, in its final determination under section 735(b), finds threat of material injury, other than threat of material injury described in paragraph (1), or material retardation of the establishment of an industry in the United States, then subject merchandise which is entered, or withdrawn from warehouse, for consumption on or after the date of publication of notice of an affirmative determination of the Commission under section 735(b) shall be subject to the assessment of antidumping duties under section 731, and the administering authority shall release any bond or other security, and refund any cash deposit made, to secure the payment of antidumping duties with respect to entries of the merchandise entered, or withdrawn from warehouse, for consumption before that date.

(c) **Security in lieu of estimated duty pending early determination of duty.**

(1) Conditions for waiver of deposit of estimated duties. The administering authority may permit, for not more than 90 days after the date of publication

of an order under subsection (a), the posting of a bond or other security in lieu of the deposit of estimated antidumping duties required under subsection (a)(3) if—

    (A) the investigation has not been designated as extraordinarily complicated by reason of—

        (i) the number and complexity of the transactions to be investigated or adjustments to be considered,

        (ii) the novelty of the issues presented, or

        (iii) the number of firms whose activities must be investigated,

    (B) the final determination in the investigation has not been postponed under section 735(a)(2)(A);

    (C) on the basis of information presented to the administering authority by any manufacturer, producer, or exporter in such form and within such time as the administering authority may require, the administering authority is satisfied that a determination will be made, within 90 days after the date of publication of an order under subsection (a), of the normal value and the export price (or the constructed export price) for all merchandise of such manufacturer, producer, or exporter described in that order which was entered, or withdrawn from warehouse, for consumption on or after the date of publication of—

        (i) an affirmative preliminary determination by the administering authority under section 733(b), or

        (ii) if its determination under section 733(b) was negative, an affirmative final determination by the administering authority under section 735(a),

and before the date of publication of the affirmative final determination by the Commission under section 735(b);

    (D) the party described in subparagraph (C) provides credible evidence that the amount by which the normal value of the merchandise exceeds the export price (or the constructed export price) of the merchandise is significantly less than the amount of such excess specified in the antidumping duty order published under subsection (a); and

    (E) the data concerning the normal value and the export price (or the constructed export price) apply to sales in the usual commercial quantities and in the ordinary course of trade and the number of such sales are sufficient to form an adequate basis for comparison.

(2) Notice; hearing. If the administering authority permits the posting of a bond or other security in lieu of the deposit of estimated antidumping duties under paragraph (1), it shall—

    (A) publish notice of its action in the Federal Register, and

    (B) upon the request of any interested party, hold a hearing in accordance with section 774 before determining the normal value and the export price (or the constructed export price) of the merchandise.

(3) Determinations to be basis of antidumping duty. The administering authority shall publish notice in the Federal Register of the results of its determination of normal value and export price (or the constructed export

price), and that determination shall be the basis for the assessment of antidumping duties on entries of merchandise to which the notice under this subsection applies and also shall be the basis for the deposit of estimated antidumping duties on future entries of merchandise of manufacturers, producers, or exporters described in paragraph (1) to which the order issued under subsection (a) applies.

(4) Provision of business proprietary information; written comments. Before determining whether to permit the posting of bond or other security under paragraph (1) in lieu of the deposit of estimated antidumping duties, the administering authority shall—

(A) make all business proprietary information supplied to the administering authority under paragraph (1) available under a protective order in accordance with section 777(c) to all interested parties described in subparagraph (C), (D), (E), (F), or (G) of section 771(9), and

(B) afford all interested parties an opportunity to file written comments on whether the posting of bond or other security under paragraph (1) in lieu of the deposit of estimated antidumping duties should be permitted.

(d) Special Rule for Regional Industries.

(1) In general. In an investigation in which the Commission makes a regional industry determination under section 771(4)(C), the administering authority shall, to the maximum extent possible, direct that duties be assessed only on the subject merchandise of the specific exporters or producers that exported the subject merchandise for sale in the region concerned during the period of investigation.

(2) Exception for new exporters and producers. After publication of the antidumping duty order, if the administering authority finds that a new exporter or producer is exporting the subject merchandise for sale in the region concerned, the administering authority shall direct that duties be assessed on the subject merchandise of the new exporter or producer consistent with the provisions of section 751(a)(2)(B).

19 USC 1673f

Sec. 737. Treatment of Difference Between Deposit of Estimated Antidumping Duty and Final Assessed Duty Under Antidumping Duty Order

(a) Deposit of estimated antidumping duty under section 733(d)(1)(B). If the amount of a cash deposit, or the amount of any bond or other security, required as security for an estimated antidumping duty under section 733(d)(1)(B) is different from the amount of the antidumping duty determined under an antidumping duty order published under section 736 then the difference for entries of merchandise entered, or withdrawn from warehouse, for consumption before notice of the affirmative determination of the Commission under section 735(b) is published shall be—

(1) disregarded, to the extent that the cash deposit, bond, or other security is lower than the duty under the order, or

(2) refunded or released, to the extent that the cash deposit, bond, or other security is higher than the duty under the order.

(b) Deposit of estimated antidumping duty under section 736(a)(3). If the amount of an estimated antidumping duty deposited under section 736(a)(3) is different from the amount of the antidumping duty determined under an antidumping duty order published under section 736 then the difference for entries of merchandise entered, or withdrawn from warehouse, for consumption after notice of the affirmative determination of the Commission under section 735(b) is published shall be—

(1) collected, to the extent that the deposit under section 736(a)(3) is lower than the duty determined under the order, or

(2) refunded, to the extent that the deposit under section 736(a)(3) is higher than the duty determined under the order,

together with interest as provided by section 778.

19 USC 1673g

Sec. 738. Conditional Payment of Antidumping Duty

(a) General Rule. For all entries, or withdrawals from warehouse, for consumption of merchandise subject to an antidumping duty order on or after the date of publication of such order, no customs officer may deliver merchandise of that class or kind to the person by whom or for whose account it was imported unless that person complies with the requirements of subsection (b) and deposits with the appropriate customs officer an estimated antidumping duty in an amount determined by the administering authority.

(b) Importer Requirements. In order to meet the requirements of this subsection, a person shall—

(1) furnish, or arrange to have furnished, to the appropriate customs officer such information as the administering authority deems necessary for determining the export price (or the constructed export price) of the merchandise imported by or for the account of that person, and such other information as the administering authority deems necessary for ascertaining any antidumping duty to be imposed under this title;

(2) maintain and furnish to the customs officer such records concerning the sale of the merchandise as the administering authority, by regulation, requires;

(3) state under oath before the customs officer that he is not an exporter, or if he is an exporter, declare under oath at the time of entry the constructed export price of the merchandise to the customs officer if it is then known, or, if not, so declare within 30 days after the merchandise has been sold, or has been made the subject of an agreement to be sold, in the United States; and

(4) pay, or agree to pay on demand, to the customs officer the amount of antidumping duty imposed under section 731 on that merchandise.

19 USC 1673h

Sec. 739. Establishment of Product Categories for Short Life Cycle Merchandise

(a) Establishment of product categories.

(1) Petitions.

(A) In general. An eligible domestic entity may file a petition with the Commission requesting that a product category be established with respect to short life cycle merchandise at any time after the merchandise becomes the subject of 2 or more affirmative dumping determinations.

(B) Contents. A petition filed under subparagraph (A) shall—

(i) identify the short life cycle merchandise that is the subject of the affirmative dumping determinations,

(ii) specify the short life cycle merchandise that the petitioner seeks to have included in the same product category as the merchandise that is subject to the affirmative dumping determinations,

(iii) specify any short life cycle merchandise the petitioner particularly seeks to have excluded from the product category,

(iv) provide reasons for the inclusions and exclusions specified under clauses (ii) and (iii), and

(v) identify such merchandise in terms of the designations used in the Harmonized Tariff Schedules of the United States.

(2) Determinations on sufficiency of petition. Upon receiving a petition under paragraph (1), the Commission shall—

(A) request the administering authority to confirm promptly the affirmative determinations on which the petition is based, and

(B) upon receipt of such confirmation, determine whether the merchandise covered by the confirmed affirmative determinations is short life cycle merchandise and whether the petitioner is an eligible domestic entity.

(3) Notice; hearings. If the determinations under paragraph (2)(B) are affirmative, the Commission shall—

(A) publish notice in the Federal Register that the petition has been received, and

(B) provide opportunity for the presentation of views regarding the establishment of the requested product category, including a public hearing if requested by any interested person.

(4) Determinations.

(A) In general. By no later than the date that is 90 days after the date on which a petition is filed under paragraph (1), the Commission shall determine the scope of the product category into which the short life cycle merchandise that is the subject of the affirmative dumping determinations identified in such petition shall be classified for purposes of this section.

(B) Modifications not requested by petition.

(i) In general. The Commission may, on its own initiative, make a determination modifying the scope of any product category established under subparagraph (A) at any time.

(ii) Notice and hearing. Determinations may be made under clause (i) only after the Commission has—

(I) published in the Federal Register notice of the proposed modification, and

(II) provided interested parties an opportunity for a hearing, and a period for the submission of written comments, on the classification of merchandise into the product categories to be affected by such determination.

(C) Basis of determinations. In making determinations under subparagraph (A) or (B), the Commission shall ensure that each product category consists of similar short life cycle merchandise which is produced by similar processes under similar circumstances and has similar uses.

(b) Definitions. For purposes of this section—

(1) Eligible domestic entity. The term "eligible domestic entity" means a manufacturer or producer in the United States, or a certified union or recognized union or group of workers which is representative of an industry in the United States, that manufactures or produces short life cycle merchandise that is—

(A) like or directly competitive with other merchandise that is the subject of 2 or more affirmative dumping determinations, or

(B) is similar enough to such other merchandise as to be considered for inclusion with such merchandise in a product monitoring category established under this section.

(2) Affirmative dumping determination. The term "affirmative dumping determination" means—

(A) any affirmative final determination made by the administering authority under section 735(a) during the 8-year period preceding the filing of the petition under this section that results in the issuance of an antidumping duty order under section 736 which requires the deposit of estimated antidumping duties at a rate of not less than 15 percent ad valorem, or

(B) any affirmative preliminary determination that—

(i) is made by the administering authority under section 733(b) during the 8-year period preceding the filing of the petition under this section in the course of an investigation for which no final determination is made under section 735 by reason of a suspension of the investigation under section 734, and

(ii) includes a determination that the estimated average amount by which the normal value of the merchandise exceeds the export price (or the constructed export price) of the merchandise is not less than 15 percent ad valorem.

(3) *Subject of affirmative dumping determination.*

(A) In general. Short life cycle merchandise of a manufacturer shall be treated as being the subject of an affirmative dumping determination only if the administering authority—

(i) makes a separate determination of the amount by which the normal value of such merchandise of the manufacturer exceeds the export price (or the constructed export price) of such merchandise of the manufacturer, and

(ii) specifically identifies the manufacturer by name with such amount in the affirmative dumping determination or in an antidumping duty order issued as a result of the affirmative dumping determination.

(B) Exclusion. Short life cycle merchandise of a manufacturer shall not be treated as being the subject of an affirmative dumping determination if—

(i) such merchandise of the manufacturer is part of a group of merchandise to which the administering authority assigns (in lieu of making separate determinations described in subparagraph (A)(i)(I)) an amount determined to be the amount by which the normal value of the merchandise in such group exceeds the export price (or the constructed export price) of the merchandise in such group, and

(ii) the merchandise and the manufacturer are not specified by name in the affirmative dumping determination or in any antidumping duty order issued as a result of such affirmative dumping determination.

(4) Short life cycle merchandise. The term "short life cycle merchandise" means any product that the Commission determines is likely to become outmoded within 4 years, by reason of technological advances, after the product is commercially available. For purposes of this paragraph, the term "out-moded" refers to a kind of style that is no longer state-of-the-art.

(c) Transitional rules.

(1) For purposes of this section and section 733(b)(1)(B) and (C), all affirmative dumping determinations described in subsection (b)(2)(A) that were made after December 31, 1980, and before the date of enactment of the Omnibus Trade and Competitiveness Act of 1988, and all affirmative dumping determinations described in subsection (b)(2)(B) that were made after December 31, 1984, and before the date of enactment of such Act, with respect to each category of short life cycle merchandise of the same manufacturer shall be treated as one affirmative dumping determination with respect to that category for that manufacturer which was made on the date on which the latest of such determinations was made.

(2) No affirmative dumping determination that—

(A) is described in subsection (b)(2)(A) and was made before January 1, 1981, or

(B) is described in subsection (b)(2)(B) and was made before January 1, 1985,

may be taken into account under this section or section 733(b)(1)(B) and (C).

Subtitle C

Reviews; Other Actions Regarding Agreements

Chapter 1—Review of Amount of Duty and Agreements
Other Than Quantitative Restriction Agreements

19 USC 1675

Sec. 751. Administrative Review of Determinations

(a) Periodic review of amount of duty.

(1) In general. At least once during each 12–month period beginning on the anniversary of the date of publication of a countervailing duty order under

this title or under section 303 of this Act, an antidumping duty order under this title or a finding under the Antidumping Act, 1921, or a notice of the suspension of an investigation, the administering authority, if a request for such a review has been received and after publication of notice of such review in the Federal Register, shall—

(A) review and determine the amount of any net countervailable subsidy,

(B) review, and determine (in accordance with paragraph (2)), the amount of any antidumping duty, and

(C) review the current status of, and compliance with, any agreement by reason of which an investigation was suspended, and review the amount of any net countervailable subsidy or dumping margin involved in the agreement,

and shall publish in the Federal Register the results of such review, together with notice of any duty to be assessed, estimated duty to be deposited, or investigation to be resumed.

(2) *Determination of antidumping duties.*

(A) In general. For the purpose of paragraph (1)(B), the administering authority shall determine—

(i) the normal value and export price (or constructed export price) of each entry of the subject merchandise, and

(ii) the dumping margin for each such entry.

(B) Determination of antidumping or countervailing duties for new exporters and producers.

(i) In general. If the administering authority receives a request from an exporter or producer of the subject merchandise establishing that—

(I) such exporter or producer did not export the merchandise that was the subject of an antidumping duty or countervailing duty order to the United States (or, in the case of a regional industry, did not export the subject merchandise for sale in the region concerned) during the period of investigation, and

(II) such exporter or producer is not affiliated (within the meaning of section 771(33)) with any exporter or producer who exported the subject merchandise to the United States (or in the case of a regional industry, who exported the subject merchandise for sale in the region concerned) during that period,

the administering authority shall conduct a review under this subsection to establish an individual weighted average dumping margin or an individual countervailing duty rate (as the case may be) for such exporter or producer.

(ii) Time for review under clause (i). The administering authority shall commence a review under clause (i) in the calendar month beginning after—

(I) the end of the 6–month period beginning on the date of the countervailing duty or antidumping duty order under review, or

(II) the end of any 6–month period occurring thereafter,
if the request for the review is made during that 6–month period.

(iii) Posting bond or security. The administering authority shall, at the time a review under this subparagraph is initiated, direct the Customs Service to allow, at the option of the importer, the posting, until the completion of the review, of a bond or security in lieu of a cash deposit for each entry of the subject merchandise.

(iv) Time limits. The administering authority shall make a preliminary determination in a review conducted under this subparagraph within 180 days after the date on which the review is initiated, and a final determination within 90 days after the date the preliminary determination is issued, except that if the administering authority concludes that the case is extraordinarily complicated, it may extend the 180–day period to 300 days and may extend the 90–day period to 150 days.

(C) Results of determinations. The determination under this paragraph shall be the basis for the assessment of countervailing or antidumping duties on entries of merchandise covered by the determination and for deposits of estimated duties.

(3) Time limits.

(A) Preliminary and final determinations. The administering authority shall make a preliminary determination under subparagraph (A), (B), or (C) of paragraph (1) within 245 days after the last day of the month in which occurs the anniversary of the date of publication of the order, finding, or suspension agreement for which the review under paragraph (1) is requested, and a final determination under paragraph (1) within 120 days after the date on which the preliminary determination is published. If it is not practicable to complete the review within the foregoing time, the administering authority may extend that 245–day period to 365 days and may extend that 120–day period to 180 days. The administering authority may extend the time for making a final determination without extending the time for making a preliminary determination, if such final determination is made not later than 300 days after the date on which the preliminary determination is published.

(B) Liquidation of entries. If the administering authority orders any liquidation of entries pursuant to a review under paragraph (1), such liquidation shall be made promptly and, to the greatest extent practicable, within 90 days after the instructions to Customs are issued. In any case in which liquidation has not occurred within that 90–day period, the Secretary of the Treasury shall, upon the request of the affected party, provide an explanation thereof.

(C) Effect of pending review under section 516A. In a case in which a final determination under paragraph (1) is under review under section 516A a liquidation of entries covered by the determination is enjoined under section 516A(c)(2) or suspended under section 516A(g)(5)(C), the administering authority shall, within 10 days after the final disposition of the review under section 516A, transmit to the Federal Register for publication the final disposition and issue instructions to the Customs

Service with respect to the liquidation of entries pursuant to the review. In such a case, the 90–day period referred to in subparagraph (B) shall begin on the day on which the administering authority issues such instructions.

(4) Absorption of antidumping duties. During any review under this subsection initiated 2 years or 4 years after the publication of an antidumping duty order under section 736(a), the administering authority, if requested, shall determine whether antidumping duties have been absorbed by a foreign producer or exporter subject to the order if the subject merchandise is sold in the United States through an importer who is affiliated with such foreign producer or exporter. The administering authority shall notify the Commission of its findings regarding such duty absorption for the Commission to consider in conducting a review under subsection (c).

(b) Reviews based on changed circumstances.

(1) In general. Whenever the administering authority or the Commission receives information concerning, or a request from an interested party for a review of—

(A) a final affirmative determination that resulted in an antidumping duty order under this title or a finding under the Antidumping Act, 1921, or in a countervailing duty order under this title or section 303,

(B) a suspension agreement accepted under section 704 or 734, or

(C) a final affirmative determination resulting from an investigation continued pursuant to section 704(g) or 734(g), which shows changed circumstances sufficient to warrant a review of such determination or agreement, the administering authority or the Commission (as the case may be) shall conduct a review of the determination or agreement after publishing notice of the review in the Federal Register.

(2) Commission review. In conducting a review under this subsection, the Commission shall—

(A) in the case of a countervailing duty order or antidumping duty order or finding, determine whether revocation of the order or finding is likely to lead to continuation or recurrence of material injury,

(B) in the case of a determination made pursuant to section 704(h)(2) or 734(h)(2), determine whether the suspension agreement continues to eliminate completely the injurious effects of imports of the subject merchandise, and

(C) in the case of an affirmative determination resulting from an investigation continued under section 704(g) or 734(g), determine whether termination of the suspended investigation is likely to lead to continuation or recurrence of material injury.

(3) Burden of persuasion. During a review conducted by the Commission under this subsection—

(A) the party seeking revocation of an order or finding described in paragraph (1)(A) shall have the burden of persuasion with respect to whether there are changed circumstances sufficient to warrant such revocation, and

(B) the party seeking termination of a suspended investigation or a suspension agreement shall have the burden of persuasion with respect to whether there are changed circumstances sufficient to warrant such termination.

(4) Limitation on period for review. In the absence of good cause shown—

(A) the Commission may not review a determination made under section 705(b) or 735(b), or an investigation suspended under section 704 or 734, and

(B) the administering authority may not review a determination made under section 705(a) or 735(a), or an investigation suspended under section 704 or 734,

less than 24 months after the date of publication of notice of that determination or suspension.

(c) Five-year review.

(1) In general. Notwithstanding subsection (b) and except in the case of a transition order defined in paragraph (6), 5 years after the date of publication of—

(A) a countervailing duty order (other than a countervailing duty order to which subparagraph (B) applies or which was issued without an affirmative determination of injury by the Commission under section 303), an antidumping duty order, or a notice of suspension of an investigation, described in subsection (a)(1),

(B) a notice of injury determination under section 753 with respect to a countervailing duty order, or

(C) a determination under this section to continue an order or suspension agreement,

the administering authority and the Commission shall conduct a review to determine, in accordance with section 752, whether revocation of the countervailing or antidumping duty order or termination of the investigation suspended under section 704 or 734 would be likely to lead to continuation or recurrence of dumping or a countervailable subsidy (as the case may be) and of material injury.

(2) Notice of initiation of review. Not later than 30 days before the fifth anniversary of the date described in paragraph (1), the administering authority shall publish in the Federal Register a notice of initiation of a review under this subsection and request that interested parties submit—

(A) a statement expressing their willingness to participate in the review by providing information requested by the administering authority and the Commission,

(B) a statement regarding the likely effects of revocation of the order or termination of the suspended investigation, and

(C) such other information or industry data as the administering authority or the Commission may specify.

(3) Responses to notice of initiation.

(A) No response. If no interested party responds to the notice of initiation under this subsection, the administering authority shall issue a final determination, within 90 days after the initiation of a review, revoking the order or terminating the suspended investigation to which such notice relates. For purposes of this paragraph, an interested party means a party described in section 771(9) (C), (D), (E), (F), or (G).

(B) Inadequate response. If interested parties provide inadequate responses to a notice of initiation, the administering authority, within 120 days after the initiation of the review, or the Commission, within 150 days after such initiation, may issue, without further investigation, a final determination based on the facts available, in accordance with section 776.

(4) Waiver of participation by certain interested parties.

(A) In general. An interested party described in section 771(9) (A) or (B) may elect not to participate in a review conducted by the administering authority under this subsection and to participate only in the review conducted by the Commission under this subsection.

(B) Effect of waiver. In a review in which an interested party waives its participation pursuant to this paragraph, the administering authority shall conclude that revocation of the order or termination of the investigation would be likely to lead to continuation or recurrence of dumping or a countervailable subsidy (as the case may be) with respect to that interested party.

(5) Conduct of review.

(A) Time limits for completion of review. Unless the review has been completed pursuant to paragraph (3) or paragraph (4) applies, the administering authority shall make its final determination pursuant to section 752(b) or (c) within 240 days after the date on which a review is initiated under this subsection. If the administering authority makes a final affirmative determination, the Commission shall make its final determination pursuant to section 752(a) within 360 days after the date on which a review is initiated under this subsection.

(B) Extension of time limit. The administering authority or the Commission (as the case may be) may extend the period of time for making their respective determinations under this subsection by not more than 90 days, if the administering authority or the Commission (as the case may be) determines that the review is extraordinarily complicated. In a review in which the administering authority extends the time for making a final determination, but the Commission does not extend the time for making a determination, the Commission's determination shall be made not later than 120 days after the date on which the final determination of the administering authority is published.

(C) Extraordinarily complicated. For purposes of this subsection, the administering authority or the Commission (as the case may be) may treat a review as extraordinarily complicated if—

(i) there is a large number of issues,

(ii) the issues to be considered are complex,

(iii) there is a large number of firms involved,

(iv) the orders or suspended investigations have been grouped as described in subparagraph (D), or

(v) it is a review of a transition order.

(D) Grouped reviews. The Commission, in consultation with the administering authority, may group orders or suspended investigations for review if it considers that such grouping is appropriate and will promote administrative efficiency. Where orders or suspended investigations have been grouped, the Commission shall, subject to subparagraph (B), make its final determination under this subsection not later than 120 days after the date that the administering authority publishes notice of its final determination with respect to the last order or agreement in the group.

(6) Special transition rules.

(A) Schedule for reviews of transition orders.

(i) Initiation. The administering authority shall begin its review of transition orders in the 42d calendar month after the date such orders are issued. A review of all transition orders shall be initiated not later than the 5th anniversary after the date such orders are issued.

(ii) Completion. A review of a transition order shall be completed not later than 18 months after the date such review is initiated. Reviews of all transition orders shall be completed not later than 18 months after the 5th anniversary of the date such orders are issued.

(iii) Subsequent reviews. The time limits set forth in clauses (i) and (ii) shall be applied to all subsequent 5–year reviews of transition orders by substituting 'date of the determination to continue such orders' for 'date such orders are issued'.

(iv) Revocation and termination. No transition order may be revoked under this subsection before the date that is 5 years after the date the WTO Agreement enters into force with respect to the United States.

(B) Sequence of transition reviews. The administering authority, in consultation with the Commission, shall determine such sequence of review of transition orders as it deems appropriate to promote administrative efficiency. To the extent practicable, older orders shall be reviewed first.

(C) Definition of transition order. For purposes of this section, the term 'transition order' means—

(i) a countervailing duty order under this title or under section 303,

(ii) an antidumping duty order under this title or a finding under the Antidumping Act, 1921, or

(iii) a suspension of an investigation under section 704 or 734, which is in effect on the date the WTO Agreement enters into force with respect to the United States.

(D) Issue date for transition orders. For purposes of this subsection, a transition order shall be treated as issued on the date the WTO Agreement enters into force with respect to the United States, if such order is based on an investigation conducted by both the administering authority and the Commission.

(7) Exclusions from computations.

(A) In general. Subject to subparagraph (B), there shall be excluded from the computation of the 5–year period described in paragraph (1) and the periods described in paragraph (6) any period during which the importation of the subject merchandise is prohibited on account of the imposition, under the International Emergency Economic Powers Act or other provision of law, of sanctions by the United States against the country in which the subject merchandise originates.

(B) Application of exclusion. Subparagraph (A) shall apply only with respect to subject merchandise which originates in a country that is not a WTO member.

(d) Revocation of order or finding; termination of suspended investigation.

(1) In general. The administering authority may revoke, in whole or in part, a countervailing duty order or an antidumping duty order or finding, or terminate a suspended investigation, after review under subsection (a) or (b). The administering authority shall not revoke, in whole or in part, a counter-vailing duty order or terminate a suspended investigation on the basis of any export taxes, duties, or other charges levied on the export of the subject merchandise to the United States which are specifically intended to offset the countervailable subsidy received.

(2) Five-year reviews. In the case of a review conducted under subsection (c), the administering authority shall revoke a countervailing duty order or an antidumping duty order or finding, or terminate a suspended investigation, unless—

(A) the administering authority makes a determination that dumping or a countervailable subsidy, as the case may be, would be likely to continue or recur, and

(B) the Commission makes a determination that material injury would be likely to continue or recur as described in section 752(a).

(3) Application of revocation or termination. A determination under this section to revoke an order or finding or terminate a suspended investigation shall apply with respect to unliquidated entries of the subject merchandise which are entered, or withdrawn from warehouse, for consumption on or after the date determined by the administering authority.

(e) Hearings. Whenever the administering authority or the Commission conducts a review under this section, it shall, upon the request of an interested party, hold a hearing in accordance with section 774(b) in connection with that review.

(f) Determination that basis for suspension no longer exists. If the determination of the Commission under subsection (b)(2)(B) is negative, the suspension agreement shall be treated as not accepted, beginning on the date of publication of the Commission's determination, and the administering authority and the Commission shall proceed, under section 704(i) or 734(i), as if the suspension agreement had been violated on that date, except that no duty under any order subsequently issued shall be assessed on merchandise entered, or withdrawn from warehouse, for consumption before that date.

(g) Reviews to implement results of subsidies enforcement proceeding.

(1) Violations of Article 8 of the Subsidies Agreement. If—

(A) the administering authority receives notice from the Trade Representative of a violation of Article 8 of the Subsidies Agreement,

(B) the administering authority has reason to believe that merchandise subject to an existing countervailing duty order or suspended investigation is benefiting from the subsidy or subsidy program found to have been in violation of Article 8 of the Subsidies Agreement, and

(C) no review pursuant to subsection (a)(1) is in progress, the administering authority shall conduct a review of the order or suspended investigation to determine whether the subject merchandise benefits from the subsidy or subsidy program found to have been in violation of Article 8 of the Subsidies Agreement. If the administering authority determines that the subject merchandise is benefiting from the subsidy or subsidy program, it shall make appropriate adjustments in the estimated duty to be deposited or appropriate revisions to the terms of the suspension agreement.

(2) Withdrawal of subsidy or imposition of countermeasures. If the Trade Representative notifies the administering authority that, pursuant to Article 4 or Article 7 of the Subsidies Agreement—

(A) (i) the United States has imposed countermeasures, and

(ii) such countermeasures are based on the effects in the United States of imports of merchandise that is the subject of a countervailing duty order, or

(B) a WTO member country has withdrawn a countervailable subsidy provided with respect to merchandise subject to a countervailing duty order,

the administering authority shall conduct a review to determine if the amount of the estimated duty to be deposited should be adjusted or the order should be revoked.

(3) Expedited review. The administering authority shall conduct reviews under this subsection on an expedited basis, and shall publish the results of such reviews in the Federal Register.

(h) Correction of ministerial errors. The administering authority shall establish procedures for the correction of ministerial errors in final determinations within a reasonable time after the determinations are issued under this section. Such procedures shall ensure opportunity for interested parties to present their views regarding any such errors. As used in this subsection, the term 'ministerial error' includes errors in addition, subtraction, or other arithmetic function, clerical errors resulting from inaccurate copying, duplication, or the like, and any other type of unintentional error which the administering authority considers ministerial.

19 USC 1675a

Sec. 752. Special Rules for Section 751(b) and 751(c) Reviews

(a) Determination of Likelihood of Continuation or Recurrence of Material Injury.

(1) In general. In a review conducted under section 751 (b) or (c), the Commission shall determine whether revocation of an order, or termination of a suspended investigation, would be likely to lead to continuation or recurrence of material injury within a reasonably foreseeable time. The Commission shall consider the likely volume, price effect, and impact of imports of the subject merchandise on the industry if the order is revoked or the suspended investigation is terminated. The Commission shall take into account—

(A) its prior injury determinations, including the volume, price effect, and impact of imports of the subject merchandise on the industry before the order was issued or the suspension agreement was accepted,

(B) whether any improvement in the state of the industry is related to the order or the suspension agreement,

(C) whether the industry is vulnerable to material injury if the order is revoked or the suspension agreement is terminated, and

(D) in an antidumping proceeding under section 751(c), the findings of the administering authority regarding duty absorption under section 751(a)(4).

(2) Volume. In evaluating the likely volume of imports of the subject merchandise if the order is revoked or the suspended investigation is terminated, the Commission shall consider whether the likely volume of imports of the subject merchandise would be significant if the order is revoked or the suspended investigation is terminated, either in absolute terms or relative to production or consumption in the United States. In so doing, the Commission shall consider all relevant economic factors, including—

(A) any likely increase in production capacity or existing unused production capacity in the exporting country,

(B) existing inventories of the subject merchandise, or likely increases in inventories,

(C) the existence of barriers to the importation of such merchandise into countries other than the United States, and

(D) the potential for product-shifting if production facilities in the foreign country, which can be used to produce the subject merchandise, are currently being used to produce other products.

(3) Price. In evaluating the likely price effects of imports of the subject merchandise if the order is revoked or the suspended investigation is terminated, the Commission shall consider whether—

(A) there is likely to be significant price underselling by imports of the subject merchandise as compared to domestic like products, and

(B) imports of the subject merchandise are likely to enter the United States at prices that otherwise would have a significant depressing or suppressing effect on the price of domestic like products.

(4) Impact on the industry. In evaluating the likely impact of imports of the subject merchandise on the industry if the order is revoked or the suspended investigation is terminated, the Commission shall consider all relevant economic factors which are likely to have a bearing on the state of the industry in the United States, including, but not limited to—

(A) likely declines in output, sales, market share, profits, productivity, return on investments, and utilization of capacity,

(B) likely negative effects on cash flow, inventories, employment, wages, growth, ability to raise capital, and investment, and

(C) likely negative effects on the existing development and production efforts of the industry, including efforts to develop a derivative or more advanced version of the domestic like product.

The Commission shall evaluate all relevant economic factors described in this paragraph within the context of the business cycle and the conditions of competition that are distinctive to the affected industry.

(5) Basis for determination. The presence or absence of any factor which the Commission is required to consider under this subsection shall not necessarily give decisive guidance with respect to the Commission's determination of whether material injury is likely to continue or recur within a reasonably foreseeable time if the order is revoked or the suspended investigation is terminated. In making that determination, the Commission shall consider that the effects of revocation or termination may not be imminent, but may manifest themselves only over a longer period of time.

(6) Magnitude of margin of dumping and net countervailable subsidy; nature of countervailable subsidy. In making a determination under section 751 (b) or (c), the Commission may consider the magnitude of the margin of dumping or the magnitude of the net countervailable subsidy. If a countervailable subsidy is involved the Commission shall consider information regarding the nature of the countervailable subsidy and whether the subsidy is a subsidy described in Article 3 or 6.1 of the Subsidies Agreement.

(7) Cumulation. For purposes of this subsection, the Commission may cumulatively assess the volume and effect of imports of the subject merchandise from all countries with respect to which reviews under section 751(b) or (c) were initiated on the same day, if such imports would be likely to compete with each other and with domestic like products in the United States market.

The Commission shall not cumulatively assess the volume and effects of imports of the subject merchandise in a case in which it determines that such imports are likely to have no discernible adverse impact on the domestic industry.

(8) Special rule for regional industries. In a review under section 751(b) or (c) involving a regional industry, the Commission may base its determination on the regional industry defined in the original investigation under this

title, another region that satisfies the criteria established in section 771(4)(C), or the United States as a whole. In determining if a regional industry analysis is appropriate for the determination in the review, the Commission shall consider whether the criteria established in section 771(4)(C) are likely to be satisfied if the order is revoked or the suspended investigation is terminated.

(b) Determination of Likelihood of Continuation or Recurrence of a Countervailable Subsidy.

(1) In general. In a review conducted under section 751(c), the administering authority shall determine whether revocation of a countervailing duty order or termination of a suspended investigation under section 704 would be likely to lead to continuation or recurrence of a countervailable subsidy. The administering authority shall consider—

(A) the net countervailable subsidy determined in the investigation and subsequent reviews, and

(B) whether any change in the program which gave rise to the net countervailable subsidy described in subparagraph (A) has occurred that is likely to affect that net countervailable subsidy.

(2) Consideration of other factors. If good cause is shown, the administering authority shall also consider—

(A) programs determined to provide countervailable subsidies in other investigations or reviews under this title, but only to the extent that such programs—

(i) can potentially be used by the exporters or producers subject to the review under section 751(c), and

(ii) did not exist at the time that the countervailing duty order was issued or the suspension agreement was accepted, and

(B) programs newly alleged to provide countervailable subsidies but only to the extent that the administering authority makes an affirmative countervailing duty determination with respect to such programs and with respect to the exporters or producers subject to the review.

(3) Net countervailable subsidy. The administering authority shall provide to the Commission the net countervailable subsidy that is likely to prevail if the order is revoked or the suspended investigation is terminated. The administering authority shall normally choose a net countervailable subsidy that was determined under section 705 or subsection (a) or (b)(1) of section 751.

(4) Special rule.

(A) Treatment of zero and de minimis rates. A net countervailable subsidy described in paragraph (1)(A) that is zero or de minimis shall not by itself require the administering authority to determine that revocation of a countervailing duty order or termination of a suspended investigation would not be likely to lead to continuation or recurrence of a countervailable subsidy.

(B) Application of de minimis standards.—For purposes of this paragraph, the administering authority shall apply the de minimis standards applicable to reviews conducted under subsections (a) and (b)(1) of section 751.

(c) Determination of Likelihood of Continuation or Recurrence of Dumping.

(1) In general. In a review conducted under section 751(c), the administering authority shall determine whether revocation of an antidumping duty order or termination of a suspended investigation under section 734 would be likely to lead to continuation or recurrence of sales of the subject merchandise at less than fair value. The administering authority shall consider—

(A) the weighted average dumping margins determined in the investigation and subsequent reviews, and

(B) the volume of imports of the subject merchandise for the period before and the period after the issuance of the antidumping duty order or acceptance of the suspension agreement.

(2) Consideration of other factors. If good cause is shown, the administering authority shall also consider such other price, cost, market, or economic factors as it deems relevant.

(3) Magnitude of the margin of dumping. The administering authority shall provide to the Commission the magnitude of the margin of dumping that is likely to prevail if the order is revoked or the suspended investigation is terminated. The administering authority shall normally choose a margin that was determined under section 735 or under subsection (a) or (b)(1) of section 751.

(4) Special rule.

(A) Treatment of zero or de minimis margins. A dumping margin described in paragraph (1)(A) that is zero or de minimis shall not by itself require the administering authority to determine that revocation of an antidumping duty order or termination of a suspended investigation would not be likely to lead to continuation or recurrence of sales at less than fair value.

(B) Application of de minimis standards. For purposes of this paragraph, the administering authority shall apply the de minimis standards applicable to reviews conducted under subsections (a) and (b) of section 751.

19 USC 1675b

Sec. 753. Special Rules for Injury Investigations for Certain Section 303 or Section 701(c) Countervailing Duty Orders and Investigations

(a) In general.

(1) Investigation by the commission upon request. In the case of a countervailing duty order described in paragraph (2), which—

(A) applies to merchandise that is the product of a Subsidies Agreement country, and

(B) (i) is in effect on the date on which such country becomes a Subsidies Agreement country, or

(ii) is issued on a date that is after the date described in clause (i) pursuant to a court order in an action brought under section 516A,

the Commission, upon receipt of a request from an interested party described in section 771(9) (C), (D), (E), (F), or (G) for an injury investigation with respect to such order, shall initiate an investigation and shall determine whether an industry in the United States is likely to be materially injured by reason of imports of the subject merchandise if the order is revoked.

(2) Description of countervailing duty orders. A countervailing duty order described in this paragraph is an order issued under section 303 or section 701(c) with respect to which the requirement of an affirmative determination of material injury was not applicable at the time such order was issued.

(3) Requirements of request for investigation. A request for an investigation under this subsection shall be submitted—

(A) in the case of an order described in paragraph (1)(B)(i), within 6 months after the date on which the country described in paragraph (1)(A) becomes a Subsidies Agreement country, or

(B) in the case of an order described in paragraph (1)(B)(ii), within 6 months after the date the order is issued.

(4) Suspension of liquidation. With respect to entries of subject merchandise made on or after—

(A) in the case of an order described in paragraph (1)(B)(i), the date on which the country described in paragraph (1)(A) becomes a Subsidies Agreement country, or

(B) in the case of an order described in paragraph (1)(B)(ii), the date on which the order is issued,

liquidation shall be suspended at the cash deposit rate in effect on the date described in subparagraph (A) or (B) (whichever is applicable).

(b) Investigation procedure and schedule.

(1) Commission procedure.

(A) In general. Except as otherwise provided in this section, the provisions of this title regarding evidence in and procedures for investigations conducted under subtitle A shall apply to investigations conducted by the Commission under this section.

(B) Time for commission determination. Except as otherwise provided in subparagraph (C), the Commission shall issue its determination under subsection (a)(1), to the extent possible, not later than 1 year after the date on which the investigation is initiated under this section.

(C) Special rule to permit administrative flexibility. In the case of requests for investigations received under this section within 1 year after the date on which the WTO Agreement enters into force with respect to the United States, the Commission may, after consulting with the administering authority, initiate its investigations in a manner that results in determinations being made in all such investigations during the 4–year period beginning on such date.

(2) Net countervailable subsidy; nature of subsidy.

(A) Net countervailable subsidy. The administering authority shall provide to the Commission the net countervailable subsidy that is likely to prevail if the order which is the subject of the investigation is revoked. The administering authority normally shall choose a net countervailable subsidy that was determined under section 705. If the Commission considers the magnitude of the net countervailable subsidy in making its determination under this section, the Commission shall use the net countervailable subsidy provided by the administering authority.

(B) Nature of subsidy. The administering authority shall inform the Commission of, and the Commission, in making its determination under this section, shall consider, the nature of the countervailable subsidy and whether the countervailable subsidy is a subsidy described in Article 3 or Article 6.1 of the Subsidies Agreement.

(3) Effect of commission determination.

(A) Affirmative determination. Upon being notified by the Commission that it has made an affirmative determination under subsection (a)(1)—

(i) the administering authority shall order the termination of the suspension of liquidation required pursuant to subsection (a)(4), and

(ii) the countervailing duty order shall remain in effect until revoked, in whole or in part, under section 751(d).

For purposes of section 751(c), a countervailing duty order described in this section shall be treated as issued on the date of publication of the Commission's determination under this subsection.

(B) Negative determination.

(i) In general. Upon being notified by the Commission that it has made a negative determination under subsection (a)(1), the administering authority shall revoke the countervailing duty order, and shall refund, with interest, any estimated countervailing duties collected during the period liquidation was suspended pursuant to subsection (a)(4).

(ii) Limitation on negative determination. A determination by the Commission that revocation of the order is not likely to result in material injury to an industry by reason of imports of the subject merchandise shall not be based, in whole or in part, on any export taxes, duties, or other charges levied on the export of the subject merchandise to the United States that were specifically intended to offset the countervailable subsidy received.

(4) Countervailing duty orders with respect to which no request for injury investigation is made. If, with respect to a countervailing duty order described in subsection (a), a request for an investigation is not made within the time required by subsection (a)(3), the Commission shall notify the administering authority that a negative determination has been made under subsection (a) and the provisions of paragraph (3)(B) shall apply with respect to the order.

(c) Pending and suspended countervailing duty investigations. If, on the date on which a country becomes a Subsidies Agreement country, there is a countervailing duty investigation in progress or suspended under section 303 or section 701(c) that applies to merchandise which is a product of that country and with respect to which the requirement of an affirmative determination of material injury was not applicable at the time the investigation was initiated, the Commission shall—

(1) in the case of an investigation in progress, make a final determination under section 705(b) within 75 days after the date of an affirmative final determination, if any, by the administering authority,

(2) in the case of a suspended investigation to which section 704(i)(1)(B) applies, make a final determination under section 705(b) within 120 days after receiving notice from the administering authority of the resumption of the investigation pursuant to section 704(i), or within 45 days after the date of an affirmative final determination, if any, by the administering authority, whichever is later, or

(3) in the case of a suspended investigation to which section 704(i)(1)(C) applies, treat the countervailing duty order issued pursuant to such section as if it were—

    (A) an order issued under subsection (a)(1)(B)(ii) for purposes of subsection (a)(3); and

    (B) an order issued under subsection (a)(1)(B)(i) for purposes of subsection (a)(4).

(d) Publication in Federal Register. The administering authority or the Commission, as the case may be, shall publish in the Federal Register a notice of the initiation of any investigation, and a notice of any determination or revocation, made pursuant to this section.

(e) Request for simultaneous expedited review under section 751(c).

(1) General rule.

    (A) Requests for reviews. Notwithstanding section 751(c)(6)(A) and except as provided in subparagraph (B), an interested party may request a review of an order under section 751(c) at the same time the party requests an investigation under subsection (a), if the order involves the same or comparable subject merchandise. Upon receipt of such request, the administering authority, after consulting with the Commission, shall initiate a review of the order under section 751(c).The Commission shall combine such review with the investigation under this section.

    (B) Exception. If the administering authority determines that the interested party who requested an investigation under this section is a related party or an importer within the meaning of section 771(4)(B), the administering authority may decline a request by such party to initiate a review of an order under section 751(c) which involves the same or comparable subject merchandise.

(2) Cumulation. If a review under section 751(c) is initiated under paragraph (1), such review shall be treated as having been initiated on the same day as the investigation under this section, and the Commission may, in accordance with section 771(7)(G), cumulatively assess the volume and effect

of imports of the subject merchandise from all countries with respect to which such investigations are treated as initiated on the same day.

(3) Time and procedure for Commission determination. The Commission shall render its determination in the investigation conducted under this section at the same time as the Commission's determination is made in the review under section 751(c) that is initiated pursuant to this subsection. The Commission shall in all other respects apply the procedures and standards set forth in section 751(c) to such section 751(c) reviews.

19 USC 1675c NOTE

FINDINGS OF CONGRESS.

Congress makes the following findings:

(1) Consistent with the rights of the United States under the World Trade Organization, injurious dumping is to be condemned and actionable subsidies which cause injury to domestic industries must be effectively neutralized.

(2) United States unfair trade laws have as their purpose the restoration of conditions of fair trade so that jobs and investment that should be in the United States are not lost through the false market signals.

(3) The continued dumping or subsidization of imported products after the issuance of antidumping orders or findings or countervailing duty orders can frustrate the remedial purpose of the laws by preventing market prices from returning to fair levels.

(4) Where dumping or subsidization continues, domestic producers will be reluctant to reinvest or rehire and may be unable to maintain pension and health care benefits that conditions of fair trade would permit. Similarly, small businesses and American farmers and ranchers may be unable to pay down accumulated debt, to obtain working capital, or to otherwise remain viable.

(5) United States trade laws should be strengthened to see that the remedial purpose of those laws is achieved.

19 USC 1675c

Sec. 754. Continued Dumping and Subsidy Offset

(a) In general. Duties assessed pursuant to a countervailing duty order, an antidumping duty order, or a finding under the Antidumping Act of 1921 shall be distributed on an annual basis under this section to the affected domestic producers for qualifying expenditures. Such distribution shall be known as the "continued dumping and subsidy offset".

(b) Definitions. As used in this section:

(1) Affected domestic producer. The term "affected domestic producer" means any manufacturer, producer, farmer, rancher, or worker representative (including associations of such persons) that—

(A) was a petitioner or interested party in support of the petition with respect to which an antidumping duty order, a finding under the

Antidumping Act of 1921, or a countervailing duty order has been entered, and

(B) remains in operation.

Companies, businesses, or persons that have ceased the production of the product covered by the order or finding or who have been acquired by a company or business that is related to a company that opposed the investigation shall not be an affected domestic producer.

(2) Commissioner. The term "Commissioner" means the Commissioner of Customs.

(3) Commission. The term "Commission" means the United States International Trade Commission.

(4) Qualifying expenditure. The term "qualifying expenditure" means an expenditure incurred after the issuance of the antidumping duty finding or order or countervailing duty order in any of the following categories:

(A) Manufacturing facilities.

(B) Equipment.

(C) Research and development.

(D) Personnel training.

(E) Acquisition of technology.

(F) Health care benefits to employees paid for by the employer.

(G) Pension benefits to employees paid for by the employer.

(H) Environmental equipment, training, or technology.

(I) Acquisition of raw materials and other inputs.

(J) Working capital or other funds needed to maintain production.

(5) Related to. A company, business, or person shall be considered to be "related to" another company, business, or person if—

(A) the company, business, or person directly or indirectly controls or is controlled by the other company, business, or person,

(B) a third party directly or indirectly controls both companies, businesses, or persons,

(C) both companies, businesses, or persons directly or indirectly control a third party and there is reason to believe that the relationship causes the first company, business, or persons to act differently than a nonrelated party.

For purposes of this paragraph, a party shall be considered to directly or indirectly control another party if the party is legally or operationally in a position to exercise restraint or direction over the other party.

(c) Distribution procedures. The Commissioner shall prescribe procedures for distribution of the continued dumping or subsidies offset required by this section. Such distribution shall be made not later than 60 days after the first day of a fiscal year from duties assessed during the preceding fiscal year.

(d) Parties eligible for distribution of antidumping and counter-vailing duties assessed.

(1) List of affected domestic producers. The Commission shall forward to the Commissioner within 60 days after the effective date of this section [effective Oct. 1, 2000] in the case of orders or findings in effect on January 1, 1999, or thereafter, or in any other case, within 60 days after the date an antidumping or countervailing duty order or finding is issued, a list of petitioners and persons with respect to each order and finding and a list of persons that indicate support of the petition by letter or through question-naire response. In those cases in which a determination of injury was not required or the Commission's records do not permit an identification of those in support of a petition, the Commission shall consult with the administering authority to determine the identity of the petitioner and those domestic parties who have entered appearances during administrative reviews conduct-ed by the administering authority under section 751.

(2) Publication of list; certification. The Commissioner shall publish in the Federal Register at least 30 days before the distribution of a continued dumping and subsidy offset, a notice of intention to distribute the offset and the list of affected domestic producers potentially eligible for the distribution based on the list obtained from the Commission under paragraph (1). The Commissioner shall request a certification from each potentially eligible affected domestic producer—

(A) that the producer desires to receive a distribution;

(B) that the producer is eligible to receive the distribution as an affected domestic producer; and

(C) the qualifying expenditures incurred by the producer since the issuance of the order or finding for which distribution under this section has not previously been made.

(3) Distribution of funds. The Commissioner shall distribute all funds (including all interest earned on the funds) from assessed duties received in the preceding fiscal year to affected domestic producers based on the certifica-tions described in paragraph (2). The distributions shall be made on a pro rata basis based on new and remaining qualifying expenditures.

(e) Special accounts.

(1) Establishments. Within 14 days after the effective date of this section [effective Oct. 1, 2000], with respect to antidumping duty orders and findings and countervailing duty orders notified under subsection (d)(1), and within 14 days after the date an antidumping duty order or finding or countervailing duty order issued after the effective date takes effect, the Commissioner shall establish in the Treasury of the United States a special account with respect to each such order or finding.

(2) Deposits into accounts. The Commissioner shall deposit into the special accounts, all antidumping or countervailing duties (including interest earned on such duties) that are assessed after the effective date of this section [effective Oct. 1, 2000] under the antidumping order or finding or the countervailing duty order with respect to which the account was established.

(3) Time and manner of distributions. Consistent with the requirements of subsections (c) and (d), the Commissioner shall by regulation prescribe the

time and manner in which distribution of the funds in a special account shall made.

(4) Termination. A special account shall terminate after—

(A) the order or finding with respect to which the account was established has terminated;

(B) all entries relating to the order or finding are liquidated and duties assessed collected;

(C) the Commissioner has provided notice and a final opportunity to obtain distribution pursuant to subsection (c); and

(D) 90 days has elapsed from the date of the notice described in subparagraph (C).

Amounts not claimed within 90 days of the date of the notice described in subparagraph (C), shall be deposited into the general fund of the Treasury.

19 USC 1675c NOTE

(c) Effective Date. The amendments made by this section shall apply with respect to all antidumping and countervailing duty assessments made on or after October 1, 2000.

Chapter 2—Consultations and Determinations Regarding
Quantitative Restriction Agreements

19 USC 1676

Sec. 761. Required Consultations

(a) Agreements in response to countervailable subsidies. Within 90 days after the administering authority accepts a quantitative restriction agreement under section 704(a)(2) or (c)(3), the President shall enter into consultations with the government that is party to the agreement for purposes of—

(1) eliminating the countervailable subsidy completely, or

(2) reducing the net countervailable subsidy to a level that eliminates completely the injurious effect of exports to the United States of the merchandise.

(b) Modification of agreements on basis of consultations. At the direction of the President, the administering authority shall modify a quantitative restriction agreement as a result of consultations entered into under subsection (a).

(c) Special rule regarding agreements under section 704(c)(3). This chapter shall cease to apply to a quantitative restriction agreement described in section 704(c)(3) at such time as that agreement ceases to have force and effect under section 704(f) or violation is found under section 704(i).

19 USC 1676a

Sec. 762. Required Determinations

(a) In general. Before the expiration date, if any, of a quantitative restriction agreement accepted under section 704(a)(2) or 704(c)(3) (if suspension of the related investigation is still in effect)—

(1) the administering authority shall, at the direction of the President, initiate a proceeding to determine whether any countervailable subsidy is being provided with respect to the subject merchandise and, if being so provided, the net countervailable subsidy; and

(2) if the administering authority initiates a proceeding under paragraph (1), the Commission shall determine whether imports of the merchandise of the kind subject to the agreement will, upon termination of the agreement, materially injure, or threaten with material injury, an industry in the United States or materially retard the establishment of such an industry.

(b) Determinations. The determinations required to be made by the administering authority and the Commission under subsection (a) shall be made under such procedures as the administering authority and the Commission, respectively, shall by regulation prescribe, and shall be treated as final determinations made under section 705 for purposes of judicial review under section 516A. If the determinations by each are affirmative, the administering authority shall—

(1) issue a countervailing duty order under section 706 effective with respect to merchandise entered on and after the date on which the agreement terminates; and

(2) order the suspension of liquidation of all entries of subject merchandise which are entered, or withdrawn from warehouse for consumption, on or after the date of publication of the order in the Federal Register.

(c) Hearings. The determination proceedings required to be prescribed under subsection (b) shall provide that the administering authority and the Commission must, upon the request of any interested party, hold a hearing in accordance with section 774 on the issues involved.

Subtitle D

General Provisions

19 USC 1677

Sec. 771. Definitions; Special Rules

For purposes of this title—

(1) Administering authority. The term "administering authority" means the Secretary of Commerce, or any other officer of the United States to whom the responsibility for carrying out the duties of the administering authority under this title are transferred by law.

(2) Commission. The term "Commission" means the United States International Trade Commission.

(3) Country. The term "country" means a foreign country, a political subdivision, dependent territory, or possession of a foreign country, and, except for the purpose of antidumping proceedings, may include an association of 2 or more foreign countries, political subdivisions, dependent territories, or possessions of countries into a customs union outside the United States.

(4) Industry.

(A) In general. The term "industry" means the producers as a whole of a domestic like product, or those producers whose collective output of a domestic like product constitutes a major proportion of the total domestic production of the product.

(B) Related parties.

(i) If a producer of a domestic like product and an exporter or importer of the subject merchandise are related parties, or if a producer of the domestic like product is also an importer of the subject merchandise, the producer may, in appropriate circumstances, be excluded from the industry.

(ii) For purposes of clause (i), a producer and an exporter or importer shall be considered to be related parties, if—

(I) the producer directly or indirectly controls the exporter or importer,

(II) the exporter or importer directly or indirectly controls the producer,

(III) a third party directly or indirectly controls the producer and the exporter or importer, or

(IV) the producer and the exporter or importer directly or indirectly control a third party and there is reason to believe that the relationship causes the producer to act differently than a nonrelated producer.

For purposes of this subparagraph, a party shall be considered to directly or indirectly control another party if the party is legally or operationally in a position to exercise restraint or direction over the other party.

(C) Regional industries. In appropriate circumstances, the United States, for a particular product market, may be divided into 2 or more markets and the producers within each market may be treated as if they were a separate industry if—

(i) the producers within such market sell all or almost all of their production of the domestic like product in question in that market, and

(ii) the demand in that market is not supplied, to any substantial degree, by producers of the product in question located elsewhere in the United States.

In such appropriate circumstances, material injury, the threat of material injury, or material retardation of the establishment of an industry may be found to exist with respect to an industry even if the domestic industry as a whole, or those producers whose collective output of a domestic like product constitutes a major proportion of the total domestic production of that product, is not injured, if there is a concentration of dumped imports or imports of merchandise benefiting from a countervailable subsidy into such an isolated market and if the producers of all, or almost all, of the production within that market are being materially injured or threatened by material injury, or if the establishment of an industry is being materially retarded, by reason of the dumped imports or imports of merchandise benefiting from a countervailable subsidy. The term "regional industry" means the domestic producers within a region who are treated as a separate industry under this subparagraph.

(D) Product lines. The effect of dumped imports or imports of merchandise benefiting from a countervailable subsidy shall be assessed in relation to the United States production of a domestic like product if available data permit the separate identification of production in terms of such criteria as the production process or the producer's profits. If the domestic production of the domestic like product has no separate identity in terms of such criteria, then the effect of the dumped imports or imports of merchandise benefiting from a countervailable subsidy shall be assessed by the examination of the production of the narrowest group or range of products, which includes a domestic like product, for which the necessary information can be provided.

(E) Industry producing processed agricultural products.

(i) In general. Subject to clause (v), in an investigation involving a processed agricultural product produced from any raw agricultural product, the producers or growers of the raw agricultural product may be considered part of the industry producing the processed product if—

(I) the processed agricultural product is produced from the raw agricultural product through a single continuous line of production; and

(II) there is a substantial coincidence of economic interest between the producers or growers of the raw agricultural product and the processors of the processed agricultural product based upon relevant economic factors, which may, in the discretion of the Commission, include price, added market value, or other economic interrelationships (regardless of whether such coincidence of economic interest is based upon any legal relationship).

(ii) Processing. For purposes of this subparagraph, the processed agricultural product shall be considered to be processed from a raw agricultural product through a single continuous line of production if—

(I) the raw agricultural product is substantially or completely devoted to the production of the processed agricultural product; and

(II) the processed agricultural product is produced substantially or completely from the raw product.

(iii) Relevant economic factors. For purposes of clause (i)(II), in addition to such other factors it considers relevant to the question of coincidence of economic interest, the Commission shall—

(I) if price is taken into account, consider the degree of correlation between the price of the raw agricultural product and the price of the processed agricultural product; and

(II) if added market value is taken into account, consider whether the value of the raw agricultural product constitutes a significant percentage of the value of the processed agricultural product.

(iv) Raw agricultural product. For purposes of this subparagraph, the term "raw agricultural product" means any farm or fishery product.

(v) Termination of this subparagraph. This subparagraph shall cease to have effect if the United States Trade Representative notifies the administering authority and the Commission that the application of this subparagraph is inconsistent with the international obligations of the United States.

(5) Countervailable subsidy.

(A) In general. Except as provided in paragraph (5B), a countervailable subsidy is a subsidy described in this paragraph which is specific as described in paragraph (5A).

(B) Subsidy described. A subsidy is described in this paragraph in the case in which an authority—

(i) provides a financial contribution,

(ii) provides any form of income or price support within the meaning of Article XVI of the GATT 1994, or

(iii) makes a payment to a funding mechanism to provide a financial contribution, or entrusts or directs a private entity to make a financial contribution, if providing the contribution would normally be vested in the government and the practice does not differ in substance from practices normally followed by governments,

to a person and a benefit is thereby conferred. For purposes of this paragraph and paragraphs (5A) and (5B), the term "authority" means a government of a country or any public entity within the territory of the country.

(C) Other factors. The determination of whether a subsidy exists shall be made without regard to whether the recipient of the subsidy is publicly or privately owned and without regard to whether the subsidy is provided directly or indirectly on the manufacture, production, or export of merchandise. The administering authority is not required to consider the effect of the subsidy in determining whether a subsidy exists under this paragraph.

(D) Financial contribution. The term "financial contribution" means—

(i) the direct transfer of funds, such as grants, loans, and equity infusions, or the potential direct transfer of funds or liabilities, such as loan guarantees,

(ii) foregoing or not collecting revenue that is otherwise due, such as granting tax credits or deductions from taxable income,

(iii) providing goods or services, other than general infrastructure, or

(iv) purchasing goods.

(E) Benefit conferred. A benefit shall normally be treated as conferred where there is a benefit to the recipient, including—

(i) in the case of an equity infusion, if the investment decision is inconsistent with the usual investment practice of private investors, including the practice regarding the provision of risk capital, in the country in which the equity infusion is made,

(ii) in the case of a loan, if there is a difference between the amount the recipient of the loan pays on the loan and the amount the recipient would pay on a comparable commercial loan that the recipient could actually obtain on the market,

(iii) in the case of a loan guarantee, if there is a difference, after adjusting for any difference in guarantee fees, between the amount the recipient of the guarantee pays on the guaranteed loan and the amount the recipient would pay for a comparable commercial loan if there were no guarantee by the authority, and

(iv) in the case where goods or services are provided, if such goods or services are provided for less than adequate remuneration, and in the case where goods are purchased, if such goods are purchased for more than adequate remuneration.

For purposes of clause (iv), the adequacy of remuneration shall be determined in relation to prevailing market conditions for the good or service being provided or the goods being purchased in the country which is subject to the investigation or review. Prevailing market conditions include price, quality, availability, marketability, transportation, and other conditions of purchase or sale.

(F) Change in ownership. A change in ownership of all or part of a foreign enterprise or the productive assets of a foreign enterprise does not by itself require a determination by the administering authority that a past countervailable subsidy received by the enterprise no longer continues to be countervailable, even if the change in ownership is accomplished through an arm's length transaction.

(5A) Specificity.

(A) In general. A subsidy is specific if it is an export subsidy described in subparagraph (B) or an import substitution subsidy described in subparagraph (C), or if it is determined to be specific pursuant to subparagraph (D).

(B) Export subsidy. An export subsidy is a subsidy that is, in law or in fact, contingent upon export performance, alone or as 1 of 2 or more conditions.

(C) Import substitution subsidy. An import substitution subsidy is a subsidy that is contingent upon the use of domestic goods over imported goods, alone or as 1 of 2 or more conditions.

(D) Domestic subsidy. In determining whether a subsidy (other than a subsidy described in subparagraph (B) or (C)) is a specific subsidy, in law or in fact, to an enterprise or industry within the jurisdiction of the authority providing the subsidy, the following guidelines shall apply:

(i) Where the authority providing the subsidy, or the legislation pursuant to which the authority operates, expressly limits access to the subsidy to an enterprise or industry, the subsidy is specific as a matter of law.

(ii) Where the authority providing the subsidy, or the legislation pursuant to which the authority operates, establishes objective criteria or conditions governing the eligibility for, and the amount of, a subsidy, the subsidy is not specific as a matter of law, if—

(I) eligibility is automatic,

(II) the criteria or conditions for eligibility are strictly followed, and

(III) the criteria or conditions are clearly set forth in the relevant statute, regulation, or other official document so as to be capable of verification.

For purposes of this clause, the term "objective criteria or conditions" means criteria or conditions that are neutral and that do not favor one enterprise or industry over another.

(iii) Where there are reasons to believe that a subsidy may be specific as a matter of fact, the subsidy is specific if one or more of the following factors exist:

(I) The actual recipients of the subsidy, whether considered on an enterprise or industry basis, are limited in number.

(II) An enterprise or industry is a predominant user of the subsidy.

(III) An enterprise or industry receives a disproportionately large amount of the subsidy.

(IV) The manner in which the authority providing the subsidy has exercised discretion in the decision to grant the subsidy indicates that an enterprise or industry is favored over others.

In evaluating the factors set forth in subclauses (I), (II), (III), and (IV), the administering authority shall take into account the extent of diversification of economic activities within the jurisdiction of the authority providing the subsidy, and the length of time during which the subsidy program has been in operation.

(iv) Where a subsidy is limited to an enterprise or industry located within a designated geographical region within the jurisdiction of the authority providing the subsidy, the subsidy is specific.

For purposes of this paragraph and paragraph (5B), any reference to an enterprise or industry is a reference to a foreign enterprise or foreign industry and includes a group of such enterprises or industries.

(5B) Categories of noncountervailable subsidies.

(A) In general. Notwithstanding the provisions of paragraphs (5) and (5A), in the case of merchandise imported from a Subsidies Agreement country, a subsidy shall be treated as noncountervailable if the administering authority determines in an investigation under subtitle A or a review under subtitle C that the subsidy meets all of the criteria described in subparagraph (B), (C), or (D), as the case may be, or the provisions of subparagraph (E)(i) apply.

(B) Research subsidy.

(i) In general. Except for a subsidy provided on the manufacture, production, or export of civil aircraft, a subsidy for research activities conducted by a person, or by a higher education or research establishment on a contract basis with a person, shall be treated as noncountervailable, if the subsidy covers not more than 75 percent of the costs of industrial research or not more than 50 percent of the costs of precompetitive development activity, and such subsidy is limited exclusively to—

(I) the costs of researchers, technicians, and other supporting staff employed exclusively in the research activity,

(II) the costs of instruments, equipment, land, or buildings that are used exclusively and permanently (except when disposed of on a commercial basis) for the research activity,

(III) the costs of consultancy and equivalent services used exclusively for the research activity, including costs for bought-in research, technical knowledge, and patents,

(IV) additional overhead costs incurred directly as a result of the research activity, and

(V) other operating costs (such as materials and supplies) incurred directly as a result of the research activity.

(ii) Definitions. For purposes of this subparagraph—

(I) Industrial research. The term "industrial research" means planned search or critical investigation aimed at the discovery of new knowledge, with the objective that such knowledge may be useful in developing new products, processes, or services, or in bringing about a significant improvement to existing products, processes, or services.

(II) Precompetitive development activity. The term "precompetitive development activity" means the translation of industrial research findings into a plan, blueprint, or design for new, modified, or improved products, processes, or services, whether intended for sale or use, including the creation of a first prototype that would not be capable of commercial use. The term also may include the conceptual formulation and design of products, processes, or services alternatives and initial demonstration or pilot projects, if these same projects cannot be converted or used for industrial application or commercial exploitation. The term does not include routine or periodic alterations to existing products, production lines, manufacturing processes, services, or other ongoing operations even if those alterations may represent improvements.

(iii) Calculation rules.

(I) In general. In the case of a research activity that spans both industrial research and precompetitive development activity, the allowable level of the noncountervailable subsidy shall not exceed 62.5 percent of the costs set forth in subclauses (I), (II), (III), (IV), and (V) of clause (i).

(II) Total eligible costs. The allowable level of a noncountervailable subsidy described in clause (i) shall be based on the total eligible costs incurred over the duration of a particular project.

(C) Subsidy to disadvantaged regions.

(i) In general. A subsidy provided, pursuant to a general framework of regional development, to a person located in a disadvantaged region within a country shall be treated as noncountervailable, if it is not specific (within the meaning of paragraph (5A)) within eligible regions and if the following conditions are met:

(I) Each region identified as disadvantaged within the territory of a country is a clearly designated, contiguous geographical area with a definable economic and administrative identity.

(II) Each region is considered a disadvantaged region on the basis of neutral and objective criteria indicating that the region is disadvantaged because of more than temporary circumstances, and such criteria are clearly stated in the relevant statute, regulation, or other official document so as to be capable of verification.

(III) The criteria described in subclause (II) include a measurement of economic development.

(IV) Programs provided within a general framework of regional development include ceilings on the amount of assistance that can be granted to a subsidized project. Such ceilings are differentiated according to the different levels of development of assisted regions, and are expressed in terms of investment costs or costs of job creation. Within such ceilings, the distribution of assistance is sufficiently broad and even to avoid the predominant use of a subsidy by, or the provision of disproportionately large amounts of a subsidy to, an enterprise or industry as described in paragraph (5A)(D).

(ii) Measurement of economic development. For purposes of clause (i), the measurement of economic development shall be based on one or more of the following factors:

(I) Per capita income, household per capita income, or per capita gross domestic product that does not exceed 85 percent of the average for the country subject to investigation or review.

(II) An unemployment rate that is at least 110 percent of the average unemployment rate for the country subject to investigation or review.

The measurement of economic development shall cover a 3–year period, but may be a composite measurement and may include factors other than those set forth in this clause.

(iii) Definitions. For purposes of this subparagraph—

(I) General framework of regional development. The term "general framework of regional development" means that the regional subsidy programs are part of an internally consistent and generally applicable regional development policy, and that regional development subsidies are not granted in isolated geographical points having no, or virtually no, influence on the development of a region.

(II) Neutral and objective criteria. The term "neutral and objective criteria" means criteria that do not favor certain regions beyond what is appropriate for the elimination or reduction of regional disparities within the framework of the regional development policy.

(D) Subsidy for adaptation of existing facilities to new environmental requirements.

(i) In general. A subsidy that is provided to promote the adaptation of existing facilities to new environmental requirements that are imposed by statute or by regulation, and that result in greater constraints and financial burdens on the recipient of the subsidy, shall be treated as noncountervailable, if the subsidy—

(I) is a one-time nonrecurring measure,

(II) is limited to 20 percent of the cost of adaptation,

(III) does not cover the cost of replacing and operating the subsidized investment, a cost that must be fully borne by the recipient,

(IV) is directly linked and proportionate to the recipient's planned reduction of nuisances and pollution, and does not cover any manufacturing cost savings that may be achieved, and

(V) is available to all persons that can adopt the new equipment or production processes.

(ii) Existing facilities. For purposes of this subparagraph, the term "existing facilities" means facilities that have been in operation for at least 2 years before the date on which the new environmental requirements are imposed.

(E) Notified subsidy program.

(i) General rule. If a subsidy is provided pursuant to a program that has been notified in accordance with Article 8.3 of the Subsidies Agreement, the subsidy shall be treated as noncountervailable and shall not be subject to investigation or review under this title.

(ii) Exception. Notwithstanding clause (i), a subsidy shall be treated as countervailable if—

(I) the Trade Representative notifies the administering authority that a determination has been made pursuant to Article 8.4 or 8.5 of the Subsidies Agreement that the subsidy, or the program pursuant to which the subsidy was provided, does not satisfy the conditions and criteria of Article 8.2 of the Subsidies Agreement; and

(II) the subsidy is specific within the meaning of paragraph (5A).

(F) Certain subsidies on agricultural products. Domestic support measures that are provided with respect to products listed in Annex 1 to the Agreement on Agriculture, and that the administering authority determines conform fully to the provisions of Annex 2 to that Agreement, shall be treated as noncountervailable. Upon request by the administering authority, the Trade Representative shall provide advice regarding the interpretation and application of Annex 2.

(G) Provisional application.

(i) Subparagraphs (B), (C), (D), and (E) shall not apply on or after the first day of the month that is 66 months after the WTO Agreement enters into force, unless the provisions of such subparagraphs are extended pursuant to section 282(c) of the Uruguay Round Agreements Act.

(ii) Subparagraph (F) shall not apply to imports from a WTO member country at the end of the 9–year period beginning on January 1, 1995. The Trade Representative shall determine the precise termination date for each WTO member country in accordance with paragraph (i) of Article 1 of the Agreement on Agriculture and such date shall be notified to the administering authority.

(6) Net countervailable subsidy. For the purpose of determining the net countervailable subsidy, the administering authority may subtract from the gross countervailable subsidy the amount of—

(A) any application fee, deposit, or similar payment paid in order to qualify for, or to receive, the benefit of the countervailable subsidy,

(B) any loss in the value of the countervailable subsidy resulting from its deferred receipt, if the deferral is mandated by Government order, and

(C) export taxes, duties, or other charges levied on the export of merchandise to the United States specifically intended to offset the countervailable subsidy received.

(7) Material injury.

(A) In general. The term "material injury" means harm which is not inconsequential, immaterial, or unimportant.

(B) Volume and consequent impact. In making determinations under sections 703(a), 705(b), 733(a), and 735(b), the Commission, in each case—

(i) shall consider—

(I) the volume of imports of the subject merchandise,

(II) the effect of imports of that merchandise on prices in the United States for domestic like products, and

(III) the impact of imports of such merchandise on domestic producers of domestic like products, but only in the context of production operations within the United States; and

(ii) may consider such other economic factors as are relevant to the determination regarding whether there is material injury by reason of imports.

In the notification required under section 705(d) or 735(d), as the case may be, the Commission shall explain its analysis of each factor considered under clause (i), and identify each factor considered under clause (ii) and explain in full its relevance to the determination.

(C) Evaluation of relevant factors. For purposes of subparagraph (B)—

(i) Volume. In evaluating the volume of imports of merchandise, the Commission shall consider whether the volume of imports of the merchandise, or any increase in that volume, either in absolute terms or relative to production or consumption in the United States, is significant.

(ii) Price. In evaluating the effect of imports of such merchandise on prices, the Commission shall consider whether—

(I) there has been significant price underselling by the imported merchandise as compared with the price of domestic like products of the United States, and

(II) the effect of imports of such merchandise otherwise depresses prices to a significant degree or prevents price increases, which otherwise would have occurred, to a significant degree.

(iii) Impact on affected domestic industry. In examining the impact required to be considered under subparagraph (B)(i)(III), the Commission shall evaluate all relevant economic factors which have a bearing on the state of the industry in the United States, including, but not limited to—

(I) actual and potential decline in output, sales, market share, profits, productivity, return on investments, and utilization of capacity,

(II) factors affecting domestic prices,

(III) actual and potential negative effects on cash flow, inventories, employment, wages, growth, ability to raise capital, and investment,

(IV) actual and potential negative effects on the existing development and production efforts of the domestic industry, including efforts to develop a derivative or more advanced version of the domestic like product, and

(V) in a proceeding under subtitle B, the magnitude of the margin of dumping.

The Commission shall evaluate all relevant economic factors described in this clause within the context of the business cycle and conditions of competition that are distinctive to the affected industry.

(iv) Captive production. If domestic producers internally transfer significant production of the domestic like product for the production of a downstream article and sell significant production of the domestic like product in the merchant market, and the Commission finds that—

(I) the domestic like product produced that is internally transferred for processing into that downstream article does not enter the merchant market for the domestic like product,

(II) the domestic like product is the predominant material input in the production of that downstream article, and

(III) the production of the domestic like product sold in the merchant market is not generally used in the production of that downstream article,

then the Commission, in determining market share and the factors affecting financial performance set forth in clause (iii), shall focus primarily on the merchant market for the domestic like product.

(v) [Repealed]

(D) Special rules for agricultural products.

(i) The Commission shall not determine that there is no material injury or threat of material injury to United States producers of an agricultural commodity merely because the prevailing market price is at or above the minimum support price.

(ii) In the case of agricultural products, the Commission shall consider any increased burden on government income or price support programs.

(E) Special rules. For purposes of this paragraph—

(i) Nature of countervailable subsidy. In determining whether there is a threat of material injury, the Commission shall consider information provided to it by the administering authority regarding the nature of the countervailable subsidy granted by a foreign country (particularly whether the countervailable subsidy is a subsidy described in Article 3 or 6.1 of the Subsidies Agreement) and the effects likely to be caused by the countervailable subsidy.

(ii) Standard for determination. The presence or absence of any factor which the Commission is required to evaluate under subparagraph (C) or (D) shall not necessarily give decisive guidance with respect to the determination by the Commission of material injury.

(F) Threat of material injury.

(i) In general. In determining whether an industry in the United States is threatened with material injury by reason of imports (or sales for importation) of the subject merchandise, the Commission shall consider, among other relevant economic factors—

(I) if a countervailable subsidy is involved, such information as may be presented to it by the administering authority as to the nature of the subsidy (particularly as to whether the countervailable subsidy is a subsidy described in Article 3 or 6.1 of the Subsidies Agreement), and whether imports of the subject merchandise are likely to increase,

(II) any existing unused production capacity or imminent, substantial increase in production capacity in the exporting country indicating the likelihood of substantially increased imports of the subject merchandise into the United States, taking into account the availability of other export markets to absorb any additional exports,

(III) a significant rate of increase of the volume or market penetration of imports of the subject merchandise indicating the likelihood of substantially increased imports,

(IV) whether imports of the subject merchandise are entering at prices that are likely to have a significant depressing or suppressing effect on domestic prices, and are likely to increase demand for further imports,

(V) inventories of the subject merchandise,

(VI) the potential for product-shifting if production facilities in the foreign country, which can be used to produce the subject merchandise, are currently being used to produce other products,

(VII) in any investigation under this title which involves imports of both a raw agricultural product (within the meaning of paragraph (4)(E)(iv)) and any product processed from such raw agricultural product, the likelihood that there will be increased imports, by reason of product shifting, if there is an affirmative determination by the Commission under section 705(b)(1) or 735(b)(1) with respect to either the raw agricultural product or the processed agricultural product (but not both),

(VIII) the actual and potential negative effects on the existing development and production efforts of the domestic industry, including efforts to develop a derivative or more advanced version of the domestic like product, and

(IX) any other demonstrable adverse trends that indicate the probability that there is likely to be material injury by reason of imports (or sale for importation) of the subject merchandise (whether or not it is actually being imported at the time).

(ii) Basis for determination. The Commission shall consider the factors set forth in clause (i) as a whole in making a determination of whether further dumped or subsidized imports are imminent and whether material injury by reason of imports would occur unless an order is issued or a suspension agreement is accepted under this title. The presence or absence of any factor which the Commission is required to consider under clause (i) shall not necessarily give decisive guidance with respect to the determination. Such a determination may not be made on the basis of mere conjecture or supposition.

(iii) Effect of dumping in third-country markets.

(I) In general. In investigations under subtitle B, the Commission shall consider whether dumping in the markets of foreign countries (as evidenced by dumping findings or antidumping remedies in other WTO member markets against the same class or kind of merchandise manufactured or exported by the same party as under investigation) suggests a threat of material injury to the domestic industry. In the course of its investigation, the Commission shall request information from the foreign manufacturer, exporter, or United States importer concerning this issue.

(II) WTO member market. For purposes of this clause, the term "WTO member market" means the market of any country which is a WTO member.

(III) European communities. For purposes of this clause, the European Communities shall be treated as a foreign country.

(iv) [Repealed]

(G) Cumulation for determining material injury.

(i) In general. For purposes of clauses (i) and (ii) of subparagraph (C), and subject to clause (ii), the Commission shall cumulatively assess the volume and effect of imports of the subject merchandise from all countries with respect to which—

(I) petitions were filed under section 702(b) or 732(b) on the same day,

(II) investigations were initiated under section 702(a) or 732(a) on the same day, or

(III) petitions were filed under section 702(b) or 732(b) and investigations were initiated under section 702(a) or 732(a) on the same day,

if such imports compete with each other and with domestic like products in the United States market.

(ii) Exceptions. The Commission shall not cumulatively assess the volume and effect of imports under clause (i)—

(I) with respect to which the administering authority has made a preliminary negative determination, unless the administering authority subsequently made a final affirmative determination with respect to those imports before the Commission's final determination is made;

(II) from any country with respect to which the investigation has been terminated;

(III) from any country designated as a beneficiary country under the Caribbean Basin Economic Recovery Act (19 U.S.C. 2701 et seq.) for purposes of making a determination with respect to that country, except that the volume and effect of imports of the subject merchandise from such country may be cumulatively assessed with imports of the subject merchandise from any other country designated as such a beneficiary country to the extent permitted by clause (i); or

(IV) from any country that is a party to an agreement with the United States establishing a free trade area, which entered into force and effect before January 1, 1987, unless the Commission determines that a domestic industry is materially injured or threatened with material injury by reason of imports from that country.

(iii) Records in final investigations. In each final determination in which it cumulatively assesses the volume and effect of imports under clause (i), the Commission shall make its determinations based on the record compiled in the first investigation in which it makes a final determination, except that when the administering authority issues its final determination in a subsequently completed investigation, the Commission shall permit the parties in the subsequent investigation to submit comments concerning the significance of the administering authority's final determination, and shall include such comments and the administering authority's final determination in the record for the subsequent investigation.

(iv) Regional industry determinations. In an investigation which involves a regional industry, and in which the Commission decides that the volume and effect of imports should be cumulatively assessed under this subparagraph, such assessment shall be based upon the volume and effect of imports into the region or regions determined by the Commission. The provisions of clause (iii) shall apply to such investigations.

(H) Cumulation for determining threat of material injury. To the extent practicable and subject to subparagraph (G)(ii), for purposes of clause (i)(III) and (IV) of subparagraph (F), the Commission may cumulatively assess the volume and price effects of imports of the subject merchandise from all countries with respect to which—

(i) petitions were filed under section 702(b) or 732(b) on the same day,

(ii) investigations were initiated under section 702(a) or 732(a) on the same day, or

(iii) petitions were filed under section 702(b) or 732(b) and investigations were initiated under section 702(a) or 732(a) on the same day,

if such imports compete with each other and with domestic like products in the United States market.

(I) Consideration of post-petition information. The Commission shall consider whether any change in the volume, price effects, or impact of imports of the subject merchandise since the filing of the petition in an investigation under subtitle A or B is related to the pendency of the investigation and, if so, the Commission may reduce the weight accorded to the data for the period after the filing of the petition in making its determination of material injury, threat of material injury, or material retardation of the establishment of an industry in the United States.

(8) Subsidies Agreement; Agreement on Agriculture.

(A) Subsidies Agreement. The term "Subsidies Agreement" means the Agreement on Subsidies and Countervailing Measures referred to in section 101(d)(12) of the Uruguay Round Agreements Act.

(B) Agreement on Agriculture. The term "Agreement on Agriculture" means the Agreement on Agriculture referred to in section 101(d)(2) of the Uruguay Round Agreements Act.

(9) Interested party. The term "interested party" means—

(A) a foreign manufacturer, producer, or exporter, or the United States importer, of subject merchandise or a trade or business association a majority of the members of which are producers, exporters, or importers of such merchandise,

(B) the government of a country in which such merchandise is produced or manufactured or from which such merchandise is exported,

(C) a manufacturer, producer, or wholesaler in the United States of a domestic like product,

(D) a certified union or recognized union or group of workers which is representative of an industry engaged in the manufacture, production, or wholesale in the United States of a domestic like product,

(E) a trade or business association a majority of whose members manufacture, produce, or wholesale a domestic like product in the United States,

(F) an association, a majority of whose members is composed of interested parties described in subparagraph (C), (D), or (E) with respect to a domestic like product, and

(G) in any investigation under this title involving an industry engaged in producing a processed agricultural product, as defined in paragraph (4)(E), a coalition or trade association which is representative of either—

(i) processors,

(ii) processors and producers, or

(iii) processors and growers,

but this subparagraph shall cease to have effect if the United States Trade Representative notifies the administering authority and the Commission that the application of this subparagraph is inconsistent with the international obligations of the United States.

(10) Domestic like product. The term "domestic like product" means a product which is like, or in the absence of like, most similar in characteristics and uses with, the article subject to an investigation under this title.

(11) Affirmative determinations by divided Commission. If the Commissioners voting on a determination by the Commission, including a determination under section 751, are evenly divided as to whether the determination

should be affirmative or negative, the Commission shall be deemed to have made an affirmative determination. For the purpose of applying this paragraph when the issue before the Commission is to determine whether there is—

(A) material injury to an industry in the United States,

(B) threat of material injury to such an industry, or

(C) material retardation of the establishment of an industry in the United States,

by reason of imports of the merchandise, an affirmative vote on any of the issues shall be treated as a vote that the determination should be affirmative.

(12) Attribution of merchandise to country of manufacture or production. For purposes of subtitle A, merchandise shall be treated as the product of the country in which it was manufactured or produced without regard to whether it is imported directly from that country and without regard to whether it is imported in the same condition as when exported from that country or in a changed condition by reason of remanufacture or otherwise.

(13) [Repealed]

(14) Sold or, in the absence of sales, offered for sale. The term "sold or, in the absence of sales, offered for sale" means sold or, in the absence of sales, offered—

(A) to all purchasers at wholesale, or

(B) in the ordinary course of trade to one or more selected purchasers in commercial quantities at a price which fairly reflects the market value of the merchandise,

without regard to restrictions as to the disposition or use of the merchandise by the purchaser except that, where such restrictions are found to affect the market value of the merchandise, adjustment shall be made therefor in calculating the price at which the merchandise is sold or offered for sale.

(15) Ordinary course of trade. The term "ordinary course of trade" means the conditions and practices which, for a reasonable time prior to the exportation of the subject merchandise, have been normal in the trade under consideration with respect to merchandise of the same class or kind. The administering authority shall consider the following sales and transactions, among others, to be outside the ordinary course of trade:

(A) Sales disregarded under section 773(b)(1).

(B) Transactions disregarded under section 773(f)(2).

(16) Foreign like product. The term "foreign like product" means merchandise in the first of the following categories in respect of which a determination for the purposes of subtitle B of this title can be satisfactorily made:

(A) The subject merchandise and other merchandise which is identical in physical characteristics with, and was produced in the same country by the same person as, that merchandise.

(B) Merchandise—

(i) produced in the same country and by the same person as the subject merchandise,

(ii) like that merchandise in component material or materials and in the purposes for which used, and

(iii) approximately equal in commercial value to that merchandise.

(C) Merchandise—

(i) produced in the same country and by the same person and of the same general class or kind as the subject merchandise,

(ii) like that merchandise in the purposes for which used, and

(iii) which the administering authority determines may reasonably be compared with that merchandise.

(17) Usual commercial quantities. The term "usual commercial quantities", in any case in which the subject merchandise is sold in the market under consideration at different prices for different quantities, means the quantities in which such merchandise is there sold at the price or prices for one quantity in an aggregate volume which is greater than the aggregate volume sold at the price or prices for any other quantity.

(18) Nonmarket economy country.

(A) In general. The term "nonmarket economy country" means any foreign country that the administering authority determines does not operate on market principles of cost or pricing structures, so that sales of merchandise in such country do not reflect the fair value of the merchandise.

(B) Factors to be considered. In making determinations under subparagraph (A) the administering authority shall take into account—

(i) the extent to which the currency of the foreign country is convertible into the currency of other countries;[,]

(ii) the extent to which wage rates in the foreign country are determined by free bargaining between labor and management,

(iii) the extent to which joint ventures or other investments by firms of other foreign countries are permitted in the foreign country,

(iv) the extent of government ownership or control of the means of production,

(v) the extent of government control over the allocation of resources and over the price and output decisions of enterprises, and

(vi) such other factors as the administering authority considers appropriate.

(C) Determination in effect.

(i) Any determination that a foreign country is a nonmarket economy country shall remain in effect until revoked by the administering authority.

(ii) The administering authority may make a determination under subparagraph (A) with respect to any foreign country at any time.

(D) Determinations not in issue. Notwithstanding any other provision of law, any determination made by the administering authority under subparagraph (A) shall not be subject to judicial review in any investigation conducted under subtitle B.

(E) Collection of information. Upon request by the administering authority, the Commissioner of Customs shall provide the administering authority a copy of all public and proprietary information submitted to, or obtained by, the Commissioner of Customs that the administering authority considers relevant to proceedings involving merchandise from non-market economy countries. The administering authority shall protect proprietary information obtained under this section from public disclosure in accordance with section 777.

(19) Equivalency of leases to sales. In determining whether a lease is equivalent to a sale for purposes of this title, the administering authority shall consider—

(A) the terms of the lease,

(B) commercial practice within the industry,

(C) the circumstances of the transaction,

(D) whether the product subject to the lease is integrated into the operations of the lessee or importer,

(E) whether in practice there is a likelihood that the lease will be continued or renewed for a significant period of time, and

(F) other relevant factors, including whether the lease transaction would permit avoidance of antidumping or countervailing duties.

(20) Application to governmental importations.

(A) In general. Except as otherwise provided by this paragraph, merchandise imported by, or for the use of, a department or agency of the United States Government (including merchandise provided for under chapter 98 of the Harmonized Tariff Schedule of the United States) is subject to the imposition of countervailing duties or antidumping duties under this title or section 303.

(B) Exceptions. Merchandise imported by, or for the use of, the Department of Defense shall not be subject to the imposition of countervailing or antidumping duties under this title if—

(i) the merchandise is acquired by, or for use of, such Department—

(I) from a country with which such Department had a Memorandum of Understanding which was in effect on January 1, 1988, and has continued to have a comparable agreement (including renewals) or superceding agreements, and

(II) in accordance with terms of the Memorandum of Understanding in effect at the time of importation, or

(ii) the merchandise has no substantial nonmilitary use.

(21) United States–Canada Agreement. The term "United States–Canada Agreement" means the United States–Canada Free–Trade Agreement.

(22) NAFTA. The term "NAFTA" means the North American Free Trade Agreement.

(23) Entry. The term "entry" includes, in appropriate circumstances as determined by the administering authority, a reconciliation entry created under a reconciliation process, defined in section 401(s), that is initiated by an importer. The liability of an importer under an antidumping or countervailing duty proceeding for entries of merchandise subject to the proceeding will attach to the corresponding reconciliation entry or entries. Suspension of liquidation of the reconciliation entry or entries, for the purpose of enforcing this title, is equivalent to the suspension of liquidation of the corresponding individual entries; but the suspension of liquidation of the reconciliation entry or entries for such purpose does not preclude liquidation for any other purpose.

(24) Negligible imports.

(A) In general.

(i) Less than 3 percent. Except as provided in clauses (ii) and (iv), imports from a country of merchandise corresponding to a domestic like product identified by the Commission are "negligible" if such imports account for less than 3 percent of the volume of all such merchandise imported into the United States in the most recent 12–month period for which data are available that precedes—

(I) the filing of the petition under section 702(b) or 732(b), or

(II) the initiation of the investigation, if the investigation was initiated under section 702(a) or 732(a).

(ii) Exception. Imports that would otherwise be negligible under clause (i) shall not be negligible if the aggregate volume of imports of the merchandise from all countries described in clause (i) with respect to which investigations were initiated on the same day exceeds 7 percent of the volume of all such merchandise imported into the United States during the applicable 12–month period.

(iii) Determination of aggregate volume. In determining aggregate volume under clause (ii) or (iv), the Commission shall not consider imports from any country specified in paragraph (7)(G)(ii).

(iv) Negligibility in threat analysis. Notwithstanding clauses (i) and (ii), the Commission shall not treat imports as negligible if it determines that there is a potential that imports from a country described in clause (i) will imminently account for more than 3 percent of the volume of all such merchandise imported into the United States, or that the aggregate volumes of imports from all countries described in clause (ii) will imminently exceed 7 percent of the volume of all such merchandise imported into the United States. The Commission shall consider such imports only for purposes of determining threat of material injury.

(B) Negligibility for certain countries in countervailing duty investigations. In the case of an investigation under section 701, subparagraph (A) shall be applied to imports of subject merchandise from developing countries by substituting "4 percent" for "3 percent" in subparagraph (A)(i) and by substituting "9 percent" for "7 percent" in subparagraph (A)(ii).

(C) Computation of import volumes. In computing import volumes for purposes of subparagraphs (A) and (B), the Commission may make reasonable estimates on the basis of available statistics.

(D) Regional industries. In an investigation in which the Commission makes a regional industry determination under paragraph (4)(C), the Commission's examination under subparagraphs (A) and (B) shall be based upon the volume of subject merchandise exported for sale in the regional market in lieu of the volume of all subject merchandise imported into the United States.

(25) Subject merchandise. The term "subject merchandise" means the class or kind of merchandise that is within the scope of an investigation, a review, a suspension agreement, an order under this title or section 303, or a finding under the Antidumping Act, 1921.

(26) Section 303. The terms "section 303" and "303" mean section 303 of this Act as in effect on the day before the effective date of title II of the Uruguay Round Agreements Act.

(27) Suspension agreement. The term "suspension agreement" means an agreement described in section [sections] 704(b), 704(c), 734(b), 734(c), or 734(*l*).

(28) Exporter or producer. The term "exporter or producer" means the exporter of the subject merchandise, the producer of the subject merchandise, or both where appropriate. For purposes of section 773, the term "exporter or producer" includes both the exporter of the subject merchandise and the producer of the same subject merchandise to the extent necessary to accurately calculate the total amount incurred and realized for costs, expenses, and profits in connection with production and sale of that merchandise.

(29) WTO agreement. The term "WTO Agreement" means the Agreement defined in section 2(9) of the Uruguay Round Agreements Act.

(30) WTO member and WTO member country. The terms "WTO member" and "WTO member country" mean a state, or separate customs territory (within the meaning of Article XII of the WTO Agreement), with respect to which the United States applies the WTO Agreement.

(31) GATT 1994. The term "GATT 1994" means the General Agreement on Tariffs and Trade annexed to the WTO Agreement.

(32) Trade representative. The term "Trade Representative" means the United States Trade Representative.

(33) Affiliated persons. The following persons shall be considered to be "affiliated" or "affiliated persons":

(A) Members of a family, including brothers and sisters (whether by the whole or half blood), spouse, ancestors, and lineal descendants.

(B) Any officer or director of an organization and such organization.

(C) Partners.

(D) Employer and employee.

(E) Any person directly or indirectly owning, controlling, or holding with power to vote, 5 percent or more of the outstanding voting stock or shares of any organization and such organization.

(F) Two or more persons directly or indirectly controlling, controlled by, or under common control with, any person.

(G) Any person who controls any other person and such other person.

For purposes of this paragraph, a person shall be considered to control another person if the person is legally or operationally in a position to exercise restraint or direction over the other person.

(34) Dumped; dumping. The terms "dumped" and "dumping" refer to the sale or likely sale of goods at less than fair value.

(35) Dumping margin; weighted average dumping margin.

(A) Dumping margin. The term "dumping margin" means the amount by which the normal value exceeds the export price or constructed export price of the subject merchandise.

(B) Weighted average dumping margin. The term "weighted average dumping margin" is the percentage determined by dividing the aggregate dumping margins determined for a specific exporter or producer by the aggregate export prices and constructed export prices of such exporter or producer.

(C) Magnitude of the margin of dumping. The magnitude of the margin of dumping used by the Commission shall be—

(i) in making a preliminary determination under section 733(a) in an investigation (including any investigation in which the Commission cumulatively assesses the volume and effect of imports under paragraph (7)(G)(i)), the dumping margin or margins published by the administering authority in its notice of initiation of the investigation;

(ii) in making a final determination under section 735(b), the dumping margin or margins most recently published by the administering authority prior to the closing of the Commission's administrative record;

(iii) in a review under section 751(b)(2), the most recent dumping margin or margins determined by the administering authority under section 752(c)(3), if any, or under section 733(b) or 735(a); and

(iv) in a review under section 751(c), the dumping margin or margins determined by the administering authority under section 752(c)(3).

(36) Developing and least developed country.

(A) Developing country. The term "developing country" means a country designated as a developing country by the Trade Representative.

(B) Least developed country. The term "least developed country" means a country which the Trade Representative determines is—

(i) a country referred to as a least developed country within the meaning of paragraph (a) of Annex VII to the Subsidies Agreement, or

(ii) any other country listed in Annex VII to the Subsidies Agreement, but only if the country has a per capita gross national product of less than $1,000 per annum as measured by the most recent data available from the World Bank.

(C) Publication of list. The Trade Representative shall publish in the Federal Register, and update as necessary, a list of—

(i) developing countries that have eliminated their export subsidies on an expedited basis within the meaning of Article 27.11 of the Subsidies Agreement, and

(ii) countries determined by the Trade Representative to be least developed or developing countries.

(D) Factors to consider. In determining whether a country is a developing country under subparagraph (A), the Trade Representative shall consider such economic, trade, and other factors which the Trade Representative considers appropriate, including the level of economic development of such country (the assessment of which shall include a review of the country's per capita gross national product) and the country's share of world trade.

(E) Limitation on designation. A determination that a country is a developing or least developed country pursuant to this paragraph shall be for purposes of this title only and shall not affect the determination of a country's status as a developing or least developed country with respect to any other law.

19 USC 1677–1

Sec. 771A. Upstream Subsidies

(a) **Definition.** The term "upstream subsidy" means any countervailable subsidy, other than an export subsidy, that

(1) is paid or bestowed by an authority (as defined in section 771(5)) with respect to a product (hereafter in this section referred to as an "input product") that is used in the same country as the authority in the manufacture or production of merchandise which is the subject of a countervailing duty proceeding;

(2) in the judgment of the administering authority bestows a competitive benefit on the merchandise; and

(3) has a significant effect on the cost of manufacturing or producing the merchandise.

In applying this subsection, an association of two or more foreign countries, political subdivisions, dependent territories, or possessions of foreign countries organized into a customs union outside the United States shall be treated as being one country if the countervailable subsidy is provided by the customs union.

(b) Determination of competitive benefit.

(1) In general. Except as provided in paragraph (2), the administering authority shall decide that a competitive benefit has been bestowed when the price for the input product referred to in subsection (a)(1) for such use is lower than the price that the manufacturer or producer of merchandise which is the subject of a countervailing duty proceeding would otherwise pay for the product in obtaining it from another seller in an arms-length transaction.

(2) Adjustments. If the administering authority has determined in a previous proceeding that a countervailable subsidy is paid or bestowed on the input product that is used for comparison under paragraph (1), the administering authority may (A) where appropriate, adjust the price that the manufacturer or producer of merchandise which is the subject of such proceeding would otherwise pay for the product to reflect the effects of the countervailable subsidy, or (B) select in lieu of that price a price from another source.

(c) Inclusion of amount of countervailable subsidy. If the administering authority decides, during the course of a countervailing duty proceeding that an upstream countervailable subsidy is being or has been paid or bestowed regarding the subject merchandise, the administering authority shall include in the amount of any countervailing duty imposed on the merchandise an amount equal to the amount of the competitive benefit referred to in subparagraph (1)(B), except that in no event shall the amount be greater than the amount of the countervailable subsidy determined with respect to the upstream product.

19 USC 1677–2

Sec. 771B.   Calculation of Countervailable Subsidies on Certain Processed Agricultural Products

In the case of an agricultural product processed from a raw agricultural product in which (1) the demand for the prior stage product is substantially dependent on the demand for the latter stage product, and (2) the processing operation adds only limited value to the raw commodity, countervailable subsidies found to be provided to either producers or processors of the product shall be deemed to be provided with respect to the manufacture, production, or exportation of the processed product.

19 USC 1677a

Sec. 772.   Export Price and Constructed Export Price

(a) Export Price. The term "export price" means the price at which the subject merchandise is first sold (or agreed to be sold) before the date of importation by the producer or exporter of the subject merchandise outside of the United States to an unaffiliated purchaser in the United States or to an unaffiliated purchaser for exportation to the United States, as adjusted under subsection (c).

(b) Constructed Export Price. The term "constructed export price" means the price at which the subject merchandise is first sold (or agreed to be sold) in the United States before or after the date of importation by or for the account of the producer or exporter of such merchandise or by a seller affiliated with the producer or exporter, to a purchaser not affiliated with the producer or exporter, as adjusted under subsections (c) and (d).

(c) Adjustments for Export Price and Constructed Export Price. The price used to establish export price and constructed export price shall be—

(1) increased by—

(A) when not included in such price, the cost of all containers and coverings and all other costs, charges, and expenses incident to placing the subject merchandise in condition packed ready for shipment to the United States,

(B) the amount of any import duties imposed by the country of exportation which have been rebated, or which have not been collected, by reason of the exportation of the subject merchandise to the United States, and

(C) the amount of any countervailing duty imposed on the subject merchandise under subtitle A to offset an export subsidy, and

(2) reduced by—

(A) except as provided in paragraph (1)(C), the amount, if any, included in such price, attributable to any additional costs, charges, or expenses, and United States import duties, which are incident to bringing the subject merchandise from the original place of shipment in the exporting country to the place of delivery in the United States, and

(B) the amount, if included in such price, of any export tax, duty, or other charge imposed by the exporting country on the exportation of the subject merchandise to the United States, other than an export tax, duty, or other charge described in section 771(6)(C).

(d) Additional Adjustments to Constructed Export Price. For purposes of this section, the price used to establish constructed export price shall also be reduced by—

(1) the amount of any of the following expenses generally incurred by or for the account of the producer or exporter, or the affiliated seller in the United States, in selling the subject merchandise (or subject merchandise to which value has been added)—

(A) commissions for selling the subject merchandise in the United States;

(B) expenses that result from, and bear a direct relationship to, the sale, such as credit expenses, guarantees and warranties;

(C) any selling expenses that the seller pays on behalf of the purchaser;

(D) any selling expenses not deducted under subparagraph (A), (B), or (C);

(2) the cost of any further manufacture or assembly (including additional material and labor), except in circumstances described in subsection (e); and

(3) the profit allocated to the expenses described in paragraphs (1) and (2).

(e) Special Rule for Merchandise with Value Added After Importation. Where the subject merchandise is imported by a person affiliated with the exporter or producer, and the value added in the United States by the affiliated person is likely to exceed substantially the value of the subject merchandise, the administering authority shall determine the constructed export price for such merchandise by using one of the following prices if there is a sufficient quantity of sales to provide a reasonable basis for comparison and the administering authority determines that the use of such sales is appropriate:

(1) The price of identical subject merchandise sold by the exporter or producer to an unaffiliated person.

(2) The price of other subject merchandise sold by the exporter or producer to an unaffiliated person.

If there is not a sufficient quantity of sales to provide a reasonable basis for comparison under paragraph (1) or (2), or the administering authority determines that neither of the prices described in such paragraphs is appropriate, then the constructed export price may be determined on any other reasonable basis.

(f) Special Rule for Determining Profit.

(1) In general. For purposes of subsection (d)(3), profit shall be an amount determined by multiplying the total actual profit by the applicable percentage.

(2) Definitions. For purposes of this subsection—

(A) Applicable percentage. The term "applicable percentage" means the percentage determined by dividing the total United States expenses by the total expenses.

(B) Total United States expenses. The term "total United States expenses" means the total expenses described in subsection (d)(1) and (2).

(C) Total expenses. The term "total expenses" means all expenses in the first of the following categories which applies and which are incurred by or on behalf of the foreign producer and foreign exporter of the subject merchandise and by or on behalf of the United States seller affiliated with the producer or exporter with respect to the production and sale of such merchandise:

(i) The expenses incurred with respect to the subject merchandise sold in the United States and the foreign like product sold in the exporting country if such expenses were requested by the administering authority for the purpose of establishing normal value and constructed export price.

(ii) The expenses incurred with respect to the narrowest category of merchandise sold in the United States and the exporting country which includes the subject merchandise.

(iii) The expenses incurred with respect to the narrowest category of merchandise sold in all countries which includes the subject merchandise.

(D) Total actual profit. The term "total actual profit" means the total profit earned by the foreign producer, exporter, and affiliated parties described in subparagraph (C) with respect to the sale of the same merchandise for which total expenses are determined under such subparagraph.

19 USC 1677b

Sec. 773. Normal Value

(a) Determination. In determining under this title whether subject merchandise is being, or is likely to be, sold at less than fair value, a fair comparison shall be made between the export price or constructed export price and normal value. In order to achieve a fair comparison with the export price or constructed export price, normal value shall be determined as follows:

(1) Determination of normal value.

(A) In general. The normal value of the subject merchandise shall be the price described in subparagraph (B), at a time reasonably corresponding to the time of the sale used to determine the export price or constructed export price under section 772(a) or (b).

(B) Price. The price referred to in subparagraph (A) is—

(i) the price at which the foreign like product is first sold (or, in the absence of a sale, offered for sale) for consumption in the exporting country, in the usual commercial quantities and in the ordinary course of trade and, to the extent practicable, at the same level of trade as the export price or constructed export price, or

(ii) in a case to which subparagraph (C) applies, the price at which the foreign like product is so sold (or offered for sale) for consumption in a country other than the exporting country or the United States, if—

(I) such price is representative,

(II) the aggregate quantity (or, if quantity is not appropriate, value) of the foreign like product sold by the exporter or producer in such other country is 5 percent or more of the aggregate quantity (or value) of the subject merchandise sold in the United States or for export to the United States, and

(III) the administering authority does not determine that the particular market situation in such other country prevents a proper comparison with the export price or constructed export price.

(C) Third country sales. This subparagraph applies when—

(i) the foreign like product is not sold (or offered for sale) for consumption in the exporting country as described in subparagraph (B)(i),

(ii) the administering authority determines that the aggregate quantity (or, if quantity is not appropriate, value) of the foreign like product sold in the exporting country is insufficient to permit a proper comparison with the sales of the subject merchandise to the United States, or

(iii) the particular market situation in the exporting country does not permit a proper comparison with the export price or constructed export price.

For purposes of clause (ii), the aggregate quantity (or value) of the foreign like product sold in the exporting country shall normally be considered to be insufficient if such quantity (or value) is less than 5 percent of the aggregate quantity (or value) of sales of the subject merchandise to the United States.

(2) Fictitious markets. No pretended sale or offer for sale, and no sale or offer for sale intended to establish a fictitious market, shall be taken into account in determining normal value. The occurrence of different movements in the prices at which different forms of the foreign like product are sold (or, in the absence of sales, offered for sale) in the exporting country after the issuance of an antidumping duty order may be considered by the administering authority as evidence of the establishment of a fictitious market for the foreign like product if the movement in such prices appears to reduce the amount by which the normal value exceeds the export price (or the constructed export price) of the subject merchandise.

(3) Exportation from an intermediate country. Where the subject merchandise is exported to the United States from an intermediate country, normal value shall be determined in the intermediate country, except that normal value may be determined in the country of origin of the subject merchandise if—

(A) the producer knew at the time of the sale that the subject merchandise was destined for exportation;

(B) the subject merchandise is merely transshipped through the intermediate country;

(C) sales of the foreign like product in the intermediate country do not satisfy the conditions of paragraph (1)(C); or

(D) the foreign like product is not produced in the intermediate country.

(4) Use of constructed value. If the administering authority determines that the normal value of the subject merchandise cannot be determined under paragraph (1)(B)(i), then, notwithstanding paragraph (1)(B)(ii), the normal value of the subject merchandise may be the constructed value of that merchandise, as determined under subsection (e).

(5) Indirect sales or offers for sale. If the foreign like product is sold or, in the absence of sales, offered for sale through an affiliated party, the prices at which the foreign like product is sold (or offered for sale) by such affiliated party may be used in determining normal value.

(6) Adjustments. The price described in paragraph (1)(B) shall be—

(A) increased by the cost of all containers and coverings and all other costs, charges, and expenses incident to placing the subject merchandise in condition packed ready for shipment to the United States;

(B) reduced by—

(i) when included in the price described in paragraph (1)(B), the cost of all containers and coverings and all other costs, charges, and expenses incident to placing the foreign like product in condition packed ready for shipment to the place of delivery to the purchaser,

(ii) the amount, if any, included in the price described in paragraph (1)(B), attributable to any additional costs, charges, and expenses incident to bringing the foreign like product from the original place of shipment to the place of delivery to the purchaser, and

(iii) the amount of any taxes imposed directly upon the foreign like product or components thereof which have been rebated, or which have not been collected, on the subject merchandise, but only to the extent that such taxes are added to or included in the price of the foreign like product, and

(C) increased or decreased by the amount of any difference (or lack thereof) between the export price or constructed export price and the price described in paragraph (1)(B) (other than a difference for which allowance is otherwise provided under this section) that is established to the satisfaction of the administering authority to be wholly or partly due to—

(i) the fact that the quantities in which the subject merchandise is sold or agreed to be sold to the United States are greater than or less than the quantities in which the foreign like product is sold, agreed to be sold, or offered for sale,

(ii) the fact that merchandise described in subparagraph (B) or (C) of section 771(16) is used in determining normal value, or

(iii) other differences in the circumstances of sale.

(7) Additional adjustments.

(A) Level of trade. The price described in paragraph (1)(B) shall also be increased or decreased to make due allowance for any difference (or lack thereof) between the export price or constructed export price and the price described in paragraph (1)(B) (other than a difference for which allowance is otherwise made under this section) that is shown to be wholly or partly due to a difference in level of trade between the export price or constructed export price and normal value, if the difference in level of trade—

(i) involves the performance of different selling activities; and

(ii) is demonstrated to affect price comparability, based on a pattern of consistent price differences between sales at different levels of trade in the country in which normal value is determined.

In a case described in the preceding sentence, the amount of the adjustment shall be based on the price differences between the two levels of trade in the country in which normal value is determined.

(B) Constructed export price offset. When normal value is established at a level of trade which constitutes a more advanced stage of distribution than the level of trade of the constructed export price, but the data available do not provide an appropriate basis to determine under subparagraph (A)(ii) a level of trade adjustment, normal value shall be reduced by the amount of indirect selling expenses incurred in the country in which normal value is determined on sales of the foreign like product but not more than the amount of such expenses for which a deduction is made under section 772(d)(1)(D).

(8) Adjustments to constructed value. Constructed value as determined under subsection (e), may be adjusted, as appropriate, pursuant to this subsection.

(b) Sales at Less Than Cost of Production.

(1) Determination; sales disregarded. Whenever the administering authority has reasonable grounds to believe or suspect that sales of the foreign like product under consideration for the determination of normal value have been made at prices which represent less than the cost of production of that product, the administering authority shall determine whether, in fact, such sales were made at less than the cost of production. If the administering authority determines that sales made at less than the cost of production—

(A) have been made within an extended period of time in substantial quantities, and

(B) were not at prices which permit recovery of all costs within a reasonable period of time, such sales may be disregarded in the determination of normal value. Whenever such sales are disregarded, normal value shall be based on the remaining sales of the foreign like product in the ordinary course of trade. If no sales made in the ordinary course of trade remain, the normal value shall be based on the constructed value of the merchandise.

(2) Definitions and special rules. For purposes of this subsection—

(A) Reasonable grounds to believe or suspect. There are reasonable grounds to believe or suspect that sales of the foreign like product were made at prices that are less than the cost of production of the product, if—

(i) in an investigation initiated under section 732 or a review conducted under section 751, an interested party described in subparagraph (C), (D), (E), (F), or (G) of section 771(9) provides information, based upon observed prices or constructed prices or costs, that sales of the foreign like product under consideration for the determination of normal value have been made at prices which represent less than the cost of production of the product; or

(ii) in a review conducted under section 751 involving a specific exporter, the administering authority disregarded some or all of the exporter's sales pursuant to paragraph (1) in the investigation or if a review has been completed, in the most recently completed review.

(B) Extended period of time. The term "extended period of time" means a period that is normally 1 year, but not less than 6 months.

(C) Substantial quantities. Sales made at prices below the cost of production have been made in substantial quantities if—

(i) the volume of such sales represents 20 percent or more of the volume of sales under consideration for the determination of normal value, or

(ii) the weighted average per unit price of the sales under consideration for the determination of normal value is less than the weighted average per unit cost of production for such sales.

(D) Recovery of costs. If prices which are below the per unit cost of production at the time of sale are above the weighted average per unit cost of production for the period of investigation or review, such prices shall be considered to provide for recovery of costs within a reasonable period of time.

(3) Calculation of cost of production. For purposes of this subtitle, the cost of production shall be an amount equal to the sum of—

(A) the cost of materials and of fabrication or other processing of any kind employed in producing the foreign like product, during a period which would ordinarily permit the production of that foreign like product in the ordinary course of business;

(B) an amount for selling, general, and administrative expenses based on actual data pertaining to production and sales of the foreign like product by the exporter in question; and

(C) the cost of all containers and coverings of whatever nature, and all other expenses incidental to placing the foreign like product in condition packed ready for shipment.

For purposes of subparagraph (A), if the normal value is based on the price of the foreign like product sold for consumption in a country other than the exporting country, the cost of materials shall be determined without regard to any internal tax in the exporting country imposed on such materials or their disposition which are remitted or refunded upon exportation.

(c) Nonmarket Economy Countries.

(1) In general. If—

(A) the subject merchandise is exported from a nonmarket economy country, and

(B) the administering authority finds that available information does not permit the normal value of the subject merchandise to be determined under subsection (a),

the administering authority shall determine the normal value of the subject merchandise on the basis of the value of the factors of production utilized in producing the merchandise and to which shall be added an amount for general expenses and profit plus the cost of containers, coverings, and other expenses. Except as provided in paragraph (2), the valuation of the factors of production shall be based on the best available information regarding the values of such factors in a market economy country or countries considered to be appropriate by the administering authority.

(2) Exception. If the administering authority finds that the available information is inadequate for purposes of determining the normal value of subject merchandise under paragraph (1), the administering authority shall determine the normal value on the basis of the price at which merchandise that is—

(A) comparable to the subject merchandise, and

(B) produced in one or more market economy countries that are at a level of economic development comparable to that of the nonmarket economy country,

is sold in other countries, including the United States.

(3) Factors of production. For purposes of paragraph (1), the factors of production utilized in producing merchandise include, but are not limited to—

(A) hours of labor required,

(B) quantities of raw materials employed,

(C) amounts of energy and other utilities consumed, and

(D) representative capital cost, including depreciation.

(4) Valuation of factors of production. The administering authority, in valuing factors of production under paragraph (1), shall utilize, to the extent possible, the prices or costs of factors of production in one or more market economy countries that are—

(A) at a level of economic development comparable to that of the nonmarket economy country, and

(B) significant producers of comparable merchandise.

(d) Special Rule for Certain Multinational Corporations. Whenever, in the course of an investigation under this title, the administering authority determines that—

(1) subject merchandise exported to the United States is being produced in facilities which are owned or controlled, directly or indirectly, by a person, firm, or corporation [*S13476] which also owns or controls, directly or indirectly, other facilities for the production of the foreign like product which are located in another country or countries,

(2) subsection (a)(1)(C) applies, and

(3) the normal value of the foreign like product produced in one or more of the facilities outside the exporting country is higher than the normal value of the foreign like product produced in the facilities located in the exporting country,

it shall determine the normal value of the subject merchandise by reference to the normal value at which the foreign like product is sold in substantial quantities from one or more facilities outside the exporting country. The administering authority, in making any determination under this paragraph, shall make adjustments for the difference between the cost of production (including taxes, labor, materials, and overhead) of the foreign like product produced in facilities outside the exporting country and costs of production of the foreign like product produced in facilities in the exporting country, if such differences are demonstrated to its satisfaction. For purposes of this subsection, in determining the normal value of the foreign like product produced in a country outside of the exporting country, the administering authority shall determine its price at the time of exportation from the exporting country and shall make any adjustments required by subsection (a) for the cost of all containers and coverings and all other costs, charges, and expenses incident to placing the merchandise in condition packed ready for shipment to the United States by reference to such costs in the exporting country.

(e) Constructed Value. For purposes of this title, the constructed value of imported merchandise shall be an amount equal to the sum of—

(1) the cost of materials and fabrication or other processing of any kind employed in producing the merchandise, during a period which would ordinarily permit the production of the merchandise in the ordinary course of business;

(2)(A) the actual amounts incurred and realized by the specific exporter or producer being examined in the investigation or review for selling, general, and administrative expenses, and for profits, in connection with the production and sale of a foreign like product, in the ordinary course of trade, for consumption in the foreign country, or

(B) if actual data are not available with respect to the amounts described in subparagraph (A), then—

(i) the actual amounts incurred and realized by the specific exporter or producer being examined in the investigation or review for selling, general, and administrative expenses, and for profits, in connection with the production and sale, for consumption in the foreign country, of merchandise that is in the same general category of products as the subject merchandise,

(ii) the weighted average of the actual amounts incurred and realized by exporters or producers that are subject to the investigation or review (other than the exporter or producer described in clause (i)) for selling, general, and administrative expenses, and for profits, in connection with the production and sale of a foreign like product, in the ordinary course of trade, for consumption in the foreign country, or

(iii) the amounts incurred and realized for selling, general, and administrative expenses, and for profits, based on any other reasonable method, except that the amount allowed for profit may not exceed the amount normally realized by exporters or producers (other than the exporter or producer described in clause (i)) in connection with the sale, for consumption in the foreign country, of merchandise that is in the same general category of products as the subject merchandise; and

(3) the cost of all containers and coverings of whatever nature, and all other expenses incidental to placing the subject merchandise in condition packed ready for shipment to the United States.

For purposes of paragraph (1), the cost of materials shall be determined without regard to any internal tax in the exporting country imposed on such materials or their disposition which are remitted or refunded upon exportation of the subject merchandise produced from such materials.

(f) Special Rules for Calculation of Cost of Production and for Calculation of Constructed Value. For purposes of subsections (b) and (e)—

(1) Costs.

(A) In general. Costs shall normally be calculated based on the records of the exporter or producer of the merchandise, if such records are kept in accordance with the generally accepted accounting principles of the exporting country (or the producing country, where appropriate) and reasonably reflect the costs associated with the production and sale of the merchandise. The administering authority shall consider all available evidence on the proper allocation of costs, including that which is made available by the exporter or producer on a timely basis, if such allocations have been historically used by the exporter or producer, in particular for establishing appropriate amortization and depreciation periods, and allowances for capital expenditures and other development costs.

(B) Nonrecurring costs. Costs shall be adjusted appropriately for those nonrecurring costs that benefit current or future production, or both.

(C) Startup costs.

(i) In general. Costs shall be adjusted appropriately for circumstances in which costs incurred during the time period covered by the investigation or review are affected by startup operations.

(ii) Startup operations. Adjustments shall be made for startup operations only where—

(I) a producer is using new production facilities or producing a new product that requires substantial additional investment, and

(II) production levels are limited by technical factors associated with the initial phase of commercial production.

For purposes of subclause (II), the initial phase of commercial production ends at the end of the startup period. In determining whether commercial production levels have been achieved, the administering authority shall consider factors unrelated to startup operations that might affect the volume of production processed, such as demand, seasonality, or business cycles.

(iii) Adjustment for startup operations. The adjustment for startup operations shall be made by substituting the unit production costs incurred with respect to the merchandise at the end of the startup period for the unit production costs incurred during the startup period. If the startup period extends beyond the period of the investigation or review under this title, the administering authority shall use the most recent cost of production data that it reasonably can obtain, analyze, and verify without delaying the timely completion of the investigation or review. For purposes of this subparagraph, the startup period ends at the point at which the level of commercial production that is characteristic of the merchandise, producer, or industry concerned is achieved.

(2) Transactions disregarded. A transaction directly or indirectly between affiliated persons may be disregarded if, in the case of any element of value required to be considered, the amount representing that element does not fairly reflect the amount usually reflected in sales of merchandise under consideration in the market under consideration. If a transaction is disregarded under the preceding sentence and no other transactions are available for consideration, the determination of the amount shall be based on the information available as to what the amount would have been if the transaction had occurred between persons who are not affiliated.

(3) Major input rule. If, in the case of a transaction between affiliated persons involving the production by one of such persons of a major input to the merchandise, the administering authority has reasonable grounds to believe or suspect that an amount represented as the value of such input is less than the cost of production of such input, then the administering authority may determine the value of the major input on the basis of the information available regarding such cost of production, if such cost is greater than the amount that would be determined for such input under paragraph (2).

19 USC 1677b–1

Sec. 773A. Currency Conversion

(a) In General. In an antidumping proceeding under this title, the administering authority shall convert foreign currencies into United States dollars using the exchange rate in effect on the date of sale of the subject merchandise, except that, if it is established that a currency transaction on forward markets is directly linked to an export sale under consideration, the exchange rate specified with respect to such currency in the forward sale agreement shall be used to convert the foreign currency. Fluctuations in exchange rates shall be ignored.

(b) Sustained Movement in Foreign Currency Value. In an investigation under subtitle B, if there is a sustained movement in the value of the foreign currency relative to the United States dollar, the administering authority shall allow exporters at least 60 days to adjust their export prices to reflect such sustained movement.

19 USC 1677c

Sec. 774. Hearings

(a) Investigation hearings.

(1) In general. Except as provided in paragraph (2), the administering authority and the Commission shall each hold a hearing in the course of an investigation upon the request of any party to the investigation before making a final determination under section 705 or 735.

(2) Exception. If investigations are initiated under subtitle A and subtitle B regarding the same merchandise from the same country within 6 months of each other (but before a final determination is made in either investigation), the holding of a hearing by the Commission in the course of one of the investigations shall be treated as compliance with paragraph (1) for both

investigations, unless the Commission considers that special circumstances require that a hearing be held in the course of each of the investigations. During any investigation regarding which the holding of a hearing is waived under this paragraph, the Commission shall allow any party to submit such additional written comment as it considers relevant.

(b) Procedures. Any hearing required or permitted under this title shall be conducted after notice published in the Federal Register, and a transcript of the hearing shall be prepared and made available to the public. The hearing shall not be subject to the provisions of subchapter II of chapter 5 of title 5, United States Code, or to section 702 of such title.

19 USC 1677d

Sec. 775. Countervailable Subsidy Practices Discovered During a Proceeding

If, in the course of a proceeding under this title, the administering authority discovers a practice which appears to be a countervailable subsidy, but was not included in the matters alleged in a countervailing duty petition, or if the administering authority receives notice from the Trade Representative that a subsidy or subsidy program is in violation of Article 8 of the Subsidies Agreement, then the administering authority—

(1) shall include the practice, subsidy, or subsidy program in the proceeding if the practice, subsidy, or subsidy program appears to be a countervailable subsidy with respect to the merchandise which is the subject of the proceeding, or

(2) shall transfer the information (other than confidential information) concerning the practice, subsidy, or subsidy program to the library maintained under section 777(a)(1), if the practice, subsidy, or subsidy program appears to be a countervailable subsidy with respect to any other merchandise.

19 USC 1677e

Sec. 776. Determinations on the Basis of the Facts Available

(a) In General. If—

(1) necessary information is not available on the record, or

(2) an interested party or any other person—

(A) withholds information that has been requested by the administering authority or the Commission under this title,

(B) fails to provide such information by the deadlines for submission of the information or in the form and manner requested, subject to subsections (c)(1) and (e) of section 782,

(C) significantly impedes a proceeding under this title, or

(D) provides such information but the information cannot be verified as provided in section 782(i),

the administering authority and the Commission shall, subject to section 782(d), use the facts otherwise available in reaching the applicable determination under this title.

(b) Adverse Inferences. If the administering authority or the Commission (as the case may be) finds that an interested party has failed to cooperate by not acting to the best of its ability to comply with a request for information from the administering authority or the Commission, the administering authority or the Commission (as the case may be), in reaching the applicable determination under this title, may use an inference that is adverse to the interests of that party in selecting from among the facts otherwise available. Such adverse inference may include reliance on information derived from—

(1) the petition,

(2) a final determination in the investigation under this title,

(3) any previous review under section 751 or determination under section 753, or

(4) any other information placed on the record.

(c) Corroboration of Secondary Information. When the administering authority or the Commission relies on secondary information rather than on information obtained in the course of an investigation or review, the administering authority or the Commission, as the case may be, shall, to the extent practicable, corroborate that information from independent sources that are reasonably at their disposal.

19 USC 1677f

Sec. 777. Access to Information

(a) Information Generally Made Available.

(1) Public information function. There shall be established a library of information relating to foreign subsidy practices and countervailing measures. Copies of material in the library shall be made available to the public upon payment of the costs of preparing such copies.

(2) Progress of investigation reports. The administering authority and the Commission shall, from time to time upon request, inform the parties to an investigation of the progress of that investigation.

(3) Ex parte meetings. The administering authority and the Commission shall maintain a record of any ex parte meeting between—

(A) interested parties or other persons providing factual information in connection with a proceeding, and

(B) the person charged with making the determination, or any person charged with making a final recommendation to that person, in connection with that proceeding,

if information relating to that proceeding was presented or discussed at such meeting. The record of such ex parte meeting shall include the identity of the persons present at the meeting, the date, time, and place of the meeting, and a summary of the matters discussed or submitted. The record of the ex parte meeting shall be included in the record of the proceeding.

(4) Summaries; non-proprietary submissions. The administering authority and the Commission shall disclose—

(A) any proprietary information received in the course of a proceeding if it is disclosed in a form which cannot be associated with, or otherwise be used to identify, operations of a particular person, and

(B) any information submitted in connection with a proceeding which is not designated as proprietary by the person submitting it.

(b) Proprietary Information.

(1) Proprietary status maintained.

(A) In general. Except as provided in subsection (a)(4)(A) and subsection (c), information submitted to the administering authority or the Commission which is designated as proprietary by the person submitting the information shall not be disclosed to any person without the consent of the person submitting the information, other than—

(i) to an officer or employee of the administering authority or the Commission who is directly concerned with carrying out the investigation in connection with which the information is submitted or any review under this title covering the same subject merchandise, or

(ii) to an officer or employee of the United States Customs Service who is directly involved in conducting an investigation regarding fraud under this title.

(B) Additional requirements. The administering authority and the Commission shall require that information for which proprietary treatment is requested be accompanied by—

(i) either—

(I) a non-proprietary summary in sufficient detail to permit a reasonable understanding of the substance of the information submitted in confidence, or

(II) a statement that the information is not susceptible to summary accompanied by a statement of the reasons in support of the contention, and

(ii) either—

(I) a statement which permits the administering authority or the Commission to release under administrative protective order, in accordance with subsection (c), the information submitted in confidence, or

(II) a statement to the administering authority or the Commission that the business proprietary information is of a type that should not be released under administrative protective order.

(2) Unwarranted designation. If the administering authority or the Commission determines, on the basis of the nature and extent of the information or its availability from public sources, that designation of any information as proprietary is unwarranted, then it shall notify the person who submitted it and ask for an explanation of the reasons for the designation. Unless that person persuades the administering authority or the Commission that the designation is warranted, or withdraws the designation, the administering authority or the Commission, as the case may be, shall return it to the party

submitting it. In a case in which the administering authority or the Commission returns the information to the person submitting it, the person may thereafter submit other material concerning the subject matter of the returned information if the submission is made within the time otherwise provided for submitting such material.

(3) Section 751 reviews. Notwithstanding the provisions of paragraph (1), information submitted to the administering authority or the Commission in connection with a review under section 751(b) or 751(c) which is designated as proprietary by the person submitting the information may, if the review results in the revocation of an order or finding (or termination of a suspended investigation) under section 751(d), be used by the agency to which the information was originally submitted in any investigation initiated within 2 years after the date of the revocation or termination pursuant to a petition covering the same subject merchandise.

(c) Limited Disclosure of Certain Proprietary Information Under Protective Order.

(1) Disclosure by administering authority or commission.

(A) In general. Upon receipt of an application (before or after receipt of the information requested) which describes in general terms the information requested and sets forth the reasons for the request, the administering authority or the Commission shall make all business proprietary information presented to, or obtained by it, during a proceeding (except privileged information, classified information, and specific information of a type for which there is a clear and compelling need to withhold from disclosure) available to interested parties who are parties to the proceeding under a protective order described in subparagraph (B), regardless of when the information is submitted during a proceeding. Customer names obtained during any investigation which requires a determination under section 705(b) or 735(b) may not be disclosed by the administering authority under protective order until either an order is published under section 706(a) or 736(a) as a result of the investigation or the investigation is suspended or terminated. The Commission may delay disclosure of customer names under protective order during any such investigation until a reasonable time prior to any hearing provided under section 774.

(B) Protective order. The protective order under which information is made available shall contain such requirements as the administering authority or the Commission may determine by regulation to be appropriate. The administering authority and the Commission shall provide by regulation for such sanctions as the administering authority and the Commission determine to be appropriate, including disbarment from practice before the agency.

(C) Time limitation on determinations. The administering authority or the Commission, as the case may be, shall determine whether to make information available under this paragraph—

(i) not later than 14 days (7 days if the submission pertains to a proceeding under section 703(a) or 733(a)) after the date on which the information is submitted, or

(ii) if—

(I) the person that submitted the information raises objection to its release, or

(II) the information is unusually voluminous or complex, not later than 30 days (10 days if the submission pertains to a proceeding under section 703(a) or 733(a)) after the date on which the information is submitted.

(D) Availability after determination. If the determination under subparagraph (C) is affirmative, then—

(i) the business proprietary information submitted to the administering authority or the Commission on or before the date of the determination shall be made available, subject to the terms and conditions of the protective order, on such date; and

(ii) the business proprietary information submitted to the administering authority or the Commission after the date of the determination shall be served as required by subsection (d).

(E) Failure to disclose. If a person submitting information to the administering authority refuses to disclose business proprietary information which the administering authority determines should be released under a protective order described in subparagraph (B), the administering authority shall return the information, and any nonconfidential summary thereof, to the person submitting the information and summary and shall not consider either.

(2) Disclosure under court order. If the administering authority denies a request for information under paragraph (1), then application may be made to the United States Customs Court for an order directing the administering authority or the Commission to make the information available. After notification of all parties to the investigation and after an opportunity for a hearing on the record, the court may issue an order, under such conditions as the court deems appropriate, which shall not have the effect of stopping or suspending the investigation, directing the administering authority or the Commission to make all or a portion of the requested information described in the preceding sentence available under a protective order and setting forth sanctions for violation of such order if the court finds that, under the standards applicable in proceedings of the court, such an order is warranted, and that—

(A) the administering authority or the Commission has denied access to the information under subsection (b)(1),

(B) the person on whose behalf the information is requested is an interested party who is a party to the investigation in connection with which the information was obtained or developed, and

(C) the party which submitted the information to which the request relates has been notified, in advance of the hearing, of the request made under this section and of its right to appear and be heard.

(d) Service. Any party submitting written information, including business proprietary information, to the administering authority or the Commission during a proceeding shall, at the same time, serve the information upon all interested parties who are parties to the proceeding, if the information is covered by a protective order. The administering authority or the Commission shall not accept any such information that is not accompanied by a certificate of service and a copy of the protective order version of the document containing the information. Business proprietary information shall only be served upon interested parties who are parties to the proceeding that are subject to protective order; however, a nonconfidential summary thereof shall be served upon all other interested parties who are parties to the proceeding.

(e) Timely Submissions [repealed]

(f) Disclosure of Proprietary Information Under Protective Orders Issued Pursuant to the North American Free Trade Agreement or the United States-Canada Agreement.

(1) Issuance of protective orders.

(A) In general. If binational panel review of a determination under this subchapter is requested pursuant to article 1904 of the NAFTA or the United States-Canada Agreement, or an extraordinary challenge committee is convened under Annex 1904.13 of the NAFTA or the United States-Canada Agreement, the administering authority or the Commission, as appropriate, may make available to authorized persons, under a protective order described in paragraph (2), a copy of all proprietary material in the administrative record made during the proceeding in question. If the administering authority or the Commission claims a privilege as to a document or portion of a document in the administrative record of the proceeding in question and a binational panel or extraordinary challenge committee finds that in camera inspection or limited disclosure of that document or portion thereof is required by United States law, the administering authority or the Commission, as appropriate, may restrict access to such document or portion thereof to the authorized persons identified by the panel or committee as requiring access and may require such persons to obtain access under a protective order described in paragraph (2).

(B) Authorized persons. For purposes of this subsection, the term "authorized persons" means—

(i) the members of, and the appropriate staff of, the binational panel or the extraordinary challenge committee, as the case may be, and the Secretariat,

(ii) counsel for parties to such panel or committee proceeding, and employees, and persons under the direction and control, of such counsel,

(iii) any officer or employee of the United States Government designated by the administering authority or the Commission, as appropriate, to whom disclosure is necessary in order to make recommendations to the Trade Representative regarding the convening of extraordinary challenge committees under chapter 19 of the NAFTA or the Agreement, and

(iv) any officer or employee of the Government of a free trade area country (as defined in section 516A(f)(10) of this title) designated by an authorized agency of such country to whom disclosure is necessary in order to make decisions regarding the convening of extraordinary challenge committees under chapter 19 of the NAFTA or the Agreement.

(C) Review. A decision concerning the disclosure or nondisclosure of material under protective order by the administering authority or the Commission shall not be subject to judicial review, and no court of the United States shall have power or jurisdiction to review such decision on any question of law or fact by an action in the nature of mandamus or otherwise.

(2) Contents of protective order. Each protective order issued under this subsection shall be in such form and contain such requirements as the administering authority or the Commission may determine by regulation to be appropriate. The administering authority and the Commission shall ensure that regulations issued pursuant to this paragraph shall be designed to provide an opportunity for participation in the binational panel proceeding, including any extraordinary challenge, equivalent to that available for judicial review of determinations by the administering authority or the Commission that are not subject to review by a binational panel.

(3) Prohibited acts. It is unlawful for any person to violate, to induce the violation of, or knowingly to receive information the receipt of which constitutes a violation of, any provision of a protective order issued under this subsection or to violate, to induce the violation of, or knowingly to receive information the receipt of which constitutes a violation of, any provision of an undertaking entered into with an authorized agency of a free trade area country (as defined in section 516A(f)(10) of this title) to protect proprietary material during binational panel or extraordinary challenge committee review pursuant to article 1904 of the NAFTA or the United States-Canada Agreement.

(4) Sanctions for violation of protective orders. Any person, except a judge appointed to a binational panel or an extraordinary challenge committee under section 402, who is found by the administering authority or the Commission, as appropriate, after notice and an opportunity for a hearing in accordance with section 554 of Title 5 to have committed an act prohibited by paragraph (3) shall be liable to the United States for a civil penalty and shall be subject to such other administrative sanctions, including, but not limited to, debarment from practice before the administering authority or the Commission, as the administering authority or the Commission determines to be appropriate. The amount of the civil penalty shall not exceed $100,000 for each violation. Each day of a continuing violation shall constitute a separate violation. The amount of such civil penalty and other sanctions shall be assessed by the administering authority or the Commission by written notice, except that assessment shall be made by the administering authority for violation, inducement of a violation or receipt of information with reason to know that such information was disclosed in violation, of an undertaking entered into by any person with an authorized agency of a free trade area country (as defined in section 516A(f)(10) of this title).

(5) Review of sanctions. Any person against whom sanctions are imposed under paragraph (4) may obtain review of such sanctions by filing a notice of appeal in the United States Court of International Trade within 30 days from

the date of the order imposing the sanction and by simultaneously sending a copy of such notice by certified mail to the administering authority or the Commission, as appropriate. The administering authority or the Commission shall promptly file in such court a certified copy of the record upon which such violation was found or such sanction imposed, as provided in section 2112 of title 28, United States Code. The findings and order of the administering authority or the Commission shall be set aside by the court only if the court finds that such findings and order are not supported by substantial evidence, as provided in section 706(2) of title 5, United States Code.

(6) Enforcement of sanctions. If any person fails to pay an assessment of a civil penalty or to comply with other administrative sanctions after the order imposing such sanctions becomes a final and unappealable order, or after the United States Court of International Trade has entered final judgment in favor of the administering authority or the Commission, an action may be filed in such court to enforce the sanctions. In such action, the validity and appropriateness of the final order imposing the sanctions shall not be subject to review.

(7) Testimony and production of papers.

(A) Authority to obtain information. For the purpose of conducting any hearing and carrying out other functions and duties under this subsection, the administering authority and the Commission, or their duly authorized agents—

(i) shall have access to and the right to copy any pertinent document, paper, or record in the possession of any individual, partnership, corporation, association, organization, or other entity,

(ii) may summon witnesses, take testimony, and administer oaths,

(iii) and may require any individual or entity to produce pertinent documents, books, or records.

Any member of the Commission, and any person so designated by the administering authority, may sign subpoenas, and members and agents of the administering authority and the Commission, when authorized by the administering authority or the Commission, as appropriate, may administer oaths and affirmations, examine witnesses, take testimony, and receive evidence.

(B) Witnesses and evidence. The attendance of witnesses who are authorized to be summoned, and the production of documentary evidence authorized to be ordered, under subparagraph (A) may be required from any place in the United States at any designated place of hearing. In the case of disobedience to a subpoena issued under subparagraph (A), an action may be filed in any district or territorial court of the United States to require the attendance and testimony of witnesses and the production of documentary evidence. Such court, within the jurisdiction of which such inquiry is carried on, may, in case of contumacy or refusal to obey a subpoena issued to any individual, partnership, corporation, association, organization or other entity, issue any order requiring such individual or entity to appear before the administering authority or the Commission, or to produce documentary evidence if so ordered or to give evidence concerning the matter in question. Any failure to obey such order of the court may be punished by the court as a contempt thereof.

(C) Mandamus. Any court referred to in subparagraph (B) shall have jurisdiction to issue writs of mandamus commanding compliance with the provisions of this subsection or any order of the administering authority or the Commission made in pursuance thereof.

(D) Depositions. For purposes of carrying out any functions or duties under this subsection, the administering authority or the Commission may order testimony to be taken by deposition. Such deposition may be taken before any person designated by the administering authority or Commission and having power to administer oaths. Such testimony shall be reduced to writing by the person taking the deposition, or under the direction of such person, and shall then be subscribed by the deponent. Any individual, partnership, corporation, association, organization or other entity may be compelled to appear and depose and to produce documentary evidence in the same manner as witnesses may be compelled to appear and testify and produce documentary evidence before the administering authority or Commission, as provided in this paragraph.

(E) Fees and mileage of witnesses. Witnesses summoned before the administering authority or the Commission shall be paid the same fees and mileage that are paid witnesses in the courts of the United States.

(g) Information Relating to Violations of Protective Orders and Sanctions.

The administering authority and the Commission may withhold from disclosure any correspondence, private letters of reprimand, settlement agreements, and documents and files compiled in relation to investigations and actions involving a violation or possible violation of a protective order issued under subsection (c) or (d) of this section, and such information shall be treated as information described in section 552(b)(3) of Title 5.

(h) Opportunity for Comment by Consumers and Industrial Users.

The administering authority and the Commission shall provide an opportunity for industrial users of the subject merchandise and, if the merchandise is sold at the retail level, for representative consumer organizations, to submit relevant information to the administering authority concerning dumping or a countervailable subsidy, and to the Commission concerning material injury by reason of dumped or subsidized imports.

(i) Publication of Determinations; Requirements for Final Determinations.

(1) In general. Whenever the administering authority makes a determination under section 702 or 732 whether to initiate an investigation, or the administering authority or the Commission makes a preliminary determination under section 703 or 733, a final determination under section 705 or section 735, a preliminary or final determination in a review under section 751, a determination to suspend an investigation under this title, or a determination under section 753, the administering authority or the Commission, as the case may be, shall publish the facts and conclusions supporting

that determination, and shall publish notice of that determination in the Federal Register.

(2) Contents of notice or determination. The notice or determination published under paragraph (1) shall include, to the extent applicable—

(A) in the case of a determination of the administering authority—

(i) the names of the exporters or producers of the subject merchandise or, when providing such names is impracticable, the countries exporting the subject merchandise to the United States,

(ii) a description of the subject merchandise that is sufficient to identify the subject merchandise for customs purposes,

(iii)(I) with respect to a determination in an investigation under subtitle A or section 753 or in a review of a countervailing duty order, the amount of the countervailable subsidy established and a full explanation of the methodology used in establishing the amount, and

(II) with respect to a determination in an investigation under subtitle B or in a review of an antidumping duty order, the weighted average dumping margins established and a full explanation of the methodology used in establishing such margins, and

(iv) the primary reasons for the determination; and

(B) in the case of a determination of the Commission—

(i) considerations relevant to the determination of injury, and

(ii) the primary reasons for the determination.

(3) Additional requirements for final determinations. In addition to the requirements set forth in paragraph (2)—

(A) the administering authority shall include in a final determination described in paragraph (1) an explanation of the basis for its determination that addresses relevant arguments, made by interested parties who are parties to the investigation or review (as the case may be), concerning the establishment of dumping or a countervailable subsidy, or the suspension of the investigation, with respect to which the determination is made; and

(B) the Commission shall include in a final determination of injury an explanation of the basis for its determination that addresses relevant arguments that are made by interested parties who are parties to the investigation or review (as the case may be) concerning volume, price effects, and impact on the industry of imports of the subject merchandise.

19 USC 1677f–1

Sec. 777A. Sampling and Averaging; Determination of Weighted Average Dumping Margin and Countervailable Subsidy Rate

(a) In General. For purposes of determining the export price (or constructed export price) under section 772 or the normal value under section

773, and in carrying out reviews under section 751, the administering authority may—

(1) use averaging and statistically valid samples, if there is a significant volume of sales of the subject merchandise or a significant number or types of products, and

(2) decline to take into account adjustments which are insignificant in relation to the price or value of the merchandise.

(b) Selection of Averages and Samples. The authority to select averages and statistically valid samples shall rest exclusively with the administering authority. The administering authority shall, to the greatest extent possible, consult with the exporters and producers regarding the method to be used to select exporters, producers, or types of products under this section.

(c) Determination of Dumping Margin.

(1) General rule. In determining weighted average dumping margins under section 733(d), 735(c), or 751(a), the administering authority shall determine the individual weighted average dumping margin for each known exporter and producer of the subject merchandise.

(2) Exception. If it is not practicable to make individual weighted average dumping margin determinations under paragraph (1) because of the large number of exporters or producers involved in the investigation or review, the administering authority may determine the weighted average dumping margins for a reasonable number of exporters or producers by limiting its examination to—

(A) a sample of exporters, producers, or types of products that is statistically valid based on the information available to the administering authority at the time of selection, or

(B) exporters and producers accounting for the largest volume of the subject merchandise from the exporting country that can be reasonably examined.

(d) Determination of Less Than Fair Value.

(1) Investigations.

(A) In general. In an investigation under subtitle B, the administering authority shall determine whether the subject merchandise is being sold in the United States at less than fair value—

(i) by comparing the weighted average of the normal values to the weighted average of the export prices (and constructed export prices) for comparable merchandise, or

(ii) by comparing the normal values of individual transactions to the export prices (or constructed export prices) of individual transactions for comparable merchandise.

(B) Exception. The administering authority may determine whether the subject merchandise is being sold in the United States at less than fair value by comparing the weighted average of the normal values to the export prices (or constructed export prices) of individual transactions for comparable merchandise, if—

(i) there is a pattern of export prices (or constructed export prices) for comparable merchandise that differ significantly among purchasers, regions, or periods of time, and

(ii) the administering authority explains why such differences cannot be taken into account using a method described in paragraph (1)(A)(i) or (ii).

(2) Reviews. In a review under section 751, when comparing export prices (or constructed export prices) of individual transactions to the weighted average price of sales of the foreign like product, the administering authority shall limit its averaging of prices to a period not exceeding the calendar month that corresponds most closely to the calendar month of the individual export sale.

(e) Determination of Countervailable Subsidy Rate.

(1) General rule. In determining countervailable subsidy rates under section 703(d), 705(c), or 751(a), the administering authority shall determine an individual countervailable subsidy rate for each known exporter or producer of the subject merchandise.

(2) Exception. If the administering authority determines that it is not practicable to determine individual countervailable subsidy rates under paragraph (1) because of the large number of exporters or producers involved in the investigation or review, the administering authority may—

(A) determine individual countervailable subsidy rates for a reasonable number of exporters or producers by limiting its examination to—

(i) a sample of exporters or producers that the administering authority determines is statistically valid based on the information available to the administering authority at the time of selection, or

(ii) exporters and producers accounting for the largest volume of the subject merchandise from the exporting country that the administering authority determines can be reasonably examined; or

(B) determine a single country-wide subsidy rate to be applied to all exporters and producers.

The individual countervailable subsidy rates determined under subparagraph (A) shall be used to determine the all-others rate under section 705(c)(5).

19 USC 1677g

Sec. 778. Interest on Certain Overpayments and Underpayments

(a) General rule. Interest shall be payable on overpayments and underpayments of amounts deposited on merchandise entered, or withdrawn from warehouse, for consumption on and after—

(1) the date of publication of a countervailing or antidumping duty order under this title or section 303, or

(2) the date of a finding under the Antidumping Act, 1921.

(b) Rate. The rate of interest payable under subsection (a) for any period of time is the rate of interest established under section 6621 of the Internal Revenue Code of 1954 for such period.

19 USC 1677h

Sec. 779. Drawback Treatment

For purposes of any law relating to the drawback of customs duties, countervailing duties and antidumping duties imposed by this title shall not be treated as being regular customs duties.

19 USC 1677i

Sec. 780. Downstream Product Monitoring

(a) Petition requesting monitoring.

(1) In general. A domestic producer of an article that is like a component part or a downstream product may petition the administering authority to designate a downstream product for monitoring under subsection (b). The petition shall specify—

(A) the downstream product,

(B) the component product incorporated into such downstream product, and

(C) the reasons for suspecting that the imposition of antidumping or countervailing duties has resulted in a diversion of exports of the component part into increased production and exportation to the United States of such downstream product.

(2) Determination regarding petition. Within 14 days after receiving a petition submitted under paragraph (1), the administering authority shall determine—

(A) whether there is a reasonable likelihood that imports into the United States of the downstream product will increase as an indirect result of any diversion with respect to the component part, and

(B) whether—

(i) the component part is already subject to monitoring to aid in the enforcement of a bilateral arrangement (within the meaning of section 804 of the Trade and Tariff Act of 1984),

(ii) merchandise related to the component part and manufactured in the same foreign country in which the component part is manufactured has been the subject of a significant number of investigations suspended under section 704 or 734 or countervailing or antidumping duty orders issued under this title or section 303, or

(iii) merchandise manufactured or exported by the manufacturer or exporter of the component part that is similar in description and use to the component part has been the subject of at least 2 investigations suspended under section 704 or 734 or countervailing or antidumping duty orders issued under this title or section 303.

(3) Factors to take into account. In making a determination under paragraph (2)(A), the administering authority may, if appropriate, take into account such factors as—

(A) the value of the component part in relation to the value of the downstream product,

(B) the extent to which the component part has been substantially transformed as a result of its incorporation into the downstream product, and

(C) the relationship between the producers of component parts and producers of downstream products.

(4) Publication of determination. The administering authority shall publish in the Federal Register notice of each determination made under paragraph (2) and, if the determination made under paragraph (2)(A) and a determination made under any subparagraph of paragraph (2)(B) are affirmative, shall transmit a copy of such determinations and the petition to the Commission.

(5) Determinations not subject to judicial review. Notwithstanding any other provision of law, any determination made by the administering authority under paragraph (2) shall not be subject to judicial review.

(b) Monitoring by the Commission.

(1) In general. If the determination made under subsection (a)(2)(A) and a determination made under any clause of subsection (a)(2)(B) with respect to a petition are affirmative, the Commission shall immediately commence monitoring of trade in the downstream product that is the subject of the determination made under subsection (a)(2)(A). If the Commission finds that imports of a downstream product being monitored increased during any calendar quarter by 5 percent or more over the preceding quarter, the Commission shall analyze that increase in the context of overall economic conditions in the product sector.

(2) Reports. The Commission shall make quarterly reports to the administering authority regarding the monitoring and analyses conducted under paragraph (1). The Commission shall make the reports available to the public.

(c) Action on basis of monitoring reports. The administering authority shall review the information in the reports submitted by the Commission under subsection (b)(2) and shall—

(1) consider the information in determining whether to initiate an investigation under section 702(a), or 732(a) regarding any downstream product, and

(2) request the Commission to cease monitoring any downstream product if the information indicates that imports into the United States are not increasing and there is no reasonable likelihood of diversion with respect to component parts.

(d) Definitions. For purposes of this section—

(1) The term "component part" means any imported article that—

(A) during the 5-year period ending on the date on which the petition is filed under subsection (a), has been subject to—

(i) a countervailing or antidumping duty order issued under this title or section 303 that requires the deposit of estimated countervailing or antidumping duties imposed at a rate of at least 15 percent ad valorem, or

(ii) an agreement entered into under section 704, 734, or 303 after a preliminary affirmative determination under section 703(b), 733(b)(1), or 303 was made by the administering authority which included a determination that the estimated net countervailable subsidy was at least 15 percent ad valorem or that the estimated average amount by which the normal value exceeded the export price (or the constructed export price) was at least 15 percent ad valorem, and

(B) because of its inherent characteristics, is routinely used as a major part, component, assembly, subassembly, or material in a downstream product.

(2) The term "downstream product" means any manufactured article—

(A) which is imported into the United States, and

(B) into which is incorporated any component part.

19 USC 1677j

Sec. 781. Prevention of Circumvention of Antidumping and Countervailing Duty Orders

(a) Merchandise completed or assembled in the United States.

(1) In general. If—

(A) merchandise sold in the United States is of the same class or kind as any other merchandise that is the subject of—

(i) an antidumping duty order issued under section 736,

(ii) a finding issued under the Antidumping Act, 1921, or

(iii) a countervailing duty order issued under section 706 or section 303,

(B) such merchandise sold in the United States is completed or assembled in the United States from parts or components produced in the foreign country with respect to which such order or finding applies,

(C) the process of assembly or completion in the United States is minor or insignificant, and

(D) the value of the parts or components referred to in subparagraph (B) is a significant portion of the total value of the merchandise,

the administering authority, after taking into account any advice provided by the Commission under subsection (e), may include within the scope of such order or finding the imported parts or components referred to in subparagraph (B) that are used in the completion or assembly of the merchandise in the United States at any time such order or finding is in effect.

(2) Determination of whether process is minor or insignificant. In determining whether the process of assembly or completion is minor or insignificant under paragraph (1)(C), the administering authority shall take into account—

(A) the level of investment in the United States,

(B) the level of research and development in the United States,

(C) the nature of the production process in the United States,

(D) the extent of production facilities in the United States, and

(E) whether the value of the processing performed in the United States represents a small proportion of the value of the merchandise sold in the United States.

(3) Factors to consider. In determining whether to include parts or components in a countervailing or antidumping duty order or finding under paragraph (1), the administering authority shall take into account such factors as—

(A) the pattern of trade, including sourcing patterns,

(B) whether the manufacturer or exporter of the parts or components is affiliated with the person who assembles or completes the merchandise sold in the United States from the parts or components produced in the foreign country with respect to which the order or finding described in paragraph (1) applies, and

(C) whether imports into the United States of the parts or components produced in such foreign country have increased after the initiation of the investigation which resulted in the issuance of such order or finding.

(b) Merchandise Completed or Assembled in Other Foreign Countries.

(1) In general. If—

(A) merchandise imported into the United States is of the same class or kind as any merchandise produced in a foreign country that is the subject of—

(i) an antidumping duty order issued under section 736,

(ii) a finding issued under the Antidumping Act, 1921, or

(iii) a countervailing duty order issued under section 706 or section 303,

(B) before importation into the United States, such imported merchandise is completed or assembled in another foreign country from merchandise which—

(i) is subject to such order or finding, or

(ii) is produced in the foreign country with respect to which such order or finding applies,

(C) the process of assembly or completion in the foreign country referred to in subparagraph (B) is minor or insignificant,

(D) the value of the merchandise produced in the foreign country to which the antidumping duty order applies is a significant portion of the total value of the merchandise exported to the United States, and

(E) the administering authority determines that action is appropriate under this paragraph to prevent evasion of such order or finding,

the administering authority, after taking into account any advice provided by the Commission under subsection (e), may include such imported merchandise within the scope of such order or finding at any time such order or finding is in effect.

(2) Determination of whether process is minor or insignificant. In determining whether the process of assembly or completion is minor or insignificant under paragraph (1)(C), the administering authority shall take into account—

(A) the level of investment in the foreign country,

(B) the level or research and development in the foreign country,

(C) the nature of the production process in the foreign country,

(D) the extent of production facilities in the foreign country, and

(E) whether the value of the processing performed in the foreign country represents a small proportion of the value of the merchandise imported into the United States.

(3) Factors to consider. In determining whether to include merchandise assembled or completed in a foreign country in a countervailing duty order or an antidumping duty order or finding under paragraph (1), the administering authority shall take into account such factors as—

(A) the pattern of trade, including sourcing patterns,

(B) whether the manufacturer or exporter of the merchandise described in paragraph (1)(B) is affiliated with the person who uses the merchandise described in paragraph (1)(B) to assemble or complete in the foreign country the merchandise that is subsequently imported into the United States, and

(C) whether imports into the foreign country of the merchandise described in paragraph (1)(B) have increased after the initiation of the investigation which resulted in the issuance of such order or finding.

(c) Minor alterations of merchandise.

(1) In general. The class or kind of merchandise subject to—

(A) an investigation under this title,

(B) an antidumping duty order issued under section 736,

(C) a finding issued under the Antidumping Act, 1921, or

(D) a countervailing duty order issued under section 706 or section 303,

shall include articles altered in form or appearance in minor respects (including raw agricultural products that have undergone minor processing), whether or not included in the same tariff classification.

(2) Exception. Paragraph (1) shall not apply with respect to altered merchandise if the administering authority determines that it would be unnecessary to consider the altered merchandise within the scope of the investigation, order, or finding.

(d) Later-developed merchandise.

(1) In general. For purposes of determining whether merchandise developed after an investigation is initiated under this title or section 303 (hereafter in this paragraph referred to as the "later-developed merchandise") is

within the scope of an outstanding antidumping or countervailing duty order issued under this title or section 303 as a result of such investigation, the administering authority shall consider whether—

(A) the later-developed merchandise has the same general physical characteristics as the merchandise with respect to which the order was originally issued (hereafter in this paragraph referred to as the "earlier product"),

(B) the expectations of the ultimate purchasers of the later-developed merchandise are the same as for the earlier product,

(C) the ultimate use of the earlier product and the later-developed merchandise are the same,

(D) the later-developed merchandise is sold through the same channels of trade as the earlier product, and

(E) the later-developed merchandise is advertised and displayed in a manner similar to the earlier product.

The administering authority shall take into account any advice provided by the Commission under subsection (e) before making a determination under this subparagraph.

(2) Exclusion from orders. The administering authority may not exclude a later-developed merchandise from a countervailing or antidumping duty order merely because the merchandise—

(A) is classified under a tariff classification other than that identified in the petition or the administering authority's prior notices during the proceeding, or

(B) permits the purchaser to perform additional functions, unless such additional functions constitute the primary use of the merchandise and the cost of the additional functions constitute more than a significant proportion of the total cost of production of the merchandise.

(e) Commission advice.

(1) Notification to commission of proposed action. Before making a determination—

(A) under subsection (a) with respect to merchandise completed or assembled in the United States (other than minor completion or assembly),

(B) under subsection (b) with respect to merchandise completed or assembled in other foreign countries, or

(C) under subsection (d) with respect to any later-developed merchandise which incorporates a significant technological advance or significant alteration of an earlier product,

with respect to an antidumping or countervailing duty order or finding as to which the Commission has made an affirmative injury determination, the administering authority shall notify the Commission of the proposed inclusion of such merchandise in such countervailing or antidumping order or finding. Notwithstanding any other provision of law, a decision by the administering authority regarding whether any merchandise is within a category for which notice is required under this paragraph is not subject to judicial review.

(2) Request for consultation. After receiving notice under paragraph (1), the Commission may request consultations with the administering authority regarding the inclusion. Upon the request of the Commission, the administering authority shall consult with the Commission and any such consultation shall be completed within 15 days after the date of the request.

(3) Commission advice. If the Commission believes, after consultation under paragraph (2), that a significant injury issue is presented by the proposed inclusion, the Commission may provide written advice to the administering authority as to whether the inclusion would be inconsistent with the affirmative determination of the Commission on which the order or finding is based. If the Commission decides to provide such written advice, it shall promptly notify the administering authority of its intention to do so, and must provide such advice within 60 days after the date of notification under paragraph (1). For purposes of formulating its advice with respect to merchandise completed or assembled in the United States from parts or components produced in a foreign country, the Commission shall consider whether the inclusion of such parts or components taken as a whole would be inconsistent with its prior affirmative determination.

(f) Time Limits for Administering Authority Determinations. The administering authority shall, to the maximum extent practicable, make the determinations under this section within 300 days from the date of the initiation of a countervailing duty or antidumping circumvention inquiry under this section.

19 USC 1677m

Sec. 782. Conduct of Investigations and Administrative Reviews

(a) Treatment of Voluntary Responses in Countervailing or Antidumping Duty Investigations and Reviews. In any investigation under subtitle A or B or a review under section 751(a) in which the administering authority has, under section 777A(c)(2) or section 777A(e)(2)(A) (whichever is applicable), limited the number of exporters or producers examined, or determined a single country-wide rate, the administering authority shall establish an individual countervailable subsidy rate or an individual weighted average dumping margin for any exporter or producer not initially selected for individual examination under such sections who submits to the administering authority the information requested from exporters or producers selected for examination, if—

(1) such information is so submitted by the date specified—

(A) for exporters and producers that were initially selected for examination, or

(B) for the foreign government, in a countervailing duty case where the administering authority has determined a single country-wide rate; and

(2) the number of exporters or producers who have submitted such information is not so large that individual examination of such exporters or producers would be unduly burdensome and inhibit the timely completion of the investigation.

(b) Certification of Submissions. Any person providing factual information to the administering authority or the Commission in connection with a proceeding under this title on behalf of the petitioner or any other interested party shall certify that such information is accurate and complete to the best of that person's knowledge.

(c) Difficulties in Meeting Requirements.

(1) Notification by interested party. If an interested party, promptly after receiving a request from the administering authority or the Commission for information, notifies the administering authority or the Commission (as the case may be) that such party is unable to submit the information requested in the requested form and manner, together with a full explanation and suggested alternative forms in which such party is able to submit the information, the administering authority or the Commission (as the case may be) shall consider the ability of the interested party to submit the information in the requested form and manner and may modify such requirements to the extent necessary to avoid imposing an unreasonable burden on that party.

(2) Assistance to interested parties. The administering authority and the Commission shall take into account any difficulties experienced by interested parties, particularly small companies, in supplying information requested by the administering authority or the Commission in connection with investigations and reviews under this title, and shall provide to such interested parties any assistance that is practicable in supplying such information.

(d) Deficient Submissions. If the administering authority or the Commission determines that a response to a request for information under this title does not comply with the request, the administering authority or the Commission (as the case may be) shall promptly inform the person submitting the response of the nature of the deficiency and shall, to the extent practicable, provide that person with an opportunity to remedy or explain the deficiency in light of the time limits established for the completion of investigations or reviews under this title. If that person submits further information in response to such deficiency and either—

(1) the administering authority or the Commission (as the case may be) finds that such response is not satisfactory, or

(2) such response is not submitted within the applicable time limits,

then the administering authority or the Commission (as the case may be) may, subject to subsection (e), disregard all or part of the original and subsequent responses.

(e) Use of Certain Information. In reaching a determination under section 703, 705, 733, 735, 751, or 753 the administering authority and the Commission shall not decline to consider information that is submitted by an interested party and is necessary to the determination but does not meet all the applicable requirements established by the administering authority or the Commission, if—

(1) the information is submitted by the deadline established for its submission,

(2) the information can be verified,

(3) the information is not so incomplete that it cannot serve as a reliable basis for reaching the applicable determination,

(4) the interested party has demonstrated that it acted to the best of its ability in providing the information and meeting the requirements established by the administering authority or the Commission with respect to the information, and

(5) the information can be used without undue difficulties.

(f) Nonacceptance of Submissions. If the administering authority or the Commission declines to accept into the record any information submitted in an investigation or review under this title, it shall, to the extent practicable, provide to the person submitting the information a written explanation of the reasons for not accepting the information.

(g) Public Comment on Information. Information that is submitted on a timely basis to the administering authority or the Commission during the course of a proceeding under this title shall be subject to comment by other parties to the proceeding within such reasonable time as the administering authority or the Commission shall provide. The administering authority and the Commission, before making a final determination under section 705, 735, 751, or 753 shall cease collecting information and shall provide the parties with a final opportunity to comment on the information obtained by the administering authority or the Commission (as the case may be) upon which the parties have not previously had an opportunity to comment. Comments containing new factual information shall be disregarded.

(h) Termination of Investigation or Revocation of Order for Lack of Interest. The administering authority may—

(1) terminate an investigation under subtitle A or B with respect to a domestic like product if, prior to publication of an order under section 706 or 736, the administering authority determines that producers accounting for substantially all of the production of that domestic like product have expressed a lack of interest in issuance of an order; and

(2) revoke an order issued under section 706 or 736 with respect to a domestic like product, or terminate an investigation suspended under section 704 or 734 with respect to a domestic like product, if the administering authority determines that producers accounting for substantially all of the production of that domestic like product, have expressed a lack of interest in the order or suspended investigation.

(i) Verification. The administering authority shall verify all information relied upon in making—

(1) a final determination in an investigation,

(2) a revocation under section 751(d), and

(3) a final determination in a review under section 751(a), if—

(A) verification is timely requested by an interested party as defined in section 771(9)(C), (D), (E), (F), or (G), and

(B) no verification was made under this subparagraph during the 2 immediately preceding reviews and determinations under section 751(a)

of the same order, finding, or notice, except that this clause shall not apply if good cause for verification is shown.

19 USC 1677n

Sec. 783. Antidumping Petitions by Third Countries

(a) **Filing of petition.** The government of a WTO member may file with the Trade Representative a petition requesting that an investigation be conducted to determine if—

(1) imports from another country are being sold in the United States at less than fair value, and

(2) an industry in the petitioning country is materially injured by reason of those imports.

(b) **Initiation.** The Trade Representative, after consultation with the administering authority and the Commission and obtaining the approval of the WTO Council for Trade in Goods, shall determine whether to initiate an investigation described in subsection (a).

(c) **Determinations.** Upon initiation of an investigation under this section, the Trade Representative shall request the following determinations be made according to substantive and procedural requirements specified by the Trade Representative, notwithstanding any other provision of this title:

(1) The administering authority shall determine whether imports into the United States of the subject merchandise are being sold at less than fair value.

(2) The Commission shall determine whether an industry in the petitioning country is materially injured by reason of imports of the subject merchandise into the United States.

(d) **Public comment.** An opportunity for public comment shall be provided, as appropriate—

(1) by the Trade Representative, in making the determination required by subsection (b), and

(2) by the administering authority and the Commission, in making the determination required by subsection (c).

(e) **Issuance of order.** If the administering authority makes an affirmative determination under paragraph (1) of subsection (c), and the Commission makes an affirmative determination under paragraph (2) of subsection (c), the administering authority shall issue an antidumping duty order in accordance with section 736 and take such other actions as are required by section 736.

(f) **Reviews of determinations.** For purposes of review under section 516A or review under section 751, if an order is issued under subsection (e), the final determinations of the administering authority and the Commission under this section shall be treated as final determinations made under section 735.

(g) **Access to information.** Section 777 shall apply to investigations under this section, to the extent specified by the Trade Representative, after consultation with the administering authority and the Commission.

Item 46

UNITED STATES: TRADE EXPANSION ACT OF 1962

(Selected provisions, as amended)

Public Law 87-794, Approved Oct. 11, 1962, 76 Stat. 872

---

19 USC 1862

Sec. 232. Safeguarding National Security

(a) Prohibition on decrease or elimination of duties or other import restrictions if such reduction or elimination would threaten to impair national security. No action shall be taken pursuant to section 201(a) or pursuant to section 350 of the Tariff Act of 1930 to decrease or eliminate the duty or other import restriction on any article if the President determines that such reduction or elimination would threaten to impair the national security.

(b) Investigation by Secretary of Commerce to determine effects on national security of imports of articles; consultation with Secretary of Defense and other officials; hearings; assessment of defense requirements; report to President; publication in Federal Register; promulgation of regulations.

(1) (A) Upon request of the head of any department or agency, upon application of an interested party, or upon his own motion, the Secretary of Commerce (hereafter in this section referred to as the "Secretary") shall immediately initiate an appropriate investigation to determine the effects on the national security of imports of the article which is the subject of such request, application, or motion.

(B) The Secretary shall immediately provide notice to the Secretary of Defense of any investigation initiated under this section.

(2) (A) In the course of any investigation conducted under this subsection, the Secretary shall—

(i) consult with the Secretary of Defense regarding the methodological and policy questions raised in any investigation initiated under paragraph (1),

(ii) seek information and advice from, and consult with, appropriate officers of the United States, and

(iii) if it is appropriate and after reasonable notice, hold public hearings or otherwise afford interested parties an opportunity to present information and advice relevant to such investigation.

943

(B) Upon the request of the Secretary, the Secretary of Defense shall provide the Secretary an assessment of the defense requirements of any article that is the subject of an investigation conducted under this section.

(3) (A) By no later than the date that is 270 days after the date on which an investigation is initiated under paragraph (1) with respect to any article, the Secretary shall submit to the President a report on the findings of such investigation with respect to the effect of the importation of such article in such quantities or under such circumstances upon the national security and, based on such findings, the recommendations of the Secretary for action or inaction under this section. If the Secretary finds that such article is being imported into the United States in such quantities or under such circumstances as to threaten to impair the national security, the Secretary shall so advise the President in such report.

(B) Any portion of the report submitted by the Secretary under subparagraph (A) which does not contain classified information or proprietary information shall be published in the Federal Register.

(4) The Secretary shall prescribe such procedural regulations as may be necessary to carry out the provisions of this subsection.

(c) Adjustment of imports; determination by President; report to Congress; additional actions; publication in Federal Register.

(1) (A) Within 90 days after receiving a report submitted under subsection (b)(3)(A) in which the Secretary finds that an article is being imported into the United States in such quantities or under such circumstances as to threaten to impair the national security, the President shall—

(i) determine whether the President concurs with the finding of the Secretary, and

(ii) if the President concurs, determine the nature and duration of the action that, in the judgment of the President, must be taken to adjust the imports of the article and its derivatives so that such imports will not threaten to impair the national security.

(B) If the President determines under subparagraph (A) to take action to adjust imports of an article and its derivatives, the President shall implement that action by no later than the date that is 15 days after the day on which the President determines to take action under subparagraph (A).

(2) By no later than the date that is 30 days after the date on which the President makes any determinations under paragraph (1), the President shall submit to the Congress a written statement of the reasons why the President has decided to take action, or refused to take action, under paragraph (1). Such statement shall be included in the report published under subsection (e).

(3) (A) If—

(i) the action taken by the President under paragraph (1) is the negotiation of an agreement which limits or restricts the importation into, or the exportation to, the United States of the article that threatens to impair national security, and

(ii) either—

(I) no such agreement is entered into before the date that is 180 days after the date on which the President makes the determination under paragraph (1)(A) to take such action, or

(II) such an agreement that has been entered into is not being carried out or is ineffective in eliminating the threat to the national security posed by imports of such article,

the President shall take such other actions as the President deems necessary to adjust the imports of such article so that such imports will not threaten to impair the national security. The President shall publish in the Federal Register notice of any additional actions being taken under this section by reason of this subparagraph.

(B) If—

(i) clauses (i) and (ii) of subparagraph (A) apply, and

(ii) the President determines not to take any additional actions under this subsection,

the President shall publish in the Federal Register such determination and the reasons on which such determination is based.

(d) Domestic production for national defense; impact of foreign competition on economic welfare of domestic industries. For the purposes of this section, the Secretary and the President shall, in the light of the requirements of national security and without excluding other relevant factors, give consideration to domestic production needed for projected national defense requirements, the capacity of domestic industries to meet such requirements, existing and anticipated availabilities of the human resources, products, raw materials, and other supplies and services essential to the national defense, the requirements of growth of such industries and such supplies and services including the investment, exploration, and development necessary to assure such growth, and the importation of goods in terms of their quantities, availabilities, character, and use as those affect such industries and the capacity of the United States to meet national security requirements. In the administration of this section, the Secretary and the President shall further recognize the close relation of the economic welfare of the Nation to our national security, and shall take into consideration the impact of foreign competition on the economic welfare of individual domestic industries; and any substantial unemployment, decrease in revenues of government, loss of skills or investment, or other serious effects resulting from the displacement of any domestic products by excessive imports shall be considered, without excluding other factors, in determining whether such weakening of our internal economy may impair the national security.

[(e)] (d) Reports by Secretary of Commerce and President.

(1) Upon the disposition of each request, application, or motion under subsection (b), the Secretary shall submit to the Congress, and publish in the Federal Register, a report on such disposition.

(2) The President shall submit to the Congress an annual report on the operation of the provisions of this section.

(f) Congressional disapproval of Presidential adjustment of imports of petroleum or petroleum products; disapproval resolution.

(1) An action taken by the President under subsection (c) to adjust imports of petroleum or petroleum products shall cease to have force and effect upon the enactment of a disapproval resolution, provided for in paragraph (2), relating to that action.

(2) (A) This paragraph is enacted by the Congress—

(i) as an exercise of the rulemaking power of the House of Representatives and the Senate, respectively, and as such is deemed a part of the rules of each House, respectively, but applicable only with respect to the procedures to be followed in that House in the case of disapproval resolutions and such procedures supersede other rules only to the extent that they are inconsistent therewith; and

(ii) with the full recognition of the constitutional right of either House to change the rules (so far as relating to the procedure of that House) at any time, in the same manner, and to the same extent as any other rule of that House.

(B) For purposes of this subsection, the term "disapproval resolution" means only a joint resolution of either House of Congress the matter after the resolving clause of which is as follows: "That the Congress disapproves the action taken under section 232 of the Trade Expansion Act of 1962 with respect to petroleum imports under _____ dated _____.", the first blank space being filled with the number of the proclamation, Executive order, or other Executive act issued under the authority of subsection (c) of such section 232 for purposes of adjusting imports of petroleum or petroleum products and the second blank being filled with the appropriate date.

(C) (i) All disapproval resolutions introduced in the House of Representatives shall be referred to the Committee on Ways and Means and all disapproval resolutions introduced in the Senate shall be referred to the Committee on Finance.

(ii) No amendment to a disapproval resolution shall be in order in either the House of Representatives or the Senate, and no motion to suspend the application of this clause shall be in order in either House nor shall it be in order in either House for the Presiding Officer to entertain a request to suspend the application of this clause by unanimous consent.

19 USC 1872

Sec. 242. Interagency Trade Organization

(a) Establishment; functions; membership and composition; participation of representatives of other agencies; meetings.

(1) The President shall establish an interagency organization.

(2) The functions of the organization are—

(A) to assist, and make recommendations to, the President in carrying out the functions vested in him by the trade laws and to advise the United States Trade Representative (hereinafter in this section referred to as the "Trade Representative") in carrying out the functions set forth in section 141 of the Trade Act of 1974

(B) to assist the President, and advise the Trade Representative, with respect to the development and implementation of the international trade policy objectives of the United States; and

(C) to advise the President and the Trade Representative with respect to the relationship between the international trade policy objectives of the United States and other major policy areas which may significantly affect the overall international trade policy and trade competitiveness of the United States.

(3) The interagency organization shall be composed of the following:

(A) The Trade Representative, who shall be chairperson.

(B) The Secretary of Commerce.

(C) The Secretary of State.

(D) The Secretary of the Treasury.

(E) The Secretary of Agriculture.

(F) The Secretary of Labor.

The Trade Representative may invite representatives from other agencies, as appropriate, to attend particular meetings if subject matters of specific functional interest to such agencies are under consideration. It shall meet at such times and with respect to such matters as the President or the Chairman shall direct.

(b) Duties. In assisting the President, the organization shall—

(1) make recommendations to the President on basic policy issues arising in the administration of the trade agreements program,

(2) make recommendations to the President as to what action, if any, he should take on reports submitted to him by the Tariff Commission [United States International Trade Commission] under section 201(d) of the Trade Act of 1974,

(3) advise the President of the results of hearings held pursuant to section 302(b)(2) [of section 301] of the Trade Act of 1974, and recommend appropriate action with respect thereto, and

(4) perform such other functions with respect to the trade agreements program as the President may from time to time designate.

In carrying out its functions under this subsection, the organization shall take into account the advice of the congressional advisers and private sector advisory committees, as well as that of any committee or other body established to advise the department, agency, or office which a member of the organization heads.

(c) Use of resources of agencies; procedures and committees. The organization shall, to the maximum extent practicable, draw upon the resources of the agencies represented in the organization, as well as such other agencies as it may determine, including the Tariff Commission [United States International Trade Commission]. In addition, the President may establish by regulation such procedures and committees as he may determine to be necessary to enable the organization to provide for the conduct of hearings pursuant to section 302(b)(2) [of section 301] of the Trade Act of 1974, and for the carrying out of other functions assigned to the organization pursuant to this section.

Item 47

UNITED STATES: TRADE ACT OF 1974

(Selected provisions, as amended)

**Public Law 93–618, Approved January 3, 1975,
19 U.S.C. §§ 2101–2487, 88 Stat. 1978.**

An Act

To promote the development of an open, nondiscriminatory, and fair world economic system, to stimulate fair and free competition between the United States and foreign nations, to foster the economic growth of, and full employment in, the United States, and for other purposes.

Be it enacted by the Senate and House of Representatives of the United States of America in Congress assembled, That this Act, with the following table of contents, may be cited as the "Trade Act of 1974".

Table of Contents

TITLE VII.   TARIFF TREATMENT OF PRODUCTS OF, AND OTHER SANCTIONS AGAINST, UNCOOPERATIVE MAJOR DRUG PRODUCING OR DRUG-TRANSIT COUNTRIES
[omitted]

---

19 USC 2102

Sec. 2.   Statement of Purposes

The purposes of this Act are, through trade agreements affording mutual benefits—

(1) to foster the economic growth of and full employment in the United States and to strengthen economic relations between the United States and foreign countries through open and nondiscriminatory world trade;

(2) to harmonize, reduce, and eliminate barriers to trade on a basis which assures substantially equivalent competitive opportunities for the commerce of the United States;

(3) to establish fairness and equity in international trading relations, including reform of the General Agreement on Tariffs and Trade;

(4) to provide adequate procedures to safeguard American industry and labor against unfair or injurious import competition, and to assist industries, firms, workers, and communities to adjust to changes in international trade flows;

(5) to open up market opportunities for United States commerce in nonmarket economies; and

(6) to provide fair and reasonable access to products of less developed countries in the United States market.

TITLE I

NEGOTIATING AND OTHER AUTHORITY

Chapter 1

Rates of Duty and Other Trade Barriers

19 USC 2111

Sec. 101.   Basic Authority for Trade Agreements

(a) **Presidential authority to enter into agreement; modification or continuance of existing duties.** Whenever the President determines that any existing duties or other import restrictions of any foreign country or the United States are unduly burdening and restricting the foreign trade of the United States and that the purposes of this Act will be promoted thereby, the President—

(1) during the 5-year period beginning on January 3, 1975, may enter into trade agreements with foreign countries or instrumentalities thereof; and

(2) may proclaim such modification or continuance of any existing duty, such continuance of existing duty-free or excise treatment, or such additional

duties, as he determines to be required or appropriate to carry out any such trade agreement.

(b) Limitation on authority to decrease duty.

(1) Except as provided in paragraph (2), no proclamation pursuant to subsection (a)(2) of this section shall be made decreasing a rate of duty to a rate below 40 percent of the rate existing on January 1, 1975.

(2) Paragraph (1) shall not apply in the case of any article for which the rate of duty existing on January 1, 1975, is not more than 5 percent ad valorem.

(c) Limitation on authority to increase duty. No proclamation shall be made pursuant to subsection (a)(2) increasing any rate of duty to, or imposing a rate above, the higher of the following:

(1) the rate which is 50 percent above the rate set forth in rate column numbered 2 of the Tariff Schedules of the United States as in effect on January 1, 1975, or

(2) the rate which is 20 percent ad valorem above the rate existing on January 1, 1975.

19 USC 2112

Sec. 102.   Nontariff Barriers to and Other Distortions of Trade

(a) Congressional findings; directives; disavowal of prior approval of legislation. The Congress finds that barriers to (and other distortions of) international trade are reducing the growth of foreign markets for the products of United States agriculture, industry, mining, and commerce, diminishing the intended mutual benefits of reciprocal trade concessions, adversely affecting the United States economy, preventing fair and equitable access to supplies, and preventing the development of open and nondiscriminatory trade among nations. The President is urged to take all appropriate and feasible steps within his power (including the full exercise of the rights of the United States under international agreements) to harmonize, reduce, or eliminate such barriers to (and other distortions of) international trade. The President is further urged to utilize the authority granted by subsection (b) of this section to negotiate trade agreements with other countries and instrumentalities providing on a basis of mutuality for the harmonization, reduction, or elimination of such barriers to (and other distortions of) international trade. Nothing in this subsection shall be construed as prior approval of any legislation which may be necessary to implement an agreement concerning barriers to (or other distortions of) international trade.

(b) Presidential determinations prerequisite to entry into trade agreements; trade with Israel.

(1) Whenever the President determines that any barriers to (or other distortions of) international trade of any foreign country or the United States unduly burden and restrict the foreign trade of the United States or adversely affect the United States economy, or that the imposition of such barriers is likely to result in such a burden, restriction, or effect, and that the purposes of this chapter will be promoted thereby, the President, during the 13-year period beginning on January 3, 1975, may enter into trade agreements with

foreign countries or instrumentalities providing for the harmonization, reduction, or elimination of such barriers (or other distortions) or providing for the prohibition of or limitations on the imposition of such barriers (or other distortions).

(2)(A) Trade agreements that provide for the elimination or reduction of any duty imposed by the United States may be entered into under paragraph (1) only with Israel.

(B) The negotiation of any trade agreement entered into under paragraph (1) with Israel that provides for the elimination or reduction of any duty imposed by the United States shall take fully into account any product that benefits from a discriminatory preferential tariff arrangement between Israel and a third country if the tariff preference on such product has been the subject of a challenge by the United States Government under the authority of section 301 of this Act and the General Agreement on Tariffs and Trade.

(C) Notwithstanding any other provision of this section, the requirements of subsections (c) and (e)(1) shall not apply to any trade agreement entered into under paragraph (1) with Israel that provides for the elimination or reduction of any duty imposed by the United States.

(3) Notwithstanding any other provision of law, no trade benefit shall be extended to any country by reason of the extension of any trade benefit to another country under a trade agreement entered into under paragraph (1) with such other country that provides for the elimination or reduction of any duty imposed by the United States.

(4)(A) Notwithstanding paragraph (2), a trade agreement that provides for the elimination or reduction of any duty imposed by the United States may be entered into under paragraph (1) with any country other than Israel if—

(i) such country requested the negotiation of such an agreement, and

(ii) the President, at least 60 days prior to the date notice is provided under subsection (e)(1) of this section—

(I) provides written notice of such negotiations to the Committee on Finance of the Senate and the Committee on Ways and Means of the House of Representatives, and

(II) consults with such committees regarding the negotiation of such agreement.

(B) The provisions of section 151 shall not apply to an implementing bill (within the meaning of section 151(b)) if—

(i) such implementing bill contains a provision approving of any trade agreement which—

(I) is entered into under this section with any country other than Israel, and

(II) provides for the elimination or reduction of any duty imposed by the United States, and

(ii) either—

(i) the requirements of subparagraph (A) were not met with respect to the negotiation of such agreement, or

(II) the Committee on Finance of the Senate or the Committee on Ways and Means of the House of Representatives disapproved of the negotiation of such agreement before the close of the 60-day period which begins on the date notice is provided under subparagraph (A)(ii)(I) with respect to the negotiation of such agreement.

(C) The 60-day period described in subparagraphs (A)(ii) and (B)(ii)(II) shall be computed without regard to—

(i) the days on which either House of Congress is not in session because of an adjournment of more than 3 days to a day certain or an adjournment of the Congress sine die, and

(ii) any Saturday and Sunday, not excluded under clause (i), when either House of Congress is not in session.

(c) Presidential consultation with Congress prior to entry into trade agreements. Before the President enters into any trade agreement under this section providing for the harmonization, reduction, or elimination of a barrier to (or other distortion of) international trade, he shall consult with the Committee on Ways and Means of the House of Representatives, the Committee on Finance of the Senate, and with each committee of the House and the Senate and each joint committee of the Congress which has jurisdiction over legislation involving subject matters which would be affected by such trade agreement. Such consultation shall include all matters relating to the implementation of such trade agreement as provided in subsections (d) and (e) of this section. If it is proposed to implement such trade agreement, together with one or more other trade agreements entered into under this section, in a single implementing bill, such consultation shall include the desirability and feasibility of such proposed implementation.

(d) Submission to Congress of agreements, drafts of implementing bills, and statements of proposed administrative action. Whenever the President enters into a trade agreement under this section providing for the harmonization, reduction, or elimination of a barrier to (or other distortion of) international trade, he shall submit such agreement, together with a draft of an implementing bill (described in section 151(b)) and a statement of any administrative action proposed to implement such agreement, to the Congress as provided in subsection (e) of this section, and such agreement shall enter into force with respect to the United States only if the provisions of subsection (e) of this section are complied with and the implementing bill submitted by the President is enacted into law.

(e) Steps prerequisite to entry into force of trade agreements. Each trade agreement submitted to the Congress under this subsection shall enter into force with respect to the United States if (and only if)—

(1) the President, not less than 90 days before the day on which he enters into such trade agreement, notifies the House of Representatives and the Senate of his intention to enter into such an agreement, and promptly thereafter publishes notice of such intention in the Federal Register;

(2) after entering into the agreement, the President transmits a document to the House of Representatives and to the Senate containing a copy of the final legal text of such agreement together with—

(A) a draft of an implementing bill and a statement of any administrative action proposed to implement such agreement, and an explanation as to how the implementing bill and proposed administrative action change or affect existing law, and

(B) a statement of his reasons as to how the agreement serves the interests of United States commerce and as to why the implementing bill and proposed administrative action is required or appropriate to carry out the agreement; and

(3) the implementing bill is enacted into law.

(f) Obligations imposed upon foreign countries or instrumentalities receiving benefits under trade agreements. To insure that a foreign country or instrumentality which receives benefits under a trade agreement entered into under this section is subject to the obligations imposed by such agreement, the President may recommend to Congress in the implementing bill and statement of administrative action submitted with respect to such agreement that the benefits and obligations of such agreement apply solely to the parties to such agreement, if such application is consistent with the terms of such agreement. The President may also recommend with respect to any such agreement that the benefits and obligations of such agreement not apply uniformly to all parties to such agreement, if such application is consistent with the terms of such agreement.

(g) Definitions. For purposes of this section—

(1) the term "barrier" includes—

(A) the American selling price basis of customs evaluation as defined in section 401a or 402 of the Tariff Act of 1930, as appropriate, and

(B) any duty or other import restriction;

(2) the term "distortion" includes a subsidy; and

(3) the term "international trade" includes—

(A) trade in both goods and services, and

(B) foreign direct investment by United States persons, especially if such investment has implications for trade in goods and services.

19 USC 2113

Sec. 103. Overall Negotiating Objective

The overall United States negotiating objective under sections 101 and 102 shall be to obtain more open and equitable market access and the harmonization, reduction, or elimination of devices which distort trade or commerce. To the maximum extent feasible, the harmonization, reduction, or elimination of agricultural trade barriers and distortions shall be undertaken in conjunction with the harmonization, reduction, or elimination of industrial trade barriers and distortions.

19 USC 2114

Sec. 104. Sector Negotiating Objectives

(a) Obtaining equivalent competitive opportunities. A principal United States negotiating objective under sections 101 and 102 shall be to obtain, to the maximum extent feasible, with respect to appropriate product sectors of manufacturing, and with respect to the agricultural sector, competitive opportunities for United States exports to the developed countries of the world equivalent to the competitive opportunities afforded in United States markets to the importation of like or similar products, taking into account all barriers (including tariffs) to and other distortions of international trade affecting that sector.

(b) Conduct of negotiations on basis of appropriate product sectors of manufacturing. As a means of achieving the negotiating objectives set forth in subsection (a) of this section, to the extent consistent with the objective of maximizing overall economic benefit to the United States (through maintaining and enlarging foreign markets for products of United States agriculture, industry, mining, and commerce, through the development of fair and equitable market opportunities, and through open and nondiscriminatory world trade), negotiations shall, to the extent feasible be conducted on the basis of appropriate product sectors of manufacturing.

(c) Identification of appropriate product sectors of manufacturing. For the purposes of this section and section 135, the United States Trade Representative together with the Secretary of Commerce, Agriculture, or Labor, as appropriate, shall, after consultation with the Advisory Committee for Trade Negotiations established under section 135 and after consultation with interested private or non-Federal governmental organizations, identify appropriate product sectors of manufacturing.

(d) Presidential analysis of how negotiating objectives are achieved in each product sector by trade agreements. If the President determines that competitive opportunities in one or more product sectors will be significantly affected by a trade agreement concluded under section 101 or 102, he shall submit to the Congress with each such agreement an analysis of the extent to which the negotiating objective set forth in subsection (a) of this section is achieved by such agreement in each product sector or product sectors.

19 USC 2114a

Sec. 104A. Negotiating Objectives With Respect to Trade in Services, Foreign Direct Investment, and High Technology Products

(a) Trade in services.

(1) In general. Principal United States negotiating objectives under section 102 shall be—

(A) to reduce or to eliminate barriers to, or other distortions of, international trade in services (particularly United States service sector trade in foreign markets), including barriers that deny national treatment and restrictions on the establishment and operation in such markets; and

(B) to develop internationally agreed rules, including dispute settlement procedures, which—

(i) are consistent with the commercial policies of the United States, and

(ii) will reduce or eliminate such barriers or distortions and help ensure open international trade in services.

(2) Domestic objectives. In pursuing the objectives described in paragraph (1), United States negotiators shall take into account legitimate United States domestic objectives including, but not limited to, the protection of legitimate health or safety, essential security, environmental, consumer or employment opportunity interests and the laws and regulations related thereto.

(b) Foreign direct investment—

(1) In general. Principal United States negotiating objectives under section 102 shall be—

(A) to reduce or to eliminate artificial or trade-distorting barriers to foreign direct investment, to expand the principle of national treatment, and to reduce unreasonable barriers to establishment; and

(B) to develop internationally agreed rules, including dispute settlement procedures, which—

(i) will help ensure a free flow of foreign direct investment, and

(ii) will reduce or eliminate the trade distortive effects of certain investment related measures.

(2) Domestic objectives. In pursuing the objectives described in paragraph (1), United States negotiators shall take into account legitimate United States domestic objectives including, but not limited to, the protection of legitimate health or safety, essential security, environmental, consumer or employment opportunity interests and the laws and regulations related thereto.

(c) High technology products. Principal United States negotiating objectives shall be—

(1) to obtain and preserve the maximum openness with respect to international trade and investment in high technology products and related services;

(2) to obtain the elimination or reduction of, or compensation for, the significantly distorting effects of foreign government acts, policies, or practices identified in section 181, with particular consideration given to the nature and extent of foreign government intervention affecting United States exports of high technology products or investments in high technology industries, including—

(A) foreign industrial policies which distort international trade or investment;

(B) measures which deny national treatment or otherwise discriminate in favor of domestic high technology industries;

(C) measures which fail to provide adequate and effective means for foreign nationals to secure, exercise, and enforce exclusive rights in intellectual property (including trademarks, patents, and copyrights);

(D) measures which impair access to domestic markets for key commodity products; and

(E) measures which facilitate or encourage anticompetitive market practices or structures;

(3) to obtain commitments that official policy of foreign countries or instrumentalities will not discourage government or private procurement of foreign high technology products and related services;

(4) to obtain the reduction or elimination of all tariffs on, and other barriers to, United States exports of high technology products and related services;

(5) to obtain commitments to foster national treatment;

(6) to obtain commitments to—

(A) foster the pursuit of joint scientific cooperation between companies, institutions or governmental entities of the United States and those of the trading partners of the United States in areas of mutual interest through such measures as financial participation and technical and personnel exchanges, and

(B) ensure that access by all participants to the results of any such cooperative efforts should not be impaired; and

(7) to provide effective minimum safeguards for the acquisition and enforcement of intellectual property rights and the property value of proprietary data.

(d) Definition of barriers and other distortions. For purposes of subsection (a), the term "barriers to, or other distortions of, international trade in services" includes, but is not limited to—

(1) barriers to establishment in foreign markets, and

(2) restrictions on the operation of enterprises in foreign markets, including—

(A) direct or indirect restrictions on the transfer of information into, or out of, the country or instrumentality concerned, and

(B) restrictions on the use of data processing facilities within or outside of such country or instrumentality.

19 USC 2115

Sec. 105.   Bilateral Trade Agreements

If the President determines that bilateral trade agreements will more effectively promote the economic growth of, and full employment in, the United States, then, in such cases, a negotiating objective under sections 101 and 102 shall be to enter into bilateral trade agreements. Each such trade agreement shall provide for mutually advantageous economic benefits.

19 USC 2116

Sec. 106.   Agreements With Developing Countries

A United States negotiating objective under sections 101 and 102 shall be to enter into trade agreements which promote the economic growth of both developing countries and the United States and the mutual expansion of market opportunities.

19 USC 2117

Sec. 107. International Safeguard Procedures

(a) A principal United States negotiating objective under section 102 shall be to obtain internationally agreed upon rules and procedures, in the context of the harmonization, reduction, or elimination of barriers to, and other distortions of, international trade, which permit the use of temporary measures to ease adjustment to changes occurring in competitive conditions in the domestic markets of the parties to an agreement resulting from such negotiations due to the expansion of international trade.

(b) Any agreement entered into under section 102 may include provisions establishing procedures for—

(1) notification of affected exporting countries,

(2) international consultations,

(3) international review of changes in trade flows,

(4) making adjustments in trade flows as the result of such changes, and

(5) international mediation.

Such agreements may also include provisions which—

(A) exclude, under specified conditions, the parties thereto from compensation obligations and retaliation, and

(B) permit domestic public procedures through which interested parties have the right to participate.

19 USC 2118

Sec. 108. Access to Supplies

(a) A principal United States negotiating objective under section 102 shall be to enter into trade agreements with foreign countries and instrumentalities to assure the United States of fair and equitable access at reasonable prices to supplies of articles of commerce which are important to the economic requirements of the United States and for which the United States does not have, or cannot easily develop, the necessary domestic productive capacity to supply its own requirements.

(b) Any agreement entered into under section 102 may include provisions which—

(1) assure to the United States the continued availability of important articles at reasonable prices, and

(2) provide reciprocal concessions or comparable trade obligations, or both, by the United States.

19 USC 2119

Sec. 109. Staging Requirements and Rounding Authority

(a) **Maximum aggregate reductions in rates of duty.** Except as otherwise provided in this section, the aggregate reduction in the rate of duty on any article which is in effect on any day pursuant to a trade agreement under section 101 shall not exceed the aggregate reduction which would have been in effect on such day if—

(1) a reduction of 3 percent ad valorem or a reduction of one-tenth of the total reduction, whichever is greater, had taken effect on the effective date of the first reduction proclaimed pursuant to section 101(a)(2) to carry out such agreement with respect to such article, and

(2) a reduction equal to the amount applicable under paragraph (1) had taken effect at 1-year intervals after the effective date of such first reduction.

This subsection shall not apply in any case where the total reduction in the rate of duty does not exceed 10 percent of the rate before the reduction.

(b) Simplification of computation. If the President determines that such action will simplify the computation of the amount of duty imposed with respect to an article, he may exceed the limitation provided by section 101(b) or subsection (a) of this section by not more than whichever of the following is lesser:

(1) the difference between the limitation and the next lower whole number, or

(2) one-half of 1 percent ad valorem.

(c) Ten-year period for commencement of reductions in rates of duty.

(1) No reduction in the rate of duty on any article pursuant to a trade agreement under section 101 shall take effect more than 10 years after the effective date of the first reduction proclaimed to carry out such trade agreement with respect to such article.

(2) If any part of a reduction takes effect, then any time thereafter during which any part of the reduction is not in effect by reason of legislation of the United States or action thereunder, the effect of which is to maintain or increase the rate of duty on an article, shall be excluded in determining—

(A) the 1-year intervals referred to in subsection (a)(2) of this section, and

(B) the expiration of the 10-year period referred to in paragraph (1) of this subsection.

Chapter 2

Other Authority

19 USC 2131

Sec. 121.   Steps to Be Taken Toward GATT Revision

There are authorized to be appropriated annually such sums as may be necessary for the payment by the United States of its share of the expenses of the Contracting Parties to the General Agreement on Tariffs and Trade. This authorization does not imply approval or disapproval by the Congress of all articles of the General Agreement on Tariffs and Trade.

19 USC 2132

Sec. 122.   Balance-of-Payments Authority

(a) **Presidential proclamations of temporary import surcharges and temporary limitations on imports through quotas in situations of fundamental international payments problems.** Whenever fundamental international payments problems require special import measures to restrict imports—

(1) to deal with large and serious United States balance-of-payments deficits,

(2) to prevent an imminent and significant depreciation of the dollar in foreign exchange markets, or

(3) to cooperate with other countries in correcting an international balance-of-payments disequilibrium,

the President shall proclaim, for a period not exceeding 150 days (unless such period is extended by Act of Congress)—

(A) a temporary import surcharge, not to exceed 15 percent ad valorem, in the form of duties (in addition to those already imposed, if any) on articles imported into the United States;

(B) temporary limitations through the use of quotas on the importation of articles into the United States; or

(C) both a temporary import surcharge described in subparagraph (A) and temporary limitations described in subparagraph (B).

The authority delegated under subparagraph (B) (and so much of subparagraph (C) as relates to subparagraph (B)) may be exercised (i) only if international trade or monetary agreements to which the United States is a party permit the imposition of quotas as a balance-of-payments measure, and (ii) only to the extent that the fundamental imbalance cannot be dealt with effectively by a surcharge proclaimed pursuant to subparagraph (A) or (C). Any temporary import surcharge proclaimed pursuant to subparagraph (A) or (C) shall be treated as a regular customs duty.

(b) **Import restrictions not imposed when contrary to national interest of United States.** If the President determines that the imposition of import restrictions under subsection (a) of this section will be contrary to the national interest of the United States, then he may refrain from proclaiming such restrictions and he shall—

(1) immediately inform Congress of his determination, and

(2) immediately convene the group of congressional official advisers designated under section 161(a) and consult with them as to the reasons for such determination.

(c) **Presidential proclamations liberalizing imports.** Whenever the President determines that fundamental international payments problems require special import measures to increase imports—

(1) to deal with large and persistent United States balance-of-trade surpluses, as determined on the basis of the cost-insurance-freight value of imports, as reported by the Bureau of the Census, or

(2) to prevent significant appreciation of the dollar in foreign exchange markets,

the President is authorized to proclaim, for a period of 150 days (unless such period is extended by Act of Congress)—

(A) a temporary reduction (of not more than 5 percent ad valorem) in the rate of duty on any article; and

(B) a temporary increase in the value or quantity of articles which may be imported under any import restriction, or a temporary suspension of any import restriction.

Import liberalizing actions proclaimed pursuant to this subsection shall be of broad and uniform application with respect to product coverage except that the President shall not proclaim measures under this subsection with respect to those articles where in his judgment such action will cause or contribute to material injury to firms or workers in any domestic industry, including agriculture, mining, fishing, or commerce, or to impairment of the national security, or will otherwise be contrary to the national interest.

(d) Nondiscriminatory treatment of import restricting actions.

(1) Import restricting actions proclaimed pursuant to subsection (a) of this section shall be applied consistently with the principle of nondiscriminatory treatment. In addition, any quota proclaimed pursuant to subparagraph (B) of subsection (a) of this section shall be applied on a basis which aims at a distribution of trade with the United States approaching as closely as possible that which various foreign countries might have expected to obtain in the absence of such restrictions.

(2) Notwithstanding paragraph (1), if the President determines that the purposes of this section will best be served by action against one or more countries having large or persistent balance-of-payments surpluses, he may exempt all other countries from such action.

(3) After such time when there enters into force for the United States new rules regarding the application of surcharges as part of a reform of internationally agreed balance-of-payments adjustment procedures, the exemption authority contained in paragraph (2) shall be applied consistently with such new international rules.

(4) It is the sense of Congress that the President seek modifications in international agreements aimed at allowing the use of surcharges in place of quantitative restrictions (and providing rules to govern the use of such surcharges) as a balance-of-payments adjustment measure within the context of arrangements for an equitable sharing of balance-of-payments adjustment responsibility among deficit and surplus countries.

(e) Broad and uniform application of import restricting actions. Import restricting actions proclaimed pursuant to subsection (a) of this section shall be of broad and uniform application with respect to product coverage except where the President determines, consistently with the purposes of this section, that certain articles should not be subject to import restricting actions because of the needs of the United States economy. Such exceptions shall be limited to the unavailability of domestic supply at reasonable prices, the necessary importation of raw materials, avoiding serious dislocations in the supply of imported goods, and other similar factors. In addition, uniform exceptions may be made where import restricting actions will be unnecessary or ineffective in carrying out the purposes of this section, such as with respect to articles already subject to import restrictions, goods in transit, or goods under binding contract. Neither the authorization of import restricting actions nor the determination of exceptions with respect to product coverage shall be made for the purpose of protecting individual domestic industries from import competition.

(f) Quantitative limitations. Any quantitative limitation proclaimed pursuant to subparagraph (B) or (C) of subsection (a) of this section on the quantity or value, or both, of an article—

(1) shall permit the importation of a quantity or value which is not less than the quantity or value of such article imported into the United States from the foreign countries to which such limitation applies during the most recent period which the President determines is representative of imports of such article, and

(2) shall take into account any increase since the end of such representative period in domestic consumption of such article and like or similar articles of domestic manufacture or production.

(g) Suspension, modification or termination of proclamations. The President may at any time, consistent with the provisions of this section, suspend, modify, or terminate, in whole or in part, any proclamation under this section either during the initial 150-day period of effectiveness or as extended by subsequent Act of Congress.

(h) Termination of tariff concessions. No provision of law authorizing the termination of tariff concessions shall be used to impose a surcharge on imports into the United States.

19 USC 2133

Sec. 123.   Compensation Authority

(a) New concessions. Whenever—

(1) any action taken under chapter 1 of title II or chapter 1 of title III; or under chapter 2 of title IV of the Trade Act of 1974; or

(2) any judicial or administrative tariff reclassification that becomes final after August 23, 1988;

increases or imposes any duty or other import restriction, the President—

(A) may enter into trade agreements with foreign countries or instrumentalities for the purpose of granting new concessions as compensation in order to maintain the general level of reciprocal and mutually advantageous concessions; and

(B) may proclaim such modification or continuance of any existing duty, or such continuance of existing duty-free or excise treatment, as he determines to be required or appropriate to carry out any such agreement.

(b) Reductions in rates of duty.

(1) No proclamation shall be made pursuant to subsection (a) of this section decreasing any rate of duty to a rate which is less than 70 percent of the existing rate of duty.

(2) Where the rate of duty in effect at any time is an intermediate stage under section 109, the proclamation made pursuant to subsection (a) of this section may provide for the reduction of each rate of duty at each such stage proclaimed under section 101 by not more than 30 percent of such rate of duty, and may provide for a final rate of duty which is not less than 70 percent of the rate of duty proclaimed as the final stage under section 101.

(3) If the President determines that such action will simplify the computation of the amount of duty imposed with respect to an article, he may exceed the limitations provided by paragraphs (1) and (2) of this subsection by not more than the lesser of—

    (A) the difference between such limitation and the next lower whole number, or

    (B) one-half of 1 percent ad valorem.

(4) Any concessions granted under subsection (a)(1) shall be reduced and terminated according to substantially the same time schedule for reduction applicable to the relevant action under section 203(e) and 204.

(c) Consideration of past violations of trade concessions. Before entering into any trade agreement under this section with any foreign country or instrumentality, the President shall consider whether such country or instrumentality has violated trade concessions of benefit to the United States and such violation has not been adequately offset by the action of the United States or by such country or instrumentality.

(d) Basic authority for trade agreements as authority for granting new concessions as compensation. Notwithstanding the provisions of subsection (a) of this section, the authority delegated under section 101 shall be used for the purpose of granting new concessions as compensation within the meaning of this section until such authority terminates.

(e) International obligations determination prerequisite to application of authority. The provisions of this section shall apply by reason of action taken under chapter 1 of title III only if the President determines that action authorized under this section is necessary or appropriate to meet the international obligations of the United States.

19 USC 2134

Sec. 124. Two-Year Residual Authority to Negotiate Duties

(a) Trade agreements. Whenever the President determines that any existing duties or other import restrictions of any foreign country or the United States are unduly burdening and restricting the foreign trade of the United States and that the purposes of this Act will be promoted thereby, the President—

    (1) may enter into trade agreements with foreign countries or instrumentalities thereof, and

(2) may proclaim such modification or continuance of any existing duty, such continuance of existing duty-free or excise treatment, or such additional duties, as he determines to be required or appropriate to carry out any such trade agreement.

(b) Maximum volume of imported articles subject to reduction of duties or continuance of duty-free or excise treatment. Agreements entered into under this section in any 1-year period shall not provide for the reduction of duties, or the continuance of duty-free or excise treatment, for articles which account for more than 2 percent of the value of United States imports for the most recent 12-month period for which import statistics are available.

(c) Maximum reduction in duties

(1) No proclamation shall be made pursuant to subsection (a) of this section decreasing any rate of duty to a rate which is less than 80 percent of the existing rate of duty.

(2) No proclamation shall be made pursuant to subsection (a) decreasing or increasing any rate of duty to a rate which is lower or higher than the corresponding rate which would have resulted if the maximum authority granted by section 101 with respect to such article had been exercised.

(3) Where the rate of duty in effect at any time is an intermediate stage under section 109, the proclamation made pursuant to subsection (a) of this section may provide for the reduction of each rate of duty at each such stage proclaimed under section 101 by not more than 20 percent of such rate of duty, and, subject to the limitation in paragraph (2), may provide for a final rate of duty which is not less than 80 percent of the rate of duty proclaimed as the final stage under section 101.

(4) If the President determines that such action will simplify the computation of the amount of duty imposed with respect to an article, he may exceed the limitations provided by paragraphs (1) and (2) of this subsection by not more than the lesser of—

(A) the difference between such limitation and the next lower whole number, or

(B) one-half of 1 percent ad valorem.

(d) Two-year period of authority. Agreements may be entered into under this section only during the 2-year period which immediately follows the close of the period during which agreements may be entered into under section 101.

19 USC 2135

Sec. 125.   Termination and Withdrawal Authority

(a) Grant of authority for termination or withdrawal at end of period specified in agreement. Every trade agreement entered into under this Act shall be subject to termination, in whole or in part, or withdrawal, upon due notice, at the end of a period specified in the agreement. Such period shall be not more than 3 years from the date on which the agreement becomes effective. If the agreement is not terminated or withdrawn from at the end of the period so specified, it shall be subject to termination or withdrawal thereafter upon not more than 6 months" notice.

(b) Authority to terminate proclamations at any time. The President may at any time terminate, in whole or in part, any proclamation made under this Act.

(c) Increased duties or other import restrictions following withdrawal, suspension, or modification of obligations with respect to trade of foreign countries or instrumentalities. Whenever the United States, acting in pursuance of any of its rights or obligations under any trade agreement entered into pursuant to this Act, section 201 of the Trade Expansion Act of 1962, or section 350 of the Tariff Act of 1930, withdraws, suspends, or modifies any obligation with respect to the trade of any foreign country or instrumentality thereof, the President is authorized to proclaim increased duties or other import restrictions, to the extent, at such times, and for such periods as he deems necessary or appropriate, in order to exercise the rights or fulfill the obligations of the United States. No such proclamation shall be made under this subsection increasing any existing duty to a rate more than 50 percent above the rate set forth in rate column numbered 2 of the Tariff Schedules of the United States, as in effect on January 1, 1975, or 20 percent ad valorem above the rate existing on January 1, 1975, whichever is higher.

(d) Retaliatory authority. Whenever any foreign country or instrumentality withdraws, suspends, or modifies the application of trade agreement obligations of benefit to the United States without granting adequate compensation therefor, the President, in pursuance of rights granted to the United States under any trade agreement and to the extent necessary to protect United States economic interests (including United States balance of payments), may—

(1) withdraw, suspend, or modify the application of substantially equivalent trade agreement obligations of benefit to such foreign country or instrumentality, and

(2) proclaim under subsection (c) of this section such increased duties or other import restrictions as are appropriate to effect adequate compensation from such foreign country or instrumentality.

(e) Continuation of duties or other import restrictions after termination of or withdrawal from agreements. Duties or other import restrictions required or appropriate to carry out any trade agreement entered into pursuant to this Act, section 201 of the Trade Expansion Act of 1962, or section 350 of the Tariff Act of 1930 shall not be affected by any termination, in whole or in part, of such agreement or by the withdrawal of the United States from such agreement and shall remain in effect after the date of such termination or withdrawal for 1 year, unless the President by proclamation provides that such rates shall be restored to the level at which they would be but for the agreement. Within 60 days after the date of any such termination or withdrawal, the President shall transmit to the Congress his recommendations as to the appropriate rates of duty for all articles which were affected by the termination or withdrawal or would have been so affected but for the preceding sentence.

(f) Public hearings. Before taking any action pursuant to subsection (b), (c), or (d), the President shall provide for a public hearing during the course of which interested persons shall be given a reasonable opportunity to be present, to produce evidence, and to be heard, unless he determines that such prior hearings will be contrary to the national interest because of the need for expeditious action, in which case he shall provide for a public hearing promptly after such action.

19 USC 2136

Sec. 126. Reciprocal Nondiscrimination Treatment

(a) Direct and indirect imports. Except as otherwise provided in this Act or in any other provision of law, any duty or other import restriction or duty-free treatment proclaimed in carrying out any trade agreement under this title shall apply to products of all foreign countries, whether imported directly or indirectly.

(b) Presidential determination of whether major industrial countries have made substantially equivalent concessions to the United States. The President shall determine, after the conclusion of all negotiations entered into under this Act or at the end of the 5–year period beginning on the date of enactment of this Act [enacted Jan. 3, 1975], whichever is earlier, whether any major industrial country has failed to make concessions under trade agreements entered into under this Act which provide competitive opportunities for the commerce of the United States in such country substantially equivalent to the competitive opportunities, provided by concessions made by the United States under trade agreements entered into under this Act, for the commerce of such country in the United States.

(c) Major industrial countries. For purposes of this section, "major industrial country" means Canada, the European Economic Community, the individual member countries of such Community, Japan, and any other foreign country designated by the President for purposes of this subsection.

19 USC 2137

Sec. 127. Reservation of Articles for National Security or Other Reasons

(a) National security considerations. No proclamation shall be made pursuant to the provisions of this Act reducing or eliminating the duty or other import restriction on any article if the President determines that such reduction or elimination would threaten to impair the national security.

(b) Action taken under other laws. While there is in effect with respect to any article any action taken under section 203 of this Act, or section 232 or 351 of the Trade Expansion Act of 1962, the President shall reserve such article from negotiations under this title (and from any action under section 122(c)) contemplating reduction or elimination of—

    (A) any duty on such article,

    (B) any import restriction imposed under such section, or

(C) any other import restriction, the removal of which will be likely to undermine the effect of the import restrictions referred to in subparagraph (B).

In addition, the President shall also so reserve any other article which he determines to be appropriate, taking into consideration information and advice available pursuant to and with respect to the matters covered by sections 131, 132, and 133, where applicable.

19 USC 2138
Omitted (no longer in effect)
Chapter 3
Hearings and Advice Concerning Negotiations
19 USC 2151

Sec. 131. Advice From International Trade Commission
(a) Lists of articles which may be considered for action.

(1) In connection with any proposed trade agreement under section 123 of this Act or section 1102(a) or (c) of the Omnibus Trade and Competitiveness Act of 1988, the President shall from time to time publish and furnish the International Trade Commission (hereafter in this section referred to as the "Commission") with lists of articles which may be considered for modification or continuance of United States duties, continuance of United States duty-free or excise treatment, or additional duties. In the case of any article with respect to which consideration may be given to reducing or increasing the rate of duty, the list shall specify the provision of this subchapter under which such consideration may be given.

(2) In connection with any proposed trade agreement under section 1102(b) or (c) of the Omnibus Trade and Competitiveness Act of 1988, the President may from time to time publish and furnish the Commission with lists of nontariff matters which may be considered for modification.

(b) Advice to President by Commission. Within 6 months after receipt of a list under subsection (a) or, in the case of a list submitted in connection with a trade agreement, within 90 days after receipt of such list, the Commission shall advise the President, with respect to each article or nontariff matter, of its judgment as to the probable economic effect of modification of the tariff or nontariff measure on industries producing like or directly competitive articles and on consumers, so as to assist the President in making an informed judgment as to the impact which might be caused by such modifications on United States interests such as sectors involved in manufacturing, agriculture, mining, fishing, services, intellectual property, investment, labor, and consumers. Such advice may include in the case of any article the advice of the Commission as to whether any reduction in the rate of duty should take place over a longer period of time than the minimum period provided for in section 1102(a)(3)(A).

(c) Additional investigations and reports requested by the President or the Trade Representative. In addition, in order to assist the President in his determination whether to enter into any agreement under section 123 of this Act or section 1102 of the Omnibus Trade and Competitiveness Act of 1988, or how to develop trade policy, priorities or other matters (such as priorities for actions to improve opportunities in foreign markets), the Commission shall make such investigations and reports as may be requested by the President or the United States Trade Representative on matters such as effects of modification of any barrier to (or other distortion of) international trade on domestic workers, industries or sectors, purchasers, prices and quantities of articles in the United States.

(d) Commission steps in preparing its advice to the President. In preparing its advice to the President under this section, the Commission shall to the extent practicable—

(1) investigate conditions, causes, and effects relating to competition between the foreign industries producing the articles or services in question and the domestic industries producing the like or directly competitive articles or services;

(2) analyze the production, trade, and consumption of each like or directly competitive article or service, taking into consideration employment, profit levels, and use of productive facilities with respect to the domestic industries concerned, and such other economic factors in such industries as it considers relevant, including prices, wages, sales, inventories, patterns of demand, capital investment, obsolescence of equipment, and diversification of production;

(3) describe the probable nature and extent of any significant change in employment, profit levels, and use of productive facilities; the overall impact of such or other possible changes on the competitiveness of relevant domestic industries or sectors; and such other conditions as it deems relevant in the domestic industries or sectors concerned which it believes such modifications would cause; and

(4) make special studies (including studies of real wages paid in foreign supplying countries), whenever deemed to be warranted, of particular proposed modifications affecting United States manufacturing, agriculture, mining, fishing, labor, consumers, services, intellectual property and investment, using to the fullest extent practicable United States Government facilities abroad and appropriate personnel of the United States.

(e) Public hearing. In preparing its advice to the President under this section, the Commission shall, after reasonable notice, hold public hearings.

19 USC 2152

Sec. 132.   Advice From Executive Departments and Other Sources

Before any trade agreement is entered into under section 123 of this Act or section 1102 of the Omnibus Trade and Competitiveness Act of 1988, the President shall seek information and advice with respect to such agreement from the Departments of Agriculture, Commerce, Defense, Interior, Labor, State and the Treasury, from the United States Trade Representative, and from such other sources as he may deem appropriate. Such advice shall be prepared and presented consistent with the provisions of Reorganization Plan Number 3 of 1979, Executive Order Number 12188 and section 141(c).

19 USC 2153

Sec. 133.   Public Hearings

(a) Opportunity for presentation of views. In connection with any proposed trade agreement under section 123 of this Act or section 1102 of the Omnibus Trade and Competitiveness Act of 1988, the President shall afford an opportunity for any interested person to present his views concerning any article on a list published under section 131, any matter or article which should be so listed, any concession which should be sought by the United States, or any other matter relevant to such proposed trade agreement. For this purpose, the President shall designate an agency or an interagency committee which shall, after reasonable notice, hold public hearings and prescribe regulations governing the conduct of such hearings. When appropriate, such procedures shall apply to the development of trade policy and priorities.

(b) Summary of hearings. The organization holding such hearing shall furnish the President with a summary thereof.

19 USC 2154

Sec. 134.   Prerequisites for Offers

(a) In any negotiation seeking an agreement under section 123 of this Act or section 1102 of the Omnibus Trade and Competitiveness Act of 1988, the President may make a formal offer for the modification or continuance of any United States duty, import restrictions, or barriers to (or other distortions of) international trade, the continuance of United States duty-free or excise treatment, or the imposition of additional duties, import restrictions, or other barrier to (or other distortion of) international trade including trade in services, foreign direct investment and intellectual property as covered by this title, with respect to any article or matter only after he has received a summary of the hearings at which an opportunity to be heard with respect to such article has been afforded under section 133. In addition, the President may make an offer for the modification or continuance of any United States duty, the continuance of United States duty-free or excise treatment, or the imposition of additional duties, with respect to any article included in a list published and furnished under section 131(a), only after he has received advice concerning such article from the Commission under section 131(b), or after the expiration of the 6-month or 90-day period provided for in that section, as appropriate, whichever first occurs.

(b) In determining whether to make offers described in subsection (a) in the course of negotiating any trade agreement under section 1102 of the Omnibus Trade and Competitiveness Act of 1988, and in determining the nature and scope of such offers, the President shall take into account any advice or information provided, or reports submitted, by—

(1) the Commission;

(2) any advisory committee established under section 135; or

(3) any organization that holds public hearings under section 133;

with respect to any article, or domestic industry, that is sensitive, or potentially sensitive, to imports.

21 USC 2155

Sec. 135. Information and Advice From Private and Public Sectors

(a) In general.

(1) The President shall seek information and advice from representative elements of the private sector and the non-Federal governmental sector with respect to—

(A) negotiating objectives and bargaining positions before entering into a trade agreement under this title or section 1102 of the Omnibus Trade and Competitiveness Act of 1988;

(B) the operation of any trade agreement once entered into, including preparation for dispute settlement panel proceedings to which the United States is a party; and

(C) other matters arising in connection with the development, implementation, and administration of the trade policy of the United States, including those matters referred to in Reorganization Plan Number 3 of 1979 and Executive Order Numbered 12188, and the priorities for actions thereunder.

To the maximum extent feasible, such information and advice on negotiating objectives shall be sought and considered before the commencement of negotiations.

(2) The President shall consult with representative elements of the private sector and the non-Federal governmental sector on the overall current trade policy of the United States. The consultations shall include, but are not limited to, the following elements of such policy:

(A) The principal multilateral and bilateral trade negotiating objectives and the progress being made toward their achievement.

(B) The implementation, operation, and effectiveness of recently concluded multilateral and bilateral trade agreements and resolution of trade disputes.

(C) The actions taken under the trade laws of the United States and the effectiveness of such actions in achieving trade policy objectives.

(D) Important developments in other areas of trade for which there must be developed a proper policy response.

(3) The President shall take the advice received through consultation under paragraph (2) into account in determining the importance which should be placed on each major objective and negotiating position that should be adopted in order to achieve the overall trade policy of the United States.

(b) Advisory committee for trade policy and negotiations.

(1) The President shall establish an Advisory Committee for Trade Policy and Negotiations to provide overall policy advice on matters referred to in subsection (a). The committee shall be composed of not more than 45 individuals and shall include representatives of non-Federal governments,

labor, industry, agriculture, small business, service industries, retailers, non-governmental environmental and conservation organizations, and consumer interests. The committee shall be broadly representative of the key sectors and groups of the economy, particularly with respect to those sectors and groups which are affected by trade. Members of the committee shall be recommended by the United States Trade Representative and appointed by the President for a term of 2 years. An individual may be reappointed to committee for any number of terms. Appointments to the Committee shall be made without regard to political affiliation.

(2) The committee shall meet as needed at the call of the United States Trade Representative or at the call of two-thirds of the members of the committee. The chairman of the committee shall be elected by the committee from among its members.

(3) The United States Trade Representative shall make available to the committee such staff, information, personnel, and administrative services and assistance as it may reasonably require to carry out its activities.

(c) General policy, sectoral, or functional advisory committees.

(1) The President may establish individual general policy advisory committees for industry, labor, agriculture, services, investment, defense, and other interests, as appropriate, to provide general policy advice on matters referred to in subsection (a). Such committees shall, insofar as is practicable, be representative of all industry, labor, agricultural, service, investment, defense, and other interests, respectively, including small business interests, and shall be organized by the United States Trade Representative and the Secretaries of Commerce, Defense, Labor, Agriculture, the Treasury, or other executive departments, as appropriate. The members of such committees

shall be appointed by the United States Trade Representative in consultation with such Secretaries.

(2) The President shall establish such sectoral or functional advisory committees as may be appropriate. Such committees shall, insofar as is practicable, be representative of all industry, labor, agricultural, or service interests (including small business interests) in the sector or functional areas concerned. In organizing such committees, the United States Trade Representative and the Secretaries of Commerce, Labor, Agriculture, the Treasury, or other executive departments, as appropriate, shall—

(A) consult with interested private organizations; and

(B) take into account such factors as—

(i) patterns of actual and potential competition between United States industry and agriculture and foreign enterprise in international trade,

(ii) the character of the nontariff barriers and other distortions affecting such competition,

(iii) the necessity for reasonable limits on the number of such advisory committees,

(iv) the necessity that each committee be reasonably limited in size, and

(v) in the case of each sectoral committee, that the product lines covered by each committee be reasonably related.

(3) The President—

(A) may, if necessary, establish policy advisory committees representing non-Federal governmental interests to provide policy advice—

(i) on matters referred to in subsection (a), and

(ii) with respect to implementation of trade agreements, and

(B) shall include as members of committees established under subparagraph (A) representatives of non-Federal governmental interests if he finds such inclusion appropriate after consultation by the United States Trade Representative with such representatives.

(4) Appointments to each committee established under paragraph (1), (2), or (3) shall be made without regard to political affiliation.

(d) Policy, technical, and other advice and information. Committees established under subsection (c) shall meet at the call of the United States Trade Representative and the Secretaries of Agriculture, Commerce, Labor, Defense, or other executive departments, as appropriate, to provide policy advice, technical advice and information, and advice on other factors relevant to the matters referred to in subsection (a).

(e) Meeting of advisory committees at conclusion of negotiations.

(1) The Advisory Committee for Trade Policy and Negotiations, each appropriate policy advisory committee, and each sectoral or functional advisory committee, if the sector or area which such committee represents is affected, shall meet at the conclusion of negotiations for each trade agreement entered into under section 1102 of the Omnibus Trade and Competitiveness Act of 1988, to provide to the President, to Congress, and to the United States Trade Representative a report on such agreement. Each report that applies to a trade agreement entered into under section 1102 of the Omnibus Trade and Competitiveness Act of 1988 shall be provided under the preceding sentence not later than the date on which the President notifies the Congress under section 1103(a)(1)(A) of such Act of 1988 of his intention to enter into that agreement.

(2) The report of the Advisory Committee for Trade Policy and Negotiations and each appropriate policy advisory committee shall include an advisory opinion as to whether and to what extent the agreement promotes the economic interests of the United States and achieves the applicable overall and principal negotiating objectives set forth in section 1101 of the Omnibus Trade and Competitiveness Act of 1988, as appropriate.

(3) The report of the appropriate sectoral or functional committee under paragraph (1) shall include an advisory opinion as to whether the agreement provides for equity and reciprocity within the sector or within the functional area.

(f) Application of federal advisory committee act. The provisions of the Federal Advisory Committee Act apply—

(1) to the Advisory Committee for Trade Policy and Negotiations established under subsection (b); and

(2) to all other advisory committees which may be established under subsection (c); except that the meetings of advisory committees established under subsections (b) and (c) shall be exempt from the requirements of subsections (a) and (b) of sections 10 and 11 of the Federal Advisory Committee Act (relating to open meetings, public notice, public participation, and public availability of documents), whenever and to the extent it is determined by the President or his designee that such meetings will be concerned with matters the disclosure of which would seriously compromise the development by the United States Government of trade policy, priorities, negotiating objectives or bargaining positions with respect to matters referred to in subsection (a) of this section, and that meetings may be called of such special task forces, plenary meetings of chairmen, or other such groups made up of members of the committees established under subsections (b) and (c) of this section.

(g) Trade secrets and confidential information.

(1) Trade secrets and commercial or financial information which is privileged or confidential, and which is submitted in confidence by the private sector or non-Federal government to officers or employees of the United States in connection with trade negotiations, may be disclosed upon request to—

(A) officers and employees of the United States designated by the United States Trade Representative;

(B) members of the Committee on Ways and Means of the House of Representatives and the Committee on Finance of the Senate who are designated as official advisers under section 161(a)(1) or are designated by the chairmen of either such committee under section 161(b)(3)(A) and staff members of either such committee designated by the chairmen under section 161(b)(3)(A); and

(C) members of any committee of the House or Senate or any joint committee of Congress who are designated as advisers under section 161(a)(2) or designated by the chairman of such committee under section 161(b)(3)(B) and staff members of such committee designated under section 161(b)(3)(B), but disclosure may be made under this subparagraph only with respect to trade secrets or commercial or financial information that is relevant to trade policy matters or negotiations that are within the legislative jurisdiction of such committee;

for use in connection with matters referred to in subsection (a) of this section.

(2) Information other than that described in paragraph (1), and advice submitted in confidence by the private sector or non-Federal government to officers or employees of the United States, to the Advisory Committee for Trade Policy and Negotiations, or to any advisory committee established under subsection (c) of this section, in connection with matters referred to in subsection (a) of this section, may be disclosed upon request to—

(A) the individuals described in paragraph (1); and

(B) the appropriate advisory committee established under this section.

(3) Information submitted in confidence by officers or employees of the United States to the Advisory Committee for Trade Policy and Negotiations, or to any advisory committee established under subsection (c) of this section, may be disclosed in accordance with rules issued by the United States Trade Representative and the Secretaries of Commerce, Labor, Defense, Agriculture, or other executive departments, as appropriate, after consultation with the relevant advisory committees established under subsection (c) of this section. Such rules shall define the categories of information which require restricted or confidential handling by such committee considering the extent to which public disclosure of such information can reasonably be expected to prejudice the development of trade policy, priorities, or United States negotiating objectives. Such rules shall, to the maximum extent feasible, permit meaningful consultations by advisory committee members with persons affected by matters referred to in subsection (a) of this section.

(h) Advisory committee support. The United States Trade Representative, and the Secretaries of Commerce, Labor, Defense, Agriculture, the Treasury, or other executive departments, as appropriate, shall provide such staff, information, personnel, and administrative services and assistance to advisory committees established under subsection (c) of this section as such committees may reasonably require to carry out their activities.

(i) Consultation with advisory committees; procedures; nonacceptance of committee advice or recommendations. It shall be the responsibility of the United States Trade Representative, in conjunction with the Secretaries of Commerce, Labor, Agriculture, the Treasury, or other executive departments, as appropriate, to adopt procedures for consultation with and obtaining information and advice from the advisory committees established under subsection (c) of this section on a continuing and timely basis. Such consultation shall include the provision of information to each advisory committee as to—

(1) significant issues and developments; and

(2) overall negotiating objectives and positions of the United States and other parties;

with respect to matters referred to in subsection (a) of this section. The United States Trade Representative shall not be bound by the advice or recommendations of such advisory committees, but shall inform the advisory committees of significant departures from such advice or recommendations made. In addition, in the course of consultations with the Congress under this title, information on the advice and information provided by advisory committees shall be made available to congressional advisers.

(j) Private organizations or groups. In addition to any advisory committee established under this section, the President shall provide adequate, timely and continuing opportunity for the submission on an informal basis (and, if such information is submitted under the provisions of subsection (g) of this section, on a confidential basis) by private organizations or groups, representing government, labor, industry, agriculture, small business, service industries, consumer interests, and others, of statistics, data and other trade information, as well as policy recommendations, pertinent to any matter referred to in subsection (a) of this section.

(k) Scope of participation by members of advisory committees. Nothing contained in this section shall be construed to authorize or permit any individual to participate directly in any negotiation of any matters referred to in subsection (a) of this section. To the maximum extent practicable, the members of the committees established under subsections (b) and (c) of this section, and other appropriate parties, shall be informed and consulted before and during any such negotiations. They may be designated as advisors to a negotiating delegation, and may be permitted to participate in international meetings to the extent the head of the United States delegation deems appropriate. However, they may not speak or negotiate for the United States.

(*l*) Advisory committees established by department of agriculture. The provisions of title XVIII of the Food and Agriculture Act of 1977 (7 U.S.C. 2281 et seq.) shall not apply to any advisory committee established under subsection (c) of this section.

(m) Non-federal government defined. As used in this section, the term "non-Federal government" means—

(1) any State, territory, or possession of the United States, or the District of Columbia, or any political subdivision thereof; or

(2) any agency or instrumentality of any entity described in paragraph (1).

Chapter 4

Office of the United States Trade Representative

19 USC 2171

Sec. 141.   Structure, Functions, Powers, and Personnel

(a) Establishment within Executive Office of the President. There is established within the Executive Office of the President the Office of United States Trade Representative (hereinafter in this section referred to as the "Office").

(b) United States Trade Representative; Deputy United States Trade Representatives.

(1) The Office shall be headed by the United States Trade Representative who shall be appointed by the President, by and with the advice and consent of the Senate. As an exercise of the rulemaking power of the Senate, any nomination of the United States Trade Representative submitted to the Senate for confirmation, and referred to a committee, shall be referred to the Committee on Finance. The United States Trade Representative shall hold office at the pleasure of the President, shall be entitled to receive the same allowances as a chief of mission, and shall have the rank of Ambassador Extraordinary and Plenipotentiary.

(2) There shall be in the Office three Deputy United States Trade Representatives and one Chief Agricultural Negotiator who shall be appointed by the President, by and with the advice and consent of the Senate. As an exercise of the rulemaking power of the Senate, any nomination of a Deputy United States Trade Representative or the Chief Agricultural Negotiator submitted to the Senate for its advice and consent, and referred to a committee, shall be referred to the Committee on Finance. Each Deputy United States Trade Representative and the Chief Agricultural Negotiator

shall hold office at the pleasure of the President and shall have the rank of Ambassador.

(3) A person who has directly represented, aided, or advised a foreign entity (as defined by section 207(f)(3) of title 18, United States Code) in any trade negotiation, or trade dispute, with the United States may not be appointed as United States Trade Representative or as a Deputy United States Trade Representative.

(c) Duties of United States Trade Representative and Deputy United States Trade Representatives.

(1) The United States Trade Representative shall—

(A) have primary responsibility for developing, and for coordinating the implementation of, United States international trade policy, including commodity matters, and, to the extent they are related to international trade policy, direct investment matters;

(B) serve as the principal advisor to the President on international trade policy and shall advise the President on the impact of other policies of the United States Government on international trade;

(C) have lead responsibility for the conduct of, and shall be the chief representative of the United States for, international trade negotiations, including all negotiations on any matter considered under the auspices of the World Trade Organization, commodity and direct investment negotiations, in which the United States participates;

(D) issue and coordinate policy guidance to departments and agencies on basic issues of policy and interpretation arising in the exercise of international trade functions, including any matter considered under the auspices of the World Trade Organization, to the extent necessary to assure the coordination of international trade policy and consistent with any other law;

(E) act as the principal spokesman of the President on international trade;

(F) report directly to the President and the Congress regarding, and be responsible to the President and the Congress for the administration of, trade agreements programs;

(G) advise the President and Congress with respect to nontariff barriers to international trade, international commodity agreements, and other matters which are related to the trade agreements programs;

(H) be responsible for making reports to Congress with respect to matters referred to in subparagraphs (C) and (F);

(I) be chairman of the interagency trade organization established under section 242(a) of the Trade Expansion Act of 1962, and shall consult with and be advised by such organization in the performance of his functions; and

(J) in addition to those functions that are delegated to the United States Trade Representative as of the date of the enactment of the Omnibus Trade and Competitiveness Act of 1988 [enacted Aug. 23, 1988], be responsible for such other functions as the President may direct.

(2) It is the sense of Congress that the United States Trade Representative should—

(A) be the senior representative on any body that the President may establish for the purpose of providing to the President advice on overall economic policies in which international trade matters predominate; and

(B) be included as a participant in all economic summit and other international meetings at which international trade is a major topic.

(3) The United States Trade Representative may—

(A) delegate any of his functions, powers, and duties to such officers and employees of the Office as he may designate; and

(B) authorize such successive redelegations of such functions, powers, and duties to such officers and employees of the Office as he may deem appropriate.

(4) Each Deputy United States Trade Representative shall have as his principal function the conduct of trade negotiations under this Act and shall have such other functions as the United States Trade Representative may direct.

(5) The principal function of the Chief Agricultural Negotiator shall be to conduct trade negotiations and to enforce trade agreements relating to United States agricultural products and services. The Chief Agricultural Negotiator shall be a vigorous advocate on behalf of United States agricultural interests. The Chief Agricultural Negotiator shall perform such other functions as the United States Trade Representative may direct.

(d) Unfair trade practices; additional duties of Representative; advisory committee; definition.

(1) In carrying out subsection (c) with respect to unfair trade practices, the United States Trade Representative shall—

(A) coordinate the application of interagency resources to specific unfair trade practice cases;

(B) identify, and refer to the appropriate Federal department or agency for consideration with respect to action, each act, policy, or practice referred to in the report required under section 181(b), or otherwise known to the United States Trade Representative on the basis of other available information, that may be an unfair trade practice that either—

(i) is considered to be inconsistent with the provisions of any trade agreement and has a significant adverse impact on United States commerce, or

(ii) has a significant adverse impact on domestic firms or industries that are either too small or financially weak to initiate proceedings under the trade laws;

(C) identify practices having a significant adverse impact on United States commerce that the attainment of United States negotiating objectives would eliminate; and

(D) identify, on a biennial basis, those United States Government policies and practices that, if engaged in by a foreign government, might constitute unfair trade practices under United States law.

(2) For purposes of carrying out paragraph (1), the United States Trade Representative shall be assisted by an interagency unfair trade practices advisory committee composed of the Trade Representative, who shall chair the committee, and senior representatives of the following agencies, appointed by the respective heads of those agencies:

(A) The Bureau of Economics and Business Affairs of the Department of State.

(B) The United States and Foreign Commercial Services of the Department of Commerce.

(C) The International Trade Administration (other than the United States and Foreign Commercial Service) of the Department of Commerce.

(D) The Foreign Agricultural Service of the Department of Agriculture.

The United States Trade Representative may also request the advice of the United States International Trade Commission regarding the carrying out of paragraph (1).

(3) For purposes of this subsection, the term "unfair trade practice" means any act, policy, or practice that—

(A) may be a subsidy with respect to which countervailing duties may be imposed under subtitle A of title VII;

(B) may result in the sale or likely sale of foreign merchandise with respect to which antidumping duties may be imposed under subtitle B of title VII;

(C) may be either an unfair method of competition, or an unfair act in the importation of articles into the United States, that is unlawful under section 337; or

(D) may be an act, policy, or practice of a kind with respect to which action may be taken under title III of the Trade Act of 1974.

* * *

Chapter 5
Congressional Procedures With Respect to Presidential Actions
19 USC 2191

Sec. 151. Bills Implementing Trade Agreements on Nontariff Barriers and Resolutions Approving Commercial Agreements With Communist Countries

(a) **Rules of house of representatives and senate.** This section and sections 152 and 153 are enacted by the Congress—

(1) as an exercise of the rulemaking power of the House of Representatives and the Senate, respectively, and as such they are deemed a part of the rules of each House, respectively, but applicable only with respect to the

procedure to be followed in that House in the case of implementing bills described in subsection (b)(1) of this section, implementing revenue bills described in subsection (b)(2) of this section, approval resolutions described in subsection (b)(3) of this section, and resolutions described in subsections 152(a) and 153(a); and they supersede other rules only to the extent that they are inconsistent therewith; and

(2) with full recognition of the constitutional right of either House to change the rules (so far as relating to the procedure of that House) at any time, in the same manner and to the same extent as in the case of any other rule of that House.

(b) Definitions. For purposes of this section—

(1) The term "implementing bill" means only a bill of either House of Congress which is introduced as provided in subsection (c) of this section with respect to one or more trade agreements, or with respect to an extension described in section 282(c)(3) of the Uruguay Round Agreements Act, submitted to the House of Representatives and the Senate under section 102 of this Act, section 1103(a)(1) of the Omnibus Trade and Competitiveness Act of 1988, or section 282 of the Uruguay Round Agreements Act which contains—

(A) a provision approving such trade agreement or agreements or such extension,

(B) a provision approving the statement of administrative action (if any) proposed to implement such trade agreement or agreements, and

(C) if changes in existing laws or new statutory authority is required to implement such trade agreement or agreements or such extension, provisions, necessary or appropriate to implement such trade agreement or agreements, either repealing or amending existing laws or providing new statutory authority.

(2) The term "implementing revenue bill" or "approval resolution" means an implementing bill or resolution which contains one or more revenue measures by reason of which it must originate in the House of Representatives.

(3) The term "approval resolution" means only a joint resolution of the two Houses of the Congress, the matter after the resolving clause of which is as follows: "That the Congress approves the extension of nondiscriminatory treatment with respect to the products of _____ transmitted by the President to the Congress on _____.", the first blank space being filled with the name of the country involved and the second blank space being filled with the appropriate date.

(c) Introduction and referral.

(1) On the day on which a trade agreement or extension is submitted to the House of Representatives and the Senate under section 102 or section 282 of the Uruguay Round Agreements Act, the implementing bill submitted by the President with respect to such trade agreement or extension shall be introduced (by request) in the House by the majority leader of the House, for himself and the minority leader of the House, or by Members of the House designated by the majority leader and minority leader of the House; and shall be introduced (by request) in the Senate by the majority leader of the Senate,

for himself and the minority leader of the Senate, or by Members of the Senate designated by the majority leader and minority leader of the Senate. If either House is not in session on the day on which such a trade agreement or extension is submitted, the implementing bill shall be introduced in that House, as provided in the preceding sentence, on the first day thereafter on which that House is in session. Such bills shall be referred by the Presiding Officers of the respective Houses to the appropriate committee, or, in the case of a bill containing provisions within the jurisdiction of two or more committees, jointly to such committees for consideration of those provisions within their respective jurisdictions.

(2) On the day on which a bilateral commercial agreement, entered into under title IV of this Act after January 3, 1975, is transmitted to the House of Representatives and the Senate, an approval resolution with respect to such agreement shall be introduced (by request) in the House by the majority leader of the House, for himself and the minority leader of the House, or by Members of the House designated by the majority leader and minority leader of the House; and shall be introduced (by request) in the Senate by the majority leader of the Senate, for himself and the minority leader of the Senate, or by Members of the Senate designated by the majority leader and minority leader of the Senate. If either House is not in session on the day on which such an agreement is transmitted, the approval resolution with respect to such agreement shall be introduced in that House, as provided in the preceding sentence, on the first day thereafter on which that House is in session. The approval resolution introduced in the House shall be referred to the Committee on Ways and Means and the approval resolution introduced in the Senate shall be referred to the Committee on Finance.

(d) **Amendments prohibited.** No amendment to an implementing bill or approval resolution shall be in order in either the House of Representatives or the Senate; and no motion to suspend the application of this subsection shall be in order in either House, nor shall it be in order in either House for the Presiding Officer to entertain a request to suspend the application of this subsection by unanimous consent.

(e) Period for committee and floor consideration.

(1) Except as provided in paragraph (2), if the committee or committees of either House to which an implementing bill or approval resolution has been referred have not reported it at the close of the 45th day after its introduction, such committee or committees shall be automatically discharged from further consideration of the bill or resolution and it shall be placed on the appropriate calendar. A vote on final passage of the bill or resolution shall be taken in each House on or before the close of the 15th day after the bill or resolution is reported by the committee or committees of that House to which it was referred, or after such committee or committees have been discharged from further consideration of the bill or resolution. If prior to the passage by one House of an implementing bill or approval resolution of that House, that House receives the same implementing bill or approval resolution from the other House, then—

(A) the procedure in that House shall be the same as if no implementing bill or approval resolution had been received from the other House; but

(B) the vote on final passage shall be on the implementing bill or approval resolution of the other House.

(2) The provisions of paragraph (1) shall not apply in the Senate to an implementing revenue bill or resolution. An implementing revenue bill or resolution received from the House shall be referred to the appropriate committee or committees of the Senate. If such committee or committees have not reported such bill or resolution at the close of the 15th day after its receipt by the Senate (or, if later, before the close of the 45th day after the corresponding implementing revenue bill or resolution was introduced in the Senate), such committee or committees shall be automatically discharged from further consideration of such bill or resolution and it shall be placed on the calendar. A vote on final passage of such bill or resolution shall be taken in the Senate on or before the close of the 15th day after such bill or resolution is reported by the committee or committees of the Senate to which it was referred, or after such committee or committees have been discharged from further consideration of such bill or resolution.

(3) For purposes of paragraphs (1) and (2), in computing a number of days in either House, there shall be excluded any day on which that House is not in session.

(f) Floor consideration in the house.

(1) A motion in the House of Representatives to proceed to the consideration of an implementing bill or approval resolution shall be highly privileged and not debatable. An amendment to the motion shall not be in order, nor shall it be in order to move to reconsider the vote by which the motion is agreed to or disagreed to.

(2) Debate in the House of Representatives on an implementing bill or approval resolution shall be limited to not more than 20 hours, which shall be divided equally between those favoring and those opposing the bill or resolution. A motion further to limit debate shall not be debatable. It shall not be in order to move to recommit an implementing bill or approval resolution or to move to reconsider the vote by which an implementing bill or approval resolution is agreed to or disagreed to.

(3) Motions to postpone, made in the House of Representatives with respect to the consideration of an implementing bill or approval resolution, and motions to proceed to the consideration of other business, shall be decided without debate.

(4) All appeals from the decisions of the Chair relating to the application of the Rules of the House of Representatives to the procedure relating to an implementing bill or approval resolution shall be decided without debate.

(5) Except to the extent specifically provided in the preceding provisions of this subsection, consideration of an implementing bill or approval resolution shall be governed by the Rules of the House of Representatives applicable to other bills and resolutions in similar circumstances.

(g) Floor consideration in the senate.

(1) A motion in the Senate to proceed to the consideration of an implementing bill or approval resolution shall be privileged and not debatable.

An amendment to the motion shall not be in order, nor shall it be in order to move to reconsider the vote by which the motion is agreed to or disagreed to.

(2) Debate in the Senate on an implementing bill or approval resolution, and all debatable motions and appeals in connection therewith, shall be limited to not more than 20 hours. The time shall be equally divided between, and controlled by, the majority leader and the minority leader or their designees.

(3) Debate in the Senate on any debatable motion or appeal in connection with an implementing bill or approval resolution shall be limited to not more than 1 hour, to be equally divided between, and controlled by, the mover and the manager of the bill or resolution, except that in the event the manager of the bill or resolution is in favor of any such motion or appeal, the time in opposition thereto, shall be controlled by the minority leader or his designee. Such leaders, or either of them, may, from time under their control on the passage of an implementing bill or approval resolution, allot additional time to any Senator during the consideration of any debatable motion or appeal.

(4) A motion in the Senate to further limit debate is not debatable. A motion to recommit an implementing bill or approval resolution is not in order.

19 USC 2192

Sec. 152. Resolutions Disapproving Certain Actions

(a) Contents of resolutions.

(1) For purposes of this section, the term "resolution" means only—

(A) a joint resolution of the two Houses of the Congress, the matter after the resolving clause of which is as follows: "That the Congress does not approve the action taken by, or the determination of, the President under section 203 of the Trade Act of 1974 transmitted to the Congress on _____.", the blank space being filled with the appropriate date; and

(B) a joint resolution of either House of the Congress, the matter after the resolving clause of which is as follows: "That the Congress does not approve _____ transmitted to the Congress on _____.", with the first blank space being filled with in accordance with paragraph (2), and the second blank space being filled with the appropriate date.

(2) The second blank space referred to in paragraph (1)(B) shall be filled as follows: in the case of a resolution referred to in section 407(c)(2) with the phrase "the report of the President submitted under section_____of the Trade Act of 1974 with respect to _____" (with the first blank space being filled with "402(b)" or "409(b)" as appropriate, and the second blank space being filled with the name of the country involved).

(b) Reference to committees. All resolutions introduced in the House of Representatives shall be referred to the Committee on Ways and Means and all resolutions introduced in the Senate shall be referred to the Committee on Finance.

(c) Discharge of committees.

(1) If the committee of either House to which a resolution has been referred has not reported it at the end of 30 days after its introduction, not counting any day which is excluded under section 154(b), it is in order to move either to discharge the committee from further consideration of the resolution or to discharge the committee from further consideration of any other resolution introduced with respect to the same matter, except no motion to discharge

> (A) may only be made on the second legislative day after the calendar day on which the Member making the motion announces to the House his intention to do so; and

> (B) is not in order after the Committee has reported a resolution with respect to the same matter.

(2) A motion to discharge under paragraph (1) may be made only by an individual favoring the resolution, and is highly privileged in the House and privileged in the Senate; and debate thereon shall be limited to not more than 1 hour, the time to be divided in the House equally between those favoring and those opposing the resolution, and to be divided in the Senate equally between, and controlled by, the majority leader and the minority leader or their designees. An amendment to the motion is not in order, and it is not in order to move to reconsider the vote by which the motion is agreed to or disagreed to.

(d) Floor consideration in the house.

(1) A motion in the House of Representatives to proceed to the consideration of a resolution shall be highly privileged and not debatable. An amendment to the motion shall not be in order, nor shall it be in order to move to reconsider the vote by which the motion is agreed to or disagreed to.

(2) Debate in the House of Representatives on a resolution shall be limited to not more than 20 hours, which shall be divided equally between those favoring and those opposing the resolution. A motion further to limit debate shall not be debatable. No amendment to, or motion to recommit, the resolution shall be in order. It shall not be in order to move to reconsider the vote by which a resolution is agreed to or disagreed to.

(3) Motions to postpone, made in the House of Representatives with respect to the consideration of a resolution, and motions to proceed to the consideration of other business, shall be decided without debate.

(4) All appeals from the decisions of the Chair relating to the application of the Rules of the House of Representatives to the procedure relating to a resolution shall be decided without debate.

(5) Except to the extent specifically provided in the preceding provisions of this subsection, consideration of a resolution in the House of Representatives shall be governed by the Rules of the House of Representatives applicable to other resolutions in similar circumstances.

(e) Floor consideration in the senate.

(1) A motion in the Senate to proceed to the consideration of a resolution shall be privileged. An amendment to the motion shall not be in order, nor shall it be in order to move to reconsider the vote by which the motion is agreed to or disagreed to.

(2) Debate in the Senate on a resolution, and all debatable motions and appeals in connection therewith, shall be limited to not more than 20 hours, to be equally divided between, and controlled by, the majority leader and the minority leader or their designees.

(3) Debate in the Senate on any debatable motion or appeal in connection with a resolution shall be limited to not more than 1 hour, to be equally divided between, and controlled by, the mover and the manager of the resolution, except that in the event the manager of the resolution is in favor of any such motion or appeal, the time in opposition thereto, shall be controlled by the minority leader or his designee. Such leaders, or either of them, may, from time under their control on the passage of a resolution, allot additional time to any Senator during the consideration of any debatable motion or appeal.

(4) A motion in the Senate to further limit debate on a resolution, debatable motion, or appeal is not debatable. No amendment to, or motion to recommit, a resolution is in order in the Senate.

(f) Procedures in the Senate

(1) Except as otherwise provided in this section, the following procedures shall apply in the Senate to a resolution to which this section applies:

(A)(i) Except as provided in clause (ii), a resolution that has passed the House of Representatives shall, when received in the Senate, be referred to the Committee on Finance for consideration in accordance with this section.

(ii) If a resolution to which this section applies was introduced in the Senate before receipt of a resolution that has passed the House of Representatives, the resolution from the House of Representatives shall, when received in the Senate, be placed on the calendar. If this clause applies, the procedures in the Senate with respect to a resolution introduced in the Senate that contains the identical matter as the resolution that passed the House of Representatives shall be the same as if no resolution had been received from the House of Representatives, except that the vote on passage in the Senate shall be on the resolution that passed the House of Representatives.

(B) If the Senate passes a resolution before receiving from the House of Representatives a joint resolution that contains the identical matter, the joint resolution shall be held at the desk pending receipt of the joint resolution from the House of Representatives. Upon receipt of the joint resolution from the House of Representatives, such joint resolution shall be deemed to be read twice, considered, read the third time, and passed.

(2) If the texts of joint resolutions described in section 152 or 153(a), whichever is applicable, concerning any matter are not identical—

(A) the Senate shall vote passage on the resolution introduced in the Senate, and

(B) the text of the joint resolution passed by the Senate shall, immediately upon its passage (or, if later, upon receipt of the joint resolution passed by the House), be substituted for the text of the joint resolution passed by the House of Representatives, and such resolution, as amended, shall be returned with a request for a conference between the two Houses.

(3) Consideration in the Senate of any veto message with respect to a joint resolution described in subsection (a)(2)(B) of this section or section 153(a), including consideration of all debatable motions and appeals in connection therewith, shall be limited to 10 hours, to be equally divided between, and controlled by, the majority leader and the minority leader or their designees.

19 USC 2193

Sec. 153. Resolutions Relating to Extension of Waiver Authority Under Section 402

(a) Contents of resolution

For purposes of this section, the term "resolution" means only a joint resolution of the two Houses of Congress, the matter after the resolving clause of which is as follows: "That the Congress does not approve the extension of the authority contained in section 402(c) of the Trade Act of 1974 recommended by the President to the Congress on _____ with respect to _____.", with the first blank space being filled with the appropriate date, and the second blank space being filled with the names of those countries, if any, with respect to which such extension of authority is not approved, and with the clause beginning with "with respect to" being omitted if the extension of the authority is not approved with respect to any country.

(b) Application of rules of section 152; Exceptions.

(1) Except as provided in this section, the provisions of section 152 shall apply to resolutions described in subsection (a) of this section.

(2) In applying section 152(c)(1), all calendar days shall be counted.

(3) That part of section 152(d)(2) which provides that no amendment is in order shall not apply to any amendment to a resolution which is limited to striking out or inserting the names of one or more countries or to striking out or inserting a with-respect-to clause. Debate in the House of Representatives on any amendment to a resolution shall be limited to not more than 1 hour which shall be equally divided between those favoring and those opposing the amendment. A motion in the House to further limit debate on an amendment to a resolution is not debatable.

(4) That part of section 152(e)(4) which provides that no amendment is in order shall not apply to any amendment to a resolution which is limited to striking out or inserting the names of one or more countries or to striking out or inserting a with-respect-to clause. The time limit on a debate on a resolution in the Senate under section 152(e)(2) shall include all amendments to a resolution. Debate in the Senate on any amendment to a resolution shall be limited to not more than 1 hour, to be equally divided between, and controlled by, the mover and the manager of the resolution, except that in the event the manager of the resolution is in favor of any such amendment, the time in opposition thereto shall be controlled by the minority leader or his designee. The majority leader and minority leader may, from time under their control on the passage of a resolution, allot additional time to any Senator

during the consideration of any amendment. A motion in the Senate to further limit debate on an amendment to a resolution is not debatable.

(c) Consideration of second resolution not in order. It shall not be in order in either the House of Representatives or the Senate to consider a resolution with respect to a recommendation of the President under section 402(d) (other than a resolution described in subsection (a) of this section received from the other House), if that House has adopted a resolution with respect to the same recommendation.

(d) Procedures relating to conference reports in the Senate

(1) Consideration in the Senate of the conference report on any joint resolution described in subsection (a) of this section, including consideration of all amendments in disagreement (and all amendments thereto), and consideration of all debatable motions and appeals in connection therewith, shall be limited to 10 hours, to be equally divided between, and controlled by, the majority leader and the minority leader or their designees. Debate on any debatable motion or appeal related to the conference report shall be limited to 1 hour, to be equally divided between, and controlled by, the mover and the manager of the conference report.

(2) In any case in which there are amendments in disagreement, time on each amendment shall be limited to 30 minutes, to be equally divided between, and controlled by, the manager of the conference report and the minority leader or his designee. No amendment to any amendment in disagreement shall be received unless it is a germane amendment.

19 USC 2194

Sec. 154. Special Rules Relating to Congressional Procedures

(a) Whenever, pursuant to section 102(e), 203(b), 402(d), or 407(a) or (b), a document is required to be transmitted to the Congress, copies of such document shall be delivered to both Houses of Congress on the same day and shall be delivered to the Clerk of the House of Representatives if the House is not in session and to the Secretary of the Senate if the Senate is not in session.

(b) For purposes of sections 203(c), 407(c)(2), and 407(c)(3), the 90-day period referred to in such sections shall be computed by excluding—

(1) the days on which either House is not in session because of an adjournment of more than 3 days to a day certain or an adjournment of the Congress sine die, and

(2) any Saturday and Sunday, not excluded under paragraph (1), when either House is not in session.

Chapter 6

Congressional Liaison and Reports

19 USC 2211

Sec. 161. Congressional Advisers for Trade Policy and Negotiations
(a) Selection.

(1) At the beginning of each regular session of Congress, the Speaker of the House of Representatives, upon the recommendation of the chairman of

the Committee on Ways and Means, shall select 5 members (not more than 3 of whom are members of the same political party) of such committee, and the President pro tempore of the Senate, upon the recommendation of the chairman of the Committee on Finance, shall select 5 members (not more than 3 of whom are members of the same political party) of such committee, who shall be designated congressional advisers on trade policy and negotiations. They shall provide advice on the development of trade policy and priorities for the implementation thereof. They shall also be accredited by the United States Trade Representative on behalf of the President as official advisers to the United States delegations to international conferences, meetings, and negotiating sessions relating to trade agreements.

(2)(A) In addition to the advisers designated under paragraph (1) from the Committee on Ways and Means and the Committee on Finance—

> (i) the Speaker of the House may select additional members of the House, for designation as congressional advisers regarding specific trade policy matters or negotiations, from any other committee of the House or joint committee of Congress that has jurisdiction over legislation likely to be affected by such matters or negotiations; and

> (ii) the President pro tempore of the Senate may select additional members of the Senate, for designation as congressional advisers regarding specific trade policy matters or negotiations, from any other committee of the Senate or joint committee of Congress that has jurisdiction over legislation likely to be affected by such matters or negotiations.

Members of the House and Senate selected as congressional advisers under this subparagraph shall be accredited by the United States Trade Representative.

(B) Before designating any member under subparagraph (A), the Speaker or the President pro tempore shall consult with—

> (i) the chairman and ranking member of the Committee on Ways and Means or the Committee on Finance, as appropriate; and

> (ii) the chairman and ranking minority member of the committee from which the member will be selected.

(C) Not more than 3 members (not more than 2 of whom are members of the same political party) may be selected under this paragraph as advisers from any committee of Congress.

(b) Briefing.

(1) The United States Trade Representative shall keep each official adviser designated under subsection (a)(1) of this section currently informed on matters affecting the trade policy of the United States and, with respect to possible agreements, negotiating objectives, the status of negotiations in progress, and the nature of any changes in domestic law or the administration thereof which may be recommended to Congress to carry out any trade agreement or any requirement of, amendment to, or recommendation under, such agreement.

(2) The United States Trade Representative shall keep each official adviser designated under subsection (a)(2) of this section currently informed regarding the trade policy matters and negotiations with respect to which the adviser is designated.

(3)(A) The chairmen of the Committee on Ways and Means and the Committee on Finance may designate members (in addition to the official advisers under subsection (a)(1)) of this section and staff members of their respective committees who shall have access to the information provided to official advisers under paragraph (1).

(B) The Chairman of any committee of the House or Senate or any joint committee of Congress from which official advisers are selected under subsection (a)(2) of this section may designate other members of such committee, and staff members of such committee, who shall have access to the information provided to official advisers under paragraph (2).

(c) Committee consultation. The United States Trade Representative shall consult on a continuing basis with the Committee on Ways and Means of the House of Representatives, the Committee on Finance of the Senate, and the other appropriate committees of the House and Senate on the development, implementation, and administration of overall trade policy of the United States. Such consultations shall include, but are not limited to, the following elements of such policy:

(1) The principal multilateral and bilateral negotiating objectives and the progress being made toward their achievement.

(2) The implementation, administration, and effectiveness of recently concluded multilateral and bilateral trade agreements and resolution of trade disputes.

(3) The actions taken, and proposed to be taken, under the trade laws of the United States and the effectiveness, or anticipated effectiveness, of such actions in achieving trade policy objectives.

(4) The important developments and issues in other areas of trade for which there must be developed proper policy response.

When necessary, meetings shall be held with each Committee in executive session to review matters under negotiation.

19 USC 2212

Sec. 162. Transmission of Agreements to Congress

(a) As soon as practicable after a trade agreement entered into under chapter 1 or section 123 or 124 has entered into force with respect to the United States, the President shall, if he has not previously done so, transmit a copy of such trade agreement to each House of the Congress together with a statement, in the light of the advice of the International Trade Commission under section 131(b), if any, and of other relevant considerations, of his reasons for entering into the agreement.

(b) The President shall transmit to each Member of the Congress a summary of the information required to be transmitted to each House under subsection (a) of this section. For purposes of this subsection, the term "Member" includes any Delegate or Resident Commissioner.

19 USC 2213

Sec. 163.   Reports

(a) Annual report on trade agreements program and national trade policy agenda.

(1) The President shall submit to the Congress during each calendar year (but not later than March 1 of that year) a report on—

(A) the operation of the trade agreements program, and the provision of import relief and adjustment assistance to workers and firms, under this Act during the preceding calendar year; and

(B) the national trade policy agenda for the year in which the report is submitted.

(2) The report shall include, with respect to the matters referred to in paragraph (1)(A), information regarding—

(A) new trade negotiations;

(B) changes made in duties and nontariff barriers and other distortions of trade of the United States;

(C) reciprocal concessions obtained;

(D) changes in trade agreements (including the incorporation therein of actions taken for import relief and compensation provided therefor);

(E) the extension or withdrawal of nondiscriminatory treatment by the United States with respect to the products of foreign countries;

(F) the extension, modification, withdrawal, suspension, or limitation of preferential treatment to exports of developing countries;

(G) the results of actions to obtain the removal of foreign trade restrictions (including discriminatory restrictions) against United States exports and the removal of foreign practices which discriminate against United States service industries (including transportation and tourism) and investment;

(H) the measures being taken to seek the removal of other significant foreign import restrictions;

(I) each of the referrals made under section 141(d)(1)(B) and any action taken with respect to such referral;

(J) other information relating to the trade agreements program and to the agreements entered into thereunder; and

(K) the number of applications filed for adjustment assistance for workers and firms, the number of such applications which were approved, and the extent to which adjustment assistance has been provided under such approved applications.

(3)(A) The national trade policy agenda required under paragraph (1)(B) for the year in which a report is submitted shall be in the form of a statement of—

(i) the trade policy objectives and priorities of the United States for the year, and the reasons therefor;

(ii) the actions proposed, or anticipated, to be undertaken during the year to achieve such objectives and priorities, including, but not limited to, actions authorized under the trade laws and negotiations with foreign countries;

(iii) any proposed legislation necessary or appropriate to achieve any of such objectives or priorities; and

(iv) the progress that was made during the preceding year in achieving the trade policy objectives and priorities included in the statement provided for that year under this paragraph.

(B) The President may separately submit any information referred to in subparagraph (A) to the Congress in confidence if the President considers confidentiality appropriate.

(C) Before submitting the national trade policy agenda for any year, the President shall seek advice from the appropriate advisory committees established under section 135 and shall consult with the appropriate committees of the Congress.

(D) The United States Trade Representative (hereafter referred to in this section as the "Trade Representative") and other appropriate officials of the United States Government shall consult periodically with the appropriate committees of the Congress regarding the annual objectives and priorities set forth in each national trade policy agenda with respect to—

(i) the status and results of the actions that have been undertaken to achieve the objectives and priorities; and

(ii) any development which may require, or result in, changes to any of such objectives or priorities.

(b) Annual trade projection report.

(1) In order for the Congress to be informed of the impact of foreign trade barriers and macroeconomic factors on the balance of trade of the United States, the Trade Representative and the Secretary of the Treasury shall jointly prepare and submit to the Committee on Finance of the Senate and the Committee on Ways and Means of the House of Representatives (hereafter referred to in this subsection as the "Committees") on or before March 1 of each year a report which consists of—

(A) a review and analysis of—

(i) the merchandise balance of trade,

(ii) the goods and services balance of trade,

(iii) the balance on the current account,

(iv) the external debt position,

(v) the exchange rates,

(vi) the economic growth rates,

(vii) the deficit or surplus in the fiscal budget, and

(viii) the impact on United States trade of market barriers and other unfair practices, of countries that are major trading partners of the United States, including, as appropriate, groupings of such countries;

(B) projections for each of the economic factors described in subparagraph (A) (except those described in clauses (v) and (viii)) for each of the countries and groups of countries referred to in subparagraph (A) for the year in which the report is submitted and for the succeeding year; and

(C) conclusions and recommendations, based upon the projections referred to in subparagraph (B), for policy changes, including trade policy, exchange rate policy, fiscal policy, and other policies that should be implemented to improve the outlook.

(2) To the extent that subjects referred to in paragraph (1)(A), (B), or (C) are covered in the national trade policy agenda required under subsection (a)(1)(B) or in other reports required by this Act or other law, the Trade Representative and the Secretary of the Treasury may, as appropriate, draw on the information, analysis, and conclusions, if any, in those reports for the purposes of preparing the report required by this subsection.

(3) The Trade Representative and the Secretary of the Treasury shall consult with the Chairman of the Board of Governors of the Federal Reserve System in the preparation of each report required under this subsection.

(4) The Trade Representative and the Secretary of the Treasury may separately submit any information, analysis, or conclusion referred to in paragraph (1) to the Committees in confidence if the Trade Representative and the Secretary consider confidentiality appropriate.

(5) After submission of each report required under paragraph (1), the Trade Representative and the Secretary of the Treasury shall consult with each of the Committees with respect to the report.

(c) ITC Reports. The United States International Trade Commission shall submit to the Congress, at least once a year, a factual report on the operation of the trade agreements program.

* * *

Chapter 8

Identification of Market Barriers and Certain Unfair Trade Actions

19 USC 2241

Sec. 181. Estimates of Barriers to Market Access

(a) National trade estimates.

(1) In general. For calendar year 1988, and for each succeeding calendar year, the United States Trade Representative, through the interagency trade organization established pursuant to section 242(a) of the Trade Expansion Act of 1962 and with the assistance of the interagency advisory committee established under section 141(d)(2), shall—

(A) identify and analyze acts, policies, or practices of each foreign country which constitute significant barriers to, or distortions of—

(i) United States exports of goods or services (including agricultural commodities; and property protected by trademarks, patents, and copyrights exported or licensed by United States persons),

(ii) foreign direct investment by United States persons, especially if such investment has implications for trade in goods or services; and

(iii) United States electronic commerce,

(B) make an estimate of the trade-distorting impact on United States commerce of any act, policy, or practice identified under subparagraph (A); and

(C) make an estimate, if feasible, of—

(i) the value of additional goods and services of the United States,

(ii) the value of additional foreign direct investment by United States persons, and

(iii) the value of additional United States electronic commerce,

that would have been exported to, or invested in, or transacted with, each foreign country during such calendar year if each of such acts, policies, and practices of such country did not exist.

(2) Certain factors taken into account in making analysis and estimate. In making any analysis or estimate under paragraph (1), the Trade Representative shall take into account—

(A) the relative impact of the act, policy, or practice on United States commerce;

(B) the availability of information to document prices, market shares, and other matters necessary to demonstrate the effects of the act, policy, or practice;

(C) the extent to which such act, policy, or practice is subject to international agreements to which the United States is a party;

(D) any advice given through appropriate committees established pursuant to section 153 and

(E) the actual increase in—

(i) the value of goods and services of the United States exported to,

(ii) the value of foreign direct investment made in, and

(iii) the value of electronic commerce transacted with,

the foreign country during the calendar year for which the estimate under paragraph (1)(C) is made.

(3) Annual revisions and updates. The Trade Representative shall annually revise and update the analysis and estimate under paragraph (1).

(b) Report.

(1) On or before April 30, 1989, and on or before March 31 of each succeeding calendar year, the Trade Representative shall submit a report on the analysis and estimates made under subsection (a) for the calendar year preceding such calendar year (which shall be known as the "National Trade

Estimate") to the President, the Committee on Finance of the Senate, and appropriate committees of the House of Representatives.

(2) Reports to include information with respect to action being taken. The Trade Representative shall include in each report submitted under paragraph (1) information with respect to any action taken (or the reasons for no action taken) to eliminate any act, policy, or practice identified under subsection (a), including, but not limited to—

(A) any action under section 301,

(B) negotiations or consultations with foreign governments, or

(C) a section on foreign anticompetitive practices, the toleration of which by foreign governments is adversely affecting exports of United States goods or services.

(3) Consultation with Congress on trade policy priorities. The Trade Representative shall keep the committees described in paragraph (1) currently informed with respect to trade policy priorities for the purposes of expanding market opportunities. After the submission of the report required by paragraph (1), the Trade Representative shall also consult periodically with, and take into account the views of, the committees described in that paragraph regarding means to address the foreign trade barriers identified in the report, including the possible initiation of investigations under section 302 or other trade actions.

(c) Assistance of other agencies.

(1) Furnishing of information. The head of each department or agency of the executive branch of the Government, including any independent agency, is authorized and directed to furnish to the Trade Representative or to the appropriate agency, upon request, such data, reports, and other information as is necessary for the Trade Representative to carry out his functions under this section. In preparing the section of the report required by subsection (b)(2)(C), the Trade Representative shall consult in particular with the Attorney General.

(2) Restrictions on release or use of information. Nothing in this subsection shall authorize the release of information to, or the use of information by, the Trade Representative in a manner inconsistent with law or any procedure established pursuant thereto.

(3) Personnel and services. The head of any department, agency, or instrumentality of the United States may detail such personnel and may furnish such services, with or without reimbursement, as the Trade Representative may request to assist in carrying out his functions.

(d) Electronic commerce. For purposes of this section, the term "electronic commerce" has the meaning given that term in section 1104(3) of the Internet Tax Freedom Act.

19 USC 2242

Sec. 182. Identification of Countries That Deny Adequate Protection, or Market Access, for Intellectual Property Rights

(a) In general. By no later than the date that is 30 days after the date on which the annual report is submitted to Congressional committees under section 181(b), the United States Trade Representative (hereafter in this section referred to as the "Trade Representative") shall identify—

(1) those foreign countries that—

(A) deny adequate and effective protection of intellectual property rights, or

(B) deny fair and equitable market access to United States persons that rely upon intellectual property protection, and

(2) those foreign countries identified under paragraph (1) that are determined by the Trade Representative to be priority foreign countries.

(b) Special rules for identifications.

(1) In identifying priority foreign countries under subsection (a)(2), the Trade Representative shall only identify those foreign countries—

(A) that have the most onerous or egregious acts, policies, or practices that—

(i) deny adequate and effective intellectual property rights, or

(ii) deny fair and equitable market access to United States persons that rely upon intellectual property protection,

(B) whose acts, policies, or practices described in subparagraph (A) have the greatest adverse impact (actual or potential) on the relevant United States products, and

(C) that are not—

(i) entering into good faith negotiations, or

(ii) making significant progress in bilateral or multilateral negotiations,

to provide adequate and effective protection of intellectual property rights.

(2) In identifying priority foreign countries under subsection (a)(2), the Trade Representative shall—

(A) consult with the Register of Copyrights, the Under Secretary of Commerce for Intellectual Property and Director of the United States Patent and Trademark Office, other appropriate officers of the Federal Government, and

(B) take into account information from such sources as may be available to the Trade Representative and such information as may be submitted to the Trade Representative by interested persons, including information contained in reports submitted under section 181(b) and petitions submitted under section 302.

(3) The Trade Representative may identify a foreign country under subsection (a)(1)(B) only if the Trade Representative finds that there is a factual basis for the denial of fair and equitable market access as a result of the violation of international law or agreement, or the existence of barriers, referred to in subsection (d)(3).

(4) In identifying foreign countries under paragraphs (1) and (2) of subsection (a), the Trade Representative shall take into account—

(A) the history of intellectual property laws and practices of the foreign country, including any previous identification under subsection (a)(2), and

(B) the history of efforts of the United States, and the response of the foreign country, to achieve adequate and effective protection and enforcement of intellectual property rights.

(c) Revocations and additional identifications.

(1) The Trade Representative may at any time—

(A) revoke the identification of any foreign country as a priority foreign country under this section, or

(B) identify any foreign country as a priority foreign country under this section,

if information available to the Trade Representative indicates that such action is appropriate.

(2) The Trade Representative shall include in the semiannual report submitted to the Congress under section 309(3) a detailed explanation of the reasons for the revocation under paragraph (1) of the identification of any foreign country as a priority foreign country under this section.

(d) Definitions. For purposes of this section—

(1) The term "persons that rely upon intellectual property protection" means persons involved in—

(A) the creation, production or licensing of works of authorship (within the meaning of sections 102 and 103 of title 17, United States Code) that are copyrighted, or

(B) the manufacture of products that are patented or for which there are process patents.

(2) A foreign country denies adequate and effective protection of intellectual property rights if the foreign country denies adequate and effective means under the laws of the foreign country for persons who are not citizens or nationals of such foreign country to secure, exercise, and enforce rights relating to patents, process patents, registered trademarks, copyrights and mask works.

(3) A foreign country denies fair and equitable market access if the foreign country effectively denies access to a market for a product protected by a copyright or related right, patent, trademark, mask work, trade secret, or plant breeder's right, through the use of laws, procedures, practices, or regulations which—

(A) violate provisions of international law or international agreements to which both the United States and the foreign country are parties, or

(B) constitute discriminatory nontariff trade barriers.

(4) A foreign country may be determined to deny adequate and effective protection of intellectual property rights, notwithstanding the fact that the foreign country may be in compliance with the specific obligations of the

Agreement on Trade–Related Aspects of Intellectual Property Rights referred to in section 101(d)(15) of the Uruguay Round Agreements Act.

(e) Publication. The Trade Representative shall publish in the Federal Register a list of foreign countries identified under subsection (a) and shall make such revisions to the list as may be required by reason of action under subsection (c).

(f) Special rule for actions affecting United States cultural industries.

(1) In general. By no later than the date that is 30 days after the date on which the annual report is submitted to Congressional committees under section 181(b), the Trade Representative shall identify any act, policy, or practice of Canada which—

(A) affects cultural industries,

(B) is adopted or expanded after December 17, 1992, and

(C) is actionable under article 2106 of the North American Free Trade Agreement.

(2) Special rules for identifications. For purposes of section 302(b)(2)(A), an act, policy, or practice identified under this subsection shall be treated as an act, policy, or practice that is the basis for identification of a country under subsection (a)(2), unless the United States has already taken action pursuant to article 2106 of the North American Free Trade Agreement in response to such act, policy, or practice. In deciding whether to identify an act, policy, or practice under paragraph (1), the Trade Representative shall—

(A) consult with and take into account the views of representatives of the relevant domestic industries, appropriate committees established pursuant to section 135, and appropriate officers of the Federal Government, and

(B) take into account the information from such sources as may be available to the Trade Representative and such information as may be submitted to the Trade Representative by interested persons, including information contained in reports submitted under section 181(b).

(3) Cultural industries. For purposes of this subsection, the term "cultural industries" means persons engaged in any of the following activities:

(A) The publication, distribution, or sale of books, magazines, periodicals, or newspapers in print or machine readable form but not including the sole activity of printing or typesetting any of the foregoing.

(B) The production, distribution, sale, or exhibition of film or video recordings.

(C) The production, distribution, sale, or exhibition of audio or video music recordings.

(D) The publication, distribution, or sale of music in print or machine readable form.

(E) Radio communications in which the transmissions are intended for direct reception by the general public, and all radio, television, and cable broadcasting undertakings and all satellite programming and broadcast network services.

(g) **Annual report.** The Trade Representative shall, by not later than the date by which countries are identified under subsection (a), transmit to the Committee on Ways and Means of the House of Representatives and the Committee on Finance of the Senate, a report on actions taken under this section during the 12 months preceding such report, and the reasons for such actions, including a description of progress made in achieving improved intellectual property protection and market access for persons relying on intellectual property rights.

TITLE II
RELIEF FROM INJURY CAUSED BY IMPORT COMPETITION
Chapter 1
Positive Adjustment by Industries Injured by Imports
19 USC 2251

Sec. 201.   Action to Facilitate Positive Adjustment to Import Competition

(a) **Presidential action.** If the United States International Trade Commission (hereinafter referred to in this chapter as the "Commission") determines under section 202(b) that an article is being imported into the United States in such increased quantities as to be a substantial cause of serious injury, or the threat thereof, to the domestic industry producing an article like or directly competitive with the imported article, the President, in accordance with this chapter, shall take all appropriate and feasible action within his power which the President determines will facilitate efforts by the domestic industry to make a positive adjustment to import competition and provide greater economic and social benefits than costs.

(b) **Positive adjustment to import competition.**

(1) For purposes of this chapter, a positive adjustment to import competition occurs when—

(A) the domestic industry—

(i) is able to compete successfully with imports after actions taken under section 204 terminate, or

(ii) the domestic industry experiences an orderly transfer of resources to other productive pursuits; and

(B) dislocated workers in the industry experience an orderly transition to productive pursuits.

(2) The domestic industry may be considered to have made a positive adjustment to import competition even though the industry is not of the same size and composition as the industry at the time the investigation was initiated under section 202(b).

19 USC 2252

Sec. 202.   Investigations, Determinations, and Recommendations by Commission

(a) **Petitions and adjustment plans.**

(1) A petition requesting action under this chapter for the purpose of facilitating positive adjustment to import competition may be filed with the

Commission by an entity, including a trade association, firm, certified or recognized union, or group of workers, which is representative of an industry.

(2) A petition under paragraph (1)—

(A) shall include a statement describing the specific purposes for which action is being sought, which may include facilitating the orderly transfer of resources to more productive pursuits, enhancing competitiveness, or other means of adjustment to new conditions of competition; and

(B) may—

(i) subject to subsection (d)(1)(C)(i) of this section, request provisional relief under subsection (d)(1) of this section; or

(ii) request provisional relief under subsection (d)(2).

(3) Whenever a petition is filed under paragraph (1), the Commission shall promptly transmit copies of the petition to the Office of the United States Trade Representative and other Federal agencies directly concerned.

(4) A petitioner under paragraph (1) may submit to the Commission and the United States Trade Representative (hereafter in this chapter referred to as the "Trade Representative"), either with the petition, or at any time within 120 days after the date of filing of the petition, a plan to facilitate positive adjustment to import competition.

(5)(A) Before submitting an adjustment plan under paragraph (4), the petitioner and other entities referred to in paragraph (1) that wish to participate may consult with the Trade Representative and the officers and employees of any Federal agency that is considered appropriate by the Trade Representative, for purposes of evaluating the adequacy of the proposals being considered for inclusion in the plan in relation to specific actions that may be taken under this chapter.

(B) A request for any consultation under subparagraph (A) must be made to the Trade Representative. Upon receiving such a request, the Trade Representative shall confer with the petitioner and provide such assistance, including publication of appropriate notice in the Federal Register, as may be practicable in obtaining other participants in the consultation. No consultation may occur under subparagraph (A) unless the Trade Representative, or his delegate, is in attendance.

(6)(A) In the course of any investigation under subsection (b) of this section, the Commission shall seek information (on a confidential basis, to the extent appropriate) on actions being taken, or planned to be taken, or both, by firms and workers in the industry to make a positive adjustment to import competition.

(B) Regardless whether an adjustment plan is submitted under paragraph (4) by the petitioner, if the Commission makes an affirmative determination under subsection (b), any—

(i) firm in the domestic industry;

(ii) certified or recognized union or group of workers in the domestic industry;

(iii) local community;

(iv) trade association representing the domestic industry; or

(v) any other person or group of persons,

may, individually, submit to the Commission commitments regarding actions such persons and entities intend to take to facilitate positive adjustment to import competition.

(7) Nothing in paragraphs (5) and (6) may be construed to provide immunity under the antitrust laws.

(8) The procedures concerning the release of confidential business information set forth in section 1332(g) of this title shall apply with respect to information received by the Commission in the course of investigations conducted under this part and part 1 of title III of the North American Free Trade Agreement Implementation Act [19 U.S.C.A. s 3351 et seq.].

* * *

(b) Investigations and determinations by commission.

(1)(A) Upon the filing of a petition under subsection (a), the request of the President or the Trade Representative, the resolution of either the Committee on Ways and Means of the House of Representatives or the Committee on Finance of the Senate, or on its own motion, the Commission shall promptly make an investigation to determine whether an article is being imported into the United States in such increased quantities as to be a substantial cause of serious injury, or the threat thereof, to the domestic industry producing an article like or directly competitive with the imported article.

(B) For purposes of this section, the term "substantial cause" means a cause which is important and not less than any other cause.

(2)(A) Except as provided in subparagraph (B), the Commission shall make the determination under paragraph (1) within 120 days after the date on which the petition is filed, the request or resolution is received, or the motion is adopted, as the case may be.

(B) If before the 100th day after a petition is filed under subsection (a)(1) of this section the Commission determines that the investigation is extraordinarily complicated, the Commission shall make the determination under paragraph (1) within 150 days after the date referred to in subparagraph (A).

(3)(A) If the Commission makes an affirmative determination under paragraph (1) and the petitioner alleges the existence of critical circumstances, the Commission shall make a determination regarding such allegation—

(i) on or before the 120th day after the day on which the petition was filed, if such allegation was included in the petition on or before the 90th day after such filing date; or

(ii) on or before the date the report required under subsection (f) regarding the determination is submitted to the President, if such allegation was included in the petition after the 90th day, and on or before the 150th day, after such filing date.

(B) For purposes of this paragraph and subsection (d)(2), critical circumstances exist if a substantial increase in imports (either actual or relative to domestic production) over a relatively short period of time has led to circumstances in which a delay in taking action under this chapter would cause harm that would significantly impair the effectiveness of such action.

(4) In the course of any proceeding under this subsection, the Commission shall, after reasonable notice, hold public hearings and shall afford interested parties and consumers an opportunity to be present, to present evidence, to comment on the adjustment plan, if any, submitted under subsection (a) of this section, and to be heard at such hearings.

(c) Factors applied in making determinations.

(1) In making determinations under subsection (b) of this section, the Commission shall take into account all economic factors which it considers relevant, including (but not limited to)—

(A) with respect to serious injury—

(i) the significant idling of productive facilities in the domestic industry,

(ii) the inability of a significant number of firms to carry out domestic production operations at a reasonable level of profit, and

(iii) significant unemployment or underemployment within the domestic industry;

(B) with respect to threat of serious injury—

(i) a decline in sales or market share, a higher and growing inventory (whether maintained by domestic producers, importers, wholesalers, or retailers), and a downward trend in production, profits, wages, or employment (or increasing underemployment) in the domestic industry,

(ii) the extent to which firms in the domestic industry are unable to generate adequate capital to finance the modernization of their domestic plants and equipment, or are unable to maintain existing levels of expenditures for research and development,

(iii) the extent to which the United States market is the focal point for the diversion of exports of the article concerned by reason of restraints on exports of such article to, or on imports of such article into, third country markets; and

(C) with respect to substantial cause, an increase in imports (either actual or relative to domestic production) and a decline in the proportion of the domestic market supplied by domestic producers.

(2) In making determinations under subsection (b) of this section, the Commission shall—

(A) consider the condition of the domestic industry over the course of the relevant business cycle, but may not aggregate the causes of declining demand associated with a recession or economic downturn in the United States economy into a single cause of serious injury or threat of injury; and

(B) examine factors other than imports which may be a cause of serious injury, or threat of serious injury, to the domestic industry.

The Commission shall include the results of its examination under subparagraph (B) in the report submitted by the Commission to the President under subsection (e) of this section.

(3) The presence or absence of any factor which the Commission is required to evaluate in subparagraphs (A) and (B) of paragraph (1) is not necessarily dispositive of whether an article is being imported into the United States in such increased quantities as to be a substantial cause of serious injury, or the threat thereof, to the domestic industry.

(4) For purposes of subsection (b) of this section, in determining the domestic industry producing an article like or directly competitive with an imported article, the Commission—

(A) to the extent information is available, shall, in the case of a domestic producer which also imports, treat as part of such domestic industry only its domestic production;

(B) may, in the case of a domestic producer which produces more than one article, treat as part of such domestic industry only that portion or subdivision of the producer which produces the like or directly competitive article; and

(C) may, in the case of one or more domestic producers which produce a like or directly competitive article in a major geographic area of the United States and whose production facilities in such area for such article constitute a substantial portion of the domestic industry in the United States and primarily serve the market in such area, and where the imports are concentrated in such area, treat as such domestic industry only that segment of the production located in such area.

(5) In the course of any proceeding under this subsection, the Commission shall investigate any factor which in its judgment may be contributing to increased imports of the article under investigation. Whenever in the course of its investigation the Commission has reason to believe that the increased imports are attributable in part to circumstances which come within the purview of subtitles A and B of title VII or section 337 of the Tariff Act of 1930, or other remedial provisions of law, the Commission shall promptly notify the appropriate agency so that such action may be taken as is otherwise authorized by such provisions of law.

(6) For purposes of this section:

(A) The term "domestic industry" includes producers located in the United States insular possession.

(B) The term "significant idling of productive facilities" includes the closing of plants or the underutilization of production capacity.

(d) Provisional relief.

(1)(A) An entity representing a domestic industry that produces a perishable agricultural product or citrus product that is like or directly competitive with an imported perishable agricultural product or citrus product may file a request with the Trade Representative for the monitoring of imports of that product under subparagraph (B). Within 21 days after receiving the request, the Trade Representative shall determine if—

(i) the imported product is a perishable agricultural product or citrus product; and

(ii) there is a reasonable indication that such product is being imported into the United States in such increased quantities as to be, or likely to be, a substantial cause of serious injury, or the threat thereof, to such domestic industry.

(B) If the determinations under subparagraph (A)(i) and (ii) are affirmative, the Trade Representative shall request, under section 332(g) of the Tariff Act of 1930, the Commission to monitor and investigate the imports concerned for a period not to exceed 2 years. The monitoring and investigation may include the collection and analysis of information that would expedite an investigation under subsection (b) of this section.

(C) If a petition filed under subsection (a) of this section—

(i) alleges injury from imports of a perishable agricultural product or citrus product that has been, on the date the allegation is included in the petition, subject to monitoring by the Commission under subparagraph (B) for not less than 90 days; and

(ii) requests that provisional relief be provided under this subsection with respect to such imports;

the Commission shall, not later than the 21st day after the day on which the request was filed, make a determination, on the basis of available information, whether increased imports (either actual or relative to domestic production) of the perishable agricultural product or citrus product are a substantial cause of serious injury, or the threat thereof, to the domestic industry producing a like or directly competitive perishable product, and whether either—

(I) the serious injury is likely to be difficult to repair by reason of perishability of the like or directly competitive agricultural product; or

(II) the serious injury cannot be timely prevented through investigation under subsection (b) of this section and action under section 203.

(D) At the request of the Commission, the Secretary of Agriculture shall promptly provide to the Commission any relevant information that the Department of Agriculture may have for purposes of making determinations and findings under this subsection.

(E) Whenever the Commission makes an affirmative preliminary determination under subparagraph (C), the Commission shall find the amount or extent of provisional relief that is necessary to prevent or remedy the serious injury. In carrying out this subparagraph, the Commission shall give preference to increasing or imposing a duty on imports, if such form of relief is feasible and would prevent or remedy the serious injury.

(F) The Commission shall immediately report to the President its determination under subparagraph (C) and, if the determination is affirmative, the finding under subparagraph (E).

(G) Within 7 days after receiving a report from the Commission under subparagraph (F) containing an affirmative determination, the President, if he considers provisional relief to be warranted and after taking into account the finding of the Commission under subparagraph (E), shall proclaim such provisional relief that the President considers necessary to prevent or remedy the serious injury.

(2)(A) The Commission shall, at the same time it makes an affirmative determination under subsection (b)(3)(A) of this section regarding the existence of critical circumstances, find the amount or extent of provisional relief that is appropriate to address such critical circumstances. The Commission shall immediately report to the President each such affirmative determination and finding.

(B) After receiving a report from the Commission under subparagraph (A), the President shall, within 7 days after the day on which the report is received and after taking into account the finding of the Commission under subparagraph (A), proclaim such provisional relief, if any, that the President considers appropriate to address the critical circumstances.

(3) If provisional relief is proclaimed under paragraph (1)(G) or (2)(B) in the form of an increase, or the imposition of, a duty, the President shall order the suspension of liquidation of all imported articles subject to the affirmative determination under paragraph (1)(C) or subsection (b)(1) of this section, as the case may be, that are entered, or withdrawn from warehouse for consumption, on or after the date of the determination.

(4)(A) Any provisional relief implemented under this subsection with respect to an imported article shall terminate on the day on which—

(i) if such relief was proclaimed under paragraph (1)(G), the Commission makes a negative determination under subsection (b) regarding injury or the threat thereof by imports of such article;

(ii) action described in section 203(a)(3)(A) or (C) takes effect under section 203 with respect to such article;

(iii) a decision by the President not to take any action under section 203(a) with respect to such article becomes final; or

(iv) whenever the President determines that, because of changed circumstances, such relief is no longer warranted.

(B) Any suspension of liquidation ordered under paragraph (3) with respect to an imported article shall terminate on the day on which provisional relief is terminated under subparagraph (A) with respect to the article.

(C) If an increase in, or the imposition of, a duty that is proclaimed under section 203 on an imported article is different from a duty increase or imposition that was proclaimed for such an article under this section, then the entry of any such article for which liquidation was suspended under paragraph (3) shall be liquidated at whichever of such rates of duty is lower.

(D) If provisional relief in the form of an increase in, or the imposition of, a duty is proclaimed under this section with respect to an imported article and neither a duty increase nor a duty imposition is proclaimed under section 203 regarding such article, the entry of any such article for which liquidation was suspended under paragraph (3) may be liquidated at the rate of duty that applied before provisional relief was provided.

(5) For purposes of this subsection:

(A) The term "citrus product" means any processed oranges or grapefruit, or any orange or grapefruit juice, including concentrate.

(B) A perishable agricultural product is any agricultural article, including livestock, regarding which the Trade Representative considers action under this section to be appropriate after taking into account—

(i) whether the article has—

(I) a short shelf life,

(II) a short growing season, or

(III) a short marketing period,

(ii) whether the article is treated as a perishable product under any other Federal law or regulation; and

(iii) any other factor considered appropriate by the Trade Representative.

The presence or absence of any factor which the Trade Representative is required to take into account under clause (i), (ii), or (iii) is not necessarily dispositive of whether an article is a perishable agricultural product.

(B) The term "provisional relief" means—

(i) any increase in, or imposition of, any duty;

(ii) any modification or imposition of any quantitative restriction on the importation of an article into the United States; or

(iii) any combination of actions under clauses (i) and (ii).

(e) Commission recommendations.

(1) If the Commission makes an affirmative determination under subsection (b)(1) of this section, the Commission shall also recommend the action that would address the serious injury, or threat thereof, to the domestic industry and be most effective in facilitating the efforts of the domestic industry to make a positive adjustment to import competition.

(2) The Commission is authorized to recommend under paragraph (1)—

(A) an increase in, or the imposition of, any duty on the imported article;

(B) a tariff-rate quota on the article;

(C) a modification or imposition of any quantitative restriction on the importation of the article into the United States;

(D) one or more appropriate adjustment measures, including the provision of trade adjustment assistance under chapter 2; or

(E) any combination of the actions described in subparagraphs (A) through (D).

(3) The Commission shall specify the type, amount, and duration of the action recommended by it under paragraph (1). The limitations set forth in section 203(e) are applicable to the action recommended by the Commission.

(4) In addition to the recommendation made under paragraph (1), the Commission may also recommend that the President—

(A) initiate international negotiations to address the underlying cause of the increase in imports of the article or otherwise to alleviate the injury or threat; or

(B) implement any other action authorized under law that is likely to facilitate positive adjustment to import competition.

(5) For purposes of making its recommendation under this subsection, the Commission shall—

(A) after reasonable notice, hold a public hearing at which all interested parties shall be provided an opportunity to present testimony and evidence; and

(B) take into account—

(i) the form and amount of action described in paragraph (2)(A), (B), and (C) that would prevent or remedy the injury or threat thereof,

(ii) the objectives and actions specified in the adjustment plan, if any, submitted under subsection (a)(4) of this section,

(iii) any individual commitment that was submitted to the Commission under subsection (a)(6) of this section,

(iv) any information available to the Commission concerning the conditions of competition in domestic and world markets, and likely developments affecting such conditions during the period for which action is being requested, and

(v) whether international negotiations may be constructive to address the injury or threat thereof or to facilitate adjustment.

(6) Only those members of the Commission who agreed to the affirmative determination under subsection (b) of this section are eligible to vote on the recommendation required to be made under paragraph (1) or that may be made under paragraph (3).* Members of the Commission who did not agree to the affirmative determination may submit, in the report required under subsection (f) of this section, separate views regarding what action, if any, should be taken under section 203.

(f) Report by commission.

(1) The Commission shall submit to the President a report on each investigation undertaken under subsection (b) of this section. The report shall be submitted at the earliest practicable time, but not later than 180 days after the date on which the petition is filed, the request or resolution is received, or the motion is adopted, as the case may be.

* Should probably be paragraph (4).

(2) The Commission shall include in the report required under paragraph (1) the following:

(A) The determination made under subsection (b) of this section and an explanation of the basis for the determination.

(B) If the determination under subsection (b) of this section is affirmative, the recommendations for action made under subsection (e) of this section and an explanation of the basis for each recommendation.

(C) Any dissenting or separate views by members of the Commission regarding the determination and any recommendation referred to in subparagraphs (A) and (B).

(D) The findings required to be included in the report under subsection (c)(2).

(E) A copy of the adjustment plan, if any, submitted under section 201(b)(4).

(F) Commitments submitted, and information obtained, by the Commission regarding steps that firms and workers in the domestic industry are taking, or plan to take, to facilitate positive adjustment to import competition.

(G) A description of—

(i) the short- and long-term effects that implementation of the action recommended under subsection (e) of this section are likely to have on the petitioning domestic industry, on other domestic industries, and on consumers, and

(ii) the short- and long-term effects of not taking the recommended action on the petitioning domestic industry, its workers and the communities where production facilities of such industry is [sic] located, and on other domestic industries.

(3) The Commission, after submitting a report to the President under paragraph (1), shall promptly make it available to the public (with the exception of the confidential information obtained under section (a)(6)(B) of this section and any other information which the Commission determines to be confidential) and cause a summary thereof to be published in the Federal Register.

(g) **Expedited consideration of adjustment assistance petitions.** If the Commission makes an affirmative determination under subsection (b)(1) of this section, the Commission shall promptly notify the Secretary of Labor and the Secretary of Commerce of the determination. After receiving such notification—

(1) the Secretary of Labor shall give expedited consideration to petitions by workers in the domestic industry for certification for eligibility to apply for adjustment assistance under chapter 2; and

(2) the Secretary of Commerce shall give expedited consideration to petitions by firms in the domestic industry for certification of eligibility to apply for adjustment assistance under chapter 3.

(h) **Limitations on investigations.**

(1) Except for good cause determined by the Commission to exist, no investigation for the purposes of this section shall be made with respect to the same subject matter as a previous investigation under this chapter, unless 1

year has elapsed since the Commission made its report to the President of the results of such previous investigation.

(2) If an article was the subject of an investigation under this section that resulted in any action described in section 203(a)(3)(A), (B), (C), or (E) being taken under section 203, no other investigation under this chapter may be initiated with respect to such article while such action is in effect or during the period beginning on the date on which such action terminates that is equal in duration to the period during which such action was in effect.

19 USC 2253

Sec. 203.   Action by President After Determination of Import Injury

(a) In general.

(1)(A) After receiving a report under section 202(f) containing an affirmative finding regarding serious injury, or the threat thereof, to a domestic industry, the President shall take all appropriate and feasible action within his power which the President determines will facilitate efforts by the domestic industry to make a positive adjustment to import competition and provide greater economic and social benefits than costs.

(B) The action taken by the President under subparagraph (A) shall be to such extent, and for such duration, subject to subsection (e)(1) of this section, that the President determines to be appropriate and feasible under such subparagraph.

(C) The interagency trade organization established under section 242(a) of the Trade Expansion Act of 1962 shall, with respect to each affirmative determination reported under section 202(f), make a recommendation to the President as to what action the President should take under subparagraph (A).

(2) In determining what action to take under paragraph (1), the President shall take into account—

(A) the recommendation and report of the Commission;

(B) the extent to which workers and firms in the domestic industry are—

(i) benefiting from adjustment assistance and other manpower programs, and

(ii) engaged in worker retraining efforts;

(C) the efforts being made, or to be implemented, by the domestic industry (including the efforts included in any adjustment plan or commitment submitted to the Commission under section 202(a)) to make a positive adjustment to import competition;

(D) the probable effectiveness of the actions authorized under paragraph (3) to facilitate positive adjustment to import competition;

(E) the short- and long-term economic and social costs of the actions authorized under paragraph (3) relative to their short- and long-term economic and social benefits and other considerations relative to the position of the domestic industry in the United States economy;

(F) other factors related to the national economic interest of the United States, including, but not limited to—

(i) the economic and social costs which would be incurred by taxpayers, communities, and workers if import relief were not provided under this chapter,

(ii) the effect of the implementation of actions under this section on consumers and on competition in domestic markets for articles, and

(iii) the impact on United States industries and firms as a result of international obligations regarding compensation;

(G) the extent to which there is diversion of foreign exports to the United States market by reason of foreign restraints;

(H) the potential for circumvention of any action taken under this section;

(I) the national security interests of the United States; and

(J) the factors required to be considered by the Commission under section 202(e)(5).

(3) The President may, for purposes of taking action under paragraph (1)—

(A) proclaim an increase in, or the imposition of, any duty on the imported article;

(B) proclaim a tariff-rate quota on the article;

(C) proclaim a modification or imposition of any quantitative restriction on the importation of the article into the United States;

(D) implement one or more appropriate adjustment measures, including the provision of trade adjustment assistance under chapter 2;

(E) negotiate, conclude, and carry out orderly marketing agreements with foreign countries limiting the export from foreign countries and the import into the United States of such article;

(F) proclaim procedures necessary to allocate among importers by the auction of import licenses quantities of the article that are permitted to be imported into the United States;

(G) initiate international negotiations to address the underlying cause of the increase in imports of the article or otherwise to alleviate the injury or threat thereof;

(H) submit to Congress legislative proposals to facilitate the efforts of the domestic industry to make a positive adjustment to import competition;

(I) take any other action which may be taken by the President under the authority of law and which the President considers appropriate and feasible for purposes of paragraph (1); and

(J) take any combination of actions listed in subparagraphs (A) through (I).

(4) The President shall take action under paragraph (1) within 60 days after receiving a report from the Commission containing an affirmative determination under section 202(b)(1) (or a determination under such section which he considers to be an affirmative determination by reason of section 330(d) of the Tariff Act of 1930); except that if a supplemental report is requested under paragraph (5), the President shall take action under paragraph (1) within 30 days after the supplemental report is received.

(5) The President may, within 15 days after the date on which he receives a report from the Commission containing an affirmative determination under section 202(b)(1), request additional information from the Commission. The Commission shall, as soon as practicable but in no event more than 30 days after the date on which it receives the President's request, furnish additional information with respect to the industry in a supplemental report.

(b) Reports to Congress.

(1) On the day the President takes action under subsection (a)(1) of this section, the President shall transmit to Congress a document describing the action and the reasons for taking the action. If the action taken by the President differs from the action required to be recommended by the Commission under section 202(e)(1), the President shall state in detail the reasons for the difference.

(2) On the day on which the President decides that there is no appropriate and feasible action to take under subsection (a)(1) of this section with respect to a domestic industry, the President shall transmit to Congress a document that sets forth in detail the reasons for the decision.

(3) On the day on which the President takes any action under subsection (a)(1) of this section that is not reported under paragraph (1), the President shall transmit to Congress a document setting forth the action being taken and the reasons therefor.

(c) Implementation of action recommended by commission. If the President reports under subsection (b)(1) or (2) of this section that—

(1) the action taken under subsection (a)(1) of this section differs from the action recommended by the Commission under section 202(e)(1); or

(2) no action will be taken under subsection (a)(1) of this section with respect to the domestic industry;

the action recommended by the Commission shall take effect (as provided in subsection (d)(2) of this section)* upon the enactment of a joint resolution described in section 152(a)(1)(A) within the 90-day period beginning on the date on which the document referred to in subsection (b)(1) or (2) of this section is transmitted to the Congress.

(d) Time for taking effect of certain relief.

(1) Except as provided in paragraph (2), any action described in subsection (a)(3)(A), (B), or (C) of this section, that is taken under subsection (a)(1) of this section shall take effect within 15 days after the day on which the President proclaims the action, unless the President announces, on the date he decides to take such action, his intention to negotiate one or more orderly marketing agreements in which case the action under subsection (a)(3)(A),

(B), or (C) of this section shall be proclaimed and take effect within 90 days after the date of such decision.

(2) If the contingency set forth in subsection (c) of this section occurs, the President shall, within 30 days after the date of the enactment of the joint resolution referred to in such subsection, proclaim the action recommended by the Commission under section 202(e)(1).

(e) Limitations on actions.

(1)(A) The duration of the period in which action taken under this section may be in effect shall not exceed 8 years.

(B) If the initial effective period for action taken under this section is less than 8 years, the President may extend the effective period once, but the aggregate of the initial period and the extension may not exceed 8 years.

(2) Action of a type under subsection (a)(3)(A), (B), or (C) may be taken under subsection (a)(1), under section 202(d)(1)(G), or under section 202(d)(2)(D) only to the extent the cumulative impact of such action does not exceed the amount necessary to prevent or remedy the serious injury.

(3) No action may be taken under this section which would increase a rate of duty to (or impose a rate) which is more than 50 percent ad valorem above the rate (if any) existing at the time the action is taken.

(4) Any action taken under this section proclaiming a quantitative restriction shall permit the importation of a quantity or value of the article which is not less than the quantity or value of such article imported into the United States during the most recent period that is representative of imports of such article.

(5) To the extent feasible, an effective period of more than 3 years for an action described in subsection (a)(3)(A), (B), or (C) of this section shall be phased down during the period in which the action is taken, with the first reduction taking effect no later than the close of the day which is 3 years after the day on which such action first takes effect.

(6)(A) The suspension, pursuant to any action taken under this section, of—

(i) [Subheadings 9802.00.60 or 9802.00.80] of the Harmonized Tariff Schedule of the United States, with respect to an article; and

(ii) the designation of any article as an eligible article for purposes of title V;

shall be treated as an increase in duty.

(B) No proclamation providing for a suspension referred to in subparagraph (A) with respect to any article may be made by the President, nor may any such suspension be recommended by the Commission under section 203(e), unless the Commission, in addition to making an affirmative determination under section 202(b)(1), determines in the course of its investigation under section 202(b) of this section that the serious injury, or threat thereof, substantially caused by imports to the domestic industry producing a like or directly competitive article results from, as the case may be—

(i) the application of subheading 9802.00.60 or subheading 9802.00.80 of the Harmonized Tariff Schedule of the United States; or

(ii) the designation of the article as an eligible article for the purposes of title V.

(f) Orderly marketing and other agreements.

(1) If the President takes action under this section other than the implementation of orderly marketing agreements, the President may, after such action takes effect, negotiate orderly marketing agreements with foreign countries, and may, after such agreements take effect, suspend or terminate, in whole or in part, any action previously taken.

(2) If an orderly marketing agreement implemented under subsection (a) of this section is not effective, the President may, consistent with the limitations contained in subsection (e) of this section, take additional action under subsection (a) of this section.

(g) Regulations.

(1) The President shall by regulation provide for the efficient and fair administration of all actions taken for the purpose of providing import relief under this chapter.

(2) In order to carry out an orderly marketing or other international agreement concluded under this chapter, the President may prescribe regulations governing the entry or withdrawal from warehouse of articles covered by such agreement. In addition, in order to carry out any orderly marketing agreement concluded under this chapter with one or more countries accounting for a major part of United States imports of the article covered by such agreements, including imports into a major geographic area of the United States, the President may issue regulations governing the entry or withdrawal from warehouse of like articles which are the product of countries not parties to such agreement.

(3) Regulations prescribed under this subsection shall, to the extent practicable and consistent with efficient and fair administration, insure against inequitable sharing of imports by a relatively small number of the larger importers.

19 USC 2254

Sec. 204. Monitoring, Modification, and Termination of Action

(a) Monitoring.

(1) So long as any action taken under section 203 remains in effect, the Commission shall monitor developments with respect to the domestic industry, including the progress and specific efforts made by workers and firms in the domestic industry to make a positive adjustment to import competition.

(2) The Commission shall submit a report on the results of the monitoring under paragraph (1) to the President and to the Congress not later than—

(A) the 2nd-anniversary of the day on which the action under section 203 first took effect; and

(B) the last day of each 2-year period occurring after the 2-year period referred to in subparagraph (A).

(3) In the course of preparing each report under paragraph (2), the Commission shall hold a hearing at which interested persons shall be given a reasonable opportunity to be present, to produce evidence, and to be heard.

(4) Upon request of the President, the Commission shall advise the President of its judgment as to the probable economic effect on the industry concerned of any extension, reduction, modification, or termination of the action taken under section 203 which is under consideration.

(b) Reduction, modification, and termination of action.

(1) Action taken under section 203 may be reduced, modified, or terminated by the President (but not before the President receives the report required under subsection (a)(2)(A) of this section) if the President—

(A) after taking into account any report or advice submitted by the Commission under subsection (a) of this section and after seeking the advice of the Secretary of Commerce and the Secretary of Labor, determines, on the basis that either—

(i) the domestic industry has not made adequate efforts to make a positive adjustment to import competition, or

(ii) the effectiveness of the action taken under section 203 has been impaired by changed economic circumstances,

that changed circumstances warrant such reduction, or termination; or

(B) determines, after a majority of the representatives of the domestic industry submits to the President a petition requesting such reduction, modification, or termination on such basis, that the domestic industry has made a positive adjustment to import competition.

(2) Notwithstanding paragraph (1), the President is authorized to take such additional action under section 203 as may be necessary to eliminate any circumvention of any action previously taken under such section.

(3) Notwithstanding paragraph (1), the President may, after receipt of a Commission determination under section 129(a)(4) of the Uruguay Round Agreements Act and consulting with the Committee on Ways and Means of the House of Representatives and the Committee on Finance of the Senate, reduce, modify, or terminate action taken under section 203.

(c) Extension of action.

(1) Upon request of the President, or upon petition on behalf of the industry concerned filed with the Commission not earlier than the date which is 9 months, and not later than the date which is 6 months, before the date any action taken under section 203 is to terminate, the Commission shall investigate to determine whether action under section 203 continues to be necessary to prevent or remedy serious injury and whether there is evidence that the industry is making a positive adjustment to import competition.

(2) The Commission shall publish notice of the commencement of any proceeding under this subsection in the Federal Register and shall within a reasonable time thereafter, hold a public hearing at which the Commission shall afford interested parties and consumers an opportunity to be present, to

present evidence, and to respond to the presentations of other parties and consumers, and otherwise to be heard.

(3) The Commission shall transmit to the President a report on its investigation and determination under this subsection not later than 60 days before the action under section 203 is to terminate, unless the President specifies a different date.

(d) Evaluation of effectiveness of action.

(1) After any action taken under section 203 has terminated, the Commission shall evaluate the effectiveness of the actions in facilitating positive adjustment by the domestic industry to import competition, consistent with the reasons set out by the President in the report submitted to the Congress under section 203.

(2) During the course of the evaluation conducted under paragraph (1), the Commission shall, after reasonable public notice, hold a hearing on the effectiveness of the action. All interested persons shall have the opportunity to attend such hearing and to present evidence or testimony at such hearing.

(3) A report on the evaluation made under paragraph (1) and the hearings held under paragraph (2) shall be submitted by the Commission to the President and to the Congress by no later than the 180th day after the day on which the actions taken under section 203 terminated.

(e) Other provisions.

(1) Action by the President under this chapter may be taken without regard to the provisions of section 126(a) of this Act but only after consideration of the relation of such actions to the international obligations of the United States.

(2) If the Commission treats as the domestic industry production located in a major geographic area of the United States under section 202(c)(4)(C), then the President shall take into account the geographic concentration of domestic production and of imports in that area in taking any action authorized under paragraph (1).

* * *

19 USC 2271

Sec. 221. Petitions

(a) **Filing of petition; publication of notice.** A petition for a certification of eligibility to apply for adjustment assistance under this subchapter [19 USC §§ 2271 et seq.] may be filed with the Secretary of Labor (hereinafter in this chapter [19 USC §§ 2271 et seq.] referred to as the "Secretary") by a group of workers (including workers in any agricultural firm or subdivision of an agricultural firm) or by their certified or recognized union or other duly authorized representative. Upon receipt of the petition, the Secretary shall promptly publish notice in the Federal Register that he has received the petition and initiated an investigation.

(b) **Hearing.** If the petitioner, or any other person found by the Secretary to have a substantial interest in the proceedings, submits not later than 10 days after the date of the Secretary's publication under subsection (a) a request for a hearing, the Secretary shall provide for a public hearing and afford such interested persons an opportunity to be present, to produce evidence, and to be heard.

19 USC 2272

Sec. 222.   Group Eligibility Requirements; Agricultural Workers; Oil and Natural Gas Industry

(a) The Secretary shall certify a group of workers (including workers in any agricultural firm or subdivision of an agricultural firm) as eligible to apply for adjustment assistance under this subchapter [19 USC §§ 2271 et seq.] if he determines—

(1) that a significant number or proportion of the workers in such workers' firm or an appropriate subdivision of the firm have become totally or partially separated, or are threatened to become totally or partially separated,

(2) that sales or production, or both, of such firm or subdivision have decreased absolutely, and

(3) that increases of imports of articles like or directly competitive with articles produced by such workers' firm or appropriate subdivision thereof contributed importantly to such total or partial separation, or threat thereof, and to such decline in sales or production.

(b) For purposes of subsection (a)(3)—

(1) The term "contributed importantly" means a cause which is important but not necessarily more important than any other cause.

(2) (A) Any firm, or appropriate subdivision of a firm, that engages in exploration or drilling for oil or natural gas shall be considered to be a firm producing oil or natural gas.

(B) Any firm, or appropriate subdivision of a firm, that engages in exploration or drilling for oil or natural gas, or otherwise produces oil or natural gas, shall be considered to be producing articles directly competitive with imports of oil and with imports of natural gas.

19 USC 2273

Sec. 223. Determination by Secretary of Labor

(a) **Certification of eligibility.** As soon as possible after the date on which a petition is filed under section 221 [19 USC § 2271], but in any event not later than 60 days after that date, the Secretary shall determine whether the petitioning group meets the requirements of section 222 [19 USC § 2272] and shall issue a certification of eligibility to apply for assistance under this subchapter [19 USC §§ 2271 et seq.] covering workers in any group which meets such requirements. Each certification shall specify the date on which the total or partial separation began or threatened to begin.

(b) **Workers covered by certification.** A certification under this section shall not apply to any worker whose last total or partial separation from the firm or appropriate subdivision of the firm before his application under section 231 [19 USC § 2291] occurred—

(1) more than one year before the date of the petition on which such certification was granted, or

(2) more than 6 months before the effective date of this chapter.

(c) Publication of determination in Federal Register. Upon reaching his determination on a petition, the Secretary shall promptly publish a summary of the determination in the Federal Register together with his reasons for making such determination.

(d) Termination of certification. Whenever the Secretary determines, with respect to any certification of eligibility of the workers of a firm or subdivision of the firm, that total or partial separations from such firm or subdivision are no longer attributable to the conditions specified in section 222 [19 USC § 2272], he shall terminate such certification and promptly have notice of such termination published in the Federal Register together with his reasons for making such determination. Such termination shall apply only with respect to total or partial separations occurring after the termination date specified by the Secretary.

19 USC 2274

Sec. 224. Study by Secretary of Labor When International Trade Commission Begins Investigation

(a) Subject matter of study. Whenever the International Trade Commission (hereafter referred to in this chapter [19 USC §§ 2271 et seq.] as the "Commission") begins an investigation under section 202 [19 USC § 2252] with respect to an industry, the Commission shall immediately notify the Secretary of such investigation, and the Secretary shall immediately begin a study of—

(1) the number of workers in the domestic industry producing the like or directly competitive article who have been or are likely to be certified as eligible for adjustment assistance, and

(2) the extent to which the adjustment of such workers to the import competition may be facilitated through the use of existing programs.

(b) Report; publication. The report of the Secretary of the study under subsection (a) shall be made to the President not later than 15 days after the day on which the Commission makes its report under section 202(f) [19 USC § 2252(f)]. Upon making his report to the President, the Secretary shall also promptly make it public (with the exception of information which the Secretary determines to be confidential) and shall have a summary of it published in the Federal Register.

19 USC 2275

Sec. 225. Benefit Information to Workers

(a) The Secretary shall provide full information to workers about the benefit allowances, training, and other employment services available under this chapter [19 USC §§ 2271 et seq.] and about the petition and application procedures, and the appropriate filing dates, for such allowances, training and services. The Secretary shall provide whatever assistance is necessary to enable groups of workers to prepare petitions or applications for program benefits. The Secretary shall make every effort to insure that cooperating State agencies fully comply with the agreements entered into under section 239(a) [19 USC § 2311(a)] and shall periodically review such compliance. The Secretary shall inform the State Board for Vocational Education or equivalent agency and other public or private agencies, institutions, and employers, as appropriate, of each certification issued under section 223 [19 USC § 2273] and of projections, if available, of the needs for training under section 236 [19 USC § 2296] as a result of such certification.

(b) (1) The Secretary shall provide written notice through the mail of the benefits available under this chapter [19 USC §§ 2271 et seq.] to each worker whom the Secretary has reason to believe is covered by a certification made under subchapter A or subchapter D of this chapter [19 USC §§ 2271 et seq. or 2331 et seq.]—

(A) at the time such certification is made, if the worker was partially or totally separated from the adversely affected employment before such certification, or

(B) at the time of the total or partial separation of the worker from the adversely affected employment, if subparagraph (A) does not apply.

(2) The Secretary shall publish notice of the benefits available under this chapter [19 USC §§ 2271 et seq.] to workers covered by each certification made under subchapter A or subchapter D [19 USC §§ 2271 et seq. or 2331 et seq.] in newspapers of general circulation in the areas in which such workers reside.

TITLE III
RELIEF FROM UNFAIR TRADE PRACTICES
Chapter 1
Enforcement of United States Rights Under Trade Agreements
and Response to Certain Foreign Trade Practices

19 USC 2411

Sec. 301.   Actions by United States Trade Representative

(a) Mandatory action.

(1) If the United States Trade Representative determines under section 304(a)(1) that—

(A) the rights of the United States under any trade agreement are being denied; or

(B) an act, policy, or practice of a foreign country—

(i) violates, or is inconsistent with, the provisions of, or otherwise denies benefits to the United States under, any trade agreement, or

(ii) is unjustifiable and burdens or restricts United States commerce;

the Trade Representative shall take action authorized in subsection (c) of this section, subject to the specific direction, if any, of the President regarding any such action, and shall take all other appropriate and feasible action within the power of the President that the President may direct the Trade Representative to take under this subsection, to enforce such rights or to obtain the elimination of such act, policy, or practice. Actions may be taken that are within the power of the President with respect to trade in any goods and services, or with respect to any other area of pertinent relations with the foreign country.

(2) The Trade Representative is not required to take action under paragraph (1) in any case in which—

(A) the Dispute Settlement Body (as defined in section 121(5) of the Uruguay Round Agreements Act) has adopted a report, or a ruling issued under the formal dispute settlement proceeding provided under any other trade agreement finds, that—

(i) the rights of the United States under a trade agreement are not being denied, or

(ii) the act, policy, or practice—

(I) is not a violation of, or inconsistent with, the rights of the United States, or

(II) does not deny, nullify, or impair benefits to the United States under any trade agreement; or

(B) the Trade Representative finds that—

(i) the foreign country is taking satisfactory measures to grant the rights of the United States under a trade agreement,

(ii) the foreign country has—

(I) agreed to eliminate or phase out the act, policy, or practice, or

(II) agreed to an imminent solution to the burden or restriction on United States commerce that is satisfactory to the Trade Representative,

(iii) it is impossible for the foreign country to achieve the results described in clause (i) or (ii), as appropriate, but the foreign country agrees to provide to the United States compensatory trade benefits that are satisfactory to the Trade Representative,

(iv) in extraordinary cases, where the taking of action under this subsection would have an adverse impact on the United States economy substantially out of proportion to the benefits of such action, taking into account the impact of not taking such action on the credibility of the provisions of this chapter, or

(v) the taking of action under this subsection would cause serious harm to the national security of the United States.

(3) Any action taken under paragraph (1) to eliminate an act, policy, or practice shall be devised so as to affect goods or services of the foreign country in an amount that is equivalent in value to the burden or restriction being imposed by that country on United States commerce.

(b) **Discretionary action.** If the Trade Representative determines under section 304(a)(1) that—

(1) an act, policy, or practice of a foreign country is unreasonable or discriminatory and burdens or restricts United States commerce, and

(2) action by the United States is appropriate, the Trade Representative shall take all appropriate and feasible action authorized under subsection (c) of this section, subject to the specific direction, if any, of the President regarding any such action, and all other appropriate and feasible action within the power of the President that the President may direct the Trade Representative to take under this subsection, to obtain the elimination of that act, policy, or practice. Actions may be taken that are within the power of the President with respect to trade in any goods and services, or with respect to any other area of pertinent relations with the foreign country.

(c) Scope of authority.

(1) For purposes of carrying out the provisions of subsection (a) or (b) of this section, the Trade Representative is authorized to—

(A) suspend, withdraw, or prevent the application of, benefits of trade agreement concessions to carry out a trade agreement with the foreign country referred to in such subsection;

(B) impose duties or other import restrictions on the goods of, and, notwithstanding any other provision of law, fees or restrictions on the services of, such foreign country for such time as the Trade Representative determines appropriate;

(C) in a case in which the act, policy, or practice also fails to meet the eligibility criteria for receiving duty-free treatment under subsections (b) and (c) of section 502 of this Act, subsections (b) and (c) of section 212 of the Caribbean Basin Economic Recovery Act (19 U.S.C. 2702(b) and (c)), or subsections (c) and (d) of section 203 of the Andean Trade Preference Act (19 U.S.C. 3202(c) and (d)), withdraw, limit, or suspend such treatment under such provisions, notwithstanding the provisions of subsection (a)(3) of this section; or

(D) enter into binding agreements with such foreign country that commit such foreign country to—

(i) eliminate, or phase out, the act, policy, or practice that is the subject of the action to be taken under subsection (a) or (b) of this section,

(ii) eliminate any burden or restriction on United States commerce resulting from such act, policy, or practice, or

(iii) provide the United States with compensatory trade benefits that—

(I) are satisfactory to the Trade Representative, and

(II) meet the requirements of paragraph (4).

(2)(A) Notwithstanding any other provision of law governing any service sector access authorization, and in addition to the authority conferred in paragraph (1), the Trade Representative may, for purposes of carrying out the provisions of subsection (a) or (b) of this section—

(i) restrict, in the manner and to the extent the Trade Representative determines appropriate, the terms and conditions of any such authorization, or

(ii) deny the issuance of any such authorization.

(B) Actions described in subparagraph (A) may only be taken under this section with respect to service sector access authorizations granted, or applications therefor pending, on or after the date on which—

(i) a petition is filed under section 302(a), or

(ii) a determination to initiate an investigation is made by the Trade Representative under section 302(b).

(C) Before the Trade Representative takes any action under this section involving the imposition of fees or other restrictions on the services of a foreign country, the Trade Representative shall, if the services involved are subject to regulation by any agency of the Federal Government or of any State, consult, as appropriate, with the head of the agency concerned.

(3) The actions the Trade Representative is authorized to take under subsection (a) or (b) of this section may be taken against any goods or economic sector—

(A) on a nondiscriminatory basis or solely against the foreign country described in such subsection, and

(B) without regard to whether or not such goods or economic sector were involved in the act, policy, or practice that is the subject of such action.

(4) Any trade agreement described in paragraph (1)(D)(iii) shall provide compensatory trade benefits that benefit the economic sector which includes the domestic industry that would benefit from the elimination of the act, policy, or practice that is the subject of the action to be taken under subsection (a) or (b) of this section, or benefit the economic sector as closely related as possible to such economic sector, unless—

(A) the provision of such trade benefits is not feasible, or

(B) trade benefits that benefit any other economic sector would be more satisfactory than such trade benefits.

(5) If the Trade Representative determines that actions to be taken under subsection (a) or (b) are to be in the form of import restrictions, the Trade Representative shall—

(A) give preference to the imposition of duties over the imposition of other import restrictions, and

(B) if an import restriction other than a duty is imposed, consider substituting, on an incremental basis, an equivalent duty for such other import restriction.

(6) Any action taken by the Trade Representative under this section with respect to export targeting shall, to the extent possible, reflect the full benefit level of the export targeting to the beneficiary over the period during which the action taken has an effect.

(d) Definitions and special rules. For purposes of this chapter—

(1) The term "commerce" includes, but is not limited to—

(A) services (including transfers of information) associated with international trade, whether or not such services are related to specific goods, and

(B) foreign direct investment by United States persons with implications for trade in goods or services.

(2) An act, policy, or practice of a foreign country that burdens or restricts United States commerce may include the provision, directly or indirectly, by that foreign country of subsidies for the construction of vessels used in the commercial transportation by water of goods between foreign countries and the United States.

(3)(A) An act, policy, or practice is unreasonable if the act, policy, or practice, while not necessarily in violation of, or inconsistent with, the international legal rights of the United States, is otherwise unfair and inequitable.

(B) Acts, policies, and practices that are unreasonable include, but are not limited to, any act, policy, or practice, or any combination of acts, policies, or practices, which—

(i) denies fair and equitable—

(I) opportunities for the establishment of an enterprise,

(II) provisions of adequate and effective protection of intellectual property rights notwithstanding the fact that the foreign country may be in compliance with the specific obligations of the Agreement on Trade-Related Aspects of Intellectual Property Rights referred to in section 101(d)(15) of the Uruguay Round Agreements Act,

(III) nondiscriminatory market access opportunities for United States persons that rely upon intellectual property protection, or

(IV) market opportunities, including the toleration by a foreign government of systematic anticompetitive activities by enterprises or among enterprises in the foreign country that have the effect of restricting, on a basis that is inconsistent with commercial considerations, access of United States goods or services to a foreign market,

(ii) constitutes export targeting, or

(iii) constitutes a persistent pattern of conduct that—

(I) denies workers the right of association,

(II) denies workers the right to organize and bargain collectively,

(III) permits any form of forced or compulsory labor,

(IV) fails to provide a minimum age for the employment of children, or

(V) fails to provide standards for minimum wages, hours of work, and occupational safety and health of workers.

(C)(i) Acts, policies, and practices of a foreign country described in subparagraph (B)(iii) shall not be treated as being unreasonable if the Trade Representative determines that—

(I) the foreign country has taken, or is taking, actions that demonstrate a significant and tangible overall advancement in providing throughout the foreign country (including any designated zone within the foreign country) the rights and other standards described in the subclauses of subparagraph (B)(iii), or

(II) such acts, policies, and practices are not inconsistent with the level of economic development of the foreign country.

(ii) The Trade Representative shall publish in the Federal Register any determination made under clause (i), together with a description of the facts on which such determination is based.

(D) For purposes of determining whether any act, policy, or practice is unreasonable, reciprocal opportunities in the United States for foreign nationals and firms shall be taken into account, to the extent appropriate.

(E) The term "export targeting" means any government plan or scheme consisting of a combination of coordinated actions (whether carried out severally or jointly) that are bestowed on a specific enterprise, industry, or group thereof, the effect of which is to assist the enterprise, industry, or group to become more competitive in the export of a class or kind of merchandise.

(4)(A) An act, policy, or practice is unjustifiable if the act, policy, or practice is in violation of, or inconsistent with, the international legal rights of the United States.

(B) Acts, policies, and practices that are unjustifiable include, but are not limited to, any act, policy, or practice described in subparagraph (A) which denies national or most-favored-nation treatment or the right of establishment or protection of intellectual property rights.

(5) Acts, policies, and practices that are discriminatory include, when appropriate, any act, policy, and practice which denies national or most-favored-nation treatment to United States goods, services, or investment.

(6) The term "service sector access authorization" means any license, permit, order, or other authorization, issued under the authority of Federal law, that permits a foreign supplier of services access to the United States market in a service sector concerned.

(7) The term "foreign country" includes any foreign instrumentality. Any possession or territory of a foreign country that is administered separately for customs purposes shall be treated as a separate foreign country.

(8) The term "Trade Representative" means the United States Trade Representative.

(9) The term "interested persons", only for purposes of sections 302(a)(4)(B), 304(b)(1)(A), 306(c)(2), and 307(a)(2), includes, but is not limited to, domestic firms and workers, representatives of consumer interests, United

States product exporters, and any industrial user of any goods or services that may be affected by actions taken under subsection (a) or (b) of this section.

(F)(i) For the purposes of subparagraph (B)(i)(II), adequate and effective protection of intellectual property rights includes adequate and effective means under the laws of the foreign country for persons who are not citizens or nationals of such country to secure, exercise, and enforce rights and enjoy commercial benefits relating to patents, trademarks, copyrights and related rights, mask works, trade secrets, and plant breeder's rights.

(ii) For purposes of subparagraph (B)(i)(IV), the denial of fair and equitable nondiscriminatory market access opportunities includes restrictions on market access related to the use, exploitation, or enjoyment of commercial benefits derived from exercising intellectual property rights in protected works or fixations or products embodying protected works.

19 USC 2412

Sec. 302. Initiation of Investigations

(a) Petitions.

(1) Any interested person may file a petition with the Trade Representative requesting that action be taken under section 301 and setting forth the allegations in support of the request.

(2) The Trade Representative shall review the allegations in any petition filed under paragraph (1) and, not later than 45 days after the date on which the Trade Representative received the petition, shall determine whether to initiate an investigation.

(3) If the Trade Representative determines not to initiate an investigation with respect to a petition, the Trade Representative shall inform the petitioner of the reasons therefor and shall publish notice of the determination, together with a summary of such reasons, in the Federal Register.

(4) If the Trade Representative makes an affirmative determination under paragraph (2) with respect to a petition, the Trade Representative shall initiate an investigation regarding the issues raised in the petition. The Trade Representative shall publish a summary of the petition in the Federal Register and shall, as soon as possible, provide opportunity for the presentation of views concerning the issues, including a public hearing—

(A) within the 30-day period beginning on the date of the affirmative determination (or on a date after such period if agreed to by the petitioner) if a public hearing within such period is requested in the petition, or

(B) at such other time if a timely request therefor is made by the petitioner or by any interested person.

(b) Initiation of investigation by means other than petition.

(1)(A) If the Trade Representative determines that an investigation should be initiated under this chapter with respect to any matter in order to determine whether the matter is actionable under section 301, the Trade

Representative shall publish such determination in the Federal Register and shall initiate such investigation.

(B) The Trade Representative shall, before making any determination under subparagraph (A), consult with appropriate committees established pursuant to section 135.

(2)(A) By no later than the date that is 30 days after the date on which a country is identified under section 182(a)(2), the Trade Representative shall initiate an investigation under this chapter with respect to any act, policy, or practice of that country that—

(i) was the basis for such identification, and

(ii) is not at that time the subject of any other investigation or action under this chapter.

(B) The Trade Representative is not required under subparagraph (A) to initiate an investigation under this chapter with respect to any act, policy, or practice of a foreign country if the Trade Representative determines that the initiation of the investigation would be detrimental to United States economic interests.

(C) If the Trade Representative makes a determination under subparagraph (B) not to initiate an investigation, the Trade Representative shall submit to the Congress a written report setting forth, in detail—

(i) the reasons for the determination, and

(ii) the United States economic interests that would be adversely affected by the investigation.

(D) The Trade Representative shall, from time to time, consult with the Register of Copyrights, the Under Secretary of Commerce for Intellectual Property and Director of the United States Patent and Trademark Office, and other appropriate officers of the Federal Government, during any investigation initiated under this chapter by reason of subparagraph (A).

(c) Discretion. In determining whether to initiate an investigation under subsection (a) or (b) of this section of any act, policy, or practice that is enumerated in any provision of section 301(d), the Trade Representative shall have discretion to determine whether action under section 301 would be effective in addressing such act, policy, or practice.

19 USC 2413

Sec. 303.   Consultation Upon Initiation of Investigation

(a) In general.

(1) On the date on which an investigation is initiated under section 302, the Trade Representative, on behalf of the United States, shall request consultations with the foreign country concerned regarding the issues involved in such investigation.

(2) If the investigation initiated under section 302 involves a trade agreement and a mutually acceptable resolution is not reached before the earlier of—

(A) the close of the consultation period, if any, specified in the trade agreement, or

(B) the 150th day after the day on which consultation was commenced,

the Trade Representative shall promptly request proceedings on the matter under the formal dispute settlement procedures provided under such agreement.

(3) The Trade Representative shall seek information and advice from the petitioner (if any) and the appropriate committees established pursuant to section 135 in preparing United States presentations for consultations and dispute settlement proceedings.

(b) Delay of request for consultations.

(1) Notwithstanding the provisions of subsection (a) of this section—

(A) the United States Trade Representative may, after consulting with the petitioner (if any), delay for up to 90 days any request for consultations under subsection (a) of this section for the purpose of verifying or improving the petition to ensure an adequate basis for consultation, and

(B) if such consultations are delayed by reason of subparagraph (A), each time limitation under section 304 shall be extended for the period of such delay.

(2) The Trade Representative shall—

(A) publish notice of any delay under paragraph (1) in the Federal Register, and

(B) report to Congress on the reasons for such delay in the report required under section 309(a)(3).

19 USC 2414

Sec. 304.   Determinations by the Trade Representative

(a) In general.

(1) On the basis of the investigation initiated under section 302 and the consultations (and the proceedings, if applicable) under section 303, the Trade Representative shall—

(A) determine whether—

(i) the rights to which the United States is entitled under any trade agreement are being denied, or

(ii) any act, policy, or practice described in subsection (a)(1)(B) or (b)(1) of section 301 exists, and

(B) if the determination made under subparagraph (A) is affirmative, determine what action, if any, the Trade Representative should take under subsection (a) or (b) of section 301.

(2) The Trade Representative shall make the determinations required under paragraph (1) on or before—

(A) in the case of an investigation involving a trade agreement, the earlier of—

(i) the date that is 30 days after the date on which the dispute settlement procedure is concluded, or

(ii) the date that is 18 months after the date on which the investigation is initiated, or

(B) in all cases not described in subparagraph (A) or paragraph (3), the date that is 12 months after the date on which the investigation is initiated.

(3)(A) If an investigation is initiated under this chapter by reason of section 302(b)(2) and the Trade Representative does not consider that a trade agreement, including the Agreement on Trade-Related Aspects of Intellectual Property Rights (referred to in section 101(d)(15) of the Uruguay Round Agreements Act), is involved or does not make a determination described in subparagraph (B) with respect to such investigation, the Trade Representative shall make the determinations required under paragraph (1) with respect to such investigation by no later than the date that is 6 months after the date on which such investigation is initiated.

(B) If the Trade Representative determines with respect to an investigation initiated by reason of section 302(b)(2) (other than an investigation involving a trade agreement) that—

(i) complex or complicated issues are involved in the investigation that require additional time,

(ii) the foreign country involved in the investigation is making substantial progress in drafting or implementing legislative or administrative measures that will provide adequate and effective protection of intellectual property rights, or

(iii) such foreign country is undertaking enforcement measures to provide adequate and effective protection of intellectual property rights,

the Trade Representative shall publish in the Federal Register notice of such determination and shall make the determinations required under paragraph (1) with respect to such investigation by no later than the date that is 9 months after the date on which such investigation is initiated.

(4) In any case in which a dispute is not resolved before the close of the minimum dispute settlement period provided for in a trade agreement, the Trade Representative, within 15 days after the close of such dispute settlement period, shall submit a report to Congress setting forth the reasons why the dispute was not resolved within the minimum dispute settlement period, the status of the case at the close of the period, and the prospects for resolution. For purposes of this paragraph, the minimum dispute settlement period provided for under any such trade agreement is the total period of time that results if all stages of the formal dispute settlement procedures are carried out within the time limitations specified in the agreement, but computed without regard to any extension authorized under the agreement at any stage.

(b) Consultation before determinations.

(1) Before making the determinations required under subsection (a)(1) of this section, the Trade Representative, unless expeditious action is required—

(A) shall provide an opportunity (after giving not less than 30 days notice thereof) for the presentation of views by interested persons, including a public hearing if requested by any interested person,

(B) shall obtain advice from the appropriate committees established pursuant to section 135, and

(C) may request the views of the United States International Trade Commission regarding the probable impact on the economy of the United States of the taking of action with respect to any goods or service.

(2) If the Trade Representative does not comply with the requirements of subparagraphs (A) and (B) of paragraph (1) because expeditious action is required, the Trade Representative shall, after making the determinations under subsection (a)(1) of this section, comply with such subparagraphs.

(c) Publication. The Trade Representative shall publish in the Federal Register any determination made under subsection (a)(1) of this section, together with a description of the facts on which such determination is based.

19 USC 2415

Sec. 305.   Implementation of Actions

(a) Actions to be taken under section 301.

(1) Except as provided in paragraph (2), the Trade Representative shall implement the action the Trade Representative determines under section 304(a)(1)(B) to take under section 301, subject to the specific direction, if any, of the President regarding any such action, by no later than the date that is 30 days after the date on which such determination is made.

(2)(A) Except as otherwise provided in this paragraph, the Trade Representative may delay, by not more than 180 days, the implementation of any action that is to be taken under section 301—

(i) if—

(I) in the case of an investigation initiated under section 302(a), the petitioner requests a delay, or

(II) in the case of an investigation initiated under section 302(b)(1) or to which section 304(a)(3)(B) applies, a delay is requested by a majority of the representatives of the domestic industry that would benefit from the action, or

(ii) if the Trade Representative determines that substantial progress is being made, or that a delay is necessary or desirable, to obtain United States rights or a satisfactory solution with respect to the acts, policies, or practices that are the subject of the action.

(B) The Trade Representative may not delay under subparagraph (A) the implementation of any action that is to be taken under section 301 with respect to any investigation to which section 304(a)(3)(A) applies.

(C) The Trade Representative may not delay under subparagraph (A) the implementation of any action that is to be taken under section 301 with respect to any investigation to which section 304(a)(3)(B) applies by more than 90 days.

(b) Alternative actions in certain cases of export targeting.

(1) If the Trade Representative makes an affirmative determination under section 304(a)(1)(A) involving export targeting by a foreign country and determines to take no action under section 301 with respect to such affirmation determination, the Trade Representative—

(A) shall establish an advisory panel to recommend measures which will promote the competitiveness of the domestic industry affected by the export targeting,

(B) on the basis of the report of such panel submitted under paragraph (2)(B) and subject to the specific direction, if any, of the President, may take any administrative actions authorized under any other provision of law, and, if necessary, propose legislation to implement any other actions, that would restore or improve the international competitiveness of the domestic industry affected by the export targeting, and

(C) shall, by no later than the date that is 30 days after the date on which the report of such panel is submitted under paragraph (2)(B), submit a report to the Congress on the administrative actions taken, and legislative proposals made, under subparagraph (B) with respect to the domestic industry affected by the export targeting.

(2)(A) The advisory panels established under paragraph (1)(A) shall consist of individuals appointed by the Trade Representative who—

(i) earn their livelihood in the private sector of the economy, including individuals who represent management and labor in the domestic industry affected by the export targeting that is the subject of the affirmative determination made under section 304(a)(1)(A), and

(ii) by education or experience, are qualified to serve on the advisory panel.

(B) By no later than the date that is 6 months after the date on which an advisory panel is established under paragraph (1)(A), the advisory panel shall submit to the Trade Representative and to the Congress a report on measures that the advisory panel recommends be taken by the United States to promote the competitiveness of the domestic industry affected by the export targeting that is the subject of the affirmative determination made under section 304(a)(1)(A).

19 USC 2416

Sec. 306. Monitoring of Foreign Compliance

(a) In general. The Trade Representative shall monitor the implementation of each measure undertaken, or agreement that is entered into, by a foreign country to provide a satisfactory resolution of a matter subject to investigation under this chapter or subject to dispute settlement proceedings to enforce the rights of the United States under a trade agreement providing for such proceedings.

(b) Further action.

(1) In general. If, on the basis of the monitoring carried out under subsection (a), the Trade Representative considers that a foreign country is not satisfactorily implementing a measure or agreement referred to in subsection (a), the Trade Representative shall determine what further action the Trade Representative shall take under section 301(a). For purposes of section 301, any such determination shall be treated as a determination made under section 304(a)(1).

(2) WTO dispute settlement recommendations.

(A) Failure to implement recommendation. If the measure or agreement referred to in subsection (a) concerns the implementation of a recommendation made pursuant to dispute settlement proceedings under the World Trade Organization, and the Trade Representative considers that the foreign country has failed to implement it, the Trade Representative shall make the determination in paragraph (1) no later than 30 days after the expiration of the reasonable period of time provided for such implementation under paragraph 21 of the Understanding on Rules and Procedures Governing the Settlement of Disputes that is referred to in section 101(d)(16) of the Uruguay Round Agreements Act.

(B) Revision of retaliation list and action.

(i) Except as provided in clause (ii), in the event that the United States initiates a retaliation list or takes any other action described in section 301(c)(1)(A) or (B) against the goods of a foreign country or countries because of the failure of such country or countries to implement the recommendation made pursuant to a dispute settlement proceeding under the World Trade Organization, the Trade Representative shall periodically revise the list or action to affect other goods of the country or countries that have failed to implement the recommendation.

(ii) Exception. he Trade Representative is not required to revise the retaliation list or the action described in clause (i) with respect to a country, if—

(I) the Trade Representative determines that implementation of a recommendation made pursuant to a dispute settlement proceeding described in clause (i) by the country is imminent; or

(II) the Trade Representative together with the petitioner involved in the initial investigation under this chapter (or if no petition was filed, the affected United States industry) agree that it is unnecessary to revise the retaliation list.

(C) Schedule for revising list or action. The Trade Representative shall, 120 days after the date the retaliation list or other section 301(a) action is first taken, and every 180 days thereafter, review the list or action taken and revise, in whole or in part, the list or action to affect other goods of the subject country or countries.

(D) Standards for revising list or action. In revising any list or action against a country or countries under this subsection, the Trade Representative shall act in a manner that is most likely to result in the country or countries implementing the recommendations adopted in the dispute settlement proceeding or in achieving a mutually satisfactory solution to the issue that gave rise to the dispute settlement proceeding. The Trade Representative shall consult with the petitioner, if any, involved in the initial investigation under this chapter.

(E) Retaliation list. The term "retaliation list" means the list of products of a foreign country or countries that have failed to comply with the report of the panel or Appellate Body of the WTO and with respect to which the Trade Representative is imposing duties above the level that would otherwise be imposed under the Harmonized Tariff Schedule of the United States.

(F) Requirement to include reciprocal goods on retaliation list. The Trade Representative shall include on the retaliation list, and on any revised lists, reciprocal goods of the industries affected by the failure of the foreign country or countries to implement the recommendation made pursuant to a dispute settlement proceeding under the World Trade Organization, except in cases where existing retaliation and its corresponding preliminary retaliation list do not already meet this requirement.

(c) Consultations. Before making any determination under subsection (b), the Trade Representative shall—

(1) consult with the petitioner, if any, involved in the initial investigation under this chapter and with representatives of the domestic industry concerned; and

(2) provide an opportunity for the presentation of views by interested persons.

19 USC 2417

Sec. 307.   Modification and Termination of Actions

(a) In general.

(1) The Trade Representative may modify or terminate any action, subject to the specific direction, if any, of the President with respect to such action, that is being taken under section 301 if—

(A) any of the conditions described in section 301(a)(2) exist,

(B) the burden or restriction on United States commerce of the denial [of] rights, or of the acts, policies, and practices, that are the subject of such action has increased or decreased, or

(C) such action is being taken under section 301(b) and is no longer appropriate.

(2) Before taking any action under paragraph (1) to modify or terminate any action taken under section 301, the Trade Representative shall consult with the petitioner, if any, and with representatives of the domestic industry concerned, and shall provide opportunity for the presentation of views by other interested persons affected by the proposed modification or termination concerning the effects of the modification or termination and whether any modification or termination of the action is appropriate.

(b) Notice; report to Congress. The Trade Representative shall promptly publish in the Federal Register notice of, and report in writing to the Congress with respect to, any modification or termination of any action taken under section 301 and the reasons therefor.

(c) Review of necessity.

(1) If—

(A) a particular action has been taken under section 301 during any 4-year period, and

(B) neither the petitioner nor any representative of the domestic industry which benefits from such action has submitted to the Trade Representative during the last 60 days of such 4-year period a written request for the continuation of such action,

such action shall terminate at the close of such 4-year period.

(2) The Trade Representative shall notify by mail the petitioner and representatives of the domestic industry described in paragraph (1)(B) of any termination of action by reason of paragraph (1) at least 60 days before the date of such termination.

(3) If a request is submitted to the Trade Representative under paragraph (1)(B) to continue taking a particular action under section 301, the Trade Representative shall conduct a review of—

(A) the effectiveness in achieving the objectives of section 301 of—

(i) such action, and

(ii) other actions that could be taken (including actions against other products or services), and

(B) the effects of such actions on the United States economy, including consumers.

19 USC 2418

Sec. 308. Request for Information

(a) In general. Upon receipt of written request therefor from any person, the Trade Representative shall make available to that person information (other than that to which confidentiality applies) concerning—

(1) the nature and extent of a specific trade policy or practice of a foreign country with respect to particular goods, services, investment, or intellectual property rights, to the extent that such information is available to the Trade Representative or other Federal agencies;

(2) United States rights under any trade agreement and the remedies which may be available under that agreement and under the laws of the United States; and

(3) past and present domestic and international proceedings or actions with respect to the policy or practice concerned.

(b) If information not available. If information that is requested by a person under subsection (a) is not available to the Trade Representative or other Federal Agencies, the Trade Representative shall, within 30 days after receipt of the request—

(1) request the information from the foreign government; or

(2) decline to request the information and inform the person in writing of the reasons for refusal.

(c) Certain business information not made available.

(1) Except as provided in paragraph (2), and notwithstanding any other provision of law (including section 552 of title 5, United States Code), no information requested and received by the Trade Representative in aid of any investigation under this chapter shall be made available to any person if—

(A) the person providing such information certifies that—

(i) such information is business confidential,

(ii) the disclosure of such information would endanger trade secrets or profitability, and

(iii) such information is not generally available;

(B) the Trade Representative determines that such certification is well-founded; and

(C) to the extent required in regulations prescribed by the Trade Representative, the person providing such information provides an adequate nonconfidential summary of such information.

(2) The Trade Representative may—

(A) use such information, or make such information available (in his own discretion) to any employee of the Federal Government for use, in any investigation under this chapter, or

(B) may make such information available to any other person in a form which cannot be associated with, or otherwise identify, the person providing the information.

19 USC 2419

Sec. 309. Administration

The Trade Representative shall—

(1) issue regulations concerning the filing of petitions and the conduct of investigations and hearings under this subchapter,

(2) keep the petitioner regularly informed of all determinations and developments regarding the investigation conducted with respect to the petition under this chapter, including the reasons for any undue delays, and

(3) submit a report to the House of Representatives and the Senate semiannually describing—

(A) the petitions filed and the determinations made (and reasons therefor) under section 302,

(B) developments in, and the current status of, each investigation or proceeding under this chapter,

(C) the actions taken, or the reasons for no action, by the Trade Representative under section 301 with respect to investigations conducted under this chapter, and

(D) the commercial effects of actions taken under section 301.

19 USC 2420

Sec. 310. Identification of Trade Expansion Priorities

(a) Identification.

(1) Within 180 days after the submission in calendar year 1995 of the report required by section 181(b), the Trade Representative shall

(A) review United States trade expansion priorities,

(B) identify priority foreign country practices, the elimination of which is likely to have the most significant potential to increase United States exports, either directly or through the establishment of beneficial precedent, and

(C) submit to the Committee on Finance of the Senate and the Committee on Ways and Means of the House of Representatives and publish in the Federal Register a report on the priority foreign country practices identified.

(2) In identifying priority foreign country practices under paragraph (1) of this section, the Trade Representative shall take into account all relevant factors, including

(A) the major barriers and trade distorting practices described in the National Trade Estimate Report required under section 181(b);

(B) the trade agreements to which a foreign country is a party and its compliance with those agreements;

(C) the medium-and-long-term implications of foreign government procurement plans; and

(D) the international competitive position and export potential of United States products and services.

(3) The Trade Representative may include in the report, if appropriate

(A) a description of foreign country practices that may warrant identification as priority foreign country practices; and

(B) a statement about other foreign country practices that were not identified because they are already being addressed by provisions of United States trade law, by existing bilateral trade agreements, or as part of trade negotiations with other countries and progress is being made toward the elimination of such practices.

(b) Initiation of investigations. By no later than the date that is 21 days after the date on which a report is submitted to the appropriate congressional committees under subsection (a)(1), the Trade Representative shall initiate under section 302(b)(1) investigations under this chapter with respect to all of the priority foreign country practices identified.

(c) Agreements for the elimination of barriers. In the consultations with a foreign country that the Trade Representative is required to request under section 303(a) with respect to an investigation initiated by reason of subsection (b), the Trade Representative shall seek to negotiate an agreement that provides for the elimination of the practices that are the subject of the investigation as quickly as possible or, if the elimination of the practices is not feasible, an agreement that provides for compensatory trade benefits.

(d) Reports. The Trade Representative shall include in the semiannual report required by section 309 report a report on the status of any investigations initiated pursuant to subsection (b) and, where appropriate, the extent to which such investigations have led to increased opportunities for the export of products and services of the United States.

TITLE IV

TRADE RELATIONS WITH COUNTRIES NOT CURRENTLY RECEIVING NONDISCRIMINATORY TREATMENT

19 USC 2431

Sec. 401. Exception of the Products of Certain Countries or Areas

Except as otherwise provided in this title, the President shall continue to deny nondiscriminatory treatment to the products of any country, the products of which were not eligible for the rates set forth in rate column numbered 1 of the Tariff Schedules of the United States on January 3, 1975.

19 USC 2432

Sec. 402. Freedom of Emigration in East–West Trade

(a) Actions of nonmarket economy countries making them ineligible for normal trade relations, programs of credits, credit guarantees, or investment guarantees, or commercial agreements. To assure the continued dedication of the United States to fundamental human rights, and notwithstanding any other provision of law, on or after the date of the enactment of this Act [enacted Jan. 3, 1975] products from any nonmarket economy country shall not be eligible to receive nondiscriminatory treatment (normal trade relations), such country shall not participate in any program of the Government of the United States which extends credits or credit guarantees or investment guarantees, directly or indirectly, and the President of the United States shall not conclude any commercial agreement with any such country, during the period beginning with the date on which the President determines that such country—

(1) denies its citizens the right or opportunity to emigrate;

(2) imposes more than a nominal tax on emigration or on the visas or other documents required for emigration, for any purpose or cause whatsoever; or

(3) imposes more than a nominal tax, levy, fine, fee, or other charge on any citizen as a consequence of the desire of such citizen to emigrate to the country of his choice,

and ending on the date on which the President determines that such country is no longer in violation of paragraph (1), (2), or (3).

(b) Presidential determination and report to Congress that nation is not violating freedom of emigration. After the date of the enactment of this Act [enacted Jan. 3, 1975], (A) products of a nonmarket economy country may be eligible to receive nondiscriminatory treatment (normal trade relations), (B) such country may participate in any program of the Government of the United States which extends credits or credit guarantees or investment guarantees, and (C) the President may conclude a commercial agreement with such country, only after the President has submitted to the Congress a report indicating that such country is not in violation of paragraph (1), (2), or (3) of subsection (a). Such report with respect to such country shall include information as to the nature and implementation of emigration laws and policies and restrictions or discrimination applied to or against persons wishing to emigrate. The report required by this subsection shall be submitted initially as provided herein and, with current information, on or before each June 30 and December 31 thereafter so long as such treatment is received, such credits or guarantees are extended, or such agreement is in effect.

(c) Waiver authority of President.

(1) During the 18–month period beginning on the date of the enactment of this Act [enacted Jan. 3, 1975], the President is authorized to waive by Executive order the application of subsections (a) and (b) with respect to any country, if he reports to the Congress that—

(A) he has determined that such waiver will substantially promote the objectives of this section; and

(B) he has received assurances that the emigration practices of that country will henceforth lead substantially to the achievement of the objectives of this section.

(2) During any period subsequent to the 18–month period referred to in paragraph (1), the President is authorized to waive by Executive order the application of subsections (a) and (b) with respect to any country, if the waiver authority granted by this subsection continues to apply to such country pursuant to subsection (d), and if he reports to the Congress that—

(A) he has determined that such waiver will substantially promote the objectives of this section; and

(B) he has received assurances that the emigration practices of that country will henceforth lead substantially to the achievement of the objectives of this section.

(3) A waiver with respect to any country shall terminate on the day after the waiver authority granted by this subsection ceases to be effective with respect to such country pursuant to subsection (d). The President may, at any time, terminate by Executive order any waiver granted under this subsection.

(d) Extension of waiver authority.

(1) If the President determines that the further extension of the waiver authority granted under subsection (c) will substantially promote the objectives of this section, he may recommend further extensions of such authority for successive 12–month periods. Any such recommendations shall—

(A) be made not later than 30 days before the expiration of such authority;

(B) be made in a document transmitted to the House of Representatives and the Senate setting forth his reasons for recommending the extension of such authority; and

(C) include, for each country with respect to which a waiver granted under subsection (c) is in effect, a determination that continuation of the waiver applicable to that country will substantially promote the objectives of this section, and a statement setting forth his reasons for such determination.

If the President recommends the further extension of such authority, such authority shall continue in effect until the end of the 12–month period following the end of the previous 12–month extension with respect to any country (except for any country with respect to which such authority has not been extended under this subsection), unless a joint resolution described in section 153(a) is enacted into law pursuant to the provisions of paragraph (2).

(2) (A) The requirements of this paragraph are met if the joint resolution is enacted under the procedures set forth in section 153, and—

(i) the Congress adopts and transmits the joint resolution to the President before the end of the 60–day period beginning on the date the waiver authority would expire but for an extension under paragraph (1), and

(ii) if the President vetoes the joint resolution, each House of Congress votes to override such veto on or before the later of the last day of the 60–day period referred to in clause (i) or the last day of the 15–day period (excluding any day described in section 154(b)) beginning on the date the Congress receives the veto message from the President.

(B) If a joint resolution is enacted into law under the provisions of this paragraph, the waiver authority applicable to any country with respect to which the joint resolution disapproves of the extension of such authority shall cease to be effective as of the day after the 60–day period beginning on the date of the enactment of the joint resolution.

(C) A joint resolution to which this subsection and section 153 apply may be introduced at any time on or after the date the President transmits to the Congress the document described in paragraph (1)(B).

(e) **Countries not covered.** This section shall not apply to any country the products of which are eligible for the rates set forth in rate column numbered 1 of the Tariff Schedules of the United States on the date of the enactment of this Act [enacted Jan. 3, 1975].

19 USC 2433

Sec. 403. United States Personnel Missing in Action in Southeast Asia

(a) **Penalty for noncooperating countries.** Notwithstanding any other provision of law, if the President determines that a nonmarket economy country is not cooperating with the United States—

(1) to achieve a complete accounting of all United States military and civilian personnel who are missing in action in Southeast Asia,

(2) to repatriate such personnel who are alive, and

(3) to return the remains of such personnel who are dead to the United States,

then, during the period beginning with the date of such determination and ending on the date on which the President determines such country is cooperating with the United States, he may provide that—

(A) the products of such country may not receive nondiscriminatory treatment,

(B) such country may not participate, directly or indirectly, in any program under which the United States extends credit, credit guarantees, or investment guarantees, and

(C) no commercial agreement entered into under this title between such country and the United States will take effect.

(b) Exception. This section shall not apply to any country the products of which are eligible for the rates set forth in rate column numbered 1 of the Tariff Schedules of the United States on the date of the enactment of this Act.

19 USC 2434

Sec. 404. Extension of Nondiscriminatory Treatment

(a) Presidential proclamation. Subject to the provisions of section 405(c), the President may by proclamation extend nondiscriminatory treatment to the products of a foreign country which has entered into a bilateral commercial agreement referred to in section 405.

(b) Limitation on period of effectiveness. The application of nondiscriminatory treatment shall be limited to the period of effectiveness of the obligations of the United States to such country under such bilateral commercial agreement. In addition, in the case of any foreign country receiving nondiscriminatory treatment pursuant to this title which has entered into an agreement with the United States regarding the settlement of lend-lease reciprocal aid and claims, the application of such nondiscriminatory treatment shall be limited to periods during which such country is not in arrears on its obligations under such agreement.

(c) Suspension or withdrawal of extensions of nondiscriminatory treatment. The President may at any time suspend or withdraw any extension of nondiscriminatory treatment to any country pursuant to subsection (a) and thereby cause all products of such country to be dutiable at the rates set forth in rate column numbered 2 of the Harmonized Tariff Schedule of the United States.

19 USC 2435

Sec. 405. Commercial Agreements

(a) Presidential authority. Subject to the provisions of subsections (b) and (c) of this section, the President may authorize the entry into force of bilateral commercial agreements providing nondiscriminatory treatment to the products of countries heretofore denied such treatment whenever he determines that such agreements with such countries will promote the purposes of this Act and are in the national interest.

(b) Terms of agreements. Any such bilateral commercial agreement shall—

(1) be limited to an initial period specified in the agreement which shall be no more than 3 years from the date the agreement enters into force; except that it may be renewable for additional periods, each not to exceed 3 years; if—

(A) a satisfactory balance of concessions in trade and services has been maintained during the life of such agreement, and

(B) the President determines that actual or foreseeable reductions in United States tariffs and nontariff barriers to trade resulting from multilateral negotiations are satisfactorily reciprocated by the other party to the bilateral agreement;

(2) provide that it is subject to suspension or termination at any time for national security reasons, or that the other provisions of such agreement shall not limit the rights of any party to take any action for the protection of its security interests;

(3) include safeguard arrangements (A) providing for prompt consultations whenever either actual or prospective imports cause or threaten to cause, or significantly contribute to, market disruption and (B) authorizing the imposition of such import restrictions as may be appropriate to prevent such market disruption;

(4) if the other party to the bilateral agreement is not a party to the Paris Convention for the Protection of Industrial Property, provide rights for United States nationals with respect to patents and trademarks in such country not less than the rights specified in such convention;

(5) if the other party to the bilateral agreement is not a party to the Universal Copyright Convention, provide rights for United States nationals with respect to copyrights in such country not less than the rights specified in such convention;

(6) in the case of an agreement entered into or renewed after the date of the enactment of this Act [enacted Jan. 3, 1975], provide arrangements for the protection of industrial rights and processes;

(7) provide arrangements for the settlement of commercial differences and disputes;

(8) in the case of an agreement entered into or renewed after the date of the enactment of this Act [enacted Jan. 3, 1975], provide arrangements for the promotion of trade, which may include arrangements for the establishment or expansion of trade and tourist promotion offices, for facilitation of activities of governmental commercial officers, participation in trade fairs and exhibits, and the sending of trade missions, and for facilitation of entry, establishment, and travel of commercial representatives;

(9) provide for consultations for the purpose of reviewing the operation of the agreement and relevant aspects of relations between the United States and the other party; and

(10) provide such other arrangements of a commercial nature as will promote the purposes of this Act.

(c) Congressional action. An agreement referred to in subsection (a), and a proclamation referred to in section 404(a) implementing such agreement, shall take effect only if a joint resolution described in section 151(b)(3) that approves of the agreement referred to in subsection (a) is enacted into law.

19 USC 2436

Sec. 406. Market Disruption

(a) Investigation by International Trade Commission; report; publication.

(1) Upon the filing of a petition by an entity described in section 202(a), upon request of the President or the Special Representative for Trade Negotiations [United States Trade Representative], upon resolution of either the Committee on Ways and Means of the House of Representatives or the Committee on Finance of the Senate, or on its own motion, the International Trade Commission (hereafter in this section referred to as the "Commission") shall promptly make an investigation to determine, with respect to imports of an article which is the product of a Communist country, whether market disruption exists with respect to an article produced by a domestic industry.

(2) The provisions of subsections (a)(3), (b)(4), and (c)(4) of section 202 shall apply with respect to investigations by the Commission under paragraph (1).

(3) The Commission shall report to the President its determination with respect to each investigation under paragraph (1) and the basis therefor and shall include in each report any dissenting or separate views. If the Commission finds, as a result of its investigation, that market disruption exists with respect to an article produced by a domestic industry, it shall find the amount of the increase in, or imposition of, any duty or other import restriction on such article which is necessary to prevent or remedy such market disruption and shall include such finding in its report to the President. The Commission shall furnish to the President a transcript of the hearings and any briefs which may have been submitted in connection with each investigation.

(4) The report of the Commission of its determination with respect to an investigation under paragraph (1) shall be made at the earliest practicable time, but not later than 3 months after the date on which the petition is filed (or the date on which the request or resolution is received or the motion is adopted, as the case may be). Upon making such report to the President, the Commission shall also promptly make public such report (with the exception of information which the Commission determines to be confidential) and shall cause a summary thereof to be published in the Federal Register.

(b) Affirmative determination. With respect to any affirmative determination of the Commission under subsection (a)—

(1) such determination shall be treated as an affirmative determination made under section 201(b) of this Act (as in effect on the day before the date

of the enactment of the Omnibus Trade and Competitiveness Act of 1988 [enacted Aug. 23, 1988]); and

(2) sections 202 and 203 of this Act (as in effect on the day before the date of the enactment of such Act of 1988 [enacted Aug. 23, 1988]), rather than the provisions of chapter 1 of title II of this Act as amended by section 1401 of such Act of 1988, shall apply with respect to the taking of subsequent action, if any, by the President in response to such affirmative determination;

except that—

(A) the President may take action under such sections 202 and 203 only with respect to imports from the country or countries involved of the article with respect to which the affirmative determination was made; and

(B) if such action consists of, or includes, an orderly marketing agreement, such agreement shall be entered into within 60 days after the import relief determination date.

(c) Products of Communist countries. If, at any time, the President finds that there are reasonable grounds to believe, with respect to imports of an article which is the product of a Communist country, that market disruption exists with respect to an article produced by a domestic industry, he shall request the Commission to initiate an investigation under subsection (a). If the President further finds that emergency action is necessary, he may take action under sections 202 and 203 referred to in subsection (b) as if an affirmative determination of the Commission had been made under subsection (a). Any action taken by the President under the preceding sentence shall cease to apply (1) if a negative determination is made by the Commission under subsection (a) with respect to imports of such article, on the day on which the Commission's report of such determination is submitted to the President, or (2) if an affirmative determination is made by the Commission under subsection (a) with respect to imports of such article, on the day on which the action taken by the President pursuant to such determination becomes effective.

(d) Petitions to initiate consultations as provided for by safeguard arrangements.

(1) A petition may be filed with the President by an entity described in section 202(a) requesting the President to initiate consultations provided for by the safeguard arrangements of any agreement entered into under section 405 with respect to imports of an article which is the product of the country which is the other party to such agreement.

(2) If the President determines that there are reasonable grounds to believe, with respect to imports of such article, that market disruption exists with respect to an article produced by a domestic industry, he shall initiate consultations with such country with respect to such imports.

(e) Definitions; factors determining existence of market disruption. For purposes of this section—

(1) The term "Communist country" means any country dominated or controlled by communism.

(2) (A) Market disruption exists within a domestic industry whenever imports of an article, like or directly competitive with an article produced by such domestic industry, are increasing rapidly, either absolutely or relatively, so as to be a significant cause of material injury, or threat thereof, to such domestic industry.

(B) For purposes of subparagraph (A):

(i) Imports of an article shall be considered to be increasing rapidly if there has been a significant increase in such imports (either actual or relative to domestic production) during a recent period of time.

(ii) The term "significant cause" refers to a cause which contributes significantly to the material injury of the domestic industry, but need not be equal to or greater than any other cause.

(C) The Commission, in determining whether market disruption exists, shall consider, among other factors—

(i) the volume of imports of the merchandise which is the subject of the investigation;

(ii) the effect of imports of the merchandise on prices in the United States for like or directly competitive articles;

(iii) the impact of imports of such merchandise on domestic producers of like or directly competitive articles; and

(iv) evidence of disruptive pricing practices, or other efforts to unfairly manage trade patterns.

19 USC 2437

Sec. 407. Procedure for Congressional Approval or Disapproval of Extension of Nondiscriminatory Treatment and Presidential Reports

(a) Transmission of nondiscriminatory treatment documents to Congress. Whenever the President issues a proclamation under section 404 extending nondiscriminatory treatment to the products of any foreign country, he shall promptly transmit to the House of Representatives and to the Senate a document setting forth the proclamation and the agreement the proclamation proposes to implement, together with his reasons therefor.

(b) Transmission of freedom of emigration documents to Congress. The President shall transmit to the House of Representatives and the Senate a document containing the initial report submitted by him under section 402(b) or 409(b) with respect to a nonmarket economy country. On or before December 31 of each year, the President shall transmit to the House of Representatives and the Senate, a document containing the report required by section 402(b) or 409(b) as the case may be, to be submitted on or before such December 31.

(c) Effective date of proclamations and agreements; disapproval of reports.

(1) In the case of a document referred to in subsection (a), the proclamation set forth in the document may become effective and the agreement set

forth in the document may enter into force and effect only if a joint resolution described in section 151(b)(3) that approves of the extension of nondiscriminatory treatment to the products of the country concerned is enacted into law.

(2) In the case of a document referred to in subsection (b) which contains a report submitted by the President under section 402(b) or 409(b) with respect to a nonmarket economy country, if, before the close of the 90–day period beginning on the day on which such document is delivered to the House of Representatives and to the Senate, a joint resolution described in section 152(a)(1)(B) is enacted into law that disapproves of the report submitted by the President with respect to such country, then, beginning with the day after the end of the 60–day period beginning with the date of the enactment of such resolution of disapproval, (A) nondiscriminatory treatment shall not be in force with respect to the products of such country, and the products of such country shall be dutiable at the rates set forth in rate column numbered 2 of the Harmonized Tariff Schedule of the United States, (B) such country may not participate in any program of the Government of the United States which extends credit or credit guarantees or investment guarantees, and (C) no commercial agreement may thereafter be concluded with such country under this title. If the President vetoes the joint resolution, the joint resolution shall be treated as enacted into law before the end of the 90–day period under this paragraph if both Houses of Congress vote to override such veto on or before the later of the last day of such 90–day period or the last day of the 15–day period (excluding any day described in section 154(b)) beginning on the date the Congress receives the veto message from the President.

19 USC 2438

Sec. 408. Payment by Czechoslovakia of Amounts Owed United States Citizens and Nationals

(a) **Renegotiation of 1974 agreement.** The arrangement initialed on July 5, 1974, with respect to the settlement of the claims of citizens and nationals of the United States against the Government of Czechoslovakia shall be renegotiated and shall be submitted to the Congress as part of any agreement entered into under this title with Czechoslovakia.

(b) **Provisional retention of gold.** The United States shall not release any gold belonging to Czechoslovakia and controlled directly or indirectly by the United States pursuant to the provisions of the Paris Reparations Agreement of January 24, 1946, or otherwise, until such agreement has been approved by the Congress.

19 USC 2439

Sec. 409. Freedom to Emigrate to Join a Very Close Relative in United States

(a) **Sanctions for emigration restrictions**. To assure the continued dedication of the United States to the fundamental human rights and welfare of its own citizens, and notwithstanding any other provision of law, on or after the date of the enactment of this Act [enacted Jan. 3, 1975], no nonmarket economy country shall participate in any program of the Government of the United States which extends credits or credit guarantees or investment guarantees, directly or indirectly, and the President of the United States shall not conclude any commercial agreement with any such country, during the period beginning with the date on which the President determines that such country—

(1) denies its citizens the right or opportunity to join permanently through emigration, a very close relative in the United State [States], such as a spouse, parent, child, brother, or sister;

(2) imposes more than a nominal tax on the visas or other documents required for emigration described in paragraph (1); or

(3) imposes more than a nominal tax, levy, fine, fee, or other charge on any citizen as a consequence of the desire of such citizen to emigrate as described in paragraph (1),

and ending on the date on which the President determines that such country is no longer in violation of paragraph (1), (2), or (3).

(b) Report to Congress concerning emigration policies. After the date of the enactment of this Act [enacted Jan. 3, 1975], (A) a nonmarket economy country may participate in any program of the Government of the United States which extends credits or credit guarantees or investment guarantees, and (B) the President may conclude a commercial agreement with such country, only after the President has submitted to the Congress a report indicating that such country is not in violation of paragraph (1), (2), or (3) of subsection (a). Such report with respect to such country shall include information as to the nature and implementation of its laws and policies and restrictions or discrimination applied to or against persons wishing to emigrate to the United States to join close relatives. The report required by this subsection shall be submitted initially as provided herein and, with current information, on or before each June 30 and December 31 thereafter, so long as such credits or guarantees are extended or such agreement is in effect.

(c) Exemption from application of section. This section shall not apply to any country the products of which are eligible for the rates set forth in rate column numbered 1 of the Tariff Schedules of the United States on the date of enactment of this Act [enacted Jan. 3, 1975].

(d) Additional exemption from application of section. During any period that a waiver is in effect with respect to any nonmarket economy country under section 402(c), the provisions of subsections (a) and (b) shall not apply with respect to such country.

19 USC 2440

REPEALED

19 USC 2441

REPEALED

TITLE V

GENERALIZED SYSTEM OF PREFERENCES

19 USC 2461

Sec. 501. Authority to Extend Preferences

The President may provide duty-free treatment for any eligible article from any beneficiary developing country in accordance with the provisions of this subchapter. In taking any such action, the President shall have due regard for—

(1) the effect such action will have on furthering the economic development of developing countries through the expansion of their exports;

(2) the extent to which other major developed countries are undertaking a comparable effort to assist developing countries by granting generalized preferences with respect to imports of products of such countries;

(3) the anticipated impact of such action on United States producers of like or directly competitive products; and

(4) the extent of the beneficiary developing country's competitiveness with respect to eligible articles.

19 USC 2462

Sec. 502.   Designation of Beneficiary Developing Countries

(a) Authority to designate countries.

(1) Beneficiary developing countries. The President is authorized to designate countries as beneficiary developing countries for purposes of this title.

(2) Least-developed beneficiary developing countries. The President is authorized to designate any beneficiary developing country as a least-developed beneficiary developing country for purposes of this title, based on the considerations in section 501 and subsection (c) of this section.

(b) Countries ineligible for designation.

(1) Specific countries. The following countries may not be designated as beneficiary developing countries for purposes of this title:

(A) Australia.

(B) Canada.

(C) European Union member states.

(D) Iceland.

(E) Japan.

(F) Monaco.

(G) New Zealand.

(H) Norway.

(I) Switzerland.

(2) Other bases for ineligibility. The President shall not designate any country a beneficiary developing country under this title if any of the following applies:

(A) Such country is a Communist country, unless—

(i) the products of such country receive nondiscriminatory treatment,

(ii) such country is a WTO Member (as such term is defined in section 2(10) of the Uruguay Round Agreements Act) and a member of the International Monetary Fund, and

(iii) such country is not dominated or controlled by international communism.

(B) Such country is a party to an arrangement of countries and participates in any action pursuant to such arrangement, the effect of which is—

(i) to withhold supplies of vital commodity resources from international trade or to raise the price of such commodities to an unreasonable level, and

(ii) to cause serious disruption of the world economy.

(C) Such country affords preferential treatment to the products of a developed country, other than the United States, which has, or is likely to have, a significant adverse effect on United States commerce.

(D) (i) Such country—

(I) has nationalized, expropriated, or otherwise seized ownership or control of property, including patents, trademarks, or copyrights, owned by a United States citizen or by a corporation, partnership, or association which is 50 percent or more beneficially owned by United States citizens,

(II) has taken steps to repudiate or nullify an existing contract or agreement with a United States citizen or a corporation, partnership, or association which is 50 percent or more beneficially owned by United States citizens, the effect of which is to nationalize, expropriate, or otherwise seize ownership or control of property, including patents, trademarks, or copyrights, so owned, or

(III) has imposed or enforced taxes or other exactions, restrictive maintenance or operational conditions, or other measures with respect to property, including patents, trademarks, or copyrights, so owned, the effect of which is to nationalize, expropriate, or otherwise seize ownership or control of such property,

unless clause (ii) applies.

(ii) This clause applies if the President determines that—

(I) prompt, adequate, and effective compensation has been or is being made to the citizen, corporation, partnership, or association referred to in clause (i),

(II) good faith negotiations to provide prompt, adequate, and effective compensation under the applicable provisions of international law are in progress, or the country described in clause (i) is otherwise taking steps to discharge its obligations under international law with respect to such citizen, corporation, partnership, or association, or

(III) a dispute involving such citizen, corporation, partnership, or association over compensation for such a seizure has been submitted to arbitration under the provisions of the Convention for the Settlement of Investment Disputes, or in another mutually agreed upon forum,

and the President promptly furnishes a copy of such determination to the Senate and House of Representatives.

(E) Such country fails to act in good faith in recognizing as binding or in enforcing arbitral awards in favor of United States citizens or a corporation, partnership, or association which is 50 percent or more beneficially owned by United States citizens, which have been made by arbitrators appointed for each case or by permanent arbitral bodies to which the parties involved have submitted their dispute.

(F) Such country aids or abets, by granting sanctuary from prosecution to, any individual or group which has committed an act of international terrorism or the Secretary of State makes a determination with respect to such country under section 6(j)(1)(A) of the Export Administration Act of 1979.

(G) Such country has not taken or is not taking steps to afford internationally recognized worker rights to workers in the country (including any designated zone in that country).

(H) Such country has not implemented its commitments to eliminate the worst forms of child labor.

Subparagraphs (D), (E), (F), (G) and (H) (to the extent described in section 507(6)(D)) shall not prevent the designation of any country as a beneficiary developing country under this title if the President determines that such designation will be in the national economic interest of the United States and reports such determination to the Congress with the reasons therefor.

(c) Factors affecting country designation. In determining whether to designate any country as a beneficiary developing country under this title, the President shall take into account—

(1) an expression by such country of its desire to be so designated;

(2) the level of economic development of such country, including its per capita gross national product, the living standards of its inhabitants, and any other economic factors which the President deems appropriate;

(3) whether or not other major developed countries are extending generalized preferential tariff treatment to such country;

(4) the extent to which such country has assured the United States that it will provide equitable and reasonable access to the markets and basic commodity resources of such country and the extent to which such country has assured the United States that it will refrain from engaging in unreasonable export practices;

(5) the extent to which such country is providing adequate and effective protection of intellectual property rights;

(6) the extent to which such country has taken action to—

(A) reduce trade distorting investment practices and policies (including export performance requirements); and

(B) reduce or eliminate barriers to trade in services; and

(7) whether or not such country has taken or is taking steps to afford to workers in that country (including any designated zone in that country) internationally recognized worker rights.

(d) Withdrawal, suspension, or limitation of country designation.

(1) In general. The President may withdraw, suspend, or limit the application of the duty-free treatment accorded under this title with respect to any country. In taking any action under this subsection, the President shall consider the factors set forth in section 501 and subsection (c) of this section.

(2) Changed circumstances. The President shall, after complying with the requirements of subsection (f)(2), withdraw or suspend the designation of any country as a beneficiary developing country if, after such designation, the President determines that as the result of changed circumstances such country would be barred from designation as a beneficiary developing country under subsection (b)(2). Such country shall cease to be a beneficiary developing country on the day on which the President issues an Executive order or Presidential proclamation revoking the designation of such country under this title.

(3) Advice to Congress. The President shall, as necessary, advise the Congress on the application of section 501 and subsection (c) of this section, and the actions the President has taken to withdraw, to suspend, or to limit the application of duty-free treatment with respect to any country which has failed to adequately take the actions described in subsection (c).

(e) Mandatory graduation of beneficiary developing countries. If the President determines that a beneficiary developing country has become a "high income" country, as defined by the official statistics of the International Bank for Reconstruction and Development, then the President shall terminate the designation of such country as a beneficiary developing country for purposes of this title, effective on January 1 of the second year following the year in which such determination is made.

(f) Congressional notification.

(1) Notification of designation.

(A) In general. Before the President designates any country as a beneficiary developing country under this title, the President shall notify the Congress of the President's intention to make such designation, together with the considerations entering into such decision.

(B) Designation as least-developed beneficiary developing country. At least 60 days before the President designates any country as a least-developed beneficiary developing country, the President shall notify the Congress of the President's intention to make such designation.

(2) Notification of termination. If the President has designated any country as a beneficiary developing country under this title, the President shall not terminate such designation unless, at least 60 days before such termination, the President has notified the Congress and has notified such country of the President's intention to terminate such designation, together with the considerations entering into such decision.

19 USC 2463

Sec. 503.   Designation of Eligible Articles

(a) Eligible articles.

(1) Designation.

(A) In general. Except as provided in subsection (b), the President is authorized to designate articles as eligible articles from all beneficiary developing countries for purposes of this title by Executive order or Presidential proclamation after receiving the advice of the International Trade Commission in accordance with subsection (e).

(B) Least-developed beneficiary developing countries. Except for articles described in subparagraphs (A), (B), and (E) of subsection (b)(1) and articles described in paragraphs (2) and (3) of subsection (b), the President may, in carrying out section 502(d)(1) and subsection (c)(1) of this section, designate articles as eligible articles only for countries designated as least-developed beneficiary developing countries under section 502(a)(2) if, after receiving the advice of the International Trade Commission in accordance with subsection (e) of this section, the President determines that such articles are not import-sensitive in the context of imports from least-developed beneficiary developing countries.

(C) Three-year rule. If, after receiving the advice of the International Trade Commission under subsection (e), an article has been formally considered for designation as an eligible article under this title and denied such designation, such article may not be reconsidered for such designation for a period of 3 years after such denial.

(2) Rule of origin.

(A) General rule. The duty-free treatment provided under this title shall apply to any eligible article which is the growth, product, or manufacture of a beneficiary developing country if—

(i) that article is imported directly from a beneficiary developing country into the customs territory of the United States; and

(ii) the sum of—

(I) the cost or value of the materials produced in the beneficiary developing country or any two or more such countries that are members of the same association of countries and are treated as one country under section 507(2), plus

(II) the direct costs of processing operations performed in such beneficiary developing country or such member countries,

is not less than 35 percent of the appraised value of such article at the time it is entered.

(B) Exclusions. An article shall not be treated as the growth, product, or manufacture of a beneficiary developing country by virtue of having merely undergone—

(i) simple combining or packaging operations, or

(ii) mere dilution with water or mere dilution with another substance that does not materially alter the characteristics of the article.

(3) Regulations. The Secretary of the Treasury, after consulting with the United States Trade Representative, shall prescribe such regulations as may be necessary to carry out paragraph (2), including, but not limited to, regulations providing that, in order to be eligible for duty-free treatment under this title, an article—

(A) must be wholly the growth, product, or manufacture of a beneficiary developing country, or

(B) must be a new or different article of commerce which has been grown, produced, or manufactured in the beneficiary developing country.

(b) Articles that may not be designated as eligible articles.

(1) Import sensitive articles. The President may not designate any article as an eligible article under subsection (a) if such article is within one of the following categories of import-sensitive articles:

(A) Textile and apparel articles which were not eligible articles for purposes of this title on January 1, 1994, as this title was in effect on such date.

(B) Watches, except those watches entered after June 30, 1989, that the President specifically determines, after public notice and comment, will not cause material injury to watch or watch band, strap, or bracelet manufacturing and assembly operations in the United States or the United States insular possessions.

(C) Import-sensitive electronic articles.

(D) Import-sensitive steel articles.

(E) Footwear, handbags, luggage, flat goods, work gloves, and leather wearing apparel which were not eligible articles for purposes of this title on January 1, 1995, as this title was in effect on such date.

(F) Import-sensitive semimanufactured and manufactured glass products.

(G) Any other articles which the President determines to be import-sensitive in the context of the Generalized System of Preferences.

(2) Articles against which other actions taken. An article shall not be an eligible article for purposes of this title for any period during which such article is the subject of any action proclaimed pursuant to section 203 of this Act or section 232 or 351 of the Trade Expansion Act of 1962.

(3) Agricultural products. No quantity of an agricultural product subject to a tariff-rate quota that exceeds the in-quota quantity shall be eligible for duty-free treatment under this title.

(c) Withdrawal, suspension, or limitation of duty-free treatment; competitive need limitation.

(1) In general. The President may withdraw, suspend, or limit the application of the duty-free treatment accorded under this title with respect to any article, except that no rate of duty may be established with respect to any

article pursuant to this subsection other than the rate which would apply but for this title. In taking any action under this subsection, the President shall consider the factors set forth in sections 501 and 502(c).

(2) Competitive need limitation.

(A) Basis for withdrawal of duty-free treatment.

(i) In general. Except as provided in clause (ii) and subject to subsection (d), whenever the President determines that a beneficiary developing country has exported (directly or indirectly) to the United States during any calendar year beginning after December 31, 1995—

(I) a quantity of an eligible article having an appraised value in excess of the applicable amount for the calendar year, or

(II) a quantity of an eligible article equal to or exceeding 50 percent of the appraised value of the total imports of that article into the United States during any calendar year,

the President shall, not later than July 1 of the next calendar year, terminate the duty-free treatment for that article from that beneficiary developing country.

(ii) Annual adjustment of applicable amount. For purposes of applying clause (i), the applicable amount is—

(I) for 1996, $75,000,000, and

(II) for each calendar year thereafter, an amount equal to the applicable amount in effect for the preceding calendar year plus $5,000,000.

(B) Country defined. For purposes of this paragraph, the term "country" does not include an association of countries which is treated as one country under section 507(2), but does include a country which is a member of any such association.

(C) Redesignations. A country which is no longer treated as a beneficiary developing country with respect to an eligible article by reason of subparagraph (A) may, subject to the considerations set forth in sections 501 and 502, be redesignated a beneficiary developing country with respect to such article if imports of such article from such country did not exceed the limitations in subparagraph (A) during the preceding calendar year.

(D) Least-developed beneficiary developing countries and beneficiary sub-Saharan African countries. Subparagraph (A) shall not apply to any least-developed beneficiary developing country or any beneficiary sub-Saharan African country.

(E) Articles not produced in the United States excluded. Subparagraph (A)(i)(II) shall not apply with respect to any eligible article if a like or directly competitive article was not produced in the United States on January 1, 1995.

(F) De minimis waivers.

(i) In general. The President may disregard subparagraph (A)(i)(II) with respect to any eligible article from any beneficiary developing country if the aggregate appraised value of the imports of such article into the United States during the preceding calendar year does not exceed the applicable amount for such preceding calendar year.

(ii) Applicable amount. For purposes of applying clause (i), the applicable amount is—

(I) for calendar year 1996, $13,000,000, and

(II) for each calendar year thereafter, an amount equal to the applicable amount in effect for the preceding calendar year plus $500,000.

(d) Waiver of competitive need limitation.

(1) In general. The President may waive the application of subsection (c)(2) with respect to any eligible article of any beneficiary developing country if, before July 1 of the calendar year beginning after the calendar year for which a determination described in subsection (c)(2)(A) was made with respect to such eligible article, the President—

(A) receives the advice of the International Trade Commission under section 332 of the Tariff Act of 1930 on whether any industry in the United States is likely to be adversely affected by such waiver,

(B) determines, based on the considerations described in sections 501 and 502(c) and the advice described in subparagraph (A), that such waiver is in the national economic interest of the United States, and

(C) publishes the determination described in subparagraph (B) in the Federal Register.

(2) Considerations by the President. In making any determination under paragraph (1), the President shall give great weight to—

(A) the extent to which the beneficiary developing country has assured the United States that such country will provide equitable and reasonable access to the markets and basic commodity resources of such country, and

(B) the extent to which such country provides adequate and effective protection of intellectual property rights.

(3) Other bases for waiver. The President may waive the application of subsection (c)(2) if, before July 1 of the calendar year beginning after the calendar year for which a determination described in subsection (c)(2) was made with respect to a beneficiary developing country, the President determines that—

(A) there has been a historical preferential trade relationship between the United States and such country,

(B) there is a treaty or trade agreement in force covering economic relations between such country and the United States, and

(C) such country does not discriminate against, or impose unjustifiable or unreasonable barriers to, United States commerce,

and the President publishes that determination in the Federal Register.

(4) Limitations on waivers.

(A) In general. The President may not exercise the waiver authority under this subsection with respect to a quantity of an eligible article entered during any calendar year beginning after 1995, the aggregate appraised value of which equals or exceeds 30 percent of the aggregate appraised value of all articles that entered duty-free under this title during the preceding calendar year.

(B) Other waiver limits. The President may not exercise the waiver authority provided under this subsection with respect to a quantity of an eligible article entered during any calendar year beginning after 1995, the aggregate appraised value of which exceeds 15 percent of the aggregate appraised value of all articles that have entered duty-free under this title during the preceding calendar year from those beneficiary developing countries which for the preceding calendar year—

(i) had a per capita gross national product (calculated on the basis of the best available information, including that of the International Bank for Reconstruction and Development) of $5,000 or more; or

(ii) had exported (either directly or indirectly) to the United States a quantity of articles that was duty-free under this title that had an aggregate appraised value of more than 10 percent of the aggregate appraised value of all articles that entered duty-free under this title during that year.

(C) Calculation of limitations. There shall be counted against the limitations imposed under subparagraphs (A) and (B) for any calendar year only that value of any eligible article of any country that—

(i) entered duty-free under this title during such calendar year; and

(ii) is in excess of the value of that article that would have been so entered during such calendar year if the limitations under subsection (c)(2)(A) applied.

(5) Effective period of waiver. Any waiver granted under this subsection shall remain in effect until the President determines that such waiver is no longer warranted due to changed circumstances.

(e) **International Trade Commission advice.** Before designating articles as eligible articles under subsection (a)(1), the President shall publish and furnish the International Trade Commission with lists of articles which may be considered for designation as eligible articles for purposes of this title. The provisions of sections 131, 132, 133, and 134 shall be complied with as though action under section 501 and this section were action under section 123 to carry out a trade agreement entered into under section 123.

(f) **Special rule concerning Puerto Rico.** No action under this title may affect any tariff duty imposed by the Legislature of Puerto Rico pursuant to section 319 of the Tariff Act of 1930 on coffee imported into Puerto Rico.

19 USC 2464

Sec. 504. Review and Report to Congress

The President shall submit an annual report to the Congress on the status of internationally recognized worker rights within each beneficiary developing country, including the findings of the Secretary of Labor with respect to the beneficiary country's implementation of its international commitments to eliminate the worst forms of child labor.

19 USC 2465

Sec. 505. Date of Termination

No duty-free treatment provided under this title [*19 USC §§ 2461* et seq.] shall remain in effect after September 30, 2001.

19 USC 2466

Sec. 506. Agricultural Exports of Beneficiary Developing Countries

The appropriate agencies of the United States shall assist beneficiary developing countries to develop and implement measures designed to assure that the agricultural sectors of their economies are not directed to export markets to the detriment of the production of foodstuffs for their citizenry.

TITLE VI

GENERAL PROVISIONS

19 USC 2481

Sec. 601. Definitions

For purposes of this Act—

(1) The term "duty" includes the rate and form of any import duty, including but not limited to tariff-rate quotas.

(2) The term "other import restriction" includes a limitation, prohibition, charge, or exaction other than duty, imposed on importation or imposed for the regulation of importation. The term does not include any orderly marketing agreement.

(3) The term "ad valorem" includes ad valorem equivalent. Whenever any limitation on the amount by which or to which any rate of duty may be decreased or increased pursuant to a trade agreement is expressed in terms of an ad valorem percentage, the ad valorem amount taken into account for purposes of such limitation shall be determined by the President on the basis of the value of imports of the articles concerned during the most recent representative period.

(4) The term "ad valorem equivalent" means the ad valorem equivalent of a specific rate or, in the case of a combination of rates including a specific rate, the sum of the ad valorem equivalent of the specific rate and of the ad valorem rate. The ad valorem equivalent shall be determined by the President on the basis of the value of imports of the article concerned during the most recent representative period. In determining the value of imports, the President shall utilize, to the maximum extent practicable, the standards of valuation contained in section 402 * * * of the Tariff Act of 1930 * * *.

(5) An imported article is "directly competitive with" a domestic article at an earlier or later stage of processing, and a domestic article is "directly competitive with" an imported article at an earlier or later stage of process-

ing, if the importation of the article has an economic effect on producers of the domestic article comparable to the effect of importation of articles in the same stage of processing as the domestic article. For purposes of this paragraph, the unprocessed article is at an earlier stage of processing.

(6) The term "modification", as applied to any duty or other import restriction, includes the elimination of any duty or other import restriction.

(7) The term "existing" means (A) when used, without the specification of any date, with respect to any matter relating to entering into or carrying out a trade agreement or other action authorized by this Act, existing on the day on which such trade agreement is entered into or such other action is taken; and (B) when used with respect to a rate of duty, the nonpreferential rate of duty (however established, and even though temporarily suspended by Act of Congress or otherwise) set forth in rate column numbered 1 of chapters 1 through 97 of the Harmonized Tariff Schedule of the United States on the date specified or (if no date is specified) on the day referred to in clause (A).

(8) A product of a country or area is an article which is the growth, produce, or manufacture of such country or area.

(9) The term "nondiscriminatory treatment" means trade treatment based on normal trade relations (known under international law as most-favored-nation treatment).

(10) The term "commerce" includes services associated with international trade.

* * *

19 USC 2483

Sec. 604.   Consequential Changes in the Harmonized Tariff Schedule of the United States

The President shall from time to time, as appropriate, embody in the Harmonized Tariff Schedule of the United States the substance of the relevant provisions of this Act, and of other Acts affecting import treatment, and actions thereunder, including removal, modification, continuance, or imposition of any rate of duty or other import restriction.

* * *

19 USC 2485

Sec. 607.   Voluntary Limitations on Exports of Steel to the United States

No person shall be liable for damages, penalties, or other sanctions under the Federal Trade Commission Act (15 U.S.C. 41–77) or the Antitrust Acts (as defined in section 4 of the Federal Trade Commission Act (15 U.S.C. 44)), or under any similar State law, on account of his negotiating, entering into, participating in, or implementing an arrangement providing for the voluntary limitation on exports of steel and steel products to the United States, or any modification or renewal of such an arrangement, if such arrangement or such modification or renewal—

(1) was undertaken prior to the date of the enactment of this Act at the request of the Secretary of State or his delegate, and

(2) ceases to be effective not later than January 1, 1975.

* * *

19 USC 2487

REPEALED

Item 48

UNITED STATES: TRADE AGREEMENTS ACT OF 1979

(Selected provisions, as amended)

Public Law 96–39, Approved July 26, 1979, 93 Stat. 144

An Act

To approve and implement the trade agreements negotiated
under the Trade Act of 1974, and for other purposes.

Be it enacted by the Senate and House of Representatives of the United
States of America in Congress assembled,

Section 1. Short Title; Table of Contents; Purposes

(a) **Short Title.** This Act may be cited as the "Trade Agreements Act of
1979".

(b) **Table of Contents.**

TITLE V.   IMPLEMENTATION OF CERTAIN TARIFF NEGOTIATIONS
[omitted]

TITLE VI.   CIVIL AIRCRAFT AGREEMENT
[omitted]

TITLE VII.   CERTAIN AGRICULTURAL MEASURES
[omitted]

TITLE VIII.   TREATMENT OF DISTILLED SPIRITS
[omitted]

TITLE IX.   ENFORCEMENT OF UNITED STATES RIGHTS
[omitted]

TITLE X.   JUDICIAL REVIEW
[omitted]

TITLE XI.   MISCELLANEOUS PROVISIONS

---

19 USC 2502

(c) Purposes. The purposes of this Act are—

(1) to approve and implement the trade agreements negotiated under the Trade Act of 1974;

(2) to foster the growth and maintenance of an open world trading system;

(3) to expand opportunities for the commerce of the United States in international trade; and

(4) to improve the rules of international trade and to provide for the enforcement of such rules, and for other purposes.

19 USC 2503

Sec. 2.   Approval of Trade Agreements

(a) Approval of agreements and statements of administrative action. In accordance with the provisions of sections 102 and 151 of the Trade Act of 1974 (19 U.S.C. 2112 and 2191), the Congress approves the trade agreements described in subsection (c) submitted to the Congress on June 19, 1979, and the statements of administrative action proposed to implement such trade agreements submitted to the Congress on that date.

(b) Acceptance of agreements by the President.

(1) In general. The President may accept for the United States the final legal instruments or texts embodying each of the trade agreements approved by the Congress under subsection (a) of this section. The President shall submit a copy of each final instrument or text to the Congress on the date such text or instrument is available, together with a notification of any changes in the instruments or texts, including their annexes, if any, as

accepted and the texts of such agreements as submitted to the Congress under subsection (a) of this section. Such final legal instruments or texts shall be deemed to be the agreements submitted to and approved by the Congress under subsection (a) of this section if such changes are—

(A) only rectifications of a formal character or minor technical or clerical changes which do not affect the substance or meaning of the texts as submitted to the Congress on June 19, 1979, or

(B) changes in annexes to such agreements, and the President determines that the balance of United States rights and obligations under such agreements is maintained.

(2) Application of agreement between the United States and other countries. No agreement accepted by the President under paragraph (1) shall apply between the United States and any other country unless the President determines that such country—

(A) has accepted the obligations of the agreement with respect to the United States, and

(B) should not otherwise be denied the benefits of the agreement with respect to the United States because such country has not accorded adequate benefits, including substantially equal competitive opportunities for the commerce of the United States to the extent required under section 126(c) of the Trade Act of 1974 (19 U.S.C. 2136(c)), to the United States.

(3) Limitation on acceptance concerning major industrial countries. The President may not accept an agreement described in paragraph (1), (2), (3), (4), (5), (6), (7), (9), (10), or (11) of subsection (c) of this section, unless he determines that each major industrial country (as defined in section 126(d) of the Trade Act of 1974 (19 U.S.C. 2136(d)) is also accepting the agreement. Notwithstanding the preceding sentence, the President may accept such an agreement, if he determines that only one major industrial country is not accepting that agreement and the acceptance of that agreement by that country is not essential to the effective operation of the agreement, and if—

(A) that country is not a major factor in trade in the products covered by that agreement,

(B) the President has authority to deny the benefits of the agreement to that country and has taken steps to deny the benefits of the agreement to that country, or

(C) a significant portion of United States trade would benefit from the agreement, notwithstanding such nonacceptance, and the President determines and reports to the Congress that it is in the national interest of the United States to accept the agreement.

For purposes of this paragraph, the acceptance of an agreement by the European Communities on behalf of its member countries shall also be treated as acceptance of that agreement by each member country, and acceptance of an agreement by all the member countries of the European Communities shall also be treated as acceptance of that agreement by the European Communities.

(c) Trade agreements to which this act applies. The trade agreements to which subsection (a) of this section applies are the following:

(1) The Agreement on Implementation of Article VII of the General Agreement on Tariffs and Trade (relating to customs valuation).

(2) The Agreement on Government Procurement.

(3) The Agreement on Import Licensing Procedures.

(4) The Agreement on Technical Barriers to Trade (relating to product standards).

(5) The Agreement on Interpretation and Application of Articles VI, XVI, and XXIII of the General Agreement on Tariffs and Trade (relating to subsidies and countervailing measures).

(6) The Agreement on Implementation of Article VI of the General Agreement on Tariffs and Trade (relating to antidumping measures).

(7) The International Dairy Arrangement.

(8) Certain bilateral agreements on cheese, other dairy products, and meat.

(9) The Arrangement Regarding Bovine Meat.

(10) The Agreement on Trade in Civil Aircraft.

(11) Texts Concerning a Framework for the Conduct of World Trade.

(12) Certain Bilateral Agreements to Eliminate the Wine-Gallon Method of Tax and Duty Assessment.

(13) Certain other agreements to be reflected in Schedule XX of the United States to the General Agreement on Tariffs and Trade, including Agreements—

(A) to Modify United States Watch Marking Requirements, and to Modify United States Tariff Nomenclature and Rates of Duty for Watches,

(B) to Provide Duty-Free Treatment for Agricultural and Horticultural Machinery, Equipment, Implements, and Parts Thereof, and

(C) to Modify United States Tariff Nomenclature and Rates of Duty for Ceramic Tableware.

(14) The Agreement with the Hungarian People's Republic.

19 USC 2504

Sec. 3. Relationship of Trade Agreements to United States Law

(a) United States statutes to prevail in conflict. No provision of any trade agreement approved by the Congress under section 2(a), nor the application of any such provision to any person or circumstance, which is in conflict with any statute of the United States shall be given effect under the laws of the United States.

(b) Implementing regulations. Regulations necessary or appropriate to carry out actions proposed in any statement of proposed administrative action submitted to the Congress under section 102 of the Trade Act of 1974 to implement each agreement approved under section 2(a) shall be issued within

1 year after the date of the entry into force of such agreement with respect to the United States.

(c) Changes in statutes to implement a requirement, amendment, or recommendation.

(1) Presidential determination. Whenever the President determines that it is necessary or appropriate to amend, repeal, or enact a statute of the United States in order to implement any requirement of, amendment to, or recommendation under such an agreement, he shall submit to the Congress a draft of a bill to accomplish the amendment, repeal, or enactment and a statement of any administrative action proposed to implement the requirement, amendment, or recommendation. Not less than 30 days before submitting such a bill, the President shall consult with the Committee on Ways and Means of the House of Representatives, the Committee on Finance of the Senate, and each committee of the House or Senate which has jurisdiction over legislation involving subject matters which would be affected by such amendment, repeal, or enactment. The consultation shall treat all matters relating to the implementation of such requirement, amendment, or recommendation, as provided in paragraphs (2) and (3).

(2) Conditions for taking effect under United States law. No such amendment shall enter into force with respect to the United States, and no such requirement, amendment, or recommendation shall be implemented under United States law, unless—

(A) the President, after consultation with the Congress under paragraph (1), notifies the House of Representatives and the Senate of his determination and publishes notice of that determination in the Federal Register,

(B) the President transmits a document to the House of Representatives and to the Senate containing a copy of the text of such requirement, amendment, or recommendation, together with—

(i) a draft of a bill to amend or repeal provisions of existing statutes or to create statutory authority and an explanation as to how the bill and any proposed administrative action affect existing law, and

(ii) a statement of how the requirement, amendment, or recommendation serves the interests of United States commerce and why the legislative and administrative action is necessary or appropriate to carry out the requirement, amendment, or recommendation, and

(C) the bill submitted by the President is enacted into law.

(3) Recommendations as to application. The President may make the same type of recommendations, in the same manner and subject to the same conditions, to the Congress with respect to the application of any such requirement, amendment, or recommendation as he may make, under section 102(f) of the Trade Act of 1974, with respect to a trade agreement.

(4) Congressional procedures applicable. The bill submitted by the President shall be introduced in accordance with the provisions of subsection (c)(1) of this section, of section 151 of the Trade Act of 1974, and the provisions of

subsections (d), (e), (f), and (g) of such section shall apply to the consideration of the bill. For the purpose of applying section 151 of such Act to such bill—

(A) the term "trade agreement" shall be treated as a reference to the requirement, amendment, or recommendation, and

(B) the term "implementing bill" or "implementing revenue bill", whichever is appropriate, shall be treated as a reference to the bill submitted by the President.

* * *

(f) Unspecified private remedies not created. Neither the entry into force with respect to the United States of any agreement approved under section 2(a), nor the enactment of this Act, shall be construed as creating any private right of action or remedy for which provision is not explicitly made under this Act or under the laws of the United States.

TITLE I
COUNTERVAILING AND ANTIDUMPING DUTIES
[See Tariff Act of 1930]

TITLE II
CUSTOMS VALUATION
[See Tariff Act of 1930]

TITLE III
GOVERNMENT PROCUREMENT
19 USC 2511

Sec. 301. General Authority to Modify Discriminatory Purchasing Requirements

(a) Presidential waiver of discriminatory purchasing require-ments. Subject to subsection (f) of this section, the President may waive, in whole or in part, with respect to eligible products of any foreign country or instrumentality designated under subsection (b), and suppliers of such products, the application of any law, regulation, procedure, or practice regarding Government procurement that would, if applied to such products and suppliers, result in treatment less favorable than that accorded—

(1) to United States products and suppliers of such products; or

(2) to eligible products of another foreign country or instrumentality which is a party to the Agreement and suppliers of such products.

(b) Designation of eligible countries and instrumentalities. The President may designate a foreign country or instrumentality for purposes of subsection (a) only if he determines that such country or instrumentality—

(1) is a country or instrumentality which (A) has become a party to the Agreement or the North American Free Trade Agreement, and (B) will provide appropriate reciprocal competitive government procurement opportunities to United States products and suppliers of such products;

(2) is a country or instrumentality, other than a major industrial country, which (A) will otherwise assume the obligations of the Agreement, and (B) will provide such opportunities to such products and suppliers;

(3) is a country or instrumentality, other than a major industrial country, which will provide such opportunities to such products and suppliers; or

(4) is a least developed country.

(c) Modification or withdrawal of waivers and designations. The President may modify or withdraw any waiver granted pursuant to subsection (a) or designation made pursuant to subsection (b).

(d) [Terminated]

(e) Procurement procedures by certain Federal agencies. Notwithstanding any other provision of law, the President may direct any agency of the United States listed in Annex 1001.1a–2 of the North American Free Trade Agreement to procure eligible products in compliance with the procedural provisions of chapter 10 of such Agreement.

(f) Small business and minority preferences. The authority of the President under subsection (a) of this section to waive any law, regulation, procedure, or practice regarding Government procurement does not authorize the waiver of any small business or minority preference.

19 USC 2512

Sec. 302. Authority to Encourage Reciprocal Competitive Procurement Practices

(a) Authority to bar procurement from non-designated countries.

(1) In general. Subject to paragraph (2), the President, in order to encourage additional countries to become parties to the Agreement and to provide appropriate reciprocal competitive government procurement opportunities to United States products and suppliers of such products—

(A) shall, with respect to procurement covered by the Agreement, prohibit the procurement, after the date on which any waiver under section 301(a) first takes effect, of products—

(i) which are products of a foreign country or instrumentality which is not designated pursuant to section 301(b), and

(ii) which would otherwise be eligible products; and

(B) may, with respect to procurement covered by the Agreement, take such other actions within the President's authority as the President deems necessary.

(2) Exception. Paragraph (1) shall not apply in the case of procurements for which—

(A) there are no offers of products or services of the United States or of eligible products; or

(B) the offers of products or services of the United States or of eligible products are insufficient to fulfill the requirements of the United States Government.

(b) Deferrals and waivers. Notwithstanding subsection (a), but in furtherance of the objective of encouraging countries to become parties to the Agreement and provide appropriate reciprocal competitive government procurement opportunities to United States products and suppliers of such products, the President may—

(1) waive the prohibition required by subsection (a)(1) on procurement of products of a foreign country or instrumentality which has not yet become a party to the Agreement but—

(A) has agreed to apply transparent and competitive procedures to its government procurement equivalent to those in the Agreement, and

(B) maintains and enforces effective prohibitions on bribery and other corrupt practices in connection with its government procurement;

(2) authorize agency heads to waive, subject to interagency review and general policy guidance by the organization established under section 242(a) of the Trade Expansion Act of 1962), such prohibition on a case-by-case basis when in the national interest; and

(3) authorize the Secretary of Defense to waive, subject to interagency review and policy guidance by the organization established under section 242(a) of the Trade Expansion Act of 1962), such prohibition for products of any country or instrumentality which enters into a reciprocal procurement agreement with the Department of Defense.

Before exercising the waiver authority under paragraph (1), the President shall consult with the appropriate private sector advisory committees established under section 135 of the Trade Act of 1974 and with the appropriate committees of the Congress.

(c) Report on impact of restrictions.

(1) Impact on the economy. On or before July 1, 1981, the President shall report to the Committee on Ways and Means and the Committee on Government Operations of the House of Representatives and to the Committee on Finance and the Committee on Governmental Affairs of the Senate on the effects on the United States economy (including effects on employment, production, competition, costs and prices, technological development, export trade, balance of payments, inflation, and the Federal budget) of the refusal of developed countries to allow the Agreement to cover the entities of the governments of such countries which are the principal purchasers of goods and equipment in appropriate product sectors.

(2) Recommendations for attaining reciprocity. The report required by paragraph (1) shall include an evaluation of alternative means to obtain equity and reciprocity in such product sectors, including (A) prohibiting the procurement of products of such countries by United States entities not covered by the Agreement, and (B) modifying the application of title III of the Act of March 3, 1933, commonly referred to as the Buy American Act. The report shall include an analysis of the effect of such alternative means on the United States economy (including effects on employment, production, competition, costs and prices, technological development, export trade, balance of payments, inflation, and the Federal budget), and on successful negotiations on the expansion of the coverage of the Agreement pursuant to section 304(a) and (b), other trade negotiating objectives, the relationship of the Federal Government to State and local governments, and such other factors as the President deems appropriate.

(3) Consultation. In the preparation of the report required by paragraph (1) and the evaluation and analysis required by paragraph (2), the President shall consult with representatives of the public, industry, and labor, and make available pertinent, nonconfidential information obtained in the course of such preparation to the advisory committees established pursuant to section 135 of the Trade Act of 1974.

(d) Proposed action.

(1) Presidential report. On or before October 1, 1981, the President shall prepare and transmit to the congressional committees referred to in subsection (c)(1) a report which describes the actions he deems appropriate to establish reciprocity with major industrialized countries in the area of Government procurement.

(2) Procedure.

(A) Presidential determination. If the President determines that any changes in existing law or new statutory authority are required to authorize or to implement any action proposed in the report submitted under paragraph (1), he shall, on or after January 1, 1982, submit to the Congress a bill to accomplish such changes or provide such new statutory authority. Prior to submitting such a bill, the President shall consult with the appropriate committees of the Congress having jurisdiction over legislation involving subject matters which would be affected by such action, and shall submit to such committees a proposed draft of such bill.

(B) Congressional consideration. The appropriate committee of each House of the Congress shall give a bill submitted pursuant to subparagraph (A) prompt consideration and shall make its best efforts to take final committee action on such bill in an expeditious manner.

19 USC 2513

Sec. 303. Waiver of Discriminatory Purchasing Requirements With Respect to Purchases of Civil Aircraft

The President may waive the application of the provisions of title III of the Act of March 3, 1933, popularly referred to as the Buy American Act, in the case of any procurement of civil aircraft and related articles of a country or instrumentality which is a party to the Agreement on Trade in Civil Aircraft referred to in section 2(c) and approved under section 2(a). The President may modify or withdraw any waiver granted pursuant to this section.

19 USC 2514

Sec. 304. Expansion of the coverage of the Agreement

(a) **Overall negotiating objective**. The President shall seek in the renegotiations provided for in article XXIV(7) of the Agreement more open and equitable market access abroad, and the harmonization, reduction, or elimination of devices which distort trade or commerce related to Government procurement, with the overall goal of maximizing the economic benefit to the United States through maintaining and enlarging foreign markets for products of United States agriculture, industry, mining, and commerce, the development of fair and equitable market opportunities, and open and nondiscriminatory world trade. In carrying out the provisions of this subsection, the President shall consider the assessment made in the report required under section 306(a).

(b) Sector negotiating objectives. The President shall seek, consistent with the overall objective set forth in subsection (a) and to the maximum extent feasible, with respect to appropriate product sectors, competitive opportunities for the export of United States products to the developed countries of the world equivalent to the competitive opportunities afforded by the United States, taking into account all barriers to, and other distortions of, international trade affecting that sector.

(c) Independent verification objective. The President shall seek to establish in the renegotiation provided for in article XXIV(7) of the Agreement a system for independent verification of information provided by parties to the Agreement to the Committee on Government Procurement pursuant to article XIX(5) of the Agreement.

(d) Reports on negotiations.

(1) Report in the event of inadequate progress. If, during the renegotiations of the Agreement, the President at any time determines that the renegotiations are not progressing satisfactorily and are not likely to result, within twelve months of the commencement thereof, in an expansion of the Agreement to cover purchases by the entities of the governments of developed countries which are the principal purchasers of goods and equipment in appropriate product sectors, he shall so report to the congressional committees referred to in section 302(c)(1). Taking into account the objectives set forth in subsections (a) and (b) of this section and the factors required to be analyzed under section 302(c), the President shall further report to such committees appropriate actions to seek reciprocity in such product sectors with such countries in the area of government procurement.

(2) Legislative recommendations. Taking into account the factors required to be analyzed under section 302(c), the President may recommend to the Congress legislation (with respect to entities of the Government which are not covered by the Agreement) which may prohibit such entities from purchasing products of such countries.

(3) Annual reports. Each annual report of the President under section 163(a) of the Trade Act of 1974 made after the date of enactment of this Act [enacted July 26, 1979] shall report the actions, if any, the President deemed appropriate to establish reciprocity in appropriate product sectors with major industrial countries in the area of government procurement.

(e) Extension of nondiscrimination and national treatment. Before exercising the waiver authority in section 301 for procurement not covered by the Agreement on the date it enters into force with respect to the United States, the President shall follow the consultation provisions of section 135 and chapter 6 of title I of the Trade Act of 1974 for private sector and congressional consultations.

19 USC 2515

Sec. 305. Monitoring and Enforcement

(a) Monitoring and enforcement structure recommendations. In the preparation of the recommendations for the reorganization of trade functions, the President shall ensure that careful consideration is given to monitoring and enforcing the requirements of the Agreement and this title, with particular regard to the tendering procedures required by the Agreement or otherwise agreed to by a country or instrumentality likely to be designated pursuant to section 301(b).

(b) Rules of origin.

(1) Advisory rulings and final determinations. For the purposes of this title, the Secretary of the Treasury shall provide for the prompt issuance of advisory rulings and final determinations on whether, under section 308(4)(B), an article is or would be a product of a foreign country or instrumentality designated pursuant to section 301(b).

(2) Penalties for fraudulent conduct. In addition to any other provisions of law which may be applicable, section 1001 of title 18, United States Code, shall apply to fraudulent conduct with respect to the origin of products for purposes of qualifying for a waiver under section 301 or avoiding a prohibition under section 302.

(c) Report to Congress on rules of origin.

(1) Domestic administrative practices. As soon as practicable after the close of the two-year period beginning on the date on which any waiver under section 301(a) first takes effect, the President shall prepare and transmit to Congress a report containing an evaluation of administrative practices under any provision of law which requires determinations to be made of the country of origin of goods, products, commodities, or other articles of commerce. Such evaluation shall be accompanied by the President's recommendations for legislative and executive measures required to improve and simplify and to make more uniform and consistent such practices. Such evaluation and recommendations shall take into account the special problems affecting insular possessions of the United States with respect to such practices.

(2) Foreign administrative practices. The report required under paragraph (1) shall contain an evaluation of the administrative practices under the laws of each major industrial country which require determinations to be made of the country of origin of goods, products, commodities, or other articles of commerce, including an assessment of such practices on the exports of the United States.

(d)–(k) [Terminated]

19 USC 2516

Sec. 306   REPEALED

19 USC 2517

Sec. 307. Availability of Information to Members of Congress Designated as Official Advisers

The Special Representative for Trade Negotiations [United States Trade Representative] shall make available to the Members of Congress designated as official advisers pursuant to section 161 of the Trade Act of 1974 information compiled by the Committee on Government Procurement under article XIX(5) of the Agreement.

19 USC 2518

Sec. 308. Definitions

As used in this title—

(1) Agreement. The term "Agreement" means the Agreement on Government Procurement referred to in section 101(d)(17) of the Uruguay Round Agreements Act, as submitted to the Congress, but including rectifications, modifications, and amendments which are accepted by the United States.

(2) Civil aircraft. The term "civil aircraft and related articles" means—

(A) all aircraft other than aircraft to be purchased for use by the Department of Defense or the United States Coast Guard;

(B) the engines (and parts and components for incorporation therein) of such aircraft;

(C) any other parts, components, and subassemblies for incorporation in such aircraft; and

(D) any ground flight simulators, and parts and components thereof, for use with respect to such aircraft,

whether to be purchased for use as original or replacement equipment in the manufacture, repair, maintenance, rebuilding, modification, or conversion of such aircraft, and without regard to whether such aircraft or articles receive duty-free treatment pursuant to section 601(a)(2).

(3) Developed countries. The term "developed countries" means countries so designated by the President.

(4) (A) In general. The term "eligible product" means, with respect to any foreign country or instrumentality that is—

(i) a party to the Agreement, a product or service of that country or instrumentality which is covered under the Agreement for procurement by the United States; or

(ii) a party to the North American Free Trade Agreement, a product or service of that country or instrumentality which is covered under the North American Free Trade Agreement for procurement by the United States.

(B) Rule of origin. An article is a product of a country or instrumentality only if (i) it is wholly the growth, product, or manufacture of that country or instrumentality, or (ii) in the case of an article which consists in whole or in part of materials from another country or instrumentality, it has been substantially transformed into a new and different article of commerce with a name, character, or use distinct from that of the article or articles from which it was so transformed.

(C) Lowered threshold for certain products as a consequence of United States–Israel Free Trade Area provisions. The term "eligible product" includes a product or service of Israel for which the United States is obligated to waive Buy National restrictions under—

(i) the Agreement on the Establishment of a Free Trade Area between the Government of the United States of America and the Government of Israel, regardless of the thresholds provided for in the Agreement (as defined in paragraph (1)), or

(ii) any subsequent agreement between the United States and Israel which lowers on a reciprocal basis the applicable threshold for entities covered by the Agreement.

(D) Lowered threshold for certain products as a consequence of United States–Canada Free–Trade Agreement. Except as otherwise agreed by the United States and Canada under paragraph 3 of article 1304 of the United States–Canada Free–Trade Agreement, the term "eligible product" includes a product or service of Canada having a contract value of $25,000 or more that would be covered for procurement by the United States under the Agreement (as defined in paragraph (1)), but for the thresholds provided for in the Agreement.

(5) Instrumentality. The term "instrumentality" shall not be construed to include an agency or division of the government of a country, but may be construed to include such arrangements as the European Economic Community.

(6) Least developed country. The term "least developed country" means any country on the United Nations General Assembly list of least developed countries.

(7) Major industrial country. The term "major industrial country" means any such country as defined in section 126 of the Trade Act of 1974 and any instrumentality of such a country.

TITLE IV
TECHNICAL BARRIERS TO TRADE (STANDARDS)

Subtitle A
Obligations of the United States

19 USC 2531

Sec. 401.   Certain Standards-Related Activities

(a) No bar to engaging in standards activity. Nothing in this title may be construed

(1) to prohibit a Federal agency from engaging in activity related to standards-related measures, including any such measure relating to safety, the protection of human, animal, or plant life or health, the environment, or consumers; or

(2) to limit the authority of a Federal agency to determine the level it considers appropriate of safety or of protection of human, animal, or plant life or health, the environment, or consumers.

(b) Unnecessary obstacles. Nothing in this title may be construed as prohibiting any private person, Federal agency, or State agency from engaging in standards-related activities that do not create unnecessary obstacles to the foreign commerce of the United States. No standards-related activity of any private person, Federal agency, or State agency shall be deemed to constitute an unnecessary obstacle to the foreign commerce of the United States if the demonstrable purpose of the standards-related activity is to achieve a legitimate domestic objective including, but not limited to, the protection of legitimate health or safety, essential security, environmental, or consumer interests and if such activity does not operate to exclude imported products which fully meet the objectives of such activity.

19 USC 2532

Sec. 402.   Federal Standards-Related Activities

No Federal agency may engage in any standards-related activity that creates unnecessary obstacles to the foreign commerce of the United States, including, but not limited to, standards-related activities that violate any of the following requirements:

(1) Nondiscriminatory treatment. Each Federal agency shall ensure, in applying standards-related activities with respect to any imported product, that such product is treated no less favorably than are like domestic or imported products, including, but not limited to, when applying tests or test methods, no less favorable treatment with respect to—

(A) the acceptance of the product for testing in comparable situations;

(B) the administration of the tests in comparable situations;

(C) the fees charged for tests;

(D) the release of test results to the exporter, importer, or agents;

(E) the siting of testing facilities and the selection of samples for testing; and

(F) the treatment of confidential information pertaining to the product.

(2) Use of international standards.

(A) In general. Except as provided in subparagraph (B)(ii), each Federal agency, in developing standards, shall take into consideration international standards and shall, if appropriate, base the standards on international standards.

(B) Application of requirement. For purposes of this paragraph, the following apply:

(i) International standards not appropriate. The reasons for which the basing of a standard on an international standard may not be appropriate include, but are not limited to, the following:

(I) National security requirements.

(II) The prevention of deceptive practices.

(III) The protection of human health or safety, animal or plant life or health, or the environment.

(IV) Fundamental climatic or other geographical factors.

(V) Fundamental technological problems.

(ii) Regional standards. In developing standards, a Federal agency may, but is not required to, take into consideration any international standard promulgated by an international standards organization the membership of which is described in section 451(6)(A)(ii).

(3) Performance criteria. Each Federal agency shall, if appropriate, develop standards based on performance criteria, such as those relating to the intended use of a product and the level of performance that the product must achieve under defined conditions, rather than on design criteria, such as those relating to the physical form of the product or the types of material of which the product is made.

(4) Access for foreign suppliers. Each Federal agency shall, with respect to any conformity assessment procedure used by it, permit access for obtaining an assessment of conformity and the mark of the system, if any to foreign suppliers of a product on the same basis as access is permitted to suppliers of like products, whether of domestic or other foreign origin.

19 USC 2533

Sec. 403.   State and Private Standards-Related Activities

(a) In general. It is the sense of the Congress that no State agency and no private person should engage in any standards-related activity that creates unnecessary obstacles to the foreign commerce of the United States.

(b) Presidential action. The President shall take such reasonable measures as may be available to promote the observance by State agencies and private persons, in carrying out standards-related activities, of requirements equivalent to those imposed on Federal agencies under section 402, and of procedures that provide for notification, participation, and publication with respect to such activities.

Subtitle B
Functions of Federal Agencies

19 USC 2541

Sec. 411.   Functions of Trade Representative

(a) In general. The Trade Representative shall coordinate the consideration of international trade policy issues that arise as a result of, and shall develop international trade policy as it relates to, the implementation of this title.

(b) Negotiating functions. The Trade Representative has responsibility for coordinating United States discussions and negotiations with foreign countries for the purpose of establishing mutual arrangements with respect to standards-related activities. In carrying out this responsibility, the Trade Representative shall inform and consult with any Federal agency having expertise in the matters under discussion and negotiation.

* * *

19 USC 2542

Sec. 412.   Establishment and Operation of Technical Offices

(a) Establishment.

(1) For nonagricultural products. The Secretary of Commerce shall establish and maintain within the Department of Commerce a technical office that shall carry out the functions prescribed under subsection (b) with respect to nonagricultural products.

(2) For agricultural products. The Secretary of Agriculture shall establish and maintain within the Department of Agriculture a technical office that shall carry out the functions prescribed under subsection (b) with respect to agricultural products.

(b) Functions of offices. The President shall prescribe for each technical office established under subsection (a) such functions as the President deems necessary or appropriate to implement this title.

19 USC 2543

Sec. 413.   Representation of United States Interests Before International Standards Organizations

(a) Oversight and Consultation. The Secretary concerned shall—

(1) inform, and consult and coordinate with, the Trade Representative with respect to international standards-related activities identified under paragraph (2);

(2) keep adequately informed regarding international standards-related activities and identify those that may substantially affect the commerce of the United States; and

(3) carry out such functions as are required under subsections (b) and (c).

(b) Representation of United States interests by private persons.

(1) Definitions. For purposes of this subsection—

(A) Organization member. The term "organization member" means the private person who holds membership in a private international standards organization.

(B) Private international standards organization. The term "private international standards organization" means any international standards organization before which the interests of the United States are represented by a private person who is officially recognized by that organization for such purpose.

(2) In general. Except as otherwise provided for in this subsection, the representation of United States interests before any private international standards organization shall be carried out by the organization member.

(3) Inadequate representation. If the Secretary concerned, after inquiry instituted on his own motion or at the request of any private person, Federal agency, or State agency having an interest therein, has reason to believe that the participation by the organization member in the proceedings of a private international standards organization will not result in the adequate represen-

tation of United States interests that are, or may be, affected by the activities of such organization (particularly with regard to the potential impact of any such activity on the international trade of the United States), the Secretary concerned shall immediately notify the organization member concerned. During any such inquiry, the Secretary concerned may solicit and consider the advice of the appropriate representatives referred to in section 417.

(4) Action by organization member. If within the 90-day period after the date on which notification is received under paragraph (3) (or such shorter period as the Secretary concerned determines to be necessary in extraordinary circumstances), the organization member demonstrates to the Secretary concerned its willingness and ability to represent adequately United States interests before the private international standards organization, the Secretary concerned shall take no further action under this subsection.

(5) Action by secretary concerned. If—

(A) within the appropriate period referred to in paragraph (4), the organization member does not respond to the Secretary concerned with respect to the notification, or does respond but does not demonstrate to the Secretary concerned the requisite willingness and ability to represent adequately United States interests; or

(B) there is no organization member of the private international standards organization;

the Secretary concerned shall make appropriate arrangements to provide for the adequate representation of United States interests. In cases where subparagraph (A) applies, such provision shall be made by the Secretary concerned through the appropriate organization member if the private international standards organization involved requires representation by that member.

(c) Representation of United States interests by federal agencies. With respect to any international standards organization before which the interests of the United States are represented by one or more Federal agencies that are officially recognized by that organization for such purpose, the Secretary concerned shall—

(1) encourage cooperation among interested Federal agencies with a view toward facilitating the development of a uniform position with respect to the technical activities with which the organization is concerned;

(2) encourage such Federal agencies to seek information from, and to cooperate with, the affected domestic interests when undertaking such representation; and

(3) not preempt the responsibilities of any Federal agency that has jurisdiction with respect to the activities undertaken by such organization, unless requested to do so by such agency.

19 USC 2544

Sec. 414.   Standards Information Center

(a) Establishment. The Secretary of Commerce shall maintain within the Department of Commerce a standards information center.

(b) Functions. The standards information center shall—

(1) serve as the central national collection facility for information relating to

    (A) standards, technical regulations, conformity assessment procedures, and standards-related activities, whether such standards, technical regulations, conformity assessment procedures, or activities are public or private, domestic or foreign, or international, regional, national, or local; and

    (B) the membership and participation of Federal, State, or local government bodies or private bodies in the United States in international and regional standardizing bodies and conformity assessment systems, as well as in bilateral and multilateral arrangements concerning standards-related activities.

(2) make available to the public at such reasonable fee as the Secretary shall prescribe, copies of information required to be collected under paragraph (1) other than information to which paragraph (3) applies;

(3) use its best efforts to make available to the public, at such reasonable fees as the Secretary shall prescribe, copies of information required to be collected under paragraph (1) that is of private origin, on a cooperative basis with the private individual or entity, foreign or domestic, who holds the copyright on the information;

(4) in case of such information that is of foreign origin, provide, at such reasonable fee as the Secretary shall prescribe, such translation services as may be necessary;

(5) serve as the inquiry point for requests for information regarding standards-related activities, whether adopted or proposed, within the United States, except that in carrying out this paragraph, the Secretary of Commerce shall refer all inquiries regarding agricultural products to the technical office established under section 412(a)(2) within the Department of Agriculture; and

(6) provide such other services as may be appropriate, including but not limited to, such services to the technical offices established under section 412 as may be requested by those offices in carrying out their functions.

(c) Sanitary and Phytosanitary Measures.

(1) Public information. The standards information center shall, in addition to the functions specified under subsection (b), make available to the public relevant documents, at such reasonable fees as the Secretary of Commerce may prescribe, and information regarding

    (A) any sanitary or phytosanitary measure of general application, including any inspection procedure or approval procedure proposed, adopted, or maintained by a Federal agency or agency or a State or local government;

    (B) the procedures of a Federal agency or an agency of a State or local government for risk assessment and factors the agency considers in conducting the assessment;

(C) the determination of the levels of protection that a Federal agency or an agency of a State or local government considers appropriate; and

(D) the membership and participation of the Federal Government and State and local governments in international and regional sanitary and phytosanitary organizations and systems, and in bilateral and multi-lateral arrangements regarding sanitary and phytosanitary measures, and the provisions of those systems and arrangements.

(2) Definitions. The definitions in section 463 apply for purposes of this subsection.

19 USC 2545

Sec. 415.   Contracts and Grants

(a) In General. For purposes of carrying out this title, and otherwise encouraging compliance with the Agreement, the Trade Representative and the Secretary concerned may each, with respect to functions for which responsible under this title, make grants to, or enter into contracts with, any other Federal agency, any State agency, or any private person, to assist such agency or person to implement appropriate programs and activities, including, but not limited to, programs and activities—

(1) to increase awareness of proposed and adopted standards-related activities;

(2) to facilitate international trade through the appropriate international and domestic standards-related activities;

(3) to provide, if appropriate, and pursuant to section 413, adequate United States representation in international standards-related activities; and

(4) to encourage United States exports through increased awareness of foreign standards-related activities that may affect United States exports.

No contract entered into under this section shall be effective except to such extent, and in such amount, as is provided in advance in appropriation Acts.

(b) Terms and Conditions. Any contract entered into, or any grant made, under subsection (a) shall be subject to such terms and conditions as the Trade Representative or Secretary concerned shall by regulation prescribe as being necessary or appropriate to protect the interests of the United States.

(c) Limitations. Financial assistance extended under this section shall not exceed 75 percent of the total costs (as established by the Trade Representative or Secretary concerned, as the case may be) of the program or activity for which assistance is made available. The non-Federal share of such costs shall be made in cash or kind, consistent with the maintenance of the program or activity concerned.

(d) Audit. Each recipient of a grant or contract under this section shall make available to the Trade Representative or the Secretary concerned, as the case may be, and to the Comptroller General of the United States, for purposes of audit and examination, any book, document, paper, and record that is pertinent to the funds received under such grant or contract.

19 USC 2546

Sec. 416. Technical Assistance

The Trade Representative and the Secretary concerned may each, with respect to functions for which responsible under this title, make available, on a reimbursable basis or otherwise, to any other Federal agency, State agency, or private person such assistance, including, but not limited to, employees, services, and facilities, as may be appropriate to assist such agency or person in carrying out standards-related activities in a manner consistent with this title.

19 USC 2547

Sec. 417. Consultations With Representatives of Domestic Interests

In carrying out the functions for which responsible under this title, the Trade Representative and the Secretary concerned shall solicit technical and policy advice from the committees, established under section 135 of the Trade Act of 1974 (19 U.S.C. 2155), that represent the interests concerned, and may solicit advice from appropriate State agencies and private persons.

Subtitle C

Administrative and Judicial Proceedings Regarding Standards-Related Activities

Chapter 1. Representations Alleging United States Violations of Obligations

19 USC 2551

Sec. 421. Right of Action

Except as provided under this chapter, the provisions of this subtitle do not create any right of action under the laws of the United States with respect to allegations that any standards-related activity engaged in within the United States violates the obligations of the United States under the Agreement.

19 USC 2552

Sec. 422. Representations

Any—

(1) Party to the Agreement; or

(2) foreign country that is not a Party to the Agreement but is found by the Trade Representative to extend rights and privileges to the United States that are substantially the same as those that would be so extended if that foreign country were a Party to the Agreement; may make a representation to the Trade Representative alleging that a standards-related activity engaged in within the United States violates the obligations of the United States under the Agreement. Any such representation must be made in accordance with procedures that the Trade Representative shall by regulation prescribe and must provide a reasonable indication that the standards-related activity concerned is having a significant trade effect. No person other than a Party to

the Agreement or a foreign country described in paragraph (2) may make such a representation.

19 USC 2553

Sec. 423.   Action After Receipt of Representations

(a) **Review.** Upon receipt of any representation made under section 422, the Trade Representative shall review the issues concerned in consultation with—

(1) the agency or person alleged to be engaging in violations under the Agreement;

(2) the member agencies of the interagency trade organization established under section 242(a) of the Trade Expansion Act of 1962 (19 U.S.C. 1872(a));

(3) other appropriate Federal agencies; and

(4) appropriate representatives referred to in section 417.

(b) **Resolution.** The Trade Representative shall undertake to resolve, on a mutually satisfactory basis, the issues set forth in the representation through consultation with the parties concerned.

19 USC 2554

Sec. 424.   Procedure After Finding by International Forum

(a) **In general.** If an appropriate international forum finds that a standards-related activity being engaged in within the United States conflicts with the obligations of the United States under the Agreement, the interagency trade organization established under section 242(a) of the Trade Expansion Act of 1962 (19 U.S.C. 1872(a)) shall review the finding and the matters related thereto with a view to recommending appropriate action.

(b) **Cross reference.**

For provisions of law regarding remedies available to domestic persons alleging that standards activities engaged in by Parties to the Agreement (other than the United States) violate the obligations of the Agreement, see section 301 of the Trade Act of 1974 (19 U.S.C. 2411).

Chapter 2.   Other Proceedings Regarding
Certain Standards-Related Activities

19 USC 2561

Sec. 441.   Findings of Reciprocity Required in Administrative Proceedings

(a) **In General.** Except as provided under chapter 1, no Federal agency may consider a complaint or petition against any standards-related activity regarding an imported product, if that activity is engaged in within the United States and is covered by the Agreement, unless the Trade Representative finds, and informs the agency concerned in writing, that—

(1) the country of origin of the imported product is a Party to the Agreement or a foreign country described in section 422(2); and

(2) the dispute settlement procedures provided under the Agreement are not appropriate.

(b) Exemptions. This section does not apply with respect to causes of action arising under—

(1) the antitrust laws as defined in subsection (a) of the first section of the Clayton Act (15 U.S.C. 12(a)); or

(2) statutes administered by the Secretary of Agriculture.

This section does not apply with respect to petitions and proceedings that are provided for under the practices of any Federal agency for the purpose of ensuring, in accordance with section 553 of title 5, United States Code, that interested persons are given an opportunity to participate in agency rulemaking or to seek the issuance, amendment, or repeal of a rule.

19 USC 2562

Sec. 442.   Consideration of Standards-Related Activities by an International Forum

No standards-related activity being engaged in within the United States may be stayed in any judicial or administrative proceeding on the basis that such activity is currently being considered, pursuant to the Agreement, by an international forum.

Subtitle D
Definitions and Miscellaneous Provisions

19 USC 2571

Sec. 451. Definitions

As used in this title—

(1) *Agreement.* The term "Agreement" means the Agreement on Technical Barriers to Trade referred to in section 101(d)(5) of the Uruguay Round Agreements Act.

(2) *Conformity assessment procedure.* The term "conformity assessment procedure" means any procedure used, directly or indirectly, to determine that relevant requirements in technical regulations or standards are fulfilled.

(3) *Federal agency.* The term "Federal agency" means any of the following within the meaning of chapter 2 of part I of title 5, United States Code:

    (A) Any executive department.

    (B) Any military department.

    (C) Any Government corporation.

    (D) Any Government-controlled corporation.

    (E) Any independent establishment.

(4) *International conformity assessment procedure.* The term "international conformity assessment procedure" means a conformity assessment procedure that is adopted by an international standards organization.

(5) *International standard.* The term "international standard" means any standard that is promulgated by an international standards organization.

(6) *International standards organization.* The term "international standards organization" means any organization—

(A) the membership of which is open to representatives, whether public or private, of the United States and at least all Members; and

(B) that is engaged in international standards-related activities.

(7) *International standards-related activity.* The term "international standards-related activity" means the negotiation, development, or promulgation of, or any amendment or change to, an international standard, or an international conformity assessment procedure, or both.

(8) *Member.* The term "Member" means a WTO member as defined in section 2(10) of the Uruguay Round Agreements Act.

(9) *Private person.* The term "private person" means—

(A) any individual who is a citizen or national of the United States; and

(B) any corporation, partnership, association, or other legal entity organized or existing under the law of any State, whether for profit or not for profit.

(10) *Product.* The term "product" means any natural or manufactured item.

(11) *Secretary concerned.* The term "Secretary concerned" means the Secretary of Commerce with respect to functions under this title relating to nonagricultural products, and the Secretary of Agriculture with respect to functions under this title relating to agricultural products.

(12) *Trade Representative.* The term "Trade Representative" means the United States Trade Representative.

(13) *Standard.* The term "standard" means a document approved by a recognized body, that provides, for common and repeated use, rules, guidelines, or characteristics for products or related processes and production methods, with which compliance is not mandatory. Such term may also include or deal exclusively with terminology, symbols, packaging, marking, or labeling requirements as they apply to a product, process, or production method.

(14) *Standards-related activity.* The term "standards-related activity" means the development, adoption, or application of any standard, technical regulation, or conformity assessment procedure.

(15) *State.* The term "State" means any of the several States, the District of Columbia, the Commonwealth of Puerto Rico, the Virgin Islands, American Samoa, Guam and any other Commonwealth, territory, or possession of the United States.

(16) *State agency.* The term "State agency" means any department, agency, or other instrumentality of the government of any State or of any political subdivision of any State.

(17) *Technical regulation.* The term "technical regulation" means a document which lays down product characteristics or their related processes and production methods, including the applicable administrative provisions, with which compliance is mandatory. Such term may also include or deal

exclusively with terminology, symbols, packaging, marking, or labeling requirements as they apply to a product, process, or production method.

(18) *United States.* The term "United States", when used in a geographical context, means all States.

19 USC 2572

Sec. 452.   Exemptions Under Title

This title does not apply to—

(1) any standards activity engaged in by any Federal agency or State agency for the use (including, but not limited to, use with respect to research and development, production, or consumption) of that agency or the use of another such agency; or

(2) any standards activity engaged in by any private person solely for use in the production or consumption of products by that person.

19 USC 2573

Sec. 453.   Reports to Congress on Operation of Agreement

As soon as practicable after the close of the 3-year period beginning on the date on which this title takes effect, and as soon as practicable after the close of each succeeding 3-year period through 2001, the Trade Representative shall prepare and submit to Congress a report containing an evaluation of the operation of the Agreement, both domestically and internationally, during the period.

* * *

Subtitle E

Standards and Measures Under the North American Free Trade Agreement

Chapter 1
Sanitary and Phytosanitary Measures

19 USC 2575

Sec. 461.   General

Nothing in this chapter may be construed—

(1) to prohibit a Federal agency or State agency from engaging in activity related to sanitary or phytosanitary measures to protect human, animal, or plant life or health; or

(2) to limit the authority of a Federal agency or State agency to determine the level of protection of human, animal, or plant life or health the agency considers appropriate.

19 USC 2575a

Sec. 462.   Inquiry Point

The standards information center maintained under section 414 shall, in addition to the functions specified therein, make available to the public relevant documents, at such reasonable fees as the Secretary of Commerce may prescribe, and information regarding—

(1) any sanitary or phytosanitary measure of general application, including any control or inspection procedure or approval procedure proposed, adopted, or maintained by a Federal or State agency;

(2) the procedures of a Federal or State agency for risk assessment, and factors the agency considers in conducting the assessment and in establishing the levels of protection that the agency considers appropriate;

(3) the membership and participation of the Federal Government and State governments in international and regional sanitary and phytosanitary organizations and systems, and in bilateral and multilateral arrangements regarding sanitary and phytosanitary measures, and the provisions of those systems and arrangements; and

(4) the location of notices of the type required under article 719 of the NAFTA, or where the information contained in such notices can be obtained.

19 USC 2575b

Sec. 463. Chapter Definitions

Notwithstanding section 451, for purposes of this chapter—

(1) Animal. The term "animal" includes fish, bees, and wild fauna.

(2) Approval procedure. The term "approval procedure" means any registration, notification, or other mandatory administrative procedure for—

(A) approving the use of an additive for a stated purpose or under stated conditions, or

(B) establishing a tolerance for a stated purpose or under stated conditions for a contaminant,

in a food, beverage, or feedstuff prior to permitting the use of the additive or the marketing of a food, beverage, or feedstuff containing the additive or contaminant.

(3) Contaminant. The term "contaminant" includes pesticide and veterinary drug residues and extraneous matter.

(4) Control or inspection procedure. The term "control or inspection procedure" means any procedure used, directly or indirectly, to determine that a sanitary or phytosanitary measure is fulfilled, including sampling, testing, inspection, evaluation, verification, monitoring, auditing, assurance of conformity, accreditation, registration, certification, or other procedure involving the physical examination of a good, of the packaging of a good, or of the equipment or facilities directly related to production, marketing, or use of a good, but does not mean an approval procedure.

(5) Plant. The term "plant" includes wild flora.

(6) Risk assessment. The term "risk assessment" means an evaluation of—

(A) the potential for the introduction, establishment or spread of a pest or disease and associated biological and economic consequences; or

(B) the potential for adverse effects on human or animal life or health arising from the presence of an additive, contaminant, toxin or disease-causing organism in a food, beverage, or feedstuff.

(7) Sanitary or phytosanitary measure.

(A) In general. The term "sanitary or phytosanitary measure" means a measure to—

(i) protect animal or plant life or health in the United States from risks arising from the introduction, establishment, or spread of a pest or disease;

(ii) protect human or animal life or health in the United States from risks arising from the presence of an additive, contaminant, toxin, or disease-causing organism in a food, beverage, or feedstuff;

(iii) protect human life or health in the United States from risks arising from a disease-causing organism or pest carried by an animal or plant, or a product thereof; or

(iv) prevent or limit other damage in the United States arising from the introduction, establishment, or spread of a pest.

(B) Form. The form of a sanitary or phytosanitary measure includes—

(i) end product criteria;

(ii) a product-related processing or production method;

(iii) a testing, inspection, certification, or approval procedure;

(iv) a relevant statistical method;

(v) a sampling procedure;

(vi) a method of risk assessment;

(vii) a packaging and labeling requirement directly related to food safety; and

(viii) a quarantine treatment, such as a relevant requirement associated with the transportation of animals or plants or with material necessary for their survival during transportation.

Chapter 2
Standards and Related Measures
19 USC 2576

Sec. 471. General

(a) No bar to engaging in standards activity. Nothing in this chapter shall be construed—

(1) to prohibit a Federal agency from engaging in activity related to standards-related measures, including any such measure relating to safety, the protection of human, animal, or plant life or health, the environment or consumers; or

(2) to limit the authority of a Federal agency to determine the level it considers appropriate of safety or of protection of human, animal, or plant life or health, the environment or consumers.

(b) Exclusion. This chapter does not apply to—

(1) technical specifications prepared by a Federal agency for production or consumption requirements of the agency; or

(2) sanitary or phytosanitary measures under chapter 1.

19 USC 2576a

Sec. 472. Inquiry Point

The standards information center maintained under section 414 shall, in addition to the functions specified therein, make available to the public relevant documents, at such reasonable fees as the Secretary of Commerce may prescribe, and information regarding—

(1) the membership and participation of the Federal Government, State governments, and relevant nongovernmental bodies in the United States in international and regional standardizing bodies and conformity assessment systems, and in bilateral and multilateral arrangements regarding standards-related measures, and the provisions of those systems and arrangements;

(2) the location of notices of the type required under article 909 of the NAFTA, or where the information contained in such notice can be obtained; and

(3) the Federal agency procedures for assessment of risk, and factors the agency considers in conducting the assessment and establishing the levels of protection that the agency considers appropriate.

19 USC 2576b

Sec. 473. Chapter Definitions

Notwithstanding section 451, for purposes of this chapter—

(1) Approval procedure. The term "approval procedure" means any registration, notification, or other mandatory administrative procedure for granting permission for a good or service to be produced, marketed, or used for a stated purpose or under stated conditions.

(2) Conformity assessment procedure. The term "conformity assessment procedure" means any procedure used, directly or indirectly, to determine that a technical regulation or standard is fulfilled, including sampling, testing, inspection, evaluation, verification, monitoring, auditing, assurance of conformity, accreditation, registration, or approval used for such a purpose, but does not mean an approval procedure.

(3) Objective. The term "objective" includes—

(A) safety,

(B) protection of human, animal, or plant life or health, the environment or consumers, including matters relating to quality and identifiability of goods or services, and

(C) sustainable development,

but does not include the protection of domestic production.

(4) Service. The term "service" means a land transportation service or a telecommunications service.

(5) Standard. The term "standard" means—

(A) characteristics for a good or a service,

(B) characteristics, rules, or guidelines for—

(i) processes or production methods relating to such good, or

(ii) operating methods relating to such service, and

(C) provisions specifying terminology, symbols, packaging, marking, or labeling for—

(i) a good or its related process or production methods, or

(ii) a service or its related operating methods,

for common and repeated use, including explanatory and other related provisions set out in a document approved by a standardizing body, with which compliance is not mandatory.

(6) Standards-related measure. The term "standards-related measure" means a standard, technical regulation, or conformity assessment procedure.

(7) Technical regulation. The term "technical regulation" means—

(A) characteristics or their related processes and production methods for a good,

(B) characteristics for a service or its related operating methods, or

(C) provisions specifying terminology, symbols, packaging, marking, or labeling for—

(i) a good or its related process or production method, or

(ii) a service or its related operating method,

set out in a document, including applicable administrative, explanatory, and other related provisions, with which compliance is mandatory.

(8) Telecommunications service. The term "telecommunications service" means a service provided by means of the transmission and reception of signals by any electromagnetic means, but does not mean the cable, broadcast, or other electromagnetic distribution of radio or television programming to the public generally.

19 USC 2581

Sec. 1102. Auction of Import Licenses

(a) In general. Notwithstanding any other provision of law, the President may sell import licenses at public auction under such terms and conditions as he deems appropriate. Regulations prescribed under this subsection shall, to the extent practicable and consistent with efficient and fair administration, insure against inequitable sharing of imports by a relatively small number of the larger importers.

(b) Definition of import license. For purposes of this section, the term "import license" means any documentation used to administer a quantitative restriction imposed or modified after the date of enactment of this Act under—

(1) section 125, 203, 301, or 406 of the Trade Act of 1974 (19 U.S.C. 2135, 2253, 2411, or 2436),

(2) the International Emergency Economic Powers Act (50 U.S.C.App. 1701–1706),

(3) authority under the notes of the Harmonized Tariff Schedule of the United States, but not including any quantitative restriction imposed under section 22 of the Agricultural Adjustment Act of 1934 (7 U.S.C. 624),

(4) the Trading With the Enemy Act (50 U.S.C.App. 1–44),

(5) section 204 of the Agricultural Act of 1956 (7 U.S.C. 1854) other than for meat or meat products, or

(6) any Act enacted explicitly for the purpose of implementing an international agreement to which the United States is a party, including such agreements relating to commodities, but not including any agreement relating to cheese or dairy products.

* * *

Item 49

UNITED STATES: TRADE AND TARIFF ACT OF 1984

(Selected provisions, as amended)

PUBLIC LAW 98–573, APPROVED OCTOBER 30, 1984, 98 STAT. 2948

An Act to amend the trade laws, authorize the negotiation of trade agreements, extend trade preferences, change the tariff treatment with respect to certain articles and for other purposes.

Be it enacted by the Senate and House of Representatives of the United States of America in Congress assembled, That this Act with the following table of contents may be cited as the "Trade and Tariff Act of 1984":

Table of Contents

TITLE VI.   TRADE LAW REFORM
[omitted]

TITLE VII.   AUTHORIZATION OF APPROPRIATIONS FOR CUSTOMS AND TRADE AGENCIES
[omitted]

TITLE VIII.   ENFORCEMENT AUTHORITY FOR THE NATIONAL POLICY FOR THE STEEL INDUSTRY
[omitted]

TITLE IX.   ELIMINATION OF BARRIERS TO INTERNATIONAL TRADE IN UNITED STATES WINE
[omitted]

TITLE III
INTERNATIONAL TRADE AND INVESTMENT
19 USC 2101 note

Sec. 301.   Short Title; Amendment of Trade Act of 1974

(a) This title may be cited as the "International Trade and Investment Act".

(b) Except as otherwise expressly provided, whenever in this title an amendment or repeal is expressed in terms of an amendment to, or repeal of, a section or other provision, the reference shall be considered to be made to a section or other provision of the Trade Act of 1974.

19 USC 2102

Sec. 302.   Congressional Statement of Purpose

The purposes of this Act are, through trade agreements affording mutual benefits—

(1) to foster the economic growth of and full employment in the United States and to strengthen economic relations between the United States and foreign countries through open and nondiscriminatory world trade;

(2) to harmonize, reduce, and eliminate barriers to trade on a basis which assures substantially equivalent competitive opportunities for the commerce of the United States;

(3) to establish fairness and equity in international trading relations, including reform of the General Agreement on Tariffs and Trade;

(4) to provide adequate procedures to safeguard American industry and labor against unfair or injurious import competition, and to assist industries, firm [firms], workers, and communities to adjust to changes in international trade flows;

(5) to open up market opportunities for United States commerce in nonmarket economies; and

(6) to provide fair and reasonable access to products of less developed countries in the United States market.

Sec. 303.   Analysis of Foreign Trade Barriers

[See Trade Act of 1974, sec. 181]

Sec. 304.   Amendments to Title III of the Trade Act of 1974 [omitted]

Sec. 305.   Negotiating Objectives With Respect to International Trade in Services and Investment and High Technology Industries

[See Trade Act of 1974, sec. 104A]

19 USC 2114b

Sec. 306.   Provisions Relating to International Trade in Services

(1) The Secretary of Commerce shall establish a service industries development program designed to—

(A) develop, in consultation with other Federal agencies as appropriate, policies regarding services that are designed to increase the competitiveness of United States service industries in foreign commerce;

(B) develop a data base for assessing the adequacy of Government policies and actions pertaining to services, including, but not limited to, data on trade, both aggregate and pertaining to individual service industries;

(C) collect and analyze, in consultation with appropriate agencies, information pertaining to the international operations and competitiveness of United States service industries, including information with respect to—

(i) policies of foreign governments toward foreign and United States service industries;

(ii) Federal, State, and local regulation of both foreign and United States suppliers of services, and the effect of such regulation on trade;

(iii) the adequacy of current United States policies to strengthen the competitiveness of United States service industries in foreign commerce, including export promotion activities in the service sector;

(iv) tax treatment of services, with particular emphasis on the effect of United States taxation on the international competitiveness of United States firms and exports;

(v) treatment of services under international agreements of the United States;

(vi) antitrust policies as such policies affect the competitiveness of United States firms; and

(vii) treatment of services in international agreements of the United States;

(D) conduct a program of research and analysis of service-related issues and problems, including forecasts and industrial strategies; and

(E) conduct sectoral studies of domestic service industries.

(2) For purposes of the collection and analysis required by paragraph (1), and for the purpose of any reporting the Department of Commerce makes under paragraph (3), such collection and reporting shall distinguish between income from investment and income from noninvestment services.

(3) On not less than a biennial basis beginning in 1986, the Secretary shall prepare a report which analyzes the information collected under paragraph (1). Such report shall be submitted to the Congress and to the President by not later than the date that is 120 days after the close of the period covered by the report.

(4) The Secretary of Commerce shall carry out the provisions of this subsection from funds otherwise made available to him which may be used for such purposes.

(5) For purposes of this section, the term "services" means economic activities whose outputs are other than tangible goods. Such term includes, but is not limited to, banking, insurance, transportation, postal and delivery services, communications and data processing, retail and wholesale trade, advertising, accounting, construction, design and engineering, management consulting, real estate, professional services, entertainment, education, health care, and tourism.

* * *

19 USC 2114c

Sec. 306. Trade in Services: Development, Coordination, and Implementation of Federal Policies; Staff Support and Other Assistance; Specific Service Sector Authorities Unaffected; Executive Functions

(1)(A) The United States Trade Representative, through the interagency trade organization established pursuant to section 242(a) of the Trade Expansion Act of 1962 or any subcommittee thereof, shall, in conformance with this Act and other provisions of law, develop (and coordinate the implementation of) United States policies concerning trade in services.

(B) In order to encourage effective development, coordination, and implementation of United States policies on trade in services—

(i) each department or agency of the United States responsible for the regulation of any service sector industry shall, as appropriate, advise and work with the United States Trade Representative concerning matters that have come to the department's or agency's attention with respect to—

(I) the treatment afforded United States service sector interest in foreign markets; or

(II) allegations of unfair practices by foreign governments or companies in a service sector; and

(ii) the Department of Commerce, together with other appropriate agencies as requested by the United States Trade Representative, shall provide staff support and other assistance for negotiations on service-related issues by the United States Trade Representative and the domestic implementation of service-related agreements.

(C) Nothing in this paragraph shall be construed to alter any existing authority or responsibility with respect to any specific service sector.

(2)(A) The President shall, as he deems appropriate—

(i) consult with State governments on issues of trade policy, including negotiating objectives and implementation of trade agreements, affecting the regulatory authority of non-Federal governments, or their procurement of goods and services;

(ii) establish one or more intergovernmental policy advisory committees on trade which shall serve as a principal forum in which State and local governments may consult with the Federal Government with respect to the matters described in clause (i); and

(iii) provide to State and local governments and to United States service industries, upon their request, advice, assistance, and (except as may be otherwise prohibited by law) data, analyses, and information concerning United States policies on international trade in services.

* * *

19 USC 2114d

Sec. 307. Foreign Export Requirements; Consultations and Negotiations For Reduction and Elimination; Restrictions on and Exclusion From Entry of Products or Services; Savings Provision; Compensation Authority Applicable

(1) If the United States Trade Representative, with the advice of the committee established by section 242 of the Trade Expansion [Act] of 1962 (19 U.S.C. 1872), determines that action by the United States is appropriate to respond to any export performance requirements of any foreign country or instrumentality that adversely affect the economic interests of the United States, then the United States Trade Representative shall seek to obtain the reduction and elimination of such export performance requirements through consultations and negotiations with the foreign country or instrumentality concerned.

(2) In addition to the action referred to in subsection (1), the United States Trade Representative may impose duties or other import restrictions on the products or services of such foreign country or instrumentality for such time as he determines appropriate, including the exclusion from entry into the United States of products subject to such requirements.

(3) Nothing in paragraph (2) shall apply to any products or services with respect to which—

(A) any foreign direct investment (including a purchase of land or facilities) has been made directly or indirectly by any United States person before October 30, 1984, or

(B) any written commitment relating to a foreign direct investment that is binding on October 30, 1984, has been made directly or indirectly by any United States person.

(4) Whenever the international obligations of the United States and actions taken under paragraph (2) make compensation necessary or appropriate, compensation may be provided by the United States Trade Representative subject to the limitations and conditions contained in section 123 of the Trade Act of 1974 (19 U.S.C. 2133) for providing compensation for actions taken under section 203 of that Act.

19 USC 2114e

Sec. 308. Negotiation of Agreements Concerning High Technology Industries

The President may enter into such bilateral or multilateral agreements as may be necessary or appropriate to achieve the objectives of this section and the negotiating objectives under section 104A(c) of the Trade Act of 1974.

* * *

TITLE IV
TRADE WITH ISRAEL
19 USC 2112 note

Sec. 402. "19 USC 2112 Note" Criteria for Duty–Free Treatment of Articles

(a)(1) Any trade agreement entered into with Israel under section 102(b)(1) of the Trade Act of 1974 may provide for the reduction or elimination of any duty imposed by the United States with respect to any article only if—

(A) that article is the growth, product, or manufacture of Israel or is a new or different article of commerce that has been grown, produced, or manufactured in Israel;

(B) that article is imported directly from Israel into the customs territory of the United States; and

(C) the sum of—

(i) the cost of value of the materials produced in Israel, plus

(ii) the direct costs of processing operations performed in Israel,

is not less than 35 percent of the appraised value of such article at the time it is entered.

If the cost or value of materials produced in the customs territory of the United States is included with respect to an article to which this subsection applies, an amount not to exceed 15 percent of the appraised value of the article at the time it is entered that is attributable to such United States cost or value may be applied toward determining the percentage referred to in subparagraph (C).

(2) No article may be considered to be an eligible Israeli article by virtue of having merely undergone—

(A) simple combining or packaging operations; or

(B) mere dilution with water or mere dilution with another substance that does not materially alter the characteristics of the article.

(b) As used in this section, the phrase "direct costs of processing operations" includes, but is not limited to—

(1) all actual labor costs involved in the growth, production, manufacture, or assembly of the specific merchandise, including fringe benefits, on-the-job training and the cost of engineering, supervisory, quality control, and similar personnel; and

(2) dies, molds, tooling, and depreciation on machinery and equipment which are allocable to the specific merchandise.

Such phrase does not include costs which are not directly attributable to the merchandise concerned, or are not costs of manufacturing the product, such as (A) profit, and (B) general expenses of doing business which are either not allocable to the specific merchandise or are not related to the growth, production, manufacture, or assembly of the merchandise, such as administrative salaries, casualty and liability insurance, advertising, and salesmen's salaries, commissions or expenses.

(c) Regulations.—The Secretary of the Treasury, after consultation with the United States Trade Representative, shall prescribe such regulations as may be necessary to carry out this section.

Sec. 403. Application of Certain Other Trade Law Provisions

(a) Suspension of duty-free treatment. The President may by proclamation suspend the reduction or elimination of any duty provided under any trade agreement provision entered into with Israel under the authority of section 102(b)(1) of the Trade Act of 1974 with respect to any article and may proclaim a duty rate for such article if such action is proclaimed under section 203 of the Trade Act of 1974 or section 232 of the Trade Expansion Act of 1962.

(b) ITC reports. In any report by the United States International Trade Commission (hereinafter referred to in this title as the "Commission") to the President under section 202(f) of the Trade Act of 1974 regarding any article for which a reduction or elimination of any duty is provided under a trade agreement entered into with Israel under section 102(b)(1) of the Trade Act of 1974, the Commission shall state whether and to what extent its findings and recommendations apply to such an article when imported from Israel.

(c) For purposes of section 203 of the Trade Act of 1974, the suspension of the reduction or elimination of a duty under subsection (a) shall be treated as an increase in duty.

(d) No proclamation which provides solely for a suspension referred to in subsection (a) with respect to any article shall be made under section 203 of the Trade Act of 1974 unless the Commission, in addition to making an affirmative determination with respect to such article under section 202(b) of the Trade Act of 1974, determines in the course of its investigation under that section that the serious injury (or threat thereof) substantially caused by imports to the domestic industry producing a like or directly competitive article results from the reduction or elimination of any duty provided under any trade agreement provision entered into with Israel under section 102(b)(1) of the Trade Act of 1974.

(e)(1) Any proclamation issued under section 203 of the Trade Act of 1974 that is in effect when an agreement with Israel is entered into under section 102(b)(1) of the Trade Act of 1974 shall remain in effect until modified or terminated.

(2) If any article is subject to import relief at the time an agreement is entered into with Israel under section 102(b)(1) of the Trade Act of 1974, the President may reduce or terminate the application of such import relief to the importation of such article before the otherwise scheduled date on which such reduction or termination would occur pursuant to the criteria and procedures of sections 203 and 204 of the Trade Act of 1974.

Sec. 404. Fast Track Procedures for Perishable Articles.

(a) If a petition is filed with the Commission under the provisions of section 201 of the Trade Act of 1974 regarding a perishable product which is subject to any reduction or elimination of a duty imposed by the United States under a trade agreement entered into with Israel under section 102(b)(1) of the Trade Act of 1974 and alleges injury from imports of that product, then the petition may also be filed with the Secretary of Agriculture with a request that emergency relief be granted under subsection (c) with respect to such article.

(b) Within 14 days after the filing of a petition under subsection (a)—

(1) if the Secretary of Agriculture has reason to believe that a perishable product from Israel is being imported into the United States in such increased quantities as to be a substantial cause of serious injury, or the threat thereof, to the domestic industry producing a perishable product like or directly competitive with the imported product and that emergency action is warranted, he shall advise the President and recommend that the President take emergency action; or

(2) the Secretary of Agriculture shall publish a notice of his determination not to recommend the imposition of emergency action and so advise the petitioner.

(c) Within 7 days after the President receives a recommendation from the Secretary of Agriculture to take emergency action under subsection (b), he shall issue a proclamation withdrawing the reduction or elimination of duty provided to the perishable product under any trade agreement provision entered into under section 102(b)(1) of the Trade Act of 1974 or publish a notice of his determination not to take emergency action.

(d) The emergency action provided under subsection (c) shall cease to apply—

(1) upon the proclamation of import relief under section 202(a)(1) of the Trade Act of 1974 "19 USC 2252";

(2) on the day the President makes a determination under section 203(b)(2) of such Act "19 USC 2253" not to impose import relief;

(3) in the event of a report of the Commission containing a negative finding, on the day the Commission's report is submitted to the President; or

(4) whenever the President determines that because of changed circumstances such relief is no longer warranted.

(e) For purposes of this section, the term "perishable product" means any—

(1) live plant provided for in subpart A of part 6 of schedule 1 of the Tariff Schedules of the United States (19 U.S.C. 1202, hereinafter referred to as the "TSUS");

(2) vegetable provided for in schedule 1, part 8, of the TSUS;

(3) fresh mushroom provided for in item 144.10 of the TSUS;

(4) edible nut or fruit provided for in schedule 1, part 9, of the TSUS;

(5) fresh cut flower provided for in items 192.17, 192.18, and 192.21 of the TSUS; and

(6) concentrated citrus fruit provided for in items 165.25 and 165.35 of the TSUS.

(f) No trade agreement entered into with Israel under section 102(b)(1) of the Trade Act of 1974 shall affect fees imposed under section 22 of the Agricultural Adjustment Act (7 U.S.C. 624).

Sec. 405.   Construction of Title

Neither the taking effect of any trade agreement provision entered into with Israel under section 102(b)(1), nor any proclamation issued to implement any such provision, may affect in any manner, or to any extent, the application to any Israeli articles of section 232 of the Trade Expansion Act of 1962, section 337 [or] title VII of the Tariff Act of 1930, chapter 1 of title II and chapter 1 of title III of the Trade Act of 1974, or any other provision of law under which relief from injury caused by import competition or by unfair import trade practices may be sought.

TITLE V
GENERALIZED SYSTEM OF PREFERENCES RENEWAL
19 USC 2461 note

Section 501.   Short Title; Statement of Purpose

(a) This title may be cited as the "Generalized System of Preferences Renewal Act of 1984".

(b) The purpose of this title is to—

(1) promote the development of developing countries, which often need temporary preferential advantages to compete effectively with industrialized countries;

(2) promote the notion that trade rather than aid, is a more effective and cost-efficient way of promoting broad-based sustained economic development;

(3) take advantage of the fact that developing countries provide the fastest growing markets for United States exports and that foreign exchange

earnings from trade with such countries through the Generalized System of Preferences can further stimulate United States exports;

(4) allow for the consideration of the fact that there are significant differences among developing countries with respect to their general development and international competitiveness;

(5) encourage the providing of increased trade liberalization measures, thereby setting an example to be emulated by other industrialized countries;

(6) recognize that a large number of developing countries must generate sufficient foreign exchange earnings to meet international debt obligations;

(7) promote the creation of additional opportunities for trade among the developing countries;

(8) integrate developing countries into the international trading system with its attendant responsibilities in a manner commensurate with their development;

(9) encourage developing countries—

(A) to eliminate or reduce significant barriers to trade in goods and services and to investment,

(B) to provide effective means under which foreign nationals may secure, exercise, and enforce exclusive intellectual property rights, and

(C) to afford workers internationally recognized worker rights; and

(10) address the concerns listed in the preceding paragraphs in a manner that—

(A) does not adversely affect United States producers and workers, and

(B) conforms to the international obligations of the United States under the General Agreement on Tariffs and Trade.

Sec. 502–506.   [See Trade Act of 1974, Title V]

* * *

Item 50

UNITED STATES: OMNIBUS TRADE AND COMPETITIVENESS ACT OF 1988

(selected provisions, as amended)

PUBLIC LAW 100–418, APPROVED AUGUST 23, 1988, 102 Stat. 1107

An Act to enhance the competitiveness of American industry, and for other purposes.

Be it enacted by the Senate and House of Representatives of the United States of America in Congress assembled,

Section 1. Short Title and Table of Contents

(a) **Short title.** This Act may be cited as the "Omnibus Trade and Competitiveness Act of 1988".

(b) **Table of contents.** (Selected Provisions)

TITLE I. TRADE, CUSTOMS, AND TARIFF LAWS

* * *

SUBTITLE C.   RESPONSE TO UNFAIR INTERNATIONAL TRADE PRACTICES

PART 1.   ENFORCEMENT OF UNITED STATES RIGHTS UNDER TRADE
AGREEMENTS AND RESPONSES TO FOREIGN TRADE PRACTICES

* * *

PART 2.   IMPROVEMENT IN THE ENFORCEMENT OF THE
ANTIDUMPING AND COUNTERVAILING DUTY LAWS

* * *

* * *

PART 3.   PROTECTION OF INTELLECTUAL PROPERTY RIGHTS

* * *

SUBTITLE D.   ADJUSTMENT TO IMPORT COMPETITION

PART 1.   POSITIVE ADJUSTMENT BY INDUSTRIES INJURED BY IMPORTS

* * *

PART 2.   MARKET DISRUPTION

* * *

PART 3.   TRADE ADJUSTMENT ASSISTANCE

* * *

* * *

SUBTITLE E.   NATIONAL SECURITY

* * *

TITLE I
TRADE, CUSTOMS, AND TARIFF LAWS
19 USC 2901 note

Sec. 1001.   Findings and Purposes

(a) **Findings.** The Congress finds that—

(1) in the last 10 years there has arisen a new global economy in which trade, technological development, investment, and services form an integrated system; and in this system these activities affect each other and the health of the United States economy;

(2) the United States is confronted with a fundamental disequilibrium in its trade and current account balances and a rapid increase in its net external debt;

(3) such disequilibrium and increase are a result of numerous factors, including—

(A) disparities between the macroeconomic policies of the major trading nations,

(B) the large United States budget deficit,

(C) instabilities and structural defects in the world monetary system,

(D) the growth of debt throughout the developing world,

(E) structural defects in the world trading system and inadequate enforcement of trade agreement obligations,

(F) governmental distortions and barriers,

(G) serious shortcomings in United States trade policy, and

(H) inadequate growth in the productivity and competitiveness of United States firms and industries relative to their overseas competition;

(4) it is essential, and should be the highest priority of the United States Government, to pursue a broad array of domestic and international policies—

(A) to prevent future declines in the United States economy and standards of living,

(B) to ensure future stability in external trade of the United States, and

(C) to guarantee the continued vitality of the technological, industrial, and agricultural base of the United States;

(5) the President should be authorized and encouraged to negotiate trade agreements and related investment, financial, intellectual property, and services agreements that meet the standards set forth in this title; and

(6) while the United States is not in a position to dictate economic policy to the rest of the world, the United States is in a position to lead the world and it is in the national interest for the United States to do so.

(b) Purposes. The purposes of this title are to—

(1) authorize the negotiation of reciprocal trade agreements;

(2) strengthen United States trade laws;

(3) improve the development and management of United States trade strategy; and

(4) through these actions, improve standards of living in the world.

Subtitle A

United States Trade Agreements

PART 1.   NEGOTIATION AND IMPLEMENTATION OF TRADE AGREEMENTS

19 USC 2901

Sec. 1101. Overall and Principal Trade Negotiating Objectives of the United States

(a) Overall Trade Negotiating Objectives. The overall trade negotiating objectives of the United States are to obtain—

(1) more open, equitable, and reciprocal market access;

(2) the reduction or elimination of barriers and other trade-distorting policies and practices; and

(3) a more effective system of international trading disciplines and procedures.

(b) Principal Trade Negotiating Objectives.

(1) Dispute Settlement. The principal negotiating objectives of the United States with respect to dispute settlement are—

(A) to provide for more effective and expeditious dispute settlement mechanisms and procedures; and

(B) to ensure that such mechanisms within the GATT and GATT agreements provide for more effective and expeditious resolution of disputes and enable better enforcement of United States rights.

(2) Improvement of the GATT and multilateral trade negotiation agreements. The principal negotiating objectives of the United States regarding the improvement of GATT and multilateral trade negotiation agreements are—

(A) to enhance the status of the GATT;

(B) to improve the operation and extend the coverage of the GATT and such agreements and arrangements to products, sectors, and conditions of trade not adequately covered; and

(C) to expand country participation in particular agreements or arrangements, where appropriate.

(3) Transparency. The principal negotiating objective of the United States regarding transparency is to obtain broader application of the principle of transparency and clarification of the costs and benefits of trade policy actions through the observance of open and equitable procedures in trade matters by Contracting Parties to the GATT.

(4) Developing countries. The principal negotiating objectives of the United States regarding developing countries are—

(A) to ensure that developing countries promote economic development by assuming the fullest possible measure of responsibility for achieving and maintaining an open international trading system by providing reciprocal benefits and assuming equivalent obligations with respect to their import and export practices; and

(B) to establish procedures for reducing nonreciprocal trade benefits for the more advanced developing countries.

(5) Current account surpluses. The principal negotiating objective of the United States regarding current account surpluses is to develop rules to address large and persistent global current account imbalances of countries, including imbalances which threaten the stability of the international trading system, by imposing greater responsibility on such countries to undertake policy changes aimed at restoring current account equilibrium, including expedited implementation of trade agreements where feasible and appropriate.

(6) Trade and monetary coordination. The principal negotiating objective of the United States regarding trade and monetary coordination is to develop

mechanisms to assure greater coordination, consistency, and cooperation between international trade and monetary systems and institutions.

(7) Agriculture. The principal negotiating objectives of the United States with respect to agriculture are to achieve, on an expedited basis to the maximum extent feasible, more open and fair conditions of trade in agricultural commodities by—

(A) developing, strengthening, and clarifying rules for agricultural trade, including disciplines on restrictive or trade-distorting import and export practices;

(B) increasing United States agricultural exports by eliminating barriers to trade (including transparent and nontransparent barriers) and reducing or eliminating the subsidization of agricultural production consistent with the United States policy of agricultural stabilization in cyclical and unpredictable markets;

(C) creating a free and more open world agricultural trading system by resolving questions pertaining to export and other trade-distorting subsidies, market pricing and market access and eliminating and reducing substantially other specific constraints to fair trade and more open market access, such as tariffs, quotas, and other nontariff practices, including unjustified phytosanitary and sanitary restrictions; and

(D) seeking agreements by which the major agricultural exporting nations agree to pursue policies to reduce excessive production of agricultural commodities during periods of oversupply, with due regard for the fact that the United States already undertakes such policies, and without recourse to arbitrary schemes to divide market shares among major exporting countries.

(8) Unfair trade practices. The principal negotiating objectives of the United States with respect to unfair trade practices are—

(A) to improve the provisions of the GATT and nontariff measure agreements in order to define, deter, discourage the persistent use of, and otherwise discipline unfair trade practices having adverse trade effects, including forms of subsidy and dumping and other practices not adequately covered such as resource input subsidies, diversionary dumping, dumped or subsidized inputs, and export targeting practices;

(B) to obtain the application of similar rules to the treatment of primary and nonprimary products in the Agreement on Interpretation and Application of Articles VI, XVI, and XXIII of the GATT (relating to subsidies and countervailing measures) [the Tokyo Round Subsidies Code, ed.]; and

(C) to obtain the enforcement of GATT rules against—

(i) state trading enterprises, and

(ii) the acts, practices, or policies of any foreign government which, as a practical matter, unreasonably require that—

(I) substantial direct investment in the foreign country be made,

(II) intellectual property be licensed to the foreign country or to any firm of the foreign country, or

(III) other collateral concessions be made,

as a condition for the importation of any product or service of the United States into the foreign country or as a condition for carrying on business in the foreign country.

(9) Trade in services.

(A) The principal negotiating objectives of the United States regarding trade in services are—

(i) to reduce or to eliminate barriers to, or other distortions of, international trade in services, including barriers that deny national treatment and restrictions on establishment and operation in such markets; and

(ii) to develop internationally agreed rules, including dispute settlement procedures, which—

(I) are consistent with the commercial policies of the United States, and

(II) will reduce or eliminate such barriers or distortions, and help ensure fair, equitable opportunities for foreign markets.

(B) In pursuing the negotiating objectives described in subparagraph (A), United States negotiators shall take into account legitimate United States domestic objectives including, but not limited to, the protection of legitimate health or safety, essential security, environmental, consumer or employment opportunity interests and the law and regulations related thereto.

(10) Intellectual property. The principal negotiating objectives of the United States regarding intellectual property are—

(A) to seek the enactment and effective enforcement by foreign countries of laws which—

(i) recognize and adequately protect intellectual property, including copyrights, patents, trademarks, semi-conductor chip layout designs, and trade secrets, and

(ii) provide protection against unfair competition,

(B) to establish in the GATT obligations—

(i) to implement adequate substantive standards based on—

(I) the standards in existing international agreements that provide adequate protection, and

(II) the standards in national laws if international agreement standards are inadequate or do not exist,

(ii) to establish effective procedures to enforce, both internally and at the border, the standards implemented under clause (i), and

(iii) to implement effective dispute settlement procedures that improve on existing GATT procedures;

(C) to recognize that the inclusion in the GATT of—

(i) adequate and effective substantive norms and standards for the protection and enforcement of intellectual property rights, and

(ii) dispute settlement provisions and enforcement procedures,

is without prejudice to other complementary initiatives undertaken in other international organizations; and

(D) to supplement and strengthen standards for protection and enforcement in existing international intellectual property conventions administered by other international organizations, including their expansion to cover new and emerging technologies and elimination of discrimination or unreasonable exceptions or preconditions to protection.

(11) Foreign direct investment.

(A) The principal negotiating objectives of the United States regarding foreign direct investment are—

(i) to reduce or to eliminate artificial or trade-distorting barriers to foreign direct investment, to expand the principle of national treatment, and to reduce unreasonable barriers to establishment; and

(ii) to develop internationally agreed rules, including dispute settlement procedures, which—

(I) will help ensure a free flow of foreign direct investment, and

(II) will reduce or eliminate the trade distortive effects of certain trade-related investment measures.

(B) In pursuing the negotiating objectives described in subparagraph (A), United States negotiators shall take into account legitimate United States domestic objectives including, but not limited to, the protection of legitimate health or safety, essential security, environmental, consumer or employment opportunity interests and the law and regulations related thereto.

(12) Safeguards. The principal negotiating objectives of the United States regarding safeguards are—

(A) to improve and expand rules and procedures covering safeguard measures;

(B) to ensure that safeguard measures are—

(i) transparent,

(ii) temporary,

(iii) degressive, and

(iv) subject to review and termination when no longer necessary to remedy injury and to facilitate adjustment; and

(C) to require notification of, and to monitor the use by, GATT Contracting Parties of import relief actions for their domestic industries.

(13) Specific barriers. The principal negotiating objective of the United States regarding specific barriers is to obtain competitive opportunities for United States exports in foreign markets substantially equivalent to the competitive opportunities afforded foreign exports to United States markets,

including the reduction or elimination of specific tariff and nontariff trade barriers, particularly—

(A) measures identified in the annual report prepared under section 181 of the Trade Act of 1974 (19 U.S.C. 2241) and

(B) foreign tariffs and nontariff barriers on competitive United States exports when like or similar products enter the United States at low rates of duty or are duty-free, and other tariff disparities that impede access to particular export markets.

(14) Worker rights. The principal negotiating objectives of the United States regarding worker rights are—

(A) to promote respect for worker rights;

(B) to secure a review of the relationship of worker rights to GATT articles, objectives, and related instruments with a view to ensuring that the benefits of the trading system are available to all workers; and

(C) to adopt, as a principle of the GATT, that the denial of worker rights should not be a means for a country or its industries to gain competitive advantage in international trade.

(15) Access to high technology.

(A) The principal negotiating objective of the United States regarding access to high technology is to obtain the elimination or reduction of foreign barriers to, and acts, policies, or practices by foreign governments which limit equitable access by United States persons to foreign developed technology, including barriers, acts, policies, or practices which have the effect of—

(i) restricting the participation of United States persons in government-supported research and development projects;

(ii) denying equitable access by United States persons to government-held patents;

(iii) requiring the approval or agreement of government entities, or imposing other forms of government interventions, as a condition for the granting of licenses to United States persons by foreign persons (except for approval or agreement which may be necessary for national security purposes to control the export of critical military technology); and

(iv) otherwise denying equitable access by United States persons to foreign-developed technology or contributing to the inequitable flow of technology between the United States and its trading partners.

(B) In pursuing the negotiating objective described in subparagraph (A), the United States negotiators shall take into account United States Government policies in licensing or otherwise making available to foreign persons technology and other information developed by United States laboratories.

(16) Border taxes. The principal negotiating objective of the United States regarding border taxes is to obtain a revision of the GATT with respect to the treatment of border adjustments for internal taxes to redress the disadvan-

tage to countries relying primarily for revenue on direct taxes rather than indirect taxes.

19 USC 2902

Sec. 1102. Trade Agreement Negotiating Authority

(a) Agreements regarding tariff barriers.

(1) Whenever the President determines that one or more existing duties or other import restrictions of any foreign country or the United States are unduly burdening and restricting the foreign trade of the United States and that the purposes, policies, and objectives of this title will be promoted thereby, the President—

(A) before June 1, 1993, may enter into trade agreements with foreign countries; and

(B) may, subject to paragraphs (2) through (5), proclaim—

(i) such modification or continuance of any existing duty,

(ii) such continuance of existing duty-free or excise treatment, or

(iii) such additional duties;

as he determines to be required or appropriate to carry out any such trade agreement.

(2) No proclamation may be made under subsection (a) that—

(A) reduces any rate of duty (other than a rate of duty that does not exceed 5 percent ad valorem on the date of enactment of this Act) to a rate which is less than 50 percent of the rate of such duty that applies on such date of enactment; or

(B) increases any rate of duty above the rate that applies on such date of enactment.

(3)(A) Except as provided in subparagraph (B), the aggregate reduction in the rate of duty on any article which is in effect on any day pursuant to a trade agreement entered into under paragraph (1) shall not exceed the aggregate reduction which would have been in effect on such day if a reduction of 3 percent ad valorem or a reduction of one-tenth of the total reduction, whichever is greater, had taken effect on the effective date of the first reduction proclaimed in paragraph (1) to carry out such agreement with respect to such article.

(B) No staging under subparagraph (A) is required with respect to a rate reduction that is proclaimed under paragraph (1) for an article of a kind that is not produced in the United States. The United States International Trade Commission shall advise the President of the identity of articles that may be exempted from staging under this subparagraph.

(4) If the President determines that such action will simplify the computation of reductions under paragraph (3), the President may round an annual reduction by the lesser of—

(A) the difference between the reduction without regard to this paragraph and the next lower whole number; or

(B) one-half of 1 percent ad valorem.

(5) No reduction in a rate of duty under a trade agreement entered into under subsection (a) on any article may take effect more than 10 years after the effective date of the first reduction under paragraph (1) that is proclaimed to carry out the trade agreement with respect to such article.

(6) A rate of duty reduction or increase that may not be proclaimed by reason of paragraph (2) may take effect only if a provision authorizing such reduction or increase is included within an implementing bill provided for under section 1103 and that bill is enacted into law.

(b) Agreements regarding nontariff barriers.

(1) Whenever the President determines that any barrier to, or other distortion of, international trade—

(A) unduly burdens or restricts the foreign trade of the United States or adversely affects the United States economy; or

(B) the imposition of any such barrier or distortion is likely to result in such a burden, restriction, or effect;

and that the purposes, policies, and objectives of this title will be promoted thereby, the President may, before June 1, 1993, enter into a trade agreement with foreign countries providing for—

(i) the reduction or elimination of such barrier or other distortion; or

(ii) the prohibition of, or limitations on the imposition of, such barrier or other distortion.

(2) A trade agreement may be entered into under this subsection only if such agreement makes progress in meeting the applicable objectives described in section 1101.

(c) Bilateral agreements regarding tariff and nontariff barriers.

(1) Before June 1, 1993, the President may enter into bilateral trade agreements with foreign countries that provide for the elimination or reduction of any duty imposed by the United States. A trade agreement entered into under this paragraph may also provide for the reduction or elimination of barriers to, or other distortions of, the international trade of the foreign country or the United States.

(2) Notwithstanding any other provision of law, no trade benefit shall be extended to any country by reason of the extension of any trade benefit to another country under a trade agreement entered into under paragraph (1) with such other country.

(3) A trade agreement may be entered into under paragraph (1) with any foreign country only if—

(A) the agreement makes progress in meeting the applicable objectives described in section 1101;

(B) such foreign country requests the negotiation of such an agreement; and

(C) the President, at least 60 days before the date notice is provided under section 1103(a)(1)(A)—

(i) provides written notice of such negotiations to the Committee on Finance of the Senate and the Committee on Ways and Means of the House of Representatives, and

(ii) consults with such committees regarding the negotiation of such agreement.

(4) The 60-day period of time described in paragraph (3)(C) shall be computed in accordance with section 1103(e).

(5) In any case in which there is an inconsistency between any provision of this Act and any bilateral free trade area agreement that entered into force and effect with respect to the United States before January 1, 1987, the provision shall not apply with respect to the foreign country that is party to that agreement.

(d) Consultation with Congress before agreements entered into.

(1) Before the President enters into any trade agreement under subsection (b) or (c), the President shall consult with—

(A) the Committee on Ways and Means of the House of Representatives and the Committee on Finance of the Senate; and

(B) each other committee of the House and the Senate, and each joint committee of the Congress, which has jurisdiction over legislation involving subject matters which would be affected by the trade agreement.

(2) The consultation under paragraph (1) shall include—

(A) the nature of the agreement;

(B) how and to what extent the agreement will achieve the applicable purposes, policies, and objectives of this title; and

(C) all matters relating to the implementation of the agreement under section 1103.

(3) If it is proposed to implement two or more trade agreements in a single implementing bill under section 1103, the consultation under paragraph (1) shall include the desirability and feasibility of such proposed implementation.

(e) Special provisions regarding Uruguay Round trade negotiations

(1) In general

Notwithstanding the time limitations in subsections (a) and (b) of this section, if the Uruguay Round of multilateral trade negotiations under the auspices of the General Agreement on Tariffs and Trade has not resulted in trade agreements by May 31, 1993, the President may, during the period after May 31, 1993, and before April 16, 1994, enter into, under subsections (a) and (b) of this section, trade agreements resulting from such negotiations.

(2) Application of tariff proclamation authority

No proclamation under subsection (a) of this section to carry out the provisions regarding tariff barriers of a trade agreement that is entered into pursuant to paragraph (1) may take effect before the effective date of a bill that implements the provisions regarding nontariff barriers of a trade agreement that is entered into under such paragraph.

(3) Application of implementing and "fast track" procedures

Section 1103 applies to any trade agreement negotiated under subsection (b) of this section pursuant to paragraph (1), except that—

(A) in applying subsection (a)(1)(A) of section 1103 to any such agreement, the phrase "at least 120 calendar days before the day on which he enters into the trade agreement (but not later than December 15, 1993)," shall be substituted for the phrase "at least 90 calendar days before the day on which he enters into the trade agreement,"; and

(B) no provision of subsection (b) of section 1103 other than paragraph (1)(A) applies to any such agreement and in applying such paragraph, "April 16, 1994;" shall be substituted for "June 1, 1991;".

(4) Advisory committee reports

The report required under section 135(e)(1) of the Trade Act of 1974 (19 U.S.C. 2155) regarding any trade agreement provided for under paragraph (1) shall be provided to the President, the Congress, and the United States Trade Representative not later than 30 days after the date on which the President notifies the Congress under section 1103(a)(1)(A) of this title of his intention to enter into the agreement (but before January 15, 1994).

19 USC 2903

Sec. 1103.   Implementation of Trade Agreements

(a) In general.

(1) Any agreement entered into under section 1102(b) or (c) shall enter into force with respect to the United States if (and only if)—

(A) the President, at least 90 calendar days before the day on which he enters into the trade agreement, notifies the House of Representatives and the Senate of his intention to enter into the agreement, and promptly thereafter publishes notice of such intention in the Federal Register;

(B) after entering into the agreement, the President submits a document to the House of Representatives and to the Senate containing a copy of the final legal text of the agreement, together with—

(i) a draft of an implementing bill,

(ii) a statement of any administrative action proposed to implement the trade agreement, and

(iii) the supporting information described in paragraph (2); and

(C) the implementing bill is enacted into law.

(2) The supporting information required under paragraph (1)(B)(iii) consists of—

(A) an explanation as to how the implementing bill and proposed administrative action will change or affect existing law; and

(B) a statement—

(i) asserting that the agreement makes progress in achieving the applicable purposes, policies, and objectives of this title,

(ii) setting forth the reasons of the President regarding—

(I) how and to what extent the agreement makes progress in achieving the applicable purposes, policies, and objectives referred to in clause (i), and why and to what extent the agreement does not achieve other applicable purposes, policies, and objectives,

(II) how the agreement serves the interests of United States commerce, and

(III) why the implementing bill and proposed administrative action is required or appropriate to carry out the agreement;

(iii) describing the efforts made by the President to obtain international exchange rate equilibrium and any effect the agreement may have regarding increased international monetary stability; and

(iv) describing the extent, if any, to which—

(I) each foreign country that is a party to the agreement maintains non-commercial state trading enterprises that may adversely affect, nullify, or impair the benefits to the United States under the agreement, and

(II) the agreement applies to or affects purchases and sales by such enterprises.

(3) To ensure that a foreign country which receives benefits under a trade agreement entered into under section 1102(b) or (c) is subject to the obligations imposed by such agreement, the President shall recommend to Congress in the implementing bill and statement of administrative action submitted with respect to such agreement that the benefits and obligations of such agreement apply solely to the parties to such agreement, if such application is consistent with the terms of such agreement. The President may also recommend with respect to any such agreement that the benefits and obligations of such agreement not apply uniformly to all parties to such agreement, if such application is consistent with the terms of such agreement.

(b) Application of congressional "fast track" procedures to implementing bills.

(1) Except as provided in subsection (c)—

(A) the provisions of section 151 of the Trade Act of 1974 (19 U.S.C. 2191) (hereinafter in this section referred to as "fast track procedures") apply to implementing bills submitted with respect to trade agreements entered into under section 1102(b) or (c) before June 1, 1991; and

(B) such fast track procedures shall be extended to implementing bills submitted with respect to trade agreements entered into under section 1102(b) or (c) after May 31, 1991, and before June 1, 1993, if (and only if)—

(i) the President requests such extension under paragraph (2); and

(ii) neither House of the Congress adopts an extension disapproval resolution under paragraph (5) before June 1, 1991.

(2) If the President is of the opinion that the fast track procedures should be extended to implementing bills described in paragraph (1)(B), the Presi-

dent must submit to the Congress, no later than March 1, 1991, a written report that contains a request for such extension, together with—

(A) a description of all trade agreements that have been negotiated under section 1102(b) or (c) and the anticipated schedule for submitting such agreements to the Congress for approval;

(B) a description of the progress that has been made in multilateral and bilateral negotiations to achieve the purposes, policies, and objectives of this title, and a statement that such progress justifies the continuation of negotiations; and

(C) a statement of the reasons why the extension is needed to complete the negotiations.

(3) The President shall promptly inform the Advisory Committee for Trade Policy and Negotiations established under section 135 of the Trade Act of 1974 (19 U.S.C. 2155) of his decision to submit a report to Congress under paragraph (2). The Advisory Committee shall submit to the Congress as soon as practicable, but no later than March 1, 1991, a written report that contains—

(A) its views regarding the progress that has been made in multilateral and bilateral negotiations to achieve the purposes, policies, and objectives of this title; and

(B) a statement of its views, and the reasons therefor, regarding whether the extension requested under paragraph (2) should be approved or disapproved.

(4) The reports submitted to the Congress under paragraphs (2) and (3), or any portion of the reports, may be classified to the extent the President determines appropriate.

(5)(A) For purposes of this subsection, the term "extension disapproval resolution" means a resolution of either House of the Congress, the sole matter after the resolving clause of which is as follows: "That the _____ disapproves the request of the President for the extension, under section 1103(b)(1)(B)(i) of the Omnibus Trade and Competitiveness Act of 1988, of the provisions of section 151 of the Trade Act of 1974 to any implementing bill submitted with respect to any trade agreement entered into under section 1102(b) or (c) of such Act after May 31, 1991, because sufficient tangible progress has not been made in trade negotiations.", with the blank space being filled with the name of the resolving House of the Congress.

(B) Extension disapproval resolutions—

(i) may be introduced in either House of the Congress by any member of such House; and

(ii) shall be jointly referred, in the House of Representatives, to the Committee on Ways and Means and the Committee on Rules.

(C) The provisions of section 152(d) and (e) of the Trade Act of 1974 (19 U.S.C. 2192(d) and (e)) (relating to the floor consideration of certain resolutions in the House and Senate) apply to extension disapproval resolutions.

(D) It is not in order for—

(i) the Senate to consider any extension disapproval resolution not reported by the Committee on Finance;

(ii) the House of Representatives to consider any extension disapproval resolution not reported by the Committee on Ways and Means and the Committee on Rules; or

(iii) either House of the Congress to consider an extension disapproval resolution that is reported to such House after May 15, 1991.

(c) Limitations on use of "fast track" procedures.

(1)(A) The fast track procedures shall not apply to any implementing bill submitted with respect to a trade agreement entered into under section 1102(b) or (c) if both Houses of the Congress separately agree to procedural disapproval resolutions within any 60-day period.

(B) Procedural disapproval resolutions—

(i) in the House of Representatives—

(I) shall be introduced by the chairman or ranking minority member of the Committee on Ways and Means or the chairman or ranking minority member of the Committee on Rules,

(II) shall be jointly referred to the Committee on Ways and Means and the Committee on Rules, and

(III) may not be amended by either Committee; and

(ii) in the Senate shall be original resolutions of the Committee on Finance.

(C) The provisions of section 152(d) and (e) of the Trade Act of 1974 (19 U.S.C. 2192(d) and (e)) (relating to the floor consideration of certain resolutions in the House and Senate) apply to procedural disapproval resolutions.

(D) It is not in order for the House of Representatives to consider any procedural disapproval resolution not reported by the Committee on Ways and Means and the Committee on Rules.

(E) For purposes of this subsection, the term "procedural disapproval resolution" means a resolution of either House of the Congress, the sole matter after the resolving clause of which is as follows: "That the President has failed or refused to consult with Congress on trade negotiations and trade agreements in accordance with the provisions of the Omnibus Trade and Competitiveness Act of 1988, and, therefore, the provisions of section 151 of the Trade Act of 1974 shall not apply to any implementing bill submitted with respect to any trade agreement entered into under section 1102(b) or (c) of such Act of 1988, if, during the 60-day period beginning on the date on which this resolution is agreed to by the _____, the _____ agrees to a procedural disapproval resolution (within the meaning of section 1103(c)(1)(E) of such Act of 1988).", with the first blank space being filled with the name of the resolving House of the Congress and the second blank space being filled with the name of the other House of the Congress.

(2) The fast track procedures shall not apply to any implementing bill that contains a provision approving of any trade agreement which is entered into under section 1102(c) with any foreign country if either—

(A) the requirements of section 1102(c)(3) are not met with respect to the negotiation of such agreement; or

(B) the Committee on Finance of the Senate or the Committee on Ways and Means of the House of Representatives disapproves of the negotiation of such agreement before the close of the 60-day period which begins on the date notice is provided under section 1102(c)(3)(C)(i) with respect to the negotiation of such agreement.

(d) Rules of House of Representatives and Senate. Subsections (b) and (c) are enacted by the Congress—

(1) as an exercise of the rulemaking power of the House of Representatives and the Senate, respectively, and as such is [sic] deemed a part of the rules of each House, respectively, and such procedures supersede other rules only to the extent that they are inconsistent with such other rules; and

(2) with the full recognition of the constitutional right of either House to change the rules (so far as relating to the procedures of that House) at any time, in the same manner, and to the same extent as any other rule of that House.

(e) Computation of certain periods of time. Each period of time described in subsection (c)(1)(A) and (E) and (2) of this section shall be computed without regard to—

(1) the days on which either House of Congress is not in session because of an adjournment of more than 3 days to a day certain or an adjournment of the Congress sine die; and

(2) any Saturday and Sunday, not excluded under paragraph (1), when either House of the Congress is not in session.

* * *

19 USC 2904

Sec. 1105. Termination and Reservation Authority; Reciprocal Non-discriminatory Treatment

(a) In general. For purposes of applying sections 125, 126(a), and 127 of the Trade Act of 1974 (19 U.S.C. 2135, 2136(a), and 2137)—

(1) any trade agreement entered into under section 1102 shall be treated as an agreement entered into under section 101 or 102, as appropriate, of the Trade Act of 1974 (19 U.S.C. 2111 or 2112); and

(2) any proclamation or Executive order issued pursuant to a trade agreement entered into under section 1102 shall be treated as a proclamation or Executive order issued pursuant to a trade agreement entered into under section 102 of the Trade Act of 1974.

(b) Reciprocal nondiscriminatory treatment.

(1) The President shall determine, before June 1, 1993, whether any major industrial country has failed to make concessions under trade agree-

ments entered into under section 1102(a) and (b) which provide competitive opportunities for the commerce of the United States in such country substantially equivalent to the competitive opportunities, provided by concessions made by the United States under trade agreements entered into under section 1102(a) and (b), for the commerce of such country in the United States.

(2) If the President determines under paragraph (1) that a major industrial country has not made concessions under trade agreements entered into under section 1102(a) and (b) which provide substantially equivalent competitive opportunities for the commerce of the United States, the President shall, either generally with respect to such country or by article produced by such country, in order to restore equivalence of competitive opportunities, recommend to the Congress—

(A) legislation providing for the termination or denial of the benefits of concessions of trade agreements entered into under section 1102(a) and (b) that have been made with respect to rates of duty or other import restrictions imposed by the United States, and

(B) legislation providing that any law necessary to carry out any trade agreement under section 1102(a) or (b) not apply to such country.

(3) For purposes of this subsection, the term "major industrial country" means Canada, the European Communities, the individual member countries of the European Communities, Japan, and any other foreign country designated by the President for purposes of this subsection.

19 USC 2905

Sec. 1106. Accession of State Trading Regimes to the General Agreement on Tariffs and Trade or the WTO

(a) In general. Before any major foreign country accedes, after the date of enactment of this Act, to the GATT 1947, or to the WTO Agreement, the President shall determine—

(1) whether state trading enterprises account for a significant share of—

(A) the exports of such major foreign country, or

(B) the goods of such major foreign country that are subject to competition from goods imported into such foreign country; and

(2) whether such state trading enterprises—

(A) unduly burden and restrict, or adversely affect, the foreign trade of the United States or the United States economy, or

(B) are likely to result in such a burden, restriction, or effect.

(b) Effects of affirmative determination. If both of the determinations made under paragraphs (1) and (2) of subsection (a) with respect to a major foreign country are affirmative—

(1) the President shall reserve the right of the United States to withhold extension of the application of the GATT 1947 or the WTO Agreement, between the United States and such major foreign country, and

(2) the GATT 1947 or the WTO Agreement shall not apply between the United States and such major foreign country until—

(A) such foreign country enters into an agreement with the United States providing that the state trading enterprises of such foreign country—

(i) will—

(I) make purchases which are not for the use of such foreign country, and

(II) make sales in international trade,

in accordance with commercial considerations (including price, quality, availability, marketability, and transportation), and

(ii) will afford United States business firms adequate opportunity, in accordance with customary practice, to compete for participation in such purchases or sales; or

(B) a bill submitted under subsection (c) which approves of the extension of the application of the GATT 1947 or the WTO Agreement between the United States and such major foreign country is enacted into law.

(c) Expedited consideration of bill to approve extension.

(1) The President may submit to the Congress any draft of a bill which approves of the extension of the application of the GATT 1947 or the WTO Agreement between the United States and a major foreign country.

(2) Any draft of a bill described in paragraph (1) that is submitted by the President to the Congress shall—

(A) be introduced by the majority leader of each House of the Congress (by request) on the first day on which such House is in session after the date such draft is submitted to the Congress; and

(B) shall be treated as an implementing bill for purposes of subsections (d), (e), (f), and (g) of section 151 of the Trade Act of 1974.

(d) Publication. The President shall publish in the Federal Register each determination made under subsection (a).

(e) Definitions. For purposes of this section

(1) The term "GATT 1947" has the meaning given that term in section 2(1)(A) of the Uruguay Round Agreements Act.

(2) The term "WTO Agreement" means the Agreement Establishing the World Trade Organization entered into on April 15, 1994 and the multilateral trade agreements (as such term is defined in section 2(4) of the Uruguay Round Agreements Act).

19 USC 2906

Sec. 1107.   Definitions

For purposes of this part:

(1) The term "distortion" includes, but is not limited to, a subsidy.

(2) The term "foreign country" includes any foreign instrumentality. Any territory or possession of a foreign country that is administered separately for customs purposes, shall be treated as a separate foreign country.

(3) The term "GATT" means the GATT 1947 (as defined in section 2(1)(A) of the Uruguay Round Agreements Act.

(4) The term "implementing bill" has the meaning given such term in section 151(b)(1) of the Trade Act of 1974.

(5) The term "international trade" includes, but is not limited to—

(A) trade in both goods and services, and

(B) foreign direct investment by United States persons, especially if such investment has implications for trade in goods and services.

(6) The term "state trading enterprise" means—

(A) any agency, instrumentality, or administrative unit of a foreign country which—

(i) purchases goods or services in international trade for any purpose other than the use of such goods or services by such agency, instrumentality, administrative unit, or foreign country, or

(ii) sells goods or services in international trade; or

(B) any business firm which—

(i) is substantially owned or controlled by a foreign country or any agency, instrumentality, or administrative unit thereof,

(ii) is granted (formally or informally) any special or exclusive privilege by such foreign country, agency, instrumentality, or administrative unit, and

(iii) purchases goods or services in international trade for any purpose other than the use of such goods or services by such foreign country, agency, instrumentality, or administrative unit, or which sells goods or services in international trade.

Subtitle B

Implementation of the Harmonized Tariff Schedule

19 USC 3001

Sec. 1201.   Purposes

The purposes of this subtitle are—

(1) to approve the International Convention on the Harmonized Commodity Description and Coding System;

(2) to implement in United States law the nomenclature established internationally by the Convention; and

(3) to provide that the Convention shall be treated as a trade agreement obligation of the United States.

19 USC 3002

Sec. 1202.   Definitions

As used in this subtitle:

(1) The term "Commission" means the United States International Trade Commission.

(2) The term "Convention" means the International Convention on the Harmonized Commodity Description and Coding System, done at Brussels on June 14, 1983, and the Protocol thereto, done at Brussels on June 24, 1986, submitted to the Congress on June 15, 1987.

(3) The term "entered" means entered, or withdrawn from warehouse for consumption, in the customs territory of the United States.

(4) The term "Federal agency" means any establishment in the executive branch of the United States Government.

(5) The term "old Schedules" means title I of the Tariff Act of 1930 (19 U.S.C. 1202) as in effect on the day before the effective date of the amendment to such title under section 1204(a).

(6) The term "technical rectifications" means rectifications of an editorial character or minor technical or clerical changes which do not affect the substance or meaning of the text, such as—

(A) errors in spelling, numbering, or punctuation;

(B) errors in indentation;

(C) errors (including inadvertent omissions) in cross-references to headings or subheadings or notes; and

(D) other clerical or typographical errors.

19 USC 3003

Sec. 1203.   Congressional Approval of United States Accession to the Convention

(a) **Congressional approval.** The Congress approves the accession by the United States of America to the Convention.

(b) **Acceptance of the final legal text of the convention by the President.** The President may accept for the United States the final legal instruments embodying the Convention. The President shall submit a copy of each final instrument to the Congress on the date it becomes available.

(c) **Unspecified private remedies not created.** Neither the entry into force with respect to the United States of the Convention nor the enactment of this subtitle may be construed as creating any private right of action or remedy for which provision is not explicitly made under this subtitle or under other laws of the United States.

(d) **Termination.** The provisions of section 125(a) of the Trade Act of 1974 (19 U.S.C. 2135(a)) do not apply to the Convention.

19 USC 3004

Sec. 1204.   Enactment of the Harmonized Tariff Schedule

(a) **[Omitted]**

(b) **Modifications to Harmonized Tariff Schedule.** At the earliest practicable date after the date of the enactment of the Omnibus Trade and Competitiveness Act of 1988 [enacted Aug. 23, 1988], the President shall—

(1) proclaim such modifications to the Harmonized Tariff Schedule as are consistent with the standards applied in converting the old Schedules into the format of the Convention, as reflected in such Publication No. 2030 and Supplement No. 1. thereto, and as are necessary or appropriate to implement—

(A) the future outstanding staged rate reductions authorized by the Congress in—

(i) the Trade Act of 1974 and the Trade Agreements Act of 1979 to reflect the tariff reductions that resulted from the Tokyo Round of multilateral trade negotiations, and

(ii) the United States–Israel Free Trade Area Implementation Act of 1985 to reflect the tariff reduction resulting from the United States–Israel Free Trade Area Agreement,

(B) the applicable provisions of—

(i) statutes enacted,

(ii) executive actions taken, and

(iii) final judicial decisions rendered,

after January 1, 1988, and before the effective date of the Harmonized Tariff Schedule, and

(C) such technical rectifications as the President considers necessary; and

(2) take such action as the President considers necessary to bring trade agreements to which the United States is a party into conformity with the Harmonized Tariff Schedule.

(c) Status of Harmonized Tariff Schedule.

(1) The following shall be considered to be statutory provisions of law for all purposes:

(A) The provisions of the Harmonized Tariff Schedule as enacted by this subtitle.

(B) Each statutory amendment to the Harmonized Tariff Schedule.

(C) Each modification or change made to the Harmonized Tariff Schedule by the President under authority of law (including section 604 of the Trade Act of 1974.

(2) Neither the enactment of this subtitle nor the subsequent enactment of any amendment to the Harmonized Tariff Schedule, unless such subsequent enactment otherwise provides, may be construed as limiting the authority of the President—

(A) to effect the import treatment necessary or appropriate to carry out, modify, withdraw, suspend, or terminate, in whole or in part, trade agreements; or

(B) to take such other actions through the modification, continuance, or imposition of any rate of duty or other import restriction as may be necessary or appropriate under the authority of the President.

(3) If a rate of duty established in column 1 by the President by proclamation or Executive order is higher than the existing rate of duty in column 2, the President may by proclamation or Executive order increase such existing rate to the higher rate.

(4) If a rate of duty is suspended or terminated by the President by proclamation or Executive order and the proclamation or Executive order does not specify the rate that is to apply in lieu of the suspended or terminated rate, the last rate of duty that applied prior to the suspended or terminated rate shall be the efffective [effective] rate of duty.

(d) Interim informational use of Harmonized Tariff Schedule classifications. Each—

(1) proclamation issued by the President;

(2) public notice issued by the Commission or other Federal agency; and

(3) finding, determination, order, recommendation, or other decision made by the Commission or other Federal agency;

during the period between the date of the enactment of the Omnibus Trade and Competitiveness Act of 1988 [enacted Aug. 23, 1988] and the effective date of the Harmonized Tariff Schedule shall, if the proclamation, notice, or decision contains a reference to the tariff classification of any article, include, for informational purposes, a reference to the classification of that article under the Harmonized Tariff Schedule.

19 USC 3005

Sec. 1205. Commission Review of, and Recommendations Regarding, the Harmonized Tariff Schedule

(a) In general. The Commission shall keep the Harmonized Tariff Schedule under continuous review and periodically, at such time as amendments to the Convention are recommended by the Customs Cooperation Council for adoption, and as other circumstances warrant, shall recommend to the President such modifications in the Harmonized Tariff Schedule as the Commission considers necessary or appropriate—

(1) to conform the Harmonized Tariff Schedule with amendments made to the Convention;

(2) to promote the uniform application of the Convention and particularly the Annex thereto;

(3) to ensure that the Harmonized Tariff Schedule is kept up-to-date in light of changes in technology or in patterns of international trade;

(4) to alleviate unnecessary administrative burdens; and

(5) to make technical rectifications.

(b) Agency and public views regarding recommendations. In formulating recommendations under subsection (a), the Commission shall solicit, and give consideration to, the views of interested Federal agencies and the public. For purposes of obtaining public views, the Commission—

(1) shall give notice of the proposed recommendations and afford reasonable opportunity for interested parties to present their views in writing; and

(2) may provide for a public hearing.

(c) Submission of recommendations. The Commission shall submit recommendations under this section to the President in the form of a report that shall include a summary of the information on which the recommendations were based, together with a statement of the probable economic effect of each recommended change on any industry in the United States. The report also shall include a copy of all written views submitted by interested Federal agencies and a copy or summary, prepared by the Commission, of the views of all other interested parties.

(d) Requirements regarding recommendations. The Commission may not recommend any modification to the Harmonized Tariff Schedule unless the modification meets the following requirements:

(1) The modification must—

(A) be consistent with the Convention or any amendment thereto recommended for adoption;

(B) be consistent with sound nomenclature principles; and

(C) ensure substantial rate neutrality.

(2) Any change to a rate of duty must be consequent to, or necessitated by, nomenclature modifications that are recommended under this section.

(3) The modification must not alter existing conditions of competition for the affected United States industry, labor, or trade.

19 USC 3006

Sec. 1206. Presidential Action on Commission Recommendations

(a) In general. The President may proclaim modifications, based on the recommendations by the Commission under section 1205, to the Harmonized Tariff Schedule if the President determines that the modifications—

(1) are in conformity with United States obligations under the Convention; and

(2) do not run counter to the national economic interest of the United States.

(b) Lay-over period.

(1) The President may proclaim a modification under subsection (a) only after the expiration of the 60-day period beginning on the date on which the President submits a report to the Committee on Ways and Means of the House of Representatives and the Committee on Finance of the Senate that sets forth the proposed modification and the reasons therefor.

(2) The 60-day period referred to in paragraph (1) shall be computed by excluding—

(A) the days on which either House is not in session because of an adjournment of more than 3 days to a day certain or an adjournment of the Congress sine die; and

(B) any Saturday and Sunday, not excluded under subparagraph (A), when either House is not in session.

(c) Effective date of modifications. Modifications proclaimed by the President under subsection (a) may not take effect before the 15th day after the date on which the text of the proclamation is published in the Federal Register.

19 USC 3007

Sec. 1207. Publication of the Harmonized Tariff Schedule

(a) In general. The Commission shall compile and publish, at appropriate intervals, and keep up to date the Harmonized Tariff Schedule and related information in the form of printed copy; and, if, in its judgment, such format would serve the public interest and convenience—

(1) in the form of microfilm images; or

(2) in the form of electronic media.

(b) Content. Publications under subsection (a), in whatever format, shall contain—

(1) the then current Harmonized Tariff Schedule;

(2) statistical annotations and related statistical information formulated under section 484(f) of the Tariff Act of 1930 (19 U.S.C. 1484(f)); and

(3) such other matters as the Commission considers to be necessary or appropriate to carry out the purposes enumerated in the Preamble to the Convention.

19 USC 3008

Sec. 1208. Import and Export Statistics

The Secretary of Commerce shall compile, and make publicly available, the import and export trade statistics of the United States. Such statistics shall be conformed to the nomenclature of the Convention.

19 USC 3009

Sec. 1209. Coordination of Trade Policy and the Convention

The United States Trade Representative is responsible for coordination of United States trade policy in relation to the Convention. Before formulating any United States position with respect to the Convention, including any proposed amendments thereto, the United States Trade Representative shall seek, and consider, information and advice from interested parties in the private sector (including a functional advisory committee) and from interested Federal agencies.

19 USC 3010

Sec. 1210. United States Participation on the Customs Cooperation Council Regarding the Convention

(a) Principal United States agencies.

(1) Subject to the policy direction of the Office of the United States Trade Representative under section 1209, the Department of the Treasury, the

Department of Commerce, and the Commission shall, with respect to the activities of the Customs Cooperation Council relating to the Convention—

(A) be primarily responsible for formulating United States Government positions on technical and procedural issues; and

(B) represent the United States Government.

(2) The Department of Agriculture and other interested Federal agencies shall provide to the Department of the Treasury, the Department of Commerce, and the Commission technical advice and assistance relating to the functions referred to in paragraph (1).

(b) Development of technical proposals.

(1) In connection with responsibilities arising from the implementation of the Convention and under section 484(e) of the Tariff Act of 1930 (19 U.S.C. 1484(e)) regarding United States programs for the development of adequate and comparable statistical information on merchandise trade, the Secretary of the Treasury, the Secretary of Commerce, and the Commission shall prepare technical proposals that are appropriate or required to assure that the United States contribution to the development of the Convention recognizes the needs of the United States business community for a Convention which reflects sound principles of commodity identification, modern producing methods, and current trading patterns and practices.

(2) In carrying out this subsection, the Secretary of the Treasury, the Secretary of Commerce, and the Commission shall—

(A) solicit and consider the views of interested parties in the private sector (including a functional advisory committee) and of interested Federal agencies;

(B) establish procedures for reviewing, and developing appropriate responses to, inquiries and complaints from interested parties concerning articles produced in and exported from the United States; and

(C) where appropriate, establish procedures for—

(i) ensuring that the dispute settlement provisions and other relevant procedures available under the Convention are utilized to promote United States export interests, and

(ii) submitting classification questions to the Harmonized System Committee of the Customs Cooperation Council.

(c) Availability of customs cooperation council publications. As soon as practicable after the date of the enactment of the Omnibus Trade and Competitiveness Act of 1988, and periodically thereafter as appropriate, the Commission shall see to the publication of—

(1) summary records of the Harmonized System Committee of the Customs Cooperation Council; and

(2) subject to applicable copyright laws, the Explanatory Notes, Classification Opinions, and other instruments of the Customs Cooperation Council relating to the Convention.

19 USC 3011

Sec. 1211. Transition to the Harmonized Tariff Schedule

(a) Existing executive actions.

(1) The appropriate officers of the United States Government shall take whatever actions are necessary to conform, to the fullest extent practicable, with the tariff classification system of the Harmonized Tariff Schedule all proclamations, regulations, rulings, notices, findings, determinations, orders, recommendations, and other written actions that—

(A) are in effect on the day before the effective date of the Harmonized Tariff Schedule; and

(B) contain references to the tariff classification of articles under the old Schedules.

(2) Neither the repeal of the old Schedules, nor the failure of any officer of the United States Government to make the conforming changes required under paragraph (1), shall affect to any extent the validity or effect of the proclamation, regulation, ruling, notice, finding, determination, order, recommendation, or other action referred to in paragraph (1).

(b) Generalized System of Preferences conversion.

(1) The review of the proposed conversion of the Generalized System of Preferences program to the Convention tariff nomenclature, initiated by the Office of the United States Trade Representative by notice published in the Federal Register on December 8, 1986 (at page 44,163 of volume 51 thereof), shall be treated as satisfying the requirements of sections 503(a) and 504(c)(3) of the Trade Act of 1974 (as in effect on July 31, 1995).

(2) In applying section 504(c)(1) of the Trade Act of 1974 (as in effect on July 31, 1995) for calendar year 1989, the reference in such section to July 1 shall be treated as a reference to September 1.

(c) Import restrictions under the Agricultural Adjustment Act.

(1) Whenever the President determines that the conversion of an import restriction proclaimed under section 22 of the Agricultural Adjustment Act from part 3 of the Appendix to the old Schedules to subchapter IV of chapter 99 of the Harmonized Tariff Schedule results in—

(A) an article that was previously subject to the restriction being excluded from the restriction; or

(B) an article not previously subject to the restriction being included within the restriction;

the President may proclaim changes in subchapter IV of chapter 99 of the Harmonized Tariff Schedule to conform that subchapter to the fullest extent possible to part 3 of the Appendix to the old Schedules.

(2) Whenever the President determines that the conversion from headnote 2 of subpart A of part 10 of schedule 1 of the old Schedules to Additional U.S. Note 2, chapter 17, of the Harmonized Tariff Schedule results in—

(A) an article that was previously covered by such headnote being excluded from coverage; or

(B) an article not previously covered by such headnote being included in coverage;

the President may proclaim changes in Additional U.S. Note 2, chapter 17 of the Harmonized Tariff Schedule to conform that note to the fullest extent possible to headnote 2 of subpart A of part 10 of schedule 1 of the old Schedules.

(3) No change to the Harmonized Tariff Schedule may be proclaimed under paragraph (1) or (2) after June 30, 1990.

(d) Certain protests and petitions under the customs law.

(1) (A) This subtitle may not be considered to divest the courts of jurisdiction over—

(i) any protest filed under section 514 of the Tariff Act of 1930; or

(ii) any petition by an American manufacturer, producer, or wholesaler under section 516 of such Act;

covering articles entered before the effective date of the Harmonized Tariff Schedule.

(B) Nothing in this subtitle shall affect the jurisdiction of the courts with respect to articles entered after the effective date of the Harmonized Tariff Schedule.

(2) (A) If any protest or petition referred to in paragraph (1)(A) is sustained in whole or in part by a final judicial decision, the entries subject to that protest or petition and made before the effective date of the Harmonized Tariff Schedule shall be liquidated or reliquidated, as appropriate, in accordance with such final judicial decision under the old Schedules.

(B) At the earliest practicable date after the effective date of the Harmonized Tariff Schedule, the Commission shall initiate an investigation under section 332 of the Tariff Act of 1930 of those final judicial decisions referred to in subparagraph (A) that—

(i) are published during the 2–year period beginning on February 1, 1988; and

(ii) would have affected tariff treatment if they had been published during the period of the conversion of the old Schedules into the format of the Convention.

No later than September 1, 1990, the Commission shall report the results of the investigation to the President, the Committee on Ways and Means, and the Committee on Finance, and shall recommend those changes to the Harmonized Tariff Schedule that the Commission would have recommended if the final decisions concerned had been made before the conversion into the format of the Convention occurred.

(3) The President shall review all changes recommended by the Commission under paragraph (2)(B) and shall, as soon as practicable, proclaim such of those changes, if any, which he decides are necessary or appropriate to conform such Schedule to the final judicial decisions. Any such change shall be effective with respect to—

(A) entries made on or after the date of such proclamation; and

(B) entries made on or after the effective date of the Harmonized Tariff Schedule if, notwithstanding section 514 of the Tariff Act of 1930, application for liquidation or reliquidation thereof is made by the importer to the customs officer concerned within 180 days after the effective date of such proclamation.

(4) If any protest or petition referred to in paragraph (1)(A) is not sustained in whole or in part by a final judicial decision, the entries subject to that petition or protest and made before the effective date of the Harmonized Tariff Schedule shall be liquidated or reliquidated, as appropriate, in accordance with the final judicial decision under the old Schedules.

* * *

Subtitle C

Response to Unfair International Trade Practices

PART 1. ENFORCEMENT OF UNITED STATES RIGHTS UNDER TRADE AGREEMENTS AND RESPONSE TO CERTAIN FOREIGN TRADE PRACTICES

[See Trade Act of 1974, sec. 301–310]

PART 2. IMPROVEMENT IN THE ENFORCEMENT OF THE ANTIDUMPING AND COUNTERVAILING DUTY LAWS

[See Tariff Act of 1930, title VII]

* * *

PART 3. PROTECTION OF INTELLECTUAL PROPERTY RIGHTS

[See Tariff Act of 1930, sec. 337]

* * *

Subtitle D

Adjustment to Import Competition

PART 1. POSITIVE ADJUSTMENT BY INDUSTRIES INJURED BY IMPORTS

[See Trade Act of 1974, secs. 201–204]

PART 2. MARKET DISRUPTION

[See Trade Act of 1974, sec. 406]

PART 3. TRADE ADJUSTMENT ASSISTANCE

* * *

Subtitle E

National Security

[See Trade Expansion Act of 1962, sec. 232]

* * *

Subtitle H

Miscellaneous Customs, Trade, and Other Provisions

PART 1. CUSTOMS PROVISIONS

* * *

TITLE V
FOREIGN CORRUPT PRACTICES AMENDMENTS; INVESTMENT; AND TECHNOLOGY

Subtitle A

Foreign Corrupt Practices Act Amendments; Review of Certain Acquisitions

* * *

PART II. REVIEW OF CERTAIN MERGERS, ACQUISITIONS, AND TAKEOVERS

50 USC App. 2170

Sec. 5021. Authority to Review Certain Mergers, Acquisitions, and Takeovers

Title VII of the Defense Production Act of 1950 (50 U.S.C.App. 2158 et seq.) is amended by adding at the end thereof the following:

authority to review certain mergers, acquisitions, and takeovers

Sec. 721. (a) Investigations. The President or the President's designee may make an investigation to determine the effects on national security of mergers, acquisitions, and takeovers proposed or pending on or after the date of enactment of this section by or with foreign persons which could result in foreign control of persons engaged in interstate commerce in the United States. If it is determined that an investigation should be undertaken, it shall commence no later than 30 days after receipt by the President or the President's designee of written notification of the proposed or pending merger, acquisition, or takeover as prescribed by regulations promulgated pursuant to this section. Such investigation shall be completed no later than 45 days after such determination.

(b) Mandatory investigations. The President or the President's designee shall make an investigation, as described in subsection (a), in any instance in which an entity controlled by or acting on behalf of a foreign government seeks to engage in any merger, acquisition, or takeover which could result in control of a person engaged in interstate commerce in the United States that could affect the national security of the United States. Such investigation shall—

(1) commence not later than 30 days after receipt by the President or the President's designee of written notification of the proposed or pending merger, acquisition, or takeover, as prescribed by regulations promulgated pursuant to this section; and

(2) shall be completed not later than 45 days after its commencement.

(c) Confidentiality of information. Any information or documentary material filed with the President or the President's designee pursuant to this section shall be exempt from disclosure under section 552 of title 5, United States Code, and no such information or documentary material may be made public, except as may be relevant to any administrative or judicial action or proceeding. Nothing in this subsection shall be construed to prevent disclosure to either House of Congress or to any duly authorized committee or subcommittee of the Congress.

(d) Action by the President. Subject to subsection (e), the President may take such action for such time as the President considers appropriate to suspend or prohibit any acquisition, merger, or takeover, of a person engaged in interstate commerce in the United States proposed or pending on or after the date of enactment of this section by or with foreign persons so that such control will not threaten to impair the national security. The President shall announce the decision to take action pursuant to this subsection not later than 15 days after the investigation described in subsection (a) is completed. The President may direct the Attorney General to seek appropriate relief, including divestment relief, in the district courts of the United States in order to implement and enforce this section.

(e) Findings of the President. The President may exercise the authority conferred by subsection (d) only if the President finds that—

(1) there is credible evidence that leads the President to believe that the foreign interest exercising control might take action that threatens to impair the national security, and

(2) provisions of law, other than this section and the International Emergency Economic Powers Act (50 U.S.C. 1701–1706), do not in the President's judgment provide adequate and appropriate authority for the President to protect the national security in the matter before the President.

The provisions of subsection (d) of this section shall not be subject to judicial review.

(f) Factors to be considered. For purposes of this section, the President or the President's designee may, taking into account the requirements of national security, consider among other factors—

(1) domestic production needed for projected national defense requirements,

(2) the capability and capacity of domestic industries to meet national defense requirements, including the availability of human resources, products, technology, materials, and other supplies and services, and

(3) the control of domestic industries and commercial activity by foreign citizens as it affects the capability and capacity of the United States to meet the requirements of national security.

(4) the potential effects of the proposed or pending transaction on sales of military goods, equipment, or technology to any country—

(A) identified by the Secretary of State—

(i) under section 6(j) of the Export Administration Act of 1979 [section 2405(j) of this Appendix], as a country that supports terrorism;

(ii) under section 6(*l*) of the Export Administration Act of 1979 [section 2405(*l*) of this Appendix], as a country of concern regarding missile proliferation; or

(iii) under section 6(m) of the Export Administration Act of 1979 [section 2405(m) of this Appendix], as a country of concern regarding the proliferation of chemical and biological weapons; or

(B) listed under section 309(c) of the Nuclear Non-Proliferation Act of 1978 on the "Nuclear Non-Proliferation-Special Country List" (15 C.F.R. Part 778, Supplement No. 4) or any successor list; and

(5) the potential effects of the proposed or pending transaction on United States international technological leadership in areas affecting United States national security.

(g) Report to the Congress. The President shall immediately transmit to the Secretary of the Senate and the Clerk of the House of Representatives a written report of the President's determination of whether or not to take action under subsection (d), including a detailed explanation of the findings made under subsection (e) and the factors considered under subsection (f). Such report shall be consistent with the requirements of subsection (c) of this Act [subsection (c) of this section].

(h) Regulations. The President shall direct the issuance of regulations to carry out this section. Such regulations shall, to the extent possible, minimize paperwork burdens and shall to the extent possible coordinate reporting requirements under this section with reporting requirements under any other provision of Federal law.

(i) Effect on other law. Nothing in this section shall be construed to alter or affect any existing power, process, regulation, investigation, enforcement measure, or review provided by any other provision of law.

* * *

TITLE VII
BUY AMERICAN ACT OF 1988
41 USC 10a note

Sec. 7001.   Short Title

This title may be cited as the "Buy American Act of 1988".

Sec. 7002.   Amendments to the Buy American Act

Title III of the Act of March 3, 1933 (41 U.S.C. 10a-10d), is amended—

(1) by redesignating sections 4 and 5 as sections 5 and 6, respectively; and

(2) by inserting after section 3 the following new section: "Sec. 4. (a) A Federal agency shall not award any contract—

"(1) for the procurement of an article, material, or supply mined, produced, or manufactured—

"(A) in a signatory country that is considered to be a signatory not in good standing of the Agreement pursuant to section 305(f)(3)(A) of the Trade Agreements Act of 1979; or

"(B) in a foreign country whose government maintains, in government procurement, a significant and persistent pattern or practice of discrimination against United States products or services which results in identifiable harm to United States businesses, as identified by the President pursuant to section 305(g)(1)(A) of such Act; or

"(2) for the procurement of a service of any contractor or subcontractor that is a citizen or national of a foreign country identified by the President pursuant to section 305(f)(3)(A) or 305(g)(1)(A) of such Act, or is owned or controlled directly or indirectly by citizens or nationals of such a foreign country.

"(b) The prohibition on procurement in subsection (a) is subject to sections 305(h) and 305(j) of such Act and shall not apply—

"(1) with respect to services, articles, materials, or supplies procured and used outside the United States and its territories;

"(2) notwithstanding section 305(g) of such Act, to an eligible product of a country which is a signatory country unless that country is considered to be a signatory not in good standing pursuant to section 305(f)(3)(A) of such Act; or

"(3) notwithstanding section 305(g) of such Act, to a country that is a least developed country (as that term is defined in section 308(6) of that Act).

"(c) Notwithstanding subsection (a) of this section, the President or the head of a Federal agency may authorize the award of a contract or class of contracts if the President or the head of the Federal agency—

"(1) determines that such action is necessary—

"(A) in the public interest;

"(B) to avoid the restriction of competition in a manner which would limit the procurement in question to, or would establish a preference for, the services, articles, materials, or supplies of a single manufacturer or supplier; or

"(C) because there would be or are an insufficient number of potential or actual bidders to assure procurement of services, articles, materials, or supplies of requisite quality at competitive prices; and

"(2) notifies the Committee on Governmental Affairs of the Senate, as well as other appropriate Senate committees, and the appropriate committees of the House of Representatives, of such determination—

"(A) not less than 30 days prior to the date of the award of the contract or the date of authorization of the award of a class of contracts; or

"(B) if the agency's need for the service, article, material, or supply is of such urgency that the United States would be seriously injured by delaying the award or authorization, not more than 90 days after the date of such award or authorization.

* * *

"(f) Nothing in this section shall restrict the application of the prohibition under section 302(a)(1) of the Trade Agreements Act of 1979.

"(g)(1) For purposes of this section with respect to construction services, a contractor or subcontractor is owned or controlled directly or indirectly by citizens or nationals of a foreign country if—

"(A) 50 percent or more of the voting stock of the contractor or subcontractor is owned by one or more citizens or nationals of the foreign country;

"(B) the title to 50 percent or more of the stock of the contractor or subcontractor is held subject to trust or fiduciary obligations in favor of one or more citizens or nationals of the foreign country;

"(C) 50 percent or more of the voting stock of the contractor or subcontractor is vested in or exercisable on behalf of one or more citizens or nationals of the foreign country;

"(D) the case of a corporation—

"(i) the number of its directors necessary to constitute a quorum are citizens or nationals of the foreign country; or

"(ii) the corporation is organized under the laws of the foreign country or any subdivision, territory, or possession thereof; or

"(E) in the case of a contractor or subcontractor who is a participant in a joint venture or a member of a partnership, any participant of the joint venture or partner meets any of the criteria in subparagraphs (A) through (D) of this paragraph.

* * *

"(h) As used in this section—

"(1) the term "Agreement" means the Agreement on Government Procurement as defined in section 308(1) of the Trade Agreements Act of 1979;

"(2) the term "signatory" means a party to the Agreement; and

"(3) the term "eligible product" has the meaning given such term by section 308(4) of the Trade Agreements Act of 1979 (19 U.S.C. 2518(4))."

* * *

Sec. 7004. Sunset Provision

The amendments made by this title shall cease to be effective on April 30, 1996, unless the Congress, after reviewing the report required by section 305(k) of the Trade Agreements Act of 1979, and other relevant information, extends such date. After such date, the President may modify or terminate any or all actions taken pursuant to such amendments.

* * *

Item 51

NORTH AMERICAN FREE TRADE AGREEMENT IMPLEMENTATION ACT

(selected provisions)

PUBLIC LAW 103–182 of December 8, 1993, 107 Stat. 2060

An Act to implement the North American Free Trade Agreement.

Be it enacted by the Senate and House of Representatives of the United States of America in Congress assembled,

SECTION 1. SHORT TITLE AND TABLE OF CONTENTS.

19 USC 3301 NOTE

(a) **Short Title**.—This Act may be cited as the "North American Free Trade Agreement Implementation Act".

(b) **Table of Contents.**

PART 2—RELIEF FROM IMPORTS FROM ALL COUNTRIES

TITLE IV—DISPUTE SETTLEMENT IN ANTIDUMPING AND COUNTERVAILING DUTY CASES

Subtitle A—Organizational, Administrative, and Procedural Provisions Regarding the Implementation of Chapter 19 of the Agreement

Subtitle D—Implementation of NAFTA Supplemental Agreements

PART 1—AGREEMENTS RELATING TO LABOR AND ENVIRONMENT

---

19 USC 3301

Sec. 2.   Definitions

For purposes of this Act:

(1) Agreement.—The term "Agreement" means the North American Free Trade Agreement approved by the Congress under section 101(a).

(2) HTS.—The term "HTS" means the Harmonized Tariff Schedule of the United States.

(3) Mexico.—Any reference to Mexico shall be considered to be a reference to the United Mexican States.

(4) NAFTA Country.—Except as provided in section 202, the term "NAFTA country" means—

(A) Canada for such time as the Agreement is in force with respect to, and the United States applies the Agreement to, Canada; and

(B) Mexico for such time as the Agreement is in force with respect to, and the United States applies the Agreement to, Mexico.

(5) International Trade Commission.—The term "International Trade Commission" means the United States International Trade Commission.

(6) Trade Representative.—The term "Trade Representative" means the United States Trade Representative.

TITLE I—APPROVAL OF, AND GENERAL PROVISIONS RELATING TO, THE NORTH AMERICAN FREE TRADE AGREEMENT

19 USC 3311

Sec. 101. Approval and Entry into Force of the North American Free Trade Agreement

(a) Approval of agreement and statement of administrative action.—Pursuant to section 1103 of the Omnibus Trade and Competitiveness Act of 1988 (19 U.S.C. 2903) and section 151 of the Trade Act of 1974 (19 U.S.C. 2191), the Congress approves—

(1) the North American Free Trade Agreement entered into on December 17, 1992, with the Governments of Canada and Mexico and submitted to the Congress on November 4, 1993; and

(2) the statement of administrative action proposed to implement the Agreement that was submitted to the Congress on November 4, 1993.

(b) Conditions for entry into force of the agreement.—The President is authorized to exchange notes with the Government of Canada or Mexico providing for the entry into force, on or after January 1, 1994, of the Agreement for the United States with respect to such country at such time as—

(1) The President—

(A) determines that such country has implemented the statutory changes necessary to bring that country into compliance with its obligations under the Agreement and has made provision to implement the Uniform Regulations provided for under article 511 of the Agreement regarding the interpretation, application, and administration of the rules of origin, and

(B) transmits a report to the House of Representatives and the Senate setting forth the determination under subparagraph (A) and including, in the case of Mexico, a description of the specific measures taken by that country to—

(i) bring its laws into conformity with the requirements of the Schedule of Mexico in Annex 1904.15 of the Agreement, and

(ii) otherwise ensure the effective implementation of the binational panel review process under chapter 19 of the Agreement regarding final antidumping and countervailing duty determinations; and

(2) the Government of such country exchanges notes with the United States providing for the entry into force of the North American Agreement on Environmental Cooperation and the North American Agreement on Labor Cooperation for that country and the United States.

19 USC 3312

Sec. 102. Relationship of the Agreement to United States and State law

(a) Relationship of Agreement to United States law.—

(1) United States law to Prevail in Conflict.—No provision of the Agreement, nor the application of any such provision to any person or circum-

stance, which is inconsistent with any law of the United States shall have effect.

(2) Construction.—Nothing in this Act shall be construed—

(A) to amend or modify any law of the United States, including any law regarding—

(i) the protection of human, animal, or plant life or health,

(ii) the protection of the environment, or

(iii) motor carrier or worker safety; or

(B) to limit any authority conferred under any law of the United States, including section 301 of the Trade Act of 1974;

unless specifically provided for in this Act.

(b) Relationship of Agreement to State Law.—

(1) Federal-State Consultation.—

(A) In General.—Upon the enactment of this Act, the President shall, through the intergovernmental policy advisory committees on trade established under section 306(c)(2)(A) of the Trade and Tariff Act of 1984, consult with the States for the purpose of achieving conformity of State laws and practices with the Agreement.

(B) Federal-State Consultation Process.—The Trade Representative shall establish within the Office of the United States Trade Representative a Federal-State consultation process for addressing issues relating to the Agreement that directly relate to, or will potentially have a direct impact on, the States. The Federal-State consultation process shall include procedures under which—

(i) the Trade Representative will assist the States in identifying those State laws that may not conform with the Agreement but may be maintained under the Agreement by reason of being in effect before the Agreement entered into force;

(ii) the States will be informed on a continuing basis of matters under the Agreement that directly relate to, or will potentially have a direct impact on, the States;

(iii) the States will be provided opportunity to submit, on a continuing basis, to the Trade Representative information and advice with respect to matters referred to in clause (ii);

(iv) the Trade Representative will take into account the information and advice received from the States under clause (iii) when formulating United States positions regarding matters referred to in clause (ii); and

(v) the States will be involved (including involvement through the inclusion of appropriate representatives of the States) to the greatest extent practicable at each stage of the development of United States positions regarding matters referred to in clause (ii) that will be addressed by committees, subcommittees, or working groups established under the Agreement or through dispute settlement processes provided for under the Agreement.

The Federal Advisory Committee Act (5 U.S.C.App.) shall not apply to the Federal-State consultation process established by this paragraph.

(2) Legal Challenge.—No State law, or the application thereof, may be declared invalid as to any person or circumstance on the ground that the provision or application is inconsistent with the Agreement, except in an action brought by the United States for the purpose of declaring such law or application invalid.

(3) Definition of State law.—For purposes of this subsection, the term "State law" includes—

(A) any law of a political subdivision of a State; and

(B) any State law regulating or taxing the business of insurance.

(c) Effect of Agreement with Respect to Private Remedies.—No person other than the United States—

(1) shall have any cause of action or defense under—

(A) the Agreement or by virtue of Congressional approval thereof, or

(B) the North American Agreement on Environmental Cooperation or the North American Agreement on Labor Cooperation; or

(2) may challenge, in any action brought under any provision of law, any action or inaction by any department, agency, or other instrumentality of the United States, any State, or any political subdivision of a State on the ground that such action or inaction is inconsistent with the Agreement, the North American Agreement on Environmental Cooperation, or the North American Agreement on Labor Cooperation.

19 USC 3315

Sec. 105.   United States Section of the NAFTA Secretariat

(a) Establishment of the United States Section.—The President is authorized to establish within any department or agency of the United States Government a United States Section of the Secretariat established under chapter 20 of the Agreement. The United States Section, subject to the oversight of the interagency group established under section 402, shall carry out its functions within the Secretariat to facilitate the operation of the Agreement, including the operation of chapters 19 and 20 of the Agreement and the work of the panels, extraordinary challenge committees, special committees, and scientific review boards convened under those chapters. The United States Section may not be considered to be an agency for purposes of section 552 of title 5, United States Code.

(b) Authorization of Appropriations.—There are authorized to be appropriated for each fiscal year after fiscal year 1993 to the department or agency within which the United States Section is established the lesser of—

(1) such sums as may be necessary; or

(2) $2,000,000;

for the establishment and operations of the United States Section and for the payment of the United States share of the expenses of binational panels and extraordinary challenge committees convened under chapter 19, and of the expenses incurred in dispute settlement proceedings under chapter 20, of the Agreement.

(c) **Reimbursement of Certain Expenses.**—If, in accordance with Annex 2002.2 of the Agreement, the Canadian Section or the Mexican Section of the Secretariat provides funds to the United States Section during any fiscal year, as reimbursement for expenses by the Canadian Section or the Mexican Section in connection with settlement proceedings under chapter 19 or 20 of the Agreement, the United States Section may retain and use such funds to carry out the functions described in subsection (a).

19 USC 3316

Sec. 106. Appointments to Chapter 20 Panel Proceedings

(a) **Consultation.**—The Trade Representative shall consult with the Committee on Ways and Means of the House of Representatives and the Committee on Finance of the Senate regarding the selection and appointment of candidates for the rosters described in article 2009 of the Agreement.

(b) **Selection of Individuals with Environmental Expertise.**—The United States shall, to the maximum extent practicable, encourage the selection of individuals who have expertise and experience in environmental issues for service in panel proceedings under chapter 20 of the Agreement to hear any challenge to a United States or State environmental law.

19 USC 2112 note

Sec. 107. Termination or Suspension of United States-Canada Free-Trade Agreement

Section 501(c) of the United States-Canada Free-Trade Implementation Act of 1988 (19 U.S.C. 2112 note) is amended to read as follows:

"(c) **TERMINATION OR SUSPENSION OF AGREEMENT.—**

"(1) *TERMINATION OF AGREEMENT.*—On the date the Agreement ceases to be in force, the provisions of this Act (other than this paragraph and section 410(b)), and the amendments made by this Act, shall cease to have effect.

"(2) *EFFECT OF AGREEMENT SUSPENSION.*—An agreement by the United States and Canada to suspend the operation of the Agreement shall not be deemed to cause the Agreement to cease to be in force within the meaning of paragraph (1).

"(3) *SUSPENSION RESULTING FROM NAFTA.*—On the date the United States and Canada agree to suspend the operation of the Agreement by reason of the entry into force between them of the North American Free Trade Agreement, the following provisions of this Act are suspended and shall remain suspended until such time as the suspension of the Agreement may be terminated:

"(A) Sections 204(a) and (b) and 205(a).

"(B) Sections 302 and 304(f).

"(C) Sections 404, 409, and 410(b).".

19 USC 3317

Sec. 108. Congressional Intent Regarding Future Accessions

(a) In General.—Section 101(a) may not be construed as conferring Congressional approval of the entry into force of the Agreement for the United States with respect to countries other than Canada and Mexico.

(b) Future Free Trade Area Negotiations.—

(1) Findings.—The Congress makes the following findings:

(A) Efforts by the United States to obtain greater market opening through multilateral negotiations have not produced agreements that fully satisfy the trade negotiating objectives of the United States.

(B) United States trade policy should provide for additional mechanisms with which to pursue greater market access for United States exports of goods and services and opportunities for export-related investment by United States persons.

(C) Among the additional mechanisms should be a system of bilateral and multilateral trade agreements that provide greater market access for United States exports and opportunities for export-related investment by United States persons.

(D) The system of trade agreements can and should be structured to be consistent with, and complementary to, existing international obligations of the United States and ongoing multilateral efforts to open markets.

(2) Report on Significant Market Opening.—No later than May 1, 1994, and May 1, 1997, the Trade Representative shall submit to the President, and to the Committee on Finance of the Senate and the Committee on Ways and Means of the House of Representatives (hereafter in this section referred to as the "appropriate Congressional committees"), a report which lists those foreign countries—

(A) that—

(i) currently provide fair and equitable market access for United States exports of goods and services and opportunities for export-related investment by United States persons, beyond what is required by existing multilateral trade agreements or obligations; or

(ii) have made significant progress in opening their markets to United States exports of goods and services and export-related investment by United States persons; and

(B) the further opening of whose markets has the greatest potential to increase United States exports of goods and services and export-related investment by United States persons, either directly or through the establishment of a beneficial precedent.

(3) Presidential Determination.—The President, on the basis of the report submitted by the Trade Representative under paragraph (2), shall determine

with which foreign country or countries, if any, the United States should seek to negotiate a free trade area agreement or agreements.

(4) Recommendations on Future Free Trade Area Negotiations.—No later than July 1, 1994, and July 1, 1997, the President shall submit to the appropriate Congressional committees a written report that contains—

(A) recommendations for free trade area negotiations with each foreign country selected under paragraph (3);

(B) with respect to each country selected, the specific negotiating objectives that are necessary to meet the objectives of the United States under this section; and

(C) legislative proposals to ensure adequate consultation with the Congress and the private sector during the negotiations, advance Congressional approval of the negotiations recommended by the President, and Congressional approval of any trade agreement entered into by the President as a result of the negotiations.

(5) General Negotiating Objectives.—The general negotiating objectives of the United States under this section are to obtain—

(A) preferential treatment for United States goods;

(B) national treatment and, where appropriate, equivalent competitive opportunity for United States services and foreign direct investment by United States persons;

(C) the elimination of barriers to trade in goods and services by United States persons through standards, testing, labeling, and certification requirements;

(D) nondiscriminatory government procurement policies and practices with respect to United States goods and services;

(E) the elimination of other barriers to market access for United States goods and services, and the elimination of barriers to foreign direct investment by United States persons;

(F) the elimination of acts, policies, and practices which deny fair and equitable market opportunities, including foreign government toleration of anticompetitive business practices by private firms or among private firms that have the effect of restricting, on a basis that is inconsistent with commercial considerations, purchasing by such firms of United States goods and services;

(G) adequate and effective protection of intellectual property rights of United States persons, and fair and equitable market access for United States persons that rely upon intellectual property protection;

(H) the elimination of foreign export and domestic subsidies that distort international trade in United States goods and services or cause material injury to United States industries;

(I) the elimination of all export taxes;

(J) the elimination of acts, policies, and practices which constitute export targeting; and

(K) monitoring and effective dispute settlement mechanisms to facilitate compliance with the matters described in subparagraphs (A) through (J).

19 USC 2112 note

Sec. 109.   Effective Dates; Effect of Termination of NAFTA Status

(a) Effective Dates.—

(1) In General.—This title (other than the amendment made by section 107) takes effect on the date of the enactment of this Act.

(2) Section 107 Amendment.—The amendment made by section 107 takes effect on the date the Agreement enters into force between the United States and Canada.

(b) Termination of NAFTA Status.—During any period in which a country ceases to be a NAFTA country, sections 101 through 106 shall cease to have effect with respect to such country.

TITLE II—CUSTOMS PROVISIONS

19 USC 3331

Sec. 201.   Tariff Modifications

(a) Tariff Modifications Provided for in the Agreement.—

(1) Proclamation Authority.—The President may proclaim—

(A) such modifications or continuation of any duty,

(B) such continuation of duty-free or excise treatment, or

(C) such additional duties,

as the President determines to be necessary or appropriate to carry out or apply articles 302, 305, 307, 308, and 703 and Annexes 302.2, 307.1, 308.1, 308.2, 300-B, 703.2, and 703.3 of the Agreement.

(2) Effect on Mexican GSP Status.—Notwithstanding section 502(f)(2) of the Trade Act of 1974 (19 U.S.C. 2462(a)(2)), the President shall terminate the designation of Mexico as a beneficiary developing country for purposes of title V of the Trade Act of 1974 on the date of entry into force of the Agreement between the United States and Mexico.

(b) Other Tariff Modifications.—

(1) In General.—Subject to paragraph (2) and the consultation and layover requirements of section 103(a), the President may proclaim—

(A) such modifications or continuation of any duty,

(B) such modifications as the United States may agree to with Mexico or Canada regarding the staging of any duty treatment set forth in Annex 302.2 of the Agreement,

(C) such continuation of duty-free or excise treatment, or

(D) such additional duties,

as the President determines to be necessary or appropriate to maintain the general level of reciprocal and mutually advantageous concessions with respect to Canada or Mexico provided for by the Agreement.

(2) Special Rule for Articles with Tariff Phaseout Periods of More Than 10 Years.—The President may not consider a request to accelerate the staging of duty reductions for an article for which the United States tariff phaseout period is more than 10 years if a request for acceleration with respect to such article has been denied in the preceding 3 calendar years.

(c) Conversion to Ad Valorem Rates For Certain Textiles.—For purposes of subsections (a) and (b), with respect to an article covered by Annex 300-B of the Agreement imported from Mexico for which the base rate in the Schedule of the United States in Annex 300-B is a specific or compound rate of duty, the President may substitute for the base rate an ad valorem rate that the President determines to be equivalent to the base rate.

19 USC 3332

Sec. 202. Rules of Origin

(a) Originating Goods.—

(1) In General.—For purposes of implementing the tariff treatment and quantitative restrictions provided for under the Agreement, except as otherwise provided in this section, a good originates in the territory of a NAFTA country if—

    (A) the good is wholly obtained or produced entirely in the territory of one or more of the NAFTA countries;

    (B)(i) each nonoriginating material used in the production of the good—

        (I) undergoes an applicable change in tariff classification set out in Annex 401 of the Agreement as a result of production occurring entirely in the territory of one or more of the NAFTA countries; or

        (II) where no change in tariff classification is required, the good otherwise satisfies the applicable requirements of such Annex; and

    (ii) the good satisfies all other applicable requirements of this section;

    (C) the good is produced entirely in the territory of one or more of the NAFTA countries exclusively from originating materials; or

    (D) except for a good provided for in chapters 61 through 63 of the HTS, the good is produced entirely in the territory of one or more of the NAFTA countries, but one or more of the nonoriginating materials, that are provided for as parts under the HTS and are used in the production of the good, does not undergo a change in tariff classification because—

        (i) the good was imported into the territory of a NAFTA country in an unassembled or a disassembled form but was classified as an assembled good pursuant to General Rule of Interpretation 2(a) of the HTS; or (ii)(I) the heading for the good provides for and specifically describes both the good itself and its parts and is not further subdivided into subheadings; or

(II) the subheading for the good provides for and specifically describes both the good itself and its parts.

(2) Special Rules.—

(A) Foreign-Trade Zones.—Subparagraph (B) of paragraph (1) shall not apply to a good produced in a foreign-trade zone or subzone (established pursuant to the Act of June 18, 1934, commonly known as the Foreign Trade Zones Act) that is entered for consumption in the customs territory of the United States.

(B) Regional Value-Content Requirement.—For purposes of subparagraph (D) of paragraph (1), a good shall be treated as originating in a NAFTA country if the regional value-content of the good, determined in accordance with subsection (b), is not less than 60 percent where the transaction value method is used, or not less than 50 percent where the net cost method is used, and the good satisfies all other applicable requirements of this section.

(b) Regional Value-Content.—

(1) In General.—Except as provided in paragraph (5), the regional value-content of a good shall be calculated, at the choice of the exporter or producer of the good, on the basis of—

(A) the transaction value method described in paragraph (2); or

(B) the net cost method described in paragraph (3).

(2) Transaction Value Method.—

(A) In General.—An exporter or producer may calculate the regional value-content of a good on the basis of the following transaction value method:

$$RVC = \frac{TV-VNM}{TV} \times 100$$

(B) Definitions.—For purposes of subparagraph (A):

(i) The term "RVC" means the regional value-content, expressed as a percentage.

(ii) The term "TV" means the transaction value of the good adjusted to a F.O.B. basis.

(iii) The term "VNM" means the value of nonoriginating materials used by the producer in the production of the good.

(3) Net Cost Method.—

(A) In General.—An exporter or producer may calculate the regional value-content of a good on the basis of the following net cost method:

$$RVC = \frac{NC-VNM}{NC} \times 100$$

(B) Definitions.—For purposes of subparagraph (A):

(i) The term "RVC" means the regional value-content, expressed as a percentage.

(ii) The term "NC" means the net cost of the good.

(iii) The term "VNM" means the value of nonoriginating materials used by the producer in the production of the good.

(4) Value of Nonoriginating Materials Used in Originating Materials.—Except as provided in subsection (c)(1), and for a motor vehicle identified in subsection (c)(2) or a component identified in Annex 403.2 of the Agreement, the value of nonoriginating materials used by the producer in the production of a good shall not, for purposes of calculating the regional value-content of the good under paragraph (2) or (3), include the value of nonoriginating materials used to produce originating materials that are subsequently used in the production of the good.

(5) Net Cost Method Must be Used in Certain Cases.—An exporter or producer shall calculate the regional value-content of a good solely on the basis of the net cost method described in paragraph (3), if—

(A) there is no transaction value for the good;

(B) the transaction value of the good is unacceptable under Article 1 of the Customs Valuation Code;

(C) the good is sold by the producer to a related person and the volume, by units of quantity, of sales of identical or similar goods to related persons during the six-month period immediately preceding the month in which the good is sold exceeds 85 percent of the producer's total sales of such goods during that period;

(D) the good is—

(i) a motor vehicle provided for in heading 8701 or 8702, subheadings 8703.21 through 8703.90, or heading 8704, 8705, or 8706;

(ii) identified in Annex 403.1 or 403.2 of the Agreement and is for use in a motor vehicle provided for in heading 8701 or 8702, subheadings 8703.21 through 8703.90, or heading 8704, 8705, or 8706;

(iii) provided for in subheadings 6401.10 through 6406.10; or

(iv) a word processing machine provided for in subheading 8469.10.00;

(E) the exporter or producer chooses to accumulate the regional value-content of the good in accordance with subsection (d); or

(F) the good is designated as an intermediate material under paragraph (10) and is subject to a regional value-content requirement.

(6) Net Cost Method Allowed for Adjustments.—If an exporter or producer of a good calculates the regional value-content of the good on the basis of the transaction value method and a NAFTA country subsequently notifies the exporter or producer, during the course of a verification conducted in accordance with chapter 5 of the Agreement, that the transaction value of the good

or the value of any material used in the production of the good must be adjusted or is unacceptable under Article 1 of the Customs Valuation Code, the exporter or producer may calculate the regional value-content of the good on the basis of the net cost method.

(7) Review of Adjustment.—Nothing in paragraph (6) shall be construed to prevent any review or appeal available in accordance with article 510 of the Agreement with respect to an adjustment to or a rejection of—

(A) the transaction value of a good; or

(B) the value of any material used in the production of a good.

(8) Calculating Net Cost.—The producer may, consistent with regulations implementing this section, calculate the net cost of a good under paragraph (3), by—

(A) calculating the total cost incurred with respect to all goods produced by that producer, subtracting any sales promotion, marketing and after-sales service costs, royalties, shipping and packing costs, and nonallowable interest costs that are included in the total cost of all such goods, and reasonably allocating the resulting net cost of those goods to the good;

(B) calculating the total cost incurred with respect to all goods produced by that producer, reasonably allocating the total cost to the good, and subtracting any sales promotion, marketing and after-sales service costs, royalties, shipping and packing costs, and nonallowable interest costs that are included in the portion of the total cost allocated to the good; or

(C) reasonably allocating each cost that is part of the total cost incurred with respect to the good so that the aggregate of these costs does not include any sales promotion, marketing and after-sales service costs, royalties, shipping and packing costs, or nonallowable interest costs.

(9) Value of Material Used in Production.—Except as provided in paragraph (11), the value of a material used in the production of a good—

(A) shall—

(i) be the transaction value of the material determined in accordance with Article 1 of the Customs Valuation Code; or

(ii) in the event that there is no transaction value or the transaction value of the material is unacceptable under Article 1 of the Customs Valuation Code, be determined in accordance with Articles 2 through 7 of the Customs Valuation Code; and

(B) if not included under clause (i) or (ii) of subparagraph (A), shall include—

(i) freight, insurance, packing, and all other costs incurred in transporting the material to the location of the producer;

(ii) duties, taxes, and customs brokerage fees paid on the material in the territory of one or more of the NAFTA countries; and

(iii) the cost of waste and spoilage resulting from the use of the material in the production of the good, less the value of renewable scrap or by-product.

(10) Intermediate Material.—Except for goods described in subsection (c)(1), any self-produced material, other than a component identified in Annex 403.2 of the Agreement, that is used in the production of a good may be designated by the producer of the good as an intermediate material for the purpose of calculating the regional value-content of the good under paragraph (2) or (3); provided that if the intermediate material is subject to a regional value-content requirement, no other self-produced material that is subject to a regional value-content requirement and is used in the production of the intermediate material may be designated by the producer as an intermediate material.

(11) Value of Intermediate Material.—The value of an intermediate material shall be—

    (A) the total cost incurred with respect to all goods produced by the producer of the good that can be reasonably allocated to the intermediate material; or

    (B) the aggregate of each cost that is part of the total cost incurred with respect to the intermediate material that can be reasonably allocated to that intermediate material.

(12) Indirect Material.—The value of an indirect material shall be based on the Generally Accepted Accounting Principles applicable in the territory of the NAFTA country in which the good is produced.

(c) Automotive Goods.—

(1) Passenger Vehicles and Light Trucks, and their Automotive Parts.—For purposes of calculating the regional value-content under the net cost method for—

    (A) a good that is a motor vehicle for the transport of 15 or fewer persons provided for in subheading 8702.10.00 or 8702.90.00, or a motor vehicle provided for in subheadings 8703.21 through 8703.90, or subheading 8704.21 or 8704.31, or

    (B) a good provided for in the tariff provisions listed in Annex 403.1 of the Agreement, that is subject to a regional value-content requirement and is for use as original equipment in the production of a motor vehicle for the transport of 15 or fewer persons provided for in subheading 8702.10.00 or 8702.90.00, or a motor vehicle provided for in subheadings 8703.21 through 8703.90, or subheading 8704.21 or 8704.31,

the value of nonoriginating materials used by the producer in the production of the good shall be the sum of the values of all nonoriginating materials, determined in accordance with subsection (b)(9) at the time the nonoriginating materials are received by the first person in the territory of a NAFTA country who takes title to them, that are imported from outside the territories of the NAFTA countries under the tariff provisions listed in Annex 403.1 of the Agreement and are used in the production of the good or that are used in the production of any material used in the production of the good.

(2) Other Vehicles and their Automotive Parts.—For purposes of calculating the regional value-content under the net cost method for a good that is a motor vehicle provided for in heading 8701, subheading 8704.10, 8704.22, 8704.23, 8704.32, or 8704.90, or heading 8705 or 8706, a motor vehicle for the

transport of 16 or more persons provided for in subheading 8702.10.00 or 8702.90.00, or a component identified in Annex 403.2 of the Agreement for use as original equipment in the production of the motor vehicle, the value of nonoriginating materials used by the producer in the production of the good shall be the sum of—

(A) for each material used by the producer listed in Annex 403.2 of the Agreement, whether or not produced by the producer, at the choice of the producer and determined in accordance with subsection (b), either—

(i) the value of such material that is nonoriginating, or

(ii) the value of nonoriginating materials used in the production of such material; and

(B) the value of any other nonoriginating material used by the producer that is not listed in Annex 403.2 of the Agreement determined in accordance with subsection (b).

(3) Averaging Permitted.—

(A) In General.—For purposes of calculating the regional value-content of a motor vehicle described in paragraph (1) or (2), the producer may average its calculation over its fiscal year, using any of the categories described in subparagraph (B), on the basis of either all motor vehicles in the category or on the basis of only the motor vehicles in the category that are exported to the territory of one or more of the other NAFTA countries.

(B) Category Described.—A category is described in this subparagraph if it is—

(i) the same model line of motor vehicles in the same class of vehicles produced in the same plant in the territory of a NAFTA country;

(ii) the same class of motor vehicles produced in the same plant in the territory of a NAFTA country;

(iii) the same model line of motor vehicles produced in the territory of a NAFTA country; or

(iv) if applicable, the basis set out in Annex 403.3 of the Agreement.

*(4) Annex 403.1 and Annex 403.2.—*For purposes of calculating the regional value-content for any or all goods provided for in a tariff provision listed in Annex 403.1 of the Agreement, or a component or material identified in Annex 403.2 of the Agreement, produced in the same plant, the producer of the good may—

(A) average its calculation—

(i) over the fiscal year of the motor vehicle producer to whom the good is sold;

(ii) over any quarter or month; or

(iii) over its fiscal year, if the good is sold as an aftermarket part;

(B) calculate the average referred to in subparagraph (A) separately for any or all goods sold to one or more motor vehicle producers; or

(C) with respect to any calculation under this paragraph, make a separate calculation for goods that are exported to the territory of one or more NAFTA countries.

(5) Phase-in of Regional Value-Content Requirement.—Notwithstanding Annex 401 of the Agreement, and except as provided in paragraph (6), the regional value-content requirement shall be—

(A) for a producer's fiscal year beginning on the day closest to January 1, 1998, and thereafter, 56 percent calculated under the net cost method, and for a producer's fiscal year beginning on the day closest to January 1, 2002, and thereafter, 62.5 percent calculated under the net cost method, for—

    (i) a good that is a motor vehicle for the transport of 15 or fewer persons provided for in subheading 8702.10.00 or 8702.90.00, or a motor vehicle provided for in subheadings 8703.21 through 8703.90, or subheading 8704.21 or 8704.31; and

    (ii) a good provided for in heading 8407 or 8408, or subheading 8708.40, that is for use in a motor vehicle identified in clause (i); and

(B) for a producer's fiscal year beginning on the day closest to January 1, 1998, and thereafter, 55 percent calculated under the net cost method, and for a producer's fiscal year beginning on the day closest to January 1, 2002, and thereafter, 60 percent calculated under the net cost method, for—

    (i) a good that is a motor vehicle provided for in heading 8701, subheading 8704.10, 8704.22, 8704.23, 8704.32, or 8704.90, or heading 8705 or 8706, or a motor vehicle for the transport of 16 or more persons provided for in subheading 8702.10.00 or 8702.90.00;

    (ii) a good provided for in heading 8407 or 8408, or subheading 8708.40 that is for use in a motor vehicle identified in clause (i); and

    (iii) except for a good identified in subparagraph (A)(ii) or a good provided for in subheadings 8482.10 through 8482.80, or subheading 8483.20 or 8483.30, a good identified in Annex 403.1 of the Agreement that is subject to a regional value-content requirement and is for use in a motor vehicle identified in subparagraph (A)(i) or (B)(i).

(6) New and Refitted Plants.—The regional value-content requirement for a motor vehicle identified in paragraph (1) or (2) shall be—

(A) 50 percent for 5 years after the date on which the first motor vehicle prototype is produced in a plant by a motor vehicle assembler, if—

    (i) it is a motor vehicle of a class, or marque, or, except for a motor vehicle identified in paragraph (2), size category and underbody, not previously produced by the motor vehicle assembler in the territory of any of the NAFTA countries;

    (ii) the plant consists of a new building in which the motor vehicle is assembled; and

    (iii) the plant contains substantially all new machinery that is used in the assembly of the motor vehicle; or

(B) 50 percent for 2 years after the date on which the first motor vehicle prototype is produced at a plant following a refit, if it is a motor vehicle of a class, or marque, or, except for a motor vehicle identified in paragraph (2), size category and underbody, different from that assembled by the motor vehicle assembler in the plant before the refit.

(7) Election for Certain Vehicles from Canada.—In the case of goods provided for in subheadings 8703.21 through 8703.90, or subheading 8704.21 or 8704.31, exported from Canada directly to the United States, and entered on or after January 1, 1989, and before the date of entry into force of the Agreement between the United States and Canada, an importer may elect to use the rules of origin set out in this section in lieu of the rules of origin contained in section 202 of the United States-Canada Free-Trade Agreement Implementation Act of 1988 (19 U.S.C. 2112 note) and may elect to use the method for calculating the value of nonoriginating materials established in article 403(2) of the Agreement in lieu of the method established in article 403(1) of the Agreement for purposes of determining eligibility for preferential duty treatment under the United States-Canada Free-Trade Agreement. Any election under this paragraph shall be made in writing to the Customs Service not later than the date that is 180 days after the date of entry into force of the Agreement between the United States and Canada. Any such election may be made only if the liquidation of such entry has not become final. For purposes of averaging the calculation of regional value-content for the goods covered by such entry, where the producer's 1989–1990 fiscal year began after January 1, 1989, the producer may include the period between January 1, 1989, and the beginning of its first fiscal year after January 1, 1989, as part of fiscal year 1989–1990.

(d) Accumulation.—

(1) Determination of Originating Good.—For purposes of determining whether a good is an originating good, the production of the good in the territory of one or more of the NAFTA countries by one or more producers shall, at the choice of the exporter or producer of the good, be considered to have been performed in the territory of any of the NAFTA countries by that exporter or producer, if—

(A) all nonoriginating materials used in the production of the good undergo an applicable tariff classification change set out in Annex 401 of the Agreement;

(B) the good satisfies any applicable regional value-content requirement; and

(C) the good satisfies all other applicable requirements of this section.

The requirements of subparagraphs (A) and (B) must be satisfied entirely in the territory of one or more of the NAFTA countries.

(2) Treatment as Single Producer.—For purposes of subsection (b)(10), the production of a producer that chooses to accumulate its production with that of other producers under paragraph (1) shall be treated as the production of a single producer.

(e) De Minimis Amounts of Nonoriginating Materials.—

(1) In General.—Except as provided in paragraphs (3), (4), (5), and (6), a good shall be considered to be an originating good if—

(A) the value of all nonoriginating materials used in the production of the good that do not undergo an applicable change in tariff classification (set out in Annex 401 of the Agreement) is not more than 7 percent of the transaction value of the good, adjusted to a F.O.B. basis, or

(B) where the transaction value of the good is unacceptable under Article 1 of the Customs Valuation Code, the value of all such nonoriginating materials is not more than 7 percent of the total cost of the good, provided that the good satisfies all other applicable requirements of this section and, if the good is subject to a regional value-content requirement, the value of such nonoriginating materials is taken into account in calculating the regional value-content of the good.

(2) Goods Not Subject to Regional Value-Content Requirement. A good that is otherwise subject to a regional value-content requirement shall not be required to satisfy such requirement if—

(A)(i) the value of all nonoriginating materials used in the production of the good is not more than 7 percent of the transaction value of the good, adjusted to a F.O.B. basis; or

(ii) where the transaction value of the good is unacceptable under Article 1 of the Customs Valuation Code, the value of all nonoriginating materials is not more than 7 percent of the total cost of the good; and

(B) the good satisfies all other applicable requirements of this section.

(3) Dairy Products, Etc.—Paragraph (1) does not apply to—

(A) a nonoriginating material provided for in chapter 4 of the HTS or a dairy preparation containing over 10 percent by weight of milk solids provided for in subheading 1901.90.30, 1901.90.40, or 1901.90.80 that is used in the production of a good provided for in chapter 4 of the HTS;

(B) a nonoriginating material provided for in chapter 4 of the HTS or a dairy preparation containing over 10 percent by weight of milk solids provided for in subheading 1901.90.30, 1901.90.40, or 1901.90.80 that is used in the production of—

(i) preparations for infants containing over 10 percent by weight of milk solids provided for in subheading 1901.10.00;

(ii) mixes and doughs, containing over 25 percent by weight of butterfat, not put up for retail sale, provided for in subheading 1901.20.00;

(iii) a dairy preparation containing over 10 percent by weight of milk solids provided for in subheading 1901.90.30, 1901.90.40, or 1901.90.80;

(iv) a good provided for in heading 2105 or subheading 2106.90.05, or preparations containing over 10 percent by weight of milk solids provided for in subheading 2106.90.15, 2106.90.40, 2106.90.50, or 2106.90.65;

(v) a good provided for in subheading 2202.90.10 or 2202.90.20; or

(vi) animal feeds containing over 10 percent by weight of milk solids provided for in subheading 2309.90.30;

(C) a nonoriginating material provided for in heading 0805 or subheadings 2009.11 through 2009.30 that is used in the production of—

(i) a good provided for in subheadings 2009.11 through 2009.30, or subheading 2106.90.16, or concentrated fruit or vegetable juice of any single fruit or vegetable, fortified with minerals or vitamins, provided for in subheading 2106.90.19; or

(ii) a good provided for in subheading 2202.90.30 or 2202.90.35, or fruit or vegetable juice of any single fruit or vegetable, fortified with minerals or vitamins, provided for in subheading 2202.90.36;

(D) a nonoriginating material provided for in chapter 9 of the HTS that is used in the production of instant coffee, not flavored, provided for in subheading 2101.10.20;

(E) a nonoriginating material provided for in chapter 15 of the HTS that is used in the production of a good provided for in headings 1501 through 1508, or heading 1512, 1514, or 1515;

(F) a nonoriginating material provided for in heading 1701 that is used in the production of a good provided for in headings 1701 through 1703;

(G) a nonoriginating material provided for in chapter 17 of the HTS or heading 1805 that is used in the production of a good provided for in subheading 1806.10;

(H) a nonoriginating material provided for in headings 2203 through 2208 that is used in the production of a good provided for in headings 2207 through 2208;

(I) a nonoriginating material used in the production of—

(i) a good provided for in subheading 7321.11.30;

(ii) a good provided for in subheading 8415.10, subheadings 8415.81 through 8415.83, subheadings 8418.10 through 8418.21, subheadings 8418.29 through 8418.40, subheading 8421.12 or 8422.11, subheadings 8450.11 through 8450.20, or subheadings 8451.21 through 8451.29;

(iii) trash compactors provided for in subheading 8479.89.60; or

(iv) a good provided for in subheading 8516.60.40; and

(J) a printed circuit assembly that is a nonoriginating material used in the production of a good where the applicable change in tariff classification for the good, as set out in Annex 401 of the Agreement, places restrictions on the use of such nonoriginating material.

(4) Certain Fruit Juices.—Paragraph (1) does not apply to a nonoriginating single juice ingredient provided for in heading 2009 that is used in the production of—

(A) a good provided for in subheading 2009.90, or concentrated mixtures of fruit or vegetable juice, fortified with minerals or vitamins, provided for in subheading 2106.90.19; or

(B) mixtures of fruit or vegetable juices, fortified with minerals or vitamins, provided for in subheading 2202.90.39.

(5) Goods Provided for in Chapters 1 Through 27 of the HTS.—Paragraph (1) does not apply to a nonoriginating material used in the production of a good provided for in chapters 1 through 27 of the HTS unless the nonoriginating material is provided for in a different subheading than the good for which origin is being determined under this section.

(6) Goods Provided for in Chapters 50 Through 63 of the HTS.—A good provided for in chapters 50 through 63 of the HTS, that does not originate because certain fibers or yarns used in the production of the component of the good that determines the tariff classification of the good do not undergo an applicable change in tariff classification set out in Annex 401 of the Agreement, shall be considered to be a good that originates if the total weight of all such fibers or yarns in that component is not more than 7 percent of the total weight of that component.

(f) Fungible Goods and Materials.—For purposes of determining whether a good is an originating good—

(1) if originating and nonoriginating fungible materials are used in the production of the good, the determination of whether the materials are originating need not be made through the identification of any specific fungible material, but may be determined on the basis of any of the inventory management methods set out in regulations implementing this section; and

(2) if originating and nonoriginating fungible goods are commingled and exported in the same form, the determination may be made on the basis of any of the inventory management methods set out in regulations implementing this section.

(g) Accessories, Spare Parts, or Tools.—

(1) In General.—Except as provided in paragraph (2), accessories, spare parts, or tools delivered with the good that form part of the good's standard accessories, spare parts, or tools shall—

(A) be considered as originating goods if the good is an originating good, and

(B) be disregarded in determining whether all the nonoriginating materials used in the production of the good undergo an applicable change in tariff classification set out in Annex 401 of the Agreement.

(2) Conditions.—Paragraph (1) shall apply only if—

(A) the accessories, spare parts, or tools are not invoiced separately from the good;

(B) the quantities and value of the accessories, spare parts, or tools are customary for the good; and

(C) in any case in which the good is subject to a regional value-content requirement, the value of the accessories, spare parts, or tools are taken into account as originating or nonoriginating materials, as the case may be, in calculating the regional value-content of the good.

(h) Indirect Materials.—An indirect material shall be considered to be an originating material without regard to where it is produced.

(i) Packaging Materials and Containers for Retail Sale. Packaging materials and containers in which a good is packaged for retail sale, if classified with the good, shall be disregarded in determining whether all the nonoriginating materials used in the production of the good undergo an applicable change in tariff classification set out in Annex 401 of the Agreement. If the good is subject to a regional value-content requirement, the value of such packaging materials and containers shall be taken into account as originating or nonoriginating materials, as the case may be, in calculating the regional value-content of the good.

(j) Packing Materials and Containers for Shipment.—Packing materials and containers in which a good is packed for shipment shall be disregarded—

(1) in determining whether the nonoriginating materials used in the production of the good undergo an applicable change in tariff classification set out in Annex 401 of the Agreement; and

(2) in determining whether the good satisfies a regional value-content requirement.

(k) Transshipment.—A good shall not be considered to be an originating good by reason of having undergone production that satisfies the requirements of subsection (a) if, subsequent to that production, the good undergoes further production or any other operation outside the territories of the NAFTA countries, other than unloading, reloading, or any other operation necessary to preserve it in good condition or to transport the good to the territory of a NAFTA country.

(*l*) Nonqualifying Operations.—A good shall not be considered to be an originating good merely by reason of—

(1) mere dilution with water or another substance that does not materially alter the characteristics of the good; or

(2) any production or pricing practice with respect to which it may be demonstrated, by a preponderance of evidence, that the object was to circumvent this section.

(m) Interpretation and Application.—For purposes of this section:

(1) The basis for any tariff classification is the HTS.

(2) Except as otherwise expressly provided, whenever in this section there is a reference to a heading or subheading such reference shall be a reference to a heading or subheading of the HTS.

(3) In applying subsection (a)(4), the determination of whether a heading or subheading under the HTS provides for and specifically describes both a good and its parts shall be made on the basis of the nomenclature of the heading or subheading, the rules of interpretation, or notes of the HTS.

(4) In applying the Customs Valuation Code—

(A) the principles of the Customs Valuation Code shall apply to domestic transactions, with such modifications as may be required by the circumstances, as would apply to international transactions;

(B) the provisions of this section shall take precedence over the Customs Valuation Code to the extent of any difference; and

(C) the definitions in subsection (p) shall take precedence over the definitions in the Customs Valuation Code to the extent of any difference.

(5) All costs referred to in this section shall be recorded and maintained in accordance with the Generally Accepted Accounting Principles applicable in the territory of the NAFTA country in which the good is produced.

(n) Origin of Automatic Data Processing Goods. Notwithstanding any other provision of this section, when the NAFTA countries apply the rate of duty described in paragraph 1 of section A of Annex 308.1 of the Agreement to a good provided for under the tariff provisions set out in Table 308.1.1 of such Annex, the good shall, upon importation from a NAFTA country, be deemed to originate in the territory of a NAFTA country for purposes of this section.

(o) Special Rule for Certain Agricultural Products. Notwithstanding any other provision of this section, for purposes of applying a rate of duty to a good provided for in—

(1) heading 1202 that is exported from the territory of Mexico, if the good is not wholly obtained in the territory of Mexico,

(2) subheading 2008.11 that is exported from the territory of Mexico, if any material provided for in heading 1202 used in the production of that good is not wholly obtained in the territory of Mexico, or

(3) subheading 1806.10.42 or 2106.90.12 that is exported from the territory of Mexico, if any material provided for in subheading 1701.99 used in the production of that good is not a qualifying good,

such good shall be treated as a nonoriginating good and, for purposes of this subsection, the terms "qualifying good" and "wholly obtained in the territory of" have the meaning given such terms in paragraph 26 of section A of Annex 703.2 of the Agreement.

(p) Definitions.—For purposes of this section—

(1) Class of Motor Vehicles.—The term "class of motor vehicles" means any one of the following categories of motor vehicles:

(A) Motor vehicles provided for in subheading 8701.20, subheading 8704.10, 8704.22, 8704.23, 8704.32, or 8704.90, or heading 8705 or 8706, or motor vehicles designed for the transport of 16 or more persons provided for in subheading 8702.10.00 or 8702.90.00.

(B) Motor vehicles provided for in subheading 8701.10, or subheadings 8701.30 through 8701.90.

(C) Motor vehicles for the transport of 15 or fewer persons provided for in subheading 8702.10.00 or 8702.90.00, or motor vehicles provided for in subheading 8704.21 or 8704.31.

(D) Motor vehicles provided for in subheadings 8703.21 through 8703.90.

(2) Customs Valuation Code.—The term "Customs Valuation Code" means the Agreement on Implementation of Article VII of the General Agreement on Tariffs and Trade, including its interpretative notes.

(3) F.O.B.—The term "F.O.B." means free on board, regardless of the mode of transportation, at the point of direct shipment by the seller to the buyer.

(4) Fungible Goods and Fungible Materials.—The terms "fungible goods" and "fungible materials" mean goods or materials that are interchangeable for commercial purposes and whose properties are essentially identical.

(5) Generally Accepted Accounting Principles.—The term "Generally Accepted Accounting Principles" means the recognized consensus or substantial authoritative support in the territory of a NAFTA country with respect to the recording of revenues, expenses, costs, assets and liabilities, disclosure of information, and preparation of financial statements. These standards may be broad guidelines of general application as well as detailed standards, practices, or procedures.

(6) Goods Wholly Obtained or Produced Entirely in the Territory of One or More of the NAFTA Countries.—The term "goods wholly obtained or produced entirely in the territory of one or more of the NAFTA countries" means—

(A) mineral goods extracted in the territory of one or more of the NAFTA countries;

(B) vegetable goods harvested in the territory of one or more of the NAFTA countries;

(C) live animals born and raised in the territory of one or more of the NAFTA countries;

(D) goods obtained from hunting, trapping, or fishing in the territory of one or more of the NAFTA countries;

(E) goods (such as fish, shellfish, and other marine life) taken from the sea by vessels registered or recorded with a NAFTA country and flying its flag;

(F) goods produced on board factory ships from the goods referred to in subparagraph (E), if such factory ships are registered or recorded with that NAFTA country and fly its flag;

(G) goods taken by a NAFTA country or a person of a NAFTA country from the seabed or beneath the seabed outside territorial waters, provided that a NAFTA country has rights to exploit such seabed;

(H) goods taken from outer space, if the goods are obtained by a NAFTA country or a person of a NAFTA country and not processed in a country other than a NAFTA country;

(I) waste and scrap derived from—

(i) production in the territory of one or more of the NAFTA countries; or

(ii) used goods collected in the territory of one or more of the NAFTA countries, if such goods are fit only for the recovery of raw materials; and

(J) goods produced in the territory of one or more of the NAFTA countries exclusively from goods referred to in subparagraphs (A) through (I), or from their derivatives, at any stage of production.

(7) Identical or Similar Goods.—The term "identical or similar goods" means "identical goods" and "similar goods", respectively, as defined in the Customs Valuation Code.

(8) Indirect Material.—

(A) The term "indirect material" means a good—

(i) used in the production, testing, or inspection of a good but not physically incorporated into the good, or

(ii) used in the maintenance of buildings or the operation of equipment associated with the production of a good,

in the territory of one or more of the NAFTA countries.

(B) When used for a purpose described in subparagraph (A), the following materials are among those considered to be indirect materials:

(i) Fuel and energy.

(ii) Tools, dies, and molds.

(iii) Spare parts and materials used in the maintenance of equipment and buildings.

(iv) Lubricants, greases, compounding materials, and other materials used in production or used to operate equipment and buildings.

(v) Gloves, glasses, footwear, clothing, safety equipment, and supplies.

(vi) Equipment, devices, and supplies used for testing or inspecting the goods.

(vii) Catalysts and solvents.

(viii) Any other goods that are not incorporated into the good, if the use of such goods in the production of the good can reasonably be demonstrated to be a part of that production.

(9) Intermediate Material.—The term "intermediate material" means a material that is self-produced, used in the production of a good, and designated pursuant to subsection (b)(10).

(10) Marque.—The term "marque" means the trade name used by a separate marketing division of a motor vehicle assembler.

(11) Material.—The term "material" means a good that is used in the production of another good and includes a part or an ingredient.

(12) Model Line.—The term "model line" means a group of motor vehicles having the same platform or model name.

(13) Motor Vehicle Assembler.—The term "motor vehicle assembler" means a producer of motor vehicles and any related persons or joint ventures in which the producer participates.

(14) NAFTA Country.—The term "NAFTA country" means the United States, Canada or Mexico for such time as the Agreement is in force with

respect to Canada or Mexico, and the United States applies the Agreement to Canada or Mexico.

(15) New Building.—The term "new building" means a new construction, including at least the pouring or construction of new foundation and floor, the erection of a new structure and roof, and installation of new plumbing, electrical, and other utilities to house a complete vehicle assembly process.

(16) Net Cost.—The term "net cost" means total cost less sales promotion, marketing and after-sales service costs, royalties, shipping and packing costs, and nonallowable interest costs that are included in the total cost.

(17) Net Cost of a Good.—The term "net cost of a good" means the net cost that can be reasonably allocated to a good using one of the methods set out in subsection (b)(8).

(18) Nonallowable Interest Costs.—The term "nonallowable interest costs" means interest costs incurred by a producer as a result of an interest rate that exceeds the applicable federal government interest rate for comparable maturities by more than 700 basis points, determined pursuant to regulations implementing this section.

(19) Nonoriginating Good; Nonoriginating Material.—The term "nonoriginating good" or "nonoriginating material" means a good or material that does not qualify as an originating good or material under the rules of origin set out in this section.

(20) Originating.—The term "originating" means qualifying under the rules of origin set out in this section.

(21) Producer.—The term "producer" means a person who grows, mines, harvests, fishes, traps, hunts, manufactures, processes, or assembles a good.

(22) Production.—The term "production" means growing, mining, harvesting, fishing, trapping, hunting, manufacturing, processing, or assembling a good.

(23) Reasonable Allocate.—The term "reasonably allocate" means to apportion in a manner appropriate to the circumstances.

(24) Refit.—The term "refit" means a plant closure, for purposes of plant conversion or retooling, that lasts at least 3 months.

(25) Related Persons.—The term "related persons" means persons specified in any of the following subparagraphs:

(A) Persons who are officers or directors of one another's businesses.

(B) Persons who are legally recognized partners in business.

(C) Persons who are employer and employee.

(D) Persons one of whom owns, controls, or holds 25 percent or more of the outstanding voting stock or shares of the other.

(E) Persons if 25 percent or more of the outstanding voting stock or shares of each of them is directly or indirectly owned, controlled, or held by a third person.

(F) Persons one of whom is directly or indirectly controlled by the other.

(G) Persons who are directly or indirectly controlled by a third person.

(H) Persons who are members of the same family.

For purposes of this paragraph, the term "members of the same family" means natural or adoptive children, brothers, sisters, parents, grandparents, or spouses.

(26) Royalties.—The term "royalties" means payments of any kind, including payments under technical assistance or similar agreements, made as consideration for the use or right to use any copyright, literary, artistic, or scientific work, patent, trademark, design, model, plan, secret formula, or process. It does not include payments under technical assistance or similar agreements that can be related to specific services such as—

(A) personnel training, without regard to where performed; and

(B) if performed in the territory of one or more of the NAFTA countries, engineering, tooling, die-setting, software design and similar computer services, or other services.

(27) Sales Promotion, Marketing, and After-Sales Service Costs.—The term "sales promotion, marketing, and after-sales service costs" means the costs related to sales promotion, marketing, and after-sales service for the following:

(A) Sales and marketing promotion, media advertising, advertising and market research, promotional and demonstration materials, exhibits, sales conferences, trade shows, conventions, banners, marketing displays, free samples, sales, marketing and after-sales service literature (product brochures, catalogs, technical literature, price lists, service manuals, sales aid information), establishment and protection of logos and trademarks, sponsorships, wholesale and retail restocking charges, and entertainment.

(B) Sales and marketing incentives, consumer, retailer, or wholesaler rebates, and merchandise incentives.

(C) Salaries and wages, sales commissions, bonuses, benefits (such as medical, insurance, and pension), traveling and living expenses, and membership and professional fees for sales promotion, marketing, and after-sales service personnel.

(D) Recruiting and training of sales promotion, marketing, and after-sales service personnel, and after-sales training of customers" employees, where such costs are identified separately for sales promotion, marketing, and after-sales service of goods on the financial statements or cost accounts of the producer.

(E) Product liability insurance.

(F) Office supplies for sales promotion, marketing, and after-sales service of goods, where such costs are identified separately for sales promotion, marketing, and after-sales service of goods on the financial statements or cost accounts of the producer.

(G) Telephone, mail, and other communications, where such costs are identified separately for sales promotion, marketing, and after-sales service of goods on the financial statements or cost accounts of the producer.

(H) Rent and depreciation of sales promotion, marketing, and after-sales service offices and distribution centers.

(I) Property insurance, taxes, utilities, and repair and maintenance of sales promotion, marketing, and after-sales service offices and distribution centers, where such costs are identified separately for sales promotion, marketing, and after-sales service of goods on the financial statements or cost accounts of the producer.

(J) Payments by the producer to other persons for warranty repairs.

(28) Self-Produced Material.—The term "self-produced material" means a material that is produced by the producer of a good and used in the production of that good.

(29) Shipping and Packing Costs.—The term "shipping and packing costs" means the costs incurred in packing a good for shipment and shipping the good from the point of direct shipment to the buyer, but does not include the costs of preparing and packaging the good for retail sale.

(30) Size Category.—The term "size category" means with respect to a motor vehicle identified in subsection (c)(1)(A)—

(A) 85 cubic feet or less of passenger and luggage interior volume;

(B) more than 85 cubic feet, but less than 100 cubic feet, of passenger and luggage interior volume;

(C) at least 100 cubic feet, but not more than 110 cubic feet, of passenger and luggage interior volume;

(D) more than 110 cubic feet, but less than 120 cubic feet, of passenger and luggage interior volume; and

(E) 120 cubic feet or more of passenger and luggage interior volume.

(31) Territory.—The term "territory" means a territory described in Annex 201.1 of the Agreement.

(32) Total Cost.—The term "total cost" means all product costs, period costs, and other costs incurred in the territory of one or more of the NAFTA countries.

(33) Transaction Value.—Except as provided in subsection (c)(1) or (c)(2)(A), the term "transaction value" means the price actually paid or payable for a good or material with respect to a transaction of the producer of the good, adjusted in accordance with the principles of paragraphs 1, 3, and 4 of Article 8 of the Customs Valuation Code and determined without regard to whether the good or material is sold for export.

(34) Underbody.—The term "underbody" means the floor pan of a motor vehicle.

(35) Used.—The term "used" means used or consumed in the production of goods.

(q) Presidential Proclamation Authority.—

(1) In General.—The President is authorized to proclaim, as a part of the HTS—

(A) the provisions set out in Appendix 6.A of Annex 300-B, Annex 401, Annex 403.1, Annex 403.2, and Annex 403.3, of the Agreement, and

(B) any additional subordinate category necessary to carry out this title consistent with the Agreement.

(2) Modifications.—Subject to the consultation and layover requirements of section 103, the President may proclaim—

(A) modifications to the provisions proclaimed under the authority of paragraph (1)(A), other than the provisions of paragraph A of Appendix 6 of Annex 300-B and section XI of part B of Annex 401 of the Agreement; and

(B) a modified version of the definition of any term set out in subsection (p) (and such modified version of the definition shall supersede the version in subsection (p)), but only if the modified version reflects solely those modifications to the same term in article 415 of the Agreement that are agreed to by the NAFTA countries before the 1st anniversary of the date of the enactment of this Act.

(3) Special Rules for Textiles.—Notwithstanding the provisions of paragraph (2)(A), and subject to the consultation and layover requirements of section 103, the President may proclaim—

(A) modifications to the provisions proclaimed under the authority of paragraph (1)(A) as are necessary to implement an agreement with one or more of the NAFTA countries pursuant to paragraph 2 of section 7 of Annex 300-B of the Agreement, and

(B) before the 1st anniversary of the date of the enactment of this Act, modifications to correct any typographical, clerical, or other nonsubstantive technical error regarding the provisions of Appendix 6.A of Annex 300-B and section XI of part B of Annex 401 of the Agreement.

TITLE III—APPLICATION OF AGREEMENT TO SECTORS AND SERVICES

Subtitle A—Safeguards

PART 1—RELIEF FROM IMPORTS BENEFITING FROM THE AGREEMENT

19 USC 3351

Sec. 301. Definitions

As used in this part:

(1) Canadian Article.—The term "Canadian article" means an article that—

(A) is an originating good under chapter 4 of the Agreement; and

(B) qualifies under the Agreement to be marked as a good of Canada.

(2) Mexican Article.—The term "Mexican article" means an article that—

(A) is an originating good under chapter 4 of the Agreement; and

(B) qualifies under the Agreement to be marked as a good of Mexico.

19 USC 3352

Sec. 302.   Commencing of Action for Relief

(a) Filing of Petition.—

(1) In General.—A petition requesting action under this part for the purpose of adjusting to the obligations of the United States under the Agreement may be filed with the International Trade Commission by an entity, including a trade association, firm, certified or recognized union, or group of workers, that is representative of an industry. The International Trade Commission shall transmit a copy of any petition filed under this subsection to the Trade Representative.

(2) Provisional Relief.—An entity filing a petition under this subsection may request that provisional relief be provided as if the petition had been filed under section 202(a) of the Trade Act of 1974.

(3) Critical Circumstances.—An allegation that critical circumstances exist must be included in the petition or made on or before the 90th day after the date on which the investigation is initiated under subsection (b).

(b) Investigation and Determination.—Upon the filing of a petition under subsection (a), the International Trade Commission, unless subsection (d) applies, shall promptly initiate an investigation to determine whether, as a result of the reduction or elimination of a duty provided for under the Agreement, a Canadian article or a Mexican article, as the case may be, is being imported into the United States in such increased quantities (in absolute terms) and under such conditions so that imports of the article, alone, constitute a substantial cause of—

(1) serious injury; or

(2) except in the case of a Canadian article, a threat of serious injury;

to the domestic industry producing an article that is like, or directly competitive with, the imported article.

(c) Applicable Provisions.—The provisions of—

(1) paragraphs (1)(B), (3) (except subparagraph (A)), and (4) of subsection (b);

(2) subsection (c); and

(3) subsection (d),

of section 202 of the Trade Act of 1974 (19 U.S.C. 2252) apply with respect to any investigation initiated under subsection (b).

(d) Articles Exempt from Investigation.—No investigation may be initiated under this section with respect to—

(1) any Canadian article or Mexican article if import relief has been provided under this part with respect to that article; or

(2) any textile or apparel article set out in Appendix 1.1 of Annex 300-B of the Agreement.

19 USC 3353

Sec. 303. International Trade Commission Action on Petition

(a) Determination.—By no later than 120 days after the date on which an investigation is initiated under section 302(b) with respect to a petition, the International Trade Commission shall—

(1) make the determination required under that section; and

(2) if the determination referred to in paragraph (1) is affirmative and an allegation regarding critical circumstances was made under section 302(a), make a determination regarding that allegation.

(b) Additional Finding and Recommendation if Determination Affirmative.—If the determination made by the International Trade Commission under subsection (a) with respect to imports of an article is affirmative, the International Trade Commission shall find, and recommend to the President in the report required under subsection (c), the amount of import relief that is necessary to remedy or, except in the case of imports of a Canadian article, prevent the injury found by the International Trade Commission in the determination. The import relief recommended by the International Trade Commission under this subsection shall be limited to that described in section 304(c).

(c) Report to President.—No later than the date that is 30 days after the date on which a determination is made under subsection (a) with respect to an investigation, the International Trade Commission shall submit to the President a report that shall include—

(1) a statement of the basis for the determination;

(2) dissenting and separate views; and

(3) any finding made under subsection (b) regarding import relief.

(d) Public Notice.—Upon submitting a report to the President under subsection (c), the International Trade Commission shall promptly make public such report (with the exception of information which the International Trade Commission determines to be confidential) and shall cause a summary thereof to be published in the Federal Register.

(e) Applicable Provisions.—For purposes of this part, the provisions of paragraphs (1), (2), and (3) of section 330(d) of the Tariff Act of 1930 (19 U.S.C. 1330(d)) shall be applied with respect to determinations and findings made under this section as if such determinations and findings were made under section 202 of the Trade Act of 1974 (19 U.S.C. 2252).

19 USC 3354

Sec. 304. Provision of Relief

(a) In General.—No later than the date that is 30 days after the date on which the President receives the report of the International Trade Commission containing an affirmative determination of the International Trade Commission under section 303(a), the President, subject to subsection (b), shall provide relief from imports of the article that is the subject of such determination to the extent that the President determines necessary to remedy or, except in the case of imports of a Canadian article, prevent the injury found by the International Trade Commission.

(b) Exception.—The President is not required to provide import relief under this section if the President determines that the provision of the import relief will not provide greater economic and social benefits than costs.

(c) Nature of Relief.—The import relief (including provisional relief) that the President is authorized to provide under this part is as follows:

(1) In the case of imports of a Canadian article—

(A) the suspension of any further reduction provided for under Annex 401.2 of the United States-Canada Free-Trade Agreement in the duty imposed on such article;

(B) an increase in the rate of duty imposed on such article to a level that does not exceed the lesser of—

(i) the column 1 general rate of duty imposed under the HTS on like articles at the time the import relief is provided, or

(ii) the column 1 general rate of duty imposed on like articles on December 31, 1988; or

(C) in the case of a duty applied on a seasonal basis to such article, an increase in the rate of duty imposed on the article to a level that does not exceed the column 1 general rate of duty imposed on the article for the corresponding season occurring immediately before January 1, 1989.

(2) In the case of imports of a Mexican article—

(A) the suspension of any further reduction provided for under the United States Schedule to Annex 302.2 of the Agreement in the duty imposed on such article;

(B) an increase in the rate of duty imposed on such article to a level that does not exceed the lesser of—

(i) the column 1 general rate of duty imposed under the HTS on like articles at the time the import relief is provided, or

(ii) the column 1 general rate of duty imposed under the HTS on like articles on the day before the date on which the Agreement enters into force; or

(C) in the case of a duty applied on a seasonal basis to such article, an increase in the rate of duty imposed on the article to a level that does not exceed the column 1 general rate of duty imposed under the HTS on the article for the corresponding season immediately occurring before the date on which the Agreement enters into force.

(d) Period of Relief.—The import relief that the President is authorized to provide under this section may not exceed 3 years, except that, if a Canadian article or Mexican article which is the subject of the action—

(1) is provided for in an item for which the transition period of tariff elimination set out in the United States Schedule to Annex 302.2 of the Agreement is greater than 10 years; and

(2) the President determines that the affected industry has undertaken adjustment and requires an extension of the period of the import relief;

the President, after obtaining the advice of the International Trade Commission, may extend the period of the import relief for not more than 1 year, if the duty applied during the initial period of the relief is substantially reduced at the beginning of the extension period.

(e) Rate on Mexican Articles After Termination of Import Relief.—When import relief under this part is terminated with respect to a Mexican article—

(1) the rate of duty on that article after such termination and on or before December 31 of the year in which termination occurs shall be the rate that, according to the United States Schedule to Annex 302.2 of the Agreement for the staged elimination of the tariff, would have been in effect 1 year after the initiation of the import relief action under section 302; and

(2) the tariff treatment for that article after December 31 of the year in which termination occurs shall be, at the discretion of the President, either—

(A) the rate of duty conforming to the applicable rate set out in the United States Schedule to Annex 302.2; or

(B) the rate of duty resulting from the elimination of the tariff in equal annual stages ending on the date set out in the United States Schedule to Annex 302.2 for the elimination of the tariff.

19 USC 3355

Sec. 305.   Termination of Relief Authority

(a) General Rule.—Except as provided in subsection (b), no import relief may be provided under this part—

(1) in the case of a Canadian article, after December 31, 1998; or

(2) in the case of a Mexican article, after the date that is 10 years after the date on which the Agreement enters into force;

unless the article against which the action is taken is an item for which the transition period for tariff elimination set out in the United States Schedule to Annex 302.2 of the Agreement is greater than 10 years, in which case the period during which relief may be granted shall be the period of staged tariff elimination for that article.

(b) Exception.—Import relief may be provided under this part in the case of a Canadian article or Mexican article after the date on which such relief would, but for this subsection, terminate under subsection (a), but only if the Government of Canada or Mexico, as the case may be, consents to such provision.

19 USC 3356

Sec. 306.   Compensation Authority

For purposes of section 123 of the Trade Act of 1974 (19 U.S.C. 2133), any import relief provided by the President under section 304 shall be treated as action taken under chapter 1 of title II of such Act.

19 USC 3357

Sec. 307.   Submission of Petitions

A petition for import relief may be submitted to the International Trade Commission under—

(1) this part;

(2) chapter 1 of title II of the Trade Act of 1974; or

(3) under both this part and such chapter 1 at the same time, in which case the International Trade Commission shall consider such petitions jointly.

PART 2—RELIEF FROM IMPORTS FROM ALL COUNTRIES

19 USC 3371

Sec. 311.   NAFTA Article Impact in Import Relief Cases Under the Trade Act of 1974

(a) **In General.**—If, in any investigation initiated under chapter 1 of title II of the Trade Act of 1974, the International Trade Commission makes an affirmative determination (or a determination which the President may treat as an affirmative determination under such chapter by reason of section 330(d) of the Tariff Act of 1930), the International Trade Commission shall also find (and report to the President at the time such injury determination is submitted to the President) whether—

(1) imports of the article from a NAFTA country, considered individually, account for a substantial share of total imports; and

(2) imports of the article from a NAFTA country, considered individually or, in exceptional circumstances, imports from NAFTA countries considered collectively, contribute importantly to the serious injury, or threat thereof, caused by imports.

(b) **Factors.**—

(1) Substantial Import Share.—In determining whether imports from a NAFTA country, considered individually, account for a substantial share of total imports, such imports normally shall not be considered to account for a substantial share of total imports if that country is not among the top 5 suppliers of the article subject to the investigation, measured in terms of import share during the most recent 3-year period.

(2) Application of "Contribute Importantly" Standard.—In determining whether imports from a NAFTA country or countries contribute importantly to the serious injury, or threat thereof, the International Trade Commission shall consider such factors as the change in the import share of the NAFTA country or countries, and the level and change in the level of imports of such country or countries. In applying the preceding sentence, imports from a NAFTA country or countries normally shall not be considered to contribute importantly to serious injury, or the threat thereof, if the growth rate of imports from such country or countries during the period in which an injurious increase in imports occurred is appreciably lower than the growth rate of total imports from all sources over the same period.

(c) Definition.—For purposes of this section and section 312(a), the term "contribute importantly" refers to an important cause, but not necessarily the most important cause.

19 USC 3372

Sec. 312.   Presidential Action Regarding NAFTA Imports

(a) In General.—In determining whether to take action under chapter 1 of title II of the Trade Act of 1974 with respect to imports from a NAFTA country, the President shall determine whether—

(1) imports from such country, considered individually, account for a substantial share of total imports; or

(2) imports from a NAFTA country, considered individually, or in exceptional circumstances imports from NAFTA countries considered collectively, contribute importantly to the serious injury, or threat thereof, found by the International Trade Commission.

(b) Exclusion of NAFTA Imports.—In determining the nature and extent of action to be taken under chapter 1 of title II of the Trade Act of 1974, the President shall exclude from such action imports from a NAFTA country if the President makes a negative determination under subsection (a)(1) or (2) with respect to imports from such country.

(c) Action After Exclusion of NAFTA Country Imports.—

(1) In General.—If the President, under subsection (b), excludes imports from a NAFTA country or countries from action under chapter 1 of title II of the Trade Act of 1974 but thereafter determines that a surge in imports from that country or countries is undermining the effectiveness of the action—

(A) the President may take appropriate action under such chapter 1 to include those imports in the action; and

(B) any entity that is representative of an industry for which such action is being taken may request the International Trade Commission to conduct an investigation of the surge in such imports.

(2) Investigation.—Upon receiving a request under paragraph (1)(B), the International Trade Commission shall conduct an investigation to determine whether a surge in such imports undermines the effectiveness of the action. The International Trade Commission shall submit the findings of its investigation to the President no later than 30 days after the request is received by the International Trade Commission.

(3) Definition.—For purposes of this subsection, the term "surge" means a significant increase in imports over the trend for a recent representative base period.

(d) Condition Applicable to Quantitative Restrictions.—Any action taken under this section proclaiming a quantitative restriction shall permit the importation of a quantity or value of the article which is not less than the quantity or value of such article imported into the United States during the most recent period that is representative of imports of such article, with allowance for reasonable growth.

TITLE IV—DISPUTE SETTLEMENT IN ANTIDUMPING AND COUNTERVAILING DUTY CASES

Subtitle A—Organizational, Administrative, and Procedural Provisions Regarding the Implementation of Chapter 19 of the Agreement

19 USC 3431

Sec. 401. References in Subtitle

Any reference in this subtitle to an Annex, chapter, or article shall be considered to be a reference to the respective Annex, chapter, or article of the Agreement.

19 USC 3432

Sec. 402. Organizational and Administrative Provisions

(a) Criteria for Selection of Individuals to Serve on Panels and Committees.—

(1) In General.—The selection of individuals under this section for—

(A) placement on lists prepared by the interagency group under subsection (c)(2)(B)(i) and (ii);

(B) placement on preliminary candidate lists under subsection (c)(3)(A);

(C) placement on final candidate lists under subsection (c)(4)(A);

(D) placement by the Trade Representative on the rosters described in paragraph 1 of Annex 1901.2 and paragraph 1 of Annex 1904.13; and

(E) appointment by the Trade Representative for service on the panels and committees convened under chapter 19;

shall be made on the basis of the criteria provided in paragraph 1 of Annex 1901.2 and paragraph 1 of Annex 1904.13 and shall be made without regard to political affiliation.

(2) Additional Criteria for Roster Placements and Appointments Under Paragraph 1 of Annex 1901.2.—Rosters described in paragraph 1 of Annex 1901.2 shall include, to the fullest extent practicable, judges and former judges who meet the criteria referred to in paragraph (1). The Trade Representative shall, subject to subsection (b), appoint judges to binational panels convened under chapter 19, extraordinary challenge committees convened under chapter 19, and special committees established under article 1905, where such judges offer and are available to serve and such service is authorized by the chief judge of the court on which they sit.

(b) Selection of Certain Judges to Serve on Panels and Committees.—

(1) Applicability.—This subsection applies only with respect to the selection of individuals for binational panels convened under chapter 19, extraordinary challenge committees convened under chapter 19, and special committees established under article 1905, who are judges of courts created under article III of the Constitution of the United States.

(2) Consultation with Chief Judges.—The Trade Representative shall consult, from time to time, with the chief judges of the Federal judicial circuits regarding the interest in, and availability for, participation in binational panels, extraordinary challenge committees, and special committees, of judges within their respective circuits. If the chief judge of a Federal judicial circuit determines that it is appropriate for one or more judges within that circuit to be included on a roster described in subsection (a)(1)(D), the chief judge shall identify all such judges for the Chief Justice of the United States who may, upon his or her approval, submit the names of such judges to the Trade Representative. The Trade Representative shall include the names of such judges on the roster.

(3) Submission of Lists to Congress.—The Trade Representative shall submit to the Committee on the Judiciary and the Committee on Ways and Means of the House of Representatives and to the Committee on Finance and the Committee on the Judiciary of the Senate a list of all judges included on a roster under paragraph (2). Such list shall be submitted at the same time as the final candidate lists are submitted under subsection (c)(4)(A) and the final forms of amendments are submitted under subsection (c)(4)(C)(iv).

(4) Appointment of Judges to Panels or Committees.—At such time as the Trade Representative proposes to appoint a judge described in paragraph (1) to a binational panel, an extraordinary challenge committee, or a special committee, the Trade Representative shall consult with that judge in order to ascertain whether the judge is available for such appointment.

(c) Selection of Other Candidates.—

(1) Applicability.—This subsection applies only with respect to the selection of individuals for binational panels convened under chapter 19, extraordinary challenge committees convened under chapter 19, and special committees established under article 1905, other than those individuals to whom subsection (b) applies.

(2) Interagency Group.—

(A) Establishment.—There is established within the interagency organization established under section 242 of the Trade Expansion Act of 1962 (19 U.S.C. 1872) an interagency group which shall—

(i) be chaired by the Trade Representative; and

(ii) consist of such officers (or the designees thereof) of the United States Government as the Trade Representative considers appropriate.

(B) Functions.—The interagency group established under subparagraph (A) shall, in a manner consistent with chapter 19—

(i) prepare by January 3 of each calendar year—

(I) a list of individuals who are qualified to serve as members of binational panels convened under chapter 19; and

(II) a list of individuals who are qualified to serve on extraordinary challenge committees convened under chapter 19 and special committees established under article 1905;

(ii) if the Trade Representative makes a request under paragraph (4)(C)(i) with respect to a final candidate list during any calendar year, prepare by July 1 of such calendar year a list of those individuals who are qualified to be added to that final candidate list;

(iii) exercise oversight of the administration of the United States Section that is authorized to be established under section 105; and

(iv) make recommendations to the Trade Representative regarding the convening of extraordinary challenge committees and special committees under chapter 19.

(3) Preliminary Candidate Lists.—

(A) In General.—The Trade Representative shall select individuals from the respective lists prepared by the interagency group under paragraph (2)(B)(i) for placement on—

(i) a preliminary candidate list of individuals eligible to serve as members of binational panels under Annex 1901.2; and

(ii) a preliminary candidate list of individuals eligible for selection as members of extraordinary challenge committees under Annex 1904.13 and special committees under article 1905.

(B) Submission of Lists to Congressional Committees.—

(i) In General.—No later than January 3 of each calendar year, the Trade Representative shall submit to the Committee on Finance of the Senate and the Committee on Ways and Means of the House of Representatives (hereafter in this section referred to as the "appropriate Congressional Committees") the preliminary candidate lists of those individuals selected by the Trade Representative under subparagraph (A) to be candidates eligible to serve on panels or committees convened pursuant to chapter 19 during the 1-year period beginning on April 1 of such calendar year.

(ii) ADDITIONAL INFORMATION.—At the time the candidate lists are submitted under clause (i), the Trade Representative shall submit for each individual on the list a statement of professional qualifications.

(C) Consultation.—Upon submission of the preliminary candidate lists under subparagraph (B) to the appropriate Congressional Committees, the Trade Representative shall consult with such Committees with regard to the individuals included on the preliminary candidate lists.

(D) Revision of Lists.—The Trade Representative may add and delete individuals from the preliminary candidate lists submitted under subparagraph (B) after consultation with the appropriate Congressional Committees regarding the additions and deletions. The Trade Representative shall provide to the appropriate Congressional Committees written notice of any addition or deletion of an individual from the preliminary candidate lists, along with the information described in subparagraph (B)(ii) with respect to any proposed addition.

(4) Final Candidate Lists.—

(A) Submission of Lists to Congressional Committees.—No later than March 31 of each calendar year, the Trade Representative shall submit to the appropriate Congressional Committees the final candidate lists of those individuals selected by the Trade Representative to be candidates eligible to serve on panels and committees convened under chapter 19 during the 1-year period beginning on April 1 of such calendar year. An individual may be included on a final candidate list only if such individual was included in the preliminary candidate list or if written notice of the addition of such individual to the preliminary candidate list was submitted to the appropriate Congressional Committees at least 15 days before the date on which that final candidate list is submitted to such Committees under this subparagraph.

*(B) Finality of Lists.—*Except as provided in subparagraph (C), no additions may be made to the final candidate lists after the final candidate lists are submitted to the appropriate Congressional Committees under subparagraph (A).

(C) Amendment of Lists.—

(i) In General.—If, after the Trade Representative has submitted the final candidate lists to the appropriate Congressional Committees under subparagraph (A) for a calendar year and before July 1 of such calendar year, the Trade Representative determines that additional individuals need to be added to a final candidate list, the Trade Representative shall—

(I) request the interagency group established under paragraph (2)(A) to prepare a list of individuals who are qualified to be added to such candidate list;

(II) select individuals from the list prepared by the interagency group under paragraph (2)(B)(ii) to be included in a proposed amendment to such final candidate list; and

(III) by no later than July 1 of such calendar year, submit to the appropriate Congressional Committees the proposed amendments to such final candidate list developed by the Trade Representative under subclause (II), along with the information described in paragraph (3)(B)(ii).

(ii) Consultation with Congressional Committees. Upon submission of a proposed amendment under clause (i)(III) to the appropriate Congressional Committees, the Trade Representative shall consult with the appropriate Congressional Committees with regard to the individuals included in the proposed amendment.

(iii) Adjustment of Proposed Amendment.—The Trade Representative may add and delete individuals from any proposed amendment submitted under clause (i)(III) after consulting with the appropriate Congressional Committees with regard to the additions and deletions. The Trade Representative shall provide to the appropriate Congressional Committees written notice of any addition or deletion of an individual from the proposed amendment.

(iv) Final Amendment.—

(I) In General.—If the Trade Representative submits under clause (i)(III) in any calendar year a proposed amendment to a final candidate list, the Trade Representative shall, no later than September 30 of such calendar year, submit to the appropriate Congressional Committees the final form of such amendment. On October 1 of such calendar year, such amendment shall take effect and, subject to subclause (II), the individuals included in the final form of such amendment shall be added to the final candidate list.

(II) Inclusion of Individuals.—An individual may be included in the final form of an amendment submitted under subclause (I) only if such individual was included in the proposed form of such amendment or if written notice of the addition of such individual to the proposed form of such amendment was submitted to the appropriate Congressional Committees at least 15 days before the date on which the final form of such amendment is submitted to such Committees under subclause (I).

(III) Eligibility for Service.—Individuals added to a final candidate list under subclause (I) shall be eligible to serve on panels or committees convened under chapter 19 during the 6-month period beginning on October 1 of the calendar year in which such addition occurs.

(IV) Finality of Amendment.—No additions may be made to the final form of an amendment described in subclause (I) after the final form of such amendment is submitted to the appropriate Congressional Committees under subclause (I).

(5) *Treatment of Responses.*—For purposes of applying section 1001 of title 18, United States Code, the written or oral responses of individuals to inquiries of the interagency group established under paragraph (2)(A) or of the Trade Representative regarding their personal and professional qualifications, and financial and other relevant interests, that bear on their suitability for the placements and appointments described in subsection (a)(1), shall be treated as matters within the jurisdiction of an agency of the United States.

(d) Selection and Appointment.—

(1) *Authority of Trade Representative.*—The Trade Representative is the only officer of the United States Government authorized to act on behalf of the United States Government in making any selection or appointment of an individual to—

(A) the rosters described in paragraph 1 of Annex 1901.2 and paragraph 1 of Annex 1904.13; or

(B) the panels or committees convened under chapter 19;

that is to be made solely or jointly by the United States Government under the terms of the Agreement.

(2) *Restrictions on Selection and Appointment.*—Except as provided in paragraph (3)—

(A) the Trade Representative may—

(i) select an individual for placement on the rosters described in paragraph 1 of Annex 1901.2 and paragraph 1 of Annex 1904.13 during the 1-year period beginning on April 1 of any calendar year;

(ii) appoint an individual to serve as one of those members of any panel or committee convened under chapter 19 during such 1-year period who, under the terms of the Agreement, are to be appointed solely by the United States Government; or

(iii) act to make a joint appointment with the Government of a NAFTA country, under the terms of the Agreement, of any individual who is a citizen or national of the United States to serve as any other member of such a panel or committee;

only if such individual is on the appropriate final candidate list that was submitted to the appropriate Congressional Committees under subsection (c)(4)(A) during such calendar year or on such list as it may be amended under subsection (c)(4)(C)(iv)(I), or on the list submitted under subsection (b)(3) to the congressional committees referred to in such subsection; and

(B) no individual may—

(i) be selected by the United States Government for placement on the rosters described in paragraph 1 of Annex 1901.2 and paragraph 1 of Annex 1904.13; or

(ii) be appointed solely or jointly by the United States Government to serve as a member of a panel or committee convened under chapter 19;

during the 1-year period beginning on April 1 of any calendar year for which the Trade Representative has not met the requirements of subsection (a), and of subsection (b) or (c) (as the case may be).

(3) Exceptions.—Notwithstanding subsection (c)(3) (other than subparagraph (B)), subsection (c)(4), or paragraph (2)(A) of this subsection, individuals included on the preliminary candidate lists submitted to the appropriate Congressional Committees under subsection (c)(3)(B) may—

(A) be selected by the Trade Representative for placement on the rosters described in paragraph 1 of Annex 1901.2 and paragraph 1 of Annex 1904.13 during the 3-month period beginning on the date on which the Agreement enters into force with respect to the United States; and

(B) be appointed solely or jointly by the Trade Representative under the terms of the Agreement to serve as members of panels or committees that are convened under chapter 19 during such 3-month period.

(e) Transition.—If the Agreement enters into force between the United States and a NAFTA country after January 3, 1994, the provisions of subsection (c) shall be applied with respect to the calendar year in which such entering into force occurs—

(1) by substituting "the date that is 30 days after the date on which the Agreement enters into force with respect to the United States" for "January 3 of each calendar year" in subsections (c)(2)(B)(i) and (c)(3)(B)(i); and

(2) by substituting "the date that is 3 months after the date on which the Agreement enters into force with respect to the United States" for "March 31 of each calendar year" in subsection (c)(4)(A).

(f) Immunity.—With the exception of acts described in section 777(f)(3) of the Tariff Act of 1930 (19 U.S.C. 1677f(f)(3)), individuals serving on panels or committees convened pursuant to chapter 19, and individuals designated to assist the individuals serving on such panels or committees, shall be immune from suit and legal process relating to acts performed by such individuals in their official capacity and within the scope of their functions as such panelists or committee members or assistants to such panelists or committee members.

(g) Regulations.—The administering authority under title VII of the Tariff Act of 1930, the International Trade Commission, and the Trade Representative may promulgate such regulations as are necessary or appropriate to carry out actions in order to implement their respective responsibilities under chapter 19. Initial regulations to carry out such functions shall be issued before the date on which the Agreement enters into force with respect to the United States.

(h) Report to Congress.—At such time as the final candidate lists are submitted under subsection (c)(4)(A) and the final forms of amendments are submitted under subsection (c)(4)(C)(iv), the Trade Representative shall submit to the Committee on the Judiciary and the Committee on Ways and Means of the House of Representatives, and to the Committee on Finance and the Committee on the Judiciary of the Senate, a report regarding the efforts made to secure the participation of judges and former judges on binational panels, extraordinary challenge committees, and special committees established under chapter 19.

19 USC 3433

Sec. 403. Testimony and Production of Papers in Extraordinary Challenges

(a) Authority of Extraordinary Challenge Committee to Obtain Information.—If an extraordinary challenge committee (hereafter in this section referred to as the "committee") is convened under paragraph 13 of article 1904, and the allegations before the committee include a matter referred to in paragraph 13(a)(i) of article 1904, for the purposes of carrying out its functions and duties under Annex 1904.13, the committee—

(1) shall have access to, and the right to copy, any document, paper, or record pertinent to the subject matter under consideration, in the possession of any individual, partnership, corporation, association, organization, or other entity;

(2) may summon witnesses, take testimony, and administer oaths;

(3) may require any individual, partnership, corporation, association, organization, or other entity to produce documents, books, or records relating to the matter in question; and

(4) may require any individual, partnership, corporation, association, organization, or other entity to furnish in writing, in such detail and in such

form as the committee may prescribe, information in its possession pertaining to the matter.

Any member of the committee may sign subpoenas, and members of the committee, when authorized by the committee, may administer oaths and affirmations, examine witnesses, take testimony, and receive evidence.

(b) **Witnesses and Evidence.**—The attendance of witnesses who are authorized to be summoned, and the production of documentary evidence authorized to be ordered, under subsection (a) may be required from any place in the United States at any designated place of hearing. In the case of disobedience to a subpoena authorized under subsection (a), the committee may request the Attorney General of the United States to invoke the aid of any district or territorial court of the United States in requiring the attendance and testimony of witnesses and the production of documentary evidence. Such court, within the jurisdiction of which such inquiry is carried on, may, in case of contumacy or refusal to obey a subpoena issued to any individual, partnership, corporation, association, organization, or other entity, issue an order requiring such individual or entity to appear before the committee, or to produce documentary evidence if so ordered or to give evidence concerning the matter in question. Any failure to obey such order of the court may be punished by such court as a contempt thereof.

(c) **Mandamus.**—Any court referred to in subsection (b) shall have jurisdiction to issue writs of mandamus commanding compliance with the provisions of this section or any order of the committee made in pursuance thereof.

(d) **Depositions.**—The committee may order testimony to be taken by deposition at any stage of the committee review. Such deposition may be taken before any person designated by the committee and having power to administer oaths. Such testimony shall be reduced to writing by the person taking the deposition, or under the direction of such person, and shall then be subscribed by the deponent. Any individual, partnership, corporation, association, organization, or other entity may be compelled to appear and be deposed and to produce documentary evidence in the same manner as witnesses may be compelled to appear and testify and produce documentary evidence before the committee, as provided in this section.

19 USC 3434

Sec. 404. Requests for Review of Determinations by Competent Investigating Authorities of NAFTA Countries

(a) **Definitions.**—As used in this section:

(1) *Competent Investigating Authority.*—The term "competent investigating authority" means the competent investigating authority, as defined in article 1911, of a NAFTA country.

(2) *United States Secretary.*—The term "United States Secretary" means that officer of the United States referred to in article 1908.

(b) **Requests for Review by the United States.**—In the case of a final determination of a competent investigating authority, requests by the United

States for binational panel review of such determination under article 1904 shall be made by the United States Secretary.

(c) Requests for Review by a Person.—In the case of a final determination of a competent investigating authority, a person, within the meaning of paragraph 5 of article 1904, may request a binational panel review of such determination by filing such a request with the United States Secretary within the time limit provided for in paragraph 4 of article 1904. The receipt of such request by the United States Secretary shall be deemed to be a request for binational panel review within the meaning of article 1904. The request for such panel review shall be without prejudice to any challenge before a binational panel of the basis for a particular request for review.

(d) Service of Request for Review.—Whenever binational panel review of a final determination made by a competent investigating authority is requested under this section, the United States Secretary shall serve a copy of the request on all persons who would otherwise be entitled under the law of the importing country to commence proceedings for judicial review of the determination.

19 USC 3435

Sec. 405.   Rules of Procedure for Panels and Committees

(a) Rules of Procedure for Binational Panels.—The administering authority shall prescribe rules, negotiated in accordance with paragraph 14 of article 1904, governing, with respect to binational panel reviews—

(1) requests for such reviews, complaints, other pleadings, and other papers;

(2) the amendment, filing, and service of such pleadings and papers;

(3) the joinder, suspension, and termination of such reviews; and

(4) other appropriate procedural matters.

(b) Rules of Procedure for Extraordinary Challenge Committees.—The administering authority shall prescribe rules, negotiated in accordance with paragraph 2 of Annex 1904.13, governing the procedures for reviews by extraordinary challenge committees.

(c) Rules of Procedure for Safeguarding the Panel Review System.—The administering authority shall prescribe rules, negotiated in accordance with Annex 1905.6, governing the procedures for special committees described in such Annex.

(d) Publication of Rules.—The rules prescribed under subsections (a), (b), and (c) shall be published in the Federal Register.

(e) Administering Authority.—As used in this section, the term "administering authority" has the meaning given such term in section 771(1) of the Tariff Act of 1930 (19 U.S.C. 1677(1)).

19 USC 3436

Sec. 406.   Subsidy Negotiations

In the case of any trade agreement which may be entered into by the President with a NAFTA country, the negotiating objectives of the United States with respect to subsidies shall include—

(1) achievement of increased discipline on domestic subsidies provided by a foreign government, including—

(A) the provision of capital, loans, or loan guarantees on terms inconsistent with commercial considerations;

(B) the provision of goods or services at preferential rates;

(C) the granting of funds or forgiveness of debt to cover operating losses sustained by a specific industry; and

(D) the assumption of any costs or expenses of manufacture, production, or distribution;

(2) achievement of increased discipline on export subsidies provided by a foreign government, particularly with respect to agricultural products; and

(3) maintenance of effective remedies against subsidized imports, including, where appropriate, countervailing duties.

19 USC 3437

Sec. 407. Identification of Industries Facing Subsidized Imports

(a) Petitions.—Any entity, including a trade association, firm, certified or recognized union, or group of workers, that is representative of a United States industry and has reason to believe—

(1) that—

(A) as a result of implementation of provisions of the Agreement, the industry is likely to face increased competition from subsidized imports, from a NAFTA country, with which it directly competes; or

(B) the industry is likely to face increased competition from subsidized imports with which it directly competes from any other country designated by the President, following consultations with the Congress, as benefiting from a reduction of tariffs or other trade barriers under a trade agreement that enters into force with respect to the United States after January 1, 1994; and

(2) that the industry is likely to experience a deterioration of its competitive position before more effective rules and disciplines relating to the use of government subsidies have been developed with respect to the country concerned;

may file with the Trade Representative a petition that such industry be identified under this section.

(b) Identification of Industry.—Within 90 days after receipt of a petition under subsection (a), the Trade Representative, in consultation with the Secretary of Commerce, shall decide whether to identify the industry on the basis that there is a reasonable likelihood that the industry may face both the subsidization described in subsection (a)(1) and the deterioration described in subsection (a)(2).

(c) Action After Identification.—At the request of an entity that is representative of an industry identified under subsection (b), the Trade Representative shall—

(1) compile and make available to the industry information under section 308 of the Trade Act of 1974;

(2) recommend to the President that an investigation by the International Trade Commission be requested under section 332 of the Tariff Act of 1930; or

(3) take actions described in both paragraphs (1) and (2).

The industry may request the Trade Representative to take appropriate action to update (as often as annually) any information obtained under paragraph (1) or (2), or both, as the case may be, until an agreement on more effective rules and disciplines relating to government subsidies is reached between the United States and the NAFTA countries.

(d) Initiation of Action Under Other Law.—

(1) In General.—The Trade Representative and the Secretary of Commerce shall review information obtained under subsection (c) and consult with the industry identified under subsection (b) with a view to deciding whether any action is appropriate—

(A) under section 301 of the Trade Act of 1974, including the initiation of an investigation under section 302(c) of that Act (in the case of the Trade Representative); or

(B) under subtitle A of title VII of the Tariff Act of 1930, including the initiation of an investigation under section 702(a) of that Act (in the case of the Secretary of Commerce).

(2) Criteria for Initiation.—In determining whether to initiate any investigation under section 301 of the Trade Act of 1974 or any other trade law, other than title VII of the Tariff Act of 1930, the Trade Representative, after consultation with the Secretary of Commerce—

(A) shall seek the advice of the advisory committees established under section 135 of the Trade Act of 1974;

(B) shall consult with the Committee on Finance of the Senate and the Committee on Ways and Means of the House of Representatives;

(C) shall coordinate with the interagency organization established under section 242 of the Trade Expansion Act of 1962; and

(D) may ask the President to request advice from the International Trade Commission.

(3) Title III Actions.—In the event an investigation is initiated under section 302(c) of the Trade Act of 1974 as a result of a review under this subsection and the Trade Representative, following such investigation (including any applicable dispute settlement proceedings under the Agreement or any other trade agreement), determines to take action under section 301(a) of such Act, the Trade Representative shall give preference to actions that most directly affect the products that benefit from governmental subsidies and were the subject of the investigation, unless there are no significant imports of such products or the Trade Representative otherwise determines that application of the action to other products would be more effective.

(e) Effect of Decisions.—Any decision, whether positive or negative, or any action by the Trade Representative or the Secretary of Commerce under this section shall not in any way—

(1) prejudice the right of any industry to file a petition under any trade law;

(2) prejudice, affect, or substitute for, any proceeding, investigation, determination, or action by the Secretary of Commerce, the International Trade Commission, or the Trade Representative pursuant to such a petition; or

(3) prejudice, affect, substitute for, or obviate any proceeding, investigation, or determination under section 301 of the Trade Act of 1974, title VII of the Tariff Act of 1930, or any other trade law.

(f) Standing.—Nothing in this section may be construed to alter in any manner the requirements in effect before the date of the enactment of this Act for standing under any law of the United States or to add any additional requirements for standing under any law of the United States.

19 USC 3438

Sec. 408. Treatment of Amendments to Antidumping and Countervailing Duty Law

Any amendment enacted after the Agreement enters into force with respect to the United States that is made to—

(1) section 303 or title VII of the Tariff Act of 1930, or any successor statute, or

(2) any other statute which—

(A) provides for judicial review of final determinations under such section, title, or successor statute, or

(B) indicates the standard of review to be applied,

shall apply to goods from a NAFTA country only to the extent specified in the amendment.

TITLE V—NAFTA TRANSITIONAL ADJUSTMENT ASSISTANCE AND OTHER PROVISIONS

Subtitle D—Implementation of NAFTA Supplemental Agreements

PART 1—AGREEMENTS RELATING TO LABOR AND ENVIRONMENT

19 USC 3471

Sec. 531. Agreement on Labor Cooperation

(a) Commission for Labor Cooperation.—

(1) Membership.—The United States is authorized to participate in the Commission for Labor Cooperation in accordance with the North American Agreement on Labor Cooperation.

(2) Contributions to Budget.—There are authorized to be appropriated to the President (or such agency as the President may designate) $2,000,000 for each of fiscal years 1994 and 1995 for United States contributions to the

annual budget of the Commission for Labor Cooperation pursuant to Article 47 of the North American Agreement on Labor Cooperation. Funds authorized to be appropriated for such contributions by this paragraph are in addition to any funds otherwise available for such contributions. Funds authorized to be appropriated by this paragraph are authorized to be made available until expended.

(b) Definitions.—As used in this section—

(1) the term "Commission for Labor Cooperation" means the commission established by Part Three of the North American Agreement on Labor Cooperation; and

(2) the term "North American Agreement on Labor Cooperation" means the North American Agreement on Labor Cooperation Between the Government of the United States of America, the Government of Canada, and the Government of the United Mexican States (signed at Mexico City, Washington, and Ottawa on September 8, 9, 12, and 14, 1993).

19 USC 3472

Sec. 532.   Agreement on Environmental Cooperation

(a) Commission for Environmental Cooperation.—

(1) Membership.—The United States is authorized to participate in the Commission for Environmental Cooperation in accordance with the North American Agreement on Environmental Cooperation.

(2) Contributions to Budget.—There are authorized to be appropriated to the President (or such agency as the President may designate) $5,000,000 for each of fiscal years 1994 and 1995 for United States contributions to the annual budget of the Commission for Environmental Cooperation pursuant to Article 43 of the North American Agreement on Environmental Cooperation. Funds authorized to be appropriated for such contributions by this paragraph are in addition to any funds otherwise available for such contributions. Funds authorized to be appropriated by this paragraph are authorized to be made available until expended.

(b) Definitions.—As used in this section—

(1) the term "Commission for Environmental Cooperation" means the commission established by Part Three of the North American Agreement on Environmental Cooperation; and

(2) the term "North American Agreement on Environmental Cooperation" means the North American Agreement on Environmental Cooperation Between the Government of the United States of America, the Government of Canada, and the Government of the United Mexican States (signed at Mexico City, Washington, and Ottawa on September 8, 9, 12, and 14, 1993).

19 USC 3473

Sec. 533.   Agreement on Border Environment Cooperation Commission

(a) Border Environment Cooperation Commission.—

(1) Membership.—The United States is authorized to participate in the Border Environment Cooperation Commission in accordance with the Border Environment Cooperation Agreement.

(2) Contributions to the Commission Budget.—There are authorized to be appropriated to the President (or such agency as the President may designate) $5,000,000 for fiscal year 1994 and each fiscal year thereafter for United States contributions to the budget of the Border Environment Cooperation Commission pursuant to section 7 of Article III of Chapter I of the Border Environment Cooperation Agreement. Funds authorized to be appropriated for such contributions by this paragraph are in addition to any funds otherwise available for such contributions. Funds authorized to be appropriated by this paragraph are authorized to be made available until expended.

(b) Civil Actions Involving the Commission.—For the purpose of any civil action which may be brought within the United States by or against the Border Environment Cooperation Commission in accordance with the Border Environment Cooperation Agreement (including an action brought to enforce an arbitral award against the Commission), the Commission shall be deemed to be an inhabitant of the Federal judicial district in which its principal office within the United States, or its agent appointed for the purpose of accepting service or notice of service, is located. Any such action to which the Commission is a party shall be deemed to arise under the laws of the United States, and the district courts of the United States (including the courts enumerated in section 460 of title 28, United States Code) shall have original jurisdiction of any such action. When the Commission is a defendant in any action in a State court, it may at any time before trial remove the action into the appropriate district court of the United States by following the procedure for removal provided in section 1446 of title 28, United States Code.

(c) Definitions.—As used in this section—

(1) the term "Border Environment Cooperation Agreement" means the November 1993 Agreement Between the Government of the United States of America and the Government of the United Mexican States Concerning the Establishment of a Border Environment Cooperation Commission and a North American Development Bank;

(2) the terms "Border Environment Cooperation Commission" and "Commission" mean the commission established pursuant to Chapter I of the Border Environment Cooperation Agreement; and

(3) the term "United States" means the United States, its territories and possessions, and the Commonwealth of Puerto Rico.

Item 52

URUGUAY ROUND AGREEMENTS ACT

(selected provisions)

SEC. 1. Short Title and Table of Contents

(a) **Short Title.**—This Act may be cited as the "Uruguay Round Agreements Act".

(b) **Table of Contents**.

19 USC 3501

Sec. 2. Definitions

For purposes of this Act:

(1) GATT 1947; GATT 1994.

(A) GATT 1947.—The term "GATT 1947" means the General Agreement on Tariffs and Trade, dated October 30, 1947, annexed to the Final Act Adopted at the Conclusion of the Second Session of the Preparatory Committee of the United Nations Conference on Trade and Employment, as subsequently rectified, amended, or modified by the terms of legal instruments which have entered into force before the date of entry into force of the WTO Agreement.

(B) GATT 1994.—The term "GATT 1994" means the General Agreement on Tariffs and Trade annexed to the WTO Agreement.

(2) HTS.—The term "HTS" means the Harmonized Tariff Schedule of the United States.

(3) International trade commission.—The term "International Trade Commission" means the United States International Trade Commission.

(4) Multilateral trade agreement.—The term "multilateral trade agreement" means an agreement described in section 101(d) of this Act (other than an agreement described in paragraph (17) or (18) of such section).

(5) Schedule xx.—The term "Schedule XX" means Schedule XX—United States of America annexed to the Marrakesh Protocol to the GATT 1994.

(6) Trade representative.—The term "Trade Representative" means the United States Trade Representative.

(7) Uruguay round agreements.—The term "Uruguay Round Agreements" means the agreements approved by the Congress under section 101(a)(1).

(8) World trade organization and WTO.—The terms "World Trade Organization" and "WTO" mean the organization established pursuant to the WTO Agreement.

(9) WTO agreement.—The term "WTO Agreement" means the Agreement Establishing the World Trade Organization entered into on April 15, 1994.

(10) WTO member and WTO member country.—The terms "WTO member" and "WTO member country" mean a state, or separate customs territory (within the meaning of Article XII of the WTO Agreement), with respect to which the United States applies the WTO Agreement.

TITLE I—APPROVAL OF, AND GENERAL PROVISIONS RELATING TO, THE URUGUAY ROUND AGREEMENTS

Subtitle A—Approval of Agreements and Related Provisions

19 USC 3511

Sec. 101. Approval and Entry into Force of the Uruguay Round Agreements

(a) Approval of Agreements and Statement of Administrative Action.—Pursuant to section 1103 of the Omnibus Trade and Competitiveness Act of 1988 (19 U.S.C. 2903) and section 151 of the Trade Act of 1974 (19 U.S.C. 2191), the Congress approves

(1) the trade agreements described in subsection (d) resulting from the Uruguay Round of multilateral trade negotiations under the auspices of the General Agreement on Tariffs and Trade, entered into on April 15, 1994, and submitted to the Congress ...; and

(2) the statement of administrative action proposed to implement the agreements that was submitted to the Congress ..., 1994.

(b) Entry Into Force.—At such time as the President determines that a sufficient number of foreign countries are accepting the obligations of the Uruguay Round Agreements, in accordance with article XIV of the WTO Agreement, to ensure the effective operation of, and adequate benefits for the United States under, those Agreements, the President may accept the Uruguay Round Agreements and implement article VIII of the WTO Agreement.

(c) Authorization of Appropriations.—There are authorized to be appropriated annually such sums as may be necessary for the payment by the United States of its share of the expenses of the WTO.

(d) Trade Agreements to Which This Act Applies.—Subsection (a) applies to the WTO Agreement and to the following agreements annexed to that Agreement:

(1) The General Agreement on Tariffs and Trade 1994.

(2) The Agreement on Agriculture.

(3) The Agreement on the Application of Sanitary and Phytosanitary Measures.

(4) The Agreement on Textiles and Clothing.

(5) The Agreement on Technical Barriers to Trade.

(6) The Agreement on Trade-Related Investment Measures.

(7) The Agreement on Implementation of Article VI of the General Agreement on Tariffs and Trade 1994.

(8) The Agreement on Implementation of Article VII of the General Agreement on Tariffs and Trade 1994.

(9) The Agreement on Preshipment Inspection.

(10) The Agreement on Rules of Origin.

(11) The Agreement on Import Licensing Procedures.

(12) The Agreement on Subsidies and Countervailing Measures.

(13) The Agreement on Safeguards.

(14) The General Agreement on Trade in Services.

(15) The Agreement on Trade-Related Aspects of Intellectual Property Rights.

(16) The Understanding on Rules and Procedures Governing the Settlement of Disputes.

(17) The Agreement on Government Procurement.

(18) The International Bovine Meat Agreement.

19 USC 3512

Sec. 102. Relationship of the Agreements to United States Law and State Law

(a) Relationship of Agreements to United States Law.

(1) United states law to prevail in conflict.—No provision of any of the Uruguay Round Agreements, nor the application of any such provision to any person or circumstance, that is inconsistent with any law of the United States shall have effect.

(2) Construction.—Nothing in this Act shall be construed

(A) to amend or modify any law of the United States, including any law relating to

(i) the protection of human, animal, or plant life or health,

(ii) the protection of the environment, or

(iii) worker safety, or

(B) to limit any authority conferred under any law of the United States, including section 301 of the Trade Act of 1974,

unless specifically provided for in this Act.

(b) Relationship of Agreements to State Law.

(1) Federal-state consultation.

(A) In general.—Upon the enactment of this Act, the President shall, through the intergovernmental policy advisory committees on trade established under section 306(c)(2)(A) of the Trade and Tariff Act of 1984 (19 U.S.C. 2114c(2)(A)), consult with the States for the purpose of achieving conformity of State laws and practices with the Uruguay Round Agreements.

(B) Federal-state consultation process.—The Trade Representative shall establish within the Office of the United States Trade Representative a Federal-State consultation process for addressing issues relating to the Uruguay Round Agreements that directly relate to, or will potentially have a direct effect on, the States. The Federal-State consultation process shall include procedures under which

(i) the States will be informed on a continuing basis of matters under the Uruguay Round Agreements that directly relate to, or will potentially have a direct impact on, the States;

(ii) the States will be provided an opportunity to submit, on a continuing basis, to the Trade Representative information and advice with respect to matters referred to in clause (i); and

(iii) the Trade Representative will take into account the information and advice received from the States under clause (ii) when formulating United States positions regarding matters referred to in clause (i).

The Federal Advisory Committee Act (5 U.S.C. App.) shall not apply to the Federal-State consultation process established by this paragraph.

(C) Federal-state cooperation in dispute settlement.

(i) When a WTO member requests consultations with the United States under Article 4 of the Understanding on Rules and Procedures Governing the Settlement of Disputes referred to in section 101(d)(16) (hereafter in this subsection referred to as the "Dispute Settlement Understanding") concerning whether the law of a State is inconsistent with the obligations undertaken by the United States in any of the Uruguay Round Agreements, the Trade Representative shall notify the Governor of the State or the Governor's designee, and the chief legal officer of the jurisdiction whose law is the subject of the consultations, as soon as possible after the request is received, but in no event later than 7 days thereafter.

(ii) Not later than 30 days after receiving such a request for consultations, the Trade Representative shall consult with representatives of the State concerned regarding the matter. If the consultations involve the laws of a large number of States, the Trade Representative may consult with an appropriate group of representatives of the States concerned, as determined by those States.

(iii) The Trade Representative shall make every effort to ensure that the State concerned is involved in the development of the position of the United States at each stage of the consultations and each subsequent stage of dispute settlement proceedings regarding the matter. In particular, the Trade Representative shall

(I) notify the State concerned not later than 7 days after a WTO member requests the establishment of a dispute settlement panel or gives notice of the WTO member's decision to appeal a report by a dispute settlement panel regarding the matter; and

(II) provide the State concerned with the opportunity to advise and assist the Trade Representative in the preparation of factual information and argumentation for any written or oral presentations by the United States in consultations or in proceedings of a panel or the Appellate Body regarding the matter.

(iv) If a dispute settlement panel or the Appellate Body finds that the law of a State is inconsistent with any of the Uruguay Round Agreements, the Trade Representative shall consult with the State concerned in an effort to develop a mutually agreeable response to the report of the panel or the Appellate Body and shall make every effort to ensure that the State concerned is involved in the development of the United States position regarding the response.

(D) Notice to states regarding consultations on foreign subcentral government laws.

(i) Subject to clause (ii), the Trade Representative shall, at least 30 days before making a request for consultations under Article 4 of the Dispute Settlement Understanding regarding a subcentral government measure of another member, notify, and solicit the views of, appropriate representatives of each State regarding the matter.

(ii) In exigent circumstances clause (i) shall not apply, in which case the Trade Representative shall notify the appropriate representatives of each State not later than 3 days after making the request for consultations referred to in clause (i).

(2) Legal challenge.

(A) In general.—No State law, or the application of such a State law, may be declared invalid as to any person or circumstance on the ground that the provision or application is inconsistent with any of the Uruguay Round Agreements, except in an action brought by the United States for the purpose of declaring such law or application invalid.

(B) Procedures governing action.—In any action described in subparagraph (A) that is brought by the United States against a State or any subdivision thereof

(i) a report of a dispute settlement panel or the Appellate Body convened under the Dispute Settlement Understanding regarding the State law, or the law of any political subdivision thereof, shall not be considered as binding or otherwise accorded deference;

(ii) the United States shall have the burden of proving that the law that is the subject of the action, or the application of that law, is inconsistent with the agreement in question;

(iii) any State whose interests may be impaired or impeded in the action shall have the unconditional right to intervene in the action as a party, and the United States shall be entitled to amend its complaint to include a claim or cross-claim concerning the law of a State that so intervenes; and

(iv) any State law that is declared invalid shall not be deemed to have been invalid in its application during any period before the court's judgment becomes final and all timely appeals, including discretionary review, of such judgment are exhausted.

(C) Reports to congressional committees.—At least 30 days before the United States brings an action described in subparagraph (A), the Trade Representative shall provide a report to the Committee on Ways and Means of the House of Representatives and the Committee on Finance of the Senate

(i) describing the proposed action;

(ii) describing efforts by the Trade Representative to resolve the matter with the State concerned by other means; and

(iii) if the State law was the subject of consultations under the Dispute Settlement Understanding, certifying that the Trade Representative has substantially complied with the requirements of paragraph (1)(C) in connection with the matter.

Following the submission of the report, and before the action is brought, the Trade Representative shall consult with the committees referred to in the preceding sentence concerning the matter.

(3) Definition of state law.—For purposes of this subsection

(A) the term "State law" includes

(i) any law of a political subdivision of a State; and

(ii) any State law regulating or taxing the business of insurance; and

(B) the terms "dispute settlement panel" and "Appellate Body" have the meanings given those terms in section 121.

(c) Effect of Agreement With Respect to Private Remedies.

(1) Limitations.—No person other than the United States

(A) shall have any cause of action or defense under any of the Uruguay Round Agreements or by virtue of congressional approval of such an agreement, or

(B) may challenge, in any action brought under any provision of law, any action or inaction by any department, agency, or other instrumentality of the United States, any State, or any political subdivision of a State on the ground that such action or inaction is inconsistent with such agreement.

(2) Intent of congress.—It is the intention of the Congress through paragraph (1) to occupy the field with respect to any cause of action or defense under or in connection with any of the Uruguay Round Agreements, including by precluding any person other than the United States from bringing any action against any State or political subdivision thereof or raising any defense to the application of State law under or in connection with any of the Uruguay Round Agreements

(A) on the basis of a judgment obtained by the United States in an action brought under any such agreement; or

(B) on any other basis.

(d) Statement of Administrative Action.—The statement of administrative action approved by the Congress under section 101(a) shall be regarded as an authoritative expression by the United States concerning the interpretation and application of the Uruguay Round Agreements and this Act in any judicial proceeding in which a question arises concerning such interpretation or application.

19 USC 3513

Sec. 103. Implementing Actions in Anticipation of Entry into Force; Regulations

(a) Implementing Actions.—After the date of the enactment of this Act

(1) the President may proclaim such actions, and

(2) other appropriate officers of the United States Government may issue such regulations,

as may be necessary to ensure that any provision of this Act, or amendment made by this Act, that takes effect on the date any of the Uruguay Round Agreements enters into force with respect to the United States is appropriately implemented on such date. Such proclamation or regulation may not have an effective date earlier than the date of entry into force with respect to the United States of the agreement to which the proclamation or regulation relates.

(b) Regulations.—Any interim regulation necessary or appropriate to carry out any action proposed in the statement of administrative action approved under section 101(a) to implement an agreement described in section 101(d) (7), (12), or (13) shall be issued not later than 1 year after the date on which the agreement enters into force with respect to the United States.

Subtitle B—Tariff Modifications

19 USC 3521

Sec. 111.   Tariff Modifications

(a) In General.—In addition to the authority provided by section 1102 of the Omnibus Trade and Competitiveness Act of 1988 (19 U.S.C. 2902), the President shall have the authority to proclaim

(1) such other modification of any duty,

(2) such other staged rate reduction, or

(3) such additional duties,

as the President determines to be necessary or appropriate to carry out Schedule XX.

(b) Other Tariff Modifications.—Subject to the consultation and layover requirements of section 115, the President may proclaim

(1) the modification of any duty or staged rate reduction of any duty set forth in Schedule XX if

    (A) the United States agrees to such modification or staged rate reduction in a multilateral negotiation under the auspices of the, and

    (B) such modification or staged rate reduction applies to the rate of duty on an article contained in a tariff category that was the subject of reciprocal duty elimination or harmonization negotiations during the Uruguay Round of multilateral trade negotiations, and

(2) such modifications as are necessary to correct technical errors in Schedule XX or to make other rectifications to the Schedule.

(c) Authority To Increase Duties on Articles From Certain Countries.

(1) In general.

(A) Determination with respect to certain countries.—Notwithstanding section 251 of the Trade Expansion Act of 1962 (19 U.S.C. 1881), after the entry into force of the Agreement with respect to the United States, if the President

(i) determines that a foreign country (other than a foreign country that is a member country) is not according adequate trade benefits to the United States, including substantially equal competitive opportunities for the commerce of the United States, and

(ii) consults with the Committee on Ways and Means of the House of Representatives and the Committee on Finance of the Senate,

the President may proclaim an increase in the rate of duty with respect to any article of such country in accordance with subparagraph (B).

(B) Rate of duty described.—The President may proclaim a rate of duty on any article of a country identified under subparagraph (A) that is equal to the greater of

(i) the rate of duty set forth for such article in the base rate of duty column of Schedule XX, or

(ii) the rate of duty set forth for such article in the bound rate of duty column of Schedule XX.

(2) Termination of increased duties.—The President shall terminate any increase in the rate of duty proclaimed under this subsection by a proclamation which shall be effective on the earlier of

(A) the date set out in such proclamation of termination, or

(B) the date the Agreement enters into force with respect to the foreign country with respect to which the determination under paragraph (1) was made.

(3) Publication of determination and termination.—The President shall publish in the Federal Register notice of a determination made under paragraph (1) and a termination occurring by reason of paragraph (2).

* * *

Subtitle C—Uruguay Round Implementation and Dispute Settlement

19 USC 3531

Sec. 121.   Definitions

For purposes of this subtitle:

(1) Administering authority.—The term "administering authority" has the meaning given that term in section 771(1) of the Tariff Act of 1930.

(2) Appellate body.—The term "Appellate Body" means the Appellate Body established under Article 17.1 of the Dispute Settlement Understanding.

(3) Appropriate congressional committees; congressional committees.

(A) Appropriate congressional committees.—The term "appropriate congressional committees" means the committees referred to in subparagraph (B) and any other committees of the Congress that have jurisdiction involving the matter with respect to which consultations are to be held.

(B) Congressional committees.—The term "congressional committees" means the Committee on Ways and Means of the House of Representatives and the Committee on Finance of the Senate.

(4) Dispute settlement panel; panel.—The terms "dispute settlement panel" and "panel" mean a panel established pursuant to Article 6 of the Dispute Settlement Understanding.

(5) Dispute settlement body.—The term "Dispute Settlement Body" means the Dispute Settlement Body administering the rules and procedures set forth in the Dispute Settlement Understanding.

(6) Dispute settlement understanding.—The term "Dispute Settlement Understanding" means the Understanding on Rules and Procedures Governing the Settlement of Disputes referred to in section 101(d)(16).

(7) General council.—The term "General Council" means the General Council established under paragraph 2 of Article IV of the Agreement.

(8) Ministerial conference.—The term "Ministerial Conference" means the Ministerial Conference established under paragraph 1 of Article IV of the Agreement.

(9) Other terms.—The terms "Antidumping Agreement", "Agreement on Subsidies and Countervailing Measures", and "Safeguards Agreement" mean the agreements referred to in section 101(d)(7), (12), and (13), respectively.

19 USC 3532

Sec. 122.   Implementation of Uruguay Round Agreements

(a) **Decisionmaking.**—In the implementation of the Uruguay Round Agreements and the functioning of the World Trade Organization, it is the objective of the United States to ensure that the Ministerial Conference and the General Council continue the practice of decisionmaking by consensus followed under the GATT 1947, as required by paragraph 1 of article IX of the Agreement.

(b) **Consultations With Congressional Committees**.—In furtherance of the objective set forth in subsection (a), the Trade Representative shall consult with the appropriate congressional committees before any vote is taken by the Ministerial Conference or the General Council relating to

(1) the adoption of an interpretation of the Agreement or another multilateral trade agreement,

(2) the amendment of any such agreement,

(3) the granting of a waiver of any obligation under any such agreement,

(4) the adoption of any amendment to the rules or procedures of the Ministerial Conference or the General Council,

(5) the accession of a state or separate customs territory to the Agreement, or

(6) the adoption of any other decision,

if the action described in paragraph (1), (2), (3), (4), (5), or (6) would substantially affect the rights or obligations of the United States under the Agreement or another multilateral trade agreement or potentially entails a change in Federal or State law.

(c) Report on decisions.

(1) In general.—Not later than 30 days after the end of any calendar year in which the Ministerial Conference or the General Council adopts by vote any decision to take any action described in paragraph (1), (2), (4), or (6) of subsection (b), the Trade Representative shall submit a report to the appropriate congressional committees describing

(A) the nature of the decision;

(B) the efforts made by the United States to have the matter decided by consensus pursuant to paragraph 1 of article IX of the Agreement, and the results of those efforts;

(C) which countries voted for, and which countries voted against, the decision;

(D) the rights or obligations of the United States affected by the decision and any Federal or State law that would be amended or repealed, if the President after consultation with the Congress determined that such amendment or repeal was an appropriate response; and

(E) the action the President intends to take in response to the decision or, if the President does not intend to take any action, the reasons therefor.

(2) Additional reporting requirements.

(A) Grant of waiver.—In the case of a decision to grant a waiver described in subsection (b)(3), the report under paragraph (1) shall describe the terms and conditions of the waiver and the rights and obligations of the United States that are affected by the waiver.

(B) Accession.—In the case of a decision on accession described in subsection (b)(5), the report under paragraph (1) shall state whether the United States intends to invoke Article XIII of the Agreement.

(d) Consultation on report.—Promptly after the submission of a report under subsection (c), the Trade Representative shall consult with the appropriate congressional committees with respect to the report.

19 USC 3533

Sec. 123.   Dispute Settlement Panels and Procedures

(a) Review by President.—The President shall review annually the panel roster and shall include the panel roster and the list of persons serving on the Appellate Body in the annual report submitted by the President under section 163(a) of the Trade Act of 1974.

(b) Qualifications of Appointees to Panels.—The Trade Representative shall

(1) seek to ensure that persons appointed to the panel roster are well-qualified, and that the roster includes persons with expertise in the subject areas covered by the Uruguay Round Agreements; and

(2) inform the President of persons nominated to the roster by other member countries.

(c) Rules Governing Conflicts of Interest.—The Trade Representative shall seek the establishment by the General Council and the Dispute Settlement Body of rules governing conflicts of interest by persons serving on panels and members of the Appellate Body and shall describe, in the annual report submitted under section 124, any progress made in establishing such rules.

(d) Notification of Disputes.—Promptly after a dispute settlement panel is established to consider the consistency of Federal or State law with any of the Uruguay Round Agreements, the Trade Representative shall notify the appropriate congressional committees of

(1) the nature of the dispute, including the matters set forth in the request for the establishment of the panel, the legal basis of the complaint, and the specific measures, in particular any State or Federal law cited in the request for establishment of the panel;

(2) the identity of the persons serving on the panel; and

(3) whether there was any departure from the rule of consensus with respect to the selection of persons to serve on the panel.

(e) Notice of Appeals of Panel Reports.—If an appeal is taken of a report of a panel in a proceeding described in subsection (d), the Trade Representative shall, promptly after the notice of appeal is filed, notify the appropriate congressional committees of

(1) the issues under appeal; and

(2) the identity of the persons serving on the Appellate Body who are reviewing the report of the panel.

(f) Actions upon Circulation of Reports.—Promptly after the circulation of a report of a panel or of the Appellate Body to members in a proceeding described in subsection (d), the Trade Representative shall

(1) notify the appropriate congressional committees of the report;

(2) in the case of a report of a panel, consult with the appropriate congressional committees concerning the nature of any appeal that may be taken of the report; and

(3) if the report is adverse to the United States, consult with the appropriate congressional committees concerning whether to implement the report's recommendation and, if so, the manner of such implementation and the period of time needed for such implementation.

(g) Requirements for Agency Action.

(1) Changes in agency regulations or practice.—In any case in which a dispute settlement panel or the Appellate Body finds in its report that a regulation or practice of a department or agency of the United States is inconsistent with any of the Uruguay Round Agreements, that regulation or

practice may not be amended, rescinded, or otherwise modified in the implementation of such report unless and until

(A) the appropriate congressional committees have been consulted under subsection (f);

(B) the Trade Representative has sought advice regarding the modification from relevant private sector advisory committees established under section 135 of the Trade Act of 1974 (19 U.S.C. 2155);

(C) the head of the relevant department or agency has provided an opportunity for public comment by publishing in the Federal Register the proposed modification and the explanation for the modification;

(D) the Trade Representative has submitted to the appropriate congressional committees a report describing the proposed modification, the reasons for the modification, and a summary of the advice obtained under subparagraph (B) with respect to the modification;

(E) the Trade Representative and the head of the relevant department or agency have consulted with the appropriate congressional committees on the proposed contents of the final rule or other modification; and

(F) the final rule or other modification has been published in the Federal Register.

(2) Effective date of modification.—A final rule or other modification to which paragraph (1) applies may not go into effect before the end of the 60-day period beginning on the date on which consultations under paragraph (1)(E) begin, unless the President determines that an earlier effective date is in the national interest.

(3) Vote by congressional committees.—During the 60-day period described in paragraph (2), the Committee on Ways and Means of the House of Representatives and the Committee on Finance of the Senate may vote to indicate the agreement or disagreement of the committee with the proposed contents of the final rule or other modification. Any such vote shall not be binding on the department or agency which is implementing the rule or other modification.

(4) Inapplicability to ITC.—This subsection does not apply to any regulation or practice of the International Trade Commission.

(h) Consultations Regarding Review of Rules and Procedures.—
Before the review is conducted of the dispute settlement rules and procedures of the that is provided for in the Decision on the Application of the Understanding on Rules and Procedures Governing the Settlement of Disputes, as such decision is set forth in the Ministerial Declarations and Decisions adopted on April 15, 1994, together with the Uruguay Round Agreements, the Trade Representative shall consult with the congressional committees regarding the policy of the United States concerning the review.

19 USC 3534

Sec. 124.   Annual Report on the WTO

Not later than March 1 of each year beginning in 1996, the Trade Representative shall submit to the Congress a report describing, for the preceding fiscal year of the

(1) the major activities and work programs of the, including the functions and activities of the committees established under article IV of the Agreement, and the expenditures made by the in connection with those activities and programs;

(2) the percentage of budgetary assessments by the that were accounted for by each member country, including the United States;

(3) the total number of personnel employed or retained by the Secretariat of the, and the number of professional, administrative, and support staff of the;

(4) for each personnel category described in paragraph (3), the number of citizens of each country, and the average salary of the personnel, in that category;

(5) each report issued by a panel or the Appellate Body in a dispute settlement proceeding regarding Federal or State law, and any efforts by the Trade Representative to provide for implementation of the recommendations contained in a report that is adverse to the United States;

(6) each proceeding before a panel or the Appellate Body that was initiated during that fiscal year regarding Federal or State law, the status of the proceeding, and the matter at issue;

(7) the status of consultations with any State whose law was the subject of a report adverse to the United States that was issued by a panel or the Appellate Body; and

(8) any progress achieved in increasing the transparency of proceedings of the Ministerial Conference and the General Council, and of dispute settlement proceedings conducted pursuant to the Dispute Settlement Understanding.

19 USC 3535

Sec. 125. Review of Participation in the WTO

(a) Report on the Operation of the WTO.—The first annual report submitted to the Congress under section 124

(1) after the end of the 5-year period beginning on the date on which the Agreement enters into force with respect to the United States, and

(2) after the end of every 5-year period thereafter,

shall include an analysis of the effects of the Agreement on the interests of the United States, the costs and benefits to the United States of its participation in the, and the value of the continued participation of the United States in the.

(b) Congressional Disapproval of U.S. Participation in the WTO.

(1) General rule.—The approval of the Congress, provided under section 101(a), of the Agreement shall cease to be effective if, and only if, a joint resolution described in subsection (c) is enacted into law pursuant to the provisions of paragraph (2).

(2) Procedural provisions.—(A) The requirements of this paragraph are met if the joint resolution is enacted under subsection (c), and

(i) the Congress adopts and transmits the joint resolution to the President before the end of the 90-day period (excluding any day described in section 154(b) of the Trade Act of 1974), beginning on the date on which the Congress receives a report referred to in subsection (a), and

(ii) if the President vetoes the joint resolution, each House of Congress votes to override that veto on or before the later of the last day of the 90-day period referred to in clause (i) or the last day of the 15-day period (excluding any day described in section 154(b) of the Trade Act of 1974) beginning on the date on which the Congress receives the veto message from the President.

(B) A joint resolution to which this section applies may be introduced at any time on or after the date on which the President transmits to the Congress a report described in subsection (a), and before the end of the 90-day period referred to in subparagraph (A).

(c) Joint Resolutions.

(1) Joint Resolutions.—For purposes of this section, the term "joint resolution" means only a joint resolution of the 2 Houses of Congress, the matter after the resolving clause of which is as follows: "That the Congress withdraws its approval, provided under section 101(a) of the Uruguay Round Agreements Act, of the Agreement as defined in section 2(9) of that Act.".

(2) Procedures.—(A) Joint resolutions may be introduced in either House of the Congress by any member of such House.

(B) Subject to the provisions of this subsection, the provisions of subsections (b), (d), (e), and (f) of section 152 of the Trade Act of 1974 (19 U.S.C. 2192(b), (d), (e), and (f)) apply to joint resolutions to the same extent as such provisions apply to resolutions under such section.

(C) If the committee of either House to which a joint resolution has been referred has not reported it by the close of the 45th day after its introduction (excluding any day described in section 154(b) of the Trade Act of 1974), such committee shall be automatically discharged from further consideration of the joint resolution and it shall be placed on the appropriate calendar.

(D) It is not in order for

(i) the Senate to consider any joint resolution unless it has been reported by the Committee on Finance or the committee has been discharged under subparagraph (C); or

(ii) the House of Representatives to consider any joint resolution unless it has been reported by the Committee on Ways and Means or the committee has been discharged under subparagraph (C).

(D) A motion in the House of Representatives to proceed to the consideration of a joint resolution may only be made on the second legislative day after the calendar day on which the Member making the motion announces to the House his or her intention to do so.

(3) Consideration of second resolution not in order.—It shall not be in order in either the House of Representatives or the Senate to consider a joint

resolution (other than a joint resolution received from the other House), if that House has previously adopted a joint resolution under this section.

(d) Rules of House of Representatives and Senate.—This section is enacted by the Congress

(1) as an exercise of the rulemaking power of the House of Representatives and the Senate, respectively, and as such is deemed a part of the rules of each House, respectively, and such procedures supersede other rules only to the extent that they are inconsistent with such other rules; and

(2) with the full recognition of the constitutional right of either House to change the rules (so far as relating to the procedures of that House) at any time, in the same manner, and to the same extent as any other rule of that House.

19 USC 3536

Sec. 126.   Increased Transparency

The Trade Representative shall seek the adoption by the Ministerial Conference and General Council of procedures that will ensure broader application of the principle of transparency and clarification of the costs and benefits of trade policy actions, through the observance of open and equitable procedures in trade matters by the Ministerial Conference and the General Council, and by the dispute settlement panels and the Appellate Body under the Dispute Settlement Understanding.

19 USC 3537

Sec. 127.   Access to the WTO Dispute Settlement Process

(a) In General.—Whenever the United States is a party before a dispute settlement panel established pursuant to Article 6 of the Dispute Settlement Understanding, the Trade Representative shall, at each stage of the proceeding before the panel or the Appellate Body, consult with the appropriate congressional committees, the petitioner (if any) under section 302(a) of the Trade Act of 1974 (19 U.S.C. 2412) with respect to the matter that is the subject of the proceeding, and relevant private sector advisory committees established under section 135 of the Trade Act of 1974 (19 U.S.C. 2155), and shall consider the views of representatives of appropriate interested private sector and nongovernmental organizations concerning the matter.

(b) Notice and Public Comment.—In any proceeding described in subsection (a), the Trade Representative shall

(1) promptly after requesting the establishment of a panel, or receiving a request from another member country for the establishment of a panel, publish a notice in the Federal Register

(A) identifying the initial parties to the dispute,

(B) setting forth the major issues raised by the country requesting the establishment of a panel and the legal basis of the complaint,

(C) identifying the specific measures, including any State or Federal law cited in the request for establishment of the panel, and

(D) seeking written comments from the public concerning the issues raised in the dispute; and

(2) take into account any advice received from appropriate congressional committees and relevant private sector advisory committees referred to in subsection (a), and written comments received pursuant to paragraph (1)(D), in preparing United States submissions to the panel or the Appellate Body.

(c) Access to Documents.—In each proceeding described in subsection (a), the Trade Representative shall

(1) make written submissions by the United States referred to in subsection (b) available to the public promptly after they are submitted to the panel or Appellate Body, except that the Trade Representative is authorized to withhold from disclosure any information contained in such submissions identified by the provider of the information as proprietary information or information treated as confidential by a foreign government;

(2) request each other party to the dispute to permit the Trade Representative to make that party's written submissions to the panel or the Appellate Body available to the public; and

(3) make each report of the panel or the Appellate Body available to the public promptly after it is circulated to members, and inform the public of such availability.

(d) Requests for Nonconfidential Summaries.—In any dispute settlement proceeding conducted pursuant to the Dispute Settlement Understanding, the Trade Representative shall request each party to the dispute to provide nonconfidential summaries of its written submissions, if that party has not made its written submissions public, and shall make those summaries available to the public promptly after receiving them.

(e) Public File.—The Trade Representative shall maintain a file accessible to the public on each dispute settlement proceeding to which the United States is a party that is conducted pursuant to the Dispute Settlement Understanding. The file shall include all United States submissions in the proceeding and a listing of any submissions to the Trade Representative from the public with respect to the proceeding, as well as the report of the dispute settlement panel and the report of the Appellate Body.

* * *

19 USC 3538

Sec. 129.   Administrative Action Following WTO Panel Reports

(a) Action by United States International Trade Commission.

(1) Advisory report.—If a dispute settlement panel finds in an interim report under Article 15 of the Dispute Settlement Understanding, or the Appellate Body finds in a report under Article 17 of that Understanding, that an action by the International Trade Commission in connection with a particular proceeding is not in conformity with the obligations of the United States under the Antidumping Agreement, the Safeguards Agreement, or the Agreement on Subsidies and Countervailing Measures, the Trade Representative may request the Commission to issue an advisory report on whether title

VII of the Tariff Act of 1930 or title II of the Trade Act of 1974, as the case may be, permits the Commission to take steps in connection with the particular proceeding that would render its action not inconsistent with the findings of the panel or the Appellate Body concerning those obligations. The Trade Representative shall notify the congressional committees of such request.

(2) Time limits for report.—The Commission shall transmit its report under paragraph (1) to the Trade Representative

(A) in the case of an interim report described in paragraph (1), within 30 calendar days after the Trade Representative requests the report; and

(B) in the case of a report of the Appellate Body, within 21 calendar days after the Trade Representative requests the report.

(3) Consultations on request for commission determination.—If a majority of the Commissioners issues an affirmative report under paragraph (1), the Trade Representative shall consult with the congressional committees concerning the matter.

(4) Commission determination.—Notwithstanding any provision of the Tariff Act of 1930 or title II of the Trade Act of 1974, if a majority of the Commissioners issues an affirmative report under paragraph (1), the Commission, upon the written request of the Trade Representative, shall issue a determination in connection with the particular proceeding that would render the Commission's action described in paragraph (1) not inconsistent with the findings of the panel or Appellate Body. The Commission shall issue its determination not later than 120 days after the request from the Trade Representative is made.

(5) Consultations on implementation of commission determination.—The Trade Representative shall consult with the congressional committees before the Commission's determination under paragraph (4) is implemented.

(6) Revocation of order.—If, by virtue of the Commission's determination under paragraph (4), an antidumping or countervailing duty order with respect to some or all of the imports that are subject to the action of the Commission described in paragraph (1) is no longer supported by an affirmative Commission determination under title VII of the Tariff Act of 1930 or this subsection, the Trade Representative may, after consulting with the congressional committees under paragraph (5), direct the administering authority to revoke the antidumping or countervailing duty order in whole or in part.

(7) Modification of action under title ii of trade act of 1974.—Section 204(b) of the Trade Act of 1974 (19 U.S.C. 2254(b)) is amended by adding at the end the following new paragraph:

"(3) Notwithstanding paragraph (1), the President may, after receipt of a Commission determination under section 129(a)(4) of the Uruguay Round Agreements Act and consulting with the Committee on Ways and Means of the House of Representatives and the Committee on Finance of the Senate, reduce, modify, or terminate action taken under section 203.".

(b) Action by Administering Authority.

(1) Consultations with administering authority and congressional committees.—Promptly after a report by a dispute settlement panel or the Appellate body is issued that contains findings that an action by the administering authority in a proceeding under title VII of the Tariff Act of 1930 is not in conformity with the obligations of the United States under the Antidumping Agreement or the Agreement on Subsidies and Countervailing Measures, the Trade Representative shall consult with the administering authority and the congressional committees on the matter.

(2) Determination by administering authority.—Notwithstanding any provision of the Tariff Act of 1930, the administering authority shall, within 180 days after receipt of a written request from the Trade Representative, issue a determination in connection with the particular proceeding that would render the administering authority's action described in paragraph (1) not inconsistent with the findings of the panel or the Appellate Body.

(3) Consultations before implementation.—Before the administering authority implements any determination under paragraph (2), the Trade Representative shall consult with the administering authority and the congressional committees with respect to such determination.

(4) Implementation of determination.—The Trade Representative may, after consulting with the administering authority and the congressional committees under paragraph (3), direct the administering authority to implement, in whole or in part, the determination made under paragraph (2).

(c) Effects of Determinations; Notice of Implementation.

(1) Effects of determinations.—Determinations concerning title VII of the Tariff Act of 1930 that are implemented under this section shall apply with respect to unliquidated entries of the subject merchandise (as defined in section 771 of that Act) that are entered, or withdrawn from warehouse, for consumption on or after

(A) in the case of a determination by the Commission under subsection (a)(4), the date on which the Trade Representative directs the administering authority under subsection (a)(6) to revoke an order pursuant to that determination, and

(B) in the case of a determination by the administering authority under subsection (b)(2), the date on which the Trade Representative directs the administering authority under subsection (b)(4) to implement that determination.

(2) Notice of implementation.

(A) The administering authority shall publish in the Federal Register notice of the implementation of any determination made under this section with respect to title VII of the Tariff Act of 1930.

(B) The Trade Representative shall publish in the Federal Register notice of the implementation of any determination made under this section with respect to title II of the Trade Act of 1974.

(d) Opportunity for Comment by Interested Parties.—Prior to

issuing a determination under this section, the administering authority or the Commission, as the case may be, shall provide interested parties with an opportunity to submit written comments and, in appropriate cases, may hold a hearing, with respect to the determination.

* * *

Subtitle D—Related Provisions

19 USC 3551

Sec. 131. Working Party on Worker Rights

(a) **In general**.—The President shall seek the establishment in the GATT 1947, and, upon entry into force of the Agreement with respect to the United States, in the, of a working party to examine the relationship of internationally recognized worker rights, as defined in section 502(a)(4) of the Trade Act of 1974, to the articles, objectives, and related instruments of the GATT 1947 and of the, respectively.

(b) **Objectives of Working Party**.—The objectives of the United States for the working party described in subsection (a) are to

(1) explore the linkage between international trade and internationally recognized worker rights, as defined in section 502(a)(4) of the Trade Act of 1974, taking into account differences in the level of development among countries;

(2) examine the effects on international trade of the systematic denial of such rights;

(3) consider ways to address such effects; and

(4) develop methods to coordinate the work program of the working party with the International Labor Organization.

(c) **Report to Congress**.—The President shall report to the Congress, not later than 1 year after the date of the enactment of this Act, on the progress made in establishing the working party under this section, and on United States objectives with respect to the working party's work program.

19 USC 3555

Sec. 135. Objectives for Extended Negotiations

(a) **Trade in Financial Services**.—The principal negotiating objective of the United States in the extended negotiations on financial services to be conducted under the auspices of the is to seek to secure commitments, from a wide range of commercially important developed and developing countries, to reduce or eliminate barriers to the supply of financial services, including barriers that deny national treatment or market access by restricting the establishment or operation of financial services providers, as the condition for the United States

(1) offering commitments to provide national treatment and market access in each of the financial services subsectors, and

(2) making such commitments on a normal trade relations basis.

(b) **Trade in Basic Telecommunications Services**.—The principal negotiating objective of the United States in the extended negotiations on basic telecommunications services to be conducted under the auspices of the is to obtain the opening on nondiscriminatory terms and conditions of foreign markets for basic telecommunications services through facilities-based competition or through the resale of services on existing networks.

(c) Trade in civil aircraft.

(1) Negotiations.—The principal negotiating objectives of the United States in the extended negotiations on trade in civil aircraft to be conducted under the auspices of the are

    (A) to obtain competitive opportunities for United States exports in foreign markets substantially equivalent to those afforded to foreign products in the United States;

    (B) to obtain the reduction or elimination of specific tariff and nontariff barriers, including through expanded membership in the Agreement on Trade in Civil Aircraft and in the US-EC bilateral agreement for large civil aircraft,

    (C) to maintain vigorous and effective disciplines on subsidies practices with respect to civil aircraft products under the Agreement on Subsidies and Countervailing Measures referred to in section 101(d)(12),

    (D) to maintain the scope and coverage on indirect support as specified in the US-EC bilateral agreement on large civil aircraft, and

    (E) to obtain increased transparency with respect to foreign subsidy programs in the civil aircraft sector, both through greater government disclosure with respect to the use of taxpayer moneys and higher financial disclosure standards for companies receiving government supports (including disclosure comparable to that required under United States securities laws).

* * *

PART 4—ENFORCEMENT OF UNITED STATES RIGHTS UNDER THE SUBSIDIES AGREEMENT

19 USC 3571

Sec. 281. Subsidies Enforcement

(a) Assistance Regarding Multilateral Subsidy Remedies.—The administering authority shall provide information to the public upon request, and, to the extent feasible, assistance and advice to interested parties concerning

(1) remedies and benefits available under relevant provisions of the Subsidies Agreement, and

(2) the procedures relating to such remedies and benefits.

(b) Prohibited Subsidies.

(1) Notification of trade representative.—If the administering authority determines pursuant to title VII of the Tariff Act of 1930 that a class or kind of merchandise is benefiting from a subsidy which is prohibited under Article 3 of the Subsidies Agreement, the administering authority shall notify the Trade Representative and shall provide the Trade Representative with the information upon which the administering authority based its determination.

(2) Request by interested party regarding prohibited subsidy.—An interested party may request that the administering authority determine if there is reason to believe that merchandise produced in a member country is benefiting from a subsidy which is prohibited under Article 3 of the Subsidies Agreement. The request shall contain such information as the administering authority may require to support the allegations contained in the request. If the administering authority, after analyzing the request and other information reasonably available to the administering authority, determines that there is reason to believe that such merchandise is benefiting from a subsidy which is prohibited under Article 3 of the Subsidies Agreement, the administering authority shall so notify the Trade Representative, and shall include supporting information with the notification.

(c) Subsidies Actionable Under the Agreement

(1) In general.—If the administering authority determines pursuant to title VII of the Tariff Act of 1930 that a class or kind of merchandise is benefiting from a subsidy described in Article 6.1 of the Subsidies Agreement, the administering authority shall notify the Trade Representative, and shall provide the Trade Representative with the information upon which the administering authority based its determination.

(2) Request by interested party regarding adverse effects.—An interested party may request the administering authority to determine if there is reason to believe that a subsidy which is actionable under the Subsidies Agreement is causing adverse effects. The request shall contain such information as the administering authority may require to support the allegations contained in the request. At the request of the administering authority, the Commission shall assist the administering authority in analyzing the information pertaining to the existence of such adverse effects. If the administering authority, after analyzing the request and other information reasonably available to the administering authority, determines that there is reason to believe that a subsidy which is actionable under the Subsidies Agreement is causing adverse effects, the administering authority shall so notify the Trade Representative, and shall include supporting information with the notification.

(d) Initiation of Section 301 Investigation.—On the basis of the notification and information provided by the administering authority pursuant to subsection (b) or (c), such other information as the Trade Representative may have or obtain, and where applicable, after consultation with an interested party referred to in subsection (b)(2) or (c)(2), the Trade Representative shall, unless such interested party objects, determine as expeditiously as possible, in accordance with the procedures in section 302(b)(1) of the Trade Act of 1974 (19 U.S.C. 2412(b)(1)), whether to initiate an investigation pursuant to title III of that Act (19 U.S.C. 2411 et seq.). At the request of the Trade Representative, the administering authority and the Commission shall assist the Trade Representative in an investigation initiated pursuant to this subsection.

(e) Nonactionable Subsidies.

(1) Compliance with article 8 of the subsidies agreement.

(A) Monitoring.—In order to monitor whether a subsidy meets the conditions and criteria described in Article 8.2 of the Subsidies Agreement and is nonactionable, the Trade Representative shall provide the administering authority on a timely basis with any information submitted or report made pursuant to Article 8.3 or 8.4 of the Subsidies Agreement regarding a notified subsidy program. The administering authority shall review such information and reports, and where appropriate, shall recommend to the Trade Representative that the Trade Representative seek pursuant to Article 8.3 or 8.4 of the Subsidies Agreement additional information regarding the notified subsidy program or a subsidy granted pursuant to the notified subsidy program. If the administering authority has reason to believe that a violation of Article 8 of the Subsidies Agreement exists, the administering authority shall so notify the Trade Representative, and shall include supporting information with the notification.

(B) Request by interested party regarding violation of article 8.—An interested party may request the administering authority to determine if there is reason to believe that a violation of Article 8 of the Subsidies Agreement exists. The request shall contain such information as the administering authority may require to support the allegations contained in the request. If the administering authority, after analyzing the request and other information reasonably available to the administering authority, determines that additional information is needed, the administering authority shall recommend to the Trade Representative that the Trade Representative seek, pursuant to Article 8.3 or 8.4 of the Subsidies Agreement, additional information regarding the particular notified subsidy program or a subsidy granted pursuant to the notified subsidy program. If the administering authority determines that there is reason to believe that a violation of Article 8 of the Subsidies Agreement exists, the administering authority shall so notify the Trade Representative, and shall include supporting information with the notification.

(C) Action by trade representative.

(i) If the Trade Representative, on the basis of the notification and information provided by the administering authority pursuant to subparagraph (A) or (B), and such other information as the Trade Representative may have or obtain, and after consulting with the interested party referred to in subparagraph (B) and appropriate domestic industries, determines that there is reason to believe that a violation of Article 8 of the Subsidies Agreement exists, the Trade Representative shall invoke the procedures of Article 8.4 or 8.5 of the Subsidies Agreement.

(ii) For purposes of clause (i), the Trade Representative shall determine that there is reason to believe that a violation of Article 8 exists in any case in which the Trade Representative determines that a notified subsidy program or a subsidy granted pursuant to a notified subsidy program does not satisfy the conditions and criteria required for a nonactionable subsidy program under this Act, the Subsidies Agreement, and the statement of administrative action approved under section 101(a).

(D) Notification of administering authority.—The Trade Representative shall notify the administering authority whenever a violation of

Article 8 of the Subsidies Agreement has been found to exist pursuant to Article 8.4 or 8.5 of that Agreement.

(2) Serious adverse effects.

(A) Request by interested party.—An interested party may request the administering authority to determine if there is reason to believe that serious adverse effects resulting from a program referred to in Article 8.2 of the Subsidies Agreement exist. The request shall contain such information as the administering authority may require to support the allegations contained in the request.

(B) Action by administering authority.—Within 90 days after receipt of the request described in subparagraph (A), the administering authority, after analyzing the request and other information reasonably available to the administering authority, shall determine if there is reason to believe that serious adverse effects resulting from a program referred to in Article 8.2 of the Subsidies Agreement exist. If the determination of the administering authority is affirmative, it shall so notify the Trade Representative and shall include supporting information with the notification. The Commission shall assist the administering authority in analyzing the information pertaining to the existence of such serious adverse effects if the administering authority requests the Commission's assistance. If the subsidy program that is alleged to result in serious adverse effects has been the subject of a countervailing duty investigation or review under subtitle A or C of title VII of the Tariff Act of 1930, the administering authority shall take into account the determinations made by the administering authority and the Commission in such investigation or review and the administering authority shall complete its analysis as expeditiously as possible.

(C) Action by trade representative.—The Trade Representative, on the basis of the notification and information provided by the administering authority pursuant to subparagraph (B), and such other information as the Trade Representative may have or obtain, shall determine as expeditiously as possible, but not later than 30 days after receipt of the notification provided by the administering authority, if there is reason to believe that serious adverse effects exist resulting from the subsidy program which is the subject of the administering authority's notification. The Trade Representative shall make an affirmative determination regarding the existence of such serious adverse effects unless the Trade Representative finds that the notification of the administering authority is not supported by the facts.

(D) Consultations.—If the Trade Representative determines that there is reason to believe that serious adverse effects resulting from the subsidy program exist, the Trade Representative, unless the interested party referred to in subparagraph (A) objects, shall invoke the procedures of Article 9 of the Subsidies Agreement, and shall request consultations pursuant to Article 9.2 of the Subsidies Agreement with respect to such serious adverse effects. If such consultations have not resulted in a mutually acceptable solution within 60 days after the request is made for such consultations, the Trade Representative shall refer the matter to the Subsidies Committee pursuant to Article 9.3 of the Subsidies Agreement.

(E) Determination by subsidies committee.—If the Trade Representative determines that

(i) the Subsidies Committee has been prevented from making an affirmative determination regarding the existence of serious adverse effects under Article 9 of the Subsidies Agreement by reason of the refusal of the member country with respect to which the consultations have been invoked to join in an affirmative consensus

(I) that such serious adverse effects exist, or

(II) regarding a recommendation to such member country to modify the subsidy program in such a way as to remove the serious adverse effects, or

(ii) the Subsidies Committee has not presented its conclusions regarding the existence of such serious adverse effects within 120 days after the date the matter was referred to it, as required by Article 9.4 of the Subsidies Agreement, the Trade Representative shall, within 30 days after such determination, make a determination under section 304(a)(1) of the Trade Act of 1974 (19 U.S.C. 2414(a)(1)) regarding what action to take under section 301(a)(1)(A) of that Act.

(F) Noncompliance with committee recommendation.—In the event that the Subsidies Committee makes a recommendation under Article 9.4 of the Subsidies Agreement and the member country with respect to which such recommendation is made does not comply with such recommendation within 6 months after the date of the recommendation, the Trade Representative shall make a determination under section 304(a)(1) of the Trade Act of 1974 (19 U.S.C. 2414(a)(1)) regarding what action to take under section 301(a) of that Act.

(f) Notification, Consultation, and Publication.

(1) Notification of congress.—The Trade Representative shall submit promptly to the Committee on Ways and Means of the House of Representatives, the Committee on Finance of the Senate, and other appropriate committees of the Congress any information submitted or report made pursuant to Article 8.3 or 8.4 of the Subsidies Agreement regarding a notified subsidy program.

(2) Publication in the federal register.—The administering authority shall publish regularly in the Federal Register a summary notice of any information submitted or report made pursuant to Article 8.3 or 8.4 of the Subsidies Agreement regarding notified subsidy programs.

(3) Consultations with congress and private sector.—The Trade Representative and the administering authority promptly shall consult with the committees referred to in paragraph (1), and with interested representatives of the private sector, regarding all information submitted or reports made pursuant to Article 8.3 or 8.4 of the Subsidies Agreement regarding a notified subsidy program.

(4) Annual report.—Not later than February 1 of each year beginning in 1996, the Trade Representative and the administering authority shall issue a joint report to the Congress detailing

(A) the subsidies practices of major trading partners of the United States, including subsidies that are prohibited, are causing serious prejudice, or are nonactionable, under the Subsidies Agreement, and

(B) the monitoring and enforcement activities of the Trade Representative and the administering authority during the preceding calendar year which relate to subsidies practices.

(g) Cooperation of Other Agencies.—All agencies, departments, and independent agencies of the Federal Government shall cooperate fully with one another in carrying out the provisions of this section, and, upon the request of the administering authority, shall furnish to the administering authority all records, papers, and information in their possession which relate to the requirements of this section.

(h) Definitions.—For purposes of this section

(1) Adverse effects.—The term "adverse effects" has the meaning given that term in Articles 5(a) and 5(c) of the Subsidies Agreement.

(2) Administering authority.—The term "administering authority" has the meaning given that term in section 771(1) of the Tariff Act of 1930 (19 U.S.C. 1677(1)).

(3) Commission.—The term "Commission" means the United States International Trade Commission.

(4) Interested party.—The term "interested party" means a party described in subparagraph (C), (D), (E), (F), or (G) of section 771(9) of the Tariff Act of 1930 (19 U.S.C. 1677(9), (C), (D), (E), (F), or (G)).

(5) Nonactionable subsidy.—The term "nonactionable subsidy" means a subsidy described in Article 8.1(b) of the Subsidies Agreement.

(6) Notified subsidy program.—The term "notified subsidy program" means a subsidy program which has been notified pursuant to Article 8.3 of the Subsidies Agreement.

(7) Serious adverse effects.—The term "serious adverse effects" has the meaning given that term in Article 9.1 of the Subsidies Agreement.

(8) Subsidies agreement.—The term "Subsidies Agreement" means the Agreement on Subsidies and Countervailing Measures described in section 771(8) of the Tariff Act of 1930 (19 U.S.C. 1677(8)).

(9) Subsidies committee.—The term "Subsidies Committee" means the committee established pursuant to Article 24 of the Subsidies Agreement.

(10) Subsidy.—The term "subsidy" has the meaning given that term in Article 1 of the Subsidies Agreement.

(11) Trade representative.—The term "Trade Representative" means the United States Trade Representative.

(12) Violation of article 8.—The term "violation of Article 8" means the failure of a notified subsidy program or an individual subsidy granted pursuant to a notified subsidy program to meet the applicable conditions and criteria described in Article 8.2 of the Subsidies Agreement.

(i) Treatment of Proprietary Information.—Notwithstanding any other provision of law, the administering authority may provide the Trade

Representative with a copy of proprietary information submitted to, or obtained by, the administering authority that the Trade Representative considers relevant in carrying out its responsibilities under this part. The Trade Representative shall protect from public disclosure proprietary information obtained from the administering authority under this part.

19 USC 3572

Sec. 282. Review of Subsidies Agreement

(a) General Objectives.—The general objectives of the United States under this part are

(1) to ensure that parts II and III of the Agreement on Subsidies and Countervailing Measures referred to in section 101(d)(12) (hereafter in this section referred to as the "Subsidies Agreement") are effective in disciplining the use of subsidies and in remedying the adverse effects of subsidies, and

(2) to ensure that part IV of the Subsidies Agreement does not undermine the benefits derived from any other part of that Agreement.

(b) Specific Objective.—The specific objective of the United States under this part shall be to create a mechanism which will provide for an ongoing review of the operation of part IV of the Subsidies Agreement.

(c) Sunset of Noncountervailable Subsidies Provisions.

(1) In general.—Subparagraphs (B), (C), (D), and (E) of section 771(5B) of the Tariff Act of 1930 shall cease to apply as provided in subparagraph (G)(i) of such section, unless, before the date referred to in such subparagraph (G)(i)

(A) the Subsidies Committee determines to extend Articles 6.1, 8, and 9 of the Subsidies Agreement as in effect on the date on which the Subsidies Agreement enters into force or in a modified form, in accordance with Article 31 of such Agreement,

(B) the President consults with the Congress in accordance with paragraph (2), and

(C) an implementing bill is submitted and enacted into law in accordance with paragraphs (3) and (4).

(2) Consultation with congress before subsidies committee agrees to extend.—Before a determination is made by the Subsidies Committee to extend Articles 6.1, 8, and 9 of the Subsidies Agreement, the President shall consult with the Committee on Ways and Means of the House of Representatives and the Committee on Finance of the Senate regarding such extension.

(3) Implementation of extension.

(A) Notification and submission.—Any extension of subparagraphs (B), (C), (D), and (E) of section 771(5B) of the Tariff Act of 1930 shall take effect if (and only if)

(i) after the Subsidies Committee determines to extend Articles 6.1, 8, and 9 of the Subsidies Agreement, the President submits to the committees referred to in paragraph (2) a copy of the document describing the terms of such extension, together with

(I) a draft of an implementing bill,

(II) a statement of any administrative action proposed to implement the extension, and

(III) the supporting information described in subparagraph (C); and

(ii) the implementing bill is enacted into law.

(B) Implementing bill.—The implementing bill referred to in subparagraph (A) shall contain only those provisions that are necessary or appropriate to implement an extension of the provisions of section 771(5B) (B), (C), (D), and (E) of the Tariff Act of 1930 as in effect on the day before the date of the enactment of the implementing bill or as modified to reflect the determination of the Subsidies Committee to extend Articles 6.1, 8, and 9 of the Subsidies Agreement.

(C) Supporting information.—The supporting information required under subparagraph (A)(i)(III) consists of

(i) an explanation as to how the implementing bill and proposed administrative action will change or affect existing law; and

(ii) a statement regarding

(I) how the extension serves the interests of United States commerce, and

(II) why the implementing bill and proposed administrative action is required or appropriate to carry out the extension. * * *

(5) Report by the trade representative.—Not later than the date referred to in section 771 (5B) (G)(i) of the Tariff Act of 1930, the Trade Representative shall submit to the Congress a report setting forth the provisions of law which were enacted to implement Articles 6.1, 8, and 9 of the Subsidies Agreement and should be repealed or modified if such provisions are not extended.

(d) Review of the Operation of the Subsidies Agreement.—The Secretary of Commerce, in consultation with other appropriate departments and agencies of the Federal Government, shall undertake an ongoing review of the operation of the Subsidies Agreement. The review shall address

(1) the effectiveness of part II of the Subsidies Agreement in disciplining the use of subsidies which are prohibited under Article 3 of the Agreement,

(2) the effectiveness of part III and, in particular, Article 6.1 of the Subsidies Agreement, in remedying the adverse effects of subsidies which are actionable under the Agreement, and

(3) the extent to which the provisions of part IV of the Subsidies Agreement may have undermined the benefits derived from other parts of the Agreement, and, in particular

(A) the extent to which member countries have cooperated in reviewing and improving the operation of part IV of the Subsidies Agreement,

(B) the extent to which the provisions of Articles 8.4 and 8.5 of the Subsidies Agreement have been effective in identifying and remedying violations of the conditions and criteria described in Article 8.2 of the Agreement, and

(C) the extent to which the provisions of Article 9 of the Subsidies Agreement have been effective in remedying the serious adverse effects of subsidy programs described in Article 8.2 of the Agreement.

Not later than 4 years and 6 months after the date of the enactment of this Act, the Secretary of Commerce shall submit to the Congress a report on the review required under this subsection.

Item 53

UNITED STATES: INTERNATIONAL EMERGENCY ECONOMIC POWERS ACT

(Selected provisions, as amended)

PUBLIC LAW 95–223, APPROVED DECEMBER 28, 1977, 91 STAT. 1625

An Act with respect to the powers of the President in time of war or national emergency.

Be it enacted by the Senate and House of Representatives of the United States of America in Congress assembled.

TITLE I

AMENDMENTS TO THE TRADING WITH THE ENEMY ACT

REMOVAL OF NATIONAL EMERGENCY POWERS UNDER THE TRADING WITH THE ENEMY ACT

Sec. 101. (a) Section 5(b)(1) of the Trading With the Enemy Act is amended by striking out "or during any other period of national emergency declared by the President" in the text preceding subparagraph (A).

(b) Notwithstanding the amendment made by subsection (a), the authorities conferred upon the President by section 5(b) of the Trading With the Enemy Act, which were being exercised with respect to a country on July 1, 1977, as a result of a national emergency declared by the President before such date, may continue to be exercised with respect to such country, except that, unless extended, the exercise of such authorities shall terminate (subject to the savings provisions of the second sentence of section 101(a) of the National Emergencies Act) at the end of the two-year period beginning on the date of enactment of the National Emergencies Act. The President may extend the exercise of such authorities for one-year periods upon a determination for each such extension that the exercise of such authorities with respect to such country for another year is in the national interest of the United States.

(c) The termination and extension provisions of subsection (b) of this section supersede the provisions of section 101(a) and of title II of the National Emergencies Act to the extent that the provisions of subsection (b) of this section are inconsistent with those provisions.

(d) Paragraph (1) of section 502(a) of the National Emergencies Act is repealed.

Wartime Authorities [omitted]

TITLE II

INTERNATIONAL EMERGENCY ECONOMIC POWERS

Short Title

50 USC 1701 note

Sec. 201.   This title may be cited as the "International Emergency Economic Powers Act".

Situations in Which Authorities May Be Exercised

50 USC 1701

Sec. 202.   (a) Any authority granted to the President by section 203 may be exercised to deal with any unusual and extraordinary threat, which has its source in whole or substantial part outside the United States, to the national security, foreign policy, or economy of the United States, if the President declares a national emergency with respect to such threat.

(b) The authorities granted to the President by section 203 may only be exercised to deal with an unusual and extraordinary threat with respect to which a national emergency has been declared for purposes of this title and may not be exercised for any other purpose. Any exercise of such authorities to deal with any new threat shall be based on a new declaration of national emergency which must be with respect to such threat.

50 USC 1702

Sec. 203.   Presidential Authorities

(a) (1) At the times and to the extent specified in section 202, the President may, under such regulations as he may prescribe, by means of instructions, licenses, or otherwise—

(A) investigate, regulate, or prohibit—

(i) any transactions in foreign exchange,

(ii) transfers of credit or payments between, by, through, or to any banking institution, to the extent that such transfers or payments involve any interest of any foreign country or a national thereof,

(iii) the importing or exporting of currency or securities,

by any person, or with respect to any property, subject to the jurisdiction of the United States;

(B) investigate, block during the pendency of an investigation, regulate, direct and compel, nullify, void, prevent or prohibit, any acquisition, holding, withholding, use, transfer, withdrawal, transportation, importation or exportation of, or dealing in, or exercising any right, power, or privilege with respect to, or transactions involving, any property in which any foreign country or a national thereof has any interest by any person, or with respect to any property, subject to the jurisdiction of the United States; and

Item 53   US: INT'L EMERGENCY ECONOMIC POWERS ACT   **1209**

(C) when the United States is engaged in armed hostilities or has been attacked by a foreign country or foreign nationals, confiscate any property, subject to the jurisdiction of the United States, of any foreign person, foreign organization, or foreign country that he determines has planned, authorized, aided, or engaged in such hostilities or attacks against the United States; and all right, title, and interest in any property so confiscated shall vest, when, as, and upon the terms directed by the President, in such agency or person as the President may designate from time to time, and upon such terms and conditions as the President may prescribe, such interest or property shall be held, used, administered, liquidated, sold, or otherwise dealt with in the interest of and for the benefit of the United States, and such designated agency or person may perform any and all acts incident to the accomplishment or furtherance of these purposes.

(2) In exercising the authorities granted by paragraph (1), the President may require any person to keep a full record of, and to furnish under oath, in the form of reports or otherwise, complete information relative to any act or transaction referred to in paragraph (1) either before, during, or after the completion thereof, or relative to any interest in foreign property, or relative to any property in which any foreign country or any national thereof has or has had any interest, or as may be otherwise necessary to enforce the provisions of such paragraph. In any case in which a report by a person could be required under this paragraph, the President may require the production of any books of account, records, contracts, letters, memoranda, or other papers, in the custody or control of such person.

(3) Compliance with any regulation, instruction, or direction issued under this title shall to the extent thereof be a full acquittance and discharge for all purposes of the obligation of the person making the same. No person shall be held liable in any court for or with respect to anything done or omitted in good faith in connection with the administration of, or pursuant to and in reliance on, this title, or any regulation, instruction, or direction issued under this title.

(b) The authority granted to the President by this section does not include the authority to regulate or prohibit, directly or indirectly—

(1) any postal, telegraphic, telephonic, or other personal communication, which does not involve a transfer of anything of value;

(2) donations, by persons subject to the jurisdiction of the United States, of articles, such as food, clothing, and medicine, intended to be used to relieve human suffering, except to the extent that the President determines that such donations (A) would seriously impair his ability to deal with any national emergency declared under section 202 of this title (B) are in response to coercion against the proposed recipient or donor, or (C) would endanger Armed Forces of the United States which are engaged in hostilities or are in a situation where imminent involvement in hostilities is clearly indicated by the circumstances; [or]

(3) the importation from any country, or the exportation to any country, whether commercial or otherwise, regardless of format or medium of transmission, of any information or informational materials, including but not limited to, publications, films, posters, phonograph records, photographs,

microfilms, microfiche, tapes, compact disks, CD ROMs, artworks, and news wire feeds. The exports exempted from regulation or prohibition by this paragraph do not include those which are otherwise controlled for export under section 5 of the Export Administration Act of 1979, or under section 6 of such Act to the extent that such controls promote the nonproliferation or antiterrorism policies of the United States, or with respect to which acts are prohibited by chapter 37 of title 18, United States Code; or

(4) any transactions ordinarily incident to travel to or from any country, including importation of accompanied baggage for personal use, maintenance within any country including payment of living expenses and acquisition of goods or services for personal use, and arrangement or facilitation of such travel including nonscheduled air, sea, or land voyages.

(c) Classified information. In any judicial review of a determination made under this section, if the determination was based on classified information (as defined in section 1(a) of the Classified Information Procedures Act) such information may be submitted to the reviewing court ex parte and in camera. This subsection does not confer or imply any right to judicial review.

50 USC 1703

Sec. 204.   Consultation and Reports

(a) Consultation with Congress. The President, in every possible instance, shall consult with the Congress before exercising any of the authorities granted by this title and shall consult regularly with the Congress so long as such authorities are exercised.

(b) Report to Congress upon exercise of Presidential authorities. Whenever the President exercises any of the authorities granted by this title, he shall immediately transmit to the Congress a report specifying—

(1) the circumstances which necessitate such exercise of authority;

(2) why the President believes those circumstances constitute an unusual and extraordinary threat, which has its source in whole or substantial part outside the United States, to the national security, foreign policy, or economy of the United States;

(3) the authorities to be exercised and the actions to be taken in the exercise of those authorities to deal with those circumstances;

(4) why the President believes such actions are necessary to deal with those circumstances; and

(5) any foreign countries with respect to which such actions are to be taken and why such actions are to be taken with respect to those countries.

(c) Periodic follow-up reports. At least once during each succeeding six-month period after transmitting a report pursuant to subsection (b) with respect to an exercise of authorities under this title, the President shall report to the Congress with respect to the actions taken, since the last such report, in the exercise of such authorities, and with respect to any changes which have occurred concerning any information previously furnished pursuant to paragraphs (1) through (5) of subsection (b).

(d) Supplemental requirements. The requirements of this section are supplemental to those contained in title IV of the National Emergencies Act.

Authority to Issue Regulations

50 USC 1704

Sec. 205. The President may issue such regulations, including regulations prescribing definitions, as may be necessary for the exercise of the authorities granted by this title.

50 USC 1705

Sec. 206. Penalties

(a) A civil penalty of not to exceed $10,000 may be imposed on any person who violates, or attempts to violate, any license, order, or regulation issued under this title.

(b) Whoever willfully violates, or willfully attempts to violate, any license, order, or regulation issued under this title shall, upon conviction, be fined not more than $50,000, or, if a natural person, may be imprisoned for not more than ten years, or both; and any officer, director, or agent of any corporation who knowingly participates in such violation may be punished by a like fine, imprisonment, or both.

50 USC 1706

Sec. 207. Savings and Provisions

(a) Termination of national emergencies pursuant to National Emergencies Act.

(1) Except as provided in subsection (b), notwithstanding the termination pursuant to the National Emergencies Act of a national emergency declared for purposes of this title, any authorities granted by this title, which are exercised on the date of such termination on the basis of such national emergency to prohibit transactions involving property in which a foreign country or national thereof has any interest, may continue to be so exercised to prohibit transactions involving that property if the President determines that the continuation of such prohibition with respect to that property is necessary on account of claims involving such country or its nationals.

(2) Notwithstanding the termination of the authorities described in section 101(b) of this Act, any such authorities, which are exercised with respect to a country on the date of such termination to prohibit transactions involving any property in which such country or any national thereof has any interest, may continue to be exercised to prohibit transactions involving that property if the President determines that the continuation of such prohibition with respect to that property is necessary on account of claims involving such country or its nationals.

(b) Congressional termination of national emergencies by concurrent resolution. The authorities described in subsection (a)(1) may not continue to be exercised under this section if the national emergency is terminated by the Congress by concurrent resolution pursuant to section 202 of the National

Emergencies Act and if the Congress specifies in such concurrent resolution that such authorities may not continue to be exercised under this section.

(c) Supplemental savings provisions; supersedure of inconsistent provisions.

(1) The provisions of this section are supplemental to the savings provisions of paragraphs (1), (2), and (3) of section 101(a) and of paragraphs (A), (B), and (C) of section 202(a) of the National Emergencies Act.

(2) The provisions of this section supersede the termination provisions of section 101(a) and of title II of the National Emergencies Act to the extent that the provisions of this section are inconsistent with these provisions.

(d) Periodic reports to Congress. If the President uses the authority of this section to continue prohibitions on transactions involving foreign property interests, he shall report to the Congress every six months on the use of such authority.

50 USC 1701 note

Sec. 208. If any provision of this Act is held invalid, the remainder of the Act shall not be affected thereby.

TITLE III
AMENDMENTS TO THE EXPORT ADMINISTRATION ACT OF 1969

[omitted]

Item 54

UNITED STATES: EXPORT ADMINISTRATION ACT OF 1979

(Selected provisions, as amended)

Public Law 96–72, Approved September 29, 1979, 93 Stat. 503

Note to the Reader

Because of space constraints, we have included only brief excerpts from the Export Administration Act. The act is rather lengthy and very detailed. Indeed, both the original act and the 1985 amendments fill more than 30 pages in U.S. Statutes at Large.

50 App. USC § 2402

Sec. 3. Congressional Declaration of Policy

The Congress makes the following declarations:

(1) It is the policy of the United States to minimize uncertainties in export control policy and to encourage trade with all countries with which the United States has diplomatic or trading relations, except those countries with which such trade has been determined by the President to be against the national interest.

(2) It is the policy of the United States to use export controls only after full consideration of the impact on the economy of the United States and only to the extent necessary—

(A) to restrict the export of goods and technology which would make a significant contribution to the military potential of any other country or combination of countries which would prove detrimental to the national security of the United States;

(B) to restrict the export of goods and technology where necessary to further significantly the foreign policy of the United States or to fulfill its declared international obligations; and

(C) to restrict the export of goods where necessary to protect the domestic economy from the excessive drain of scarce materials and to reduce the serious inflationary impact of foreign demand.

(3) It is the policy of the United States (A) to apply any necessary controls to the maximum extent possible in cooperation with all nations, and (B) to encourage observance of a uniform export control policy by all nations with which the United States has defense treaty commitments or common strategic objectives.

(4) It is the policy of the United States to use its economic resources and trade potential to further the sound growth and stability of its economy as well as to further its national security and foreign policy objectives.

(5) It is the policy of the United States—

(A) to oppose restrictive trade practices or boycotts fostered or imposed by foreign countries against other countries friendly to the United States or against any United States person;

(B) to encourage and, in specified cases, require United States persons engaged in the export of goods or technology or other information to refuse to take actions, including furnishing information or entering into or implementing agreements, which have the effect of furthering or supporting the restrictive trade practices or boycotts fostered or imposed by any foreign country against a country friendly to the United States or against any United States person; and

(C) to foster international cooperation and the development of international rules and institutions to assure reasonable access to world supplies.

(6) It is the policy of the United States that the desirability of subjecting, or continuing to subject, particular goods or technology or other information to United States export controls should be subjected to review by and consultation with representatives of appropriate United States Government agencies and private industry.

(7) It is the policy of the United States to use export controls, including license fees, to secure the removal by foreign countries of restrictions on access to supplies where such restrictions have or may have a serious domestic inflationary impact, have caused or may cause a serious domestic shortage, or have been imposed for purposes of influencing the foreign policy of the United States. In effecting this policy, the President shall make reasonable and prompt efforts to secure the removal or reduction of such restrictions, policies, or actions through international cooperation and agreement before imposing export controls. No action taken in fulfillment of the policy set forth in this paragraph shall apply to the export of medicine or medical supplies.

(8) It is the policy of the United States to use export controls to encourage other countries to take immediate steps to prevent the use of their territories or resources to aid, encourage, or give sanctuary to those persons involved in directing, supporting, or participating in acts of international terrorism. To achieve this objective, the President shall make reasonable and prompt efforts to secure the removal or reduction of such assistance to international terrorists through international cooperation and agreement before imposing export controls.

(9) It is the policy of the United States to cooperate with other countries with which the United States has defense treaty commitments or common strategic objectives in restricting the export of goods and technology which would make a significant contribution to the military potential of any country or combination of countries which would prove detrimental to the security of the United States and of those countries with which the United States has defense treaty commitments or common strategic objectives, and to encourage other friendly countries to cooperate in restricting the sale of goods and technology that can harm the security of the United States.

(10) It is the policy of the United States that export trade by United States citizens be given a high priority and not be controlled except when such controls (A) are necessary to further fundamental national security, foreign policy, or short supply objectives, (B) will clearly further such objectives, and (C) are administered consistent with basic standards of due process.

(11) It is the policy of the United States to minimize restrictions on the export of agricultural commodities and products.

(12) It is the policy of the United States to sustain vigorous scientific enterprise. To do so involves sustaining the ability of scientists and other scholars freely to communicate research findings, in accordance with applicable provisions of law, by means of publication, teaching, conferences, and other forms of scholarly exchange.

(13) It is the policy of the United States to control the export of goods and substances banned or severely restricted for use in the United States in order to foster public health and safety and to prevent injury to the foreign policy of the United States as well as to the credibility of the United States as a responsible trading partner.

(14) It is the policy of the United States to cooperate with countries which are allies of the United States and countries which share common strategic objectives with the United States in minimizing dependence on imports of energy and other critical resources from potential adversaries and in developing alternative supplies of such resources in order to minimize strategic threats posed by excessive hard currency earnings derived from such resource exports by countries with policies adverse to the security interests of the United States.

* * *

50 App. USC § 2403(c)

Sec. 4(c). Foreign Availability

In accordance with the provisions of this Act, the President shall not impose export controls for foreign policy or national security purposes on the export from the United States of goods or technology which he determines are available without restriction from sources outside the United States in sufficient quantities and comparable in quality to those produced in the United States so as to render the controls ineffective in achieving their purposes, unless the President determines that adequate evidence has been presented to him demonstrating that the absence of such controls would prove detrimental to the foreign policy or national security of the United States. In complying with the provisions of this subsection, the President shall give strong emphasis to bilateral or multilateral negotiations to eliminate foreign availability. The Secretary and the Secretary of Defense shall cooperate in gathering information relating to foreign availability, including the establishment and maintenance of a jointly operated computer system.

50 App. USC § 2404

Sec. 5. National Security Controls

(a) **Authority.** (1) In order to carry out the policy set forth in section 3(2)(A) of this Act, the President may, in accordance with the provisions of this section, prohibit or curtail the export of any goods or technology subject to the jurisdiction of the United States or exported by any person subject to the jurisdiction of the United States. * * *

50 App. USC § 2405

Sec. 6.   Foreign Policy Controls

(a) Authority. (1) In order to carry out the policy set forth in paragraph (2)(B), (7), (8), or (13) of section 3 of this Act, the President may prohibit or curtail the exportation of any goods, technology, or other information subject to the jurisdiction of the United States or exported by any person subject to the jurisdiction of the United States, to the extent necessary to further significantly the foreign policy of the United States or to fulfill its declared international obligations. The authority granted by this subsection shall be exercised by the Secretary, in consultation with the Secretary of State, the Secretary of Defense, the Secretary of Agriculture, the Secretary of the Treasury, the United States Trade Representative, and such other departments and agencies as the Secretary considers appropriate, and shall be implemented by means of export licenses issued by the Secretary.

(2) Any export control imposed under this section shall apply to any transaction or activity undertaken with the intent to evade that export control, even if that export control would not otherwise apply to that transaction or activity.

(3) Export controls maintained for foreign policy purposes shall expire on December 31, 1979, or one year after imposition, whichever is later, unless extended by the President in accordance with subsections (b) and (f). Any such extension and any subsequent extension shall not be for a period of more than one year.

(4) Whenever the Secretary denies any export license under this subsection, the Secretary shall specify in the notice to the applicant of the denial of such license that the license was denied under the authority contained in this subsection, and the reasons for such denial, with reference to the criteria set forth in subsection (b) of this section. The Secretary shall also include in such notice what, if any, modifications in or restrictions on the goods or technology for which the license was sought would allow such export to be compatible with controls implemented under this section, or the Secretary shall indicate in such notice which officers and employees of the Department of Commerce who are familiar with the application will be made reasonably available to the applicant for consultation with regard to such modifications or restrictions, if appropriate.

(5) In accordance with the provisions of section 10 of this Act, the Secretary of State shall have the right to review any export license application under this section which the Secretary of State requests to review.

(6) Before imposing, expanding, or extending export controls under this section on exports to a country which can use goods, technology, or information available from foreign sources and so incur little or no economic costs as a result of the controls, the President should, through diplomatic means, employ alternatives to export controls which offer opportunities of distinguishing the United States from, and expressing the displeasure of the United

States with, the specific actions of that country in response to which the controls are proposed. Such alternatives include private discussions with foreign leaders, public statements in situations where private diplomacy is unavailable or not effective, withdrawal of ambassadors, and reduction of the size of the diplomatic staff that the country involved is permitted to have in the United States.

(b) Criteria. (1) Subject to paragraph (2) of this subsection, the President may impose, extend, or expand export controls under this section only if the President determines that—

(A) such controls are likely to achieve the intended foreign policy purpose, in light of other factors, including the availability from other countries of the goods or technology proposed for such controls, and that foreign policy purpose cannot be achieved through negotiations or other alternative means;

(B) the proposed controls are compatible with the foreign policy objectives of the United States and with overall United States policy toward the country to which exports are to be subject to the proposed controls;

(C) the reaction of other countries to the imposition, extension, or expansion of such export controls by the United States is not likely to render the controls ineffective in achieving the intended foreign policy purpose or to be counterproductive to United States foreign policy interests;

(D) the effect of the proposed controls on the export performance of the United States, the competitive position of the United States in the international economy, the international reputation of the United States as a supplier of goods and technology, or on the economic well-being of individual United States companies and their employees and communities does not exceed the benefit to United States foreign policy objectives; and

(E) the United States has the ability to enforce the proposed controls effectively.

(2) With respect to those export controls in effect under this section on the date of the enactment of the Export Administration Amendments Act of 1985 [enacted July 12, 1985], the President, in determining whether to extend those controls, as required by subsection (a)(3) of this section, shall consider the criteria set forth in paragraph (1) of this subsection and shall consider the foreign policy consequences of modifying the export controls.

(c) Consultation with industry. The Secretary in every possible instance shall consult with and seek advice from affected United States industries and appropriate advisory committees established under section 135 of the Trade Act of 1974 before imposing any export control under this section. Such consultation and advice shall be with respect to the criteria set forth in subsection (b)(1) and such other matters as the Secretary considers appropriate.

(d) Consultation with other countries. When imposing export controls under this section, the President shall, at the earliest appropriate opportunity, consult with the countries with which the United States maintains export controls cooperatively, and with such other countries as the

President considers appropriate, with respect to the criteria set forth in subsection (b)(1) and such other matters as the President considers appropriate.

(e) Alternative means. Before resorting to the imposition of export controls under this section, the President shall determine that reasonable efforts have been made to achieve the purposes of the controls through negotiations or other alternative means.

(f) Consultation with the Congress. (1) The President may impose or expand export controls under this section, or extend such controls as required by subsection (a)(3) of this section, only after consultation with the Congress, including the Committee on Foreign Affairs of the House of Representatives and the Committee on Banking, Housing, and Urban Affairs of the Senate.

(2) The President may not impose, expand, or extend export controls under this section until the President has submitted to the Congress a report—

(A) specifying the purpose of the controls;

(B) specifying the determinations of the President (or, in the case of those export controls described in subsection (b)(2), the considerations of the President) with respect to each of the criteria set forth in subsection (b)(1), the bases for such determinations (or considerations), and any possible adverse foreign policy consequences of the controls;

(C) describing the nature, the subjects, and the results of, or the plans for, the consultation with industry pursuant to subsection (c) and with other countries pursuant to subsection (d);

(D) specifying the nature and results of any alternative means attempted under subsection (e), or the reasons for imposing, expanding, or extending the controls without attempting any such alternative means; and

(E) describing the availability from other countries of goods or technology comparable to the goods or technology subject to the proposed export controls, and describing the nature and results of the efforts made pursuant to subsection (h) to secure the cooperation of foreign governments in controlling the foreign availability of such comparable goods or technology.

Such report shall also indicate how such controls will further significantly the foreign policy of the United States or will further its declared international obligations.

* * *

(h) Foreign availability. (1) In applying export controls under this section, the President shall take all feasible steps to initiate and conclude negotiations with appropriate foreign governments for the purpose of securing the cooperation of such foreign governments in controlling the export to countries and consignees to which the United States export controls apply of any goods or technology comparable to goods or technology controlled under this section.

(2) Before extending any export control pursuant to subsection (a)(3) of this section, the President shall evaluate the results of his actions under paragraph (1) of this subsection and shall include the results of that evaluation in his report to the Congress pursuant to subsection (f) of this section.

(3) If, within 6 months after the date on which export controls under this section are imposed or expanded, or within 6 months after the date of the enactment of the Export Administration Amendments Act of 1985 [enacted July 12, 1985] in the case of export controls in effect on such date of enactment [enacted July 12, 1985], the President's efforts under paragraph (1) are not successful in securing the cooperation of foreign governments described in paragraph (1) with respect to those export controls, the Secretary shall thereafter take into account the foreign availability of the goods or technology subject to the export controls. If the Secretary affirmatively determines that a good or technology subject to the export controls is available in sufficient quantity and comparable quality from sources outside the United States to countries subject to the export controls so that denial of an export license would be ineffective in achieving the purposes of the controls, then the Secretary shall, during the period of such foreign availability, approve any license application which is required for the export of the good or technology and which meets all requirements for such a license. The Secretary shall remove the good or technology from the list established pursuant to subsection (1) of this section if the Secretary determines that such action is appropriate.

* * *

(j) Countries supporting international terrorism. (1) A validated license shall be required for the export of goods or technology to a country if the Secretary of State has made the following determinations:

(A) The government of such country has repeatedly provided support for acts of international terrorism.

(B) The export of such goods or technology could make a significant contribution to the military potential of such country, including its military logistics capability, or would enhance the ability of such country to support acts of international terrorism.

(2) The Secretary and the Secretary of State shall notify the Committee on Foreign Affairs of the House of Representatives and the Committee on Banking, Housing, and Urban Affairs and the Committee on Foreign Relations of the Senate at least 30 days before issuing any validated license required by paragraph (1).

(3) Each determination of the Secretary of State under paragraph (1)(A), including each determination in effect on the date of the enactment of the Antiterrorism and Arms Export Amendments Act of 1989 [enacted December 12, 1989], shall be published in the Federal Register.

(4) A determination made by the Secretary of State under paragraph (1)(A) may not be rescinded unless the President submits to the Speaker of the House of Representatives and the chairman of the Committee on Banking, Housing, and Urban Affairs and the chairman of the Committee on Foreign Relations of the Senate—

(A) before the proposed rescission would take effect, a report certifying that—

(i) there has been a fundamental change in the leadership and policies of the government of the country concerned;

(ii) that government is not supporting acts of international terrorism; and

(iii) that government has provided assurances that it will not support acts of international terrorism in the future; or

(B) at least 45 days before the proposed rescission would take effect, a report justifying the rescission and certifying that—

(i) the government concerned has not provided any support for international terrorism during the preceding 6-month period; and

(ii) the government concerned has provided assurances that it will not support the acts of international terrorism in the future.

* * *

(p) Effect on existing contracts and licenses. The President may not, under this section, prohibit or curtail the export or reexport of goods, technology, or other information—

(1) in performance of a contract or agreement entered into before the date on which the President reports to the Congress, pursuant to subsection (f) of this section, his intention to impose controls on the export or reexport of such goods, technology, or other information, or

(2) under a validated license or other authorization issued under this Act,

unless and until the President determines and certifies to the Congress that—

(A) a breach of the peace poses a serious and direct threat to the strategic interest of the United States,

(B) the prohibition or curtailment of such contracts, agreements, licenses, or authorizations will be instrumental in remedying the situation posing the direct threat, and

(C) the export controls will continue only so long as the direct threat persists.

* * *

(r) Expanded authority to impose controls. (1) In any case in which the President determines that it is necessary to impose controls under this section without any limitation contained in subsection (c), (d), (e), (g), (h), or (m) of this section, the President may impose those controls only if the President submits that determination to the Congress, together with a report pursuant to subsection (f) of this section with respect to the proposed controls, and only if a law is enacted authorizing the imposition of those controls.

* * *

50 App. USC § 2406

Sec. 7.   Short Supply Controls

(a) Authority. (1) In order to carry out the policy set forth in section 3(2)(C) of this Act, the President may prohibit or curtail the export of any goods subject to the jurisdiction of the United States or exported by any person subject to the jurisdiction of the United States. In curtailing exports to carry out the policy set forth in section 3(2)(C) of this Act, the President shall allocate a portion of export licenses on the basis of factors other than a prior history of exportation. Such factors shall include the extent to which a country engages in equitable trade practices with respect to United States goods and treats the United States equitably in times of short supply.

* * *

(3) In imposing export controls under this section, the President's authority shall include, but not be limited to, the imposition of export license fees.

* * *

(g)(3)(A) If the President imposes export controls on any agricultural commodity in order to carry out the policy set forth in paragraph (2)(B), (2)(C), (7), or (8) of section 3 of this Act, the President shall immediately transmit a report on such action to the Congress, setting forth the reasons for the controls in detail and specifying the period of time, which may not exceed 1 year, that the controls are proposed to be in effect. If the Congress, within 60 days after the date of its receipt of the report, adopts a joint resolution pursuant to paragraph (4) approving the imposition of the export controls, then such controls shall remain in effect for the period specified in the report, or until terminated by the President, whichever occurs first. If the Congress, within 60 days after the date of its receipt of such report, fails to adopt a joint resolution approving such controls, then such controls shall cease to be effective upon the expiration of that 60-day period.

(B) The provisions of subparagraph (A) and paragraph (4) shall not apply to export controls—

(i) which are extended under this Act if the controls, when imposed, were approved by the Congress under subparagraph (A) and paragraph (4); or

(ii) which are imposed with respect to a country as part of the prohibition or curtailment of all exports to that country.

* * *

50 App. USC § 2415

Sec. 16.   Definitions

As used in this Act—

(1) the term "person" includes the singular and the plural and any individual, partnership, corporation, or other form of association, including any government or agency thereof;

(2) the term "United States person" means any United States resident or national (other than an individual resident outside the United States and employed by other than a United States person), any domestic concern (including any permanent domestic establishment of any foreign concern) and any foreign subsidiary or affiliate (including any permanent foreign establishment) of any domestic concern which is controlled in fact by such domestic concern, as determined under regulations of the President;

(3) the term "good" means any article, natural or manmade substance, material, supply or manufactured product, including inspection and test equipment, and excluding technical data;

(4) the term "technology" means the information and know-how (whether in tangible form, such as models, prototypes, drawings, sketches, diagrams, blueprints, or manuals, or in intangible form, such as training or technical services) that can be used to design, produce, manufacture, utilize, or reconstruct goods, including computer software and technical data, but not the goods themselves;

(5) the term "export" means—

(A) an actual shipment, transfer, or transmission of goods or technology out of the United States;

(B) a transfer of goods or technology in the United States to an embassy or affiliate of a controlled country; or

(C) a transfer to any person of goods or technology either within the United States or outside of the United States with the knowledge or intent that the goods or technology will be shipped, transferred, or transmitted to an unauthorized recipient;

(6) the term "controlled country" means a controlled country under section 5(b)(1) of this Act;

(7) the term "United States" means the States of the United States, the District of Columbia, and any commonwealth, territory, dependency, or possession of the United States, and includes the Outer Continental Shelf, as defined in section 2(a) of the Outer Continental Shelf Lands Act (43 U.S.C. 1331(a)); and

(8) the term "Secretary" means the Secretary of Commerce.

Item 55

U.S. DEPARTMENT OF COMMERCE, REGULA-
TIONS APPLICABLE TO ANTIDUMPING
AND COUNTERVAILING DUTY CASES

19 C.F.R. Part 351

§ 351.401 In General

(a) Introduction. In general terms, an antidumping analysis involves a comparison of export price or constructed export price in the United States with normal value in the foreign market. This section establishes certain general rules that apply to the calculation of export price, constructed export price and normal value. (See section 772, section 773, and section 773A of the Act.)

(b) Adjustments in general. In making adjustments to export price, constructed export price, or normal value, the Secretary will adhere to the following principles:

(1) The interested party that is in possession of the relevant information has the burden of establishing to the satisfaction of the Secretary the amount and nature of a particular adjustment; and

(2) The Secretary will not double-count adjustments.

(c) Use of price net of price adjustments. In calculating export price, constructed export price, and normal value (where normal value is based on price), the Secretary will use a price that is net of any price adjustment, as defined in § 351.102(b), that is reasonably attributable to the subject merchandise or the foreign like product (whichever is applicable).

(d) Delayed payment or pre-payment of expenses. Where cost is the basis for determining the amount of an adjustment to export price, constructed export price, or normal value, the Secretary will not factor in any delayed payment or pre-payment of expenses by the exporter or producer.

(e) Adjustments for movement expenses—

(1) Original place of shipment. In making adjustments for movement expenses to establish export price or constructed export price under section 772(c)(2)(A) of the Act, or normal value under section 773(a)(6)(B)(ii) of the Act, the Secretary normally will consider the production facility as being the "original place of shipment. However, where the Secretary bases export price, constructed export price, or normal value on a sale by an unaffiliated reseller, the Secretary may treat the original place from which the reseller shipped the merchandise as the "original place of shipment."

(2) Warehousing. The Secretary will consider warehousing expenses that are incurred after the subject merchandise or foreign like product leaves the original place of shipment as movement expenses.

(f) Treatment of affiliated producers in antidumping proceedings—

(1) In general. In an antidumping proceeding under this part, the Secretary will treat two or more affiliated producers as a single entity where those producers have production facilities for similar or identical products that would not require substantial retooling of either facility in order to restructure manufacturing priorities and the Secretary concludes that there is a significant potential for the manipulation of price or production.

(2) Significant potential for manipulation. In identifying a significant potential for the manipulation of price or production, the factors the Secretary may consider include:

(i) The level of common ownership;

(ii) The extent to which managerial employees or board members of one firm sit on the board of directors of an affiliated firm; and

(iii) Whether operations are intertwined, such as through the sharing of sales information, involvement in production and pricing decisions, the sharing of facilities or employees, or significant transactions between the affiliated producers.

(g) Allocation of expenses and price adjustments—

(1) In general. The Secretary may consider allocated expenses and price adjustments when transaction-specific reporting is not feasible, provided the Secretary is satisfied that the allocation method used does not cause inaccuracies or distortions.

(2) Reporting allocated expenses and price adjustments. Any party seeking to report an expense or a price adjustment on an allocated basis must demonstrate to the Secretary's satisfaction that the allocation is calculated on as specific a basis as is feasible, and must explain why the allocation methodology used does not cause inaccuracies or distortions.

(3) Feasibility. In determining the feasibility of transaction-specific reporting or whether an allocation is calculated on as specific a basis as is feasible, the Secretary will take into account the records maintained by the party in question in the ordinary course of its business, as well as such factors as the normal accounting practices in the country and industry in question and the number of sales made by the party during the period of investigation or review.

(4) Expenses and price adjustments relating to merchandise not subject to the proceeding. The Secretary will not reject an allocation method solely because the method includes expenses incurred, or price adjustments made, with respect to sales of merchandise that does not constitute subject merchandise or a foreign like product (whichever is applicable).

(h) Treatment of subcontractors ("tolling" operations). The Secretary will not consider a toller or subcontractor to be a manufacturer or producer where the toller or subcontractor does not acquire ownership, and does not control the relevant sale, of the subject merchandise or foreign like product.

(i) Date of sale. In identifying the date of sale of the subject merchandise or foreign like product, the Secretary normally will use the date of invoice, as recorded in the exporter or producer's records kept in the ordinary course of business. However, the Secretary may use a date other than the date of invoice if the Secretary is satisfied that a different date better reflects the date on which the exporter or producer establishes the material terms of sale.

§ 351.402   Calculation of export price and constructed export price; reimbursement of antidumping and countervailing duties

(a) Introduction. In order to establish export price, constructed export price, and normal value, the Secretary must make certain adjustments to the price to the unaffiliated purchaser (often called the "starting price") in both the United States and foreign markets. This regulation clarifies how the Secretary will make certain of the adjustments to the starting price in the United States that are required by section 772 of the Act.

(b) Additional adjustments to constructed export price. In establishing constructed export price under section 772(d) of the Act, the Secretary will make adjustments for expenses associated with commercial activities in the United States that relate to the sale to an unaffiliated purchaser, no matter where or when paid. The Secretary will not make an adjustment for any expense that is related solely to the sale to an affiliated importer in the United States, although the Secretary may make an adjustment to normal value for such expenses under section 773(a)(6)(C)(iii) of the Act.

(c) Special rule for merchandise with value added after importation—

(1) Merchandise imported by affiliated persons. In applying section 772(e) of the Act, merchandise imported by and value added by a person affiliated with the exporter or producer includes merchandise imported and value added for the account of such an affiliated person.

(2) Estimation of value added. The Secretary normally will determine that the value added in the United States by the affiliated person is likely to exceed substantially the value of the subject merchandise if the Secretary estimates the value added to be at least 65 percent of the price charged to the first unaffiliated purchaser for the merchandise as sold in the United States. The Secretary normally will estimate the value added based on the difference between the price charged to the first unaffiliated purchaser for the merchandise as sold in the United States and the price paid for the subject merchandise by the affiliated person. The Secretary normally will base this determination on averages of the prices and the value added to the subject merchandise.

(3) Determining dumping margins. For purposes of determining dumping margins under paragraphs (1) and (2) of section 772(e) of the Act, the Secretary may use the weighted-average dumping margins calculated on sales of identical or other subject merchandise sold to unaffiliated persons.

(d) Special rule for determining profit. This paragraph sets forth rules for calculating profit in establishing constructed export price under section 772(f) of the Act.

(1) Basis for total expenses and total actual profit. In calculating total expenses and total actual profit, the Secretary normally will use the aggregate of expenses and profit for all subject merchandise sold in the United States and all foreign like products sold in the exporting country, including sales that have been disregarded as being below the cost of production. (See section 773(b) of the Act (sales at less than cost of production).)

(2) Use of financial reports. For purposes of determining profit under section 772(d)(3) of the Act, the Secretary may rely on any appropriate financial reports, including public, audited financial statements, or equivalent financial reports, and internal financial reports prepared in the ordinary course of business.

(3) Voluntary reporting of costs of production. The Secretary will not require the reporting of costs of production solely for purposes of determining the amount of profit to be deducted from the constructed export price. The Secretary will base the calculation of profit on costs of production if such costs are reported voluntarily by the date established by the Secretary, and provided that it is practicable to do so and the costs of production are verifiable.

(e) Treatment of payments between affiliated persons. Where a person affiliated with the exporter or producer incurs any of the expenses deducted from constructed export price under section 772(d) of the Act and is reimbursed for such expenses by the exporter, producer or other affiliate, the Secretary normally will make an adjustment based on the actual cost to the affiliated person. If the Secretary is satisfied that information regarding the actual cost to the affiliated person is unavailable to the exporter or producer, the Secretary may determine the amount of the adjustment on any other reasonable basis, including the amount of the reimbursement to the affiliated person if the Secretary is satisfied that such amount reflects the amount usually paid in the market under consideration.

(f) Reimbursement of antidumping duties and countervailing duties—

(1) In general.

(i) In calculating the export price (or the constructed export price), the Secretary will deduct the amount of any antidumping duty or countervailing duty which the exporter or producer:

(A) Paid directly on behalf of the importer; or

(B) Reimbursed to the importer.

(ii) The Secretary will not deduct the amount of any antidumping duty or countervailing duty paid or reimbursed if the exporter or producer granted to the importer before initiation of the antidumping investigation in question a warranty of nonapplicability of antidumping duties or countervailing duties with respect to subject merchandise which was:

(A) Sold before the date of publication of the Secretary's order applicable to the merchandise in question; and

(B) Exported before the date of publication of the Secretary's final antidumping determination.

(iii) Ordinarily, under paragraph (f)(1)(i) of this section, the Secretary will deduct the amount reimbursed only once in the calculation of the export price (or constructed export price).

(2) Certificate. The importer must file prior to liquidation a certificate in the following form with the appropriate District Director of Customs:

I hereby certify that I (have) (have not) entered into any agreement or understanding for the payment or for the refunding to me, by the manufacturer, producer, seller, or exporter, of all or any part of the antidumping duties or countervailing duties assessed upon the following importations of (commodity) from (country): (List entry numbers) which have been purchased on or after (date of publication of antidumping notice suspending liquidation in the Federal Register) or purchased before (same date) but exported on or after (date of final determination of sales at less than fair value).

(3) Presumption. The Secretary may presume from an importer's failure to file the certificate required in paragraph (f)(2) of this section that the exporter or producer paid or reimbursed the antidumping duties or countervailing duties.

§ 351.403 Sales used in calculating normal value; transactions between affiliated parties

(a) Introduction. This section clarifies when the Secretary may use offers for sale in determining normal value. Additionally, this section clarifies the authority of the Secretary to use sales to or through an affiliated party as a basis for normal value. (See section 773(a)(5) of the Act (indirect sales or offers for sale).)

(b) Sales and offers for sale. In calculating normal value, the Secretary normally will consider offers for sale only in the absence of sales and only if the Secretary concludes that acceptance of the offer can be reasonably expected.

(c) Sales to an affiliated party. If an exporter or producer sold the foreign like product to an affiliated party, the Secretary may calculate normal value based on that sale only if satisfied that the price is comparable to the price at which the exporter or producer sold the foreign like product to a person who is not affiliated with the seller.

(d) Sales through an affiliated party. If an exporter or producer sold the foreign like product through an affiliated party, the Secretary may calculate normal value based on the sale by such affiliated party. However, the Secretary normally will not calculate normal value based on the sale by an affiliated party if sales of the foreign like product by an exporter or producer to affiliated parties account for less than five percent of the total value (or quantity) of the exporter's or producer's sales of the foreign like product in the market in question or if sales to the affiliated party are comparable, as defined in paragraph (c) of this section.

§ 351.404 Selection of the market to be used as the basis for normal value

(a) Introduction. Although in most circumstances sales of the foreign like product in the home market are the most appropriate basis for determining normal value, section 773 of the Act also permits use of sales to a third country or constructed value as the basis for normal value. This section clarifies the rules for determining the basis for normal value.

(b) Determination of viable market—(1) In general. The Secretary will consider the exporting country or a third country as constituting a viable market if the Secretary is satisfied that sales of the foreign like product in that country are of sufficient quantity to form the basis of normal value.

(2) Sufficient quantity. "Sufficient quantity" normally means that the aggregate quantity (or, if quantity is not appropriate, value) of the foreign like product sold by an exporter or producer in a country is 5 percent or more of the aggregate quantity (or value) of its sales of the subject merchandise to the United States.

(c) Calculation of price-based normal value in viable market—

(1) In general. Subject to paragraph (c)(2) of this section:

(i) If the exporting country constitutes a viable market, the Secretary will calculate normal value on the basis of price in the exporting country (see section 773(a)(1)(B)(i) of the Act (price used for determining normal value)); or

(ii) If the exporting country does not constitute a viable market, but a third country does constitute a viable market, the Secretary may calculate normal value on the basis of price to a third country (see section 773(a)(1)(B)(ii) of the Act (use of third country prices in determining normal value)).

(2) Exception. The Secretary may decline to calculate normal value in a particular market under paragraph (c)(1) of this section if it is established to the satisfaction of the Secretary that:

(i) In the case of the exporting country or a third country, a particular market situation exists that does not permit a proper comparison with the export price or constructed export price (see section 773(a)(1)(B)(ii)(III) or section 773(a)(1)(C)(iii) of the Act); or

(ii) In the case of a third country, the price is not representative (see section 773(a)(1)(B)(ii)(I) of the Act).

(d) Allegations concerning market viability and the basis for determining a price-based normal value. In an antidumping investigation or review, allegations regarding market viability or the exceptions in paragraph (c)(2) of this section, must be filed, with all supporting factual information, in accordance with § 351.301(d)(1).

(e) Selection of third country. For purposes of calculating normal value based on prices in a third country, where prices in more than one third country satisfy the criteria of section 773(a)(1)(B)(ii) of the Act and this section, the Secretary generally will select the third country based on the following criteria:

(1) The foreign like product exported to a particular third country is more similar to the subject merchandise exported to the United States than is the foreign like product exported to other third countries;

(2) The volume of sales to a particular third country is larger than the volume of sales to other third countries;

(3) Such other factors as the Secretary considers appropriate.

(f) Third country sales and constructed value. The Secretary normally will calculate normal value based on sales to a third country rather than on constructed value if adequate information is available and verifiable (see section 773(a)(4) of the Act (use of constructed value)).

§ 351.405   Calculation of normal value based on constructed value

(a) Introduction. In certain circumstances, the Secretary may determine normal value by constructing a value based on the cost of manufacture, selling general and administrative expenses, and profit. The Secretary may use constructed value as the basis for normal value where: neither the home market nor a third country market is viable; sales below the cost of production are disregarded; sales outside the ordinary course of trade, or sales the prices of which are otherwise unrepresentative, are disregarded; sales used to establish a fictitious market are disregarded; no contemporaneous sales of comparable merchandise are available; or in other circumstances where the Secretary determines that home market or third country prices are inappropriate. (See section 773(e) and section 773(f) of the Act.) This section clarifies the meaning of certain terms relating to constructed value.

(b) Profit and selling, general, and administrative expenses. In determining the amount to be added to constructed value for profit and for selling, general, and administrative expenses, the following rules will apply:

(1) Under section 773(e)(2)(A) of the Act, "foreign country" means the country in which the merchandise is produced or a third country selected by the Secretary under § 351.404(e), as appropriate.

(2) Under section 773(e)(2)(B) of the Act, "foreign country" means the country in which the merchandise is produced.

§ 351.406   Calculation of normal value if sales are made at less than cost of production

(a) Introduction. In determining normal value, the Secretary may disregard sales of the foreign like product made at prices that are less than the cost of production of that product. However, such sales will be disregarded only if they are made within an extended period of time, in substantial quantities, and are not at prices which permit recovery of costs within a reasonable period of time. (See section 773(b) of the Act.) This section clarifies the meaning of the term "extended period of time" as used in the Act.

(b) Extended period of time. The "extended period of time" under section 773(b)(1)(A) of the Act normally will coincide with the period in which the sales under consideration for the determination of normal value were made.

§ 351.407   Calculation of constructed value and cost of production

(a) Introduction. This section sets forth certain rules that are common to the calculation of constructed value and the cost of production. (See section 773(f) of the Act.)

(b) Determination of value under the major input rule. For purposes of section 773(f)(3) of the Act, the Secretary normally will determine the value of a major input purchased from an affiliated person based on the higher of:

(1) The price paid by the exporter or producer to the affiliated person for the major input;

(2) The amount usually reflected in sales of the major input in the market under consideration; or

(3) The cost to the affiliated person of producing the major input.

(c) Allocation of costs. In determining the appropriate method for allocating costs among products, the Secretary may take into account production quantities, relative sales values, and other quantitative and qualitative factors associated with the manufacture and sale of the subject merchandise and the foreign like product.

(d) Startup costs.

(1) In identifying startup operations under section 773(f)(1)(C)(ii) of the Act:

(i) "New production facilities" includes the substantially complete retooling of an existing plant. Substantially complete retooling involves the replacement of nearly all production machinery or the equivalent rebuilding of existing machinery.

(ii) A "new product" is one requiring substantial additional investment, including products which, though sold under an existing nameplate, involve the complete revamping or redesign of the product. Routine model year changes will not be considered a new product.

(iii) Mere improvements to existing products or ongoing improvements to existing facilities will not be considered startup operations.

(iv) An expansion of the capacity of an existing production line will not qualify as a startup operation unless the expansion constitutes such a major undertaking that it requires the construction of a new facility and results in a depression of production levels due to technical factors associated with the initial phase of commercial production of the expanded facilities.

(2) In identifying the end of the startup period under clauses (ii) and (iii) of section 773(f)(1)(C) of the Act:

(i) The attainment of peak production levels will not be the standard for identifying the end of the startup period, because the startup period may end well before a company achieves optimum capacity utilization.

(ii) The startup period will not be extended to cover improvements and cost reductions that may occur over the entire life cycle of a product.

(3) In determining when a producer reaches commercial production levels under section 773(f)(1)(C)(ii) of the Act:

(i) The Secretary will consider the actual production experience of the merchandise in question, measuring production on the basis of units processed.

(ii) To the extent necessary, the Secretary will examine factors in addition to those specified in section 773(f)(1)(C)(ii) of the Act, including historical data reflecting the same producer's or other producers' experiences in producing the same or similar products. A producer's projections of future volume or cost will be accorded little weight.

(4) In making an adjustment for startup operations under section 773(f)(1)(C)(iii) of the Act:

(i) The Secretary will determine the duration of the startup period on a case-by-case basis.

(ii) The difference between actual costs and the costs of production calculated for startup costs will be amortized over a reasonable period of time subsequent to the startup period over the life of the product or machinery, as appropriate.

(iii) The Secretary will consider unit production costs to be items such as depreciation of equipment and plant, labor costs, insurance, rent and lease expenses, material costs, and factory overhead. The Secretary will not consider sales expenses, such as advertising costs, or other general and administrative or non-production costs (such as general research and development costs), as startup costs.

§ 351.408   Calculation of normal value of merchandise from non-market economy countries

(a) Introduction. In identifying dumping from a nonmarket economy country, the Secretary normally will calculate normal value by valuing the nonmarket economy producers' factors of production in a market economy country. (See section 773(c) of the Act.) This section clarifies when and how this special methodology for nonmarket economies will be applied.

(b) Economic Comparability. In determining whether a country is at a level of economic development comparable to the nonmarket economy under section 773(c)(2)(B) or section 773(c)(4)(A) of the Act, the Secretary will place primary emphasis on per capita GDP as the measure of economic comparability.

(c) Valuation of Factors of Production. For purposes of valuing the factors of production, general expenses, profit, and the cost of containers, coverings, and other expenses (referred to collectively as "factors") under section 773(c)(1) of the Act the following rules will apply:

(1) Information used to value factors. The Secretary normally will use publicly available information to value factors. However, where a factor is purchased from a market economy supplier and paid for in a market economy currency, the Secretary normally will use the price paid to the market economy supplier. In those instances where a portion of the factor is purchased from a market economy supplier and the remainder from a nonmarket economy supplier, the Secretary normally will value the factor using the price paid to the market economy supplier.

(2) Valuation in a single country. Except for labor, as provided in paragraph (d)(3) of this section, the Secretary normally will value all factors in a single surrogate country.

(3) Labor. For labor, the Secretary will use regression-based wage rates reflective of the observed relationship between wages and national income in market economy countries. The Secretary will calculate the

wage rate to be applied in nonmarket economy proceedings each year. The calculation will be based on current data, and will be made available to the public.

(4) Manufacturing overhead, general expenses, and profit. For manufacturing overhead, general expenses, and profit, the Secretary normally will use non-proprietary information gathered from producers of identical or comparable merchandise in the surrogate country.

351.409 Differences in quantities

(a) Introduction. Because the quantity of merchandise sold may affect the price, in comparing export price or constructed export price with normal value, the Secretary will make a reasonable allowance for any difference in quantities to the extent the Secretary is satisfied that the amount of any price differential (or lack thereof) is wholly or partly due to that difference in quantities. (See section 773(a)(6)(C)(i) of the Act.)

(b) Sales with quantity discounts in calculating normal value. The Secretary normally will calculate normal value based on sales with quantity discounts only if:

(1) During the period examined, or during a more representative period, the exporter or producer granted quantity discounts of at least the same magnitude on 20 percent or more of sales of the foreign like product for the relevant country; or

(2) The exporter or producer demonstrates to the Secretary's satisfaction that the discounts reflect savings specifically attributable to the production of the different quantities.

(c) Sales with quantity discounts in calculating weighted-average normal value. If the exporter or producer does not satisfy the conditions of paragraph (b) of this section, the Secretary will calculate normal value based on weighted-average prices that include sales at a discount.

(d) Price lists. In determining whether a discount has been granted, the existence or lack of a published price list reflecting such a discount will not be controlling. Ordinarily, the Secretary will give weight to a price list only if, in the line of trade and market under consideration, the exporter or producer demonstrates that it has adhered to its price list.

(e) Relationship to level of trade adjustment. If adjustments are claimed for both differences in quantities and differences in level of trade, the Secretary will not make an adjustment for differences in quantities unless the Secretary is satisfied that the effect on price comparability of differences in quantities has been identified and established separately from the effect on price comparability of differences in the levels of trade.

§ 351.410 Differences in circumstances of sale

(a) Introduction. In calculating normal value the Secretary may make adjustments to account for certain differences in the circumstances of sales in the United States and foreign markets. (See section 773(a)(6)(C)(iii) of the Act.) This section clarifies certain terms used in the statute regarding circumstances of sale adjustments and describes the adjustment when commissions are paid only in one market.(b) In general. With the exception of the allowance described in paragraph (e) of this section concerning commissions paid in only one market, the Secretary will make circumstances of sale adjustments under section 773(a)(6)(C)(iii) of the Act only for direct selling expenses and assumed expenses.

(c) *Direct selling expenses.* "Direct selling expenses" are expenses, such as commissions, credit expenses, guarantees, and warranties, that result from, and bear a direct relationship to, the particular sale in question.

(d) *Assumed expenses.* Assumed expenses are selling expenses that are assumed by the seller on behalf of the buyer, such as advertising expenses.

(e) *Commissions paid in one market.* The Secretary normally will make a reasonable allowance for other selling expenses if the Secretary makes a reasonable allowance for commissions in one of the markets under considerations, and no commission is paid in the other market under consideration. The Secretary will limit the amount of such allowance to the amount of the other selling expenses incurred in the one market or the commissions allowed in the other market, whichever is less.

(f) *Reasonable allowance.* In deciding what is a reasonable allowance for any difference in circumstances of sale, the Secretary normally will consider the cost of such difference to the exporter or producer but, if appropriate, may also consider the effect of such difference on the market value of the merchandise.

§ 351.411   Differences in physical characteristics

(a) *Introduction.* In comparing United States sales with foreign market sales, the Secretary may determine that the merchandise sold in the United States does not have the same physical characteristics as the merchandise sold in the foreign market, and that the difference has an effect on prices. In calculating normal value, the Secretary will make a reasonable allowance for such differences. (See section 773(a)(6)(C)(ii) of the Act.)

(b) *Reasonable allowance.* In deciding what is a reasonable allowance for differences in physical characteristics, the Secretary will consider only differences in variable costs associated with the physical differences. Where appropriate, the Secretary may also consider differences in the market value. The Secretary will not consider differences in cost of production when compared merchandise has identical physical characteristics.

§ 351.412   Levels of trade; adjustment for difference in level of trade; constructed export price offset

(a) *Introduction.* In comparing United States sales with foreign market sales, the Secretary may determine that sales in the two markets were not made at the same level of trade, and that the difference has an effect on the comparability of the prices. The Secretary is authorized to adjust normal value to account for such a difference. (See section 773(a)(7) of the Act.)

(b) *Adjustment for difference in level of trade.* The Secretary will adjust normal value for a difference in level of trade if:

(1) The Secretary calculates normal value at a different level of trade from the level of trade of the export price or the constructed export price (whichever is applicable); and

(2) The Secretary determines that the difference in level of trade has an effect on price comparability.

(c) Identifying levels of trade and differences in levels of trade—

(1) Basis for identifying levels of trade. The Secretary will identify the level of trade based on:(i) In the case of export price, the starting price;

(ii) In the case of constructed export price, the starting price, as adjusted under section 772(d) of the Act; and

(iii) In the case of normal value, the starting price or constructed value.

(2) Differences in levels of trade. The Secretary will determine that sales are made at different levels of trade if they are made at different marketing stages (or their equivalent). Substantial differences in selling activities are a necessary, but not sufficient, condition for determining that there is a difference in the stage of marketing. Some overlap in selling activities will not preclude a determination that two sales are at different stages of marketing.

(d) Effect on price comparability—

(1) In general. The Secretary will determine that a difference in level of trade has an effect on price comparability only if it is established to the satisfaction of the Secretary that there is a pattern of consistent price differences between sales in the market in which normal value is determined:

(i) At the level of trade of the export price or constructed export price (whichever is appropriate); and

(ii) At the level of trade at which normal value is determined.

(2) Relevant sales. Where possible, the Secretary will make the determination under paragraph (d)(1) of this section on the basis of sales of the foreign like product by the producer or exporter. Where this is not possible, the Secretary may use sales of different or broader product lines, sales by other companies, or any other reasonable basis.

(e) Amount of adjustment. The Secretary normally will calculate the amount of a level of trade adjustment by:

(1) Calculating the weighted-averages of the prices of sales at the two levels of trade identified in paragraph (d), after making any other adjustments to those prices appropriate under section 773(a)(6) of the Act and this subpart;

(2) Calculating the average of the percentage differences between those weighted-average prices; and

(3) Applying the percentage difference to normal value, where it is at a different level of trade from the export price or constructed export price (whichever is applicable), after making any other adjustments to normal value appropriate under section 773(a)(6) of the Act and this subpart.

(f) Constructed export price offset—

(1) In general. The Secretary will grant a constructed export price offset only where:

(i) Normal value is compared to constructed export price;

(ii) Normal value is determined at a more advanced level of trade than the level of trade of the constructed export price; and

(iii) Despite the fact that a person has cooperated to the best of its ability, the data available do not provide an appropriate basis to determine under paragraph (d) of this section whether the difference in level of trade affects price comparability.

(2) Amount of the offset. The amount of the constructed export price offset will be the amount of indirect selling expenses included in normal value, up to the amount of indirect selling expenses deducted in determining constructed export price. In making the constructed export price offset, "indirect selling expenses" means selling expenses, other than direct selling expenses or assumed selling expenses (see § 351.410), that the seller would incur regardless of whether particular sales were made, but that reasonably may be attributed, in whole or in part, to such sales.

(3) Where data permit determination of affect on price comparability. Where available data permit the Secretary to determine under paragraph (d) of this section whether the difference in level of trade affects price comparability, the Secretary will not grant a constructed export price offset. In such cases, if the Secretary determines that price comparability has been affected, the Secretary will make a level of trade adjustment. If the Secretary determines that price comparability has not been affected, the Secretary will not grant either a level of trade adjustment or a constructed export price offset.

§ 351.413 Disregarding insignificant adjustments

Ordinarily, under section 777A(a)(2) of the Act, an "insignificant adjustment" is any individual adjustment having an ad valorem effect of less than 0.33 percent, or any group of adjustments having an ad valorem effect of less than 1.0 percent, of the export price, constructed export price, or normal value, as the case may be. Groups of adjustments are adjustments for differences in circumstances of sale under § 351.410, adjustments for differences in the physical characteristics of the merchandise under § 351.411, and adjustments for differences in the levels of trade under § 351.412.

§ 351.414 Comparison of normal value with export price (constructed export price)

(a) Introduction. The Secretary normally will average prices used as the basis for normal value and, in an investigation, prices used as the basis for export price or constructed export price as well. This section explains when and how the Secretary will average prices in making comparisons of export price or constructed export price with normal value. (See section 777A(d) of the Act.)

(b) Description of methods of comparison—

(1) Average-to-average method. The "average-to-average" method involves a comparison of the weighted average of the normal values with

the weighted average of the export prices (and constructed export prices) for comparable merchandise.

(2) Transaction-to-transaction method. The "transaction-to-transaction" method involves a comparison of the normal values of individual transactions with the export prices (or constructed export prices) of individual transactions for comparable merchandise.

(3) Average-to-transaction method. The "average-to-transaction" method involves a comparison of the weighted average of the normal values to the export prices (or constructed export prices) of individual transactions for comparable merchandise.

(c) Preferences.

(1) In an investigation, the Secretary normally will use the average-to-average method. The Secretary will use the transaction-to-transaction method only in unusual situations, such as when there are very few sales of subject merchandise and the merchandise sold in each market is identical or very similar or is custom-made.

(2) In a review, the Secretary normally will use the average-to-transaction method.

(d) Application of the average-to-average method—

(1) In general. In applying the average-to-average method, the Secretary will identify those sales of the subject merchandise to the United States that are comparable, and will include such sales in an "averaging group." The Secretary will calculate a weighted average of the export prices and the constructed export prices of the sales included in the averaging group, and will compare this weighted average to the weighted average of the normal values of such sales.

(2) Identification of the averaging group. An averaging group will consist of subject merchandise that is identical or virtually identical in all physical characteristics and that is sold to the United States at the same level of trade. In identifying sales to be included in an averaging group, the Secretary also will take into account, where appropriate, the region of the United States in which the merchandise is sold, and such other factors as the Secretary considers relevant.

(3) Time period over which weighted average is calculated. When applying the average-to-average method, the Secretary normally will calculate weighted averages for the entire period of investigation or review, as the case may be. However, when normal values, export prices, or constructed export prices differ significantly over the course of the period of investigation or review, the Secretary may calculate weighted averages for such shorter period as the Secretary deems appropriate.

(e) Application of the average-to-transaction method—

(1) In general. In applying the average-to-transaction method in a review, when normal value is based on the weighted average of sales of the foreign like product, the Secretary will limit the averaging of such prices to sales incurred during the contemporaneous month.

(2) Contemporaneous month. Normally, the Secretary will select as the contemporaneous month the first of the following which applies:

(i) The month during which the particular U.S. sale under consideration was made;

(ii) If there are no sales of the foreign like product during this month, the most recent of the three months prior to the month of the U.S. sale in which there was a sale of the foreign like product.

(iii) If there are no sales of the foreign like product during any of these months, the earlier of the two months following the month of the U.S. sale in which there was a sale of the foreign like product.

(f) Targeted dumping—

(1) In general. Notwithstanding paragraph (c)(1) of this section, the Secretary may apply the average-to-transaction method, as described in paragraph (e) of this section, in an antidumping investigation if:

(i) As determined through the use of, among other things, standard and appropriate statistical techniques, there is targeted dumping in the form of a pattern of export prices (or constructed export prices) for comparable merchandise that differ significantly among purchasers, regions, or periods of time; and

(ii) The Secretary determines that such differences cannot be taken into account using the average-to-average method or the transaction-to-transaction method and explains the basis for that determination.

(2) Limitation of average-to-transaction method to targeted dumping. Where the criteria for identifying targeted dumping under paragraph (f)(1) of this section are satisfied, the Secretary normally will limit the application of the average-to-transaction method to those sales that constitute targeted dumping under paragraph (f)(1)(i) of this section.

(3) Allegations concerning targeted dumping. The Secretary normally will examine only targeted dumping described in an allegation, filed within the time indicated in § 351.301(d)(5). Allegations must include all supporting factual information, and an explanation as to why the average-to-average or transaction-to-transaction method could not take into account any alleged price differences.

(g) Requests for information. In an investigation, the Secretary will request information relevant to the identification of averaging groups under paragraph (d)(2) of this section and to the analysis of possible targeted dumping under paragraph (f) of this section. If a response to a request for such information is such as to warrant the application of the facts otherwise available, within the meaning of section 776 of the Act and § 351.308, the Secretary may apply the average-to-transaction method to all the sales of the producer or exporter concerned.

§ 351.415   Conversion of currency

(a) In general. In an antidumping proceeding, the Secretary will convert foreign currencies into United States dollars using the rate of exchange on the date of sale of the subject merchandise.

(b) Exception. If the Secretary establishes that a currency transaction on forward markets is directly linked to an export sale under consideration, the

Secretary will use the exchange rate specified with respect to such foreign currency in the forward sale agreement to convert the foreign currency.

(c) Exchange rate fluctuations. The Secretary will ignore fluctuations in exchange rates.

(d) Sustained movement in foreign currency value. In an antidumping investigation, if there is a sustained movement increasing the value of the foreign currency relative to the United States dollar, the Secretary will allow exporters 60 days to adjust their prices to reflect such sustained movement.

§ 351.501   Scope

The provisions of this subpart E set forth rules regarding the identification and measurement of countervailable subsidies. Where this subpart E does not expressly deal with a particular type of alleged subsidy, the Secretary will identify and measure the subsidy, if any, in accordance with the underlying principles of the Act and this subpart E.

§ 351.502   Specificity of domestic subsidies

(a) Sequential analysis. In determining whether a subsidy is de facto specific, the Secretary will examine the factors contained in section 771(5A)(D)(iii) of the Act sequentially in order of their appearance. If a single factor warrants a finding of specificity, the Secretary will not undertake further analysis.

(b) Characteristics of a "group." In determining whether a subsidy is being provided to a "group" of enterprises or industries within the meaning of section 751(5A)(D) of the Act, the Secretary is not required to determine whether there are shared characteristics among the enterprises or industries that are eligible for, or actually receive, a subsidy.

(c) Integral linkage. Unless the Secretary determines that two or more programs are integrally linked, the Secretary will determine the specificity of a program under section 771(5A)(D) of the Act solely on the basis of the availability and use of the particular program in question. The Secretary may find two or more programs to be integrally linked if:

(1) The subsidy programs have the same purpose;

(2) The subsidy programs bestow the same type of benefit;

(3) The subsidy programs confer similar levels of benefits on similarly situated firms; and

(4) The subsidy programs were linked at inception.

(d) Agricultural subsidies. The Secretary will not regard a subsidy as being specific under section 771(5A)(D) of the Act solely because the subsidy is limited to the agricultural sector (domestic subsidy).

(e) Subsidies to small-and medium-sized businesses. The Secretary will not regard a subsidy as being specific under section 771(5A)(D) of the Act solely because the subsidy is limited to small firms or small-and medium-sized firms.

(f) Disaster relief. The Secretary will not regard disaster relief as being specific under section 771(5A)(D) of the Act if such relief constitutes general assistance available to anyone in the area affected by the disaster.

§ 351.503 Benefit

(a) *Specific rules.* In the case of a government program for which a specific rule for the measurement of a benefit is contained in this subpart E, the Secretary will measure the extent to which a financial contribution (or income or price support) confers a benefit as provided in that rule. For example, § 351.504(a) prescribes the specific rule for measurement of the benefit of grants.

(b) *Other subsidies.*—

(1) *In general.* For other government programs, the Secretary normally will consider a benefit to be conferred where a firm pays less for its inputs (e.g., money, a good, or a service) than it otherwise would pay in the absence of the government program, or receives more revenues than it otherwise would earn.

(2) *Exception.* Paragraph (b)(1) of this section is not intended to limit the ability of the Secretary to impose countervailing duties when the facts of a particular case establish that a financial contribution (or income or price support) has conferred a benefit, even if that benefit does not take the form of a reduction in input costs or an enhancement of revenues. When paragraph (b)(1) of this section is not applicable, the Secretary will determine whether a benefit is conferred by examining whether the alleged program or practice has common or similar elements to the four illustrative examples in sections 771(5)(E)(i) through (iv) of the Act.

(c) *Distinction from effect of subsidy.* In determining whether a benefit is conferred, the Secretary is not required to consider the effect of the government action on the firm's performance, including its prices or output, or how the firm's behavior otherwise is altered.

(d) *Varying financial contribution levels.*—

(1) *In general.* Where a government program provides varying levels of financial contributions based on different eligibility criteria, and one or more of such levels is not specific within the meaning of § 351.502, a benefit is conferred to the extent that a firm receives a greater financial contribution than the financial contributions provided at a non-specific level under the program. The preceding sentence shall apply only to the extent the Secretary determines that the varying levels of financial contributions are set forth in a statute, decree, regulation, or other official act; that the levels are clearly delineated and identifiable; and that the firm would have been eligible for the non-specific level of contributions.

(2) *Exception.* Paragraph (d)(1) of this section shall not apply where the statute specifies a commercial test for determining the benefit.

(e) *Tax consequences.* In calculating the amount of a benefit, the Secretary will not consider the tax consequences of the benefit.

§ 351.504 Grants

(a) *Benefit.* In the case of a grant, a benefit exists in the amount of the grant.

(b) Time of receipt of benefit. In the case of a grant, the Secretary normally will consider a benefit as having been received on the date on which the firm received the grant.

(c) Allocation of a grant to a particular time period. The Secretary will allocate the benefit from a grant to a particular time period in accordance with § 351.524.

§ 351.505 Loans

(a) Benefit.—

(1) In general. In the case of a loan, a benefit exists to the extent that the amount a firm pays on the government-provided loan is less than the amount the firm would pay on a comparable commercial loan(s) that the firm could actually obtain on the market. See section 771(5)(E)(ii) of the Act. In making the comparison called for in the preceding sentence, the Secretary normally will rely on effective interest rates.

(2) "Comparable commercial loan" defined.—

(i) "Comparable" defined. In selecting a loan that is "comparable" to the government-provided loan, the Secretary normally will place primary emphasis on similarities in the structure of the loans (e.g., fixed interest rate v. variable interest rate), the maturity of the loans (e.g., short-term v. long-term), and the currency in which the loans are denominated.

(ii) "Commercial" defined. In selecting a "commercial" loan, the Secretary normally will use a loan taken out by the firm from a commercial lending institution or a debt instrument issued by the firm in a commercial market. Also, the Secretary will treat a loan from a government-owned bank as a commercial loan, unless there is evidence that the loan from a government-owned bank is provided on non-commercial terms or at the direction of the government. However, the Secretary will not consider a loan provided under a government program, or a loan provided by a government-owned special purpose bank, to be a commercial loan for purposes of selecting a loan to compare with a government-provided loan.

(iii) Long-term loans. In selecting a comparable loan, if the government-provided loan is a long-term loan, the Secretary normally will use a loan the terms of which were established during, or immediately before, the year in which the terms of the government-provided loan were established.

(iv) Short-term loans. In making the comparison required under paragraph (a)(1) of this section, if the government-provided loan is a short-term loan, the Secretary normally will use an annual average of the interest rates on comparable commercial loans during the year in which the government-provided loan was taken out, weighted by the principal amount of each loan. However, if the Secretary finds that interest rates fluctuated significantly during the period of investigation or review, the Secretary will use the most appropriate interest rate based on the circumstances presented.

(3) "Could actually obtain on the market" defined.—

(i) In general. In selecting a comparable commercial loan that the recipient "could actually obtain on the market," the Secretary normally will rely on the actual experience of the firm in question in obtaining comparable commercial loans for both short-term and long-term loans.

(ii) Where the firm has no comparable commercial loans. If the firm did not take out any comparable commercial loans during the period referred to in paragraph (a)(2)(iii) or (a)(2)(iv) of this section, the Secretary may use a national average interest rate for comparable commercial loans.

(iii) Exception for uncreditworthy companies. If the Secretary finds that a firm that received a government-provided long-term loan was uncreditworthy, as defined in paragraph (a)(4) of this section, the Secretary normally will calculate the interest rate to be used in making the comparison called for by paragraph (a)(1) of this section according to the following formula:

$$i_b = [(1-q_n)(1+i_f)^n/(1-p_n)]^{1/n} - 1$$

where:

n = the term of the loan;

i_b = the benchmark interest rate for uncreditworthy companies;

i_f = the long-term interest rate that would be paid by a creditworthy company;

p_n = the probability of default by an uncreditworthy company within n years; and

q_n = the probability of default by a creditworthy company within n years.

"Default" means any missed or delayed payment of interest and/or principal, bankruptcy, receivership, or distressed exchange. For values of p_n, the Secretary will normally rely on the average cumulative default rates reported for the Caa to C-rated category of companies in Moody's study of historical default rates of corporate bond issuers. For values of q_n, the Secretary will normally rely on the average cumulative default rates reported for the Aaa to Baa-rated categories of companies in Moody's study of historical default rates of corporate bond issuers.

(4) Uncreditworthiness.—(i) In general. The Secretary will consider a firm to be uncreditworthy if the Secretary determines that, based on information available at the time of the government-provided loan, the firm could not have obtained long-term loans from conventional commercial sources. The Secretary will determine uncreditworthiness on a case-by-case basis, and may, in appropriate circumstances, focus its creditworthiness analysis on the project being financed rather than the company as a whole. In making the creditworthiness determination, the Secretary may examine, among other factors, the following:

(A) The receipt by the firm of comparable commercial long-term loans;

(B) The present and past financial health of the firm, as reflected in various financial indicators calculated from the firm's financial statements and accounts;

(C) The firm's recent past and present ability to meet its costs and fixed financial obligations with its cash flow; and

(D) Evidence of the firm's future financial position, such as market studies, country and industry economic forecasts, and project and loan appraisals prepared prior to the agreement between the lender and the firm on the terms of the loan.

(ii) Significance of long-term commercial loans. In the case of firms not owned by the government, the receipt by the firm of comparable long-term commercial loans, unaccompanied by a government-provided guarantee, will normally constitute dispositive evidence that the firm is not uncreditworthy.

(iii) Significance of prior subsidies. In determining whether a firm is uncreditworthy, the Secretary will ignore current and prior subsidies received by the firm.

(iv) Discount rate. When the creditworthiness of a firm is considered in connection with the allocation of non-recurring benefits, the Secretary will rely on information available in the year in which the government agreed to provide the subsidy conferring a non-recurring benefit.

(5) Long-term variable rate loans.—

(i) In general. In the case of a long-term variable rate loan, the Secretary normally will make the comparison called for by paragraph (a)(1) of this section by relying on a comparable commercial loan with a variable interest rate. The Secretary then will compare the variable interest rates on the comparable commercial loan and the government-provided loan for the year in which the terms of the government-provided loan were established. If the comparison shows that the interest rate on the government-provided loan was equal to or higher than the interest rate on the comparable commercial loan, the Secretary will not consider the government-provided loan as having conferred a benefit. If the comparison shows that the interest rate on the government-provided loan was lower, the Secretary will consider the government-provided loan as having conferred a benefit, and, if the other criteria for a countervailable subsidy are satisfied, will calculate the amount of the benefit in accordance with paragraph (c)(4) of this section.

(ii) Exception. If the Secretary is unable to make the comparison described in paragraph (a)(5)(i) of this section or if the comparison described in paragraph (a)(5)(i) of this section would yield an inaccurate measure of the benefit, the Secretary may modify the method described in paragraph (a)(5)(i) of this section.

(6) Allegations.—

(i) Allegation of uncreditworthiness required. Normally, the Secretary will not consider the uncreditworthiness of a firm absent a specific allegation by the petitioner that is supported by information establishing a reasonable basis to believe or suspect that the firm is uncreditworthy.

(ii) Government-owned banks. The Secretary will not investigate a loan provided by a government-owned bank absent a specific allegation that is supported by information reasonably available to petitioners indicating that:

(A) The loan meets the specificity criteria in accordance with section 771(5A) of the Act; and

(B) A benefit exists within the meaning of paragraph (a)(1) of this section.

(b) Time of receipt of benefit. In the case of loans described in paragraphs (c)(1), (c)(2), and (c)(4) of this section, the Secretary normally will consider a benefit as having been received in the year in which the firm otherwise would have had to make a payment on the comparable commercial loan. In the case of a loan described in paragraph (c)(3) of this section, the Secretary normally will consider the benefit as having been received in the year in which the firm receives the proceeds of the loan.

(c) Allocation of benefit to a particular time period.—

(1) Short-term loans. The Secretary will allocate (expense) the benefit from a short-term loan to the year(s) in which the firm is due to make interest payments on the loan. In no event may the present value (in the year of receipt of the loan) of the amounts calculated under the preceding sentence exceed the principal of the loan.

(2) Long-term fixed-rate loans with concessionary interest rates. Except as provided in paragraph (c)(3) of this section, the Secretary normally will calculate the subsidy amount to be assigned to a particular year by calculating the difference in interest payments for that year, i.e., the difference between the interest paid by the firm in that year on the government-provided loan and the interest the firm would have paid on the comparison loan. However, in no event may the present value (in the year of receipt of the loan) of the amounts calculated under the preceding sentence exceed the principal of the loan.

(3) Long-term fixed-rate loans with different repayment schedules.—

(i) Calculation of present value of benefit. Where the government-provided loan and the loan to which it is compared under paragraph (a) of this section are both long-term, fixed-interest rate loans, but have different grace periods or maturities, or where the shapes of the repayment schedules differ, the Secretary will determine the total benefit by calculating the present value, in the year that repayment would begin on the comparable commercial loan, of the difference between the amount that the firm is to pay on the government-provided loan and the amount that the firm would have paid on the comparison loan. In no event may the total benefit calculated under the preceding sentence exceed the principal of the loan.

(ii) Calculation of annual benefit. With respect to the benefit calculated under paragraph (c)(3)(i) of this section, the Secretary will determine the portion of that benefit to be assigned to a particular year by using the formula set forth in § 351.524(d)(1) and the following parameters:

A_k = the amount countervailed in year k,

y = the present value of the benefit (see paragraph (c)(3)(i) of this section),

n = the number of years in the life of the loan,

d = the interest rate on the comparison loan selected under paragraph (a) of this section, and

k = the year of allocation, where the year that repayment would begin on the comparable commercial loan = 1.

(4) Long-term variable interest rate loans. In the case of a government-provided long-term variable-rate loan, the Secretary normally will determine the amount of the benefit attributable to a particular year by calculating the difference in payments for that year, i.e., the difference between the amount paid by the firm in that year on the government-provided loan and the amount the firm would have paid on the comparison loan. However, in no event may the present value (in the year of receipt of the loan) of the amounts calculated under the preceding sentence exceed the principal of the loan.

(d) Contingent liability interest-free loans.—

(1) Treatment as loans. In the case of an interest-free loan, for which the repayment obligation is contingent upon the company taking some future action or achieving some goal in fulfillment of the loan's requirements, the Secretary normally will treat any balance on the loan outstanding during a year as an interest-free, short-term loan in accordance with paragraphs (a), (b), and (c)(1) of this section. However, if the event upon which repayment of the loan depends will occur at a point in time more than one year after the receipt of the contingent liability loan, the Secretary will use a long-term interest rate as the benchmark in accordance with paragraphs (a), (b), and (c)(2) of this section. In no event may the present value (in the year of receipt of the contingent liability loan) of the amounts calculated under this paragraph exceed the principal of the loan.

(2) Treatment as grants. If, at any point in time, the Secretary determines that the event upon which repayment depends is not a viable contingency, the Secretary will treat the outstanding balance of the loan as a grant received in the year in which this condition manifests itself.

§ 351.506 Loan Guarantees

(a) Benefit.—

(1) In general. In the case of a loan guarantee, a benefit exists to the extent that the total amount a firm pays for the loan with the government-provided guarantee is less than the total amount the firm would pay for a comparable commercial loan that the firm could actually obtain on

the market absent the government-provided guarantee, including any difference in guarantee fees. See section 771(5)(E)(iii) of the Act. The Secretary will select a comparable commercial loan in accordance with § 351.505(a).

(2) Government acting as owner. In situations where a government, acting as the owner of a firm, provides a loan guarantee to that firm, the guarantee does not confer a benefit if the respondent provides evidence demonstrating that it is normal commercial practice in the country in question for shareholders to provide guarantees to their firms under similar circumstances and on comparable terms.

(b) Time of receipt of benefit. In the case of a loan guarantee, the Secretary normally will consider a benefit as having been received in the year in which the firm otherwise would have had to make a payment on the comparable commercial loan.

(c) Allocation of benefit to a particular time period. In allocating the benefit from a government-provided loan guarantee to a particular time period, the Secretary will use the methods set forth in § 351.505(c) regarding loans.

§ 351.507   Equity

(a) Benefit.—

(1) In general. In the case of a government-provided equity infusion, a benefit exists to the extent that the investment decision is inconsistent with the usual investment practice of private investors, including the practice regarding the provision of risk capital, in the country in which the equity infusion is made. See section 771(5)(E)(i) of the Act.

(2) Private investor prices available.—

(i) In general. Except as provided in paragraph (a)(2)(iii) of this section, the Secretary will consider an equity infusion as being inconsistent with usual investment practice (see paragraph (a)(1) of this section) if the price paid by the government for newly issued shares is greater than the price paid by private investors for the same (or similar form of) newly issued shares.

(ii) Timing of private investor prices. In selecting a private investor price under paragraph (a)(2)(i) of this section, the Secretary will rely on sales of newly issued shares made reasonably concurrently with the newly issued shares purchased by the government.

(iii) Significant private sector participation required. The Secretary will not use private investor prices under paragraph (a)(2)(i) of this section if the Secretary concludes that private investor purchases of newly issued shares are not significant.

(iv) Adjustments for "similar" form of equity. Where the Secretary uses private investor prices for a form of shares that is similar to the newly issued shares purchased by the government (see paragraph (a)(2)(i) of this section), the Secretary, where appropriate, will adjust the prices to reflect the differences in the forms of shares.

(3) *Actual private investor prices unavailable.* If actual private investor prices are not available under paragraph (a)(2) of this section, the Secretary will determine whether the firm funded by the government-provided equity was equityworthy or unequityworthy at the time of the equity infusion (see paragraph (a)(4) of this section). If the Secretary determines that the firm was equityworthy, the Secretary will apply paragraph (a)(5) of this section to determine whether the equity infusion was inconsistent with the usual investment practice of private investors. A determination by the Secretary that the firm was unequityworthy will constitute a determination that the equity infusion was inconsistent with usual investment practice of private investors, and the Secretary will apply paragraph (a)(6) of this section to measure the benefit attributable to the equity infusion.

(4) *Equityworthiness.*—

(i) *In general.* The Secretary will consider a firm to have been equityworthy if the Secretary determines that, from the perspective of a reasonable private investor examining the firm at the time the government-provided equity infusion was made, the firm showed an ability to generate a reasonable rate of return within a reasonable period of time. The Secretary may, in appropriate circumstances, focus its equityworthiness analysis on a project rather than the company as a whole. In making the equityworthiness determination, the Secretary may examine the following factors, among others:

(A) Objective analyses of the future financial prospects of the recipient firm or the project as indicated by, inter alia, market studies, economic forecasts, and project or loan appraisals prepared prior to the government-provided equity infusion in question;

(B) Current and past indicators of the recipient firm's financial health calculated from the firm's statements and accounts, adjusted, if appropriate, to conform to generally accepted accounting principles;

(C) Rates of return on equity in the three years prior to the government equity infusion; and

(D) Equity investment in the firm by private investors.

(ii) *Significance of a pre-infusion objective analysis.* For purposes of making an equityworthiness determination, the Secretary will request and normally require from the respondents the information and analysis completed prior to the infusion, upon which the government based its decision to provide the equity infusion (see, paragraph (a)(4)(i)(A) of this section). Absent the existence or provision of an objective analysis, containing information typically examined by potential private investors considering an equity investment, the Secretary will normally determine that the equity infusion received provides a countervailable benefit within the meaning of paragraph (a)(1) of this section. The Secretary will not necessarily make such a determination if the absence of an objective analysis is consistent with the actions of reasonable private investors in the country in question.

(iii) Significance of prior subsidies. In determining whether a firm was equityworthy, the Secretary will ignore current and prior subsidies received by the firm.

(5) Benefit where firm is equityworthy. If the Secretary determines that the firm or project was equityworthy (see paragraph (a)(4) of this section), the Secretary will examine the terms and the nature of the equity purchased to determine whether the investment was otherwise inconsistent with the usual investment practice of private investors. If the Secretary determines that the investment was inconsistent with usual private investment practice, the Secretary will determine the amount of the benefit conferred on a case-by-case basis.

(6) Benefit where firm is unequityworthy. If the Secretary determines that the firm or project was unequityworthy (see paragraph (a)(4) of this section), a benefit to the firm exists in the amount of the equity infusion.

(7) Allegations. The Secretary will not investigate an equity infusion in a firm absent a specific allegation by the petitioner which is supported by information establishing a reasonable basis to believe or suspect that the firm received an equity infusion that provides a countervailable benefit within the meaning of paragraph (a)(1) of this section.

(b) Time of receipt of benefit. In the case of a government-provided equity infusion, the Secretary normally will consider the benefit to have been received on the date on which the firm received the equity infusion.

(c) Allocation of benefit to a particular time period. The benefit conferred by an equity infusion shall be allocated over the same time period as a non-recurring subsidy. See § 351.524(d).

§ 351.508   Debt Forgiveness

(a) Benefit. In the case of an assumption or forgiveness of a firm's debt obligation, a benefit exists equal to the amount of the principal and/or interest (including accrued, unpaid interest) that the government has assumed or forgiven. In situations where the entity assuming or forgiving the debt receives shares in a firm in return for eliminating or reducing the firm's debt obligation, the Secretary will determine the existence of a benefit under § 351.507 (equity infusions).

(b) Time of receipt of benefit. In the case of a debt or interest assumption or forgiveness, the Secretary normally will consider the benefit as having been received as of the date on which the debt or interest was assumed or forgiven.

(c) Allocation of benefit to a particular time period.—

(1) In general. The Secretary will treat the benefit determined under paragraph (a) of this section as a non-recurring subsidy, and will allocate the benefit to a particular year in accordance with § 351.524(d).

(2) Exception. Where an interest assumption is tied to a particular loan and where a firm can reasonably expect to receive the interest assumption at the time it applies for the loan, the Secretary will normally

treat the interest assumption as a reduced-interest loan and allocate the benefit to a particular year in accordance with § 351.505(c) (loans).

§ 351.509 Direct Taxes

(a) Benefit.—

(1) Exemption or remission of taxes. In the case of a program that provides for a full or partial exemption or remission of a direct tax (e.g., an income tax), or a reduction in the base used to calculate a direct tax, a benefit exists to the extent that the tax paid by a firm as a result of the program is less than the tax the firm would have paid in the absence of the program.

(2) Deferral of taxes. In the case of a program that provides for a deferral of direct taxes, a benefit exists to the extent that appropriate interest charges are not collected. Normally, a deferral of direct taxes will be treated as a government-provided loan in the amount of the tax deferred, according to the methodology described in § 351.505. The Secretary will use a short-term interest rate as the benchmark for tax deferrals of one year or less. The Secretary will use a long-term interest rate as the benchmark for tax deferrals of more than one year.

(b) Time of receipt of benefit.—

(1) Exemption or remission of taxes. In the case of a full or partial exemption or remission of a direct tax, the Secretary normally will consider the benefit as having been received on the date on which the recipient firm would otherwise have had to pay the taxes associated with the exemption or remission. Normally, this date will be the date on which the firm filed its tax return.

(2) Deferral of taxes. In the case of a tax deferral of one year or less, the Secretary normally will consider the benefit as having been received on the date on which the deferred tax becomes due. In the case of a multi-year deferral, the Secretary normally will consider the benefit as having been received on the anniversary date(s) of the deferral.

(c) Allocation of benefit to a particular time period. The Secretary normally will allocate (expense) the benefit of a full or partial exemption, remission, or deferral of a direct tax to the year in which the benefit is considered to have been received under paragraph (b) of this section.

§ 351.510 Indirect Taxes and Import Charges (Other Than Export Programs)

(a) Benefit.—

(1) Exemption or remission of taxes. In the case of a program, other than an export program, that provides for the full or partial exemption or remission of an indirect tax or an import charge, a benefit exists to the extent that the taxes or import charges paid by a firm as a result of the program are less than the taxes the firm would have paid in the absence of the program.

(2) Deferral of taxes. In the case of a program, other than an export program, that provides for a deferral of indirect taxes or import charges, a benefit exists to the extent that appropriate interest charges are not

collected. Normally, a deferral of indirect taxes or import charges will be treated as a government-provided loan in the amount of the taxes deferred, according to the methodology described in § 351.505. The Secretary will use a short-term interest rate as the benchmark for tax deferrals of one year or less. The Secretary will use a long-term interest rate as the benchmark for tax deferrals of more than one year.

(b) Time of receipt of benefit.—

(1) Exemption or remission of taxes. In the case of a full or partial exemption or remission of an indirect tax or import charge, the Secretary normally will consider the benefit as having been received at the time the recipient firm otherwise would be required to pay the indirect tax or import charge.

(2) Deferral of taxes. In the case of the deferral of an indirect tax or import charge of one year or less, the Secretary normally will consider the benefit as having been received on the date on which the deferred tax becomes due. In the case of a multi-year deferral, the Secretary normally will consider the benefit as having been received on the anniversary date(s) of the deferral.

(c) Allocation of benefit to a particular time period. The Secretary normally will allocate (expense) the benefit of a full or partial exemption, remission, or deferral described in paragraph (a) of this section to the year in which the benefit is considered to have been received under paragraph (b) of this section.

§ 351.511 Provision of Goods or Services

(a) Benefit.—

(1) In general. In the case where goods or services are provided, a benefit exists to the extent that such goods or services are provided for less than adequate remuneration. See section 771(5)(E)(iv) of the Act.

(2) "Adequate Remuneration" defined.—

(i) In general. The Secretary will normally seek to measure the adequacy of remuneration by comparing the government price to a market-determined price for the good or service resulting from actual transactions in the country in question. Such a price could include prices stemming from actual transactions between private parties, actual imports, or, in certain circumstances, actual sales from competitively run government auctions. In choosing such transactions or sales, the Secretary will consider product similarity; quantities sold, imported, or auctioned; and other factors affecting comparability.

(ii) Actual market-determined price unavailable. If there is no useable market-determined price with which to make the comparison under paragraph (a)(2)(i) of this section, the Secretary will seek to measure the adequacy of remuneration by comparing the government price to a world market price where it is reasonable to conclude that such price would be available to purchasers in the country in question. Where there is more than one commercially available world market price, the Secretary will average such prices to the extent practicable, making due allowance for factors affecting comparability.

(iii) World market price unavailable. If there is no world market price available to purchasers in the country in question, the Secretary will normally measure the adequacy of remuneration by assessing whether the government price is consistent with market principles.

(iv) Use of delivered prices. In measuring adequate remuneration under paragraph (a)(2)(i) or (a)(2)(ii) of this section, the Secretary will adjust the comparison price to reflect the price that a firm actually paid or would pay if it imported the product. This adjustment will include delivery charges and import duties.

(b) Time of receipt of benefit. In the case of the provision of a good or service, the Secretary normally will consider a benefit as having been received as of the date on which the firm pays or, in the absence of payment, was due to pay for the government-provided good or service.

(c) Allocation of benefit to a particular time period. In the case of the provision of a good or service, the Secretary will normally allocate (expense) the benefit to the year in which the benefit is considered to have been received under paragraph (b) of this section. In the case of the provision of infrastructure, the Secretary will normally treat the benefit as non-recurring and will allocate the benefit to a particular year in accordance with § 351.524(d).

(d) Exception for general infrastructure. A financial contribution does not exist in the case of the government provision of general infrastructure. General infrastructure is defined as infrastructure that is created for the broad societal welfare of a country, region, state or municipality.

§ 351.512   Purchase of Goods. [Reserved]

§ 351.513   Worker-Related Subsidies

(a) Benefit. In the case of a program that provides assistance to workers, a benefit exists to the extent that the assistance relieves a firm of an obligation that it normally would incur.

(b) Time of receipt of benefit. In the case of assistance provided to workers, the Secretary normally will consider the benefit as having been received by the firm on the date on which the payment is made that relieves the firm of the relevant obligation.

(c) Allocation of benefit to a particular time period. Normally, the Secretary will allocate (expense) the benefit from assistance provided to workers to the year in which the benefit is considered to have been received under paragraph (b) of this section.

§ 351.514   Export Subsidies

(a) In general. The Secretary will consider a subsidy to be an export subsidy if the Secretary determines that eligibility for, approval of, or the amount of, a subsidy is contingent upon export performance. In applying this section, the Secretary will consider a subsidy to be contingent upon export performance if the provision of the subsidy is, in law or in fact, tied to actual or anticipated exportation or export earnings, alone or as one of two or more conditions.

(b) Exception. In the case of export promotion activities of a government, a benefit does not exist if the Secretary determines that the activities consist of general informational activities that do not promote particular products over others.

§ 351.515 Internal Transport and Freight Charges for Export Shipments

(a) Benefit.—

(1) In general. In the case of internal transport and freight charges on export shipments, a benefit exists to the extent that the charges paid by a firm for transport or freight with respect to goods destined for export are less than what the firm would have paid if the goods were destined for domestic consumption. The Secretary will consider the amount of the benefit to equal the difference in amounts paid.

(2) Exception. For purposes of paragraph (a)(1) of this section, a benefit does not exist if the Secretary determines that:

(i) Any difference in charges is the result of an arm's-length transaction between the supplier and the user of the transport or freight service; or

(ii) The difference in charges is commercially justified.

(b) Time of receipt of benefit. In the case of internal transport and freight charges for export shipments, the Secretary normally will consider the benefit as having been received by the firm on the date on which the firm paid, or in the absence of payment was due to pay, the charges.

(c) Allocation of benefit to a particular time period. Normally, the Secretary will allocate (expense) the benefit from internal transport and freight charges for export shipments to the year in which the benefit is considered to have been received under paragraph (b) of this section.

§ 351.516 Price Preferences for Inputs Used in the Production of Goods for Export

(a) Benefit.—

(1) In general. In the case of a program involving the provision by governments or their agencies, either directly or indirectly through government-mandated schemes, of imported or domestic products or services for use in the production of exported goods, a benefit exists to the extent that the Secretary determines that the terms or conditions on which the products or services are provided are more favorable than the terms or conditions applicable to the provision of like or directly competitive products or services for use in the production of goods for domestic consumption unless, in the case of products, such terms or conditions are not more favorable than those commercially available on world markets to exporters.

(2) Amount of benefit. In the case of products provided under such schemes, the Secretary will determine the amount of the benefit by comparing the price of products used in the production of exported goods to the commercially available world market price of such products, inclusive of delivery charges.(3) Commercially available. For purposes of

paragraph (a)(2) of this section, commercially available means that the choice between domestic and imported products is unrestricted and depends only on commercial considerations.

(b) Time of receipt of benefit. In the case of a benefit described in paragraph (a)(1) of this section, the Secretary normally will consider the benefit to have been received as of the date on which the firm paid, or in the absence of payment was due to pay, for the product.

(c) Allocation of benefit to a particular time period. Normally, the Secretary will allocate (expense) benefits described in paragraph (a)(1) of this section to the year in which the benefit is considered to have been received under paragraph (b) of this section.

§ 351.517 Exemption or Remission Upon Export of Indirect Taxes

(a) Benefit. In the case of the exemption or remission upon export of indirect taxes, a benefit exists to the extent that the Secretary determines that the amount remitted or exempted exceeds the amount levied with respect to the production and distribution of like products when sold for domestic consumption.

(b) Time of receipt of benefit. In the case of the exemption or remission upon export of an indirect tax, the Secretary normally will consider the benefit as having been received as of the date of exportation.

(c) Allocation of benefit to a particular time period. Normally, the Secretary will allocate (expense) the benefit from the exemption or remission upon export of indirect taxes to the year in which the benefit is considered to have been received under paragraph (b) of this section.

§ 351.518 Exemption, Remission, or Deferral Upon Export of Prior-Stage Cumulative Indirect Taxes

(a) Benefit.—

(1) Exemption of prior-stage cumulative indirect taxes. In the case of a program that provides for the exemption of prior-stage cumulative indirect taxes on inputs used in the production of an exported product, a benefit exists to the extent that the exemption extends to inputs that are not consumed in the production of the exported product, making normal allowance for waste, or if the exemption covers taxes other than indirect taxes that are imposed on the input. If the Secretary determines that the exemption of prior-stage cumulative indirect taxes confers a benefit, the Secretary normally will consider the amount of the benefit to be the prior-stage cumulative indirect taxes that otherwise would have been paid on the inputs not consumed in the production of the exported product, making normal allowance for waste, and the amount of charges other than import charges covered by the exemption.

(2) Remission of prior-stage cumulative indirect taxes. In the case of a program that provides for the remission of prior-stage cumulative indirect taxes on inputs used in the production of an exported product, a benefit exists to the extent that the amount remitted exceeds the amount of prior-stage cumulative indirect taxes paid on inputs that are consumed in the production of the exported product, making normal allowance for

waste. If the Secretary determines that the remission of prior-stage cumulative indirect taxes confers a benefit, the Secretary normally will consider the amount of the benefit to be the difference between the amount remitted and the amount of the prior-stage cumulative indirect taxes on inputs that are consumed in the production of the export product, making normal allowance for waste.

(3) Deferral of prior-stage cumulative indirect taxes. In the case of a program that provides for a deferral of prior-stage cumulative indirect taxes on an exported product, a benefit exists to the extent that the deferral extends to inputs that are not consumed in the production of the exported product, making normal allowance for waste, and the government does not charge appropriate interest on the taxes deferred. If the Secretary determines that a benefit exists, the Secretary will normally treat the deferral as a government-provided loan in the amount of the tax deferred, according to the methodology described in § 351.505. The Secretary will use a short-term interest rate as the benchmark for tax deferrals of one year or less. The Secretary will use a long-term interest rate as the benchmark for tax deferrals of more than one year.

(4) Exception. Notwithstanding the provisions in paragraphs (a)(1), (a)(2), and (a)(3) of this action, the Secretary will consider the entire amount of the exemption, remission or deferral to confer a benefit, unless the Secretary determines that:

(i) The government in question has in place and applies a system or procedure to confirm which inputs are consumed in the production of the exported products and in what amounts, and to confirm which indirect taxes are imposed on these inputs, and the system or procedure is reasonable, effective for the purposes intended, and is based on generally accepted commercial practices in the country of export; or

(ii) If the government in question does not have a system or procedure in place, if the system or procedure is not reasonable, or if the system or procedure is instituted and considered reasonable, but is found not to be applied or not to be applied effectively, the government in question has carried out an examination of actual inputs involved to confirm which inputs are consumed in the production of the exported product, in what amounts, and which indirect taxes are imposed on the inputs.

(b) Time of receipt of benefit. In the case of the exemption, remission, or deferral of prior stage cumulative indirect taxes, the Secretary normally will consider the benefit as having been received:

(1) In the case of an exemption, as of the date of exportation;

(2) In the case of a remission, as of the date of exportation;

(3) In the case of a deferral of one year or less, on the date the deferred tax became due; and

(4) In the case of a multi-year deferral, on the anniversary date(s) of the deferral.

(c) Allocation of benefit to a particular time period. The Secretary normally will allocate (expense) the benefit of the exemption, remission or deferral of prior-stage cumulative indirect taxes to the year in which the benefit is considered to have been received under paragraph (b) of this section.

§ 351.519 Remission or Drawback of Import Charges Upon Export

(a) Benefit.—

(1) In general. The term "remission or drawback" includes full or partial exemptions and deferrals of import charges.

(i) Remission or drawback of import charges. In the case of the remission or drawback of import charges upon export, a benefit exists to the extent that the Secretary determines that the amount of the remission or drawback exceeds the amount of import charges on imported inputs that are consumed in the production of the exported product, making normal allowances for waste.

(ii) Exemption of import charges. In the case of an exemption of import charges upon export, a benefit exists to the extent that the exemption extends to inputs that are not consumed in the production of the exported product, making normal allowances for waste, or if the exemption covers charges other than import charges that are imposed on the input.

(iii) Deferral of import charges. In the case of a deferral, a benefit exists to the extent that the deferral extends to inputs that are not consumed in the production of the exported product, making normal allowance for waste, and the government does not charge appropriate interest on the import charges deferred.

(2) Substitution drawback. "Substitution drawback" involves a situation in which a firm uses a quantity of home market inputs equal to, and having the same quality and characteristics as, the imported inputs as a substitute for them. Substitution drawback does not necessarily result in the conferral of a benefit. However, a benefit exists if the Secretary determines that:

(i) The import and the corresponding export operations both did not occur within a reasonable time period, not to exceed two years; or

(ii) The amount drawn back exceeds the amount of the import charges levied initially on the imported inputs for which drawback is claimed.

(3) Amount of the benefit.—

(i) Remission or drawback of import charges. If the Secretary determines that the remission or drawback, including substitution drawback, of import charges confers a benefit under paragraph (a)(1) or (a)(2) of this section, the Secretary normally will consider the amount of the benefit to be the difference between the amount of import charges remitted or drawn back and the amount paid on imported inputs consumed in production for which remission or drawback was claimed.

(ii) *Exemption of import charges.* If the Secretary determines that the exemption of import charges upon export confers a benefit, the Secretary normally will consider the amount of the benefit to be the import charges that otherwise would have been paid on the inputs not consumed in the production of the exported product, making normal allowance for waste, and the amount of charges other than import charges covered by the exemption.

(iii) *Deferral of import charges.* If the Secretary determines that the deferral of import charges upon export confers a benefit, the Secretary will normally treat a deferral as a government-provided loan in the amount of the import charges deferred on the inputs not consumed in the production of the exported product, making normal allowance for waste, according to the methodology described in § 351.505. The Secretary will use a short-term interest rate as the benchmark for deferrals of one year or less. The Secretary will use a long-term interest rate as the benchmark for deferrals of more than one year.

(4) *Exception.* Notwithstanding paragraph (a)(3) of this section, the Secretary will consider the entire amount of an exemption, deferral, remission or drawback to confer a benefit, unless the Secretary determines that:

(i) The government in question has in place and applies a system or procedure to confirm which inputs are consumed in the production of the exported products and in what amounts, and the system or procedure is reasonable, effective for the purposes intended, and is based on generally accepted commercial practices in the country of export; or

(ii) If the government in question does not have a system or procedure in place, if the system or procedure is not reasonable, or if the system or procedure is instituted and considered reasonable, but is found not to be applied or not to be applied effectively, the government in question has carried out an examination of actual inputs involved to confirm which inputs are consumed in the production of the exported product, and in what amounts.

(b) *Time of receipt of benefit.* In the case of the exemption, deferral, remission or drawback, including substitution drawback, of import charges, the Secretary normally will consider the benefit as having been received:

(1) In the case of remission or drawback, as of the date of exportation;

(2) In the case of an exemption, as of the date of the exportation;

(3) In the case of a deferral of one year or less, on the date the import charges became due; and(4) In the case of a multi-year deferral, on the anniversary date(s) of the deferral.

(c) *Allocation of benefit to a particular time period.* The Secretary normally will allocate (expense) the benefit from the exemption, deferral, remission or drawback of import charges to the year in which the benefit is considered to have been received under paragraph (b) of this section.

§ 351.520   Export Insurance

(a) Benefit.—

(1) In general. In the case of export insurance, a benefit exists if the premium rates charged are inadequate to cover the long-term operating costs and losses of the program.

(2) Amount of the benefit. If the Secretary determines under paragraph (a)(1) of this section that premium rates are inadequate, the Secretary normally will calculate the amount of the benefit as the difference between the amount of premiums paid by the firm and the amount received by the firm under the insurance program during the period of investigation or review.

(b) Time of receipt of benefit. In the case of export insurance, the Secretary normally will consider the benefit as having been received in the year in which the difference described in paragraph (a)(2) of this section occurs.

(c) Allocation of benefit to a particular time period. The Secretary normally will allocate (expense) the benefit from export insurance to the year in which the benefit is considered to have been received under paragraph (b) of this section.

§ 351.521   Import Substitution Subsidies. [Reserved]

§ 351.522   Green Light and Green Box Subsidies

(a) Certain agricultural subsidies. The Secretary will treat as non-countervailable domestic support measures that are provided to certain agricultural products (i.e., products listed in Annex 1 of the WTO Agreement on Agriculture) and that the Secretary determines conform to the criteria of Annex 2 of the WTO Agreement on Agriculture. See section 771(5B)(F) of the Act. The Secretary will determine that a particular domestic support measure conforms fully to the provisions of Annex 2 if the Secretary finds that the measure:

(1) Is provided through a publicly-funded government program (including government revenue foregone) not involving transfers from consumers;

(2) Does not have the effect of providing a price support to producers; and

(3) Meets the relevant policy-specific criteria and conditions set out in paragraphs 2 through 13 of Annex 2.

(b) Research subsidies. In accordance with section 771(5B)(B)(iii)(II) of the Act, the Secretary will examine the total eligible costs to be incurred over the duration of a particular project to determine whether a subsidy for research activities exceeds 75 percent of the costs of industrial research, 50 percent of the costs of precompetitive development activity, or 62.5 percent of the costs for a project that includes both industrial research and precompetitive activity. If the Secretary determines that, at some point over the life of a particular project, these relevant thresholds will be exceeded, the Secretary will treat the entire amount of the subsidy as countervailable.

(c) Subsidies for adaptation of existing facilities to new environmental requirements. If the Secretary determines that a subsidy is given to upgrade existing facilities to environmental standards in excess of minimum statutory or regulatory requirements, the subsidy will not qualify for non-countervailable treatment under section 771(5B)(D) of the Act and the Secretary will treat the entire amount of the subsidy as countervailable.

§ 351.523   Upstream Subsidies

(a) Investigation of upstream subsidies.—

(1) In general. Before investigating the existence of an upstream subsidy (see section 771A of the Act), the Secretary must have a reasonable basis to believe or suspect that all of the following elements exist:

(i) A countervailable subsidy, other than an export subsidy, is provided with respect to an input product;

(ii) One of the following conditions exists:

(A) The supplier of the input product and the producer of the subject merchandise are affiliated;

(B) The price for the subsidized input product is lower than the price that the producer of the subject merchandise otherwise would pay another seller in an arm's-length transaction for an unsubsidized input product; or

(C) The government sets the price of the input product so as to guarantee that the benefit provided with respect to the input product is passed through to producers of the subject merchandise; and

(iii) The ad valorem countervailable subsidy rate on the input product, multiplied by the proportion of the total production costs of the subject merchandise accounted for by the input product, is equal to, or greater than, one percent.

(b) Input product. For purposes of this section, "input product" means any product used in the production of the subject merchandise.

(c) Competitive benefit.—

(1) In general. In evaluating whether a competitive benefit exists under section 771A(b) of the Act, the Secretary will determine whether the price for the subsidized input product is lower than the benchmark input price. For purposes of this section, the Secretary will use as a benchmark input price the following, in order of preference:

(i) The actual price paid by, or offered to, the producer of the subject merchandise for an unsubsidized input product, including an imported input product;

(ii) An average price for an unsubsidized input product, including an imported input product, based upon publicly available data;

(iii) The actual price paid by, or offered to, the producer of the subject merchandise for a subsidized input product, including an imported input product, that is adjusted to account for the countervailable subsidy;

(iv) An average price for a subsidized input product, including an imported input product, based upon publicly available data, that is adjusted to account for the countervailable subsidy; or

(v) An unadjusted price for a subsidized input product or any other surrogate price deemed appropriate by the Secretary.

For purposes of this section, such prices must be reflective of a time period that reasonably corresponds to the time of the purchase of the input.

(2) Use of delivered prices. The Secretary will use a delivered price whenever the Secretary uses the price of an input product under paragraph (c)(1) of this section.

(d) Significant effect.—

(1) Presumptions. In evaluating whether an upstream subsidy has a significant effect on the cost of manufacturing or producing the subject merchandise (see section 771A(a)(3) of the Act), the Secretary will multiply the ad valorem countervailable subsidy rate on the input product by the proportion of the total production cost of the subject merchandise that is accounted for by the input product. If the product of that multiplication exceeds five percent, the Secretary will presume the existence of a significant effect. If the product is less than one percent, the Secretary will presume the absence of a significant effect. If the product is between one and five percent, there will be no presumption.(2) Rebuttal of presumptions. A party to the proceeding may present information to rebut these presumptions. In evaluating such information, the Secretary will consider the extent to which factors other than price, such as quality differences, are important determinants of demand for the subject merchandise.

§ 351.524   Allocation of Benefit to a Particular Time Period

Unless otherwise specified in §§ 351.504–351.523, the Secretary will allocate benefits to a particular time period in accordance with this section.

(a) Recurring benefits. The Secretary will allocate (expense) a recurring benefit to the year in which the benefit is received.

(b) Non-recurring benefits.

(1) In general. The Secretary will normally allocate a non-recurring benefit to a firm over the number of years corresponding to the average useful life ("AUL") of renewable physical assets as defined in paragraph (d)(2) of this section.

(2) Exception. The Secretary will normally allocate (expense) non-recurring benefits provided under a particular subsidy program to the year in which the benefits are received if the total amount approved under the subsidy program is less than 0.5 percent of relevant sales (e.g., total sales, export sales, the sales of a particular product, or the sales to a particular market) of the firm in question during the year in which the subsidy was approved.

(c) "Recurring" versus "non-recurring" benefits.—

(1) Non-binding illustrative lists of recurring and non-recurring benefits. The Secretary normally will treat the following types of subsidies as providing recurring benefits: Direct tax exemptions and deductions; exemptions and excessive rebates of indirect taxes or import duties; provision of goods and services for less than adequate remuneration; price support payments; discounts on electricity, water, and other utilities; freight subsidies; export promotion assistance; early retirement payments; worker assistance; worker training; wage subsidies; and upstream subsidies. The Secretary normally will treat the following types of subsidies as providing non-recurring benefits: equity infusions, grants, plant closure assistance, debt forgiveness, coverage for operating losses, debt-to-equity conversions, provision of non-general infrastructure, and provision of plant and equipment.

(2) The test for determining whether a benefit is recurring or non-recurring. If a subsidy is not on the illustrative lists, or is not addressed elsewhere in these regulations, or if a party claims that a subsidy on the recurring list should be treated as non-recurring or a subsidy on the non-recurring list should be treated as recurring, the Secretary will consider the following criteria in determining whether the benefits from the subsidy should be considered recurring or non-recurring:

(i) Whether the subsidy is exceptional in the sense that the recipient cannot expect to receive additional subsidies under the same program on an ongoing basis from year to year;

(ii) Whether the subsidy required or received the government's express authorization or approval (i.e., receipt of benefits is not automatic), or

(iii) Whether the subsidy was provided for, or tied to, the capital structure or capital assets of the firm.

(d) Process for allocating non-recurring benefits over time.—

(1) In general. For purposes of allocating a non-recurring benefit over time and determining the annual benefit amount that should be assigned to a particular year, the Secretary will use the following formula:

$$A_k = \frac{y/n + [y - (y/n)(k - 1)]d}{1 + d}$$

Where:

A_k = the amount of the benefit allocated to year k,

y = the face value of the subsidy,

n = the AUL (see paragraph (d)(2) of this section),

d = the discount rate (see paragraph (d)(3) of this section), and

k = the year of allocation, where the year of receipt = 1 and $1 \leq k \leq$ n.

(2) AUL.—

(i) In general. The Secretary will presume the allocation period for non-recurring subsidies to be the AUL of renewable physical assets for the industry concerned as listed in the Internal Revenue Service's ("IRS") 1977 Class Life Asset Depreciation Range System, as updated by the Department of Treasury. The presumption will apply unless a party claims and establishes that the IRS tables do not reasonably reflect the company-specific AUL or the country-wide AUL for the industry under investigation, subject to the requirement, in paragraph (d)(2)(ii) of this section, that the difference between the company-specific AUL or country-wide AUL for the industry under investigation and the AUL in the IRS tables is significant. If this is the case, the Secretary will use company-specific or country-wide AULs to allocate non-recurring benefits over time (see paragraph (d)(2)(iii) of this section).

(ii) Definition of "significant." For purposes of this paragraph (d), significant means that a party has demonstrated that the company-specific AUL or country-wide AUL for the industry differs from AUL in the IRS tables by one year or more.

(iii) Calculation of a company-specific or country-wide AUL. A calculation of a company-specific AUL will not be accepted by the Secretary unless it satisfies the following requirements: the company must base its depreciation on an estimate of the actual useful lives of assets and it must use straight-line depreciation or demonstrate that its calculation is not distorted through irregular or uneven additions to the pool of fixed assets. A company-specific AUL is calculated by dividing the aggregate of the annual average gross book values of the firm's depreciable productive fixed assets by the firm's aggregated annual charge to accumulated depreciation, for a period considered appropriate by the Secretary, subject to appropriate normalizing adjustments. A country-wide AUL for the industry under investigation will not be accepted by the Secretary unless the respondent government demonstrates that it has a system in place to calculate AULs for its industries, and that this system provides a reliable representation of AUL.

(iv) Exception. Under certain extraordinary circumstances, the Secretary may consider whether an allocation period other than AUL is appropriate or whether the benefit stream begins at a date other than the date the subsidy was bestowed.

(3) Selection of a discount rate.

(i) In general. The Secretary will select a discount rate based upon data for the year in which the government agreed to provide the subsidy. The Secretary will use as a discount rate the following, in order of preference:

(A) The cost of long-term, fixed-rate loans of the firm in question, excluding any loans that the Secretary has determined to be countervailable subsidies;

(B) The average cost of long-term, fixed-rate loans in the country in question; or

(C) A rate that the Secretary considers to be most appropriate.

(ii) Exception for uncreditworthy firms. In the case of a firm considered by the Secretary to be uncreditworthy (see § 351.505(a)(4)), the Secretary will use as a discount rate the interest rate described in § 351.505(a)(3)(iii).

§ 351.525   Calculation of Ad Valorem Subsidy Rate and Attribution of Subsidy to a Product

(a) Calculation of ad valorem subsidy rate. The Secretary will calculate an ad valorem subsidy rate by dividing the amount of the benefit allocated to the period of investigation or review by the sales value during the same period of the product or products to which the Secretary attributes the subsidy under paragraph (b) of this section. Normally, the Secretary will determine the sales value of a product on an f.o.b. (port) basis (if the product is exported) or on an f.o.b. (factory) basis (if the product is sold for domestic consumption). However, if the Secretary determines that countervailable subsidies are provided with respect to the movement of a product from the port or factory to the place of destination (e.g., freight or insurance costs are subsidized), the Secretary may make appropriate adjustments to the sales value used in the denominator.

(b) Attribution of subsidies.

(1) In general. In attributing a subsidy to one or more products, the Secretary will apply the rules set forth in paragraphs (b)(2) through (b)(7) of this section.

(2) Export subsidies. The Secretary will attribute an export subsidy only to products exported by a firm.

(3) Domestic subsidies. The Secretary will attribute a domestic subsidy to all products sold by a firm, including products that are exported.

(4) Subsidies tied to a particular market. If a subsidy is tied to sales to a particular market, the Secretary will attribute the subsidy only to products sold by the firm to that market.

(5) Subsidies tied to a particular product.

(i) In general. If a subsidy is tied to the production or sale of a particular product, the Secretary will attribute the subsidy only to that product.

(ii) Exception. If a subsidy is tied to production of an input product, then the Secretary will attribute the subsidy to both the input and downstream products produced by a corporation.

(6) Corporations with cross-ownership.

(i) In general. The Secretary normally will attribute a subsidy to the products produced by the corporation that received the subsidy.

(ii) Corporations producing the same product. If two (or more) corporations with cross-ownership produce the subject merchandise, the Secretary will attribute the subsidies received by either or both corporations to the products produced by both corporations.

(iii) Holding or parent companies. If the firm that received a subsidy is a holding company, including a parent company with its own operations, the Secretary will attribute the subsidy to the consolidated sales of the holding company and its subsidiaries. However, if the Secretary finds that the holding company merely served as a conduit for the transfer of the subsidy from the government to a subsidiary of the holding company, the Secretary will attribute the subsidy to products sold by the subsidiary.

(iv) Input suppliers. If there is cross-ownership between an input supplier and a downstream producer, and production of the input product is primarily dedicated to production of the downstream product, the Secretary will attribute subsidies received by the input producer to the combined sales of the input and downstream products produced by both corporations (excluding the sales between the two corporations).

(v) Transfer of subsidy between corporations with cross-ownership producing different products. In situations where paragraphs (b)(6)(i) through (iv) of this section do not apply, if a corporation producing non-subject merchandise received a subsidy and transferred the subsidy to a corporation with cross-ownership, the Secretary will attribute the subsidy to products sold by the recipient of the transferred subsidy.

(vi) Cross-ownership defined. Cross-ownership exists between two or more corporations where one corporation can use or direct the individual assets of the other corporation(s) in essentially the same ways it can use its own assets. Normally, this standard will be met where there is a majority voting ownership interest between two corporations or through common ownership of two (or more) corporations.

(7) Multinational firms. If the firm that received a subsidy has production facilities in two or more countries, the Secretary will attribute the subsidy to products produced by the firm within the country of the government that granted the subsidy. However, if it is demonstrated that the subsidy was tied to more than domestic production, the Secretary will attribute the subsidy to multinational production.

(c) Trading companies. Benefits from subsidies provided to a trading company which exports subject merchandise shall be cumulated with benefits from subsidies provided to the firm which is producing subject merchandise that is sold through the trading company, regardless of whether the trading company and the producing firm are affiliated.

§ 351.526   Program-Wide Changes

(a) In general. The Secretary may take a program-wide change into account in establishing the estimated countervailing duty cash deposit rate if:

(1) The Secretary determines that subsequent to the period of investigation or review, but before a preliminary determination in an investigation (see § 351.205) or a preliminary result of an administrative review or a new shipper review (see §§ 351.213 and 351.214), a program-wide change has occurred; and

(2) The Secretary is able to measure the change in the amount of countervailable subsidies provided under the program in question.

(b) Definition of program-wide change. For purposes of this section, "program-wide change" means a change that:

(1) Is not limited to an individual firm or firms; and

(2) Is effectuated by an official act, such as the enactment of a statute, regulation, or decree, or contained in the schedule of an existing statute, regulation, or decree.

(c) Effect limited to cash deposit rate.—

(1) In general. The application of paragraph (a) of this section will not result in changing, in an investigation, an affirmative determination to a negative determination or a negative determination to an affirmative determination.

(2) Example. In a countervailing duty investigation, the Secretary determines that during the period of investigation a countervailable subsidy existed in the amount of 10 percent ad valorem. Subsequent to the period of investigation, but before the preliminary determination, the foreign government in question enacts a change to the program that reduces the amount of the subsidy to a de minimis level. In a final determination, the Secretary would issue an affirmative determination, but would establish a cash deposit rate of zero.

(d) Terminated programs. The Secretary will not adjust the cash deposit rate under paragraph (a) of this section if the program-wide change consists of the termination of a program and:

(1) The Secretary determines that residual benefits may continue to be bestowed under the terminated program; or

(2) The Secretary determines that a substitute program for the terminated program has been introduced and the Secretary is not able to measure the amount of countervailable subsidies provided under the substitute program.

§ 351.527   Transnational Subsidies

Except as otherwise provided in section 701(d) of the Act (subsidies provided to international consortia) and section 771A of the Act (upstream subsidies), a subsidy does not exist if the Secretary determines that the funding for the subsidy is supplied in accordance with, and as part of, a program or project funded:

(a) By a government of a country other than the country in which the recipient firm is located; or

(b) By an international lending or development institution.

†